ALSO BY STEPHEN WALSH

Stravinsky: A Creative Spring
Russia and France, 1882–1934

The Lieder of Schumann

Bartók Chamber Music

The Music of Stravinsky

Stravinsky: Oedipus Rex

STRAVINSKY:

THE SECOND EXILE

STRAVINSKY

THE SECOND EXILE

FRANCE AND AMERICA, 1934–1971

STEPHEN WALSH

ALFRED A. KNOPF

New York   2006

THIS IS A BORZOI BOOK PUBLISHED BY ALFRED A. KNOPF

www.aaknopf.com
Published in Great Britain by Jonathan Cape Ltd., London.

Knopf, Borzoi Books, and the colophon are registered
trademarks of Random House, Inc.

Library of Congress Cataloging-in-Publication Data
Walsh, Stephen, [date]
Stravinsky : the second exile : France and America, 1934–1971 / Stephen Walsh.
p. cm
Includes bibliographical references and index.
ISBN 0-375-40752-9
1. Stravinsky, Igor, 1882–1971.   2. Composers—Biography.   I. Title.
ML410.S932W355 2006
780'.92—dc22
[B]   2005047231

Manufactured in the United States of America
First Edition

For Mary

Towards great persons use respective boldnesse.

—GEORGE HERBERT

CONTENTS

ACKNOWLEDGMENTS

MANY OF THOSE whose names figure in the acknowledgments for the first volume have been at least as important to the second. In particular I should like to repeat my thanks to the Paul Sacher Stiftung in Basle and its expert staff, to the library staff of Cardiff University, and to my colleagues in the Cardiff University Music Department, without whose support—personal as well as institutional—neither volume could ever have been written. The Paul Sacher Stiftung kindly gave me permission to quote from and reproduce a large number of documents and photographs in its possession. The Cardiff Music Department helped me with research money, and I was also supported by research grants from the AHRB and the Leverhulme Trust and by a year's sabbatical under the AHRB's research leave scheme. Among the many other libraries and archives to which I am indebted, I should particularly mention the Harry Ransome Humanities Research Center at the University of Texas at Austin, the Department of Special Collections at UCLA, the Butler Library of Columbia University, the Stiftung Archiv der Akademie der Künste in Berlin, the London Library, the newspaper section of the British Library at Colindale, and the Music Division of the Library of Congress. In addition to those individuals mentioned in the introduction to volume I, I should like to thank Petra Kupfer and Carlos Chanfón (Paul Sacher Stiftung) and Linda Ashton (HRC, Austin) for their particular and unstinting help.

I have made heavy demands on the time and patience of busy friends and colleagues. Anthony Powers, Arlene Sierra, Mark Almond, Shirley Hazzard, and Colin Slim all read the manuscript, pointed out errors or imprecisions, and suggested improvements. I am deeply grateful to them all. Others who have helped me, in a variety of often extremely substantial ways, are Gilbert Amy, the late Arthur Berger, Thomas Bösche, Pierre Boulez, Marilee Bradford, David Bray, Sally Cavender, Dorothy L. Crawford, Paolo Dal Molin, Teresa D'Arms, Valérie Dufour, Christopher Flood, Anthony Holden, Stephanie Jordan, Charles M. Joseph, Andrew Kemp, Lyudmila Kovnatskaya, William Kraft, Lourdes Lopez, Alan Maclean, John McClure, Russell McCulloh, Noëlle Mann, Belinda Matthews, David Matthews, Edward Mendelson, Carol Merrill-Mirsky, Roger Nichols, Susan Palmer, David Raksin, Nancy Reynolds, Sir Adam Ridley, Julia Rosenthal, Ann Schreffler, Stanislav Shvabrin, Nigel Simeone, the late Leonard Stein, Jonathan Stone, Irina Vershinina, Claudia Vincis, and Jerry and Helen Young. I repeat that these are merely my more recent benefactors, in addition to those already named in volume one.

The second volume has had one major category of help not available to the first. Stravinsky's own close family, who had initially preferred to distance themselves from the project, changed their minds (as I believe) when they saw that it was not simply a new painting of old pictures. In particular I should like to thank the composer's daughter, Milène Marion, and place on record the kindness of his late daughters-in-law, Denise Strawinsky and Françoise Stravinsky, in welcoming me to their homes and talking to me at great length about him. The composer's grandson, John Stravinsky, was no less hospitable, and also gave me a huge amount of material assistance, kept me informed about the emergence of new letters and documents, allowed me to read everything in his possession, and, as in the first volume, allowed me to quote from private letters and copyright materials. Without his support, the first volume could not have been published in its intended form, but the second volume could scarcely even have been written. I am hugely indebted to him and his wife, Dava.

Writings by Isaiah Berlin are reproduced with permission of Curtis Brown on behalf of The Isaiah Berlin Literary Trust © 2004 by The Isaiah Berlin Literary Trust.

Extracts from *Goodbye to Berlin, Lost Years,* and *Diaries* by Christopher Isherwood, published by Chatto & Windus, are reprinted by permission of The Random House Group Ltd.

Letters of Chester Kallman are quoted by permission of the literary estate of Chester Kallman.

Writings by Lincoln Kirstein are © 2006 by the New York Public Library (Astor, Lenox, and Tilden Foundations) and are quoted by permission.

Quotations from *And Music at the Close* by Lillian Libman are copyright © 1972 by W. W. Norton & Company, Inc., and are used by permission of W. W. Norton & Company, Inc.

Writings by Francis Steegmuller are quoted with the kind permission of Shirley Hazzard Steegmuller.

Extracts from the writings of Dylan Thomas are reprinted by permission of David Higham Associates and Harold Ober Associates.

For permission to quote from other copyright materials, I should like to thank the following: Pierre Boulez, Martin Duberman, the Fondation Internationale Nadia et Lili Boulanger, Leopold Godowsky, Doris Halsey (for the Huxley Literary Estate), Marie Iellatchitch-Strawinsky, Nicholas Jenkins,

Milène Marion, Edward Mendelson, Madeleine Milhaud, Daniel Milhaud, Dominique Nabokov, Marie-Victoire Nantet, Oliver Neighbour, Fabio Rieti, Marion Sapiro, Myriam Scherchen, and Jeff Towns.

I reiterate with sorrow my abiding debt to my Moscow colleague, Viktor Varunts, who continued to supply me with Russian-language material from the composer's and other archives until his tragic death from a heart attack soon after his arrival in New York at the start of a Fulbright scholarship in September 2003. Varunts's three published volumes of Stravinsky's Russian-language correspondence are a wonderful memorial to a great scholar, a memorial edged only with the sadness that the two additional volumes that he was preparing survive—and seem likely to remain—only in draft form. I was nevertheless able to make use of the correspondence intended for these volumes, which Varunts had supplied to me before his death, alas without the commentaries and appendixes which adorn the published volumes.

My debt to my wife and family hardly needs stating but is partly and inadequately expressed in the dedications of the two volumes. Living with somebody else's obsession is probably even worse than living with one's own. I can't thank them enough, and will not try.

When the first volume, *Stravinsky: A Creative Spring*, came out in 1999–2000, my mother was already too poor-sighted to read it. One day, a fairy godfather arrived in the person of Nigel Davis, a High Court judge who, in his not very considerable spare time, did voluntary work visiting the elderly and housebound. He struck up what seemed at the time a somewhat unlikely friendship with my mother, and since then has spent several hours on most Saturday afternoons reading her son's book to her and (I'm slightly afraid) discussing its contents. I am moved by his kindness every time I think about it, and can only hope that he will not blench at the realization of what still remains. A creative spring: all right. But a second exile? That's a lot more Saturday afternoons.

STEPHEN WALSH
Welsh Newton, September 2005

A NOTE ON TRANSLATIONS

As in the first volume, I have used my own translations of all foreign-language material for which I have had access to the original texts, but I have again adopted the procedure of referencing published English translations in the endnotes. Reference to a published translation does not mean that I have quoted it in my own text.

ENTR'ACTE: A HOUSE DIVIDED

EUROPE in 1934 was like a fault line in the earth's crust. Life went on its calm, untroubled way, in the manner of a road that traversed unseen rifts and dormant volcanoes, its course interrupted now and then by smoking crevasses beyond which the tarmac ran ahead to the gray horizon. In Germany, an aged president was succeeded by one younger and more ambitious. In France, riots flared and a foreign king was assassinated. In Vienna, in Munich and Berlin, in Moscow and Leningrad, political murder became almost a daily routine. But for the nameless multitude, life remained a drudgery of the commonplace or worse. The hungry children, one writer observed, "went sniffing to chilly schools to be taught by dispirited teachers on reduced salaries, but still the schools were not closed; the bankrupt railways and steamship lines ran diminished but punctual services; hotels stayed open not to make profits but to mitigate losses; the road traffic lost something of its newness and smartness and swiftness, but still it flowed." Yet war "was manifestly drawing nearer, in Eastern Asia, in Eastern Europe, it loitered, it advanced, it halted, and no one displayed the vigour or capacity needed to avert its intermittent unhurrying approach."[1]

In a first-class compartment of the Paris–Grenoble express one August afternoon, a short, slightly built man of fifty-two was reading with the concentrated attention of someone to whom such journeys—and that journey in particular—were no novelty. Recently come from London, he was returning to his family in Isère, where for some years they had rented a minor château in the little town of Voreppe. Had the train crossed a border, his passport would have revealed him as a Frenchman; but in neither look, dress, nor speech was he exactly French. On the contrary, some element of caricature in his features—the nose, the lips, the ears, all somehow larger and more pronounced than might have been allocated by a strictly equitable Providence—combined with a certain overdone elegance in his tailoring to hint at more remote, Eastern European, perhaps Jewish, origins. He might have been a Baltic count turned bank manager, or one of the myriad Georgian princes and generals who had descended on Paris after the Revolution and reinvented themselves as stockbrokers or impresarios. Actually he was neither Georgian nor Balt, nor had he Jewish blood—a fact of which he had been at somewhat exaggerated pains to inform those to whom such things increasingly mattered in the 1930s. He was pure Slav, a Russian from old St. Petersburg, the great-grandson of Polish castellans and Tsarist Privy Councillors, and, less respectably, a composer whom some radical spirits regarded as the most important of his generation. His latest work, a setting of a neo-Homeric melodrama by André Gide, had horrified well-spoken Frenchmen by its flagrant butchery of their language in the interests of musical character. His own spoken French emerged from somewhere deep in the caverns of the earth, saturnine and slow and by no means always correct.

As so often with exiles, Igor Stravinsky's personality seemed to mold itself to its environment. The insecurities of his childhood he had learnt to conceal behind a severe expression and a courtly manner. But the severity could at any moment dissolve into a huge grin like a burst of sunshine on a darkened hillside, and the courtliness was no more than a veil for a sharp wit and a vivid sense of the absurd. In Paris, where he had kept a pied à terre for the past fourteen years and where he had recently taken the lease on a large apartment at the smart end of the rue du Faubourg Saint-Honoré, he was much cultivated in those circles on the fringes of high society for whom modern art was a chic and preferably not too gloomy accessory of the life of leisure. His mistress, Vera Sudeykina, a charming Russian former actress and occasional theatre costumière, moved effortlessly in this artistic-cum-intellectual milieu, even though she was entirely without means of her own and often had scarcely enough ready cash to feed the electricity meter at her flat in the sixteenth arrondissement. Her husband, long since dismissed, had been a painter and stage designer, and in the time of her fidelity she had drawn up a list of what she termed the "Duties of an Artist's Wife": to force him to work, "even with a stick," to love his work, to inspire in him new ideas, to know his work and keep it in order, to greet each new work with wonder, to know how to contemplate his work, and to be herself physically perfect and "his model forever."[2] She should be, in short, his muse. Exactly how some of these duties would transfer to the art of music might seem problematical, but in essence they remained the same. As far as Paris was concerned, Igor and Vera were, in the vulgar parlance of a later age, an item, but they were also an adornment, a pair who graced the social and artistic stage on which they walked and whose frequently protracted absences from it were regretted.

The other half of Stravinsky's life—the half toward which he was travelling that August afternoon—was very different in tone. His wife, Catherine (a first cousin whom he had known since he was eight), consciously preserved a family hearth of a specifically Russian character, a kind of *dvoryan-skoye gnezdo,* Turgenev's "nest of gentle folk," a household that included her mother-in-law, her two daughters, now in their early twenties, and two sons (when not otherwise occupied in Paris), together with the children's old *nyanya* Madubo Svitalski, and assorted day servants. Here Stravinsky could find the peace and stability he needed in order to compose. Katya understood this need and dedicated her entire effort to satisfying it, notwithstanding her husband's open infidelity and his despotic insistence that she accept it and even, in certain respects, connive at it. There was about her nothing of the muse; she made inspiration possible, but had no thought of creating it. At the same time she struggled for her children, and tried to make up for the emotional gap left by their father's lengthy absences, of whose cause they were by now aware. For some years she had suffered intermittent attacks of tuberculosis, a disease apparently inherited from her maternal grandfather by way of her mother, both of whom had died of it. Illness and sorrow had gradually induced in her a spirit of intense piety, which found expression in a constant study of the Orthodox holy book, the *Dobrotolyubiye,* the frequent invocation of saints, and a growing fondness for sacred relics and images about the house. There was no resident priest at Voreppe, as there had been in the last family home, in Nice, perhaps because of the children's open distaste there for Father Nikolay Podosenov, with his lank hair, dirty cassock, and revolting table manners, or perhaps simply because, deep in the Isère countryside, there was no Orthodox priest to be found. But you could not be in the house for ten minutes without being aware of the faint odor of sanctity, a whiff of candles and incense, some hint of spirituality in the air.

Stravinsky relished this atmosphere and found it conducive to work, though his own piety was selective and, like his behavior, somewhat irregular. Icons adorned his piano and a crucifix hung round his neck, but he went infrequently to confession and as a matter of habit attended mass only at Christmas, at Easter, and on his birthday. Religious observance was a personal matter. But he talked much about the life of the spirit and read widely in devotional literature. His art, he considered, was a divine grace. "Why do they blame me for my gifts?" he would say. "They should blame God." His lifestyle, on the other hand, was his own concern. Each of these different things belonged in a channel of its own, but at the end of each of them was the single thing that mattered most to him: his music. As for his children, he loved them in his own way, worried about them, and bullied them to lead their lives in a manner that suited his view of things, which was, when all was said and done, an old-fashioned, White Russian, autocratic view. It was a view Katya, in her gentle, undemonstrative way, shared, and on this, as on much else, there was little or no disagreement between them. Only on the one big thing did they part company; and for that there seemed to be no cure.

Stravinsky's divided life was now of thirteen years' standing and it had settled into a routine. When he was composing, he would go home, shut himself in his studio all morning, appear promptly for meals, spend part of the afternoon with his family, then work on until dinnertime. Sometimes the pattern would be broken by visits of one kind or another, and it would vary in intensity. But in its essential, calming regularity it never changed, for the good reason that he needed it so. Work would be interrupted for long conducting tours abroad or necessary trips to the capital, for concerts, recordings, meetings with publishers, or on some less compelling pretext simply to enable him to be with Vera. Then he would become a rich Parisian, live expensively, keep late hours and intellectually or artistically amusing company, and compose only spasmodically. When he toured, Vera would go as his companion; they would travel first class and put up at the best hotels. As a conductor or pianist he could command high fees because his music had made him not liked but notorious, and audiences came to peer at this unexpectedly diminutive, surprisingly normal-looking creator of musical earthquakes. Unfortunately of late a different kind of earthquake had threatened to disrupt these smooth, lucrative progresses. The political mood in Germany, hitherto the most reliable platform for the newest music, had turned against everything that was modern and foreign; economic conditions to the east had become unstable. Even in France and Italy, where politics and art were still officially on good terms, enthusiasm for the new was tempered by anxiety and the fear of risk. Financial insecurity, the terror of the exile and the torment of the artist, once again roamed the countryside like an immigration officer, demanding to see your passport and your work permit.

Stravinsky's own music had never openly involved itself in the worries of its creator's daily life, and certainly never in the politics of the world beyond. Since the explosion of *The Rite of Spring* more than twenty years before, it had cultivated an increasingly detached, impassive tone. Its composer would have agreed with Jacques Maritain that "the tedium of living and willing stops at the door of every studio."[3] In 1916, while the opposing armies were slaughtering tens of thousands of young men on the Somme, Stravinsky had sat in a turret room in a small town on the shores of Lake Geneva and written a song-and-dance piece about farmyard animals. After the war, settled now in France, he perfected a cool, objective, formalist language that seemed studiously to deny any possible emotional engagement or nervous instability. The homosexual Tchaikovsky, while his ill-conceived marriage was disintegrating in 1877, had composed an intense, romantic opera dramatizing the very situation that had led to the disaster. But when

Stravinsky fell passionately in love with Vera Sudeykina in 1921, he celebrated with a mild comedy based on a style parody by Pushkin about the servant problem in early nineteenth-century St. Petersburg. He then followed this with a series of neoclassical instrumental works, an opera-oratorio about Oedipus in which the characters were masked and inert throughout, and a *ballet blanc* for string orchestra on the birth and apotheosis of Apollo. While Communists and Royalists fought pitched battles in the Place de la Concorde in early 1934, Stravinsky was putting the finishing touches on one of his most serene masterpieces, a large-scale dance drama about Persephone, the pomegranate, and the origin of the seasons. If these great works had any single message for the sublunary world, it could only be that disorder—whether political or psychic—must be neutralized through stern formal control and a refusal of facile emotion.

Now the Stravinskys had decided to move to Paris. Their children were grown up, and increasingly frustrated by the boredom and emptiness of genteel rural life. Katya was constantly ill and in need of more sophisticated medical care than could ever be provided by country doctoring. Anna Stravinsky, her mother-in-law, was eighty, and growing frail, though outwardly in good enough health. As for Anna's son, he must have felt some pull toward the focus of things, some desire to be fully in contact with the heart of the country of which he and Katya were now citizens. Paris would not solve the central problem of his existence; it would aggravate it, pulling the two halves uncomfortably close, like opposite magnetic poles forced reluctantly together. It would not help his bookings, either, and it would if anything hinder his composing. Perhaps he was himself simply weary of the interminable travel, the incessant journeys like this nine-hour trip to Grenoble. Perhaps he had made up his mind to challenge the division in his life, to negate it by sheer force of will. Or perhaps, in his inmost heart, he sensed that Paris was no more than a staging post on some longer, as yet unmapped journey.

STRAVINSKY:

THE SECOND EXILE

A GENTLE AND A FREE SPIRIT ▬

IN THE SUMMER OF 1934, Stravinsky celebrated his new nationality by writing his memoirs. Ever since the seed had been sown on a car journey from Biarritz to Paris in 1932, it had been assumed that he would have a collaborator, and probably that the collaborator would be his old friend from the Diaghilev years Walter Nouvel.[1] In fact Nouvel's role in the *Chroniques de ma vie* was never openly acknowledged, and nothing much survives to tell us exactly what it was, apart from a contract awarding him a quarter of the book's proceeds in recognition of his part in "establishing a French text," together with a series of receipts. Remembering Stravinsky's businesslike attitude to collaborators, one can take it that a quarter allocation represented a fairly substantial contribution; but to assert unequivocally that the autobiography was ghost-written by Nouvel[2] is greatly to overstate what we know. When Prokofiev and Pierre Souvtchinsky called on Stravinsky in Voreppe at the end of August, they found him writing both the memoirs and a new piece for two pianos (this was the large-scale work left hanging at the start of 1933 when the *Persephone* commission came along). Nouvel was there too, but working—according to Prokofiev—on a book about Diaghilev.[3] Six months later Katya Stravinsky talks, in a letter to her husband on tour in the U.S.A., about "your finishing your little book by the time you arrive,"[4] and their younger son, Svetik (Soulima),[5] who was often present, remembers the collaboration as something like free dictation, in which Stravinsky would walk up and down in his study reminiscing and developing ideas in Russian which Nouvel would then convert into literate French.[6]

Whoever wrote the actual text, Stravinsky certainly put a lot of time and effort into it. The main evidence for this is not anything in the book itself, but the striking absence of other work from the period when it was being written. Compositionally the seventeen months between finishing *Persephone* in January 1934 and the first movement of the Concerto for Two Solo Pianos in June 1935 were by far his leanest time since the start of his studies with Rimsky-Korsakov more than thirty years before. Of course, there were plenty of distractions, as there always had been in his complicated family and professional life. The summer was disrupted by recordings and illness, and by the impending move from Voreppe, which eventually happened at the end of September. The vast new apartment in the rue du Faubourg Saint-Honoré was a challenge to even the Stravinskys' home-making prowess. And there were the usual autumn concerts. Stravinsky had tinkered with the new concerto in the spring, after the *Persephone* performances, and he pulled it out again, more productively, back in Voreppe in early August. But by December, when he handed the first part of his *Chroniques* to the Paris publisher Denoël and Steele and set off with his duo partner, the violinist Samuel Dushkin, on a recital tour of eastern and southern France, the first movement was still in fragments, and it stayed that way until after his return from the United States the following April. Of any other movement there was still no sign.

The French tour, from Liège to Lyons via Strasbourg, Mulhouse, Toulon, Monte Carlo, and Marseilles, was a natural, if not particularly lucrative, response to the effective closure of Germany to Stravinsky's music.[7] But all his instincts told him that a second American tour was the only serious practical alternative, and he had in fact appointed a New York agent for just that purpose a whole year before, in September 1933. Alexander Merovitch was a maddeningly vague, likable, but self-important entrepreneur, fond of expatiating on the complexities of New York concert life and his own somewhat airy-fairy schemes for introducing great artists like Stravinsky to the American public, but apparently much less interested in fixing firm, precise itineraries within specified budgets. For Stravinsky, nevertheless, he had the inestimable virtue of being Russian, and this seems to have calmed the composer as first September, then October, 1934 passed without clear information about bookings for a tour that was supposed to begin in early January. In the end Merovitch came up with an itinerary a mere three weeks before Stravinsky and Dushkin sailed from Villefranche on the SS *Rex*, on 27 December; but for Igor's optimistic hope (which he confided to Katya) of bringing home a hundred and fifty thousand francs at the end of the three-and-a-half-month trip, the outlook was far from good.[8]

Compared with the reasonably compact visit of a decade earlier, Merovitch had laid on a wasteful and exhausting tour that involved much back-tracking and several empty weeks. His grumbles about the difficulties of New York life had proved only too justified, and he had failed to book Stravinsky a single Philharmonic concert in the city of his greatest 1925 success. On the other hand, he had organized things in such a way that the two musicians had to go twice to Chicago, the second time on a branch from Washington, D.C. (750 miles away), and travel from Indianapolis to

St. Louis (250 miles to the west) via New York (700 miles to the east). From St. Louis they would then journey two thousand miles to San Francisco, and give a recital on the day of their arrival. All these trips, of course, were by rail, with Stravinsky bearing the cost of both his and Dushkin's tickets as well as all their accommodation and Dushkin's fees. Stravinsky's letters home have not surfaced, but there is curiously little echo in either Katya's or Vera's voluminous letters of any complaint on his part about what must have been a gruelling and sometimes futile-seeming sixteen weeks. At the end of it all, Merovitch was firmly engaged to organize the next tour the following season, and would actually have done so had he not suffered a mental breakdown in November, become violent, and had to be confined in an asylum.9

Arriving from the storm-tossed Atlantic in early January 1935, Stravinsky lingered for a week in New York with Dushkin, giving much the same half-theatrical press interviews as ten years before, and taking part in chamber concerts at the League of Composers and the Plaza Hotel, before setting off to Chicago, which was to be their base for concerts both there and in Milwaukee and Minneapolis (a mere 450 miles away) over the next ten days. As on Stravinsky's previous visit, there was a reception and concert at the Chicago Arts Club, followed by a string of symphony concerts with programs carefully selected to massage provincial vanities without discommoding unpracticed ears. Thus an evening of *Pulcinella* (Pergolesi et al.), the Divertimento from *The Fairy's Kiss* (Tchaikovsky), *Petrushka,* and *The Firebird* (folk song) was welcomed by the critic of the *Milwaukee Wisconsin News* as proof of Stravinsky's gifts as a tunesmith (whereas the New York *Town Crier* had deduced from his other work that "like most lesser composers of great talent [Stravinsky] is an inferior melodist").10

Of course, the success of these concerts was gratifying, with packed halls and largely sympathetic reviews which accepted his musical importance without question and praised his conducting for its energy and precision.11 Yet it must have been hard to view with much pleasure the prospect of another three months of this kind of thing. The programs with Dushkin, in Minneapolis, Toledo, and points west, were inevitably unvaried, restricted as they were to Stravinsky's own music for violin and piano.12 Whereas in Paris money was still to some extent in the hands of people with educated and progressive taste, in provincial America much larger sums were dispensed by the wives of bankers and industrialists who were attracted as much by the notoriety of the European artistic lion as by anything particular to do with his work. Then there was the question of language. For while the Russian-American Dushkin spoke native English, Stravinsky could still do no better than half-understand it and reply in French or German.13 Worse still were the interminable and unvarying hotels, where the phone never stopped ringing and people you hardly knew walked into your room at any hour of the day practically without knocking.

One January morning in Chicago, Stravinsky received a letter that was like a shaft of sunlight out of this leaden sky. It was an invitation to stay in Los Angeles, where he had concerts in late February, from someone claiming to be an old friend from St. Petersburg. "Dear Igor," it began, "I had wanted to start this letter 'deeply respected Igor Fyodorovich, you probably don't remember me,' but then it struck me that that was stupid, you might forget the giddiest successes of your premieres, but you would never forget your own youth and all our mutual friends: F. A. Luther, N. Richter, Misha Yelachich, Oreus, Bilibin, Andrey Rimsky-Korsakov, and the rest."[14] It was the first indication Stravinsky had had that the journey west would not inevitably take him beyond contact with a world he knew and understood. Alexis Kall may not have been the most distinguished alumnus of the St. Petersburg Conservatoire and the Rimsky-Korsakov Wednesdays, but he had survived and made an artistic life for himself outside Russia, in which respect he was much more like Stravinsky than any of the "mutual friends." A pianist with academic credentials, and a formidable linguist, Kall had a doctorate from Leipzig but had held a university teaching post in St. Petersburg until driven out by the Revolution. He had then taught for a year in Tokyo before fetching up in Los Angeles in 1919 and starting what he grandly christened the Institute of Musical Art, with himself as director. There he gathered about him a school of adoring and in some cases talented, predominantly female, piano pupils. A large, avuncular, bibulous, cigar-puffing, rather seedy bachelor, Kall was not without some hint of the aging faun in his portly benevolence. But like so many émigré Russians, he had adapted only in part to this profoundly alien environment, and the house to which he was inviting his old friend, in South Gramercy, three or four miles from downtown Los Angeles, was a modest, slightly unkempt, and exceedingly un-American establishment, small and cozy—as Kall euphemistically described it—with a Chekhovian patch of grass where tea could be drunk, and well-to-do Russian neighbors who would happily lend Igor their chauffeur-driven cars, since Kall had no car and did not drive.[15]

Stravinsky's reply was not quite a refusal, but it doubted whether Kall could also find room for Dushkin, whom the composer would not abandon: "He's my great friend," he wrote, "and has agreed to accompany me everywhere, even to cities where we're not both playing."[16] Once Kall (whose "cozy little *domik*" turned out to have nine rooms) had warmly extended his invitation to include the violinist, all difficulties evaporated and Stravinsky could accept without hesitation.[17] It was a decision he never regretted.

When he next wrote to Kall, "dorogoy [dear] Alexey [*sic*] Fyodorovich" had become "milïy [dearest] Woof"—a nickname supposedly due to Kall's way of expressing surprise or mild physical distress. Bumping along in the train from Los Angeles to Denver six weeks later, Stravinsky would write of his

> warm feelings of heartfelt friendship ripened by twelve days of Californian sun. How I can thank you for them I don't know. I only know that it's a long, long time since I've felt so spiritually well and at ease as in your company and thanks to your endless touching attentions. May God give you good health and me once again the pleasure of staying with you.[18]

Kall was gifted with the power of calming waters. There was something reassuring about this "huge, gentle Russian,"[19] with his tactful, convivial manner and spontaneous generosity. Women, including his students, confided in him, often revealing to him their most intimate emotional secrets. Perhaps men like Stravinsky did the same, if not in correspondence, then in person. In any case, he sensed even before their reunion that Kall would be a sympathetic intermediary in those matters of musical planning that were awkward to deal with from a distance; and so, in his very first letter, he asks him to discuss his Los Angeles programs with Otto Klemperer, the resident conductor of the Philharmonic Orchestra, and to find out the rehearsal schedule from him. The fact that, as it gradually transpired, Kall was far from being a reliable organizer was a matter of secondary importance. Although Stravinsky affected to hate inefficiency in his professional agents, what he feared most was their deviousness and hostility (imagined or otherwise) and their insufficient care over his interests, and it was his needs in these respects that he constantly strove to satisfy by delegating business matters to close—often the very closest—friends and relations. So Woof, though in a sense his oldest friend apart possibly from Valechka Nouvel, became the latest in a long line of associates for whom affection meant errands and practical responsibilities, as well as the more usual intimacies and convivialities.

All this was still several weeks in the future. From Toledo the two travelling musicians had steamed back across Ohio to Pittsburgh, then back again to Indianapolis, then turned on their tracks a third time to head for New York, where Stravinsky was to conduct the General Motors Symphony Orchestra on 3 February. This curious event, one of a series sponsored by General Motors in which conductors were specifically not allowed to direct their own music, was thus devoted to Russian music other than Stravinsky (though an excerpt from *Petrushka* and his arrangement of the "Song of the Volga Boatmen" were somehow smuggled into a program of popular Tchaikovsky and Glinka, the first time that he had conducted music by these composers).[20] As a modest revenge, he made a short speech in English at the start of the concert, apparently his first public attempt at the language, in which he expressed his pleasure at conducting a program of works by the great Russian composers, from whom, he added, "I consider myself descending in some ways directly."[21]

For two weeks they had no other concerts. Instead, Stravinsky signed copies of his scores and records at Schirmer's (the New York agent of Schott and Co.) and lunched with René Auberjonois's son Fernand, eating wild rice and talking about bison hunting.[22] The day after his concert, he went to see the visiting Cleveland semistaged production of Shostakovich's *Lady Macbeth of the Mtsensk District* under Artur Rodzinski. He had already heard and liked the young Soviet composer's First Symphony. But the opera, which *Pravda* would soon anathematize as "Muddle Instead of Music,"[23] made a no less baleful impression on the great Russian outcast. "It's nothing but doom and gloom," he told San Francisco's Russian-language newspaper a week or two later. "This kind of tragic realism would be excusable in an old man disillusioned with life, but from a youngster of twenty-eight something more cheerful might have been expected."[24] Moscow could not have put it more succinctly.

Carl Engel, onetime head of the Music Division of the Library of Congress and now president of the Schirmer publishing house, had talked Stravinsky into the book-signing session, then made amends by throwing a big reception in his honor. It was one of those glamorous, faceless world-of-art events where you might meet everybody or nobody. Among the musical grandees invited for their notability rather than any connection with or interest in the guest of honor was the composer-pianist Leopold Godowsky; and with him was his daughter Dagmar, a former silent-film star now grounded by the talkies and, in her late thirties, no longer quite the svelt femme fatale who had played opposite Valentino in *A Sainted Devil*. Dagmar, according to her memoirs, had left at least one husband and a trail of broken hearts and ruined lives from Hollywood to Paris and Berlin. Her conquests had included Chaplin, Hayakawa, Heifetz, Rubinstein. Stravinsky, however, had somehow eluded her. And now here he was in front of her, talking to her father about "everything in the world but music" while she smoldered, attending "not to what he was saying [the conversation was in Russian], but to that voice . . . a very deep basso, and vibrant . . . like far-off thunder."[25] Impulsively, she invited him to tea. "My tea was small," she notes modestly. "I had, besides Stravinsky, Otto Klemperer, Mischa Elman, Artur Schnabel, David and Lisette Sarnoff, Emanuel Feuermann, Artur Rubinstein, and, of course, [her father] Popsy."

Dagmar had a way of collecting celebrities and insinuating herself into their lives. When Stravinsky and Dushkin arrived in Washington in the last week of March, there she was too; and whoever threw a party for the visiting musicians, Dagmar would get herself invited and somehow, every time, she would find herself next to Stravinsky. At the end of their stay, while her father flew back to New York with Engel, Igor asked her to go with him on the train. But then, instead of the hoped-for passionate declarations, he told her only about his tragic life and the illness of his wife and children. In the dining car, a friend of Dagmar's at the next table sensed electricity. "She would indeed have been shocked to discover," Dagmar confesses disarmingly, "that for once all the sparks were emanating from me. It was a most disappointing trip."[26] But that was not the end of Dagmar.

From New York, early in February, Stravinsky and Dushkin had headed west once more. In St. Louis on the 10th they combined forces with the local symphony orchestra in front of an audience of three thousand, interspersing duo items with orchestral works, including the Divertimento, and donating a third of their fee to the orchestra's pension fund. The concert had started twenty minutes late because Stravinsky overslept in his hotel, and perhaps it was remorse at such a rare lapse into the strictly unprofessional that prompted him to add another hundred-dollar donation at the end of the evening. As for Sam, it was his first public outing for a fortnight. But this changed abruptly in San Francisco, where they played in the Opera House and at Stanford University on consecutive days, then at Carmel two days later, before finally reaching Los Angeles on the evening of the 17th.

The next morning, in Kall's house, Stravinsky gave his first West Coast conference for the English-language press, with Sam as interpreter. The modern world, he told California, had had enough of great long works and program music. "Contemporary composers write abstract music, that is pure music, and pack so much into a small work that it is suited to the minds of today."[27] He himself was constantly striving for compression; and he cited the string-orchestral *Apollo* (which was in his Los Angeles programs) as an example of reduced scoring, and the Duo Concertant, which he and Sam would be playing in their recital on the 28th, as a recent case of formal economy, while studiously omitting to mention that his very latest completed score was a narrative work for larger forces and on a bigger scale than anything apart from *Oedipus Rex* that he had written since *The Nightingale*. Did he find any change in America in the ten years since he was last there? Yes, and so much, indeed, that he had no doubt the experience would eventually reflect in his music.

As it turned out, America *would* soon be changing his music, in ways he can hardly have had in mind that February morning in South Gramercy. But by 1935, in any case, no student of Stravinsky's newspaper interviews would have thought of taking anything he told a press conference at face value. On the one hand, he was merely relaying old dogmas to a new audience; on the other, he was reacting to a naïveté he detected in the automatic questions, teasing their assumptions, deliberately outraging their proprieties. For instance, jazz, which in 1925 had been the most interesting modern music around, was now very old hat. But what jazz was he talking about? Was this the considered judgment of someone who had visited cellar clubs in Greenwich Village or spent time on the Chicago Black Belt? Did it embrace popular so-called jazz, the music of Gershwin, for instance, or the recent Irving Berlin, whose *Top Hat* was about to hit the screen more or less as Stravinsky was speaking? Or was it simply that what had seemed a new and offbeat enthusiasm a decade earlier had now come to seem jejune and conventional, and ripe for rejection, like opera in 1913 or folk Russianism in 1920?

No doubt the frisson provoked by such remarks was, and was meant to be, a direct anticipation of the likely effect of Stravinsky's music on what was still a somewhat provincial audience. "In the light of the latest advances in musical theory," wrote one critic of the Stravinsky/Dushkin recital at the Philharmonic on the 28th, "there is nothing particularly disturbing about these pieces of Stravinsky [the *Suite italienne,* the Divertimento, the Duo Concertant, and smaller transcriptions]. But to a public like ours, which has been nourished on the Melba toast and spumoni of the Romantics, the bitter herbs of the Russian were a bit biting."[28] What most excited Los Angeles about Stravinsky was his celebrity, not its cause. "Only the recent visit of Einstein," the *Times* reported a day or two later, "has created such interest,"[29] and the rehearsals with the Philharmonic Orchestra, which Stravinsky conducted in a bizarre but brilliantly effective mixture of French, German, Russian, and English, were almost as widely reported as the concerts.[30] Philharmonic Hall was sold out for both evenings with the LAPO, and the reception was uproarious, with an ovation at the end that lasted a full half-hour. As in Chicago, Stravinsky had been careful not to test the cultural frontiersmen's endurance too far. He offered them only *Petrushka* and *Firebird,* together with the two little orchestral suites and *Apollo;* and even this last work (which as a matter of fact Klemperer had already programmed the previous season) caused puzzlement, needing "study and more frequent hearings to be fully appreciated."[31]

But if Stravinsky's work struck Los Angeles as obscure, he himself was prepared to take an interest, and more than an interest, in L.A.'s own far from obscure artistic produce. Once again, it was Kall who had suggested the contact and undertook to make the arrangements. "It struck me," he had written, "that you should without fail visit a *Movie-studio,* such as Metro-Goldwyn, Paramount, Universal, etc. And you need to be received in suitable fashion. This is necessary not for fun or diversion, but *strictly for business.* Even if they ask you for just one scene (a ballet!), believe me it pays more than conducting symphonies."[32]

Kall duly set up visits to studios, and arranged to introduce the composer to Edward G. Robinson, Chaplin, and others. On the Wednesday after his arrival Stravinsky called on Robinson in his "ersatz Tudor mansion"[33] and added his signature to the collection on the soundboard of the actor's Steinway grand. Later, Robinson threw a reception for Stravinsky, and the two were photographed by and with Kall. There was a guided tour of the MGM studios in Culver City with the company's senior composer, Herbert Stothart; and Stravinsky made a speech in German to the assembled staff of the music department, with Merovitch, who had joined them in Los Angeles a few days earlier, interpreting. He even shook hands with Louis B. Mayer, who remarked tersely, "I am a man like all the others, but I have a lot to do," and passed on. Whether or not this encounter satisfied Kall's concept of "strictly for business," at least it proved, as Stravinsky told a reporter in Rome three months later, "that Mr. Mayer was not a myth."[34]

On the whole, it was a moderately inauspicious start to what was to become an eventful but ultimately barren association with the silver screen. Stravinsky, who adored the movies as a consumer, must quickly have seen that professionally they were not his world—seen it even in the eyes of MGM's salaried musicians, a team of fluent, multitalented hacks some of whom probably felt indifference, if not out-and-out hostility, to this intrusion by a "genius" who patently lacked their applied skills. For his part, he could not suppress a mild disdain for this music factory, not least because its most obvious effect—in the "business" sense—was to do composers like himself out of the royalties they might reasonably expect to earn from the use of their existing music as accompaniment to films. Events were to prove, of course, that if the studios did try to use Stravinsky's existing music for that purpose, they did so at their peril. As for the idea that they might interest themselves in what he now, in the 1930s, was willing to offer them on his own terms, that was an illusion that would take time to fade.

On the face of it, his meeting with Chaplin, probably at the Robinson reception, held out some promise. The idea of a collaboration seems to have occurred to them both, but it was Stravinsky who first sensed its impracticality and, perhaps precisely because he loved and understood Chaplin's genius, saw that their artistic ideas did not coincide. In his autobiography, Chaplin outlines an elaborate scenario which he says he invented on the spur of the moment in response to a suggestion by Stravinsky that they collaborate on a film. The setting is a nightclub, with a Passion play as floor show, while the tables occupied by the customers symbolize various aspects of mankind's disinclination to let God interfere with his pleasures. At the moment of crucifixion, a drunk protests that "they're crucifying Him! And nobody cares!" but is thrown out, as Chaplin explains, "for upsetting the show."[35] This idea must have emerged at least in part from some prior discussion, however cursory, about religion and art; but its moralizing, sententious tone was essentially alien to Stravinsky's cast of thought, and the representation of Christ on stage at once struck him as sacrilegious—as he told Chaplin, to the actor's considerable surprise.

Exactly when this idea was broached is not completely certain. Later in 1935, Chaplin wrote to Stravinsky's Mainz publisher, Willy Strecker, with a proposition which, in principle, the composer thought "not at all utopian, but very, very difficult to realize particularly if I decide not to go to America this year."[36] When he did eventually return to Los Angeles, in March 1937, he and Chaplin met again at dinner at the Robinsons' house, and it may conceivably have been on that occasion that the actor devised his crucifixion scenario. Back in Europe, Stravinsky continued to press Chaplin on the idea of a collaboration, both directly and through Dushkin, who was still in the States. But, as Chaplin admits, "my enthusiasm had cooled off and I became interested in making a film of my own."[37] Quietly the project died.

After almost a fortnight in Los Angeles, and fortified by a party thrown in their honor by another new friend, Mildred Bliss, the music-loving wife of a former U.S. ambassador to Argentina, Robert Woods Bliss, the two musicians waved goodbye to Kall and the West Coast at the start of March, and set off back into the cultural wastelands of the Midwest. Colorado Springs heard them on the 3rd. On the 4th, in the state capital, Stravinsky made a short speech in questionable English to an audience that he characterized as "the artistic elite of Denver";[38] at Fort Worth on the 6th their efforts were greeted with "amiable and bewildered enthusiasm." And so the tour continued its somewhat aimless course. From Texas they picked their way to Boston, where on the 15th Stravinsky at last presented his most recent work, *Persephone,* to an American audience. As usual there was stormy applause and the composer was recalled many times to the rostrum. Still more encouragingly, the East Coast press for once proved equal to this latest manifestation of Stravinsky's protean creative spirit. The *New York Times* critic, Olin Downes, found it "more integrated and consistent in style than perhaps any other score of Stravinsky's late period . . . One of the most distinguished and inspired of Stravinsky's compositions since *Le Sacre du printemps,* and in a large measure a vindication of his later tendencies"— this from the critic who had found *Apollo* "too eclectic and too anachronistic in various places to give the listener any confidence in the composer or the authenticity of his inspiration."[39] Alas, Downes's conversion to the "synthetic" style, as he neatly called it, was no more than temporary. Hearing *Persephone* a second time in New York less than a year later, he decided that its virtues were inadequate "to palliate the aridities and banalities which encumber all too many pages" and spoke of "a lack of invention which not all the technic and style in the world can conceal."[40]

From Boston to Washington, they yet again passed through New York, spending almost a week without giving a single concert.[41] On the other hand, their two Washington recitals (on 24 March and 9 April) were split by a long excursion to Chicago, where they were forced to cancel at the last minute because Stravinsky was laid low by a heavy cold.[42] Thus the rambling tour wound slowly to its close. Yet he accepted it all without much complaint. Sitting in the Lowell Hotel in New York on the way back to Washington at the start of April, he composed a long letter to Ernest Ansermet that reserves most of its bile for an extended denunciation of Shostakovich's opera, but adds that "luckily that isn't all there is in the United States, which has made a very good impression on me this time."[43] One inevitably wonders what was the basis of that impression. He had been away longer than in 1925, had travelled enormously farther, and had made less money. He had, it was true, had Dushkin's company throughout, and there had been the heartwarming interlude with Kall, something quite outside his experience of ten years ago, when he had seen hardly anything but hotel rooms and strangers on trains. On the whole, his music had been well played. With the possible exception of St. Louis, he had worked only with the best American orchestras: Chicago, Los Angeles, Boston. Yet he cannot have been satisfied with the spread of his music across these vast distances. His repertory had been dominated by the early ballets, eked out by "easy" later works like *Pulcinella, The Fairy's Kiss,* and the little suites, while in New York he had performed not a single complete work of his own. It seems impossible that his Hollywood contacts can yet have figured significantly on his mental balance sheet.

Meanwhile, the news from home was confusing, disturbing, and worse. As Vera put it in her last letter before Igor boarded the *Île de France* for Le Havre on 13 April: "Surprises await you."[44]

THE POET OF MONTPARNASSE

Two women wept for Igor in his absence. While the long separation was bad for Vera Sudeykina, since she was unused to it, in most ways it was worse for Katya. She was Igor's wife, but knew that she did not possess him as a wife should, and would not fully possess him even when he came home. Her health was poor. It was true that she had her family as a consolation and that they now lived in a big, luxurious apartment close to the center of things, instead of lost and forgotten deep in the country, while Vera had a lonely domestic life in a small Passy flat that was not even properly heated all the time, since money was short and she was economizing. But Katya had also profound humiliations to endure on Vera's account. Not only did Igor make his mistress an allowance, but he expected Katya to hand the money over in person, which she dutifully did, meeting Vera at the bank and talking to her for a while in the car afterwards. Any resentment or bitterness she may have felt at this atrocious act of self-immolation she typically sublimated by telling Vera that "she wanted to kiss me and . . . that she was thinking of me." The good-hearted Vera was very touched, but seems not to have suffered any more troublesome perturbations.[1]

In any case she was never entirely lonely. In fact she had so many visitors that she would often complain that her time was not her own.[2] For Katya, on the other hand, family life was sometimes as much a trial as a consolation. Her children were now grown up—Milène, the youngest, had her twenty-first birthday in January 1935—but their lives were unsettled and their direction unsure. Milène was studying to be a singer, and lived for her weekly lessons with Monsieur Alberti, perhaps because he believed in her and wanted her to audition for musicals, while Katya only worried about the disappointment that might thereby be in store.[3] Milène's older sister, Mika, had a flair for design and made marble papers for bookbinding while taking life classes and classes in fashion drawing; but she was often unwell, and when she was well she was bored. Though not conventionally pretty, she had a Slavic handsomeness, with broad cheekbones and a narrowing, defiant gaze; and she had her suitors (including, for a while, the younger brother of Serge Lifar).⁴ But she seemed at times to be in search of some-thing "higher," something that Katya once described tactfully to Igor as "a suitable milieu."⁵ One day, when their aunt Irina Terapiano invited the two sisters to a meeting of one of the Russian literary societies and introduced them to a circle of young Russian writers and poets, Mika was in seventh heaven, as if she had suddenly found something she had been looking for for a long time.⁶

The girls' brothers knew better what they wanted from life, but they were feeling their way quite unsteadily toward it. Theodore was hard at work on a series of portraits, including one of Pierre Souvtchinsky, another of a cer-tain Mademoiselle Guerzoni, and a third—to his grandmother's dismay—of a model who came several times to pose nude for him at the Faubourg. It was the kind of work in the midst of which, for various reasons, he could begin to forget that the girl he loved had coolly announced her engagement to another man.⁷ Theodore was the healthy one of the four, for all his peri-tonitis the previous summer. His younger brother, Soulima, had been diag-nosed as tubercular a year earlier after collapsing from exhaustion and cancelling recitals in Switzerland, and had spent the first three months of 1934 in the sanatorium of Sancellemoz, at Plateau d'Assy in Haute-Savoie.⁸ By the summer he had recovered, and by September he was back on the concert platform. That month, while Katya assembled packing cases at Voreppe, Igor had taken his pianist son to Venice, where they had per-formed the Capriccio together in a Biennale concert and met Alban Berg, whose *Der Wein* was having its Italian premiere in the same program, con-ducted by Hermann Scherchen.⁹

Soulima, though, needed not so much to capitalize on his father's emi-nence as to break free of it, and this he still had not managed. It happened that he was booked the very next month to play the Concerto for Piano and Wind Instruments under Scherchen at the so-called Musico-Dramatic Work Days in Strasbourg. Two or three days before the concert on the 24th of October, Igor was surprised by a letter from Soulima complaining bitterly about Scherchen's conducting: "Scherchen is terrible," the young man wrote, "and everything he does is disgusting."¹⁰ But while the musician in Igor instinctively defended Scherchen, unable to believe that he could be as bad as Soulima claimed, his loyalties would have been more severely tested had he known Scherchen's opinion of his work and Soulima's playing of it. The concerto, the conductor told his wife, "remains what it always was: an inadequate piece . . . [which] doesn't sound, and Igor's son plays it boringly—he strikes one as the anxious child of a bad, hard-hearted father . . . a poor, empty young man, who never once braves the revolt he craves."¹¹ Obviously there had been some kind of incident at rehearsal. Scherchen had a notoriously evil temper, and he would have been quite capable of turning on Soulima and dressing him down on some pretext or other in front of the whole orchestra. So when he wrote again after the performance praising both music and pianist, Stravinsky filed the correspondence in an envelope marked "H. Scherchen, his hypocrisy, my answer, and the performance of my concerto by Nini [Soulima] under Scherchen's direction."[12] Yet Scherchen's change of heart was genuine, however much fueled by vanity. "The concert was magnificent," he confided to his wife, "[but] my big success is the son, whom I've released into himself from the ground up, so that his playing is unrecognizable as that of the same person."[13]

Now, with Igor off in America, Soulima was having his own private European tour. A January recital in Amsterdam only seemed to confirm his dependence on his father's prestige. The audience was poor and the response cold. But once he got away from the standard circuit, to the Yugoslav cities of Belgrade, Novi Sad, and Zagreb, and as far afield as the Bulgarian capital, Sofia, he found himself basking in praise and admiration intended purely for him. It helped that he was surrounded in Belgrade by Yelachich cousins: Zhenya and Gavriyil (the two youngest Pavlovka brothers) lived in the Serb capital, and their cousin Alexey—the cause of so much trouble at Pechisky long ago—came up specially from Skopje.[14] So warm was the atmosphere, in fact, that Soulima fell in love with a Serbian girl and could barely be enticed back to Paris in time for his debut recital in the Salle Gaveau at the end of March 1935.

Igor was kept abreast of all these events by Katya's letters. She wrote twice a week: newsy, homely missives that might strike a casual reader as otiose and wearisome, but that met a specific need, even demand, of her autocratic husband. That he himself replied rather less often (and was chided for it) is not particularly significant. He wrote as seldom to Vera—to judge by her no less frequent grumbles. Busy and constantly on the move, distracted by social pressures, not to mention—as Vera only half-jokingly suggested[15]—the odd flirtation, he had neither time nor inclination to correspond at length and in duplicate across thousands of miles of land and ocean. Katya and Vera could (and did) share such communications as they received. He, nevertheless, expected to be kept informed about his wife's and children's doings. It was all part of his need to feel that his family hearth was intact and secure: the profound desire of the exile for stability and rootedness, the artist's need to preserve a safe haven for his work, but not least his overpowering urge, as the son of his father, to know and to regulate.

Soon after he set sail for New York, there was a significant development in the business, and hence domestic, lives of his Belyankin in-laws. After years of litigation, they were at last to receive some part of the restitution on their Ustilug estate, and Grigory went straight to Warsaw in January to settle the matter. He came back with two hundred thousand francs from his wife's land, twenty thousand for the Stravinskys from the Rovno distillery, a new suit and overcoat for himself, and his long beard freshly trimmed. This was good but not overwhelming news for the Belyankins' numerous creditors, some of whom would get paid while others would be kept firmly in the dark about the whole outcome. Some of the money was going to prop up Grisha's latest Parisian catering venture, an ur-Russian establishment called the Café de la Paix, but there was enough left over to pay for a larger apartment in their block just behind the Théâtre des Champs-Élysées, which was big enough to serve their domestic needs as well as for Ira to run her dressmaking business in reasonable comfort.[16] Vera, who to her occasional irritation had become a universal aunt to the distressed Russian gentry of Paris, helped them move in at the beginning of February, enduring their squabbling and shouting partly for Ira's sake, partly for Igor's, partly out of a congenital inability to refuse help to anyone, friend or foe.[17]

Everyone went to Vera, for advice or to cry on her shoulder, or to grumble about the cold or about wives or husbands. She specialized in neurotic women friends with suicidal tendencies. Georgette (the princesse Mestchersky) was deserted by her husband, became hysterical, and had to be given valerian drops. But when Vera upbraided her husband on the phone, he simply remarked, "You are the only woman who knows how to talk to me." Vera's niece Kirsta would get drunk at parties and pester the men, regardless of their age or sexual persuasion. Then there was Ansermet's mistress Elena Hurtado, a singer who had been taking lessons from Milène's teacher, Alberti. One night at dinner at Vera's she got drunk and lay on the sofa laughing hysterically, to the intense disapproval of Valechka Nouvel, a fastidious homosexual who loathed ostentatious displays of femininity. But Hurtado's nervousness was understandable. A few days earlier, hearing that the singer was visiting her husband, Marguérite Ansermet had tried to gas herself and been taken to a hospital in Geneva screaming, "Ernest, please come, I adore you!" The saintly Katya declared herself baffled at Hurtado's presence in Geneva at such a moment. But to the more worldly Vera, all was clear.[18]

Vera was also cast in the role of adviser to the Stravinsky children, who occasionally found their mother's precepts restrictive, however lovingly expressed. The boys would go and play bridge at Vera's rue du Ranelagh flat; or Mika would come with Milène, or alone. Though she said nothing to Igor, Vera may have been the first person Mika told that she had fallen in love with a Russian poet she had met at the club with Aunt Irina. Under any circumstances, such a development might have perturbed her possessive and watchful father. But it was complicated by the fact that the poet in question, Yury Mandelstam, was a Jew. Katya had quickly grasped the situation.

A week or so after the meeting at the Russian society, the Terapianos, Mandelstam, and another young writer spent an evening at the Faubourg. Katya was down with flu and kept to her bed, but she heard all about it afterwards from the other children. One of the writers was Jewish, she informed Igor in Los Angeles, "and, they say, a very sympathetic and good person, and Irina said that at heart he's really a Christian."[19] A week later, Mika herself wrote:

> Don't suppose that I'm immediately going to tell you I'm in love, though it seems to me I'm not far off that condition. But the main change is that I've acquired my own circle of friends, two of whom I get on with particularly well . . . I've suddenly found myself in a world that's utterly new to me—a literary world mostly of young writers, poets and critics. The young ones are very fresh in spirit, not backward-looking but, on the contrary, very advanced. At first I was afraid of feeling rather *dépaysée* in this environment, but to my surprise I met such sympathetic people that I immediately felt at home with them . . . And I think that these two whom I already know better are trying very hard to get to know *me* better and see me more often.
>
> I don't know what you'll think of all this, but you can't imagine how happy it makes me. I feel as if I were entering a new phase of my life. . . .[20]

What Stravinsky thought when he read Mika's letter we do not know. But his subsequent behavior sheds revealing light on the relationship between what might be termed "automatic" White Russian anti-Semitism and the flesh-and-blood reality of love and friendship. Katya was absolutely clear that what counted was personal goodness and proper spiritual direction, both of which she found in Yury from the moment she herself first met him in May. But this emphatically did not mean that race ceased to be an issue, since the bedrock of Russian attitudes remained the instinctive feeling that Jewishness in some way precluded those virtues, so that for the Jew an exceptional moral and spiritual discipline was called for. Yury, she found,

> is as I imagined really a hundred percent Jewish in face, expression, and gesture . . . I had at once sensed in him not just a good but an utterly good person, to whom we could without fear and with complete confidence entrust our Mikushka. And what I felt before I set eyes on him has been strengthened and confirmed now that I've got to know him. It's obvious that he's intelligent and kind and loves Mika in a good way, with true feeling, and Mikusha says that he's tremendously fond of his par-

ents, which also speaks well for him. In general, their relationship and the way they behave toward each other made the very best impression on me.[21]

Igor had by that time already met Yury and reacted in the same way. "I was glad to hear," Katya had written, "that Y[ury] Vl[adimirovich] made rather a good impression on you. That's already a good start. And as for the sense of his race, I think that will all disappear of its own accord and in any case will feel different when you get used to the man himself and get to know his good qualities, of which it seems to me he has a lot."[22] Mika, she now added, "is so infinitely grateful to you for your attitude and that you are so nice to her Yury."[23] Not all their relations were able to grasp the distinction. Ira Belline would make a visible effort to be polite, but avoided conversation, while Katya's Nosenko cousin Vera refused to have anything to do with him and told Katya frankly that she hoped it would all fall through. "I can't be angry with her, though," Katya said, "and only feel sorry for her that she harbors such opinions, attitudes and feelings toward Jews."[24]

Yury Mandelstam was not just a personable and serious-minded young man, however, but already, at the age of twenty-six, a published poet with two collections to his name, and a third about to appear when he met Mika. He was also a critic and essayist whose work was becoming known in émigré circles, and who had published in French-language journals such as the *Revue de France*. Stravinsky's attitude to the emigration had long been equivocal. He was on good enough terms with Irina Terapiano and her husband, Yury, himself a poet of some note, with Pierre Souvtchinsky and others, but he kept his distance from Russian artistic cliques like the Zelyonaya Lampa and Krug, or the émigré cafés in Montparnasse, which were a focus of Mandelstam's existence. But if he knew Mandelstam's work (and we can certainly assume that he made sure he got to know it), he must have recognized some kinship of view with his own music of the twenties and thirties. Mika's new friends all ran with the so-called Perekryostok (Crossroads) group of neoclassicists, for whom aesthetic values such as clarity and simplicity were paramount, and whose great hero was Pushkin. The composer of *Mavra* and the Octet could scarcely have hoped for an artistically more congenial son-in-law.[25]

But there was another possible objection to Mika's marriage, one which had nothing to do with Mandelstam and everything to do with her. Like her mother and to a lesser extent her younger brother, Mika was tubercular, and the disease had chosen that winter of 1935 to break out with renewed force. Perhaps Paris was partly to blame. It was their first winter in the north since 1920, and moreover there was a flu epidemic raging, to which first Theodore, then Katya succumbed, while Mika and Soulima both nursed disagreeable coughs. Katya's letters of these January and February weeks begin to recall Igor's childhood letters to his parents, with their relentless chronicling of every ailment, every symptom, every medication. But beneath the stupefying clinical data, sinister undercurrents flow. Katya's flu lingered and lingered, and as February turned to March she took to her bed once again with severe tracheitis and an inflammation of the pleura brought on by coughing. For a time she tried to conceal the true situation from her husband; but by mid-March it was clear that her tuberculosis had been reactivated and, worse still, that Mika was showing an alarming tendency in the same direction. On the 21st Katya took the train to Le Fayet, under the northwestern slope of Mont Blanc, and for the first but by no means last time drove by taxi up the winding road to Plateau d'Assy and the sanatorium of Sancellemoz, where Soulima had already spent the early part of the previous year. Her sister, Lyudmila Belyankin, accompanied her.

It was a disagreeable reminder of their time at Leysin in 1914, and Katya could not forget that the immediate cause of that earlier relapse had been the birth of Milène. If Mika were now to get married and become pregnant, would she not run at least as great a risk? Yet to marry and not attempt to have children would be a grotesque aberration for the Orthodox Stravinskys, and especially so for Katya, whose devoutness and piety had intensified in recent years. On the other hand it was plain that any significant delay to the wedding would equally distress Mika and just as surely aggravate her illness. That August she wrote to her father from Sancellemoz, where she in her turn had been sent two months before by the Paris doctors to join her mother. She and Yury were bubbling over with their plans for his baptism in the coming weeks, their wedding in October, and their subsequent life together in a Paris flat living on his somewhat uncertain income from writing and editing.

> Dear, darling Papochka! You'll understand our impatience. . . . I can't begin to describe to you what's going on in our hearts. But I confess that it will be very sad and difficult if we have to wait till next year, since November is the Christmas fast and during the fast you can't marry. Help us. Everything hangs on your consent; please talk it over with Yury. As for me, I've got another three boring weeks without him, and the month I spent with him here was so wonderful and good![26]

They did not wait. On the day Katya and Mika returned from Sancellemoz, 12 September 1935, Yury was baptized into the Russian Orthodox Church, and six weeks later the couple were married in the little upstairs Russian church in the rue d'Odessa, Montparnasse.[27]

. . .

STRAVINSKY HAD ARRIVED from New York at Le Havre on the 19th of April and been met by Vera with the latest domestic news. Of Katya's move to Sancellemoz he already knew from his sister-in-law. But anything specific about Yury Mandelstam had been kept from him, and he had not been told that his eldest son was also courting: the Mademoiselle Guerzoni he had been painting, a twenty-year-old Genevoise called Denise, herself the daughter of a Swiss painter by the name of Stéfanie Guerzoni. From Paris Igor went straight to Sancellemoz for a long talk with Katya about their children. On such occasions, her concern was always to calm him so that his work would not be disturbed by family anxieties. But he could not be detached about the present circumstances. Neither he nor Katya knew Denise, and Igor had never been instinctively relaxed about their sons' elective affinities. As for Mandelstam, whom equally neither of them had yet met, the composer would have been less than human if he had not been perturbed at the apparent suddenness of Mika's choice. Leaving aside his own feelings, he knew that his mother would have to be told and could not be expected to approve. Returning to Paris, he made up his mind to try and talk Mika out of Yury. There was a tense interview in his study at the Faubourg. But Mika was made of the same stuff as her father, and she returned his recriminations in kind. "Don't bully me!" she shouted, so loudly that her voice could be clearly heard in the hallway outside. "What about you and Vera?" That, in Stravinsky's opinion, was quite a different matter. But he could not make headway with his elder daughter from so morally weak a position. She would not listen to him, would not have her feelings overruled in this way, and she gradually wore him down.[28] Perhaps he was even half-pleased to be defeated for once. When he met Yury a day or two later he liked him. And Denise, too, charmed both him and Katya. "How good she is," Katya exclaimed, "so pure and simple in every way."[29] Soon Mika was telling her mother that, despite being horribly busy, Igor was "in a good mood and being very nice," while Lyudmila Belyankin and Irina Terapiano both noticed that he was "somehow completely changed, so even-tempered, placid and kind." They variously put this down to an improved liver and to a healthier spirit; but it may just have been a sense of relief.[30]

Four weeks before his return, the first volume of *Chroniques de ma vie* had come out in Paris, and he was now hard at work with Valechka on the second. Volume 1, which the London publisher Victor Gollancz had told Stravinsky was too serious and too short for British tastes, took the reader to 1920 and the move from Morges to Carantec.[31] Volume 2, up to *Persephone*, would be swiftly completed and in the shops in time for Christmas 1935.

Many Parisians who hurried out to buy the first installment that March will have hoped for a colorful account of life in prerevolutionary Russia, or sensational revelations about Diaghilev and his ballet company, or fresh anecdotes about Debussy or Ravel; others may have looked for some insight into the personal, emotional—perhaps even sexual—life of the great composer; yet others, for some clear explanation of his artistic goals and baffling changes of style. Simpler souls merely hoped to learn what manner of man was the creator of *The Rite of Spring.* Would he explode off the page like his music? Or would he remain an enigma, like Petrushka, thumbing his nose at his readers before vanishing in a puff of ambiguous harmony?

Would a new, unexpected, more vivid Stravinsky emerge? That least of all. "As I read these *Chroniques,*" Boris de Schloezer reported,

> I seemed to be hearing one of his latest works: clean, precise, dry, and sharp-edged; here and there a little, very little, emotion expressed in carefully chosen, measured terms. In the course of this half-century covered by the two volumes of the *Chroniques,* there has been the war, the Russian Revolution, communism; our whole existence, our whole intellectual and moral life has been turned upside down; of these events, one catches no echo in the book, or rather, the author invokes them only incidentally insofar as they have affected his changes of abode or the rhythm of his work.[32]

Most, though not all, reviewers were disconcerted by the book's cool, almost bureaucratic account of a life which, by any normal standards, had been strikingly eventful and diverse. For the philosopher Gabriel Marcel, there did not exist "a more desiccated book than this.

> When the author speaks to us about emotion, about the distress he felt in this or that situation, for example on the death of his father, we take his word for it. But nothing of such emotions has passed into this chronicle, in which one will find only factual information together with a few instructive professions of faith.[33]

Marcel speculates that Stravinsky is practically incapable of communicating with his own inner self; and he cites the composer's remark (about *The Rite of Spring*) that he feels "absolutely unable, after twenty years, to recall the feelings which animated me when I wrote that score."[34]

> It is clear to me [Marcel goes on], that Stravinsky tends to set up as a general rule a deficiency that is personal to him: the absence of affective

memory, that affective memory which not only appears in Tolstoy or Proust, but which, I am personally convinced, is a principle of the majority of authentic musical masterpieces.

So for the lay musician-philosopher, as for the professional critic de Schloezer, the book is a direct extension of the music. But for Marcel it merely confirms in words what he has already suspected from the notes: that Stravinsky is artistically defective, inauthentic, and—not to mince words—bankrupt.

Had Marcel been more sympathetically disposed to Stravinsky's music, he might have made more critically constructive use of a shrewd initial observation. A casual reader of the *Chroniques* could well simply have assumed that their chilly uncommunicativeness was the natural tone of the musician ill at ease with having, for once, to express himself in words, even if he might also have noted with a certain disquiet that, in what was to become the most notorious passage in the book, Stravinsky insists that music itself is "by its very nature, essentially powerless to *express* anything at all, whether a feeling, an attitude of mind, a psychological mood, a phenomenon of nature, etc. . . ."[35] After all, if Stravinsky preferred to keep his feelings (and by extension his more intimate thoughts) to himself, did that necessarily mean he was a bad composer?

But Marcel's point about affective memory is much more suggestive in relation to the music than he seems to have realized. When we listen to a classical symphony, memory plays much the same essential role in our understanding of the discourse as it does when we read a novel by Jane Austen or a poem by Keats. But with Stravinsky, even when he adopts so-called classical forms, one often feels that something different is taking place in relation to the passage of events. Although this is hard to describe precisely, it sometimes does seem as if the sounds and ideas are isolated incidents without a past or a future in the usual narrative sense but with an exceptionally intensified present. They are like greatly expanded instants, looked at, perhaps, in a succession of different ways, like a series of photographs of one object in changing lights, but seldom with that sense of moving toward a dimly perceived conclusion that one gets with, say, a motion picture or a story. Memory, as a tool for understanding the past and the present or predicting the future, seems to play a much reduced role. Sequence becomes more arbitrary, less rational or logical. While the music explodes like an expanding universe, time stands still.

Stravinsky himself was to take up "time" and examine it more systematically, under the influence (especially) of contemporary French thinking, in his Harvard lectures four years later. Since then the question of time in his music has been widely and earnestly discussed, and books about musical time have ignored him at their peril. If Stravinsky's music, as is often said, created a new sensibility, then time—past, present, and future—was the main medium through which it did so.

However, there is little of any of this in *Chroniques*, beyond a few hints, and a certain psychological and emotional detachment for which one of the leading French philosophers of the day hit on an explanation that happened to be provocative. In point of fact, the things supposedly remembered in the autobiography are often either commonplace or emblematic, and there is hardly any affectionate penetration into the remembered past, not because Stravinsky was incapable of such a thing, but because he had neither the time nor the inclination to get so involved in the process of writing. Similarly, the artistic revelations and descriptions of method in the book are disappointing and on the whole evasive, simply because he did not care to discuss the creative process with strangers or even, by this time, with close acquaintances. The portraits of friends and collaborators are thin and for the most part ritualistic. Nearly everybody comes well out of the book, while those like Arthur Lourié who, for personal or artistic reasons, happened to be out of favor in 1935, are mentioned either not at all or only in passing. There is an obvious reason for this. Stravinsky was a hardworking artist in a swiftly contracting market, and he could not afford to be on bad terms with those whose goodwill he needed. The most rounded portrait is of Diaghilev, who was dead; the most disparaging is of Nijinsky (as choreographer), who was safely out of circulation in a Swiss mental hospital.[36] Early collaborators like Benois and Roerich found to their surprise that their part in the creative process had been conveniently forgotten or trivialized. Benois, for instance, is mentioned only as the designer of *Petrushka* and *The Nightingale*, never as (in any sense) their co-scenarist, while Ramuz and Cocteau get better recognition presumably because their contributions had been textual, published, and therefore beyond denial. Meanwhile, influential conductors like Koussevitzky and Monteux are praised, blandly or otherwise, despite past bloodlettings. Koussevitzky must have been quite relieved to find himself exonerated for the fiasco of the *Symphonies of Wind Instruments*: victim, like the work itself, "of circumstances in which no conductor in the world could have made good."[37]

At the time, naturally enough, these and other eccentricities were noticed for the most part only by their victims or beneficiaries, and nobody seems to have minded, either, that *Chroniques* was so unforthcoming about its author's family background or his personal and domestic life. After all, he had for some time been playing down the Russian origins of his work, and repositioning himself as a cosmopolitan modern artist with the world as his oyster. These days, if anything, he wrote as a Frenchman. And it was a picture happily accepted by his readers in France and elsewhere, if only because they had got used to it, could be at ease with it, and—to be blunt— knew no better. In the words of Florent Schmitt, Stravinsky's oldest French friend but one who rated no more (if no less) than a single mention in the book:

> Our catastrophically disordered times put nothing in its proper place. So thanks be to the incomparable musician of *Petrushka,* the *Rite, Nightingale,* and *Les Noces,* for coming forward in person, with all the authority bestowed by his work, to tell us in firm and measured tone the history of that work, constructed from day to day with the patience of genius and in the shadow of the varying fortunes that all life incurs, with the mystery inherent in all creation, but with the simplicity of the greatest beings confronted with that mystery which inheres in all things, which is dominant in art, and which is perhaps its most powerful lever, but not its explanation.[38]

Such lofty platitudes may not have been Stravinsky's style, but they suited his book. They implicitly backed up his warning that the reader should not "seek in these pages for any aesthetic doctrine, a philosophy of art, or even a romantic description of the pangs experienced by the musician in giving birth to his creations, or of his rapture when the Muse brings him inspiration."[39] *Chroniques* is in many ways an opinionated book: it holds forth about conductors, about the gramophone, Bayreuth, expression, interpretation, choreography, Tchaikovsky, Beethoven, English musicians, and other matters. But it offers no system and no thesis, beyond that of the artist as arbiter of his own work, and here it is as coherent, as pitiless, and as movingly direct as any of Stravinsky's musical works. "At the beginning of my career as a composer," it concludes,

> I was a good deal spoiled by the public. Even such things as were at first received with hostility were soon afterwards acclaimed. But I have a very distinct feeling that in the course of the last fifteen years my written work has estranged me from the great mass of my listeners. They expected something different from me. Liking the music of *L'Oiseau de Feu, Petroushka, Sacre,* and *Les Noces,* and being accustomed to the language of those works, they are astonished to hear me speaking in another idiom. They cannot and will not follow me in the progress of my musical thought. What moves and delights me leaves them indifferent, and what still continues to interest them holds no further attraction for me. . . .
> Their attitude certainly cannot make me deviate from my path. I shall

assuredly not sacrifice my predilections and my aspirations to the demands of those who, in their blindness, do not realize that they are simply asking me to go backwards. . . .[40]

Only then, in his very final paragraph, does Stravinsky perhaps confirm Marcel's intuition about his supposed lack of "affective memory."

I live neither in the past nor in the future. I am in the present. I cannot know what tomorrow will bring forth. I can only know what the truth is for me today. That is what I am called upon to serve, and I serve it in all lucidity.[41]

Whatever this may tell us about the composer's aesthetics, it must rank as one of the most compelling assertions of artistic conscience ever made. However much of the rest of the book Valechka wrote, these final pages were surely the work of the composer himself, pen in hand.

A FORTNIGHT after docking at Le Havre in April 1935, Stravinsky reopened his sketchbook for the two-piano work he had started at Voreppe two and a half years before. There were several substantial fragments of an allegro movement, but little evidence of structure or continuity, and even now he could not give the music his full attention. Not only was his entire family, it seemed, either sick or lovesick, but he had somehow managed to punctuate the month of May with a trip to Copenhagen and a pair of concerts in Bologna and Rome. Not until June, after a brief visit to Katya at Sancelle-moz, could he properly clear his desk and start turning the jigsaw puzzle into a piece of music,

More than twenty years had passed since he had told Romain Rolland, at Vevey, that he disliked Beethoven, and thirteen since he had rebuffed Proust on the same topic. These days he sided firmly with the angels against "the stupidity and drivel of fools who think it up to date to giggle as they amuse themselves by running [Beethoven] down."[1] Of course, the Beethoven he had himself formerly denounced had been less a composer than an idea: at first, a symbol of the German overlord, then later a creature of the Parisian art-loving intelligentsia. And to be fair, Stravinsky was still, in 1935, at war with this tendency of intellectuals to harness the great symphonist to this or that philosophical, social, or political cause. For him, what mattered about Beethoven was the sheer quality of his musical material and the single-minded force with which he molded every ingredient into monumental structures where the purely ornamental played little or no part. This was a strictly creative obsession of Stravinsky's. Beethoven's was, in general terms, the kind of music he now wanted to write himself. So Beethoven piano sonatas, borrowed from Soulima's collection, rang out through the Faubourg apartment, and when pianists like the young American Beveridge Webster came, they would have to play them too.[2] A copy of the great man's death mask was ordered from Mainz, and the *Grosse Fuge* spun endlessly on the gramophone.[3] To combat the difficulty he had had at Voreppe testing the music for two pianos on one, he acquired a Pleyel double piano, like the ones used for *Les Noces* in 1923, and each day he and Soulima would sit facing each other at this instrument and try out what he had written.[4]

The curious thing is that the brilliant, pulsating sonata movement that emerged from the jigsaw puzzle those few June days has only the most generalized flavor of Beethoven or any other classical composer. Stravinsky later claimed to have been studying Brahms as well.[5] But here again there was no question of invoking a Brahmsian style as such. What took his eye was Brahms's way of constructing certain types of music, especially keyboard variations like the solo-piano Handel set (op. 24) or the duo version of the so-called Haydn Variations (op. 56b), which he might equally have used as a model for two-piano writing. Brahms's variations are severely formulaic and, even at their most complex, still follow the classical idea of a simple repeated pattern with enrichments of texture and harmony. Stravinsky liked this repetitive patterning. One day when Webster was playing Beethoven's op. 110 piano sonata, Valechka started grumbling about its incessant A-flats. But for Igor that was what was so marvelous, the fact that Beethoven wasn't afraid to go on and on with the same chord. He was fascinated, too, by the intricate trelliswork of shorter and shorter subdivisions in variation movements like the Arietta finale of op. 111, where the embroidery of very simple ideas generates strange, sometimes conflicting inner rhythms.[6]

The Concerto for Two Solo Pianos, as the new piece was called, explores these devices in a completely individual way, and with no trace of pastiche and certainly no musical borrowing. Discreetly, it initiates a new phase in Stravinsky's work, in which questions of style are more and more subordinated to the overriding force of the musical idea, and any "classicism" in the writing is confined to general concepts of form, the rigorous treatment of thematic material, and an overall severity of manner. It was all a matter of discourse, as the composer tried—with somewhat limited success—to explain to the audience at the first performance a few months later. In a concerto with two equal soloists and no accompaniment, the natural medium for the debate or contest implied by the title was counterpoint—by which he simply meant the close interweaving of themes, without any of the empty pyrotechnics of the typical romantic concerto. Of course, that might mean "no contest," since counterpoint is an integrative, not confrontational, procedure—which is why fugue, the ultimate expression of contrapuntal thinking, is so rarely found in classical or romantic concertos.[7] But the real point was that Stravinsky's title was simply a convenience, adopted because of a certain "public" quality in the music's tone that ruled out the other obvious title, "Sonata." The counterpoint, on the other hand, was an essential part of the conception.[8]

After completing the first movement in June, he worked for a full month on the more relaxed and decorative Notturno second movement, then again put the score aside in order to finish off the second volume of *Chroniques*. Only at the start of August did he get down to the most challenging part of the concerto, a set of variations culminating in a full-blown fugue like the ones at the end of Beethoven's op. 110 and Brahms's Handel variations. But whether because writing a fugue for two pianos presented special difficulties or because he was undecided about the shape of the ending, or even possibly because he had not planned a separate variation movement at all, he wrote the fugue first, then the slow Preludio which introduces it, and finally the four preceding variations. He may simply have meant to insert a variation episode between the fugue and its inversion, like the Arioso episode in op. 110, then found that the break in mood was too abrupt—Beethoven's fugue is broad and reflective, but Stravinsky's is thrusting and, by nature, unstoppable. At all events, in attaching his variations to the front of the prelude and fugue, he "forgot," creatively speaking, to present the theme, which crystalizes gradually as the variations gather pace and only emerges decisively as a theme in the fugue itself. There is something faintly artificial about this procedure, as if a series of notes were being worked into preexisting music. In places it even suggests Schoenberg and his linear patterns. Nevertheless, the effect of the theme at the start of the fugue is so powerful that one immediately understands what Stravinsky meant when he told Soulima that "it's much better to wait for the theme."9

All this time, Katya was confined to Sancellemoz, and when Igor visited her for his birthday on the 18th of June, Mika went with him and was herself promptly admitted as a patient. Within days, her tuberculosis, too, had been confirmed. So there they were, mother and daughter, caught in that strange upper world so hauntingly described by Thomas Mann in *The Magic Mountain*. The huge modern hospital occupied its own slope looking away from the plateau toward the low, wooded mountain known as the Prarion and, beyond, the massif of Mont Blanc. From that side it was like Mann's Sanatorium Berghof, "with so many balconies that from a distance it looked porous, like a sponge."10 Already it was one of several similar establishments dotted around the wooded slopes on the northwestern side of the Arve Valley, each with its own specialisms, but each depending on the virtues of pure mountain air and water; clear, direct sunlight; clinical hygiene; and a remote, monotonous regime to alleviate the various symptoms of infected lungs, strained nerves, arthritic joints, and other perils of modern and not-quite-so-modern urban civilization. You could sit on your balcony or walk in the woods that ran right up to the hospital grounds; you could sleep or read or write letters. You could even at a pinch be allowed out for the night. But in practice, patients—then as now—were expected to obey doctors' orders, lead a quiet life, and adhere to strict rules. In the sanatorium the doctor was god, and his edicts and diagnoses were spoken of with the awed gratitude of doomed acolytes. The residents resigned themselves to indefinite stays relieved by frequent assurances of eventual cure. As Mann's Joachim Ziemmsen warns his cousin: "Wait a bit. You've only just come. Three weeks are nothing at all, to us up here—they look like a lot of time to you, because you are only up here on a visit, and three weeks is all you have. Get acclimatized first—it isn't so easy, you'll see."[11] At Sancellemoz, time stood still, and so, it sometimes seemed, did the condition of its inmates.

Katya settled willingly if not easily into this pattern of benign, authoritarian tedium. For years she had been sustained through a prolonged and incurable infirmity in her emotional life by an unshakable Christian faith, which as her physical health declined turned increasingly toward pious resignation. At home, in Biarritz, in Nice, Voreppe, and now Paris, she had endured the burden of Igor's double life in the interests of the stable family home that he, as much as any of the family, needed. She had forced herself to befriend his mistress, whether as an act of mortification or because to have refused this solace to his own sense of wrongdoing would have risked driving him away altogether. While she had always disliked and where possible avoided the social consequences of his fame, she had never compromised the integrity of their home life so far as it was in her power to determine its character and content. Shy and retiring though she was, she had never been afraid to involve Igor in domestic or family problems; and he, perhaps surprisingly, had accepted them without reluctance or irony. For all his huge infidelity, he remained profoundly, impeccably dynastic, while Katya's role had been the still, dependable center, the guardian, the focus of continuity.

Now, at Sancellemoz, she could only exercise these functions at a distance and through almost daily letters that are less like written communications than intimate conversation, full of clinical detail, accounts of the boring daily round, family news, money worries, trivial pieties, and the occasional admonition.[12] The Stravinskys had never spared each other their full medical reports, so why should Katya, whose illness was dangerous and under close clinical scrutiny, refrain from recording the daily temperature changes, the frequencies of coughing and blood-spitting, the X-rays, the pneumothoraxes, and all the other gruesome data of sanatorium life? In the slow tempo of Sancellemoz, in any case, such things took on greater significance, marking out the long hours and days into a quietly dramatic routine. Katya had leisure to occupy herself with their children's emotional lives. While Mika happily received letters and visits from her betrothed in Paris, who was preparing for baptism under instruction from a rather dry catechist called Father Vassily, Milène had fallen in love with her singing teacher and was resisting her father's efforts to detach her from him. But when she was eventually persuaded to leave Paris and appeared at Sancelle-moz with her cousin Ganya Belyankin, she was soon engaged in a mild flir-tation with a certain Marquis d'Anoville. Meanwhile, Soulima's unwanted Serb girlfriend had turned up in Paris. "What's to be done?" Katya wrote anxiously to her husband. "Our children are now at the age when they will be involved in all sorts of amorous relationships. I understand that all these worries are difficult for you what with your work and travels, but one has somehow to keep an eye on them."[13]

Igor did try to keep an eye on them, even though—as Katya knew better than anyone else—he was always at his least calm when preoccupied by composition.[14] As he grappled with his concerto fugue and prepared for a Scandinavian recital tour with Dushkin at the end of September, he worried quite as much as his wife about his family's health and romantic entangle-ments. His mother, who had naturally moved into the Faubourg apartment with them, had also been a source of anxiety. Now turned eighty, she had been suffering from a nervous ailment, and her hair had started falling out. But when the question of a wig came up, Igor muttered something about the expense, and in the end Katya proposed a kind of installment plan whereby Anna would repay the cost of the wig out of her weekly allowance.[15] Unfortunately, Stravinsky was going through one of his periodic bouts of penny-pinching. His American tour had earned him much less than he had expected, he had no conducting dates in France or Germany, and now he was having to stump up for not one but three rooms at Sancellemoz on top of the enormous Faubourg rent, the four or five servants, and an allowance to Vera; and meanwhile his children, instead of working, were getting mar-ried and falling ill. Yury Mandelstam might be something of a figure in émigré literary circles, but he hardly earned any money. True, Theodore had been painting and had a "successful" vernissage in Paris in June, but with-out actually selling any pictures.[16] And then, no sooner had Katya and Mika returned to Paris in time for Yury's baptism on the 12th of September than Theodore's intended, Denise Guerzoni, went down with pleurisy and a severe kidney ailment. No wonder Katya's letters began to take fright at the least extra expense, even those involved in essential medical tests; and no wonder that, helpless as she was to change these circumstances for the bet-ter, she could only "pray to God for help . . . and at the same time ask him to give me that 'holy indifference'—la sainte indifférence—about which St. Francis of Sales talks so much."[17]

STRAVINSKY HAD abandoned his intention of touring the U.S.A. again that coming winter,[18] and instead he found himself caught up in aspects of

Parisian musical and intellectual life that one might suppose, at first glance, to have held little interest for him. The principal agent of this change was his friend Nadia Boulanger; but the decisive event was the death of the composer Paul Dukas in May 1935.

Nadia had been teaching at the École Normale de Musique ever since it was founded by Alfred Cortot and Auguste Mangeot in 1919. She was in many ways the obvious successor to Dukas's chair of composition—had indeed been famously teaching composition both at the École and privately in her rue Ballu flat—but there were difficulties connected with the undeniable fact that she was not (or at least no longer) herself a composer, to say nothing of the even more undeniable misfortune that she was a woman. The École Normale was and remains, in both its virtues and its defects, a peculiarly French kind of institution. Founded with the specific aim of providing high-quality tuition in the theory, history, and practice of music to gifted students of any age or nationality, with no existing paper qualifications and not much money, it depended more than the Conservatoire on its ability to sell its wares on the open market; and in practice this meant humoring the prejudices of an essentially conservative, middlebrow clientele. The board's solution was to appoint Nadia to the chair, but to give her a distinguished and reassuringly male co-professor in the person of Stravinsky. Cortot's letter confirming Stravinsky's appointment in September 1935 envisages him as "inspecting" Nadia's composition course and "participating in her analyses of the works of the Masters."[19] But it is clear that his real function was simply to legitimize her appointment in the eyes of the lay world.

Her biographer Léonie Rosenstiel suggests that

> someone as proud as Nadia could only have been incensed by the situation that resulted. She would be expected to be subservient to Stravinsky when he appeared in "her" classroom and relinquish control to him meekly, the moment he arrived.[20]

Stravinsky was nevertheless presumably her recommendation, and if she did feel momentary pangs of injured pride, she knew perfectly well that whatever theoretical authority his appointment gave over her, he would never dream of exercising it. After all, he had never taught composition, had no interest in analysis, and was far too busy composing and performing to waste time poking his nose into her classes. All that was required of him was that he should take a composition class of his own once a month. Sometimes this would involve discussion of works presented by the students, sometimes discussion of his own music, which Nadia would play at the piano, pointing out salient features as she went along, while Stravinsky supplied the occasional confirmatory apothegm. With the student works, his method was to try and improve weak spots in the same way as he composed his own music, by trial and error at the piano. It must have been a strange experience for the young composers (who included the eighteen-year-old Dinu Lipatti) to have their inspirations assayed by this clinical, chord-by-chord method, so bizarrely at odds with sound conservatoire practice based on linear, grammatical thinking away from the piano. But it was the only kind of tuition the master could or would offer.[21]

Meanwhile his own concerto was scheduled for a series of performances on 21 and 22 November in the Salle Gaveau by a very different kind of further-educational enterprise, the so-called Université des Annales, a society which put on talks, readings, discussions, and lecture-recitals for a membership consisting mainly of well-heeled ladies of a self-improving disposition. From the intellectual heights of the *Nouvelle Revue française* and the Paris Russian-language paper *Posledniye novosti,* Boris de Schloezer was inclined to adopt a condescending tone toward this kind of event: "The speakers at these sessions are usually recognized celebrities—academics of the present or future, fashionable writers, professors, and with their largely female audience they have to maintain the tone of a refined *causerie.*"[22] But that was by no means Stravinsky's style. Instead, he mapped out a rather straight-faced, studiously nonconfessional disquisition under the highly misleading title "Mes Confidences," by way of prelude to the actual first performance of his severely unchatty concerto, after which Soulima was to end the hour-long presentation by playing the *Three Movements from Petrushka.*[23]

Apart from his description of the new concerto, most of Stravinsky's "confidences" were lifted with minor modifications from *Chroniques,* including some prefatory remarks on the relationship between effort and inspiration, the familiar account of the origins of *Petrushka,* and an admonition to the audience to think of the piano version of that ballet, not as a reduction of the orchestral score, but as a piano work in its own right. Some of these ideas, admittedly, were from the as-yet-unpublished second part of the autobiography. On the new work, he confined himself to a few generalities about the concerto as a genre and a brief program note about the music, ending with a stern injunction to any sentimentally inclined members of his audience not to look for hidden meanings in the music, or "for anything other than its actual constituents."[24] The audience at all three performances apparently cheered this evasive little speech to the echo, but its effect on the critics was merely to inspire their regret at the supposed absence of those very elements Stravinsky did not want them to look for. "Certainly," Robert Brussel lamented in *Le Figaro,* "the first movement bears in its outward form the imprint of authority and mastery. But I prefer the mysterious poetry which floats on the nocturne, the Beethovenian vehemence of the third and fourth variations, and everything that the prelude to the fugue exudes in its plays of sonority and voluptuous plenitude."[25] As for Boris de Schloezer, after his assault on *Persephone* eighteen months before, he was happy to acknowledge "the perfection of workmanship, the rigorous logic, the suppleness and complexity of the polyphonic tissue," and so forth.

> But what's missing, as in all Stravinsky's recent works, is some essential element of mystery—mystery in that sense which is impossible to define, what I call the gratuitous but others call chance. Everything is "made," admirably made, but this very perfection proves that it is impossible in art to be solely beholden to oneself, to one's will, one's intelligence, that you have to know how to accept with humility and trust what may be given you, what you are incapable of understanding and justifying.[26]

Stravinsky, it seems, had been at such pains to play down individual expression and play up the virtues of objective order and construction that he was in danger of being taken too literally even by his most intelligent critics. True, he had for years made war on inspiration, in the vulgar romantic sense of the term. But no careful reader of the first part of *Chroniques,* for instance, could doubt that he nevertheless accepted inspiration under a different guise, that of the "trouvaille" or "découverte."[27] For him inspiration was a matter of "finding," and this process of discovery was both a delight and, precisely, something given—in de Schloezer's sense—which the composer had to "know how to accept with humility and trust." Sometimes Stravinsky's *homo faber* explanations might seem to reduce art a little too easily to the level of cabinetmaking or regular mealtimes. But after all, these were merely images. As Stravinsky had assured an interviewer in Trieste a few years earlier:

> I use the word "appetite" in a more spiritual sense—that is, as St. Augustine used it, speaking of the appetites of the soul, which exalts and sublimates itself the greater its appetite for light and God. Now—Stravinsky concludes—all our senses, both our imaginative faculty and our musical ear's appetite for sounds, would be sterile without light, grace, and the guidance which comes to us from above. To be worthy we must pray in the purest manner—that is, strip the entire soul of its inferior appetites.[28]

Perhaps, though, what de Schloezer regretted more than the loss of that wild, unpredictable element in Stravinsky's musical language was the loss of its effect on audiences and critics. In middle age, the great revolutionary had become an establishment icon. As he left the Salle Gaveau that November afternoon, de Schloezer wistfully recalled "the battles we have fought for Stravinsky, and how dazzled we were by each work of his . . . The concerto will please some, irritate or sadden others, but the time of furies and enthusiasms is alas well and truly past."[29]

On the Saturday following this premiere, there was to have been an election to the chair at the Académie des Beaux-Arts left vacant by Dukas's death, but a postponement had been requested by one of the academicians, Jacques-Emile Blanche, who had a special interest in one of the candidates but could not be present on that date. Blanche's preferred candidate was none other than his old friend Igor Stravinsky.

Of all the great cultural institutions of the world, the Institut de France—of which the five academies are the main constituents—was and remains one of the most byzantine in its workings and the most obscure in its purpose. Like almost everything in France today, it originated—or at least acquired its modern form—in the Revolution, and its philosophy is Napoleonic: language, art, and science are a state concern, and between them they form a subgroup of learning and civilized values. Unfortunately the idea that the finest artists and writers—by implication the necessary alumni of such an institute—would automatically interest themselves in an Academy of Fine Arts or a guild for the preservation of the French language (which is essentially the role of the Académie française) is the purest fantasy. One might as well imagine a conference of hermits or a sunshine holiday for arctic explorers. The inevitable fate of the Institute has been to attract minor or unsuccessful figures who have known how to manipulate the system, and who—since new members are elected by the academicians themselves—have often made it their business to ensure that on the comparatively rare occasions when a first-rate artist has offered himself for election, somebody less threatening has been voted in instead.

The idea that Stravinsky might stand had originated with Gabriel Pierné, himself an academician and a symbolic figure in Stravinsky's association with France, since it was he who had conducted the first performances of *The Firebird* in 1910. Pierné's motives can only be guessed at. He may genuinely have wanted to enhance the musical membership of the Académie des Beaux-Arts, which at the time was particularly rich in nonentities (Gustave Charpentier and the ninety-one-year-old Charles-Marie Widor were the least obscure); he may conceivably have hoped to clinch Stravinsky's own commitment to his new French citizenship; or there may have been some more refined political intention. He may even have been inspired by the twenty-fifth anniversary of the *Firebird* premiere on 25 June.[30] By involving Stravinsky's painter friend Blanche, he will have hoped to gain support from the nonmusical academicians, whose votes, far outnumbering those of the musicians, would be decisive. Stravinsky later claimed that "I stood as a candidate solely on the insistence of a few friends, whom I felt it impossible to refuse a gesture of deference toward a venerable French institution to which they themselves belong and to which, in their opinion, I could be useful."[31] But he can hardly have been indifferent to the prestige and hence presumably security that membership would confer, nor can he have failed to be impressed that, so early in his citizenship, the notoriously chauvinist French were laying such honors out for his inspection. For a short time, his head was turned.

From November, the election was postponed to mid-January 1936, and early that month Stravinsky embarked on the laborious and, on the face of it, somewhat humiliating courtesy calls on the academicians which protocol required. Blanche may have led him to believe that his election would be a formality, in which case the visits would lose their supplicatory tone and become merely ceremonial.[32] But if so, he reckoned without the internal politics of the Academy, and above all without its *esprit de chapelle*—its fierce protectiveness toward its own marks of distinction and their possessors. "Mr. Stravinsky's supporters forgot to tell him," Camille Mauclair wrote later, "[that] for entry into the Académie des Beaux-Arts, it is almost indispensable to be a Prix de Rome, and professor in a school or conservatoire. Talent only comes later." Also, "it is better not to have had big successes in the theatre or even concerts, self-esteem and rivalry being part of human nature."[33] No sooner was Stravinsky's candidacy being generally reported than more comfortable alternatives began to be found: Henri Busser (a former friend of Debussy and orchestrator of his *Printemps*), Marcel Samuel-Rousseau, and finally Stravinsky's own old friend Florent Schmitt. All were past winners of the Prix de Rome, and all held Conservatoire professorships except Schmitt, who was a mere ex-director of the Lyons Conservatoire but in other ways, presumably, a more plausible face-saving opponent. According to Mauclair, a novelist and art historian who was also well connected musically, Schmitt agreed to run as a joke, and perhaps did not expect to be elected, being, apart from his musical successes, a well-known journalistic snapper at the heels of the Institute itself.

As might have been expected, Stravinsky's Russian origins and recent naturalization were soon being canvassed against him. Somebody dredged up a law—passed in July 1934, only a few weeks after he had become French—whereby foreign-born citizens were not permitted to hold state-paid office for ten years after their naturalization. But was an academy *fauteuil* an "office" in this sense? Academicians received an annual stipend of six thousand francs, but that was an honorarium and imposed no duties.

For the most part, the Parisian press ridiculed what was self-evidently at best a bureaucratic expedient, at worst an organized attack on Stravinsky's candidacy; but the question was also widely asked why an artist of Stravinsky's originality and independence should even want to fit himself into the *habit vert*—the green uniform which academicians traditionally pass on to their successors—and sit alongside "colleagues the most obscure of whom once wrote [of] *Les Noces:* 'Absurd ballet. Absurd music.' "

> To want to chomp at the same manger as this colleague you really need a strong stomach, when your name is Stravinsky and you've just brought out the second volume of your *Chroniques de ma vie*—a work so lofty, a work so beautiful, a work as far removed from the academic spirit as it is humanly possible to get. For the *fauteuil* my money is all on Florent Schmitt . . . Florent is not academic, but he is inoculated; he didn't die of the Prix de Rome, and he won't die of the Institut.[34]

The nationality issue was quickly resolved in Stravinsky's favor, though not before his two sponsors had let him know that, in their opinion, it would be fatal to his candidacy, and had summarily urged him to withdraw.[35] Of course, this was yet another pretext. With Schmitt on the ballot paper, Stravinsky had no chance, but with Stravinsky there too, Schmitt might very well not win, and that would, for Pierné, be the worst of all possible worlds. Stravinsky was not to be persuaded into so undignified an exit; but in the end it made no difference.[36]

Schmitt duly won, and Stravinsky was eventually abandoned by all his supporters. In the five ballots on the 25th of January a solid core of a dozen or so academicians voted for Samuel-Rousseau, a composer of exceptional obscurity even by Academy standards, but whose composer father many of them had known. Stravinsky got five votes out of thirty-two, then four out of thirty-three, after which his support switched *en bloc* to Schmitt, presumably in order to thwart Samuel-Rousseau. Stravinsky was left to nurse his injured dignity in a lengthy apologia printed by *Le Jour* on the Monday after the ballot, a curious piece in which he takes particular umbrage at the *Figaro* critic, Guermantes, for having in effect doubted the Academy's relevance to an artist of his stature. "It naturally isn't a question," Guermantes had written, "of despising honors. But there are some works of Stravinsky's which themselves seem to say no to them."[37] Unfortunately, he also—gently—accused Stravinsky of betraying his youth in seeking such honors. This touched the composer on a raw spot, after the remarks of de Schloezer and others about his concerto. "I'm not ashamed of my age nor at all frightened of it," he countered:

It's the age at which Bach composed his best cantatas, Beethoven his last symphonies, and Wagner—whom I mention to please the Wagnerites— his *Mastersingers*. There's nothing more odious than the shameful grovelling of the old before the young, their criminal flatteries, dictated above all by the fear of seeming out-of-date. Do these old folk consider the cruel deceptions they lay up for the young when, egoistically, instead of guiding them, they shower praise on them one day, only to drop them the next? There's no merit in being young. It's a state, and a passing one. As Goethe said, the great art in life is to survive.[38]

FEW CAN have doubted that Stravinsky would survive as a composer. But as a performer his prospects, in Europe at any rate, looked bleak. In the eight months of 1935 after his return from the U.S.A. he had only four orchestral concerts, compared with thirty or so in the whole of 1930. The Salle Gaveau lecture-recitals in November were his only Paris engagement. Germany was a complete blank, in spite of Strecker's best efforts behind the scenes on his behalf. Even Italy, which was still nominally well disposed to his music, and where, at the end of May, he was again received by Mussolini (as well as by his son-in-law Count Ciano, the minister of propaganda), could offer him only one concert in Bologna and one in Rome; and even that single Roman concert was spoilt by the cancellation of *Persephone* because Ida Rubinstein had fallen ill, so that Stravinsky found himself conducting a program unlike any other in his entire career, with *Petrushka* and *Firebird* topped up by two of Debussy's Nocturnes ("Nuages" and "Fêtes") and a memorial performance of Dukas's *Apprenti sorcier*.[39] As for the gramophone, his six-year Columbia contract had come to an end with the London *Les Noces* and Paris *Ragtime* in July 1934, by which time falling profits had led to a merger of Columbia and HMV, and such generous deals were no longer on offer to commercially risky composers like him. Instead Polydor, the export wing of Deutsche Grammophon, booked him and Dushkin to record the Violin Concerto as a one-off project in the Salle Pleyel at the end of October 1935. This was to be almost his last Paris recording, and his last anywhere for practically another two and a half years.

Since 1928, when the world economy had seemed relatively secure and record companies had felt bullish about the prospects of electrical recording, a great deal had changed in the marketplace, and Stravinsky had changed with it. These days he was openly skeptical about the value of armchair listening, whether through the gramophone or the radio. He still maintained that his recordings could be treated as documents of his intentions, and he still routinely recommended them as guides to would-be performers of his music. But he made no secret of his dislike of the "on-off switch" mentality bred by mechanical transmission and reproduction. "Indeed, it is in just this incredible facility," he wrote in the second part of his *Chroniques*, which was just going to press as he recorded the Violin Concerto,

> this lack of necessity for any effort, that the evil of this so-called progress lies . . . The radio has got rid of the necessity which existed in Bach's day for getting out of one's armchair. Nor are listeners any longer impelled to play themselves, or to spend time on learning an instrument in order to acquire a knowledge of musical literature. The wireless and the gramophone do all that . . . For the majority of listeners there is every reason to fear that, far from developing a love and understanding of music, the modern methods of dissemination will have a diametrically opposite effect—that is to say, the production of indifference, inability to understand or appreciate or to undergo any worthy reaction.[40]

Probably as he contemplated the apparent decline in interest in his own work, and its failure to excite the old enthusiasm even among sympathetic connoisseurs, he was tempted to see himself as an early victim of the more-equals-less culture, though in his heart he knew perfectly well that the trouble lay much deeper, in circumstances beyond day-to-day commercial control. He did not yet understand (and in this he was by no means alone) that the problems were or would soon be worldwide, and it seemed only natural to direct his hopes back out over the Atlantic.

The early-1936 American tour was still theoretically on as late as mid-November, but Merovitch's breakdown that month laid bare a hopelessly underplanned itinerary, and Stravinsky risked losing precious European dates if he delayed cancellation any longer. In any case, he now had other irons in the fire. There was talk of a South American trip in the (northern) spring of 1936; and there was also the possibility of a ballet commission for New York the following year, which might entail his presence and could be worked into a more carefully planned concert tour with a new agent. Meanwhile he could accept concerts in Italy and Spain for the coming early spring, and Strecker might even engineer some German performances of the new concerto.

In the six years since Diaghilev's death, Stravinsky's sole creative contact with staged ballet had been in the hybrid *Persephone*, a work which—even had Diaghilev lived—would hardly have done much to restore their good relations, so damaged by that earlier Rubinstein piece, *The Fairy's Kiss*. The summer before *Persephone*, George Balanchine had tried unsuccessfully to reestablish himself in Paris as a star ballet master and choreographer, through a short-lived company called Les Ballets 1933, which the English millionaire-aesthete Edward James had sponsored as a vehicle—or more precisely a bait—for his unfaithful dancer wife, Tilly Losch.[41] Stravinsky had attended the opening night that June, which included the first performance of Weill's *Seven Deadly Sins,* with Losch as bad Anna, Weill's own estranged wife, Lotte Lenya, as good Anna, and choreography by Balanchine. What the Russian composer thought of the company as a whole is not recorded, but it hugely impressed a young American enthusiast called Lincoln Kirstein, who also, like James, happened to be rich enough to consider setting up a dance company of his own, and who—unlike him—had felt predestined to leave his mark on ballet, ever since, one day in Venice in 1929, he had stumbled across an Orthodox funeral that turned out to be that of Diaghilev himself.[42] Kirstein was tall and gangly, and though he had scratched a few dance lessons from the great Fokine, it was in the cause of elementary knowledge rather than mature practice. He was to remain an intellectual of the dance, but an organizer of a determination amounting to genius, an irascible and impulsive force carried along by sheer passionate energy and love of ballet.

Kirstein had met Balanchine during the company's brief London run and invited him to New York, and there, at the very start of 1934, they opened the first-ever School of American Ballet—precisely so-called—in a fourth-floor studio on Madison Avenue. More than a year was spent training and refining young dancers who were utterly unused to the intense discipline of professional ballet and who were at first bemused by Balanchine's freewheeling, highly unacademic method of impromptu choreography. But by March 1935 the American Ballet was deemed ready for its first public New York season, and a few months later the still immature company was—somewhat to its own astonishment—invited by the new general manager of the Metropolitan Opera, Edward Johnson, to be the house's resident ballet troupe. It must have been at about this time that Kirstein or, more likely, Balanchine conceived the idea of commissioning a completely new ballet score from Stravinsky, exactly as Diaghilev had done for the second season of the nascent Ballets Russes when it became evident that musical arrangements and potpourris were betraying the brilliant innovations in choreography, dance, and design. Early in August Nicolas Nabokov, who had been seeing a lot of Balanchine in New York, wrote to Stravinsky from his summer home in Alsace, mentioning the project and suggesting a meeting in Paris.[43] As yet there was no subject and no firm contract, partly because nobody was sure where the money would come from, but mostly because the Met, having appointed the company as an opera ballet, simply had—or said it had—no room in its schedules for evenings of pure ballet.

Curiously, the delay—though not its cause—was also just as with *The Firebird*. With the premiere of the Concerto for Two Solo Pianos behind him, Stravinsky started sketching what would eventually become *Jeu de cartes* in early December 1935, before he even knew that his score would be needed.

4

AN ENEMY OF DEMOCRACY

WHILE STRAVINSKY'S past and forthcoming North American tours were to some extent commercial affairs, enabled, certainly, by the support of rich enthusiasts but largely set up by agents or orchestral managers, his first visit to South America, in 1936, was brought about entirely by the passion and energy of one woman, the Argentine writer, editor, and publisher Victoria Ocampo. They had met for the first time in Paris in 1929, through Ansermet, who knew her well from his annual Buenos Aires seasons.[1] It was her first visit to Europe since 1913–14, when as a strikingly beautiful and recently married young woman of twenty-three she had sat in the front stalls at the premiere of *The Rite of Spring* and struggled with the four-hand reduction on the piano in her room at the Hotel Meurice.[2] By July 1934, when Stravinsky again ran into her in London, she had long since shed her husband and established herself, to the dismay of her cultivated but traditional-minded family, as Argentina's most prominent New Woman. She had openly rejected the conventional values of the Argentine governing, land-owning, conquistador class to which she belonged by birth; she had interested herself, in the teeth of provincial disapproval, in the new art and new writing of the twenties and thirties, and in 1931 had founded and edited a literary review called *Sur* (South) as a vehicle for this enthusiasm. She even built herself a functional, Corbusier-style house in the smart Buenos Aires neighborhood of Palermo Chico and invited Le Corbusier himself to visit the capital, admire her design, and even consider building more in the same vein along the banks of the River Plate; only, as she laments in her *Testimonios*, "I couldn't find people who were enthusiastic enough about Le Corbusier's projects to risk money on them."[3]

In 1934, Victoria's interest in Stravinsky was focused on two of his own current projects. When he told her about his *Chroniques,* she at once offered to bring the book out in Spanish at the new Sur publishing house which she had grafted onto the review the previous year; and when they talked about *Persephone,* she suggested that he come in person to Buenos Aires and conduct it, with her (she was, among other New Womanish things, a trained actress) speaking the title role.[4] From the composer's point of view, her passion for his music was both flattering and useful. She was a woman of formidable personality, charm, and taste; she was clever; but she also had money and influence, and she talked about Argentina as if her mere wanting to arrange things there would be enough to remove all obstacles. True to form, Stravinsky was soon harnessing her energy in his negotiations with the Teatro Colón in Buenos Aires, and it was through her that he eventually met the director of the Colón, Athos Palma, in Paris at the end of February 1936, by which time an intensive spring tour—also involving Rio de Janeiro and the Uruguayan capital, Montevideo—was more or less tied up and Victoria booked for several *Persephones*. After Ida Rubinstein, Stravinsky was surely sincere when he told his Argentine hostess that he was looking forward to performing the work with her. "But," he warned, "I shall be pitiless over the coordination of the spoken text with the musical text: aren't you frightened?"[5]

Four years before, he had half-planned an Argentine trip with Vera, and there had been a second, quite well-developed project in 1933. This time Soulima would be travelling with him, to partner him in the two-piano concerto, to appear as soloist in the Piano Concerto and Capriccio, and to give recitals on his own account. It was a big opportunity, if not necessarily one to enhance Soulima's sense of his artistic and professional independence of his father. But it would mean that Igor had a travelling companion, and it would bring vicarious comfort to Soulima's mother, whose illness, more serious and threatening than in 1932, weighed heavily on Igor's heart, and probably on his conscience as well.[6] In the middle of January, after a four-month respite in Paris, poor Katya was summoned back to the wintry heights of Sancellemoz, like the young man in *The Fairy's Kiss* borne away to the Eternal Dwellings by the Ice Maiden. As for Vera, Victoria must have made it abundantly clear that so irregular a companion would never be received by the straitlaced Argentines, and she may even have hinted that she herself already had quite enough social troubles in Buenos Aires—what with her divorce, her independent lifestyle, her notorious taste for modern art and progressive thinking—without adding to them a taint of sexual bohemianism. Vera was thrown into deep gloom by this impending separation, and it initiated the first and probably last serious test of their fifteen-year-old relationship.

Fortunately for Soulima, his father's touring schedule in the early spring provided several opportunities to polish up his South American repertoire. There were concerts in Italy and Spain and even a trip to the English seaside resort of Bournemouth. Better still, the situation in Germany was looking more hopeful. Strecker had secured an invitation for them to play the two-piano concerto at the "alternative" Nazi ISCM Festival at Baden-Baden in early April, and there was talk of concerts in Frankfurt, where Rosbaud was taking advantage of what the German press was beginning to call Stravinsky's "rehabilitation" to arrange a broadcast performance of the concerto complete with introductory talk.[7] Strecker took this rehabilitation very seriously—so seriously, in fact, that at his persuasion the composer accepted a thirty-six percent cut in his proposed fee for Baden-Baden, being, as he told Strecker, "very touched by the part you are playing in my reappearance in Germany, this Germany that was always so attentive to my music."[8] Alas for such sentiments, Rosbaud soon found himself under attack from local Nazi elements and was forced to withdraw the Frankfurt invitation. The Baden-Baden performance, on the 4th of April, survived, presumably because of the Nazis' desire to maintain the international credentials—such as they were—of their alternative festival, a mere four weeks after Hitler's Wehrmacht had marched back into the officially demilitarized Rhineland. But it was the last time Stravinsky would perform in public in Germany for a small matter of fifteen and a half years.

Frankfurt was not the only casualty of political conditions among his and Soulima's concerts during these months. After playing the two-piano concerto in Milan in February and in Rome a fortnight later, they were forced to forgo a third concert in Genoa because of what Katya called an "unpleasant occurrence";[9] and then, lo and behold, something similar happened in Madrid a few days later. One can only speculate what these occurrences may have been, but they were probably of a political nature. Spain had gone to the polls on 16 February, and the victory of the Popular Front was followed by violent incidents, in Madrid and elsewhere, provoked almost equally by the defeated right-wing Falange and by various amnestied political prisoners of the Left. In fact, such was the popular turmoil in Spain—and not least in Catalonia, whose nationalist leader, Luis Companys, was among those amnestied—that it may seem surprising that the Stravinskys' two Barcelona concerts went ahead as planned on 12 and 15 March. But the atmosphere as Igor experienced it—or at least as he reported it—was calm, despite Katya's fears to the contrary.[10] "As always," he assured Charles-Albert Cingria in a Paris radio interview a week later, "in a country where something is happening, one notices absolutely nothing. Appearances in the street were completely normal."[11] Cingria, who had been summarily arrested and imprisoned without trial by Mussolini's police in Rome ten years earlier, might well have muttered something under his breath about his friend's powers of observation.[12] But Stravinsky was in any case probably not being altogether candid. He must himself have witnessed, or at least been aware of, the huge popular demonstration in Rome that greeted the Italian victory at Mount Alaji in Ethiopia at the end of February. Katya had seen a picture of the celebrations in *Paris-Soir* and was sufficiently struck by the spectacle to mention it in a letter to her two travellers.[13] But Igor's instinctive reaction to such manifestations was to will them out of existence, surely realizing that they boded no good for the general peace and quiet he so valued. He still admired Mussolini enough to present him with an inscribed copy of the second volume of *Chroniques* together with "a small gold medal representing Napoleon and Marie Louise," but he nowadays knew better than to advertise such gifts, and perhaps it even occurred to him that the Duce's African adventure was unlikely to benefit the good order of Italian civic life.[14] One thing that clearly did not much trouble him—incomprehensible though this may seem to us today—was that unarmed Ethiopian peasants were being slaughtered.

The sea crossing from Boulogne to Rio, starting on the 9th of April 1936, took twelve days, with stops at Vigo, Lisbon, and Funchal. At Rio they spent a day ashore, then sailed on to Santos (the port for São Paulo), then for two more days to Montevideo, before finally crossing the vast River Plate estuary to Buenos Aires on the 24th.[15] Having embarked in spring, they arrived in autumn, but a distinctly Mediterranean autumn—warm, sunny, and dry. They must have hoped to get ashore without delay and start to flesh out their mental images of urban South America, with its curious blend of the familiar and the strange, the stately and the ramshackle, its elegance and squalor, confronting one another, even then, with a violence both shocking and outmoded to the northern eye. But the press were too quick for them, and almost before they could gather up their belongings they found themselves surrounded on deck by photographers and reporters anxious as ever to put a face and a set of opinions to one of the most famous names in music. It seems that Victoria had omitted to brief Stravinsky on the political nuances of the situation, and he may have been caught unawares. Perhaps he felt lightheaded so far from home, as if he were talking to moon men; or he may have felt goaded into a certain contrariness by recent experiences in Germany and Spain. Whatever the cause, even he must have been startled by the apparent irrelevance but stark, simple truth of the headline above the report in the left-wing paper *Crítica* the next morning: STRAVINSKY ES ENE-MIGO DE LA DEMOCRACIA.

What on earth had he told them? He only had to read the various interviews to remind himself. He had been answering questions about his favorite modern composers, a rum lot, as usual: Conrad Beck (whom he happened to have met in Baden-Baden three weeks before); Vittorio Rieti, a friend and disciple; Goffredo Petrassi, whom he had seen in Rome. Debussy he venerated, of course. Who else? Well, he was very fond of Manuel de Falla. And then out it came:

I admire his profoundly religious spirit, and this pleases me, because with faith you can create great works. You'll know that when the Republic came in in Spain, Falla was made an honorary citizen of Granada, but feeling that a town which burnt down convents and churches was a sacrilegious town, he replied: "I believe in Christ; and so I don't accept such honors." Beautiful, don't you think? And I find it beautiful because materialism is something very far from me. It's what has stopped me going back to my country. To give one's life for a material paradise I find unworthy of mankind; by contrast, I understand perfectly the ideal which inspires the Crusades, for example. Politics leaves me remote from its oscillations. I am neither realist nor republican. But yes, I am anti-parliamentarian. I can't stand it, as a horse couldn't put up with a camel . . .[16]

At this point in Madrid, shots might have been fired. In Buenos Aires there was merely the fury of a press which reflected at a fairly safe distance the quarrels then threatening to tear Europe apart. *Crítica,* for instance, was enraged by Stravinsky's remark that the music of the Soviet Union didn't count as art "because it is simply propaganda." The composer, it felt, was ignorant of the most elementary facts that it was every citizen's duty to know. Hadn't he heard that things had now changed in Russia, the Writers' Association had been dissolved and "art is recovering the climate of freedom in which masterpieces can begin to flourish"?[17] In any case, the writer pointed out with rather more justice, it was hardly tactful to arrive as the guest of a state-run theatre and before even setting foot on land denounce the political system under which, at least nominally, that theatre flourished. But the Catholic paper *Criterio* defended the maestro. His words showed "his understanding of the kind of revolution needed for salvation in our time. He knows that creative toil is for man an imitation of the work of God, and man must turn to God if he wants to find strength to imitate with fulfillment."[18]

Stravinsky was in Argentina for over three weeks and the press continued to snap at his heels. The next bone of contention was his supposed (and admittedly somewhat bizarre) refusal to allow his concerts to be broadcast, in a huge country where—as one pained commentator observed—radio had helped raise the level of musical culture in remote areas where families would tune in eagerly to hear the latest program from the Colón.[19] Another, less temperate columnist bafflingly headlined an article mainly about Mussolini and the Spanish prime minister, Manuel Azaña, with what was practically an article in its own right excoriating Stravinsky as "a pinhead with a rudimentary brain, and a nose for a bargain: a villainous composer, bad conductor, and worse pianist," who had come to Argentina in order to suck its exchequer dry.[20] What his hostess said or thought about such invective left no echo in their correspondence, but she was probably much too chic either to be disconcerted by her guest's opinions or to notice the reactions of the Fourth Estate. She was far from thinking as he did. She had long since renounced the church, and though no Communist (of any stripe), she was an instinctive progressive and candid feminist—in a country where women still could not vote and until recently had been legally not much better than their husbands' chattels. But she also knew quite enough artists and writers not to expect their opinions to coincide with hers or each other's. A woman who could find equal room in her heart for Ortega y Gasset, Tagore, Huxley, Maritain, and, later, Camus and Graham Greene was not likely to be put out by the perversities of an exiled White Russian. "What mattered to me," she said in an interview near the end of her life,

> was talent, not politics. Each person held the right to think as he wished in that zone. Of course those who put themselves at the service of a party and made "propaganda" for it dropped immediately to another level. There's no reason to name names. And let it be noted that I refer to propaganda, not to an honest expression of opinions (even though they may appear mistaken to us).[21]

Though also an admirer of Gandhi's antimaterialism, and notoriously abstemious in her personal habits (she was, for instance, teetotal, and imposed this abstinence on all but her most imperious guests), Victoria never disowned the Ocampo estate. She had first thought of putting Igor and Soulima up in the family home at San Isidro, then considered the "Corbusier" house in Palermo Chico, but it was already let. In the end they stayed in another of her town houses, in the Calle Tucumán, a place of unhappy memories for her because she had lived there in the dead years of her marriage after 1914, when she and her too-conventional husband had occupied the same building but scarcely communicated. Yet it had also resonated to music she had heard in Europe. "How happy I am," she told Igor, "that you are in the house where your music has been so much played (mainly on records, of course) . . . the house to which I returned from my Europe trip in 1913 with the score of *The Rite*."[22] There was a piano for Soulima's practice; and he needed it, as he had eight concerts in three weeks, including a pair of solo recitals, two performances of the two-piano concerto complete with Igor's lecture and his own solo items, and three concerto appearances under his father, in one of which he was giving both the Piano Concerto and the Capriccio—something Stravinsky senior had invariably refused to do. Igor's program was still heavier. His Colón concerts, with *The Rite*, *Apollo*, and the *Symphony of Psalms*, among much else, were interspersed with ballet performances, including *The Fairy's Kiss* revived in person by its original choreographer, Bronislava Nijinska.

Essentially none of this music was new to Buenos Aires, where Anser-met had worked for several seasons, always programming major works by Stravinsky. But that naturally did not prevent what one paper called a "numerous and well-qualified audience"[23] from turning out to witness the great iconoclast at first hand, and presumably the reports of his reactionary politics did no harm at all to his box office. He may himself have been mildly relieved to find that the press reviews of the opening Colón concert on the 28th ignored such questions and instead treated him as an interna-tional master whose works were admired and whose conducting was of course authoritative, even if the orchestral playing was not always of the best quality. Even Soulima's performance of the Piano Concerto was treated without condescension: "a pianist of rare quality and extraordinary musical intelligence," the *Nación* called him, which must have been a huge comfort to a young musician who, barely six weeks before in Barcelona, had lost his way and all but come to grief in this same concerto.[24]

The sole novelty of the three weeks was the concert performance of *Perse-phone* with Victoria herself in the title role, at the climax of the visit on 17 May. She had claimed not to be deterred by the composer's admonitions about rhythm, but instead she scared herself by going down with flu less than a week before the performance, then panicked when she found she could not hear the orchestra—even in the "perfect sound box" of the Colón.[25] Yet the performance seems to have gone extremely well, and Victo-ria declaimed her lines "with a French articulation and accent of unsurpass-able purity" in which "Gide's mystical essence and exaltation emerged in all their significance, thanks to the fine qualities of this consummate artist."[26] Whatever the composer may have thought of this description of the text, he surely agreed with the assessment of Victoria's delivery, since he soon after-wards persuaded her, against her better judgment, to rejoin them in Rio so that he could program further performances there early in June.[27] On the 19th, he and Soulima crossed back to Montevideo, where there were more concerts before they again set sail on the 27th, with Victoria and her sister Angelica, up the coast of Uruguay and Brazil back to Rio.

"Do you remember," Victoria wrote to Igor almost eighteen years later,

> our voyage to Rio? Your cold on the boat? My fear of catching it? The rehearsals which gave you so much trouble with the English tenor who trembled with fear and gave himself confidence by beating time with his score? Our lunches and dinners at the Copacabana? The evening at the G's (the garden with the huge palm trees. It's now the Argentine embassy at Rio)? The variegated chorus-singers? The heat? The pine-

apples? The seafood at night? Your way at table of putting your napkin on your head, like a turban, when the orchestra was playing (and what an orchestra!)? The scent of the East in the air? Your way of saying to me: "She has a bad character . . ."?[28]

At the time, though, she recalled only "the disagreements and the heat and the inedible food and the monkeys."[29] They did *Persephone* two or three times in the Teatro Municipal, and Victoria contributed some readings to their recital program with the two-piano concerto. Then, on Victoria's very last evening, the "bad character," Dagmar Godowsky, turned up in person.

Dagmar's memory, too, tended to romanticize. She had come down from New York with the pianist Josef Hofmann and his wife, Betty, and put up at the Copacabana in complete ignorance, she claimed, that Stravinsky was so much as in the same hemisphere. Then the phone is supposed to have rung. "Dagmar! This is Stravinsky." "Stravinsky! Where are you, in Paris or New York?" "Right here at the Copacabana. I'm here with my son Soulima. Will you dine with us tonight?" "I'd *adore* to."[30] But Dagmar had in reality soon sniffed Stravinsky out, and tried to invite him for cocktails. "I've called you often but never have any luck."[31] Then, after the last *Persephone* on 10 June, her luck suddenly changed. Perhaps after the performance Victoria went early to bed, since she was returning to Buenos Aires the next day. Dagmar reported, no doubt truthfully, that Stravinsky asked her to dine. But somehow he missed her at the Copacabana, and after a good deal of to-ing and fro-ing they all ended up at the Hotel Gloria, with the Hofmanns, in intense heat and humidity. "It was," she says with more than her usual accuracy, "an unfortunate decision."[32]

Stravinsky had first heard Hofmann in St. Petersburg more than thirty years before, when his "serious, precise, and finished playing filled me with such enthusiasm that I redoubled my zeal in studying the piano."[33] Since then they had met in New York, and they had crossed the Atlantic together at the end of 1934, "at which time," Stravinsky told Craft, "I discovered that he had a querulous character and drank heavily, and that the latter made the former worse."[34] Now in the Brazilian heat, they ate little but drank much, and Stravinsky was moved by the atmosphere and the alcohol to enthuse once again about Hofmann's playing and what it had meant to him. The reaction was unexpected. Hofmann became apoplectic. He certainly could not say the same for Stravinsky's music. In fact he detested it, and he despised Stravinsky as a musician. "You've taken music back a hundred years. You are terrible. You are a menace!"[35] Somehow a worse scene was averted; the Stravinskys coldly departed, and Hofmann was left to face Dagmar's furious resentment. The next day, she and the Stravinskys dined again; there were explanations, walks through old Rio, visits to the zoo, the botanical gardens, the parks and caves. Igor magnanimously invited the Hofmanns to his final concert on the 12th. But the pianist was unrepentant. "I'm glad," he muttered, "I'm glad I said what I did."[36]

Did Stravinsky go to bed with Dagmar in Rio, as Craft maintains?[37] Dagmar, to do her credit, does not openly claim so, though she did soon find herself falling in love with this fascinating genius whose music, she admits, did not on the whole greatly please her. Craft, however, whose information on such matters presumably comes from Vera, implies that the affair was common gossip by the summer of 1936, and he finds coded statements to this effect in Dagmar's book.[38] Stravinsky was obviously more than capable of infidelity: and if unfaithful to Katya, why not to Vera? Craft has even hinted at an affair with Victoria Ocampo, who had admitted to Coco Chanel, in 1929, that she was jealous of Coco's relationship with Stravinsky.[39] But whereas Dagmar was a loose cannon, Victoria was an aristocrat of carefully regulated indiscretions, who would surely never have countenanced misbehavior under Soulima's eyes. A mutual attraction there may have been, and something of the sort would help account for Victoria's mildly irresponsible excursion to Rio. Throughout these years, though, her emotional life centered on someone quite different, an Argentinian whose anonymity, in her six-volume autobiography, is studiously preserved: he is almost invariably "J," at most "Julián." Ansermet's daughter, Anne, who knew Victoria in Buenos Aires, regarded her in such matters as "prudent and honest, and even if one never saw her lover, she let no one remain unconscious of his existence."[40] Victoria recorded that "J" was not gifted himself but had faith in her talents, and this was the unconventional basis of their understanding. "If [his virtues] had been limited to attractions of a physical or sexual order, my relationship [with him] would have endured as long as a rose—a single morning. I can now speak about this with special knowledge from other experiences."[41] Whether Stravinsky was ever one of them remains a matter for speculation.

For Vera these possibilities were no doubt painful, and she skirted round them in her letters. At the best of times Igor's affections were subject to mood. "Your goodbye was hasty," she had complained when he left, "not very tender, and at the last moment you did not call me 'Sobachkina' [dear little doggie]."[42] The infrequency of his letters sometimes saddened her too. But she continued to involve herself in his family affairs. She would walk in the Bois de Boulogne with Theodore and listen to his anxieties about Denise's liver, or drive out with the two of them and Milène to Meudon and drink fresh milk at a farm. As soon as Igor was back Theodore and Denise were going to get married, and Vera was eager to approve. She already knew what he subsequently told Victoria:

My feelings toward my children, and especially my sons, are of that well-known type in which joy at seeing them happy is offset by a bitterness at parting that is infinitely painful to me. So don't be surprised to see me counting Theodore's marriage among the other cares which never cease to harass me.43

Vera may have become so gloomy about their relationship while he was away that she embarked on an affair with one of her oldest admirers, Baron Fred Osten-Saken, a scion of the aristocratic Balt family which had included one of Igor's school friends. Baron Fred had known Vera since her Moscow and Berlin days, and remained her loyal courtier in thirties Paris, both in her old rue du Ranelagh flat and now in the new apartment in the parallel rue de l'Assomption to which she moved while Igor was in South America.44 Then, later that summer, long after Igor's return, Fred was with her at Wiessee, in Bavaria, where she was taking a cure for high blood pressure.45 But such episodes should perhaps be understood as an aspect of Vera's generosity to suffering friends, of whom she had more than her fair share. A few days after Igor left Paris in April, she arranged to meet Arthur Lourié for lunch, but at the last minute he telephoned to cancel. Then two weeks later she ran into him in the street, looking the color of his green overcoat and clearly in need of moral, not to say financial, support. Some trouble had blown up between him and Stravinsky, trouble in which Vera felt powerless—or unwilling—to intervene. Exactly what this was, however, we do not know.46

Igor returned on the 24th of June to a Paris that was shaking with collective terror after the Nazi occupation of the Rhineland in March. Fear of war alternated almost daily with fear of revolution, and after Léon Blum's election victory in early May at the head of a Popular Front which included Communists, dread of a Communist takeover persisted, especially of course among White Russians, who detested the new government and probably agreed with the right-wing slogan "Better Hitler than Léon Blum." Katya's letters show that the Stravinskys were sympathetic to Pierre Laval, the French prime minister, who resigned in January amid protests over the pro-Mussolini peace plan for Abyssinia. Even after Blum's victory, strikes continued to break out, bread was scarce, petrol unobtainable, and, Vera wrote, Jews were afraid to leave their homes for fear of right-wing reprisals. "Some say that in a few days all this will be over," she added, "but we Russians, remembering the revolution, think otherwise."47

Soon after Igor's return a curious light was thrown on these events by a project in Berlin for a production of *The Soldier's Tale* by the so-called Jüdischer Kulturbund (Jewish Cultural Association), a "ghetto" organization that was officially sanctioned but whose performances were attended only by Jews and reviewed only in the Jewish press. Strecker saw this as a sign that the composer's Baden-Baden concert in April had "broken the boycott," but he advised against approval, since *The Soldier's Tale* was still regarded as Bolshevik in Nazi circles, and the production would merely revive allegations that Stravinsky was himself a Jew. When he heard, however, that the Reichstheaterkammer had approved the production, Strecker changed his tune. He now advised Stravinsky to give his approval and make a special reduction in the performance fee, since if it became known that a performance permitted by the Nazis had been stopped by the composer, there could be a disagreeable reaction abroad, especially in America, where Jewish opinion was influential. No wonder the poor composer, as usual mainly anxious not to lose German royalties, was left confused by his publisher's Realpolitik. But he gave permission, and the production duly took place on 4 November, to mixed reactions that partly justified Strecker's initial hesitation. One critic regretted a work "that lets man be destroyed by life's adversities"; another compared it—worryingly—to the Jewish Schoenberg's *Pierrot lunaire*. All agreed that the performance was excellent; but how far any of this affected Stravinsky's German reputation in the longer run remained (and remains) an open question.[48]

Theodore duly married his young Roman Catholic bride on 29 June 1936, in the upstairs chapel in the rue d'Odessa in which Mika and Yury had wed eight months before. A service of Catholic benediction followed at Montrouge, on the south side of Paris.[49] Katya was released from Sancellemoz for the occasion, but three weeks later she went back there with Milène, who was herself now displaying mild symptoms of the family disease.[50] Within weeks, her profoundly tubercular sister had announced that she was pregnant, in open defiance of her doctors' orders. Igor, apparently suffering from nothing more infectious than worry, took refuge, for neither the first nor the last time, in composition.

It was nearly a year since Balanchine had raised the matter of a new ballet, and there was still no firm contract and no clear idea of a subject. Back in the winter, Stravinsky had made substantial sketches for an opening scene, and even played some of the music to Katya before she left for Sancellemoz in mid-January.[51] But by late February, Balanchine was still waiting on the Met, and for most of the next four months Stravinsky was on tour and essentially unable to compose.[52] On his return from South America in late June, he found waiting for him a letter from Balanchine that was still no more than hopeful about a commission but was starting to hint at subject matter. Stravinsky may not have realized that the choreographer was smarting from the failure of his danced production of Gluck's *Orpheus and Eurydice* three weeks before—the only proper chance the Met had so far given him to do more than provide divertissements in existing productions of operas like *Faust* and *Carmen*—and was desperate to set a new and significant work in motion almost regardless of plot, an issue which in any case never greatly bothered him. He now mentioned Andersen, and specifically his tale "The Flowered Ball." But the composer had had enough of fairy tales, and in any case, he remarked loftily, "I must tell you that I have never yet composed ballet music without knowing the subject in advance . . . The ballet I am now composing is not a divertissement in the sense you warn me against; my ballet has a definite and wholly intelligible subject with light intrigue . . ."[53]

This was probably untrue. The evidence, on the contrary, is that he had been composing either to an abstract plan or to a partially known but as yet unformulated plot. Soon after the approach from Nabokov in August 1935, he had tried to involve Cocteau in a collaboration on what was presumably this ballet, and Cocteau had even supplied a text (whether preexisting or specially written), which he told the composer to alter as much as he liked.[54] But this can hardly have been the "card-game plot" which Stravinsky later claimed to have proposed to Cocteau, nor does it exactly look as if Cocteau declined to collaborate, as the composer also claimed:[55] or rather, if the text was preexisting, it cannot have been Stravinsky's idea; but if it was specially written, then its author had obviously not declined. Several months later, after South America, the composer again solicited the writer's help in fixing a subject and working out a scenario; there was a meeting, but again apparently with no result.[56] Toward the end of July Anna Stravinsky wrote to her daughter-in-law that Igor doubted whether Cocteau would prove useful or "help [him] in [his] difficulty."[57] Up to this point, there is no reference to card games in any surviving correspondence about the new ballet.

When the idea came to him one evening in a fiacre, he was so pleased— he later told an interviewer—that he invited the cab driver to have a drink with him.[58] Such delight argues a long period of uncertainty. Now, with Cocteau finally ruled out, he did something curious: he invited the assistance of a certain Nikita Malayev, a young friend of Soulima's based in Marseilles. "Why did you consider Malayev?" Katya asked. "Is he qualified for that kind of work?"[59] Or did Stravinsky simply yield to pressure from his younger son, who wanted to help a gifted friend of a certain neurasthenic— even suicidal—tendency, as we learn from Katya's letters of the following April?[60] At all events, Malayev duly came to Paris in mid-August, and within a week the subject was finalized and ready to be acknowledged for the first time in a letter to Willy Strecker, who, with the persistent difficulties of the Édition Russe in Paris, was now rapidly emerging as Stravinsky's main and most energetic publisher.[61] Almost at the same moment, coincidentally, Kirstein's partner Edward Warburg (another enthusiast with a rich father) had come up with clear financial terms for the commission—five thousand dollars for a one-year exclusivity for the American Ballet, including two performances conducted by Stravinsky himself.[62] At last the game was on.

At the start of September Stravinsky visited Katya in Sancellemoz, then went to Alsace with Vera for a few days of what Katya herself indulgently called "Nachkur" (that is, rest, after Vera's blood-pressure treatment at Wiessee).[63] Thereafter he settled down in the Faubourg to concentrated work on *Jeu de cartes*. He labored steadily on the second of the three tableaux—or "deals," as he had decided to call them—dispatching the score to Strecker in (not always complete) sections so that copying and publication could be well in hand by his planned departure for America in mid-December.[64] By November, what with interruptions for concerts in Zurich and Winterthur and, later, Naples, he was under almost the same intensity of pressure as eight years before with *The Fairy's Kiss*. "I work all day long," he told Strecker, "almost without rest. I sleep well, I eat well, and withal I suffer atrociously (in my sympathetic nervous system) from the bad weather."[65] Meanwhile Malayev elaborated the libretto: the so-called argument, or plot outline, as well as the detailed scenario, much of which figures in the draft score that Stravinsky completed on the 3rd of December. Perhaps because the card-playing idea had been entirely his own and hard-won, Stravinsky afterwards clung to it with an obstinacy in defiance of the fact that the early musical ideas had been conceived without plot and that Balanchine was in any case notoriously uninterested in anecdotal ballets. Of course, in one sense *Jeu de cartes* remains abstract, since the dramatis personae are playing cards and the plot is a game of poker. But the scenario, with its Alice-like battles between hearts and spades, its strutting, perfidious joker, and its abrupt triumph of good over evil, is a curious relapse into anecdotalism for the composer of *Apollo,* his one previous American ballet commission. Strecker grumbled at having to print the synopsis in the score, feeling that it would inhibit choreographers. But Stravinsky dug his heels in, and the argument—though not the bar-by-bar scenario—duly featured in the early published editions.[66]

The music itself nevertheless lacks recognizable anecdote and has on the face of it little to do with the poker action, notwithstanding the assertion in *Themes and Conclusions* that the trombone figure that accompanies the opening theme is an imitation of the croupier's "Ein neues Spiel, ein neues Glück" remembered from the German casinos of Stravinsky's childhood.[67] In fact the theme itself (though admittedly not the trombone figure) was one of the earliest pencil sketches for the work, on a sheet dated 2 December 1935 and headed "Jeu de Cartes" in a (probably later) red crayon.[68] Stravinsky himself was never a serious poker player, and seldom gambled, though like most people he played cards as a social pastime, and later in life became addicted to patience (solitaire).[69] The real meaning of this score harks back to that earlier Balanchine collaboration *Apollo,* which had used a more or less schematic scenario as the pretext for a modern re-creation of the form of classical ballet, complete with solo variations, pas d'action, and a culminating pas de deux for the principal dancers. The detailed scenario (though not the score) of *Jeu de cartes* reveals a similar framework, if one with a more narrative flavor, faintly reminiscent of Tchaikovsky, with elements of divertissement thrown in—as Stravinsky had hinted to Balanchine. Though not conventionally tuneful, it suggests a certain well-behaved "tunefulness," as in the opening brass theme, the flute tune of the pas d'action, or the march theme of the second deal. Very unusually for Stravinsky, there are actual or virtual quotations from other composers: Rossini's *Barber of Seville* Overture in the third deal, Ravel's *La Valse* earlier in the same tableau, and Johann Strauss's *Die Fledermaus* in the second, among others less blatant.

What Stravinsky seems to be aiming at here is some encapsulation of the idea of a "popular" ballet, without the austerities and intellectualisms of *Apollo* or the two-piano concerto. He had probably just missed the opening season of the American Ballet in New York in March 1935. But if he talked to Balanchine about the school or those opening performances later that month, he may well have formed the mental picture of a company not yet fully attuned to the esoteric refinements of post-Imperial ballet. In place of the intricacies of *Apollo* and the rich multilayerings of *Persephone, Jeu de cartes* offers a simple, direct, slightly brash, studiously conventional image of modern dance theatre. It uses a "normal" (roughly, Beethoven) orchestra, "a single set, and some simple costumes."[70] The form is episodic, the harmony and rhythm bold and uncomplicated, the orchestration brilliant but on the whole unsurprising, the drama inconsequential. More than any other large-scale work by Stravinsky since *The Firebird,* it feels aesthetically "safe." How far this reflects some concept of thirties Americanism, how far a particular stage in the composer's own artistic life, will emerge in the light of his works of the next decade, all of them commissioned by or written for Americans. It certainly cuts a slightly incongruous figure as his first work written wholly as a Frenchman.

5

DEATH DEALS . . .

For his third U.S. tour, Stravinsky had the biggest network of unpaid helpers even he had ever assembled. Sam Dushkin, who had married a girl from Cleveland in January 1936, had been watching over his interests in New York, keeping him up to date on the Merovitch crisis, briefing him on Merovitch's likely successor, Richard Copley, and acting as go-between with Balanchine and Kirstein over the *Jeu de cartes* commission. Meanwhile Dagmar was back on the warpath, offering to make herself useful by booking hotels, meeting him off the boat, and generally acting as unofficial personal assistant. In Los Angeles "dear fat doctor Kall" liaised with Klemperer and the impresario Merle Armitage, who was effectively managing Stravinsky's West Coast appearances. Even poor Malayev, having exhausted his usefulness as scenarist, was now detailed to ship to New York two cases of fine claret, which Stravinsky had either forgotten to take with him or made the mistake of assuming would be widely available in post-Prohibition America.[1]

The French liner *Normandie* docked in New York on Christmas Eve 1936, three weeks before his first concert. But there were important matters to attend to in the meantime. The *Jeu de cartes* score had preceded him by three weeks, and Balanchine had already choreographed the first two deals by the time the composer arrived. Irene Sharaff's costume and stage designs were also largely ready. Lincoln Kirstein, who had perhaps met Stravinsky in Paris in 1933 but was now getting to know him for the first time, found his response to these preparations "as courtly as it was terrifying." Sharaff's designs, based on a set of medieval playing cards, he dismissed as too definite in period and too decorative in manner, and instead he demanded "the banal colors of a deck of ordinary cards, forms and details so simple as to be immediately recognizable." The choreography seems to have pleased him, but some parts he found too prodigal in invention, and here, "instead of so much variety in the pictures he preferred a repetition of the most effective groupings."[2] The austerity and formalism he sought were of course nothing new in his work, but it looks as if his collaborators may have been disoriented by the anecdotalism of the scenario. Having fussed over its elaboration, Stravinsky now had to reimpose the necessary simplification.

After a few days in New York, he took a night train to Toronto, where, on 5 January, he conducted for the first time on Canadian soil. In itself it was no epoch-making event, not even indeed a full concert, since, after he had led the Toronto Symphony Orchestra in the suites from his first two ballets, the orchestra's permanent director, Ernest McMillan, conducted Brahms. But it gave the local press their first chance to interrogate the monster and to discover—as Los Angeles had discovered two years before—that he was a normal human being who looked like a diminutive if nattily dressed bank clerk, loved the cinema, was tired of jazz, and liked Hemingway. Stravinsky had been taking a Berlitz English-language course in Paris; but he still preferred to be interviewed in French, and his claim that "he likes reading the English and American writers best" should perhaps, at this stage, be taken as a broad compliment to his hosts rather than an expression of simple truth.[3] His one significant observation was the prophecy that "art in Spain will be held back one hundred years by the present civil war" and that "all art is retarded by revolution,"[4] a remark which reiterated his profound distrust of disorder, even in a cause to which he was in principle sympathetic. On his way back to New York he visited Niagara Falls and burst out: "It's something like a revolution—it's terrible."[5]

Where Merovitch had failed to book him a single concert with the New York Philharmonic, Copley had arranged no less than six in a fortnight— the familiar scheme of Thursday and Friday evenings and Sunday afternoon in Carnegie Hall, the same concert with minor variations, followed by a second trio, with a different program, the following week. For the first set, Soulima's young friend Beveridge Webster played the Capriccio and Mozart's G-major Piano Concerto, K. 453, and Stravinsky conducted *Fireworks* and *Petrushka*, plus Weber's *Turandot* Overture alternating with Rimsky's *Sadko* Intermezzo—the first time he had programmed music by anyone else in New York.[6] The second week's concerts were built round *The Rite of Spring*, his North American debut in the piece, along with *The Firebird* suite and Tchaikovsky's Third Symphony. As before, Stravinsky received ovations from packed houses but a somewhat mixed press, which generally found him to be a clear, incisive, efficient, honest but unspectacular performer. "To say that he is an incandescent leader, a mage, a master of that incalculable gift of revelation which a leader has or hasn't—to say that would be absurd," the *Herald Tribune* critic, Lawrence Gilman, insisted.[7] And Olin Downes of the *Times*, after admitting that *The Rite* "came close to being the most thrilling interpretation of the work that we have heard in this city," added in mock astonishment that "all this was done by a little scientific-looking man with eye-glasses, who rose from time to time on his heels and beat the measure, frequently in wide windrow motions to be certain that the orchestra understood him."[8] None of the reviews give more than a general flavor of Stravinsky's impact on the New York Philharmonic at this difficult moment in its history, after the resignation of Toscanini the previous April and the abortive move to appoint Furtwängler in his place. The first half of the 1936–7 season had been entrusted, very successfully, to the young Englishman John Barbirolli, a musician of utterly different character from either Toscanini or Stravinsky (according to one account, Stravinsky's first rehearsal was actually held up while Barbirolli said goodbye to the orchestra).[9] A recording survives of the Sunday concert in the first Stravinsky set (17 January), including both concertos, but alas not of the *Rite of Spring* program. As for the Capriccio, which New York was hearing for the first time since 1931, there was the usual damning with faint praise. According to the *Herald Tribune*, "its cleverness and whimsicality, while still apparent, have paled to a noticeable extent since six years ago; there are moments when one is conscious of a sense of length."[10] Downes described it illuminatingly as "ugly, tedious, irritating music."[11]

There followed a series of forays into the interior: a recital with Dushkin in Montreal, another in Worcester, Massachusetts, and, in between, a Town Hall recital that was greeted with quite astounding obtuseness by the bemused New York press ("The program opened," wrote one, "with a 'Suite Italienne' on themes by Tschaikowsky, which did not impress one hearer as being particularly Italian or Tschaikowskian").[12] Somehow, amid all these concerts, Stravinsky drafted a two-minute piece for radio orchestra, which he later christened Praeludium for Jazz Band (though it included strings) and which years later he told his publisher was written at the request of a band leader called Reichman, "who wanted it in full property, I disagreed, and there it was."[13] The piece is a ragbag of things heard in Manhattan bars and clubs, including perhaps "Smoke Gets in Your Eyes." But though intriguing as the master's first on-the-spot creative response to American music—and composed at a time when he was telling everyone that jazz was done for—its musical interest is extremely slight.

From New York the duo headed west to Ohio, gave a pair of recitals in Columbus on 8 and 9 February, then later in the month went on tour with the Cleveland Orchestra in a program that included, most intriguingly, Tchaikovsky's *Pathétique* Symphony and, at Severance Hall, Bach's Third Brandenburg Concerto. In these remote parts, the composer was still, as on his previous visits, treated something like a two-headed dog or a bearded lady. "If you would see this provocative figure in the flesh," gasped one newsman, "go to Severance Hall next week." The *Cleveland Press* headline— IGOR STRAVINSKY—SMALL BODY BUT A GIANT BRAIN—perfectly encapsulated the image of a stunted alien with freakish intellectual powers, while the paper's cartoonist, James Herron, added his own impression of the composer-conductor as a goggle-eyed automaton jerking around in front of a page of the Danse russe from *Petrushka*.[14] Yet the Clevelanders had seen and heard Stravinsky twelve years before and were being no more severely tested this second visit: the Violin Concerto in place of *The Song of the Nightingale*, and *Petrushka* for *Fireworks*, hardly amounted to a voyage into the unknown.

For Stravinsky himself, the human, earthly side of life had, these past few weeks, been asserting itself in no uncertain terms. The news from home was as disturbing as ever in the past. Early on 18 January, when he will have been sipping his evening cocktail in New York's Sulgrave Hotel after the Sunday-matinee Philharmonic concert, Mika gave birth to the daughter she had so longed for and Igor and Katya had so dreaded, knowing that her own life was being placed in the balance. Not that Mika had bothered herself in the least about such trifles. While pregnant, she had merrily taken twelve-mile hikes in the mountains with Yury, and now she went on foot to the hospital before enduring a seventeen-hour labor from which she emerged the happiest mother anyone could remember and ready, as she told Vera, "to do it all over again."[15] Katya, true to family tradition, worried over seemingly trivial defects in the child's health and physique: her stomach, her complexion, and of course—in view of her ancestry—her nose, which, as Katya calmly reminded Igor, would be the ultimate insignia of her Jewishness. But the little Catherine—or Kitty, as everyone called her from the start—was the unhappy herald of another misfortune than the ones she seemed marked out for. Less than three weeks after she was born her great-aunt Lyudmila Belyankin suffered a catastrophic stroke, and on the 10th of February, surrounded by her distraught family, at the age of only fifty-seven, died.

Of all exiled Russians, the Belyankins were the least equipped to cope with such a disaster. Ganya—epileptic and sickly—could barely do more than fend for himself and work on homely things. Hardly anybody was buying Ira's dresses, despite a complimentary review recently in *Le Jour*. As for Grigory, his habitually disordered world lay in fragments. The Café de la Paix was no more, while his latest venture, yogurt making, had depended crucially on Lyudmila's calm business head and her reassuring smile. To run anything of the kind on his own was quite beyond him. He had a weak heart. The Polish money had alleviated but by no means cured his chronic indebtedness, and now, just when he was beginning to feel that the world owed him a peaceful retirement, his sole emotional support had been brutally kicked away. The Belyankins were so poor and everything so untidy, Katya wrote, that "there's nothing to lay your hands on, neither clothes, nor blankets nor sheets."[16] Needless to say, she in her grief had to pay the doctor's bill, and later she gave three thousand francs toward the funeral expenses. "We buried her today," she wrote on the 12th,

> in the Russian cemetery at Ste Geneviève-des-Bois, forty kilometers outside Paris . . . The cemetery is just a large segment of a field enclosed within walls, without a single tree for the time being, but today, in the sunny, bright spring weather, it was very nice there and we all are comforted to think that she is lying there, among Russians, far away from the city, in the middle of a field.[17]

Stravinsky had reached Detroit when he received Katya's telegram, and Cleveland by the time Katya's and Vera's letters arrived. Both women took it for granted that he would be profoundly shaken by the news. Milochka was not only his sister-in-law but a cousin to whom he had been close since Ustilug days, and for him blood really was thicker than water. In his way he loved all the Belyankins. Milochka's daughter Ira, his favorite, would, he knew, be overwhelmed with grief, not least because she had quarrelled with her mother over Yury Mandelstam; but now, Katya reported, she had become a reformed character, was calmly taking over domestic responsibilities, going to church, and even behaving well toward Yury, whom she had previously loathed. Above all, from so far away he could feel the coming together of the different strands of his life. Vera had dropped everything to help the Belyankins, not only out of friendship for Ira but from genuine affection for Milochka. "This is the first time that I have witnessed the death of someone close to me," she wrote, "and I cannot get over it."[18] Her liberal upbringing and easygoing nature had not prepared her for the Dostoyevskian torments of an Orthodox death in exile, but while she therefore sometimes adapted uneasily to the mortuary tone of the Belyankin household, her innate goodness overcame all difficulties except the most fundamental one of her own relationship with the two families, and for that it was now much too late.

In a series of letters to Katya, Igor reflected on the bereavement.[19] And it was at this precise moment, on the 3rd of March, that he jotted down his first idea for a new symphony he had decided to write a month or so before, perhaps as a result of his New York concerts or even (though one hesitates to talk about outside inspiration where Stravinsky is concerned) after hearing about Kitty. The sketch theme, written on hotel notepaper in Evanston, Illinois, is at the same time an offshoot of the Rossini quotation in the final tableau of *Jeu de cartes* and an obvious precursor of the main theme of the Symphony in C.[20] Stravinsky had mentioned this project in a letter to Strecker at the end of January,[21] and probably it had already been discussed with Bruno Zirato, the assistant manager of the New York Philharmonic, as an inducement to engage Stravinsky again the following winter. At any rate, Copley later told Dushkin that Zirato would only want Stravinsky if he could have the symphony (adding, still less kindly, that he would only want Dushkin if he could have Stravinsky).[22] But the composer, under pressure from Katya not to tie himself down with deadlines, declined a formal commission, and there the matter for the time being rested.[23]

He and the Dushkins at last reached Los Angeles on the 8th of March.[24] At the railway station they were met by an impressive reception committee, including Otto Klemperer (who had been away from L.A. at the time of their visit in 1935); Theodore Kosloff, an ex-Diaghilev dancer well-known for his Hollywood Bowl productions and work in films; Alexis Kall; and—rather encouragingly—Boris Morros, head of music at Paramount Pictures.

The idea for a film collaboration had come this time from Merle Armitage, who had discovered that Morros was a graduate of the St. Petersburg Conservatoire and yet another voice (however faintly recalled) from Stravinsky's past.[25] But now the former movie actress Dagmar Godowsky decided on a pincer movement, and wired Morros on the 10th that he should at all costs book Stravinsky. Three days later, the two musicians dined together and drew up a contract under which Paramount would supply Stravinsky with scenarios, from which he would choose one to compose at the not inconsiderable fee of twenty-five thousand dollars.[26] The contract itself was vague about the actual process, but Stravinsky later told reporters that the intention was for him to propose a subject that would be worked up by staff writers into a screenplay for which he would then compose music, after which the filming itself would take place. Unfortunately this interesting—if, for Hollywood, somewhat optimistic—idea was understood differently by different interviewers. One quoted Stravinsky as saying that "the story and the setting and all the rest will be written around the music, and the music will be composed in terms of the sound film. Thus the whole production will be conceived as a unit."[27] Another heard him say that "I have left them my subject. They have given it to a noted writer. If I like what he does with it, I will then develop the story and music into an artistic unity."[28] A French journalist who cornered him in the Faubourg Saint-Honoré soon after his return to Paris elicited the view that

> the time has come when music must stop being the accompaniment to film. It can in certain cases provide the theme, underline the scenario, make sense of a cinematographic work and doubtless even inspire it . . . So I've suggested to our Hollywood friends that I provide them with the score for a film in the same way that one gives a ballet score to the scenarist. They are very excited by this proposition.[29]

Whether the basic idea was for a kind of World of Art cinema in which all the elements would cohere, or simply for a film in which the composer would call the tune, it got nowhere, though Stravinsky was serious enough about it to let it be known that the symphony was being put aside until the film score was done.[30] Morros was supposed to turn up in New York in April with a worked-up scenario, but never appeared, and although he did contact Copley after Stravinsky's departure, the trail eventually went dead. Stravinsky later told an admiring Darius Milhaud that Morros had rejected his demand that his music, once delivered, should not be tampered with, and he had therefore refused to sign.[31] Certainly he did not sign; the draft contract was never executed. More remarkable is that Morros, a working Hollywood musician, so much as contemplated such a bizarre transaction. He must have assumed that the score, once in his hands, would be his to manipulate as he pleased. But it remains odd that this rather obvious difficulty did not surface at their first dinner.[32]

For Stravinsky the failure was all the more galling because the two-year-old Chaplin project was also still theoretically alive but in practice just as elusive. After dining at the Robinsons' with Chaplin, Paulette Goddard, and George Gershwin that March, he preserved the idea that Chaplin was serious about a collaboration, and it was only after several months of vain transatlantic correspondence involving Dushkin, Strecker, and Robinson himself that he at last came to share Robinson's opinion that Chaplin was simply untrustworthy, and promiscuous in his attitude to such commitments.[33] He was learning a painful lesson about the fickle Hollywood mentality of gushing enthusiasm for high culture and intellectual respectability. Of course he was starstruck. It was flattering, even for the world's most famous composer, to receive, as he had done, requests for autographed copies of his *Chroniques* from Douglas Fairbanks and Marlene Dietrich.[34] Yet he knew perfectly well what the silver screen was really made of. Precisely at this time another aspect of Hollywood possessiveness—its artistic kleptomania—was invading his life in the form of a lawsuit he had instigated in 1936 against Warner Bros. for the "misuse" of his music in a detective film in which excerpts from *The Firebird* were used as leitmotif for a seduction, interspersed with fragments of a Viennese waltz. Such litigation nearly always proved painful, not only because Stravinsky's rights were often questionable (the courts already knew that the material interest in *Firebird* was vested in Jurgenson's former agent, Forberg, who had as a matter of fact sold the soundtrack rights to Warner Bros.), but also because his grumbles tended to look trivial to judges who did not share his pure ethical code where music was concerned. In this particular case the court found for him over the misuse, but showed its contempt for the principle at stake by awarding him damages of one franc.[35]

As before, Stravinsky and Dushkin stayed with Kall in Los Angeles. But their visit was shorter than in 1935, and there were fewer bookings, thanks to the financial crisis that had beset the Philharmonic Orchestra after it had shown a deficit of $156,000 at the close of the previous season.[36] In the end Armitage himself backed Stravinsky's pair of concerts in the Shrine Auditorium, but not without misgivings in view of the somewhat unusual character of the program. The first half would be conventional enough: the Divertimento followed by the *Firebird* suite. But for the second half the orchestra had engaged Kosloff—an old Petersburg crony of Kall's—to choreograph and dance the title role in a staged version of *Petrushka*.[37] Kosloff was a prominent and influential figure in Hollywood dance, but his reputation with serious balletomanes was, Armitage reported, "only so-so."[38]

Where Stravinsky was concerned, Kosloff had nevertheless been taking his duties seriously. For months before the performances he virtually withdrew from the real world in order to be free to imagine himself back into Benois's St. Petersburg, and when rehearsals began he made his two hundred and fifty dancers practice for hours to Stravinsky's own *Petrushka* recording. The same care was lavished on the (anonymous) costumes. And it does seem that, whatever may have been the quality of the playing by an orchestra whose very existence had been under threat, the show itself was so spectacular—and so spectacularly promoted—that the auditorium was packed for both performances and produced a healthy profit for Armitage and the Philharmonic. Kosloff, one critic wrote (with an eye, perhaps, to future billings), "blended action, waves of color and individual dances in a glittering parade of entertainment, which dazzled the eye and charmed the senses."[39] This was modern music as only Tinseltown could understand and appreciate it.

A few days later the two musicians shook the Los Angeles glitter off their heels and set off northward up the West Coast. A recital at Santa Barbara on the 16th was followed by half a concert in San Francisco, consisting of the West Coast premiere of the *Symphony of Psalms* (coupled with Rossini's Stabat Mater conducted by Hans Leschke—though the orchestra's regular conductor, Pierre Monteux, was present and introduced Stravinsky to the orchestra).[40] They then proceeded to Tacoma and Seattle for three further recitals, and the backwoods atmosphere deepened. The concerts were a success, Stravinsky told Kall,

> but God, the things you overhear! Just like what you heard in Santa Barbara—you remember, when someone told you he understood nothing in the entire concert (after performances of things like *Pulcinella* and the *Fairy's Kiss* Divertimento, the *Firebird* Scherzo and Lullaby, and the

Russian Dance from *Petrushka*—really baffling stuff), but understood only that Stravinsky the violinist had a remarkable accompanist (Stravinsky?). And this in 1937. It's obvious it'll be the same in 4937, since recent history teaches us that a century or so ago Napoleon had never heard of Beethoven, his contemporary.[41]

On 1 April they gave their last West Coast recital in Seattle and headed back eastward to New York. Stravinsky had reason to feel optimistic about his work. *Jeu de cartes* was coming up; he at last had the prospect of a serious and lucrative film project; and after that he would write his symphony. If only everybody's health could be better; if only the world could be less confused emotionally and politically. And now there was an even bigger anxiety: he himself was coughing. It had started, of all places, in Los Angeles. For weeks he had been suffering from a persistent, debilitating colitis. Then suddenly, every morning, there would be a coughing fit, brought on, it seemed, by the notorious drafts in halls like the Shrine. Samples were taken, tests made, and his worst fears confirmed; he himself had the dread disease that had been ravaging his family and that both he and Katya had presumably inherited from their Kholodovsky mothers. It was no mild attack. Soon after arriving in New York he began coughing blood, and his doctor ordered him to bed and allowed him up only for essential rehearsals and performances. Worse still, he had for a time to give up smoking, after nearly forty years of the habit. "It never rains but it pours," he grumbled to Kall as he also reported to him Morros's failure to put in an appearance in New York.[42]

All the same, he was less in bed than medical science would have liked. He went with Dagmar to Gian Carlo Menotti's *Amelia Goes to the Ball* on the 11th, and Paul Hindemith spotted him four days later at the New York premiere of his *Schwanendreher* viola concerto, sitting in the front row and looking "very decorative and detached," but afterwards telling everyone what an important piece it was.[43] Daily rehearsals for *Jeu de cartes* (or *The Card Party*, as Kirstein had decided to call it) lasted six hours, and Stravinsky was assiduous in his attendance; he would even, Kirstein recalled, take the pianist (sixteen-year-old Leo Smit) back to his hotel in the evening to work on tempi. He was as vigorous a rehearser as ever. "He would slap his knee like a metronome for the dancers, then suddenly interrupt everything, rise and, gesticulating rapidly to emphasize his points, suggest a change."[44] He and Balanchine were working closely together for the first time (their collaboration on *Apollo* nine years earlier having been intermittent at best),[45] but they clearly understood each other from the start. Balanchine always choreographed at rehearsal, working from the merest outline of a scenario and preferring to respond directly to the music; so while he retained the skeletal narrative of Stravinsky's three deals, he largely ignored the anecdotal stage directions. Indeed, the composer's account of the ballet a few months later to an interviewer from the Paris paper *Le Jour* reads more like a report on Balanchine's approach than a description of his own original intentions: "a work," he called it, "in which the saltatory essence, the act of dancing, would be respected. You can introduce into dance any kind of movement, on condition that you respect what I call the 'canons' of dance, its immutable laws, if you like."46 This is certainly not incompatible with Balanchine's own remark that in *Jeu de cartes* he "used the bodies of the dancers to feel out [the] volatile quality of the rhythm."47

For the American Ballet the two evenings, the 27th and 28th of April, were every bit the success Kirstein had hoped for. Stravinsky himself conducted performances which—since the orchestra consisted mainly of Philharmonic players—were probably on a reasonably high level. The Met was packed, the audience smart, the enthusiasm almost tangible, and the financial loss much smaller than might have been feared. Admittedly the press was tepid or worse: the music critics largely negative or condescending, the dance critics equivocal about Balanchine and baffled by the music. One music columnist (Julian Seaman) chose to interpret the lack of anecdote in the choreography as helplessness in the face of such sterile music—music that was "barren of ideas, bleak and meagre, and occasionally downright cheap."48 He liked only Sharaff's designs, described by another critic as "a green card table whose surface stretched from the proscenium floor to the upper reaches of the backdrop, defying both perspective and gravitation. Upon it, and in front of it, hearts, spades, diamonds and clubs shuffled and dealt themselves."49 Perhaps significantly, Stravinsky continued to dislike the designs, even in their revamped form, but "greatly admired" Balanchine's dances.50 One naturally takes this disagreement to mean that Seaman was simply unhappy with the modernisms, such as they were, in the score and the ballet. Ironically, his dance colleague on the *Daily Mirror,* Irving Deakin, was scathing about the picturesque, figurative elements in Alice Halicka's settings for *The Fairy's Kiss,* which was also on the program in a new production by Balanchine, even though the music obviously cries out for such treatment. Meanwhile, the music critic of the *New York American,* Winthrop Sargeant, rather enjoyed the new ballet (which "showed Stravinsky in his lustiest and most cleverly vaudevillian manner"), but took the opportunity to inform his readers that *Apollo,* the remaining work on the bill, "has always impressed this reviewer as one of the most tiresome of all Stravinsky's scores."51

Success or failure, the short "Stravinsky Festival" was a mere stay of execution for the American Ballet. It showed New York what Balanchine was capable of, but it also proved that mainstream opera houses like the Met were no more ready to take ballet seriously on his terms than the Maryinsky had been to accept Diaghilev thirty-six years before. *Jeu de cartes* was the company's last new ballet; within less than a year of its premiere the Met terminated their association, and a few months later the company ceased to exist.

On the 5th of May Stravinsky sailed for Europe on the *Paris*. Among his fellow passengers was Nadia Boulanger, who had been in the States on a one-month lecture and concert tour, but had also, she told him, been to see a Los Angeles acquaintance of his in Washington, Mildred Bliss. For some reason, Nadia had taken it on herself to arrange a commission for her composer hero, whether because of some hint he had himself dropped or through an unprompted rush of sympathy for his difficult and deteriorating family circumstances.[52] The Blisses had authorized her to convey to him a request for a new chamber-orchestral work to celebrate their thirtieth wedding anniversary the following year, and to be performed in their Georgetown mansion, Dumbarton Oaks. The fee would be two thousand five hundred dollars.[53]

Stravinsky could see at once that this was a reliable and manageable commission: neither a casual offer which depended on the caprice of some film mogul nor, on the other hand, a major commitment of the kind Katya had persuaded him against. The suggestion was for a work "of Brandenburg Concerto dimensions," which implied a small orchestra and no more than fifteen minutes of music.[54] Unfortunately, though actually now feeling much better and hardly coughing at all, he was still under strict doctors' orders. "I'm feeling very well but very bored," he told Dagmar. "I'm not allowed to smoke, not allowed to do any music, have to go to bed early, lie down a lot . . . a nice life, eh?"[55] Then, scarcely was he out of bed from what he assumed to be a stomach infection at the start of June than he had to step in at short notice and conduct the *Symphony of Psalms* in the Théâtre des Champs-Élysées in place of Monteux, who was himself ill.[56]

But he was growing restless, having done no serious composition for six months. Was there, he asked Nadia—who was conducting on the same program—any firm news from Washington? Another intriguing possibility had come up at a recent meeting in Paris with Leonid Massine, who was trying to raise American money for a commission for the Ballet Russe de Monte Carlo. They had been talking about Shakespeare, and in particular the comedies; Massine favored *Much Ado About Nothing*. But Stravinsky now proposed an altogether richer concept which he had already, as with *Jeu de cartes*, "handed to a very gifted young writer to work up."

> It has to be something like a monument to Shakespeare, a kind of choreographic action inspired by a series of his tragedies—"Shakespeariana"

perhaps, with a speaker narrating to the audience the course of the action, act by act or scene by scene. I'm only a bit cross that in the phrase in your letter—"as soon as there's something positive on this, I'll let you know at once, and very much hope this project will come off"—I don't sense the necessary confidence in my participation in your new and interesting affair . . .[57]

But Massine never did find the backing he needed for this remarkable scheme, which would have combined certain aspects of Stravinsky's past—the Cocteau narrator, the Diaghilev salad—with ceremonial elements that would surely have interested Balanchine and Kirstein. Two months later he despairingly suggested that Stravinsky might like to write the piece anyway "in his spare time," a commodity that, alas, played little if any part in the calendar of Stravinsky's life.[58] By this time, in any case, he had begun composing his Washington concerto, and though he probably visited Massine on his private island off Positano in September, the ballet idea quietly died.[59]

There now began what he later described to Kall as the "terrifying summer" of 1937.[60] For the first time for six years they were renting a house in the country, in the village of Monthoux, above Annemasse in the Haute-Savoie: a minor château, the former residence of the bishops of Annecy, but now run as a pension by a somewhat decrepit-looking and none-too-well-groomed Russian prince and his wife, who themselves did the cooking and—so far as it was done at all—the cleaning. The château stood peacefully in its own little park, with the village church on a low knoll behind, and to one side a dignified but less grand building which, it turned out, housed the ancient episcopal library. Here, amid the calf bindings and illuminated parchments, the composer promptly installed himself and his piano, and he was soon hard at work.[61]

They were a sickly party, the Stravinskys, that summer, but with the exception of poor Milochka Belyankin they were at least complete. For Igor that was the point. He could bury himself in his composing and rage if he was disturbed. But when he emerged from his studio, he wanted to know that the whole tribe was assembled. It was the instinct of the patriarch, but it was also the natural anxiety of the husband and father who sensed that at any moment fate might start picking his family off like so many homesteaders surrounded by wolves. And this was no mere fantasy. Katya's lungs were getting worse, despite the supposed benefits of the air at six hundred meters. His own were, perhaps, slightly improved; but instead his doctor had now found scarred ulcers in his stomach and intestine and had slapped him straight back onto a severe diet. Part of the trouble was that the Stravinskys had too many doctors specializing in too many ailments, real or imaginary. In Paris they had fallen into the clutches of a Russian "healer" who had prescribed cigarettes for the nonsmoking Anna's giddiness and breathing exercises for Katya's tuberculosis. At Monthoux a doctor from Annemasse cast a baleful eye on the dietary arrangements in the château kitchen, took one look at Katya, and without hesitation packed her off to Sancellemoz. Mika, however, was nowhere to be seen. When the doctor had left, Denise found her hiding in her room. She had started to cough again.[62]

As the summer advanced, the composer became miserably aware of the thickening cloud that hung over his family. Reporting to Cingria on Katya's declining health, he confessed to being "worried and unhappy" about it.[63] "One day, two days, she is better, then three days less good," he told Sam Dushkin, in a letter whose edgy and querulous tone reveals as much as its contents about the strain he was under.[64] For him, of course, Monthoux was by no means pure holiday. He was already writing the Washington piece, while grumbling to Sam about the Blisses' delay in paying the first installment of his fee; and he was mulling over a short homage to Ramuz for his sixtieth birthday the next year, based on a charmingly whimsical poem supplied by Cingria under the title "Petit Ramusianum harmonique."[65] Nor was all his business correspondence with or about America. He was soon also involved in an exchange with Werner Reinhart about a possible German edition of Chroniques to be brought out by Atlantis Verlag in Zurich; and there was much to-ing and fro-ing with Strecker and with agents in Frankfurt about Jeu de cartes and possible winter concerts in Germany. As before, he seemed quite blind to political realities in that country, even though at this very time he was pasting up his scrapbooks with newspaper cuttings of Nazi leaders in comic poses, which he embroidered with rude captions.[66] When the Chroniques translation arrived in mid-August he instantly noticed that cuts had been made (in his satirical description of Bayreuth and in a passage praising Jewish violinists), and though he knew perfectly well why, he pretended that the problem could be solved by footnotes referring to the uncut French edition.[67] No doubt, the fact of the memoirs being available in Germany at all was a sign of Stravinsky's rehabilitation there.[68] But he was still finding it hard to accept how qualified that rehabilitation would have to be.

Meanwhile, in his episcopal library at Monthoux, he was once again "inside the whale," mentally insulated from the quotidian world. Sitting at the piano he had had brought up from Geneva, he played Bach and gradually evolved the intricate rhythmic and contrapuntal style of the first movement of the brilliant E-flat concerto grosso that would be his response to the Bliss commission. He must still have had the Third Brandenburg Concerto, which he had conducted in Cleveland in February, buzzing round inside his head. The reference at the start of his own concerto is unmistakable, though short of actual quotation; and there are other hints later on. But in reality the music owes not much more to Bach than its starting point—the idea of a pair of melodic figures very closely worked against versions of each other and with a strong metric impulse which Stravinsky, unlike Bach, varies at the dictates of his increasingly subtle melodic alterations. The first movement is not very long, and is lightly scored for a fifteen-piece chamber orchestra only passingly related to any of Bach's (with clarinet but no oboe and, above all, no kind of keyboard continuo). Yet the craftsmanship is so refined that it may well have taken him at least his seven weeks at Monthoux to write it. Many composers would be happy to produce in a lifetime anything as exquisite, for instance, as the little fugato halfway through the movement.

When Katya moved to Sancellemoz at the beginning of September, Igor and Milène went with her, but stayed only a night or two before descending gloomily to their château, leaving her to the all-too-familiar sanatorium round of thermometers and injections and short, slow constitutionals. Igor was due in Venice to conduct *Jeu de cartes* at the Biennale on the 12th. So Monthoux came to its scheduled end, the family returned to Paris, and Igor climbed into the Turin sleeper at Geneva on the 7th. In Venice he would be meeting Vera, and afterwards they would head south for a holiday in Positano before depositing him again at Sancellemoz at the end of the month.

The 1937 Venice festival was the brainchild of Stravinsky's old friend Alfredo Casella, himself a keen Fascist yet touchingly optimistic about the prospects for modern music under the Duce's increasingly pro-Nazi dispensation.[69] Casella prided himself on having eliminated from the festival "all those mediocrities who had previously infiltrated the programs,"[70] and though this tactic inevitably got him into trouble with the nonentities in question, it was true that the 1937 program was strong. For instance, Stravinsky conducted his new ballet (its European premiere) plus the Divertimento in a Teatro Goldoni concert (12th September) which included Markevitch's *Flight of Icarus* as well as Milhaud's *Suite provençale* and Vittorio Rieti's Second Piano Concerto (played by Marcelle Meyer), works which would soon effectively be outlawed by the anti-Semitic legislation of 1938.[71] Earlier on, festival audiences (possibly including Stravinsky) had heard Bartók's recent, masterly *Music for Strings, Percussion, and Celesta,* Schoenberg's Suite, op. 29, Prokofiev's *Lieutenant Kijé,* and the Third Piano Sonata of Szymanowski, who had died of tuberculosis in March.[72] Italian public life still preserved an aristocratic, royalist façade, and in the interval of his own concert Stravinsky and the other composers taking part were presented to Princess Maria of Piedmont in her box. The next day he and Vera headed south.

The lure of the Amalfi coast, apart from its climate and scenery, was an invitation from Mikhail Semyonov, the former St. Petersburg critic who had been a member of Diaghilev's entourage in Rome in 1917. Semyonov had bought and renovated a tumbledown mill near Positano, where he lived with his mistress and entertained visiting Russian artists and intellectuals. It was said that he was in the habit of sitting naked on his terrace soaking up sun and communing with nature, with, always to hand, "a wine-bottle of industrial dimensions—also for his health."[73] Into this world of cultivated debauchery, Igor, Vera, and Ira Belline—who had come down from Paris to join them—slipped without effort, and only fled back to Naples and Rome when the weather became inimical to sunbathing. Whether the conversation suited them as much will have depended on how far it touched on politics. "Forgive my pressing you [to invite Ira]," Stravinsky had written to Semyonov, "but I regard you more as family than as a kind, like-minded acquaintance, even though you might be considered a 'leftist,' which can't be said of me, since those who know me well realize that I have no truck with that world."[74] Katya was more prosaic. "However tempting it may be to lie in the sun on the beach, I hope you won't, as it could be very bad for your lungs, liver and nerves. Perhaps there's a big rock where you can lie in the shade . . ."[75] She wanted him to spend some of his Venice concert money in Rome, on a new coat, in case the weather turned cold.[76]

Back in Sancellemoz, Stravinsky wrote on 29 September to ask Strecker if he had heard anything about Ansermet's performance of *Jeu de cartes* in Vevey two days earlier.[77] But he had the date wrong: Ansermet was conducting the work for the first time in October, with the main Geneva performance on the 27th. On the 12th he wrote to the composer suggesting that to play the ballet complete in a concert risked baffling the ordinary listener, and proposing cuts that would reduce the score by a third but give it a more comprehensible symphonic form.[78] Stravinsky's response was curt. "What particularly astonishes me," he replied, "is that you should try to convince me personally to make cuts in it, me who have just conducted this work in Venice and have told you with what pleasure the audience greeted it . . . I don't really think that your audience is less intelligent than the one in Venice."[79] Meanwhile, Ansermet had already written countermanding his request. Having played the music through at rehearsal, he said, he was convinced. Nevertheless, he still wanted to cut some fifty-eight bars of the March.[80] Stravinsky, by now in London (where he had himself just conducted *Jeu de cartes* "without cuts" at a Courtauld-Sargent concert in the Queen's Hall), wrote back in a fury:

> The absurd cut you ask for *cripples* my little march, which has its form and structural meaning in the composition as a whole . . . But you're not *chez vous,* my dear, I had never said to you—"Here you are, have my

score, do what you like with it"—I repeat, either you play *Jeu de cartes* as it is or you don't play it at all.[81]

This dressing down, relatively mild though it was, was more than Ansermet could endure. In an eight-page letter of circuitous and sometimes obscure philosophical reasoning—which in tone, if not tendency, somewhat anticipates his massive postwar "proof" that atonal music was an affront to human consciousness[82]—he attempted to justify what, on the most generous view, was an untenable position. In the end he seems to have irritated himself by the impotence of his own arguments, and the letter ends with an outburst of righteous indignation which seems frankly calculated to put an end to their twenty-five-year friendship.

> Insofar as you put up with others conducting your works, they will inevitably acquire a conviction about them equal to yours, and you are in no position to treat them as mindless or imbeciles. And if I can't discuss questions like these with you on a plane of mutual confidence, and without being received with your brutalities, it would be better to bring this conversation, as you say, to a full stop.[83]

Stravinsky did not deign to reply to this tirade, but instead decorated the letter with exasperated marginalia, then put the whole matter aside. Ansermet duly conducted an abbreviated version of the ballet, cautiously billed as "Music from the Ballet *Jeu de cartes*," in his Geneva concert, which was broadcast ("I shall be listening," Stravinsky had warned him).[84] Apart from a formal note from Ansermet sixteen months later, it was to be their last communication for more than a decade.

The rift is hard to explain on rational grounds. Craft suggests that the quarrel went deeper than the issue of cuts in a single score, but if so there is scant evidence as to the true cause.[85] Stravinsky, who had had a desperately anxious few months, certainly reacted jumpily to Ansermet's request, perhaps aware that his reservations about the work's abstract form were to some extent justified. On the other hand, Ansermet's rambling self-defense suggests a growing and somewhat unstable egotism of which there had also been signs in his treatment of his wife and his affair with Elena Hurtado. Just at this time he was beginning to interest himself in questions of musical psychology and aesthetics, and was bringing his old training as a mathematician to bear on the idea that the validity of this or that musical language could be logically demonstrated by reference to the affective structure of the brain.[86] But whatever the virtues of this kind of reasoning, it was remarkably naïve to imagine that it would weigh with a composer against the character or design of his own works. It was like trying to prove to a man in love that his feelings were logically unsound.

Whatever its flaws, in any case, *Jeu de cartes* had become a good draw for concert bookings. In London Stravinsky conducted it twice that October, and took the opportunity of spending the weekend before the concerts with his old friend Lord Berners at his ancestral home at Faringdon, in Berkshire. (Vera—or Madame Sudeykina, as the eccentric but well-bred English peer insisted on calling her—was with Igor on this visit, and afterwards she sent Berners some dyes for coloring his pigeons.)[87] Later that autumn he took the new work to Amsterdam, Naples, and the Baltic capitals Tallinn and Riga, with a public French radio concert in Paris in between.[88] One of the many Stravinsky doctors, a certain E. Sobeysky, attended the radio concert and, from his seat, watched Anna Stravinsky, "the only person in the hall who didn't clap but nevertheless felt very deeply the delight of the audience."[89]

Somehow in the interstices Stravinsky managed to work on the new concerto, finishing the first movement on the 24th of October, and the allegretto second movement by early January. The performance was scheduled for May, but any thoughts he may have entertained of conducting it himself were rapidly fading. Copley had simply not managed to set up a U.S. tour for early 1938, not least because Stravinsky himself had raised so many obstacles; he had refused to accept a symphony commission, and had opposed the idea of any more joint recitals with Dushkin—largely in response to Dushkin's own grumbles at no longer being recognized in New York as an artist in his own right, but solely as the rear end of a pantomime horse called Stravinsky-Dushkin. In a moment of pure, joyful fantasy, there had been talk of an Australian tour instead. But reality soon triumphed over the mad idea of spending three months on board ship and heaven knew how many weeks on tour to pay for them, with so much sickness at home. In the end he settled for Christmas at the Faubourg Saint-Honoré in the bosom of his ailing family, including Theodore and Denise, who had spent so much money on medicine and doctors for Denise that there was now nothing left. Mika's temperature was once more the subject of daily bulletins. Katya's condition continued to worsen. Had his English advanced that far, Stravinsky might well have thought of Tennyson's *In Memoriam A. H. H.* (xxix, 1–4):

> *With such compelling cause to grieve*
> *As daily vexes household peace,*
> *And chains regret to his decease,*
> *How dare we keep our Christmas-eve . . .*

Yet the decease, when it came, was outside the family. Three days after Christmas, Maurice Ravel died of a progressive and agonizing brain condition known as Pick's Disease, which had slowly incapacitated him over the past five years. The two composers had been on comparatively distant, though not unfriendly, terms since Ravel had reacted coolly to Stravinsky's beloved *Mavra* fifteen years before. Even so, Stravinsky responded promptly, if in somewhat official tones, to a request from *L'Intransigeant* for an obituary ("France loses in him one of her great musicians, one whose prestige is recognized throughout the world");[90] he went to view the body, and he attended the funeral in Levallois. Ravel "lay on a table draped in black, with a white turban round his head (which had been shaved for trepanning), dressed in a black suit, white gloves on his hands, arms at his sides. His face was pale, with black brows but an expression of seriousness and majesty."[91] Never in his life did Stravinsky treat death with anything less than a sense of awe.

As for Christmas that year, he kept only the Western date with his family. On Christmas Eve Old Style, 6 January 1938, he once again left Paris, this time for Rome.

6

... AND WINS

THE ROMAN TRIP, for a radio concert on the 10th of January 1938, had been arranged at little more than twenty-four hours' notice, and probably Stravinsky accepted only because of a desperate shortage of concert bookings to pay his rapidly growing doctors' bills. He was grateful, too, that Italy still seemed unequivocally friendly to his music, whereas the German situation—rehabilitation or not—was in practice more and more confused. Strecker was constantly advising him to accept this or that engagement in order to reinforce his position against the influential voices that were speaking out against his music. So when Telefunken invited him to record *Jeu de cartes* with the Berlin Philharmonic Orchestra early in 1938, Strecker was insistent that the company's huge prestige in Germany made the booking unrefusable.[1] Stravinsky duly proceeded to Berlin in the third week of February, and on the 21st put onto disc the best but, to the morally and politically sensitive, most infuriating of all his prewar recordings. The question of whether it was or was not ethical to appear to endorse a regime that was openly violating and humiliating Jews like his own daughter's husband seems not to have occupied him to any noticeable extent. It was more important that the thousand-mark fee would help pay for that daughter's urgently needed medical treatment.

Mika had suddenly become so ill in January that she had had to return to Sancellemoz, taking Kitty with her and leaving Yury to struggle on alone with his writing and editing in Paris. Then, toward the end of March, the sanatorium doctors decided that the mountain air was doing her more harm than good and sent her back to Paris, where, as her father wearily informed Strecker, "we shall look after her better and more attentively than in a sanatorium with so many sick people."[2] The atmosphere in the Faubourg had grown tenser and more wretched. "I live in terrible anguish," he told Dagmar, a month after Mika's return home.[3] Yet, as usual with him, the music he wrote during this unhappy time was innocent of all taint of suffering or self-pity. The middle movement of the E-flat concerto, which he imagined at an appreciably sprightlier pace than is today often adopted, is a cool study in pattern variation, with what feels like a duple-time melody played off against a triple-time beat, and with plenty of internal shifts governed by the changing lengths of the phrases. The finale, though more elaborate and in places more strident, derives essentially from the same kind of thinking. It is music with two overriding attributes: on the one hand, a joyful ebullience that constantly strives to break out of the conventional framework; on the other hand, the sheer benign control that, calmly and without apparent tyranny, prevents it from doing so.

Stravinsky was spending even more time than usual with Vera, and with those who made up her circle, like Baron Fred, now restored to his former role as courtier-in-waiting, and Arthur Lourié, who was often at lunch or dinner at Vera's.[4] Whatever the earlier difficulty between him and Igor, it evidently had been patched up. Just before Christmas, Stravinsky had sent Lourié a *pneu* warmly inviting him to call,[5] and though the old intimacy was no longer there, relations must have been good or the meetings would simply have been avoided. On the 6th of March, the two friends lunched at Vera's, two days after Stravinsky had conducted *Jeu de cartes* and the *Symphony of Psalms* in the Salle Gaveau and a fortnight before Lourié's *Sinfonia dialectica* was down for performance in the Salle Pleyel. Did they talk about each other's music, or just Stravinsky's, or did they simply avoid the subject? A month or so later they again dined together; but thereafter there is no recorded meeting. In September Lourié wrote, anxiously seeking information about Stravinsky's family situation,[6] and it must have been at about this time that, in some moment of bitterness or irritation, he let slip to Theodore a few salacious details about Vera's life in St. Petersburg during the Stray Dog period, when the two of them had shared an apartment with her future husband Sergey Sudeykin and his then wife, Olga Glebova.[7] As luck would have it, Igor was at that very time showing resentment at what he saw as Theodore's excessive attentiveness toward his in-laws, and on the subject of divided loyalties Theodore also had something to say. There were angry phone conversations and on at least one occasion Igor hung up on his son.[8] The coolness between them lasted for several months. But the chill that descended on Igor's friendship with Arthur Lourié never lifted.[9]

He and Vera also went to concerts. They would sit with Marie-Laure de Noailles in her box at the Sérénade concerts of the marquise de Casa Fuerte,[10] or go to the Salle Pleyel to hear Marcelle Meyer play Rieti's latest piano concerto. They went to many plays and even more films. They heard Prokofiev play his First Piano Concerto, and dined with him afterwards—the last time, as it turned out, that the two great Russian composers, who had been friends in their violent Russian way for almost thirty years, would meet.[11] But they never heard any Stravinsky. It was only a few months since Igor had been grumbling to *L'Intransigeant* about the neglect of his music in

Paris,[12] and it was still true that his stage works, especially, were largely forgotten in his home city. The *Oedipus Rex* in his French radio concert in
December was, Boris de Schloezer thought, its first performance in Paris
since Diaghilev had put it on in 1927.[13] But when Jacques Rouché, the manager of the Opéra, expressed a desire to stage *Jeu de cartes* in a production by
Lifar, Stravinsky rejected the idea out of distaste for Lifar, while tactfully
explaining to interviewers that the music was "too recent" and would have
to be choreographed by Balanchine.[14] In the end Rouché agreed on a "Festival Stravinsky" comprising *Pulcinella, The Fairy's Kiss,* and *The Firebird,* not
that it made much difference, since, despite his promise to put these works
on by June, nothing of the kind seems to have happened. So after all, the
composer's only conducting was the Salle Gaveau concert in March and his
Berlin recording. Just before Berlin, he and Soulima recorded the two-piano
concerto for French Columbia, but this too was not issued, and instead it sat
in the Columbia archives until 1951.[15]

The Washington concerto was at last finished on the 29th of March, dangerously close (considering the distance and the decision to print score and
parts in advance) to the first performance, now fixed, Nadia wrote from
Philadelphia, for the start of May. Since the composer would not be going to
America, Nadia was in charge of all the arrangements, and she would also
be conducting the performance. Strictly speaking, the premiere at Dumbarton Oaks on 8 May was a private affair, with a starchy Georgetown audience
of wedding-anniversary guests, many of whom will have found the program
of Stravinsky alternating with Bach rather heavy going for such a jolly occasion. There was the Duo Concertant, played by Dushkin and Webster; some
Bach cantata extracts sung by Hugues Cuénod and Doda Conrad; and then
finally Nadia stepped up and conducted the concerto, with Dushkin leading
the fifteen-piece band: an efficient rather than invigorating performance, if
one is to trust the Washington press, whose authority in the matter of
Stravinsky's latest music was admittedly a trifle suspect.

Nadia, more demanding and certainly not prone to blow her own trumpet, told Stravinsky that "the Concerto was played honestly, *well,* really
well—and was, I think, *understood.*"[16] The Blisses were of course delighted,
and Mildred at once fired off a beautifully ambiguous telegram to the composer: PERFORMANCE CONCERTO DUMBARTON OAKS WORTHY OF THE WORK.[17]
Admirable work, admirably played, Stravinsky understood; but he was baffled by the title. "It wasn't Nadia who conducted," he wrote distractedly to
Strecker, "for reasons they don't give me. Illness? Or was she at the last
minute afraid of not knowing the work well enough? According to Mrs.
Bliss's cable it was a certain Dumbarton Oaks who conducted."[18] A few days
later, the confusion was explained. Mildred had unilaterally decided that

"Concerto in E-flat" was too anonymous a title for a work of hers, so what more natural than to give it the name of the house in whose gracious and lofty music-room it was first performed?[19] Stravinsky was happy enough to accede to his patroness's wishes about the title, though Strecker disliked it "since in both French and German it sounds like the noises of ducks or frogs."[20] But he was not so sure about Dushkin's idea that he might emulate Bach by writing a whole series of "Dumbarton Oaks" concertos. "Let us not think about all the perspectives that might be opened up by a new Frederick the Great," he wrote to Strecker, temporarily mixing up his potentates, "but content ourselves with carefully correcting the mistakes (plentiful enough) in the instrumental parts."[21]

Just over a month later, on the 16th of June, Stravinsky himself conducted the European—as well as public—premiere at a Sérénade concert in the Salle Gaveau. Predictably enough, the reaction was very different from the polite but guarded enthusiasm of Washington. On the one hand, a full house of the type that was becoming commonplace for high-profile new music concerts—a mixture of socialites, professional musicians, fellow composers, and progressive, thinking art-lovers—cheered the concerto (played twice) to the rafters. On the other hand, the critics generally excoriated it. Like de Schloezer reflecting on the Concerto for Two Solo Pianos, they could not endure the spectacle of a composer whose music had once started riots composing such a lucid, classical, un-shocking piece. "Why does Stravinsky go on writing," enquired one, "if he no longer wants to say anything?"[22] "To see a hall in delirium," said another, "and to remain insensible to its cause; to understand a perfectly clear work but not to understand the enthusiasm it provokes, is a melancholy and acidulated pleasure."[23] Yet the problem was often one of expectation rather than perception. A fortnight or so earlier, Manuel Rosenthal had conducted a twenty-fifth-anniversary performance of *The Rite of Spring*, and both the impact and the historic significance of that work were fresh in everyone's mind.[24] How could Stravinsky, of all people, not want to renew his language, preferably with violence, every time he put pen to paper? The disturbing thing about the Concerto in E-flat was precisely that "one hasn't at all the impression of any question of failure:

> on the contrary, it's a question of a deliberate limitation, of a quite decided will to abandon all his riches. While keeping a sense of proportion, one thinks of those Brahmans who, on some internal prompting, renounce everything that constitutes the richness of their life and go off, their hands empty, dressed only in an old tunic inherited from a grandfather, along desert paths. This is moving when it simply concerns a

human being. But when it's a matter of creating a musical work, it's penury taking control.[25]

Though damning in intention, this is in itself a not inaccurate account of Stravinsky's creative aims at this period, and it raises specific questions that he would soon have occasion to elaborate in a nonmusical form.

The most strident polemics, though, came from Boris de Schloezer himself, who, while claiming that "I would willingly have forgone talking about this Concerto for small orchestra," in fact reviewed it at some length in three different places.[26] Not since the early thirties had de Schloezer bothered to discuss Stravinsky's new music as such. Instead he aired theories about it. In his *Vendredi* review of the Concerto for Two Solo Pianos, for instance, he had suggested that Stravinsky was these days content to manufacture his works on the basis of his own expertise and intelligence alone, and no longer had any truck with inspiration, with anything "given."

> I may be wrong, but I imagine that if Stravinsky were to receive a gift of this kind, he would examine it and check it, so much and so well that he would end up letting it slip. At bottom, on the evidence of his music, he has confidence only in himself and in his prodigious technique, and thus realises in the aesthetic domain a sort of "pelagianism."[27]

Now of the *Dumbarton Oaks* concerto he wrote that

> Stravinsky has always been a "composer" . . . ; but in the past, in "composing," he deployed a fantasy, an audacity, a subtlety which, I freely admit, dazzled us. Now he has arrived at the most dismal, the flattest academicism. Yet Stravinsky is playing his role; he remains true, cannot but remain true, to himself, he must obey the diabolical dialectic of his evolution.[28]

If such attacks proved anything, it was how right Stravinsky had always been to try to escape from the shadow of his own early works: from the concept of perpetual revolution and the dependably disagreeable which it sometimes seemed they imposed. If transparent, brilliantly made works like *Jeu de cartes* and the Concerto in E-flat were going to be torn to shreds simply because their lucidity made it appear that they contained nothing new, then the composer would never again be in the position to build on his own mature achievements. Yet it was in many cases precisely the most intelligent and sympathetic musical minds that were thinking this way. Ansermet, having been guardedly critical of *Jeu de cartes,* was candidly horrified by its successor. "If you insist that I play Stravinsky's 'Dumbarton Oaks' concerto," he wrote to Reinhart,

> I'll do it, but I beg you not to, as I'm dismayed by this score, which I have in my hand, and which I find desperately empty and boring. It's really the first frankly bad thing I've seen by Stravinsky. I shall not give it [in Geneva].[29]

No doubt Ansermet was still feeling cross with his old friend; but after all, this new opinion was consistent with the one that had caused the breach in the first place. The fact is that these various judgments did genuinely hint at a looming crisis for the comfortable, settled neoclassicism of the 1930s, however unjust the criticisms of individual works may now seem. In the event, circumstances would conspire to lead Stravinsky out of it by a route that he could hardly have predicted at the time of *Dumbarton Oaks*. But it would be by no means an easy or straightforward journey.

DAGMAR GODOWSKY had been working at full throttle on Stravinsky's interests in New York, but there was disappointingly little to show for her efforts. The Morros plan had faded out. She was in touch with both the New York Philharmonic and the recently formed NBC Symphony Orchestra, but Copley was yet again having difficulty putting together a tour that would be lucrative enough to justify the time and travel. The one promising approach from the States had come from Walt Disney's agent, Harry Fox, who wanted permission to use music from *The Firebird* to accompany part of an animated cartoon film. Stravinsky, well aware of his tenuous hold on the rights in his first ballet, once again had dreams of a collaboration in which music he would compose specially would mesh with Disney's animations. But these were still inchoate ideas. Then suddenly, out of the blue, Dagmar turned up in Paris, claiming to have been caught on board saying goodbye to friends when the *Britannic* weighed anchor in New York harbor. Though she had made no films since the silent era, her arrival did not go unnoticed. Photographers and reporters tracked her, no doubt not without her connivance, to her Paris hotel, where she told them that she was planning to take a slimming cure at Brides-les-Bains. The truth, which to his certain relief she did not mention to the newsmen, was that she had come to see Igor.

Stravinsky himself may have been displeased at her arrival, but he cannot have been wholly surprised. Back in February she had written him what was probably no more than a passionate reminder of past conversations.

My only love. I love you *so* madly and am *so* happy when I hear from you and your last letter was so specially sweet and I still simply couldn't pull myself together to write to you, my darling . . . My blood pressure is low (80) but it would certainly go up if I were to see you . . .[30]

Now, in the middle of May, she turned up unannounced at the Faubourg, just as he was about to leave with Soulima for a concert in Brussels on the 19th. This was too much to endure, and—roughly or gently—he gave her short shrift. Back at her hotel, she poured out her despair:

But once in my life—my beloved one—have I felt such utter misery as today—To have you send me away, when all I care about is you—all my dreams, all my life means you—is hard to bear. I understand your motive and will respect it, but emotionally I don't see how I will carry the burden. It is sad to love someone to whom one is merely an incident. And it is really you to blame who made me feel as I do. Now it is too late—No matter what you do to me, it can't alter the fact that it is you around whom my whole life revolves—And you send me away—coldly, unfeelingly with only one thought—not to complicate your life. I am not reproaching you—but only myself, that *I* wasn't capable of making *you* care. If only religion would help, but nothing, nothing seems to be able to stop the terrible pain in my heart.[31]

A day or two later, while he was away in Brussels, there was a phone call from another woman out of his recent, but also more distant, past: Ida Rubinstein. Ida had yet another new idea for a stage work which would give her fresh opportunities to develop her talents as a *diseuse,* and when Stravinsky returned her call it transpired that the target of her literary attentions this time was Paul Claudel.[32] Like Gide in 1933, Claudel was by no means unknown to him. They had first met in Paris before the war,[33] then during the war in Switzerland, where the author of *Partage de midi* was sometimes a fellow guest at Ramuz's, and to judge from Stravinsky's conversations, which often mention Claudel casually, they met socially a good deal thereafter. According to Craft,[34] Stravinsky disliked Claudel from their first meeting—which would not be surprising, as the playwright was difficult and quick-tempered—and he was certainly not much in sympathy with his particular kind of intellectual dogmatism. It seems, nevertheless, to have been Claudel who suddenly took against Stravinsky when they met for lunch at Ida's early that June. "I do not take to him," he noted in his diary, and he told Milhaud that "I actually didn't get on with Stravinsky, [but] I don't particularly mind, since during the conversation he developed for my benefit some implausible ideas about music and art."[35] Perhaps Stravinsky lectured him on Wagner and Berlioz, about whom Claudel had recently published an article, "The Wagnerian Poison," that had annoyed him.[36] Stravinsky was himself no Wagnerite by this time, but, as he scribbled in the margin of the article, "it really isn't worth rejecting Wagner in order to exalt the beauties of . . . Berlioz—it's too stupid." Unfortunately, Berlioz reminded him too much of the St. Petersburg of his youth, where the French composer had been God. But he always in any case reacted against the musical asseverations of literary men; he, a musician, had the right to detest Wagner precisely because he understood the scale of Wagner's genius. Literary critics of the Bayreuth master did not have that right.

Ida was clear from the start that she wanted a big stage work with a choir and speaking parts, but though possible subjects were aired at the lunch, no decision was made. Stravinsky wanted a Homeric myth in the line of *Persephone,* and he proposed the legend of Prometheus. Claudel was only interested in religious subjects of a moralizing tendency, and he suggested the Apocryphal Old Testament story of Tobit. A few days later, Claudel attended Stravinsky's Sérénade concert and experienced a revelation that put their meeting in a different perspective. It seemed that literary men understood perfectly well after all. "What an Elysian language you make music speak!" Claudel wrote:

> What perfection! What sovereign elegance! The concentration of the entire soul in what is heard obviates the need for words, ideas, even feelings, leaving attention only for the divine voices, which make music together, and separate only in order to recombine. But how to introduce a foreign element into this superior and self-sufficient world? The chief impression that I retain from yesterday evening, one of the most beautiful in my artistic life, is one of intimidation.[37]

He nevertheless announced a week later that he was starting on "the work you requested," still without saying what it was about. Stravinsky, who had not paid much attention to Claudel's views on the matter and merely stood by his own opposition to the staging of scriptural stories, took it for granted that it was Prometheus. Claudel's response was as dismissive as his reaction to Stravinsky's music had been fulsome. No, the subject was not Prometheus but Tobit. "Not for the world," he added sadistically, "would I again poke my nose into that antique pagan frippery, worn to a thread, and reminiscent only of Offenbach." Small wonder that the composer of *Oedipus Rex* and *Apollo* later remembered Claudel without much affection. At the time, however, they preserved a cordial tone. "We were not made to collaborate," Claudel suggested. "You are too great a musician, and we could never have penetrated each other's mind." As to that, replied the musician, "the only obstacle I saw, as you know very well, was the choice of a subject from scripture."[38] But on this occasion the writer saw more clearly. Stravinsky reserved his venom for poor Ida, telling Strecker that she was to blame for the rejection of Prometheus, and that he had broken off negotiations over the biblical story, "conveying to her my regret at having wasted a month on her for nothing when she knew from the beginning of our talks that I would not and could not do her a stage piece on a subject of that type."[39]

There is no sign that current affairs or politics at large figured in the conversation at Ida's. And yet the omission would have been astonishing. Claudel had been heavily engaged a year earlier in a row with a group of Catholic writers of the Left—including Maritain, Mauriac, Gabriel Marcel, Emmanuel Mounier, and Jacques Madaule—who had invited him to sign an open letter of protest at the bombing of Guernica in April 1937. Essentially, Claudel's line had been that to condemn the atrocity without decisively establishing Franco's complicity (which was questioned by some) amounted to connivance at the thousands of murders of Catholic priests by republicans, against which no protest had been made.[40] Stravinsky, who was pro-Franco, pro-clerical, and not overburdened with humanitarian scruples of a more general kind, would certainly have sided with Claudel on this issue, though whether he would have gone so far as to publicly endorse his open manifesto on the subject, as its author may have suggested, is another question.[41]

Any reference to the Nazis at Guernica would have brought up Stravinsky's chief political grouse of the moment: the exhibition of so-called *Entartete Musik*—"Degenerate Music"—which had just opened in the Kunstpalast in Düsseldorf, and in which *The Soldier's Tale* was among the prize exhibits. This curious event, which echoed the previous year's Munich exhibition of "Degenerate Art," was in fact little more than a sideshow in the weeklong *Reichsmusiktage,* an official celebration of Nazi-approved music, musical aesthetics, and musicology, organized under the patronage of the minister of propaganda, Joseph Goebbels. Outwardly, *Entartete Musik* was a compendium of those aspects of modern music that were excluded from the Music Days; it had sections on jazz, school music, and atonal theory, and a room of listening alcoves where you could hear excerpts from works by Hindemith, Weill, Berg, and others at the touch of a button—a situation purposely designed, of course, to emphasize the "incoherence" of the music in question. But the exhibition also had the political function of propitiating the Nazi *Kulturgemeinde* run by Goebbels's most dangerous rival, Alfred Rosenberg, which is why a mere two days before *The Soldier's Tale* and the *Chroniques de ma vie* were pilloried as degenerate in Düsseldorf, *Persephone* was performed in Braunschweig and the recently published German edition of *Chroniques* remained on sale in bookshops everywhere, as if Stravinsky's "rehabilitation" had never come into question.[42]

The inconsistency was typical of Goebbels's somewhat pragmatic approach to propaganda, as opposed to Rosenberg's unflinching ideological purity, but not surprisingly this distinction was lost on Stravinsky, who at once fired off a letter of protest to Willy Strecker[43] and was soon engaged in a laborious correspondence through various cultural and diplomatic channels in an attempt to secure some kind of retraction from the Nazi authorities.[44] He had come to the conclusion, mainly on the basis of press cuttings and hearsay, that he was the victim of a conspiracy on the part of German musicians; but he also noted with alarm that he was still being described in press reports as a Jew, an error that concerned him—he told one harassed French official—only because he knew the importance that was now attached to such questions in Germany.[45] He seems not to have noticed that other composers targetted by *Entartete Musik* (including Hindemith and Berg) were also gentiles, or to have grasped the fact that his music was still being played at all in the Reich only because it suited Goebbels to encourage an air of uncertainty at home while parading his cultural liberalism abroad. In any case, there was no longer any serious likelihood that Stravinsky would be engaged to conduct there. To do him justice, none of these intricacies was ever explained to him by his publisher, who was perhaps himself in the dark. As late as January 1939, Strecker wrote to him that "I can happily inform you that your position in Germany is apparently completely reestablished. You will be played and nobody will raise any objections."[46] The following June, less than three months before war was declared, Telefunken contacted Strecker about the possibility of Stravinsky recording his first three ballets for them.[47] If such relatively well-placed Germans could delude themselves to such an extent, it is hardly surprising that Stravinsky himself continued to dwell in cloud-cuckoo-land.

His reaction does nevertheless now strike one, with all allowances made, as grotesque. How could so subtle and intelligent a man abase himself in such a manner before a regime which, as he knew perfectly well, made no consideration of matters of art but was simply engaged in a policy of suppression and manipulation? It is almost as if he accepted the principle of political interference as long as it was not turned against him, an attitude that would have found little favor with his teacher, Rimsky-Korsakov, who had been sacked from his post for supporting his students' protests against the arbitrary closure of the Conservatoire.[48] For Stravinsky, such anti-authoritarian behavior was not quite impossible; but it ran sharply counter to his instincts.

On the very day that *Entartete Musik* opened in Düsseldorf, he had written to the official Italian concert agency, the Centro Lirico Italiano, suggesting Rieti's Second Piano Concerto for inclusion in a program he was contracting for Turin radio in early December 1938.[49] It was a policy of the Ministry of Popular Culture that twenty-five percent of such concerts should be devoted to music by Italian composers. So Stravinsky, who probably knew hardly any non-operatic Italian music later than Pergolesi, naturally offered the one work he had heard recently, which happened to be by a friend and in the repertoire of another friend, Marcelle Meyer. Unfortunately he neglected to brief himself about recent tendencies in racial attitudes in Italy; and he overlooked the fact that Rieti was a Jew.

There now ensued a bizarre fencing match between Stravinsky and the C.L.I., who wrote on the 3rd of June informing him that Rieti's concerto was not acceptable and inviting him to choose something else. On the 13th Stravinsky wrote back declining to drop the Rieti; on the 22nd the C.L.I. replied insisting on the change, the next day the composer again wrote a refusal, the C.L.I. insisted again, and finally on the 26th Stravinsky broke off negotiations and cancelled the concert—an almost unheard-of step for him to take purely on programming grounds. The curious aspect of all this is that Stravinsky never showed any sign of understanding why Rieti's work could not be included, and no reason was ever given by the C.L.I. or by the radio (E.I.A.R.). Rieti was fulsome in his thanks to Stravinsky for taking such a stand, but his own letter is coy, if unambiguous, on the crucial point:

> The fact that these gents at the E.I.A.R. wouldn't give you any explanation of the reason for their refusal is entirely symptomatic of their cause's bad conscience. It goes without saying that this reason, which they so carefully conceal, is in its turn merely a pretext behind which lurk the tendencies and interests of the diehards, that is, against what they call "modern music."[50]

Rieti obviously knew better than most that the tide was rising against Jews in Italy. By September, his son was being denied schooling and his parents had lost their jobs. "I shall soon leave," he wrote.[51] But if Stravinsky had indeed been standing on a point of moral principle, rather than artistic integrity or simple loyalty, it was one that the C.L.I. found it ludicrously easy to circumvent. On the 8th of July they resumed the negotiations as if for a completely different engagement. This time they offered Stravinsky a concert based entirely on his own works, except that he could if he liked include music by an earlier Italian composer. The hint that *Pulcinella* would, for the present purposes, count as an Italian work was palpable, and it was duly taken. Stravinsky accepted at once to conduct *Apollo*, the Capriccio (with Soulima), *The Song of the Nightingale*, and *Pulcinella* in Turin on the 2nd of December.[52]

THE MENACING summer of 1938 wore on, and for the Stravinskys there was to be no respite. Early in July even Vera fell briefly ill, with a throat infection so severe that Igor suggested (wrongly) that it might be diphtheria. As for Mika, her condition had scarcely improved since her return from Sancellemoz in March, but in the middle of July it suddenly took a turn for the worse and she endured ten days of agonized coughing, night after night, that left her exhausted and thin, a mere shadow of the radiant mother of eighteen months before. Igor could hardly bear to see his adored elder daughter suffer such horrors, and he would go off to lunch with Vera, or take her to some cinema, and earth his misery into her inexhaustible sanity and good humor. In August there was another, less acute crisis, and the doctor reassured them all that Mika's condition was not dangerous. "He has a very convincing manner," Igor wrote, without irony, to his eldest son.[53] But outside in the streets of Paris you could almost touch the sense of danger. Ever since the annexation of Austria in March, Hitler had been eyeing his Sudetenland border with Czechoslovakia, a country with which France had a treaty of mutual assistance; then at the end of August, amid frightening signs of German mobilization, the British prime minister, Neville Chamberlain, warned Hitler that an attack on Czechoslovakia could mean war. On the 24th of September, the day that the Czechs rejected Hitler's Godesberg Memorandum by which they were supposed to cede the entire Sudetenland to Germany, France mobilized more than half a million reservists. It was the closest Europe had been to war since 1918.

In Paris they sat glued to their radio sets, listening to speeches by Hitler and Chamberlain and nervously leafing through railway timetables. Everyone knew what Hitler had done to Guernica; now the French capital would certainly be high on his list. Many of Vera's friends were leaving; a feeling of panic was everywhere.[54] But in the rue du Faubourg Saint-Honoré two women were quietly, slowly dying. Both Mika and Katya were in bed, Katya having gone down with pneumonia, and Igor was so anxiously busy helping Milène and Madubo nurse them that for two weeks he hardly went out. On the day of the mobilization, Ramuz's old publisher Henri-Louis Mermod threw a lunch for the novelist's sixtieth birthday, the occasion for which Stravinsky had written his little single-line setting of verses from Charles-Albert Cingria's *Petit Ramusianum harmonique*. But the composer could not face the company, perhaps above all could not face Ansermet, who would be there, talking nonstop, lecturing him about his latest music.[55]

A few days later Paris heaved a sigh of relief as the four powers signed the Munich agreement which effectively blackmailed the Czechs into handing the Sudetenland over to Germany. Now all would be well. And for a time there was even a slight lifting of the clouds over the Stravinsky apartment. Katya's pneumonia eased; Mika was well enough to talk on the phone to Charles-Albert.[56] Igor started dining out again and spending time with Vera, walking with her in the Bois de Boulogne or going for late suppers at the Café Weber. Victoria Ocampo and her sister Angelica were in Paris, and Igor and Vera saw them often, including at one disastrous dinner at Vera's when Victoria aroused Charles-Albert's fury by speaking condescendingly about his musical judgments, an incident that provoked a storm of wounded indignation in his next letter to Stravinsky.[57]

However, the return to social normality proved only a lull. One evening in November, Igor arrived at Weber's in a state of terrible agitation.[58] Mika had had a relapse, and meanwhile he had to leave the next evening (the 22nd) for Rome, where he had a pair of concerts before going to Turin for his E.I.A.R. booking. Perhaps he should have cancelled his trip, but sickness had for so long been a routine in his family that he might as well give up altogether if he was to change his plans every time somebody coughed blood. So off he and Soulima duly set, late on the 22nd of November. It was the wrong decision. Mika was having some good nights and some bad, but the incessant coughing was taking its toll on the rest of her body; she had become horribly thin, ate little, and had difficulty breathing, and her heart was showing the strain. Yury had moved into Soulima's room, but he could only watch helplessly—the epitome of the loving, unpractical, bookish poet—as his wife drifted away from him. On the 29th her coughing intensified, and it was clear that such suffering could have only one conclusion. At five in the morning of the 30th it came. Igor and Soulima had arrived in Turin when Theodore's telegram reached them, and not until late in the evening did they get back to Paris. The family was assembled; Mika was still lying on the bed where she had died. Kitty was with Madubo. One part of the long-drawn-out tragedy had ended.[59]

Yury Mandelstam was bewildered by his loss. He wrote a poem in Mika's memory and sent it to his father-in-law.[60] Though moved by the poem and by the letter that accompanied it, Stravinsky would not agree to Kitty staying with her father, whom he regarded as too abstracted and unworldly to be a suitable custodian for so young a child. Not surprisingly, Yury took a different view, and there was briefly tension between them.[61] But Stravinsky's patriarchal inclinations were by no means undermined by his daughter's death, and he would brook no argument. As he explained to Kall, who had written to him in ignorance of his bereavement, Mika had "left us her little two-year-old darling, as well as, unfortunately, her very needy husband, and I cannot refuse to take them under my wing."[62] So Yury was set up in a bed-sitter, and little Kitty was dispatched with Madubo to Leysin—of all too significant memory—to live with their doctor cousin Vera Nosenko, who specialized in children's diseases.

Mika was buried near her aunt Milochka in the field-cemetery at Sainte-Geneviève-des-Bois, and Katya left her bed for long enough to attend. But it was a rare adventure that would not be repeated. Theodore had persuaded his father to dismiss the Russian "healer," whose mantra that tuberculosis was not an infectious disease was already showing catastrophic signs of being not quite correct.[63] The new doctor ordered Katya to the Pyrenees for a fresh variety of mountain air, but she was already, in mid-December, too ill to travel such a distance. At the end of the month, Igor and Soulima hurried back to Turin to give their postponed concert. As for any thought of America, that was now out of the question. Igor had made a few fitful sketches for his symphony, but he was no nearer to a commission or a date for its performance. By New Year the work had not advanced at all substantially, and when Copley pressed him about a tour the following winter he hardly knew what to reply, in view of his wife's condition.[64]

The matter was resolved for him with brutal swiftness. By the end of January, Katya was perceptibly weaker, racked by a relentless and exhausting cough that now threatened to turn into influenza. All through the month of February she lay in bed in the Faubourg, nursed by her family, her mind wandering over her childhood and those happy years of her marriage before illness and grief took up residence in their house. She had been for so long the calm, steady focus of their existence, the one who molded their lives and gave direction to their being while their father excited them with his spasmodic presence, it was natural that her dying should seem no more than a perpetuation. On the 1st of March 1939, a Sunday, Igor quietly slipped away to Vera, and Katya was heard to whisper: "Today I should have liked him to understand me as he has always understood me." It was their penultimate parting. The next day, at two in the afternoon, discreetly and without fuss as she had always lived, she groaned, leant sideways, and died on Denise's arm. Igor had called his mother in, knowing the end was in sight. Afterwards he stood alone by the bed for long minutes, gazing at his wife, needing, it seemed, to be still and know.[65]

After the funeral service in the alternative Russian church in the rue Boileau and the now-familiar trek to Sainte-Geneviève-des-Bois, Vera Nosenko lined up the whole surviving family in the Faubourg apartment and inspected them one by one with her stethoscope. The diagnosis was shattering. Milène: badly infected—off to Sancellemoz. Igor: badly infected—off to Sancellemoz. Denise: badly infected—off to Sancellemoz. Theodore and Soulima: not so bad. Theodore would naturally go with his wife to the sanatorium, but Soulima was allowed to stay in Paris with

Madubo and Baba Anna. They would move into Denise's mother's apartment in the rue Antoine Chantin (where Theodore and Denise had been living), while the Faubourg apartment was being disinfected. So, a mere ten days after Katya's death, Stravinsky drew the shutters and locked the door of his most luxurious but ill-fated home, and set off for the last time to the chilly heights and gloomy balconies of the Plateau d'Assy.[66]

ANNA STRAVINSKY had grieved for so many of her family that death no longer affected the severe set of her expression or the perpetual mourning of her dress. She had buried a husband and two sons, a granddaughter and two nieces, one of them her beloved daughter-in-law. She had left another son in Russia. In more than sixteen years in France, she had preserved the dignity and distance appropriate to the granddaughter of a Privy Councillor of Tsar Nicholas I. She had looked on her celebrated musician son and, on the whole, found him wanting. She did not much like his music, and still felt, perhaps, that the law would have been a more civilized as well as more useful vocation. She was somewhat mystified, to say the least, by his social activities, and disapproving of the free and easy ways of his children. Now the world seemed to be preparing to blow itself to pieces. It was time for her to leave. Always the healthiest of the Stravinsky family, she did not deign even now to fall seriously ill as they had done. Instead, with just enough pneumonia to satisfy the registrar of births and deaths, she collected up her frailties, and on the 7th of June, two months short of her eighty-fifth birthday, stoically died.[67] It was the last, and doubtless the least, of Igor's three great sorrows.

7

TO THE MAGIC MOUNTAIN ■

IN ACCOUNTS OF Stravinsky's life, the tragedies of the nine months that preceded the outbreak of war are passed over in a curiously detached way, like preordained events, a regrettable but necessary condition of his final emancipation from the stifling restrictions of his bourgeois Russian background.

It seems doubtful that he himself understood things in quite that way, then or for a long time afterwards. This past of his, this home that seemed not quite a home: they were still the focus of his consciousness. When Katya died, he was so distraught that his children heard him sobbing at night, and for the brief time that remained at the Faubourg they took it in turns to share his bedroom and keep him company.[1] After his mother's death, he wrote without false pathos to René Auberjonois from Sancellemoz. "My house, my family is destroyed—I no longer have anything to do in Paris. . . ."[2] So much for France, for Soulima, even for Vera. Life had for the second time in a quarter century taken its secateurs and snipped him off at the stem; and when a growing plant is cut, it bleeds.

Somehow, amid all the sickening and dying, amid the fear and tension and the confused alarms of struggle and flight, he again had to concentrate on work.[3] As 1939 dawned, he had no musical projects except the symphony, and no commission even for that. European concert bookings had all but dried up. America he could plan only for next winter. Then in late February, with Katya also nearing her end, his New York agent, Richard Copley, died suddenly, leaving his affairs in the inexperienced hands of his daughter. And just then, at the lowest point, the tide began slowly to turn.

Nothing had been heard from Disney for months, but at some time in the autumn of 1938 there came word that he wanted to use, not *The Firebird*, but *The Rite of Spring* for a sequence about prehistoric animals in a full-length animated cartoon film. Somebody had brought a recording of *The Rite* to one of Disney's Hollywood planning meetings in September, and he had got very excited and begun, as was his wont, to visualize the setting, with "dinosaurs, flying lizards, and prehistoric monsters." "*Fantasia* was made at a time," he later recalled, "when we had the feeling that we had to open the doors here, . . . that we could do some very exciting, entertaining, and beautiful things with music and pictures and color:"4 the time, he might have added, when *Snow White* was making him so much money at the box office that he felt able to test the market for somewhat more esoteric fare. In this ambition, as we have seen, he was not alone. Stravinsky's agreement with Morros had been founded on a similarly optimistic view of the potential for cinema as an integrated art form, which is why, when he was originally approached by Disney's agent, his first idea had been to compose music specially for use with the animations.5 He certainly had no real artistic interest in the use of an existing score; in these circumstances his concern was purely financial.

The contract that his New York lawyer, Maurice Speiser, signed with Disney early in January 1939 reflected, as much as anything, his desperate family situation at the time. For a consideration of six thousand dollars, it surrendered every vestige of control over the use to which his music could be put. It allowed Disney to use the score in whole or in part, and to adapt, change, add to, or subtract from it "all as shall appear desirable to the Purchaser in its uncontrolled discretion."6 Disney could put what images he liked to the music and he could call the resulting film what he liked. In other words, he could do exactly what Warner Bros. had been taken to court for doing, but he had Stravinsky's permission, which in any case he only needed for worldwide distribution, since in the U.S.A. the music was in the public domain.7 Disney and his conductor, Leopold Stokowski, made the most of these concessions. They cut the score by a third, and they completely reorganized what was left to fit the scenario of dinosaurs roaming the primal Earth, culminating in a tremendous battle between the stegosaurus and the tyrannosaurus, accompanied not by the Sacrificial Dance that concludes Stravinsky's score, but by the more remorseless (and much shorter) Dance of the Earth that ends the first part. Stravinsky was consulted on none of these changes, of course, and they came as a surprise to him when he saw the finished film eighteen months or so later.

He himself had somehow managed, during Katya's last illness, to get down to serious work on his symphony, even though there was still no sign of a commission or a first performance. In fact, the only premiere in sight was a curious echo from the past in Brussels, where a score of the still unperformed *Zvezdoliki* had turned up after being bought at a London auction by the Conservatoire. The piece received its very first performance, twenty-seven years late, at a public concert of the national radio on the 19th of April, 1939.8 Two days before, at Sancellemoz, the long first movement of the symphony was completed in short (compressed) score. By the end of the month Stravinsky was composing the "Larghette concertante" slow movement. And while Bach had supplied him with the starting point for the Dumbarton Oaks concerto, he was now again deeply immersed in the classical models that had been his inspiration for the two-piano concerto. When Soulima arrived at Sancellemoz at the end of June, he found his father installed in a two-room suite with a piano, well away from the other inmates. He was bubbling over with enthusiasm for certain passages in the late symphonies of Haydn and Mozart. He was in ecstasies over the "incredible freedom of harmony and voice-leading" in one phrase of the slow movement of the *Jupiter* Symphony, and the unequal phrase lengths here and there in the Andante of Haydn's *London* Symphony; and while neither these nor any other classical works are directly quoted in his own symphony, the sense of breaking out from strict conventions certainly is an important, if rather unpredictable, element of the Symphony in C, as Stravinsky eventually called his work.[9]

As usual, his unpaid agents were working vigorously on his behalf. Nadia Boulanger and Sam Dushkin had both sailed (separately) for New York in January, and they were soon colluding on a plan whereby the manuscript of the new symphony would be bought for the Library of Congress with money provided by Mrs. Bliss and others. In Chicago, Nadia discussed this question with John Alden Carpenter's second wife, Ellen Borden, and in March she wrote to say that Mrs. Carpenter and Mrs. Bliss were prepared jointly to guarantee a commission by the Chicago Symphony Orchestra.[10] This was the state of affairs when, at the end of March, there came a quite different proposal that once again pushed the symphony into the background and even for a time threatened its American prospects altogether.

Once again, Nadia was the catalyst. During the first half of March she was conducting in Boston and teaching Harvard students at Gerry's Landing, the Cambridge home of the university's professor of fine arts, Edward Forbes. Forbes was *ex officio* chairman of the committee for the Charles Eliot Norton Chair of Poetry, an endowed post that was filled each year by some—usually literary—star who was invited to give a series of formal public lectures backed up by private classes or seminars for postgraduate students in the relevant subject. In the fourteen years since the endowment of the chair, it had never been occupied by a musician, though music was expressly mentioned in the terms of the bequest as an eligible case of "poetic expression in language." It therefore seems highly possible that the final decision to invite Stravinsky came out of Forbes's conversations that March with Nadia, mostly—it is true—conducted in the small hours or during the brief moments when Nadia, who often taught from breakfast-time until after midnight, paused to gulp down a cup of coffee or a cheese sandwich.[11] On the 21st of March Forbes told the Harvard president that Stravinsky had been "selected." Six days later the choice was approved, and Forbes wrote to the composer formally proposing that he take up the chair, at a salary of nine thousand dollars for six or eight lectures and the associated classes.[12]

Though his doctors were pleased with him and he was putting on weight, and though he was technically an outpatient at the sanatorium, Stravinsky still had to ask their clinical permission before he could accept. Dr. Tobé, the director, could be a stern taskmaster, especially in view of the somewhat less than satisfactory recent statistics involving the Stravinsky family and lung disease. But after a few days' consideration, aided no doubt by much studying of temperature charts, X-rays, and pulse counts, the composer was allowed to accept the Harvard post, in addition to some concerts in Italy in May and September to which he was already committed. He duly wired Forbes his provisional agreement on 11 April, and ten days later he wrote a long letter to Alexis Kall in Los Angeles:

> You probably don't know what has happened to me since my terrible loss, which I told you about and to which you responded with a kind letter. Three months after the death of my daughter Lyudmila, my wife also died of the same frightful consumption as my daughter. It is hard for me to write to you about this new and dreadful blow which has struck me— I have lost the thing that was dearest to me in life.

After explaining about the Harvard post, he went on:

> You told me last time that I could count on your help, that you would go with me and fuss over me like a faithful friend. So I turn to you with this request. I shall arrive in New York at the end of September alone—you will meet me on the jetty, and we will go to live in Cambridge together (for seven months). I will go off to my concerts from there and you will always go with me to help me and comfort me. Agreed? . . . I have to tell you frankly that the thought of spending this winter with you in my painful loneliness of spirit is very appealing to me; and I would be exceptionally happy if, your health permitting, you found it possible to satisfy my request.[13]

At the best of times, Stravinsky did not like public speaking. However sharp and amusing in conversation, however fascinated by language, he was not particularly gifted with words in the systematic form of lecturing or writing, and he was ill and in deep mourning. The thought of a lecture series in the northern states in winter must have depressed him almost beyond measure, yet he simply could not afford to turn down such a lucrative post, with all the possibilities it offered for concert bookings in the interstices of his professorial duties. Even when it transpired, some months later, that the philanthropic ladies who had been putting up money for the Chicago commission had backed out when they heard about his well-paid Norton chair, he felt no special regrets.[14] The symphony might, as Strecker hoped, be commissioned instead by the BBC, or by some other American orchestra. The Harvard chair might never come up again; and meanwhile, not for the first time, dear old Woof would be there to make life bearable.

The only questions were, what should the lectures be about, what language should they be in, and how was he to get them written? Stravinsky was by no means averse to the elaboration of musical or even philosophical concepts, as many pages of his *Chroniques* had shown. But as a notoriously volatile creative musician, he had never reconciled himself to structured thought, nor been prepared to shape his work according to a preconceived aesthetics. In the twenties, while Arthur Lourié had been doing his best to locate his music in relation to certain more or less precise tendencies, Stravinsky had contradicted himself almost daily in press interviews and, in his music, had skipped from style to style and from one technique to another, with infuriating disregard for what ordinary human beings understood as artistic or intellectual consistency. For a series of linked papers, then, what he needed was a collaborator like Nouvel, a sympathetic thinker who, on the basis of an agreed plan, could assemble his ideas into a coherent text with a beginning, a middle, and an end, which he could then read out, in his picturesque, deeply accented basso French (since English, in so public an arena, was still beyond him) to the Harvard audience. As it happened, he had been seeing a good deal in recent months of his old friend Pierre Souvtchinsky, a highly literate and well-read musical egghead who, by a convenient coincidence, had just written and was about to publish an article on the subject of Music and Time in a special Stravinsky edition of the *Revue musicale*. The trouble with Souvtchinsky was that, like Stravinsky himself, he was Russian, whereas what was needed was a text in refined, idiomatic French. Of course, Souvtchinsky might draft the lectures and then have them revised by some French writer; or the French writer might himself establish a text, perhaps with background help from Souvtchinsky.

There were other pending contributors to the *Revue musicale* issue who might qualify, including André Schaeffner, the author of a book on Stravinsky which, on the whole, he liked, and several other friends, including Cingria, and the music critic Alexis Roland-Manuel. Cingria, though, was unreliable and factious, and a highly idiosyncratic writer with whom Stravinsky may instinctively have felt it unwise to get professionally involved. In any case, he was not a trained musician.[15] Roland-Manuel, though, was a more solid figure, a composer as well as a critic, and the author of a sympathetic and intelligent review of the *Chroniques* three years before. A converted Jew, like Lourié, he was similarly a friend and disciple of Maritain (his godfather), but a more humane thinker who, while sharing the formalist and artisanal attitudes of the neo-Thomists, could view them in a gently ironic light. "We shall not hesitate to point out to our intransigent Aristotelian," he had remarked about Stravinsky's views on expression, "that the musical work is inevitably expressive. Whether he likes it or not, it expresses its author." But he had admired the recent music, "in which the dogged precision of the artisan reveals to us, perhaps on the boundaries of tension and calculus, the delights of spiritual delectation."[16] Stravinsky had dined with him several times in recent months, and after two of these suppers Roland-Manuel had written up tidy notes on the master's conversation, much as Romain Rolland had done all those years ago at Vevey and on the Thünersee steamer. Only, Roland-Manuel's record was lively without spite. He noted Stravinsky's "appetite—his need for concrete realities:

> "If Czechoslovakia, the S.D.N., or the USSR had any substantial reality, they would have other names; France doesn't call itself Britanno-Normando-Languedoc, etc." He had heard a lecture by Sunerwein which told him nothing. Abstractions weighed in the balance by an impartial and tolerant man. Nothing more tedious. A plague on tolerance! A bad photo of Hitler, a gesture caught on the wing, a pose, a tic, a tone of voice, teach him more and strike him with a livelier jolt than generalities. "When someone squashes a mouse in front of me, its movements and cries affect me and move me, the idea pursues me for hours. When I read that twenty thousand Chinese have died in a flood, I'm no more moved than by a perturbation on the planet Mars."[17]

Later, they discussed the article Roland-Manuel was writing for the *Revue musicale*, and the critic had just written to report that he was writing the piece up when the Harvard invitation reached Sancellemoz.[18]

Forbes pressed for eight lectures, but Stravinsky from the start insisted that he would be able to manage no more than six.[19] After accepting the post, he quickly contacted Souvtchinsky, commissioned him to help draft the lectures, and discussed with him the question of the French text and who would write it. They must have talked on the telephone, since Souvtchinsky's letter of 26 April is the first written document of the arrangement, by which time he had drawn up a detailed plan for eight lectures, shown it to Roland-Manuel, and fixed for him to visit Stravinsky at Sancellemoz.[20] The critic arrived on the 29th, and in the next six days they elaborated and refined, and in some respects modified, Souvtchinsky's draft, making extensive notes which, when he went back to Paris on the 5th,

Roland-Manuel used as a basis for writing up each lecture in deliverable French. At the end of May, with probably four of the lectures written, and with Stravinsky back from his concerts in Milan and Florence, Roland-Manuel returned to Sancellemoz for what was meant to be a fortnight of intensive work but was interrupted by Anna's death and her funeral on the 10th of June. The two men would sit on the balcony of Stravinsky's room looking out toward Mont Blanc, and while the composer attempted to clarify his ideas, Roland-Manuel would annotate his own drafts and try to grasp the logical sequence of thought.[21] Meanwhile Forbes, an obstinate negotiator who liked things to be done correctly, was still naming eight possible lecture dates. But on the 17th Stravinsky put an end to that particular argument by sending his definitive list of six titles. Four days later Souvtchinsky wrote to him that the lectures were finished, then two days after that corrected himself by sending notes for a revised ending to the fifth lecture, on Russian music, which he himself had composed and which Soulima had been busy translating into rough French for Roland-Manuel's benefit.

So although the final French texts were entirely written by Roland-Manuel, the real pattern of the collaboration was much more intricate than that suggests. The influence of Souvtchinsky would be obvious even without his own original outlines, recently unearthed in Paris. For instance, the discussion of ontological and psychological time in the second lecture is heavily indebted to Bergson by way of Souvtchinsky's *Revue musicale* essay, "La Notion du Temps et la Musique,"[22] and in fact a lot of the terminology comes from that article. In general, the abstract thinking about music as a phenomenon and a language, and about issues of style, form, and perception, is pure Souvtchinsky, and not characteristic of Stravinsky at all. Souvtchinsky also did nearly all the background research for the lengthy denunciation of Soviet music in the fifth lecture (how else could Stravinsky have known about the operas of Deshevov and Gladkovsky?). On the other hand, the classic description of the composition process in the third lecture, many of the passing remarks on style in the fourth, and the by now familiar assault on conductors and virtuosos in the sixth, are all inimitably, unforgettably Stravinskian, and in fact were partly lifted from a radio interview he had given with Serge Moreux in Paris the previous December.[23] Here the reader feels himself at once in the presence of someone for whom the creative act is completely without drudgery. "In the course of my labors," he explains, "I suddenly stumble upon something unexpected. This unexpected element strikes me. I make a note of it. At the proper time I put it to profitable use." And when he expands the idea, the image is so peculiar that one might almost suspect him of a deliberate tease, if one did not know from listening to his music and studying the way he wrote it that it is the exact, unvarnished, wonderfully and inspiredly shameless truth.

One does not contrive an accident: one observes it to draw inspiration therefrom. An accident is perhaps the only thing that really inspires us. A composer improvises aimlessly the way an animal grubs about. Both of them go grubbing about because they yield to a compulsion to seek things out. What urge of the composer is satisfied by this investigation? The rules with which, like a penitent, he is burdened? No: he is in quest of his pleasure . . .[24]

On the philosophical level, these ideas still admittedly show the influence of Maritain. Maritain's hero, *homo faber*—man the maker—is here, as is the "idea of the work to be done," the concept of the artist as artisan that figures also in Roland-Manuel's *Revue musicale* article, "Démarche de Strawinsky."[25] It is equally apparent that Stravinsky—or Souvtchinsky or Roland-Manuel—has been reading Valéry's *Poetics*. Valéry, like Stravinsky, starts off with a quest for the etymology of the word "poétique," and he too comes back to the simple act of making, which is the root meaning of the Greek word *poiein*. But whereas Valéry characteristically pursues this idea of art as an activity, rather than a family of objects, to its logical consequences for our thinking about value, about process and effect, and about the relationship between the artist and his public, Stravinsky soon loses interest in the theoretical aspect of what, for him, is simply a handy definition of what he himself is up to. His attitude to the public is entirely conditioned by the joy he himself derives from the creative act. So while Valéry explores in painstaking detail the inevitable chasm between the maker and the consumer ("there is no viewpoint capable of taking in both functions at once"), Stravinsky rather tetchily sees the listener as a partner in his joy, "free to accept or refuse participation in the game" but not thereby in any way entitled to act as judge and jury.[26]

It is this odd mixture of pedantry, irritability, and artistic candor that gives the *Poétique musicale (Poetics of Music)* its unique flavor. The dogmatic tone often comes across as little more than a smoke screen for the airing of heterodox tastes of the sort calculated to enrage serious critical opinion in Paris, while probably merely baffling the average Harvard music student. Only the composer of *The Rite of Spring* and *Apollo* would cite reviews of Gounod's *Faust* as an example of the ineptitude of music critics, or remark that "there is more substance and true invention in the aria 'La Donna è mobile' . . . than in the rhetoric and vociferations of [Wagner's] *Ring*."[27] But then while the intellectual context and genre of the *Poetics* are clearly French, the coloring and mentality are often wayward and disaffected—in a word, *émigré*. There is a certain piquancy in the image of the great Russian composer (together with his Russian guru) using the Cartesian methodology of a French music critic to undermine so many of the conventional assumptions of French teaching and criticism about the nature of composition and the role of the artist. It would, though, have taken a very acute listener at the time to see in this anything beyond the instinctive eccentricity of genius.

All this time, Stravinsky had been struggling to get on with the slow movement of his symphony. Three times he had to break off: twice for Roland-Manuel's visits, and once for his own fortnight-long trip to Italy; but the music shows no traces—or at least no damaging traces—of interruption. At the end of May, just before the critic's long second visit, he drafted the double-speed middle section, with its shanty-like horn and violin tune, which does have exactly the feeling of a sudden "find" in the midst of a related if qualitatively different music. But one might not describe it in this way without help from the _Poetics_. Later, after his mother's death, he worked for a month, on and off, completing and refining the movement. Then he again put the score aside, having already made up his mind in April that he would compose the remaining two movements in America, by which time, presumably, he would know who would be giving the first performance.[28]

Souvtchinsky had been hard at work behind the scenes writing the Russian music lecture and advising on the other five. Then suddenly he found himself entangled in a Stravinsky family crisis that, for once, had nothing to do with lungs or, for that matter, mistresses. Almost routinely, Stravinsky had invited Soulima to come with him to Italy in May, and for the first time ever, Soulima had declined. He had his reasons, he explained airily, adding with a touch of pomposity: "I assure you that it is better so, and if you disagree now, one day you will see that I was right."[29] He had confided in Souvtchinsky, who urged the composer, in his next Sancellemoz letter, to "give credit to his spirit of independence, even if it could have come out at a better moment."[30] The moment, however, was precisely the issue, for while Igor raged at Soulima for "not thinking of me at the most difficult time of my life, nor of how terribly lonely I would be in Italy,"[31] Soulima's action was clearly no less connected with his mother's death and some pent-up revulsion at the treatment to which she had been subjected, even if it also, as Souvtchinsky began to speculate in the course of long conversations with a young man whom previously he had scarcely known, arose from an agony of self-doubt, and an almost pathological lack of confidence in his own abilities as a pianist and musician.[32]

Soulima was twenty-eight and, in his father's shadow, was starting to feel that life had passed him by. Igor remarked irritably but none too perceptively that Soulima "generally does not have to fight his own way, since actually he made it a long time ago."[33] But Souvtchinsky preferred to take a more analytical view. Soulima, he declared, was deeply immature and mentally sick, and his aggressive and suspicious behavior was due to chronic insecurity and lack of self-assurance. "I repeat, this is a kind of mental wound or injury, and to take offense or get cross with him about it makes no more sense than to be angry about a broken leg or lung disease. . . . I didn't understand his condition at first; he's very proud and reticent and good at concealing his inner perplexity." Souvtchinsky had heard Soulima at the piano and was not impressed. "I will speak frankly: he played to me and I must honestly say that there is something 'inadequate' about his playing, both technically and even musically. He himself is well aware of this, of course. The whole question is—how to help him?"34

Poor Soulima, trapped between a loving, authoritarian genius of a father and a clever amateur psychologist afraid—as he himself admitted35—of upsetting the father by too casual an attitude to the son's problems: how could he hope to survive at all? Igor was all too ready to accept Souvtchinsky's diagnosis, and quite unready to suppose that Soulima, after a winter of horrors, simply needed space and reassurance. He understood only that his own wishes were being challenged just when he himself felt in the greatest need of calm, unquestioning love. "Everything you write about him," he replied to Souvtchinsky, "disturbs and unsettles me to the depths. . . . I have never tyrannized any of my children, and have never even had it in mind to tyrannize them, but it is from every point of view and in all circumstances absolutely unacceptable that my grown-up children, who are financially utterly dependent on me, disregard rights which belong to me and not to them." Even so, his own wounded heart went out to his younger son, and in his anger he never failed in affection. He begged Souvtchinsky "to see Svetik and talk to him, and don't just fob him off with good advice but also send him something nice which he needs and which he cannot get from me because of the distance which separates us and because a letter only makes up for a hundredth part of a conversation."36

Whatever Souvtchinsky said or did, it had a good effect, since Igor soon calmed down, Soulima wrote a friendly, newsy letter discreetly avoiding the troubles,37 and by the end of June he was visiting his father with Madubo and taking an intense interest in the new symphony. Unfortunately for family relations in general, he was not the last visitor Igor received that summer at Sancellemoz.

Ever since Lyudmila Belyankin's final illness, Vera had behaved with typical loyalty and spontaneous warmth toward all the Belyankins and Stravinskys. Temperamentally she was as different from them all, except perhaps Ira, as it was possible to imagine. Where they were intense and insecure, emotional, devout, and in some ways enclosed and old-fashioned, she was open, confident and happy, affectionate, colorful, slightly prosaic, ready to make light of almost any difficulty. It was impossible not to love her. Yet at times her directness could show an astonishing lack of grasp or tact. There was the occasion at the *Persephone* premiere when she had sat openly at the back of the family box in full view of the audience, with Katya and Anna sitting at the front. Naturally she attended Katya's funeral, and when she ushered Igor to her car at the end of the ceremony she was think-ing of his comfort and convenience, and it obviously did not occur to her that she was coming between him and his family at a moment of shared grief.[38] Even Vera, though, knew that she could not simply turn up at San-cellemoz two or three weeks after Katya's death. Some decent pause was *de rigueur*. But who was to decide what was decent? For Igor, four months was already too long, while Vera would be easygoing on this question as on all others; but for Stravinsky's children, with their troubled attachment to old values and their passionate devotion to their dead mother, Vera's arrival on the 9th of July was a good deal too soon.[39]

She arrived to find Igor in a terribly agitated state. Theodore and Denise had made a scene about Vera, and had either gone off in a huff or been sent away in disgrace, depending on whom you asked.[40] Igor was now telling them to find somewhere to spend the summer as far as possible from San-cellemoz; but instead, to his intense annoyance, they had put up at a hotel in Yvoire on the southern shore of Lake Geneva, which he regarded as alto-gether too close for comfort. Meanwhile, Milène had suddenly taken a turn for the worse, had undergone a pneumothorax operation leading (almost inevitably, Dr. Tobé said) to pleurisy, and was now extremely sick with a nightly temperature of 102.[41]

The composer himself was physically much better, but deeply disturbed by all these family anxieties and at the same time tending to get upset at the things he was reading about himself in the June issue of the *Revue musicale*. What had started out as a Stravinsky celebration had, in his opinion, turned into a polemic, and the only articles he would admit to liking were Souv-tchinsky's and Schaeffner's. The rest was "tasteless and distorted . . . all quite pitiful, if not always intentionally, at least in the realization. Nothing *substantial*, nothing really *serious* is said to the advantage of my art. What untalented babble by Messiaen. I'm appalled by it all and prefer not to speak or think about it any more. I can imagine Schloezer's triumph!"[42] Worst of all was a long article by Lifar, prefaced by a few pages of smooth talk about Stravinsky's genius, but then launching into an extended denunciation of his ballets as fundamentally undanceable and even "positively anti-dance."[43] Probably it had reached Lifar's ears that Stravinsky had blackballed him as a producer of *Jeu de cartes*, a work that, he now decided, was sour grapes: "an anti-dance ballet *par excellence*." And he stated without reserve that "Stra-vinsky has always been a complete stranger to the ballet and has done everything in his power to impoverish it from the dance point of view."

There was some stirring in the Stravinsky ranks at this. Souvtchinsky and Roland-Manuel threatened to write to the *Revue* dissociating themselves from the whole issue of the journal, and Souvtchinsky muttered about getting something into the gossip magazine *Candide*. But Valechka Nouvel argued that the publicity would suit Lifar down to the ground; the musicologists failed to get the support of any other contributors, and, as usual, nothing happened.[44]

Throughout July and August, the composer languished at Sancellemoz with Milène, whose health slowly began to improve, and Vera, who occasionally took to her bed with this or that minor ailment or perhaps merely to avoid being conspicuous. Vera did not much like Denise, but she liked Theodore and was soon working on Igor to make up his quarrel with his elder son. At some point in late July the two of them drove to Yvoire in her car and there was a happy reconciliation.[45] A few days later, Soulima reappeared at the sanatorium. The remnants of the broken family suddenly seemed to be coming together again.

Igor had now finished his slow movement and was quietly writing up the orchestral score, while at the same time plotting the complexities of his American trip.[46] His latest plan was to embark at the end of September, having accepted to conduct a concert at the Venice Biennale on the 4th of that month. Vera's hopes of travelling with him had been dashed by the seeming impossibility of a Nansen passport holder obtaining a U.S. visa, so he would sail alone and be met by Kall on the quay at New York, exactly as he had originally suggested. Forbes, after losing the battle over the number of lectures, was being awkward about accommodation for Kall, who was prevented by some obscure Harvard regulation from sharing Stravinsky's College House lodgings, while the alternative Eliot House was excluded because of a rule against playing the piano in the mornings, Stravinsky's time for composing. They even briefly considered renting a flat with a housekeeper, until Igor learnt from Serge Koussevitzky that servants were a scarce and expensive commodity in the egalitarian U.S.A.—a salutary lesson for the composer of *Mavra*, which, as it happened, was on the program for Venice. In the end, nothing was settled. They would simply arrive at Cambridge and find accommodation on the spot. Forbes, it seemed, was washing his hands.

It was easy in Sancellemoz to get completely wrapped up in your own concerns and forget about the world outside, and certainly easier to worry about the meaning of a Greek verb or the price of lodgings in Massachusetts than about the significance of a military victory in Spain or a territorial threat in Poland. From time to time, Stravinsky had news from Paris. Gavriyil Païchadze, who had long since stopped publishing new work but who still acted as go-between in matters of concern to the Édition Russe, had written in April that Paris was once more in a state of fear and confusion after Hitler's annexation of what was left of Czechoslovakia the previous month.[47] But Willy Strecker had more or less ceased to mention politics in his letters, which could have been construed as a bad sign by anyone more politically alert than the Stravinskys. When Strecker came to Sancellemoz in August to pick up the score of the symphony slow movement, he again either said nothing or spoke honeyed words, since two days later (by which time Hitler's threats against Poland had made war inevitable) Stravinsky was writing to Roland-Manuel that war seemed unlikely despite the fact that Soulima had been called up as a reservist and had had to cut short his stay at the sanatorium.[48] From Paris, Soulima himself wrote that "the idea is gaining ground that Mussolini will side with England and France" and that Valechka "is certain there will not be war."[49] But by now, even Igor had the wind up and had already written to Mario Corti doubting whether he could come to Venice as he had heard that the frontiers were being closed.[50] Then finally a gnomic letter arrived from Roland-Manuel:

> This wind of madness blows on to a paradoxically calm world. It isn't the panic of last year. The disquiet hides at the bottom of hearts, but it is at the bottom of hearts that we need to find the peace which passes all happiness. It is at such moments that you make the distinction between what is troubling you and the one necessary thing, and it is in the one necessary thing that are reconciled the love of God and our loves for each other insofar as they remain, these loves, of the order of charity. Brotherly love is decidedly the best of what there is on earth. This is sufficient to tell you that now more than ever my thoughts go toward you, dear friend, with all my cordial affection.[51]

Two days later, on 2 September, Igor was discharged from Sancellemoz for the last time. On the 3rd, Britain and France declared war on Germany.

OPTIMISM now had to be replaced by realism, and practical questions needed to be asked and answered. Stravinsky had booked a two-way passage on the *Île de France*, with the intention of returning to Paris in May. But with German U-boats already active in the Atlantic, he was seriously doubting whether he ought to sail at all. On the very first day of war the Germans sank the British liner *Athenia*, with the loss of more than a hundred of its fourteen hundred passengers, including a number of Americans; and while Hitler, who was terrified of breaching American neutrality, denied responsibility for the attack, few believed his "theory" that Churchill, the First Lord of the Admiralty, had ordered the sinking so as to bring the United States into the war. In the end Stravinsky decided to go all the same, influenced by his desperate need of the Harvard emolument and the fees from the concerts and recordings that Copley's successor, Charles Drake, had set up for him in the gaps between lectures. It still remained, however, to decide when he would sail and by what ship, since regular timetables and bookings had been suspended; when and how Vera would join him; and whether they would return to France or stay for the time being in America.

Igor had in any case to plan for a long absence. The Faubourg flat, which had not been lived in since Katya's death, was paid off and vacated, and the contents put into a warehouse, except for Igor's manuscripts, which were placed in a bank.52 He then moved into the apartment in the rue Antoine-Chantin, Theodore having by now been called up to the army at Le Mans. But already the air-raid sirens were going off every night, so after two nights of struggling down into the cellar with his bedding, Igor decamped to Nadia Boulanger's country house at Gargenville, arriving unannounced with a carload of suitcases and still clutching his gas mask.53 From this none too convenient distance, thirty miles or so northwest of Paris, he did his best (with Vera's help in the city) to put his financial affairs in order, while waiting for news of berths and trying not to panic every time a U-boat sank an Allied warship, which happened nineteen times in the first half of the month. His clumsy and more than somewhat insensitive idea was to set up a single bank account, with Vera, his two sons, and Madubo as signatories, which was a little like feeding the cat and the dog in the same bowl.54 At the very least he failed to allow for the perfectly natural influence of a daughter-in-law in such situations. It was to prove an unfortunate, if not quite disastrous, miscalculation.

Gargenville was distant from Paris, but it was by no means cut off socially. For one thing, Nadia surrounded herself with pupils and ex-pupils during the summer, and not all of them had yet dispersed. Edward Forbes's son, Elliot, had been there, and Forbes senior himself turned up to see Stravinsky and discuss Harvard plans. For another thing, the outbreak of war had had an instantly centrifugal effect on Parisian society. Paul Valéry was a neighbor, and he and Stravinsky met several times, at Gargenville and at Valéry's house at Juziers nearby, and talked about music. The composer showed the poet his lecture texts, unashamed—or unaware—of the obvious if superficial parallel with Valéry's own Cours de Poétique (which Valéry, however, noticed at once and hastened to point out to Gide).55 Stravinsky teased the Wagner-loving poet about The Ring, which, he insisted, he would happily sacrifice in its entirety "for the theme of the Fox Movietone News."56 There was music-making, and an atmosphere at once cerebral and Elysian and as far removed as possible from the sirens and the blackouts and the U-boats and all the other terrors and anxieties of the phony war. "I will write again," Nadia told Poulenc, "to tell you about Stravinsky and Valéry and those extraordinary hours in the annals of drama, luminous, messengers of the future."[57] But she apparently never did.

Forbes had found Stravinsky still in a highly unsettled state, and he returned to Harvard half-prepared for a cancellation, with Valéry, naturally enough, as substitute.[58] The composer, though, was no longer thinking of withdrawing, but was merely waiting for a boat. On the 21st of September, after several changes of plan, he at last left Paris for Bordeaux, travelling with another pupil of Nadia's, Katherine Woolf, who, "though not rich," he told Theodore gratefully, "has upgraded to first class so as not to leave me alone with that crowd of unknown Americans."[59] A crowd it was, on the *Manhattan*, when she sailed on the 22nd. Even in first class, they were five to a cabin, and a U-boat would have reaped a heavy harvest, including Arturo Toscanini, who, according to a report in *Le Jour*, refused to take to his berth at night and instead paced the decks in a fury.[60] But there were no U-boats, and the *Manhattan* slipped quietly into New York Harbor on the last day of the month, discharging her passengers to their unknown fate on the peaceful continent of North America.

8

THE POETICS OF SURVIVAL

KALL WAS WAITING on the quay as arranged, and they were quickly ensconced together in the Hotel Sulgrave on East 67th Street. But no sooner had the composer wired Forbes to announce that he would arrive at Harvard on the 3rd of October than he went down with flu; and no sooner was he on the mend than Kall succumbed in his turn, and what with one thing and another it was the 10th before they reached Cambridge. The first lecture was fixed for the 18th and they still had nowhere to live, so Forbes invited them to stay a few nights at Gerry's Landing while they looked for an apartment, and then, when they predictably failed to find anything that met the composer's stringent needs, he agreed to lodge them in his house, at an agreed rent, for a trial period during the autumn. Space was hardly a problem for the Forbeses, for Gerry's Landing was a large, comfortable three-story house with a big garden. But the two Russian musicians cannot have been the easiest of houseguests, and the pernickety Forbes might well have been excused a twinge of relief at having agreed to the reduction from eight lectures to six, with long absences for concert tours in between.[1]

The lectures themselves were to take place in the New Lecture Hall (now the Lowell), a solid, turn-of-the-century edifice on the edge of the main Harvard campus. The lecturer spoke into a microphone, from a raised platform, to an audience distributed between a conventional auditorium and a long balcony that curved round the inside of the building. These Norton lectures were no dusty academic affair, but an event in the Boston social calendar, and the Stravinsky visit attracted a particularly chic audience, at least for the opening lecture. Half an hour before the start, "early intellectuals trickled in, to be sure of a seat . . .

> Then followed a rush of more intellectuals—Harvard and Radcliffe esthetes all. . . . Next came the big names of the Harvard music department, with their wives. This kind of an audience was what we had expected—musicians and music lovers from in and around the University. But then, to our amazement, black, sleek limousines began to drive

up to the New Lecture Hall, Beacon Hill dowagers, radiating white hair, evening dresses, diamonds, and dignity entered and added a *ton* of glamour to the affair. No sooner had we settled down to Beacon Hill than the New Lecture Hall rustled again. This time it was for Koussevitzky. . . . Eager, tense, the audience waited for Stravinsky.[2]

In the composer swept, followed by Edward Forbes, both of them dressed as for a concert, in white tie and tails. A brief introduction by Forbes, applause, a handshake, a bow, and Stravinsky set off nervously on the first lecture— the "Prise de Contact," or "Getting Acquainted," as the English summary supplied to the audience more amiably put it. Behind him, Forbes sat with a second copy of the text, in case any pages got muddled. Nobody will ever know how many of that first, or indeed the subsequent five, audiences understood the master's slow, heavily accented French. Kall himself suggested that "the large audiences . . . accepted [the printed synopses] out of courtesy and habit rather than of necessity,"[3] but other observers were less sanguine. That most telltale sign, laughter, argued the other way. "To Stravinsky's witticisms," one cynic noted, "the audience reacted like a grove of aspens; a few trees quivered at first, and eventually the foliage of the whole grove was alive."[4] Press reports occasionally revealed imperfect comprehension. The *Christian Science Monitor* reviewer made much of Stravinsky's attacks on Wagner, which, he maintained, "fairly tumbles down the educational set-up of Cambridge itself . . . [and] blows a hole, I daresay, in Harvard's own music department." But he misquoted the joke about endless melody in the third lecture ("the perpetual becoming of a music that never had any reason for starting"), and thought that Stravinsky was praising Verdi's *Falstaff* at Wagner's expense, when in fact he was regretting the influence of Wagner on late Verdi.[5]

At the end of the first lecture, though, there was wild applause, a very deep bow, another handshake, and Stravinsky "breezed out, his tails flying behind."[6] Afterwards, there was a reception attended by various university luminaries, musical and otherwise, including several former and current students of Nadia whose names Stravinsky had, for tactical reasons, jotted down on scraps of paper.[7] Among them were Walter Piston, by now a Harvard associate professor in composition, and a young Russian-born composer by the name of Alexei Haieff, who had been in Nadia's class at Gerry's Landing the previous spring and had met Stravinsky at her house in Gargenville barely six weeks before.

The second and third lectures followed on the next two Wednesdays, and between them Stravinsky embarked on the twice-weekly seminars with Piston's composition students that were the other part of his duties as Norton Professor. Like his École Normale classes of four years before, these were more like group-therapy sessions than classes in the conventional sense. He made little attempt at formal teaching and imposed no syllabus. Instead, each student in turn would present his latest opus, and Stravinsky would ooh and aah, pick out the things he liked, suggest improvements, remark on rhythmic or harmonic effects or defects, and sometimes play and talk about music of his own, usually speaking in French with Kall as interpreter. They were the kind of class in which, later, it is difficult to say exactly what has been studied. And yet, like Stravinsky's own weekly lessons with Rimsky-Korsakov, they left the mark that comes from intimate contact with an extraordinary individual who understands the importance of discipline and taste to any serious creative work, but who does not seek to dominate or bully in the matter of style. Perhaps more surprisingly, Stravinsky enjoyed himself at least as much as did the students. "Of course, the lectures were like concerts," he told an interviewer at the end of his professorial stint, "the performance was given and then an 'au revoir.' But the meetings with students in between the lectures, those were the good things which filled me with the best impression of interest. . . . Those young men who came to see me were so serious, not only filled with literary interest but with professional music interest as well. I was enchanted." Harvard, he added, was "a nursery of good manners and good taste."[8] Naturally it helped that so many of these young Harvard composers, and even some of their teachers, were sympathetic to his work and above all seemed to know it well. It was a curious reminder of that day in Berlin in 1922 when George Antheil had led him to suppose that America was full of bright young composers who adored his music.[9] It had taken a mere seventeen years for Antheil's white lie to become at least a quarter true.

Stravinsky and Kall stayed in Cambridge for exactly eight weeks before setting off on their winter travels. The composer's schedule left him ample time for writing, but in fact work on the symphony proceeded slowly, and there is some evidence that the exact style of the continuation was causing him headaches, whether because of the six-month break in composition, the unfamiliar strain of teaching, or simply the change of environment. Whatever the cause, the four-and-a-half-minute Allegretto third movement is as intricate in its detailing as anything in the *Dumbarton Oaks* concerto, and inevitably more complex because of the larger forces involved. In both cases the music flies off at a tangent to the classical—or baroque—sphere in which it supposedly originated. At this time, and months later, Stravinsky was still telling interviewers that the symphony was to be classical in character and severe in form, but at Gerry's Landing that autumn he was grappling with a music that was doing its best to evade the obvious implications of a Haydn minuet or a Beethoven scherzo, and it looks as if the creative discipline this entailed was slowing him down more than he might have cared to admit.

As relief from these labors, he would go for gentle afternoon strolls with Kall, a very different business from the brisk walks in the grounds at Ustilug or Voreppe simply because Woof was stout and unfit and not given to rapid movement: a heavy smoker and drinker, and a sufferer from various more or less debilitating ailments that were already beginning to take their toll on his physical vigor and mental alertness. Not that Stravinsky was far behind him when it came to unhealthy habits. Since Sancellemoz, he was back to forty cigarettes a day, retained his fondness for claret, and sometimes overate. At the beginning of November Dagmar drove all the way from New York to Boston for Igor's Cambridge concert on the 4th, bearing a consignment of wine for her two favorite Russians; and probably on that occasion they all ate too much. As the by no means sylphlike ex-movie star grumbled to Woof, "I lose everything but weight and my cold"; and neither she nor Kall was in the habit of exercising in front of an open window, as the trim, wiry Stravinsky still did every morning.[10] As for the Boston social circuit, that was less a relaxation than an unstated contractual obligation. There was a stiff dinner at the house of the Harvard president, James B. Conant, with a lot of professors and university dignitaries, which was perhaps the occasion on which Stravinsky turned to his escort, Walter Piston, just before they arrived and suggested: "Let's go somewhere and have a sausage." But he evaded the worst formalities of Back Bay society by the simple expedient of declining invitations, on the convenient—if not wholly truthful—pretext that he was too busy.[11]

One Boston invitation he did not turn down was to dine with Sergey and Natalie Koussevitzky on the 20th of November, a week or so before he was due to conduct the Boston Symphony Orchestra in a series of concerts in Providence and Boston itself. The Koussevitzkys, of all his Russian acquaintances, were among the most sympathetic and least censorious toward his association with Vera and his plan to marry her as soon as she could divorce Sudeykin. And he now knew enough about American provincial society to know that, if she came to the States, there could be no acceptable arrangement outside marriage.

Almost since arriving in Cambridge, he had been receiving anguished letters from her about the hardships of Paris in wartime, the wretchedness of old friends like Valechka Nouvel and Fred Osten-Saken, the lack of heating, the shortages, her experiences with divorce lawyers, and above all the seeming impossibility of obtaining a U.S. visa and even a French exit permit now that emergency regulations were in force. These regulations changed all the time, but were also much embroidered by rumor. There were laws against foreigners leaving, against women leaving, against French citizens marrying non-French citizens abroad; the French would not issue return visas to America, but America routinely refused visas to anyone without a return visa; and so on. For her divorce, Vera needed her birth certificate, the only copy of which was in Georgia because she had taken Georgian citizenship on her escape from the Soviet Union in 1920; she might try to prove that Sudeykin never legally divorced his previous wife, Olga, or (more difficult) that her own marriage to him was unconsummated, but in either case it would help to have her own previous divorce papers, which (needless to say) were in the possession of her husband in New York. To get almost any documentation she needed a new identity card, as was now required of all foreigners, but issue was slow and alphabetical, so it would benefit her to change from Sudeykina to her maiden name, de Bosset, which, however, she could not do quickly without the very papers she needed for her divorce.[12]

It so happened that Natalya Koussevitzky's much younger half sister, Tanya, and Tanya's husband Joseph Iorgy were at the Koussevitzkys' in Boston that evening. Iorgy had just been appointed U.S. delegate-general of the Union Féminine Française, and Stravinsky seized the opportunity to point out to him the possible benefits to the UFF in America of so well-connected a Parisienne and her even better-connected French fiancé. Iorgy had contacts with the French military authorities, and he could supply letters that would enable Vera—with a certain amount of footwork and a well-placed charitable donation—to obtain a visa swiftly and without bureaucratic interference. Igor wanted her to do all this at once and not wait until spring; the divorce could be arranged in America. As ever, his will was paramount.[13]

He had ample evidence of opposition to that will, and not only on the part of immigration officials and divorce lawyers. A few weeks after his departure from Paris, his son Theodore had come to Paris from Le Mans and, without consulting his co-signatories, transferred all but a token sum in the joint bank account to an account in his own name at a bank in Le Mans. He did this, he told Vera, because he had heard a rumor that the bank in question (the ultra-solid Crédit Commercial) was in danger of failing. But Vera, remembering the incident at Sancellemoz, saw in it the hand of Denise, who, she alleged, had organized the transfer out of a desire to exercise control. Everyone was so furious with Theodore that the money had to be returned and he went around for weeks with his tail between his legs. Meanwhile his father fired off at him a letter of such grinding, inflexible reproof that Vera refused to forward it and in due course persuaded Igor to allow her to burn it.[14]

That Denise was the *éminence grise* behind this calculated snub to Vera can hardly be doubted. For all her gentle disposition and sweet charm, she was a woman of character and spirit, not without a certain consciousness of rectitude, and inclined—like any young wife—to be touchy about her husband's standing in family circles, not to mention in his case artistic ones. Theodore, as the eldest child, deserved better of his father than to be placed on an equal footing of financial responsibility with the woman who, for nearly eighteen years, had cuckolded his dying mother; and it did not improve matters that he had personally been on friendly terms with her, been helped by her, even been watched over by her, nor that he was still, at the age of thirty-two, financially partly dependent on his father. Vera had for some time understood that Denise resented her, and she seems to have reciprocated the dislike, as far as was in her nature. Recently, in her letters to Igor, she had been lauding Soulima to the skies, sharing his wide-eyed accounts of life in the barracks at Cosne-sur-Loire, near Nevers, whither he had been conscripted, and praising his positive, enthusiastic attitude to work that he could easily have found soul-destroying. She knew perfectly well that all this would be balm to Soulima's father, who had been deeply agitated by his quarrel with his younger son earlier in the year. Vera had also sided with Madubo in a separate dispute, over whether the ex-governess stayed in Paris and kept the Antoine-Chantin flat warm for Soulima on his weekends off, or went to Le Mans to keep house for Denise and Theodore. Madubo—and Vera on her behalf—naturally preferred Paris, where she had fewer duties, greater independence, and more fun. Still, Denise might well reason that Madubo, in her late forties, was effectively pensioned by Stravinsky and could hardly object to a little cleaning and cooking for his childless son and daughter-in-law. To the easygoing and still somewhat bohemian Vera, this was bourgeois opportunism writ large. What Igor thought about it, nobody seems to have troubled to find out; but the money transfer left him "tormented in my soul," and when Denise sent him condolences on the first anniversary of Mika's death, it left him "with a heavy heart, for I do not believe her any more."[15]

In these matters, Vera was to blame only, perhaps, in failing to understand the natural currents of feeling of those who, this side of sainthood, were bound to wake up some mornings and feel that, on the whole, the world would be a more acceptable place without the likes of Madame Sudeykina. But how could she understand such a thing? Herself so devoid of bitterness, so easy in her view of the world, so generous yet so little beholden to others, she knew almost nothing of the ordinary horrors of family life. As for the extraordinary horrors of being the children of an egocentric, possessive, unfaithful genius, these she could see perfectly and help to moderate as well as she could. But she would always remain in some way outside them, in some way above them, vulnerable in their sufferers' affections to any passing squall of unfavorable circumstance. She would be, after all, a stepmother, but of grown-up children who could act and reflect but not escape.

BY THE TIME Vera reached his headquarters, Iorgy's military contact had been transferred, and it was only through Païchadze that she managed to trace him and make the arrangements for her visa. In spite of this delay, she suddenly had the papers she needed just after Christmas, and she made up her mind to leave at once on one of the fast but expensive Italian liners, rather than pay less for slightly more comfort on a later, slower American boat. On New Year's evening 1940 she dined with Ira Belyankin in the restaurant at the Gare de Lyon, then took the night train for Genoa, sharing a couchette as far as Chambéry. Her boat ticket was two-way, but the return half was token—a third-class passage for fifty dollars—and it must have occurred to her that it would be a long time before she saw Ira, or any of the Belyankins, or her future stepchildren again. They receded from view: Milène cut off in Sancellemoz, Soulima playing at soldiers in Cosne, Theodore licking his wounds in Le Mans, Kitty—the only grandchild—sent to Switzerland while her father, whom Vera had wined and dined after the *panikhida* for Mika a month before, sat in a café in Montparnasse, playing cards, writing poetry, and from time to time editing the literary pages of *Vozrozhdeniye.* War had not yet come to France, but its effects were everywhere to be seen.[16]

New York was another planet. Stravinsky and Kall had arrived well before the *Rex* docked on the 12th of January, and the sense of freedom and a new start lasted as far as the Great Northern Hotel, where Vera and Igor checked into separate rooms and he could not visit her in hers because they were not married.[17] In the Park Lane Cafeteria—another astonishing concept to a Parisienne—he could bring her up to date with his Harvard experiences and his recent trip to the West Coast, where he had conducted two concerts for Monteux in San Francisco the week before Christmas, then gone on to stay with Kall in Los Angeles, seen Balanchine—who was working in Hollywood—and visited the Disney studios with him to examine the models for *Fantasia* and listen to the *Rite of Spring* part of the soundtrack.[18] Since arriving in New York he had been working on a series of concerts with the Philharmonic, including a program of unadulterated Tchaikovsky.[19] The next thing now—curiously, in view of Le Mans—was an exhibition of Theodore's pictures organized at the Perls Gallery by the indefatigable and everhopeful Dagmar.[20] Then they were all off to Pittsburgh for more concerts, before Igor went back to Harvard to be a professor once more and Vera headed south to stay with her old Paris friend Georgette in Charleston.[21] The problem of her divorce and American social conventions still stood between them and an uncomplicated future.

At the Webster Hall Hotel in Pittsburgh, Igor tried checking them in as Mr. and Mrs. Stravinsky; but their passports betrayed them, and the embarrassment was all the keener for the fact that the Websters in question were the family of Soulima's pianist friend Beveridge, whose brother had just met them at the station and was standing beside them as they registered. So for more than two weeks of January in what Vera thought a "sad, provincial city full of factories,"[22] they kept separate rooms and a platonic façade, while Igor worked on his symphony and rehearsed Fritz Reiner's orchestra in *Apollo, Jeu de cartes,* and the two early ballet suites. His Syria Mosque concerts on the 26th and 28th were his début appearances as a conductor in the smoky city, and after the first concert he made a speech to the members of the Musicians' Club praising their orchestra and the musical life of America in general. "You see before you a happy man," he assured them, without telling them all the reasons.[23] But a week later, back in New York, the happy man had to watch his intended steam away to South Carolina while he faced a chilly journey in the opposite direction. There had been more hotel troubles. A reporter had traced them to the Great Northern and started asking indiscreet questions about their relationship, after which they had hastily changed hotels, tempers had become frayed, and Igor had ended up having a row, on some pretext or other, with poor Woof.[24]

The second block of Harvard lectures was timetabled to begin in March, but the semester, and with it the composition seminars, was starting up again in early February and the professor was required to be in residence. So there was nothing for it but to beard the New England winter in its lair. On the 14th of February so much snow fell in Cambridge that for two or three days nothing moved and it was a relief to get away by train to Chicago on the 18th for another series of concerts, especially as a Chicago premiere for the symphony was back on the schedule for the autumn, Mrs. Bliss and Mrs. Carpenter having at last found the extra money to guarantee the commission as well as the purchase of the manuscript.[25] Admittedly, Stravinsky still had quite a lot of the music to compose; but Harvard in the spring would be a stimulating environment, and if the weather continued bad, so much the better for indoor work, not least because he had now decided to cut the Gordian knot of American prudery and marry Vera as soon as he could get her in front of a New England justice of the peace.

After her month in the south, Vera reached Boston on the 2nd of March, and the next day she and Igor drove out fifteen miles to Bedford, Massachusetts, to file a notice of intention to marry, a drive which must for him have conjured up strange memories of a similar winter journey in an open droshky thirty-four years before.[26] And just as Igor and Catherine had prevaricated about their exact relationship at Novaya Derevnya in 1906, so Igor now told lies about Vera's history of marriage and divorce. Briefly, he testified that Vera had married Sudeykin in 1918 and divorced him at Tiflis in February 1920. These fabrications were either believed or "believed" by the probate judge, who probably had little choice but to issue the desired divorce certificate. The couple were married in a civil ceremony in Bedford, in the house of a Harvard professor of Russian named Timothy Teracuzio, on 9 March, a year and a week after the death of Stravinsky's first wife. The sole competent living witness to the truth, Vera's husband in New York, did not in this case emerge from the shadows.[27]

Between the lie and the act, Stravinsky directed two chamber concerts, one in Boston and one in Cambridge. The programs were the same: the Octet, *Dumbarton Oaks,* the *Soldier's Tale* suite, and the two-piano concerto, which he played with a former piano pupil of Kall's, Adele Marcus, and Mildred Bliss came up from Washington to hear her "house" concerto and to discuss the symphony commission with the composer.[28] In Cambridge, the concert on the 8th—fortunately a non-ticketed affair—had been arranged for the Paine Hall, but demand proved so great that it was moved late in the day to the larger Sanders Theater. A certain irony in this would not have been lost on Stravinsky when he strode into the New Lecture Hall for his fourth lecture on the 13th. The auditorium was less than half full, as if, faced with the choice between the composer's music and his musicology, Boston and Harvard had decisively opted for the former. Or perhaps it was simply that the novelty of his speaking presence had worn off. Attendance remained modest for the last two lectures. The studiedly controversial fifth lecture on the 20th, with its prolonged attack on Soviet music, was preached to an already partly converted audience of expatriate Russians and academic Russianists, many of whom, nevertheless, found Stravinsky's (or Souvtchinsky's) thinking excessively dogmatic, while local critics were disappointed that he said so little about the Russian music they knew, including his own.[29] At the final lecture after the Easter break, on 10 April, he was "enthusiastically applauded by his small, though appreciative, audience, and he took curtain calls at the end in the manner of an admired performer."[30] But a cheering mob of excited students would have made a more gratifying culmination.

After the wedding, Vera and Igor had moved out of the Forbes's into the Hemenway Hotel on the Back Bay Fens in Boston, and there they stayed for the rest of their time in New England. They had been mulling over their future, and had decided that to return to Europe in May would be both pointless and fraught with practical difficulties. The war, instead of ending within weeks as everyone always seemed to think wars would, was grumbling on, and though the news from France so far was unsettling rather than catastrophic, it was clear that concert work in Europe that year would be negligible, while Igor had his own grim memories of what happened to royalty payments and hire fees at such times. Immediately after his 13 March lecture, he had caught the night train to New York to take part in a concert organized in Town Hall by the Blisses in aid of French war relief, a concert for which he was donating his services on condition that a percentage of the money was earmarked for French artists.[31] There was not much point in his returning to Paris merely to be himself once again the beneficiary of precisely this kind of American charity. In the States he still seemed able to attract work and command decent fees. Boston itself, thanks to Koussevitzky, liked him, as both composer and performer. He and Adele Marcus played in Exeter, New Hampshire, just after their New York show, and there was a series of concerts with the Boston Symphony at the end of March.[32] And if his lectures had sown any doubts about the durability of his appeal to American audiences, they were firmly dispelled by the Boston concerts, every one of which was packed to the doors for programs dominated by difficult or problematical works like *Oedipus Rex* and *Apollo*. Now he had concerts in New York, in the course of which he would be recording *Petrushka* and *The Rite of Spring* with the Philharmonic, his first-ever sessions for the Columbia parent company, which had recently been taken over by CBS, had a new policy of recording with American orchestras, and was about to turn the whole philosophy of marketing classical records on its head by literally halving the price of a twelve-inch disc from two dollars to one.

But if they wanted to stay in the United States, the question of visas would rear its head once more. It turned out that Igor's temporary visa as the holder of a French passport could routinely be renewed for six-month periods, but Vera had a Nansen passport and had come to America under a so-called "Titre d'identité et de voyage," which could not be renewed.[33] What happened if they wanted to leave the United States and then come back in? This was no hypothetical question, because while he was in New York Stravinsky had met Carlos Chávez, the conductor of the Orquesta Sinfónica de México, who wanted him to conduct in Mexico in July. He simply did not dare leave with Vera unless he was certain they could both return. The only serious alternative was to come in permanently, under the American immigration quota system, and to file for U.S. citizenship on reentry. But Robert Bliss now terrified Stravinsky by announcing that there was a waiting list of at least eight months on the Russian quota—a waiting list one could not get on from within the United States.[34] For the second time in less than six months, the world's immigration bureaucracy seemed to have them by the throat.

Anxiety over these troubles made Stravinsky irritable, and it was just at this moment that things started going wrong with Kall. Igor himself had always been able to put up with the muddles and eccentricities of his helpers if he found them personally congenial; but the cold weather seemed to have affected Kall, who was drunker and more disorganized than ever in the past, added to which Igor was no longer a grass-widower but a newly married man whose wife, however easygoing, would not like to see her husband's affairs being run by an alcoholic. There was another, complicating factor. Dagmar had been busy in New York fixing Igor's Columbia bookings and concert dates in return for a commission. But Dagmar liked to mix business with passion, and she was still in undiminished pursuit of her client, with Kall as go-between and confidant. "Woof, dear," she urged, "write to me *as promised* right away and I shall destroy at once *as promised.*— Am *so* anxious to hear how 'he' is . . . I haven't had one drop of alcohol since you left—I *will* become again beautiful. I pray your cough has left you. It seems only what one loves leaves one though. . . ."[35] At other times, Dagmar and Kall would talk on the phone, and after one of these conversations Kall made a scene of some kind with Stravinsky.[36] Whether or not Kall was playing Pandarus as Dagmar hoped, his ineptitude as an organizer was unlikely to help her cause. At the end of March, when he and the Stravinskys set off for New York, he left the rail tickets at the hotel and lost two suitcases and a wallet at Grand Central Station when they arrived. Igor lost his temper, and it began to look as if their happy winter together would end in tears.[37]

Dagmar, fortunately, was a more dependable planner, and she had set up the Carnegie Hall concerts and recordings, together with all necessary press coverage, with dedicated efficiency. From the start, she had been instrumental in persuading Columbia's classical music director, Moses Smith, to record Stravinsky, and it was probably her fixing that tied the sessions in with a concert series—the composer's second with the New York Philharmonic that year—including his two great early ballets.[38] In the space of a week he conducted four concerts with what was surely America's best orchestra and probably, therefore, the best in the world at that particular moment when Europe's finest had been decimated by conscription and anti-Semitism. On the 4th of April, he recorded both *The Rite of Spring* and *Petrushka* (the short suite, starting with the "Tour de passe-passe"), in two heavy Carnegie Hall sessions that left him dripping and exhausted. Yet, whatever the strain of recording nearly fifty minutes of the most arduous and complicated modern music in five hours, the results set new standards for both works. Compared to the almost routine precision of postwar performances, they may lack absolute rhythmic security. On the other hand, for brilliance of sound and for sheer physical, balletic energy, they were unmatched in their day, and they still have a unique immediacy and authenticity that must have been a shattering experience to new listeners who acquired these discs in the early forties. Particularly in *The Rite of Spring,* there are grounds for thinking that the 1940 recording established a view of the music that effectively rendered earlier versions (including of course Stravinsky's own) obsolete. The fact that the recordings were themselves of outstanding modern quality and could be bought very cheaply also naturally did the music's dissemination no harm.

The Harvard semester still had a month to run, but Igor's route back to Boston lay via Washington, where the Blisses had set up a meeting with the director of the U.S. Visa Division and a lunch at the French Embassy, with a view to smoothing over the formalities of his and Vera's quota application. A certain added urgency may have crept into the deliberations with the news, which arrived during the embassy lunch, that the Germans had occupied Denmark and were at that moment launching an attack on Oslo. The next day, at Harvard, Stravinsky delivered his final lecture, and the day after that he started work on the finale of the symphony. He still had seminars to give, and even a few private lessons. But on 6 May the Forbeses threw a farewell party, and on the 7th the three Russians—husband, wife, and secretary—left Boston Harbor on a ship bound for New York, the first leg of a honeymoon trip that would eventually take them by a circuitous route to California. Before leaving, Igor wrote to his children describing his recent schedule and raising an issue that had been worrying him ever since he had received a letter from Yury Mandelstam announcing that he had himself remarried. "I was struck," he told Theodore,

> by the suddenness of the news of Yura Mandelstam's remarriage, which he told me by letter. By marrying Vera, I have regularized before the world and the laws of humanity the nineteen years of our union, but with him it's quite another matter, only a year after Mikusha's death.[39]

A brave son might have pointed out that Yury had at least waited for his wife to die. But above all there is a certain defiance in the composer's statement, a claim for special status, even while its gratuitousness (since the matter had not been raised by Theodore) suggests a bad conscience. This double image of his moral position apparently had not perished with Katya but remained with him, haunting and enriching his feelings, until—decades later—he followed her to the grave.

. . .

THEY WERE in Manhattan for a week, planning the next stage of their cruise and catching up with important people in Igor's life: his doctor (Garbat); his New York publisher, Ernest Voigt, editor in chief of Schott's U.S. representative, Associated Music Press; and useful local friends like the Dushkins. It should have been an agreeable time, constructive yet relaxed, but the news from Europe was such as to murder sleep. On the 10th of May, the Nazis invaded the Low Countries on the pretext of protecting their neutrality, and within five days not only had Holland surrendered, but the Wehrmacht had crossed the Meuse at Sedan, smashed the defending French army, and headed swiftly for the Channel. Seldom can a honeymoon trip have taken place under such dark shadows of anxiety. On the 15th, with no letup in the flow of frightening news, Igor and Vera embarked with Kall and a new assistant, Grigory Golubeff, on the *Seminole* bound for Galveston.⁴⁰ The idyll of sailing into warm blue seas in spring was regularly shattered by news of what seemed to them the destruction of the Europe they knew. On the 21st, the day they docked at Galveston, came reports that the Germans had reached Abbeville, trapping the British Expeditionary Force and a large part of the French and Belgian armies in the coastal region of Flanders. They did not have the heart to make their intended trip to the Grand Canyon, but instead took a train direct from Houston to Los Angeles, where they arrived on the 23rd "like refugees," as Vera noted in a burst of empathy with France as she was imagining it.⁴¹

They spent their first night at Kall's house in South Gramercy, but what had been for Igor a cozy and congenial refuge now struck his wife as mean, dirty, and uncomfortable. It had suffered greatly in its owner's absence and with the passing years. Bills had been left unpaid, there was no electricity or gas, and the telephone had been cut off. It was all somehow symptomatic of poor Woof's slow disintegration, and Igor, who had had almost eight months of his secretary's company, could not resist telling him so. There was a quarrel, which was then patched up well enough for them to stay with a roof over their heads. But it was the more imperative for them to find a house or apartment of their own, if only as a temporary recourse for the two months until Mexico, after which, as properly registered immigrants, they could look for something permanent. The decision to stay in America was now irrevocable. With the Nazis in France and advancing on Paris, there could be no thought of an early return.

In the days that followed, they were driven round the more salubrious parts of Los Angeles by friends, looking for somewhere to live: by Otto Klemperer, who was entering one of his manic phases and must have made a somewhat nerve-wracking chauffeur;⁴² by a piano pupil of Kall's named Dorothy McQuoid, whom Stravinsky had met on his December visit; and by the dancer Adolph Bolm, who had settled on the West Coast with his wife, Beata, and been appointed resident choreographer of the Hollywood Bowl. Bolm's latest Bowl project was a stage production of *The Firebird* that coming August—with designs by Nicholas Remisoff, who had collaborated with Bolm on the Washington *Apollo* in 1928—and this he now pressed Stravinsky to agree to conduct. Stravinsky said something like: "I will conduct your *Firebird* if you will be my guarantor in my application for U.S. citizenship." And so it was settled.

In 1940, Los Angeles was already a sprawling and confusing city, and there were many immigrants looking for houses that summer.[43] It took them ten days to find one they liked, at 124 South Swall Drive in Beverly Hills, an unassuming single-story house in one of the gridded streets that run south off Wilshire Boulevard. So desperate were they by this time that they signed on the spot, and within three days they had moved in, with such belongings as they had with them. Thus their Californian life together stumbled into motion: two more Russians in a city created by migration and rapidly filling up with Europeans in flight from a conflict which, it was increasingly being said, spelt the end of civilization as they knew it and the beginning of a new European Dark Age. On the very day that the Stravinskys found their house, Paris was bombed by the Luftwaffe for the first time, and eleven days later, on the 14th of June, the German army took possession of the grandest and most desirable real estate even they had yet violated. The swastika flew from the Eiffel Tower and, the next day, the Palace of Versailles. A week later, France fell. Of the Stravinskys scattered around the French provinces, nothing was known.

Between the news bulletins on the one hand and the peculiarly detached Hollywood social world on the other, Stravinsky could again turn to his symphony finale. For the first time there was real pressure to finish the work, now firmly scheduled for Chicago in November. But he seems in any case to have had no difficulty reentering the music's particular world each time he took up the score, and though the symphony is diverse in character, it shows few outward signs of its disjointed manufacture. Perhaps the slightly self-conscious finale references to the main theme of the first movement (an atypical device for Stravinsky) could be seen as a symptom of anxiety, but only with inside knowledge, since musically it makes perfect sense. On the other hand, the main finale theme, with its curious suggestion of Tchaikovsky or Rimsky-Korsakov, derives from an idea Stravinsky had scribbled on the back of a telegram form, then rejected, the previous autumn—an idea that eventually resurfaced in the "Pas d'Action" of the *Danses concertantes*.[44]

Outside working hours, the Stravinskys slipped effortlessly into the round of star-studded garden parties, charity teas, and drive-in dinners that were Los Angeles's special contribution to civilized life. They saw a good deal of Edward G. Robinson, an old but never intimate friend (to whom they remained "Mr. and Mrs. Stravinsky"); there were Marlene Dietrich, Josef von Sternberg, Erich Remarque, Cecil B. De Mille, Hedda Hopper, Max Steiner, and an ever-expanding credit sequence of Hollywood names, some of whom doubtless wondered who exactly this diminutive Russian and his large but still-beautiful wife were, while others certainly knew enough to hope that his intellectual eminence and artistic genius would rub off on them. These days they were both speaking passable English, Vera having studied assiduously in Paris the previous autumn; and their rich, sonorous accents were far from out of place in that land of the immigrant and the B-feature thriller. There is no particular evidence that, at so early a stage, they were bored by these gleamingly vapid, self-congratulatory gatherings. What is certain is that the climate suited them after Northern Europe and New England, which—Igor complained to one reporter—had only two seasons: winter and the Fourth of July. In many subtle ways, California soon began to affect their temper as well as their health. In Beverly Hills, surrounded by celluloid showbiz smiles in the unbroken sunshine, even Igor's hitherto inscrutable camera-face started to soften and the wonderful radiance which his family and friends had always known made its belated début in photographs.

Six weeks after settling into South Swall Drive they set off for Mexico, having at last managed—through interminable meetings with lawyers—to secure quota allocations without needing to leave the country before applying. It was, all the same, no token visit. Chávez had arranged for Stravinsky to conduct no fewer than four concerts with his Orquesta Sinfónica, and he was also booked to record his Divertimento for RCA Victor. Either because of the immigration rules or because there was no air service, they had to make the seventeen-hundred-mile journey by train, via El Paso and Guadalajara, a languid four-day trek with delays for paperwork and innumerable stops at wayside halts to take on peasants with their bundles, their babies, and their guitars. Mexico City itself, with its nearby Aztec ruins and its rim of volcanic mountains, was more than worth the discomfort, and Stravinsky liked working with the excitable but disciplined Mexican musicians. The concerts went well. But when it came to the recording session, it turned out that radio interference had broken in on the tape, and it could not be used.[45]

The final concert was on 4 August, and on the 5th they again boarded the train for Los Angeles, travelling this time with an immigration lawyer via Nogales on the border with Arizona. Here, on 8 August, it was necessary to leave the train and submit to medical examination and a lengthy form-filling process. One of the immigration officers asked Stravinsky if he wanted to change his name; "well, most of them do," he drawled when Stravinsky chortled at the suggestion.[46] The inquisition lasted three hours—a long wait in the scorching early afternoon heat of the Arizona desert, but a short enough time, in all conscience, in which to change the direction of one's life. When the U.S. consul eventually drove them to their train on the Arizona side of the border, they were not yet Americans; but they had embarked on a process that, after five years and barring accidents, would bring them to that desirable state. When they in due course got back to South Swall Drive, it felt, Vera said, like coming home.[47]

AT LAST there was news of the family in Europe. Theodore and Milène had both written, and there was a letter from Rieti, who had left Paris just before the German takeover and was now in New York. He had seen Soulima at Nevers and found him in good heart. "But I think our France is really done for, alas," he added.[48] Theodore had moved to the region of Toulouse, in unoccupied France, though whether voluntarily or by evacuation was not clear. His father was now worrying desperately about how they would all survive the coming winter, since Milène had written from Sancellemoz that she had no money and was unable to get access to the Paris bank account.[49] He had already sent fifty dollars via Vera's friend Olga Sallard, but he had no idea whether it had arrived; and now he wanted to send more. He was desperate for news of Soulima and Madubo (this was before Rieti's letter came), and anxious about Kitty in her mountain fastness at Leysin: "I suppose," he told Theodore, "that [Aunts Vera and Olga] are offended that I didn't send them an offical announcement of my marriage with Vera."[50] Even in wartime, there was to be no excuse for failure to communicate.

At this nervous moment, when so little was known and outcomes were shrouded in mist, he at long last finished his Symphony in C—of all his works the one that bears covert witness to the most terrible and tragic events. Later that day, the 17th of August, he stepped onto the stage of the Hollywood Bowl to rehearse his *Firebird*, in the form of its short 1919 suite, with Bolm's troupe and the Los Angeles Philharmonic.[51] The change of mood could hardly have been more abrupt. He had attended concerts at the Bowl and endured the queues of cars and the nightmare of parking, to say nothing of the doubtful advantages of listening in the open air, the polyphony of nature noises and distant traffic, the cool air and the rustle of fur coats, but he had never conducted there before, and he had certainly not seen the Bowl as it would be for the concert on the 27th. For the danced part of the program, Remisoff had designed a screen of brightly painted and brilliantly lit shrubbery to conceal the orchestra. At the end of *The Firebird* the bushes slid sideways "to reveal a fairy-tale city that reached into a rainbow" and the Firebird "mounted the topmost tower in triumph over all the monsters, kikimoras and boliboshki who had been so terrifying in their chartreuse, green, devil-red and bright blue costumes." Even the audience was invited to contribute to this spectacular Russian *son et lumière*. Before *The Firebird* began the lights were extinguished, and the eighteen thousand patrons held lighted matches above their heads, "like a vast field of fireflies."[52] In the interval the critic Deems Taylor made a speech in which he claimed that Bolm had choreographed the suite because the complete ballet score was in Paris and "he doubted the propriety of asking for it at present."[53]

Such events were comforting to Stravinsky's sense of belonging in this new and remote land, but they could not disguise the fact that his future there as a working composer was at best uncertain. He had no commissions nor prospect of any. From Europe he could expect nothing. Since the spring, his music had been under a formal Nazi ban, so the more countries Hitler invaded, the fewer would perform his work.[54] In any case, the distribution of royalties (especially from Schott and Édition Russe) was bound to be curtailed, as it had been in the last war. So if he wanted to earn his living by his pen as well as his baton, he would have to adapt to the environment in which he found himself, an environment in which the serious composer was an object of prestige rather than comprehension, and in which commercial criteria held almost universal sway.

Accordingly, early in October, he again visited Paramount, toured the studios, and lunched with the new music director, Louis Lipstone. A few days later, on the 12th, he attended a screening of *Fantasia* at the Disney studios, an experience that sorely tested his goodwill toward what was, after all, very much the "intellectual" end of the Hollywood spectrum.[55] He knew, of course, that his score had been cut and reorganized; but he now had to confront the dinosaurs in all their animated grotesquerie, and watch the conductor, Leopold Stokowski, walk up and down a color-lit staircase and shake hands with Mickey Mouse. Yet however distasteful he may have found this whole performance,[56] he swallowed his pride and, a few days later, entered into negotiations with Disney over possible film animations of other works of his. On the 28th of October, before *Fantasia* had even been shown to a paying audience,[57] he signed a new contract for the exploitation of *The Firebird, Renard,* and *Fireworks,* an option for which he was paid $1,500. Had Disney ever used any of these works, there would have been more cash, but he never did.[58]

Stravinsky had also discovered that it was possible to make money by allowing his works to be adapted in band arrangements, with or without voice, and a few days before the Paramount visit he had made an agreement with an arranger called Gregory Stone, under which Stone was authorized to make adaptations from various Stravinsky works, including the three early ballets and *Pulcinella,* in return for a fifty percent royalty and an acknowledgment of the composer's "editorship."[59] This might seem to conflict with Stravinsky's supposed reluctance to allow any music he wrote for films to be adapted or orchestrated by other hands; but he appears to have felt differently about existing works, especially where the agreement was under his control and did not place him at the mercy of some large, philistine institution. It may nevertheless have been at Stone's suggestion that he spent several days in early October writing a tango specifically with a view to commercial exploitation.[60] Although the Tango is often regarded as a piano piece, the three-line sketch is actually the short-score of a work for band or instrumental ensemble, and the object was to add words to it and turn it into a popular song.[61] It is this commercial intention that accounts for the straightforward dance-hall metrical regularity of the piece, compared with the quirky stylizations of the tango in *The Soldier's Tale*—a concession that shows a hitherto unheard-of readiness on Stravinsky's part to compromise in order to break into the marketplace.

Nothing of the kind leapt to the ear when he conducted the premiere of the Symphony in C, "composed to the glory of God [and] dedicated to the Chicago Symphony Orchestra on the occasion of its fiftieth anniversary," in Chicago's Orchestra Hall on the 7th of November.[62] To some, a half-hour symphonic work by Stravinsky was still too baffling a phenomenon to call forth more than bemused admiration. A few were struck by the ease with which the new work kept company with popular old scores like *The Firebird* and *Petrushka,* but that was more the case with the first two movements than the last two. "The symphony's immediate appeal," one critic found, "undoubtedly lessens as it goes on, for the fugue in the third movement plumbs depths which are not easy for a listener to reach on his first try. The fourth movement, too, is a great deal more recondite than the two which open the work."[63] Others were content merely to enjoy the feeling that, for a few short hours, their city was the center of the musical universe, "a privilege," one wrote, "which Chicago will not cease to value."[64]

It was too much to expect the Chicago press to notice the most remarkable fact about the symphony: that it was the first concert work for orchestra without soloist or voices, not counting arrangements or suites, that Stravinsky had written since *Fireworks* (which happened to be on the program with it). In this simple and obvious sense, it marked a return to something he was conventionally regarded as having rejected. Once before, in 1925, he had thought of writing a symphony, but had dropped the idea in favor of *Oedipus Rex,* an opera that had nevertheless reinstated the symphony orchestra in his work after years of wind bands and small mixed ensembles.[65] This time the idea had not been dropped, though it might well have been if Stravinsky and Claudel had not fallen out over their Ida Rubinstein commission. But the two symphony projects had one other significant thing in common; both, so far as one can judge, were conceived in America, and with American concert life in the foreground of Stravinsky's field of musical vision. What this would have meant to the 1925 symphony can only be guessed at. What it meant to the Symphony in C is writ large in the music.

Conducting symphony concerts all over provincial America, Stravinsky had become conscious of the intensely conservative world he was invading, and what an incongruous figure he cut in it. He entered it as a tiger might enter a cat's home: a creature not wholly out of place, yet for all that rather frightening and not ideally to be admitted too often. What sort of work might he himself contribute to such a culture? The obvious answer was a symphony: a symphony in C, of course—like Beethoven's first and Mozart's last, the purest, most archetypal, most classical, above all least frightening kind of orchestral concert work. When questioned about the new piece by nosy Boston reporters, he had concocted a technical explanation of the title: it was neither in C major nor in C minor but simply in C, and "instead of all chords gravitating towards one final tonic chord, all notes [would] gravitate towards a single note."[66] Leaving aside the accuracy of this description (it was not accurate), it studiously missed the point. This was a work that would start out from the *image* of the symphony—something rooted in the consciousness of anyone who had ever attended what was still called a "symphony" concert. Like the post-Brandenburg *Dumbarton Oaks* concerto, it would pay ritual homage to the various forms and procedures locked up in that basic image: it would employ a Beethoven-sized orchestra and have four movements, sonata forms, first and second subjects, recognizable key sequences, and all the rest of the baggage of the symphonic program-note. But behind all that, and eventually in front of it, it would be doing something essentially different. It would be pursuing Stravinskian methods through the prism of the symbolic idea, just as earlier works like the Piano Sonata or even *Oedipus Rex* had done. Like all his so-called neoclassical works, in other words, it was an exercise in modelling—in taking some strong idea as the starting point for a personal creative journey like any other. Hence the apparent change of focus as the work proceeded, a change actually no greater, allowing for the difference in scale, than in *Dumbarton Oaks;* and hence the greater difficulty—greater modernity perhaps—that sensitive critics experienced in the last two movements.

The symphony included the last music Stravinsky conceived and composed in Europe, and for all its American affiliations, it was a fitting climax to his life as a European, just as the Harvard lectures had embodied certain academic and polemical aspects of French thought. And just as the well-bred Gallic framework of the lectures concealed an individuality of a distinctly un-Cartesian type, so the symphony was in reality a most curious and unclassical addition to the classical repertoire it smilingly and reassuringly claimed to represent. The one thing one could safely say about it was that it knew where it stood in relation to that repertoire. From the outposts of the West, that certainty would for a long time be hard to recapture.

9

A HOUSE IN THE HILLS

STRAVINSKY was not returning to Los Angeles from Chicago, but planned instead to spend the next three months in the East, conducting, socializing, and living out of suitcases. He and Vera gave up the Beverly Hills house, and for the second consecutive winter they did without a fixed abode. In Chicago they stayed for two weeks with the composer John Alden Carpenter and his wife, but rather as in a hotel, coming and going as they pleased and rarely seeing their hosts.[1] Igor had three concerts with the orchestra, always with the new symphony, which—he told Nadia—went beautifully, even though there had been terrible trouble with mistakes in the printed orchestral materials.[2] He also sat in on a rehearsal of his host's own recent symphony. And they went to see a triple bill put on by a new company called Ballet Theatre, which had been set up in 1939 by a well-to-do young dancer by the name of Lucia Chase.

From Chicago, they proceeded to Cincinnati, where Eugene Goossens was now the orchestra's chief conductor. There were more performances of the symphony, and the audiences were so enthusiastic that, after *The Rite of Spring* in the second concert, they went on cheering and refused to leave. But by the 26th of November they were in New York, and there were still more reunions. Balanchine was there with a new young wife, Brigitta Hartwig (the dancer Vera Zorina); they saw Dushkin and Rieti and the painter Pavel Tchelitcheff, who had designed Nabokov's *Ode* for Diaghilev and Balanchine's Schubert ballet *Errante* for Les Ballets 1933; and they lunched with Serge Denham, the manager of the latest incarnation of the old Ballet Russe de Monte Carlo. They even went to Harlem and listened to the swing bands.[3] It was all cheerfully remote from the concert circuit and New York was numbingly unlike Los Angeles. In Cincinnati it had been unseasonably warm, but in Manhattan it was snowing hard in good time for Christmas, and as the festive season approached Igor promptly went down with a heavy cold that by Christmas Day itself was threatening to turn into full-blown flu. Just as in the old days in St. Petersburg, it was enough to keep him indoors for a week, until New Year's Day 1941, when he and Vera went to Central Park and fed the squirrels.[4]

Behind all this jollity and pampering, there was hard professional planning. Balanchine, who had for years been choreographing concert music but had never risked anything of the kind with Stravinsky, had now got his agreement to turn the Violin Concerto into a ballet for a one-off triple bill being promoted by Sol Hurok under the aegis of the provocatively titled Original Ballet Russe. At the same time Lucia Chase's manager, Richard Pleasant, had commissioned Stravinsky to make a chamber-orchestral arrangement of the so-called "Bluebird" pas de deux in the third-act divertissement of Tchaikovsky's *Sleeping Beauty*, for inclusion in the rival Ballet Theatre's coming February season of chamber ballets. So while using New York as a base for conducting trips to Minneapolis, Washington—his first appearance there with an orchestra—and Boston (where Nadia, who had arrived from Europe two months before and was teaching at the Longy School, threw a party for them at Gerry's Landing), Igor spent his time going through the concerto with Sam Dushkin, rehearsing the ballet in the icy-cold 51st Street Theatre with Balanchine, and mulling over the score of Tchaikovsky's pas de deux.[5] On 22 January he conducted the first of three performances of *Balustrade*, as the new ballet was called.[6] A fortnight later, having completed the Tchaikovsky arrangement and banked five hundred dollars for his modest pains, he once again boarded a train with Vera bound for Los Angeles.

In each of his previous Stravinsky ballets, Balanchine had leant toward an abstract rendering of plot, whether the scenario was inherently neutral and architectural, as in *Apollo*, or detailed and anecdotal, as in *Jeu de cartes* and *The Fairy's Kiss*, which he had also staged in the 1937 Met season. But *Balustrade* was from start to finish abstract; there was, simply, no plot, and the choreography, which Balanchine composed while listening to a record of the concerto,[7] was a direct response to the music in terms of movement, texture, and dynamic contour. In this, it curiously resembled dance routines of the kind Balanchine had been composing in Hollywood. And it had one other disconcerting property: whereas narrative dancing was a continuous interweaving of gesture and response, as in a play, *Balustrade* was rather a succession of linked dialogues, parallel to the ones in the music.[8] "Its novelty," Edwin Denby wrote,

> is that it is not complex at each moment, in the manner we are accustomed to. The individual part has almost no countermovement, no angular breaking of the dance impulse or direction. The impulse is allowed to flow out, so to speak, through the arms and legs, which delin-

eate the dance figure lightly, as it were in passing. As they do in our show dancing . . . Once more, dancing like any living art has moved ahead of what we had come to think of as the modern style; and this time without even any manifestos to warn us.9

Another sympathetic reviewer admitted that it was "scarcely a pretty piece."10 But Stravinsky himself remembered the ballet, which was never revived, as "one of the most satisfactory visualizations of any of my works."11 Tchelitcheff's designs were barely more allusive than the music: "a white balustrade [presumably the source of the title] flanked by a couple of thin, conventionalized trees,"12 and his costumes began "after the first minute or so [to] look like a bunch of rags cutting the line of the body at the knee, obscuring the differentiation of steps, and messing up the dance."13 But even Denby had to acknowledge that "it was right of the management to take a first-rate painter for a work of this kind; an artist's mistake is infuriating but it isn't vulgar."

The fact was that Tchelitcheff, whatever his flair for stage design, disliked the theatre and could never reconcile himself to its ephemerality. Moreover he was increasingly allergic to what he called "ballet-ivanich"—roughly, "son of *Firebird*"—and he refused point blank to design a new Stravinsky ballet for Denham: "Just thinking about all those 'ballets russes,' invoking poor Sergey Pavlovich, makes me feel sick," he told the composer. "I'm sure Diaghilev would never have formed his company if he had known what his precedent would lead to."14 Whether he exempted Balanchine from these strictures is not clear. He had stayed away from the dress rehearsal and the first night, pleading a "high fever," but he then praised Stravinsky's music without saying a word about the choreography. It was as if he would have agreed with Claudel that music of the purity and self-containedness of Stravinsky's simply left the attendant artist with nothing to contribute; and in any case Tchelitcheff, like Claudel, was hardly by nature an "attendant," whereas Balanchine seemed completely without artistic vanity, accepted— even relished—the subsidiarity and evanescence of the dance, and liked to renew his work rather than revive it. "What is *Balustrade*?" he asked years later.

> Stravinsky never wrote *Balustrade;* he wrote *Violin Concerto.* The ballet should be announced as what it is. Then the musicians can come, the young people who love music and who want to hear the composition— they'll know what they're getting. They don't have to look at the ballet if it bores them, they can just listen to the music. And that's fine with me, that's wonderful.15

THE FIRST THING the Stravinskys did when they got to Los Angeles on the 9th of February was take rooms in the Château Marmont, a luxury apartment block designed like a medieval castle in the Laurel Canyon area of Sunset Boulevard, a favorite base for the less-domesticated Hollywood stars and their hangers-on. For the Stravinskys, the idea was to spend a few days there while they looked for a more permanent home in the area; but what with satisfying the first need of West Coast life—to buy a car—and rehearsing for concerts with the LAPO in Los Angeles and San Diego, they were slow to begin serious househunting and soon decided on a month's lease on a Château Marmont apartment. They then realized that, as the previous May, rented accommodation would be hard to find and that, for the first time in either of their lives, they would have to take out a mortgage and buy a house. Within days of this momentous and nerve-wracking decision, they had found what Vera described in her diary as "a cozy house on a hill"[16] but was, to be more exact, a cramped, secluded single-story cottage with a steep-sloping front garden behind tall hedges near the top of a twisty residential lane called North Wetherly Drive, a mile or so on the Beverly Hills side of the Marmont. You could walk in three or four minutes down to Sunset Boulevard, with its attenuated sprawl of shops, offices, and restaurants, and you could even walk back up again, if you were fit and did not mind the curious scrutiny of neighbors not themselves much accustomed to journeys on foot. The Stravinskys, too, now had their secondhand Dodge, and, though Igor himself did not drive (had not driven for fifteen years or more), Vera had passed her American test the previous summer and enjoyed being at the wheel. She did not, though, much care for suburban Los Angeles. Igor thought the house "ravishing," but Vera disliked the absence of any local center, the lack of small shops and cafés, the immaculate front lawns on which children never played and dogs never misbehaved, and the enclosed social life where nobody ever dropped in uninvited.[17] As an image of the free world, it was undeniably somewhat disappointing.

They moved in on the 6th of April, and on the 7th the hot water system failed and the gas cooker broke down. Somehow they coped; but for Parisian apartment-dwellers, used to concierges and maids and maintenance staff, it was disconcerting to be suddenly alone in a quiet American street with nobody they could call on except by telephone in a language they had not yet fully mastered. Within a few weeks they had hired two gardeners and a cook, but they too were Russians, who spoke little or no English and brought them no nearer to the community. Their most frequent non-Russian contacts in the early days, in fact, were Igor's dentist, who had embarked on a draconian course of extractions and bridge-building in the neglected interior of his mouth, and an aspiring middle-aged composer named Earnest Andersson, who had contacted him at the Château Marmont, offered him temporary accommodation in his house, and booked him for a series of lessons in the course of which he was to help Andersson "learn good manners in composition by watching how I rewrite his symphony from the foundations up."[18] During the next two years, Andersson became something of a fixture at 1260 North Wetherly Drive. They met more than two hundred times, so often, in fact, that one suspects Stravinsky of having prolonged the course for the sake of the twenty-five dollars per lesson, which he badly needed not only for his own well-being, as we shall shortly see. He later told an interviewer that he had himself learnt a lot in the process.[19] But poor Andersson hardly had time to profit from the experience, for in June 1943, six months after the final lesson, he suddenly died. "All this is very sad," Stravinsky lamented superstitiously after seeing Andersson in his coffin, "and just shows I shouldn't teach."[20]

Gradually they began to build up a small circle of Russian, and even non-Russian, acquaintances. On the Russian side there were the Bolms and the painter and theatre designer Eugene Berman, whom Vera had known in Paris but who had come to California, it was said, in pursuit of the film actress Ona Munson after seeing her in *Gone with the Wind;*[21] also their doctor, Prince Galitzin, who like many of their professional advisers was also (or primarily) a friend and drinking companion. Kall had fallen out of true intimacy, partly because of the drink, partly because he had the rare gift of inspiring Vera's distaste; but he came occasionally and sometimes brought Russian books. A postcard from the Stravinskys in El Paso, on the way to Mexico in July, thanks him for poems by Akhmatova and Blok, as well as, more surprisingly, Pushkin's *Onegin.*[22] It was through Berman, who specialized in lesbians, that a former, passing acquaintanceship with the playwright Mercedes de Acosta began to turn into a close friendship soon after they moved to North Wetherly Drive. And friendship with Mercedes soon brought them into contact with her reputed lover Greta Garbo, and so back to the inevitable self-congratulatory Hollywood star-circuit, which flattered but did not enrich. Mercedes was witness to a certain mellowing in Stravinsky's personality during these early Hollywood years. In France, where she had met him through Prince Argutinsky, she had "thought him conceited and ungracious," but now she warmed to both him and Vera.[23] Many of those who had known him in Europe noticed that he became gradually more relaxed, less despotic, on the open-necked West Coast. Mercedes would nevertheless learn in due course that not all his ice had been melted by the Californian sun.

Then there were musician friends like Sol Babitz, a violinist in the

LAPO. A Brooklyn Jew of Russian descent, Babitz was a clever thinker about violin technique, contributed a brilliant column on string-playing to the musicians's federation journal, *International Musician,* and like Dushkin would often advise Stravinsky on violinistic matters. There were half-unexpected neighbors, like the inescapable Dagmar, who moved to Beverly Hills soon after them and came round one day for what Vera called "having things out" but Dagmar called "remembering."[24] Vera, who knew all about Dagmar but had not met her before, tactfully absented herself, only to return several hours later to find Dagmar still remembering and not having had things out. To suggest that Vera was jealous would be absurd, but she may well have read this ebullient ex–movie star as a potential nuisance. In the next weeks and months they were often at parties with Dagmar, who nearly always got drunk, sometimes paralytically. At one of her own lavish dinners, she and her maid drank so much that they passed out and a doctor had to be summoned. "The men behaved better," Vera noted drily in her diary.[25]

Finally, a few doors down Wetherly Drive, another old Paris friend, the Baroness Catherine d'Erlanger, had bought a house, much larger than theirs, eccentrically decorated and furnished from the stock-in-trade of antique and flea markets, and inhabited—apart from its owner—mainly by cats.

Though spacious in its way, the Stravinskys' new house had few rooms and lacked the thick-walled privacy of Igor's huge European apartments in Morges or Nice or Paris. Fortunately, it also lacked their density of population. Behind the single large living room, which fronted on to a verandah and the sloping lawn, was a smaller room, with a sofa and large numbers of books, which would in due course serve as a spare bedroom. As he had always done in new premises, Igor quickly had his studio set up, at the other end of a narrow passage out of the sitting room, with a pair of upright pianos, both in mediocre condition and usually out of tune; and here he was soon at work amid the familiar organized clutter of pens, pencils, colored inks, erasers, photographs, icons, ornaments, stravigor stave-rollers, stopwatches, and music paper. There were fragmentary sketches of a work in hand, a score for a chamber orchestra similar (though not identical) to the one he had used for his Tchaikovsky arrangement, as if he had planned to write an original piece for Ballet Theatre's chamber repertoire; or it may have been the piece he had at some point mentioned to Tchelitcheff. In fact the exact concept of the *Danses concertantes* was slow to emerge. A sketch for a set of variations made at the time of the Tango back in October might well suggest an idea for a ballet, and this may have remained the intention until, in March, Rieti wrote to tell him (mistakenly) that Ballet Theatre was closing down and merging with Lincoln Kirstein's Ballet Caravan for a tour of

South America that summer.[26] At all events, when Werner Janssen got wind of the piece in September 1941 it was still unattached, though two-thirds written, and he was able to commission it as a concert work for the orchestra he had recently founded in Los Angeles precisely for the performance of bright new works of this type.[27]

From his sun-drenched Hollywood hillside, Igor kept track of events in Europe and, while he never shared the Paris-born Nadia's agonized sense of guilt at having fled the country of Joan of Arc, he did worry ceaselessly about his family stranded there.[28] Nadia had seen Soulima in good spirits at Vichy, which was encouraging news in one sense and discouraging in another, since the collaborationist Vichy government was behaving in a more and more Nazi-like, xenophobic way. Luckily by the time Stravinsky heard, in May 1941, that Vichy was deporting Jews and others in large numbers, he already knew that Soulima was in Paris and taking part in concerts;[29] he had given a Salle Gaveau recital in January, taken one of the piano parts in *Les Noces* under Charles Munch at the Conservatoire in early March, and appeared as soloist in Scriabin's Piano Concerto at the Châtelet later that month. Igor remained blissfully unaware that in April Soulima had also asked a Nazi acquaintance in Paris to enquire of Willy Strecker whether he might be able to arrange concert work in Germany, a request Strecker was forced to refuse because he mistakenly believed Soulima to be a French citizen.[30] Theodore, meanwhile, had managed to arrange an exhibition in Toulouse, but regular work was unobtainable in Villemur-sur-Tarn, where he and Denise were living, and money had become a desperate problem. In midsummer, Igor's fears about the Vichy regime proved only too justified when Theodore was interned, as an enemy alien, in the concentration camp at Recebedou, where he was left virtually without food for four days and was only released when a local farmer came looking for hands to help with the haymaking.[31]

Since the winter, Igor had been frantically in search of ways of sending money and provisions to his three children, as well as to Kitty Mandelstam and Ira Belyankin, and to the Nosenko sisters in Switzerland, who were in charge of Kitty and were also paying the upkeep of Berthe Essert's grave in Lausanne. He was meeting Milène's fees at Sancellemoz and Kitty's at Leysin. Some of his European funds, he wrote to Theodore in June, were still accessible, but for the rest he was having to find devious ways of transmitting money from the neutral U.S.A. to combatant France, which was both difficult and technically illegal.[32] This usually involved French or Italian friends in America instructing relatives in Europe according to some agreed code. For instance, Darius Milhaud, who had recently taken up a post at Mills College in Oakland (near San Francisco) would instruct his mother in Aix-en-Provence to "give [Theodore] Strawinsky news of his father, as you did recently. All well."[33] Later, when the American censor became suspicious, the formula was changed to "Just seen Stravinsky. Health as usual. Transmit children."[34] For Darius's mother, in Vichy France, the transaction was at first not much more than an inconvenience; but when the Nazis occupied the whole of France in November 1942, the money transfers assumed a far more dangerous complexion. Mme. Milhaud (who was seventy-five, had just had a cataract operation, and was generally in poor health) had seventy German soldiers billeted on the ground floor of her family house at L'Enclos.[35] Later, the whole house was seized and the remarkable lady was transferred to a clinic, where, in January 1944, she died. On her instructions, however, the Stravinsky payments continued, while the composer gradually—and, it must be said, on terms somewhat generous to himself—repaid the money to her son in California.[36]

The trouble was that, exactly as he had feared, Igor's own normal income was threatening to dry up altogether. After February 1941, and apart from Werner Janssen, Los Angeles seemed to lose interest alike in his conducting and in his music, while the so-called music industry itself remained all too alive to the prestige of his name. In May he signed an endorsement for a "radio-phonograph" made by Stromberg-Carlson, which was then marketed as the "Igor Stravinsky Autograph Model" at the exalted price of four hundred dollars. But the charming and elegant couple pictured in the company's advertisement in intimate enjoyment of their "Stravinsky Autograph" would have been hard pressed to find their nominal hero or his music on the Los Angeles billboards during these troubled times. Indeed his sole conducting date anywhere until almost the end of the year was a return visit to Mexico in July, where, thanks to Chávez's energy and enthusiasm, he directed a pair of concerts of his music (including the symphony), and re-recorded the Divertimento. Meanwhile in the States it was the potboiling little Tango that was attracting the most interest. At the end of March, Sam Dushkin had included a transcription for violin and piano in his Town Hall recital, and three months later, while Stravinsky was in Mexico and Mercury were still trying to resolve the problem of the lyric, the jazz clarinettist Benny Goodman conducted an orchestral arrangement in a Philadelphia concert: a very poor performance, Leonard Feist (of Mercury) wrote to the composer, "and poorly publicized. There were ten thousand jitterbugs who came only to hear Goodman's band."[37] The press, however, foresaw a bright future for the new piece; "it might," one even thought, "become a rival of Ravel's Bolero as a public favorite."[38]

To add insult to these various injuries, a substantial part of Stravinsky's royalty income was being blocked by Édition Russe's New York agent, Galaxy. The irony of this particular situation was that all or most of his ERM works were in the public domain in the U.S.A., while Galaxy were refusing to pass on his income from sales and rentals on the grounds that their contract was not with Stravinsky but with ERM's Paris representative Païchadze, a French resident with whom it was regrettably not permitted for them to do business. Igor's fury at this bland obstructiveness was compounded by the fact that he was in regular contact with ERM's proprietor, Koussevitzky, who was at that very moment in the process of booking him to conduct a composition class at the Berkshire Music Center at Tanglewood in the summer of 1942. Unfortunately, Koussevitzky was not in possession of any legal documentation with which to override Païchadze's authority. Why, Stravinsky asked despairingly, could Galaxy not make *ex gratia* payments for the time being, as Associated were doing in respect of his (unfortunately more modest) Schott royalties?[39] As with most expressions of the ordinary man's bewilderment at the bureaucratic mentality, the question went unanswered and no money was forthcoming.

In the midst of all these anxieties and clashes of culture, Stravinsky suddenly took one of the most extraordinary decisions of his life. In an access of goodwill toward his new hosts, and out of a desire to write what he called "a work of national importance," he made an arrangement for chorus and orchestra of "The Star-Spangled Banner" and invited Mercury to publish it.[40]

Early that July, Earnest Andersson was coming for a lesson almost every day, but he did not come on the 4th of July, and instead Stravinsky spent the day making the arrangement, apparently at Andersson's suggestion.[41] He had, of course, sometimes conducted the anthem at the start of his American concerts, and he must often have thought that he could improve on the standard arrangement, especially when he found out that the Federal law establishing the tune as the national anthem said nothing about any particular harmonization.[42] Perhaps, he suggested to Feist, Congress might even standardize his version by law. In any case, the premiere was fixed for Washington in early September, President Roosevelt would be there and the manuscript would be presented to him. The composer would waive all performance fees and rejected the obvious solecism of dedicating to the American people what, in the best sense, was already theirs.

Feist was enthusiastic, even though Stravinsky's generosity over fees meant that Mercury would make hardly any money on the deal. After all, it indicated "a background of feeling towards this country and a sense of service" that Feist could not but reciprocate.[43] He grew more nervous, admittedly, when it turned out that he would have to print "eight different versions in this slightly speculative market."[44] What he meant, of course, was that it would be optimistic to expect choirs or orchestras to replace their copies of the traditional arrangement with a new and—to be frank—somewhat more challenging version of an anthem which, in any case, most of them knew by heart. He may also have foreseen positive resistance to

Stravinsky's arrangement, even though it was less a complete reharmonization than a freewheeling gloss on the familiar text—a sort of Pulcinellification, with some scrunchy added notes here and there and a few quirks in the bass line.

The harmonization was duly copyrighted, but it proved too much for the White House, who swiftly but politely declined to participate. The first performance was thus delayed until 14 October, when Andersson's son-in-law, James Sample, conducted it at the end of a concert by the WPA Symphony Orchestra and Chorus in the Embassy Auditorium, Los Angeles. The anthem was sung three times, and there were no protests, though "the audience seemed loath to join [in]."[45] Stravinsky himself planned to conduct it for the first time at his St. Louis concerts just before Christmas, but it seems that there was adverse comment during rehearsals and he promptly withdrew the arrangement, on the pretext that the parts were full of mistakes or the score unavailable, according to which newspaper you read. He did, however, conduct it in San Francisco three weeks later, by which time the published materials were available. If there were grumbles, they were isolated and unimportant. Even the fact that the United States had been at war for a month did not arouse the patriotic guard dogs of the vulnerable West Coast. As for any hint that the arrangement might be illegal, that was far from the composer's or his publisher's mind.[46]

By the start of December 1941, the *Danses concertantes* were complete except for the short fifth movement, which in any case was to be an exact reprise of the work's opening pages with a stitched-up ending, and this Stravinsky wrote in January after his two concerts in San Francisco. The finished score is dated the 13th, but Vera's diary notes that finishing touches were still being added on the 14th, before the score went for copying.[47] Just over three weeks later, on the 8th of February, he conducted the premiere with Janssen's orchestra in the mock-Renaissance Wilshire Ebell Theatre, his first-ever appearance in that particular hall, and for him a happy début, since he found Janssen's players first rate and strongly approved his unusual generosity in granting five full rehearsals for the twenty-minute *Danses* plus the well-known *Pulcinella* suite.[48]

The work itself, though, raised some puzzling issues for the Los Angeles press that were not much elucidated by Sol Babitz's article in the program maintaining that Stravinsky's neoclassicism was these days a matter of "reliving the music of the past in a new way . . .

> Stravinsky's means is music, his subject, the music of others. Here he is in the tradition of Bach harmonizing the themes of others; van Gogh repainting famous Rembrandts and Millets in his own style, and Chapman rendering Homer. Not judgment but sympathy is the

purpose of these men. Their "imitations" are as good or better than the originals. . . .[49]

And he quoted Stravinsky's own account of his procedure: "After studying many pages of a certain composer, I begin to sense his musical personality and signature. Like a detective, I reconstruct his musical experience." Reviewing the performance for *Modern Music,* Alfred Frankenstein wondered how much of this was "official." "Stravinsky," he noted, "said nothing even remotely similar during the hour I spent with him over the score." What he did say was that "the attention span of today's audience is limited, and the problem of the present-day composer is one of condensation. To say the essential and say it quickly—that's what counts."[50] *Danses concertantes* is certainly, as Isabel Morse Jones found, "compressed, abrupt, and moves rapidly from one idea to another before satiety. Part of it is satire and part sentiment but all of it is concentrated energy, rhythmically exact, highly intense."[51] Its speed and concentration are those of *Dumbarton Oaks;* but its anecdotalism and fondness for half-quotation are an abstracted form of a tendency that had first emerged in *Jeu de cartes,* where however there was a plot, if of a stylized kind. *Danses concertantes* was, by contrast, a disembodied ballet, a card-index ballet, with entries for standard elements such as "pas d'action," "variations," and "pas de deux," and shorthand references to more or less relevant composers like Tchaikovsky, Delibes, Schubert (the "marche militaire" at fig. 161), and Bach.

In the end, however, all this missed the point. *Danses concertantes* might, when you went into it, seem a derivative or off-the-peg kind of score; but its sound and texture were entirely Stravinskian (of the late-thirties period)—sharp, economical, and above all highly refined. The music might pick up unused bits of the Symphony in C, but it had a tautness and intricacy not, on the whole, typical of that work. Balanchine later drew attention to its rhythmic complexity, which comes not from irregular meters like the ones in *The Rite of Spring* and *Les Noces,* but instead from the disruption of simple meters, like the way the shanty-tune of the horn rides across the three-four time of the first variation.[52] Done with due precision, it made an excellent concert piece. But it was only a matter of time before it found its way onto the stage.

While Stravinsky was at work on the *Danses concertantes,* in mid-November, a letter had arrived from a certain Dmitry Borodin in Long Island, telling him that Yury Stravinsky had died in Leningrad the previous May at the age of sixty-two.[53] Igor had not seen his sole surviving brother for thirty-three years, and had not even corresponded with him to any significant extent, but Katya had kept in touch with his wife, Yelena Nikolayevna, and through her it was known that Yury had been suffering from angina pectoris since the mid-thirties.[54] Lately he had become deeply depressed, and weighed down by the drudgery of his work inspecting and listing Leningrad's historic buildings. It was just as well, Yelena later told Igor, that he had not lived to see the horrendous bombardment of those buildings by the Nazis and had been spared the nightmare of the blockade, which had begun later that summer. He had died at work in her arms, and those of their daughters, Tanya and Xenya.[55]

A *panikhida* service for Yury was hastily arranged in the little Russian church in downtown Hollywood, where there had already been a service for Katya in March and would soon be one for Mika at the end of November. It is hard to know what Igor actually felt about the loss of this already long-lost sibling, beyond his sense of what was right at such moments. He told Theodore that "this death has caused me profound grief."[56] Yet to dwell on the past was scarcely in his nature; and though he had grown fond of his sister-in-law and through her of Yury himself after their marriage, and been charmed by Tanya when she came to Nice in 1925, he lacked the ability— even perhaps the will—to hold on to such affections through so many empty years. At bottom Yury had never been his favorite brother; if any- thing, living as he still did at No. 66 Kryukov Canal, he reminded Igor of gloomy and difficult times. And he stood for Russia: old, unfriendly Russia, but also new, frightening Soviet Russia, the Russia that was grinding down his fellow artists and had ground Yury down too—just as it was now in its turn being ground down by the German army. It all doubtless proved how right he had been not to go back.

The day before Stravinsky received Borodin's letter, he was telephoned from New York by Balanchine, who had been approached by Ringling Brothers and Barnum and Bailey's Circus to choreograph a polka for the circus elephants, and wanted Stravinsky to compose the music. Stravinsky told him that he could not write even a short piece before March, because of the Janssen project.[57] All the same he certainly tinkered with the idea long before that. He noticed that by an odd coincidence there were polka rhythms everywhere in the *Danses concertantes,* and at about Christmastime he started sketching ideas for the elephant piece while still working on the ending of the *Danses.* Then, as soon as that work was finished, he rapidly composed the *Circus Polka* as a piano solo and completed the draft score by the 5th of February. The point about this, for him, slightly unusual way of working was that Ringling would need a score for a circus band, and for the first time in his life Stravinsky did not feel equal to the task. So he approached the best-known Hollywood arranger of the day, Robert Rus- sell Bennett, and Bennett recommended a young composer called David Raksin—a pupil of Schoenberg, as it turned out, and already an experi- enced filmwriter—who duly orchestrated the polka for the bizarre combination of wind and percussion instruments (including hammond organ) that Ringling had assembled for their circus performances.[58]

As a piece of barefaced opportunism, the *Circus Polka* would be hard to beat. A few years later Stravinsky gratefully accepted a Canadian radio interviewer's suggestion that the piece was a musical equivalent of the circus paintings of Toulouse-Lautrec,[59] but at the time he was mainly concerned to write it as quickly as possible for the biggest fee Balanchine could get him.[60] Later still, he reconstructed the original phone conversation in terms of an imaginary aesthetic discrimination. "I wonder if you'd like to do a little ballet with me, a polka perhaps," Balanchine is supposed to have said. "For whom?" "For some elephants." "How old?" "Very young." (After a pause) "All right. If they are very young elephants, I will do it."[61] As for the music, the piece galumphs amusingly enough through vestiges of rhythmic ideas from the *Danses concertantes* reimagined for pachyderms, with an unexpected nod at one point toward Tchaikovsky's Fourth Symphony, and ending with a heavily underlined and quotation-marked parody of the same Schubert march that he had merely hinted at in the Janssen score.[62]

In fact the ballet—which Stravinsky never saw—was danced, when the circus opened at New York's Madison Square Garden on the 9th of April, by fifty elephants in pink tutus, all apparently of mature age, like the fifty girls who sat atop them. At their head, lovely Vera Zorina rode in on Old Modoc, the chief and oldest elephant.

> As carefully as if La Zorina were spun glass—which she is!—the giant deposited her in the center of the forest of elephants, and when she had completed her exquisite pirouetting upon the sawdust picked her up and carried her away. But not before she had handed [Modoc] a huge bunch of American Beauties, which he promptly coiled up in his trunk like a commuter filing his copy of *The New York Sun* under his arm to read after dinner.[63]

The impression that the elephants took Balanchine's *Circus Polka* in their stride was nevertheless perhaps misleading. "Aside from the dancing of old Modoc," one observer wrote,

> "Display no. 18" was not a pretty act. The ballet skirts made the bulls appear ridiculous. The music didn't suit them. In spite of some of the stunts which they are made to perform, elephants are dignified animals. They respond instantly to waltz tunes and soft, dreamy music, even to some military numbers of a particular circusy tempo. The involved music of Stravinsky's "Elephant Ballet" was both confusing and frightening to them. It robbed them of their feeling of security and confidence

in the world about them—so alien to their native condition of life. It would have taken very little at any time during the many performances of the ballet music to cause a stampede.[64]

Fortunately there was no stampede except to the box office, and though the Ringlings never revived the piece after the first season, the publicity it attracted served them well until, after less than two months, the band was paid off because of a pay dispute, and the circus continued with gramophone recordings, which of course precluded the Stravinsky ballet.[65]

From the composer's point of view, such commissions were lucrative but artistically frustrating. He could and did use the *Circus Polka* as a bait for Associated Music Press, hoping to persuade them to take him on as a directly contracted composer, which would avoid the problem of blocked royalties; but musically it was not at all what he wanted to write.[66] Instead, his thoughts were turning in a completely new direction. Early in April he began sketching an orchestral work that soon evolved into a symphonic movement of a character strikingly unlike anything in his recent music. The movement was built up episodically from obscure beginnings, and without any clear sense of order; but already in the early sketches there are a kinetic energy and a certain harmonic ferocity quite different from the clumping rhythms and raucous dissonance of the *Circus Polka,* or the brisk needle-point refinement of the *Danses concertantes.* At one point the music explodes into a violent C major Allegro. Later a piano is added to the orchestra and begins to articulate hard, diamantine rhythms and brittle textures that might suggest an altogether earlier, more "Stravinskian" Stravinsky. From nowhere, and in a matter of ten weeks or so, the master has created out of nothing, and in the most unpropitious circumstances, the first part of what will in due course grow into one of his greatest works, the Symphony in Three Movements.

What did he think he was writing at the time? Outside the sketches there is no contemporary record of the piece, but another of his musician friends, the composer Alexandre Tansman, later reported hearing him play through well-developed fragments of the sketches and describe them as part of "a symphonic work with a piano concertant."[67] Much later still, Stravinsky told Robert Craft that he had originally been thinking in terms of a concerto for orchestra, a type of writing in which different instruments or groups of instruments are thrown into prominence in the manner of a stage play, where a narrative or argument is articulated through a pattern of dialogues.[68] If so, he was deliberately confronting in an abstract form a problem that had been at the core of his orchestral writing for a decade or more: how to reconcile an essentially sectional style like that of his early ballets and songs with the needs of a complex and integrated symphonic discourse of the classical type that had begun to provide him with his stylistic models in the early twenties. The terms "concerto" and "concertante" resonate like a litany through his works of the thirties and early forties. The Symphony in C had clearly been an attempt—whether or not wholly successful—to force this dramatic, oppositional way of thinking into symphonic, dialectical molds. But the 1942 essay seems in some significant way different. Here the conception is quite openly sectional, and the ideas as they emerge in the sketches bear no perceptible relation to the sequence of the music Stravinsky eventually settled on. For instance, the strident opening was a late discovery, and the brilliant, pulsating music that follows was originally conceived in the position it occupies later in the movement, which is presumably why (as Craft points out[69]) the actual opening only comes back at the very end of the movement, which was in fact written last.

It was entirely typical of the composer of *Renard* and the Octet to respond to Pearl Harbor, the U.S. declaration of war, and the whole apparatus of air-raid sirens, blackouts, and searchlights that soon became part of West Coast life, by absorbing himself in the problems of symphonic form. Yet, curiously, this merciless opponent of music as the representation of nonmusical images was soon describing the result as war music, in which it was possible to find repercussions of "this our arduous time of sharp and shifting events, of despair and hope, of continual torments, of tension, and at last cessation and relief."[70] This was admittedly a postwar description applied to the whole symphony. Years later still, Stravinsky supposedly elaborated it into a full-blown program inspired, in the case of the first movement, by scenes from a war documentary about China, including one episode "conceived as a series of instrumental conversations to accompany a cinematographic scene showing the Chinese people scratching and digging in their fields."[71] If that sounds far-fetched, one might be tempted to take out the words "Chinese people" and substitute "chickens." On 25 April, three weeks after the first sketch for the symphonic movement, Stravinsky registered for war-defense work, as he was required to do by law, and in due course this involved building and stocking a hen coop and starting a kitchen garden. Everybody hated the cocks, which had a bad habit of crowing at four in the morning and soon had to be given away. But Igor grew fond of the hens; "I like their rhythmic clucking," he told one reporter,[72] and it is more than tempting to suppose that particular sound memorialized in, for instance, the ostinato piano figuring at 66 in the symphony's first movement.[73]

Whatever its inspiration, the piece clearly reflects a desire to escape from the treadmill of more or less unsuitable hackwork commissions that were continuing to assail him. The film industry was still trying desperately to grab hold of his name, while evading his high-minded conditions. In March he had been visited by Morris Stoloff, director of music for Columbia Pictures, with a proposal that he write music for a film about the Norwegian landings called *The Commandos Strike at Dawn*. Then later in the spring he was approached by the ultimate film mogul, Samuel Goldwyn, who was planning another war film *(North Star)*, about the Nazi invasion of Russia, and also by Louis B. Mayer, with whom he dined at the end of May in connection with a project for Russian War Relief.[74] The Goldwyn and Mayer encounters gave birth to some mildly amusing anecdotes about money, but little or no film music.

> *Goldwyn:* I understand it's twenty-five thousand you want? *Stravinsky:* Whatever my agent says. *Goldwyn:* Well, you have to have an arranger. *Stravinsky:* What's an arranger? *Goldwyn:* An arranger! Why, that's a man who has to arrange your music, who has to fit it to the instruments. *Stravinsky:* Oh. *Goldwyn:* Sure, that'll cost you $6,000. And it'll have to come off your $20,000. *Stravinsky:* I thought it was $25,000.[75]

The Norway film was more promising for a time, and Stravinsky probably worked on a score for it. The music for *North Star* was eventually provided by Aaron Copland, but Stravinsky was involved for long enough to turn his mind to the question of what kind of music he, as a Russian, ought to be writing for such a subject. In both cases there would eventually be a residue to be used up one way or another in concert works.

It was symptomatic of his insecure and unsettled frame of mind that for a time in February 1942 he even seriously considered a project with Massine to compose a ballet for Serge Denham on excerpts from Donizetti. Denham told Rieti that the idea had been Stravinsky's, though it was surely in fact Massine's; and the sweet-natured Italian took fright at the thought that his own recent Bellini ballet, *The Night Shadow* (of which Stravinsky was perfectly well aware), might be accused of plagiarism.[76] Fortunately for Rieti, Massine, who was supposed to come up with suggestions for suitable Donizetti excerpts, was so long in doing so that Stravinsky, still believing his summer to be fully occupied with the Columbia film, more or less abandoned the project.[77] Soon afterwards he cancelled his planned visit to Tanglewood that summer for the same optimistic reason, that he was expecting the Norway film to be quickly followed by the Russian one.[78]

THAT JUNE he celebrated his sixtieth birthday. It was an altogether more subdued affair than his fiftieth, and not only because not a single member of his own family was now within five thousand miles of him. The war was a real, if ghostly presence: occasional air-raid warnings and rumors of

Japanese shelling from offshore. Family news from Europe was not much less upsetting than its frequent absence. Milène had left Sancellemoz and was staying with Theodore; Milène had had a relapse and gone back to Sancellemoz; Milène (most worryingly of all) had got engaged to a fellow patient, a step apparently as inevitable—not to say fatal—as marrying your first cousin if your parents were also first cousins. Igor had lost one daughter too recently to be anything but disturbed by the marriage of the other. Every time he thought of little Kitty, he told Theodore, he had sad memories of Mika.[79] Soulima was presumably still in Paris, but he seldom wrote. Milène wired and asked for money.

Made devout once again by anxiety and fear, Igor was going to church more often than before. There were the inevitable *panikhidas,* the Easter duties, and other important dates in the Orthodox calendar. On his birthday he and Vera took communion, a habit that was to remain with him and turn the occasion into something closer to a penance than a celebration.[80] In 1942, at least, that was appropriate enough. "One day," a friend would write at the end of the war, "it will be universally recognized that [Stravinsky's] white house in the Hollywood hills . . . which was regarded by some as an ivory tower, was just as close to the core of a world at war as the place where Picasso painted *Guernica.*"[81]

After church they drove to Big Bear Lake, in the San Bernardino Mountains, and went boating.

THE NORWEGIAN film project finally broke down in early July 1942, either because Stravinsky was as usual unwilling to fit in with Hollywood's whirlwind production schedules, or because the music that he had in fact written was not liked. At any rate, the eight-minute, four-movement, orchestral piece that he put together apparently from the sketches within about two weeks of the collapse of negotiations would have cut a bizarre figure in a war film about commandos, although it might have suited a travelogue on country life in Norway. Stravinsky did suggest to Ernest Voigt, in his still uncertain English, that the pieces "could be no doubt very actual" (that is, topical);[1] but the title he gave the little suite—*Four Norwegian Moods*—implies no such ambition, even allowing for the linguistic error of "moods" for "modes," which he himself later pointed out.[2] The real intention is indicated by the standard French title, "Quatre pièces à la norvégienne"—four pieces in Norwegian style.[3]

Stravinsky had decided that the best way to write music that Hollywood could understand was to use folk tunes and stray as little as possible from their native idiom. Virtually all the material in the *Norwegian Moods* comes from a published nineteenth-century collection called *The Norway Music Album*, which he found in a secondhand bookshop in Los Angeles.[4] It was in no sense a scholarly tome, but rather a popular anthology of songs and piano pieces in arrangements by Grieg, Lindeman, and their contemporaries, and in pinching the tunes Stravinsky also pinched the drawing-room style of the arrangements—a style familiar enough from Grieg's *Lyric Pieces*, though Stravinsky later denied the connection.[5] As usual he gingered up the harmonies a little, dislocated the rhythms, and orchestrated the music in a crisp and highly differentiated style more like Glinka than Grieg. But the modernization is painless and slightly routine—scarcely challenging or provocative, as it was in *Pulcinella*.

The piece has a certain importance in that it marks out procedures that were to prove useful to him during an awkward two years of adjustment and insecurity as a new immigrant. In fact, while working on the Norwegian materials, he had also been tinkering with a volume of Russian tunes—Bernard's *Pesni russkago naroda* (Songs of the Russian People)— which may have turned up at the same time in the same bookshop or in the public library.[6] He probably leafed through the collection in a more or less nostalgic spirit, thinking of his homeland under the Nazi boot. Then, just when he was turning his attention to the Norway film, he decided for some reason to make similar workings from the Bernard volume. Exactly what he wrote at this stage is hard to establish, but by the time the film commission fell through on 8 July he had concocted enough music, in the form of a draft sonata for two pianos, for Nadia Boulanger to plan a private run-through at Bloomington, Indiana, later that summer. Alas, disaster struck, as she wrote on the 15th:

> Since yesterday, a struggle between despair and rage! As I told you, I wanted to give an (informal) try-out at Indiana University, Bloomington. When I briefed my pupil, I told him: *private* performance, while insisting that *he publish nothing* until I give him an *exact* text for the program. In the excess of his joy, the idiot has indeed published nothing except the one thing that he was not supposed to say—and has announced the premiere of your Sonata. I have just sent him a furious note informing him that, barring some kind of miracle, we can no longer play the sonata.[7]

There is no particular evidence that Nadia had suggested to Stravinsky the idea of a two-piano sonata, but it seems a distinct possibility, despite his own later memory that the piece was not commissioned and that he originally conceived it for one piano and only switched to two to avoid confusion in the texture of criss-crossing melodic lines.[8] In fact, the earliest surviving version of the eventual three-movement sonata seems to consist of two short pieces laid out like songs without words, with the melody on the top stave and the "accompaniment" on two staves underneath. Both pieces were copied out of *Pesni russkago naroda,* but with the harmonies and barrings Stravinskyized, exactly as in the *Norwegian Moods.* One of them survives as the middle section of the finale of the published sonata, completed eighteen months later; the other remains in manuscript as a kind of sad memory, more than just a copy, something less than a finished, independent movement.[9] Most critics have taken it for granted that Stravinsky's interest in the *Pesni russkago naroda* was prompted by his need for Russian material for the Goldwyn film *North Star,* Lillian Hellman's account of a Nazi attack on a communal farm in Soviet Ukraine. But the existence of an early form of the Sonata for Two Pianos—a work almost entirely derived from the Bernard collection—argues against this. When he did start thinking about *North Star,* he probably turned to the Russian songs; but that was still several months in the future, and his active interest in the film was to be relatively short-lived.

Meanwhile, he was virtually becalmed creatively, unable to bury himself in his big concerto for orchestra—if such it was to be—but at the same time unsettled in his commercial plans, with no conducting dates before January, and utterly without firm creative projects. The nearest he came to a finished product those late summer months of 1942 was the publication in August of the original French text of the *Poétique musicale*, and even this was not greatly to his satisfaction, since he had hoped for a parallel text edition and could not see the point of an American publication of the lectures in French.[10] The irony was that he had withdrawn from Tanglewood on the assumption that his time would be taken up with film projects, and instead all he had to do was orchestrate the *Circus Polka* and the concerto movement, both of which he finished by mid-October.[11] Then in November he had planned a run-through of the *Circus Polka* in its new symphonic version, but he went down with flu and it had to be cancelled. Just when the situation in Europe was worsening to a frightening degree, with the total Nazi occupation of France and a murderous battle raging round Stalingrad, it was beginning to seem as if his own brave new world was turning into a bundle of empty promises.

Among their growing circle of friends in Hollywood were the playwright and novelist Franz Werfel and his wife, Alma Mahler. That November they lunched and dined together,[12] and a certain common intellectual ground emerged between the two artists that to some extent belied their apparently incompatible backgrounds, Werfel being a product of that *Jugendstil* expressionism that Stravinsky had been publicly rejecting, on and off, for the past twenty years. Of course in faraway Los Angeles such differences shrank into insignificance compared with their shared plight as intellectual refugees from the Old World. One evening at the Werfels' a few months later, Stravinsky met Thomas Mann for the first time since the twenties, and had a long conversation with him about Schoenberg.[13] But there was more to the connection than solidarity among castaways. Werfel, though not a musician (unlike his wife), loved music passionately, and especially Verdi, whose letters he had edited and about whom he had written a novel. He had also, like Mahler before him, converted from Judaism to Catholicism, and he had recently fallen under the spell of St. Bernadette. His novel about the visionary of Lourdes, *The Song of Bernadette*, had just come out (unlike the *Poétique*) in English as well as its original German, and that autumn he presented the Stravinskys with a copy of each edition. The book was about to be filmed by Twentieth Century–Fox. Perhaps they might commission Stravinsky to compose the music?

Whether the *Bernadette* idea was ever anything more than an after-dinner proposition between gentlemen is impossible now to establish. The trouble with all Stravinsky's wartime film projects is that (except in the case of *Fantasia*) no contract was ever signed, and the only evidence of negotiations is a diary entry here or there, a passing reference in a letter to a publisher, a few sketches in an archive, and the composer's reminiscences. Of the Werfel film, Stravinsky remarked that he had liked the idea but found the terms unacceptable.[14] Whether or not he was ever seriously considered by the studio for a film that so signally called for precisely the kind of soft-centered music that he was famous for not writing, the score was eventually produced by Fox's head of music, Alfred Newman. Three months later, on the 15th of February, 1943, Stravinsky began composing music that he later maintained had been intended for the "Apparition of the Virgin" scene in the film, but which by mid-March, when it was completed, had turned into the second of his concerto-for-orchestra movements—a piece of great subtlety and refinement, but about as suited to the climactic moment of a film about the intervention of God in the life of a peasant girl as it would have been to accompany the sinking of the *Titanic* or Moses's descent from Mount Sinai.

Oddly enough, only three days before starting this movement, he had drafted another piece that he later insisted was meant for a film: hunting music with prominent horn-calls and cascading string figures. This time the film in question was *Jane Eyre*, another Twentieth Century–Fox blockbuster, which would be starring Orson Welles as Mr. Rochester. According to Stravinsky, Welles had personally urged him to write the music "for his *Jane Eyre*," though in fact the film was not his (unlike *Citizen Kane* or *The Magnificent Ambersons*); he was merely in it. Nevertheless Stravinsky did for a time work on ideas for the film; he copied out tunes from a collection of English songs, and he made notes about the scenario. Whether he read the novel as he claimed, or indeed the film script, may be doubted, since he unblinkingly described his only actual piece of music as "for one of the hunting scenes," of which there is not a single one in Charlotte Brontë's novel and only one in the film—a typical Hollywood confection in which Jane first encounters Rochester on the hunting field.[15] Still more curious is the fact that the piece, as drafted that February, is not film music at all but a well-formed concert piece in A-B-A form, complete with a second theme that, in an earlier sketch, was labeled "Song for Bessie" (presumably Jane's childhood nurse, a character unconnected with Rochester). This movement would soon figure as the central panel in the orchestral triptych called *Ode*, which Stravinsky wrote in memory of Natalie Koussevitzky, who had died in January 1942. But no such work had yet been mentioned, much less commissioned, in February 1943; and this jolly, ebullient piece is in any case hardly music one would naturally associate with such a commission.

Work on *Jane Eyre*, whatever it was, doubtless followed the final collapse of discussions about *North Star* in January. On the 7th, Igor had paid a visit to Sam Goldwyn and had taken home Hellman's script to read overnight. It was, he reported next morning, "a veritable *Schlafmittel*" (sleeping draught), and he disliked it so much that, without quite being ready to drop out there and then, he was soon hoping that Goldwyn would not accept his as usual somewhat inflexible terms. His hopes were gratified, and by the 18th the deal was off.[16] How much work he had actually done on *North Star* before reading the script is, once again, a matter for speculation, but since there is a gap of almost three months during which he otherwise composed nothing at all, it looks as if he was at least tinkering with possible material for the Russian subject, which he already knew about in general terms. He still had the *Pesni russkago naroda* to hand, and he had the sonata draft that Nadia had probably in the end not played at Indiana, but which he himself did play through with the French pianist-composer Marcelle de Manziarly, when they saw her at the Sachses' farm in Santa Barbara in October 1942.[17] That autumn and early winter he sketched other music, all of it based on songs from the Bernard collection, and all of it in due course reused in works that today form part of the Stravinsky canon: specifically the Sonata for Two Pianos, which he returned to and elaborated toward the end of 1943, and an as yet unthought-of work, the *Scherzo à la russe*, eventually composed in 1944.

These various folk-derived scores form an island of naïve charm at the very heart of Stravinsky's early American years. In one sense they seem like a throwback to his late twenties and thirties, when folk song, real or imaginary, had been a common thread through his greatest works, from *Petrushka* to the *Symphonies of Wind Instruments*. But the similarity is superficial. The tunes in these wartime pieces are accepted for what they are, dressed up in a Stravinskian manner, but never for a minute treated as ammunition in a full-scale assault on the very foundations of musical language, as the folk material had been in *The Rite of Spring* or *Les Noces* or *Renard*. Instead, as with the *Four Norwegian Moods*, the Russian pieces take in elements from the style of the published arrangements, which were nineteenth-century salon pieces with no serious claim to authenticity at all. It was rather as if Stravinsky had used settings from the *New National Songbook* or Cecil Sharp's arrangements of English or American folk songs as the basis for more or less free adaptations of his own. In this sense these Hollywood leftovers still partake of a certain vestigial neoclassicism; they are style copies, attempts to fuse local color, popularism, and a sprinkling of modernism. They show how Stravinsky thought it might be possible for him to write film music; but they also show how badly he got it wrong.

While working on *North Star*, he was not wholly without prospects as a performer. Later in January 1943 he went to San Francisco to conduct a new Ballet Theatre production of *Petrushka* with Massine in the title role; and there would be six weeks in New York in the spring. But for the most part he and Vera stayed at home and cultivated their friends, their chickens, and, until its sad demise that February, their parrot. Their circle still had an essentially émigré complexion with a strong Russian bias. Since the summer of 1942, Rachmaninov had been a neighbor and had sent his spies to find out whether a social contact would be welcomed at 1260 North Wetherly Drive. It was, and the Stravinskys had duly dined at the Rachmaninovs' in Beverly Hills—one of those classic encounters between artists of similar background but radically different outlook that one feels ought to change the course of civilization. For most of the evening, however, the two most famous Russian musicians of the twentieth century "talked about managers, concert bureaus, agents, ASCAP [the American performance-rights agency that Stravinsky had recently, after much heart-searching, joined], and royalties."[18] A few days later, Rachmaninov arrived on his colleague's doorstep with a huge jar of honey, a product for which Stravinsky had confessed a liking.

Alas for this newfound amity and sweetness, Rachmaninov was already dying of a rapidly advancing melanoma. In February 1943, the great pianist-composer collapsed after a recital in Knoxville and arrived home at Beverly Hills in an ambulance. Five weeks later he was dead.

As far as American acquaintanceships were concerned, the Stravinskys were still mainly limited to a few old friends, to showbiz, and to professional contacts of one kind or another. Many of the latter were composers, ex-pupils of Nadia, like Copland, or Arthur Berger, whom Igor had met at a rehearsal for *Danses concertantes* in Los Angeles but who by 1943 was in New York writing music criticism and editing a music journal called *Listen;* or David Diamond, a nervy, quarrelsome character who had fought tooth and nail with Nadia in Paris but who admired Stravinsky so much that he happily ran errands for him on the East Coast, tracking down scores that were unobtainable in California and reporting on New York performances of his music.[19] There was Alexei Haieff, the Boulanger pupil whom Stravinsky had met at Harvard, and whom, when he saw him again in New York that spring, he helped in some way or other with his new symphony.[20] Equally there were West Coast musicians like Sol Babitz or the pianist Leonard Stein. Stein was unusual among Stravinsky's acquaintances in being an associate of Schoenberg, who lived a mere eight miles away in Brentwood Heights but with whom Stravinsky still had absolutely no contact.

Their closest American friends, however, were a handful of music-loving non-musicians, who tended to include professional advisers like their new lawyer, Aaron Sapiro, a former army sergeant-major, cousin of Tansman, and a huge, even at times oppressive admirer of Stravinsky's music. Above all there was the ex-banker Arthur Sachs—a board member of the New York Philharmonic Orchestra—and his French wife, Georgette, who lived in Santa Barbara on an estate called Rayben Farm with a well-appointed guest cottage where their friends could stay in comfort and with a measure of independence. The Sachses were the focus of a social life that preserved a certain old-fashioned style. There were often visitors from the East, including the Blisses (who had a house of their own in Santa Barbara), Nadia herself, and other former pupils, including Marcelle de Manziarly and Richard Hammond, who had helped try to secure Stravinsky's American copyright in the early twenties.[21] This circle was so congenial, so much of a home-from-home compared with shapeless and heartless Los Angeles, that for a time Igor and Vera seriously contemplated moving to Santa Barbara and spent several weeks there with that end in view in the autumn of 1943.[22] They did not move, however, perhaps because, for a peripatetic musician (as Stravinsky still partly regarded himself) Santa Barbara, a hundred miles north of Los Angeles, was simply too remote and provincial to be a permanent home, rather than an occasional weekend retreat.

That spring of 1943, in showery New York for the first time for two years, he might have reflected that from a certain angle Los Angeles could seem provincial in its turn. In Manhattan, even—perhaps especially—in wartime, one felt the proximity of Europe. Where else, apart from Paris, could one dine with Tchelitcheff, Léger, and André Maurois, practically on consecutive nights? Where else could one run into Beecham and Koussevitzky and Ziloti, the three conductors to whom Stravinsky perhaps owed most, whether or not he might care to admit it? Vladimir Golschmann, a former Diaghilev conductor, was giving the East Coast premiere of the *Danses concertantes*, and Stravinsky spent many hours coaching him in the work, in the interstices of his own heavy schedule conducting at the Met for Ballet Theatre, who had brought the Massine-Bolm *Petrushka* from the West Coast and were reviving Balanchine's *Apollo*. Busy as it was musically and socially, however, it was a somewhat restricted visit artistically, and it would have been almost wholly unproductive if Koussevitzky had not come to see him early in April and presented him with a commission of a thousand dollars for an orchestral work, to be paid for by a new fund Koussevitzky had established in memory of his wife.[23]

For almost forty years Natalie Koussevitzky had been the engine of her husband's career. In Russia before the revolution, it had been her money, inherited from her Ushov family tea business, that had supported his orchestra and his publishing house. In the West, she had set herself up as the power behind the throne, bullying her husband's biographers, like

Lourié, and his musical assistants, like Nicholas Slonimsky, whom she once called "a dirty Odessa Jew" to his face.[24] She was, Slonimsky recalled, "an imperious-looking woman who rarely spoke, and when she compressed her taciturn lips, she reminded one of an owl at her silent watch." Stravinsky, who seems not to have disliked her as much as he distrusted her husband, said that she unfortunately always looked cross, "like a hen, even when in good humor."[25] Curiously enough, chickens were once again much in his mind while he was composing the music in her memory. In February, three or four days after he had drafted the *Jane Eyre* hunting piece that later found its way into the memorial work, almost the entire Stravinsky chicken population were found dead in their run. Three months later, on the couple's return from New York, Vera recorded the arrival of fifteen new chicks; and on 9 June, the day Igor started the "Eulogy" of the *Ode*, she noted that he also composed "verses on the chicken coop theme."[26] Whether these were musical or poetic verses, and whether or not they had any connection with the *Ode*, is impossible to tell.

In fact the first music Stravinsky composed when he got home in May was the "Epitaph," eventually the final movement of the three. At this point he called the work *Triads*, perhaps because the instruments in the "Epitaph" are grouped in threes and the music is very transparently scored, so that the groupings are clear and in some sense emblematic. He then turned to the solemn, fugue-like "Eulogy," which became the first movement. Finally, before sending Koussevitzky the finished score on 9 July, he added the hunting piece, under the title "Eclogue," not perhaps without a twinge of doubt about its suitability to an elegiac context, since his covering letter calls it a "concert champêtre" and describes it, tendentiously, as "open-air music, a principle defended with such passion by the departed one, and so brilliantly realized by you at Tanglewood."[27] The idea was that Stravinsky would himself conduct the first performance when he came to Boston the following January; but Koussevitzky liked the piece so much that he decided on the spur of the moment to program it in his own Boston concert on 8 October. The score and orchestral parts were far from ready when Stravinsky heard this unwelcome news two weeks before the event. He had not forgotten the disaster of Koussevitzky's *Symphonies of Wind Instruments* in London twenty-two years before. But it was impossible to object. All he could do was alert Hugo Winter, his new editor at AMP,[28] to the urgency now surrounding the copying and checking of the performance materials, note the time of the coast-to-coast broadcast, and cross his fingers.

Koussevitzky's difficulty with new music lay essentially in his inability to learn a work from a score, and in the fact that he could not play the piano well enough to pick his way through one—however laboriously—in private. So except when he used a practice pianist (a role performed for him by

Slonimsky for some years in the twenties), he would arrive at a first orchestral rehearsal without much idea how a new piece was meant to sound. Nevertheless the fiasco of the *Ode* premiere, as entertainingly reported by the author of *Themes and Conclusions,* was by no means entirely his fault.[29] It is true that the trumpeter played his solo in the "Epitaph" in the wrong key; but that was because the composer, in his haste, had written the part out at the sounding pitch, failing to allow for the fact that on the B-flat trumpet it would come out a tone lower. It is also true that the performance ended in a mild cacophony, because the AMP copyist had misread two lines (or systems) of the manuscript full score as if they were one, which meant that six bars on the penultimate page were played simultaneously with the next six. But this only came about because of an oddity in the manuscript itself. It so happened that the first six bars in question were for oboes, clarinet, and horns, while the next six were for timpani and strings, so that at first glance the whole thing looked like an ordinary six bars of full score. To add to the confusion, Stravinsky had even written them out so that the barlines in the two systems lined up precisely. In the nature of the music's style, even the resulting concatenation of sounds was improbable rather than impossible: as Stravinsky himself told Koussevitzky, "the blurring was not too disturbing, for the two lines played together are almost integrated in the same mode." One might well suspect that Stravinsky himself had been momentarily fooled by the uniform and symmetrical character of his own writing.[30]

In any case, and whatever he may have said in later years, he took full responsibility at the time. After firing off a routine if slightly barbed congratulatory telegram ("Just heard *Ode* in your most penetrating performance. Profoundly touched . . ."),[31] he looked more closely at his score and saw with horror that the fault was his. He, the composer, had produced a misleading manuscript, and moreover he had failed to read the proofs with sufficient care. On the 11th he sent Koussevitzky a detailed explanation in English complete with errata sheet, and on the 12th he did what one might have supposed unthinkable: he wrote, in Russian, a second, more personal letter of abject apology to this conductor whom he had so often, in private, spoken of with derision.

> *Errare humanum est:* to err is human. So I think you will forgive me. But what I can't forgive myself is that I tormented your ears through my absurd carelessness, or rather absent-mindedness, in checking the parts. This is very, very disagreeable to me, my dear.[32]

A few days after sending the *Ode* in July, Stravinsky had conducted the Massine-Bolm *Petrushka* in the Hollywood Bowl, his second appearance there. Two days after that, on the 15th, there was an intimate but probably none too cheerful Russian lunch at North Wetherly Drive with Vasily Kibalchich, the former director of the Geneva Russian choir that had sung the first performance of *Les Noces,* and an even older friend, Alexis Kall. Kall's immoderate lifestyle, which had come between him and the Stravinskys three years earlier, had at last begun to catch up with him. He was suffering from diabetes, bad circulation, and severe leg pains, and the prognosis was bad. Six weeks later, poor Kall went into the Cedars of Lebanon Hospital with a gangrenous foot, and his left leg was amputated above the knee. For months afterwards he needed further treatment; for a time he went around in a wheelchair, then a year or so after the operation he had a prosthetic leg fitted. One hopes that at least his sense of humor remained intact. On his nameday (perhaps in July 1944), Igor and Vera sent him a short note of congratulations appended to a quotation from Igor's children's song about the bear whose leg is cut off by an old peasant but who makes himself a new one out of limewood and comes and gobbles up the old peasant and his wife. "Creak, my leg; creak, my limewood leg," goes the song, in a tone of grim jollity.[33]

Having finished the *Ode* in July, and having nothing new on the stocks apart from the incomplete concerto for orchestra, Stravinsky again took up the two-piano sonata that Nadia had hoped to perform the previous summer. Exactly what that early version had amounted to is hard now to establish for certain, but what he drafted in July and August 1943 was what became the first movement of the work in its final form. Curiously, he also made an orchestral draft of part of this same music, dating it 12 August. Craft says that it was another piece of aborted film music.[34] But the sketches give no such indication, and the orchestration may just as well have been an attempt at another section of the concerto. The only Hollywood project still being discussed at this stage was a bizarre Warner Bros. film about Gershwin in which Stravinsky was to play himself in a scene in which Gershwin asks him for lessons but, on learning Gershwin's income, Stravinsky demands lessons from him instead.[35] But for this there was no suggestion that Stravinsky should compose any music.

In any case, the two-piano work soon took over, and by October Stravinsky had drafted the first movement and sketched a finale, with one of the earlier three-stave pieces incorporated as a middle section. All the music was extensively based on tunes from *Pesni russkago naroda,* which strongly suggests that the new material derived at least in part from music originally intended for *North Star.* As before, however, any cinematic character it may ever have had is quite undetectable in what remains: placid, equable music, devoid of narrative elements, and with even its folkish ingredients homogenized to the point where its precise ethnic origins—unacknowledged by the composer—went unnoticed for almost forty years.[36]

Toward the end of October, with the two-piano work still unfinished, the Stravinskys went to Santa Barbara for a month. Koussevitzky had been pressing Igor to include *The Rite of Spring* in his Boston concerts in January, and although nervous about rehearsal time he had at last agreed, perhaps partly out of a desire to make up for the *Ode* fiasco.[37] He nevertheless remained edgy about the idea, not least because, being out of touch with Païchadze and not on speaking terms with Galaxy, he had no access to new or cleaner performance materials and above all no proprietorial shoulder to lean on in his difficulty. He had in mind a radical solution. He planned a new version of the work's technically and notationally most problematic movement, the Danse sacrale. He would get Nadia Boulanger, who was staying at the Sachses', to help him, and he would hand the revised score to AMP for publication—a recourse that was open to him because *The Rite of Spring* was in the public domain in America.[38] Nadia would be useful in other ways, too. Stravinsky had agreed to give a lecture at the University of Chicago on his way home from Boston, and he desperately needed her help excerpting the *Poétique* and turning it into usable English, since John Nef, Chicago professor of economics and chairman of the Moody Foundation lecture committee, wanted him to deliver it in that language.[39]

The revisions to the Danse sacrale were merely the latest stage in a process that had gone on since the first performances in 1913. Even the first published orchestral score of 1921 was different in many important details from the manuscript from which Monteux had conducted the riotous premiere, and since then there had been new published revisions and a great many tinkerings in pencil or blue crayon that had never figured in any printed score. This was the music that, Stravinsky claimed much later, he had been able to play but not write down.[40] Its difficulties were inherent in its revolutionary musical language. But it was also extremely hard for an orchestra to perform, and some of the changes had been designed to make it less so. At the same time, Stravinsky kept having new ideas about particular effects; he would cut out a gong here or a timpani thwack there, he would remove or reinstate tricky string pizzicatos, and he would constantly reposition the barlines or connect the notes in different ways so as to make the score easier to read. Yet when people asked him to simplify the actual music or reduce the size of the orchestra, he always claimed it was impossible, that he had tried and given up. The music was what it was, and that was that.[41]

The Santa Barbara revision followed this pattern. The only crucial difference was that, because he had ditched Galaxy (and therefore Édition Russe), there was no question of printing from old plates, and since new ones would have to be made anyway the whole notation could be rethought. For instance, he could, and did, change the basic note value from a semiquaver (sixteenth) to a quaver (eighth), though he characteristically forgot to alter the metronome mark accordingly, so that the score would have made nonsense if the mistake had not been obvious. As for the revisions to the orchestration, many of them reflected his own recent performances, especially his New York recording of 1940, where the excellence of the orchestra had evidently justified taking certain risks. The trouble with this version, from the practical point of view, was that, since it involved only one movement, anyone performing the whole work would still have to hire material from Galaxy/ERM and would be understandably reluctant to pay a second hire charge for the AMP Danse sacrale. The value of the revision might be, more simply, as a guide to the composer's latest intentions. Its importance—another matter—would remain that it was the first of a whole series of revisions of his works which, while partly motivated by the practicalities of the marketplace or copyright law, ended in musical reassessments, sometimes of a quite radical kind. They soon became a favorite aspect of the Stravinsky myth: the myth of revision for copyright—like all the best myths, a half-truth at the very most.

In spite of all this hard work, *The Rite* was not given in his January concerts in Boston, and instead he conducted the Symphony in C, *Pulcinella*, *Jeu de cartes,* and a string of first performances: the concert premiere of the *Circus Polka* (in its symphonic dress), the first performance anywhere of the *Four Norwegian Moods,* and the East Coast premiere of his arrangement of "The Star-Spangled Banner." Everything went off calmly enough in Cambridge's Sanders Theatre on the 13th and Boston's Symphony Hall on the 14th, but by the second Boston concert on the 15th word had got about, and to his astonishment the composer was visited in his dressing-room by a policeman and warned that if he conducted his "Star-Spangled Banner" that evening he would be in breach of a Massachusetts state law banning performance of the national anthem in any "embellished" form. The anthem was duly omitted and no further action taken. But the incident soon established itself as yet another myth, in which Stravinsky was supposedly arrested, held in police custody for several nights, and even photographed full-face and in profile for police records.[42] It soon emerged that the police reading of the law was in any case suspect, to say the least. What was actually forbidden was to play the anthem in part, or "as dance music, as an exit march, or as a part of a medley of any kind." Stravinsky's arrangement, of course, infringed none of these prohibitions, "unless," Nadia's friend Winifred Johnstone suggested, "the fact that a few indignant and conservative members of that Friday audience departed at the first strains [put it] under the heading of 'Exit March.' "[43]

From Boston, they proceeded (via New York) to Chicago, where, on the 20th of January, Stravinsky presented his lecture "Composing, Performing,

Listening," reading from a heavily annotated typescript that cannot much have eased the nervous strain of delivering a formal lecture in English for the first time. He and Nadia had somehow managed to knock together a coherent hour-long discourse from the six-hour *Poétique*, basing themselves mainly on the third lecture, about his working method as a composer, and the sixth, on the duties of the performer, together with an expanded ending about the role of the listener in the whole process. Much of this is little more than a précis of relevant parts of the *Poétique* turned into colorful and occasionally, it must be said, barely comprehensible English, such as in the image of art as a product of human artifice rather than nature, which seems to have been offered to the bemused audience in the Leon Mandel Assembly Hall as: "For if art does not drop from heaven as a bird's song, it is unfailingly so be it only the simplest of modulations correctly realized."[44] One can only hope that this sounded intelligent in Stravinsky's richly accented *basso profondo* English, and with its convolutions somewhat absorbed into those of his own personality and presence.

Not only the language, but to some extent also the tone of Stravinsky's remarks about the performer-listener axis was discreetly modified in Chicago, compared with the severe admonitions of the Harvard text. After four years away from France and French absolutism, he seems to have resigned himself to an at least marginally more benign view of the role of the interpreter, insisting that "nothing worthy to live is done without enthusiasm, love and joy" (in the *Poétique* "loving care" had been deemed sufficient), and quoting with approval Apollinaire's praise of good taste, Gauguin's distinction between technique and natural flair, and Cocteau's famous epigram about "the secret of knowing how far one can go too far." A marginal note in Stravinsky's hand even admits that in the realms of tempo and dynamics the performer is *"u sebya doma"* ("on home ground"). As for the listener, who had received short shrift at Harvard, he too is now required to commit himself actively, to give of himself in a loving and sympathetic spirit, and to accept joyfully the assaults on his habits of mind that all worthwhile music will make. Whether, as has been suggested, such changes of nuance were due to the influence of Nadia Boulanger and "her sense of the practical importance of the subject,"[45] or alternatively to the effects of four years amid the easygoing pragmatism of American daily life, is an intriguing but of course insoluble question.

The day after the lecture, Stravinsky practiced what he preached by taking part, in a spirit of "enthusiasm, love and joy," in a concert of his music organized by Remi Gassman of the university's music department. For no more than half his official fee, he played the Duo Concertant (with the violinist John Weicher) and the two-piano concerto (with Willard McGregor), and he also conducted a performance of the suite from *The Soldier's Tale*, in defiance of his habitual refusal to play and conduct in the same concert. More-over, he went to considerable pains to ensure the success of the occasion, supplying the players with recordings of the works in advance, and making himself available for rehearsals at all kinds of unsavory hour. Vera's diary reveals that he spent the greater part of their three-day stay in Chicago rehearsing for this concert.[46] Two days later they were in Madison, Wiscon-sin, where Igor repeated his lecture for the benefit of the Dominican sisters of Edgewood College, an invitation set up by Nadia, who had pupils there.

By the 27th they were back in Hollywood ("what joy to come home," Vera enthused), and within three days he was once again hard at work on his much interrupted but now almost complete piano-duo sonata.

11

THE BROAD WAY AND
THE STRAIT GATE

FOR SOME MONTHS now, and at least since the landings in southern Italy in September 1943, the Stravinskys had kept track of the progress of the war by pasting up large-scale maps of Europe and marking the Allied advances with colored pins. Isolated as they were from the vortex of events, they could watch the drama of the rescue of European civilization unfold as though on a screen, like the war films to which Americans flocked and for which Igor had never quite written the music. But local tremors from the far-off earthquake were comparatively slight. Blackouts, fuel rationing, and censorship were minor inconveniences when set beside the death and destruction one read about in the newspapers every day. They meant that permission was needed to drive to Santa Barbara; they meant afternoon concerts; and they meant writing family letters in French rather than Russian, to avoid the appearance of code or the suspiciously incomprehensible. When Western Union rang on New Year's Day 1944 to say that a telegram to Theodore, who had been living in Switzerland since the occupation of the south, had been suppressed on grounds of security, it was annoying rather than deeply worrying.[1] And yet the anxiety of extreme distance is never to be discounted, and Igor had good reason to be anxious about the scattered remnants of his family.

Worry gave life a provisional quality and made it hard to settle down to large-scale projects. So instead of finishing the concerto for orchestra, he worked on a set of variations as central movement for the two-piano sonata, again taking his theme from Bernard. He seems to have gone out of his way to create music of an unclouded harmonic texture, yet the workmanship is deceptively intricate and in some ways quite unlike anything he had tried before. The secret lies in the tune itself, which, though melodically plain, has a curiously fluid, seamless phraseology that Stravinsky emphasizes by repeating it twice against two upside-down versions of itself. The sense of discourse is not unlike that of late-medieval polyphony. In the same way the variations seem to hint at the keyboard writing of Bach, and especially the *Goldberg Variations*, a work that as it happens Stravinsky was on the lookout for but did not possess, though he did own Wanda Landowska's recording.[2] When he completed the sonata with this movement on 11 February, it had been on his desk, in one form or another, for more than eighteen months. Yet like the two-piano concerto, which had also had a disrupted gestation, it betrays few signs of hesitancy or unevenness. It may be a minor work, but it is the minor work of a great master, who can relax without falling into the casual or inconsequential.

A few days after finishing it, and precisely when he must have been wondering what to compose next, he received a letter from Mercedes de Acosta inviting him to write the music for a stage production of her play *The Mother of Christ*.[3] Religious subjects, she pointed out, were all the rage in Hollywood at that moment, as if Igor and Vera hadn't noticed, having sobbed their way through *The Song of Bernadette* only a week or so before. But Mercedes was no Franz Werfel, and her proposition was accompanied by a hard-cash offer of impressive dimensions: ten thousand dollars plus thirty percent of the takings, on condition that the score be ready by the 1st of September. It says a great deal for Stravinsky's powers of artistic resistance that, while agreeing to the idea in principle, he attached a condition of his own that he must have known Mercedes would be unlikely to accept. He insisted that Our Lady (who after all was presumably the play's central character) be represented on the stage not by a human actress but by a light. In fact the tone of his letter suggests that they had previously discussed the idea in person and that Mercedes's letter was by way of a formal contract. She had already expressed doubts about the light ("too hackneyed"). By the time they next had a chance to discuss alternative possibilities, other commissions had come up, and the intriguing prospect of a neo-Bachian theatre score by Stravinsky was lost forever.

Early in March 1944, he was approached by an MGM staff composer, Nathaniel Shilkret, with another proposal for a religious work: a collaborative piece based on episodes from the Book of Genesis. The motivation for this bizarre enterprise remains obscure. Shilkret's intention seems to have been to make not a film but a gramophone recording, on six 78-rpm discs, and since Stravinsky's contribution was to occupy only one of the twelve sides, it looks as if Shilkret had eleven other composers in his sights, including himself. In the event there were six others. Schoenberg wrote a wordless choral-orchestral prelude, Shilkret himself composed the Creation, Tansman composed Adam and Eve, Milhaud Cain and Abel, Castelnuovo-Tedesco the Flood, Ernst Toch the Covenant of the Rainbow, and Stravinsky brought up the rear with the Tower of Babel.[4] The story was to be told by a narrator, while the chorus and orchestra supplied what was supposed to be background music. According to Tansman, Shilkret envisaged the work "almost cinematographically, as an external synchronization of the text with the musical atmosphere"[5]—in other words, with the music as a kind of soundtrack to the biblical readings. But just as Stravinsky had opposed the direct representation of the Virgin Mary, so he fought tooth and nail against any musical characterization of God. "Music," Tansman reports him as having argued, "should illustrate nothing whatsoever. Such is not its function, and in this case less than ever."[6]

In fact *Babel*, as Stravinsky composed it in the three or four weeks after the meeting described by Tansman, is true to some but not all of this typically extreme statement of principle. Obviously he did not seriously believe that music could never be illustrative, in the sense of responding directly to a visual or narrative stimulus; countless pages of *Oedipus Rex* and *Persephone* make nonsense of the idea. He was simply standing out against the crude pictorialism that was the stock-in-trade of Hollywood composers like Shilkret, and that no money on earth would induce him, Stravinsky, to essay. The refusal to portray God is another kind of taboo altogether, and a much more interesting one, since it had significant musical consequences that resonate through later, more substantial works. In *Babel* there are two kinds of text. On the one hand there is the spoken narrative (verses 1–5 and 8–9), where Stravinsky uses Shilkret's speaker, accompanied by orchestral writing that is at least broadly descriptive, especially at the point where the Lord scatters the people across the face of the Earth and the music scurries about in suitably bewildered figurations. But when the Lord speaks, in verses six and seven, the music takes on a marmoreal calm, and suddenly we are in the presence of the divinely impersonal. Rather than have the speaker pronounce God's words, Stravinsky sets them for male chorus in two homophonic (that is, fully aligned) parts—an effect of real power and originality, despite the restricted anecdotal context. That he was engaged by the problems posed by this commission is also suggested by the harmonic style, which refers back to procedures he had largely abandoned with the neoclassical works of the early twenties, procedures that belong deep in his musical past. The main exception had been the *Symphony of Psalms*—also, of course, a religious work. Another exception—not religious—was still on his desk: the as-yet-incomplete concerto for orchestra. But *Babel* was the first public signal that a change might be in process.

Stravinsky finished the draft score on the 29th of March and the full score two weeks later. For a seven-minute piece it was good going; but he had scarcely drawn breath before the next commission landed on his doormat in a letter from his AMP editor, Hugo Winter. This time the approach was from the Blue Network radio station on behalf of the bandleader Paul Whiteman, who wanted a short, easy-listening piece, to go on one or two sides of a record (the timings of 4'20" or 8'40" were specified).[7] The fact that a popular musician like Whiteman should ask Stravinsky for a soft-centered work might seem to be further evidence of the extent to which the American commercial world regarded him primarily as a Big Name, without having much clue about the sort of music he wrote. But Whiteman had been involved with so-called symphonic jazz for more than twenty years, at least since the *Rhapsody in Blue*, and must have been well aware that he would not get a popular work in the normal sense from Stravinsky.[8] The composer himself was not put off by this one-and-only condition. Once again he liked the thousand-dollar fee (or "advance," as Whiteman wanted to call it); he liked the absence of technical restrictions of the *Babel* variety;[9] and above all he liked the fact that, as he probably realized at once, he had material on hand that he could easily adapt to Whiteman's needs.

Exactly how much of the *Scherzo à la russe* existed before 11 April 1944, when Stravinsky first heard about the commission, is curiously hard to establish. At some stage, probably in the autumn of 1943, he worked on a two-piano version of the main scherzo and first trio, perhaps with some idea of incorporating them into the sonata he was writing at that time. Meanwhile, the second trio had existed for two pianos, quite separately, at least since the previous January. All the material for these pieces comes, like that of the sonata, from Bernard, but if, as Stravinsky himself later claimed,[10] the scherzo started life as music for *North Star,* then it must all have been written by that January of 1943 (when the film project fell through), which is certainly possible but fails to explain the two-piano form of many of the drafts. The best explanation might be that the themes were first worked for the film, then reworked for two pianos at a time when the eventual form of the sonata was still unclear. Stravinsky says that the film version was exactly the same as the *Scherzo à la russe* in its version for symphony orchestra, but this is certainly wrong.[11] The band version came directly from the two-piano drafts, and the orchestral score was made some months later.[12]

In any case, writing the music up for band took several weeks of May and June 1944, a fact only partly attributable to the unfamiliar medium. Whiteman's band was much more like a misshapen symphony orchestra than the circus band for which Stravinsky had had to call in David Raksin to arrange the *Circus Polka*. It had strings and wind in a fairly normal balance, except that saxophones replaced the clarinets and bassoons. Otherwise, the only "oddities" were the guitar and the fact that Whiteman had a flautist who could also play the saxophone (there was no mandolin, Stravinsky's memory notwithstanding[13]). There were questions of balance to resolve, but musically the writing was simple and repetitive—"very *Petrushka* 1944," Milhaud thought it, judging from the two-piano version[14]—and even the little canon in the first trio was child's play compared with the imitative writing in the sonata variations. It is, one feels, on the refined instrumentation of such episodes that Stravinsky expended the most effort. He was still at work on that in the first week of June, when the next showbiz commission arrived in the shape of a telegram from the Broadway impresario, songwriter, and nightclub owner Billy Rose.[15]

By this time it might have struck him that he was in danger of sliding into a creative trough, dragged down by the commercial world's seemingly unquenchable thirst for the credit attached to his artistic fame. It may or may not have been the Rose commission that led him to turn down a request a week later for a cello concerto from the director of the Kansas Symphony Orchestra, Efrem Kurtz.[16] He had never liked the cello as a solo instrument anyway, and after all, Rose was asking for a ballet, which certainly *was* his kind of thing, if not entirely in the sense understood by Rose. The new work was wanted for a Broadway revue called *The Seven Lively Arts,* and although the pitch of the show would certainly be elevated by the normal standards of New York revue (it would have Alicia Markova and Anton Dolin as dancers, and Rose was even commissioning a series of paintings by Salvador Dalí for the Ziegfeld Theatre lounge), the "lively arts" would mostly not be the ones that Diaghilev and Benois used to dream of combining in their *Mir iskusstva* days: there would be comedians, Cole Porter songs, a jazz combo, and the inevitable chorus line. The atmosphere would be that of a revue, with audience to match. Rose was investing a huge sum of money in the show, more than a million dollars according to one report. Even so, he nearly fainted when Stravinsky demanded fifteen thousand dollars for a single season's performance rights. In the end they agreed on five thousand, plus two hundred dollars for each week in which the show ran; but Rose must have wondered if he had been misinformed about the unworldliness of great artists.[17]

What Stravinsky undoubtedly liked about Rose was his clear specification of what he did and did not want. Rose's original idea had been to transplant into his revue a shortened version of the second act of *Giselle,* which Markova had been dancing for Hurok at the Met. But Markova had jibbed, and instead Rose had approached Kurt Weill, then, when Weill declined and at his suggestion, Stravinsky, to supply a fifteen-minute score "after" *Giselle* for a theatre orchestra of forty exactly itemized players.[18] What Weill—even in his Broadway incarnation—would have made of this pallid-sounding task can only be imagined, but for Stravinsky it was as natural as the air he breathed. A week or so after the initial approach, Dolin himself called on him at Wetherly Drive, and between them they concocted a semi-abstract scenario, loosely derived from *Giselle,* Act 2, complete with timings and suggested musical references (including pages from *Coppelia* and *Swan Lake* as well as *Giselle,* all of which scores Stravinsky borrowed from Dolin). The piece would be called *L'Étoile* ("The Star"), as a tribute to Markova's preeminence as Adam's ill-fated heroine. Within days of this meeting, however, Stravinsky suddenly remembered past battles with Ramuz and others over the derivation of concert suites from stage works, and he wrote to Winter arguing for a title that Dolin would not be able to claim as his when the music migrated to the concert hall. The neutral but suggestive *Scènes de ballet* seems to have been devised expressly to avoid that danger.[19]

On the afternoon of Dolin's visit, on the 16th of June, Balanchine also came to work with Stravinsky at his house.[20] He and Rieti had conceived the idea of a choreographic version of *Danses concertantes* for a new ballet company they were proposing to set up in New York.[21] Then Balanchine had for some reason turned against the Rieti idea, and by early June was arguing in favor of Denham's Ballet Russe, whose dancers, he said, were superior and whose terms were less demanding.[22] In fact Stravinsky attended Balanchine's rehearsals in late June and found his dancers poor; then, a few days later, when Eugene Berman came with his designs for the production, Stravinsky took against them so abruptly that he left the room and went back to his score for Billy Rose. After all, it cannot have been easy to move between two such different abstract projects. While *Scènes de ballet* was, by its very nature, a showcase presentation of the essence of romantic ballet by a pair of spotlit soloists, Balanchine was interested only in movement as a virtual construct in its own right, inspired by music, but with its own autonomous laws, and performed by a company of individuals, "like characters in a garden, [. . .] who communicate, respond, who modify and return without losing their distinctness."[23]

Stravinsky was in any case under pressure to complete his new score. He had three months in which to compose and copy a quarter of an hour of orchestral music—not a huge task, but for him a steady enough rate of production. On two separate occasions in August he was again conducting *Petrushka* in the Bowl, and in between he attended other Bowl concerts, including one in which the twenty-six-year-old Leonard Bernstein conducted *Firebird* (disappointingly, Vera noted),[24] and another directed by Dimitri Mitropoulos, who later came to dinner and stayed until two in the morning discussing the Orthodox church. And these same three months had been marked out by fate as the most critical and frightening of the entire European war so far. When British and American troops landed in Normandy on the 6th of June, the Stravinskys bought an assortment of French guidebooks to help them follow the progress of the invasion. Among the expatriate community in Los Angeles, the anxiety was almost tangible. Igor's fears for his family were compounded by the fact that he had little news of Soulima, who was still in Paris, while all he knew of Milène was that she had married a fellow consumptive at Sancellemoz in the spring. Only Theodore, now in Geneva, was presumably safe. Kitty, in

Leysin, was also out of Hitler's reach, whatever the smaller microbes might have in store for her. Above all she—like the rest of her family—was for now spared the news that her Jewish father, Yury Mandelstam, had been deported in July 1943 from the transit camp in the Paris suburb of Drancy, where he had been incarcerated after his arrest fifteen months previously, and sent in a cattle truck to the Polish mining town of Jaworzno, near Katowice. There, on the 18th of October, 1943, in unknown circumstances, he had perished, leaving his sickly daughter an orphan at the age of six.[25]

As the Allied troops advanced slowly through northern France, Stravinsky gradually assembled his ballet about a ballet about a girl who turns into a fairy. To say that he was unaware of the world outside his studio would be a grotesque perversion of his view of the meaning and function of music. Yet there remains something disturbing about the degree of detachment involved in this case, apparently so much greater than the isolationism of *Renard* (where a new language was being forged out of fragments of the old), and if anything thrown into relief by its sudden abandonment in the work's final two minutes. By the time the French Second Armored Division and U.S. Fourth Infantry entered Paris on the 25th of August, *Scènes de ballet* was complete in draft, apart from a few particulars. On the 23rd, the day the Nazis actually fled the French capital, Stravinsky kept breaking off work on the Apotheosis to listen to the radio news,[26] and he appended to the final draft page the laconic inscription "Paris n'est plus aux allemands"—Paris is no longer in German hands. The music inflates from the simple "finale" of the original outline into a peroration as extended as, and a great deal more grandiose than, the equivalent ending of the *Symphony of Psalms* or *The Fairy's Kiss,* and it culminates in a sequence of uncouth fortissimo chords that can only be understood as a response, so to speak outside the frame of the work, to events that have not concerned it, still do not concern it, and in some way betray its innocence. Rose himself was maintaining that his revue had nothing to do with the war, though he did also later claim that, by opening in New York on the third anniversary of Pearl Harbor, he was "paying tribute to the nation's strength and stability."[27] But few who understood the ways of Broadway will have lent much credence to that.

Whatever the effects on his music, the physical restrictions imposed by war were playing havoc with Stravinsky's ability to attend and participate in his own first performances. Early in August, Nadia Boulanger and Richard Johnson had at last played the Sonata for Two Pianos in its definitive form to the Dominican sisters at Edgewood College, who heard it "with devotion" in appalling heat. Then on the 8th, Nadia and Robert Tangeman gave what was curiously billed as the "official private premiere" at the university at Bloomington, Indiana, thus at last fulfilling Nadia's promise and intention of two years earlier. "How the two pianos sound," Nadia had enthused. "We are preparing a Palestrina mass for the feast of St. Dominic [8 August], and the mass and sonata shed mutual light on one another."[28] The comparison must have delighted Stravinsky, who had worked hard on the sonata's seemingly effortless texture of flowing polyphony and had probably said as much to Nadia in conversation.

The performance even brought another, more modest commission his way. Among the supporting musicians at Edgewood had been Germain Prévost, the violist in the Pro Arte Quartet, who had played Stravinsky's *Concertino* in Paris in the Wiéner retrospective of December 1923 and again in Brussels in 1924.[29] The quartet had come to the U.S.A. in 1940, but its leader, Alphonse Onnou, had died at Madison that same year, and Prévost—anxious and homesick for Belgium, where he had left his wife and children—nourished the idea of commissioning and performing a work in Onnou's memory. Alas, he had no money to spare except his hundred-dollar fee for playing at Edgewood. Nadia urged Igor to agree.[30]

A few weeks later, toward the end of October, he at last performed the sonata with her as part of a short program of two-piano works to go with a repeat of his Chicago lecture at Mills College. They played the *Scherzo à la russe* and the *Circus Polka;* and Madeleine and Darius Milhaud (now in a wheelchair because of chronic arthritis) threw a party for twenty-five professors and their wives "[and] the most interesting people" in Mills College, Vera noted drily.[31] The most interesting people did however include at least one who caught and held Stravinsky's attention: a young associate from Berkeley called Manfred Bukofzer, who talked learnedly about medieval music and played them some of his recordings.[32] Then, back in Hollywood on the 27th, Igor composed the beautiful and intimate *Elegy for solo viola* for Prévost, placing at its heart a fully worked fugue in two parts, worthy of Bach in its skillful suggestion of a polyphonic texture within the limitations of what is essentially a melody instrument.[33]

Meanwhile Whiteman's Blue Network transmission of the *Scherzo à la russe* on the 5th of September had failed to reach the West Coast, and Stravinsky had to wait for an acetate recording that AMP made for him from the broadcast. When he did hear it, he found the performance mediocre and much too fast.[34] He was absent too, of course, from the ballet premiere of *Danses concertantes,* in the New York City Center five days later. That would soon be remedied, however, when Denham's company came to the West Coast at the start of December, and Stravinsky would himself—as it turned out—be in the pit.[35]

The echoes from New York were disconcertingly contradictory. According to Denham, the new ballet was greeted with "wild acclamation."[36] But Balanchine was not yet the godlike figure in Manhattan that he later became, and it was still considered chic among hard-bitten pressmen to describe his choreography as "twinkle-toed mathematics," "almost totally devoid of dancing," "an illustrated exercise book,"[37] and so forth, just as the recent Stravinsky could safely be written off as anti-dance and even (so rapidly had New York's critics now caught up with the latest styles), "gravely démodé, belonging to that avant-gardisme of about 1925 which is now as quaint as grandmother's antimacassar."[38] These studious imbecilities were happily counteracted by a pair of brilliant notices from the *Tribune*'s dance critic, Edwin Denby, who was perfectly conscious of the "rare luxury" of having "a ballet composer, a choreographer and a ballet decorator [Berman] so eminent that each in his field can be called the best in the world." Denby grasped at once something exceptional in Balanchine's relation to the music, and his remarks amount to the first detailed perception of the intimacy of the choreographer's response to Stravinsky's writing.

> Astonishing is the ease with which Balanchine understands the flow of the unsymmetrical periods of the music and gives them a visual grace and a logic that illuminates the musician's musical intentions. The music is delicious instrumentally, but it is very firm in its melodic and rhythmic logic, and the absence of any rhetoric gives it a gentle serenity that is strangely bewitching. It is that rarity, a modest masterpiece.[39]

Unlike his colleagues, Denby was not at all put out by Balanchine's rejection of narrative.

> The dance is like a conversation in Henry James, as surprising, as sensitive, as forbearing, as full of slyness and fancy. The joyousness of it is the pleasure of being civilized, of being what we really are, born into a millennial urban civilization. This is where we are and this is what the mind makes beautiful.[40]

Compared with Louis Biancolli's "I can be wrong [but] I merely like ballet that heads somewhere," this was penetrating indeed.[41]

Stravinsky naturally soon began to receive inside reports as well. "The choreography is perfect," Berman wrote, "at once noble, gay, roguish, always marvellously designed and composed." The company itself was the best since Diaghilev: calm and serene, no hanging of heads, everything ready for curtain-up. Needless to add, the success had gone down badly in the trade. "Among the other Ballet Russe companies, everyone is now against you and Balanchine, and they say that Hurok is doing everything he can to scupper Denham and bad-mouth *Danses concertantes* and especially your music."[42] No doubt Berman was making trouble on his own account, but still Stravinsky began to worry about all these goings-on in his absence;

about the way his music was being handled by Denham's new young conductor whose name he didn't know (intelligently, Rieti said; timidly according to others: the conductor was Emanuel Balaban[43]); and about the fate of his *Scènes de ballet,* to be conducted by God knew whom. He half expected—hoped—that Rose would invite him to do it;[44] then, when he heard it would be a certain Maurice Abravanel, he claimed ignorance of this pupil of Kurt Weill's whom he had, in fact, met (Hugo Winter reminded him) at the Paris premiere of the *Mahagonny Songspiel* and *Der Jasager* in 1932.[45]

Rose had arranged a pre-Broadway run of *The Seven Lively Arts* in the form of public rehearsals in the Forrest Theatre, Philadelphia, opening on 27 November. On the 30th, the composer received a long telegram from Dolin, reporting a "great success," confessing to one or two cuts, and imploring him to rescore the soupy trumpet melody in the Pas de deux for strings and to strengthen the orchestra in the Apotheosis. "Please believe me," the telegram concluded, "this is important and then I know ballet will be tremendous."[46] Stravinsky promptly wired Abravanel: "Refuse to consider Dolin's extremely shocking suggestions of crippling my music by cuts and reorchestrations to obtain what he calls tremendous success being entirely satisfied with merely great success mentioned in his wire today."[47] Three days later Abravanel telephoned. He assured Stravinsky that there was no question of rescoring his music, but there were practical reasons why cuts were needed. The male dancers in the corps de ballet were what he called "hoofers"—tap-dancers who could skip around in four-four time for as long as you liked, but who simply could not manage the five-eight of their opening dance. This piece had already been cut in Philadelphia, and the conductor wanted Stravinsky's approval for the same cut in the Broadway run.[48]

Naturally it was Rose who was calling for these changes. When Abravanel had first played him the music he had wanted "to cut everything that was not Markova." Then in the performances he noticed that in the pas de deux on Cole Porter's "Easy to Love" there were constant bursts of applause, whereas in Stravinsky's ballet the audience sat on their hands until the end. To his mind, this was a defect, and the remedy lay in the pit. Abravanel, by his own account, refused to accept alterations in the scoring, and Dolin backed him up in front of Rose but then double-crossed him with his telegram to Stravinsky. The conductor knew perfectly well, of course, that Stravinsky's *schmalz*-free scoring was wrong for a Broadway show, but he could not bring himself to side with Rose's philistinism.[49] Dolin simply disliked the music: "Its only merit," he wrote later, "was it was short, and Alicia danced in it."[50] It seems not to have occurred to him that Stravinsky, who had year after year fought Diaghilev off over such matters, might not agree with him.

The composer did nevertheless consent to the excision of the opening dance, provided the performance was billed as excerpts;[51] and so it duly was when the show opened at the Ziegfeld on the 7th of December. Even incomplete, *Scènes de ballet* attracted a highbrow leavening of the usual revue clientele, but they cannot have enjoyed themselves all that much. For one thing, the work was badly placed at the beginning of the second half, which meant that the audience were still struggling to their seats after it had started. For another, it was merely one rather modest ingredient in what one critic appetizingly described as "an opulent grab-bag of entertainment."[52] There were comedy sketches by Moss Hart played by Beatrice Lillie, there were new songs by Cole Porter (including "Every Time We Say Goodbye"), there was a talkative M.C. and a standup comic, and an extravagant set piece called "Billy Rose Buys the Metropolitan Opera House," which ended with Benny Goodman and his band playing in the Diamond Horseshoe; and the whole show lasted nearly until midnight. "Stripped of its fancy wrappings," *Time* magazine lamented, "*The Seven Lively Arts* is oversized and overstuffed. At times the whole thing seems less like the seven lively arts (which presumably include dressmaking and sex) than like seven luxury hotels."[53] Mercedes de Acosta, who had moved to New York to take up a job at the Office of War Information, attended the opening and was appalled by the sight of Rose himself standing in the foyer dispensing bad champagne "to fat Jewish women, and fat Christian women too, all dripping in mink coats and bosoms dripping in orchids."[54] She thought Porter's music poor and Dolin's choreography banal. Markova was too much the dying swan; the orchestra played too loud. But in spite of everything, Igor's ballet "shone out like a star on a dark night." No doubt life was hard in the Office of War Information, but with all allowances made, Stravinsky was probably fortunate to be two thousand miles away that night.

The show ran for 183 performances, but long before it closed Rose—previously so keen to enrich the sound—now tried to save money by reducing the orchestra. "Except for your composition," he wrote to Stravinsky, in a much-misquoted telegram,

> there is nothing in the Cole Porter score that requires a forty-piece orchestra. Robert Russell Bennett assures me he can reorchestrate the Porter music very effectively for twenty-eight men. This will mean a saving to me of $60,000 on the year. As a practical man of the theatre I hope you can appreciate my problem and reorchestrate your composition for this smaller number of men. Otherwise I would have no choice but to replace it with other music. I would very much like to retain it and if you are willing to do this will wire you the new instrumentation.[55]

At first, Stravinsky did his best to avoid reworking his orchestration, and instead suggested that Rose use a two-piano version, with the pianos on the stage—a bizarre throwback to the design idea of *Les Noces*. In the end, however, they compromised by dropping the tuba, one of the trombones, and seven out of twenty strings.[56] Probably, with the audience still tripping over one another's feet and the music cut to about ten minutes, the difference was in any case not too noticeable. In its reduced form, *Scènes de ballet* was still in the show on the 3rd of February, when Stravinsky conducted it complete for the first time in a Carnegie Hall concert with the New York Philharmonic, so that, as that was a Saturday, an energetic Manhattan enthusiast could have heard most of it three times that day, including the Rose matinée, if so inclined.

As 1944 drew toward its close, Stravinsky must surely have surveyed his year's work with mixed feelings. He had kept busy and he had made money; but the musical results were a curious and, on the face of it, aimless miscellany, mostly written to other people's specifications, or using up material he might not have considered but for the imagined needs of the silver screen. Meanwhile his big orchestral work had not advanced beyond its second movement, and he had conducted nothing since January apart from a handful of ballet performances. Even a brief spell conducting run-through performances with a pick-up orchestra of Hollywood musicians had come to an end after the occasion in May 1943 when so many players had failed to turn up to a rehearsal of *Dumbarton Oaks* that he had walked out in dudgeon.[57]

Yet whatever he may have thought of American commercial and musical life in general and its effects on his work in particular, he was inevitably being drawn more and more into its fabric, and discovering more of its variety. Social activities were still dominated by the tedious Hollywood round. A fortnight after the liberation of Paris, Elsa Maxwell threw what she called a "victory" party for the beautiful and famous of Los Angeles, with glittering fashions and diamonds but, Vera confessed to Mercedes, "no brains or soul."[58] But while the Stravinskys still saw a good deal of fellow expatriates like Artur Rubinstein, the Werfels, and the Milhauds, and stuck to their close Russian friends like the film actor Vladimir Sokolov and his wife Lisa, or Eugene Berman, or Adolf Bolm and his wife, Beata (who worked for a time as Igor's secretary), they seem in some ways to have begun to feel, in themselves, more American than before. Many years had passed since the composer had cultivated the image of a dandy, with his check plus-fours and mustard-colored pullovers. His early-forties persona, at least in photographs, is more that of a prosperous businessman—though he would have denied at least the adjective—who has no particular desire, perhaps no need, to distinguish himself from his well-to-do surroundings. Most remarkably, his politics had turned turtle. Having watched the destruction of ordered society in Europe by precisely those right-wing forces he had believed destined to protect it, he now candidly sided with the political "strength" of his adopted home and became, practically overnight, a new-deal democrat. When Roosevelt won his fourth term in November 1944, the Stravinskys, though they did not have the vote, could and did thank heaven,[59] and after his death they happily transferred their allegiance to his successor. "As far as I am concerned," the composer would now say, "they can have their generalissimos and Führers. Leave me Mr. Truman and I'm quite satisfied."[60]

One day in late February 1944 a letter had arrived from a young New York musician called Robert Craft, asking certain technical questions to do with the performance of *The Soldier's Tale* and other matters.[61] Craft was a twenty-year-old Juilliard conducting student who had decided at the age of twelve that his life's ambition was to study with Stravinsky, but who was still, eight years later, frustrated by the fact that Stravinsky's work did not figure in the Juilliard syllabus.[62] His letter was a desperate personal thrust at his target, like Tatyana's to Eugene Onegin. And its immediate outcome was nearly as unhappy since, although Stravinsky did not, like Onegin, reply in stern schoolmasterly tones, the friendly reply he did dictate to Beata Bolm was never posted, for the supposed reason that he suddenly became afraid that Craft's own handwritten letter, which he was enclosing because he deduced its author had not kept a copy, might get lost. This explanation is so unlikely—bearing in mind that Stravinsky had only to extract Craft's letter and post his own—that one automatically looks for another: that Stravinsky simply forgot to post it, later found it, and kept it, as he kept most pieces of paper, on file. The more interesting question is whether the "fear of loss" story was concocted by Stravinsky to excuse his oversight, or by Craft to evade its implications. Craft wrote again a few weeks later, without apparently referring to his earlier letter; but for the time being thereafter, the correspondence faltered.[63] Stravinsky often received letters from musicians, young and old, and there was little beyond evident enthusiasm to distinguish Craft's from countless others. Their first communications were, simply, unimpressively one-sided.

Two of Stravinsky's closest musician friends in Hollywood, Sol Babitz and the composer Ingolf Dahl, a refugee from Nazi Germany who was undergoing a course of study with Nadia and had worked with Stravinsky on the piano reduction of *Danses concertantes*, had recently become involved in a new concert venture in Hollywood called "Evenings on the Roof." The concerts had been started in 1939 by a passionate, impoverished young music-loving idealist by the name of Peter Yates and his pianist wife Frances Mullen, in a specially built loft-chamber cantilevered out over their decrepit hillside bungalow in Silverlake. In 1942 the monthly concerts had moved to the Assistance League Playhouse in central Hollywood, and two years later they had moved again to a studio of KFWB radio, just off Sunset Boulevard. Yates was an explorer with a mission, not merely to fill a gap in Los Angeles's limited and conservative musical life—"a veritable Sahara," he called it, "of artistic incomprehension"—but more especially to present a new type of concert where unusual music of all kinds would be played by musicians dedicated to what they were doing, at low admission cost, without consideration of profit, and with a minimum of ostentation. Early audiences had been tiny and select, but by the time Stravinsky attended his first Roof concert (as they continued to be called) on 6 March 1944, audiences of two or three hundred had become normal.[64]

Los Angeles being what it was, "unusual music" was a much wider category than it would have been in London or New York; and though Yates had started out as an apostle of modernism, he had also begun to delve into what came to be known as "early music" (pre-Bach), while at the same time making an exhaustive personal study of the lesser-known works of the classical masters: Mozart, Haydn, Beethoven. Among other things, he was a pioneer of the composer retrospective; he programed whole concerts of Bartók and Ives—whose music was little known and greatly feared on the West Coast—and whole series of Beethoven sonatas. But he was also a vigorous mixed-programmer, a repertory opportunist who was not afraid to mix the seemingly incompatible and challenge the audience's knowledge of its own taste. Stravinsky went to hear Babitz play a Mozart violin sonata, but he also heard a Haydn piano sonata and, more remarkably, keyboard pieces by Gibbons, Byrd, and Purcell, played by Yates's resident early music specialist, Wesley Kuhnle, on a harpsichord he had built himself.[65]

It would be fanciful to suggest that this or any other single encounter with ancient music had a significant effect on Stravinsky's own creative thinking. For twenty-five years he had been modeling himself on music of the early eighteenth century. Jacques Handschin, the Swiss medievalist, had been a good friend in the early thirties. He knew Nadia Boulanger's investigations into early baroque vocal chamber music, had lapped up Cingria's *Pétrarque* with its remarks about the Renaissance instrumental *canzona*, and had recently composed something like a *canzona* of his own in the slow movement of the two-piano sonata, based on a barely recognizable Russian folk song. It is perfectly true that within a few weeks of hearing Kuhnle play, he and Vera were listening to Landowska's recording of the *Goldberg Variations,* and trying to acquire the music.[66] But far more interesting than these apparently chance encounters with, after all, unrelated old music is a connection that was forming in his mind between the styles and techniques of pre-classical music in general and the context in which such techniques were most comprehensively displayed—the music of the medieval Catholic Church.

Exactly when he began composing a Kyrie and Gloria for mixed chorus and ten wind instruments is uncertain, but he was definitely working on the Gloria just before Christmas 1944, and probably on the Kyrie just before that.[67] Although they were not his first sacred music of 1944, these two movements stand apart from *Babel* for the simple reason that there is no evidence of a commission for them, and the presumption therefore is that Stravinsky wrote them on some inner prompting. Craft thought that a spiritual crisis was involved, but if so, the two Mass movements are its only outward and visible sign.[68] It is perhaps natural for the nonbeliever to assume that sudden expressions of faith must have some powerful psychological origin. But Stravinsky had never stopped being a devout, somewhat credulous believer since the time in the twenties when he had forced his entire family to kneel and pray in front of their domestic icons,[69] or the years of Katya's illness, when her letters had been peppered with invocations to the saints, and they had, as a family, followed the dissident Church in Exile to its chapel above a garage in the rue d'Odessa. Now, at 1260 North Wetherly Drive, the icons still graced the walls and desk, the *panikhidï* still came round with grim regularity, and Christmas, Easter, and birthdays—if not always other festivals—were honored as much in church as at the dinner table. Stravinsky was and remained profoundly superstitious, a literal believer—as Craft often later recorded—in the person of the devil and the actuality of holy relics. Only the context had changed. Vera, so far from sharing Katya's intense piety, was a happy rationalist who went to church when Igor went and stayed away when—increasingly often—he stayed away. Thus the tone of religious life at Wetherly Drive was very different from its tone at the Faubourg. There it had centred on Katya, while Igor was the wayward element. Here it focused on Igor, and fluctuated with his waywardness.

As communicants, they never wavered from the Orthodox Church, but as in the past Stravinsky's intellectual interest in Christianity was essentially Catholic. His Orthodox reading was confined to the prayers and precepts of the *Dobrotolyubiye*—the Russian version of the Greek *Philokalia*—with its injunctions to a humbler and more ordered spiritual life. "What shall we say of the belly, the queen of passions? If you can slay it or half kill it, keep a tight hold." "Nothing is more ruinous than talkativeness, and more harmful than an uncontrolled tongue; and nothing is more destructive and disorganizing to the treasure of the soul." "Increasing knowledge of God decreases knowledge of all else." To subdue the activities of the mind, the tongue, and the digestion was a pious goal but, for the thinking, drinking man, not necessarily a consistent or desirable one. From the twenties on, Igor and Katya had read Maritain and Aquinas (especially the *Summa Theologiae*), Bossuet, Francis of Sales, and much else in the great central tradition of Catholic theology that sought to reconcile the brain and the spirit.[70] Igor had run into Maritain at his Chicago lecture early in 1944; they had dined and talked, surely, about the Thomist aspects of the *Poétique* and their residue in the Chicago text. Later in the year he had made the acquaintance, through Nadia, of a Québecois priest named Elzear Fortier, who had given him Bossuet's *Élévations sur les mystères* in return for a copy of the two-piano sonata, which Fortier had heard at Edgewood College.[71]

Whether these contacts, scattered as they were and in any case not essentially new, explain the Mass settings might be doubted. They merely reveal an openness and, in some respects, a preference. Having spent more than a year dancing to commercial tunes, and producing—as he must have felt— nothing of the first rank, Stravinsky may simply have experienced an urge to write something of a more detached and spiritual character. What more natural than to turn to the liturgy: to imagine a music that would be sung in church, not in the manner of a concert, but as a humble enrichment of a solemn observance? That would be a suitably austere pleasure. But if he were to write for the Russian Church, he would have to forgo instruments, which were forbidden in the Orthodox rite. In any case, a work for the Russian liturgy—and to a Slavonic text—would sink without trace outside that liturgy. With music, as with theology, the Orthodox tradition was narrow and restrictive, while the Catholic Church offered precedents of an unbelievable wealth and variety, from the severest to the most sumptuous, and from the simplest to the most technically and intellectually complex. It was in this direction, especially, that his thoughts were now beginning to turn.

It would be good to know more about the meeting with Bukofzer at Mills that October. Craft reports that while writing the Kyrie and Gloria Stravinsky was immersed in the music of the fourteenth-century composers Guillaume de Machaut and Jacopo da Bologna, though Stravinsky himself claimed (in conversations recorded by Craft) not to have known any Machaut—or at any rate not his only surviving Mass—until later, and not to have been influenced at all by early models.[72] This latter claim, like others of the same kind, is hard to take seriously. Herbert Murrill long ago pointed out the remarkable similarity of flavor between passages in Stravinsky's Gloria (as well as in the later Sanctus) and an early fifteenth-century Mass setting by Perusio (Matteo da Perugia).[73] His examples show the same decorative, incantatory manner, with an intricate and very fluid rhythmic relationship between the different parts—entirely vocal in the Matteo Mass, vocal and instrumental in Stravinsky's. Murrill was not suggesting that Stravinsky copied this or any other particular work, only that he seems consciously to have adopted a certain general style—that of the Ars Nova—to go with his strict concept of a musical liturgy. The music comes, so to speak, complete with the image of chanting monks, candlelit misericords, and echoing vaults. But the vision is neither romanticized nor a retreat into the past. As with all his modelings, Stravinsky is concerned to reinvent his own language by oblique reference to other styles and techniques; their appeal lies in their severity and impersonality, and not in any impressionistic suggestiveness.

He must have planned a complete Mass from the outset, but for various reasons he got no farther than the Gloria before he was once again diverted by the insistent call of Mammon.

12

DISTANT CLASHES OF ARMS

THAT YEAR'S New York trip was to be twice as long as its predecessor, fully six weeks. They set off by train on the 24th of January 1945, traveling with Arthur and Georgette Sachs, and by the 30th, Stravinsky—with his usual feverish January cold—was in the thick of rehearsals in Carnegie Hall. The concerts (on the first four days of February) were his first with the New York Philharmonic for almost five years, and unlike his 1940 programs they painted a bizarre picture of the great composer in wartime. Half of each was devoted to Glinka's *Ruslan* overture and Tchaikovsky's Second Symphony, while the Stravinsky halves were various permutations of the recent semi-potboilers—the *Four Norwegian Moods,* the *Circus Polka,* the *Scènes de ballet,* alongside the *Ode,* all of them new to the Manhattan concert platform—together with Beveridge Webster playing the piano concerto, a piece Virgil Thomson reckoned had not been heard in New York since Stravinsky himself played it there in 1925.[1]

All this was welcome enough money in the bank. But the New York stay was important for another reason; it put him back in touch with the machinery of the music business, just at the moment when the war seemed to be coming to an end and a certain modest optimism was in the air. For more than two years since August 1942, the whole recording industry in the U.S.A. had been crippled by a strike of the American Federation of Musicians; but by November 1944, with war restrictions on materials starting to relax, the record companies could no longer justify holding out against the AFM demands for a proper distribution of royalties, and that month both Columbia and RCA Victor came to terms with the Federation.[2] On the 5th of February, the day after his last New York concert, Stravinsky went back to Carnegie Hall to record the four recent works he had just been conducting, and on the same day he signed a nonexclusive recording contract with Columbia.

It was an early example of the type of concert-recording deal that later became something like a blood-transfusion system for concert life. The circumstances, however, reflected a particular reality of the political structure of music in New York, since Arthur Judson, the all-powerful manager of the Philharmonic, was also co-founder and a major stockholder of CBS, and Goddard Lieberson, who had produced Stravinsky's 1940 recordings with the NYPSO, was now director of Masterworks at Columbia. Ten days after signing for Lieberson, Stravinsky lunched with Judson's assistant, Bruno Zirato, and accepted a commission for what was optimistically described as a "victory" symphony, at a fee of five thousand dollars, to be premiered by the orchestra in January 1946.3 The new work was not added to the Columbia contract until August 1945 at the earliest. But two whole movements of it already existed, in the form of the symphonic Allegro and Andante supposedly intended for his concerto for orchestra, and Stravinsky may have made a snap decision that only one more movement was needed to round off this long-projected but never properly formulated work. A few days after the Zirato lunch, there was a heavy session at AMP, at which Stravinsky almost certainly put pressure on Gretl Urban to start acting as his main publisher, rather than as a somewhat cautious agent for Schott. For years he had been assuring her that he had no exclusive contract with Schott and was therefore free to offer his new works to whom he pleased.4 His lawyer, Sapiro, had, with what was to prove a characteristic blend of sycophantic wheedling and injured rectitude, bullied AMP into signing a deal with Chappell of London, to whom Stravinsky had already sold the two-piano sonata and the viola *Elegy.* Meanwhile, Stravinsky had seen Koussevitzky, heard nothing but bad news about the Galaxy squabble, and learnt that the great man was thinking of backing out of music publishing altogether, selling his catalogue and transferring his rights.5 The company's Berlin offices had been destroyed by Allied bombing in 1944, and for the second time in less than thirty years the old Russische Musikverlag—Édition Russe—had effectively been put out of business as a result of what had once seemed a shrewd and strategic choice of headquarters.

For all the worrying condition of his publishing contracts, Stravinsky returned to Hollywood in the second week of March with a clearer idea of the work to be done. The symphony, already by far his most powerful and complex piece of writing since the mid-thirties, could now presumably be completed, without fear of its again being pushed aside by footling, money-spinning commissions. He also planned to rescore one of those commissions, the *Scherzo à la russe,* for symphony orchestra, and after that he would finish the Mass. But the publishing trade had by no means finished with him. He and Vera had been home for barely two weeks when he was contacted by Lou Levy, the president of Leeds Music Corporation, with a proposal about his three most famous ballets, *Firebird, Petrushka,* and *The Rite of Spring,* all of which were still in the public domain in the U.S.A.6 It had come to Levy's notice that Stravinsky was about to acquire U.S. citizenship, and he had also somehow found out that Koussevitzky might be interested in selling the Édition Russe catalogue. If Stravinsky could revise or rewrite these pieces sufficiently to distinguish the new versions from the old, it would then be possible to re-copyright them in the U.S.A. under the protection of the composer's citizenship; and if Koussevitzky would sell, then such protection as *Petrushka* and *The Rite of Spring* enjoyed abroad would likewise accrue to Leeds.[7]

Despite this comparatively simple equation, it was *Firebird*—a score not published by ERM—that came first out of the hat, and for reasons not hard to fathom. Of all Stravinsky's works, it was the only one that could conceivably be called popular in the normal sense of the term, and while its potential earnings were hard to establish (precisely because it was in the public domain in the States, and its score and materials had naturally been pirated there), it was a reasonable bet that it was played more in the U.S.A. alone than were the other two ballets in Europe and America combined. Moreover, Levy may have had a concealed motive, in the shape of an intention to plunder Stravinsky's most conventionally melodious score for popular hit tunes. Leeds were certainly much less enthusiastic about the two later ballets than their opening gambit had implied. Their initial contract with Stravinsky in early May related only to *Firebird,* and they were soon indicating, ever so sweetly, that they would rather wait and see how the first ballet went before doing anything about the second.[8] Sapiro, who had attended the early Leeds meetings, was swiftly reduced to a tone of pious apoplexy. He was shocked that "people like yourselves can treat one of the greatest creative musicians of this last century with the same kind of light disdain that you use towards the ephemeral writers of Broadway brass."[9] Levy must have been surprised to encounter a lawyer who based his arguments on aesthetic value judgments, but he would doubtless have replied—if a reply had been called for—that Sapiro should not have let his client sign the contract if he disliked its terms.

Meanwhile, word had got out that Stravinsky was revising *Firebird,* and within minutes, it almost seemed, Levy's hunch was being proved right. Goddard Lieberson wanted to record the new version; then Lucia Chase wanted to use it as the basis for a new ballet, with choreography by Bolm, to be staged by Ballet Theatre in the autumn.[10] Stravinsky had finished his reorchestration of the *Scherzo à la russe* at the end of May. So now after all, instead of completing his symphony finale, he had to take up what amounted to further hack rewriting, and spend time on a work that belonged to his most distant past, a work he had so often grumbled at having to conduct, and one he even claimed he had never really wanted to compose at all. The sole consolation, he told Theodore several months later, was that he could "at last get rid of those superfluous pantomimes willed on me by Fokine."[11] But that was not quite true. What he in fact did was altogether more time-saving and practical. He simply expanded the 1919 suite (with its reduced orchestra) by adding to it six or seven minutes of the superfluous pantomimes, reorchestrated from the full score. He pointedly—and regrettably—did not include such brilliantly distinctive movements as the Magic Carillon and the Dialogue and Intercession that follow it, presumably because they did not easily reduce for the smaller orchestra. The 1945 suite is to all intents and purposes the 1919 suite, extended to make it copyrightable, and diffused to make it danceable. What it is not is a compressed and lightened version of the whole ballet, which would have been a marvelous idea but would simply have taken Stravinsky too long to do.

While he was thus detained in the land of the bellyboshkies and the demon Kashchey, the world of mortals had been busy slaying its own monsters. By early May Hitler was dead and the Russians were ensconced amid the ruins of Berlin. The day before the formal German surrender, the Stravinskys went, as they often did, to a newsreel cinema and were profoundly shaken by film of Nazi atrocities. On VE Day, the 8th of May, they patriotically hoisted a flag over their house. For them, unlike many others, the end of the war did not mean an imminent return to Europe; they had, for the time being at least, cast their lot with America and the Americans. But it did mean—or so they must have hoped—reestablishing contact, and the possibility of travel. France, especially, beckoned. Paris, as it happened, had already begun some kind of postwar life straight after her own liberation, without waiting for the final destruction of the Nazi machine elsewhere.

Already at the start of January, Stravinsky had received enquiries from the French capital about the availability of his recent music for performance. French radio were planning, among other things, a seven-concert festival of his music conducted by Manuel Rosenthal, as a symbolic celebration of that which the Nazis had most energetically suppressed. Meanwhile Roger Desormière wanted to include the *Danses concertantes,* a work as yet unheard in Europe, in a Salle Gaveau concert in late February. This was all very encouraging, not least in view of Stravinsky's grumbles about the neglect of his music in Paris in the late thirties. If it crossed his mind to wonder about musical conditions and attitudes in France after four years of brutal occupation and four subsequent months of turbulent and sometimes murderous settling of scores, he said and wrote nothing about it. As news trickled through, a picture soon formed of frightening events and terrifying consequences; of an unprecedented atmosphere of social and artistic crisis that threatened not only his family but his music. Yet its manifestations were strange, and attached themselves to seemingly unworthy or innocent objects. Like Wordsworth, he looked on Paris

> *as doth a man*
> *Upon a volume whose contents he knows*
> *Are memorable, but from him locked up,*
> *Being written in a tongue he cannot read.*[12]

It was several weeks before he began to hear how the concerts were going. At the end of March, after three of the Rosenthal concerts and the Desormière performance, Poulenc sent Milhaud an update on Paris musical life. "The rise of [Olivier] Messiaen," he reported, "is the most important musical event. You'll find, in fact, that this musician—genuinely remarkable, despite his impossible literary jargon—is surrounded by a fanatical sect. The Messiaenists are very 'against Stravinsky last period.' For them, Igor's music stops with the *Rite*. They whistled at *Danses concertantes,* a work I adore."[13] In fact the Gaveau demonstration had been fairly discreet: "timid murmurs," Claude Rostand had called them.[14] But for the third radio concert at the fabled Théâtre des Champs-Élysées on the 15th of March, there was a more numerous claque armed with whistles and, according to one report, a hammer, which was twice wielded so noisily that the orchestra stopped playing.[15] The culprits, it seemed, were a group of Conservatoire students in the top gallery; and although Henri Sauguet observed, tongue-in-cheek, that this merely proved that "academicism always protests against novelty,"[16] he knew as well as anyone else that it was not Stravinsky's novelty that had enraged these students from Messiaen's harmony class, but on the contrary the banal and outworn insipidities, as they saw them, of his neoclassical works. They nevertheless heard out *Jeu de cartes* in silence, ignored the early *Faun and Shepherdess,* then vented their entire fury on the humble *Four Norwegian Moods,* shouting and booing, banging and whistling, for most of its eight minutes. By contrast the *Symphony of Psalms,* which ended the concert, was again uninterrupted, the students having perhaps by that time gone home to an early bed.

As Parisian demonstrations go, it was a feeble and rather insignificant affair, and it might well have passed unnoticed if the press had not taken sides and turned an obscure aesthetic quarrel, of a type much cherished in French intellectual circles, into a public controversy in which Messiaen camp followers like André Jolivet and the young composer Serge Nigg (apparently one of the whistlers) traded journalistic punches with such Stravinsky devotees as Poulenc and Yves Baudrier under headlines like "Assez de Strawinsky" and "Vive Strawinsky."[17] Messiaen himself held his peace and was probably not even party to either the incident or the argument. The intellectual hero of the protesters was not a "Messiaeniste" at all, but a "Schoenbergiste," a Polish composer and conductor by the name of René Leibowitz, who had recently arrived in Paris from Vichy and had mounted a private performance of Schoenberg's long and forbidding wind quintet to which several of Messiaen's class managed to gain admittance, including a brilliant, hot-headed nineteen-year-old named Pierre Boulez. Boulez had seized on Leibowitz's notion that the only possible way forward for a modern composer lay through "the entirely conscious and rigorous application of a thoroughgoing discipline which has command of all the possibilities of chromatic polyphony," and that this discipline was only to be found in Schoenberg's serial technique.[18] Boulez had been "very nice," Messiaen told Joan Peyser, when he first entered the class in 1944. "But soon he became angry with the whole world. He thought everything was wrong with music. The next year he discovered the serial language and converted to it with immense passion, judging it the only viable grammar."[19] Boulez was already thinking, and would soon write, that "all non-serial composers are *useless*."[20] In the shadow of such a dogma, Stravinsky's neo-classical music—and his *Norwegian Moods* especially—was obviously fit only for the junk heap.

Mulling over the newspaper cuttings a few weeks later, Stravinsky was bemused by the whole affair, having not even realized that the broadcast concerts had had a live audience. It was one thing to start a riot against *The Rite of Spring*, violent music in a threatening new language. "But why the *Norwegian Moods?*" he asked Rosenthal in some puzzlement.[21] He naturally knew nothing of the deadly earnestness of the new French modernism, an attitude that held Cocteau's flippant epigrams in near-homicidal contempt. Above all, he remained largely ignorant of the Schoenberg connection, which he might perhaps have understood better, remembering Lourié's original antithesis at the time of *Apollo*.[22] The newspapers talked about Messiaen, since it was well known that the rowdies were members of his class. The Paris publisher Roland Bourdariat, who was proposing to bring out a new French edition of the *Poétique*, mentioned that "for the Messiaenistes, the greatest modern composer is Schoenberg," but almost in the same breath satirized them as a "coterie of ridiculous disciples, whom [Messiaen] hypnotizes and preaches to in a pseudo-mystical jargon whose nauseating religiosity barely conceals a sensuality of unprecedented vulgarity."[23] As a characterization of the pro-Schoenberg position it was worse than useless. For the time being, Stravinsky seems to have concluded vaguely that the whole thing was a Communist plot, until he was disabused of this by his old friend André Schaeffner.[24]

Much more disturbing for Igor than this distant clash of arms were certain rumors that began to reach him about his younger son's Paris activities during the Occupation. After the fall of France, Soulima had been demobilized from Nevers and had gone back to Paris and settled in his older brother's flat. Concert work had been scarce, but not unobtainable; there had been the occasional recital, he had taken a piano part in *Les Noces* under Charles Munch, and the solo part in Scriabin's piano concerto, and had even presented a lecture about his father at the Lycée Musicale et Dramatique, playing the piano sonata, the *Petrushka* movements, and the studies, op. 7, despite the supposed ban on all these works. Then, early in 1944, he had given a radio talk on Stravinsky and expatiated on his "taste for the concrete, that quest for the authentic in all things that gives the least of his actions such an extraordinary intensity."[25] Suddenly, after the departure of the Germans, there were no more engagements. Soulima wrote to his father in March 1945 that he was being professionally ostracized and treated as a collaborator. For a time it even seemed that he might have to be denazified, which would mean investigation and possibly a trial.[26] To Igor, this was as baffling as the treatment of his *Norwegian Moods*, and far more upsetting. Was it really so dreadful for a musician to give concerts in whatever situation he found himself in? How else was he supposed to live? Were the Parisians expected to do without music just because they were occupied by a foreign power? "I live in hope," he wrote to Milhaud, "that this will not last forever and that these people will understand, once passions have cooled, that they are carrying their zeal too far."[27]

Early in 1945, Francis Poulenc had provided Milhaud with a detailed account of wartime goings-on in Paris that revealed the niceties and dangers of a situation which, in some ways, was outside the comprehension of a pragmatist like Stravinsky. France was being torn apart by forces that went well beyond the refined quantification of individual actions: the sense of national humiliation, the search for scapegoats, the settling of personal and institutional scores. "The number of people deported or shot [by the Germans] is alas impossible to tally," Poulenc wrote. "One needed a good deal of agility to keep out of trouble without giving anything in return." Not all had succeeded. Honegger had been "a bit weak," Cocteau *"un peu léger"* (easygoing); Jacques Rouché, at the Opéra, had behaved well but was hopelessly compromised by his wife's lack of tact and his daughter's overt fascism, and was forced to step down. Marcelle Meyer's husband had made a fortune from sequestrations of Jewish property, and they had both had to flee: "A pity," Poulenc reflected, "as she was playing better than ever." Pierre Bernac had "nearly killed himself teaching so as to avoid having any dealings with the radio."[28] There was at first no mention of Soulima. Then, later on, it began to come out. Like his father he had shown a pragmatic streak where the Nazis were concerned. As well as giving concerts and broadcasts, he had played for lectures by Heinrich Strobel at the German Institute. "Perhaps not very serious," Poulenc added, "but a bit much, all the same." Igor's return, he thought, would put things right, though he doubted whether Soulima was a good enough pianist to reopen the doors that mattered.[29] Had it emerged about the young man's attempt to fix concert appearances in Germany early in the Occupation, his outlook in postwar Paris would have been grim indeed.[30] But luckily for Soulima, Strecker kept this matter to himself. As for the German Institute concerts, Soulima later claimed to have acted out of friendship for Strobel, whom he knew from the Voreppe days, and who had himself been forced out of Germany because his wife, Hilde, was Jewish. Soulima had even concealed Hilde from the Nazis in his apartment. Alas, such refinements were quickly lost in the tortured atmosphere of post-liberation France. Soulima never defended himself publicly, and perhaps, on the whole, it was just as well.[31]

At about the time of the Strecker approach, Soulima had fallen in love with a married French woman called Françoise Bon, who had left her army-officer husband and was studying law in Paris. For some time now she and Soulima had been living together, and by the spring of 1945—though still not free to remarry—she was expecting a baby by him. An earlier rumor that Milène had had a child had proved false. But it was precisely this unreliable flow of worrying news that Igor found hardest to support and that decided him that, if he and Vera were going to stay in America, he would have to bring his children out to be close to him there. It was the patriarchal urge that had last been satisfied at Monthoux, in that ill-fated summer of 1937 when sickness and decay had infected the very air. Now it was Milène and her new husband, André Marion, who were ill and in need. As soon as the money could be found, they must come and get better—as Igor had done—in California.[32]

The last and most curious dispatch from France had to do with Bourdariat's interest in the *Poétique,* and was a disconcerting reminder of the psychological distance the world had travelled since the winter of 1940. The fifth lecture of the six, "The Avatars of Russian Music," composed before the outbreak of war and delivered under the shadow of the Nazi-Soviet pact, was a swingeing if not very well-directed attack on Soviet policy toward music and the arts, and by implication on the Soviet Union itself. In 1941, however, the U.S.S.R. had perforce changed sides, and in 1945 was part of the victorious Western Alliance. This difficulty had, for some reason, passed unnoticed at the time of the Harvard publication of the original French text in 1942; indeed, it was still being ignored by Harvard as their thoughts turned once more to an English translation early in 1945. But in Paris such questions were complicated by France's ambiguous and subordinate position in the Alliance, and, to cut a long story short, Bourdariat wanted to leave the problematical chapter out, "all the more because there is a high risk of its being banned [and with it the whole book] by the military censorship."[33]

Stravinsky bade temporary farewell to his Russian revenge without much of a qualm. In the last four years he had been feeling his roots more strongly once again as he tried to keep track of the devastation of his native city and the slow reversal of fortunes since the raising of the siege. Not that he can have expected Stalin to change his spots after the war, or even thought very hard about that likelihood. With him, attitudes to such matters were entirely ruled by feeling, and blood was always thicker than water. At the time of *North Star* he had immersed himself in arrangements of Russian folk tunes, along precisely the lines that he had mocked in his "Avatars" lecture as "this fad for folklore" and "the unfailingly conventional and often suspect harmonizations of these folk songs."[34] At the same time he had involved himself in Russian war relief. Now on 16 May, barely a week after the end of the European war, he agreed to conduct his *Firebird* suite (not yet in its revised form) without fee at an American-Russian friendship concert in Los Angeles's Shrine Auditorium, attended by Soviet delegates to the recent San Francisco conference of the United Nations. It was a starchy sort of occasion; the mayor of Los Angeles greeted the Russians, Edward G. Robinson made a speech, and Otto Klemperer conducted Prokofiev's *Alexander Nevsky* cantata without enthusiasm.[35] But the mere act of participation showed the degree of change in the wind; it might not last, but for the moment it was unmistakable.

As for the new *Firebird* suite, its completion in June by no means put an end to the tensions and ill feeling prompted by the legalistic nature of its conception.[36] Sapiro was having a field day with the (as he at least thought) wily Leeds executives, demanding contracts and accusing them of "deliberate bad faith" over the allocation of payments for the production by Ballet Theatre.[37] Undeterred by this barrage, Leeds's Hollywood manager, Aaron Goldmark, now came up with a fresh proposition. He had been approached by the clarinettist and bandleader Woody Herman to act as go-between in persuading Stravinsky to compose a work specially for Herman's band— the Herd, as it was known in the trade. Stravinsky agreed to write a seven-and-a-half-minute piece by the end of December for a fee of two thousand dollars.[38]

For the time being he was burying his head in the sand and finishing off the finale of his "Victory" symphony, a movement of stunning complexity and brilliance that must have been mapped out and partly composed in the spring for him to have brought it so swiftly to an end, as he did, on the 7th of August. The previous day, the Americans had dropped their first atom bomb on Hiroshima, and Craft has observed that on the 7th Stravinsky made a subtle change to the last chord to lend it greater finality, and invented the dismissive rhythmic gesture that so superbly concludes this most volcanic of all his concert works.[39] The curious thing is that, in his much later description of the supposed war-program of the finale ("goose-stepping soldiers," and so forth), Stravinsky does not so much as mention Hiroshima or the Japanese, who in fact surrendered three days after the symphony's completion.[40] If the work celebrates any particular victory, it must be this one. In truth, though, its music is not of that kind.

A month or so after he had completed the fair copy of the Symphony in Three Movements, as he had finally decided to call it,[41] a brief report on the Herman commission appeared in the show-business broadsheet *The Bill-board,* couched in the typical language of Tin Pan Alley, to the effect that "Igor Stravinsky, noted classical composer, has agreed to write a special composition titled *The Ebony Concerto* for Woody Herman's ork [*sic*]. . . . Stravinsky is expected to bring forth something of a new era in music expression for the modern day 20-piece dance band of the jump type Woody Herman leads."[42] After reading this masterpiece, Stravinsky took umbrage and tried to withdraw, but he was dissuaded by the ever-judicious Sapiro, who was able to use Herman's embarrassment over the leak as a lever in the subsequent negotiations.[43] However, what really upset him about the *Billboard* report was probably the final paragraph, which had nothing to do with Herman but contained the bald announcement that "Kermit Goell, lyric writer, is doing a couple of pop songs based on themes from Stravinsky's *Firebird Suite.*" Here, no doubt, was the real object of the Leeds connection. Whether Stravinsky knew about it, had agreed to it, but did not expect the fact to be blurted from the housetops, or alternatively was learning about it for the first time from the columns of *The Billboard,* is by no means clear. The subsequent history of the affair suggests the former. But in any case there was little he could do except grumble, or relinquish a lucrative commission, since *Firebird*—as has many times been noted—was public property in America and its music was fair game to anyone who cared to make use of it. Stravinsky might succeed in recopyrighting the suite, if he could somehow persuade orchestras and ballet companies to prefer his revised version, but the individual tunes (not all of them in any case composed by him) were quite out of his reach.

Ballet Theatre, at least, were using the new suite for their Met production that October, conducted by Jascha Horenstein. It seems likely in fact that the choice of "pantomime" links, which are what mainly distinguish it from the popular 1919 version, came out of discussions with Bolm and Hurok's representative, the former dance critic Irving Deakin.[44] But however much the new *Firebird* score may have been tailored to Bolm's conception, the results did not measure up to the degree of integration Edwin Denby had observed in Balanchine's *Danses concertantes* the previous year. Part of the trouble was Marc Chagall's décors, which were so sumptuous and fantastic that everything else was overwhelmed, Markova in the title role was made to look insignificant, and the playing was scrappy, partly because—as Horenstein reported in an anguished telegram the day after the premiere—the Leeds orchestral parts were "simply horrible[,] manuscripts done by non-professional copyists[,] worse than anything ever experienced."[45] As for *Apollo,* revived in Balanchine's choreography (rather than Bolm's, which presumably was lost), the performance had been ruined by the mediocre playing of a too-small string orchestra. "The conclusion," Rieti reported, "is that Ballet Theatre 'stinks.' "[46] So Hurok's machinations against Denham had not helped his own project, and for the time being it was Denham who was in Stravinsky's good books and had his ear. At the end of November in Los Angeles, the composer attended the Ballet Russe opening night, even though *Pulcinella* was being danced in a truncated form and under a title *(Commedia balletica)* to which he might have been expected to take exception. After the show he and Vera dined amicably with Denham.[47]

For much of November 1945 Stravinsky worked on the *Ebony Concerto,* whose main hazard as far as he was concerned was its scoring for a small swing band very different in character from the jazz orchestra for which he had composed the *Scherzo à la russe.* There would be a clarinet solo for Herman, and the band was otherwise dominated by choirs of saxophones and trumpets, with harp, piano, guitar, and drums, but no strings except the ubiquitous bass. Apart from the orchestral parts in the *Scherzo,* he had never written for saxophone before, and he needed to have the fingering explained to him by a saxophonist (a precaution that shows the importance he attached to an exact sense of the instruments he wrote for).[48] He was, he confessed to Nadia early in the month, "a bit unnerved in view of the short time available, and the fact that I am unfamiliar with this sort of thing."[49] And yet he had already by that time finished the first movement, a piece which cunningly adapts the rhythmic-ostinato style of Stravinskian neoclassicism to the jazz clichés he had picked up from Herman's records. By the 13th the bluesy slow movement was also finished. There was then a minor but significant interruption. Nathaniel Shilkret had at last managed to place his *Genesis* suite, in a concert by Janssen's orchestra in the Wilshire-Ebell Theatre on the 18th, and Stravinsky attended three afternoons of rehearsals, as well as of course the concert itself, in which Janssen combined the composite work with Beethoven's *Egmont* overture and an eightieth-birthday performance of Sibelius's First Symphony.

Musically, the performance was as frustrating as such occasions invariably are. The forty-five-minute bundle of scores had consistency of neither style nor treatment, some composers having opted merely to illustrate the spoken text, while others (including Milhaud and Stravinsky himself) attempted a greater dramatic or symbolic intensity. The prelude, for orchestra with wordless chorus, an authentic and uncompromising piece of late, serial Schoenberg, certainly fell into this latter category: "the prelude," as one later critic remarked, "to something only [Schoenberg himself] could have composed,"[50] but followed in the event by Shilkret's account of the Creation, which Isabel Morse Jones called "straightforward picture-music [written] with the devices which film and radio experience has taught him."[51] *Babel* must have made a confusing ending to this potpourri of what Morse Jones somewhat vaguely called "the modern idiom," not least because Edward Arnold's narration was often inaudible even above Stravinsky's comparatively discreet scoring.

Two weeks before the concert, Shilkret and Janssen had arranged a lunch for the participating composers, but Stravinsky seems not to have attended. Nor did he and Schoenberg meet at the rehearsals. At the dress rehearsal they chose, according to Leonard Stein (who was with Schoenberg), "to remain on opposite sides of the hall," and the same thing happened at the concert.[52] At the rehearsal, Stein recalled,

> Not a word was exchanged. I left the hall with Schoenberg just at the completion of Stravinsky's piece. Only one sentence was forthcoming from Schoenberg when I asked him what he thought of the piece. "It didn't end; it just stopped."

But if Schoenberg and Stravinsky did not meet at such an obvious opportunity, it can only have been because they did not want to, whether out of fear, or simple shyness, or some awkwardness engendered by old hostilities or the polemics of their various acolytes (not including Stein, who had copied the parts for the revised Danse sacrale and remained on a friendly footing with both masters). They had, as it happened, almost met less than three months before at the funeral of Franz Werfel, one of the few others who had managed, through his wife Alma Mahler, to remain on terms with both composers, and who yet seems never to have attempted a reconciliation. At the cemetery, Stravinsky observed Schoenberg's "angry, tortured, burning face," but no words were exchanged.[53] Perhaps the anger was, or seemed, personal in intent. Unfortunately, Stravinsky's is the only account.

In spite of his anxieties about the genre, he had finished the *Ebony Concerto* by the 10th of December, three weeks ahead of schedule, and the next day he embarked on yet another work of revision, this time of only part of a work, and one which he had hardly so much as glanced at for well over a decade. In addition to his coming January Carnegie Hall concerts with the symphony premiere, he was conducting the NYPO in a late-evening half-hour broadcast of the *Symphony of Psalms* in the CBS Invitation to Music series on the 30th on WABC. But because the broadcast would be live and the symphony was only twenty-one and a half minutes long, a filler was needed, and for some reason Stravinsky's mind fell on the final chorale of the *Symphonies of Wind Instruments,* a work that he had never conducted, that had not been published except as a piano reduction, and for which no performing materials existed in the U.S.A. In one day, working from a copy of the original piano reduction as published in 1920 by the *Revue musicale* for its Debussy memorial, he rescored this three-minute piece for a wind ensemble without clarinets, instruments not required for the *Symphony of Psalms.*[54]

What prompted him to think of this work, apparently so remote from his current creative preoccupations? One answer is that it is less remote than it seems. He had just been writing a piece in which trumpets dialogue with saxophones, and the melodies rock back and forth just as they do in the *Symphonies* chorale, albeit in a style as urban-modern as that of the *Symphonies* is ethnic-antique. It is just possible, in other words, that the chorale was actually suggested by his work on the *Ebony Concerto.* On the other hand, the Kyrie and Gloria of a year before are actually quite close in atmosphere to this almost forgotten quarter-century-old music for wind. There was another, more mundane factor. A week or so earlier, he had had a wire from Koussevitzky, urging him to meet Ralph Hawkes, the director of the London publishing house Boosey and Hawkes, with whom Koussevitzky was in the process of negotiating a deal for the sale of the Édition Russe catalogue, and who was visiting Los Angeles over Christmas. With such a meeting in view, and in the light of his unsettled relations with AMP, his growing disillusion with Leeds, and his fury over the unresolved situation with Galaxy, Stravinsky's instinct would certainly have been to take stock of his own ERM catalogue and brief himself on the likely details of any discussion with Hawkes. The existence of an unpublished, undistributed, and virtually unperformed nine-minute instrumental score, which could now be kept out of the hated U.S. public domain, is most unlikely to have escaped his notice.

The ERM sale was already a foregone conclusion. Koussevitzky himself had long since lost interest in his publishing operation and had been effectively running it down since the mid-thirties. These days his great enthusiasm, apart from conducting, was for the educational work of the Berkshire Music Center at Tanglewood, to which he had tried without success to entice Stravinsky. ERM in Europe had in any case been fatally damaged by the war both in Germany (Berlin and Leipzig)—where its offices had as in 1914 been politically isolated even before they were bombed—and in Paris, where the Occupation throttled practically the entire catalogue, consisting as it did mainly of music by modern Russians not looked on with favor by the Nazis. At least the Paris operation was theoretically intact. Amid the ruins of the German capital it was more a case of rescuing what could be rescued. Nicolas Nabokov, himself an ERM composer, had been in Berlin since August working as civilian cultural adviser to the American military government, and in October he wrote Koussevitzky a progress report on his efforts to have the cellars of the wrecked Russische Musikverlag offices in the Martin Luther Strasse dug out for surviving scores and orchestral parts while at the same time trying to protect the position of the old office chief, F. V. Weber, who was destitute and without work. Nabokov's short-term aim was to index the materials and set up an emergency catalogue for occupied Germany. But as a longer-term publishing proposition, the RMV was to all intents and purposes dead.

Stravinsky lunched with Hawkes on the 28th of December, 1945, and on that same day he and Vera took the oath as U.S. citizens, sponsored by Edward G. Robinson, who in the course of the proceedings turned out not to be a proper citizen himself—to have been, in fact, an illegal immigrant for the past forty years.[55] His testimony, however, was merely the visible sign of a hidden network of venial untruths. Not only had Igor made a fraudulent statement about Vera's supposed divorce from Sudeykin in Tiflis in 1920 (a statement that also falsely claimed it to have been her first marriage), but Vera herself lied about her age in her naturalization papers, stating that she was fifty-three rather than fifty-six. What was crucially truthful, on the other hand, was their intention, as the certificate put it, "to reside permanently in the United States (when so required by the Naturalization Laws of the United States)."[56] With the war over, this was a more momentous decision than it might previously have seemed. Many of the distinguished refugees who had formed part of their world were going back to Europe. Nadia Boulanger sailed for France three days after the naturalization, bearing with her packages of food for her starving compatriots, a photographic copy of the manuscript of Stravinsky's symphony finale, and baby clothes for Soulima and Françoise, and leaving behind her old car, which she was donating to the Stravinskys. Others would soon follow. But Igor and Vera themselves were becoming not less but more settled. Their household was growing again. They had a new, vaguely genteel Russian housekeeper named Yevgenia Petrovna but usually known—mysteriously— as Mrs. Gates. Vera was now much occupied with a new project of her own, a small gallery on La Cienega Boulevard called La Boutique, which she had opened in partnership with Lisa Sokolov at the end of August. They presented select exhibitions of modern art (starting in December with Tchelitcheff), but also of various artefacts and collages that Vera herself made out of painted stones, dried sponges, and other more or less unlikely materials.[57] Igor had been offered a new European commission (his first since *Persephone*): a string piece for the twentieth anniversary of Paul Sacher's Basle Chamber Orchestra.[58] After a lifetime of moving house, and seven thousand miles from his starting point, he seemed to have found a home.

· · ·

FEW CAN have been prepared for the sheer impact of the Symphony in Three Movements, when Stravinsky conducted its premiere in Carnegie Hall on 24 January 1946. In one sense, of course, it was more gratifyingly Stravinskian than anything he had composed since, at the latest, *Oedipus Rex*: it was rhythmic, aggressive, strident—a Scythian wind blowing in from the Russian steppes. But that was precisely the difficulty. It was a kind of music that Stravinsky had recently abandoned in favor of soft-centered commercial parodies like *Scènes de ballet*, which—just to confuse matters further—was again in the Carnegie program. One could doubtless understand it as simply the latest turn in the Stravinsky zigzag; one could call it (rather unconvincingly) a "Victory" symphony, as Zirato had done, or a "War" symphony, as the critics were more inclined to do. None of this, however, helped locate it in the composer's notoriously unpredictable and changeable oeuvre.

It would certainly have helped to know (as the Carnegie Hall audience did not) that the symphony had been more than three years in the writing and that at various times its composition had got badly entangled with Stravinsky's various commercial projects. The first movement, after all, was closer in time to the finale of the Symphony in C than to its own finale, and in many respects its music related stylistically to certain preoccupations in Stravinsky's music of the thirties rather than to any of the motley collection of Americana that he had brought to the same hall a year before. For instance, its descent from the concerto for two pianos would have been apparent to anyone familiar with that little-played masterpiece. At the same time it might have been clear that the finale was not an expression of the excitement of the end of the war but the solution to a formal problem: how to unite two movements, one of them violent and with a percussive piano solo, the other delicate and bardic, with a solo for harp. Stravinsky probably only approached this problem in quite those terms after receiving the commission; but it was a problem that, in some ways, recalled the troubled history of the Symphony in C, where, for all that work's brilliance, it had been less decisively solved.

Like many of the greatest works of art, the Symphony in Three Movements is a work of synthesis. True, it recaptures the Scythian fury of *The Rite of Spring*, but in no sense is it a revisionist score. Like all Stravinsky's main works of the thirties and early forties, it channels energy into counterpoint, a kind of writing where the individual parts enjoy a certain autonomy but within what might be called socially defined limits—like an intense and animated conversation whose participants talk across one another but who each still manage to take account of what the others say. The wildly independent instrumental lines in the introduction to *The Rite of Spring,* which retain, in Peter Hill's apt phrase, "a reptilian indifference to one another," for that very reason tend to sound—and no doubt were meant to sound—inhuman and pitiless.59 But the symphony finale, with its dazzling fugal and imitative exchanges, breathes a refinement that civilizes the ferocity, without in any way drawing its sting. It is neoclassicism without fancy dress and come of age.

13

ORPHEUS IN A NEW GUISE

THE SYMPHONY CONCERTS were the focus of that winter's Manhattan stay; after all, the Symphony in Three Movements was Stravinsky's first orchestral work ever to be premiered on the New York concert platform. But they were by no means its only excitement. Early in February he went to Baltimore to conduct the symphony orchestra and give his Chicago lecture at the Peabody Conservatory, where both Nadia and Nicolas Nabokov had been teaching during the war. Then on the 8th he took part, without fee, in a Carnegie Hall recital in aid of the New York Philharmonic's pension fund, playing the Duo Concertant with Joseph Szigeti—a partnership whose brief but distinguished life had begun in Hollywood in October with a recording of the Duo for Columbia, and ended there seven months later with a recording of the so-called "Russian Maiden's Song" from *Mavra*.[1] Still more enticing was the prospect of Woody Herman's premiere of the *Ebony Concerto* in March. Stravinsky would be gone by then, but he was taking care to make his intentions clear before quitting the East Coast.

Herman must originally have assumed that he would do the concerto as a band piece without conductor, but Stravinsky's floating meters proved too much for players used to working their syncopations against a rigid barline, and soon a conductor was engaged in the person of the NYPO's permanent associate conductor, Walter Hendl. Hendl was Stravinsky's own choice, but his real alter ego in ensuring a properly literate performance was Alexei Haieff, the young composition pupil of Nadia's whom he had met at Harvard at the start of his lecture series in 1939. Haieff had since become a regular New York helper, who would book hotels for Igor and Vera, would meet them at the railway station, and had even been engaged by AMP—not very successfully—as copyist for the Symphony in C.[2] But the *Ebony Concerto* sealed their intimacy. The thirty-one-year-old Haieff worked tirelessly with Herman's players, partly with the intention of conducting the work himself in subsequent performances for which Hendl was unavailable. His letters praised the band's " 'humbleness' and seriousness of approach to the work . . . , such that one could only wish that all orchestras had the same attitude."[3] In return, Stravinsky gave him a reference for a Guggenheim Fellowship, which—no doubt in consequence—he duly received that spring. The fact was that Haieff was a composer and musician with whom Stravinsky felt comfortable. It was not just that the young man wrote his kind of music—though the debt was easy enough to spot; Haieff also had a deep and abiding love for Stravinsky's work, and he talked as if he understood it. Best of all, he was Russian, born in Blagoveshchensk near the Sino-Siberian border, which meant that they could communicate quickly and semi-intuitively in what amounted to a private language, in a word or a phrase, about people or music or social situations, a facility Stravinsky had not previously encountered in an American musician of Haieff's generation.

On the day of the *Ebony* premiere, the 25th of March 1946, Igor and Vera arrived home at North Wetherly Drive from concerts in San Francisco, at the end of a punishing tour that more than anything so far resembled their European travels of the late twenties and early thirties. After attending a performance of *The Fairy's Kiss* danced by Balanchine's pupils at the School of American Ballet, they had taken the night train with Haieff to Boston, where Igor had concerts in Symphony Hall and at Cambridge.[4] They had then abandoned him to the tender mercies of Herman's Herd, had gone by train to Miami and from there flown to Havana for a ten-day stay that had almost turned into a state visit, including a courtesy call by President Aixala, a pair of concerts, and a hundred-mile journey by private train, in tropical heat, for a three-day holiday on a sugar plantation.[5] Later there had been another long train journey via New Orleans to Dallas, where they lost their baggage and Vera had to go on an emergency shirt-buying expedition for her husband. After a single concert in Dallas they flew to San Francisco, and thence home.[6] As a concert tour it was the beginning of a postwar odyssey that would make a sizable annual dent in Stravinsky's composing schedule but would accumulate an income, as well as a degree of limelight, which he continued to find indispensable to maintaining the high subsistence level to which they had become used. Artistically such tours would often seem quite pointless, and this one was hardly an exception. Everywhere it was *Firebird,* as often as not *Petrushka,* one or more of the recent potboilers, and perhaps *Pulcinella* or the Tchaikovsky-based Divertimento, or else Tchaikovsky's own Second Symphony and Glinka's *Ruslan* overture, which Olin Downes had insultingly, but not without a certain perverse logic, described as the best work in Stravinsky's Carnegie Hall concert of a year ago.[7] Of course, Downes was not a serious critic. And yet Stravinsky could easily have found himself wondering what he was doing on a rostrum in Cuba conducting a second-class orchestra in a second-rank and not particularly brief Russian symphony of the nineteenth century, while a tricky new piece of his own was being prepared and performed by other hands a thousand miles away.

Of the *Ebony Concerto* he picked up a recording on the radio four days after the event, but the balance was poor and naturally the peculiar atmosphere of a Carnegie Hall jazz concert was missing. Marcelle de Manziarly described the unusual audience: "a lot of youngsters chewing gum and swaying to the music's rhythms."[8] Haieff reported that in the hall the balance was good and the performance accurate if timid, since Herman was ill at ease with the unfamiliar idiom—"like a frightened man," Stravinsky told Marcelle on the evidence of the broadcast.[9] Haieff himself had had to take over from Hendl conducting performances in Baltimore and Boston: his "directoral rebirth," he called it, with a naïve pride that it had not gone badly, Herman had been pleased, and he had even been paid a fee. For Stravinsky, though, it was worrying that he would himself be recording the piece with "Voody" in Hollywood in the summer, when the swaying and the gum-chewing and the whole concert euphoria would vanish behind the simple question of whether the musicians could play the work properly or not.

He had still not quite made up his mind about the Sacher commission. His initial reaction had been that he was too busy,[10] presumably because his preliminary contract with Boosey and Hawkes, drawn up at the start of January, included an undertaking on his part to revise *Petrushka* for a (slightly) reduced orchestra by the 1st of April—a timetable that in any case his trip to Havana rendered impossible. Then in February in New York, Berman had pressed him to write incidental music for Robinson Jeffers's version of Euripides's *Medea,* a project that was still theoretically afloat at the end of March, when the actress Judith Anderson came to see him at Wetherly Drive in order to discuss it.[11] Stravinsky had probably assumed that the *Petrushka* revision—like the new *Firebird* suite—would be a largely mechanical process, one of those afternoon activities that he liked to engage in while being read to by some amenable slave. But then as he worked on it, it began to turn into a complete retexturing—a thorough rethinking of the score in the spirit of his recent music, with a sharper delineation of sonorities and less reliance on rhythmic washes of harmony. So when April came, he took heart from the fact that the Boosey contract was held up by technical matters (including the size of his own emolument),[12] abandoned the *Petrushka* deadline, and accepted Sacher, naming a fee of $2,500, which gave the Swiss conductor, for all his wife's Hoffmann–La Roche millions, a most disagreeable surprise in his turn.[13]

Stravinsky's idea was to write his string piece before a conducting trip to Mexico that he had planned for the second half of July,[14] then finish *Petrushka* in the late summer. Before Mexico, nevertheless, he worked on both scores, at least if Aaron Sapiro was telling the strict truth when he announced to Hawkes early in July that three of the four tableaux were done.[15] Stravinsky was understandably anxious to copyright his new version as quickly as possible. He was constantly being confronted with evidence of the abuse to which his public-domain works were subjected by American orchestras and dance companies. For instance, it turned out that Massine's recently formed touring company, Ballet Russe Highlights, had been playing excerpts from *Petrushka* in the American provinces with a hugely reduced orchestra, and with no authorization from the composer whatsoever. This emerged only because Massine now needed his permission to use part of the work in a play called *A Bullet in the Ballet,* a backstage whodunnit in which a series of dancers in the role of Petrushka were murdered one after the other, and which was going on the stage in England. Massine was disappointed to learn that even Stravinsky's "reduced" score needed sixty-eight players, whereas the English pits could accommodate no more than forty-five. Reluctantly, Stravinsky gave his former colleague the permission he sought, on condition that the program explicitly dissociated him from the result.[16]

In the event, the Concerto in D, as the new string piece was called, was practically if not quite ready before Mexico, and the complicated new *Petrushka* score not until October.[17] Stravinsky had struggled with *Ebony,* but his "Basler" concerto finds him so much on home ground that one could even wish for a little more grit in the oyster, to turn a very polished demonstration of modern classical technique into something urgent and out of the way. To call the *Ebony Concerto* the better piece would be a perversion of critical values; and yet in overcoming a more bizarre and difficult set of challenges, it emerged in some respects as the more distinctive and personable of the two works. The string concerto is exactly the kind of score Sacher must have expected: a clinching if lightweight expression of the neoclassical spirit, immaculate and inscrutable. For the first time in his long career, Stravinsky was starting to do what his admirers wanted, walking the tightropes they stretched for him, or—to subvert Schopenhauer's image of genius—hitting the targets they pointed out.[18]

It was much the same in May, when Lincoln Kirstein invited him to write a work for the School of American Ballet.[19] Stravinsky had already spent part of April working with Balanchine on the latter's idea of the Orpheus legend as subject, apparently unconcerned at the too-evident logic of the great neoclassicist crowning his ballet career with the archetypal Greek musical myth. The final details of the scenario were worked out between them when Balanchine visited the West Coast in June; but it was an essentially smooth, linear process, a true meeting of great minds. Balanchine had composed a Russian acrostic on the name "Igor" for Stravinsky's sixty-fourth birthday, a little chorale that Stravinsky promptly copied out and reharmonized.[20] On the ballet, they worked together like friends planning a holiday. It was such a pleasure to be with Stravinsky, Balanchine later told his biographer Bernard Taper, "because he's a happy man." They agreed on the essentially practical nature of artistic work, priding themselves "on being disciplined craftsmen, able to apply themselves to a job of work and produce it in good fashion and on time."[21] Stravinsky's working notes, which itemize the action from start to finish complete with detailed timings ("Begin with Eurydice's funeral: Orpheus stands for a ½ minute immobile; friends arrive with gifts, offer condolence, and leave 1½ [minutes]"), confirm this beyond doubt.[22] It was all quite without the personal and aesthetic tensions of the composer's last major theatrical collaborations, with Gide and Cocteau, not least because Balanchine instinctively deferred to Stravinsky, who was twenty-two years his senior and the unquestioned master.

In 1939 Stravinsky had arrived in America as a guest lecturer, but he had stayed as a refugee, a suppliant for admission to a land that did not obviously want or need him even if it sometimes condescended to recognize the value of his name. For Europe he was by then simply an outsider. Virtually the whole continent east of the Rhine and south of the Alps was or soon would be closed to him and his music, and France—even before the Nazis came—had shown time and again that it did not greatly value his presence. Seven years on, all that had changed. Now an American citizen, he was fast turning into a Masterwork—as he later announced himself to the Columbia series director Schuyler Chapin.[23] France at least thought him worth another riot or two. Above all, Germany was preparing to make handsome amends for its years of darkness. Willy Strecker had written in January, his first letter for almost six years, reporting on the destruction of Mainz and of the Schott printing works and warehouses, but sensing an optimism in German musical life.[24] Three months later, seven months later, the Symphony in C was at the printers, was printed; interest in Stravinsky was huge and growing, many performances were planned, a German edition of the *Poétique* was needed, and so forth.[25] Surely the Master would soon arrive in person.

It was a question that he was naturally asking himself, but reports of the destruction and paralysis of European life—whether from Strecker or Nabokov or from friends in France or England—were not very encouraging to the cautious and insecure exile that lurked behind his fearless creative façade. Ordinary luxuries were said to be unobtainable. He himself had for some time been dispatching food parcels to a whole battery of European friends, including the widow of his old priest, Nikolay Podossenov, Katya's cousin Olga Nosenko-Schwartz, Vera's friend Olga Sallard, and RMV's Berlin manager, F. V. Weber. The political situation was tense. America itself was crippled by strikes for much of 1946—his own Columbia recording of the *Symphony of Psalms* in February had been postponed because of one. On the other hand he was desperately anxious to see his children and grandchildren, not one of whom he had set eyes on since 1939. There was terrifying news of his Pavlovka Yelachich cousins, several of whom had found themselves in Yugoslavia when the Germans arrived in 1941. Zhenya, the closest to Igor in age and his companion in tarantula hunting at Pechisky, had been murdered in Belgrade by Cetnik partisans, Zhenya's younger brother Ganya had been killed there by a German bomb, and young Alyosha—whom Stravinsky remembered being "confiscated" by Aunt Yekaterina at Pechisky[26]—had been murdered by the Croat Ustase. Igor's oldest cousin, Nikolay, the Pavlovka tease, had been arrested by the N.K.V.D. in 1936, sent to the gulag, and later shot. In Igor's mind, the urge to gather his family around him grew all the stronger with such reports.

By the end of June he and Vera had bought another house near their own, and Vera was busy having it furnished and decorated ready for Milène and André and the faithful Madubo, as soon as their journey could be organized. In a certain sense, this was the easiest decision to take and (more important) impose, because the Marions, after years in a sanatorium, were without means of support and could scarcely refuse to come even if they had wanted to. With Theodore and Soulima matters stood rather differently. Theodore had settled in his wife's native Geneva, and he was becoming a Roman Catholic and adopting his orphan niece, Kitty. They had no desire to cross the Atlantic. Soulima meanwhile had resumed his career in Paris, still amid a palpable atmosphere of recrimination. Whenever Nadia wrote she made a point of including praise of Soulima's playing and of Françoise and their little son Zizi (Jean), whom Igor was impatient to meet, having been sent a photograph that he described gushingly to Nadia as "superbe, ravissant, tellement brave."[27] Yet neither son could be certain of self-sufficiency in the immediate term. Theodore was still waiting on a work permit from the notoriously recalcitrant Swiss, and he had meanwhile touched his father for a two-hundred-dollar subsidy, which Igor sent somewhat querulously and with a short homily to his thirty-eight-year-old son on the subject of his behavior toward his younger brother.[28] Soulima had received an equivalent sum from Païchadze out of the composer's undistributed wartime royalties.[29] But his own professional prospects in France remained murky and unpredictable.

IGOR AND VERA were away in Mexico for three weeks of July and August 1946, travelling by train with their friends the Sokolovs: the film actor Vladimir and his wife Lisa, Vera's business partner. As in Havana, there were concerts and guided trips, to the shrine of Our Lady at Guadalupe and the pre-Columbian city of Cholula. But on the journey home, Lisa Sokolov went down with jaundice and was so ill that when they got to Los Angeles she had to be taken to the car in a wheelchair. Alexei Haieff had come west for the summer, and luckily he was there to meet them at the station and relieve the strain with his lively and obliging disposition. His main task that summer was to help prepare for Stravinsky's recording of the *Ebony Concerto* two weeks later. But he stayed on until October, living in what was to be Milène's house, and helping with musical chores, including perhaps the score of *Petrushka*, which was Stravinsky's only remaining project until he started *Orpheus* in October, just after Haieff's return to New York. Haieff became exceptionally close to Igor and Vera during this two-month visit. Back in Manhattan he performed the usual sub-Stravinskian errands, booking hotels ready for their arrival in December, fixing rehearsals, and so forth, and then duly reported back, adding: "I've said everything except what I meant to say at the start, which is that I love you both unendingly and am so grateful for your kindness, and for the refuge, and for all the wonderful time I've spent with you."[30] It was a relationship that might have grown into something unique, only fate had other plans for them all. Lisa Sokolov, meanwhile, did not immediately recover from her illness, and when the Stravinskys went east for two months at the start of December, Vera simply had to close La Boutique down.

One day at the Farmers' Market on Fairfax Avenue, at about the time of Alexei's departure, Stravinsky was spotted by two young Belgian women who claimed to have met him at a party and now flirtatiously reintroduced themselves. They were Claire and Sylvia Nicolas, the nieces of Aldous Huxley's Belgian wife Maria; and Huxley himself was with them, came up, and presented himself as "a friend of Victoria Ocampo's."[31] They had in fact met briefly once before, through Victoria, in London in 1934. But in Los Angeles they had missed one another, partly because the Huxleys had been living up in the Mojave Desert at Llano and more recently at Wrightwood, in the San Gabriel Mountains, and merely kept a pied-à-terre in Beverly Hills. Now they at once struck up a friendship, based less on a common worldview than on some less readily definable mutual fascination, and they began to meet regularly, at first on the Huxleys' routine expeditions to the Farmers' Market, then socially at each other's houses and elsewhere. In November, the Stravinskys spent a day at Wrightwood, and later they entertained Maria's sculptor sister and the two daughters, and the twenty-one-year-old Claire, who was a writer, interviewed the composer for a magazine called *Junior Bazaar*. For Igor it all amounted to a soft landing in the world of Anglo-Saxon culture, which, on the whole, he had so far avoided—not just because Huxley's in-laws were Francophone Belgian but because Huxley was him-

self a polyglot who conversed with complete fluency in French. For the Huxleys it was a refreshing antidote to what Robert Craft later called the "sover-
eignty of scientific rationalism" in Aldous's own conversation.[32] "Today,"
Maria Huxley wrote to their son, Matthew, a year or so later, "we had a most
delightful dinner with the Stravinskys. . . . I must say it was delightful to listen to Stravinsky. He pours out—what he pours is very intelligent—it is
often very new—sometimes quite difficult to explain, but always
immensely worth listening to and the French, not perfect, is intelligent and
colorful." They talked about books and pictures. Eugene Berman was there,
and showed his drawings ("competent," Maria thought, "but not nice.
Somehow—méchant . . ."). And Vera cooked "a vegetarian dinner for
Aldous, just right, simple, good. She is so easy and very nice."[33]

Stravinsky completed his revision of *Petrushka* on the 14th of October
1946, and six days later made his first sketches for *Orpheus.* Much of the
ballet's character had already been fixed in his discussions with Balanchine.
They had worked out a sequence of dances and a scenario derived from a
copy of Ovid and a classical dictionary, which also supplied some of the
dance titles,[34] and they had agreed on timings and tempos. At one point
Balanchine had suggested modeling the action on that of a seventeenth-
century opera.[35] But that simply meant that the action, though more eventful than that of *Apollo,* was to be stereotyped, or ritualized, in the same kind
of way. Its main features would be the ones that everyone knows about
Orpheus, with some embroidery; the narrative would be poised, statuesque,
and with anecdote reduced to a minimum.

In fact, as Robert Craft has observed, *Orpheus* turned out a far more pan-
tomimic, less danced, ballet than *Apollo.*[36] He compares it with *Persephone,*
with its similar setting and heavy dependence on mime, and as it happens
Persephone was on Stravinsky's mind as he started writing the new ballet,
since he was planning a broadcast with Madeleine Milhaud in the title role
and wanted to get hold of the manuscript score, which was still in a bank
vault in Paris. But in truth the music of *Orpheus* is both drier and stiller than
that of its Ovidian predecessor. The opening scene—the first music Stravinsky composed—has Orpheus standing "motionless, with his back to the
audience," while "friends pass, bringing presents and offering him sympathy."[37] The music is like a slow chorale prelude with a counter-melody for
harp and two brief interjections of wind chords (for the friends). Later, a
series of formal dances is punctuated by curiously inert narrative episodes,
as the oddly named Angel of Death (or Dark Angel) leads Orpheus to the
nether regions and the "tormented souls . . . implore [Orpheus] to continue
his song." These interludes preserve the quality of chorale, if sometimes
with more intricate counterpoint. For instance, in the last scene, where
Orpheus's severed head sings on and Apollo presents the singer's lyre to

heaven, the opening music is enriched by a fugue for two horns with an extra part for a trumpet—a strange and austerely beautiful effect.

Stravinsky himself is supposed to have denied any influence of early music on *Orpheus*,[38] and it is true that there is no obvious stylistic reference in the sense that *Dumbarton Oaks* might suggest Bach or *Oedipus Rex* Verdi. Yet it is hard to avoid the feeling that his growing excitement with strict contrapuntal technique in recent works like the Symphony in Three Movements, the *Elegy*, and the unfinished Mass is a signal just as definite in its way as the hints at sonata form and the key of E-flat in the Octet. How appropriate to represent Orpheus, the primal musician, through the most esoteric ways of writing, and to cloak them in an atmosphere of cabbalistic secrecy. And yet as with the original neoclassicism, the allusions go well beyond the obvious schoolroom techniques or idioms. There is a good deal of fugue in *Orpheus*, but there are many other places where some flavor of counterpoint or some curious figuration suggests an antique music, without one being able to put one's finger on precisely what it is. Stravinsky expressly denied Monteverdi, yet the brass writing in the Interlude after Eurydice's death or in the Apotheosis irresistibly suggests the composer of the *Vespers*, as well as certain of Schütz's *Symphoniae sacrae*, even though it has not the faintest flavor of baroquism in any more conventional sense. Similarly, there is not much in *Orpheus* to make the casual listener think of medieval music, apart perhaps from the trumpet and violin melody in the Apotheosis, which Stravinsky himself thought sounded like a medieval fiddle.[39] Nevertheless he was in touch with Manfred Bukofzer—his Berkeley medievalist of two years before—while composing it, and in April 1947, when half the score was still unwritten, Bukofzer sent him an essay on the isorhythmic motet.[40] The pas de deux, which was written soon afterwards, contains some of the most intensely polyphonic writing in the whole ballet and has rhythmic motives that might have been suggested by medieval practice; but an antique flavor is lacking, and the music sounds more like an astringent, purified version of a neo-romantic piece like Barber's *Adagio*.

Stravinsky worked on *Orpheus* for some six weeks, but he had then to break off for what was becoming his annual midwinter trip to the East Coast. They stopped in Chicago (on the 5th of December 1946) and visited an exhibition of English painting at the Art Institute (including, Vera noted, works by Hogarth, Constable, and Turner).[41] From New York they went straight to Montreal for a pair of concerts with the local orchestra; then, after Christmas, there were side trips to Cleveland, where the audience, Vera recorded, was "very rich and very dull," and Philadelphia, where the concerts were so successful that, just as after the Paris *Rite of Spring* in 1914, they needed a police escort back to their hotel.

In New York, Stravinsky again conducted a late-night broadcast of the

Symphony of Psalms, and this time—the strike having been settled—he managed also to record it, on the 19th of December, the day after the broadcast. But he had no public concerts. He saw a good deal of Haieff, dined with Victoria Ocampo, with Rieti, and with the Milhauds. Above all, he spent many hours with Balanchine, discussing *Orpheus,* but especially helping plan a new staging of *Renard* that Balanchine was choreographing for his latest venture with Kirstein, an exclusive-sounding but none-too-glamorous enterprise called Ballet Society.

Ballet Society had opened its doors in November 1946 in the improbable surroundings of the Central High School of Needle Trades, with the world premiere of a specially commissioned ballet by Hindemith called *The Four Temperaments.* The new staging of *Renard,* on the other hand, was booked for the marginally more suitable Hunter College Playhouse in mid-January, on a bill with Paul Bowles's *Pastorela,* Haieff's Divertimento, and a display of Javanese dancing. The program was typical of Kirstein's new society in its early days. The whole intention, as the society's publicity put it, was "the encouragement of the lyric theatre by the production of new works."[42] Admission to performances was open only to members, profit was not an issue, and the press were not invited but instead bought their own tickets and published rather sheepish, uninformative notices that indicated the importance they attached to the venture without quite revealing why. The society's conductor was the Belgian-born Leon Barzin, but Stravinsky auditioned the singers and attended rehearsals while he was in Manhattan, as well as both performances (on the 13th and 14th of January). After the first night there was a supper party in the apartment of Lucia Davidova, an old Russian acquaintance of Vera's and a notable Balanchine groupie, an occasion so bibulous that when Stravinsky turned up at the Columbia studios at ten the next morning to rehearse for his coming broadcast of *Persephone,* he was still drunk.[43]

Until that December, Robert Craft had not been back in touch since their interrupted exchange of letters in 1944, but he quietly missed nothing of Stravinsky's doings in New York. He had of course heard the first performance of the Symphony in Three Movements and was in Carnegie Hall for the recital with Szigeti and Arrau. Quite apart from his excitement at the music, whose composer (he later claimed) was neither admired nor much studied at the Juilliard School, his sharp eye and mind recorded vivid images of Stravinsky's manner and physique: the unusual speed of his walk to and from the rostrum, his brisk, punctilious platform presence, his way of acknowledging the audience, "unsmiling and aloof, . . . his right hand above his heart and with a single deep bow."[44] Now Craft had somehow talked his way into the *Renard* rehearsals, as well as into the rehearsals and studio performance of *Persephone,* a little-known work that was still only published in vocal score. He was intrigued by Stravinsky's rehearsal technique. The composer would dash up and down the aisle with a towel round his neck, grumbling in French at Barzin or shouting directions to Balanchine in his deep-throated Russian. He would leap onstage and demonstrate the required actions to the dancers. Always that same amazing quickness and athleticism, like those of a bird.[45]

For the *Renard* sessions, Craft stationed himself just behind Stravinsky in his stalls seat, and then on the day of the *Persephone* performance, in the short break between the final rehearsal and the broadcast, he sneaked into a photograph of Stravinsky examining the score with a group of young musicians, including the *Ebony* conductor, Walter Hendl, the composer Lukas Foss, and Claudio Spies, a Boulanger pupil and a close friend of Craft's from the previous summer at Tanglewood. But Stravinsky was unaware of Craft and they did not meet.[46] Nervous and unself-assured, the young man behaved like a lover-from-afar, shadowing his idol from the stage door to his car, hanging around at rehearsals, hoping for some miraculous introduction, but not daring to put himself forward or declare himself in any way. And like many a seemingly hopeless lover, he possessed only the courage of the pen. This was what had helped him to write in 1944, fabricating some pretext about cornet articulations in *The Soldier's Tale* and about wanting to borrow scores. This very Christmas, he had written again with an enquiry about unpublished works, but Stravinsky, who received many such letters and now had a new publisher to whom he could refer nuisance correspondence, replied briefly from Hollywood in February with the address of his editor, Hans Heinsheimer, of Boosey and Hawkes, 668 Fifth Avenue.[47]

The new contract had been signed in New York in January 1947, and by a neat coincidence the very first work that would bear the exclusive Boosey and Hawkes imprint, the Concerto in D for strings, had its first performance on the 21st of that same month, conducted by Paul Sacher in distant Basle, while its composer was conducting yet another second-rate orchestra in Glinka, Tchaikovsky and his own early ballets in Buffalo.[48] From upstate New York, they went home via San Antonio, Texas, where Stravinsky conducted, and where they visited Randolph Field (the Air Force equivalent of West Point) and the maestro again took up his baton to rehearse the Air Force band. But amid these very American experiences, his mind kept straying to Europe. For some time he had been intending to cross back in May, but the plan was complicated by the impending arrival of Milène and André, who had at last received their quota allocation and could be expected to sail within a couple of months. The problem, he wrote to Mildred Bliss from San Antonio, was André's medical history, which might lead to his being sent to Ellis Island and force Igor and Vera to postpone their departure for Europe. Could she, he pleaded, pull strings in order to avoid any such tiresomeness? She could, and within a week had done so.⁴⁹ However, his other anxieties about the coming summer were not so easily laid to rest.

When he resumed work on _Orpheus_ early in February, he may have already half-sensed that time was short to complete the thirty-minute score by the autumn, when Balanchine was planning to stage the new ballet. At least that was the main reason he gave to Heinsheimer when he informed him a month later that he had abandoned his European plans for that year.⁵⁰ Yet hidden between the lines of this March letter were other worries. His own health, he admitted, was good these days; but was this not an oblique reference to a previous letter from the publisher warning him that living conditions in London were appalling, that it was cold, and with constant power cuts and severe food shortages? Ralph Hawkes's advice that Stravinsky send himself food parcels in advance might almost have been calculated to shake the comfort-loving composer's confidence in the wisdom of his journey.⁵¹ Then there was the issue of Paris and its likely reception of his music. It was true that Nadia had been writing for months about "those who matter among the young [French] musicians knowing perfectly well whence comes the light";⁵² but dear Nadia could never quite see beyond the circle of her own prejudices, and there was something undeniably disconcerting in her well-meant remark about the idiocies that were going around Paris, "the theories, the systems—ravings [that] lead a frenzied dance." A long letter had come from Pierre Souvtchinsky that put such epithets in an altogether more painful light. The state of music in France, he wrote, "is complicated and confused. . . .

> For us to succeed, it will be necessary to work carefully and farsightedly, since the enemies of your music (our enemies) are unfortunately cleverer and more "up-to-date" than some of our friends. Naturally, none of these opinions have anything to do with you or your work, but it's impossible not to worry about the damage to the new generation and necessary to help that generation find the right path once more.⁵³

There was a certain bravado in Stravinsky's reply. He quoted Mark Twain: "It's difference of opinion that makes horse races," but he also reported on a visit he had had a month before from Yves Baudrier, from whom he had derived an utterly depressing picture of French music and musical thought. Baudrier had brought a recording of Messiaen's _Trois petites liturgies_, and Stravinsky was moved to a decidedly un-Twain-like expression of disgust: "Why write such tedious stuff? Who needs it? Your 'progressive' Belgian . . . is probably in ecstasy, since César Franck (that compatriot of Messiaen's) is rather hard to listen to nowadays. So that's how they swap an old bore for a new one! But why does Lalique have to be more interesting than Wagner?"⁵⁴

More to the point, if Stravinsky optimistically supposed that Messiaen's faintly unctuous and far from atonal *Liturgies* were the starting point for the young Parisian progressives, Souvtchinsky's next letter would have come as a severe disappointment.

> Lately in Paris (as everywhere, I suppose) there has emerged a youthful school of "atonalists" which, with all its heresies, has unfortunately attracted a very talented circle of youngsters. I've got into a "love-hate" relationship with this group, since I find that when it comes to culture these musical "Trotskyites" are very interesting. The group has broken with Messiaen and is, of course, much more interesting than he is. . . .[55]

This was not quite the music to Stravinsky's ears that Souvtchinsky may have hoped, and there may even have passed through his mind the ghost of a memory of prewar Russia and his reluctance to subject himself to the disputes and name-calling that his own reappearance there would have occasioned. By an odd coincidence, Souvtchinsky had actually announced in his previous letter that he and his wife, Marianna, had made up their minds not to go back to Russia but to become French citizens instead. Whatever Stravinsky thought of this particular decision, he seems not to have replied a second time. A shadow fell across his friendship with Souvtchinsky, so recently revived.[56] And he did not for now return to France.

On the 4th of April, Milène phoned from New York; they had arrived and were well. Four days later, they were in Los Angeles and settling into the house Igor had set up for them. They seemed radiantly happy, he informed Nadia, and he himself was overjoyed to see them and once again have family around him, his first sight of any blood relation—near or distant—for almost eight years.[57] André Marion was admittedly a very different type from his previous son-in-law. Where Yury Mandelstam had been a bookish, poetic, unworldly, and profoundly unpractical Russian Jew, André turned out to be a businesslike, matter-of-fact Frenchman, culturally a shade provincial, by no means uneducated, but nothing of an aesthete or a literary sophisticate. As with many Frenchmen, there was a certain air of native superiority about him, not always softened by an ability to laugh at himself. Milène was and remained utterly devoted to him, but his entry into the Stravinsky household was not without its difficulties, since his interests were not essentially artistic and he understandably did not take kindly to being patronized by intellectuals. Olga Sallard, who had observed him for a short time in Paris, had taken against him and warned Vera of his tendency, as she saw it, to bully Milène and suppress her artistic abilities. Worse, André did not get on with Madubo, of whom—Olga claimed—he was in fact somewhat scared.[58]

Within days of welcoming the newcomers, Igor and Vera were away on their travels once again. Though Europe was off the itinerary, there were associated East Coast bookings that, for various reasons, the composer did not want to abandon. He had agreed to conduct two concerts at Dumbarton Oaks at the end of April, transparently as a quid pro quo for Mrs. Bliss's string-pulling in the matter of Ellis Island; and he was also recording the *Dumbarton Oaks* concerto in New York on the 28th for a small company called Keynote. This would not have been precluded by his Columbia agreement, which was nonexclusive. But as it happened, that contract had expired in February, and Stravinsky had no immediate plans to renew it.[59] He was furious with Goddard Lieberson about the non-release of several recordings (including the *Ode* and *Circus Polka,* which had been sitting on the Columbia shelves for two whole years), and he was fidgeting under Lieberson's claim that he was being blocked by his superiors. As usual, he could not, or would not, understand the commercial factors that inevitably governed such decisions, but always took them as specific, if not actually malicious, conspiracies against his music. What had seemed good, friendly, even jocular relations with Columbia's chief producer were rapidly turning sour.

They were away on this occasion for no more than a fortnight, including the best part of five days on railway trains; but it was to be a journey more productive than could ever have been measured by favors repaid or money earnt. As on the previous trip, they stopped off in Chicago, this time in both directions, and went to exhibitions. The Institute was still preoccupied with British artists. On the outward journey it was Henry Moore. On the way home—the 2nd of May—there was a Hogarth show, including the entertaining and instructive series of prints known as "The Rake's Progress."[60] Stravinsky's attention was particularly arrested by these pictures, and not simply on account of their artistic merit or historical interest, but because he was on the lookout for a subject for an opera.

Precisely when he decided to compose his first-ever full-length theatre piece is a matter for conjecture, but it may well have been in New York in January 1947 when he saw Hawkes and signed the definitive version of his new publishing agreement. The five-year contract provided for an annual guarantee of ten thousand dollars, rising to twelve thousand after two years, and this meant that from 1949 onward he would be assured an annual sum more than double the commission fee for the Symphony in Three Movements. It must have struck either him or Hawkes at once that under these circumstances it was at least possible to contemplate a work that would effectively shut out other commissions for a minimum of two years.[61] He would be able to put behind him once and for all those frustrating wartime years when he had bounced from one potboiler to the next, and his own most serious projects, like the symphony and the still unfinished Mass, had constantly been pushed aside because nobody was asking for them, or to be more exact, paying for them. But there was also a more specific impulse. Hawkes was full of a new British venture called the English Opera Group, which had emerged from the previous season's Glyndebourne production of Benjamin Britten's chamber opera *The Rape of Lucretia*. Britten was setting up the EOG with the specific aim of creating a repertory of English-language opera for small forces, and when Stravinsky reacted with interest to this whole scheme, Hawkes was quick to take the possibility back to the Group's founder. That April, before Stravinsky had set eyes on the Hogarth series, Hawkes sent him the EOG prospectus, "just to keep you reminded of the fact that they are more than interested in your idea of a new piece."[62]

By the 4th of May, they were home, and Igor was taking out his twice-interrupted *Orpheus* score. Seven weeks later he wrote to Hawkes that "as to composing a new operatic work, you are right—impossible for some time to come. As soon as I finish *Orpheus,* I have to complete my *Mass*."[63] He had barely thought about an English-speaking librettist for any such new work, and he was already planning his postponed European tour for 1948.

At that very moment, on the 23rd of May, the author of Stravinsky's first ever non-Russian theatre text, C. F. Ramuz, died in Lausanne after an operation for sclerosis. They had not seen each other for nine years, since Stravinsky had failed to turn up to Mermod's lunch for Ramuz's sixtieth birthday, though in truth they had been slowly drifting apart for years before that, their friendship constantly undermined by the painful question of *Soldier's Tale* royalties and by growing artistic differences. The composer's response to a request by the *Suisse Contemporaine* for a tribute was curiously lacking in warmth. "Do not ask me to write. . . . Facts reconstructed by memory are deformed if invoked during a state of grief. That grief is still fresh and too precious for me to renounce at will. . . ."[64] It might have been an epitaph for a whole period of his existence, a time once vivid, now best forgotten. He did not, it is true, much love the past. The present, for him, was always too immediate and compelling; and now, moreover, the future was bright.

14

THE EYE OF THE NEEDLE

THE CANCELLATION of their European trip left the summer of 1947 free of burdensome commitments, and Stravinsky could give his whole attention to writing the second half of *Orpheus*, and to settling the Marions into their new home. Balanchine had been in Paris since March, working as ballet master at the Opéra while Lifar, who had held the post throughout the Occupation, was being investigated for collaboration. Meanwhile the idea of an autumn premiere had been dropped, and Kirstein was looking for a theatre for an opening in April 1948. The Metropolitan, he thought, would be suitably distinguished but hopelessly expensive, and when he tried to circumvent this problem by slipping *Orpheus* into the spring program of Lucia Chase's Ballet Theatre he found himself embroiled in a row between her and Hurok, who still held the concession for ballet promotion at the Met. In the end he had to settle for City Center, a huge former Shriners temple on Fifty-fifth Street with seating for two thousand, but a cramped stage, a narrow pit, mediocre acoustics and sight lines, and the general atmosphere of a municipal hall decorated by Ali Baba.

Though originally commissioned for the dance school, *Orpheus* had naturally been taken over as a star project of the newly formed Ballet Society. Kirstein, who was much given to laying out elaborate but idealistic plans, imagined the society as "the repository of the classic productions of your works, done by George and you. . . .

> We want to have in our permanent repertory *Apollo, Jeu de cartes, Baiser de la fée, Renard, Balustrade, Orpheus*, those other ballets of yours which you wish revived, and, we sincerely hope, new works when you write them. I feel that Balanchine is the Petipa *de nos jours;* he alone has brought the great tradition of western theatrical dancing to its possible high peak. His repertory, and that is largely based on your scores, is the single stable repertory. He deserves a frame where it can be well presented, and all my efforts are toward securing it.[1]

He also longed to entice Pavel Tchelitcheff, the designer of *Balustrade,* back to the stage. Tchelitcheff still claimed to detest the theatre but had profound ideas about *Orpheus,* with which he bombarded Kirstein from his summer retreat in Arizona. Alas, no sooner had Stravinsky finished his score in late September than Tchelitcheff once more turned against the whole project, resenting, as Kirstein reported, "George's inability to think in mystical terms; he [Tchelitcheff] sees the drama of *Orpheus* as the story of man and his soul; Orpheus as Bacchus, as Apollo, as the artist-scientist-magician; and here we are, making it into a ballet-ivanich."[2] Not until January did they settle on Isamu Noguchi as a designer who could think sculpturally, but by this time Kirstein had eaten the dust of Manhattan indifference to new work. "Frankly," he moaned, "no one but Balanchine, Barzin and I care whether we live or die;

> it is of accidental or superficial interest to everyone else; people simply don't give a damn, and what we do is well done, and it costs money, and I have no more of my own left, so it is an agony to ask other people to help, knowing that there is no social prestige for them through us; we do unpopular things, etc; but we struggle along.[3]

Stravinsky received these various dispatches with a good grace but without obvious involvement. Long gone were the World of Art days when design ideas were part and parcel of the musical conception, as with *Petrushka* and *The Nightingale,* and even with *Oedipus Rex.* Stravinsky had a high opinion of Tchelitcheff as a stage designer, but one shudders to think how he must have reacted to the prospect of a Jungian visualization of his *Orpheus,* a work that moves so inscrutably through that legend's accumulated tangle of myth and meaning. "When you wrote *Orpheus,* did you think about classical Greece?" a critic once asked him. "I thought about strings," he replied;[4] and it is true that his letters of the time say more about the number of instruments needed (forty-three) than about the work's symbolism. Nor can he have forgotten that, less than twenty years before, Benois had refused to design the final scene of *The Fairy's Kiss* without some sight of the music. Yet here was Tchelitcheff promoting a whole psychological concept without the least idea of the sound or rhetoric of the score.

As for collaboration, in any case, Stravinsky's sights were now set elsewhere; he needed to find a librettist for his opera, and he needed to decide what kind of work it was to be. He had gone with Huxley to the West Coast premiere of Britten's *Rape of Lucretia* in June, hoping to learn something about the EOG from the character of its source opera. But alas it was a very amateurish staging by local performers, he reported sadly to Hawkes, and he made no comment about the music.[5] What was at issue, of course, was

Family tea at the orangery, Voreppe, 1933: Catherine and
Igor Stravinsky, Anna Stravinsky, Walter Nouvel, Ira Belline,
Soulima, and Theodore

Catherine Stravinsky with her granddaughter, Kitty, 1937

Milène and Mika (Lyudmila)
Stravinsky in the 1930s

Mika with her husband,
Yury Mandelstam, Château de
Monthoux, 1937

With Victoria Ocampo,
onboard ship, Montevideo
to Rio de Janeiro, 1936

With Nadia Boulanger, onboard the *Paris* from New York to Le Havre, 1937

Igor and Vera Stravinsky in Cincinnati, November 1940

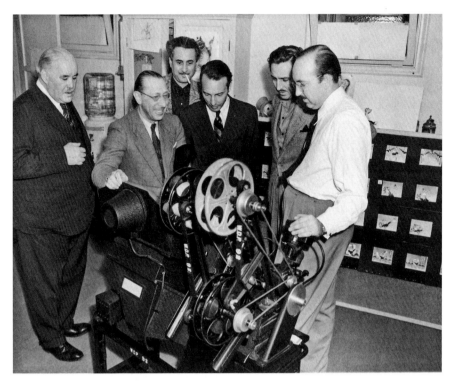

In the Disney Studios, Hollywood, with Alexis Kall (far left),
Balanchine (center), and Walt Disney (to Balanchine's left), 1939

With George Martin, Dagmar Godowsky, and Mercedes de Acosta,
Hollywood, c. 1941

Rehearsing *Ebony Concerto* with Woody Herman and band, New York, February 1946

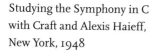

Studying the score of *Persephone* with James Fassett and Robert Craft, who has sneaked into the photograph, New York, 1947

Studying the Symphony in C with Craft and Alexis Haieff, New York, 1948

Stravinsky arrives in Venice for *The Rake's Progress,* September 1951, with Auden (left) and Kallman, and greeted by the Biennale director, Ferdinando Ballo (right). Vera Stravinsky is behind Auden; Robert Craft is in the background right.

Opening scene of *The Rake's Progress,* Venice, 1951

Rehearsing *The Rake's Progress*, Venice, 1951

With Jean Cocteau, Paris, 1952

Dylan Thomas at a book signing in New York, 1952

Christopher Isherwood and Aldous Huxley, Los Angeles, 1954

With Ernst Roth, Venice,
probably 1956

Listening to Craft rehearsing
the *Canticum sacrum*, Venice,
San Marco, September 1956

the intended scale of his own work and probably also its subject. On these matters, he kept his counsel until the completion of *Orpheus* on 23 September, after which he promptly announced to Hawkes that he had decided on the Hogarth subject and that on Huxley's advice he intended to invite W. H. Auden to write the libretto.[6] He had some experience of Auden's work in performance. He had seen the GPO film *Night Mail* (with Auden's verse commentary and Britten's music) only two or three weeks before the *Rape,* and he must have talked with Huxley about this short but brilliantly successful collaboration; Huxley may or may not have known that Auden had written other texts for Britten, including the libretto for his operetta *Paul Bunyan.* The central question was: could Auden write a verse libretto, not just in the sense of rhyming quatrains but in the larger sense of discrete formal structures governed by strict conventions, something Stravinsky had originally found himself insisting on twenty years before when Cocteau had appeared with his blank-verse first draft of *Oedipus Rex*? That Auden could concoct musical verse of a certain kind was obvious from *Night Mail,* whatever the weight or significance of the lines. It was the quality of mind and technique behind these jig-jogging couplets that Stravinsky needed confirmed by Huxley, by now his *vade mecum* on all matters to do with English literature and culture generally.

Whether or not this *Rake's Progress* would be for the English Opera Group was a question that occupied Hawkes (who was also Britten's publisher) more than it did Stravinsky. The EOG, Hawkes wrote at the end of September, would be very interested in a chamber opera but only if there were no chorus.[7] Stravinsky, however, doubtless understood at once that he would not get a proper commission fee from a new young company playing to small audiences on a public subsidy; so why commit himself to a type of work that, outside that company, would have such limited usefulness? The whole point about a full-length opera by Stravinsky in, say, 1950 was that there would be international competition to stage its premiere. In any case the Hogarth, with its varied and crowded urban setting, cried out for a well-populated stage, and that, in the end, meant precisely the chorus that EOG would want to avoid. So Stravinsky's Rake was left to make his own way, although, as we shall see, some aspects of the original chamber-opera idea survived in the work as it gradually took shape.

Before thinking of writing any operatic music, however, he had his Mass to finish, a debt only to his own muse, since for a work of this kind there was no chance of a commission and not even much prospect of a performance. True, the two existing movements had been sung in February to an enthusiastic Harvard audience, with the accompaniment arranged for two pianos by Claudio Spies and conducted by Irving Fine. But when Spies had tried to get up a performance with wind instruments a month later, attendance at rehearsal had been so halfhearted that he had had to abandon the project.[8] Stravinsky had authorized but not heard Fine's performance, and in fact it was almost three years since he had worked on the piece at all, a break in composition longer than with any work since he had taken up *The Nightingale* in July 1913. Fine had certainly not been able to respect one particular requirement that the composer only told Hawkes about in September: the fact that the soprano parts were supposed to be sung by children.[9] This stipulation, so impracticable for West Coast, or even East Coast, America in the forties, reflected the unworldly spirituality and medieval remoteness of the original inspiration, which seems to have welled up out of the commercial ghastliness of Stravinsky's artistic environment in 1944. That environment had changed, but not entirely for the better. The tintinnabulation of the cash register remained the defining ambient sound in postwar Los Angeles; and it was never far from Stravinsky's ears, whatever he might happen to be composing.

That summer, having lost faith in Columbia's willingness to release his recordings, he had signed an exclusive three-year contract with RCA Victor, and for several days in September—just as he was finishing *Orpheus*—he was in the Republic Studios in Hollywood, recording the *Danses concertantes*, the Divertimento, and the *Scherzo à la russe*, three works that for some reason had been left out of his Columbia contract in 1945.[10] So far so good. But when it came to rival publishers, the situation was by no means without its annoyances. Against Boosey and Hawkes he had no serious complaints; they were taking an interest both in his new works and in reprinting the old ones. It was Leeds, whose original idea it had been to establish new copyrights, who were now giving him trouble. And it was no consolation that the trouble was largely of his own making.

It all went back to the old *Billboard* announcement about the pop songs that were being made out of two tunes from *Firebird*.[11] After the debacle of the Ballet Theatre *Firebird* in October 1945, Stravinsky's irritation with Leeds had boiled over in arguments about accounting and proof-setting, which at one point in July 1946, thanks to Aaron Sapiro's bullishness over such matters, had almost come to court. Later the whole thing had been patched up, and in May 1947 Stravinsky had actually signed a contract for the adaptation of the oboe tune in the Khorovod (the "Princesses' Round Dance") as a popular song called "Summer Moon," with lyrics this time by a certain John Klenner. The composer was to receive an advance of one dollar but a twenty-five percent royalty on sales, which he and his lawyer evidently expected to be considerable. Three months later, Sapiro wrote to Aaron Goldmark authorizing Leeds to exploit "Summer Moon," and adding a sententious aside about "the thousands of people who may perhaps be humming and whistling this melody from the *Firebird Suite* all over America, much as they hummed and whistled and sang the famous Andante from Tschaikowsky's Fifth Symphony after it was adapted from one of the world's great classics."[12]

Unfortunately it turned out that, while looking forward to the income, Stravinsky had not expected his name to be directly associated with the commodity. It was one thing to describe the song as "adapted from Stravinsky's *Firebird*," quite another to label it "adapted by Stravinsky from his own *Firebird*," as Leeds had (of course, quite knowingly) done. Once again Sapiro bared his teeth. A disclaimer appeared in the *Los Angeles Times*,[13] and this time the long-threatened suit against the enterprising but not overscrupulous publisher was duly instituted. "It is as difficult for you to understand a man like Stravinsky," Sapiro told Lou Levy amiably, "as it is for a skunk to understand a lion."[14] But while never at a loss for words, Sapiro was for the second time to prove wanting in practical experience of contract law. The case grumbled on expensively for nearly a year, and in the end the court decided that while Leeds should not have used the wording they had, Stravinsky should not have sued on tort (that is, non-contractual injury) but on contract. "We *worked*," Sapiro ruefully told his famous client (for whom he indeed worked, and without fee), "but the result is nil—and costly!"[15]

While Leeds were doing their best to exploit Stravinsky's reputation, Hawkes was merely anxious to consolidate his work as a marketable product in its proper form. The first thing he discovered about the ERM catalogue was that many of the items listed were in fact unobtainable.[16] For ten years or more Païchadze had been prevented—whether by political and economic circumstances or by the caprice of his proprietor—from running an effective day-to-day publishing business, and the Occupation, followed by the destruction of the Berlin offices, had hammered the final nails into the coffin. The only solution, Hawkes felt, was to reprint everything, while at the same time establishing new copyrights, which would now be valid in America since Stravinsky was a U.S. citizen. In many cases, he told the composer, only the barest alterations were needed. In *Oedipus Rex*, for instance, it would be enough to revise the performance markings, dynamics, and editor's notes. Much of the necessary work could even be done by an amanuensis without so much as bothering the composer.

The snag in all this was that over the years Stravinsky had made many revisions to his works that had never reached print: blue or red pencil markings in his own conducting scores, corrections of misprints, altered phrasings, and so forth. The *Firebird* revision had admittedly been not much more than an expanded version of an old suite; but the new *Petrushka* was a radical retexturing, based partly on old changes, partly on new ones. Once he had started looking at the score, he had wanted to work it over thoroughly; and the result was like a painting whose colors had been completely reorganized: Picasso's *Demoiselles d'Avignon* recolored in the style of his *Woman in a Blue Dress*. Hawkes was also desperate for a revised version of *The Rite of Spring*, of which there were several printed editions (in many respects incompatible with one another) but no definitive score. The idea of reducing or in any way reconstructing its orchestration *à la Petrushka* made Stravinsky feel weak at the knees, but a cleaned-up text was obviously desirable. Then there were the various orchestral scores that had never come out at all: *Oedipus* and *The Fairy's Kiss, Persephone,* and above all the *Symphonies of Wind Instruments,* which Stravinsky had never conducted, and of which he possessed no score at all except a battered old proof from 1933—recently sent by Soulima from Paris—with Ansermet's (sometimes wrong) corrections all over it.[17]

He had been looking through this work and had decided, he told Hawkes, "to rewrite it [and] make it easier for performers as well as for audiences, and that without sacrificing any of my intentions."[18] The idea may have been in the back of his mind ever since he had rescored the final chorale as a filler for his radio concert in January 1946. But if so, a more recent communication had brought it forward. A few weeks earlier, Robert Craft had been in touch again, enquiring about precisely this score, which he wanted to perform with his Chamber Arts Society in New York, but which of course he had been unable to obtain there.[19] This time, Stravinsky could not refer his young correspondent to Boosey and Hawkes, since he knew that they had no better materials for the *Symphonies* than he had himself. In any case, Craft had made it hard for him to avoid writing a more detailed reply than in the past, by offering (rather than simply sending) him a copy of a recording of the Piano Concerto that Soulima had recently made in Paris and that Craft had acquired through Marcelle de Manziarly.[20] This shrewd tactic worked better than he can have thought possible. Returning to New York at the start of September from Hancock, Maine, after dropping out of Monteux's conducting class there, he was astonished to find Stravinsky's reply waiting for him, and so nervous at what it might contain that he left it unopened for several hours.[21] What he read when he finally plucked up the courage to take it out of its envelope was friendly if not particularly encouraging. No, there was no material for the *Symphonies;* but yes, "I shall be more than glad receiving Sviatoslav's record of my Piano Concerto, which you so generously offer me." Craft had mentioned the autumn premiere of *Orpheus,* and Stravinsky expressed surprise that he was unaware of the postponement to April. Finally, Craft had—again very shrewdly—recommended some reading matter, especially T. E. Hulme's *Speculations,* which Stravinsky did not know, and Souvtchinsky's recent essay on his music, which he did.[22]

It was like threading a needle. Twice the cotton snags on the eye, the third time, by some instinctive correction between brain and hand, it slips through. Craft's timing on this occasion had been immaculate. Stravinsky had just been looking at his notoriously intractable *Symphonies,* and hey presto, along comes a conductor offering to perform it. The young man is determined; he has written before. And he gets things done. Had Stravinsky not recently heard good reports of a Juilliard performance of his Octet under, surely, this same young conductor?[23] Nor was that all. The conductor read books, and had with his first shot come up with an intriguing suggestion that gave the highly literate but not preeminently anglophone composer a twinge of guilt. Even with Huxley, his closest English-speaking friend outside music, Stravinsky's conversation was French, but in fact ranged so wide that Huxley's superiority in Anglo-Saxon fields of enquiry was not much more noticeable than his superiority in all other fields except music. Craft, on the other hand, seemed to be hinting at ideas and avenues of thought that Stravinsky himself had neglected for too long.

In the course of the next weeks and months, the correspondence burgeoned. Craft sent the concerto recording, along with tactful words of praise for Soulima's performance, and further reading suggestions.[24] Stravinsky confided (early in October) that he was rewriting the *Symphonies* and would like the work played when complete, and he vouchsafed some uninhibited criticism of Leonard Bernstein's recent recordings of the Octet and *The Soldier's Tale,* to which Craft had also referred. "I am praying those records would never be published," he remarked, in the picturesque English of North Wetherly Drive.[25] There was a sense here of an alliance being forged, an enlisting of aid through shared indiscretion. But it was also clear that Craft knew these works and was an observant critic. For instance, he had spotted, and questioned, Bernstein's use of pedal timpani in *The Soldier's Tale.* He also turned out to be an efficient sleuth when Stravinsky asked him to find out why his *Dumbarton Oaks* recording was unobtainable in Los Angeles record shops; the vinylite discs, Craft learnt, had come out in blisters, and were now being repressed in an alloy.[26] At last, when Stravinsky indicated at the end of October that his reorchestration of the *Symphonies* was practically complete, Craft boldly invited him to conduct the piece himself in a Chamber Arts Society concert in the near future, and Stravinsky promptly wired back his acceptance.[27] More remarkably, he offered to conduct without fee, as he informed Ralph Hawkes, "to help that young and gifted Robert Craft and by the way to hear myself how it sounds."[28]

Auden, meanwhile, had reacted enthusiastically to the idea of collaborating on an opera. As with Craft, the time was ripe. "I don't think I am overanxious about the future," he had written to Ursula Niebuhr from his room in Greenwich Village a month or so earlier, "though I do quail a bit sometimes before the probability that it will be lonely."[29] He had completed *The*

Age of Anxiety, his immense reflection on this very theme, the previous November; now, for the opera-loving poet, a *Rake's Progress* might suggest an invigorating satyr-play on a not unrelated topic. Its moral implications at any rate resonated with the ethical, Christian strain in his own recent work, and Stravinsky himself, writing early that October, was careful not to dictate too many details of plot (the Hogarth series itself being loose in narrative continuity). "Please," he insisted, "do feel absolutely free in your creative work on the chosen theme. Of course there is a sort of limitation as to form in view of Hogarth's style and period. Yet make it as contemporary as I treated Pergolesi in my *Pulcinella.*" Had he known that Auden was already thinking in terms of the Seven Deadly Sins, and had a vision of the Bedlam scene as a coronation service in which the hero is anointed with a chamber pot (since "piss is the only proper chrism"),[30] he might have felt less indulgent on the question of theme. He was, though, adamant about the type of opera he wanted to write. "Bear in mind that I will compose *not* a musical drama, but just an opera with definitely separated numbers connected by spoken (not sung) words of the text, because I want to avoid the customary operatic recitative."[31]

After a brisk exchange of letters, it became obvious that working together at such a distance on so complicated a project would be impossible; there were too many unconnected strands. Stravinsky wanted a "Choreographic Divertissement" in the first act finale; Auden was suggesting an Aristophanic parabasis (where the chorus would address the audience directly) between the acts. So the composer wired for him to come to Hollywood, expenses paid, for a few days in November, Auden duly turned up on the 11th, and for a week they chipped away at the scenario and some aspects of the text. In outline, and considering the vagueness of the initial idea, their work together comes remarkably close to the finished version. The two acts originally envisaged by Stravinsky became—and would remain—three (though with a different scene distribution), and the spoken text was after all replaced by recitative, with piano accompaniment. The characters are not yet named, and there is no bearded lady, only an ugly duchess. But in essence the story is complete: of the young wastrel who, led astray by an inheritance communicated to him by a diabolical servant, abandons his faithful country bride for the fleshpots of London, grows bored to the point at which he marries the ugly duchess for her money, loses it all in a ludicrous business venture (involving, at this stage, a machine that turns water into gold; later it will be stones into bread), escapes the devil's clutches by beating him at cards, but ends up in a madhouse, where he is visited by his country bride and then dies of a broken heart when she goes away. This first scenario also contains many musical descriptions and indications for dialogue (partly in French), many of which were retained. The divertissement has disappeared, but Auden's parabasis has shifted to the end, where the characters address the audience in the manner of a Mozartian epilogue.

It was Stravinsky's first literary collaboration for nearly fifteen years, and possibly his most congenial since *The Nightingale* with Stepan Mitusov almost thirty-five years before. Like Mitusov, Auden was infinitely adaptable and self-effacing, and like him believed that it was "the librettist's job to satisfy the composer, not the other way round."[32] But Auden was also a versifying genius who could turn any practical requirement into memorable poetry; like Stravinsky himself he had a brilliant associative mind that was quick to see the familiar in the strange, the new in the old; and he was someone for whom the dividing line between the earnest and the satirical or the poetic and the banal was often hard to detect. "Tristan and Isolde," he would say, "were unloved only children";[33] or "Don Giovanni was a certain type of male homosexual"; or "Roosevelt developed paralysis in order to become President."[34] Such remarks can seem juvenile in print, and there *was* something schoolboyish about Auden, but attached to a mental quickness and a range of allusion that were conversationally dazzling. Stravinsky claimed to have been puzzled by such inconsistencies: the apparent conflict, for instance, between reasoned argument and the belief in astrology or "the telepathic powers of cats."[35] But the truth was that Stravinsky's own built-in contradictions, though culturally very different, chimed well with Auden's. He too, while addicted to clarity and an almost mathematical precision in his own work, had the religious superstitions of an Italian peasant. Just as Auden was a fluent Carrollian nonsense versifier, so Stravinsky was obsessed with dictionaries and with words and etymologies for their own sake, without regard to their sense. In his case, it was the old Russian tension between system and fantasy, in Auden's the English public schoolboy's distaste for intellect and sensibility, even his own. Once they grasped this similarity-in-contrast, they got on splendidly.

In certain inessential ways, Auden fitted less well into the Stravinskys' lives. For one thing, he was too tall for the guest couch in the den next-door to the composer's studio, and had to sleep with his feet propped up on a chair, "like the victim of a more humane and reasonable Procrustes."[36] He was also unkempt, and careless about personal hygiene, qualities which struck a discordant note in the somewhat bourgeois environment that Igor and Vera had created for themselves in trim North Wetherly Drive. According to the housekeeper, Mrs. Gates, the soap and towels put out for him in the den remained unused, and when the Sokolovs came to dinner on his final evening, Lisa remarked on his dirty fingernails. "Who was that extraordinary woman?" Auden asked Stravinsky when the guests had left.[37] And certainly there was nothing of La Boutique about the great English poet, however delightful he and Vera may have found each other in all other respects.

Stravinsky took Auden to an amateur production of Mozart's *Così fan tutte,* not for pleasure (there was no orchestra, only a piano accompaniment), but strictly to acquaint him at first hand with the kinds of model he was interested in for the *Rake.* He had already started planning his musical references. Before Auden's arrival he had attended performances of *The Marriage of Figaro* and *Don Giovanni* by the visiting San Francisco Opera, and had written to Hawkes asking him to send the orchestral scores of these works, as well as *Così* and *The Magic Flute,* "this genuine source of inspiration for my future opera."[38] But *Così* was his particular favorite at this juncture, perhaps partly because (as with his sources for *Mavra* a quarter-century before) it was by far the least well known of the late comedies, but also no doubt because of its rich ensembles and schematic narrative. The manipulative elements in the story must have caught his interest as well, notwithstanding the more obvious relevance of *Don Giovanni,* with its graveyard scene, its retributive ending, and its cautionary epilogue. There would be other models for the *Rake.* Stravinsky was soon sending for Handel oratorios (curiously enough as models for the setting of English[39]), and *The Beggar's Opera*—a work Hogarth himself saw and painted and that may have influenced his *Rake* series.[40] But Mozart, though strictly too late for the subject, remained paramount.

Stravinsky also took Auden to a performance of Lorca's last play, *La casa de Bernarda Alba* (with music by Milhaud), and afterwards there was a small party at North Wetherly Drive with, among the guests, the stage director John Houseman. Houseman was busy organizing support for the composer Hanns Eisler, who had been hauled up before the House Committee on Un-American Activities and charged with having concealed his links with the Communist Party when he reentered the U.S.A. in 1940. Stravinsky had recently seen and liked the Eisler-Brecht play *Galileo,* and he agreed to lend his name to a sponsorship committee of American composers for a concert of Eisler's music at Hollywood's Coronet Theatre in December.

Stravinsky seldom made political gestures, and the ones he did make he usually lived to regret. The Eisler sponsorship was no exception. His support for his German colleague was certainly genuine, since he went out of his way to write to him praising *Galileo* some weeks after seeing it, and immediately after the House Committee hearing at the start of October.[41] But his intentions were probably quite vague: pro-composer, perhaps still residually pro-Russian-Allies (Communist or not), certainly not pro-Communist as such. It was only after the appearance in *New Republic* of a brilliant but provocative article by Martha Gellhorn denouncing the "Un-

Americans," as she labelled the Committee's examiners, that the more alert members of the nonpolitical community saw a faint but distinct red light. Virgil Thomson, for instance, wrote cautiously to Bette Odets declining to sign a petition in Eisler's support, on the grounds that it contained "statements about matters of which I have no knowledge. . . . I am deeply sorry for him, but the best I can do is to certify his musical and intellectual achievements. I know nothing about his character and private life, having met him only once or twice and that briefly."[42] Stravinsky could have said much the same, but he failed to see the intricacies of the situation until Aaron Sapiro—prompt as ever with his advice—warned him that he was being used by "the Communist crowd" (since the Gellhorn article had been posted to subscribers in the same envelope as the Eisler concert program) and urged him to withdraw his support for the concert.[43] This, to his credit, Stravinsky was unwilling to do, but he did write to the *Los Angeles Times* on the 12th of December insisting that his interest in the concert was apolitical and purely musical. Unfortunately, his letter failed to appear before the concert on the 14th, and instead the paper ran a news item on the 13th that specifically identified him as heading "the list of internationally noted composers" who were sponsoring the event. At this point, he wrote to Houseman, "the only thing I could do to protest was not to attend the concert."[44]

ONCE AGAIN work on the Mass had been held up, this time by the decision to rewrite the *Symphonies of Wind Instruments,* and he probably made little progress on the choral work before completing the *Symphonies* revision toward the end of November 1947, shortly after Auden left for New York. What was involved in the wind piece was similar to his work on *Petrushka* the previous year. In substance the music remained virtually the same, but from start to finish it was radically retextured, rephrased, and rebarred, and the result was to make it drier, clearer, and more astringent. In the revised version, the thin, nasal tone of oboes and bassoons colors the music where, in the original, the fruitier sound of the clarinets and horns was more prominent. The phrases are now shorter and more staccato, and the shorter bars increase the number of accents and so break up the flow of the old melodic lines. Most intriguingly of all, Stravinsky experimented with his harmonies by adding bass notes whose sole purpose seems to be to reinforce notes at the top of the chords through a process of overtone resonance—in the way that one matches colors in a room by picking out particular tones in a carpet or chair cover. The subtlety of these changes is astonishing, and it tells us a great deal about Stravinsky's priorities as a composer: his concern for the exact spacing and timing of chords and the correct placing of accents. It also perhaps indicates why he had never himself conducted the *Symphonies,* and even why it had never been published. He simply had not been happy with it in its original scoring, but had had neither opportunity nor incentive to rework it.

In one other respect, the revised score is deeply revealing of Stravinsky's creative attitudes; it bears out a remark he had made in the *Poetics of Music* about the role of sheer accident in the compositional process. "If his finger slips," he had said there, "[the true creator] will notice it; on occasion he may even draw profit from something unforeseen that a momentary lapse reveals to him."[45] In revising the *Symphonies,* as we saw, he had to work from a proof copy of the original with Ansermet's corrections. But in fact the music was so strange, so richly unconventional, that some of these corrections were actually mistakes based on wrong assumptions about what was likely. It seems that, in 1947, Stravinsky either failed to notice the errors, or else decided that he liked them after all. For whatever reason, the revised score accepts quite a few details that can be proved beyond doubt to have originated in mistakes, though whether this is "profit" or loss is, of course, another question.[46]

Having completed this task, and some other less extensive revisions, he was at last free to resume work on the Mass. He had scarcely touched it for three years, unless (which is possible) the little two-part vocal canon he tossed off as a sixtieth-birthday present ("Hommage") for Nadia on the 16th of September was a discarded sketch. He may still have had some difficulty picking up the liturgical mood, after several weeks immersed in another wind score of a superficially similar but in many ways profoundly different character. On 10 December he wrote to Hawkes asking for copies of Palestrina masses, presumably as models for his own, and the next day he broke off, for reasons that are hard to fathom, to compose a sombre little piece for string quartet apparently inspired by the proposed graveyard scene in the opera (and eventually used as prelude to that scene). This piece, too, with its oscillating, chantlike melodic figuration, could be a discarded fragment of the Mass, though there is no external evidence beyond the fact that he was probably working at the time on the "Sanctus," which is similarly and intensively based on rocking figures worked in four-part polyphony.[47]

Then, just when this creative difficulty was perhaps approaching resolution, he was again distracted by visitors. First René Leibowitz, the *éminence grise* of the Paris anti-Stravinsky demonstrations, turned up requesting an interview to discuss the Symphony in Three Movements and "certain problems relative to your music in general." Stravinsky had been warned by André Schaeffner against this "stateless arriviste,"[48] but for some reason agreed to talk to him. Leibowitz rewarded his hospitality with a vicious attack in the left-wing *Partisan Review.*

Stravinsky writes slowly, meticulously, every day at regular hours, with the cold determination and control of an engineer [. . .]. These works are brilliantly made as far as craftsmanship goes, and every note seems to be the result of absolute lucidity. But behind these frozen and sometimes readymade patterns (or rather, these petrified sound forms, put together with such diabolical skill) there is nothing except perhaps the illusion of music. In Stravinsky's hands the musical materials are like stone, wood, or leather. The complete work is, in the long run, a grouping of diverse elements which *sounds* because it is made of sounds but which only conveys the deadly *Maya* of a musical work.[49]

Leibowitz naturally also visited Schoenberg, and his article is above all a confrontation of the one composer with the other, like Lourié's of twenty years before, but now heavily weighted against Stravinsky. While Stravinsky's recent music displayed "an ever increasing mastery and control applied to less and less significant musical problems," Schoenberg's was "full of renewal, dominated by passion, boldness and risk."

It is an incredible sight to watch a composer who for fifty years has been the exponent of musical economy, now unfold an amazing abundance of ideas without ever falling into chaos or disorder. Every new work has an absolute novelty of its own. The wild and utterly fresh features of the *Survivor from Warsaw* . . . demonstrate a vitality and creative strength which are almost inconceivable: it is frankly a masterpiece.[50]

The sole, qualified consolation for Wetherly Drive was that Leibowitz's comparison was a Manichaean one between the light and the dark, God and the Devil: two undoubted powers. He had heard the recording of *Genesis,* and concluded that, whatever he might think about Schoenberg and Stravinsky, "not one of the other participants betrays the slightest ability to write a coherent piece of music."

A week after Leibowitz's visit, Nicolas Nabokov came for Christmas, arriving by train with Balanchine. Since the end of the war he had been in Berlin with the U.S. military government, but he had been back in New York since January, Stravinsky had seen a good deal of him there in April, and their friendship had grown closer than before. For twenty years Nika had been a bird of passage in Stravinsky's life. At first, at the time of *Apollo* and *Ode,* he had been very much the junior composer, to be patronized and, on occasion, reprimanded; later he had acted as go-between with Balanchine over the commissioning of *Jeu de cartes,* and during the war there had been occasional meetings on the East Coast. Somehow this first Californian stay was different. Stravinsky had badly wanted the visit, had been urging Nika to come for more than a year, and was now candidly delighted to see this tall, benign, cosmopolitan forty-four-year-old Russian, with his lop-sided smile and his mop of prematurely graying black hair. "Please don't change your mind," Igor had written. And naturally there were errands; bring some Handel scores, bring your own Pushkin cantata ("Auden admires it very much"), bring some Bols Dutch gin ("unobtainable here"); above all: "Do you know Robert Craft—to all appearances a serious man [. . .]. Get in touch with him and let me know what you think of him."[51]

Nabokov spent five days in Hollywood, sleeping on the same couch as his friend Auden had so recently done, and after he left he immortalized the visit in a long article in *Atlantic Monthly*.[52] He was unique among Stravinsky's surviving prewar Russian friends in being a composer, and although Igor's interest in his music was never much more than (and occasionally somewhat less than) polite, it remained a sort of bond between them. It is true that, when Stravinsky suggested looking at Nabokov's latest scores, he was rather too easily persuaded to show his visitor his own instead. He played through *Orpheus*, drawing attention to the curious way in which the closing fugue keeps breaking off, "like a kind of . . . compulsion, like something unable to stop . . . Orpheus is dead, the song is gone, but the accompaniment goes on."[53] Then they looked at the work-in-progress on the Mass, presumably the Sanctus and the Credo. Nika, feeling tired, sat down on a sofa, while Stravinsky continued to fuss over his score. Soon he had forgotten all about his visitor. "He was playing the same passage over and over again. It looked as if he were testing the quality of what he had written. He was remeasuring the interval relations and recalculating the rhythmical patterns. His head and body jerked and bobbed and he was quite distinctly humming the words of the Mass."[54]

Since settling in America, Stravinsky—always a keen patron of zoos—had become a lover of domestic animals of various kinds. Nika met the cat, Vaska, and the aviary of house-birds, not all of whom spent the day in cages. ("Be careful," Stravinsky warned him when Pópka the parrot started delousing his hair, "you know what birds do on people's heads.") They sampled Igor's cellar, in which *vin ordinaire* did not figure prominently: at lunch they drank Mouton Rothschild '37, while Nika briefed them on the political situation in Europe—a continuing worry of his host's, because of his need to decide for or against a tour there the next summer.[55] Constantly in his mind was the terror of a new war or revolution and of being stranded in France or Germany without means of returning home. In October their Wetherly Drive neighbor Baroness d'Erlanger had written from Venice about the ruinous state in which she had found her house there, and about the growing threat of bolshevism in Italy, where strike after strike was being fomented by Communist infiltrators of the trade unions.[56] Willy Strecker had just written assuring Stravinsky that, despite the awfulness of conditions in Germany, life was going on in a surprisingly lively and constructive way. But then, he was trying to persuade the composer to participate in a Stravinsky Festival in Bayreuth, of all places, in July or August, and was obviously painting as rosy a picture as he could.[57] In any case, whatever Nika told them that Christmas, he must have been noncommittal on the question of a European trip, since a week after his departure they were still equivocating, telling the Milhauds (who were now themselves back in Paris) that they were coming, and Olga Sallard that they might not be.[58] Not until mid-March, after much hesitation over contracts, and after successively booking then cancelling ship berths and airline seats, did fear finally overcome the spirit of adventure and their minds turn instead to the possibility of Soulima, Françoise, and little Zizi taking ship for America.[59]

ROBERT CRAFT's object in inviting Stravinsky to conduct the revised *Symphonies* had patently been to get Stravinsky, rather than to get the premiere of the *Symphonies,* but it did look, all the same, as if that is what the April performance would be. Then something unexpected, yet bizarrely appropriate, happened: the work's oldest advocate and most practiced exponent, Ernest Ansermet, turned up in New York, intending to conduct the *Symphonies* in the original version in a radio concert with the NBC Symphony Orchestra at the end of January. It was almost exactly ten years since the quarrel over *Jeu de cartes,* and Ansermet knew little about Stravinsky's wartime doings and nothing at all about the new version of the *Symphonies.* When he saw it, on his arrival in Manhattan in the second week of January, he expressed himself somewhat coolly, and indicated that he would rather conduct the version he knew, "unless you would rather I gave the new one."[60] Stravinsky certainly would rather, however, and Ansermet was happy to oblige. With the new score in hand, he proceeded to bombard the composer with detailed questions about it, questions that revealed yet again the problems and pitfalls of establishing correct texts for so radical a musical language. Stravinsky nevertheless answered everything patiently, if not always accurately, and after listening to Ansermet's broadcast performance on the 31st, cabled his enthusiastic congratulations and thanks.[61]

Much had altered in both musicians' lives since they had parted in angry correspondence in 1937. Yet in one particularly catastrophic way their paths had run along parallel tracks. Ansermet, too, had lost his wife and married another, younger one. There, however, the similarity ended. Marguérite Ansermet had died in 1940 in an agony that was moral and emotional as well as physical, since her husband had pursued his affair with the increasingly neurotic Elena Hurtado to the bitter end, and it was only when Hurtado had subsequently abused Marguérite's memory to his face that Ernest had broken with her, "even though I knew very well the drama that this would inevitably provoke. One day in February 1942, Elena killed herself in front of me by swallowing several tubes of phenobarbitone. The poor woman ought never to have met me, but I equally could not sacrifice my life to no purpose." He had remarried four months later. "It seems to me," he went on, "that I owed you this frightful narrative; you've been too involved in my life, you and Vera, for me not to confess it all at the moment that we meet again."[62]

It was curious how the egotism still in some ways shone through what was evidently meant to be an admission of guilt. After talking about his orchestra in Geneva, the conductor brought up the old issue of his phenomenological study of music that had originally triggered his diatribes about *Jeu de cartes*. He foresaw a book on the subject. "If this book comes out, I wouldn't want it to shock you, but I know that there are certain essential points that we don't approach in the same way, and I wouldn't want these differences to prevent your being aware that my admiration for what you do and my affection for you have not changed." Thus the thinker addresses the maker. Stravinsky, who in any case seldom wrote discursive letters these days, was probably glad of a genuine excuse—that he was shortly leaving for San Francisco—for sending nothing but a night letter in reply. "Glad have your moving letter. Too bad no more time left for correspondence. . . ."[63]

THE SAN FRANCISCO date was followed by a ten-day trip to Mexico City and a pair of concerts in Los Angeles in mid-March. It was his first appearance at the L.A. Philharmonic for seven years, and while the centerpiece was the abrasive Symphony in Three Movements, the rest of the program was a familiar selection from the "easy" Stravinsky of wartime potboilers and the Divertimento (studiously billed as "1949 version," though the changes to the prewar score were minimal indeed). On 15 March 1948, three days before the first concert, he at last completed his Mass, and on the 28th they set off for the East Coast, travelling via Chicago and Pittsburgh to Washington, where they were due to meet Auden to discuss his completed libretto and certain contractual matters on the 31st.

Auden had, as he put it in his note covering the dispatch of the first act, "taken in a collaborator, an old friend of mine in whose talents I have the greatest confidence."[1] He did have confidence in Chester Kallman's talents, more perhaps than was fully justified. But to call him an old friend was a distinct if permissible clouding of the truth. Auden and Kallman had been lovers since soon after their first meeting, at an evening of the League of American Writers in New York in 1939. Chester was now twenty-seven, wavy-haired, blond, chubby-faced, a serious poet in his own right, and above all a passionate and knowledgeable opera lover who brought to this first of several operatic collaborations an instinct for the genre that Auden did not strictly possess. Stravinsky was disconcerted to learn that there was a co-author whose existence had been kept from him, but he never seems to have minded, or even noticed, differences in style or quality that might have disturbed him if his English had been more acute. For instance, of the three scenes in Act 1, Auden wrote the first half of the first scene and the whole of the second, Kallman the rest;[2] and while Kallman's verses are consciously operatic (like highly polished translations from some Italian original), Auden's are precise, stylized English poetry, beautifully conceived for patterned musical setting, but, as Stravinsky did quickly observe, not amenable to conventional operatic manipulations of the kind that routinely destroy scansion and rhyme schemes. The libretto was brilliant, he agreed with Hawkes, but "from time to time a little bit complicated for musical purposes." Moreover, its language was sometimes self-consciously arcane, with its budding groves and pliant streams, and its Cyprian Queen whose "genial charm translates our mortal scene." There were plenty of things here that needed explaining to a self-taught and still somewhat hesitant anglophone like Stravinsky.

Above all, something had happened to the governing idea behind the scenario. Before going to California, Auden had been frankly baffled by the task of converting Hogarth's vague morality into a narrative for the stage. He had, as we saw, some notion of associating the seven characters with the Seven Deadly Sins, with the hero as Pride crowned as Lucifer in the final scene. "But what *am* I going to do with the plot?" he enquired helplessly of his secretary, Alan Ansen.[3] Then in discussion with Stravinsky a clear, if inconsistent, story had begun to emerge, in which the still unnamed hero, having sacrificed simple rustic happiness for a rich but loveless urban marriage and doubtful success in business, unexpectedly outwits the villain-devil only to die of a broken heart in the madhouse. But once Auden had chewed over the scenario with Kallman, a more incisive theme crystallized, which he set out in a letter accompanying the second act.

> Have made a few slight alterations in our original plot in order to make each step of the Rake's Progress unique, i.e.:
>
> Bordel—Le plaisir.
> Baba—L'acte gratuit.
> La Machine—Il désire devenir Dieu.[4]

Instead of the Ugly Duchess, Rakewell (as he had become) would now marry the bearded lady, Baba the Turk, and he would do so, not for money or title, but as an existential act: precisely, that is, because he had no reason to. Having thereby escaped the "twin tyrants of appetite and conscience," as his diabolical servant, Nick Shadow, dubs the basic motives of human conduct, he would in the third act play God by inventing a machine that could magically transform stones into bread. Baba would in due course create as many problems for the composer as she solved for the librettists. As a plot mechanism, she introduced an element of implausibility that bothered lovers of operatic verisimilitude,[5] while as a character she had to be sentimental and warmhearted in a way that here and there threatened to reduce the drama to the level of soap opera. However, the real problem of Baba was that she looked dangerously like a bad homosexual joke (Kirstein told Craft that she was modelled on the bearded painter Christian Bérard),[6] but one without consequences, a mere jest, as Baba describes herself to Anne.

Stravinsky seems not to have protested about these difficulties, and was only troubled by technical questions such as how to integrate Baba into Tom and Anne's duet in the second act without convulsing the audience with untimely laughter.7 But that was in the future, and for the time being he apparently expressed no formal reservations about Baba herself.

The Washington meeting with Auden had been fixed because he was sailing for Europe only a day or two after Stravinsky was due in New York, and for similar reasons of shortage of time Robert Craft was coming from New York to discuss arrangements for their Town Hall concert on 11 April. Craft arrived at the Raleigh Hotel on the morning of the 31st to find Auden waiting impatiently in the lobby, because "the night train from Pittsburgh was late, and the Stravs aren't receiving yet."8 This accidental encounter was probably fortunate for Craft, since it enabled him to break the ice with Auden before entering the Stravinskys' suite, and to appear, therefore, as a useful intermediary with the idiosyncratic and to them not always comprehensible English poet. At all events the meeting was a success. Auden had brought a revised version of the libretto, and Stravinsky insisted that a toast be drunk in the form of small tumblers of scotch all round. Feeling less nervous, Craft began to observe his host: his tiny stature but broad shoulders and huge hands, his way of slapping his knee in frustration when a reply failed to satisfy him, above all his taste for categorical and unanswerable propositions like (of Beethoven's Violin Concerto) "that D-sharp in the first movement is such an ugly note," to which, even in his lubricated state, Craft found it difficult to respond adequately. Nevertheless after a substantial, well-irrigated lunch and a solitary afternoon walk along the Potomac, he returned for dinner to what he felt was a warm and sympathetic welcome. The Stravinskys, he sensed, had taken a liking to him, and—not much less important—perceived in him a usefulness that went beyond the musical qualities and enthusiasms that his letters had already revealed.

Craft was later inclined to emphasize the practical grounds for this openness so early in their acquaintance. Though now settled in America, Stravinsky could not feel confident of his reputation there, which continued to depend on the activities of a handful of well-disposed (mainly immigrant) conductors and a limited coterie of admirers, likewise in many cases Europeans and many of them composers of a distinctly sub-Stravinskian cast. His own conducting remained confined largely to "soft-centered" works like the two early ballets, the Pergolesi and Tchaikovsky pasticcios, and the wartime commercial parodies. Now here was a young New Yorker who seemed to know all his music, in some cases better than he knew it himself, and was itching to perform hitherto unprogrammable scores like the *Symphonies of Wind Instruments* and *Dumbarton Oaks* or technically forbidding ones like the Symphony in C. It turned out, besides, that this same young man was not only highly literate and well read, but that he knew how to talk about books, could hold his own with so brilliant a literary gossip as Auden, and not least had a fascination for the pure mechanics of language that—like Stravinsky's own—was amusingly just this side of the unbearably pedantic, while always hinting at the importance of exactitude and economy, criteria which, as a composer, he had always set above all others. "Delighted you enjoy reading dictionaries," Stravinsky had written a few weeks before, in reply to the gift of a copy of Dr. Johnson, "so do I."9 From all this, he might naturally have concluded that Craft was just the person to assist him in the delicate task of setting Auden's beautiful verse to music that, at the very least, did not do unintentional damage to its rhythm or accentuation.

Yet none of this would have counted for a great deal if he had not taken personally to Craft, had not experienced that quickening of sympathy and interest that we occasionally feel toward others in ways that are ultimately inexplicable—neither passionate nor sensual, but quietly tingling, a pleasure of recognition. On the face of it Craft was not at all Stravinsky's type. The descendant of educated but steady Kingston (New York) businessmen, he was not cosmopolitan, not in any sense "old-world," not forthright, certainly not authoritative or autocratic, did not have the gift of tongues, above all knew almost nothing about Russia or the Russians. He was not even intellectual, in the usual sense of that much-abused term. He had, rather, a lateral brain, fed by astonishing powers of recall and a speed of association that appealed and enlivened in a way that stark reason could not. As a young American he was far from "typical." He was not cool, but edgy, even vulnerable, likeable only sometimes and not by all, complex, quick, almost Jewish but apparently (like Stravinsky) with no Semitic blood. If Stravinsky warmed to this unusual character, it was not only because he saw in it qualities he needed, but also and at least as much because he grasped that it was a character that needed him. The sense of being used had become all too familiar since his arrival in America. The sense of being needed, and by a gifted man younger than his own children, was not at all familiar, and it left a strong and agreeable impression that, as events were to show, he was increasingly anxious to explore.10

Auden went straight back to New York, but Craft hung around in Washington, sitting in on Stravinsky's rehearsals with the National Symphony Orchestra and going with him and Vera to a Mozart concert at Dumbarton Oaks. On the 3rd he flew to New York, but he was back in the capital for Stravinsky's matinee concert the next day, and later they took the same night train to New York. During the next month, Craft was a constant item in the Stravinsky retinue. At first there were rehearsals for their joint Town Hall concert, interspersed with lunches with Haieff, who was also much in attendance and who, Craft later recalled, did his best to smooth the young man's path and "cover up for my gaucheness and inadequacies."[11] Later there were the preparations for the premiere of *Orpheus* at the end of April, and it was at this point that Craft began to belong obviously to the Stravinsky circle, since there was now no immediate reason for his continued presence. But the path was still sometimes thorny. On one occasion, he decided to repay the composer's hospitality by taking him, Vera, and Lisa Sokolov (who was also with them in Manhattan) out to lunch, without having yet learnt enough about Stravinsky's somewhat elevated standards in such matters. At the Town and Country restaurant there was no wine list and the specialty was that curious American muffin known as the popover. Vera dissuaded her husband from walking out, but she recorded it laconically in her diary as an "unsuccessful luncheon."[12] In spite of this debacle, Craft went with them that same day to a production of *Oedipus Rex* at the Juilliard School, and there the atmosphere was strained for a quite different reason. As an ex-student, he sensed guiltily that his former teachers looked on him as an interloper in this exalted company, as if the incident of the Hunter College photograph had become the key to his entire life.[13]

They stepped before the public together for the first time the day before the Town Hall concert, in a live radio "Stravinsky Tribute" with Balanchine and Kirstein.[14] But the concert was the significant debut. Stravinsky's presence transformed the audience, as Craft had known it would. Friends and associates like the Balanchines, Nicolas Nabokov and his new wife, the novelist Stark Young, Pavel Tchelitcheff, together with what Virgil Thomson called "the musico-intellectual world,"[15] turned out to hear the Master conduct his *Symphonies* and *Danses concertantes*. But if they were also in some measure curious to take a look at the young conducting graduate who had talked him into gracing so inauspicious an event, the same could not be said of the hard-bitten Manhattan critics, who volunteered little or nothing on Craft's conducting of the difficult Symphony in C and failed to notice that the Capriccio all but broke down when the soloist, Elly Kassman, missed a bar in the finale.[16] Thomson instead discoursed airily on neoclassicism; and Stravinsky was so disappointed by this that he penned an instant complaint, which, in turn, drew from the *Tribune* critic a second review praising Craft's musicianship while noting his lack of "platform elegance."[17]

The day they arrived in New York, the Stravinskys had dined with Auden, and there they for the first time met his co-librettist, Chester Kallman. Luckily they got on well with him from the start, and they even found that, in some ways, Auden was more relaxed and amenable when Chester was there, being entertaining in the extrovert, slightly theatrical way that came naturally to him. It was nevertheless, Vera recorded, a "strange dinner," whether because of the food or the company is not wholly clear.[18] The two poets already had a new idea for a libretto—something about Berlioz, Mendelssohn, and Rossini, though if they mentioned it (as Auden did the very next day at lunch with his secretary)[19] Stravinsky must surely have raised his hand and begged to be left in peace with the existing text, of which he had, after all, not yet composed a note. Two days later Auden and Kallman sailed for Europe, where they stayed for a time in England, and then proceeded for the summer to Ischia, where Auden had taken a house at Forio.

Stravinsky's own next port of call was the studio of Isamu Noguchi, the designer of *Orpheus*. After Tchelitcheff's defection, Kirstein had turned against the idea of hiring a painter, and he had decided on Noguchi precisely because he was a sculptor with, as Kirstein told Stravinsky, "a charming delicacy and justice of handling forms; they are not wildly original, but he creates space and airiness, and this is what Balanchine wants."[20] Noguchi, in other words, would not trouble them with any heavy ideas of his own about the Orpheus legend, but would create a neutral, abstract geometry that would coalesce with Balanchine's integrated choreographic style. The sculptor showed Stravinsky his *Orpheus* maquette, a "wonderful construction," as Vera called it,[21] of spheroids and hat stands, with paper cutout figures for the dancers. They would have been less happy if Noguchi had produced his finished masks, which—it transpired—blocked the dancers' vision and made them look like baseball catchers.[22] But these they were spared until the first dress rehearsal in City Center on the 26th, two days before the premiere, when it was still possible to adjust the masks but too late to change the concept.

Lucia Chase had resolved her dispute with Hurok, and Ballet Theatre's Met season was already running as the preparations for *Orpheus* reached their climax. A mere eight days before the Ballet Society opening, Balanchine himself took the baton and conducted the orchestra for his own Tchaikovsky ballet *Theme and Variations;* then on the 26th Stravinsky conducted *Apollo,* a work Kirstein would himself have liked to pair with the new ballet. It was as if Chase had gone out of her amiable way to steal Ballet Society's thunder. But Kirstein still held by far the strongest card.

Ballet Society opened its own season at City Center on 28 April 1948, with the world premiere of *Orpheus* (with Nicholas Magallanes in the title role, Maria Tallchief as Eurydice, and the composer conducting), together with three other Balanchine works: *Renard, Symphonie concertante* (based on Mozart's K. 364), and a curious little piece of plastique in which a pair of dancers (Tanaquil Le Clercq and Patricia McBride) tied themselves in elegant knots to the austere strains of Stravinsky's viola *Elegy.* Kirstein had relaxed his members-only policy, and though the first night was still restricted, the press were invited and for the subsequent three performances tickets were sold, a change that released the critics from their village-wedding politeness and gave them back their judicial role. There were the now-familiar disagreements about the Balanchine manner. While, for some, it hardly amounted to dancing at all, others sensed the intimacy of the relationship between the suppressed eloquence of the score and the plainness of the choreography. The *Times* dance critic, John Martin, saw in the whole work the quintessence of the Greek concept of ritual tragedy. "The music," he wrote, "is remote, hieratic, tender with the memory of distant emotion, purified and distilled by time and perspective," and Balanchine had "treated it with the utmost simplicity" and "told the story with complete directness and a minimum of ornamentation."[23] Martin's *Tribune* colleague, Walter Terry, was firmly of the "dancing? what dancing?" school of Balanchine criticism, but the paper made amends by running a separate piece by Virgil Thomson, who loved the music and, as a composer himself, understood that "only the repose of thorough concentration ever produces a work so abundant in its variety and withal so restrained in style."[24]

No one, friend or foe, pointed out that the Orphic tragedy of the Greeks was in fact a very violent phenomenon, and that in consciously introverting this quality Stravinsky had adopted what was psychologically, if not stylistically, a hypermodern, post-Freudian view of the legend. This Orpheus stands, at the outset, "motionless, with his back to the audience," and even his dismemberment by the Bacchantes is played out, for much of its length, mezzo-forte and half in secret, as if veiled by the large tulle curtain that figures prominently in the stage directions, and that Balanchine was only able to procure by the last-minute acquisition from an unknown sponsor of a thousand dollars in cash.[25] The image, musically as well as dramaturgically, is of a legend that retains beauty but has lost force and immediacy, one that we witness with the superior detachment of a post-legendary age, or like the children in Auden's account of Breughel's *Icarus*, "who did not specially want it to happen," and the ship that had "somewhere to get to and sailed calmly on."[26] But for Stravinsky it seems clear that the element of sublimation was at bottom religious, and that therein lay the deeper significance of his importing of devices like canon and fugue, which belonged symbolically to the musical language of an ancient time when old men really did wait reverently and passionately for the miraculous birth. It was much as when *Apollo* had prompted Boris de Schloezer to predict, from the note of renunciation he detected in that ballet, that Stravinsky's next work would be a Mass.[27] This time, his next work would be—was already—just that.

Kirstein was so delighted with the outcome of his commission that he promptly wrote to ask Stravinsky to undertake another after *The Rake's Progress*. "*Apollo,*" he revealed, "was actually my start in musical education; it was a door through which I passed into the music of the past, and out of which I heard the music of the present and the future. . . . To me *Orpheus* is the second act of a great lyric-drama."[28] For a third act he suggested—somewhat predictably—"the maturity of Apollo. . . . At least let us talk about it." But as de Schloezer had himself enquired on that earlier occasion twenty years before: "is our logic that of the artist?"

Just over a week later, Stravinsky was back in Hollywood and embarking at last on the composition of Auden's first scene, starting as he intended to continue, with an unashamed accent on Anne Trulove's opening definite article ("THE woods ARE green"), thereby twisting the poet's iamb into a trochee. Craft had been left behind in New York with various duties, including editorial work on *Orpheus* and the compilation of a reading list to help sustain Stravinsky in his English-language studies, but also with a firm invitation to come and stay at North Wetherly Drive later in the summer. For forty years, Stravinsky had been delegating tasks that he found irksome or inconvenient or simply too expensive or remote. Now with "Bobe," as he had quickly become, there was a qualitative change, and errands were allocated without inhibition, as a quid pro quo, no doubt, for the leg-up he had received in his career, for meals bought and introductions given, yet essentially not for these reasons at all, but rather, simply, as the natural flow and return of a more particular affection, exactly as if this clever, sensitive, and efficient young man had been specially laid on by Providence to soothe the eight-year pangs of son-starvation. For in truth Craft had come on the scene at an amazingly providential moment. For two years running, Stravinsky had hoped and planned to greet his family in Europe, and for two years he had been denied. Now at this very moment his younger son, Soulima, was making final arrangements to fly to America with the wife and child his father had never seen. He would actually arrive in New York on—or almost on—his father's sixty-sixth birthday. Igor Stravinsky's paternal instincts were on maximum alert.[29]

There was nothing particularly unusual about his writing to Craft at the start of June, asking him if he would go to La Guardia to meet Soulima off the plane and see him safely to his Manhattan hotel.[30] In fact it was the most natural thing in the world. Either Rieti or Sam Dushkin would normally have gone to the airfield, but both were going to be out of town. And while it was true that they both knew Soulima well and could talk to him in French, Craft more than made up for his deficiencies in these departments by his willingness and dependability, and by the fact that Stravinsky already felt close enough to him to trust him with family responsibilities. The closeness is almost tangible in his and Vera's letters to the young conductor. They are direct, simple, warm, and devoid of formality. Igor's "it would be wonderful if you could meet them there and help them at their arrival" is in marked contrast to the often slightly officious tone of his instructions to others. In a second letter he confides to Craft his contempt for "the ridiculous old man" (Koussevitzky) and his anxiety about the way American choirs will sing his Mass: "you are right in mistrusting the ppppp-fffff technic of this kind of organization."[31] As for Vera, Craft had had the impression in New York that she was puzzled by him and had befriended him chiefly for Igor's sake, knowing his thirst for acceptance by intelligent and well-informed young Americans. Now, though, she talks to him like a favorite aunt. She asks him about Isherwood and the identity of the characters in his autobiography, adding without irony "you know everything—that is why I ask *you*."[32] She lists her stepson's various names: Sviatoslav, Svetik, Nini, Soulima—and she gently repeats the invitation to Hollywood. It seems that they have already half-adopted Craft, for what he is as well as for what he knows.

For some time Stravinsky had been putting heavy pressure on his pianist son to come to the States, using a technique that derived partly from his own impatient and authoritarian nature. Think seriously about it, he told Soulima, but decide quickly; I don't want to wait. At the back of his mind, no doubt, were the difficulties he knew his son to be experiencing in Paris in the shadow of his wartime activities. Life and work would be better and easier for Soulima in America, and there need be no backward glances. But Igor was in any case an instinctive patriarch, and he would have transported all his children and installed them in North Wetherly Drive if money and space had permitted, whatever their circumstances in Europe.

They themselves, it was true, wavered in their acquiescence to such plans. Theodore had his painting work in Geneva, and though money was often short they had a house and friends there; they felt, Denise said, "decidedly Europeans,"[33] and it suited them to be outside the Stravinsky gravitational field. Meanwhile in Beverly Hills, Milène and André were finding life less amenable. After barely three months, André's problems with Madubo had reached the point at which she decamped to North Wetherly Drive and refused to go back until the cramped arrangements there made it inevitable. No doubt André was, as Olga Sallard had suggested, an uncongenial employer. But as always there were two sides to the argument. Now in her mid-fifties, Madubo was still finding it hard to break her lifelong habit of treating Milène as a child, while the Marions in their turn, feeling that Madubo had been dumped on them and unable to assign her a role in their lives, tended to treat her as an unwanted guest in their house. Matters were made worse by the fact that André had no job and few prospects; his health was indifferent, his temper volatile, and he resented the lack of privacy in his own home. At one point he even consulted Stravinsky's lawyer Aaron Sapiro about how he might legally evict the poor woman.[34] How Stravinsky himself reacted to such developments can only be guessed, but he certainly occupied himself with the Marions' troubles. Vera's diary often refers to serious talks, heart-to-hearts, and plans involving the unlucky pair. Nevertheless the situation was still unresolved when the Soulima Stravinskys arrived in Hollywood in the fourth week of June and installed themselves in a flat that Igor and Vera had rented for them from the Sokolovs and had furnished partly with objects brought from the Sachs mansion in Santa Barbara.

Their arrival could hardly have been worse timed. On the 22nd, the very day that they stepped onto a train in New York, Lisa Sokolov, who had seemed to recover from her Mexican jaundice of two years before, suddenly and quite unexpectedly died of a heart attack. Lisa was not only Vera's business partner but her best Californian friend, and the atmosphere that greeted Soulima and his family when they got off the train at Pasadena and drove to the bereaved widower's flat in Holloway Drive must have been muted indeed. Nevertheless the auguries for the newcomers were at least better than for the Marions. Stravinsky had managed to arrange a handful of performing dates for his son, including the Capriccio in a concert he was himself conducting at Red Rocks, Colorado, in four weeks' time. Robert Craft would be meeting them in Denver, then coming on later to spend a week or two in Hollywood.

When they reached the Brown Palace Hotel in Denver on the 19th, it was soon clear that Craft was not in Colorado exclusively for the scenery or the music-making. Stravinsky had actually composed only about half of the first scene of the *Rake* (up to the end of Nick's arioso "Fair lady, gracious gentlemen"), but what he now needed from his new young helper was detailed technical advice about the setting of the libretto as a whole. He had composed an English text only once before, in *Babel,* and even there the sung text had been limited to a few biblical lines for two-part male chorus, in which mistakes of prosody were either inaudible or unimportant. It was one thing, he realized, to misaccentuate a language like French, which he knew well and the effect of whose maltreatment he could calculate in advance; it was quite another thing to mangle an original English text by a great poet in a work lasting three hours simply because he was ignorant of its finer points. He accordingly made Craft go through the whole text with him in great detail, reading it aloud and answering questions about meaning and intonation. It was a vital piece of collaboration, and one that must have convinced Stravinsky that he had found in this young man a priceless assistant who could, so to speak, focus all the different types of help that he had in the past sought from a variety of musicians, writers, factotums of one kind or another—in fact, whoever happened to be available. No doubt in his partisan enthusiasm he in some respects overrated Craft, as he had always tended to overrate the advice he solicited. Nevertheless, it was an astonishing stroke of luck that, just when he needed an educated anglophone musician with a flair for words and a strong literary instinct who adored his music, fate should have sent one along. That this same person should also be a sensitive soul with emotional needs that fitted his own must have seemed little short of miraculous.

For a new visitor, Denver has always been a surprising city. Immediately to the west stands the highest massif of the Rocky Mountains, the source of huge electric storms that, to this day, can set off a chain reaction of havoc to U.S. domestic air transport, for which Denver is a major nexus. Yet this most forbidding of mountain ranges provided, in the summer of 1948, the setting for some curiously rarefied artistic experiences. The Stravinsky concert with the Denver Symphony Orchestra (the Capriccio plus the usual amalgam of Glinka, Tchaikovsky, and Tchaikovsky *à la* Stravinsky) took place on the 23rd of July in an open-air theatre called Red Rocks, in the foothills twenty miles west of the city; and after rehearsing there in scorching July heat the day before the concert, they drove on to the old gold-mining town of Central City for *Così fan tutte* in the town's unexpected Victorian opera house—perhaps Stravinsky's first orchestral encounter with what Craft calls his "favorite opera of the time."[35] Finally, at the university at Boulder, there was Virgil Thomson's opera about Susan B. Anthony, *The Mother of Us All,* with its consciously naïve, repetitious setting of Gertrude Stein. Stravinsky loathed every reduplicated minute but could not leave because Thomson himself—a friend and an influential critic—was present. On the other hand, Soulima's wife, Françoise, a sophisticated Frenchwoman with little taste for the *faux-naïf,* became convulsed with mirth and was forced to make a rapid exit.[36]

Though unimpressed by the Rockies, Stravinsky was intrigued by the ethnic impedimenta of old America, and it may partly have been the native art in the Denver Museum, intermingling with his memories of peasant Russia, that prompted him to insist that instead of coming straight to Hollywood, Craft should go by train to Mexico City, study the villages and the baroque churches, then fly on to Los Angeles the following week.[37] Craft thus reached North Wetherly Drive only on the 30th, three days after his hosts, and he missed the spectacle of Stravinsky fidgeting to escape from another, very different musical agony: Mahler's Eighth Symphony conducted in the Hollywood Bowl by Eugene Ormandy. Just as it was important not to offend Thomson, so it was hard to evade the hospitality of the Bowl, especially since Stravinsky had attended a dinner given by Ormandy in honor of Mahler's widow only three weeks before. As distinguished guests, the Stravinskys would be seated prominently near the front of the amphitheater, so that discreet departure was out of the question. Igor would shuffle and mutter and Vera would whisper sharply in Russian that they *could not leave.* No wonder Stravinsky rechristened the composer "malheur." His attitude to such music is one of many possible starting points for an understanding of his own.[38]

Craft stayed for ten days, sleeping on the "Procrustes" couch, mentally photographing the house and studio, and lunching or dining out with various members of the Stravinsky circle: with Babitz and Dahl; Eugene Berman; the flamboyant Anglo-Catholic priest James McLane; the composer's favorite West Coast doctor, Maximilian Edel; and naturally with the Soulima Stravinskys and the Marions, whose new idea of buying a restaurant may well have been discussed in his presence. Igor and Vera took him to the Farmers' Market and the Forest Lawn Memorial Park—the original of Evelyn Waugh's Whispering Glades in *The Loved One,* which the composer had already read in *Horizon* and admired.[39] Stravinsky played Craft his Mass, and what existed of the *Rake,* on one of the out-of-tune pianos in the studio, groping for the chords and gesturing for Craft to help with notes that were beyond his stretch. Craft was struck by what he saw as Stravinsky's complete lack of indolence, and astonished to realize that the sixty-six-year-old Master needed the reassurance of his twenty-four-year-old guest's praise. He also noticed that the bookshelves were dominated by Russian and French literature, including a ninety-eight-volume set of Voltaire. He must have commented on this, because within forty-eight hours he had been whisked off to the Pickwick Book Store with a blank check and an instruction to restock the shelves with books in English, the exact selection, of course, being left to him.[40] Then on the 9th of August he flew back to New York, conscious of having "sat at the feet of a man whose horizons were broader and further away than those of other men,"[41] even if they did still need broadening in one or two respects. He had a new plan for a Town Hall concert the following February, in which Stravinsky had agreed to conduct the premiere of the Mass.

Stravinsky had been in touch with Hawkes about this particular scheme while Craft was in Hollywood. He was trying to insist on a New York premiere under his own direction because of the unusual problems the work presented, problems of vocal color and articulation, since the kind of choir envisaged was not the average choral society that might attempt the *Symphony of Psalms* but rather a superior church choir or large vocal consort, preferably with children's voices or a very light, vibratoless female timbre, a type of choir that would never before have sung any Stravinsky. In effect he was urging the publisher to forgo immediate profit by declining earlier performances, so that the composer could, as he put it, "establish *my own tradition.*"[42] Not surprisingly, Hawkes was evasive. There had been enquiries, as Stravinsky had indicated to Craft, from choirs in New York and Washington, neither of whom fitted his mental image of the work's sound, and now there was a proposal from Ansermet to conduct it in Milan in the autumn. Hawkes seems to have argued (his letter is lost) that such a premiere would not harm Stravinsky's priority. But Stravinsky was trying and failing to imagine what his austere liturgy would sound like in the sumptuously profane surroundings of La Scala, and perhaps at the same time trying to reconcile its cool objectivity with Ansermet's self-centered lucubrations on phenomenology and the "essential points which we do not approach in the same way."43 He did not succeed; but nor did he manage to prevent the performance.

Ansermet duly gave the premiere as part of an orchestral concert, alongside Mozart's late E-flat symphony, Malipiero's Third, and Debussy's *Iberia,* on the Scala stage on the 27th of October, under conditions that were much as Stravinsky had feared. The chorus was more than a hundred strong with, of course, women sopranos and altos, and the conductor himself admitted that while he could teach them the notes, after years of *Aida* the austere church style was beyond them.44 In other words they sang it like opera, full-throatedly and vibrantly, *con passione.* It was just as hard to teach motet manners to the audience and the press. The occasion was like an opera gala, and after the Stravinsky there were cheers answered by hissing. As for the critics, they seemed at a loss to account for the music's curious reversion to a medieval style. One of them referred to its "impudent modernism," and detected "a certain flavor of jest, something between the ironic and the balletic."45 Stravinsky's old friend Domenico de' Paoli described it, confusingly, as "a work of humility and submission and diabolical pride."46 But there was nothing from Ansermet himself for almost a month, and when it came it proved, Stravinsky told Craft,

> a very empty letter, indeed, excuses for writing so late, not a word, of course, about his personal reaction to the work (neither about that of the public). The only thing he said was: "singers, instrumentalists and the conductor did their best" [*sic*]. How very kind of them!47

Craft's own departure in August had left a hole in Wetherly Drive life which for various reasons Stravinsky's children were unable or unwilling to fill. Soulima, wisely and deliberately, was building a career for himself and was careful not to get drawn into the ferocious vortex of his father's work. True, he had concerts in Los Angeles that depended more or less on the family connection. He gave a solo recital for the Evenings on the Roof, then a week later, in early October, took part in a Roof Stravinsky evening in the Wilshire Ebell Theatre, a concert which for some reason his father did not attend.48 No doubt even his New York broadcast of Mozart's C major piano concerto (K. 503) the previous month was entirely due to Igor's Columbia connections, and it must have been clear to him that he would soon have to cut the umbilical cord, whatever the consequences. As for the Marions, they were still bouncing from one project to the next: from the restaurant to a sweetshop, from the sweetshop to a French delicatessen—each one as dependent as the next on some kind of financial input from Milène's father. From Igor's point of view, they were a presence that was as disturbing in one respect as it was delightful in another. Not for a minute would he have withdrawn his support or encouragement; but from the point of view of his own work, they were for the time being undeniably somewhat of a distraction.

The fact that something was lacking is painfully evident in his correspondence with Craft that autumn. "Yes, am glad to hear from you," he wrote on one occasion, "for I too miss you greatly. Please, do come at Christmas, please, please! Please answer YES."[49] His letters now begin "Dearest Bob" and close with "Love" or "Love-Kisses," a formula that Stravinsky must have realized carried more impact than its conventional Russian equivalent, *obnimayu* (I embrace [you]). The more elaborate effusions are admittedly quite rare amid the barrage of commissions that is the real content and purpose of the letters. But it would be a great mistake to interpret the shows of affection as in some way distinct from—or an emollient to—the use to which the competent young man was unashamedly being put. On the contrary, it is precisely in the trust he places in Craft that Stravinsky's affection comes out most forcibly, implying as it does a complete confidence in his ability to act as he himself would act, to understand the relative importance of this or that concern, and above all to do so on the basis of a deep knowledge of the central fact of the music. While Soulima the musician-son was backing away from the vortex, Craft the musician-arriviste seemed to be welcoming it, revelling in it, and to all outward appearances able to survive in it. In view of Stravinsky's deep self-centeredness, this contrast is quite enough to explain the difficult family situation that gradually began to develop—a situation which Stravinsky should have foreseen but certainly did not will, and which eventually came close to destroying all but the central character of the drama himself.

There were so many things in his life that needed the on-the-spot attention of an efficient and loving slave. That autumn there were plans for Craft's own concerts, including *Mavra* at the end of December and the Mass (to be conducted by the composer) at the end of February; there was Soulima to meet at the airport and see safely to his rehearsals for the Mozart concerto and the performance itself; there was Boosey and Hawkes to keep in order over the publication of the Mass and the small matter of their printed list of his works. "Enclosed," he wrote to Craft, a new nonsense from B & H which they probably call *catalogue*. Even as a proof it is not acceptable. In order to avoid writing them a letter with high words which they deserve, please explain them, as you can, their utmost stupidity and neglect. You will be an Angel![50]

Craft could indeed be tactful in such matters; and he could also explain gently to Minna Lederman, the editor of *Modern Music*, why Stravinsky preferred not to have his new opera, still largely unwritten, discussed in her forthcoming anthology of essays on his theatre music, however desirable this might seem to everyone else.[51]

Finally, the young man had become a crucial go-between in Stravinsky's difficult relations with the recording industry. For a year or more the composer had been grumbling about Columbia's failure to release all the recordings he had made for them, but now the dagger was being twisted in his breast by another strike in the industry, this time caused by a dispute over union welfare funds. Early in June 1948, he wrote abusively to Lieberson disputing his claim that the releases were being blocked by his superiors, and Lieberson was so incensed that he in as many words invited Stravinsky to take his problems to RCA Victor and leave them there.[52] Stravinsky had chosen a bad moment to pick a quarrel with Columbia, who, that very spring, had announced their revolutionary new LP (33 rpm) records but were still by no means certain of winning a marketing war against RCA Victor's 45 rpm extended-play discs. Lieberson did not hesitate to remind the Master that his recent works had not exactly burnt themselves into the popular consciousness. So it seemed just as well that *Orpheus* and the Mass were booked to be recorded in February 1949 by RCA. Then in October, with the strike still not settled, Stravinsky's RCA producer, Dick Gilbert, blithely informed him that he had moved over to Columbia.[53] The composer made the best of it. "I am very pleased," he told Gilbert pointedly, "to find myself a good friend at Columbia."[54] It was no less pleasant, though, to have someone as well-informed, not to say personally involved, as Craft to negotiate face to face with Gilbert's successor, Richard A. Mohr, over such awkward matters as side-breaks and numbers of recording sessions, in which his authority as a musician might be seen as outweighing his lack of direct practical experience.

JUST AT this moment, when Stravinsky was discovering for the first time the joys of a reliable organizer, nemesis struck down one of his last and least reliable. For some years now, Alexis Kall had been an infrequent visitor to North Wetherly Drive, partly because of his own poor health since his leg amputation, partly no doubt because of Vera's impatience with his drinking habits. But on his seventieth birthday this last February the Stravinskys had risen to the occasion and dispatched a congratulatory telegram. To be exact what they sent was a night letter, but that was out of consideration for his finances rather than theirs, since they sent it collect. "Dearest Woof, too bad not to be present on your birthday celebration. We wish you many happy returns . . ."[55]

It was to be their penultimate gesture, and there were no returns. On the 7th of September 1948, Kall died, and three days later they attended his funeral.

16

A FAMILY HAPPY IN ITS OWN WAY ■

SINCE ROBERT CRAFT's return to New York in August 1948, Stravinsky had been working away quietly on the first act of the *Rake*. By early October the first scene was finished and he was starting the Brothel scene, with its coded religious imagery and somewhat less veiled allusions to the street life of Hogarth's London. But progress, though steady, was slower than he (and above all his publisher) would have liked.[1] Hawkes was already pondering the venue for the first performance before the opening scene was written, and while he was dreaming of Covent Garden, the composer was held up by the need for an extra verse of poetry in the second chorus of Roaring Boys and Whores.[2] Auden was proving brilliantly adept at manufacturing additional or variant text. Nevertheless the opera's composition stretched away into a dark and uncertain future, and Stravinsky may already have been half-regretting the commitment it entailed. On the 15th of October he wrote to Hawkes ruling out a European tour until the opera was finished, which he knew would be at least two years hence.[3]

To say that the work was giving him stylistic anxieties would probably be an exaggeration, but there is evidence that the subject matter and the kind of text Auden and Kallman had matched to it were between them taking him along musical paths somewhat different from those he imagined when he first conceived the idea. From the start his prime model had been Mozart; he had requested Mozart operas in score and was taking every opportunity to see and hear them onstage, and Craft dutifully told Auden that what had so far been written (in August) was "very Mozartian."[4] But that was at best a half-truth. For one thing, end-rhyme in English is by its nature more obtrusive than in Italian (whose inflected vowel-endings are naturally recurrent); and for another thing, Auden was sometimes modelling himself on a style much closer to the popular verse in *The Beggar's Opera* than to anything in da Ponte. In such cases the challenge for Stravinsky was to avoid falling into the kind of four-square jog-trot that bedevils that epoch-making but musically trivial work, and to do so by dodging what are in part linguistic traps in a language with which he was no more than half-familiar. The problem is already apparent in Tom's first aria, "Since it is not by merit," with its consciously Augustan patterning, but it intensifies in the second scene, where Mother Goose's entourage naturally express themselves in doggerel, albeit of a subtle, even elegant variety. At these points, the music had to preserve a demotic tone without lapsing into coarseness or naïveté. By an odd coincidence, Craft was this very autumn preparing a New York concert performance of Stravinsky's one earlier opera whose text in some ways foreshadowed Auden's stylizations, his Pushkin one-acter, *Mavra*. The difference was that in 1922, with *Mavra*, the whole idea of modelling had been new and surprising, whereas by the time of the *Rake* it was what Stravinsky's audience (including perhaps his librettists) had come to expect. So there was a conceivable danger that the new opera would slip into a comfortable rut of the predictable: updated ballad opera with Mozartian attachments.

Stravinsky did not discuss such matters, certainly not in letters. But he knew that his recent music was regarded in some quarters as old-fashioned, head-in-the-sand, or worse, and not only by a handful of student modernists in liberated Paris. Nicolas Nabokov had replied to Leibowitz's poisonous article in *Partisan Review*, but not all that convincingly, and as always in such cases the reply had given Leibowitz a second platform on which to reinforce his accusations. "The fact," he remarked smugly, "that a theoretical defense of a composer who betrays a total creative impotence turns out to be equally impotent [. . .] is not astonishing."[5] It would certainly have been wiser to leave Leibowitz's attack to gather dust in those relatively little-read left-wing pages. But a much more dangerous adversary was at this precise moment bringing out, in Germany, a book-length demolition of the whole basis of Stravinskian aesthetics that would transfer the arguments from the murky depths of the analysis class to the sunlit uplands of philosophy, psychology, and political sociology. To what extent Stravinsky was aware of Theodor W. Adorno's *Philosophie der neuen Musik* at the time of its publication in Frankfurt at the end of 1948 is hard to establish; but he certainly knew Adorno's name, not only as that of a critic on the Berlin *Neue Musik Zeitung* at the time of the Kroll *Oedipus Rex* in 1928,[6] but also probably as a friend of Thomas Mann's in Los Angeles in the forties. Stravinsky had met the novelist from time to time since the end of the war, and Mann had adapted certain of Stravinsky's childhood memories from the *Chroniques* for Adrian Leverkühn, the composer-hero of his recent novel *Doctor Faustus*.[7] Adorno's connection with *Doctor Faustus* was much closer, since he had provided Mann with the technical information about Schoenberg's twelve-note method that had formed the basis of Leverkühn's compositional "system."

Like Leibowitz, but for somewhat different reasons, Adorno regarded

Schoenberg as the model of a true progressive. He would not necessarily have agreed with Mann's diagnosis of the "system" as the product of a diabolical possession, but he did regard its difficult or disagreeable aspects—its atonal harmonies and impenetrable textures—as an inevitable reflection of the violence and confusion of the modern world. Above all, he saw in Schoenberg's evolution an honest and authentic response to the historic needs of individual expression through music. By contrast, he launches a comprehensive, psychologically based attack on Stravinsky and all his works, accusing him in Freudian terms of regression and infantilism, of a pseudo-primitivism masking a sadomasochistic "joy in self-denial," of a reactionary anti-individualism that "sneers at the tradition of humanistic art" and "does not identify with the victim [in *Petrushka*], but rather with the destructive element." Everything in his music is dismissed as inauthentic. Neoclassicism is simply "traditional music combed in the wrong direction." Even expression, which Stravinsky himself had claimed to reject, is here and there tolerated by his music, "so long as it is no longer true expression, but merely the death-mask thereof." As for the borrowed styles, they "pay for their accessibility not by revealing the true nature of form, but by hovering meaninglessly over the surface of aesthetic form." "The will to style replaces style itself and therewith sabotages it." And as with regressive tendencies in Freud, the primary impulse is fear. It is out of fear that Stravinsky "spares himself the tormenting self-animation of the material" and thus arrives at "the aesthetic transfiguration of the reflective character of present-day man. . . .

> His neo-classicism fashions images of Oedipus and Persephone, but the employed myth has already become the metaphysics of the universally dependent, who neither want nor need metaphysics. They mock the very principle thereof. Therewith objectivism designates itself as that which it fears and the proclamation of which constitutes its entire content.[8]

Much of what Adorno says about Stravinsky strikes one as true, or at least plausible, and the one (admittedly all-embracing) disaster of the whole critique—apart from its notoriously impenetrable prose—is its unremitting hostility. Stravinsky was no doubt "regressive," "anal," and artistically self-denying. That fear and insecurity lay behind many of his aesthetic (and indeed social) attitudes can hardly be gainsaid. Yet out of this "psychosis"—as Adorno would have called it—he created a body of work that has enriched countless lives and continues to do so more than thirty years after his and Adorno's deaths. Adorno, of course, knew perfectly well that this would be the case. In essence, his attack on Stravinsky is an attack on the whole of modern bourgeois culture, to which he saw Stravinsky's music as subservient, while Schoenberg's music alone had resisted commodification and the marketplace, and achieved a kind of negative virtue "more by its denial of any meaning in organized society, of which it will have no part, [. . .] than by any capability of positive meaning within itself." The fatuity of this remark as a critical judgment from within "organized society" has not prevented Adorno from exerting an overpowering influence on postwar German cultural thought and, more recently, the cultural philosophy programs of Anglo-American universities. But it does also partly explain why the whole shooting match was rejected out of hand by its nominal winner. "So modern music has a philosophy," Schoenberg wrote to the German critic Hans Heinz Stuckenschmidt.

> It would be enough if it had a philosopher. He attacks me quite vehemently in it. Another disloyal person. . . . I have never been able to bear the fellow . . . now I know that he has clearly never liked my music. . . . It is disgusting, by the way, how he treats Stravinsky. I am certainly no admirer of Stravinsky, although I like a piece of his here and there very much—but one should not write like that.[9]

A few months later, in April 1949, Stuckenschmidt was in Los Angeles, and, after lunching with Mann, called on Schoenberg in Brentwood Park and later took George Antheil and his wife to dine there. Mann had warned him not to refer to the lunch, and *Faustus* was not mentioned. What surprised the visitor more was that a few days later Stravinsky invited him to tea at North Wetherly Drive and specifically asked after Schoenberg. He admired Schoenberg, he said, and regretted that they met only occasionally "in a third place," a fact that he attributed to the influence of "the ladies."[10] The picture is irresistible of the two great composers pulling down their hats, turning up their collars, and sloping off without their wives' knowledge for clandestine meetings in Joe's Cafe. Alas, Stravinsky was being either polite or self-exculpatory in the presence of a guest he knew to be a true friend and admirer of Schoenberg's. As for Adorno, it seems unlikely that his name came up in either house.

Nobody gave Stravinsky Adorno's book for Christmas in 1948, and instead he had to make do with a slim volume that his own Theodore had been writing about his music under the title *Le Message d'Igor Strawinsky*. It was a book that started no arguments and studiously avoided depth psychology, but it pleased its subject, partly because it reflected closely his own attitudes to his work, partly out of simple fatherly pride. It was, he told Theodore, the first book about his music ("and there have been plenty") that entirely satisfied him. "If you only knew what rubbish has gone into print about me," he wrote,

> But I like your book not because it's an apologia (Tansman's is also an apologia, but God, what a bore, unintelligent and unconvincing; poor Tansman is expecting a letter from me about it, but what can I say?), but above all because your apologia has an entirely solid basis, both ethically and aesthetically.[11]

"FATHER WILL PLAY Rake's score to you and Auden, *nobody* else," Soulima wrote to Craft on the 23rd of January 1949. "So keep it in absolute secret, don't tell anybody (even Rieti or Nabokoff, for instance) anything that can reveal it."[12] Stravinsky had at last completed the draft score of Act 1 on the 16th, and a week later he and Vera set off for the East Coast by way of Houston, where he was conducting on the 31st. They finally steamed into Penn Station early on the 3rd of February, and that same evening the composer played the first act through at the apartment of the violinist Alexander Schneider.

Somehow Nabokov had found out and was there with his wife, Patricia, as well as Balanchine, Auden, and Craft, who did his best to turn the pages of the draft score while Stravinsky groaned out the vocal parts. The atmosphere was tense. In recent years Stravinsky had lost the habit of such tryouts, disliked the presence of outsiders, and was irritated by Auden's non-musician's way of talking during the performance. Yet when the librettist proposed that Anne be allowed to take a high C at the end of her cabaletta, Stravinsky's sole objection was that the vowel was wrong, whereupon Auden promptly wrote something more singable.[13]

At this juncture, New York was no more than a staging post on a curiously parochial conducting tour Stravinsky had fixed with the Boston Symphony Orchestra, starting in Cambridge on 8 February, then taking in Boston itself and, after a repeat performance in Carnegie Hall, striking out beyond Manhattan to Newark and Brooklyn. Thanks to Koussevitzky's influence, the repertoire for these concerts was more uncompromising than often of late. Soulima had been engaged, at his father's urging,[14] to play the Capriccio and Piano Concerto, and there were also the first concert performances of *Orpheus,* together with the *Ode* and the Basle concerto. As a matter of routine, Craft travelled with them, and he not only participated in their socializing but was even beginning to exercise some influence on it. For instance, he seems to have decided that it would be fun for the Stravinskys to meet Evelyn Waugh, since they had expressed enthusiasm for his books; and he had accordingly—with a touch of the same bravado that had taken him to the Stravinskys' door in the first place—arranged for the three of them to dine with the novelist and his wife, Laura, the day after their arrival in New York.[15]

It was an early example of those faintly contrived Meetings of the Great that pepper Craft's diaries and that one often suspects of having been arranged at his suggestion and for his benefit. His account of the dinner is brilliant and convincing. Waugh showed not the slightest sign of being intimidated by his famous and twenty-years-older host, but typically sought to exert control by rejecting courtesies: he refused any aperitif, denied conversational ability in French, denounced the U.S. Constitution, and expressed interest only in American methods of burial, while claiming (untruthfully, of course) that he himself had "arranged to be buried at sea." At dinner, in a small and crowded Italian restaurant, Stravinsky tried politely to relate his own recent work to the theme of Waugh's lecture tour (the Catholic writers Chesterton, Ronald Knox, and Graham Greene) by describing his Mass and inviting the couple to the forthcoming performance. To this the novelist's deathless—and alas characteristic—response was "All music is positively painful to me."[16]

Once the Boston Symphony tour was out of the way, rehearsals began in earnest for the Mass concert in Town Hall on the 26th of February. Craft had managed to find at the Church of the Blessed Sacrament that New York rarity, a choir with boy trebles to sing the new work, and had also booked Soulima to play his father's solo sonata and the double concerto with Beveridge Webster. Although Stravinsky was conducting the Mass, Craft took some of the rehearsals, and the schedule was punishing. In the four days before the concert, Stravinsky was recording *Orpheus* and the Mass under his contract with RCA, together with his unaccompanied settings of the Lord's Prayer and the Ave Maria in new Latin versions made specially for the Town Hall concert (but with the same Catholic intention as the Mass) and sung by a small and slightly squeaky adult chorus prepared by Robert Shaw.[17]

Despite these pressures, the concert went well enough, and Stravinsky was able to feel vindicated in his insistence on children's voices in the Mass, even if, as he reported to Nadia Boulanger, "they were not quite first-rate, [since] unlike in Europe, there is no tradition here of choir schools for discanti and alti. I had to opt for children, nevertheless, as the presence of women, however perfect, in the music of my Mass would be a much more serious mistake (for the sense and spirit of this music) than the imperfection of a chorus of children."[18] As leavening for the musical items, Auden stepped up and read three of his poems, including the subtle and intricate and, in some of its byways, curiously Stravinskian "In Praise of Limestone":

Not to lose time, not to get caught,
Not to be left behind, not, please! to resemble
The beasts who repeat themselves, or a thing like water
Or stone whose conduct can be predicted, these
Are our Common Prayer, whose greatest comfort is music
Which can be made anywhere, is invisible,
And does not smell.[19]

The poet fidgeted nervously as he read, twice wiped his nose on his cuff, but gripped the audience's attention, Craft noted, "by sheer force of intellect."[20] Then Stravinsky, ignoring the stern injunction about the beasts, conducted the Mass twice, just as he had repeated the *Symphonies* in the same hall the previous year.

It was no secret, of course, that Stravinsky and Auden were working on an opera together. Yet it was impossible to imagine, from the intriguing miscellany of this concert, what on earth it would be like. Auden's poetry, though suggestive of musical ideas, was hardly such as could actually be set to music, while the austere incantations of the Mass were miles from any normal person's image of the operatic, as Stravinsky had been quick to point out when confronted with Ansermet's Milan premiere. The privileged few who had heard the run-through of the *Rake* at Schneider's three weeks before might have picked up a resonance of the opera's first scene, with its tendrils of what would eventually be oboe and bassoon sound, just as in the Mass. They might even have been aware of a dawning element of redemptive ceremony in Tom and Anne's opening duet. But comparison would have ended there. The Mass certainly did sow important seeds for Stravinsky, but they were not on the whole seeds that would germinate under greasepaint or in the glare of footlights. For the time being the work came to rest in the shape of a neoclassical medievalism, a mixture no more bizarre, perhaps, but also not obviously more forward-looking than the neoclassical commercialism of the works that had immediately preceded it.

Leaving New York by train at the end of February, the Stravinskys crisscrossed America on their way home, stopping for "wonderful concerts" in Urbana and, once again, Denver.[21] Soulima was with them, and he played the piano concerto with real success in both cities. Craft stayed behind in New York. He had concerts of his own planned, including an April *Les Noces* and further performances of the Mass, but he would be coming to Hollywood in June, this time for three full months, to begin the task of sorting and identifying the contents of several large boxes of manuscripts that had at last arrived from the bank vault in Paris, where they had been gathering dust for the past ten years.[22]

By quitting New York when he did, Stravinsky narrowly missed getting involved with a much-publicized official visit to the city by a seven-man delegation from the Soviet Union to what was grandly called the First Cultural and Scientific Congress for World Peace. On the 13th of March Olin Downes wired him in Hollywood asking him to add his name to an open telegram from American musicians specifically welcoming the composer Shostakovich to the United States as a member of the delegation. But Stravinsky was unimpressed by Downes's arguments about "symbolizing the bond which music can create among all peoples," and he wired back that "all my ethic and esthetic convictions oppose such gesture." A few days later, when asked by a West Coast reporter if he would take part in a debate with Shostakovich, he retorted: "How can you talk to them? They are not free. There is no discussion possible with people who are not free."[23]

This dignified response was less straightforward than it seemed. Stravinsky had known all about the Peace Congress from Nicolas Nabokov, who was organizing an action group to oppose the propaganda of the Soviet delegation, and had already enlisted Stravinsky as a member of his "international" sponsorship committee.[24] When a speech allegedly by Shostakovich was read out by an interpreter, in his presence, to a large audience in the Waldorf-Astoria Hotel on 26 March, condemning Western music in general as decadent and bourgeois, and Stravinsky in particular as having "betrayed his native land and severed himself from his people by joining the camp of reactionary modern musicians,"[25] it was Nabokov who stood up and asked Shostakovich if he agreed personally with Soviet denunciations of Stravinsky, Schoenberg, and Hindemith, whereupon Shostakovich "was handed a microphone, and, looking down at the floor, said in Russian: 'I fully agree with the statements made in *Pravda.*' "[26] But Shostakovich's role in this charade was in any case of secondary importance. Like all White Russians in postwar America, Stravinsky had long since made his choice, and he was certainly not going to jeopardize his hard-won status as a loyal American by the slightest appearance of supporting a pro-Communist propaganda exercise. On this point, the lawyer Sapiro had given him firm advice at the time of the Eisler case two years before; and it was Sapiro again who drew a line under the Waldorf affair by issuing a press release that Stravinsky had decided "that public controversy is not his field; and that he should refrain from the unnecessary continuation of such controversies."[27]

At North Wetherly Drive there now began a long period of calm, during which Stravinsky had no conducting engagements except for a single production of *The Soldier's Tale* at UCLA in June. He worked on the second act of the *Rake* in an atmosphere as near as he had yet come, in America, to the *coeur du foyer*—the bosom of the family—that had meant so much to him in prewar France. André Marion had for the time being given up "enterprise," and was working as his father-in-law's secretary. Soulima gave occasional concerts, and was meanwhile completing a ballet based, *Pulcinella*-fashion, on the keyboard sonatas of Domenico Scarlatti. Theodore, in far-off Switzerland, was being employed—on a twenty percent commission—as agent for the sale of certain of his father's manuscripts, picked out from the boxes that had gone to Hollywood. Now and then, however, these apparently smooth waters were ruffled by gusts of emotion. Early in April, news came of the death of Igor's oldest friend, Valechka Nouvel, who had long been living in something close to destitution in Paris. "His death," the composer told Theodore, "didn't surprise us . . . and upsets me less than his life in recent years—that slow, agonizing process of decline, both physical and, I think, mental."[28] Meanwhile, poor Madubo, having fallen out with the Marions, had moved in with the Soulimas in Holloway Drive and was now engaged in a battle of wills with the sweet-tempered but strong-minded Françoise. One day in April the charge detonated, and Madubo was once more cast into outer darkness.[29] The reasons for this particular quarrel have long vanished into oblivion, but it surely reflected some new aspect of Soulima's problem of subservience. He adored his father and had never, it seemed, escaped the overpowering magnetic force of his will. Now here he was living in a house rented by him, driving a car bought by him, living with a nanny imposed by him, and—the crowning irritant for which Soulima had only himself to blame—writing a ballet that everyone would say was an inferior imitation, based on music that Soulima loved but in which nothing could persuade his father to take any interest.[30]

Craft's arrival on 1 June injected a new and volatile ingredient into this unstable mixture. On the face of it his role was purely professional, though unpaid. He was there to sort manuscripts, a task that called for skills which, of the children, only Soulima remotely possessed but that it would hardly have been possible, in the circumstances, for him to perform.[31] Craft's real position, though, was plainly supra-professional. Both Igor and Vera had already developed an affection for him that went well beyond ordinary friendship and verged at times on the parental. In letters, even where the contents were businesslike, the tone was nearly always noticeably tender. This feeling—as it became apparent—was not resented by the Stravinsky children, but if anything shared. "Everybody here eager to see you soon," the composer wrote with patent sincerity at the end of April.[32] Soulima had good reason to echo such sentiments, knowing the praise that Craft had heaped on his recording of the Piano Concerto, and recalling how charming he and Françoise had found him in New York. Craft, for his part, had liked Soulima from the start, had been touched by his politeness, and felt no sense of competition between them. Soulima, after all, was a pianist, he a conductor; as for any questions of family, they were far from his or anyone else's thoughts.

As before, Craft slept at first in the Procrustean den, but then he moved into the studio, where there was a more comfortable couch on which Stravinsky would himself take his afternoon naps. Both arrangements were purely temporary, however. Soulima had landed a summer job as a piano teacher at the Music Academy of the West in Santa Barbara, and Craft was to move into the Holloway Drive apartment at the start of July. From there each day he would walk the few blocks to 1260 North Wetherly Drive in time for breakfast, and he was always included in its nonstop social and musical life. One day early on, David Diamond came to lunch, and they ate a kulebyaka cooked by Vera and listened to Stravinsky recordings.[33] A week or two later, at the UCLA *Soldier's Tale* in Royce Hall, they ran into Bronislava Nijinska, who had danced in *L'Après-midi d'un faune* and *The Rite of Spring* but had now grown stout and showed her age. There were visits from Koussevitzky and from Ralph Hawkes, who was still energetically plotting a British premiere for the *Rake* and whom Craft found a notably aggressive man; and there were trips to Santa Barbara to see and hear Soulima, and to San Diego, from where they crossed into Mexico for a bullfight at Tijuana, a ceremony that thrilled Stravinsky at least as much as in the old days at Bayonne.[34]

When Craft arrived in June, the Paris manuscripts were still in their boxes on the floor, but he soon had them out on the sitting-room table and began slowly to go through them, listing the finished scores and identifying and cataloguing the sketches. His excitement was intense. For years he had loved Stravinsky's music above any other and had sought out copies of his works at a time when many were out of print or unobtainable. Two years before, he had written to Stravinsky asking him for a copy of the *Symphonies of Wind Instruments,* in vain; now here was the original, calligraphic autograph score, intriguingly marked up in pencil and red ink, an exquisite composition draft, and a whole bundle of sketches more or less clearly traceable to this same work. Here were *Les Noces* in all kinds of fragmentary versions, a composition score of *Oedipus Rex* with the opening pages composed back to front, the autograph vocal score of *Renard* without the opening and closing march, the full score of *The Fairy's Kiss* completed in near-panic at the end of October 1928, less than four weeks before the premiere. Many famous scores were missing, either because Stravinsky had given them away, or because (as with *The Rite of Spring*) their publishers had claimed them, or because they had been left in Europe for sale by Theodore. But there were pages of unidentified, sometimes unidentifiable sketches, and several small leather- or cloth-bound notebooks containing annotations for works of the First War years and just afterwards, sketches whose exact intention Stravinsky had clearly often not immediately known. Some bore titles that hinted at unknown works, like the *Cinq pièces monométriques,* most but not all of which went into the Octet. On one occasion Craft asked Stravinsky to identify a tiny duet for two instruments, but he was unable to remember it, and instead added a punning title on the spot: *Lied ohne Name[n] für zwei Fagotten* [bassoons]—"Song without a name, for I've forgotten [what]."[35]

Stravinsky himself, though he walked past the table several times a day, seemed completely uninterested in the contents of the boxes.[36] It was as if he felt no vestige of nostalgia about these mortal remains of his struggles of the spirit. To him they were a source of income and nothing more, and in those days of postwar austerity and economic neurosis there was little market for any but the most famous or spectacular manuscripts, and of these the most likely were still in Europe. But it went farther than that: he was not even greatly interested in the music itself. His own preoccupation was always with the work he was writing at the time, as he repeatedly told interviewers who asked him to name his favorite among his own works. To an extraordinary extent he was an artist and human being who lived in the present, with neither past nor future. Gabriel Marcel had accused him of lacking "affective memory,"[37] and though Marcel's intention had been hostile, the observation itself was shrewd enough. Above all, Stravinsky had in his own opinion good reason not to wish to revisit his personal history—a history of exile and bereavement, of divided emotions and a family life that, as it receded in time, seemed to take on an ever darker and more menacing color.

The present was both more agreeable and more dependable, and above all it was American. That was where Craft came in: but not only Craft. Russians like Balanchine and Nabokov, Sokolov and the Bolms still played a huge part in the Stravinskys' lives, sometimes just by virtue of being Russians. They all talked more spontaneously and vividly in Russian and could say things in that language—scatological and otherwise—that they could not express in any other, as well as using it as a convenient code for private communications, a habit to which Igor was prone, often in circumstances where it could give offense. But his intellectual focus had shifted away from Russians, and even—now that so many fellow émigrés had gone back or were preparing to go back to Europe—away from the French and the Germans, to newer English friends who, for one reason or another, had settled in California and showed no particular inclination to leave. Such was Aldous Huxley, whom (with his wife, Maria) Craft was able to observe closely when they all dined together one evening in late July; and such also was Christopher Isherwood, who was at the Farmers' Market one August day with the Huxleys, and who came to dinner at North Wetherly Drive ten days later with his lover, the photographer Bill Caskey.

This was the Stravinskys' first encounter with the author of *Goodbye to*

Berlin, and it went well from the start. Isherwood was in many ways like the Christopher of his novels; he was receptive rather than voluble; vital, not cerebral; open to experience: "a camera with its shutter open, quite passive, recording, not thinking."[38] In Isherwood's own opinion, Stravinsky must have found his company relaxing compared to the "chilling" intellectualism of Huxley's, and his "appetite for good wine and liquor and food, his lack of pretense about his sex life and also indeed his preference for a devotional form of religion [. . .] agreeably 'Russian.' "[39] When he and Caskey arrived for dinner on 20 August, Stravinsky greeted them with the suggestion that "we listen to my Mass before we get drunk."[40] On a similar occasion a few months later, Isherwood got drunk without musical preamble, and remembered lying on the floor, gazing up at the very tall, very blind Huxley, who was tactfully ignoring him while he discussed aesthetics with Stravinsky in French.[41]

Just as Craft could talk to Auden, he was at home in the literary and intellectual world of Auden's old friend and former collaborator. He could shine in it. He had read everything Isherwood had published, was hugely articulate, in his nervy, associative way, and his cleverness and encyclopedic knowledge "didn't annoy Christopher, [who] had an entirely different set of pretensions—to intuition, psychological insight, sensibility, etc.—which Bob was prepared to respect."[42] With Huxley it was different. Huxley's conversational form was the monologue, and his erudition was such that even Craft was, by his own frequent admission, silenced. The philosopher-novelist, like Philip Quarles in *Point Counter Point,* could discourse in his unexpectedly squeaky voice on every conceivable subject except (in this company) music: on every aspect of history and anthropology, on the latest findings in microbiology, on linguistics, astronomy, astrology, religion, mythology, and poetry, on the sexual habits of the frog, on techniques for improving the defective vision of the eye and the mind. Stravinsky, according to Craft,[43] valued Huxley as a walking encyclopedia who could save him from hours of futile (if admittedly pleasurable) rummaging through dictionaries and encyclopedias; but Huxley's scientific rationalism consorted ill with the composer's "mystagogic view of human existence,"[44] and when they all went for tea and carrot cake at the Huxley's sub-baronial King's Road residence, Craft thought him intimidated by the Friends-of-the-Earth atmosphere, the London-club separation of wives and husbands, and the absence of hard liquor.[45]

Craft's reports of these encounters, insofar as they are genuinely contemporary,[46] certainly suggest a mild inferiority complex where Huxley was concerned. He as good as admits this in a later note to his diaries (labelled "Postscript 1965" in the original edition of *Dialogues and a Diary,* then disarmingly relabelled "Postscript 1994" in the second edition of *Chronicle of a*

Friendship[47]), but he never corrects the impression that Stravinsky was bewildered by Huxley's personality and cultivated his friendship only out of some mutual attraction of genius, or even simply out of intellectual snobbery. That the two great men met so often, in fact, proves that the attraction was personal, and that intellectual differences did not interfere on that level, any more than they had done between Stravinsky and Valéry or Ocampo. Why else would Vera have telephoned one evening to solicit an invitation, since "they could not bear going to another cinema"?[48] Igor to some extent drew social sustenance from the admiration of the famous, but this was hardly an overt factor with Huxley, whose musical tastes were classical and who had written disparagingly about Stravinsky's music in the twenties. As for Huxley's rationalism, it was tempered (much more than his brother Julian's) by a preoccupation with the paranormal, various brands of hysteria, and "alternative" patterns of thought. "Has anyone ever detested humanity more?" he would ask admiringly about the nineteenth-century German caricaturist and epigrammatist Wilhelm Busch, a hero of Stravinsky's, too.[49] Of course, there was a scientific slant to all this; even the irrational and destructive were phenomena to be studied, and the Devil was of interest precisely because people like Stravinsky believed in him and (presumably) acted on that belief. Yet, as Craft himself observes, Huxley was credulous in his own way and took seriously all kinds of metaphysical quackery and pseudo-science.[50] The difference lay, perhaps, between Stravinsky's instinctive acceptance of the supernatural and Huxley's need to explain it positivistically. But that still left a great deal of common ground for them to explore from their very different starting points.

Throughout the summer, work continued on the second act of the *Rake*. As always, Stravinsky composed in the mornings, closeting himself behind the double doors of his studio, and the evidence of Craft's diaries for this period is that composition was still proving somewhat intractable, since he reports Stravinsky as being usually in a bad mood when he emerged at lunchtime, which in later years was by no means always the case.[51] Matters were not helped by an attack of neuritis in his right arm, which lasted several weeks in July, kept him awake at night, and prevented him from playing the piano—an essential element in his composing method.[52] In the afternoons, he was writing up the full score of the first act, and at such times Craft took over the old family task of reading to him. Craft was also enlisted as correspondence secretary, a duty he either shared with or inherited from André Marion (who in any case took it up again when he left). It was bad luck for André that, so soon after assuming this function, he should be displaced by an American who could write fluently and was familiar with the musical world with which the bulk of the correspondence was concerned. This was the first sign that the newcomer might interpose himself, intentionally or otherwise, between Stravinsky and his family, and it unfortunately happened just at a time when André, having cast about unsuccessfully for a livelihood, was finding his feet and making himself useful to his loving but despotic father-in-law. Not that the secretarial role was in itself agreeable. The post came early, and Stravinsky expected to deal with it before starting composition, a fact which made him impatient and sometimes ill-tempered. Craft came to dread this part of the day, and he soon understood why Vera would prefer to have breakfast and go out in the car rather than face the sour expression and unreasonable resentments of her consort.[53]

Exactly how Craft coped with these moods is far from clear. That he was at first sometimes upset by them is hardly surprising. Once, when the phone rang, he failed to reach it before Stravinsky emerged in a fury from his studio, shouting for it to be answered *immediately*. It was the first time that he had spoken sharply to his new young assistant, and the shock was such that Craft walked out of the front door and would have left for good if Vera had not talked him into staying. On another, later, occasion, Vera sent him into the studio with a message and, after knocking, he entered tremulously to find the Master praying in front of his personal icon. This time there was no open expression of anger, but Craft was made to feel that he had trespassed on sacred ground, had broken some fundamental law of the household. Noise and physical interruption were the twin prohibitions of the Stravinsky studio. "He notices," Craft recorded in his journal, "noises heard by no one else."[54] As for the day-to-day sounds dreaded by all working musicians, like pneumatic drills or the tinkling ice-cream vans of summer afternoons, such things were torture to him, and it was because of the inevitability of these intrusions in a city like Los Angeles that he always composed with his studio windows shut, even in the hottest July weather.[55]

At the start of September, after the Tijuana *corrida*, Craft flew back to New York, but he left, now, unwillingly and with a lump in his throat. Vera took him to the Greyhound bus terminal, but after she had driven away his courage failed him; claiming to have lost his bus ticket, he pursued her back to North Wetherly Drive in a taxi, and it was only the following evening, the 6th, that he could finally bring himself to leave Los Angeles by plane.[56] Stravinsky had just been composing Anne's arioso in the second scene of Act 2: "O heart be stronger . . . No step in fear shall wander, nor in weakness delay." A few weeks later, he was once again in difficulties, this time with the scene in which Baba, from her sedan chair, continually interrupts Anne and Tom's duet of lost love. Baba was supposed to interject spoken lines, but Stravinsky found it impossible to integrate these into the duet without risking the music becoming drowned by audience laughter. So instead, he asked Auden to supply verse lines for Baba to sing, thereby turning the duet into a trio.[57] Once more, Auden obliged without hesitation, and Stravinsky then rapidly composed the ensemble that was to remain both musically and psychologically the most intricate and sustained movement in the whole opera. At the trio's climax, where Anne, forever abandoned, "exits hurriedly," Stravinsky achieved a superb dramatic irony by attaching the empty shell of Tom's "love" for Baba to a stately but unfeeling Chaconne, culminating in the ludicrous *coup de théâtre* of her unveiling.

At this point he must at last have felt in control of his stylistic means, whatever the anxieties of the preceding year. The scene resembles the Act I finale of *Don Giovanni* in its integration of formal dance elements with a dramatic situation that is in part ceremonious, in part chaotic, and in part absurd, and like a typical Mozart finale it abandons the so-called *secco* recitative (with keyboard) that elsewhere provides the conversational interludes between arias and ensembles, in favor of a continuous musical montage that propels the action swiftly to its climax.[58] Whether in writing this music he was in any sense conscious of a summing-up after thirty years of what he would still have refused to call "neoclassicism" is a moot point. Conscious of his models he undoubtedly was, and conscious, too, that the process was essentially the same (though the models were different) as in the key works of the start of that whole phase, *Pulcinella* and especially *Mavra*. But there are no open letters about the *Rake*, no apostrophes to Mozart at the expense of later music, and certainly no attempt to "locate" the opera in relation to public expectation, as in his article on Tchaikovsky which *Figaro* had published just before the premiere of *Mavra* in 1922.[59] There is perhaps some tension in the *Rake* between what might be thought of as the "automatic" aspects of neoclassical writing and the perennial need to master what had never ceased to be difficult techniques, to write well, as Maritain would have put it; but these are private, workshop matters. The progress of the *Rake*— as everybody including the composer joked *ad nauseam*—was a progress toward the mastering of, rather than by, the classical simplicity and elegance that had been its inspiration. And this is perhaps why the music increases in density as it goes along, and why in the end the final act would turn out appreciably the longest and most involved of the three.

CRAFT HAD ORGANIZED no fewer than three major concerts with his Chamber Arts Society in New York that autumn, including a string of difficult Stravinsky rarities—*Renard, Persephone,* and the U.S. premieres of *Zvezdoliki* and the complete *Pulcinella;* and since Stravinsky's friends had always kept him informed about East Coast performances of his music, they naturally reported to him on the Craft concerts. It was known, of course, that the young conductor was on more than visiting terms with the composer, and—whether or not for this reason—many of the reports were favorable. Auden risked a reservation about the voices in *Renard* ("a bit frightened"[60]); the critic and composer Arthur Berger, whom Stravinsky regarded as a good friend of his music and a supporter of Craft, complained in his *Tribune* review that the *Persephone* concert on the 21st of November had stretched the young conductor beyond his abilities.[61] More painfully than either of these, Vittorio Rieti at first delayed writing at all, then wrote mainly in praise of Balanchine's "overwhelming" new production of *Firebird,* and added simply: "I'm sorry that I can't be as enthusiastic about Craft's work in his last two concerts; and that's why I didn't write."[62] Pressed by Stravinsky, he elaborated: everything had been rigorous but lacking in vitality. *Renard,* in particular, was "dead." As for Berg's *Chamber Concerto,* it had seemed interminable, people had walked out, Craft had carried on relentlessly, then the music had suddenly stopped and nobody had known if it was over or not.[63]

It was curious how things went in symmetry. Less than three months before, Soulima's Scarlatti ballet *(The Mute Wife)* had been played in New York to a uniformly mediocre press and it had been Craft who had found himself writing tactfully to Soulima's father.[64] Now Soulima was wanting to leave the West Coast altogether and try to establish himself in New York, while Craft could hardly wait to cut his ties with Manhattan and move to the West Coast for good. After his October concert he flew back to Los Angeles for a week. Then in mid-December, after conducting concert performances of *Mavra* and Monteverdi's *Orfeo,* he disbanded the Chamber Arts Society and headed west by bus, at almost precisely the moment that Soulima, Françoise, and little Zizi left Hollywood for New York.

It seems doubtful whether Igor Stravinsky understood this as the simple changing of places that it can easily seem in retrospect. He knew why Soulima wanted to leave, but he did not approve and probably never altogether forgave what he saw as a betrayal.[65] Craft, on the other hand, he needed for reasons that had nothing much to do with family and everything to do with music. Yet in filling one gap, Craft almost inevitably filled several others. He became "family" in a different, perhaps more functional sense, but he displaced nobody, until the accumulation of circumstances presented him with what amounted to a *fait accompli,* by which time it was too late to resist.

17

DEATH OF A PROPHET ▄

ALTHOUGH STRAVINSKY was his great love, Robert Craft was also a keen student of Schoenberg and the Second Viennese School, of certain other (preferably unfashionable) strains of twentieth-century music, and of all kinds of so-called early music, especially of the late renaissance and early baroque. He was a musician who flourished above all in ungrazed pasture, but in 1949 that was still, as Peter Yates had found, a broad terrain inhabited by several great composers and many little-known masterpieces. His October Town Hall concert had included Berg and Falla as well as Stravinsky, and in December there had been Monteverdi, still at that time generally regarded as a prehistoric figure. His closer involvement with Stravinsky had not in the least dulled his enthusiasm for other brands of the remote and exploratory.

Los Angeles, for its part, was not quite the cultural desert it had begun to seem in the war years and just afterward. Even Schoenberg's seventy-fifth birthday had been celebrated. Izler Solomon had conducted Berg's *Chamber Concerto* (originally composed for Schoenberg's fiftieth) at a Roof concert, and on the actual birthday, 13 September 1949, the series had mounted a whole Schoenberg evening, including *Pierrot Lunaire,* the Cello Concerto, and the world premiere of the violin *Phantasy,* played by Adolf Koldofsky and Leonard Stein. Soulima Stravinsky remembered attending with his father, though Vera's diary records a dinner that evening at the house of the painter Eugene Lourié and says nothing about the concert.[1] But they certainly did go six weeks later to a concert at which Harold Byrnes conducted the First Chamber Symphony, and Schoenberg read out a speech—written in huge letters on many sheets of paper, because of his failing eyesight— publicly accepting the Freedom of the City of Vienna.[2] It was later alleged that at a reception after the concert the two composers came within an ace of meeting but that as Stravinsky approached, Schoenberg was whisked away by the Austrian consul to meet someone else.[3] Stravinsky never referred to this incident, but he did remember the concert as the last occasion on which he set eyes on the Viennese master. A month after arriving in

Los Angeles that December, Craft went to a Schoenberg matinée in the County Museum; but Stravinsky stayed at home.4

Between Stravinsky and certain of Schoenberg's followers there was no such difficulty. In August 1949 he had gone with Craft to an ISCM concert of twelve-note music and renewed his old acquaintance with Ernst Krenek, whom he had first met when Krenek came to Nice in the 1920s.5 These days, the composer of the jazzy *Jonny spielt auf* was much preoccupied with, and liked to talk about, serial manipulations of a more or less complicated kind, but though Stravinsky still knew absolutely nothing about such techniques they did not in themselves constitute a social obstacle. Nor was he invariably cautious about rival reputations. When Benjamin Britten came to Los Angeles with Peter Pears in November, Stravinsky went to both of their concerts and entertained them at North Wetherly Drive. Their meeting seemed the most natural thing in the world, and it was only as a result of something that happened at the time that a trace of poison entered into their subsequent attitudes to one another. Britten later put it about that Stravinsky, while claiming (truthfully) to have seen *The Rape of Lucretia,* seemed unaware that it contained recitative with piano.

> When was Stravinsky himself going to write a full-length opera, asked Britten. "I have one in progress even now," said the old master. "But opera, not music drama, is my interest—and I shall write it in closed forms." "Just as I did in *Lucretia,*" said Britten. "Not at all," said Stravinsky. "My opera will have *secco* recitative accompanied only by piano, not by orchestra!" Britten was dumbfounded [. . .] Either the master was a liar, or a fool.6

Had Stravinsky slept through *Lucretia,* or had he simply misheard Britten's remark? Why, if it comes to that, did Britten ask his question about full-length opera? He must have known, from Hawkes or any one of several other sources, that Stravinsky's EOG plan had long since turned into a big opera; it was actually common knowledge. At all events, something took place that unsettled the older composer, to judge from the ambivalence of his account of the visit to Nabokov. "We listened for a whole week here to Auntie Britten and Uncle Pears," he wrote.

> Well, we'll talk about it when we meet. Britten himself makes a very nice impression and has a huge success with an audience. He has an unquestionable talent as a performer (especially at the piano).7

In the few days since Britten's departure, Stravinsky had been to see *Albert Herring* and had very clearly disliked it. Perhaps the central joke in Eric

Crozier's libretto, about the male May Queen, struck an uncomfortable chord with him after Kirstein's remarks about Baba the Turk;[8] or perhaps Britten had said something about Auden as a librettist, or even—since Britten these days was paranoid where his old collaborator was concerned—about Auden as a person.[9] All one can say with confidence is that Britten's account of the conversation is incomplete, but in what respect, it is impossible at this distance to make out.

It must in fairness be added that when he saw *Albert Herring*, and certainly by the time he was writing to Nabokov, Stravinsky was suffering from a duodenal ulcer. On the 16th of December his doctor put him on a milk-only diet for two days, then, just when he was recovering his temper, he went down with a heavy cold and once again retired to bed, leaving Craft to deal with an irritating correspondence with Boosey and Hawkes about the *Symphonies of Wind Instruments* and a supposed revision of *The Rite of Spring*.[10] It was two years since Stravinsky had sent Hawkes his revised score of the *Symphonies*. Since when nothing had been heard until this very month, when Boosey's chief editor, Erwin Stein, suddenly produced an old set of 1930s proofs from ERM's Paris office, apparently quite unaware that the revision existed.[11] On the other hand, the publishers had for months been pestering Stravinsky to produce a corrected score of *The Rite of Spring* for them to copyright like *Petrushka,* something that only interested him if they were able to incorporate his 1943 revision of the Danse sacrale (which belonged to AMP), since he continued to maintain that a reduced-orchestra *Rite* was impossible. When Craft in his turn went down with pleurisy at the start of January, Stravinsky's frustration boiled over in a thoroughly old-fashioned diatribe directed at Hawkes, and on another subject altogether, the question of the first performance of *The Rake's Progress*.

For well over a year Hawkes had been plotting a British premiere, either at Covent Garden itself or by the Garden (Royal Opera) company at the Edinburgh Festival. On the whole this suited Stravinsky, who wanted a small house and an English-speaking audience and was implacably opposed to Rudolf Bing's desire to have the work for his first season (1950–51) at the Met, a much bigger house than Covent Garden, and a vastly bigger one than Edinburgh's King's Theatre.[12] But there were snags. David Webster, of Covent Garden, kept pressing for a 1950 premiere until Stravinsky irritably insisted that the work could not be ready before 1951. Then the question of a conductor arose. Stravinsky had no commission for the opera, nor was he likely to get one from a house like the Royal Opera, which had no such funds at its disposal; so his only hope of a fee remotely commensurate with the work's scale was to conduct it himself. But that would mean going to Europe in 1951, and he was still by no means certain he wanted to commit himself to the trip. In any case, as Hawkes incautiously hinted, Webster might well not want to book an expensive guest conductor when he had a salaried music director, Karl Rankl, with experience as a conductor of new music.[13] This was altogether too much for Stravinsky, who began rapidly to cool toward the whole idea of a British *Rake*. "I have been interested," he wrote crossly to Hawkes, in his own unmediated English,

> in creating myself the original tradition of my opera and in cashing on my personal appearance to compensate for my loss of income during the time I work for nothing composing it, as this work is a non-commissioned one. I see that from now on I shall not expect any help from the sources we had considered.[14]

Hawkes tried to insist that he was by no means ruled out as conductor, but the damage was done and Stravinsky was soon looking for alternative theatres, especially in America, while merely continuing to pay lip service to Hawkes's British schemes.

He was now composing the final scene of Act 2, in which Tom, sent to sleep by Baba's chatter, dreams of a machine that can turn stones into loaves of bread. Such a machine, at this particular moment, would doubtless have pleased Stravinsky as much as it pleased his feather-brained hero. And meanwhile, Tom and Baba's curious marriage had its real-life counterpart at the end of January in the composer's own living room, where Eugene Berman and the film actress Ona Munson—"a necrophiliac homosexual and a lesbian," as Craft noted in his diary[15]—were married by a judge, with Craft himself as best man. Five days later, Stravinsky composed Tom's "My wife? I have no wife. I've buried her," which ends the second act of the opera; and five days after that he, Vera, and Craft set out, for the first time, to drive in their old Dodge to New York.

The direct route from Los Angeles across the central states is some two and a half thousand miles long and might be traversed, in that pre-freeway age, in six or seven days. But the Stravinskys had decided to follow the southern fringe of the country to Miami and Key West, then drive up the Eastern Seaboard to New York, a total distance of nearly four thousand miles through some of the most mournful and unvarying terrain that even an experienced rail-traveller from Tsarist Russia would ever have seen. Craft later described the journey in matter-of-fact terms.[16] There was trouble over money, since some hotels would not take checks, but in truth there were several days on which money was hardly an issue, there being nowhere to spend it. Driving through the empty Texan sierra between El Paso and Del Rio, they found nowhere to eat and soon finished off the supplies provided for the trip by Mrs. Gates. Stravinsky, who had long years ago given up driving, sat in the passenger seat and took the occasional swig of claret or armagnac. At Del Rio the only available rooms were in a brothel. Later they drove twelve hundred miles across the flatlands of the Missisippi delta and Florida, down through the Everglades from St. Petersburg to Miami, then on another hundred and fifty miles along the causeway to Key West, only to find that the hotels were full and they had to drive back to Miami for the night. They finally arrived in New York City on 18 February after twelve days of solid driving. Three days later, Stravinsky was conducting *Firebird* at City Center.

Sitting together in the Dodge for hours on end, day after day, with Vera and Craft taking turns at the wheel, they talked about many things, and as they talked they grew more and more intimate. Stravinsky was not particularly interested in his young friend's middle-class, upstate New York background, nor was he very attentive to the admittedly somewhat monotonous scenery, even though the object of the drive had been for him and Vera to see the country of which they were now in their fifth year as citizens. Instead Craft prompted him to talk about his own family in Russia before the revolution, about Rimsky-Korsakov and Diaghilev and what life had been like in old St. Petersburg. They discussed books: literature and philosophy, words, music, and ideas. Perhaps they talked about religion; and perhaps, even, it was on this trip that Craft first realized that he could disagree with Stravinsky "and survive," as Vera put it, which few of his older friends had ever been able to do.[17] Conversing in so easy, natural a fashion without the intrusion of telephones or appointments, without the possibility of work or the threat of visitors, they could begin to feel close in a way subtly different from the proximity of parents and children or brothers and sisters, who may live together all their lives without ever exploring each other's ideas on anything more profound than the temperature of the bathwater or the time it takes to boil an egg.

Having conducted a single performance of *Firebird* and another of *Orpheus* for Kirstein's still-fledgling New York City Ballet, Stravinsky settled into a long, concertless Manhattan stay interrupted only by a trip to Urbana and St. Louis in mid-March. For Kirstein, the ballet performances were emblematic, since the new company had actually risen from the ashes of the old Ballet Society in the autumn of 1948 thanks to the patronage of a certain Morton Baum, chairman of the City Center finance committee. Baum had gone to see *Orpheus* out of semi-official curiosity and been so bowled over that he had at once proposed that Kirstein re-form his society as a resident company with the direct financial support of the Center. But though Kirstein dropped frequent gentle reminders to Stravinsky about his next ballet commission, and even came up with ideas for subject matter (his latest suggestion was the *Bacchae*),[18] he knew there was no realistic chance of an agreement until the *Rake* was finished. So instead he now proposed that the *Rake* itself be given its first production at the Center.[19] This hardly seemed a serious idea, since City Center had its own resident opera company with very limited resources, and in any case it would be difficult to imagine a less suitable venue for so intimate a work. Stravinsky, though, was prepared to favor any U.S. theatre that could meet his financial conditions, and it was true that in the past Kirstein had never failed to find the backing he needed for even the most harebrained projects. At the end of March, the composer received a visit from the A&P grocery millionaire and art lover, Huntington Hartford, who was a Kirstein possible to finance either a City Center production, or conceivably a Broadway run like that of Menotti's *The Medium* (in 1947), or his *Consul,* which had recently opened at the Ethel Barrymore and was likewise, to Stravinsky's intense irritation, settling in for a long stay.[20] Unfortunately, Hartford wanted to hear the music, while Stravinsky was unwilling to be judged (as he saw it) by a non-musician. In the end, Craft arranged for Billy Rose to be spirited into a piano run-through of the first two acts, which Stravinsky and Marcelle de Manziarly gave in her Manhattan apartment on the 20th of April. As they played, Craft kept his eyes on Rose's face, and it soon dawned on him that the *Rake* had no chance of commercial backing.[21]

Stravinsky had been working with Auden on details of the libretto before Auden's departure for Europe at the end of March 1950. They had tried out the episode of the bread machine, with practice timings for its entrance and exit, and they had devised a bidding sequence for the auction scene that was to open Act 3.[22] But Stravinsky seems to have become generally disillusioned about the opera's prospects. According to Craft, he even for a brief time thought of postponing its completion in order to write the music for a ballet about St. Francis that Clare Booth Luce, the author of the scenario, described to him—perhaps at Kirstein's instigation—at a cocktail party in late March.[23] He was now more or less openly hostile to Hawkes's British plans, not least because Berman, who was in London for the revival of Ashton's *Scènes de ballet* (for which he had designed the sets), was writing him black letters about the standard of performance there, the bad food, and the horrible weather.[24] Such things made him more than ever determined—as he wrote to Theodore a few weeks later—to insist on a premiere in America, where he could personally supervise the preparations without having to endure "six weeks of poverty in London."[25] Hawkes was also hinting at France, Italy, or Germany; but after all, the opera was going to be sung in English; and in any case he could not think of the *Rake* in vast, ceremonious houses like La Scala or the Paris Opéra, where, moreover, money was short for such projects.[26]

They lingered on in New York for the whole of April. Stravinsky had recordings for RCA at the start of the month, including the Piano Concerto with Soulima, who was bubbling with excitement, having just been offered a post as professor of piano at the University of Illinois, Urbana.[27] At the end of April, Craft reconvened the Chamber Arts Society for a concert that included Schoenberg's *Serenade* and Webern's Concerto for Nine Instruments, as well as Stravinsky's early Russian songs; but Stravinsky himself was ill, according to Craft's later memory, and unable to attend.[28] They did go together to a Carnegie Hall concert in which Mitropoulos conducted Schoenberg's *Survivor from Warsaw*. To what extent this enthusiasm of Craft's was beginning to chip away the ice can only be imagined. From the Warsaw ghetto to Hogarth's London—whatever they may have had in common of cruelty and deprivation—remained aesthetically an unbridgeable gulf.

The return drive to Los Angeles was by a more direct and northerly route, and they were home within nine days. It was a trip through American folklore, cinematic and otherwise, and hugely to the Stravinskys' taste. They saw the South Dakota badlands, Deadwood, and the Little Bighorn, drove through Yellowstone Park, and spent their last night in Monterey on the Pacific coast. In Gillette, Wyoming, they sat in an audience of cowboys in a fleapit cinema and watched a bad Western, an image to put beside that of Rimsky-Korsakov playing Glinka's *Life for the Tsar* on the lounge piano in the Niagara Hotel almost ninety years before.[29] But alas, Hollywood offered no escape from the problems of New York. As Stravinsky embarked on composing the scene in which the bankrupt Tom's possessions are sold off, he was more and more conscious of the extent to which the two years already spent on the opera and the year that still remained were eroding his own finances. There were minor items of good news. Hawkes wrote at one point to announce that the French royalties, blocked for more than a year by postwar exchange regulations, had at last been cleared.[30] No doubt it was comforting to learn from his librettists on Ischia that apart from Mozart and Beethoven, "Stravinsky is the most played on the European radio."[31] But for him the real news about Europe was that his dependants there were showing little sign of achieving self-sufficiency. Olga Sallard, for instance, seemed as happy to accept his money as she was to feed Vera with vaguely discreditable information about his children.[32] Above all, his granddaughter, now thirteen, had scarcely improved in health and still needed expensive medical care, which her grandfather was paying for through the sale of his manuscripts. "Alas, what you write about our Kitty," he told Theodore,

> has not yet eased my constant state of alarm, although I should like to hope that you will manage to protect her from the worst. Her improvement in weight, appetite and general appearance nourishes this hope in

me. [But] the old terrible gaping wound in my life of eleven years ago, which was gradually healing, has started to nag at me again. . . . I'm so glad that you and Soulima could meet and have a good talk. Whenever shall I have that joy myself? But I'm a complete prisoner of my opera; until I finish it I can't plan anything. . . .³³

In this tense and anxious condition he nevertheless composed what is in many ways the most brilliant and certainly the most entertaining scene in the entire opera. The problem of Baba, it is true, was never completely solved. The wonderful idea of her being revealed as the final lot in the sale and resuming her "Rage" aria where she had left off in the previous scene, when Tom had covered her head like a parrot's at bedtime, is somewhat dissipated by her sentimental change of heart toward Anne. But the choruses and Sellem's aria are a dazzling achievement for a composer who had never written for a genuinely participatory stage chorus, and whose last proper tenor aria before the *Rake* had been for Oedipus almost a quarter of a century before. The technique is magisterial. The rapid changes of pace and intensity—notoriously the hardest part of composing for the lyric stage—work like a dream. And when he turned to the graveyard scene in October or early November, he at once found the sinister and ritualistic tone to match, a switch of mood for which Mozart's *Don Giovanni* was the only conceivable model. But while the working of these two scenes, and the way they interlock musically, reveal the hand of a master, they did not come easily or fluently. Not until the very end of 1950 did he complete the second scene with Tom's deranged closing verse of the ballad song, "With roses crowned, I sit on ground." As usual, he rolled up what he had composed and sent it off to the publishers, even though there was still a whole scene, an epilogue, and an overture to be written.

During all these months, the only working interruptions had been a trip to Colorado to conduct two concerts in the inaugural Aspen Festival at the end of July, and a series of concerts in San Francisco in mid-December. In the big tent at Aspen he conducted twice, the first time in jeans, as his suitcase had been delayed by a rail strike;³⁴ and it was also during a rehearsal at Aspen that he brought down his baton expecting to hear the opening of Tchaikovsky's Second Symphony and was regaled instead by a tune he did not recognize but which turned out to be "Happy Birthday to You," played in honor of one of the players' wives, who had just had a baby.³⁵ The trip otherwise was something of a holiday. They had again gone by car, making a huge detour via Portland, Seattle, and Coeur d'Alene in Idaho, before travelling down to Colorado through the Rockies. Between concerts, they drove off to Santa Fe, where they stayed with the piano-duo couple Victor Babin and his wife, Vitya Vronsky, watched the corn dance at San Domingo Pueblo, and visited Frieda Lawrence and Mabel Dodge at Taos.

These huge and often arduous sightseeing adventures into wild or lonely terrain had become a feature of their life with Craft, whether at his instigation or simply because his presence as a young, dependable cicerone and reserve driver gave them the confidence to sally forth in a way that might otherwise have daunted them. Some weeks before the Aspen trip, they had driven out the two hundred or so miles to Sequoia National Park with Isherwood and Caskey, and gazed up at the 280-foot General Sherman tree. "That's very serious," said Stravinsky solemnly, and Craft felt so good in the dry mountain air that he drove them the whole way home that same evening, arriving at two in the morning, "quite silly with exhaustion."[36] Then early in September they again headed up into Oregon with Milène and André. They went to Gold Beach, and Crater Lake with its deep, clear blue water, and were away five days.

When they got home on the 12th there was a telegram waiting; Ralph Hawkes had died of a heart attack four days before at his home in Connecticut, at the age of fifty-two. For Stravinsky it was a disagreeable reminder of the sudden death of Ernest Oeberg in 1925, for although the choleric and at times ruthless Hawkes had not become a close friend, his surefooted professionalism had been indispensable at a time of complex and difficult negotiations, and—for the composer—drastic forward commitments. At this precise moment, with the *Rake* approaching completion and the issue of its first performance hanging in the air like an outsize question mark, Hawkes's loss was doubly disturbing, and Stravinsky was soon writing anxiously to Ernst Roth, the director of Boosey and Hawkes's London office, wanting to know who would be taking over in New York.[37] When he learnt that it would be Hawkes's young assistant Betty Bean, he was pleased enough to be dealing with a known quantity, whatever doubts he may have harbored as to her experience or likely toughness. A more subtle anxiety, with the Connecticut-based Hawkes gone, was which office would assume the overriding authority. The Bean arrangement strongly suggested that the answer would be London.

At the time of Hawkes's death, Stravinsky was still strongly in favor of an American premiere for the *Rake,* and the leading contender as far as he was concerned was now the little old Victorian theatre in Central City, Colorado, where they had seen *Così fan tutte* in 1948, and whose director, Frank Ricketson, was offering good money for him to supervise and conduct the first performance.[38] Hawkes had been well aware of this situation, but he had nevertheless continued negotiating with various European houses on the basis of a possible world premiere, and apparently without much regard for Stravinsky's frequently expressed hostility to large theatres in non-anglophone cities. By October, La Scala was being announced as firm for the following autumn, and Covent Garden as nearly so, with what would therefore possibly be the premiere. Yet Stravinsky had categorically rejected an approach that very June from the Milan intendant, Antonio Ghiringhelli, even though Ghiringhelli was offering to stage the work in English and with Stravinsky conducting.[39]

As for London, Stravinsky had had further unsettling news about Covent Garden from Lincoln Kirstein, who had taken the New York City Ballet to England for an August season and was spitting venom at the conservatism of the British press and the chilly arrogance of the London ballet aristocracy. Kirstein praised Tyrone Guthrie, whom Hawkes had mentioned months before as a possible director for the *Rake,* and he named the Earl of Harewood as a man of influence who could pull strings on the work's behalf. But his account of the critics' reaction to Balanchine was so lurid (*Firebird* had been "peed on in every part of the intellectual press"), and his portrait of the arts establishment's loathing of "the way we sabotaged your music and [our] violation of the late holy Fokine" so angry, that Stravinsky could have been forgiven for then and there making up his mind never to let the British within earshot of his new opera. Kirstein was planning a Stravinsky ballet festival for a commercial London theatre such as Drury Lane the following spring, and he was imagining the composer there in person "to be icy and polite, and have those dead eels and kippered herrings come around and say well, maybe you have some rights even in your, alack-a-day, non-Russian scores."[40] This was not, however, a vision that was likely to appeal to the hypersensitive composer. Kirstein's account he claimed to find "very comforting and you and George come out as the happy winners, despite all traps laid in your path by the old London press idiots and the new British chauvinists," but his only reaction to the festival plan was that "London would be impossible," while the idea of a *Rake* production there he simply ignored.[41]

Kirstein was the kind of organizer—what the French aptly call an *animateur*—who never lets go of a project until it has been comprehensively explored and pronounced irretrievably dead. Above all, he was making sure that Stravinsky did not forget that he, Kirstein, was first in the queue to commission the next work after the *Rake,* and his way of ensuring this was to keep proposing new subjects until he hit on one that the composer was unable to resist. *Apollo architectons* and the *Bacchae* had come and gone.[42] Now Kirstein had been talking in London to T. S. Eliot, and after Eliot had expressed enthusiasm for *Orpheus,* Kirstein had opportunistically asked him to suggest a sequel. Eliot had been shy of doing anything of the kind, but he had later not only somewhat hesitantly suggested his own *Sweeney*

Agonistes as a subject, but had even seemed interested in a collaboration. Partly no doubt for tactical reasons, Kirstein affected to see this as the most natural suggestion imaginable, though he might well have wondered how the fragmentary Aristophanic (as Eliot called it) doggerel of these two unfinished scenes could conceivably be turned into a dance scenario, even by their own author (who would no doubt have new ideas about them). Stravinsky, as before, held his peace.[43]

It must have been the growing confusion of all these apparently conflicting plans, aggravated by Hawkes's death and a lack of immediate confidence in his successors' ability to grasp the special needs of the situation, that drove Stravinsky to the decision that eventually led to the *Rake* being premiered in a city and theatre not previously discussed, and which for a time threatened to drown the whole project in waves of recrimination and legal wrangling. In November, just when it looked as if the Ricketson deal might be falling through, there came a new and financially more dazzling proposal from the University of Southern California, who offered Stravinsky a commission fee of ten thousand dollars, with the possibility of an extra five thousand if he would also conduct the performances.[44] It was a deal first suggested by Hawkes on the strength of USC's highly regarded opera school, of which the German producer Carl Ebert, one of the original founders of Glyndebourne, was director.[45] For Stravinsky, of course, it had the added virtue of being a mere taxi-ride from his own home. With all these things in its favor, it is not at once clear why the project melted away within a few weeks of crystallizing. Perhaps USC, who wanted the production for autumn 1952, were put off by Stravinsky's insistence on 1951. In any case, as it faded it left echoes, the clearest of which was a true realization on his part of what the premiere might be worth in crude monetary terms.

Just at that moment, a letter arrived from Nicolas Nabokov, recently returned from Europe, where he had been elected president of a new American-funded anti-Soviet organization with the magnificent title of Congress for Cultural Freedom. Feeling in the mood for further organizing, Nabokov had gone on from Berlin—where the Congress had met—to Rome, had discussions with the music chief of Italian Radio (RAI), Mario Labroca, and persuaded him that the *Rake* should be premiered in Italy under the auspices of the RAI, either at the Florence or the Venice festival or at La Scala, in return for a one-off fee to the composer of twenty thousand dollars.[46] Nabokov seems to have had no particular brief for these discussions, and he admitted to Stravinsky that he had plucked the sum of money out of the air. On the other hand it was Stravinsky who, in his own letter to Labroca, at once stated a preference for Venice. The Fenice had, as it happened, expressed an interest in the *Rake* before he had composed so much as a note of it, and he had himself mentioned Venice to Hawkes in 1949.[47] There was every reason why he should want the Fenice—it was a small theatre with excellent acoustics, and the city was one he knew well and had loved ever since his first visit there with Diaghilev in 1912. But nobody had in fact said anything definite about Venice until Auden mentioned it casually, out of the blue, early that same December of 1950: "the ideal premiere would be La Fenice, don't you think."[48] As for the fee, Auden was not alone in being taken completely unwares by its scale and precise intention.

The objections to La Serenissima were obvious enough. It had no adequate opera company, the organization of the Biennale was notoriously shambolic, and the question of language remained. When Roth, Boosey and Hawkes's London director heard toward the end of January that Stravinsky had accepted Venice behind his back, his first reaction was that it would be a miracle if the curtain ever went up on *The Rake's Progress* at the Fenice at all.[49] He quickly realized, however, that whatever might eventually happen operatically in Venice was as nothing compared to the histrionics he would have to endure in the intervening months. After all the discussions about Edinburgh and London, and all the more recent American proposals, the European premiere had finally been promised to Covent Garden for December 1951, with a continental premiere at La Scala immediately afterwards. Both houses, he told the composer, would be "very annoyed" about the Fenice agreement.[50] But even he underestimated the full impact Italy's highly politicized musical life would have on a dispute of this kind. Ghiringhelli, the Milan intendant, at once threatened legal action, his fury if anything intensified by Stravinsky's bungling attempt to console him by offering him the Italian-language premiere while describing La Scala as a house of "an essentially national [that is, not international] character."[51] Soon Ghiringhelli was threatening to bring the matter of the twenty thousand dollars before the Italian parliament, which naturally had the power to refuse exchange clearance for such a sum.[52] Roth tried desperately to broker a collaboration between La Scala and the Biennale. He endured interminable meetings in Rome and Milan, entirely Latin in tone and temperature, with Ghiringhelli, Labroca, and Ferdinando Ballo, the director of the Biennale— meetings that even at one point involved the director general of Italian radio, Giulio Razzi. The Italian consul in Los Angeles cabled Ghiringhelli urging him to make terms with Ballo.[53] But by the end of May, with the premiere contracted for the second week of September, there was still no agreement. Ballo kept wiring optimistic news, and by mid-June it was clear that a settlement really was near. But Ghiringhelli maintained the tension until the very last minute, and it was only on the 20th of June, a mere twelve weeks before the premiere, that Roth was able to confirm a definitive agreement under which La Scala would itself produce the *Rake* in English at the Fenice in September and would then take it into their own repertoire for performances in Italian during the winter. "There have been," Roth reported drily, "many harsh words."[54] And he pressed Stravinsky, for the sake of good relations, to agree to conduct concerts at La Scala in October, after the Venice performances, at a concessionary fee.

When David Webster heard about the Venice deal from the composer's own lips, he nearly fainted, Stravinsky told Roth.[55] From Covent Garden a chilly Anglo-Saxon fog spread slowly over the whole affair, the planned December production was withdrawn, and for twenty-eight years *The Rake's Progress* simply ceased, as far as the Royal Opera was concerned, to exist.[56]

While Roth thus dealt with the enraged Ghiringhelli, Stravinsky was composing the final scene of his opera, set in a madhouse. He had hoped to finish the whole work before flying to Cuba, where he had concerts booked in early March, but by the day of their departure, the 20th of February, he had not got beyond Tom's "Madmen, where have you hidden her?," just before the end of Act 3 scene 3, which still left the epilogue and a short prelude to be written. Seemingly untroubled by the interruption, he then set off by road with Vera and Craft in their new Buick for Miami, from where they flew to Havana. They stayed one week, then drove home after an absence of fully three.

It was almost as if Stravinsky had decided that if the world was going to obstruct the performance of this most time-consuming of his works, he would not exert himself to finish it. He had tried to explain to Roth that the Venice deal would mean that he could afford to complete the opera that year, but that otherwise he would have to shelve it and accept a new commission.[57] After three years of being a "prisoner" of his opera, as he had grumbled to Theodore, he was feeling intensely protective about the money it was going to earn him. So when Auden wrote suggesting that he and Kallman might be entitled to a cut of the twenty thousand dollars, Stravinsky replied unblinkingly that, since the money was not a commission fee but a payment for preparing and conducting the premiere, there was no question of a percentage. Of course, he wanted Wystan and Chester to be there in Venice, but alas it was not his responsibility "to provide for your active role with Kallman."[58]

This dispute, like all the others, eventually landed on Roth's desk. Auden made what trouble he could about the technicalities of the situation, but was eventually appeased by a payment for expenses, free tickets, and a participation in rehearsals. The incident must all the same have confirmed him in his original character assessment of Stravinsky, "in whose case, obviously, the mother figure is money,"[59] and it was much used against the composer in later years, especially by highminded critics who took literally a footnote in his published correspondence to the effect that he was "pretending that the $20,000 for the opera . . . was not a commission (which he would have had to share with the librettists) but a fee for conducting the premiere."[60] But Auden and Kallman had received payment for the libretto at the outset (in the form of an advance on royalties), and they would have had neither a contractual nor even a clear moral right to any share in a commission fee, whatever their rights in the matter of royalties or performance dues.[61] Stravinsky obviously nevertheless feared the apparent ambiguity of a commission fee negotiated so late in the process, which is why he insisted that "I have not sold La Biennale anything but my conducting."[62] Later, he was more cautious in his dealings with Auden from the start, and as we shall see the world may thereby have been deprived of a second collaboration between them.

In addition to the twenty thousand, he also had high hopes of a deal over the recording rights for the first performance. His exclusive contract with RCA had expired the previous summer, and he had been looking around for some new association, possibly out of disillusion with RCA's lingering commitment to the 45-rpm extended-play record.[63] For a time it looked as if Cetra-Soria, a small but progressive Italian company with good contacts at RAI, would be well placed to make the recording. Then, when Soria backed out, there was a brief flirtation with Decca. The difficulty was that both companies understandably wanted to market the discs as soon as possible, while Roth was shrewdly insisting that to do this would be to undermine the local broadcasting rights on which many opera houses depended for the production of new works.[64] Stravinsky, on the other hand, was working on the assumption that no studio recording of such a long work was likely in the foreseeable future, and he was anxious not to miss what he saw as an artistic as well as a commercial opportunity.[65] His bizarre solution, not for the first time, was to get his lawyer, Aaron Sapiro, to write one of his "I'd hate to think you didn't have my client's best interests at heart" letters to Roth, throwing in a number of hugely speculative statistics that the canny publisher had little difficulty in politely demolishing.[66] The final straw in this curious but in the short term unproductive episode snapped when Roth discovered that British Decca, with whom he had been dealing, and American Decca, with whom Stravinsky had been dealing, were completely different companies. By that time it was too late to conclude a new agreement, and though RAI kept a recording of the first performance, Roth got more than his wish and it was not released commercially for another thirty years.

Amid all this hocus-pocus, as André Marion later called it,[67] Stravinsky quietly finished the opera that had dogged his footsteps for the past three and a half years. The epilogue, with its flippant moralizing tone in the manner of *Don Giovanni,* was completed on the 7th of April, and the brief invocatory prelude to Act I a few days later. On the 3rd of May, the composer parcelled up the orchestral scores of these movements and sent them off to Erwin Stein in London.

Typically, a new work of such length and importance would have been cast, and the director and designer engaged, long before this. But it was impossible to sign contracts with busy and expensive solo artists while the performance itself remained uncertain. Carl Ebert had long been envisaged as director, ever since the USC plan had come and gone the previous autumn. Stravinsky felt safe with Ebert, who had been staging operas since his time as intendant of the Berlin Städtische Oper in the early thirties, and while Auden—who had aspirations to direct the *Rake* himself[68]—made difficulties, the composer stuck to his guns and Ebert was duly booked, though it was late in July before he received a contract from the sluggish Italian bureaucrats.[69] For the designs Stravinsky had wanted Eugene Berman, with his penchant for neo-baroque curlicues, but Venice could not make it worth the indigent painter's while to fly from New York to Italy, and after the French artist Balthasar Balthus and the Englishman John Piper had for one reason or another likewise fallen out of the reckoning, the composer had to accept the *fait accompli* of two Italian designers, Gianni Ratto and Ebe Colciaghi.[70] As for the musicians, by July most of the cast was fixed: in fact all except the title role, for which Stravinsky, intent on an anglophone tenor, eventually unearthed a Hollywood operetta singer named Robert Rounseville, a friend of the Baroness Catherine d'Erlanger and fresh from starring in Michael Powell's film of Offenbach's *Tales of Hoffmann*. Rounseville must have been quick of study, since he had barely four weeks—including a few days with the composer in New York at the start of August—to learn the lengthy and difficult part before rehearsals began later that month. The question of a reserve conductor—since Stravinsky refused to conduct anything but the premiere—was even more nerve-wracking. Not until he arrived in Naples in mid-August did he learn the identity of his deputy, Ferdinand Leitner. It was much as Roth had warned: in Venice it was always a matter of good fortune if the curtain rose at all.

OBSESSED, as ever, with his own health, Stravinsky was also acutely sensitive to the ill health of others, as if conscious of some need to propitiate the gods who watched over the territory between life and death. Condolences or a get-well message, where appropriate, would invariably precede all else even in a business letter. The death of a friend or associate, past or present, was like a memento mori, a warning of his own mortality as he approached his biblical quota of years. When André Gide died in February 1951, Stravinsky was visibly upset and for a long time silent, even though he had not set eyes on his *Persephone* collaborator since the ill-fated run-through at Ida Rubinstein's seventeen years before.[71] He even expressed grief—perhaps of a more ritualistic kind—at the death of his fellow Rimsky-Korsakov pupil Max Steinberg when he heard about it that March, more than four years after the actual event, and more than a quarter-century after he had avoided Steinberg in Paris in 1925.[72] Eugenia Errazuriz (killed in a road accident in Chile), Serge Koussevitzky, and Adolph Bolm—who had been "declining before my eyes," Stravinsky told Soulima, and died in his sleep one April morning—all went to their graves during the first half of 1951.[73] But the most momentous death was reserved for July, when Arnold Schoenberg died of heart failure on Friday the 13th at his home in Brentwood Park. Stravinsky, who had not communicated with Schoenberg since 1919, at once sent a telegram to his widow: "Deeply shocked by saddening news of terrible blow inflicted to all musical world by loss of Arnold Schoenberg. Please accept my heartfelt sympathy."[74]

What Stravinsky really thought of Schoenberg at this precise moment is far from clear. Craft has asserted that, in the first year or two of his association with Stravinsky, Schoenberg's name was seldom if ever mentioned in the house, and mutual friends such as David Diamond, Ingolf Dahl, Klemperer, or even Milhaud, tended to keep quiet about their dual loyalty.[75] But this is not quite believable; or, if it was true, it can only have been because Stravinsky himself found it awkward to go against the persona long since created for him by factious associates like Arthur Lourié or, on the other side, René Leibowitz. The ice may have formed too thick to break. Nevertheless Stravinsky had discussed Schoenberg with Stuckenschmidt, and he had attended the Freedom of Vienna concert. When Craft went to Mitropoulos's Carnegie Hall performance of *A Survivor from Warsaw* in April 1950, Stravinsky, who was in New York, must have known about it, and when the young man called on Schoenberg three months later, it was Vera who drove him there.[76] No doubt Stravinsky disliked such of Schoenberg's music as he had heard; but he cannot any longer have been unaware that many of the musicians in whose company he spent so much time admired the Viennese master and his so-called "school." In April 1951, Mitropoulos's concert performance of Berg's *Wozzeck* had been broadcast, and they had all sat and listened.[77] But Craft is silent about Stravinsky's reaction.

Six days after Schoenberg's death, the Stravinskys dined at Alma Mahler-Werfel's house, and they were there when Anna Mahler arrived with Schoenberg's death mask (which she herself had sculpted), and unwrapped it for their inspection.[78] Stravinsky had just begun a new work, a song for mezzo-soprano to an anonymous Elizabethan poem taken from the first volume of Auden's recently published *Poets of the English Language:*

The maidens came
When I was in my mothers bower.
I had all that I wolde.
The baily berith the bell away,
The lilly, the rose, the rose I lay, . . .

Auden had given him the five compact volumes as a Christmas present, and had perhaps drawn his attention to the marvelous series of "anonymous lyrics and songs" on pages 426–431 of volume I as the possible starting point for a songbook that would build on the word-setting techniques he had evolved in *The Rake's Progress.* Or Stravinsky may have asked for poems of a progressive character, to judge by a letter Auden wrote to Craft in mid-September with further suggestions from all five chronological volumes, including lyrics by Philip Sidney, Campion, Herrick, Pope, Blake, and Christina Rossetti.[79]

None of these later ideas was ever taken up, but Stravinsky's music for "The maidens came" is in many respects that of a starting point. The whole song is a model of melodic simplicity and clarity combined with an intricacy of rhythm obviously inspired by the fascinating and elaborate imagery of the poem. The curious unaccompanied apostrophe to the "Right mighty and famous / Elizabeth, our quen princis" is set boldly and simply in C major, as if for the white notes of a piano, but in a metric style that cuts across the idiosyncratic scansion of the poem by bringing "Elizabeth" up into the previous line and then spreading out the rest of her original line so that it occupies the same metric space as its elongated predecessor. Most strikingly, the piece is a study in the ancient technique of strict melodic imitation known as canon. At the start, the cor anglais copies the flute, a seventh lower and in inversion (upside down), and later, at "The baily berith the bell away," the soprano and flute are in strict canon, again by inversion, with a freer imitation in the oboe. The lines weave perceptible patterns, like the rose branches in a Schongauer Madonna.

How much of the song Stravinsky wrote before setting off for New York at the end of July is not clear from the sketches. But it is somehow pleasing that even this fragment existed to carry forward the *Rake* style before anybody had heard or seen the opera itself. It might seem a very innocent little seed; but a seed it undoubtedly was.

18

THE TIME-TRAVELLER COMES ASHORE

CRAFT WAS to have travelled to New York by train with the Stravinskys, but at the last minute he went down with severe stomach pains and was whisked into the Cedars of Lebanon Hospital with suspected polio. The diagnosis was neither confirmed nor, in so many words, denied; but it was a week before he was well enough to fly east, and he must for a time have even wondered whether he would get to Europe at all. He reached New York with only two days to spare before the SS *Constitution* sailed for Naples on the 7th of August.

No doubt the symptoms were in part nervous in origin, and in any case they seem to have had no noticeable consequences. Instead, as they approached the Azores four days out, Stravinsky suddenly collapsed with pneumonia, brought on, he maintained, by the intermittent blasts of air from the ship's somewhat primitive air conditioning.[1] He was still ailing when they docked at Naples on the 15th, and the following Tuesday, when the illness persisted, his doctor ordered him to bed for the rest of the week. Rehearsals for the *Rake,* due to start in Milan, were postponed. It was a distinctly subdued, low-spirited return to European soil.

The pneumonia had, however, one fortunate result. The travellers were met on the quay by Auden and Kallman, by Leitner, the reserve conductor, and by Theodore, Denise, and their fourteen-year-old niece and adoptive daughter, Kitty. Igor had not set eyes on his eldest son for almost twelve years, and though his illness robbed him of all but the gentlest Neapolitan sightseeing, it repaid him with time to spend with his family while Craft, who was on his first visit to Europe, nosed round the city, took the bus to Pompeii and Sorrento, visited Auden and Kallman on Ischia and the Blue Grotto on Capri, and for once enjoyed the riches of his new life without its sometimes wearying obligations. Not until the 26th was Stravinsky pronounced fit to take the train north to Milan, where to their astonishment they were greeted at the Hotel Duomo by cheering crowds undeterred by the fact that the train had arrived two hours late.[2]

In the south they had already come face to face with the agonizing contrasts of postwar Europe—contrasts for which nothing in the America they knew had seriously prepared them. Poverty and Naples were historic companions, of course, but the violent bombardments of 1943 had left a moral and physical wreckage that eight years had done little to repair. For the first time in their lives, the well-heeled Stravinskys were made to feel uneasy, even a little frightened, by the deprivation through which they passed. Milan was more modern-feeling, and it was comforting to be reminded that, whatever the young bloods of the Messiaen set might think, Stravinsky was still a celebrity in cultivated Europe, just as on his prewar tours when he had routinely been met at railway stations by photographers and local dignitaries bearing bouquets. In any case, Milan meant rehearsals more than sightseeing, and though they might visit the cathedral and the Sforza castle, or lunch at Bellaggio or Certosa di Pavia, the important thing now was to teach the *Rake* to the Scala orchestra and English pronunciation to its chorus. The language coaching was delegated to Auden, who made no complaint about this necessary task but grumbled furiously about Ebert's production, which "could hardly be worse if the director were Erwin Piscator and the singers were climbing and descending ladders," and about Stravinsky's conducting ("he can't conduct . . . doesn't know the score . . . is deaf"[3]). For the composer it certainly was in some ways a process of discovery. He would sometimes rehearse at unnecessary length out of sheer curiosity to experience the orchestral sound imagined for so long at the piano. When they proceeded to Venice a week before the opening, he mostly preferred to sit in on Leitner's rehearsals rather than take his own. Not until the first dress rehearsal in the Fenice on the 9th of September did he conduct a proper run-through on his own account.[4]

The atmosphere in Venice was a disagreeable reminder of Naples and its extremes of poverty and disaffection. A vigorously Communist city, it reeked of an anti-Americanism as unmistakable as the exhalations of its canals and gutters. The wealthy sailed in in their yachts and the smart hotels did good business, but for the wretched Venetians such things were no better than a sideshow at which they might be permitted to gawp, preferably from a safe distance behind a rope. As a symbol of these disparities, *The Rake's Progress* could hardly have been better chosen. Its costume drama about a rich wastrel who marries a bearded lady and tries to make bread out of stones epitomized the incurable frivolity of the international rich, and the fact that its composer was known to have been paid fifty times the average annual income just to come and conduct it was calculated to send a shiver down the spine of even the moderate left-wing press. When the audience itself began to forgather, and the conductors, opera managers, modern-music addicts, composers, and publishers began, in Nicolas Nabokov's words, to mingle with "the most elegant and snobbish set of international café society and titled owners of Venetian palaces,"⁵ the picture was complete and the stage set for a crucial showdown between the World of Art and the world of painful modern reality.

Whatever the standing of the Fenice as an international opera house, the annual music festival (for some reason known as the Biennale) was rapidly acquiring a prestige that would, in the next few years, give it real importance as a showcase for new work and star performers. Only three days before the *Rake* premiere, Victor de Sabata had conducted a stunning Verdi *Requiem* in the Fenice, with Elisabeth Schwarzkopf (Stravinsky's Anne Trulove) among the soloists. On the night of *The Rake's Progress,* in stifling sirocco heat, the jam of gondolas and *motoscafi* at the theatre's canal entrance was so great, and the crush of old friends in the foyer so intense, that the start was delayed for more than half an hour and it was nine thirty-five by the time Stravinsky sped to the rostrum, spread his arms to acknowledge the audience's ecstatic welcome, and gave the downbeat for the opening E-major chord of the fanfare-prelude. He was understandably nervous. He had been absent from Europe for twelve years, he had seldom conducted stage opera and not at all since *The Nightingale* at La Scala in 1926, and the *Rake* was a long and deceptively complicated work, full of tricky cues and awkward tempo changes—not difficult in the *Rite of Spring* sense, but in its own way unforgiving and, as he knew perfectly well, underprepared. From the start the audience fidgeted and rustled their programs, trying to grasp crucial details of the plot—the dead uncle, the catechism, the bearded lady—from the sometimes involved poetry and convoluted action of the libretto. The composer's initial insistence on a premiere in an anglophone city may well have come back to haunt him, since only three of his Venice soloists were native English-speakers, the chorus might as well have been singing in Swahili, and in neither case could the Italian audience be expected to understand more than the occasional phrase.⁶

Somehow the opera trundled along, kept alive by the quality of the Scala orchestra, the excellence of individual performances—Schwarzkopf's Anne, Hugues Cuénod's auctioneer Sellem—and above all by Stravinsky's own presence, which imparted a sense of excitement and uniqueness to the whole occasion. Details were often untidy or worse; there were missed entries, wrong notes, and sloppy rhythms, attributable partly to Stravinsky's inexperience at cueing the stage, partly to the singers' own unfamiliarity with the idiom. Ebert had been able to do little more by way of stage direction than simply get the work on, sometimes in the teeth of Auden's unconcealed animosity during production rehearsals. As for Ratto's sets, they were too Italian and too stately. "With a house as grand as [Trulove's]," Auden had remarked, "the Rake would be better off marrying the daughter right away and forgoing his progress."⁷ They were also too complicated. To the composer's annoyance, there were unscripted pauses for scene changes, to add to the excessively long intervals during which the audience spilled out into the Campo San Fantin and discussed the music's stylistic borrowings and Mme. Schwarzkopf's unforgettable top C over their grappa and *caffè espresso*. By the time Stravinsky swung into the moralistic epilogue, it was one o'clock and not a few of the audience had gone home. The majority that remained gave him a huge ovation with twenty or more curtain calls, and the newspaper headlines the next day duly reported "uno straordinario successo" and "un avvenimento d'arte." But the small print of the local reviews, which Vera spirited away before the maestro could be troubled by them, told a different, more intricate story.

On the whole, the Italian critics were willing to allow Stravinsky the mastery of his craft, at least as regards the fine detail of the new work, even if there were complaints that it was, as Guido Pannain put it, "a flightless opera [*senza voli*], constructed piece by piece, which you listen to without abandon, without ever being taken over by it, but with curiosity, sometimes with annoyance, while at the same time admiring its skillful, painstaking craftsmanship."⁸ They were, however, almost universally puzzled by the music's synthetic qualities, its seemingly pointless reanimation of dead conventions. Pannain detected in the *Rake* "the artifice of an essay in imitation, [. . .] an industrialized eighteenth century. A return to past forms? Yes, but in the manner of a collector: a reflective meditation, without spontaneity and limited in its initiative." His *Giornale* colleague grumbled at the whole implication that the dramatic relationship between stage action and music could be reduced to such purely conventional terms, an error, he went on, "compounded by a worn out invention which certainly cannot compare with that of an 'Oedipus Rex' or a 'Persephone' [notwithstanding] joyous pages of an exquisite intimacy, and others of a life-giving wit, the product of a lucky hand which manages to transform into music whatever it touches."⁹ Behind such qualifications there lurked an evident fear of what it later became normal to call "irrelevance," whether social or aesthetic. The Milan critic, Franco Abbiati, saw in the *Rake* "an act of birth and a certificate of death, a declaration of love and a sign of impotence, a miracle of open-mindedness and a triumph of conventionality." It was "everything and nothing, everything that has for centuries existed within the orbit of melodrama, nothing that can stand comparison with all that those centuries have given us—nothing, that is, which might open up the hope of a substantial renewal of dramatic expression."¹⁰ And Teodoro Celli ended a long and by no means unfriendly review by identifying "the fearful sadness which issues from this score, technically so rigorous and 'perfect,' as if it were the proof of some theorem in geometry," and concluding that the opera was nevertheless "the document of a sentimental shame which verges on the pathological."[11]

In their apparently perverse way, these observations touch on an aspect of the *Rake* that had dogged Stravinsky's heels ever since he had begun work on the opening scene almost three and a half years before. From the start, the idyllic tone of the lovers' duet had demanded a clarity of style and texture that seemed to contradict the whole idea of modernism; but then the urban scenes, with their references to Mozart and ballad opera, had insisted on an equivalent, almost demotic, simplicity—the simplicity of a sublimated eighteenth-century popular music. Now, it was perfectly true that "simplification" had always been one of the battle cries of a certain kind of neoclassicism, the kind that reacted against the exaggerated complexity of high romanticism. But in 1951 that was no longer an issue with "progressive" artists. The real problem of postwar neoclassicism was rather the question of how a synthetic style could proceed at all in a world that, as many felt, had rejected the past and was yet again in search of new expressive tongues and new technical resources. Listening to the *Rake*, with its arias and recitatives, its breezy, lyrical tunes and smooth tonal harmonies, one might imagine that in his seventieth year Stravinsky had at last made his peace with his audience, opted out of the stylistic battle, and would soon be retiring to his Hollywood garden to grow begonias. On any contemporary view, the *Rake* looked and sounded like the end of the long road from *Pulcinella* and the Octet. Those critics who sensed its undiminished vitality naturally assumed that its denial of modernism would be decisive for future work. "Stravinsky," remarked one, "is going in the direction of melody. . . . He will probably be the Verdi of the second half of the twentieth century." Another interpreted the opera as "Stravinsky's warning to other composers that they must not be incomprehensible to the public. The era of ferocious dissonance is ended. Whether this work contains the seeds of life, however, is too early to decide."[12] But if not here, where? The most curious thing of all is that, three decades after *Mavra* and more than two after *Apollo*, nobody seems to have expected to be surprised by Stravinsky anymore. The only question left was whether, creatively, he would live and do more of the same, or simply turn over and die.

IT WAS IN Venice that, so far as his old friends and admirers were concerned, Stravinsky effectively returned to Europe. At the Hotel Bauer Grünwald, he and Vera installed themselves in the vast and airy Royal Suite, looking out over Santa Maria della Salute toward the Giudecca, and the indispensable piano was winched up to the first floor from the Rio di San

Moisè at the side of the hotel. Auden was less fortunate. The Scala management had deposited him in a cramped upper room without a bath, and he soon appeared in the Stravinsky suite weeping with mortification, and was promptly found something better through the good offices of the head porter, a part-time composer by the name of Luigi Tortorella. Craft, in his own smaller first-floor room, accepted his menial position, understandably, with a better grace.[13]

Well before the first night, the reunions began. Nadia Boulanger and Marcelle Meyer were there early from Paris. Igor Markevitch appeared, and Stephen Spender, who was in Venice on Auden's account but soon befriended the composer. The premiere itself brought an avalanche of old acquaintance: Nabokov and Boris Kochno, Leopold Survage and Marya Freund, Marie-Laure de Noailles, Domenico de' Paoli, Paul Collaer, and Charles-Albert Cingria, among many others.[14] "The master and I melted into each other's arms," Cingria told a friend, "and we chewed the fat at some length."[15] After the performance, the hardier or more excitable among them repaired with Stravinsky to the Taverna la Fenice, talked about the music and the performance and played spot-the-derivation, until dawn rose over San Marco and they staggered wearily to their beds.[16] But through all these proceedings, the composer seems to have preserved a certain detachment from his past. When Vera and Craft took a vaporetto to the San Michele cemetery the day after the premiere to put flowers on Diaghilev's grave, Stravinsky superstitiously refused to go with them. Venice might be the most beautiful city in the world, but it was also one of the most frightening, especially for someone like Stravinsky, who (like Diaghilev himself) could not swim, and for whom a city of canals was an only half-agreeable reminder of his childhood in St. Petersburg. Looking across the Giudecca or back from San Giorgio Maggiore toward the Piazzetta, he could almost imagine himself on the Palace Embankment by the Neva looking out toward Vasilevsky Island and the Peter and Paul Fortress. Then again, if Venice was redolent of childhood, it also often made you think of death. Even Craft found that the Lido conjured up Mann's famous novella, a book Stravinsky disliked. The whole place was like an epitome of old Europe, fascinating and irresistible, but somehow finished. If the composer ever, on this trip, thought of moving back permanently, the idea was fleeting and did not take root. Vera was another matter. She by this time detested Los Angeles, liked New York, but really wanted nothing better than to go back to her old friends in Paris, a city Igor did not even want to visit. In such matters her will was never law, and as usual she accepted the inevitable with a wistful shrug of the shoulders.

That same day following the first performance there was a pompous little ceremony in the City Hall at which Stravinsky was officially welcomed to

La Serenissima and thanked for his opera by the mayor.[17] On the 13th he sat in the audience while Leitner conducted an altogether tidier, less nervy, and no doubt less interesting second performance of the *Rake*. Their remaining ten days in Venice were a much-needed holiday. They went to Torcello, with its unforgettable mosaics, and Chioggia, at the southern end of the lagoon, where the people were if anything even poorer than in the city but knew who their visitor was and applauded him as he came ashore. Later they drove to Padua and Vicenza and had tea with the Grand Duchess Marie Pavlovna (cousin of Tsar Nicholas II) at the Villa Malcontenta, one of the Veneto properties of their Wetherly Drive neighbor, the Baroness d'Erlanger. Since their chauffeur was another Russian aristocrat, Baron Raffaello de Banfield Tripcovich, who also drove them in his Lancia to Ravenna and Ferrara before returning them to their Royal Suite at the Bauer Grünwald, it may well have crossed their minds that, whatever Europeans in general thought of modern art, they knew how to treat modern artists. It was their first real taste of VIP life on the grand scale, and they rather enjoyed it.[18] But reality called, and on the 23rd of September they finally left Venice for Milan and the start of a very different kind of tour.

Stravinsky's two concerts in La Scala at the end of the month were the quid pro quo for Ghiringhelli's backing down over the *Rake,* and for the fact that the composer would not be staying to conduct the Milan performances of the opera itself at the end of the year. The main part of the autumn tour, however, was through Germany and German Switzerland, and was the outcome of much pressure from Strecker and, more recently, Heinrich Strobel, now the music director of the Südwestfunk—the South-West German Radio—at Baden-Baden. Since Ralph Hawkes's death the previous September, Strecker had been engaged in heavy discussions with AMP and a battery of New York lawyers in the hope of securing for Schott some kind of joint agreement over Stravinsky's music, and with it a permanent deal to replace his Boosey and Hawkes contract, which was due to expire at the end of 1951. The negotiations (which came to nothing, Strecker thought, because of the bullying tactics of AMP's attorneys) partly indicated Stravinsky's extreme nervousness about the situation at Boosey's after Hawkes's death, but they also reflected the energy of German regrowth and the determination of administrators there to reassert the richness and efficient organization of the German cultural scene after the desert years of the Third Reich. Bringing Stravinsky back to Germany was a vital symbolic act for the regeneration of the country's musical life.

The tour started in Cologne, where he conducted a public concert of the *Symphonies of Wind Instruments, Apollo,* and *Oedipus Rex* with the North-West German Radio Orchestra, and also recorded the *Symphonies* and *Oedipus Rex* for Columbia, with whom he had signed a new exclusive contract only six weeks earlier in Naples.[19] Such a program showed at once the serious intentions and elastic resources of the new German radio stations, in stark contrast with the wreckage of the city's buildings and bridges. The radio building itself, Craft noted, was still under construction, but the orchestra and chorus were alike of a high standard. On the 9th of October they took the *Rheingold Express* to Baden-Baden, where Stravinsky conducted a single concert with the Südwestfunk orchestra that same day, but otherwise spent his time in the mild air and soothing environment of the Black Forest spa town trying to shake off an attack of laryngitis picked up in draughty Cologne.

As the guest of two successive radio orchestras, Stravinsky was invited to listen to recent recordings of which they were especially proud. Thus "kleine Modernsky," as Schoenberg had once satirically dubbed him, found himself in a Cologne studio with Robert Craft, listening probably for the first time to major orchestral works by the Viennese master, in the shape of the Violin Concerto, and the "Dance round the Golden Calf" from *Moses und Aron,* which Scherchen had premiered in a Darmstadt concert three months before. What Stravinsky thought of this orgiastic but hypersophisticated music, history does not relate. Craft reports only that he listened "attentively" and displayed no reaction.[20] But Baden-Baden had a far more disconcertingly esoteric experience in store for him. On the day after his own concert there on the 14th, Strobel ushered him into a listening room of the Südwestfunk and played him recordings of music by Webern, Pierre Boulez, and others from the radio station's extensive tape library. Whether or not Stravinsky had met Webern in Vienna at the ISCM reception in 1926, there is no evidence that he had ever heard a note of his music.[21] His encounter now with the late orchestral *Variations,* op. 30, one of Webern's most mysterious and attenuated works, must have been at best puzzling, and it may have been as much because of the music's strangeness as for anything more specific in its impact that Stravinsky twice asked for it to be repeated. He also heard a recording of Boulez's recent *Polyphonie X,* which Hans Rosbaud had conducted at the Donaueschingen Festival the previous week. He listened in a state of bewilderment to the furious complexities of this dense chamber-orchestral piece in which every element was governed by serial thinking, and of which Rosbaud's far from accurate performance was accompanied by hoots of laughter, catcalls and at one point a blast from a police whistle. By comparison, Hans Werner Henze's Third Symphony and Krenek's Violin Concerto, which Strobel also probably played him, will have sounded agreeably old-fashioned, though both are in one way or another post-Schoenbergian in spirit and technique, and essentially unlike anything Stravinsky had heard in America.[22]

Meanwhile Nicolas Nabokov, having acted as midwife for the Venice

Rake, was incubating a plan for a festival of twentieth-century music in Paris the following spring, under the auspices of the Congress for Cultural Freedom. The idea was for a kind of grand retrospective of the first half of the century, and naturally Stravinsky was to figure prominently. Nabokov hoped to secure the French premiere of the opera, he wanted Balanchine to stage *The Rite of Spring,* and he wanted Stravinsky himself to conduct a concert of his works. His intentions, which he later claimed to have formulated in detail during an eleven-hour transatlantic flight in May, were in every sense high-minded, but he knew enough about Paris—and probably (despite his subsequent denials) about the politics and CIA funding of the CCF—not to expect to get his way without obstruction.[23] As designer for the *Rite* he had hoped to get Picasso, but Picasso's Communist sympathies and his recent anti-American, *Guernica*-like canvas *Massacre in Korea* ruled him out, while Tchelitcheff, whom Stravinsky favored, was still refusing to work in the theatre. As for the *Rake,* it turned out that the Opéra already had a contract for the Paris premiere, and Nabokov's only hope was for some kind of co-production. At this point, Nabokov turned up in Baden-Baden, and on 12 October Stravinsky signed an agreement to direct three separate events in Paris for a fee of four and a half thousand dollars plus two thousand for expenses. Then just over a week later, in the Deutsches Museum in Munich, he again conducted *Oedipus Rex,* and it must have been the success of this performance (which still survives on tape) that decided him to offer Nabokov *Oedipus* instead of *The Rite of Spring.*[24]

For more than two months they had been wandering round Italy, Germany, and now Switzerland, and from the very start Stravinsky had never been quite well. His Cologne laryngitis had turned into flu. Baden-Baden had been a partial rest cure, but even so when they reached Geneva on 24 October he was still getting mild temperatures, which he had already used as a pretext for cancelling a concert he was to have given in Lausanne. In his mind, Switzerland remained the natural home of the chronically ill. Vera Nosenko had written from Leysin in the hope of calling on them, and Igor had shuddered at the memory of those snowy heights where Katya had first been treated for tuberculosis, and at the thought of the debt of honor he owed to this kindhearted but not hugely loved cousin-in-law who had looked after his sickly granddaughter throughout the war years. The visit could not be avoided. On 2 November they went to Lausanne and paid their respects to Vera and her older sister Olga, the companions of his Ustilug summers of half a century ago. The last time he had seen Vera, in 1939, she had pressed a stethoscope to his chest, and perhaps she did the same again now. She might as well have done at any rate; the information would have been less distressing but still probably not altogether welcome.[25]

In Geneva they saw much of Theodore and Denise, but could not be accommodated by them, and instead put up at the smart Hôtel des Bergues, on the Rhône at the point where it flows on out of the lake. At Theodore's, predictably enough, they met a new doctor, Maurice Gilbert, who at once, like so many of the Stravinskys' professional advisers, became a friend as well as a physician and took them on a tour of Fribourg and the Vaud, ending up at Les Tilleuls in Clarens, the birthplace of *The Rite of Spring*. Somewhat uncharacteristically, they went about Geneva by public transport, and one day they ran into Ansermet on a tram.[26] Later he and they dined together, but though relations were amicable, the old intimacy eluded them, not just because of memories of *Jeu de cartes* or the more recent awkwardness over the Mass premiere, but because Ansermet in person had become judicial and intellectually obstinate, and his enthusiasms—formerly so dependable—now often seemed provisional or subject to analysis. "It's clear," Stravinsky had written to Theodore, "that he's impossible to get on with."[27] Matters were not helped by the fact that, since Ansermet had programmed *Orpheus* in a pair of concerts the previous week, pressure had been put on the composer not to include it in his own concert on 4 November. He insisted on doing so, however, and pointedly absented himself from Ansermet's concert four days before. Stravinsky, too, could be obstinate.

The most important reunion, though, was with Theodore himself. Their long separation had ended in Naples; but the Geneva meetings were probably more relaxed, if only because the *Rake* and the German concert tour were now over and done with and, after all, Theodore was at home here and could enjoy his father's and stepmother's company in a calm domestic environment. One might suppose that those who observed them at close hand would be anxious to record how it was: the joys and hesitations, the tensions and stiffnesses, the entire manner of the forty-four-year-old son toward his devoted but despotic father. But there is nothing of the kind in Craft's published diaries, nor in the reports that Vera sent back to Theodore's sister in Los Angeles. In the latest and fullest version of his chronicle, Craft mentions that Theodore was on the quay at Naples with Denise and Kitty but says not one word about them, though he must surely have been curious at the time.[28] His Geneva diary refers to the Ansermet meeting and Dr. Gilbert; but the only family name that figures is Vera Nosenko's, which is included merely to record Stravinsky's irritation at having to visit her.[29] Of course, the *Chronicle of a Friendship* is a published "work," much preoccupied with the famous and describable, brilliant in its way if somewhat self-conscious like all such documents, and demonstrably false as a contemporary record in the sense that the various published texts differ substantially one from another. If no cloud of suspicion hung over the subsequent relations between Stravinsky's family and his American companion, one might not give the omission a second thought. As it is, it will gradually and inevitably assume a certain significance.

Before flying back to the States, Stravinsky had concert bookings in Rome and Naples, and in the event he gave an extra concert in Rome, at the Teatro Argentina on the 19th of November, in aid of the victims of the Po Valley floods. Chester Kallman was alone on Ischia, Auden having returned to New York from Venice, and he and the Stravinskys met and for the first time, according to Craft, became intimate.[30] Kallman was hoping to be invited to help stage the *Rake* at La Scala, and had been tinkering with the work's theatrical detailing. He had even come up with what he called "a very private extra scene. [. . .] It's to open the third act and be between Mother Goose, Trulove and Sellem . . . We can reveal that Mother Goose and Trulove go off together at the end."[31] The point of this particular little jest was that in the Venice production there had been a long pause between the first two scenes of the final act, the auction and the graveyard, and to avoid this problem in future it would be necessary either to move the auction scene to the end of the second act or to add some front-of-curtain business to cover the scene-change. In their Naples discussions in November, Stravinsky must have argued for the former solution, since Kallman wrote to him soon afterwards specifically refuting it, and Stravinsky acknowledged his arguments, while insisting that "*I will not accept* any stops between scenes as it was in Venice."[32]

Their first transatlantic flight, starting from Rome on the 21st of November, was a protracted, complicated, and exhausting affair. Earlier in the year, Charles Blair had set a new record of just under eight hours for the opposite, west-east, crossing; but the Rome airliner made stops in Paris (where there was time for them to have dinner at the airport with Arthur Sachs), Shannon, Gander, and Boston, was in the air for some fourteen hours, and finally put down at Idlewild a full thirty hours after initial takeoff.[33] Not surprisingly Stravinsky, who was in any case scared of flying, arrived at the Lombardy in an edgy mood, took against the expensive "modernized" discomfort of a hotel they had used before and liked, and checked for the first time into the Gladstone, on East 52nd Street, which thereafter became their regular Manhattan base. Yet within hours he was standing up in front of the New York City Ballet orchestra, rehearsing *The Fairy's Kiss* for a performance a mere three days later.[34]

Lincoln Kirstein had at last abandoned his efforts to mount the *Rake* on Broadway, and had instead returned to the charge on the promised new ballet. The latest idea for a subject was a pageant set in "a vast ballroom in space," in which assorted gods and demigods—Zeus, Apollo, Prometheus, and others—would present a kind of history of the dance, from the pavane to the polka, leading up to "a big jazz finale."35 The ballet would be called *Terpsichore.* Kirstein sent Stravinsky a draft scenario at the end of November, and it is obvious from his letter that the idea had already been discussed, probably when Stravinsky was in New York on his way to Venice at the start of August. No doubt it was discussed again now. Stravinsky spent several evenings at the ballet; he saw *Tyl Ulenspiegel* (the Balanchine version, not the long-lost Nijinsky ballet), Bartók's *Miraculous Mandarin,* and his own Basle concerto danced as *The Cage,* a new Jerome Robbins ballet about insect Amazons. But there were too many other distractions for him to settle on anything specific at this moment. During December they went many times to the Metropolitan Opera, as guests of Rudolf Bing, with whom Igor was now in serious negotiations for precisely that big-stage *Rake* premiere which he had always previously insisted on opposing. And meanwhile, Auden was pressing him on the matter of a second operatic collaboration. The latest project was a one-act adaptation of George Peele's satirical drama *The Old Wives' Tale,* another by-product, like "The maidens came," of Auden's work on the *Poets of the English Language.* He and Stravinsky mapped out a scenario in December in New York,36 and by March, with Kallman back from Ischia, the libretto of *Delia,* as it was to be called, was complete. But there was a snag. With the Venice twenty thousand dollars still fresh in everyone's mind, the librettists were insisting on a formal contract, and meanwhile the composer was flatly refusing to compose a note without a firm commission and money on the table.37

He thus arrived home on New Year's Day without a major project in view. Either the ballet or the opera might come next, but neither was settled either contractually or as regards subject. *Delia* was going to be an expensive commission, and when Betty Bean approached the directors of the Aspen Festival, they were enthusiastic but pointed out that the combined fee was five times the figure mentioned to them by another, unnamed but "well-known" composer. Meanwhile, Sam Dushkin had come up with a possible symphonic commission by an anonymous patron whose identity he never revealed but who must likewise have been struck dumb by Stravinsky's fee of fifteen thousand dollars, since nothing more was heard from that quarter. In some ways more intriguing, because more specific, was a suggestion from an English filmwriter called Simon Harcourt-Smith that Stravinsky should compose music for a film of the *Odyssey.* Harcourt-Smith had suitably Homeric ideas for the project. His ideal Odysseus was Douglas Fairbanks Jr., and the script, when it landed on the Wetherly Drive doormat, proved to be rich in wide-screen incident: "Wagner, not Stravinsky," Craft said when invited to read it and give his opinion.38 It soon emerged, however, that Harcourt-Smith was not the only pebble on the Ithacan beach, and when Michael Powell came in mid-March to discuss what was evidently in essence the same project, he had quite other ideas about scripting and casting, and promised that Dylan Thomas would be involved.

What these various and interesting proposals could not conceal was that in a certain sense Stravinsky was becalmed. It was as if the huge effort involved in composing a full-length opera had left him limp and exhausted, just as conversation can die when a topic that has dominated it for too long suddenly reaches some natural conclusion. The only work in hand was the songbook, or "mezzo-soprano cycle," as Auden had called it,[39] for which "The maidens came" had already been drafted, and he seemed in no immediate hurry to take that up again. In the whole of January the only music he composed was an innocent little improvization theme for Marcel Dupré, the organist of Saint-Sulpice in Paris, which he dispatched via Nadia Boulanger on the 8th.[40] A week later he conducted a concert of his own chamber works in the Royce Hall, on the UCLA campus. It might almost have been another benefit for flood victims. The rain came down in torrents, Sunset Boulevard was blocked by a mud slide, and the concert was delayed for an hour because the first trombonist (who was in every piece except the *Dumbarton Oaks* concerto) could not cross a ravine carved across the road by the floods.[41] As if the weather were not bad enough, a more potent misery entered their lives. Huxley suddenly announced that Maria had breast cancer and had already—on the 12th—had a mastectomy. By the end of the month her condition had been diagnosed as terminal, but Aldous himself either did not know the truth or was unable, in his rational mind, to accept it. They did their best to divert him. He came to lunch often, and to the UCLA concert, and continued to take refuge in his vast and sometimes inconsequential erudition. "In a few more weeks," he wrote to Maria's sister Jeanne, "I think that M will be back to normal, able to do everything . . ."[42]

Early in February Stravinsky reopened his first volume of *Poets of the English Language* and started work on a setting of "Westron winde," a mysterious little poem about wet weather and lost love. A few days later, on the 8th, he turned a couple of pages and composed the first line of "Tomorrow shall be my dancing day," a carol of uncertain antiquity cast in the form of an autobiography of Christ. The setting of the first line remains inchoate in the sketch, but Stravinsky quickly found something like a definitive music for the line that in different forms serves as refrain to each of the eleven verses, "To call my true love to my dance." On the same page of sketches there is also some practice counterpoint involving canon. He had recently once again been immersing himself in old music of various kinds and periods, from Bach's "48" backwards. He and Craft had just been playing through Heinrich Isaac's *Choralis Constantinus* on the piano, and on the day of the first "Westron winde" sketch, they spent the evening at the Huxleys' and listened to music by the fifteenth-century French master Dufay.[43] He had also heard Hugues Cuénod's recent recording of the *Leçons de Ténèbres* of Couperin, and had written to him pleading to know where he could get hold of the printed music.[44] Then on the 12th he attended a rehearsal of Schoenberg's Suite, op. 29, which Craft was due to conduct at a Roof concert a couple of weeks later. After the rehearsal Craft tried to explain to him how the music was made, but found it hard, at first, to overcome his prejudices, and, perhaps, his instinctive distaste for the idiom.[45]

It was always Stravinsky's advice to young composers to "find a model,"[46] and no doubt he was at this moment practicing what he preached. But for once the old music did not afford him what he needed. Eric Walter White once suggested that "Tomorrow shall be my dancing day" was reminiscent of the *Leçons de Ténèbres,* but the comparison (no doubt prompted by Stravinsky) argues unfamiliarity with Couperin's elegant baroque "Lamentations" and above all with their peculiar form, which Stravinsky stored up and copied only much later on.[47] For the moment, it was the Schoenberg (rather than Webern's Quartet, op. 22, which was also on Craft's program) that, against all probability, caught his imagination.[48]

The Suite was in fact one of the few Schoenberg works that he claimed to have heard before (in Venice in 1937). But whereas a quarter-century before he had assured readers of the *Daily Mail* that "Schoenberg is one of the greatest creative spirits of our age," by the late thirties he was describing him as

> a chemist of music more than an artistic creator. His investigations are interesting, since they tend to expand the possibilities of auditory pleasure, but just as with Haba, the discoverer of quarter-tones, they have more to do with the quantity than with the quality of the music.[49]

In 1936, Stravinsky had almost certainly not heard any of Schoenberg's serial music, but he had had it described to him, mostly by hostile judges such as Lourié.[50] In the circumstances, his opinion is much what one would expect. Schoenberg had devised a method that involved taking the twelve different notes in the octave, arranging them in a certain order, then using that order—or series—as a fixed template for the melodic and harmonic material of an entire work. Put so crudely, it sounded about as pointless artistically as change-ringing. You could play the series forwards, backwards, or upside down, or the upside-down version backwards, and you could do all these things starting on any note you liked. Every music student has experienced that moment of despair on first hearing Schoenberg "explained" in these terms, that feeling of disbelief that anyone would bother to write, listen to, or study music conceived in such a way. What Craft achieved with Stravinsky was simply what any sensible music teacher would at once see as necessary: he transmitted his own enthusiasm for the actual music, and only then, when pressed, showed how the music and the method interacted—how this particular music came out of this particular set of procedures, exactly as one might do in analyzing a Josquin motet or a Bach fugue. After all, only a simpleton really imagines that large-scale pieces of music can be written without any structural or thematic scaffolding. The one question that matters is whether the music itself makes one want to find out how it is made.

Stravinsky never grew to like Schoenberg as much as Craft did, but as regards its musical substance the scales fell from his ears. The Suite, written in the mid-twenties, is a rich, strongly wrought, if sometimes hard-working piece, not always felicitous in its scoring (for three clarinets, piano, and string trio), but, from the very first chord, musically compelling. Stravinsky knew at once that it could not be ignored. And suddenly its method began to intrigue him. For much of the day after the first rehearsal, he practiced writing canons—a device fundamental to serialism; and the day after that they dined with Thomas Mann and surely discussed Schoenberg. "Tradition," Stravinsky remarked, "carries the good artist on its shoulder as St. Christopher carried the Lord," an observation that fits Schoenberg at least as well as himself.[51] The following Sunday (the 17th of February), he drafted part of the canonic setting of the penultimate verse of "Tomorrow shall be my dancing day," then went to another rehearsal of the Suite. Musically, there is not even a remote similarity between Schoenberg's work and what Stravinsky was writing, yet there cannot be any doubt that Stravinsky was in a sense using the Suite as a model.[52] Soon afterwards, the main theme of the opening emerged, apparently spontaneously, from a phrase of "The maidens came," and for some reason Stravinsky decided to treat it as a series.[53] It has eleven notes, including several duplicates (unlike a true Schoenberg "row," in which there are always twelve different notes), and this lends it a simple, tonal flavor completely unlike any serial melody by Schoenberg. By the time Craft conducted his performance of the Suite at the University of Southern California on the 24th, the long carol setting, for tenor, two flutes, and a cello, was practically complete in outline. Stravinsky still had no clear idea of what he was writing. He had one three-minute song, one fifteen-minute one, and a fragment of a third, and he had been so absorbed in the intricacies of the work that he had not even noticed, for instance, that his flautists were being expected to play for a quarter of an hour almost without drawing breath.[54] He had not decided whether he was writing a song cycle or, if so, how many songs it would contain.[55] Never in his life had he been so detached from any idea of the final product.

Toward the end of February 1952, he took to his bed with a bad dose of flu and had to wire Carlos Chávez in Mexico City, postponing a pair of concerts he was to have conducted there in the second week of March. Instead, on the 8th, they drove out for lunch at Palmdale, in the Mojave Desert, and on the way back Stravinsky did something else that he had never done before: he broke down and wept. He was finished as a composer, he said; the *Rake* would be his last work. What was more, he felt exposed by Schoenberg's mastery and incriminated by the years in which he, Stravinsky, had written serialism off as some kind of fin de siècle number-mysticism or chemical experimentation.[56] He almost seemed to be adopting Leibowitz's opinion of his recent music as "the deadly *Maya*" of art, compared with the "amazing abundance," the "vitality and creative strength" of late Schoenberg.[57] It was a frightening moment of emptiness and fear for a man whose life had for fifty years been founded on composition, but who had also known the terrors of rejection and insecurity.

Casting about for a remedy, Craft suggested that instead of fighting his creative block head-on, he should reorchestrate an early work such as the string-quartet Concertino, which, he maintained, was admired by progressives but which might benefit from more varied instrumentation and would make a useful concert piece.[58] Stravinsky at once took this advice. Two days after the Palmdale confession, he told Roth that he was working on a transcription of the Concertino for twelve instruments, and also on an arrangement for small orchestra of the accompaniment to his early Verlaine songs, of which there in fact already existed a version with standard orchestra, performed by his brother Gury as long ago as 1914, but never published.[59] For Roth these two somewhat marginal pieces of work meant more trouble than they were perhaps worth, since both originals were the property of other publishers, who would automatically own publication rights in any arrangement. Stravinsky, naturally enough, was more interested in their practical creative value. The Concertino, especially, is no simple transcription, but a typically inventive piece of rewriting which makes capital out of unexpected aspects of the quartet movement.[60] Though not particularly likable as sound and arguably, for a short piece, too kaleidoscopic in coloring, it nicely symbolizes its composer's abiding creative energy and opportunism, and it sounds as if the task gave him pleasure.

Stravinsky chose the scoring from the instruments needed for a Los Angeles Chamber Orchestra concert he had agreed to conduct in the autumn, and in which he had decided to include his new songs and the old Octet.[61] So the Concertino is linked to the evolving shape of the songbook, and Stravinsky worked on them side by side. A fortnight after Palmdale he rewrote "Westron winde" as a duet for the two voices (mezzo-soprano and tenor) that he now needed for the other songs, and then, after his postponed Mexican tour in the last week of the month, he scored "The maidens came" for flutes, oboes, and a cello, as in the carol. At last he was beginning to make sense of what he was writing. He was soon telling Craft that the vocal pieces would be interspersed with a series of instrumental chorales.[62] Later, the chorales themselves became vocal. The work would be a semi-sacred Cantata about death and rebirth, love and the seasons, with the long carol, or "Sacred History," at its center, and braced at its four "corners" by verses of the "Lyke-wake Dirge" composed for a small female choir. Thus Christ's Nativity, Passion, and Resurrection would be framed by the recurrent *memento mori* of "This ae nighte," like the panels of a Last Judgment or a Romanesque arch with Christ in Glory surrounded by human souls in various states of redemption or damnation. And as so often in late medieval work, the beauty and simplicity of the conception would conceal an immense intricacy and even cerebration in the craftsmanship.

On Palm Sunday, the 13th of April, the grateful composer presented Craft with a manuscript page from "The maidens came," the exquisite wedding piece out of which the Cantata had sprung, inscribing it "To Bob whom I lob."[63]

> *And through the glasse window*
> *Shines the sone.*
> *How shuld I love and I so young?*

The next day Craft himself conducted another Schoenberg score, the Serenade, op. 24, a work that passingly resembles the Cantata in some formal respects, having seven movements with a serial vocal movement (a setting of a Petrarch sonnet) at its center. That Saturday, the 19th, Stravinsky completed his arrangement of the Concertino. For him, the Easter Vigil had, that year, a special significance.

19

COUNT ONE, COUNT TWO,
COUNT TWELVE

WHILE STRAVINSKY had been engaged in a struggle with his artistic identity, Nicolas Nabokov had been doing battle with the more tangible, but in
some ways no less slippery, bureaucracy of the Parisian musical world over
the question of the French premiere of the *Rake*. At the Opéra there was the
usual problem of knowing who exactly was in charge and what were his
true intentions. Maurice Lehmann, the director, had an exclusive agreement with Boosey and Hawkes for the French premiere, which would
expire in July 1952, and this seemed to be in Nabokov's favor. But Lehmann
wanted Stravinsky to take the baton, while Stravinsky had announced, in
December, that for reasons of his own he declined to conduct the *Rake* in
Paris.[1] At one point Roth even floated the bizarre idea that he might at least
direct one act.[2] Then Stravinsky changed his mind and agreed to conduct
the whole opera for the small matter of five thousand dollars.[3] Nobody
seems to have taken this offer very seriously, and the next idea was that
Roger Desormière, a prewar friend of Stravinsky's and an experienced hand
at his music, might conduct instead. Unfortunately Desormière, a card-
carrying Communist, seemed unlikely to agree to take part in an anti-
Communist event, and it was for the same reason still more doubtful
whether Nabokov, or for that matter the Opéra, could engage him. Thus the
plan foundered partly on the political question and partly, Roth thought, on
Nabokov's lack of diplomatic subtlety,[4] and the *Rake* was duly postponed, as
Nabokov noted with a faint sneer, in favor of Rameau's *Les Indes galantes*.[5]

Stravinsky was understandably nervous about his Paris appearances, his
first anywhere in France since 1938. Paris had never been kind to his music,
and now it was as far as he knew the epicenter of a ferocious avant-garde
neomodernism which had already made trouble for works of his and of
which he had felt disconcerting tremors in the SWF studios in Baden-
Baden. That may have been why he had decided to conduct *Oedipus Rex*
rather than *The Rite of Spring*—of evil Parisian memory, though popular
with the modernists—and why he had asked for an old friend, Jean
Cocteau, to speak the narrations and design the staging. Cocteau responded

in a sympathetic spirit. Although he had invented the original visual concept of *Oedipus,* he had never seen the work staged, and now his new idea was to replace the static, two-dimensional tableau (with the singers onstage) with a series of *tableaux vivants* set on a platform behind the orchestra, and revealed and hidden at selected moments by a drop curtain with, as Jean described it, "a rather violent picture painted on it."[6] The tableaux would be presented by a trio of masked dancers, and Cocteau intended to construct the masks himself, with the help of a team of theatrical craftsmen, out of whatever materials came to hand: raffia for the hair, ping-pong balls for Oedipus's eyes, old cork panelling, discarded photographic lamps, and so forth.[7]

What he wanted, he explained to Stravinsky, was a series of aggressive images that nevertheless did not interfere with the music.

> I feel that we should leave to the oratorio its oratorio style. [. . .] The illustration will be no more than allusive, for since the opera isn't being put on as an opera, it would be a serious mistake to duplicate for the eye the action meant for the ear. [. . .] Your work is of such force that a visual pleonasm cannot be made of it. What is needed is a number of presentations to underline the grandeur with a calm violence. No one could understand better than you how impossible it is for us to acquiesce in the stupidity of an audience to which we are condemned by "galas."[8]

Poor Jean had just come from a society dinner at which the hostess, a maharani, wore "pink veils and fifty million francs' worth of pearls around her neck." "It is for this ridiculous public," he noted in his diary, "that I am preparing the production of *Oedipus Rex*."[9] But even Stravinsky, while professing a liking for his ideas,[10] was slow to understand the degree of detachment he intended between the scenario and the tableaux, which were to follow the oratorio "at a considerable distance."[11] Stravinsky had gathered that the singers would be involved in the tableaux. Had he known the tableaux' titles—which included "The Sadness of Athena," "The Sphinx," "The Oedipus Complex," and "The Three Jocastas" (mother, wife, and queen)—he would surely have got the point, though he might have been less sure of the effect.[12] His incomprehension made Cocteau nervous. "I am still worried," he noted in mid-April, "about this work for a luxury audience and a theatre booked in advance. Since Stravinsky doesn't seem to want my *tableaux* to be used during the oratorio, I will make them coincide with my texts. All I want is to finish this disagreeable work and get away."[13]

After a few days in New York, Stravinsky flew into Paris at Orly on 29 April 1952. He was en route initially for Geneva, where Theodore had persuaded him to attend a production of *The Rake's Progress* for which he had made the designs; but there was time at Orly for a program meeting with Nabokov, and Stravinsky also hoped to see Cocteau. "Where's Jean?" he demanded as he came off the plane.[14] But Jean was at Montsouris working on his masks, and Stravinsky flew on to Switzerland without seeing him or them. The Geneva *Rake,* conducted by Samuel Baud-Bovy, was its French-language premiere, but apart from Cuénod's Sellem, Craft found it "very provincial [and] underprepared," and seems once more to have noticed nothing about Theodore's family except that Kitty's adoption had recently been completed.[15]

The next day they were back in Paris for the CCF festival and attending another sort of premiere, the first French stage performance (by the visiting Vienna State Opera) of Berg's *Wozzeck.* Vera noted the event in her diary in big letters,[16] but beyond this it is hard to discern the exact character of the impression made on her husband by this great but, one would think, essentially alien masterpiece. When Craft, in his own diary, has Stravinsky praise the apparent spontaneity of a work "compounded of strict formal devices," one might suspect that it is the diarist speaking, just as the lengthy Berg critique in the *Conversations,* a few years later, is clearly the writer's—not the converser's—work.[17] The Stravinskys shared their box that night and dined afterwards with Albert Camus, who—for all his pianist wife—had no ear for the music and insisted on discussing Büchner's play.[18] It was evidently another of those occasions when great men meet and talk because, like Virgil and Dante, great men must meet and talk, or be reported as having talked, in quotable utterances. Camus later, unsuccessfully, tried to interest Stravinsky in a ballet scenario by René Char.[19] Nevertheless, Stravinsky did feel intellectually drawn to him, because of his recently published attack on the Stalinist wing of French socialism in *L'Homme révolté.* "He is the only person in France," he told Theodore, "who can stand up to Sartre, who has a very powerful brain, but for whom, unfortunately, I have absolutely no sympathy."[20] Whether this kind of issue came up between them, aside from its embodiment in the figures of Wozzeck and his tormentors, we unfortunately do not know.

Two days later, on 5 May, Stravinsky and Cocteau at last met again, for the first time for thirteen years. "He is unchanged," Cocteau recorded. "As soon as you begin talking to this man, everything is numbers, and disorder ceases." The two of them dined alone, and Cocteau explained his staging to the composer, with the help of diagrams on the tablecloth. The next day they met again at the theatre, where Cocteau was already rehearsing his three dancers, and Stravinsky started talking about Powell's idea for a film of the *Odyssey,* trying to arouse his collaborator's interest. But Cocteau was wary of the unpredictable degree of commitment involved in such a project.[21] Though pleased to hear that Stravinsky had had difficulty getting tickets for his *Orphée* film in the States, he had become deeply skeptical about popular or indeed fashionable success, and knew that his *Oedipus* would win him no friends in Paris. He longed to walk out onto the stage of the Théâtre des Champs-Élysées, and instead of the familiar "Spectateurs, vous allez entendre . . . ," shout, "Poor fools, enjoy your filth. I'm clearing out, and you won't ever hear from me again."[22] The real trouble was that the Parisian public, like certain types of venomous snake, could sense the artist's unease in their regard and tended to react accordingly.

In their first week there, thanks to the scope of Nabokov's festival, the Stravinskys had ample reminders of the factious nature of artistic life in the French capital. A few days after *Wozzeck* they went to a concert in the Comédie des Champs-Élysées at which Olivier Messiaen and Pierre Boulez played Boulez's *Structures Ia* for two pianos. Having already heard *Polyphonie X*, Stravinsky can hardly have been surprised at the uncompromising complexity and ferocity of this work in which every element—including rhythm, dynamics, and even types of attack and articulation—is serially organized; and from his own past experience, he may actually have felt some sympathy for the composer when a girl in the audience started clapping ironically, a young man leapt across the auditorium, slapped her in the face, and was promptly led away by a policeman.[23] The pianists, however, took the whole incident in their stride and carried on playing; there was, Boulez remarked casually to John Cage, "some disturbance of a mildly irritating kind."[24] In fact, the provocation was plainly deliberate, the music's aggression being logically unconnected with its intellectualism. The next day, by an odd quirk of planning, the Stravinskys found themselves in the main Théâtre des Champs-Élysées listening to Monteux conducting *The Rite of Spring,* exactly as he had done on another May night thirty-nine years before; but there was no riot, nobody was attacked, and the police were not needed.

There were to be two performances of *Oedipus Rex,* of which Stravinsky was conducting only the first, on the 19th. The second performance, on the 20th, was under Hans Rosbaud, who, with typical apostolic fervor, was playing it in a double bill with Schoenberg's *Erwartung.* Stravinsky, who had wanted to play *Oedipus* on its own with an interval between the acts, but had been persuaded by Nabokov to add *Scènes de ballet* as a curtain-raiser, went to Rosbaud's rehearsal of *Erwartung,* which he had never heard before, and cordially disliked it.[25] Fifteen years later he told Craft that he was pleased at the coupling of Schoenberg's work with his,[26] but as usual with the conversation books (and leaving aside the question of authorship), one has to understand such remarks entirely within their own context. By the sixties, the Stravinsky image was that of a sage of modernism and an omniscient if waspish chronicler of the great trends to which he himself belonged. But in 1952, he would have had good reason not to be so pleased. Rosbaud's double bill would inevitably attract the young progressives, in respect of whom he was already feeling vulnerable and insecure, leaving him with the "gala" audience so despised by Cocteau, the pashas and maharanis, the princesses and the bankers and the whole international set.

At his performance, everything went reasonably well, the opera (with Léopold Simoneau as Oedipus and Eugenia Zareska as Jocasta) was adequate and well sung, and the production—camp as it was—warmly received apart from some titters, Craft noted, when Cocteau declaimed that "the *tableau vivant* [for the scene with the Messenger and the Shepherd] represents the Oedipus complex."[27] But if the post-cubist mannerism of Cocteau's large masks, with their angular ears and noses and popping eyes, pleased the middle-aged art buffs of the first-night audience, for whom cubism and surrealism conjured up memories of the Picasso and Matisse of their youth, they were a provocation to the neomoderns at Rosbaud's double bill, who had come to hear *Erwartung* but either to miss or to mock *Oedipus Rex* after the interval. At one point, when Cocteau rose to narrate, there was an outburst of whistles and boos from the upper regions of the house, and instead of his set speech—and not daring the fantasy rebuke of his dreams—he said, in a voice different from that of the Speaker: "Stravinsky and I have always worked with great respect for the public. We ask for the same respect in return."[28] Then at the end, the booing resumed but was increasingly swamped by the applause, so that Cocteau, from the stage, believed the approval to be in the ascendant, while Craft, in the stalls, was conscious of an unassuaged "war between the claques," backed up by shouts of "enough of Cocteau."[29] By this time, in any case, Stravinsky himself had long since fled back to his hotel. "I know my way out of this theatre," he remarked acidly as he left.[30]

They lingered on in Paris for almost another week. Stravinsky had to conduct an orchestral concert on the 22nd, with Monique Haas playing his Capriccio, and Fred Goldbeck, who was in charge of the chamber music programs of the CCF festival, had booked Craft to conduct Walton's *Façade* on the 24th. On their last evening (the 25th) they trooped off dutifully with Nadia Boulanger to the Salle de l'Ancien Conservatoire for a concert of *musique concrète* (music made from manipulations of tape-recorded sounds). According to Craft, they soon retreated to Nadia's apartment in the rue Ballu for dinner;[31] but Stravinsky's own account suggests a less dismissive reaction.

Endless pieces whose substance was a mélange of sounds and noises. . . . The participants were professional composers, very antipathetic, and amateurs, "revolutionaries," rather sympathetic. A lady next to me raged in the intermission, declaring that this "music" was horrible. I had . . . a great desire to ask her: "But how do you know, Madame?" Was she acquainted with other examples that were not so bad?[32]

He himself must nevertheless have left Paris the next day (for concerts in Belgium and at the Holland Festival) with mixed feelings about his own position on the European new-music stage. As far as Nabokov's festival went, he could be satisfied that *Oedipus Rex* had stood its ground as a major representative of "L'Oeuvre du XXe Siècle." Yet it was painfully evident that this very "standing" placed it beyond the pale for a whole new generation of young enthusiasts. He was uncomfortably aware that the protests at the second performance were partly directed at his music's semi-official status, as opposed to the outlandishness and hence progressiveness of *Erwartung*. Moreover, this confirmed an impression he had formed in Germany the previous autumn that, whatever his prestige as a historic figure and modern-art grandee, he was by way of being regarded as a back number by those who saw postwar music as a new adventure with a minimum of historical baggage. It was horribly likely that the young man who had hit the girl at the *Structures* concert was also among the whistlers and booers at *Oedipus*—had perhaps even been one of the rowdies at the Rosenthal concerts seven years before. Igor had not forgotten Souvtchinsky's worrying enthusiasm for that "talented circle of youngsters, [. . . the] musical 'Trotskyites.' "[33] In Paris he had avoided Souvtchinsky, mainly for that reason.[34] But what if Boulez himself were one of Pyotr Petrovich's permanent international revolutionaries? It was a distinctly disagreeable thought.

The flight from old Amsterdam to New on the 9th of June was also, paradoxically, a flight from such anxieties. Before leaving America, Stravinsky had ordered a new Buick, the one disadvantage of which was that it had to be collected in Flint, Michigan. So from New York they flew—the three of them plus Alexei Haieff—to Detroit, and the next day they took a taxi to Flint, sixty-five miles to the northwest, where they picked up the Buick and drove off into the northern hinterland of the Midwest. It was another of their long detours round the edge of the United States. On 18 June in Duluth, at the far western end of Lake Superior, they celebrated Stravinsky's seventieth birthday in a restaurant that served only iced Beaujolais—not necessarily in itself a solecism on a hot summer afternoon in Minnesota, but enough of an irritant, for the claret-loving composer, to provoke one of his most petulant displays of restaurant hostilities.[35] From Duluth they drove for a thousand miles along U.S. 2, before cutting north into Canada via the winding and precipitous Going-to-the-Sun Road through Glacier National Park. "I despise mountains," Stravinsky announced defiantly, "they tell me nothing," as if by visiting them at all he were posing a question.[36] After almost a fortnight of beating the bounds in this fashion, they arrived home on the 29th, and Stravinsky had once again to confront his own anxieties.

Whether because of his Paris experiences or, more probably, because his work on the Cantata was beginning to ferment in his unconscious, he now had a completely new idea for an instrumental piece on which he was desperate to get down to work. It was at this point that he abandoned his intention to write instrumental chorales in the vocal work and decided to deploy the nine verses of the "Lyke-wake Dirge" as a frame for the solo movements that he had already written. The music being the same for every verse (apart from the changing harmonies at the end of each pair), he was able to compose the entire text in a single day. Early that morning, 21 July, a minor earthquake had struck Los Angeles, and several objects in the house were smashed. But Stravinsky's lyke-wake is an amiable, unapocalyptic, almost neutral piece of writing, studiously evading Whinnymuir and the Brigg o'Dread, and with none of the scurryings and wailings of Britten's brilliant setting in his Serenade, which Stravinsky told the critic Lawrence Morton he did not know.[37] The next day he started to compose the music that was by now at the forefront of his mind, and that he saw as the real way out of his technical and stylistic impasse.

The curious thing about the first movement of this new work, the Septet, is nevertheless that to all outward appearances it reverts to a chamber-instrumental style that had been second nature to him at least since the Dumbarton Oaks concerto of fifteen years earlier. In fact the opening even somewhat resembles the start of that work. It has the same irresistible vitality, the same eventfulness of texture, the same miraculous balance and economy of effort and movement. The only obvious reference to recent experience lies in the choice of instruments. Stravinsky's Septet, like the one in Schoenberg's Suite, is grouped round a piano, with a string trio on the one hand, and a wind trio (clarinet, horn, and bassoon in place of Schoenberg's three clarinets) on the other. There seems no question of any stylistic influence. Schoenberg's churning, embattled counterpoint is answered by a jolly explosion of rhythmic conversation, and the glowering E-flattish atonality of the Suite is laughed off by Stravinsky's unabashed key of A minor-major. The music bursts out like water from a broken main. And this ease does seem, for once, to have come easily. The movement, with its deceptive intricacy of inner voicing (including a dazzling little fugue by way of development section) took only just over a fortnight to compose—slow enough for Schoenberg, but quick for Stravinsky, whose speed of production seldom matched that of the resulting music. Four days after finishing it, on the 12th of August, he conducted Soulima in the Capriccio in a poorly rehearsed, mediocrely played Hollywood Bowl concert.[38] Then he turned at once to the second movement of his Septet.

In reality, there was more to the first movement than would have met the casual ear. The music is a wonderful example of what Stravinsky later called "a rare form of kleptomania."[39] Without being in the least serial in Schoenberg's sense, it steals all kinds of device—little melodic imitations, inversions (upside-down copies), augmentations (slowed-down copies)—from the secret drawer of serial technique. For instance, at the very start, the bassoon mimics the clarinet at exactly half speed. The second movement, however, is more systematic. Schoenberg was once again in the air at Wetherly Drive, since Craft had begun rehearsing items for a series of four Evenings on the Roof concerts in his memory, and as before Stravinsky was frequently in attendance. Craft had been explaining something about the application of note-rows, and had written out the series of Schoenberg's Wind Quintet on a sheet of music manuscript paper. On the other side of the sheet, Stravinsky then devised a series of his own, using the opening of his Septet as a starting point, rather in the way that a schoolboy invents a secret code by writing down his own name then adding the unused letters of the alphabet to make a complete set. The only difference is that Stravinsky, instead of limiting himself to twelve notes, used sixteen; as in the Cantata, he repeated several notes, but in all included only eight of the possible twelve. The resulting "theme" he then proceeded to use as the scaffolding—or ground bass—for the eight variations of his passacaglia second movement.[40]

From the start, the intention behind this movement was cerebral and methodical, and it took him considerably longer to write. For once there were relatively few distractions, and only one short trip (to Vancouver at the start of October). Craft had moved in April from the Sokolov house into a small house owned by the Baroness d'Erlanger just behind her own home at 1218 North Wetherly Drive, and he was now a mere three minutes' walk away. He and his explanations, as well as his rehearsals, became part of the landscape of the passacaglia. Yet still the music is not remotely Schoenbergian. The young conductor had shown Stravinsky how Schoenberg used his series to make chords as well as melodies;[41] but Stravinsky seems to have been uninterested in that aspect of the method, and his passacaglia is almost entirely made out of superimposed imitative melodies, always with a strong rhythmic profile. With or without its sixteen-note row, it feels much closer to the Bach of the C minor passacaglia, or even *The Art of Fugue,* than to anything modern and Viennese, while even in its densest passages (such as the seven-part final variation) the lines are invariably distinct, something that certainly cannot always be said of Schoenberg.

The main problem with the Septet, from its composer's point of view, was the by now all-too-familiar one that it had not been commissioned. Meanwhile, those projects that might have commanded fat advances hung fire. The libretto for *Delia* had arrived in April, and Craft had read it aloud to Stravinsky; but they had quickly agreed that, money or no money, it was too much of an Elizabethan fantasy to boil down for operatic use.[42] As for the proposed new Kirstein work, the New York City Ballet had been in Paris in May, and Stravinsky had conducted the company there in a performance of his *Orpheus*. But Kirstein was not on the tour, having stayed at home to tend his sick mother. When she died at the end of July, Balanchine wrote to him advising caution in his desire to create new repertoire at too great a pace, and now—as late summer turned to autumn—there was silence on the whole issue.[43] The *Odyssey* film, likewise, seemed to have faded out. Stravinsky had met Harcourt-Smith in Paris and found him as unappealing as his script, but he liked Powell and had enjoyed his films, especially *The Red Shoes,* which made him feel homesick for Monte Carlo.[44] He particularly liked Powell's idea of a collaboration with Dylan Thomas. But Powell, like Kirstein, had gone quiet. Instead David Adams, who had taken charge of Boosey's New York office after Betty Bean had—for reasons not known at North Wetherly Drive—been eased out in the spring, was trying to interest Stravinsky in composing music for a one-hour ballet film "about a lonely little window-cleaner," to be made by a Manhattan advertising agency.[45] Balanchine was said, mistakenly, to be involved, and doubtless that was the main reason why Stravinsky did not reject this quaint proposal out of hand. When the mistake was revealed, the project rapidly collapsed.

Early in November, he finished off his passacaglia, and a few days later, on the 11th, he conducted the Cantata, together with the new Concertino arrangement, *Danses concertantes* and the *Pulcinella* suite, in a Los Angeles chamber orchestra concert in Royce Hall. He had gone out of his way to engage strong singers, even to the extent of subsidizing Hugues Cuénod— the brilliant Venice Sellem—to come to the West Coast and sing the long tenor solo.[46] The hall was packed and the audience enthusiastic. Yet it was in many ways a puzzling event. Stravinsky seemed to have become so wrapped up in his contrapuntal devices, especially in the long tenor "Ricercar," that he had most uncharacteristically forgotten about certain elementary practicalities of performance. Not only was the carol relentless and exhausting to sing, but it was tiring and even somewhat tedious to listen to. One critic admitted that "the most invigorating sound I heard was a restive neighbor winding his watch,"[47] and even the sympathetic *Los Angeles Times* critic Albert Goldberg suggested that

Perhaps only a musician can appreciate the extreme technical discipline involved in such an experiment. It makes no obvious appeal to anything within the average listener's range of experience, yet by its very starkness it creates a perfect setting both historically and musically for the old English texts involved. Once again, it would seem, Stravinsky has opened new paths for others to follow.[48]

The remark was more perceptive than Goldberg himself knew. Word had somehow got out that Stravinsky was interesting himself in serial devices. More than a week before the premiere, Darius Milhaud had written to enquire: "Is it true you've used a twelve-note row? It would interest me a lot to know if this is true, and if so, how you treat it."[49] Strictly, of course, it was not true. The only row in the Cantata was eleven-note and unashamedly tonal, and though its technical apparatus was certainly in part prompted by Schoenberg, Stravinsky himself was far from ready to admit as much openly. A few weeks later, when asked by a New York journalist if it was true that he was "embracing twelve-tone atonal principles," he replied firmly that "certain twelve-tone things I like, certain I don't."

> For instance, I have tremendous respect for the discipline imposed on the twelve-tone man. It is a discipline that you find nowhere else. But on the other hand there are too many twelve-tone swindlers working today. [. . .] Not, of course, Schoenberg, Berg or Webern. These are masters, wonderful musicians, luxury composers. But some others do not hear what they are writing.

This kind of discipline, he added, could easily become a prison.

> Twelve-tone composers have to use the twelve-tones. I can use five, eleven, six—anything I like. I am not obliged to use more. I do as I wish in the scale or mode I prefer. I am also able to work in series, like the atonalists, if I want to. But what is important is that I do not have to.[50]

What Goldberg had spotted, however, was that in its essential character the Cantata was simply a continuation of earlier tendencies in Stravinsky's music with a few new twists. Naturally enough, there was the desire to carry on setting English texts after *The Rake's Progress;* but on the other hand, there was an asceticism that harked back to the pre-*Rake* Stravinsky of the Mass and (though Goldberg did not mention it) *Orpheus.* He drew attention to the music's deliberately limited harmonic range, and to its melodic debt to Gregorian chant, and he indicated that the contrapuntal devices were those of music of the same period as the poems, the fifteenth and sixteenth centuries—a point he may have got from the composer himself, who was letting it be known that he had been studying Heinrich Isaac: "He is my honey, my daily bread. I love him. I study him constantly. And between his musical thinking and writing and my own there is a very close connection."[51] In such company, the work's serial element hardly seemed worth mentioning at all.

Esoteric the Cantata may have been, or—as the *Daily News* critic Mildred Norton put it more candidly—a "mercilessly dull, wholly unleavened essay in boredom,"[52] but it turned out to have unexpected power to arouse indignation. The trouble was an unobtrusive line in the sixth of the eleven verses of "Tomorrow shall be my dancing day," exactly at the halfway point of the poem:

> *The Jews on me they made great suit,*
> *And with me made great variance,*
> Because they lov'd darkness rather than light,
> *To call my true love to my dance.*[53]

There must have been some early sign of a wounded reaction to this passage, since Stravinsky promptly wired Boosey and Hawkes: "To avoid biased comments from narrow minded groups necessary state clearly Christian character Cantata adding to Ricercar 2nd parenthetical subtitle quote Sacred History unquote."[54] It was soon evident that such a response was too technical to meet the case, since the Christian character, far from distancing the offense, was exactly its cause. "As one of those who presumably 'lov'd darkness rather than light,' " wrote one *Daily News* reader,

> [. . .] I was shocked and offended as a human being, who has not forgotten the voices of the millions of innocents of all creeds and races, choked by the hands of the fanatics and tyrants, who segregated, hated, incited and destroyed through centuries until today.
>
> If this be "light," then let me remain in the darkness, and preserve the dignity, endurance, patience and tolerance of my fathers, as well as their faith in a better and more brotherly world. In that spirit I repudiate any work that reflects a bigoted and narrow outlook, and as a musician I am saddened beyond words by the spectacle of a man who—admired as a great composer—has shrunk in his stature to the level of those who kneel in pious devotion, yet hammer still another nail into the bleeding body of Him who died to redeem the world.[55]

Stravinsky would no doubt have replied that, in setting a sixteenth-century poem as a "virtual" entity, he should not feel obliged to alter any sentiment or shade of sentiment it contained in order to fit his own views (whatever they may have been in 1952) or the finer feelings of any imaginable listener. The poem had been set many times before and printed without expurgation in countless anthologies, including Auden's. As Peter Yates wrote a few months later, "I believe that we have hunted anti-semitism far enough through the poems of T. S. Eliot and Ezra Pound without holding it up for abhorrence in the words of a sixteenth century Anonymous."[56] Yet, so soon after Auschwitz and Dachau, the issue understandably remained, for many, so painful as to cloud reasoned argument and forbid artistic license. Even to a converted Jew, like (presumably) the *Daily News* correspondent, the line was as much an incitement to pogroms as it was a recrucifixion of Christ, and even the clearheaded Yates had to admit that "the stanza does jar, and I should be happier to see it altered to characterize the nature of the persecutors rather than their race." In fact, although the East Coast premiere five weeks later kept the authentic text (and duly drew down on the Cantata the anathema of the Jewish paper *Congress Weekly*[57]), it was for many years thereafter usually performed in New York with the words modified. Stravinsky seems never to have objected to such alteration, and Richard Taruskin is probably right that in setting it in the first place he scarcely even noticed the offending lines.[58]

After the Cantata premiere there was little immediate chance of resuming work on the Septet. The next day, Vera was booked in for a thyroid operation, and although Igor described the surgery to Nabokov as "long rather than serious,"[59] she was in hospital for eight days and remained convalescent when Stravinsky set off with André Marion (who was still working as his secretary) for concerts and recordings in Cleveland on 6 December. In Cleveland they had a two-day visit from Soulima, Françoise, and Zizi, looking—as Igor reported to Vera—"very *Ladies' Home Journal* in style."[60] Having had nothing much to do with children for twenty-five years (and even then having been well protected against his own), he found his little grandson noisy but fun, as he rushed round the hotel corridors playing cowboys and Indians, talking bad French, and mixing it up with American slang. The Cleveland Orchestra, similarly, he found too noisy and not adept at the "almost chamber-music quality," as he called it, of the Symphony in C, though the recording he made with them in Severance Hall on the 14th shows at least that this difficult work held relatively few terrors for them on any technical level. On the 15th he and André flew on to New York, and five days later Vera and Craft arrived by train to join them.

The main purpose of this latest New York visit was to assist in the preparation of the U.S. premiere of *The Rake's Progress*, which Fritz Reiner was to conduct at the Met in February. But meanwhile Stravinsky had a concert of his own. On 21 December he conducted New York premieres of the Cantata and the Concertino in Town Hall, again with Cuénod but with Jennie Tourel in place of Marni Nixon, who had sung in Los Angeles. Not surprisingly, Stravinsky's first new concert music for six years attracted a big, highbrow audience, a "turn-out of New York's musical and intellectual public such as this reporter [Virgil Thomson] has not witnessed in some years." The reaction, though, was inscrutable. Thomson himself praised the music's "weight" and "ritual quality," but his compliments were full of ifs and buts, and it was evident that he was unsure of the work's effect. "Its power to move people," he noted cautiously, "cannot be known yet; it has not been heard enough." The packed house, he added, "listened with absorption, [but] reserved judgment in its intermission talk."[61]

In the following Sunday's *Tribune*, Thomson elaborated on this theme of inscrutability, pointing out that nobody he knew had really warmed to the piece, and yet nobody was prepared to blame Stravinsky for this disconcerting fact. He tried, without much conviction, to explain it by reference to the composer's past neoclassical work, and he drew a comparison with the Mass, the last new Stravinsky piece to have been heard in Manhattan. What he apparently did not think of doing, curiously enough, was to compare the Cantata with the *Rake*, which he may not yet have heard but must surely have known from the published score. Almost everything that is stylistically strange about the Cantata—including its fascinating but idiosyncratic word-setting and its curious "flatness" of harmony and form—is best understood as an attempt to build experimentally on the opera. Its balancing technical intricacies (which Thomson tended to wave away as "gothic ingenuities") have other origins as well, of course, but are not in themselves at all hard to understand. It is almost as if Thomson, himself the author of works of a studied, agonizing simplicity, wanted to ignore this new complicating aspect of Stravinsky's music altogether.[62]

Stravinsky and Thomson were personally on good terms, though Stravinsky loathed his colleague's music and had fidgeted his way through *Four Saints in Three Acts* the previous April (as he had through *The Mother of Us All* in Boulder in 1948) mainly out of diplomatic expedience. One evening early in Stravinsky's New York stay, Thomson threw a dinner party in his Chelsea Hotel apartment and invited Stravinsky, and also the young French composer whose *Structures* he had heard in Paris and whose *Polyphonie X* Craft had recently conducted at a Roof concert in Los Angeles. Pierre Boulez was in New York with the Compagnie Renaud-Barrault. "Everyone," Boulez later told his biographer Joan Peyser, "waited for the clash between Stravinsky and me because of my past polemics against him."[63] But there is in fact little evidence that Stravinsky knew anything about Boulez's connection with the Rosenthal disturbances in Paris in 1945. Souvtchinsky had not mentioned his name, and because he had recently been out of touch with

Souvtchinsky, Stravinsky was unaware of Boulez's verbal assaults on his neoclassical music in various articles in the Paris music journal *Contrepoints*.[64] Boulez relates, with a certain pride, that he quarreled at Thomson's party with the conductor Jean Morel about *Carmen,* and that Morel left in a huff. Boulez and Stravinsky, on the other hand, got on—Thomson himself recalled—"like comets."[65] "The two of them sat talking on a sofa, in spite of milling guests, for two straight hours."[66] What did they talk about? Perhaps not *Structures* and surely not *The Rake's Progress* ("What ugliness!" Boulez had exploded in a letter to Cage after hearing its premiere on the radio[67]). The most likely topic was Webern. Boulez was writing a short article about his music for the *Tribune* by way of introduction to an ISCM all-Webern concert on the 28th of December, and since Stravinsky was now a candid admirer of the most austere of the three modern Viennese masters, there would have been no difficulties on that ground. The Stravinskys duly went to the ISCM concert with Craft (who was uncharacteristically critical, in his diary, of Webern's obsession with "limitations": "architecture with no furniture," he called it[68]). The irony of the fact that Boulez's Webern article appeared next to Thomson's second article about the Cantata would have struck nobody at the time, except perhaps their respective authors.[69]

Now twenty-seven, Boulez could be provocative and quarrelsome; he could not let disagreement on what he saw as fundamental issues pass without retaliation. Yet he was susceptible to lifestyle, that element of opulence combined with fine taste that Stravinsky himself had aspired to, as a matter of course, since the early Diaghilev days of automatic first-class travel and bon vivant dining. It was an aspect of Boulez that Cage, who had drawn close to him in an intense correspondence of shared technical and aesthetic ideas, was finding hard to come to terms with. With him, Cage told Joan Peyser, "things had to be exactly where they should be. I was still terribly poor. I wanted to make poverty elegant but Pierre was not interested in that. What he wanted was an excellent richness. Everything had to be exactly right, aesthetically right."[70] But with all these complications, Boulez had one set of irresistible qualities: he was charming, intelligent, and quick. Starved of Gallic urbanity and sophistication behind his West Coast stockade, Stravinsky reacted instinctively to this lively, magnetic, and above all intensely musical Frenchman. The Frenchman was no less attracted. After Stravinsky had left Thomson's dinner, Boulez stayed on for several hours "in a very excited state," almost like a man who has just fallen in love.[71]

Perhaps not all of Stravinsky's social life would have impressed the young French composer by its "excellent richness." On Boxing Day he, Vera, and Craft dined with Auden and Kallman in their decrepit fifth-floor apartment on Seventh Avenue, and Craft noted in detail the squalor of empty bottles and dirty glasses and crockery, and the filth in the bathroom, which disoriented Vera to such an extent that she unthinkingly flushed away a dish of brown liquid that turned out to have been Chester's chocolate pudding.[72] Auden continued to gratify a certain need for the bohemian in Stravinsky, which, all the same, he preferred to keep at a safe distance in the personalities of others. It was his vicarious form of *nostalgie de la boue*. Yet Auden famously combined lack of physical hygiene with a mental, moral purity that at times approached the old-maidish. A few weeks after the Christmas dinner, he walked out of *Pal Joey* in disgust at its bawdiness. "There are three cardinal rules," he would say: "don't take somebody else's boyfriend unless you've been specifically invited to do so, don't take a drink without being asked, and keep a scrupulous accounting in financial matters."[73]

STRAVINSKY began sitting in on rehearsals for the *Rake* early in January, but he was so stimulated by his meeting with Boulez that he broke his normal habit of not composing in hotel bedrooms and got to work on the finale of his Septet—already begun at home in November during Vera's thyroid crisis. The piece was a gigue, like the finale of Schoenberg's Suite and beyond question intended as a sort of answer to that movement. For Stravinsky, a gigue had to dance, and Schoenberg's didn't. From the first notes of the viola's opening theme, the music pulsates with an energy and a vibrancy of rhythm and color that utterly belie the fact that from start to finish it is composed in strict fugal style, complete with an inversion of the fugue at the halfway mark (like the ones in Beethoven's late A-flat piano sonata and Stravinsky's own two-piano concerto) and a double fugue by augmentation—that is with a second, half-speed fugue on top of the original quick one—by way of coda. The music is admittedly not serial (though it well could be). Instead it uses a "repertoire" of notes—in effect an unordered set—derived from the eight different notes of the sixteen-note row in the passacaglia, which supplies whatever melodic and harmonic unity a movement of such irresistible impetus needs. Luckily, the music made out of these devices is a great deal less arid, hugely more exciting, than the mere description of the devices themselves. It invites direct comparison with Bach, who, of all great contrapuntalists, was able to make fugues leap with joy.

Stravinsky completed the Septet on the 21st of January, by which time he had been attending *Rake* rehearsals for a fortnight. Fritz Reiner was one of the few conductors whom he unreservedly respected, and while Reiner had been the natural choice to conduct the *Rake*, since he was the Met's musical director and a Stravinsky enthusiast, it was a choice that the composer had strongly urged. Working with him, however, was not always a comfortable experience. At rehearsal, Reiner could be irritable and even downright rude, and at one point, Craft reports, he as good as told Stravinsky to shut up.[74] This was certainly not an injunction Stravinsky was likely to heed for long. When orchestral rehearsals began, the composer "admonished Reiner to make the orchestra play more softly and with shorter note values,"[75] which is exactly what he had told the Cleveland Orchestra at his own December rehearsals, as a surviving recording shows. Stravinsky would sit immediately behind Reiner and from time to time interrupt.[76] Several months after the premiere, *Esquire* ran an account by Martin Mayer of the recording sessions that Stravinsky conducted (with the Met cast) in early March, which alleged that "Stravinsky himself came across the continent to quarrel with conductor Fritz Reiner about the proper way to perform the music," a suggestion that so upset the composer that he sent a specific disclaimer to the editor (and to Reiner himself). "I never," he insisted, "approached my work with him in a quarrelling spirit and—on the contrary—all decisions made by him always met with my full support. And I am glad to add that all his ideas and suggestions proved in the light of the experience to have been master-minded by one of the most talented conductors of our time."[77]

All the same, Mayer's observation that Stravinsky liked the recording better than the production was probably accurate. The Met staging, by Balanchine with designs by Horace Armistead, was stolid and conventional, and it clearly reflected Balanchine's feeling that the stage was too large and the acoustics too gross for the work.[78] To fill the space, he felt obliged to use a bigger chorus and more ostentatious choreography than the opera called for, while Reiner had doubled up the woodwind as well as substituting a piano for Stravinsky's harpsichord in the recitatives (which, as a matter of fact, Stravinsky himself had also done in Venice). For the recording, of course, Stravinsky restored the correct numbers of woodwind, and the harpsichord. He and Reiner had a stronger cast and a better orchestra than at the Fenice. Yet it can hardly have comforted him to read in the *New York Times,* the morning after the premiere on 14 February 1953, that the performance came "nearer the ideal representation of the opera than any production the work has received in lyric theatres of European cities," by way of justifying what amounted to a complete demolition of every musical and dramaturgical aspect of the opera.[79] No doubt he reflected that Olin Downes—for it was he—would have demolished the work under whatever circumstances it had been given. The fact that his review betrayed not a shadow of insight into the aesthetic bases of the opera, nor a shred of information as to its background in Stravinsky's own work, would have seemed proof enough of that.

The composer was booked to conduct the opera himself three months later with student performers of the Boston University Opera Workshop, directed by Sarah Caldwell. But in the intervening weeks there was little time for repose. Immediately after the Met opening, he had a concert in Baltimore (on the 18th), followed by a series with the New York Philharmonic at the end of February. Between recording sessions for the *Rake,* he coached the New Music Quartet in his own quartet pieces and music by Webern for a private concert at the home of the critic Arthur Berger.[80] On the 11th of March they flew back to Los Angeles, where Stravinsky spent several days rewriting the cimbalom part of *Renard* for piano, for a performance at a Roof concert on the 30th. He naturally felt that, the good cimbalomist being an even rarer animal than the good viola player of orchestral folklore, the work would receive more performances if that instrument were excluded. The curious fact is that *Renard* has remained a comparative rarity, but *Renard* with piano almost an extinct species. The mystery of popularity is not so easily reduced to a matter of accessibility.

The day after the Roof concert, Stravinsky flew to Havana with André, conducted a pair of concerts there in intense heat, then flew on to Caracas for further concerts, before proceeding to Boston via New York. While he was away, a Gordian knot was cut in Hollywood, and Gertrud and Nuria Schoenberg—the composer's widow and daughter—were invited to dinner by Vera Stravinsky. "This should have happened twenty years ago," Mrs. Schoenberg remarked, but added that "the fault was not Schoenberg's and not Stravinsky's, but that of intermediaries," a suggestion only partly contradicted by the fact that Vera had deemed it wise to invite them for the first time in Stravinsky's absence.[81]

The Boston *Rake* involved the composer in his most difficult series of rehearsals for many years, partly because of the inexperience of the students, partly because the two performances—on the 17th and 18th of May—had been double cast. At one point, the tension became so great that he completely lost his temper with the harpsichordist, Ralph Kirkpatrick, who was having difficulty following his beat, and ordered him out of the hall.[82] In the end the experience made him ill. In the heat of Havana he had suffered nausea and diarrhea; in New York, on the way to Boston, he had gone down with flu. The first Boston performance nevertheless went extremely well, and Stravinsky was delighted with his idea of transferring the auction scene to the end of the second act—a change that his librettists and Balanchine had opposed. The second performance, however, was insecure or worse, and the next day he was assailed by colitis, promptly cancelled his next concert in Chicago, and retired to his bed at the Sheraton Hotel.

There, on the 22nd of May, he received an important visitor.

DYLAN THOMAS had been giving readings and lectures in America on and off for more than three years, but Stravinsky had not set eyes on him. Vera had attended one of his early performances, at Urbana in March 1950, and at about that time Auden had talked enthusiastically about his poetry but despairingly about his physical condition.[1] The first suggestion of a collaboration had come from Michael Powell. Powell's idea of a film version of the *Odyssey* had survived the Harcourt-Smith project, and by January 1953 was for the moment taking the more specific and contained form of a filmed "tale" (in the manner of Powell's recent *Tales of Hoffman*) based on the Nausicaa episode in Homer's epic.[2] The intention was to commission Thomas to write the script, while Stravinsky would compose a prelude, a pair of dances, and perhaps some brief vocal numbers. Stravinsky was delighted with the whole idea, and he wanted Roth (his go-between with Powell) to negotiate a quick deal on exact terms that he communicated to the publisher in mid-January.[3] Perhaps his terms were too exact—or too exacting—since he wanted twelve thousand dollars for twelve minutes of chamber-ensemble music, and he wanted to retain the film and television rights. In any case, and for whatever reason, nothing more was ever heard from Powell, who did not have settled financial backing and may, like Billy Rose before him, have expected a less worldly response to his go-ahead ideas from a fellow progressive.

That spring was exceptionally busy even by Stravinsky's standards, and by the time he got to Boston in early May he seems to have forgotten all about the film project. Since finishing the Septet, he had been travelling a good deal and in indifferent health, and he had barely even had time to worry about his complete lack of firm commissioned work. Then, out of the blue, Sarah Caldwell suggested that, since he was so impressed with her Boston students, he might consider writing a new opera for them.[4] This was an instantly attractive idea; Boston had not balked at his conducting fee, and might not balk at an expensive commission. Craft told Caldwell that Stravinsky would never again write a full-length piece like the *Rake,* but might well agree to something shorter—something on the scale of the ill-fated _Delia_. Whom would he want as librettist? Why, who better than Dylan Thomas, the finest living writer of English—or at least of poetic, musical English, the master of the singing, lilting phrase and the resonant polyphony of images? Thomas was in the States and could be traced through his American fixer, the Boston poet and university teacher John Malcolm Brinnin.

Thomas had been in New York for a month, finishing off _Under Milk Wood_ and taking part in its first public reading, at the Poetry Centre on Lexington Avenue, on 14 May. But he was giving a poetry reading at Amherst on the 20th, and he came on to stay with Brinnin in Boston the next day. On the 21st Caldwell wired him at Brinnin's with a provisional commission for a libretto to be set by Stravinsky and suggesting that he contact the composer at his Boston hotel. The following morning, Thomas duly presented himself in Stravinsky's suite at the Sheraton.[5]

Stravinsky, still suffering from colitis, received him in bed, and there was some awkwardness due to what seemed to be nervousness on Thomas's part and a determination not to allow himself to be bracketed, on either literary or sexual grounds, with the other British writers the composer said he knew. Auden he admired, and he spoke well of the _Rake_ libretto but regretted its wordiness and overuse of verbal conceits. He recited Yeats, "the greatest lyric poet since Shakespeare."[6] Stravinsky gave him a tumbler of scotch, which in Craft's opinion relaxed him, and he began to talk about his ideas for a libretto—ideas which, curiously enough, were already in a fair state of development. Apparently there were two distinct concepts, though he elaborated only one of them, which was based on the idea of a new creation of the world by "the only man and woman alive on earth." He described it in detail to Brinnin later.

> These creatures might be visitors from outer space who, by some cosmic mischance, find themselves on an earth recently devastated and silenced by global warfare; or they might be earthlings who somehow have survived an atomic miscalculation. In either case, they would re-experience the whole awakening life of aboriginal man. They would make a new cosmogony. Confronted with a tree pushing its way upward out of radioactive dust, they would have to name it, and learn its uses, and then proceed to find names and a definition for everything on earth. The landscape would be fantastic—everything shaped and coloured by the dreams of primitive man—and even the rocks and trees would sing.[7]

Stravinsky liked the idea and promptly invited Thomas to visit him in Hollywood in the autumn to work it out more fully. No doubt he noticed how the prehistoric theme seemed tailor-made for the composer of *The Rite of Spring,* even though Dylan can hardly have expected a reversion to any such idiom.[8] Stravinsky may also have sensed the biblical connotations: the resonances of Genesis, the casting out of Adam and Eve, Noah and the Flood. As for Dylan himself, he was working himself into an excited state, about the subject, about working with Stravinsky, about the money he would earn. Back in Brinnin's apartment, he prowled around the room, chain-smoking, outlining the project, his imagination on fire.[9] That day or the day after he wrote to his wife, Caitlin, in lyrical terms about the collaboration. "We can get a boat from London, direct but slow, to San Francisco, & then fly to Los Angeles in an hour or so. Outside Hollywood, in a huge easy house in the hills, we're to stay for the month with Stravinsky. I've seen him, just now, in Boston, and we've thought of an opera and it is—for me—so simple that the libretto can be written in the time we're there. That's not just optimistic: it *can,* & will be."[10]

Many years later, Craft maintained that he had felt from the moment Thomas walked into the Stravinskys' room that there would be no collaboration.[11] Unfortunately his various descriptions of the meeting are bedevilled by hindsight and a familiar penchant for the editorialized reminiscence. Thomas, he reports in one account, had his left arm in a sling.[12] Yet not only did Thomas not have his arm in a sling (he broke it a few days later in New York), but Craft never saw him in that condition. As so often where Dylan's health was concerned, a certain image of the tubby, drunken, red-nosed, cartoon-strip Welshman tends to color the portrait. Another of Craft's thumbnail sketches suggests that the poet's edginess portended an attack of delirium tremens, kept at bay only by the hair of the dog—the stiff whisky.[13] His own explanation that he was tormented by gout is treated as another aspect of the same joke; for the chronic alcoholic, indeed, there is no escape from affectionate ridicule. But we now know that Thomas's true condition was no better understood by his doctor than by his mythologists, and that when he told Stravinsky that the cure for gout was worse than the disease, he spoke more truly than he knew. The twice-weekly painkilling cortisone injections, combined with increasing doses of morphine, were slowly but surely killing him by aggravating the diabetes that he himself had known about for years but had neglected to mention to his friends or, more especially, to the expensive Manhattan society quack into whose hands he had carelessly if optimistically placed himself.[14]

Toward the end of May, Stravinsky and Craft returned to New York, and from there set off on another of their long drives home, this time taking a route through the middle of the United States, via St. Louis, Oklahoma, and Albuquerque, reaching Los Angeles on the 4th of June. While they were on the road, telegrams were flying back and forth between Nicolas Nabokov in

Paris and André Marion in Hollywood. Victoria Ocampo had been falsely implicated in an assassination attempt against the Argentine dictator Juan Perón and incarcerated in the women's prison of Buen Pastor in Buenos Aires. Nabokov was demanding Stravinsky's signature to a public protest by leading figures in the art world;[15] but by the time Stravinsky could get round to expressing his usual cautious attitude to joint protests Mme. Ocampo had been released, though she continued to be harassed by Perón's agents and for more than two years was refused a passport or any other of the necessary means for foreign travel. When the question arose of her speaking Persephone in Stravinsky's planned Columbia recording later that summer, the composer was himself doubtful because, as he put it, "[Vera] Zorina is Mrs. Lieberson" (and wanted the part herself),[16] but when a Turin performance came up soon afterwards, Ocampo had eventually to refuse because she was "a prisoner in her own country for having committed the crime of thinking freely."[17]

Meanwhile, Dylan Thomas had flown home to Wales and was back in the Boat House at Laugharne, his arm still in a sling, but "thinking a lot about the opera and [having] a number of ideas—good, bad, and chaotic."[18] Whether Stravinsky had any ideas we do not know, but he was undoubtedly eager to pursue the collaboration, and he pressed Thomas to come to California in the early autumn. "If you can accommodate yourself," he wrote, "on the convertible sofa in our living room—our home is rather small unfortunately—you will be our most welcomed guest and you and I could work out something very authentic."[19] So much for the huge easy house in the hills. Unfortunately, Boston University was needing time to raise the necessary funds for the commission, and at the end of June Stravinsky wrote encouragingly to the music faculty agreeing to wait until November for the final decision, and insisting that "we will not deliver a work involving an outrageously expensive staging (not another *Aida*, for example). We can be committed to deliver a work whose production will require only a limited chamber ensemble, a limited number of characters and small chorus numbers. It might eventually be possible to quantify all this in the agreement."[20] Thus the parameters for the work were laid down by the composer himself, almost as a factor in the negotiations. That he was desperately anxious to secure the commission cannot seriously be doubted.

All the same, he could not start without a libretto, and in any case the colonic pains of which he had recently been complaining had now been diagnosed as prostatic in origin, and he was booked into the Good Samaritan Hospital for a prostatectomy in late July. Such an operation stands like a wall blocking out the future. So instead of starting anything substantial, he was casting around for casual work to occupy the coming weeks. He had already, during June, been tinkering with finished scores. He had written a band arrangement of the Tango (a piece originally meant as a song with band accompaniment), to go in a concert of his so-called jazz music planned for the Roof autumn season, and he had made a piano duet version of the Septet, apparently for no better (or worse) reason than to enable him to play it with Craft, as he had always in the past played four-hands with Soulima.[21] It may have been the Tango instrumentation, which included a guitar, that gave him the idea of arranging a pair of his old Russian songs— "The Drake" and "Sektantskaya," both from the 1919 set—with accompaniment for that instrument. Or it may have been Craft's suggestion. Vera had recently bought a guitar and was learning to play it, and no doubt its technique and peculiarly soft, intimate sonority were the subject of discussion at North Wetherly Drive. Early in July, Craft drew Stravinsky's attention to the first of the Shakespeare sonnets in *Poets of the English Language*, "Musick to heare," and suggested he make a setting for soprano with flute, harp, and guitar. Barely two weeks later, the new song had been composed—but for mezzo-soprano, with flute, clarinet, and viola—and the arrangement of the two Russian songs sketched, for the ensemble proposed by Craft.[22]

The Shakespeare song is a curious little exercise in pocket-serialism for the voice. When Schoenberg or Webern wrote for voice, they habitually treated it as a virtuoso instrument that could be "played" like a clarinet or a violin. But Stravinsky was fascinated, as ever, by the instrument's particular limitations; and he was sensitive, as he always claimed, to the exact quality of melodic intervals and to the tendency of singers to be vague about the pitch of a note if they were not given proper clues. It was precisely for this reason that he had insisted on writing an accompanied Mass, which could therefore not be used in the Orthodox liturgy. In the same way "Musick to heare" is serial, but never at all atonal. The series has only four notes and is clearly in G major-minor (just as the Septet had been in A minor-major). The accompaniment apes discreetly the typically jagged outlines of Webern; but they are a mask for tonal figures that have nothing to do with serialism or expressionism or any of the other isms of the Second Viennese School. Viola and clarinet split up a C major scale between them; the singer performs some modest, ladylike zigzags; and every line of the song ends on a nice clean open fifth, like a piano tuner checking his temperament. Whatever Stravinsky thought of Schoenberg's method, it is quite obvious from this unpretentious piece that he had no interest at all in his style.

On the 23rd of July, a week after showing Craft the completed draft of "Musick to heare," Stravinsky went into hospital for his operation. He was understandably frightened of it, and though clinically it went well, it left him, according to Craft, perceptibly older and slower, less sure on his feet, and for some time subject to dizzy spells.[23] It also made him unreasonably bad-tempered. A fortnight before the operation, the question had come up of his old article about Diaghilev, ghosted by Nouvel back in the mid-thirties, never published in its original French, but now being considered for publication by *Atlantic Monthly,* for a fee of five hundred dollars, in an English translation that Mercedes de Acosta had made in 1946. The journal was hoping to persuade Stravinsky to extend the article by answering a series of questions, but when Stravinsky offered to write the extra pages himself in return for a net five hundred, and Mercedes pointed out that this would leave nothing for either her (as translator) or her agent, Stravinsky dug in his heels and returned the article unextended.[24]

It was the day he was being admitted to Good Samaritan, but Mercedes knew nothing of all that, and she was not one to take such petty mean-nesses lying down. She wrote a direct and reproachful reply,[25] and only a few days later, having heard about the prostatectomy from Natasha Nabokov, wrote again to Vera, asking her to explain the situation to her husband, but refusing to give in on what she called Igor's "very bad habit of always con-sidering only himself when money is concerned."[26] Stravinsky was furious. "Read your letter to Vera," he wired back. "Let Atlantic Monthly take article as is for 400 and let me not hear of it any more because my time costs more than what they can ever pay."[27] The article duly appeared, without addition, as "The Diaghilev I Knew," in the November *Atlantic.* But it seems doubtful whether Stravinsky ever quite forgave Mercedes her sharp character analy-sis, and though she and Vera stayed in touch, the only subsequent commu-nications from Igor were grumbles to do with royalties in the original French text, which came out in *Figaro littéraire* soon after the translation.[28]

He was in hospital for ten days, but weak for much longer, and he could scarcely work for another month. He may have toyed with the Shakespeare song, or contemplated another one or two. He looked at the score of Brit-ten's *Gloriana* (sent at his request by Lesley Boosey), interested above all, no doubt, in its word-setting.[29] He went to a lecture by Gerald Heard on the concept of "abandon," lunched with Isherwood, dined with Huxley and his tame fakir, Tara Bey, and went to a Walton concert in the Hollywood Bowl.[30] It was all a curious cross-section of expatriate West Coast Englishry. Mean-while he was informing his British publisher, Ernst Roth, that "I will never go to either Vienna or Berlin for reasons you may guess."[31] Roth did not have to guess the reasons. He knew perfectly well that Stravinsky was terri-fied of being stranded on the wrong edge of civilization in the event of war or revolution, still widely expected in those tense years of the Cold War. However much they might dislike Hollywood (and Vera, especially, detested it), they felt safe there; for them, it was the right edge.

Then suddenly at the end of August, practically on the same day, the question of commissions began to unravel. On the 26th Stravinsky wrote again to Dylan Thomas. He explained that he would not know about the Boston money until the autumn, but suggested that they might discreetly start work in any case, then if the Boston deal went through they would be under way, and if it did not, they would have something to sell elsewhere. He urged Dylan to come to Hollywood as soon as possible.[32] However, the very next day, a letter arrived from Lincoln Kirstein, who had at last found the money (from the Rockefeller Foundation) to pay for a ballet commission. He could offer ten thousand dollars for a work up to forty-five minutes long, and he was again promoting the idea of an Apollo sequel: "Apollo Architectons: builder of shelters and bridges."[33] Without hesitation, Stravinsky accepted this new commission in principle, and asked for more details about the subject: "The title is not enough for me to start with. [. . .] The reason for my insisting on this is that I want to start working on this ballet right away instead of starting on some more intricate projects which can wait."[34] Then a mere twenty-four hours later he wrote again. He had now decided that the Apollo-Orpheus-Apollo idea imposed too slow a prevailing tempo for an evening's ballet, and instead he suggested a completely different program made up of Scènes de ballet and Pulcinella, with, in between, the new ballet, for which he now put forward the Nausicaa episode from the Odyssey, exactly as originally proposed by Powell for their film collaboration with Dylan Thomas.[35]

Behind this mild duplicitousness, there plainly lurked some anxiety about his own Thomas project. Dylan had never replied to his June letter, the Boston money was uncertain, and, whatever he might say to Dylan about having "something of our own to produce and for which we should well be able to find an underwriter," he had no intention of embarking on a two-year operatic project—as he knew it would be—without some kind of advance money.[36] This was precisely the reef on which Delia had foundered. Then again there was the question of health. He was too soon out of hospital not to remember that Dylan himself had not looked well, had complained of gout and doctors, famously had a drink problem, and had subsequently fallen downstairs and broken his arm. Obviously the composer's safest tactic was to accept the Kirstein commission, which he could count on, and assume that, even if the Boston money were forthcoming, he would have to wait for the libretto, by which time the new ballet would be well in hand and its completion foreseeable.

The question of subject, though, was not so easily resolved. Neither Kirstein nor Balanchine liked the Nausicaa idea. It had charm but no outcome, since once Odysseus has been welcomed by Nausicaa's father, Alcinous, the princess herself fades out of the story. On the other hand Balanchine's own ideas were becoming more and more grandiose. He wanted, Kirstein reported, "a ballet which would seem to be the enormous finale of a ballet to end all the ballets the world has ever seen." One version of this might be "a competition before the gods; the audience are statues; the gods are tired and old; the dancers re-animate them by a series of historic dances, [. . .] courante, bransle, passepied, rigaudon, menuet, etc. etc. It is as if time called the tune, and the dances which began quite simply in the sixteenth century took fire in the twentieth and exploded."[37] To back up this idea, Kirstein was sending a copy of a recent critical edition of de Lauze's seventeenth-century dance manual, *Apologie de la danse,* which included music examples by the contemporary theorist Marin Mersenne.[38] None of this met Stravinsky's need for precise specifications, those limitations which, he told Kirstein, "generate the form." So instead he simply washed his hands of subject, and decided to compose a " 'Concerto for the dance' for which George will create a matching choreographic construction."[39] Nevertheless, many details of Balanchine's idea stuck in his mind and in due course found their reflection, suitably transformed, in the new ballet.

Still he could not start work. For one thing, he was writing two more Shakespeare settings, this time of songs from the plays, which, as before, he found in the Auden anthology: "When dasies pied" (from *Love's Labour's Lost*) and "Full fadom five" (from *The Tempest*). These he completed on 6 October. For another thing, he had by no means given up on the Thomas project. Dylan had eventually written from Laugharne on 22 September that he would be in New York in the second half of October and could come to Hollywood at the end of that month, but that he had no money to pay for the West Coast trip. "I'll have to work these things out the best I can," he added disingenuously, "and I mustn't bother you with them now. [. . .] The *main* thing, I know, is for me to get to you as soon as possible, so that we can begin—well, so that we can *begin,* whatever it will turn out to be. I've been thinking an awful lot about it."[40] Stravinsky, who had already started extending his house precisely to accommodate essential guests like Thomas, promptly offered to fix him reading engagements to help pay his fare. "I am as eager as you are," he insisted, "to actually see 'our' (yes) work started."[41] Yet Thomas still seems privately to have been shy about the project. In any case he did not, as promised, write from New York when he arrived there on the 20th of October. A week later, having heard nothing, Stravinsky wrote again, pressing him to come and as good as promising him reading dates to cover the fare. "You know," he added, "that you will be my guest here and therefore you do not have to worry about your living expenses. Do come, the weather is beautiful, too much maybe . . . we live in short sleeves . . . Please drop me a line."[42]

Stravinsky was not to know that the real reason that Dylan had not written from New York was that he was ill. Since arriving there, he had been leading his usual irregular life, with too little food and sleep, and from time to time too much drink. But the long-accepted theory that he was destroying himself with alcohol is, as we saw, no longer tenable. The likely cause of his illness was diabetes, untreated for many years, and aggravated by increasing injections of cortisone and (later) morphine, and by regular doses of benzedrine, prescribed for alcoholism and supposed delirium tremens by his "Dr. Feelgood" (the sinisterly named Milton Darwin Feltenstein), and all counterindicated for diabetics. Early on 5 November 1953, Dylan was brought into St. Vincent's Hospital in a coma apparently induced by a huge intake of whisky the previous night, but in fact probably the direct result of a series of morphine injections administered by Feltenstein later on the 4th. Four days later he died, without regaining consciousness, and with his wife, Caitlin, still trying to talk her way out of the mental institution to which she had been committed when she had turned violent and hysterical at his bedside the previous day.[43]

The news reached Wetherly Drive within little more than an hour by telegram from a London newspaper seeking a tribute from Stravinsky, whose plan to collaborate with Thomas was widely known despite the poet's promise a mere seven weeks before "not to tell anyone about it."[44] Stravinsky went into his studio, closed the door, and wept.[45]

HE HAD already started planning his new ballet, but had as yet sketched no music. On 19 October Craft had conducted the Roof concert of so-called Stravinsky jazz, including *Ragtime* with piano instead of cimbalom, the new version of the Tango, and the world premiere of the *Praeludium* "for jazz ensemble," written in 1937 for something more like a "radio orchestra," and discreetly revised for this first performance.[46] Still not fully recovered from his operation, Stravinsky then promptly went down with flu; and what with this illness, the all-too-brief uncertainty over Thomas, and a four-day tour he had planned with the Los Angeles Philharmonic in mid-November, there was precious little time for concentrated work before he flew to New York with Milène and André just before Christmas. As far as actual composition went, he managed only to sketch a brief fanfare for three trumpets which he may or may not already have envisaged as the ballet's opening.[47] Otherwise the year wound to its close with nothing to show creatively since the completion of the Septet in January, apart from one or two stalled projects, a tiny set of songs, and a few minor revisions. It was his most frustrating year, and his sickliest, since he had left France. Fortunately the auguries for 1954 were better.

They were in Philadelphia for concerts around Christmas, then returned to New York, where Stravinsky had recordings at the end of January. In between, he conducted the Septet for the first time at Dumbarton Oaks on the 23rd. It seems to have gone down well enough—smartly played by an ensemble that included the clarinettist David Oppenheim and the pianist Ralph Kirkpatrick, now evidently restored to favor after the contretemps in Boston. But not surprisingly the occasion passed without much notice, and it was left to Richard RePass, writing in the British monthly *The Musical Times,* to point out the work's importance (as compared, in his opinion, with *The Rake's Progress,* which was being revived at the Met that very week amid general apathy). "The septet," he wrote, "is a fascinating piece of music, full of intricate polyphony and exciting rhythmic effects. Perhaps the most extraordinary side to it is the close resemblance of the style to the twelve-note method of Schönberg . . ."[48] To so much as notice this fact was quite impressive; to admire it was positively prophetic. A few days later, in New York, Stravinsky recorded the work with the same performers under his Columbia contract, adding the Octet and *Soldier's Tale* suite for good measure.

Craft seems to have opted out of this winter's New York visit partly because he was conducting Roof concerts in mid-January and early February, and partly because he was embarking on a project to record the complete works of Webern for Columbia only ten days after Stravinsky's return. But a certain pattern is worth remarking. Craft had gone late to New York, missing Cleveland, the previous December, and he had also missed the trip to Cuba and Venezuela in April. On every occasion, Vera had stayed behind with him. The reason, no doubt, was perfectly simple. It boiled down to family. For Igor to travel with Milène and André was a chance to be with them in a way that was not quite possible at home, where André was the secretary and Milène a visitor; and though he disliked travelling alone, needing company and all kinds of attention and support on tour, especially when conducting, he was by no means inseparable from either his wife or his young musical assistant, notwithstanding the impression one might get from the various published chronicles (entirely from the pen or under the editorship of Craft himself).

The exact situation is admittedly by no means easy to read. Whether by accident or design, Stravinsky's children flit in and out of Craft's writings on these early years like tolerated presences but without open hostility, even if certain nuances (especially to do with poor Madubo) show them in a disagreeable light. Such colorings, though, are editorial, the product of attitudes that emerged later. There is no contemporary evidence, in early 1954, that Craft thought poorly of, or was on poor terms with, any of Stravinsky's children. We cannot, for instance, tell—without sight of an original, authentic text of his diaries—whether the omission of Theodore from the account of the Swiss visit in 1952 was a decision of the diarist or the editor. Nor can we say what was the children's true attitude to Craft in those years. It would certainly have been strange for them to have had no hostile feelings whatever toward the younger man who had, in a sense, usurped their position in their father's household. And it would have been equally remarkable if they had viewed with complete equanimity the woman who had displaced their own mother, under circumstances of such atrocious pain and humiliation to her. No doubt their feelings, like so much intense emotion, were confused. They may have both loved and resented Vera, liked and resented Craft; and that complication of sentiments was very likely reciprocated in one form or another. Of only one thing can we be certain: Vera Stravinsky and Robert Craft were an axis in their minds. They were that part of their father which, whatever else happened, did not belong to them.

Stravinsky himself saw little of his children these days except for Milène, who still lived nearby. But the dispersal of his family by no means reduced his patriarchal need of their dependence. Soulima, now firmly settled in Urbana, was slowly rebuilding his concert career but at the age of forty-three had still not fully escaped from his father's gravitational field. That January he was booked to play the Piano Concerto and Capriccio under Stravinsky's baton in Chicago. Barely a month before the concert, his father cabled him about an extra date with the same program at Milwaukee, taking it for granted that Soulima would make himself available, and when his son told him that he had a Mozart concert elsewhere, he replied angrily that "you must decide whom you prefer: Mozart or me." It was a typical piece of emotional blackmail, and Soulima could not resist. He cancelled his Mozart date and played for Stravinsky. But he paid the price. The Mozart engagement was not repeated; there was tension between father and son, and they never again appeared on the concert platform together.[49]

Stravinsky not unnaturally considered that securing concert dates for Soulima was the best way of helping him financially. It hardly seems to have crossed his mind that in the long run it might have the opposite effect. Nor did it occur to him to refuse direct fiscal aid when his children asked for it, merely on the grounds that they ought to be supporting themselves. Craft was later inclined to suggest that at such times it was usually Vera who intervened on her stepchildren's behalf, just as she had (certainly) poured oil on the troubled waters of Theodore's bank transfers in 1939. But this is at best an oversimplification. When Theodore asked his father for money to build a garage onto his Geneva house in 1952, Stravinsky was forced to refuse, but with unconcealed reluctance, simply because he could not afford it. He was seventy years old, he reminded Theodore, and dependent on conducting—a power that might fail him at any time—to enable him to maintain a "good but modest" standard of living. He was, he said, "sincerely distressed at being unable to fulfil your request. . . . Please don't be angry with me, but try and understand my situation."⁵⁰ In the end when Theodore persisted, he did send three thousand francs—about a third of the amount Theodore had asked for.⁵¹ It was conscience money, and accompanied by mild reproaches, but it seems unlikely that Vera was directly responsible, since she had been in hospital for her thyroid operation, and barely able to talk, for several days.

Craft's place in the composer's affections and budgeting was essentially different from that of his children. He certainly never received a tiny fraction of the fifteen thousand dollars Stravinsky gave to each of his offspring to purchase a house after the war, and he was paid no salary (until much later) for what had gradually evolved into an undivided professional commitment. When he moved into the Baroness's house, the composer paid half his rent, and since he took all his meals at no. 1260, he had relatively few basic living costs, especially for as long as he could pay his own share of the rent by reading to his increasingly eccentric and decrepit landlady.⁵² As for pocket money, Stravinsky was constantly trying to wangle paid work for him, just as he had pulled strings for Soulima before the war and continued to do for Theodore after it.⁵³ He would put him forward as a program annotator or translator, and he was even beginning to recommend him as a stand-in or support conductor.⁵⁴ When they travelled together, he would pay the young man's fares and hotel bills, albeit in "steerage" class and often in the cheapest rooms. But any idea that Craft was milking the situation financially would be absurd. Of course he was enjoying a glamorous existence in the shadow of one of the world's great men and in the company of many others. He was the object of female attention, to which he was far from immune, to put it no more strongly; and he was seeing the world and forming an extraordinary network of social and professional contacts. But by 1953 he was nearly thirty years old; he knew—or suspected—that his privileged position with Stravinsky was making him an object of envy and ridicule; he had no money and no career. It was surely time for him to move on.

Why did he stay? One part of the answer is that, just when he was weighing up all these factors and seriously thinking of taking to the road, Stravinsky fell ill—so ill, in fact, that few if any of his many doctors would have counted on his living more than another year or two. His prostate operation aged him to the extent that he gave up his daily exercises, lost his speed of foot, and for the first time began to look and behave like a septuagenarian. He was frequently, inexplicably unwell. To leave at that moment, Craft felt, was simply not possible.⁵⁵ Perhaps he reasoned that his imprisonment would not be indefinitely prolonged. But there was something else as well.

The fact was that Stravinsky had come to depend on him, not just emotionally, but musically as well, and this was such an astonishing, flattering, inspiring thing that no young musician with blood in his veins could have dreamt of decamping at that moment without waiting to see how the situation would develop. From the day he had moved to Wetherly Drive, Craft had advised on matters such as the accentuation of English verse (in the *Rake* and the Cantata), the choice of texts (for the Shakespeare songs), even the technical capabilities of the trumpet—his own instrument. He had talked Stravinsky out of his creative block, had demonstrated serial technique to him, and could legitimately regard the composer's latest masterpiece, the Septet, as in some measure a product of his own influence. At this very moment, with Dylan Thomas so recently dead and Stravinsky away on the East Coast, Craft had an idea for a commemorative piece based on "Do not go gentle into that good night," the villanelle Thomas had written when his father was dying in 1951. Early in January 1954 he wrote to Stravinsky in New York, suggesting a setting of the poem for voice and string quartet, and when Stravinsky arrived home at the start of February he set to work almost at once composing exactly the piece the young man had outlined.[56] Meanwhile Craft himself was preparing the *Three Songs from William Shakespeare* with the mezzo-soprano Grace-Lynn Martin for their first performance in a Roof concert on 8 March, a program in which he was also conducting the West Coast premiere of the Septet. On this occasion he would be literally acting as representative of the composer, who was away in Seattle on yet another concert trip with André. It was certainly no exaggeration to say that Stravinsky was coming to depend on his young American assistant.

Stravinsky completed the setting of "Do not go gentle" on the 14th of March, echoing the severe rhyme scheme of the villanelle with his own strictest piece of serial writing so far. The work has a row of only five notes, but as with Schoenberg repetitions are avoided and the treatment would seem much more "classical" to ears attuned to the Viennese style than anything Stravinsky had written before. The next day, the critic Lawrence Morton, who had taken over the running of the Evenings on the Roof for the next season and was rechristening them the "Monday Evening Concerts," wrote to him about his complicated plans for the opening program in September, which was to be a Dylan Thomas memorial.[57] Stravinsky's tribute would be done, but also a Bach cantata and a series of early baroque works including a repeat performance of Schütz's "Fili mi, Absalon," with its highly structured accompaniment for four trombones—a piece that Craft had recently conducted in a Roof concert. Having set the son's admonition to his dying father, Igor liked the idea of matching King David's lament for his son with a solemn dirge of his own for the same four trombones. So on the 21st of March he composed the "Dirge-Canons," as he called them, for trombones and string quartet, using the same series as for the song and placing them as a prelude.

Four days later he and Vera took off for New York, this time with Milène and André as well as Craft in tow, on the first stage of a two-and-a-half-month European tour, their third in less than four years.

21

COMPETITION OF THE GODS

AFTER THE SPECTACULAR success of his Paris festival in 1952, Nicolas Nabokov had been enthusiastically planning a sequel to take place in Rome eighteen months later, in the autumn of 1953. The focus was broadly the same: "Music in Our Time." But to lend it intellectual credibility (and no doubt to open a few additional purses), he was attaching it to a conference with the modest title "The Situation of Music in the Twentieth Century." Stravinsky, he optimistically hoped, might accept the presidency of the Advisory Board, and would participate in discussions, perhaps give a talk, as well as conduct performances of his works.[1] Such a hope was naturally the purest fantasy. Stravinsky would only agree to be president if there were no duties, and he would only come at all if he could arrange a European concert tour.[2] The upshot of all this was that Nabokov found himself acting as his friend's European agent, for which service Stravinsky paid him a commission while contributing little of significance to the Rome festival apart from conducting two fairly conventional orchestral concerts and presenting the prize in the composers' competition.

The arrangements were dogged by bad luck from the start. In the early stages of planning, Nika's marriage to Patricia Blake collapsed.[3] Then, when he postponed the festival to April 1954, he ran into difficulties with the Italian authorities over the programming of concerts in Holy Week. Stravinsky's first concert—an essentially profane affair framed by *Orpheus*, the *Scènes de ballet*, and *Firebird*—had to be moved at a late stage from 15 April to the 14th because Rome Radio refused to broadcast a secular concert on Maundy Thursday. In general, Roman officialdom proved quite as obstructive as its Parisian counterpart. When Stravinsky and Craft turned up at the Opera for Henze's *Boulevard Solitude* in lounge suits rather than dinner jackets, they were refused admittance until Stravinsky revealed his identity, whereupon an exception was made for him but not for Craft. Nabokov did his dignified best, as Festival Director, to overrule the doorman, but when that failed he simply rolled up his sleeves and punched the man in the eye. It was all to no avail. Craft was not admitted, Stravinsky declined to enter without him, and the two of them went back to their hotel with Vera. They thus missed a scandal which, in terms of sheer noise and audience hostility, was fully the equal of a well-remembered riot in the Théâtre des Champs-Élysées forty-one years before.4

Stravinsky had met Henze at the opening reception two or three days earlier, and had asked him about his attitude to serialism and how he had used the technique in his recent work. According to Henze, Stravinsky himself was still unsure about it, and if anything somewhat skeptical. Perhaps he was wary of associating himself too directly, talking to a German composer, with what was still widely regarded as a Germanic way of doing things; and he was certainly cautious about his own standing with the young generation of European progressives, among whom he doubtless numbered Henze, a onetime student of the hated Leibowitz. It was true that he had not yet composed anything with a twelve-note row; but then Henze's own use of the method was flexible, to put it mildly, and in fact *Boulevard Solitude* was a roundly eclectic piece with roots in the semipopular theatre of Weill and the allusive atonality of Berg, as Stravinsky will have realized when he heard the second performance (this time overdressed in a dinner jacket) a few nights later.5

There were several other concerts while they were in Rome. They heard Milhaud conduct Satie's *Socrate*—a piece whose unvarying gait Stravinsky inevitably found monotonous—and they went to what Craft described as a "dreadful concert" of works by Britten, Prokofiev, and Poulenc, in the Foro Italico.6 In another Foro concert, Craft conducted Stravinsky's Septet, and in yet another, they heard Peter Racine Fricker's second violin concerto, and Stravinsky scribbled a warning to his neighbor, Stephen Spender, to "fasten your seat belt."7 But they spent as much time out of Rome as in it. They went to Frascati, in the Alban Hills, the monster park of the Orsinis at Bomarzo and the Villa Farnese at Caprarola, the Etruscan tombs at Cerveteri, and the gardens at Ninfa.8 They felt at home in Italy, and for a time seriously thought of moving there: according to Craft, who (in memory at least) firmly included himself in these plans, it was as usual Stravinsky's medical needs that ultimately prevented them from doing so. Being in Rome, with its ancient stones and small trattorias, its vibrant social activity, brought out Vera's loathing of the trimmed lawns and endless boulevards of faraway Los Angeles, a city in which—as she announced in something more than an undertone at an American Academy reception—"there is no one to talk to."9

Her husband had to be in Turin for rehearsals of *Persephone* on the 19th; but while André went with him as secretary and factotum, the others took a slower route by car through Tuscany to Siena, and on to Milan and Lugano, where they arrived in time for Stravinsky's concert in the Kursaal with the local radio orchestra on the 28th. Oddly enough, Craft's published diary makes no mention of this parting of ways, and you can also read it without the faintest suspicion that the Marions are anywhere but back home in Beverly Hills. Igor is with Vera and Craft again at the Thyssen collection on the shores of Lake Lugano, and they proceed together by train from Stresa to Geneva, where they are pursued by photographers from *Paris-Match*. Then, after two nights in Geneva, they are in Baden-Baden for rehearsals and recordings, before flying from Frankfurt via London to New York. Only when a telegram arrives for Vera in London from Igor in Geneva do we realize that there has been another separation; and still there is no hint of the family gathering that is in fact at the heart of the composer's Genevan stay: the presence together, for the first time in fifteen years, of Stravinsky, Theodore and Denise, Milène and Kitty, together with the son-in-law whom he has never previously so much as seen in the same room with his Swiss son and daughter-in-law.[10]

Craft had preceded Stravinsky to Baden-Baden for recordings with the Südwestfunk Orchestra on 5 May. Meanwhile Stravinsky was due in Cologne for a concert on the 10th, before himself going on to Baden-Baden to conduct the radio orchestra; but by that time Craft would be on his way back to the American West Coast, where he had been engaged as musical director of the festival at Ojai, a small health resort in the hills north of Los Angeles. What seems mildly curious about these arrangements is that the Europe-loving Vera, instead of continuing the tour with Igor, was travelling back with Craft. It looks as if she either did not want to intrude on her husband's family party in Geneva, or (more plausibly, since otherwise she could have rejoined him in Cologne) for some reason did not want to travel with André, who would be acting as Stravinsky's assistant for the rest of the trip. The most likely explanation of all, though, is that she was fussing about Craft's having to look after himself on his own at Ojai. This had evidently annoyed Stravinsky. "Was it worthwhile," he wrote to her petulantly when he heard that the festival's production of *Apollo* (which Craft was due to conduct) had been cancelled because of an injury to the choreographer: "All your bother and worry and rush at the hotel in Rome? What an absurdity. I'm furious, and have been thinking about it since yesterday evening and can't reconcile myself to it."[11] As for him, he never even reached Cologne. Three days after Craft and Vera had left, he bought a bottle of mouthwash from a Geneva chemist's shop, gargled with it, and suffered an immediate and violent throat reaction. In fact he was in such pain, and so voiceless, that he promptly cancelled his Cologne concert and postponed his appearance in Baden-Baden. The bottle, it turned out, had been wrongly labelled, and contained formaldehyde.

As chance would have it, André also fell ill in Geneva, and when his father-in-law eventually left for Baden-Baden and, a few days later, London, it was Theodore who went with him.[12] The London trip was his first since 1937, and, frankly, he went without enthusiasm, as a gesture to his publisher, in order to conduct a single concert in the Royal Festival Hall and to receive the gold medal of the Royal Philharmonic Society. Despite—or because of—the venerable history of that society, the fee of five hundred pounds was (so he calculated) below his normal minimum rate, and would be subject to what he regarded as "outrageous" local taxation.[13] But then the British have always regarded their ancient awards as in some sense dishonored by commerce, and Stravinsky was certainly by no means the first great composer, nor probably the last, to discover that veneration and remuneration were, in London, seen as opposites. Nevertheless, on the 27th of May 1954 he solemnly accepted the RPS medal, together with a conductor's baton with silver handle and tip, said to have been used by Haydn.[14] The next day he and Milène flew back to Geneva, collected André, then took off again for Lisbon, where he had concerts on the 5th and 8th of June. It was his first proper visit to the Portuguese capital, and, like many before him, he was charmed by the lightness of its coloring: "light pink, light green, light gray—silver white," he told Craft.[15] "The air is exceptionally transparent," he reported to Vera, "the colors of the landscape, the sky, the streets, the flowers are extraordinary, as if they had gorged themselves on mescalin—unbelievable."[16]

Stravinsky flew into Los Angeles on the 11th in a musically hyperactive state. Craft records that he insisted on a musical evening and that they played a four-hand arrangement of Bach's Canonic Variations on "Vom Himmel hoch." He also claims to have suggested that Stravinsky transcribe the piece for instrumental ensemble.[17] It seems that on the long flight (without the company and stimulus of his musical alter ego) the composer had been trying to organize his creative agenda in his own mind. The Dylan Thomas tribute was still in hand but more or less complete and needing only tidying up, perhaps an additional page or two composed. Then there was the Kirstein ballet—not yet seriously begun, and still somewhat obscure as to its subject matter. To complicate matters, among the letters that awaited him on his return was a commission from the new director of the Venice Biennale, Alessandro Piovesan, for a thirty- to forty-minute choral work to be performed in St. Mark's Cathedral that coming September (which was plainly absurd) or in 1955.[18] But this approach cannot have been entirely unexpected; its musical conditions were too well tailored to Stravinsky's specific needs and interests not to have been the result of actual discussions with somebody in tune with his current thinking. For instance, Piovesan envisaged the new work as forming the second half of a concert whose first half would contain works by the late-sixteenth-century Venetian composer Giovanni Gabrieli, conducted by Craft. The letter even referred specifically to "evangelical or biblical texts." Clearly Piovesan had taken soundings; and his most likely contact, apart from Stravinsky or Craft themselves, was Nabokov.

The idea that Stravinsky may already have been planning a sacred work of some kind is borne out by subsequent events. Within ten days he had accepted Piovesan's commission, named a fee of twelve thousand dollars (plus three thousand for conducting the premiere), and indicated that only a select group of instruments—not a full orchestra—would be involved.[19] Such decisiveness was not quite normal with him. Several months later, while Piovesan was still trying to raise money for the commission, Craft told him that Stravinsky had begun a St. Mark Passion, though when Piovesan mentioned this in a letter to the composer, the reply was evasive.[20] In fact the Schütz-like Dirge-Canons in the Thomas memorial piece already suggest a fascination with the sonority of late-Renaissance or early Baroque brass music, of the kind Craft had recently been exploring in Roof programs and was planning to explore further in the memorial concert in September. The days in Rome, the saturation with the sound and atmosphere of Italian churches, the sacral power emanating from the Vatican and St. Peter's: one can imagine all these as influences on the particular creative image that lay behind the initial conception of the *Canticum sacrum.*

Meanwhile Stravinsky concentrated on other work. Soon after getting home that June, he completed the *In Memoriam Dylan Thomas* by adding a second set of Dirge-Canons as a postlude, with the trombones playing the string music from the original set, and the strings the trombone music.[21] It was the closest he had yet come to Webern's practice of eliminating waste by constant reduplication and self-referencing, though there is not much similarity in the actual musical language, which studiously avoids Webern's way of scattering the melodic line across the different registers like so many flashes on a radar screen. He also worked on a series of arrangements. He completed his flute, harp, and guitar version of the two Russian songs of 1919, then decided (in August) to add "Tilimbom" and "Gusi-Lebedi" ("The ducks, the swans, the geese . . .") from the *Three Children's Tales* of 1917 to make a new set of *Four Songs.*[22] He rewrote the piano accompaniment of his early Balmont songs (1911) for the same ensemble as he had used in the original version of the *Three Japanese Lyrics,* and finally made a radical revision of his four Russian women's choruses—the *Podblyudniye*—with a completely new accompaniment for four horns.[23] The object of these occasionally somewhat curious instrumentations was above all practical. They were designed, at least in thought, to be included in the Monday Evening Concerts, an institution Stravinsky had come to regard with huge affection, especially now that it was being run by his friend Lawrence Morton, and with Craft as one of its regular and most influential conductors. "An organization that puts on a program like that," he had told Morton after the opening autumn concert in 1953, "is going to be a dedicatee of my next piece," and he duly honored the promise by dedicating his Shakespeare songs to Peter Yates and the Evenings "as a tribute to their artistic achievement during sixteen seasons of concerts."[24] In particular, the bizarre idea of adding horns to the unaccompanied female voices of the *Podblyudniye* looks as if it was prompted by the availability of those instruments in the band for Strauss's early wind suite, which Craft was conducting that coming autumn. Stravinsky told Douglas Gibson at Chester's that the intention was simply to make the choruses easier to sing.[25] Not surprisingly, such arguments cut little ice with his poor, harassed publishers, who were being invited to bring out even less marketable versions of works that they were already hardly able to justify keeping in print in the first place.

As far as the new ballet was concerned, of course, all this was simply so much displacement activity. The project was still suffering, as Stravinsky had so often grumbled in the past, from a shortage of precise specification, since even a dance symphony has to have a form, and that form must depend at least partly on dance criteria. Fortunately, help was at hand. Balanchine was arriving in Los Angeles early in July with the New York City Ballet for a season at the Greek Theatre. He would bring with him the last five thousand dollars of the commission fee, and it would be Stravinsky's chance to pin him down, not on subject matter as such, but on questions of dramaturgy and architecture. They met several times, as Stravinsky reported to Kirstein, and "established the whole structure of [the] new ballet."[26] By early August Stravinsky was composing in earnest, and by the 12th they had settled on a title:[27] *Agon*, the Greek for "contest" (the sketches have it in Greek capital letters, with a long "o" (omega), so that the second syllable rhymes with "bone"). One recalls that an early idea for the (or at least a) ballet was Eliot's *Sweeney Agonistes*, but there seems to be no deeper connection. Balanchine's idea of a contest is on the face of it a highly abstracted, schematic affair involving twelve solo dancers (four male, eight female) in varying combinations whose starting positions are represented by stick men drawn by the composer at appropriate places in the draft plan they drew up together. Balanchine thought of it as "less a struggle or contest than a measured construction in space, demonstrated by moving bodies set to certain patterns or sequences in rhythm and melody."[28]

Such pure dance geometry might have been the cue for a first proper essay in twelve-note serialism; but in fact the models were not quite as constructivist as that description might suggest. At some stage of their discussions, Balanchine had brought up his old idea of a competition before the aging gods, with its series of historic dances exploding—as Kirstein had put it—into the twentieth century.[29] Stravinsky still had the copy of De Lauze's *Apologie de la danse* that Kirstein had sent him, and they probably mapped out the work in terms of the sixteenth- and seventeenth-century dances represented there. The music examples included a sarabande, a gaillarde, and several versions of the French popular dance known as the branle, or bransle: the "bransle simple," or single bransle, the quick "bransle gai," and the oddly named "bransle à mener ou de Poitou," a kind of early minuet with three-bar phrases; and there was a picture of two trumpeters playing a bransle. In Stravinsky's scheme, the first part of the ballet would be a "Pas de Quatre" based on the trumpet fanfare he had composed the previous December, and followed by a "Double" and "Triple Pas de Quatre," for eight and twelve dancers respectively—titles that pun on the old musical sense of "double" as a "variation" (like the ones in Handel's "Harmonious Black-smith"). The long second part would be a sarabande and gaillarde, in the form of a *pas de trois,* followed by a string of different types of branle (also *pas de trois*), and ending with a "Pas de Deux," just at the point where that episode usually figures in Romantic ballets. This would then run into the final part, a more up-to-date set of duos and trios, cast as a quick-moving sequence of angular modern dances culminating in a return to the opening fanfares.

Whether or not Stravinsky planned *Agon* quite so explicitly that summer of 1954 (and he certainly did know more or less how long it would be[30]), there is no mistaking the resemblance of this musical dramaturgy to the scheme outlined by Kirstein the year before. Balanchine, it is true, had long since abandoned—if he had ever entertained—any idea of Handelian gods surrounded by baroque statues and an ornate proscenium. He would be content with dancers in rehearsal tights on a bare stage. But Stravinsky was obviously intrigued by the musical concept of antique dances in a hyper-modern setting—a neoclassicism that would transform the modelling process as well as the model. He duly marked up his De Lauze and, while there are no clear quotations, the sense of allusion—rhythmic as well as melodic—remains extremely strong. We may be a long way from the Pulcinellification of Mersenne, but not so far that the outline of a phrase or the turn of a rhythm cannot sometimes, here and there, be recognized.

For a while the music came quite rapidly, and by the day of the Monday Evenings' Dylan Thomas tribute, the 20th of September, the first part was virtually complete, despite the distraction of a three-day trip to Las Vegas toward the end of August, for some reason, with his doctor, Max Edel. Closeted in his studio at one end of the house, he was nevertheless surrounded by at least the spiritual echoes of musics remote from one another in time. Craft was not only rehearsing the program for the Thomas concert, which included madrigals by his latest hero, the Neapolitan mannerist Gesualdo,

Schütz's "Fili mi, Absalon" and various other Baroque pieces, as well as the *In Memoriam Dylan Thomas* (for which Stravinsky himself coached the tenor, Richard Robinson), but he was also preparing more Webern, which he had persuaded Columbia's director of repertoire, David Oppenheim, to let him record in September with some of the artists who were also involved in the memorial concert. Rehearsals took place, sometimes during the day, in the sitting room at North Wetherly Drive, like some daily domestic reenactment of Balanchine's vision of the passage of centuries.[31] When they started recording, Stravinsky—as he had done in February—sat in on the sessions.

Oppenheim had already agreed a recording session for the new Stravinsky piece, together with the Shakespeare songs, and was even willing to let Craft conduct these works, on the principle, as he told Stravinsky, that "in this series we are making absolutely authentic performances under the supervision of yourself." "Perhaps," he added, with a shrewd eye to the seventy-two-year-old composer's future, "we should continue that way."[32] Hitherto, Stravinsky had not automatically seen Craft in quite this kind of role, though he certainly had confidence in him as a conductor of his music. At the Evenings the young man was rapidly establishing himself as an efficient and well-organized conductor of obscure or difficult modern music like Webern and Schoenberg, and equally of the kind of early music that lay outside the usual orbit of small choirs or baroque orchestras. He had prepared the Shakespeare songs in the composer's absence, had conducted the West Coast premiere of the Septet, and was now being entrusted with the *In Memoriam*. It was true that his manner at rehearsal was apt to be abrasive, and not all the players liked him. But somehow his enthusiasm and musicality overrode such difficulties, and on the occasions when they did not, he was protected by the feeling that Stravinsky's support for the concerts would not be jeopardized by the dissatisfaction of a few replaceable individuals.[33]

The concert on the 20th of September 1954 marked a watershed in this and other ways. It was Craft's first major Stravinsky premiere, and—taken as a whole, with its Gesualdo and other Renaissance and Baroque items—it was a statement about the historical context within which Stravinsky wished his music to be understood. Perhaps this connection did not strike the majority of the audience, to whom his new "atonal" manner was still too strange for its antique connotations to stand out. Those closer to the composer, like Huxley, who sat with him as usual in the front row and stepped up to give a short talk about Dylan Thomas as a lyric poet, may have seen Craft's presence on the podium as a kind of focus of the new direction. There may even have been some—acute, or merely cynical—who realized the extent to which the program was a survey of Craft's own past and future influence on the composer. The purest form so far of Stravinskian serialism rubbed shoulders with solemn, lapidary motets and ricercars from the late Renaissance, and weirdly dissonant Gesualdo madrigals that Craft and Morton had themselves extracted from manuscripts in the Library of Congress.[34] Of course, Stravinsky's interest in old music long predated his association with Craft, but the intensity of the latter's enthusiasm and its practical outcome in concerts that Stravinsky attended meant that its sound was suddenly a presence in his creative ear in a way that it had seldom been before.

The concert was also a pointer toward a new and somewhat altered Evenings regime. Peter Yates had withdrawn at the end of the previous season, and had insisted on taking the old Roof title with him. As director of the Monday Evening Concerts, Morton was projecting a more solidly structured, less bohemian, more professional type of season, with fewer concerts but a less hand-to-mouth, less "underground" mentality. Craft would play a bigger part in the program planning, and he would conduct something like half of the concerts. The memorial itself was quite a grand affair. The County Auditorium was packed and the atmosphere emotional. A recording was played of Dylan himself reading three of his poems including "Do not go gentle," and the *In Memoriam* setting, with its Dirge-Canon frame, was performed twice.[35]

Partly as a result of this concert and the planning that had gone into it, Morton himself became more intimate with the Stravinsky household. They had first met in 1941, but had only become friends in 1953 when Craft (who knew Morton through his association with Yates) brought him to Wetherly Drive to discuss the possibility of altering the anti-Semitic passages in the Cantata for a performance at a Roof concert the following March.[36] Morton, himself a Jew, was a music critic and musicologist, but he must quickly have overcome Stravinsky's prejudices as to the musicality of those trades, since he was soon being asked for his advice, or at least his ear, on artistic matters. A day or two after finishing his setting of the Thomas poem, Stravinsky had played it through as usual to Craft;[37] but by the time he had composed the Dirge-Canons a week later, Craft was in New York, and it was Morton who was summoned to act as captive audience. Stravinsky, he found,

> played it at the piano, very badly, and he sang the tenor part himself, in a composer's voice. This was not a performance, but it was accompanied by a running verbal analysis of the serial structure. [. . .] At one point in the preluding dirge-canons, he paused to say in a conspiratorial whisper, "Here I cheated the row—I did not like the harmony."

After handing out whisky, Stravinsky added that

> it was still difficult to "unlearn" tonality and that he still felt the pull towards a tonal center. [. . .] "But I do resist the academic approach, except that I find it very interesting to 'experience' [. . .] the serial method in my *Dylan Thomas* piece, so long as the harmony is correct. I must have the correct harmony!"[38]

IT REMAINED Stravinsky's intention to finish *Agon* before starting on the Venice commission, if it came through, or something else if it did not. He had promised Kirstein as much in August, and when Paul Sacher had written a fortnight earlier offering a new Basle commission, he had not even troubled to respond.[39] As for Piovesan, he was still battling with the labyrinthine Italian bureaucracy to find the money to pay Stravinsky's advance. Having heard about the St. Mark Passion, he implored Stravinsky not to abandon the idea, which he considered a huge attraction for recalcitrant Venetian committees.[40] At this point, the end of November, the composer was not even thinking about Venice. *Agon* was now complete to the end of the "Gaillarde" in the middle of the second part, a piece so exquisitely intricate and individual in its conception that one can scarcely imagine its being written in any state other than complete mental absorption. Basing himself very loosely on the Mersenne gaillarde in De Lauze, Stravinsky weaves a surreal musical tapestry from behind which the dance is no more than faintly heard, like costumed figures glimpsed through a series of colored gauzes lit at an angle. Everything about the music is improbable, from the idea of setting the actual gaillarde tune as a strict canon between harp and mandolin (the two most disembodied yet least cerebral instruments in Stravinsky's orchestra), to the eccentric notion of turning the string section upside down, with a pair of double basses at the top and a viola-cello quartet groaning away underneath in thick C major harmonies of a kind that would probably have sent his old teacher, Vasily Kalafati, into a rage of offended propriety. Like much of *Agon*, the "Gaillarde" is music that studies every known procedure in a mirror, inverting everything, offering us a world we can "see" but not enter, understand but not inhabit. The most astonishing thing about it is that once we have seen it we can neither forget it nor deny it. Like every work of imaginative genius, it changes our minds and perceptions forever.

On the day Stravinsky finished the "Gaillarde," the 29th of November, Bonnie Murray sang the new version of the Balmont songs at an Evenings concert, conducted by Ingolf Dahl, and the twenty-year-old Marilyn Horne, a member of the vocal ensemble for Craft's Gesualdo recording, gave the U.S. premiere of the three little "Souvenir de mon enfance" songs (likewise in their orchestral version).[41] Whether or not Stravinsky attended is uncertain, but if he did, he must have been as conscious as anyone in the audience of the remoteness of these songs from the music he was writing at that moment. He was drafting a short *pas de trois* by way of coda to the "Gaillarde," but this time, instead of taking a model from Mersenne, he was sketching a miniature violin concerto in the style of Berg. Early in November he had written to the head of Boosey's German office in Bonn, Edgar Bielefeldt, asking him to send a copy of the orchestral score of Berg's concerto;[42] and presumably it was sent, since the violin figuration in the Coda, with its strings of bravura sixths, bears an obvious family resemblance to the smooth thirds and sixths that, in Berg's case, reflect the conscious quasi-tonal design of the series. Stravinsky's piece, too, is serial, though the violin writing does not depend on that fact. The series is even a twelve-note one, the first example in any work by Stravinsky, although the point is largely symbolic as there is no proper dodecaphonic (twelve-tone) working, only a succession of brisk play-throughs, in a rhythmic style that again, somewhat oddly, recalls the Berg.

On 4 December, the day before he drafted the first part of the Coda, he had written to Piovesan what amounts to a protocol of an agreement to compose the St. Mark Passion that the Biennale director so earnestly desired. His wording, though, was ambiguous. "Agree, then, from this moment" it ran, "that it is this 'Passion' which should form the object of your negotiations [that is, with Piovesan's Venetian backers], and of our possible contract."[43] In other words, call it a Passion for the sake of diplomacy, but it might well not be one in the end. No less significantly, the letter makes no mention of the work's duration, though Piovesan had specified "thirty to forty minutes" in his commission. Whether it was this letter, or something to do with the novelty of the *pas de trois* Coda, that led him to write to Kirstein ten days later suggesting a meeting in New York the following month in order to "discuss some important technical problems in connection with my *Agon*," is a matter for conjecture, but it seems likely that he had already decided to request a postponement of the ballet.[44] In the intervening days he had been away in San Francisco, conducting *Petrushka* with the touring London Festival Ballet, and he had had time to reflect on the relative possibilities of the two commissions. Piovesan wanted his choral work, which Stravinsky still probably intended to last at least half an hour, for the 1956 Biennale. *Agon* was scheduled for earlier in 1956. But Stravinsky may have reasoned that, since the ballet commission was in the bag and he had actually received all of the fee, it would be more politic to guarantee the Venice work for that year (to help Piovesan raise the money) and put

Agon off until 1957. He could, of course, present the issue of twelve-note technique as a pretext—a "technical problem"—and perhaps even not a wholly imaginary one, since a serial ballet was undeniably a riskier, more speculative venture than was a serial choral work (assuming it was going to be one), which would have the whole long history of medieval, Renaissance, and late Baroque polyphony, to say nothing of Pythagorean and Boethian number theory and Schoenberg's own late choral works, as spiritual precedent. In any case, it seems clear that, by the time he and Vera climbed onto the plane for Portland, Oregon, at the start of a short concert tour that would touch on New York before returning them home via Atlanta at the start of February, he had firmly made up his mind to shelve the ballet in favor of the Passion, or cantata, or whatever it might turn out to be. The agreement he reached with Kirstein and Balanchine, when they lunched together in Manhattan on 24 January, was little more than a formality.

The Passion idea was certainly genuine. In New York, the day after the Kirstein lunch, he discussed the project with Auden, who suggested some possible text sources but did not conceal his dismay on learning that Stravinsky had thought of using the Picander libretto, which was all that survived of the St. Mark Passion of Bach.[45] The trouble was that they would not be back at North Wetherly Drive until 5 February, and they would be off again on a two-month European tour a month later. In the absence of a firm Venetian contract, and knowing the perils of Italian bureaucracy, it was hard for Stravinsky to start work with any conviction on a new commission at such a moment, and impossible to carry on with the old one. For several weeks he was in a creative limbo. When Charles Munch wrote from Boston inviting him to compose a short piece for Monteux's eightieth-birthday concert in April, he expressed ritualistic doubts as to whether he would have the time, but in fact soon produced a convulsive one-minute orchestral canon on "Happy birthday to you"—the piece that had surprised and irritated him at his Aspen rehearsal five years before—and offered it to Munch under the gently ironic title *Greeting Prelude*.[46] That month Craft was again rehearsing and recording Webern, and Stravinsky's birthday piece is a more or less open skit on Webern's prismatic arrangement of Bach's six-part Ricercar in the *Musical Offering*, except that, like most of Stravinsky's Webernisms, it has an energy and physicality lacking in the model.

They set off once more for the East Coast on 5 March 1955, going first by train to Pittsburgh, where Stravinsky had a pair of concerts, before flying on to New York on the 13th. It had not been a productive month, but it had been a tragic one. Within hours of each other in mid-February, Eugene Berman's film-star wife, Ona Munson, committed suicide and Maria Huxley died of the cancer that had wracked her for the past three years. The Stravinskys had to comfort both husbands, but Huxley, who dined with them two days after Maria's funeral, was the more difficult subject, since he was, it seemed, no more capable of facing the reality of his wife's death than he had for a long time been of accepting the likelihood of her dying. At the dinner her name was not so much as mentioned, and almost a fortnight later, when Isherwood came to supper with his young partner, Don Bachardy, Stravinsky told them that Huxley had still not referred to Maria's death in his presence.[47] By contrast Gerald Heard, whose Sunday-morning sermons in the Ivar Street Buddhist Temple they all continued to frequent, appalled the Stravinskys with his unconcealed glee at her demise. "How much happier she will be," he had chortled less than a week before she died, "out of the body."[48]

With a nice sense of symmetry, they returned to Europe through Lisbon, then hired a car and drove across southern Spain to Madrid, where Stravinsky conducted a concert, visited the Escorial, and called on the philosopher Ortega y Gasset.[49] From Madrid they flew to Rome, where the composer promptly took to his bed with flu and missed the opening of Vera's first ever one-woman show of her paintings at the Obelisco Gallery at the end of March. He recovered in time to conduct a radio concert in the Foro Italico a week later, but was then assailed by diverticulitis, spent two days in the hospital, and emerged only just in time to attend the special vernissage that Vera had laid on for his benefit. It was thirty years almost to the day since Katya had been hospitalized in the Eternal City with the pleurisy that heralded the final onset of her long-drawn-out terminal illness.

Piovesan had at last managed to produce a draft contract for the Venice commission, and he had turned up in Rome early in April to discuss the finer points. A youngish man, in his mid-forties, courteous, smiling, simple in his manner, he made a very different impression from the slightly condescending, self-important bureaucratic types who tended to be in charge of major events, in Italy as elsewhere. His effectiveness, though, remained to be proven. Curiously, the contract referred to a "Passion according to St. Mark," but said nothing about its length, perhaps because it had not occurred to those drafting it that a Passion setting could be anything but very long.[50] Piovesan must also have raised a doubt over the availability of St. Mark's, after all, for what would amount to a "profane" concert; and since the acoustical properties of that cavernous and sepulchral building were bound to be a factor in the music Stravinsky composed to be played there, he decided to go straight to Venice to sound out alternatives. Santa Maria della Salute proved too resonant (though not more so, surely, than San Marco itself); the gothic church of the Frari was drier, and you could make out the rapid semiquaver passages of an accompanied motet by Giovanni Croce reasonably well.[51] The musicians were laid on by Piovesan, but Stravinsky no doubt indicated what kind of music would provide the best index for his own needs. Croce was a transitional composer—a prede-cessor of Monteverdi as *maestro di capella* at St. Mark's—whose highly sec-tional motets combine the brilliant modern (that is, Baroque) instrumental style with the more stately Renaissance vocal idiom associated with the dou-ble galleries of St. Mark's. At the very least, Stravinsky was already includ-ing Venetian church architecture, and possibly Venetian church music, in his mental image of the new work. Soon he was starting to talk about what Craft calls his "musico-theological-architectural concepts,"[52] and it must have been at this moment that the idea of a narrative, English-language Pas-sion finally faded away and was replaced by a more severely exhortatory sequence with Vulgate (Latin) texts.

After concerts in Baden-Baden and Lugano, Stuttgart and Mannheim, with a visit to Webern's grave at Mittersill in between, they flew back to Los Angeles by the so-called polar route (over Greenland) and arrived home on the 6th of May. Stravinsky at once cast around for texts, and within barely a week he was describing the new work to Roth as a "sacred concerto for soloists, chorus and limited instrumental ensemble, based on the Gospel of St. Mark and fragments of the Old Testament (Psalms)."[53] At that month's Ojai Festival, in his second year as director of music, Craft was conducting Monteverdi's *Vespers,* a work well known to musicologists but still at that period very seldom performed, and this time Stravinsky was in the audi-ence, as well as conducting a concert of his own despite severe arthritis in his left leg. By the last week of May, however, they were firmly reinstalled at North Wetherly Drive, and within a fortnight Stravinsky had drafted the short, intonation-like "Dedicatio" for two male voices and three trombones that opens the *Canticum sacrum.*

22

AN ECHO CHAMBER
BY CANDLELIGHT

APART FROM short excursions, Stravinsky scarcely moved from Wetherly Drive throughout the summer and autumn of 1955, and the *Canticum sacrum* was written without a break during those six months. Domestically, it was not the easiest of times. André Marion, who had been working as his father-in-law's secretary, had now taken a job in a travel agency, and for a while Stravinsky had to handle routine correspondence on his own. Vera, it seems, had encouraged André to break away, but Igor was annoyed by what he saw as a challenge to his authority, and when Gerald Heard's companion, Michael Barrie, came one day in July to discuss taking on some of the work, Igor kept him waiting, then brusquely refused to see him.[1]

It was typical of him that he could see only the inconvenience and—as he imagined—slight to himself in what was in truth a wholly natural bid for independence on André's part. Igor must have been aware that Marion and Craft, since working together amicably enough on the translation of Theodore's *Message d'Igor Strawinsky* three years before, had been getting on less well, whether or not because (as the family automatically assumed) Craft and Vera had been systematically undermining Marion's position, which—the argument continued—was in some way interpreted as a threat to Craft's. Such possibilities are, of course, latent in any clash of personalities, but in this case there is no particular evidence that André left for any more sinister reason than the simple desire to better himself.

As ever, Stravinsky, absorbed by the technical aspect of his new score, was able to close his studio door on all such troubles. Before composing the "Dedicatio," he had worked out a schematic ground-plan recognizably like that of a church—in fact like that of St. Mark's itself. As Craft himself pointed out in an early article about the *Canticum,* the five main movements were like the five domes of the basilica.[2] You went in through the vestibule (the "Dedicatio") and then proceeded round the building, passing under the large central dome (alias the three-part middle movement), returning to the exit by way of the first dome, which you experienced of course in the opposite direction.[3] The text was even more scrupulously planned. Jesus's admonition "Go ye into all the world" was answered at the end by St. Mark's "And they went forth"; at the center were the three virtues—faith, hope, and charity, but in the reverse order—with "Caritas" (spiritual love) preceded by carnal love in the form of a passage from *The Song of Songs,* and "Faith" followed by the casting out of the Devil: "Lord, I believe; help thou mine unbelief."

Everything about the setting of the opening text, "Euntes in mundum," was purpose-built for St. Mark's. The loud choral exclamations with brass semiquavers in the Gabrieli manner were interrupted by soft passages for organ, to let the cathedral's booming echo clear, and one could imagine the brass players themselves disposed around the famous galleries, even though there is nothing in the music to indicate who would stand where. After writing this brilliant piece in June, Stravinsky then spent the first part of July working on the subtle and intricate tenor aria "Surge aquilo," from the *Song of Songs.* For some reason, the enticing poem ("Let my beloved come into his garden, and eat his pleasant fruits") inspired in him the desire to write cerebrally. For the first time he composed an entire movement based on a twelve-note row, adopting for the purpose a slightly modified form of the row he had already used in the puckish coda to the "Gaillarde" in *Agon,* but with strikingly different results. The tenor line exudes sensuality, as well as a certain airiness, almost like Oedipus's music in the last work Stravinsky had composed to a profane Latin text.

He completed the "Surge aquilo" on 20 July 1955, and three days later they all dined with the Kreneks at their house at Tujunga, an hour away in the far north of Los Angeles. They had recently been seeing Krenek more often than before, enjoying long musical conversations about theoretical matters in which he was expert, especially serial technique, Monteverdi, and the complex polyphonic music of the high Renaissance (he had written a book and an important technical paper on Ockeghem).[4] Krenek, a learned, courteous Viennese Jew, would play them tapes of his own latest works, or older pieces he thought would interest Stravinsky, like his prewar opera *Karl V* or his choral *Lamentatio Jeremiae Prophetae,* in which he had invented some particularly esoteric rotational procedures that he was at pains to analyze for their benefit. Curiously enough, Stravinsky, who had never liked discussing his own music in analytical terms, seems to have found these sessions stimulating. He even discussed his own work-in-progress with Krenek, if not analytically, at least to the extent of describing the music in general terms or showing him the text. When he talked about his latest cantata, or "sacred concerto," Krenek at once came up with a suitably ceremonious Latin title: *Canticum Sacrum Ad Honorem Sancti Marci Nominis,* which Stravinsky liked so much that he adopted it forthwith.[5]

After recording the new version of the Russian choruses and the *Three*

Little Songs (with Marilyn Horne) on the 28th, and after a three-day trip to Yosemite at the start of August, he got down to work on the tripartite central movement of the *Canticum*. At this point, the music takes on a significantly new aspect. The energetic and the sensual are alike discarded, in favor of a certain catechistic tone which is already established in the organ solo at the start of "Caritas," a plain, twelve-note melody of a quite nondescript rhythmic profile and based on a new series. In the same way, the choral setting of the words from Deuteronomy, "Diliges Dominum"—"Thou shalt love the Lord thy God with all thine heart"—is like the reading-out of school regulations: strict, unmodulated, and with a strong sense of the difficulty of things. The expression relaxes a little in the two later sections, "Spes" and "Fides," but so to speak under the same rubric: always the organ solo warning us of serious matters and the vocal lines constrained by the necessity of good order.

These three short pieces, jointly titled "Exhortations to the Three Virtues," are the first music Stravinsky composed in which one is strongly conscious of the influence of Webern, and on the whole it must be said that the effect is inhibiting, even though there is little trace of a Webern sound as such. It is the severe, relentless way of working, and the hesitant rhythmic design, that derive from the most recondite of the three masters of the so-called Second Viennese School. Webern was much in evidence at North Wetherly Drive these days. Craft was steadily recording his way through the whole oeuvre, and Stravinsky would sit in on rehearsals and studio sessions and sometimes help with the editing. Moreover, the tenth anniversary of Webern's death was coming up in September, and Stravinsky had recently penned a short but glowing tribute by way of foreword to a special Webern issue of the Universal Edition house magazine, *Die Reihe*. "We must hail not only this great composer, but also a real hero," he had written. "Doomed to a total failure in a deaf world of ignorance and indifference he inexorably kept on cutting out his diamonds, his dazzling diamonds, the mines of which he had such a perfect knowledge."[6] Considering that Stravinsky himself had figured prominently in that "deaf world of ignorance and indifference," this must count as one of the most bizarre voltes-faces in music history, as if Brahms had suddenly announced in 1885 that Wagner was a misunderstood genius and had started composing music dramas.

Like Berg, Webern had been an early pupil of Schoenberg in Vienna, and when Schoenberg had begun writing serial music in the early twenties, Webern had soon followed him—had even preceded him in certain respects. But whereas Schoenberg and Berg never wholly broke with their expressionist past but went on writing a music of the long phrase and the agonized gesture, Webern was drawn farther and farther into a black hole of esoteric serialism, in which every gesture was compressed to an extreme, every phrase rationalized, every note given weight in a highly attenuated sound-space. After the war, when progressive young composers were looking for a rational, contained answer to the chaos in which most of them had grown up, Webern's compact, highly organized, emotionally inscrutable late works shone for them like a beacon in the darkness, and it certainly did no harm to his image that these works were almost wholly unknown outside a small circle of friends and initiates, that they lacked every imaginable ingredient of popularity, and that their composer had been shot dead at Mittersill by a trigger-happy American sentry four months after the end of the European war. For a young conductor of Craft's predilections, Webern was at once a cause and an opportunity. Nobody knew or cared about his music; Craft loved it and would make it known. His Los Angeles performances were nearly all West Coast—and in some cases U.S.—premieres, and the recordings he embarked on in 1954 were, in almost every case, the music's gramophone début. Finally, Webern, like Krenek, had been a student of early music, had edited part of the *Choralis Constantinus* of Heinrich Isaac (died 1517),[7] and so combined in his own work the twin intellectual preoccupations, with the very old and the very new, that were hypermodernism's answer to the charge that it had abandoned all contact with the past.

Whether it was the spontaneous result of the last two or three years' exposure to Webern in Craft's concert programs and recordings, or whether there was any definite pressure from him to study and imitate, is hard to decide. Craft's own testimony is highly ambiguous. In his diary for 1956 he remarked that nobody "could lead *that* horse to water, if it didn't want to go, let alone make it drink";[8] but in an article published long after Stravinsky's death he claimed to have suffered from Bloom's "anxiety of influence," "because I *had* directed Stravinsky. [. . .] for, in truth, every Stravinsky opus, after and including *Three Songs from William Shakespeare* (1953), was undertaken as a result of discussions between us."[9] Of course, these statements are not quite contradictory, bearing in mind the crucial rider about the horse, "if it didn't want to go." Yet if the *Canticum sacrum* was written in the light of discussions with Craft, then it would be distinctly odd if the question of a Webernian technique had not formed part of those discussions. As for the *Die Reihe* statement, the only telling evidence that Craft did not simply write it himself might seem to be the strange and irritating grammatical error in the much-quoted final phrase, which ought to read "of whose mines . . . ," with a double genitive. As we shall see in due course, where Craft is concerned such quibbles are something more than mere pedantic exhortations to linguistic virtue.

Stravinsky completed the third of his own Exhortations, "Fides," on 30 September, then spent much of October on the so-called "Brevis Motus Cantilenae," the "help thou mine unbelief" setting for baritone and chorus (which really is quite brief), and the next three weeks after that turning "Euntes in mundum" back-to-front to make the final section of the whole work. He completed this largely mechanical process on 21 November 1955; and having finished the whole work, he was able to confirm what he had already warned Roth to expect—namely that, far from being "thirty to forty minutes" long, the *Canticum* was barely more than a quarter of an hour of music.[10] This was, as Stravinsky knew, a serious discrepancy. Piovesan had almost certainly secured the commission fee by inflating the likely scale of the work, and even at the expected length of thirty minutes he was worried about the shape of the concert and the reaction of city fathers who were quite used to valuing pictures by the square foot, and who moreover were having to curtail the festival budget severely to meet Stravinsky's demands. Now it turned out that they would be getting only half a canvas, while Stravinsky's somewhat airy initial solution to the problem of filling the program was simply to perform the new work twice.[11] In desperation, Piovesan suggested to Roth that the Maestro might at least consider composing one additional ten-minute movement, and conduct a complete program of his own sacred works, including the Mass and the *Symphony of Psalms*.[12] But the Maestro would have none of either of these ideas. The symphony, he told Roth, would overpower the *Canticum sacrum*, while the mere thought of performing his Mass as a concert piece in a Catholic church had suddenly become anathema to him.[13] As for extending the *Canticum*, that was obviously impossible on artistic grounds, but in case Piovesan should start making insinuations about the amount of work that had gone into its writing, he advised Roth not to let him know that the score was finished for at least another four months.[14] Meanwhile he had decided to transcribe Bach's famous organ variations on "Vom Himmel hoch" for the *Canticum sacrum* orchestra, and this (as he claimed) twenty-five-minute work he was prepared to throw in free of charge.[15]

For all his unusual niceness, Piovesan was, when all was said and done, an Italian man of the theatre trapped between an autocratic composer and an army of soulless and wily bureaucrats. "One will have to talk to him carefully," Roth said, "because he is a bit of a showman," knowing that, as with the *Rake*, he was the one who would have to do most of the talking.[16] So off he duly set for Venice in January 1956, hoping to pacify Piovesan as he had once pacified Ghiringhelli. But to his surprise Piovesan pleaded illness, like an opera star, and refused to see him.[17] Obviously, Roth told Stravinsky, he is very upset—a deduction that, by this time, the composer was well able to make for himself. "Am in a situation I hope will never be repeated," Piovesan had wired melodramatically to Roth,[18] and Stravinsky realized that the time had come for some further gesture on his part. With breathtaking pomposity, and not a little disingenuity, he chided Piovesan for entertaining unreasonable expectations:

> If you and your organization ever expected a substantially longer piece it shouldn't have been commissioned from me at this time because the contrapuntal line of my music today—which is by no means an unknown fact—makes it a must to keep the duration of a composition strictly within rigid limits. This is due to the requirements and possibilities of the human ear and because this kind of music is of the densest kind. This incidentally means also that it is the one which takes the hardest work to compose. To illustrate my point I will refer you to the works of Schoenberg, Webern, etc.[19]

He nevertheless offered to accept a reduced honorarium of ten thousand dollars, and to waive his conducting fee, concessions that clearly show that he was aware of some element of chicanery on his own part. "I do not believe," Piovesan responded ambiguously through Roth, "that there is any proposal capable of changing the course of events." He admitted that no duration had been specified in the contract; but if Stravinsky refused to include his Mass, he—Piovesan—could also be awkward about the inclusion of a motet by Gesualdo, a disreputable Neapolitan composer whom the Venetians could hardly be expected to welcome on so important a program in their cathedral.[20] And, rather grandly, he ignored Stravinsky's offer, instead announcing (prematurely, as it transpired) that the first half of the contracted twelve thousand dollars had now, in late February, been paid into the composer's bank.[21]

It was unfortunate, in some ways, that the *Canticum* had been composed so much in one breath and so far from reality. It had not come easily; quite the opposite, its composition had been an intricate, hardworking process, and for once Stravinsky had lost sight of practicalities. It was clearly true, as he told Piovesan, that his music had become very compressed, whether through the shortwindedness of old age or because of the concentration imposed on him by the serial technique, which he was not yet handling with complete fluency. But events would prove that compression did not inevitably mean brevity, even to a composer in his mid-seventies.

At the same time, the whole issue of the rest of the program showed a similar detachment from reality. The idea that two performances of so severe and forbidding a work in one concert could possibly either compensate the promoters or (more important) please the audience was obviously sheer fantasy. As for the "Venetian" items that Stravinsky had placed at the start of the program (Gabrieli, Monteverdi, Schütz, and the rogue Gesualdo), he clearly had never had any intention of conducting these himself, but always meant to leave them to Craft, who had conducted several programs of such music at recent Monday Evenings. He as good as admitted this later when he explained to Roth that "Craft has a great deal of experience conducting and recording this music, whereas I have none."[22] He had not, however, made this plain at the outset, and Piovesan was understandably annoyed when he found out. Once again he pleaded with Stravinsky to conduct an entire program of his own works, and promised to find an outside engagement for Craft.[23] Then, when Stravinsky agreed to add the Mass to his two performances of the *Canticum* plus the Bach arrangement, but only if this rather short concert took place in the Fenice, Piovesan with difficulty persuaded his superiors to accept Craft *and* the Fenice, whereupon Stravinsky smoothly expressed a preference for St. Mark's.[24] He had in effect won the war of nerves. As late as June 1956, neither the exact date nor the venue had been settled for the performance in September; but the composer eventually got his way, the concert was at last agreed for St. Mark's, and half of it was conducted by Craft, only the second time he had shared a rostrum with Stravinsky since their early concerts for the Chamber Arts Society.[25]

IN PRINCIPLE, Stravinsky had wanted to finish the *Canticum sacrum* by the end of November 1955, because he intended as usual to spend December and part of January on the East Coast. There was even some vague plan to live for six months of 1956 in Europe, perhaps with a view to settling there in due course for good.[26] More immediately there were concerts in New Orleans and (with the usual geographical profligacy) Cleveland, where he was also recording *The Fairy's Kiss*, before reaching New York in the middle of December.

For once the New York trip seems to have been motivated by nothing more urgent than the need for a change from the monotony of West Coast life.[27] "Going back to L.A, *hélas*," Vera lamented in her diary for 11 January, after a month of energetic dining out and theatre-going, punctuated by the usual bouts (in Igor's case) of unexplained illness.[28] As far as business was concerned, nothing much happened beyond a lunch with his Columbia producer, David Oppenheim, and meetings with the company's lively and sociable new publicity director, Deborah Ishlon. But while there were neither concerts nor recordings and his only formal engagement was a ceremony at the Finnish consulate on the 4th at which he was presented with the Sibelius Medal, he by no means wasted his time. Having promised Piovesan a transcription of "Vom Himmel hoch," he now had to carry out what was at the very least a laborious process entailing creative decisions.

Before embarking on it—and perhaps by way of preparation—he made an arrangement for two recorders of Ann's lullaby in the final scene of *The Rake's Progress,* a task that involved a reduction from three parts to two in the solo verses and a still more drastic condensation of the short choral interludes.[29] He then turned at once to the Bach. From the start he refused to confine himself to a straight instrumentation of the organ work, with its increasingly elaborate canonic embroidery of the well-known chorale tune. Already in the first variation, which he worked on after Christmas, there is a certain impatience with the plain act of orchestration and an inability to resist little touches of his own, an added canon for bassoon and cor anglais, extra fragments of harp melody or string pizzicato, and, at the very start of the second variation, a countermelody for trombone.

When they returned to Los Angeles, he took these two variations with him. He then composed the remaining three in draft form by early February, but it was the end of March before he completed the admittedly quite complicated, but after all largely derivative, orchestral score. Why the delay? Certainly there were distractions. Soon after getting home from New York, he had been offered ten thousand dollars to make and record an abbreviated version of *Petrushka* to accompany a television cartoon film,[30] and though he excused himself with the pure-minded Nadia Boulanger ("Yes sir, it's certainly reprehensible, but also explicable when you think of the taxes they so pitilessly squeeze out of us"[31]), there was really no sensible reason to refuse such a commission with a work that for thirty years or more had earned him nothing in the United States and that even now the producers could—as they were careful to hint—have used free of charge provided they chose the unrevised original and did not distribute the film outside America. Acceptance meant that Stravinsky could select the excerpts, compose the new links, and conduct the result, which he duly did in a Los Angeles studio at the beginning of March.[32]

What he must have been itching to do was restart work on *Agon,* as yet only half-composed and still scheduled for production in February 1957. The earliest dated sketch from this period is on a full draft of the second dance, the "bransle gai," completed on the 8th of June. But he must have been working on these dances for several weeks before that, since he probably composed them in order, and there are extensive serial workings and the usual rough sketches and drafts for both pieces. There was one interruption of a week or so in May for the Ojai Festival, of which Craft was again musical director. On the 27th Craft conducted the first performance of the "Vom Himmel hoch" arrangement, and Stravinsky himself took the baton for a rare concert performance of *Les Noces.* Otherwise he probably devoted the whole of April and May to *Agon,* starting with the canonic trumpet duet that begins the "bransle simple" and openly suggests the types of movement and texture, though certainly not the harmony, of Bach's variations. The work was unusually intricate, since he was combining a variety of note-ordering techniques (different in each dance) with his usual process of modelling. For instance, the sketches show that the rhythm of the "bransle simple" was at first taken from the dance of that name in Mersenne, though it would be hard to detect this fact from the final version.[33] As so often with Stravinsky, it is the richness and apparent promiscuity of reference that give the music its peculiar feeling of transparent depth, as if it were a series of perspex sheets laid against one another and lit (as Debussy had once said of *Parsifal*) from behind.[34]

That Easter, just when Stravinsky was taking up *Agon* once again, Deborah Ishlon came up with a new promotional idea, perhaps originally prompted by a rather unsatisfactory documentary film they had gone to see in New York of him rehearsing and conducting *The Soldier's Tale*.[35] She wanted to send a photographer to take pictures of him at work; but more particularly she had had the idea of recording him reading extracts from his published writings.[36] It says a good deal for her persuasive powers and personal charm that Stravinsky did not simply reject this latter proposal out of hand. On the contrary, he declared himself "very interested in it" and eager "to do it at a later date." The trouble was that there was nothing he had written that he would now care to associate himself with in that kind of way. What he meant was that there was nothing that, in his new anglophone, American existence, he felt would adequately represent his character and thinking, or would belong, whether implicitly or explicitly, to the latest developments in his music. "It would certainly be of more interest to you," he told Ishlon, "to have a statement from me in my own style and from my present point of view. I will try to write this during the free time on our travels, and I can work on it with Bob Craft during our concert tours."[37]

The publicity director, however, was not willing to wait on such a vague eventuality, and as soon as the Stravinskys arrived in New York in mid-June, at the outset of the European trip that would take them to Venice in September, she appeared with a tape recorder and a set of questions, recorded the composer's answers, then wrote them up in part and sent the typescript for his approval the very next day. It was, she assured him, "an exact transcription of your own delightful phrases and ideas, [and] reads, I think, with the precision and charm of your own conversation."[38] No doubt he had prompted her as to what questions he cared to answer; he may even have had written notes. The remarks themselves would have surprised no one who knew the *Poetics* or had heard the Chicago lecture. Their interest lies in their tone of voice, so to speak, and their choice of language. One has no difficulty in sensing, through these written words, what Huxley had meant when he wrote that "Stravinsky's talk has a curious and fascinating quality all its own."[39] You can hear, for the first time, the deep Russian accent, the idiosyncratic, not always quite accurate, use of English, and the vivid, always surprising wit and concreteness of imagery.

To be a good listener you must acquire a musical culture, as in literature. You must be familiar with the history and development of music, you must listen. The person with the subscription ticket for concerts, he is not necessarily a musically cultured person. He is musical only because the music is performed in front of him. To receive music you have to open the ears and wait, not for Godot, but for the music; you must feel that it is something you need. Some let the ear be present and they make no effort to understand. To listen is an effort, and just to hear is no merit. A duck hears also.

The larger the audience, the worse. I have never attached much importance to the collective mind and collective opinion. You can imagine what collective opinion looks like. Especially in America, they like to speak and work with masses. But music is not a moral activity, to render the masses more happy. Music cannot deal with such things. Music never was for the masses. I am not against masses. But please do not confuse the value of the music which is addressed from ear to ear with the value of music addressed from one ear to a million ears. That doesn't mean for millions, but for each of the millions. Don't make the mistake of merely multiplying.

No audiences are good anywhere, but the major level, the best musical level, is that of the Germans. They have a higher level of listeners because of their musical history and musical culture. You can think how it was in the seventeenth and eighteenth centuries. The people who listened to music were much more learned; music was for them a language which they knew well. They knew not only by passive listening but by active playing. Everybody played—harpsichords, organs, flutes, violins. They had the habit of music played with their own hands, not only by ears. Now we hear music by the gramophone. This gives maybe more people a connection with music, but the result is not the same because the passive is not the active.

Accustomcy to music is a fact with which we have to count. We think that very difficult works like all the last works of Beethoven are better understood now. No, people are simply more accustomed to them. It isn't that they understand better. People are not shocked by dissonances. Otherwise, why should we write them? And shocking really means striking. To be merely shocking is vulgar. It could not be the legal goal merely to be shocking. Music should be striking.

A composer thinks about the audience, but not primarily. If you think about audience, you don't think about your work. You think about a reaction which will come from certain things. If the audience is yourself, that is quite different. To be yourself the audience is difficult; it is difficult to multiply yourself. To become an audience by imaginary multiplication does not give you new value.

Where is music going? How can we see the direction? Even going very high we can see very little. The higher we go, the less we see, because we are far away. If we are very close we see only a part of the mountain. We can judge about some facts. But to draw a conclusion is another thing. We can never be absolutely right.[40]

The latest idea was for these remarks to be included in an article in *Newsweek*. Whether Ishlon also still intended them to be published as a recording is not entirely clear, but in any case Stravinsky seems to have decided not to let the text be printed, and there the matter might have rested but for the energetic Miss Ishlon's firm conviction, as she told the composer, "that you should write—or talk—a book."[41]

After a week in Manhattan they sailed, as the previous year, for Lisbon. Two days out from New York, a cable announced that Madubo had died in Switzerland.[42] The news was more disturbing than unexpected, since she had been slowly dying of an agonizing though long-undiagnosed cancer for almost a year. But for the Stravinskys pain at her loss was compounded by a nagging sense of guilt over their past treatment of her. They had brought her to California, but she had never settled down there; and while it was perfectly true—as Stravinsky told her brother—that the main problem had been her own inability to come to terms with the fact that her former charges were no longer naughty children, he could not shake off a feeling of responsibility for what had been, for all of them, an unhappy episode.[43] Madubo had gone back to Switzerland in 1954, and Vera and Craft had visited her in Berne in April 1955, and endured what Vera recorded as a "very emotional" day with her.[44] The composer could only salve his conscience by the gift of money. He had contributed to her hospital expenses, and now he helped pay for her funeral. But it was a very abstract recompense for almost forty years of devotion tainted, at the end, by a sense of neglect.

From Lisbon they embarked on four weeks of pure holiday, albeit of that peculiarly gruelling, self-improving variety that saps the intellect and leaves the body screaming for mercy. "What one has to suffer," Huxley exclaimed when he heard about the trip, "in the name of culture."[45] Travelling with Lawrence Morton, they continued by boat from Lisbon to Barcelona, then on to Naples and Palermo, and eventually, in excruciating heat, to Patras, from where they drove for seven hours to Delphi. The next day, on the road to Athens, they passed the Oedipus crossroads, in a wide-open landscape not at all like the narrow defile that the composer had imagined as the setting for Oedipus's enraged slaughter of the unknown but obstructive old man.[46] But then Stravinsky, usually such an eager and attentive tourist, was in a grumpy mood and made unwell by the heat, and soon after reaching Athens he took to his bed and did not go with Craft and Morton to Nauplia. From Athens they escaped (perhaps at the suggestion of Robert and Mildred Bliss, who were making the same move) to Istanbul, where they spent a week seeing the city and enduring the disconcerting blend of luxury and squalor inseparable at that time, and to some extent still, from five-star tourism in Eastern lands. One night (in the Hilton Hotel) Craft was kept awake by bedbugs, and captured three of them in an envelope that Vera, the next morning, painstakingly tipped out onto the reception desk in front of a crowd of the hotel's clientele.[47] Small wonder that when the four travellers finally chugged into the Serenissima from Piraeus and Brindisi on 30 July, and despite the unremitting heat, Vera recorded in her diary, "What a *bonheur*! to be in Venice!"[48]

It is clear from Morton's brief accounts of this trip[49] and from Craft's diaries, especially, that the Stravinskys were Baedeker travellers *par excellence*. They would insistently visit the major sites, sometimes journeying considerable distances and enduring real discomfort, but invariably returning to the security of a good hotel and a first-class dinner. Not for them the sheep's-eye stew and the rough palliasse at the end of a nine-hour walk through hill country. At Stravinsky's age such things would certainly have been absurd; yet one is constantly struck by the laborious routines even of well-to-do tourism in their case. Craft stands there with the guidebook or discoursing learnedly from his astonishing memory of what he has read in advance, while the Stravinskys inspect the mosaics, remark on their likeness to Torcello or their inferiority to Ravenna.[50] In suits and ties, with the temperature in the high nineties, they struggle round Delphi, or stagger up the Acropolis, returning as often as not to hotels whose comfort is most clearly expressed in their price. To many of their friends the pace seemed excessive. Huxley, who had done more than his fair share of rough travel but was no hotel-hopper, found their postcards from Greece more disturbing than reassuring: "So much heat and attendant ills," he wrote.[51] Arriving in Venice for what might seem like a rest six weeks before the *Canticum* premiere, they continued the round of churches, villas, and art galleries, lunches and dinners, in the greater relaxation of a settled and familiar environment, and now with Eugene Berman, who had settled in Rome after his wife's suicide, as a specialist guide. But they must have felt, in some way, that enough was enough, since Stravinsky promptly announced to his publisher that they had decided to cancel a planned visit to Egypt in the autumn, not—to be sure—in the interests of repose, but in order for him to accept a conducting date in Hamburg.[52]

Morton was struck by the energy and perceptiveness of the Stravinskys' sightseeing; and he also noted that Stravinsky never stopped composing, even when on tour.[53] In the past, as we have seen, this had not been the case. In France before the war, he had composed at home and, to some extent, in his Paris studio, but he had seldom if ever written music in hotel bedrooms. Since the war he had sometimes composed in hotels. The Septet was completed in one, and the first two variations of "Vom Himmel hoch" were transcribed in the same one. But when actually travelling, as in Greece and Turkey in 1956, Stravinsky probably still did not compose, unless he perhaps toyed with note-rows or serial charts on long flights or train journeys. In Venice that year, however, he made up his mind to work. As soon as they were ensconced in the Hotel Bauer-Grünwald, a piano was ordered, and a few days later it arrived and was winched up to his bedroom, exactly as at the time of the *Rake*.[54] The hotel staff watched this procedure somewhat nervously, no doubt imagining that the air would from now on be rent by cascades of Lisztian arpeggios and shrieks of Wagnerian frustration.[55] In fact, though Stravinsky's way of composing was altogether more discreet, it does seem that some difficulty arose about his working in his bedroom, since by the end of August he had moved down two floors into the stale smoke of the hotel's cellar bar and was working on the "bransle double" at a pink grand piano by the light of an angle lamp.[56] The image is at least as bizarre as that of *The Rite of Spring* taking shape in a suburban Swiss rooming house. There is little enough of the nightclub about any single page of *Agon*, but the "bransle double" was certainly the least smoochy so far, its rhythms articulated by jagged, serial string melodies more suggestive of a pole-vaulting contest than cheek-to-cheek dancing. In Balanchine's original scheme, Stravinsky had evidently reached the point at which "the dances which began quite simply in the sixteenth century took fire in the twentieth and exploded."[57] For him it was the critical moment in the whole work, the moment at which his new, esoteric compositional technique had to be invested with a vibrant physicality alien to the music of its inventors and only found spasmodically, if at all, in a handful of works by younger composers—Boulez's *Structures*, Stockhausen's *Kontra-punkte*—that he had heard but not studied.[58]

Rehearsals for the *Canticum sacrum* began in the Fenice on 30 August. It had finally been settled that the actual performance would take place in St. Mark's on 13 September, and although Stravinsky and Craft had called on the Patriarch of Venice, Cardinal Roncalli (the future Pope John XXIII), a month before the concert to request permission for the profane use of the cathedral, the visit was a formality and a refusal not in question.[59] But rehearsals did not move to St. Mark's until three days before the concert, at which point it became evident that whatever allowances Stravinsky may have made for the cavernous acoustics were insufficient. "We need blotting paper, not echo chambers," he muttered to Craft.[60] The music's precisions and refinements were drifting up into the domes and mingling with the timeless echoes that seem to hang in those vast spaces without the necessity of any initiating sound from below. The *Canticum,* however neo-Venetian in some respects, simply did not partake of the stately, slow-pulsed harmonies that the composers of three and a half centuries before had found suitable for a building where chords run like colors in a bowl of water.

Stravinsky had at least never had any illusions about the likely quality of the performers. He had expressed his anxieties about the ability of the Fenice choir and orchestra to cope with the work's difficult and unfamiliar idiom in a letter to Roth in early May, adding that "I have never heard trombones and trumpets in any Italian orchestra of the calibre I need."[61] Craft, who took nearly all the rehearsals, duly found the music to be too difficult for the local performers, though there was no such reservation about the soloists, Richard Lewis and Gérard Souzay.[62] By any measurable standard, the concert was destined to be a nerve-wracking occasion. The cathedral, in a glow of red candlelight, was packed with the Great and the Good for what was said to be the first concert in St. Mark's for three hundred years, and was certainly the first high-profile Stravinsky premiere since the *Rake,* here in Venice exactly five years before. When Craft came on to open proceedings with music by the Gabrielis, Monteverdi and Schütz, he bowed ceremoniously to Cardinal Roncalli, who was ringed by what one newspaper described as "other high authorities of the international ecclesiastical, political and artistic world."[63] The atmosphere was tense and noisy, as is often the way in crowded churches especially in Italy, where piety is not normally felt to entail silence. Photographers roamed about; flashbulbs popped in all directions. Only when, during the first piece, a flashbulb fell from one of the balconies and went off like a cannon did the audience go comparatively quiet and the music come genuinely to the front of the acoustical stage. But in truth the audience was waiting for the new work and its composer. Craft was experiencing for the first time the consciousness, if not the actual sound, of the words being mouthed behind his back: "Where is Stravinsky? Who is this young man?"

The *Canticum sacrum* was, in the event, played twice, once before and once after the interval, and Stravinsky conducted both performances—almost as much, in total, as he had conducted it in rehearsal. According to Craft himself, the performances were uneasy, because Stravinsky had rehearsed so little and the musicians were unaccustomed to his beat. "There was nothing about the choral singing," Peter Heyworth reported in the London *Observer*, "that suggested that we were hearing the work in favourable conditions," a roundabout way of saying that the choir was execrable.[64] The concert ended, no less muddily, with the "Vom Himmel hoch" transcription, also conducted by Stravinsky. In the cathedral itself neither applause nor (as the *Corriere* reviewer pointedly noted) protest was permitted.[65] But the Cardinal had arranged for the concert to be relayed into the piazza outside, and when Stravinsky emerged from the basilica, a shade reluctantly, at the end of the concert, there was a spontaneous outburst of clapping and cheering from the still considerable crowd who had heard the music and had waited in the warm Venetian evening for a glimpse of its composer.[66]

Moved by what he instinctively knew to be a genuine, not a polite or snobbish, enthusiasm, Stravinsky walked slowly across the great square toward the Taverna La Fenice.

23

THE ETERNAL FOOTMAN ■
HOLDS HIS COAT

EVER SINCE the Cantata, it had been well known in the trade, and to some extent more widely reported, that Stravinsky was flirting with serial technique, but on the whole the rumors had not been borne out in practice. For the musical world at large, serialism still meant twelve-note rows like the ones in Schoenberg, and it meant atonality—music with no sense of key, music which made you grit your teeth and wish it would stop. Nothing of the kind had come from Stravinsky. The Cantata itself had proved somewhat esoteric and learned, but neither technically nor stylistically was it anything like Schoenberg; and since then he seemed to have composed rather little, and mainly small-scale pieces consistent with the general impression that he was quietly winding down and growing old with grace. The *Canticum sacrum* was a rebuke to such ideas, and it at first caused something close to consternation in the Stravinsky camp, just as Erwin Stein had predicted it would.[1] For here, irrefutably, was a serious and important score by the great supposed enemy of Schoenbergism substantially made out of twelve-note rows; and, at least to the casual or untutored ear, much of it was atonal.

On the whole the newspaper men who flocked to Venice that September were well briefed and knew what to expect. "Stravinsky has gone dodecaphonic!" exclaimed one French critic, halfway through a long review which showed that the change was no surprise to him, however much it might disconcert his readers.[2] The sophisticated Peter Heyworth made hardly anything of the work's serial elements in his London *Observer* notice, beyond drawing attention to the influence of Webern on the "Surge aquilo" (fluidly sung by the British tenor Richard Lewis). And even this, he insisted, was "no more than a half-truth."

> Stravinsky seems condemned to wander the face of Western music, but where he has seized hold of a technique or of a manner it has not been for purposes of pastiche but to gain, as it were, a point of departure for a genius that has no roots other than its own individuality. If in "Surge

aquilo" the hand of Webern is apparent, there is also a liturgical austerity about the vocal line. Yet all this is curiously inessential. A cuckoo among composers, Stravinsky has an astonishing ability to make other men's nests his own, so that the final impression left by this song is not of an odd amalgam of styles but of a severe yet deeply expressive lyricism, highly characteristic of Stravinsky and of no one else.[3]

For a review of a difficult work in a poor first performance, this was very shrewd. It was exactly true that, while technically hybrid, the *Canticum sacrum* breathed its own air, just as Stravinsky's music had always done, whatever its apparent points of reference. Heyworth may well have attended rehearsals as well as the concert. But no doubt the physical context of the premiere itself—the Byzantine architecture, the candles, the stately Venetian motets, the Patriarch in his scarlet habit, the chattering grandees, the lapping Adriatic nearby—all helped draw attention away from the crude mechanics of the rule of twelve, and made it easier to locate this austere yet vibrant music within the glowing hieratic tradition of the Eastern church, with which, after all, Stravinsky's work had often rubbed shoulders in the past. The names of old masterpieces like *Les Noces*, the *Symphony of Psalms*, the Mass, were on many lips. On the other hand, as another, less excitable Frenchman, Fred Goldbeck, observed,

> the real find of Stravinsky's *Canticum*—a find not of technique but of style—is to have passed from analogy to synthesis. And, medievalism for medievalism, troubled age (ours) for troubled age (that of the birth of Venice), everything fades into irrelevance, as if Stravinsky had discovered that the twelve-note technique could turn into the technique of a style strangely akin to that of a Byzantine mosaic: in the orchestra, the carousel of disjointed intervals is laid out like a metallic background—compartmentalized, multicolored—from which the cantilena of solo or choral voices emerges in fixed and enigmatic figures like the figures of Ravenna—discretely terrifying and discretely seductive like the glances of Justinian and Theodora.[4]

Most strikingly of all, the *Canticum* press bore witness to a drastic change in Stravinsky's standing in the European worldview. Five years before, *The Rake's Progress* had been eyed with a certain condescension, as the effusion—however accomplished—of an aging master left behind by an irretrievably altered world. Now suddenly, he was once more the pathfinder, the challenging, esoteric genius, the dazzling synthesizer of past, present, and future. Knowledgeable critics like Heyworth and Goldbeck—sympathetic to the new music and inclined to be hostile to revisionism—

were even prepared to admit to not having grasped everything in the *Canticum*. Heyworth was baffled by the "Virtues" section but took it for granted that further, better hearings would "make its exceedingly intricate structure apparent to the ear as well as to the eye." Stravinsky himself might be pleased, but could hardly be astonished, by this transformation. After all, it was precisely out of the misery of rejection that he had evolved the new style in the first place, so there was no need to be surprised at its success with its target audience. Some, naturally, would ridicule him as a mere straw in the wind. There would be mutterings among the Stravinskian old-stagers, who would see the *Canticum* as a betrayal of thirty years of shoulder-to-shoulder opposition to Vienna and all its works. Robert Craft would be identified as the evil influence, the seducer, the serpent with the forbidden fruit. All this would come to pass. But no matter what anyone thought about it, Stravinsky was back where he belonged, in the vanguard of European music, and once more asserting his mastery. As Poulenc, who disliked the idea of twelve-note music and had mixed feelings about the *Canticum sacrum*, wrote to Henri Hell after the premiere: "I'd still be happy to write like that at 72."[5]

A FEW DAYS after the premiere, the party split up. Stravinsky was conducting in Montreux on the 25th—a concert fixed for him by Theodore—while Craft had a recording session in Turin on the same day. So the composer duly set off for the Vaud in his son's car, and a day or two later Vera and Craft took the train to Turin. On the 26th they met up again in Berlin, where Stravinsky had yet another concert in the Titania Palast the following Tuesday, 2 October 1956—his first public appearance in the old German capital since 1931. On the day of their arrival, however, he felt unwell and asked Craft to take over his evening rehearsal with the radio orchestra.[6] This had happened before, and was never thought cause for alarm. But the concert went badly from the start. The orchestra—the strings especially—struggled with ensemble and intonation throughout the first movement of the opening work on the program, the Symphony in C. Then suddenly, near the end of the movement, Stravinsky dropped his hands and stopped conducting. Somehow the orchestra got to the end, but for several minutes the composer did not raise his arms to start the Larghetto. There was an awkward pause. Then he seemed to recollect himself, the music resumed, and by some half-conscious, half-instinctive process he managed to shepherd this awkward and intricate work to some kind of acceptable conclusion.

For the rest of the concert and throughout the next day and a half Stravinsky behaved as if nothing out of the way had occurred.[7] He felt numb, he said, on his right side, his speech was slurred, and he was visibly having difficulty with balance and coordination. Yet not until almost forty-eight hours after his blackout on the rostrum, by which time they had flown to Munich, did Craft manage to override his refusal to be examined by a doctor. The diagnosis was chilling. He had suffered a serious stroke, and a second one, still more severe, was possible and might be fatal. Yet even now, incredibly, he did not go to hospital. Instead he spent a day with Karl Amadeus Hartmann, the director of the Musica Viva series in Munich, and enjoyed a high-protein dinner cooked specially for him by the chef of the Hotel Vier Jahreszeiten. His Munich concert on the 10th was cancelled. But only when Maurice Gilbert arrived from Geneva and talked to the local specialist was Stravinsky finally persuaded to abandon his Swiss tour and, on that same 10 October, enter the Red Cross Hospital in Munich. There he stayed for more than five weeks, forced into an unwilling quiescence while the world shook at events in Budapest, Warsaw, and Suez. Vera stayed with him, sustained by tranquillizers, terrified of the future, desperate to go home. Letters flowed in from friends urging him to rest, to give up conducting, to save himself for composition. Eugene Berman wrote to Craft, insisting that he, or Vera, or even Theodore, should act.[8] The newspapers hovered. After a month, the patient received a visit from the holy trinity of the avant-garde—Boulez, Stockhausen, Nono—as if they hoped for a "Weihekuss," a consecrating kiss, like Beethoven's on the child Liszt.

For Craft, the whole episode was in some ways as disturbing as for its protagonist. For seven years he had lived and travelled with the Stravinskys, and on more than one occasion he had come close to deciding it was time to move on.[9] On the day the composer tottered out of his hospital bed for the first time—the 20th of October—Craft turned 33. He had no dependable work, no career, and a reputation as something between a minder and a *famulus* that, among fellow musicians, earned him envy and disapproval as much as respect. Many of Stravinsky's older musical friends regarded him as a troublemaker whose influence had driven a wedge between them and the composer. Yet, as he admits in his published diaries, he did not want to leave.[10] For one thing, the Stravinskys now needed him more than ever, and he was too entangled in their lives simply to consult his own professional interests and go. He was surely by now conscious of a definite sense of family rivalry with Stravinsky's children. He is careful to record in his diary that, when he returned to Munich with Theodore and Denise after a three-day absence substituting for Stravinsky as conductor in Lausanne, Vera told him, in Theodore's hearing, that the composer was longing to see him, Craft, but did not want to see his eldest son.[11] As an expression of Stravinsky's (as opposed to his wife's) wishes, the story is frankly incredible, but what is very striking is that Craft was so ready to believe, not to mention report it. Elsewhere he drops a heavy hint that the reason he and Vera had not travelled with Stravinsky to Montreux was that Theodore was with him, even though less than a month later Craft was perfectly happy to drive with Theodore from Lausanne to Munich.[12] No doubt one reason for the Montreux split was the purely practical question of car passenger space. Another simple explanation is that it was specifically Vera who, for some reason, would not travel with Theodore and Denise.

Two weeks after returning from Lausanne, Craft was due in Paris, where he was conducting the *Canticum sacrum,* the Bach variations, and some late Webern for Boulez's Domaine Musical series in the Salle Gaveau. This was not a stand-in engagement but a deal struck directly, with Stravinsky's approval, between Craft and Boulez, who had written to Craft in July requesting the French premiere of the *Canticum,* and suggesting that it be recorded at the same time.[13] The approach seems to have come out of the blue, since Boulez had not been in touch with the Stravinskys since their meeting at Virgil Thomson's in New York in December 1952. There had even been bad blood between them, at least of a vicarious, unspoken kind, also involving Souvtchinsky and that old Stravinsky bugbear, Parisian musical politics, which was no doubt why Boulez had preferred to communicate initially with Craft, rather than beard the lion in person.

The old trouble with Souvtchinsky had never been resolved. Stravinsky still associated him with the group of young French composers whom Souvtchinsky himself had unguardedly described as "enemies of your music" who were "unfortunately cleverer and more 'up-to-date' " than some of its friends,[14] and he also had not forgiven his old colleague for—as he thought—siding with the Parisian faction that had ostracized Soulima after the liberation.[15] In Paris in May 1952 he had ignored Souvtchinsky's invitation to arrange a meeting,[16] and barely a year later Souvtchinsky had edited two volumes of essays under the umbrella title *Musique Russe* that seemed to confirm his worst fears. Among the essays was a hugely extended and detailed analysis of *The Rite of Spring* by none other than Pierre Boulez, sympathetic enough in its painstakingly arithmetical way, but ending with some general observations about Stravinsky's subsequent works that at once raised the specter of Souvtchinsky's musical Trotskyites and the disturbances at the Rosenthal concerts in 1945. "It is impossible," Boulez had written,

> not to reflect with a certain anguish on the Stravinsky "case." How to explain, after *Les Noces,* that rapid exhaustion which comes out in a sclerosis of every element: harmony and melody (ending in a kind of fake academicism), and even rhythm, where a painful atrophy is to be seen developing? . . . His technical defects have left their mark on his rhythmic discoveries, and prevented their realization: technical defects of

The Eternal Footman Holds His Coat

every type, in the domain as much of language as of [musical] development. Logically Stravinsky should not have been content with a system clogged up with composite and anarchizing formulae. . . . For the rest, we can ignore this swapping of conjuring roles—in which the object vanishes the magician—since there did once exist a true Stravinsky domain. . . .[17]

"There is no more risk of my being charmed by Boulez," Stravinsky had fulminated to Nadia Boulanger on reading this diatribe, "than he claims to be by me."[18] But that was not all. The volume also contained an introductory essay on Russian music by Souvtchinsky himself, between whose lines Stravinsky seemed to detect still more weasel words.

> Stravinsky requires of music that it be a living and active synthesis of the domains of the intelligence and the spirit, while assigning to sensibility and sensuality (lyricism) the role of a mere resultant. This conception has had and continues to have a more general import; it remains valid, in a sense, for the aspirations of the young music of our time that is no longer *with* Stravinsky; but while it could have been a particularly effective influence on Russian music, this tendency has been deliberately opposed. . . .

And so on, about Soviet music. But then, a few lines down, there was reference to "the effective presence of Stravinsky's work," together with a footnote indicating that "obviously this means, above all, Stravinsky's great works, such as *The Rite of Spring, Les Noces, The Nightingale* . . ."[19] So that was it! Souvtchinsky pretended to talk about Stravinsky's music as a whole, but was then careful not to admire anything that might put him at odds with his beloved young turks. Suddenly, no mention of *Oedipus Rex* or *Apollo,* or *Persephone,* music which the singer-philosopher had once professed to love. Stravinsky's pen tasted the poison and passed it on. "Salon careerism," he told Nadia, "is alive and well."[20]

Souvtchinsky and Boulez had by that time been intimate friends for five years or more, possibly even since 1946, when Boulez remembered Souvtchinsky coming up to him at a symposium at which he had spoken, and proposing that they meet again to discuss the issues raised.[21] Souvtchinsky was clearly on the lookout for a new intellectual cause. He would turn up at Leibowitz's in order to find out more about Schoenberg and serialism. In Boulez he sensed an exceptional mind, but one as yet unformed, undirected, an inchoate genius possessed of a fierce, intolerant energy that, with proper guidance, could change the world. Souvtchinsky in effect appointed himself Boulez's mentor. They would talk for hours on the telephone, and

Souvtchinsky would use all his formidable knowledge of the psychology of genius and the historical evolution of music to press on Boulez the role of the Chosen One, "the predestined musician," who would allow the new generation of composers "at last to achieve awareness of itself and of its historical worth; for it is always an event—a creator—who, by his arrival on the scene, his presence, the assertion of his gifts, his judgement, makes everything suddenly once again clear and visible, near and far."[22]

Above all, Souvtchinsky was a source of social, financial, and literary contacts for the young Frenchman. He introduced him to Cocteau's and Stravinsky's old friend Count Etienne de Beaumont (Radiguet's Comte d'Orgel) and to Suzanne Tézenas, an old-style *beau monde* patroness with a taste for the ultramodern, whose companion of many years, the fascist writer Pierre Drieu la Rochelle, had committed suicide at the end of the war rather than face trial as a collaborator. Then in 1953, the year of *Musique russe*, Souvtchinsky took Boulez to a performance of Berlioz's *Troyens* conducted by Hermann Scherchen, and introduced the two musicians. Scherchen agreed to lend his weight to the new avant-garde concert organization that Souvtchinsky and Boulez were putting together for the coming season; and it was Scherchen who duly conducted the inaugural concert of the Domaine Musical in the Théâtre du Petit Marigny in January 1954.[23]

At the nadir of his relations with Stravinsky, Souvtchinsky was thus inextricably entangled with Boulez and the whole post-Webern, post-Messiaen axis of young radical composers whose music would be the heart and soul of the early Domaine Musical concerts and was beginning to set up spheres of influence through institutions like the Darmstadt Summer School and the annual festival at Donaueschingen, in the Black Forest. From time to time Stravinsky's Paris spies sent him morose reports of the goings-on in this circle. "I assure you," Nabokov wrote after attending a Domaine concert in March 1956, "all this is quite bad and depressing. It's so many gnawed bones instead of music. Boulez's *Marteau sans maître* sounds at best like Burmese or Siamese music, except that there it's natural, while here it's artificial (if skilful). As for Stockhausen and Nono, it's a lot of tedium in a small space."[24] But Nika was for once behind the times. He seems only just to have caught up with the fact that Stravinsky was himself now writing serial music,[25] while Boulez's approach to Craft that summer was certainly prompted by the knowledge that the Master's latest progeny was likely to be such as might safely grace Domaine programs that were forever closed to anything with the taint of neoclassicism.

CRAFT WAS in Paris by the 3rd of November, and he lunched with Boulez the next day, a Sunday. They got on well, having much in common musically if not temperamentally. Boulez, so earnestly modernist in public, had a fun-loving, undergraduate side in private. He played the Andante theme of Schoenberg's Violin Concerto on the upright piano in his mansard flat near the Bastille with a spoof Brahms accompaniment, and he talked about the George Washington music at the end of the *Ode to Napoleon* as "pure César Franck."[26] Presumably there were no such jests at the expense of the serial Stravinsky, though Craft must have suspected that they, too, were part of the young Frenchman's social repertoire in other company. But Boulez had a charming, agreeable way with him that dissolved mistrust, so that Craft could be struck by his observation that "writers are in a worse way than composers, Mallarmé and Joyce having done it all," without seeing the implied barb against Stravinsky and Schoenberg, whom Boulez had long since attacked in print for, precisely, failing to do it all—failing, that is, to realize the full consequences of the revolution they had initiated.[27]

On the Wednesday, Boulez haled Craft off to lunch with Souvtchinsky, obviously in the conscious hope of rebuilding bridges. Craft's account of the meeting is one of the best half-dozen pages in his published diary.[28] Souvtchinsky expatiated, in his voluble, authoritative White Russian way, about Stravinsky's character, his obsession with money, his weakness for Fascism and fear of Communism, his failure to grasp the central musical issue of his time—the overriding importance of Schoenberg. From Souvtchinsky's lips, Craft heard for the first time in detail about Arthur Lourié's role in Stravinsky's life in the twenties and thirties, and learnt the full horror of Soulima's wartime activities, in particular how he had written to Strecker in 1941 to try to secure German concert bookings. The nervy young American had the courage to take issue with the elderly Russian over some of these matters, sensing both a taste for hyperbole and a certain bitterness mixed in with the avant-garde Parisian attitudinizing. But he did not leap to Soulima's defense, or contradict Souvtchinsky's description of Theodore as a boor, merely reporting his remark—delivered apparently without irony—that "in all fairness, to know that one has *those* genes is a burden."[29]

Did this fascinating conversation ever in fact take place? One supposes that at least some of it did. Souvtchinsky loved psychologizing and enjoyed the role of "pilot fish," as Boulez put it, to young voyagers.[30] But he cannot have mentioned Soulima's wartime letter to Strecker, for the simple reason that he cannot have known it existed, unless he had had illicit Nazi contacts of his own during the war.[31] In the same way Poulenc's remark, supposedly brought up at the lunch by Craft, that Stravinsky was "too old for the new hats he tries on in the *Canticum sacrum*"[32] is surely in fact an embroidered quotation from a letter Poulenc had written to his niece in March 1956 but which was not published until many years later.[33] In other words, the conversation looks like a reconstruction, for whatever reason, in the light of subsequent information. In no sense is it a reliable account of an actual meeting.

A day or two after the Souvtchinsky lunch, Boulez flew to Munich and visited Stravinsky in the hospital, but the next day he missed his flight back to Paris and he was not at the Salle Gaveau to stage-manage Craft's Domaine concert on the 10th. The Gaveau was packed and the audience, Craft reported, enthusiastic.[34] But he had had low expectations of the actual performances ever since his first rehearsal with the choir, and it may even have crossed his mind that Boulez's absence had about it some element of self-preservation. French choirs were notoriously weak and often uncooperative into the bargain, and to confront one, on inadequate rehearsal, with a program that included the *Canticum sacrum,* the "Vom Himmel hoch" transcription, and both Webern cantatas, verged on the suicidal. Craft was fortunate, in all probability, to get through without major embarrassments. It was an early-evening concert, and when it was over he lingered for only a few minutes before hurrying off to the Gare de l'Est for the Munich sleeper. Boulez, arriving by the next flight, got to the Salle Gaveau soon after eight, just in time to help clear away the music stands.[35]

ALTHOUGH out of bed for a short time each day, Stravinsky was not well enough to leave the hospital for another four weeks. He would shuffle round the hospital garden on the arm of one of the sisters, or occasionally take a turn round the block.[36] He was still smoking, but much less than before. The idea that he might soon once again conduct would have struck any casual acquaintance as absurd. Berman had written to Craft imploring him to prevent the composer from fulfilling his engagement in Rome at the end of November, but the concert had not been cancelled by the time Stravinsky was discharged from hospital on the 17th of November, and a few days later he and Vera duly boarded the express for the Italian capital, where Craft would meet them from another engagement of his own in Vienna.[37]

When friends had told Stravinsky to his face that he should conduct less, he had been in the habit of replying that he could not afford to,[38] and it was a wretched irony of this latest illness that, just when the arguments for cutting back started to look irresistible, the reasons for not doing so became unanswerable. All his life, medical charges had been a substantial item of expenditure, but now they would soar into the stratosphere; and it would no longer be a case of settling the bill with the prestige of his friendship. In every city there would be specialists, "crouched like gardeners to pay," as Nick Shadow put it agreeably in *The Rake's Progress.* As soon as he got to Rome, he was examined by a neurologist and a hematologist, who pronounced his blood pressure too high and ordered him to cancel his New York engagements in January. Then in London a week or two later there was more phlebotomy, and a consultation with the great clinical neurologist, Sir Charles Symonds, who made the gloomiest prediction thus far. It so happened that Stravinsky had woken up in his hotel that morning (7 December) feeling numb in his right side. Symonds diagnosed a basilar stenosis (a narrowing of the arteries at the base of the skull) and warned that a second stroke could well be imminent and would, in his opinion, be fatal. Polycythemia (a superfluity of red corpuscles over white) he considered a likely but not certain contributory cause. He actually informed Vera that her husband had only "a fair chance" of surviving more than six months, and he told the husband himself that smoking had probably brought on the thrombosis, whereupon Stravinsky at last reluctantly but definitively gave up the habit.[39]

Yet notwithstanding all this medical head-shaking and finger-wagging, he had managed to conduct the *Canticum sacrum* at the Teatro Eliseo in Rome a week before without significant mishap. He had initially been very nervous and had ducked out of his first rehearsal with the orchestra, then, on the evening of the concert, lost his nerve over the "Vom Himmel hoch" variations and asked Craft to take over in that work. The latter noted that the composer's beat in the *Canticum* was erratic, but that he—Craft—somehow managed to coordinate the performance from the wings, presumably without Stravinsky noticing. In fact, Stravinsky was so euphoric at this triumph over bodily frailty that he stayed up half the night at the post-concert reception, kept going dangerously by his own adrenaline, by plentiful doses of alcohol, and presumably, for nearly the last time, by nicotine.[40]

In London, nevertheless, he did not conduct, having withdrawn from a BBC concert in the Festival Hall and the London premiere of the *Canticum sacrum* at an ICA concert in St. Martin-in-the-Fields. Craft both rehearsed and directed the St. Martin's concert on the 11th, while Stravinsky consulted his doctors and endured the December fog. Nobody, though, seems to have said anything about peace and quiet. On his Paris visit, Craft had set up for the journey from Rome to London one of those between-train days that crowd a week's worth of work and socializing into twelve anxious hours. He himself was recording the *Canticum* and the Bach variations with his Domaine Musical performers. They were met at the station by Boulez and Souvtchinsky, and for the first time for more than seventeen years Stravinsky talked face-to-face with the friend who had stood by him so loyally just before the war, then—as he had obviously felt—so lightly betrayed him just after it. We do not know what was said or if the encounter was in any way troubled.[41] But the composer's mood was by no means unreservedly conciliatory. At the recording session, he ran into another old friend, Alexander

Tansman, who was likewise in his bad books for having written to him at the time of the Cantata protesting at the anti-Semitism of its "Sacred History." Tansman remained unforgiven, and Stravinsky cut him dead.[42]

Somehow London was socially more comfortable, less fraught with old antagonisms, yet no less stimulating in its own way. Stravinsky had scarcely been in England since the thirties, and he was still partly under the influence of Kirstein's diatribes against the British arts establishment at the time of the New York City Ballet's Covent Garden season in 1950.[43] The reality in 1956 was altogether different. For one thing, the musical standards in London turned out, unexpectedly, to be superior to those in Italy or—to judge by Craft's reports—Paris. The Elizabethan Singers, one of those well-trained, quick-learning small professional choirs in which London was beginning to specialize, sang the Mass stylishly and without fuss, while the amateur London Bach Society choir coped more than adequately with the *Canticum sacrum*. No less important, Stravinsky found himself among kindred spirits. William Glock, who had organized the ICA concert, was an attentive host and a knowledgeable one, with a genuine—not merely polite—enthusiasm for new music. Glock drove them to Hampton Court, and he threw a reception attended by old friends like Edward Clark and his wife, the composer Elisabeth Lutyens, and sympathetic new people like Michael Tippett, a composer whose own work was at that precise moment entering a Stravinskian phase. Nicolas Nabokov appeared at the Savoy with Isaiah Berlin, and Stephen Spender brought T. S. Eliot for tea. These were perhaps not in themselves momentous encounters; in fact the Eliot tea party, as separately reported by Craft and Spender, seems to have been as slow and viscous as the motion of Stravinsky's blood, which he described to the two poets while "moving his hands as though moulding an extremely rich substance."[44] But all these meetings were in some sense indicative of a certain acknowledged status in the Anglo-Saxon world. There were, it appeared, advantages to being a Grand Old Man widely thought to be on his last legs. It was a situation well worth preserving.

New York was no less foggy than London when they sailed in, several days late, on the 21st of December. Stravinsky was desperate to get home and resume work on *Agon*, which Kirstein was now intending to stage in the City Ballet's autumn season but which was already half-committed for a concert premiere in Los Angeles at the time of the composer's seventy-fifth birthday in June.[45] But having ignored his Italian doctor's advice to cancel his New York concerts, he was effectively trapped on the East Coast for a whole month. Admittedly the concerts themselves were good for morale at this particular juncture. Stravinsky once again left most of the rehearsing to Craft, but he conducted the concerts with growing confidence and vitality, and was rewarded afterwards—if that is the right expression—by a huge throng of admirers in the Carnegie Hall green room and a milling crowd of fans at the stage door.

New York had not seen him on the podium for four years (since, that is, before his prostatectomy), and no doubt the "warmth and affection" that, according to the *Times* headline, greeted his reappearance, came as much from the fact that he was known to have been ill and was visibly aged as from any newfound affection for his music. "Igor Stravinsky was in Carnegie Hall last night conducting a concert of his own music," one critic declared, adding sententiously: "The person for whom that is not enough is an enemy of art."[46] Yet nobody seemed to feel any need to condescend or make allowances about the performances. Craft observed that at the opening concert on 10 January *Persephone* went exceptionally slowly and took almost an hour (whereas the composer's studio recording a few days later is if anything on the quick side and lasts barely fifty-three minutes).[47] But such details generally went unnoticed in a work that, as the reviews demonstrated, was little known in Manhattan. From a musical point of view, it seemed, the master was still in good shape and mentally alert, less balletic on the rostrum than in the past, maybe, but as ever "meticulous, precise, beating time and signaling cues without mannerisms. . . . All he was after was to let his music speak for him."[48] Perhaps the Bach variations, which New York was hearing for the first time, were slightly overrated as original work ("far more Stravinsky than it is Bach"), as if to dignify the occasion beyond its real deserts. And if, as the same critic insisted, the NYPO's playing and the Westminster Choir's singing were no better than routine, he seemed not remotely to be suggesting that that might have been Stravinsky's fault.

The goodwill was positively cloying. Whether it would survive the realization that the master was not only far from dead but was actually embarking on a new and distinctly awkward creative phase: that was another matter.

RETURNING TO LOS ANGELES on 26 January 1957, Stravinsky at once resumed work on *Agon*. According to his own timings, painstakingly worked out for Balanchine's benefit and studiously recorded on a separate sheet of paper, the music so far written lasted twelve and a quarter minutes; but that was for three-quarters of the entire three-part scheme, which had originally been supposed to last twenty-six. As with the *Canticum sacrum,* the septuagenarian composer was embarrassing himself by the growing concentration of his musical thought, and it scarcely helped that, now that the moment had arrived to "explode"—as Kirstein had put it—into the twentieth century, his preferred model was that arch-compressor, Anton Webern. The "Pas de deux" he now began to write would be as far as possible from the lyrical periods of his last two essays in the genre—in *Scènes de ballet* and *Orpheus*. Instead it would mysteriously translate the rarefied musical hieroglyphics of late Webern into a dance idiom—hesitant at first, then increasingly bold and impulsive, a vivid image of the mental transformed into the physical.

By nevertheless carefully respecting the conventional sequence, with solos for each dancer framed by their duos, Stravinsky was able to preserve the traditional function of the "Pas de deux" as a moment of intensification and repose. The music is intricate but reflective, and it is by far the longest dance in the whole work, playing for the best part of six minutes (including the short Interlude that precedes it). The orchestration, though, is light and airy. "My score," he later told his Boosey and Hawkes editor, "is not an orchestra score but an instrumental score,"[1] and he composed the piece in three weeks and dispatched it to Boosey's New York office on 15 February. At this point there came yet another, and in its way remarkably suggestive, interruption.

On the day the Stravinskys had spent in Paris on their way to London early in December, Souvtchinsky had set up a meeting at the Ritz between Craft, Boulez, and Gérard Worms, the proprietor of a Monaco publishing house called Éditions du Rocher. Worms wanted Craft to write a book about

Stravinsky, and he wanted Stravinsky himself to write an introduction; but when Craft put this idea to him later that same day, the composer typically declined to write anything of his own, and instead proposed a dialogue in the form of a series of questions and answers. In the back of his mind, no doubt, was Deborah Ishlon's recent suggestion that he "should write— or talk—a book,"[2] and he may also have reflected, or been reminded by Craft, that his seventy-fifth birthday was looming, a time when interviews would be requested, reminiscences sought, statements demanded. The world would want to be told once more about the premiere of *The Rite of Spring*, about Rimsky-Korsakov, Diaghilev, and Debussy, about how Stravinsky composed his own music and what he thought of other people's. Why not take the opportunity to put together a text of this kind under Craft's informed and sympathetic prompting? The whole thing could be handled conversationally, without the stupid and unhelpful questions so often put by journalists, and above all without significant loss of time from his own increasingly crowded schedule, and it could be published widely in many languages and publications as well as in the commissioned French volume.

Exactly when and under what circumstances Craft began to assemble these dialogues is hard now to establish, since hardly any draft material survives from the initial stages. By early March 1957, however, a series of "Answers to Thirty-Six Questions" had been compiled and dispatched to Deborah Ishlon, who was acting as agent for the dialogues and who acknowledged their receipt by telegram on the 11th.[3] Boulez had just arrived in Los Angeles for the performance of his *Marteau sans maître* planned for a Monday Evening concert on 18 March, and he read the dialogue over and offered to translate it into French. But it can hardly be true that, as Craft claims, much of it was written during Boulez's visit "and under his influence."[4] The only unmistakable sign of Boulez's influence on Stravinsky's remarks is in his answer to the question, "What piece of music has most attracted you from a composer of the younger generation?" to which he replies, "*Le Marteau sans maître* by Pierre Boulez," a choice which may or may not have reflected the young Frenchman's West Coast visit, since Stravinsky certainly already knew the work from the recording that Boulez had given Craft when they first met in Paris in November.[5] The obsession with Webern that comes out in several answers—for instance, the claim that "an entirely new principle of order is found in the Webern songs which in time will be recognised and conventionalised," or the seemingly arbitrary comparison of his own habit of composing at the piano with that of the Viennese composer[6]—has less to do with Boulez directly than with the whole musical environment at Wetherly Drive since Craft had started recording the entire oeuvre two or three years before and Stravinsky had modelled his own serial manner (in the "Surge aquilo" of the *Canticum sacrum*) on Webern's. Even the final dithyramb to Webern as a divine essence of music ("the *juste de la musique*"), though it was sent to Ishlon a few days later and may therefore seem to reflect conversation with Boulez, is no different in tone from the panegyric Stravinsky had penned for *Die Reihe* in 1955.[7] In any case, of all the first series of "Answers," this is the only one that, for some obscure reason, was omitted from the Rocher volume when it came out the following year.[8]

Boulez, who was in America with the Barrault company, had arrived in Hollywood at the beginning of March from a visit to a friend in San Francisco. He told his biographer Joan Peyser (as he later told the present author) that he passed through Los Angeles in order to assist in preparing the *Marteau* performance, which as a matter of fact Craft was slated to conduct, but that the rehearsals were so chaotic, and in particular Craft was having such difficulty with the constant pauses and tempo changes in the long fourth movement, that the musicians implored Boulez to take over and direct the performance himself.[9] Craft has maintained, on the other hand, that it was always the intention for Boulez to conduct, and he even refers specifically to a letter of January 1957 in which Boulez announces that Lawrence Morton has invited him to do so.[10] This letter, if it ever existed, is mysteriously absent from both Stravinsky's and Craft's consultable archives. Boulez's surviving letters to Craft discuss his series of UCLA lectures in early March, and the possibility of his attending the *Marteau* concert, but they say nothing about his conducting or rehearsing it.[11] The date was admittedly brought forward for his convenience. In one letter, Craft offered him the baton—whether out of courtesy or nervousness—but he declined.[12] The plain fact seems to be that Craft was down to conduct but withdrew because of the work's extreme difficulty, and that Boulez not only took over but managed to prepare the performance a week earlier than scheduled to fit his own Barrault commitments. Craft conducted Tallis's *Lamentations*, and the program also included Stockhausen's tape work, *Gesang der Jünglinge*.[13]

Whatever the circumstances of his arrival, and whatever was talked about during his stay, Boulez's visit was a huge success so far as Wetherly Drive was concerned. Stravinsky was bewitched almost equally by his musicality, his professionalism, his quickness of mind, and his subtle Gallic charm. At the concert, just as the *Marteau* was about to begin, Stravinsky lost his score, and Boulez held up the performance until it was found.[14] They dined together several times (including once—an irresistible picture—with Marlene Dietrich), and they all went to a "marvellously interesting" lecture Boulez gave at UCLA in connection with a symposium on modern music in which both he and Craft took part. The whole experience was a shot in the arm for the provincial West Coast. Stravinsky told Nika

Nabokov that "both as man and musician, [Boulez] made a splendid impression on us all and on the musicians he conducted,"[15] and to Nadia Boulanger he was still more effusive.

> Boulez made an excellent impression on us all: an absolutely top-class musician, highly intelligent, he has fine manners and is probably a generous man. His *Marteau,* which he conducted so well here, is an admirably well-organized score, comprehensible to both ear and eye, for all its complications (counterpoint, rhythm, meter). Without feeling at home with this music of Boulez, I find it frankly preferable to a lot of things by his generation.[16]

Admittedly, both Nika and Nadia were inclined to be skeptical about Boulez, who—whatever his obvious talent—stood out against everything that gave substance to their musical instincts. Scarcely a year had passed since Nabokov had described *Marteau* to Stravinsky as "so many gnawed bones,"[17] and though Nadia was more indulgent, being well aware of Boulez's musical brilliance, she could not bring herself to say anything better of his work than that it contained "no trickery or bluff."[18] She may have hoped that contact with Stravinsky would mellow the young turk, perhaps even convert him to more civilized ways. She had talked to him about his Hollywood trip, which, she optimistically suggested to Stravinsky, would "have a big influence on him."[19]

No sooner had Boulez left than Stravinsky started coming under pressure to provide more questions and answers for hungry publishers. Herbert Weinstock, of the New York house Knopf, wanted to bring out a new edition of the old *Chronicle of My Life* with updated autobiographical material and a section of dialogue, but Stravinsky was adamant that he would not answer any more questions until he had finished *Agon.*[20] He now had only a few weeks in which to complete the score in time for the concert premiere in June, and, as he assured Nabokov, "this music doesn't at all lend itself to haste."[21] Nevertheless on the 26th of April 1957 he at last completed the draft score of this much-interrupted masterpiece of stylistic time-travelling, and a week later he posted to David Adams the final section of the full score.[22] At about the same time, he sent Balanchine a copy of the piano reduction, with the serial workings helpfully indicated, not, of course—as he had claimed with the bracketings in his earlier serial scores—because he had forgotten to rub them out, but because the technical intricacies of the music would be an important aspect of the ballet's dramaturgy for this choreographer who, on the whole, rejected storytelling and conventional figurative imagery.[23]

With *Agon* finished, Stravinsky found himself staring, for the first time since the Septet, at an empty commissions diary. At any rate it was almost empty. There was, as we shall shortly see, a whisper of a new Venice project. Moreover for the past three years Paul Sacher had been pursuing him for a new work for his Basle Chamber Orchestra, and it was true that at the third time of asking, in May 1956, Stravinsky had more or less promised but without agreeing any details.[24] Now, as he worked on the final pages of his ballet, he replied almost casually to Sacher's fourth annual enquiry, to the effect that another string piece like the Concerto in D would cost at least five thousand dollars.[25] He certainly cannot have expected Sacher to balk at such a fee. Yet there is something curiously unenthusiastic—something bland and unpromising—about the suggestion, so un-Stravinskian in its implication that he might have the remotest interest in a formulaic proposal of this kind. Sacher must have sensed it, too, and hastened to reply that the work need not limit itself to string orchestra. "What about choir and soloists?" the composer suggested. Why not? Sacher had actually programmed the *Canticum sacrum* for Basle the following month.[26] Vocal music was in the air.

There were various reasons why vocal commissions had suddenly become attractive to Stravinsky. Although *Agon* had provided him with a canvas on which to work out some of the consequences of serialism for his own way of writing, it was the *Canticum sacrum* that had satisfied a certain feeling that all these canons and inversions and number manipulations led inexorably toward the setting of sacred texts, just as the medieval and Renaissance composers who had brought these techniques to a pitch of complexity had used them exclusively in the service of church music and the liturgy. He had been playing and studying their work for well over a decade, but it was only now, with a genuinely modern equivalent of their methodology under his hands, that he felt drawn to emulating them fully on his own terms. As we saw earlier, the key to this linkage was Webern. He was now trying to get hold of Webern's 1909 edition of Isaac's *Choralis Constantinus* (part 2), in order to study its elaborate canonic settings of the Mass liturgy, but also presumably to find out how Webern had explained his own enthusiasm for this esoteric music, so seemingly distant from the preoccupations of late Romanticism and the Sezession.[27] Webern, after all, had never remotely aped the Renaissance style of polyphony, and when he eventually started writing canons of his own, toward the end of the First World War, their style was uncompromisingly modern and dissonant, in a way that suggested that the strict imitation was what counted with him, and that any chords that resulted were a mere fortunate or unfortunate accident.

Stravinsky, on the other hand, minded desperately about the chords and harmonies his music contained. When he composed at the piano, such muffled sounds as could be faintly heard in adjacent rooms were more often than not isolated chords—chords repeated over and over again, with minute adjustments, until both the sound and the harmony were, to his ear, perfectly tuned. No wonder his interest in polyphonic music was matched by an enthusiasm for the rich harmonies of the early Baroque—composers like Schütz, Gabrieli, and Monteverdi, whose music generally avoided the intricacies of the old polyphony but relished the sheer dramatic thrill of a sonorous chord or, occasionally, an excruciating discord. In the past two or three seasons, Craft had conducted a good deal of this music at the Monday Evenings, culminating, just recently, in two almost absurdly contrasted settings of *Lamentations* texts: Couperin's ornate third *Leçon de Ténèbres*, and the solemnly expressive consort setting by Tallis.[28] Now Craft had a new project. He was preparing to record an album of motets and madrigals by Carlo Gesualdo, the Neapolitan prince who in 1590 famously murdered his wife and her lover, and whose music became not much less notorious for its extravagant dissonances and bold vocal polyphony. Craft had got hold of a microfilm of the second part of Gesualdo's *Sacrae cantiones* (1603), a collection of six- and seven-part motets of which, however, the bass parts and the so-called sextus, or sixth, parts were lost. Starting with the single seven-part motet, "Illumina nos misericordiarum," he had made up a score out of the five surviving part-books, and he now persuaded Stravinsky—fresh from posting off the last batch of material for *Agon*—to complete the score by adding the two missing parts.[29]

For a musicologist, whose aim would presumably be to come as close as possible to the composer's likely intentions, this would be a tall order, especially with a style as deviant and unpredictable as Gesualdo's. For Stravinsky, in a certain sense, it was easier, since he could always invoke artistic license for any tasteful digressions of his own, and he could cite the waywardness of the original style in support of all but the most improbable vagaries. Craft in fact claims that none of Stravinsky's harmonies would have been impossible for Gesualdo;[30] but this is misleading (the clashing Sextus line in the opening bars already behaves in a way that Gesualdo would not have thought of), and in any case it misses Stravinsky's point, which was surely to put himself into Gesualdo's musical shoes without abandoning some favorite sounds of his own—or perhaps to put Gesualdo into *his* musical shoes, while accepting the constraints of the five authentic parts that could not be altered. The result was a strange but eminently comprehensible and very beautiful piece of space-age polyphony, which somehow managed to look sufficiently like a serious realization to merit an eventual place in the collected Gesualdo edition, and which continues to be cited in the scholarly literature as if Stravinsky had miraculously transformed himself into a scholar while remaining at the same time a creative genius.[31]

It was one thing, of course, to spend a day or two adding a pair of lines to a five-minute piece by somebody else, quite another to embark on a full-scale choral work of his own with, presumably, a tight deadline. As in 1956, the second half of the year was badly blocked by a planned European tour. And before that he was committed to something that, as the time approached, he began increasingly to dread. The first performance of *Agon* was scheduled for a joint Monday Evenings and Los Angeles Festival concert on the 17th of June; the 18th was his seventy-fifth birthday, which would in fact be spent (along with the 19th) recording *Agon* and the *Canticum sacrum;* and for several days before that he had agreed to subject himself to the ordeal of being filmed and interviewed in his own home by an NBC television crew, for a program to be called "A Conversation with Igor Stravinsky." He grumbled to Roth about this "terrible loss of time in my birthday period."[32] So, having practically come to an agreement with Sacher, he again postponed a final decision on the new piece, and steeled himself for the celebrations.

He had done his best to avoid the NBC visitation, first by his usual method of demanding an outrageous fee ($7,500 for two or three days' filming), then by claiming that his doctors had ordered him to rest.[33] Somehow these little difficulties were overcome, and at the end of May the NBC producer, Robert Graff, turned up at North Wetherly Drive and spent the day there, discussing the contents of the program and the mechanics of the actual filming. A fortnight later, the crew arrived—no fewer than twenty-seven of them, Stravinsky told Roth.[34] They installed their own generator, wrapped the house in canvas, and closed Wetherly Drive to traffic. They then moved all the living-room furniture around in order to provide alternative views of Stravinsky's "studio," since they did not have mobile equipment and in any case Stravinsky would not let them film in his real studio. For three whole days, life moved on a different planet. Graff had produced a scenario for the program, complete with questions that Craft was supposed to ask Stravinsky on camera and to which Stravinsky had composed short scripted replies. "How do musical ideas occur to you?—Well, sometimes in the bathroom." "Do you write them down?—Sometimes." "Which of the older composers do you like best? "The older the better." And so on. Although, as one specialist has observed, these answers "were right on the mark in capturing the composer's dry wit," they were not used in the program, which cleaved to "family values" and had no room for shades of irony.[35] Instead a more serious, if conventional, view of creativity was promulgated. Craft asked Stravinsky scripted questions about craftsmanship, about conducting, about music itself. Stravinsky sat at the piano "composing," and the two of them leafed through manuscripts together. Craft, on his own admission, was terrified and tongue-tied by the whole process, and at one point Stravinsky, apparently sensing this, reached across and patted him reassuringly on the hand.[36] But Stravinsky, despite his apprehensions, was in his element, acting up to the cameras, happily abetting a theatricalized image of the great composer. After all, as he reminds his viewers, "I am the son of an actor, and the theatre is in my blood."[37]

On the very day that filming ended, they rehearsed *Agon,* and three days later Craft directed its first performance in the UCLA Royce Hall, along with the *Canticum sacrum* (its U.S. premiere) and the *Symphonies of Wind Instruments,* while Stravinsky himself conducted the Bach variations and the *Symphony of Psalms.* It was altogether a gala occasion. President Eisenhower sent a message, which was read out; scrolls were presented from various august bodies; Franz Waxman, the L.A. Festival director, opened the concert with Stravinsky's *Greeting Prelude;* and Aldous Huxley made a speech. Isherwood, who was in the audience, had his creative camera fully trained: Craft, "pale as a lily and quite beautiful in his exhaustion" as if "purged through hard work and so curiously innocent and good"; Igor, "limp with sweat but wonderfully svelte," conducting "with the most graceful, campy gestures, like a ballerina"; Vera and her "sweetly lovable dazed innocent fatness."[38]

"Of course," the novelist, who loathed concerts, added, "I didn't enjoy the music. It seems chiefly to consist of nervous stabbing sounds, the creakings and squeaks of a door swinging in the wind . . ." Igor himself, had he read his friend's diary, might well have felt that such insights qualified him to be a music critic ("Do music critics perform a useful function?" Graff had asked. Stravinsky: "They think so."[39]) But in general, as a matter of fact, the local reviews were neither unfavorable nor obtuse. Admittedly the *Los Angeles Times* critic, Albert Goldberg, thought the *Canticum sacrum* "recondite and uncompromising," but he was engrossed by *Agon,* with its "characteristic rhythmic vitality [and] endless imagination for musical surprise."[40] Alfred Frankenstein, of the *San Francisco Chronicle,* found both works "completely and instantly enchanting." *Agon* he thought "one of Stravinsky's wittiest, most effervescent compositions . . . a ballet score that clicks its heels, bows formally, and proceeds to enact a ritual in highly complex rhythms and with an utterly bewildering array of coloristic inventions. . . ." "You might think," he went on, "that after fifty years of research and discovery in the blending and contrasting of instrumental sounds, Stravinsky would run out of new orchestral piquancies, but 'Agon' suggests that he has only just begun." And Frankenstein drew attention to the astonishing use of the mandolin, as an example of Stravinsky's ability to "imagine every component of the orchestra in a new way every time he sets to work."[41] This was exactly right. Purely as sonority, and quite apart from its pulsating energy and dazzling control of form, the music proclaimed in every bar the

activity of a sound-inventor without rival even among the younger generation of avant-garde composers for whom instrumental color, texture, and
the invention of new sounds were a vital expression of their rejection of the
past.

The next day—his actual birthday, as he nowadays chose to convert the
Old Style date—he recorded *Agon* for Columbia, this time conducting it
himself apparently without ill effects or undue difficulty; and the day after
that he similarly recorded the *Canticum sacrum*. The performances are, for
the most part, crisp and assured, though no doubt much edited and, as
always from now on, likely to include takes from rehearsals conducted by
Craft.[42] The next day Craft left for Boston, where he was conducting a pair of
Stravinsky concerts (including the Capriccio with Soulima); and a fortnight
or so later Igor and Vera went by train to Santa Fe, where *The Rake's Progress*
was being staged to inaugurate a new open-air theatre and a new summer
opera festival. No wonder Stravinsky had been hesitant about Basle; and no
wonder Nika Nabokov wrote to him at the end of June, not for the first time,
in alarm at his schedule of work and travel and its likely effect on his
health.[43] Yet Nabokov was hardly in a position to offer counsel in such matters. He had already written on the day of the *Agon* premiere, referring to a
scheme he had in mind for the composer to conduct in Japan, and conveying to him a commission from Rolf Liebermann, the newly appointed
musical director of Hamburg Radio, to write and conduct a twenty-minute
work for a European Cultural Conference in that city in September 1958.
Everything, he assured Stravinsky, would be done properly, and "not in the
sort of *zuppa inglese* atmosphere of Venice."[44] The fee would be five thousand dollars, plus half that figure for conducting. Once again Stravinsky
hesitated. Would he have the time? He had already started on another commission, long promised, and now necessarily shelved for six months. "Too
bad," he lamented modestly, "I do not feel able to compose interesting
music in Mozart's speed."[45]

What, though, was this long-promised commission? One's first thought
is that Stravinsky was using the half-agreed Sacher project as a lever to
ensure the most favorable terms from Hamburg. After all, he had made no
similar excuse to Sacher, and he had told Roth (without mentioning any
other project) that he was postponing Sacher because of Europe. Yet there is
good reason to believe that he had indeed started another work, and that his
hesitation sprang from the fact that it had not yet been formally contracted
and the money for it was still uncertain. Nabokov's joke about *zuppa inglese*
was much too near the bone for comfort. Stravinsky actually was writing another work for Venice, and he already knew its subject and general
character.

Six months before, in Rome, Stravinsky had received a visit from the

Biennale director, Piovesan, who had come, Craft notes in his diary, "to discuss the commission for the Scuola di San Rocco."[46] What happened after that is to some extent a matter for speculation. Stravinsky heard nothing further from Piovesan except New Year's greetings, and we may assume that, as with the *Canticum sacrum*, the director was engaged in a protracted struggle with his bureaucratic superiors and had meanwhile simply gone to ground. Despite this silence, after finishing *Agon* early in May, Stravinsky certainly started thinking about the Venice commission, and by the end of that month at the latest he had decided on a text. We know this because the subject is mentioned in the first British publication of the "Answers to Thirty-six Questions" (reduced mysteriously to thirty-four), which came out in the July 1957 issue of *Encounter*, and must therefore have been in press early in June. Asking Stravinsky about the harmonic implications of his serial method, Craft refers to "your new *Tenebrae* service," in terms suggesting that some of its music already existed.[47] The point about harmony in the new work may admittedly have been a guess on Craft's part, but in any case the reference proves the existence of the idea. Moreover the intention to write a choral setting of the *Lamentations* texts, which Stravinsky had heard sung in recent months to music by Couperin and Tallis, and which he had discussed before that with Krenek in connection with his own setting, explains his anxiety to establish that Sacher would, if need be, accept a choral work for Basle, and it also explains Stravinsky's stalling tactics. He was still hoping for a Venice commission, but was preparing an escape route for the new work in case, as seemed increasingly probable, Piovesan let him down.

Not much if anything had been written, all the same, by the time they went to Santa Fe, a two-week visit that Stravinsky may well by now have been beginning to regret. The whole idea had come from their friend Mirandi Masocco, whom they had known since their first trip to New Mexico in 1950, and who had been responsible for introducing them to Frieda Lawrence and taking them to the corn dance at San Domingo. Mirandi, a tough, warmhearted, dry-humored Venice-born jewelry designer, had offered to persuade Stravinsky to come to Santa Fe, and had succeeded, characteristically, by the direct approach. She had described the conductor John Crosby's plans for the new opera house and for inaugurating it with the *Rake*, and when Stravinsky had expressed interest, she had simply got on a plane and flown to Hollywood to show him the designs. Mirandi knew how to combine boldness with a certain relaxed formality. Soon after the Stravinskys arrived at Santa Fe, she invited them to dinner at the house of Brink Jackson and entertained them in style but without imposing official guests on them. They met the novelist Paul Horgan, a couple of retired headmistresses from Pennsylvania, and Jackson's bouncy pair of labrador retrievers.[48]

Craft was conducting the opera, but Stravinsky involved himself as usual in rehearsals and took an interest in every aspect of the production. As at the Venetian premiere, there was a piano in place of the harpsichord, but this time the composer rewrote certain passages to suit the modern instrument.[49] It was typical of him that, where a youthful venture was in question and there was enthusiasm for his work but no apparent intention to overexploit his name and presence, he gave himself unstintingly to the common effort. He took a liking to Santa Fe. It was true that it had its off-duty-Hollywood aspect. The adobe houses and yucca-clad mountainsides concealed a chic diaspora of retired film stars and fashionable artists, who exhibited in a string of smart local galleries (where Mirandi had even organized a show of Vera's paintings); and the social atmosphere was only incidentally related to the Pueblo culture that had made the region famous. On the other hand, the air—like Mirandi—was dry, warm, and invigorating, and the climate was on the whole settled, though by a curious twist of fate it rained hard on the first night of the *Rake* and the opening had to be postponed. The one thing that did not suit Stravinsky was the altitude—seven thousand feet—which dangerously boosted his red corpuscle count.[50] But above all, Santa Fe was interested in his music and wanted to commission him to write a new opera.

From the semi-desert of New Mexico, they travelled to the verdant landscape that enfolded the medieval hall and model cottages of Dartington, in South Devon, arriving there by way of New York and Plymouth on 7 August. As in Santa Fe, it was Craft who was doing the work, conducting several concerts (including *The Soldier's Tale* narrated by Christopher Hassall), while Stravinsky was present, on the invitation of the summer school's director, William Glock, as an icon, a walking legend, a slice of history. Perhaps not surprisingly, he was growing a little bored with this role. He loved the Devonshire countryside, got on well with his English hosts, and was amused by the things one did in rural England, like drinking in pubs and looking at old churches. But when all was said and done, the countryside was not for him a place of prolonged entertainment. In this respect he and Vera (not to mention Craft) were strictly urban animals, drawn to art galleries and restaurants, theatres and a certain variety of social intercourse. It was a relief to get back to London and to be setting off from there for Paris and Venice, even though none of these cities was offering him any performances of his music—not, at any rate, until he returned to Paris to conduct the European premiere of *Agon* in mid-October.[51]

In London that August they put up at the Dorchester, and it was there that the first documented sessions of "conversations" took place whose results would eventually emerge in printed form. Already the so-called 36 Answers (in fact either thirty-four or thirty-five) had appeared in journals in America, England, and West Germany, but we have no record of the way they were put together.[52] For some reason, these London sessions, and others that followed in Venice in September, have come down to us, albeit in fragmentary form, on sheets of hotel letterhead or odd scraps of paper. They reveal, above all, the essential authenticity of the process in its early stages. This is not to say (nor does Craft himself claim) that the "interviews" took place in exactly the form in which they were published. Sometimes he would put questions, which Stravinsky would answer either in writing or, presumably, viva voce. At other times, Craft would simply devise questions to go in front of casual remarks or reminiscences, obiter dicta, anecdotes— what he calls the composer's table talk. Of such cases there is little or no record prior to a typescript, corrected usually by Craft but with occasional marks by Stravinsky. But the evidence of the surviving written replies is that Craft's editing mostly consisted of improving Stravinsky's English and cutting out errors, indiscretions, or—now and then—unacceptable opinions. For instance, Stravinsky's famous account of the origin of the "Petit concert" theme in *The Soldier's Tale* (which he dreamt being played by a Gypsy fiddler to her child) is here more or less verbatim, in his hand.[53] Craft prompts him by formulating the general question about how he gets his musical ideas, then reminding him of the—evidently oft-told—dream story. Stravinsky then writes out his answer in Russian, and finally (no doubt with Craft's help) in English on the other side of the paper. On another sheet he tells (in French) the story of his half-remembered visit to Modigliani with Bakst in 1912 or 1913. But his suggestion that Modigliani failed to paint him because of the war and his death in 1920 was edited out, perhaps because a portrait (done from memory) had meanwhile turned up.[54] Another famous remark about Mahler in St. Petersburg—that "Mahler impressed me greatly, himself, his conducting, and his music"—was added by Craft to Stravinsky's own account of foreign musicians in St. Petersburg (and for some reason lost its final term in print).[55] None of this alters one's basic feeling that in essence this first series of dialogues, as it gradually came out in various excerpts and languages culminating in the definitive book form as *Conversations with Igor Stravinsky,* is a fair reflection of his thoughts and memories at that time, even if the language is too slick and versatile, too innocent of the mistakes and eccentricities of his actual speech, as preserved (for instance) in the Ishlon transcript or in countless recordings and films. But as we shall see, the matter would not always be so simple.

They were in Paris for no more than forty-eight hours, but the hours were crowded, and even in one respect decisive. Boulez played through

Stockhausen's *Klavierstuck XI* in his flat, and later they dined with Giacometti, whom Boulez had asked to draw Stravinsky for the cover of the *Agon* recording that Rosbaud was due to make just before the Domaine Musical premiere in October. Most significant of all, Nabokov was in Paris, and with a brilliant solution to Stravinsky's dilemma over the Hamburg commission. The composer was worried about Piovesan; but wait— Nabokov's own Congress for Cultural Freedom was now going to have its conference, precisely, at the 1958 Venice Biennale. As usual there would be concerts. So what could be simpler than for him to book the Hamburg radio orchestra, and for the orchestra to include the new work as part of the agreement? Stravinsky could conduct it in Hamburg soon afterwards, and as for Venice, Piovesan could be in or out of the deal, as he chose. At any rate, the discussions must have taken some such turn, though even when Stravinsky met Liebermann in Venice a fortnight later, the Biennale's active participation in the Hamburg scheme was still uncertain, and the protocol for an agreement that Stravinsky drew up with North German Radio on 13 September makes no reference to a Venice performance. This aspect of the project crystallizes only with the NDR's formal offer of nearly a month later.[56]

Nevertheless the conversation with Nabokov gave Stravinsky the impulse he needed to start work in earnest on his *Tenebrae* setting, and practically on the day they reached Venice he descended to the cellar nightclub of the Bauer Grünwald, where he had worked on *Agon* the year before, and took up the Latin text from Jeremiah. *Incipit lamentatio Jeremiae Prophetae*— "Here beginneth the lamentation of the Prophet Jeremiah." Like Tallis and Couperin before him, he set the "incipit" and also the Hebrew letters at the start of each verse: "Aleph," "Beth," and so on. If the "bransle double" of *Agon* had consorted strangely with the stale smoke and the upturned chairs, how much odder these austere lacerations of the exiled Jewish spirit in that paradise bar of the great Serenissima. On the 15th of September, when the master was photographed at work by Gjon Mili, he was probably composing the "Quomodo sedet," with its muttered, anxious choric chant and its curiously dislocated duet for flügelhorn and tenor.[57] This is surely the music of that other famous dream in the *Conversations*, in which the intervals in the new work appeared to him as an "elastic substance" stretched between the notes and weighed down at each end by "a large testicular egg."[58] Generally speaking, the thing that distinguishes one serial work from another is the particular coloring it derives from the arrangement of its intervals—the ups and downs, that is, of the row thought of as a melody. In one way or another, these intervals constantly recur, if not quite with the precision of Proust's "little phrase," at least as a kind of atmosphere, or defining color, like the rise and fall of a familiar voice. This was an attribute Stravinsky had so far always evaded, since, although he had written serial music using twelve-note rows, he had never based a long work on a single series, as had been Schoenberg's invariable practice. In fact, he had never started off a work with twelve-note writing at all—the serial workings in *Agon* and the *Canticum sacrum* came in inner movements, and all his earlier pieces had used partial series or series with repeated notes. But *Threni*, as he decided to call his *Tenebrae* on the day of the Mili photograph,[59] was dodecaphonic from the start; and from the start, Stravinsky does things quite differently from Schoenberg, or even Webern, "weighing" the intervals in his row like an assayer, tossing them from hand to hand, turning them over, subtracting one element and adding another, until the whole makeup of the music seems almost cruelly clear and peremptory. The famous opacity of Schoenberg is completely absent. This is par excellence an objectified music, take it or leave it.

Yet even here, appearances can be deceptive. Stravinsky was soon telling Craft that his use of the flügelhorn may have been suggested by the playing of the jazz trumpeter Shorty Rogers.[60] So perhaps the cellar bar was not such an incongruous workshop after all.

At the end of September they set off for Paris by way of Baden-Baden, where Rosbaud was preparing the Paris *Agon* with the radio orchestra, and also—on 8 October—making a commercial recording. In engaging the Sudwestfunk orchestra for the Domaine Musical, Boulez had taken a calculated financial risk, well aware that on strict budgetary grounds the organization could not afford such an extravagant gesture, but convinced that no Parisian orchestra would be likely to do the work justice, and anxious to avoid any repetition of the previous year's troubles with the *Canticum sacrum*. In the same spirit, he had booked the two-thousand-seat Salle Pleyel, and he had agreed, this time, to pay Stravinsky's hefty fee, even though the master would conduct only *Agon*, while the rest of the program—the orchestral pieces by Webern and Berg (both op. 6), and Schoenberg (op. 16)—would be taken by Rosbaud himself.

For Stravinsky it was an occasion almost as nerve-wracking as the *Canticum* premiere in St. Mark's: his public debut with *Agon*, and in front of a packed hall in a city that had often in the past seemed hostile to his music. Moreover, for all the excellence of the orchestra, his solitary rehearsal with them in the Salle Pleyel had gone uneasily, with all kinds of rhythmic and ensemble problems, which the composer struggled to resolve while Craft fidgeted irritably in the stalls. Somehow the actual performance came out reasonably well, the audience was ecstatic, the press, with some notable exceptions, sympathetic.[61] But this was Paris, and as ever it was difficult to disentangle the good and bad opinions from the political posturing and the aesthetic point-scoring. It was widely assumed that Stravinsky was being used by Boulez for the publicity value of his name, and as a weapon in his ongoing war against neoclassicism and the Boulanger traditionalists. For the pro-Boulez Antoine Goléa, the whole affair was a promotional triumph for the Domaine Musical and its presiding genius. "Not even the most loyal friends of the 'Domaine Musical,' " he wrote, "would dream of attributing the sell-out to anything other than the desire of the crowd and the snobs to see Stravinsky again in the flesh. But all the same, compared to 1952 . . . something had changed. A sensational element had meanwhile intervened: the interest Stravinsky had shown in serial music . . . It was the rout of all those who, for thirty years, had carried Stravinsky on the shoulders of their neoclassical faith, had made him their beacon, their standard-bearer."[62] One critic, who had carried Stravinsky on his metaphorical shoulders for a good deal longer than that, heard and repudiated these "derisive sniggers of the adolescent hotheads who regard *Agon* as a masterpiece and despise *Firebird* and *Petrushka*." "They will not prevent me," the composer's old Apache friend Emile Vuillermoz wrote tragically,

> from representing the feelings of Stravinsky's first friends, the faithful comrades-in-arms of the heroic time of his Paris débuts, all those who have been pushed out of the "serial" gala in favor of the snobs of Panurge and who are grief-stricken at the latest evolution in taste and technique of a genius who, at the end of his marvelous career, wastes his time on crazy undertakings and pointless challenges and seems to make it a point of honor to deny his past every time he writes a new score.[63]

AT WHATEVER point he eventually read such diatribes, Stravinsky would have paid them little heed. He never, of course, denied his past in quite Vuillermoz's sense, though he often misrepresented it in print. It was delightful to him to have achieved a popular success, in Paris of all places, with a work that at the same time propelled him into controversy and, to cap it all, was well received by bright young musicians. At Suzanne Tézenas's reception after the performance he was in sparkling form and stayed up until three. The next day there was a birthday party at Nabokov's. Nika was waiting for him at the door with "a cake crowned with candles in his hands. Igor Stravinsky grabbed it, held it over his head and entered the drawing-room, applauded by the guests, singing: 'Happy birthday to me. . . . ' "[64]

Above all, Stravinsky felt intellectually revitalized. Boulez, who had just recorded the two existing movements of his Third Piano Sonata, was at the height of his enthusiasm for Mallarmé's *Livre* and presented Stravinsky with a copy of Jacques Schérer's study of that work.[65] They discussed the relevance of Mallarmé's *coup de dés* to Boulez's recent music; and they talked about Klee with Giacometti, who had started to draw Stravinsky.[66] Something of Stravinsky's partly undigested engagement with these subjects emerges in the *Conversations*, where he quotes Klee on Schoenberg's *Pierrot lunaire* and reports on Boulez's latest concepts of form—a passage presumably compiled during these Paris days.[67] By an irony that would have appealed to Vuillermoz, the first edition of *Conversations* printed it opposite an early photograph of Igor and Katya Stravinsky with Rimsky-Korsakov in his Zagorodny apartment in St. Petersburg, and it is impossible not to be struck by the thought that Stravinsky was as impressionable at seventy-five as he had been at twenty-five.

Then, as if to clinch the old master's new youthfulness, they went by train and car to Donaueschingen, the little town in the Black Forest whose modern-music festival had, since 1950, turned itself into the country retreat of the serial avant-garde, under the auspices of Heinrich Strobel and the Sudwestfunk in Baden-Baden. The mere suggestion of programming neoclassical Stravinsky in fifties Donaueschingen would have aroused merriment or worse, but *Agon* was of course another matter, and the composer duly conducted it there on the 19th. The next day, in Zurich, he signed a firm contract for the Venice *Threni* with Liebermann and Piovesan before flying on to Rome for yet another performance of *Agon*, this time conducted by Craft. By the 26th they were back in Paris, and on the 29th they sailed from Le Havre.

25

HE HATH SET ME IN DARK PLACES ▬

AFTER A GOOD DEAL of vacillation, Kirstein had finally made up his mind to stage *Agon* with Balanchine's choreography in New York at the end of November. He had intended to mount an ambitious autumn festival of Stravinsky ballets, with the composer conducting at least one or two of them.[1] But as 1957 advanced, it gradually became apparent that no such festival was likely to happen, and by September Stravinsky had even come to the conclusion that *Agon* itself would not be done.[2] Balanchine had lost practically a year's work since his fourth wife, Tanaquil Le Clercq, had been struck down by polio the previous October, but he had nevertheless turned up at the Los Angeles concert premiere of *Agon,* and he and the composer had spent a day together working on the score and discussing how it might be danced. Now Balanchine had gone silent once again; and by the time he wired Stravinsky in the second week of October, inviting him to a charity performance of the new ballet on the 26th of November in aid of polio victims, the composer had decided that he needed to be back home by the 14th in order (though he implied a more pressing and specific reason to Balanchine) to resume work on *Threni.*[3]

Why did he not change his plans and stay an extra fortnight in New York? The reason is sometimes given that he deliberately avoided the premiere because he expected it to fail.[4] No doubt he did not anticipate any sensational success. But while he certainly had reservations about one or two details of Balanchine's staging, there is no evidence that he was anxious about its artistic effect as a whole. He was irritated with Kirstein for having cancelled most of the planned festival without consultation, and he may well have felt sulky at being treated in such an offhand way, by no means for the first time.[5] He had heard only through his lawyer-agent that Kirstein could not afford to book him to conduct the ballet.[6] He agreed with some reluctance to attend one of Balanchine's rehearsals two days before leaving for Los Angeles; but once in the studio, he reacted with his usual ebullient energy and enthusiasm, offering strong, constructive advice, and frequently exploding in praise of the young dancers.[7] Later he described the occasion to Souvtchinsky with whom he was now back on good terms after their Paris reunion the previous December. "Balanchine," he reported, "showed me his dances in rehearsal. Superb. There won't be any scenery, and to tell the truth none is needed, though it's a shame there are no costumes either, since dancing in practice kit has been done in other ballets and is no longer very convincing."[8] Above all, though, he insisted he was simply unable to hang around in New York after an absence of four months. They had had a "nice" week at sea, and a "tiresome" week in Manhattan.[9] It was time to catch up with things at home.

He thus missed one of the most spectacular successes of his entire career. Whatever Kirstein may have cancelled, he had actually laid on a dazzling all-Stravinsky evening for the new ballet, programming it not only with *Apollo* and *Orpheus,* as always intended, but also with *Firebird* in Balanchine's choreography of the 1945 suite. After the charity evening, Soulima wired his enthusiasm for the new work,[10] and one or two reviews appeared, notably that of John Martin in the *New York Times,* by no means always a wholehearted friend of Balanchine or the New York City Ballet, but now enthralled by the intricacy and ingenuity of the collaboration and the wizardry of the dancing.[11] But it was only after the official premiere on 1 December that the full extent of the triumph became clear. *Agon* was greeted with wild acclaim by the packed City Center audience, and with something approaching rapture by a press that, in the past, had often expressed itself coolly about Balanchine's particular genre of anti-narrative dance. Edwin Denby (a dependable supporter) wrote that "the balcony stood up shouting and whistling when the choreographer took his bow. Downstairs, people came out into the lobby, their eyes bright as if the piece had been champagne."[12] As for the work itself, Louis Biancolli, who had detested *Danses concertantes* ("an illustrated exercise book"), was fully reconciled to what he now praised as "the very anatomy of dance" and "a living textbook on the art of blending music and motion."[13] The *Tribune* critic, Walter Terry, found simply that "for sheer invention, for intensive exploitation of the human body and the designs which it can create, 'Agon' is quite possibly the most brilliant ballet creation of our day, at least in that area usually described [. . .] as 'abstract dance.' True, 'Agon' is not warm, not overtly human, but its very coolness is refreshing and it generates excitement because it totally ignores human foibles, dramatic situation, and concentrates wholly upon the miracle of the dancing body."[14] A few days later Kirstein wrote to the composer that the ballet was so successful that they had put in six extra performances,[15] and Diana Adams, who had danced the "Pas de deux" with Arthur Mitchell, wrote of their "pleasure and excitement in performing *Agon.* I wish it were on each program. We are still not 'note-perfect' but we seize Kopeikine [Balanchine's rehearsal pianist] and the stage at every opportunity and our concentration is intense, so we improve! The audience response is tremendous, they seem to love it, and several more performances have been added. I do hope you have seen the notices, they were marvelous. Congratulations, and thank you for our beautiful, beautiful score."[16]

The composer was so delighted by all this that when Balanchine wrote soon afterwards to Boosey's claiming an exclusivity in *Agon* and challenging the publisher's right to allow it to be staged at La Scala, Milan, Stravinsky most uncharacteristically supported his claim, which was certainly not based on any written contract and which contradicted Stravinsky's own previous agreement to the Milan production. He was motivated, he said, partly by gratitude, but was in any case "quite uninterested" in anyone but Balanchine putting the work on.[17]

ON THE DAY of the charity premiere of *Agon*, Stravinsky had his mind on an utterly different type of dodecaphony and another form of duet writing. For several days he had been working on the first part of *Threni*. In Venice he had got as far as the setting of the letter "Beth," and now, back at Wetherly Drive, he was manipulating a pair of unaccompanied solo tenors in the "Plorans ploravit" and "Vide, Domine": "She weepeth sore in the night, and her tears are on her cheeks . . . See, O Lord, and consider; for I am become vile." From here he soon moved on to the letter "Caph," with its curious vocal monosyllables supported by polyphonic writing for strings, and by Christmas he had started on the second part of the whole work, the "Querimonia," or "Complaint," where the prophet portrays himself as abandoned by God. In some ways the instrumental music Stravinsky was evolving for the *Lamentations* was the closest he had yet come to the attenuated, needlepoint textures of mature Webern; but the vocal writing was fundamentally unlike anything by the Second Viennese School. In designing his twelve-note row, he had gone out of his way to build into it the very property that Schoenberg had been at such pains to avoid: a sense—however faint and evanescent—of key. Elsewhere in the house, Craft was again rehearsing for a Monday concert: sacred vocal music of the fifteenth and sixteenth centuries by Josquin, Lassus, and Gesualdo; and *Threni* itself at times almost bears traces of some distant choral liturgy, imperfectly overheard. In fact, with its long stretches of unaccompanied voice, it even recalls the Orthodox services at which, of late, Stravinsky had been a somewhat infrequent attender. At any rate "the miracle of the dancing body" is here as remote as New York is from Los Angeles.

Threni was well ahead of schedule for its Venice premiere, now fixed for September, and the only trouble—as with the *Canticum sacrum*—was its length. But this time the score was turning out not shorter, but considerably longer than expected. Already in the second week of January, with the music barely half-written, Stravinsky was warning Liebermann about the extra length, and suggesting a program for the Venice concert (*Threni* plus the Mass and *Symphonies of Wind Instruments*), which shows that he feared—because of the amount of still-unset text—that it was likely to end up nearly twice as long as the twenty minutes stipulated by the commission.[18] Whatever the reason for this new miscalculation—whether it was the rigidity of the serial technique or the sheer length of a text being composed, so to speak, litany-fashion, line by line—Stravinsky was once again inclined to be evasive on the subject, and when a month later Nabokov relayed to him Craft's report that the duration might be as much as forty minutes, he denied it firmly. *Threni,* he insisted, "is gradually nearing completion [he had only the final section, "De Elegia Quinta," to compose] and its length is still far from what Bob, exaggeration-prone as ever, tells you."[19] But the exaggeration-prone Bob had merely been conveying information given him by the Master himself. On the 19th of March, two days before the actual completion of the "short" score, he updated Nabokov to the effect that the whole work lasted only twenty minutes, "despite IS's prediction a month ago." Instead of the *Symphonies,* they were now proposing the Tallis *Lamentations* with, most intriguingly, a canonic prelude, interlude, and postlude for instruments by Stravinsky, and a Lassus motet, "Laudate Dominum," transcribed by him for orchestra.[20] Alas for these shining hopes, *Threni* did turn out to last upwards of half an hour, as Stravinsky finally admitted to Liebermann a few days later;[21] nothing came of the bonus works, and the whole episode proved only that the composer, usually so sure-footed over timings, was for once confused about the structural effect of this difficult new style, pursued relentlessly from start to finish and for the most part at slowish tempo.

In Paris, Boulez was also having to juggle programs for the planned Domaine Musical performance of *Threni* in November on the basis of these erratic predictions. But he was to some extent distracted by performances of his own music. In December, his lavishly scored René Char cycle *Le Visage nuptial* had had its belated premiere in Cologne, more than a decade after the completion of its original chamber version, and he was now working on a complicated idea for a mixed orchestral and electronic piece to be done at Donaueschingen in the autumn.[22] Souvtchinsky had attended the Cologne premiere, and reported back to Stravinsky. "Boulez," he announced, "turned overnight into some sort of Mahler, and everyone was open-mouthed with astonishment, including our friend Scherchen [who was conducting]." Souvtchinsky himself had found it all very sumptuous, in its jingling, tinkling, twittering way, and he saw the work as a kind of Schoenberg *Gurre-*

lieder in Boulez's development.[23] Despite these slightly barbed compliments, Stravinsky greeted the score with something approaching rapture when it arrived from the publisher a few weeks later. "Oh Boulez!" he wrote. "You've given me such a beautiful present!" He longed to hear the music, about which Souvtchinsky had spoken so enthusiastically. At the same time he was anxious to learn whether Boulez had managed to secure the Cologne radio orchestra for *Threni,* since he knew that the Sudwestfunk were otherwise committed, likewise at Donaueschingen.[24]

Over the Venice premiere, there had been no lack of communication from Liebermann and Nabokov, but Piovesan had again gone silent and was refusing to answer letters. By February they needed to be engaging singers; and there was the nice, helpless Biennale director, as usual with "no money, no power, and no authority to sign contracts," as Stravinsky grumbled to Nabokov.[25] Afterwards, it was as if the complaint had echoed round the caverns of doom. A week later Craft, who had flown to New York after repeating Tallis's *Lamentations* at a Monday concert, phoned to report that Piovesan had died suddenly of pneumonia—aged only fifty—on the very day of Stravinsky's letter, as the composer superstitiously admitted when he next wrote to Nika.[26] For some reason, Wetherly Drive took this death more personally than might have been thought likely from their frequent tirades against Piovesan's dilatoriness. Stravinsky mourned, Craft told Nabokov, "for two black weeks," while he himself found it so cruel and unjust that he had no desire ever to go back to Venice.[27] Nika came to the conclusion that Piovesan had suffered at the hands of his fellow bureaucrats "precisely because he was such a good man . . . the one astonishingly decent, intelligent, and kind person I came across in that black hole of musical operators."[28] But Stravinsky's mood had also another cause. The weekend after Craft's phone call, a telegram brought news of the death of Willy Strecker. For Stravinsky, this was a more genuinely personal loss, since Strecker had for nearly thirty years acted as a strong business adviser and energetic supporter when times were hard and decisions difficult. He had been less in evidence of late, certainly, but Igor had not forgotten his steady support in the thirties or his vigorous promotion of his music amid the ruins of postwar Germany. "I'm overwhelmed by this death," he told Sam Dushkin (who had first come into his life through Strecker), "to the point of being unable to go on with this letter."[29] "Perhaps at our age," he wrote, more stoically, to Nika, "it is natural to pass away like that, but it causes nevertheless a very painful reaction."[30] As for Piovesan, all he could do was send money to the director's widow, who was without means and had a little son.

With *Threni* finished, the question now arose as to what he would write next. The thought that he might at last hang up his Stravigor seems never to have occurred to him, but at the same time he plainly had no overriding urge to compose one thing rather than another. He had established that Sacher would accept a choral work, but had then proceeded to write that work for Venice, meanwhile calmly informing Sacher that his commission would have to wait until the season after next.[31] Santa Fe were still hoping for an opera for their 1959 season, but were having difficulty raising the fee; Kirstein was already angling for a new ballet. In one way or another these were distant prospects, and as for Sacher, he was suffering the fate of the dependable suitor down the ages. It was a role he accepted with the best possible grace. He was even prepared to act as go-between for a rival Basle commission, in the shape of a request from the university for a cantata setting of its medieval Latin charter to mark its five-hundredth anniversary in 1960. Still more remarkable, Stravinsky did not turn this unprepossessing commission down flat, but instead temporized while, for honor's sake, upping the fee from seven to ten thousand dollars. Not until late May did he inform the university that he could not write their cantata; and on the same day he wrote to Sacher, postponing *his* work for yet another year.[32]

The reason for all these maneuverings was the usual one. A better offer had come up, but was not yet firm; and since "better" in this case meant "better paid," the contractual question was paramount. Once again it was Nabokov who broke the stalemate. Would Stravinsky, he wrote in mid-March, write a fifteen- or twenty-minute concerto for a good young Swiss pianist, for fifteen thousand dollars paid by a Swiss industrialist and hotel tycoon by the name of Karl Weber?[33] Like a dog with a juicy new bone, Stravinsky at once became furtive. He would write the concerto, on condition that the deal was kept secret and the U.S. revenue evaded by having the fee paid direct into his Basle bank account. But he was curious about Weber's motives. Obviously, the pianist was a "tyotka" (a "queer"), or Weber would hardly stump up that kind of money on his behalf.[34] Nabokov hastened to correct him. The pianist was a woman: in fact she was the tycoon's wife, Margrit. The Webers were typical cultivated Swiss, and owned a big chain of hotels and a magnificent collection of paintings. Nabokov knew about them through the Hungarian conductor Ferenc Fricsay, who had suggested the commission and was hoping to conduct the new work. According to Rolf Liebermann, Nika reported, Frau Weber was a perfectly competent pianist.[35]

Stravinsky had composed nothing specifically for piano (except orchestral parts and the Septet) for almost fifteen years, and there is no evidence that he had been planning anything of the kind now. His mind was still running on vocal—preferably sacred—music. But he quickly entered into the spirit of this new idea. On about the day that he received Nabokov's reassuring second letter, he attended a Monday Evening Concert and heard Leonard Stein play four of Stockhausen's *Piano Pieces* (nos. 1, 2, 3, and 5) and the three Schoenberg pieces, op. ii. Two days later he wrote to David Adams in New York, asking him to send a score of Schoenberg's Piano Concerto.[36] Stockhausen's refined, diamantine piano textures must have intrigued him as a less drastic—or at least less Dionysian—solution than Boulez's (in his sonatas and *Structures*) to the question of how to write serially for the instrument, but at the same time it looks as if he wanted the most recent possible advice on the combination of piano and orchestral sound from the fountain of truth. The lyrical elegance of Schoenberg's gloss on the Viennese concerto tradition may have surprised him, but in the end it gave him little more than a distant point of departure. It was utterly remote from his interests musically. The Stockhausen pieces had much more to do with the kind of instrumental sound-world that had been crystallizing here and there in his own most recent music, however little he may have known (or cared) about their complex sub-serial manipulations of pitch and of rhythmic and dynamic values.

As far as actual serial technique was concerned, there was a model closer to home and more able and willing to explain itself. It was nearly three years since they had talked to Krenek about the rotating series in his *Lamentatio Jeremiae Prophetae*, but it was only in recent months that the score had at last come out in a printed edition. Krenek had sent a copy that very December, just as Stravinsky was starting work on the second part of his own *Lamentations* settings. The preface included a chart that indicated how Krenek had varied his note-row according to a strict cycle of rotations, rather like one of those country dances in which the front couple peels off to the back and the remaining couples move up one place. The musical equivalent of this choreography also involved adjustments of pitch so that the rotated rows all started on the same note. Stravinsky was fascinated by these manipulations, and he drew connecting lines and arrows on Krenek's chart, as if plotting cavalry movements at Austerlitz. Writing his own "Querimonia" in *Threni*, he tinkered vaguely with a few rotations of the country-dance variety; but it seems to have struck him only several months later, when he started to think about his new Weber commission, that Krenek's chart would make a good starting point for a much farther-reaching process, no less rational in its way than the serialization-of-everything methods of the European young bloods, but at the same time beautifully irrational and, within musical limits, unpredictable. At this point he drew his own chart and his own set of cavalry movements. The stage was set for the last and in some respects most hair-raising sidestep in almost fifty years of evading the expectations of his most fervent admirers and virulent detractors.[37]

By the end of May 1958 he had made up his mind to compose the concerto, even though the agreement with Weber was by no means signed and sealed. He knew that, if by any mischance the Swiss deal fell through, he would still have a highly marketable work, one that he could sell to Sacher, or even possibly to Kirstein. It was true that when Nabokov made this latter suggestion to Balanchine a few weeks later, the choreographer hated the idea.[38] But Nika was a tireless networker, and his contacts were second to none. The new director of the Cologne Opera, Oscar Fritz Schuh, had asked his advice about a big Stravinsky festival that he hoped to organize with various German radio stations in the winter of 1959–60, and Nabokov had pounced. "I at once said," he reported to Stravinsky, "that such a framework would be the best opportunity for you to conduct the new piano concerto, and I am sure the fat Germans would pay you a good fee for the rights of a world premiere. If not, they would obviously want to commission you to write a new piece. I told Schuh he would have to book Bob as organizer, conductor and bibliographer, and George as ballet master."[39] Schuh might have been forgiven for taking to his heels at this point, and it says much for Stravinsky's vast prestige in Germany as well as for Nabokov's extraordinary charm and persuasive power that, on the contrary, his interest was aroused, he later went to Venice to meet Stravinsky, and he was still discussing a Stravinsky opera cycle with Nabokov in November, long after the clinching of the Weber agreement.[40] Nabokov, moreover, did not come empty-handed from such talks. Stravinsky paid him a 10 percent commission on the piano concerto fee, and Nika got a lavish production of his own recently completed opera, *Rasputin's End,* in Cologne a year later.[41]

Stravinsky now naturally wanted to get down to composing the music, but this time his health intervened. The polycythemia diagnosed in December 1956 had been controlled by frequent and regular bloodlettings, but this had begun to produce alarming side effects, and at the end of May 1958 he was forced to spend ten days in the Cedars of Lebanon hospital having treatment for a bleeding ulcer. As ever, his medical life at this time was a social and philosophical, as well as strictly clinical, phenomenon. His current doctor, Sigfrid Knauer, was a practitioner of holistic medicine who used homeopathy and acupuncture alongside more conventional treatments, performed diagnoses with the help of a pendulum, and (according to Craft, who was also for a time treated by him) believed in "rejuvenation by the ingestion of minced fetuses."[42] Knauer had the added advantage—particularly for the holistic physician to a holistic composer—that he spoke Russian. But at Cedars of Lebanon there were other doctors, who put Stravinsky on a course of blood transfusions and radioactive phosphorus injections, which, he said, would probably make him light up like a firefly.[43]

No sooner was he out of hospital than he had to prepare his early song cycle *The Faun and the Shepherdess* and a staged performance of *Mavra* for a concert in the Royce Hall of UCLA on 16 June. It must have been a curious feeling to confront these relics of past stylistic anxieties just when he was thinking himself into the modernism of composers not yet born when *Mavra* had been new and shocking. All the same, he was unwilling to concede the irrelevance of his beloved little opera, inextricably associated for him with his dawning passion for Vera. In fact the whole occasion roused him to a most uncharacteristic fit of nostalgia. Writing a few days later to Souvtchinsky on the fiftieth anniversary of the death of his teacher Rimsky-Korsakov, he related to him the story that he had recently also told Craft about Nadezhda Rimsky-Korsakov's spiteful remark at her husband's funeral that "we still have Glazunov," and then proceeded to rail against the Los Angeles audience's incomprehension of *Mavra*.

> It's my impression that, even with a clearcut performance of this transparent and uncomplicated music, it only gets through to the odd listener, while the rest hear nothing and merely whisper and giggle like idiots when Mavra comes on in high boots and hussar's trousers under his skirt. All the same you and I need to have a particular talk about *Mavra*. I don't think (even though I'm now busy with other problems) that its place in music is as unimportant as Boulez probably thinks or as Ravel thought.[44]

Whatever the importance of *Mavra*, it would be hard at first to trace the smallest direct connection between it and the music he was now starting to compose. By the 9th of July he had managed to write some two minutes of his new concerto—the first of five *Movements*, as it turned out: two minutes which became three by the simple device of adding a repeat sign to the end of the first section. Apart from a few isolated moments in *Threni*, he had written nothing like it before. It was not just the technique that was intricate; the music itself breathed the rarefied atmosphere of the extreme post-Webern European avant-garde. The instrumental lines floated free through an atonal ether, devoid of recognizable melody, harmony, or rhythm, their notes scattered like the random flashes on an optometrist's screen. It was music so obviously designed to place its author in relation to a group of admired younger composers, that any cool, well-informed observer might have mistaken it, on a casual glance, for an attempt at parody that had turned by accident into a serious and extended exercise.

Stravinsky was certainly taking his usual pains to make the music as refined and precise as he could. From the very first gesture on the flute, an idea that turns into a two-note chord identical to the one that had opened *Les Noces,* the delicacy and individuality of the writing are beyond argument. Uncomplicated it may not be, but transparent it remains. Here and there a soft open fifth chord, like some far-off fanfare, marks off the short sentences that seem to be the septuagenarian's way of rethinking a kind of music that, in more youthful hands, had tended toward aggression, relentlessness, and excess. In fact, the more one looks at these opening bars of *Movements*, the more one becomes intrigued at the manner of the theft: so shameless yet elegant, like Mozart pinching from early Wagner. Hardly less remarkable is the fact that the music betrays neither anxiety nor uncertainty. Plainly Stravinsky had lost none of that "thirst for renunciation" and "faculty for renewal" that Boris de Schloezer had detected thirty years before in *Apollo*.[45] Issues of style and continuity, motivation, sincerity, and the rest of the baggage of popular criticism simply did not interest him. He just got on with the process of making.

NOT MUCH TIME now remained before their departure for Europe and the Venice premiere of *Threni*, scheduled for late September. Craft was conducting in Santa Fe, but the Stravinskys were going direct to New York, meeting up with him on the way. They were in Manhattan by 23 July 1958, and six days later they sailed for Genoa on the *Cristoforo Colombo*, reaching Venice on the 9th. Their early arrival to some extent betokened a holiday. "This year the pederasts outnumber the pigeons," Stravinsky remarked, like some character in E. M. Forster arriving at the usual boardinghouse.[46] But it was self-mockery, of course. He had had a muted spinet installed in his room at the Bauer, and he was soon at work on the second of the *Movements*, music that introduces little trembling figures for harp and piano that may even have been half-suggested by the instrument on which they were being composed.[47] Toward the end of the month Craft went off to Hamburg, where he had the difficult task of preparing the performers for the Venice concerts: not just the new work, but also *Oedipus Rex*, the *Symphonies of Wind Instruments*, and *The Rite of Spring*, a score he had never conducted before.[48] He is soon sending back detailed bulletins, full of extravagant praise of *Threni*, which he now considers a masterpiece, Stravinsky's best work since the *Symphonies of Wind Instruments*, and—along with the Webern cantatas—the best choral music of the twentieth century, having previously described it to Nabokov as puzzling and, by virtue of its "museum" instrumentation, virtually unprogrammable. It is not hard, but arduous and, of course, completely out of place at the Venice Biennale, where there is little sympathy for the truly modern, but instead they are performing "junk by Hindemith and Bartók." In any case, the Hamburg radio orchestra has little concept of exact rhythm and all too little experience of playing Stravinsky.[49]

But if he reveres the masterwork, he is not always so very gentle with the master. His letters are not quite those of an assistant, certainly not those of an employee (justly, since Stravinsky paid him no salary, and perhaps did not always even pick up his hotel bill: Craft grumbles at one point that he owes the Bauer five hundred dollars). He as good as instructs the composer to stay free on the evening of his return to Venice and not to attend other concerts, by way of revenge against the Hamburg chorus master and the orchestra's regular conductor, Hans Schmidt-Isserstedt, who did not attend Craft's rehearsals. From Brussels, where he is preparing Stravinsky's Mass, among other things, for a concert in Huy, he grumbles furiously about the place, the people, and his cramped, uncomfortable lodgings, making it abundantly clear that he is only there at all because he has no other source of income. This tone of brusque, querulous intimacy might come as a shock to anyone expecting filial respect or a natural hierarchy to the relationship. It no longer, however, surprised Craft himself. Only a month before, he had drawn up a ruthless inventory of his own defects, describing himself as "feckless, irresolute, physically and mentally indolent, yet impulsive . . . [and] a scold." With devastating self-awareness, he put forward possible titles for his books: "Collected Carpings," "Cavils of a Curmudgeon," "With Microscope and Tweezers." He was promiscuous, sybaritic, fickle in argument, and above all a conflicting instance of what Walpole had intended as a distinction when he remarked that "this world is a comedy to those that think, a tragedy to those that feel."[50] He was capable, nevertheless, of sincere affection. Returning to Brussels to conduct *Threni* at the Exposition Universelle in early October, and living in the house of a banker friend whose daughter he was courting, he admitted to the Stravinskys: "How lucky I am to have been with you these ten years . . ."[51]

It was a relief for Craft to get back to Venice in mid-September, and probably a relief to have him back. The *Threni* premiere was only a week away, and in between Stravinsky was conducting *Oedipus Rex* and *The Rite of Spring* in the Fenice.[52] Venice was momentarily the center of the intellectual universe. Nabokov had tied in the *Threni* premiere with a conference on "tradition and renewal" in the arts, and the city was even fuller than usual of thinkers and feelers. Auden was there, and Spender, and Virgil Thomson; Craft glimpsed A. J. Ayer and E. M. Forster on the Piazza San Marco.[53] Isaiah Berlin, whom they had met briefly with Spender in London in December 1956, came to the Fenice concert on the 19th, and afterwards wrote Stravinsky a four-page letter so verbosely and gushingly enthusiastic that he instantly regretted it and begged Nabokov to retrieve it at all costs.[54] The sense of art and mind coming together was almost palpable as the *Threni* premiere approached.

The performance was being given on the 23rd in the upper hall, the Sala dell'Albergo, of the Scuola Grande di San Rocco, beneath the sumptuous but suitably patriarchal gaze of Tintoretto's fantastic Old Testament ceiling and surrounded by his New Testament series on the walls, which so baffled

Ruskin by its apparent haste and carelessness of execution.[55] As with the *Canticum sacrum,* Stravinsky had conducted only the final rehearsals, and they had not gone notably well. A special run-through had been arranged that afternoon for the benefit of the press, who had been locked out of the working rehearsals; but even now there were frequent stops that demonstrated, as one Italian diarist noted, how "the good work of training and preparation by the young Craft was thrown to the winds by the still younger Stravinsky, always insecure, always in search of himself."[56] At the concert itself, Stravinsky was in sole charge. He conducted the *Symphonies of Wind Instruments,* the *In Memoriam Dylan Thomas,* and the Bach Variations, then, after the interval, *Threni.* An audience of five or six hundred—mainly press, the international set, local grandees, and a handful of first-nighters able and willing to pay twenty dollars for a seat—crammed into the long rectangular salon, deadening the acoustics, and exposing still more the spareness and severity of Stravinsky's Jeremiad. According to one Italian critic, "The select audience . . . gave composer and performers the most enthusiastic reception, both during the concert and at the end."[57] But Peter Heyworth noticed only "a little perfunctory clapping while most of the *élégants* rushed for the doors. Stravinsky never appeared to take a bow, so that the remainder of us made our way disconsolately down that imposing staircase feeling that due respect had hardly been paid to the greatest of living composers, or to the impressive new work that he had just presented to the world."[58]

The fact is that, even for hardy spirits and under ideal conditions, *Threni* is a tough nut to crack. "I'm afraid it's a big bore," the composer himself had told Morton, only half-jokingly, "but it will be good to bore my enemies."[59] One can look at the score, or even listen to a recording, and sense how wonderful much of its music might sound in some imaginary performance heaven. But Stravinsky's performance was not good; it was tentative and without pace, the vocal soloists were fairly strong, but the chorus lacked assurance, and the music plodded from section to section.[60] So judgment of the work's stature needed a certain musical acumen allied to an unfailing confidence in Stravinsky's artistic authority. Heyworth, an old Stravinsky hand, found much to admire but also a lack of variety in the contrapuntal texture. Poulenc, who was also present, told Pierre Bernac that "*Threni* is austere but authentic Stravinsky. Alas he conducted it very badly. But despite everything it was very moving. The Venetian audience was indescribably coarse, getting up as soon as the last bar ended. [. . .] Plenty of musicians. Press average. The horrible Goléa [music critic of the Paris journal *Carrefour*] yelled out 'it's not a concert, it's a cemetery.' "[61] But Poulenc, though not sympathetic to Stravinsky's serialism, was musician enough and a large enough character to grasp the music's unique personality breaking through the more or less servile mechanics of the twelve-note technique. It was too much to expect such discrimination from the average Italian reviewer, whose knowledge of Stravinsky's recent music was probably not much greater than his knowledge of Webern or, for that matter, Schoenberg. The critic of the *Gazettino,* for instance, after excusing himself for being unable to comment on particulars without a score, ventured the general impression "that Stravinsky, having dedicated himself entirely, at least in this work, to dodecaphony, has written a radically dodecaphonic work, Webernian and Schoenbergian, and has adopted the most extreme intellectual positions, laying out a score that is as complex, difficult and calculated as it is musically and poetically devoid of value, meaning or impact."[62] With professional help of this caliber, it is perhaps not surprising that the *élégants* made for the exit.

The day after the premiere, Stravinsky went by car to Lugano with his son Theodore and Ernst Roth, and from there by train to Zurich, where he was starting a brief Swiss concert tour of *Threni* performances, in unlikely combination with Beethoven's Choral Symphony under Schmidt-Isserstedt. In Zurich he met Karl Weber and his pianist wife for the first time. Venice, when they returned there on the 1st of October, was under water, and they picked their way across the piazzas and along the canals on duckboards. Within days, however, they were off again, this time to Hamburg, where the Venice concert was being repeated in the circumstances for which it had originally been commissioned. Stravinsky had told Lawrence Morton that the Swiss performances had gone better than the premiere,[63] but it seems likely that the Hamburg performance was the best, and it was certainly here that both the work and its composer were treated with the respect that Heyworth had missed in Venice. At the start of the concert, when Stravinsky walked to the rostrum, the whole audience in the Musikhalle rose to their feet, and at the end there was a huge ovation, in which the performers joined.

Their next stop was Baden-Baden and, from there, Donaueschingen, where Boulez was conducting his latest work, *Poésie pour pouvoir,* a technically ambitious setting for tape and live performers of an astonishingly fierce, imprecatory poem by Michaux. Curiously enough, Craft does not say in any of his various accounts of the visit whether they heard this beautiful but ultimately unsuccessful work (which Boulez afterwards withdrew), though he admits to Stockhausen's triple-orchestral *Gruppen,* which Rosbaud conducted with Boulez and Stockhausen in a morning concert on the same day, 19 October.[64] They had already dined with the two young composers, themselves still on friendly terms, in Baden-Baden, but seem not to have gathered anything from Boulez about the preparations for the

Domaine Musical *Threni* in Paris the following month. They already knew that he had been unable to secure the services of any of the German radio orchestras and had had to fall back on the Lamoureux, a Paris orchestra with limited experience in modern music (though it had recently played Boulez's own eight-minute *Doubles,* and was, he rather alarmingly claimed, well intentioned and hardworking).[65] Stravinsky was also aware that Roth had been slow to provide orchestral materials for Paris, not wanting to print a second set before the first performance, in case of changes.[66] What he may not have realized was that Boulez had been unable to honor his undertaking to handpick and prepare the singers (a promise he had made "because here one can't trust anyone to be sufficiently strict"[67]), but had instead delegated the task to an agent. His own schedule had become atrociously demanding, and he had been wearing himself out "composing, writing, conducting, organizing—all in a kind of frenzy."[68] He had realized only a few weeks before that the vocal solos in *Threni* needed professional singers, not chorus members.[69] Now soloists had been booked, but he himself had been too preoccupied with Donaueschingen to work with them.

However little of this came out at the Baden-Baden dinner, all will have become brutally clear within minutes of the start of the composer's first Paris rehearsal on the 9th of November. In between there had been a delightful trip to Florence, where Stravinsky had a pair of concerts at the end of October, and a disagreeable stay in Vienna (for *Oedipus Rex* at the Staatsoper), a city that he and Vera detested and had in fact succeeded in avoiding since 1930. Craft was ill and in discomfort from a suspected appendicitis. The omens were not propitious. In Paris, from the start, nothing went right. The young choir of the Jeunesses Musicales could not sing *Threni* and did not improve; the soloists were uneven and unreliable. Boulez implored Stravinsky to be more demanding with the singers, "but he was in a benign mood, and convinced me that it was not necessary to harass them."[70] It then transpired that the orchestral parts had not arrived for Schoenberg's *Variations,* which Craft was down to conduct (with Webern's *Passacaglia*) in the first half of the concert. The only recourse was to substitute the three string-orchestral pieces from Berg's *Lyric Suite,* even though they were plainly too hard for the Lamoureux strings to master at such short notice. In despair (Craft later claimed) he, Vera, and Nadia Boulanger implored Stravinsky to cancel.[71] He refused. Boulez himself urged him to be more considerate of the players, who were frequently left to sit on their hands while the choir practiced an awkward passage, or some other section of the much-fragmented orchestra rehearsed.[72] It was all in vain. Stravinsky seemed in the grip of some fatalistic demon, compelling him to a new Paris scandal like the one that had clinched his notoriety all those many years before. With Jeremiah he seemed to be saying:

He hath set me in dark places, as they that be dead of old . . .
Remembering mine affliction and my misery, the wormwood and the gall,
My soul hath them still in remembrance, and is humbled in me.
This I recall to my mind, therefore have I hope.

The Lord came not to his rescue, and the concert, in the Salle Pleyel on
14 November, was an unmitigated disaster from start to finish. The orchestra was more or less at sea throughout the first half, and it did not help—in
the opinion of at least one critic—that Craft conducted the Webern and
Berg items without the clarity that the underprepared players needed.[73] But
at least the music remained roughly intact. *Threni* was not so fortunate. It
actually broke down on more than one occasion, despite Boulez's having
concealed himself among the chorus in order to cue their entries, and several of the unaccompanied vocal ensembles dissolved into chaos. Stravinsky himself got more and more nervous, his beat increasingly vague.
Somehow the performance staggered to a conclusion, and the audience,
who must all have realized that the cacophony to which they had just been
subjected was not deliberate, prepared to acknowledge the composer in a
manner appropriate to his artistic stature rather than to the monstrosity
they had just witnessed. As the applause began, Stravinsky nodded perfunc-
torily in the general direction of the auditorium, then retreated to the wings
and shut himself in his dressing-room, refusing all entreaties, from Boulez
and others, to return to the rostrum and take a bow. At this point the mood
in the audience turned less friendly. The shouts of "*Vive* Stravinsky!"
increasingly mixed with jeers and hisses as the poor musicians were left, in
effect, to take full responsibility for the debacle. Backstage, Stravinsky
yelled at Boulez that he would not go out and that he would never again
agree to conduct in Paris. At last he emerged from the dressing room,
ignored the inevitable cluster of admirers, and left the hall alone.

Outside, two elderly Russians approached him, one of them Sonya
Botkine, only surviving daughter of Nicholas II's last doctor, niece of
Bakst, and a close friend from the early Diaghilev years. "Master, you
remember . . . ?" she prompted in Russian. "Nichevo ne pomnyu: I remember nothing," he snapped, as he sank into his car.[74]

26

THE PILOT FISH AT SEA

FOR THREE consecutive years now, the Domaine Musical had provided a platform for Stravinsky's newest work, and while the ultimate effect on the composer was to confirm him in his hatred of Parisian musical life, Paris itself nourished a profound ambivalence toward its most famous living ex-citizen. On the very night of the *Threni* concert, and almost as if he had not noticed the ghastliness of the performance, the scourge of the *Symphony of Psalms,* Boris de Schloezer, wrote to Stravinsky praising "the grandeur of this score, its formal unity, its austerity, its beauty in the refusal of all com-promise, all effect, all sensual seduction, all personal effusion."[1] But for Stravinsky's oldest Paris friends the picture was a lot more complicated. Poulenc had summed up their confusion after hearing the double Venice *Canticum sacrum* on the radio. After the first performance, he had asked himself whether, "if this wasn't signed Stravinsky, they would be crying masterpiece," but after the second he had decided that "nobody else could write like that." He concluded, nevertheless, that serialism had given Stravinsky nothing, and put it all down to the "bad influence of Craft."[2] Dar-ius Milhaud now went much farther. "Igor's dodecaphony," he told Paul Collaer, "reminds me of Ravel's polytonality . . . The coquetry of great men wanting to show that they're on the latest boat. It does take a certain courage. What's sinister in Igor's case is that the Domaine Musical make use of him but don't trust him. Too bad. That's what happens when you invite the Devil (Robert Craft) into your home."[3]

Craft's influence was no less manifest on the Pleyel book-stall, which gave prominent display to the volume of articles and conversations that he and Souvtchinsky had been assembling for almost two years, and which Rocher had at last brought out a week or so earlier under the title *Avec Stravinsky.* Nobody flicking through this book, with its articles by Boulez and Stockhausen, its "Entretiens d'Igor Stravinsky avec Robert Craft" (expanded, now, from thirty-six to ninety-two questions and answers), and its array of analytical texts—notably on the most recent scores—by Craft himself, could have failed to notice that a certain image was being cultivated, the image of a great master lending the full weight of his work and artistic authority to the "mainstream" European avant-garde. The book, so to speak, was of one mind with the music. Of other composers, the most frequently invoked was Webern, of whose music Stravinsky had literally known nothing before the advent of Craft. Serialism was now confidently assumed to be the one true path. "Masterpieces aside," Stravinsky remarked at one point, "it seems to me the new music will be serial," and when asked to name the most interesting work by a young composer, he inevitably chose Boulez's *Marteau sans maître*.[4]

Boulez, for his part, was prepared to acknowledge Stravinsky's patriarchal status in conjunction with the sainted Webern, but only insofar as he disowned his old following. "After an encounter with the dead," Boulez wrote in his own brief but trenchant contribution, "the living reflect and change course; and in so doing they smash out the mythology that collects like dirt in the cracks of inferior minds."[5] The sense of what the French call a "cénacle," a closely knit artistic circle, was almost tangible. But the full hidden force of the situation would only have become clear if you had picked up another new book on the Pleyel stall, Goléa's *Rencontres avec Pierre Boulez*, and read on its second page about Boulez's participation in the demonstrations against the neoclassical Stravinsky in the post-liberation concerts of 1945.[6] It was a measure of the extent to which Stravinsky had "changed course" that he was now on the march precisely with his former assailants. And it was a measure of the way he had been maneuvered into that position that he seems for the moment to have been no more than dimly aware of that fact. Of Goléa's book—or at any rate of its contents—he remained blissfully ignorant until, as friends sometimes do, Souvtchinsky in the same breath revealed and denounced it to him.[7]

After his initial rage, he evidently bore Boulez no particular grudge for the *Threni* debacle. From Rome, where he was conducting a fortnight after the Pleyel concert, he wrote his young colleague a perfectly amiable letter, pressing for rapid payment of his fee (for tax reasons) and ending with "mille amitiés de nous tous et à bientôt."[8] Then, in London to conduct the British premiere of *Agon* in a BBC concert in the Festival Hall on the 10th of December, he was able to drown his injuries in the unqualified homage that he could count on these days from the English capital. There was a cocktail party at Faber and Faber, who were about to publish the British edition of the *Conversations*, and the *Observer* threw a lunch at the Connaught at which Stravinsky—possibly to his surprise (since the guest list was controlled by Craft)—found himself opposite Harold Nicolson, and not far from the novelist Henry Green and the newspaper's editor, David Astor, a man not famous for his interest in modern music. Isaiah Berlin was at the Connaught lunch as well, and the next day they all proceeded to Oxford and lunched at Berlin's Headington house among a party of academic grandees that included the philosopher Stuart Hampshire, Lord David Cecil, and the historian Maurice Bowra. Such parties no doubt tended to reflect Craft's enthusiasms as much as Stravinsky's; or rather, insofar as the enthusiasms were Stravinsky's, they were ones he had acquired from Craft. But his acquisitive mind was more than ready to adapt to what might have seemed random intellectual situations; and his creative mind rarely if ever slept.

This sociable mood was rudely disturbed at Christmas—by which time the Stravinskys were back in New York—by a long letter from Souvtchinsky. He had already tried several times, he said, to put pen to paper, but had been unable to bring himself to remind Stravinsky of what he knew had been a very unhappy time in Paris. He now, however, felt obliged to inform him of "an extremely painful and disagreeable matter" to do with Boulez, *Threni,* and Goléa's *Rencontres.* "When I mentioned Goléa's book to Boulez, in your presence, I hadn't read it," he continued. "Now I have, and one thing is clear. This book was written with Boulez's consent and with his closest involvement." What had caught Souvtchinsky's eye was not the account of the 1945 protests, but a passage much later in the book where Goléa alleges that, in engaging Stravinsky to conduct *Agon* at the Domaine Musical in 1957, Boulez had been motivated primarily by the desire for publicity.[9] "Can this mean," Souvtchinsky demanded, "that Boulez actually made use of your name for his own self-promotion? And is this why he did none of the things he should have done for the performance of *Threni?*" Why he never stirred from Baden to choose the singers or to see that they were in a fit state to sing the music? Why he was now refusing to publish any kind of a rebuttal? "Dear Igor Fyodorovich, you may take an indulgent view of all this if you wish. I cannot, since for me you represent a value that is sacred, in the plainest and highest sense of the word." Souvtchinsky insisted that he was not seeking in the slightest to influence Stravinsky's feelings toward Boulez. "Indeed, I hope they won't change. But as for me, I've communicated to him that my friendly relations with him are now broken off." "What's very sad," he concluded, "is that his moral condition coincides with his music: his conflict with Strobel, his latest works, his rivalry with Stockhausen—it all shows that on this level something has happened, something that bodes no good."[10]

If Souvtchinsky expected the composer to be shocked by these revelations, he was to be disappointed. Stravinsky admired Boulez and enjoyed his company, but he did not entirely trust him (after the "Stravinsky demeure" article), and he certainly knew better than to expect so active and successful a figure to be exempt from the normal conditions of Paris musical politics. "Forget about the ghastly Goléa and his victim, Boulez," he advised Souvtchinsky. "Get used to the idea that for Boulez success has always depended on others: Strobel, Goléa, and tomorrow there'll be someone else, and the day after tomorrow, and so on. The only thing to do is forget it as quickly as possible."[11] Nevertheless, his own feelings toward Boulez for a while cooled perceptibly. Craft was soon telling Nabokov that the two composers had broken over the issue,[12] and it is at least true that Stravinsky did not communicate with Boulez for more than two months after Souvtchinsky's letter. In New York he was preoccupied with the U.S. premiere of *Threni*, which Craft conducted in Town Hall on 4 January, and with the recording for Columbia, which he himself conducted immediately afterwards. But the New York *Threni* was so brilliantly successful that it seems to have reignited the composer's irritation with Boulez over the Paris fiasco. "The ovations were never-ending," he reported to Souvtchinsky, "and I don't doubt that if the Parisians had heard this performance, their attitude to the work and to me would have been very different." And he could not resist adding that "it is with no feeling of gratitude toward Boulez that I shall remember my stay in Paris. How is it that someone so clever, sensible and honest did not have the courage to admit his Baden-Baden negligence and say 'mea culpa.' "[13]

The object of this censure remained—or so it seems—blissfully unconscious of his senior Russian colleagues' concern for his moral well-being. To Stravinsky he wrote with apparent unconcern about the "great pleasure of having seen him in Paris, despite the black shadow of those idiotic soloists, who forced us to give them lessons in elementary solfège!"[14] Later, there were cheerful postcards, signed jointly with Strobel, Stockhausen. and Mme. Tézenas, from Cologne, where Boulez was conducting *Renard*.[15] Not until almost the end of February did he at last write in a tone that indicated some awareness that the idiotic soloists might have been the cause of any more lasting injury. He had recently, he says, had his attention drawn to the Goléa book, "since there was a phrase in it that might wound you and make you altogether doubt my sincerity." The phrase was, of course, the one about the "publicity coup." "I beg you to believe," Boulez was suddenly pleading, "that I never had any such intention, and that I esteem you too highly—and, by the way, myself enough also—not to play such a ridiculous Barnum and Bailey role." His real hope, he added (thus tactfully repairing any extra damage left by Goléa's reference to the 1945 demonstrations), had been to make "public recompense for all the misunderstandings that had previously kept us apart."[16]

Had Boulez really only just found out what was in the book? Or had he simply, and not unreasonably, failed to predict the impact of one half-flippant expression by a notoriously caustic critic on the delicate sensibilities of a proud but insecure fellow genius? Stravinsky had certainly at first assumed that Boulez and Goléa were hand in glove. But in truth the *Ren-*

contres issue was a complete red herring. Stravinsky was complaining, not about anything in the book, but about Boulez's failure to apologize for the *Threni* nightmare. So who had told Boulez that Stravinsky was offended about the book? The answer, naturally, is Souvtchinsky. It was Souvtchinsky who was energetically "breaking" with his young hero, or so he told Stravinsky, though in fact he never did anything of the kind, but continued to cultivate good relations with Boulez, precisely as he was doing with Stravinsky. To Stravinsky he was careful to write that "in order to avoid getting your name mixed up in this affair, I am even prepared not to tell Boulez that I have written to you."[17] Not only did he not tell Boulez he had written, he apparently did not for some weeks so much as mention to him the imagined cause of offense. Only toward the end of February, by which time Boulez may well have been wondering about Stravinsky's continuing silence, did Souvtchinsky confront him with the "coup de publicité" and its supposed consequences. Souvtchinsky's own account of their meetings to Stravinsky makes bizarre reading.

> I had two conversations with him, and in all we talked for eight hours. . . . I always supposed that "hysterical scenes" only happened with characters in Dostoyevsky, but it turns out they're available to French musicians too. Boulez threw a tantrum by any standards Dostoyevskian. He sobbed, screamed, banged his fists, tore his hair, grumbled, threatened. He would crush and destroy everyone; he alone knew and understood everything. It was a terrible spectacle. . . . But despite everything, I'm convinced it was a *cold* fit. Neither of us persuaded the other. He will go on as before with his electronic music, his Mallarmé, writing for Strobel, and bossing everyone around.[18]

Whether or not one believes this colorful description, it is far from clear that it had anything to do with Stravinsky. Boulez had long been an obsession of Souvtchinsky's, but recently he had become preoccupied with what he regarded as the younger man's careerism, his ambitions as a conductor and entrepreneur, his growing involvement with Germany. Boulez, he claimed, could not bear to be opposed.[19] But neither did Souvtchinsky enjoy the loss of influence all this implied for him. The Goléa affair looks like nothing so much as a bid to reassert control by fomenting trouble for Boulez in an influential quarter. And if this is true, fate chose a strategic moment to deal Souvtchinsky another useful card at precisely this juncture.

It came in the form of a paragraph by Goléa on the *Threni* concert in an article on the "Paris Music Industry," in the February issue of the German periodical *Neue Zeitschrift für Musik*.[20] The review, such as it was, was brief and to the point. As far as *Threni* was concerned, Goléa made no comment on the music, shrugged his shoulders at the poor performance (since "we have known for almost forty years that Stravinsky is no great conductor"), and merely reproached him for leaving the performers to take the blame. He then turned his guns on the composer's hapless assistant. "In the first half of the concert," he sneered, "Robert Craft, who for ten years has swum cheerfully in Stravinsky's wake, 'conducted,' if one can call it that, the *Passacaglia*, op. 1, of Webern and the three string-orchestral movements from Berg's *Lyric Suite*; it was a catastrophe, to the point where even the most hardened opponent of the 'New Music' will have been clear that it was not the music, but the 'conductor,' who was responsible for the works' shipwreck."

Whether or not Boulez had seen this review when he wrote his letter of apology to Stravinsky (he later implied that he had not), Stravinsky this time did not need either him or Souvtchinsky to tell him about it, being himself a subscriber to the journal. Bitter as he must have felt at the attack on his own conducting, the assault on Craft's was still more painful to him, coming as it did so soon after the triumph of the New York *Threni*. Craft was *his* conductor, *his* exponent, *his* mouthpiece. Fatherly affection aside, it was psychologically important to him that this young American who had come to him and stayed with him of his own free will should be accepted as a musician of international caliber—a kind of household talisman against the Bernsteins and the Stokowskis, the Markevitches and (nowadays) the Ansermets, whom he so much feared and, officially at least, detested. Robert Craft, he once remarked, was the best conductor of his old works, of his new works, and of the works he had yet to write.[21] Reservations about the young man's performances were not welcome at North Wetherly Drive, and Pierre Souvtchinsky had certainly not forgotten this when he told Stravinsky that "among young musicians, Boulez rates (and fears!) only Craft and Stockhausen. He spits on the rest. . . ."[22] Doubtless it was a lie, but it was a white lie. And now here was this malicious Frenchman Goléa hitting Craft where it hurt most, at the level of simple competence. After all, what kind of modern specialist was it who could not, with a professional orchestra, get up a half-respectable performance of a source-work like Webern's *Passacaglia*, even at short notice? The master took up his pen:

> Your reviewer of the Paris concert in which I conducted my *Threni* . . . is guilty of vicious injustice. The responsibility for the fiasco of that concert is the Domaine Musical's, and your reviewer, as the author of a vulgar book which is in part a history of that organization, is close enough to it to know the truth, which is that the Domaine Musical did not prepare the concert as it promised to do. Your reviewer's remarks about R. Craft are also vicious and unjust since he knows perfectly well that

R. Craft was obliged to sight-read Berg's *Lyric Suite* and perform it only after two hasty and incomplete rehearsals, and that if the Venice performance of *Threni* was better than the Paris [as Goléa had observed], the reason is that R. Craft prepared it, in fact, did what the Domaine Musical did not do.

But having composed this neat riposte, he began to worry about its effect, and he decided instead to submit it first to Souvtchinsky for his approval.[23] Souvtchinsky did not think it the right approach. It seems that he was determined to subject Boulez to the aftershocks for as long as he could, and he accordingly advised Stravinsky to insist that Boulez write personally to the *NZfM*, dissociating himself from Goléa's remarks and explaining the circumstances in detail. Goléa, he claimed, was busy ingratiating himself with the Lamoureux's chief conductor, Igor Markevitch, and was hoping to drive a wedge between the Lamoureux and Stravinsky.[24] Quite why this should have worried Stravinsky, who had already stated categorically that he would never again conduct in Paris, is not entirely clear. Nevertheless he accepted the advice, withdrew his own letter, and, having told Souvtchinsky on 9 March that he would not press Boulez to write, for fear of embittering him, in fact did so on the 10th, in a stiff and somewhat chilly letter in which he represented it as Boulez's moral duty to challenge Goléa's review.[25]

The Machiavellian aspect of these goings-on may seem sufficiently complicated, but the whole situation becomes positively Byzantine when one includes in the equation the crucial and unquantifiable element of emotion. Souvtchinsky, it appears, was possessive of Boulez; Stravinsky was cross with him but still fascinated by him musically and intellectually, and personally fond of him. Having praised *Le Marteau sans maître* in print, he had now, however, come to the conclusion that Boulez was not much interested in his own recent music, and certainly not in *Threni*, which he had just conducted in Munich, but which he talked about purely in terms of numbers of performers and seating arrangements.[26]

Meanwhile, Robert Craft was going through his own personal dark night of the soul. Shattered by his traumatic experience in the Salle Pleyel, a concert that, because of his subservient position, he had been powerless to abort, he now had to endure an attack on his competence that, if it became widely known, would be seized on by his enemies as proof of their contention that he was merely using Stravinsky as a free ride to unmerited success. What was almost worse, Stockhausen had recently been in New York at the start of a U.S. concert and lecture tour, and had been loudly abusing Craft's recent recording of his *Zeitmasse* to anyone who would listen, including influential people at Columbia such as David Oppenheim and, no doubt, Goddard Lieberson. Craft badly needed the reassurance of Boulez's oft-expressed admiration, and when the French composer lowered the barriers with his letter of apology, the waters of Craft's anguish flowed into the empty channel. While Stravinsky's manner remained defensive, Craft could—unofficially, so to speak—reveal his true sensibilities. They had, he told Boulez, suspected him at North Wetherly Drive of manipulating Goléa, but the *NZfM* review had changed their minds. Stravinsky *had* meant to reply to the review, but, not wanting to damage the Domaine Musical, had decided to ask Boulez to do so instead. As for Craft himself, his insecurities had now reached fever pitch; he had (he claimed) attacked Boulez in print without meaning to, had received a curt letter in reply, but now wanted his love and friendship back on an even stronger footing than before. His own "Rencontres" with the French master had been profoundly rewarding and productive, and so too had Stravinsky's. Finally, in a near-frenzy of unguarded enthusiasm, he offered Stravinsky for a Paris concert a year hence, including "the new piano concerto," despite the composer's vow never to mount a rostrum in that city again.[27]

Boulez's reply was charming, generous, and sympathetic, but perhaps not impeccably sincere.[28] He too had been anxious about their relationship and was relieved by Craft's attitude. Stockhausen's behavior he could not comprehend, and he deeply regretted any damage to Craft's relations with Columbia, "which had yielded, among other things, the irreplaceable complete Webern." He knew nothing about Goléa's review, but would certainly have something to say about it, since "you are my friends, and I do not put up for long with my friends' being attacked, least of all in a questionable manner." On the same day he wrote to Stravinsky about the Munich *Threni* without referring to Goléa at all, but—prompted by the skeptical composer—he wrote again three weeks later that he had seen the article, agreed it was unacceptable, and had in fact already drafted a reply that was at that moment being translated into German. He would send it to Stravinsky as soon as it was ready; and they would meet in Copenhagen, where Stravinsky would be receiving the Sonning Prize toward the end of May.[29]

It was typical of Stravinsky that he could seem completely taken up with a painful dispute of this kind, yet continue working as if nothing had happened. Back from New York in mid-January, he at once returned to work on the new piano concerto, *Movements*, taking it up where he had left off in Venice, at the start of the third movement. For all the music's abstract spareness, it did not come quickly, and it took him most of a month to complete these eighteen bars of music—a working rate (if one thinks only in terms of what was kept) of a mere handful of notes a day. In music, as in all utterance, significant compression is one of the hardest things to achieve.[30] Drafting the remaining two movements took much of the next five weeks. But as he composed, he began to have doubts—not about the music itself (his creative certainty seems not to have wavered)—but about how it would be received by the Webers, who had committed a large sum of money on the assumption, presumably, that a Stravinsky concerto would sound like *The Rake's Progress,* or at worst the more presentable bits of *Agon.* After finishing the third movement he sent Frau Weber part of the short score so that she could familiarize herself with the strange idiom.[31] Now, with the work almost fully drafted, he actually offered to release her from the commission and return the advance "if the style and technique are alien to you."[32] This was perhaps a less dangerous offer than it sounded, since Liebermann had started taking an interest in the new work as a possible showpiece for the well-to-do Berlin Festival in September or for the ISCM Festival in Cologne the following June, and there was still also, of course, Sacher waiting in the wings for whatever Stravinsky might choose to offer him. In any case there was no need to worry. Margrit Weber soon replied that she had no desire to withdraw. She was convinced that the concerto was a masterpiece, even while admitting that it presented rhythmic difficulties of a kind she had not previously encountered, "having never played such a work before."[33]

Apart from the still-undecided Sacher project, there remained a hope that Santa Fe would commission an opera. Their Mycenas of the year before, an oil tycoon by the name of Senutovitch, had proved a broken, or at least slightly bent, reed. But John Crosby was optimistic about foundation money—Ford or Rockefeller—and by March he was talking in serious contractual terms, offering twenty thousand dollars to the composer, and the same sum to his librettist, who was to be none other than T. S. Eliot.[34] This suggestion must have come from Stravinsky himself, but Eliot, whose own verse is so rich in musical allusion, was evasive when it came to working with musicians, and he was soon assuring Stravinsky that he was unqualified for such a task, could not read music, had no operatic ideas, and was frankly wary of treading where Auden—a more musical person, in his opinion—had supposedly failed with *The Rake.*[35] With *Movements* now nearing completion, Stravinsky replied in April that he, too, had no intention of writing another opera like *The Rake,* and certainly not for twenty thousand dollars. He was thinking more along the lines of "a cantata, or static stage piece (genre my *Oedipus Rex*), a shorter work than an opera and one more suitable to my present non-operatic musical thought. Perhaps a Greek-subject piece in a contemporary reinterpretation—a Christian morality play."[36] In due course, Eliot responded politely but still without great enthusiasm to this new idea: "If and when the subject comes to you and in any case when you have further thoughts about the subject, I should be delighted to hear from you again on this matter."[37] But it was obviously going to be an uphill struggle.

Eliot had shown a more spontaneous interest (with his Faber hat on) in the conversation-book idea, which the composer had mentioned to him more than a year before, on the pretext of seeking his advice about the contents and organization of the manuscript.[38] At that stage—January 1958—the questions and answers had already appeared, in one or another compact version, in magazines like *Atlantic Monthly* and *Encounter,* in German as a supplement to an omnibus edition of the *Chroniques* and *Poetics,* and in French as a pamphlet sold on the Pleyel book-stall at the *Agon* concert.[39] The first installment of a somewhat larger series was about to appear in the German music journal *Melos.*[40] And now various New York publishers were pressing Stravinsky to expand the conversations into a book of reminiscences, perhaps in the form of an updated edition of the *Chroniques.*[41] By early 1958 his own objections to this idea (which he saw as a nuisance to his composing schedule) had been overcome, probably by some kind of pincer movement on the part of Craft himself and Deborah Ishlon, who was almost certainly responsible for whipping up rival enthusiasms among publishers in New York for the entirely new kind of publication a book of conversations would represent, and when Eliot saw an initial manuscript in March and pleaded for it to be given to Faber, publication in America by Doubleday was practically a settled intention.[42] Only the precise form of the book remained to be teased out of the disparate material that had gradually evolved around the original set of questions.

The problem was partly one of length. Exactly how much material Eliot saw in March 1958 is hard to establish, but it was probably less than the sixty-four questions and answers that eventually appeared in *Melos* in 1958, or the ninety-two in the French volume *Avec Stravinsky,* which came out in time for the disastrous *Threni* concert in November. There the questions make fifty-eight pages of a book that includes a good deal of other material, some of it of a technical character unsuitable for the lay reader. There would indeed be more questions (another twenty-five or so, as it turned out). But the book was still going to be perilously thin for hard covers. One possibility was to add a selection of the letters Stravinsky still possessed from major figures like Debussy, Ravel, and Satie. Another was to include a "diary" section, ostensibly by Stravinsky, but in fact written by Craft in the composer's persona: the so-called Venetian Journal, which figures intriguingly in the correspondence relating to the *Conversations* but which never came out in that original form.[43] The journal nevertheless brought to a head the question of titling and attribution of the book as a whole. Craft was trying his best to stay in the background—whether out of native shyness or from a feeling that the book would do better as Stravinsky's unaided work. He doubtless suspected that he would be accused of manipulating the answers and even of having simply written the whole text on his own. Anyone who knew Stravinsky at all well would surely know at once that this was not his English, even if the memories and opinions might be more or less safely trusted. Yet Craft's name could hardly be left off altogether. Obviously he had asked the questions and at least edited the answers. His role had to be defined with some care.

Stravinsky had his own views on this important matter. "The title of the book," he wrote to Debbie Ishlon,

> is "Conversations with Igor Stravinsky by Robert Craft," and at the end of the Venetian Diaries the words "written for Igor Stravinsky by Robert Craft" must appear. . . . This isn't Bob, who is in fact at fault the other way in not wanting his name on anything. But he did write the book, it is his language, his presentation, his imagination, and his memory, and I am only protecting myself in not wanting it to appear as though I write or talk that way. It's not a question of ghost writing but of somebody who is to a large extent creating me.[44]

In some respects this goes too far. Craft admitted in a letter to his Faber editor that he had written the journal in such a way as to contrive a diary personality on Stravinsky's behalf,[45] and no doubt the language of the actual *Conversations*—so crisp, immaculate, and severe—is also in large measure his contrivance. It certainly has little flavor of the foreign, and no trace of the idiosyncratic *basso profondo* drolleries of the composer's English-language conversation. It is too wordy, and in a sense too intellectual—not, certainly, too quick or intelligent, but too dialectically organized, at bottom too Anglo-Saxon, too sensible. On the other hand, to ascribe to Craft the element of memory in the biographical parts of the book is plainly absurd. For all the many errors of fact and distortions of viewpoint, there is too much here that Craft simply could not have known, even well enough to get them wrong. Why Stravinsky misrepresented his past (especially his Russian past) in so many small—and some larger—ways that can now be checked in letters and diaries not available in the fifties is a slightly different question, though not wholly unconnected with the depiction of a persona that, preferably, had severed its links with that past. The Stravinsky of the *Conversations* is a supremely up-to-date, learned, almost omniscient figure, versed in the latest tendencies of the musical avant-garde and with well-formed views on the history and aesthetics of modern music, a ready definition of his own neoclassicism (a concept he would not have given the time of day to in 1930), and an opinion on every aspect of art, old and new. For such a thinker, the Russia of Rimsky-Korsakov was a simple irrelevancy, a mere accident, no more than a landing place for the parachutist from the stars. It certainly was not convenient to exaggerate its importance as a formative influence on the composer of *The Rite of Spring*, to say nothing of *Threni* or the *Movements*.

On the whole these problems escaped the notice of reviewers when *Conversations with Igor Stravinsky* was published in early May 1959. Nearly everyone was dazzled by the wit and articulateness of a musician who could reminisce so entertainingly about figures as great and varied as Rimsky-Korsakov and Debussy, Schoenberg and Diaghilev, who had seen Ibsen, met Rodin and Monet and Proust, and had amusing yet pertinent anecdotes to relate about them all. In the sections on composing and modern music, Stravinsky's erudition and, on the other hand, his technical and aesthetic self-awareness, were all accepted with admiration and without question. "Here," one reviewer asserted, "is a musician who *knows*."[46] The fact that Stravinsky had never previously known or cared much about the music of his contemporaries and had never in his life theorized about method or about art, except in the most general terms, troubled no one, even while several reviewers quoted with approval his insistence that he was "a doer, not a thinker."[47] The composer had come to terms with his past, the old musical time-traveller had simply at last come out in prose, and that was that. Here and there his revisionist enthusiasm for Webern and Schoenberg attracted comment. One writer went so far as to wonder if this was cause or effect of Craft's own admiration for these composers, as evinced by his concerts and recordings.[48] But the book's authorship was never an issue. One reviewer is even supposed to have claimed, with no more than ritual incredulity, that the two finest modern writers of English prose were now both Russians: Vladimir Nabokov (the author, recently, of *Lolita*) and Igor Stravinsky.[49]

Today, nearly fifty years after its publication, and at a time when the book is available only in a form that destroys its original integrity and posthumously reconstructs both its prose and its factual and intellectual substance, it is more important than ever to see the *Conversations* as a document of its time.[50] Its opinions on modern music and art, on the act of composition, and on the crucial importance of serialism and the semi-divine status of its leading practitioners, above all reflect Stravinsky's own creative direction and preferences at that period. Insofar as they differ from or conflict with previous (or indeed later) attitudes, it is because Stravinsky was under new and overpowering influences, but that does not alter the fact that, at that time, he thought this way. The thinking is no more invalidated by the apparent lack of intellectual independence than the music is invalidated by its seemingly craven up-to-dateness. They are both what they are, and both, curiously enough, remain entirely personal and unique. There is no serious case for arguing that at this stage Craft represented his own views as Stravinsky's, whatever the extent of the hidden influence. The same is broadly true of the biographical parts of the book. The fact that they devote no more than six or eight pages to Stravinsky's Russian background, but thirty or forty to the early Diaghilev years and the Russian Ballet, reflects not only the basis of his fame but also the continuing prestige of the main works from that time. The neoclassical works, which Boulez and Co. so despised, are glossed over in a tone that reads horribly like an apologia, in answer to Craft's itemization of the works "the young *avant-garde*" did and did not like—this from a composer notoriously intolerant of any criticism of his music from whatever source.[51] But in presenting a series of letters from Debussy, Stravinsky is careful to identify the French master as the composer to whom he and his contemporaries owed the most—which is demonstrably untrue but was guaranteed to please the young Paris avant-garde.[52] After all, how could he have answered "Rimsky-Korsakov," which, in his case, would have been more truthful, if not the whole truth?

NICOLAS NABOKOV's latest scheme for Stravinsky was a tour of Japan, fixed for the spring of 1959. The trip had originally been tied in with a music festival Nabokov was organizing there, but the festival had been postponed, leaving the composer stranded with a series of concert dates, which simply became paymaster for an extended tour of the Far East.

Like their Greek holiday of three years earlier, the Japanese trip reads like a highly organized assault course alleviated by the occasional overwhelming or unforgettable experience. At Honolulu, on the outward flight, they visited Pearl Harbor, then flew on to Manila and Hong Kong, where they drove round the New Territories and as far as the Chinese border, before finally flying to Japan on 5 April, eleven days after leaving Los Angeles. They were appalled by Tokyo. "A horrible city," Stravinsky reported to Souvtchinsky. "No streets, only back-yards. Roads in a dreadful state. No architecture. Nine million inhabitants! They say that the orchestras are very bad and provincial. Thank you very much!"[53] As for many new arrivals in Japan from the West, the first impression was of a chaotic, overheated capitalist society whose traditional culture hid behind closed doors. When the doors opened, you removed your shoes and entered a different world. For Stravinsky, this double-sided aspect of Japanese life struck home with full force when they attended a performance at the Kabuki-za Theatre and watched one of the traditional dance-plays from the Kabuki repertory, *Kanjincho*. For any alert Western visitor, the visual aspect of Kabuki is thrilling even if he has no notion of what is taking place, doesn't understand the language, or cannot grasp the meaning of the intensely stylized gestural idiom. But the sound-world is almost as striking, with its astounding use of what we would call extended voice—every kind of vocal effect from free lyrical melody, through speech-song, down to groans and shrieks—accompanied by the shamisen (lute-like but twangier), with bamboo flute or transverse noh flute in attendance, and a whole range of percussion, from the wooden clappers that announce the start and finish of the performance, to the drums, bells, and gongs that punctuate it along the way. Stravinsky was riveted by particular effects like the drum glissando and by the flute, with its subtle deviations of pitch; but he was just as excited by the integration of music and gesture, by what he called the play's "rhythmical orderliness," and surely also by the element of ritual, which must have reminded him of works of his own— *Renard, Les Noces*—where ritual actions are articulated through singing, instrumental music, and dance.⁵⁴ In his own diary that night he recorded the visit in two words: "Kabuki!!! Formidable!!!" and he told a journalist in Osaka that "he had been inspired by Kabuki music and indicated strongly that several musical ideas already are forming in his head."⁵⁵ By what may or may not have been coincidence, it was on the very day of this theatre visit that he wrote to Eliot about his idea for "a static stage piece" on a Greek or Christian subject done as a morality play.⁵⁶ Kabuki is not exactly static, but its discourse is anti-logical, and even its "realism" is highly emblematic.

In Osaka, by which time Nabokov had joined them, they also went to a Noh play and to the Bunraku puppet theatre. But the Noh, which had so impressed Britten three years before, was altogether too motionless for Stravinsky, at times literally static, as when the only two characters onstage stood for half an hour without moving while the chorus sang a semi-inaudible chant.⁵⁷ By contrast, the Stravinskys' complaints about Japan, after less than a fortnight in the country, were growing ever more audible. "Have seen lots of the Stravinskys and Bob Craft," Nabokov wrote to Liebermann from Tokyo. "They *hate* their trip and are grumbling bitterly."⁵⁸ Craft mused half-facetiously that Igor hated it less than Vera did because the Japanese did not expect tips, and because—being himself of Japanese dimensions—he actually fitted the country better.⁵⁹ Yet for him, as much as for the others, the culture was difficult and the art and architecture—apart from Kabuki, and the gagaku music they heard at the Imperial Palace toward the end of the trip—disappointing. As for his own concerts—one in Osaka at the start of May, and two in Tokyo the following week—they seem to have gone reasonably well; at least no disasters are recorded in any of their various diary reports. Klaus Pringsheim, writing in the English-language paper *Mainichi*, called the final Tokyo concert "a unique artistic event in the history of the Japanese capital" and noted that "the near-capacity audience accorded him a hero's triumphant welcome."⁶⁰

Locally, the occasion was symbolic. Less than fourteen years had passed since Hiroshima, less than three since Japan's admission to the United Nations. But it was a symbolism that meant little to the Russian-American visitors. They flew back to California on 9 May in a mood of relief that was only intensified when an engine failed on their final stage from Seattle, and they landed with their heads in their arms, their hearts in their mouths, and their undercarriage in a sea of foam. "Fortunately usual landing," Stravinsky noted laconically in his diary.[61]

27

A STRANGE CONCOCTION ▬

In the ten days before they were due to set off again for Copenhagen, Stravinsky let his *Movements* draft lie, and instead wrote another piece altogether, a miniature trio for flute, clarinet, and harp in memory of Prince Max Egon zu Fürstenberg, the founder and patron of the Donaueschingen Festival, who had died while the Stravinskys were in Japan.[1] Igor had no very personal grounds for mourning the prince any more than countless other generous and agreeable hosts and patrons. But Boulez had asked him to contribute what he called a "frontispiece" to a memorial concert he was planning of music by Webern;[2] and Stravinsky had a particular reason for wanting to oblige his French colleague at that moment, because in the same letter Boulez at last reported having seen the Goléa review in the *NZfM* and having written a stern but chilly reply, designed, he claimed, to settle the matter once and for all and to leave no room for those damaging polemics so beloved of French critics. The letter was being typed out, and Boulez would bring it to Copenhagen to show to Stravinsky.

Meanwhile Stravinsky was writing his frontispiece, or *Epitaphium* as he called it, using three of the instruments Boulez would have on tap for his program of middle-period Webern. The music—composed between the 14th and 16th of May 1959—could almost have come from unused fragments of the *Movements;* it has the same scattered appearance and disjointed texture, and the sonorities are ones favored also in the piano work: for instance, the bass register of the harp, which Stravinsky had begun to hear as specifically funereal, like a muffled drum.[3] He also said that the flute-clarinet duet started out as a flute duet, for which there are several precedents in *Movements*. There is no sign of this change in the Basle sketch, but it does confirm his remark that the idea of a bass-treble dialogue (or "funeral responses") between harp and wind only occurred to him after he had written the first fragment for flute and clarinet. In fact the harp music looks as if it was drafted as a whole quite separately from the wind music, the two types then being dismembered and interleaved to make the dialogue. Looking at the score of *Epitaphium*, with its little boxes of music laid out apparently at random on a single page, it is hard to resist the feeling that Stravinsky was mimicking the appearance of aleatoric (chance) works like Boulez's Third Piano Sonata or Stockhausen's Piano Piece XI, where the sequence of such boxes is partly at the performer's discretion. But it hardly needs adding that, in Stravinsky, there is no such discretion and the order is fixed.

A few days later he flew to Copenhagen, a return journey of more than twenty-four hours for less than a six-day stay. On the face of things, this might seem a more than usually dotty expedition for a man in his late seventies and in indifferent health, but then the Léonie Sonning Music Prize was a more than usually prestigious endowment. Stravinsky was to be its first recipient, and it will not have escaped his notice that the first recipient of the parent award—the Sonning Prize endowed a few years earlier by Léonie's late husband, the Danish writer Carl Johann Sonning—had been Winston Churchill. No doubt he was also influenced by the fifty thousand Danish crowns of the award itself.[4] In any case he duly accepted the prize and conducted a concert in the Tivoli Gardens on 25 May. But the visit was useful and important in other ways, too. Rolf Liebermann made the short journey from north Germany to persuade Stravinsky to give the first performances of *Movements* to Hamburg and Cologne the following June; and on the last day in the Danish capital the Webers appeared and several hours were spent correcting mistakes in the manuscript.

Most important of all, Boulez turned up with a draft of his letter to the *NZfM*. From Stravinsky's point of view it was a reasonably satisfactory text.[5] It drew attention to the poor quality of the Jeunesse Musicale chorus and the unprofessionalism of the soloists; it at least half-exonerated Craft for the Berg and Webern disasters (referring to the insufficient rehearsal "for which it would be unjust to blame Robert Craft alone"). It stopped short of a personal attack on Goléa of the kind Stravinsky had launched in his own aborted letter; but then Stravinsky recognized—if not without bitterness—that Boulez could not risk offending the powerful French critic or being cast as a troublemaker in the highly politicized German new-music world.[6] Indiscretions there rarely went unpunished. Only recently, Boulez had been quoted in *Melos* as having suggested, in an introductory talk before his Munich *Threni*, that Stravinsky had been shamed into composing such music by the monastic character of Webern, a "pretty *bon mot*," as the German critic called it, though Boulez naturally denied it ("If I utter *bons mots*," he assured Stravinsky, "I hope they are prettier than that").[7]

In his by now chronic cynicism about the real feelings of the European avant-garde toward his music, Stravinsky seems to have been happy to keep his personal friendship with Boulez separate from the more complex question of professional loyalty. "What a joy to see you in Copenhagen," he told him when he next wrote; [8] and to Souvtchinsky he sighed: "Poor Boulez, it's not very jolly to be surrounded by such people."[9] But the indulgent words concealed a question mark, since Stravinsky went on to talk about Stockhausen in a tone of resigned reproach that implicitly included Boulez.

> He knows me so little, and my music interests him so little. He belongs naturally to a generation which needs biologically to be hostile to me. What to do? I can't change it and won't think or speak ill of him for it, but will simply regret that it's so and that it's useless to expect any reciprocity on his part.

It was left to Souvtchinsky to interpret this lament in his own way. "Believe me," he wrote, "Stockhausen truly values and understands you, but he's a bit gauche, in a way rather uncouth. Moreover he's now going through some drama in his relations with Boulez. . . . I hope that Boulez wrote his letter and it didn't stay a draft; perhaps it's naughty of me, but I greatly mistrust him."[10] Then some weeks later: "He's very taken up with his conducting career. . . . I must say that relations with him have become extremely difficult: he talks only about himself and his plans, but I'm very much afraid that these plans are more organizational than creative. I shall be glad if I'm wrong . . ."[11]

Back in Hollywood, Stravinsky was for a time deep in preparations for a concert performance of *The Nightingale* that he was conducting for the Los Angeles Festival in UCLA's Royce Hall in the middle of June;[12] then he set to work to complete the *Movements*, starting—for some reason—by rewriting the fifth movement. One inevitably wonders how he could pass from the Scriabinesque indulgences of the early opera to the complex serial rotations and compressed, fragmented syntax of this latest score without some tremor of self-questioning, some at least momentary feeling of stylistic vertigo. But if he felt any such anxiety, it remained unspoken. Instead he became absorbed by the technology of his rotations, working from charts that gave him melodies and chords almost as mechanically as a computer program—almost as mechanically, one might say, as a Japanese nightingale—but which nevertheless cost him, he insisted, "a gigantic effort."[13] Not surprisingly, he loathed Shostakovich's rambling, epic Eleventh Symphony, which he heard conducted by Franz Waxman at another festival concert: "an hour of aesthetically and technically primitive junk," he called it in a letter to Souvtchinsky.[14] And when Douglas Gibson asked him to contribute to a collaborative set of piano variations on a theme by Falla to mark Chester's centenary, he replied dustily that he was too busy and that in any case Gibson (who was naturally not expecting to pay) couldn't afford him.[15]

As usual, the problem was that his working time was threatened by his travel plans. At the end of June they were off to Santa Fe, where he was due to conduct *Threni* in the Catholic cathedral on 12 July; then they would be back in Hollywood for a mere six weeks before their now more or less ritual absence of several months in Europe and New York. In Santa Fe, Paul Horgan, the festival board member who had this time been instrumental in setting up the visit, had arranged for a room with a muted piano to be placed at Stravinsky's disposal in a secluded outbuilding of the archbishop's palace.[16] But one might doubt whether much composing was done. Craft, who was due to conduct Donizetti's *Anna Bolena,* had arrived a few days earlier and had managed to fall during a rehearsal and dislocate his right arm. When the Stravinskys arrived, he was in hospital with his arm in plaster. Horgan paints a touching, gently satirical picture of their reunion, with everyone close to tears not only, it transpired, because of the accident, but also because the visitors were distressed at the (by their valetudinarian standards) somewhat irregular accommodation they had been given in the house of the local poet Witter Bynner. A persuasive fixer, Horgan found them rooms in La Fonda, Santa Fe's adobe equivalent of the Savoy; and thereafter, with Craft able to rehearse but not conduct *Anna Bolena* and also involved in preparing *Threni* and Bach's *Trauer-Ode* for the cathedral concert, Horgan was much in Stravinsky's company and able to scrutinize the more intimate sides of his personality as if he were himself the principal character in a novel about "the unexpectedly homely and affectionate Great Russian Artist."[17]

The portrait is the tenderest and most three-dimensional of the many left by writers for whom Stravinsky's musical genius was a mystery alleviated, if not illuminated, by the colorful intensity yet vulnerability of his person. As always, there are the copious whiskies and idiosyncratic diets, the tiny, gnomelike stature, the large ears, the pantomime English, and the sudden, unforgettable smiles, emerging like the sun from behind a cloud on a windy day. But there is something more penetrating, too. "His social sense was great," Horgan observed, "and if a passing vagary of health, or a stupid letter, say, had upset him, he strove to conceal a state of irritability.

> I rarely saw him in an abstracted or absent mood—until the end. [. . .] With waiters as well as importunate hunters, he showed the same royal sort of courtesy, and I thought this politeness was the other side of his medal of personality—that caustic brilliance and sarcasm which could operate when there was anything worthy of calling it forth. [. . .] His general style [. . .] was concentrated, impacted, densified, to the greatest degree. In all its expressions, from the idlest personal in conversation to the utmost significant in composition and performance, there was a total absence of vulgarity. To be with him was to be conscious that one

was within the field of energy of genius, even during its lapses into rest-ful triviality. [. . .] Even with the growing familiarity of years, I never lost something of awed restraint; but it was one of his powers that he never needed explanations—he could feel what one felt, and if there was some-thing genuine behind it, he was aware of that, too, and accepted what could not easily find expression when he knew it to be compact of both respect and love, with a pinch of intelligence thrown in.[18]

After the performance of *Threni*, Horgan went with Stravinsky to his dress-ing room. The composer was edgy and, it seemed, angry about something, but then Horgan noticed that it was more like "mortal disappointment." "It is never good enough!" the composer muttered as he struggled with his cufflinks. "But I thought it wonderfully beautiful!" the novelist insisted. "Oh my God, the mistakes you did not hear!" In the end, Horgan explains this bitterness as a kind of postcoital emotional detumescence. "A surge of compassion beyond presumption went through me but I knew of no way to reassure him." Yet when Stravinsky arrived at the reception Horgan had laid on, "I saw a master of transformation [. . .] he was smiling widely, not quite bowing but inclining himself forward, taking in the whole room. He looked fifteen years younger." Mirandi Masocco embraced him: "I loved it, it's so catchy. I hummed it all the way over here," and Stravinsky was delighted by her not-quite-mock philistine directness.[19]

The performance was certainly not alone among early (or even later) *Threnis* in its wrong notes. Craft's New York premiere had been perhaps the least inaccurate, though its great success with the audience is by no means proof of that. Barely a month before Santa Fe, William Steinberg's London premiere had been described by the reliable David Drew as "brave but imperfect."[20] But Santa Fe had one big thing in its favor: unlike all previous performances, it was given in a church. The city's curious nineteenth-century, neo-Romanesque cathedral—part adobe, part sandstone—was a far cry, as Horgan admitted, from St. Mark's, but it provided the right devo-tional atmosphere and nearly ideal acoustics, with just enough wash in the sound to moisten the edges of Stravinsky's desiccated vocal lines and severe, unyielding instrumentation. The liturgical flavor was enhanced by the decorum of a church performance, with no applause.[21] The composer was led to the rostrum in silence, "like a bride being conducted to the altar in an Orthodox Jewish ceremony."[22] The archbishop was present, and he introduced himself to Vera, though hardly knowing what to say to her. "Do you know," she remarked, to mask his awkwardness, "that this is Schiapa-relli 'Shocking Pink' you are wearing?" "Oh? Indeed? How interesting. Yes." "You see?" she added, "We match exactly."[23]

Stravinsky did manage to complete *Movements* during the subsequent six weeks in Hollywood. In fact, by the end of July he had finished the fourth movement, and on the same day he dated the whole work on the draft.[24] Two days later, however, Craft wrote to Glenn Watkins that Stravinsky was "adding" a fifth movement: that is, presumably, the second rewrite that Stravinsky refers to in *Memories and Commentaries*.[25] Then, having made this revision, he decided to add four short linking interludes to suture the five movements together. By 15 August the whole work was at last complete, and it was at this point that the composer stood back from the strange concoction—so utterly unlike anything he had ever written before—and decided that he could not bear to wait until the following June to find out whether it would make sense in performance. So he at once informed Margrit Weber that he had decided to bring the premiere forward and give it in New York in December, since "I do not want this very concentrated and fine work to be flanked by 'modern music' I know nothing about; and I think it absolutely imperative that the work be repeated immediately after it is played the first time."[26] At the same time he wrote to Liebermann, who was predictably furious at the loss of his premiere: "Why New York, of all places?" he sulked.[27] Well, there were various excuses: the Webers' convenience, the composer's timetable and health, and so forth. What Stravinsky did not mention was that, since no New York orchestra would want the new concerto at such short notice, he would have to promote the concert and take the financial risk himself. For this task he would need a dependable manager. At Santa Fe he had met and liked the Opera's publicity officer, Lillian Libman. She seemed to know her job. Accordingly, Craft now wrote to her inviting her to manage and promote not one, but three Stravinsky concerts in Manhattan that coming December and January.[28]

Nothing more seems to have been said about the Santa Fe commission, and by early August Stravinsky was beginning to evolve other plans for his collaboration with Eliot. The main catalyst for the change was Robert Graff, who had directed the NBC film of Stravinsky at home on his seventy-fifth birthday. The composer had lunched with Graff in New York in January and discussed the possibility of working with Balanchine on a new "story" ballet devised specially for television. Now Balanchine was in Los Angeles, and the two of them had begun to examine this idea in more detail. Neither was much interested in anything Graff would regard as a "story" ballet. "In fact," Stravinsky told the director, "even another abstract ballet (like *Agon*) is not in the line of my present thought.

> However I do have in the mind a theatrical work with scenic and choreographic elements and with a story or myth subject, ancient and known to everyone. I do not yet see the exact *form* of this work, whether it will employ a chorus, what kind of instrumentation, whether or not a narra-

tor, but I do think it might be theatrically, if not musically, closer to my *Oedipus Rex* and *Persephone* than to any other works of mine.[29]

He expected Eliot to be the librettist, and was actually planning to start work with him in London that very September. A few days later he wrote to Eliot himself in somewhat different terms.

> All commissioners have in mind a work of one's past they want repeated, but the very reference to a past work helps one to realize how unrepeatable it is. I have been considering the story of Noah. I can imagine a dramatic work in it involving narration (as in my *Oedipus Rex*), singing—a chorus, the voices of Noah and his sons and perhaps of an angel—and scenic and choreographic elements. It might follow the form of a medieval morality play, for example, with narration used to connect [a] sequence of "set" pieces, instrumental and vocal numbers, pure, i.e. spoken, verse (what delightful animal rhymes you could do, for example), dance. And the morality play appeals to me not only because it would permit this kind of diversity but also because it suggests a stylization and a symbolism. We cannot put Christ on the stage, but Noah, the second Adam, has also been Christ to the Christian mind, and the drunkenness of Noah, Christ's Passion. Here anyway is a subject I hope you will consider.[30]

Leaving aside the unorthodox theology (which resuscitates a specifically late medieval idea about Noah), it is noticeable that, while expressly rejecting self-repetition in his own case, Stravinsky assumes it without question in Eliot's. This may be one reason why Eliot wrote back in mainly negative terms, though without quite dismissing the collaboration out of hand. He had "done" Old Possum and *Murder in the Cathedral* (though he refrained from saying so). He was now engrossed in a new play of his own.[31]

Stravinsky had not lost sight of the Boulez letter. Each month he checked his copy of the *NZfM*, and by August the letter had still not appeared.[32] Instead, in the middle of the month, a letter from Boulez arrived at North Wetherly Drive, enclosing a new and much shorter version of the *NZ* text, now translated into German. Boulez's covering letter excused the delay, explained that he had made the translation with Strobel and sent it to the *NZ*, but said not a word about the abbreviation.[33] Stravinsky was furious. "You know German well enough," he replied, "to realize that this isn't a translation of the article you handed me in Copenhagen. It's a German version, shortened (to a third of the French), smoothed out and toned down beyond recognition . . . I'm surprised by all this, for I expected a very different attitude on your part given our friendly and cordial relations. That is why I sign this letter with much bitterness and disillusion."[34] Had Boulez expected any other reaction? From the swiftness of his recantation, it seems that he had. He protested that he had merely followed Strobel's advice to keep the letter neutral and avoid controversy; but he now saw his miscalculation and was sending the *NZ* a translation of the full text. He implored Stravinsky, in the Gallic manner, to believe in the "undeniable fidelity" of his feelings, "and—less solemnly—in everything, in life and work, that unfailingly binds us."[35] Stravinsky was reassured and told Boulez so.[36] The letter went off and duly appeared, with only slight modifications, in the October *NZ*, though Stravinsky curiously enough failed to notice it and was still, in late January, grumbling to Souvtchinsky that it had not yet been printed.[37]

When a friend divorces for the second or third time, one inevitably suspects—if only in private—that the friend is in some way to blame. Yet if one examines the many "breaks" in Stravinsky's long career—with the Rimsky-Korsakovs, with Bakst, Benois, Diaghilev, Ansermet, Lourié—one often feels that the great composer was more sinned against than sinning. He suffered, no doubt, from an incorrigible expectation that his closest associates would put loyalty to him above all other considerations. In this he was perhaps naïve, perhaps tyrannous, and the speed and absoluteness of his vengeance when the expectation was dashed tended to reflect those qualities. With Boulez, though, matters were less simple. For one thing, the break was temporary, and cordial relations were soon resumed, even if they never returned to quite the unguarded warmth of their pre-*Threni* state. For another thing, the puzzling behavior of Pierre Souvtchinsky has to be taken into account.

Souvtchinsky, as we saw, had given Stravinsky a distorted account of his relations with Boulez earlier in the year. By August, this duplicity had assumed Iago-esque dimensions. Throughout the summer he had written negatively about Boulez in letters to Stravinsky.[38] Now, when Stravinsky sent him the abbreviated *NZ* text, Souvtchinsky felt free to elaborate. He was, he said, not surprised. Strobel could not let Boulez damage him with the German musical press, and Boulez, for his part, was protecting his relations with Goléa. In his—Souvtchinsky's—opinion, Boulez had written two letters, one for Stravinsky's eyes, the other for the journal (this was a curious allegation, since Stravinsky had just reported to him the contrary). In any case he was thoroughly disillusioned with his young friend and had told him so in no uncertain terms. "So far," he added, "I've had no reply to this letter and don't expect one.

> But I don't trust him any more and I'm sure that, having embarked on a
> course of the most banal careerism, he will go on climbing regardless of

the consequences and without remorse. But what I find inexpressibly painful is that he has not been ashamed to display to you his new rules of life. When I see you I'll tell you a lot else about this "metamorphosis." Just don't trust him!39

That was on 22 August. On the 23rd Souvtchinsky wrote to the "careerist" in person.

> Thank you for your letter, to which the word "magnificent" applies a thousand times more than to mine. I thank you for it with all my heart, for it's true: there was "something" of a break between us which is repaired, for me at any rate, in the friendship and admiration that I have for you and which will remain one of the "essential" bases for what I call my "existence." That is how it is, and it cannot be otherwise, in spite of all the traps life may yet reserve for us.

On the subject of Stravinsky, Souvtchinsky offered some words of fatherly wisdom. He had advised Boulez not to get mixed up in the Goléa affair (even though, as we saw, he had urged Stravinsky to insist that Boulez reply in person to the *NZfM*40), but now that that had happened, he felt it necessary to explain Stravinsky's reaction.

> You are one of the most intelligent men I know, and this being so, allow me to say one thing: you lack psychology. Stravinsky's relationship with you is a passionate one; and there is also an issue of conscience. I know (because I'm a bit *au courant* in this affair) that he has for you a sort of adoration. This adoration now seems to him betrayed and even abused. You are also for him the Webern of our time, that Webern of whom he was ignorant in the past and towards whom he now feels like a repentant sinner. He wants you to love him, as he would have wanted Webern to love him. . . . Obviously [he] wanted the *Threni* business cleared up, but believe me, above all he expected from you a demonstration of friendship which would have "obliterated" the hateful attack by Goléa.

Instead, Souvtchinsky went on, Boulez had presented him with two different versions of his letter, and Stravinsky had inevitably wondered about the motives for the change. "Not to conceal anything from you, I had the same feeling." So, he urges, "set your Valkyries and their husbands to work organizing a Stravinsky festival, under your direction of course; but in my view you owe him an explanation. After all, I don't know whether a real creature is more vulnerable at the start of his career, or at its apogee . . ."41

As an exercise in manipulation this letter must be accounted a masterpiece. Boulez, certainly, had been slapdash over the *NZ* letter. He had hoped to avoid trouble with Goléa and with Strobel; he had delayed, vacillated, temporized. Yet his behavior had been essentially open. It was Souvtchinsky who had played a double game. He had known Stravinsky intimately since before Boulez was born; he shared his background and his language. He knew precisely how Stravinsky reacted to attacks on his work, and he knew what the composer expected of his friends. His analysis of Stravinsky's feelings toward Boulez rings utterly true; and this was not something that had suddenly dawned on him—he had realized it from the moment he read Goléa's *Rencontres* and saw the opportunity to drive a wedge between the two composers, a wedge which he, Pierre Souvtchinsky, could then withdraw at the moment of his own choosing. This may seem harsh, but it is the only lucid conclusion to draw from the known circumstances and the available correspondence.

Boulez duly wrote to Stravinsky early in September, expressing his relief that his decision to reinstate the original letter had restored their friendship.[42] Soon afterwards Souvtchinsky wrote that he had advised a small cut, "a phrase that altered everything to Goléa's advantage" (it was a remark about Boulez having nothing to set against Goléa's "feelings" other than his own).[43] He did not mention that a still smaller phrase had been inserted, qualifying his correction of Goléa, the words "wenn auch contre coeur"—"if indeed reluctantly." Stravinsky, when he at last read the printed text, did not overlook this tiny adjustment, nor fail to see it in the worst possible light.[44] As for Boulez, he had not quite learnt that he could not be friends both with Stravinsky and with those whom Stravinsky saw as his enemies.

STRAVINSKY's first European concert in the autumn of 1959 was in Naples in mid-October. Nevertheless they set off from Hollywood at the end of August, and after a few days in Princeton, where they had a meeting with Graff and took part in a symposium on modern music, they flew on to London for the discussions with Eliot. Of what exactly transpired at their dinner on 6 September we know frustratingly little, Craft's diary entry being largely taken up with table talk.[45] All we know is that Eliot agreed to go on thinking about the project and to talk about it again in November.[46] Meanwhile the Stravinsky party proceeded to Edinburgh, purely as guests of the festival—the first time any of them had been to Scotland. Venice, where they arrived on the 17th, was likewise unadulterated holiday, at least as far as conducting was concerned. Leonard Bernstein was there with the NYPO, and he offered Stravinsky a commission on behalf of the orchestra for the opening of the the Philharmonic Hall in Lincoln Center. But Stravinsky's thoughts were not at all in that direction. Hearing Bernstein conduct his own *Age of Anxiety* symphony in the Fenice, Stravinsky abandoned ship after the first few minutes and returned, perhaps, to his own work, which consisted of adding missing parts to two more Gesualdo motets, this time six-part ones, "Da pacem, Domine" and "Assumpta est Maria."[47]

His earlier Gesualdo completion, the seven-part "Illumina nos," had been made essentially as a practical exercise for performance. But this time there was also a scholarly motive, at least of a secondhand kind. Three months before, Craft had been approached by Glenn Watkins, a young Gesualdo specialist at the University of North Carolina, who was co-editor of the collected edition of that composer's music then being published in Hamburg.[48] Watkins had found errors in the bass lines of Craft's recording of Gesualdo's *Responsoria,* but he was also covetous of the *Sacrae cantiones* material Craft had used for the same recording, and when Craft duly sent him copies of his part-books, Watkins quickly discovered that, in the defective six-part motets, not two but only one part needed realizing. He worked out the missing voice himself; but later he sent his realization to Stravinsky, with the suggestion that he make one of his own.[49] It was this task, partly mechanical (because the canons, once traced, were strictly self-fulfilling), partly creative (because Stravinsky, as we saw, did not scruple to superimpose his own stylistic image onto Gesualdo's) that occupied him during late September in Venice.[50]

Apart from this piece of creative musicology, as one might call it, the only certain musical product of the month in Venice was a tiny two-part instrumental canon of his own, sketched on the 10th of October. The little fragment looks like a brief demonstration of the automatic nature of canonic writing in serial music like Webern's, where the imitative character of the lines is a built-in result of the technique. But Stravinsky actually had a particular commission in mind. A certain Marcelle Oury, who was in the process of editing for publication her correspondence with the painter Raoul Dufy, had written to the composer asking him, apparently quite idly, about his attitude to Dufy's work.[51] We do not know what, or if, Stravinsky replied, but we do know, from another source, that Mme. Oury wanted to commission a short piece from him to go into her book to illustrate, so to speak, Dufy's love of music, both in itself and as a subject for painting. Having failed, it seems, to entice Stravinsky on her own account, she tried again through the new young manager of Boosey and Hawkes's Paris office, Mario Bois, who had just met Stravinsky for the first time on his way through Paris from London to Venice. Bois does not claim that Stravinsky wrote his Double Canon "Raoul Dufy in Memoriam" at his instigation. On the contrary, he advised Mme. Oury that Stravinsky would be most unlikely to take on such a commission, and he suggested that she try Poulenc instead. Yet the fact remains that Stravinsky did write the piece, did dedicate it to the memory of Dufy (whom he had never met), and did complete it—as a piece for string quartet—late in November 1959. Poulenc's tribute, a little Apollinaire song called "Le Puce," was not composed until the spring of 1960, at the earliest.[52]

From Venice they flew to Rome, then drove on south to Naples with Berman and the photographer Robert Bright, whose presence accounts for well-known publicity photographs of the composer and Craft at Paestum and the town of Gesualdo (Vera having stayed in Venice). Their Naples concert in the Teatro San Carlo on the 18th was followed by one in Bologna four days later. But Stravinsky did not react well to this renewed activity, and in Bologna he suffered what may have been a mild stroke, though he nevertheless conducted his half of the program on the 22nd. For a day or so he could barely stand upright. For most of the trip he had been plagued by gastric troubles, which reached a climax when, having double-dosed himself against diarrhea, he had to endure a stormy crossing of the English channel followed by a train breakdown. Somewhat the worse for wear, they reached London on the evening of the 27th of October, ten hours late.

Not surprisingly they made straight for Harley Street; there were the usual blood tests, and another consultation with Sir Charles Symonds, who, in December 1956, had not expected Stravinsky to see out 1957. This time, unexpectedly, the great neurologist pronounced his health much improved, seemed unconcerned by the lameness and the stiff right arm that had persisted from the Bologna attack, and gave him permission to conduct.[53] This was, of course, purely clinical advice. Stravinsky himself was less than sanguine about directing with a partly incapacitated conducting arm; yet he seems not to have seriously considered cancelling either of the two difficult BBC concerts that William Glock had lined up for him: a studio recording of *Oedipus Rex* and the awkward and taxing Symphony in C; and a late-evening concert performance of *Oedipus Rex* in the Festival Hall on 9 November, an event that had started out as a *faute de mieux,* since the normal concert times were all booked, but had grown into a cult occasion, a rare chance to hear a famous work that had still never been professionally staged in London, conducted by its composer, and with Cocteau himself, these days the darling of the arty cineaste coffee-bar circuit, reading the narration.

As it turned out, Stravinsky conducted without apparent discomfort. The press noticed nothing untoward, and even Paul Horgan, who was in London and had dined with the Stravinskys and Eugene Goossens the previous evening, seems to have been unaware of any grounds for disquiet.[54] "A Memorable Oedipus Rex," the *Times* voted it, adding by way of footnote that "M. Cocteau undemonstratively set the various scenes," and that "the tactful sincerity with which he delivered his last line, 'Adieu, Oedipe; on t'aimait,' was a concert in itself."[55] This tribute to the author's modesty will have surprised those who knew him, and certainly it must have astonished Horgan, who had been mesmerized by Cocteau's posturing histrionics during the performance, the way he gestured to the audience before the work started, gazed ostentatiously about him during the music, missed several cues, then leapt to his feet, ready for the applause, well before the final soft orchestral unisons had died away. Horgan felt that Stravinsky was infuriated by Cocteau's antics, and implies that the two co-authors scarcely met outside the performance (though they must have talked long enough for Stravinsky to complain about his lameness, since Cocteau wrote to him a few days later advising him to look after his legs and recommending hot foot baths[56]). The composer had not yet pronounced his famous anathema on "the speaker device, that disturbing series of interruptions" or in particular dismissed the narrator's very last phrase—precisely the "on t'aimait"— as "a journalist's caption and a blot of sentimentality wholly alien to the manners of the work."[57] But perhaps it was this very performance—and even this very review—that prompted him to express himself in quite that way a mere two or three years later.

NERVOUS STRAIN may have been a factor in the composer's poor health that autumn of 1959, and no doubt it was the need for rest that decided the Stravinskys to return to New York by sea rather than air. It was more than forty years since Stravinsky's involvement in the failed promotion of *The Soldier's Tale*. Craft's experience as a concert organizer was more recent but, on the whole, scarcely more encouraging. Now they were together promoting not one but three separate professional concerts, including several difficult modern scores and a variety of complex baroque vocal works, while engaged on a complicated European tour, and with a manager they scarcely knew. Lillian Libman was expected to book a large orchestra for *Movements* and *The Rite of Spring,* and for complex, practically unknown masterpieces like Schoenberg's *Die glückliche Hand* and Webern's op. 6 orchestral pieces, as well as a dependable choir and soloists for Schütz, Gesualdo, and Bach; somehow timetable adequate rehearsals for these disparate and unrelated forces; and at the same time stay within a ridiculously tight budget. Admittedly Karl Weber had agreed to underwrite the *Movements* premiere, and since Columbia were supposed to be recording all the works, there would presumably be support, whether logistical or financial, from that quarter as well. But Columbia were proving curiously reluctant to come forward with a material contribution, even after Goddard Lieberson had happily agreed, at Libman's suggestion, to lend the company's name as having "The Honor to Present . . ." Eventually they did contribute about a tenth of the overall cost, and they made studio recordings of the major Stravinsky works except *Movements,* for which Mrs. Weber could not get a release from her contract with Deutsche Grammophon.[58] But the negotiations were tense and at times acrimonious, and the human chemistry frothed and bubbled and hissed like a laboratory in a science fiction film.[59]

Lillian Libman ran a small agency from an upstairs office on Madison Avenue, and some of her business methods recall those of Milo Minderbinder in Joseph Heller's *Catch-22,* who made money by buying eggs for seven cents each and selling them for five. Libman's particular version of this loss-leading procedure was to use Stravinsky's name to persuade expensive musicians to perform for hardly any fee, then to waive a large part of her own percentage while meeting many of the office costs involved in securing the reductions. As a businesswoman she was a curious though perhaps not wholly uncommon mixture of the tough and the maternal. In her brief acquaintance with Stravinsky, she had fallen under the spell of his big Russian smile and his aura of vulnerability. Craft, she soon realized, was effectively in charge of practical arrangements, had an astonishing but volatile grasp of detail, took many decisions on his own account while appearing to consult the composer's interests, and read all Stravinsky's mail.[60]

Quickly, she began to feel a personal attachment to this improbable troika. Her letters—calm, efficient, businesslike—end with endearments like "I miss you" or "deepest affection to you."[61] Letters and telephone calls flew back and forth between New York and Europe throughout October. And perhaps it was a certain possessiveness in her nature that aroused the irritation of those around her who, as she herself put it, felt "a prior claim" on the maestro. One such was certainly Deborah Ishlon, whose role as Columbia's publicity director inevitably brought her into either collusion or collision with Stravinsky's new agent. Debbie, Lillian clearly felt, was jealous of her, saw her as a rival, and sought control by making executive decisions in relation to the Columbia association without consulting the Libman office.[62] In her memoirs, Libman is tactfully silent about the quarrel, but Craft—in a postscript to his own chronicle—draws attention to it and implicitly blames her.[63] There is also a curious entry in Vera Stravinsky's diary for December describing an incident in which Lillian and her husband turned up at the Hotel Pierre in New York late on the 31st wanting to wish them all a happy New Year, and making it clear that the visit was importunate and unwelcome. However, this is not a genuine diary entry but a gratuitous report, out of keeping with the normal character of what is typically an engagement diary with brief journal annotations. It bears suspicious features. The top half of the page for 31 December has been cut out, and the text—in English in Vera's hand—starts below the cut, then runs back on to the 30th. Whatever has been excised must have referred to another incident that displeased her (since in the surviving text she declares herself "again *unzufrieden* [unhappy]") but which the wielder of the scissors did not want preserved. Moreover, the existing entry is the only one for the whole of November and December, almost as if the diary had gone missing at the end of October, then turned up—perhaps packed and sent home in the wrong suitcase, or left in a Paris hotel and then sent on.[64]

By New Year 1960, in any case, the first of the three concerts had taken place, and had gone off well, at least as far as Stravinsky himself was concerned. On 20 December a sold-out Town Hall heard him conduct an English-language *Les Noces* with four leading American composers—Foss, Barber, Sessions, and Copland—playing the four pianos, exactly as in the recording, which, as a matter of fact, was made the next day; and, by way of bizarre contrast, they also heard the little *Epitaphium* and the world premiere of the Dufy Double Canon played by the Galimir Quartet. The rest of the program was admittedly less notable, with Craft, who had told Lillian that he was "sick of all-Stravinsky concerts and did not wish to conduct them," instead reverting to baroque music in the form of Monteverdi and a long, early, and not very characteristic Bach cantata (BWV 131).[65] "Its performance," in the opinion of the *Tribune* critic, Paul Henry Lang, "was insufferably dull, [and] I am afraid that this recherché antiquarianism is a high price to pay to hear Stravinsky."[66] Warming to his theme, Lang also noted waspishly that "since Mr. Stravinsky's present monitors won't permit the great composer to be exhibited in just any company, mixed programs are restricted to the three departed coryphees of Viennese dodecaphony, or to some highly respectable museum pieces." Thus, before Stravinsky conducted *The Rite of Spring* at the second concert in Carnegie Hall two weeks later, Craft duly stepped up and delivered the op. 6 orchestral pieces of Berg and Webern, respectively, and Schoenberg's *Accompaniment to a Film Scene* (*Die glückliche Hand* having been abandoned on grounds of cost). And when the *Movements* premiere came along in Town Hall on the 10th, Craft offset this strange novelty with Bach's *Trauer Ode* and motets by Schütz, Monteverdi, and Gesualdo, including "Assumpta est Maria" in Stravinsky's completion.[67] Happily, Lang had himself grown sick of what he would probably have called "all-Craft" concerts, and instead sent his assistant, Jay Harrison, who had just published an interview with Craft and was more in tune with his ideas.[68]

Movements, like *Les Noces*, played to a packed but subdued house, "startled into bashfulness," according to Libman, "so startled, in fact, that the sparse applause did not warrant a repetition of the work, as had been originally planned."[69] Even the critics admitted to not understanding the arcane music in every detail, but for the most part gave it the benefit of the doubt—

a concession rarely extended by their lordly predecessors, the late Olin Downes and his colleagues. One reason for caution may well have been the presence of *The Rite of Spring* in the same series. "Not of course," Harrison observed, "that the two works have the least in common, the one being innovational in its new-found uses for tonality, while the 'Movements' are, in its creator's words, 'anti-tonal.'

> The fact is, however, that no music after "Le Sacre" was quite the same, and it may be that "Movements" may stand as a similar point of departure. Certainly, those involved in the development of serial methodology must now face the truth that doodling in tone will not do; before them this morning is the image of a man who has proved beyond question that atonality is the business of genius and not the preserve of those who, lacking talent for anything else, find the adoption of twelve-tone disciplines a handy way of remaining up-to-date.[70]

Margrit Weber had learnt her solo by heart and played it with a certain stolid precision, one note after another—as Craft reported to Mario Bois—without regard to the shape or phrasing of the music.[71] Rehearsals had been tense; at one point the composer had brought his hand down hard on the score to the accompaniment of "a vocal explosion, *crescendo:* 'No . . . NO . . . NO!!!.' "[72] And this was a worry to the composer, because she had exclusivity in the work for another year, and had plans for further performances not involving him. Still, the modest public and critical *succès d'estime* at least made it slightly more bearable that, despite Libman's best efforts, the concerts had left him several thousand dollars out of pocket, as he reported mournfully to Boulez three days after the last of them. A fourth concert, tentatively arranged for the 23rd, had long since been cancelled.

It was little more than a paper disaster. On the day of the Carnegie Hall concert, Stravinsky made a ten-minute recording for television in a CBS "Leonard Bernstein and the New York Philharmonic" program and earned four thousand dollars—double his net loss on the concerts—for conducting a few excerpts from *The Firebird*.[73] On the same program, a brilliant, idiosyncratic Canadian pianist named Glenn Gould played the first movement of Bach's D minor concerto, and the two musicians met briefly. Bernstein linked the program with some remarks about "the role of conductors, instrumentalists and soloists to freely interpret the composer's music as the artist felt it, and to perform the music in that manner."[74] But Stravinsky had probably left the studio by then.

"THERE ARE MANY who believe," Jay Harrison had written, "that Robert Craft holds the most enviable position in the world of music. He is Igor Stravinsky's closest friend, his confidant, amanuensis, spokesman and fellow conductor."[1] Enviable or not, Craft's position increasingly aroused ill feeling. Lang's review was symptomatic. Without mentioning Craft by name, he plainly suggested that Stravinsky was being manipulated and that third parties were using him to advance their own careers. Some of the composer's oldest friends grumbled among themselves that they no longer had direct access to him but were constantly running up against this young Cerberus, who answered the phone, read all Stravinsky's letters, and organized his diary. Darius Milhaud, who had been responsible for the joke about the Devil and Craft, had recently managed to see Igor and Vera "*without* Craft." "You know," he wrote to Poulenc, "that one is never sure if one can get near him or not these days." But they had contrived a meeting at Jascha Heifetz's in Pacific Palisades. They had found Stravinsky much aged, and with an "end of the road" feeling about him. "We were very sad, Mady and I, to see him in this state, but we spent an exquisite afternoon with a rediscovered Igor, and without his frightful Mentor."[2] Even Stravinsky's own family found themselves cast as supplicants. "We learned gradually," Soulima told Thor Wood many years later, "that things were done through Craft. Craft wanted something. He told Vera, Vera told Igor and Igor had his reaction accordingly. That was the pattern."[3]

Craft was omnipresent. Concert promoters who wanted to book Stravinsky were now routinely forced to accept the younger man as part of the deal, just as, in earlier times, they had often been put under pressure to take Soulima as soloist or (which still sometimes happened) Theodore as stage designer. Few of these promoters would have engaged Craft at that time on the strength of his own reputation or experience as a conductor; but it was no less obvious that without him Stravinsky could scarcely have persevered as a conductor at all. It was like a miniature ecosystem. The whole cycle depended on a combination of high fees, a low-paid assistant, and tax-deductible expenses. Since his stroke in 1956, Stravinsky had felt unequal to the physical and mental strain of preparing and conducting whole concerts. But part concerts were not in question; they were hopeless promotionally and unhelpful logistically. The system depended on the undiluted idea of the "Stravinsky Concert," and the advantage of Craft was that he could be dripped into that idea—like water into strong beer—without detracting noticeably from its flavor. The fee was to all intents and purposes appearance money, so it was immaterial that Craft did the lion's share of the rehearsing; and since audiences mostly had little idea who this young man was in any case, his presence on the rostrum was no more than a teasing distraction from the star turn. As long as they had a substantial and sufficiently thrilling view of the master himself, they were reasonably content.

These considerations also applied, if rather differently, in the recording studio. You could not on the whole sell records of Craft conducting Stravinsky; or rather, you could not sell records described as conducted by Craft. But since the distinction between rehearsal and performance was less clear-cut in the studio than in the concert hall, and since, above all, the conductor of a recording was not on view, the role of the assistant was more fluid and in the end probably greater. By 1960, Craft was not only preparing the performances of which Stravinsky would then conduct the official takes, he was also editing final versions, often alone with a studio technician.[4] There is some evidence that the recording of *Petrushka*, in February 1960, was produced under these conditions.[5] At their disposal would be, of course, the official takes; but there would also be "rehearsal" takes, since it was normal practice to run tape for whole sessions, without regard to who was conducting; so, cutting rooms being what they were, it seems virtually certain that takes conducted by Craft would regularly have found their way onto records eventually issued as conducted by Stravinsky. No recording logs were kept, so such matters cannot now be checked. But it is hard to suppose that Craft would not have availed himself of rehearsal takes to plug inadequacies in the composer's performances if the alternative was to issue a defective performance or else scrap an entire project.

Craft's role as a conductor was thus large and, in the nature of things, growing; but it was covert. The suggestion that he was engaged in some cynical scheme to advance his own conducting career simply does not bear scrutiny. On the contrary, his attachment to Stravinsky may well have served to block whatever prospects he might have had as a conductor in his own right, since it made it appear that he could only get work through that channel. Friends warned him of the danger;[6] his answer was that he was well aware of it but could not abandon the Stravinskys—that he was too necessary to them. And in a sense it was true. Without Craft, Stravinsky could not have toured, could scarcely have accepted concert dates, and could have recorded only with difficulty. He might have stayed at home, composed more, worried less, and lived more frugally, except that, but for Craft, his creative life might well have ended when he was seventy. In indifferent health, deprived of any strong raison d'être, he might then and there have wasted away and died, full of years and respectable honor, but left behind by history and forgotten by the young, to whom he so desperately wanted to remain important. To those friends and colleagues who expressed astonishment at the composer's schedule and urged him to moderate it, Craft could, and perhaps did, reply that retirement would kill Stravinsky more swiftly than any amount of work or travel. Or perhaps he claimed that the matter was not in his hands, that he was merely the agent of Stravinsky's and Vera's own wishes. This would surely have been no better than half true. For both—or all three—of them there was something inexorable in the situation, something none of them could alter without fatally undermining the other two.

As far as Craft was concerned, what was taking place was something like a process of absorption into Stravinsky's personality. Nervy, emotionally insecure, a prey to resentment and self-loathing, he was finding it possible to escape from himself only by creating a persona partly borrowed from unused fragments of Stravinsky. This persona soon assumed a fascinating life of its own. One of its favorite activities was writing letters to newspapers, something that Stravinsky himself had rarely done in the past. Its first excursion into this medium may well have been the draft letter to the *NZfM* that Stravinsky had shown to Souvtchinsky in March 1959 but had never actually sent to the journal itself. Early in February 1960 another, much longer, missive winged its way to the editor of the *Saturday Review*, "correcting" a number of errors in an earlier letter to the editor about Stravinsky's attitude to Disney's adaptation of *The Rite of Spring* for *Fantasia*.[7] The fact that most of the corrections are either misleading or simply wrong does not, of course, prove that Stravinsky did not write the letter.[8] But the corrective form itself, and the fact that its information is partly derived from an examination of old documents (in this case a contract), to say nothing of the brilliantly assured English, point strongly to the hand of that other persona. It was an idiom that Craft would later make definitively his own, but at this early stage the precise authorship is hard to establish for certain. One is only sure that Stravinsky himself did not simply sit down, as most people would, and knock out a text of his own.

A few weeks after the publication of this letter, the joint persona reappeared in the more rounded and substantial form of a second volume of conversations, under the title *Memories and Commentaries*. Like the first volume, the new book was a sparkling mixture of reminiscence and opinion, but with more emphasis, now, on autobiography. In particular it contains

Stravinsky's first account of his childhood, his home and family, his schooling, university, and early musical tuition, plus further reminiscences of Diaghilev, Nijinsky, the Ballets Russes, and various Russian composers he had known.[9] There is also a musical section, including some mildly technical discussion (with music examples), and finally a section called "Three Operas," with correspondence about *The Nightingale* (with Benois, its first designer), *Persephone* (with Gide), and *The Rake's Progress* (with Auden, including also the draft first scenario). There is a lot here that Craft could not have known, and although Stravinsky's memory is unreliable, selective, and sometimes downright tendentious, the biases are consistent with his known attitudes pre-Craft. For instance, his remark that "I never could love a bar of [Scriabin's] bombastic music," though disingenuous, repeats an opinion he had been putting about for almost forty years, while his jaundiced picture of his home life as a child is much as he had described it to Souvtchinsky when they met in Berlin in 1922.[10]

Even so, the evidence of the surviving drafts (fewer for *Mem* than for *Conv*) is that most of the actual texts were written by Craft, sometimes with crude errors or sheer inventions that Stravinsky corrected on the typescript.[11] Moreover, the discussion of musical issues increasingly reflects preoccupations of Craft's own: the fussing over rhythmic constructivism in Stockhausen's *Gruppen,* the detailed parallels between textural intricacies in *Movements* and the complexities of fifteenth-century polyphony, the quotations from Huizinga and the letters of Webern. Not that Stravinsky necessarily did not know or talk about such things; but the kind of suave, scholarly, organized thinking seems to belong to a more detached, professorial mind, a mind attracted by the omniscience of the academy rather than the candid prejudices of the artist's workshop: the mind, perhaps, of that other persona. By now, one feels, Craft is beginning to cobble together the composer's table talk, occasionally bulking it out with answers to actual questions, linking it with threads of his own devising, and enlivening it with the verbal acrobatics of the born writer. One cannot yet say that Stravinsky himself is absent or misrepresented. But the conditions are established under which he will later be able to recede into the background, and then, later still, vanish completely.

For the time being, Craft is the one who stays in the shadows. Whether you look at the conversations or the letters, the recordings or the concerts, his presence is elusive. He is the "Robert" of Lillian Libman's memoirs, with his "talent for dematerializing at airports, docks, and hotels."[12] But there was also a much more definite, tangible Robert. This was the real Craft, who took the day-to-day decisions on contracts and itineraries, warded off callers, dominated mealtime conversation with his seemingly boundless college-boy erudition, his quick, lateral brain, and his encyclopedic memory; the hypertense, excitable Craft who sometimes astonished colleagues and bystanders by the abrupt rudeness of his manner to orchestral players, even to Stravinsky himself, and who certainly did not meekly acquiesce, as a paid factotum might do, in the wishes or needs of his employer. There was even something disturbing in the apparent contrast between his coolly deferential way of addressing, or referring to, Igor and Vera—"Mr. Stravinsky" and "Madame"—and the sometimes abrasive closeness of his relationship with them, like that of a widowed son-in-law. The avoidance of first names seemed to draw attention to his reluctance to adopt the still more intimate forms of address that would have been appropriate. Yet some thought their mutual affection went beyond that of ordinary blood relatives. Close friends noticed that he and Vera sometimes held hands, and that Stravinsky was upset by it.[13] Stephen Spender, who adored all three of them, thought that they were "all in love with each other, like the characters in a Henry James novel."[14]

This closeness certainly caused pain, and in due course it would cause trouble. Madame, whose affection for Craft had grown at least maternal and included a powerful strain of possessiveness, had to watch and endure a trail of affairs with nubile young girls, one or two of which did in fact come close to marriage. She was not invariably calm about it. The chic and beautiful Vera, now somewhat stout but with her radiant social charm apparently untarnished by her seventy years, could in private be offhand and uncommunicative if she chose. By the people they met and the life they led she was frequently bored to distraction. She loathed hotels and concert tours and detested California, and though she still loved painting and painted well, she must have known that the effortless exhibitions, the crowded vernissages and easy sales, were in honor more of her husband's work than of her own. She can hardly have enjoyed seeing the talented, attractive, yet deeply vulnerable Craft courting and being courted by lovely girls with titled mothers or rich fathers—girls with whom she sometimes had to share long car journeys and to whom she must needs make herself agreeable.

Craft, to judge by what he later wrote, idealized both Vera and her marriage: "as nearly perfect a match as can be imagined."[15] His tenderness toward her leaps off the page, in his descriptions of her art, her personality, above all her closeness and importance to her husband's music. Not once does he separate them; he drives no posthumous wedges. But that there were domestic explosions cannot be doubted, and as often as not it was Craft who exploded. On one occasion, in a rage about something, he hurled a score at Stravinsky, and when Milène, who was present, asked her father why he put up with such behavior, he merely shrugged helplessly.[16] Ingolf Dahl's wife, Etta, told Lawrence Morton about a row at a rehearsal for *Les Noces* in the Royce Hall in June 1960. Stravinsky had wanted to make a point to Craft, who was conducting, but "Bob just let him stand there apologetically for four minutes while he dressed down the percussion in dreadfully insulting language."[17] With all such tales, needless to say, one has to remember the possible motives of the tellers. Etta Dahl, as her letter shows, disliked Craft, whether because she felt he had displaced her husband in Stravinsky's counsels or for some less tangible reason. Denise Strawinsky, who claims to have witnessed the score-throwing incident, had obvious grounds for resenting Craft's influence over her father-in-law (which is not of course to say that she did resent it). A more neutral witness, nevertheless, is Morton himself. He had no evident ulterior motive and seems to have remained on good terms with Craft, who later trusted him with highly indiscreet confidences. But when Stravinsky dedicated his *Eight Instrumental Miniatures* to Morton in 1962, Morton rhetorically asked himself why, and surmised that it was "maybe because I am not rude to him as Craft is . . ."[18]

Morton liked Craft personally, but became increasingly annoyed by his manner to the outside world, which he attributed to "envy of his betters."[19] Why this should have made Craft short-tempered with Stravinsky is open to question, but Stravinsky himself made up his mind that it was due to his inability to match Craft's erudition. He even wrote himself a curious little note to this effect: "Suffering constantly from his (RC) simultaneous respect and vexation. The latter—result of my total ignorance which upsets him and me even more. If I would be able only to accept this my ignorance as a fact, to recognize it and behave accordingly, my amour propre would disappear and I will not suffer any more. What a relief! March 26/60."[20] It is difficult to decide which is more bizarre: the explanation or the act of writing it down and dating it, as if it were a message in a bottle from Odysseus on Calypso's island. But it hardly takes a psychoanalyst to see that the real Homeric parallel is with Oedipus, and that Craft's occasional aggressiveness is typically filial and prompted by resentment at the powerful father figure's slowness and obstructiveness. But then, to reduce such a relationship to Freudian generalities is certainly not the way to understand its intricacies. The fact is that, by 1960, Craft's affection for Stravinsky was tinged with ferocity; that a number of people observed this and attached their own meaning to it; and that in due course these interpretations began to imply a certain view of the young man's relations with Vera as well as with Igor.

Within Stravinsky's own family, the Craft situation had long since been accepted, even if not exactly liked. Why should the children of a first marriage be at ease with the second wife or with what amounts to an adoptive stepbrother from an utterly different social and cultural milieu? And yet relations with Vera had remained warm and contacts with Craft apparently equable. Milène, living nearby, saw her father most, probably several times a week, and when he was away on tour they corresponded in a manner that now seems completely natural and loving, invariably in French, a language with which she was these days more at home than with Russian. Her letters often mention Vera, never with the slightest hint of rancor. Sometimes she wrote to Vera, who herself wrote at least as often as her husband. Milène thanks her for sending a book of photographs from Italy: "How kind of you to send it me. You must have thought when you saw it, 'That's just right for Milène,' and that's what really pleased me most."[21] André was still working for a local travel agent, while helping with Wetherly Drive correspondence after hours. Two or three years earlier there had been a disagreeable incident over Venice hotel bookings that André was supposed to be handling through his Hollywood agency but that Stravinsky had unwittingly short-circuited by writing direct to the hotel. André had sent a sharp note of complaint, and a chill had descended on their relations, which only lifted when Milène interceded with a long and tender apologia for her husband, imploring her father not to hold his lack of finesse against him.[22] In reporting such exchanges, Craft is apt to give the impression that they were recurrent and that Stravinsky regarded his children and their spouses as at best a nuisance that had to be endured.[23] But that is because he for the most part ignores the voluminous evidence of Stravinsky's actual and—when one reads the correspondence in extenso—very obvious love and concern. One might add that his accounts of such incidents (and there will be more of them) have a nasty flavor of triumphalism, of using access to print in order to damage those who, not being publishable writers, have no reasonable means of reply. Perhaps he has been fortunate that this was the case, since it is a game that more than one can play.

One of Craft's favorite targets has been the fact that the children received frequent cash subsidies from their father, some volunteered, some solicited. It would certainly have been bizarre if the composer, who by 1960 had a six-figure income, had not made gifts to his children, two of whom were in America at his behest, while the other was a struggling artist with a wife and adopted daughter, both of whom enjoyed indifferent health. This son, moreover, often did concert-agency work for his father in Europe, which meant that payments to him were tax deductible. If sons' requests for money from their rich parents were routinely to become the subject of disapproving footnotes in learned publications, the world would certainly grind rapidly to a halt on its axis. In any case, the issue was more complicated than that. Stravinsky was also using Theodore as agent for the sale of certain of his manuscripts to European buyers, transactions that he was anxious to avoid attracting the attention of the U.S. revenue service. Possibly Craft was unaware of the details of these sales, since Stravinsky instructed Theodore always to write to him in Russian where bank transactions were in question,[24] and it may even be that this circumstance induced mild feelings of paranoia in a man who had become so used to sifting and filtering the composer's correspondence, yet who, remarkably enough, seems never to have made the slightest effort to learn his language. Stravinsky could be a fierce taskmaster over such commissions, and harsh words sometimes flew back and forth across the Atlantic Ocean because in the father's opinion the son had misconstrued his instructions, or had acted on his own authority or in a highhanded manner. He remained touchy on money questions, perhaps because he was nervous about the doubtful legality of his proceedings, or because he remembered Theodore's subterfuge over the family money just before the war.[25] Nevertheless he duly paid Theodore a fair commission for anything he sold; and he duly deducted that sum from his taxes under some other guise.

STRAVINSKY had at last told Sacher in November 1959 that he would be starting the long-promised commission that coming February, by which time he would be back in Hollywood after the New York concerts; but he was as yet unable to say what kind of work it would be. For the Eliot project he was still thinking of Noah and had started leafing through the York Miracle Plays. But there was no question of this for Sacher, and meanwhile the Graff project hung fire presumably because of Eliot's continuing reluctance to commit himself. Stravinsky had even had other biblical ideas. As an alternative to Noah, he had as we saw been thinking about Tobias and the Angel, the very subject that, twenty years before, Claudel had wanted and he had not.[26] He had also recently been approached by an organization called the Festival of Faith and Freedom for an hour-long "oratorio-symphony" on a New Testament subject, and he had counter-proposed a thirty-minute setting of the Seven Last Words.[27] Nothing had come of that particular commission, but the general idea lingered, and by the time they got back to Los Angeles at the end of January, a rather different New Testament subject was taking shape in his mind, based on the martyrdom of St. Stephen in the Acts of the Apostles. On the 29th he announced it to Sacher as a twenty-minute cantata and demanded the impressive sum of twenty thousand dollars "in view of punitive taxes."[28]

This seemingly unmotivated piece of blackmail was in fact intimately linked to the television project. Nothing was yet signed with Graff, but Stravinsky knew that he would be able to ask a big fee for such a high-profile work, and since Graff was now talking about a production date in March 1961, the composer needed to make up his mind quickly which of the two commissions should take precedence. He accordingly made encouraging but noncommittal noises to Graff while waiting on Sacher;

then, when Sacher replied in mid-February raising no difficulty about the fee, he let Graff know that the TV commission would have to wait a year.[29] This was inconvenient for Graff, who had just left NBC to take up the presidency of an independent production company called Sextant, and who wanted to sell an option in the new work to CBS. Soon he and Lillian Libman, acting for the composer, were locked in heady negotiations about the whole character of the work, the time scale, the involvement of Balanchine and Craft, and naturally the vexed question of rights, for which there were few if any precedents with a composer of Stravinsky's standing. Graff showed his impatience. At one point in April he issued a press release calling the work a ballet and announcing a recording date in the summer of 1961. Stravinsky reacted with irritation on both counts. He had always refused to compose a ballet, he reminded Libman, and repeated what he had long since told Graff, that the concept was hybrid, like *Persephone*, with dancing only in certain episodes such as the scene of Noah's drunkenness—a new idea taken from the famous sculpture on the southeast angle of the Doge's Palace in Venice. As for the completion date, Stravinsky spelled out how little time his schedule allowed him. In the whole of 1960 he had only eight weeks left for composition. To write on a large scale was barely possible for him any longer, to write to a tight deadline still less so. He refused, in a word, to sign to any delivery date before 1962.[30] Somehow Libman got round these difficulties. The contract, that May, still effectively specified late summer 1961 (in that the work had to be "staged, choreographed, rehearsed and videotaped" by the 1st of January 1962), though Stravinsky knew he could not meet such a deadline; it gave him twenty-five thousand dollars and Craft two and a half thousand plus another two if he ended up conducting; and all this for twenty-five minutes' music and a "documentary" appearance in an introductory film about the work. Craft, for one, was already earning his share. In New York in early May he had a series of meetings with Graff in which he explained in some detail the character and design of the work Stravinsky envisaged, the ideas behind it, and how it would adapt to the needs of television.[31] In return, Sextant got generous exclusivities: so generous, in fact, that when Ernst Roth saw the agreement he nearly had apoplexy. "Sign nothing till I see you in Venice," the publisher wrote anxiously at the beginning of July.[32] Not for the first time in his long life, Stravinsky had been selling somebody else's property.

He had meanwhile started sketching his Basle cantata in early February; but there had then come an unexpected, apparently unplanned interruption. Possibly because he was having difficulty imagining himself back into a feasible vocal idiom from the abstractions of *Movements*, he started making an instrumental transcription of a set of three madrigals by Gesualdo. No doubt the immediate trigger for this self-imposed task was the recent issue of a selection of the madrigals conducted by Craft himself. But Craft seems not to have been responsible for the idea of the arrangements, for all Stravinsky's dedication in the score: "To Bob, who forced me to do it, and I did it." On the contrary, Craft told Glenn Watkins, Stravinsky had done the work without his knowledge. What was more, he had found it one of the hardest things he had ever attempted, "a definition of what is vocal and what instrumental."[33] It turned out that what could seem radical and challenging when sung tended to sound pallid when transferred to instruments. So Stravinsky had found himself spicing up the counterpoint, switching parts, adding dissonances, and eventually even to an appreciable extent recomposing the originals. Having completed the exercise in mid-March, and noticing that 1960 was the four-hundredth anniversary of Gesualdo's birth, he promptly labelled it ceremoniously *Monumentum pro Gesualdo di Venosa ad CD annum,* then turned once again to his Sacher cantata.[34]

Whether or not Stravinsky saw his Gesualdo arrangement as a study for the cantata, there is little or nothing in the cantata itself to suggest a connection. The instrumental introduction to the first movement is in the same style as *Movements*—it even has a spiky little flute solo early on—and when the six-part choir enters, singing Pauline texts about faith and hope selected by Craft[35] from Romans and Hebrews, its music is not much less angular melodically, just rhythmically less intricate. What is not clear is how far, at this stage, Stravinsky had mapped out the whole work. The "Sermon," as he called the first movement, was probably finished by early May, after which he embarked fairly promptly on the longer second movement, a quasi-dramatic account of the stoning of St. Stephen, from The Acts of the Apostles. It was the first time he had set English words since *In Memoriam Dylan Thomas,* and he seems not to have found it all that easy to reconcile a straightforward narrative with the "anti-tonalism" (as he liked to call it) of his latest idiom. At least half the words are declaimed by a speaker, somewhat in the manner of his miniature wartime cantata, *Babel,* and a device which, barely a year earlier, he had denounced in print.[36] Nevertheless by the end of June he was able to report to Ernst Roth that he had written much of the "Narrative," but had not yet orchestrated it.[37] The problem, as ever, was that the second half of the year was going to be the nomadic half, and this year they would literally be away for six months, in various parts of the northern and southern hemispheres. He now knew the work's title: *A Sermon, a Narrative, and a Prayer;* but he also knew that, having composed nearly half of it, he had no hope of finishing the other half until 1961.[38]

Just as he was grappling with the vocal implications of this new advanced style of his, he "felt the air," in Stefan Georg's phrase, "of other planets."[39] A letter arrived from a twenty-two-year-old conductor in Kiev by the name of

Igor Blazhkov, begging him to send copies of his works, most of which were still unobtainable in the Soviet Union. Blazhkov described the dismal situation in Soviet music, dominated by apparatchiks from Stalinist times who were scared of anything new and still expended much of their energy blackening the names of composers like Prokofiev, Myaskovsky, Shostakovich, and Stravinsky himself. It grieved him, he said, to have to write in this way; but he was not without hope "that in some ten or fifteen years all this will be a distant memory. And we will achieve this—we, the young! Oh! We have marvelous young people!"[40]

By an odd coincidence, this was the second such approach Stravinsky had had from the U.S.S.R. within a matter of months. Back in September, just when Blazhkov was posting his letter in Kiev, Souvtchinsky had passed on a similar request from the Moscow pianist Mariya Yudina.[41] Now, Yudina was a personage very different from Blazhkov. Though unknown in the West, she was a prominent musician and a notorious figure in the Soviet Union, sixty years old, and with a long history of speaking out in favor of precisely the kind of music that Blazhkov was longing to advocate on behalf of young Kiev. She had continued to play and defend modern piano music, including Stravinsky's and Schoenberg's, and in the early days had even, according to Souvtchinsky, broken with Max Steinberg, her composition teacher and Stravinsky's estranged fellow Rimsky-Korsakov pupil, over this very issue. The Soviet authorities had adopted the tactic of treating her as not quite right in the head. She was a kind of *yurodivy*—a holy fool—in an age when any show of religiosity was officially forbidden. It was even said that she would sometimes kneel down and pray in the street. But to Souvtchinsky her importance was more practical. While nominally professor of chamber music at the Moscow Conservatoire, she used her position to promote modern music and had at her disposal "fine instrumentalists and many young composers, thirsting to get to know and study the 'new' music." She was just the kind of disadvantaged musician Stravinsky should be trying to encourage.

Stravinsky may not have realized the fact, but Blazhkov and Yudina were alike, in their different ways, a symptom of a gradual change in the artistic climate in the Soviet Union since Stalin's death in 1953. Ten years earlier a letter like Blazhkov's would have been unpostable; it would have been stopped, opened, and read, and the consequences for its writer might well have been fatal. The mere fact of receiving such a letter with such contents was evidence of a significant cultural shift, however depressing the situation it described. Unfortunately the most recent news about the Soviet art scene had been dominated by the aftermath of the award of the Nobel Prize to Boris Pasternak for his novel *Doctor Zhivago* in 1958. In fact it was on Pasternak's recommendation that Yudina had written to Souvtchinsky. But pressure had been exerted on Pasternak to refuse the award, and now he was being charged with treason, as Nika Nabokov had informed Stravinsky in September.[42] Stravinsky himself disliked *Zhivago*: "pure *peredvizhnichestvo* [nineteenth-century realism]," he called it, adding that it was "strange to read this in the century of James Joyce."[43] If such a novel was regarded as subversive—albeit for its contents rather than its style—what hope was there for his music (old or new), which satisfied hardly any of the criteria apparently thought desirable by the Soviet cultural trendsetters? He did send scores to both Yudina and Blazhkov, and continued to do so; but it was more out of generosity to struggling admirers than in any serious hope that it would do him or his music much good in the long run.

SANTA FE in July 1960 focused on a new production of *Oedipus Rex* directed by Hans Busch, with Stravinsky conducting, and again there was a "free" cathedral concert, this time with the *Symphony of Psalms*.[44] But all this was little more than a prelude to an extended and, in the view of many of his friends, pointless trip to Mexico and South America in the late (northern) summer. Roth declared himself "stupefied" by the thought of the tour;[45] when it was over Souvtchinsky asked Vera how she could survive "this brutal touring schedule."[46] In fact the idea of the trip had started as a holiday in Argentina at the invitation of Victoria Ocampo. Stravinsky was supposed to be the guest of a film festival in Buenos Aires, which would pay his travel costs but impose no duties and require no public appearances. At some point in January, he started having doubts; on the 27th he wrote to Ocampo that he might have to cancel on doctors' orders, and on the same day he told Souvtchinsky that the trip was off.[47] Yet a month later he again wrote to Souvtchinsky that they had been invited for a six-week concert tour and were going. Craft maintained afterwards that the true motive for the trip was to see Ocampo and other friends in Argentina and Chile and for Vera to visit her stepmother in Buenos Aires.[48] But when Isherwood dined with them in late March he found that Vera was dreading the tour; Craft had hepatitis, and claimed he did not want to go and that only Stravinsky himself was wedded to the idea.[49] Vera's own diagnosis was that Igor was "so accustomed to being a great celebrity that he feels he has to keep making public appearances."[50] Meanwhile, Mirandi Masocco had told Isherwood that Craft "is the one who's determined that it shall go through!"[51]

The real reason for the sudden volte face in February and the subsequent reluctance to withdraw was almost certainly once again financial. Within weeks of the cancellation of the Argentine holiday, Lillian Libman had negotiated an extremely lucrative contract with a Lima-based concert agent called Oscar Alcazar for a seven-week tour, which, if carried out to the letter, would have earned Stravinsky more than forty thousand dollars.[52] It was in every sense a celebrity affair. Libman was good at organizing the VIP aspects of airport lounges and hotel check-ins and at dealing with awkward agents and obstructive bureaucrats. At every airport they were greeted by cheering crowds, reporters, photographers. At their first port of call, Mexico City, a posse of government ministers and embassy officials, delegations of musicians and orchestra representatives "marched onto the airfield followed by a huge crowd of fans who broke through the tapes and, waving American and Mexican flags, shouted '*Viva* Stravinsky!' Above this roar of welcome, a high-school band, stationed at the head of the lane that led to the terminal building, rendered a *fortissimo* version of excerpts from *Petrushka*."[53] Stravinsky adored these demonstrations and played along with them like a ham actor, saluting the crowd, posing for the cameras, and saying quotable things in praise of his hosts. But behind the scenes, what was said was often less quotable. When it came to payment, Alcazar sometimes proved awkward, and there were rows.[54] The altitude in Mexico and, especially, Bogotá (nearly nine thousand feet above sea level) was troublesome, and the orchestras were mediocre or worse. Craft, who conducted all the rehearsals on the tour, thought the Lima orchestra the worst ever.[55] In Santiago, the horn player came in on a glaringly wrong note in his solo at the start of the finale of *The Firebird,* and in Buenos Aires the final tableau of *Petrushka* broke down and had to be restarted. At least in the Argentine capital the political rows of 1936 were quite forgotten, and the government invested Stravinsky with the Order of Maya (omitting, regrettably, to invite his wife to the ceremony). Nevertheless by the time they reached Rio de Janeiro on 4 September they had had enough of hotels, orchestras, braided officials, and quarrelsome agents, and they decided to abort the rest of the tour and fly straight to New York, abandoning their concerts in Rio and Caracas.

If the South American tour was artistically worthless and financially disappointing, the two-and-half-month European trip that followed was if anything even less productive. True, in Venice Stravinsky conducted the first performance of his *Monumentum pro Gesualdo* on 27 September. And Venice had a style of its own. In Mexico City he had been given a fireman's lift up the back stairs to the stage of the Bellas Artes, but in Venice he was borne up to the Sala del Scrutinio of the Doge's Palace in a sedan chair carried by two strong men. Yet his unsolicited seven-minute recomposition of music by a composer previously rejected by the Venice Biennale would never have justified an Atlantic crossing on its own; and otherwise there was nothing but a pair of concerts in Genoa in mid-November, one in

Rome, and one in Palermo in December, which, when it came to the point, Stravinsky could not face and cancelled on the pretext of having to return to New York for blood tests.[56]

It is also true that in Venice he could compose, even if, as he once remarked, it was hard to compose his "dry" music in such a humid place.[57] After the *Monumentum* concert he worked on the "Narrative" of his Basle cantata, and by the time they left Venice at the start of November he had finished the whole movement in fair copy. He loved Venice for its own sake, even when—as on this visit—it was under water for a lot of the time, northern Italy having once again had heavy rains that autumn. They were so happy here that they started thinking of moving back to Europe for good, something they had contemplated from time to time over the past four or five years but had usually decided against for fear of European doctors. Vera had never made any bones about wanting to live in Paris again.[58] There had been a moment when Igor had taken definite steps to acquire a house in Monaco.[59] The latest scheme was to move to Campione, on the Swiss shore of Lake Lugano but actually an Italian enclave, a notorious tax haven that encouraged rich foreign residents. The only snags from Stravinsky's point of view were that there were few if any houses to be bought there (so he would have to live in an apartment), and that he would probably have to give up his American citizenship to avoid U.S. taxes.[60]

In the end nothing ever came of these ambitious ideas. As the composer contemplated the swollen canals of Venice, no fiscal ark floated into view. All that rose from the waters was the title of his next work: not *Noah*, of course, but *The Flood*.

SINKING THE ARK ▬

STRAVINSKY could not swim, and somewhere in his consciousness he feared the rising waters. In his third book of conversations, completed in draft by the autumn of 1960, he recalled the floods to which St. Petersburg—itself a canal city—was prone, and the intimations of death he had felt there in the wheeling of the seagulls. In Thomas Dekker's prayer book *Foure Birds of Noah's Ark* he found a prayer that struck a chord:

> Oh My God, if it Bee Thy Pleasure to cut me off before night, yet make me, my Gracious Shepherd, for one of Thy lambs to whom Thou wilt say "Come you blessed," and clothe me in a white robe of righteousness, that I may be one of those singers who shall cry to Thee, Alleluia.[1]

He would use this prayer, not in *The Flood,* but for the final part of his Basle cantata, in the spirit of a funerary intercession for St. Stephen, whose martyrdom has just been described in the "Narrative." Meanwhile, on the ship that bore them from Le Havre to New York in the first week of December, he and Craft polished the libretto for *The Flood* itself, a text that says curiously little about water or rain but a good deal about boats.

Early in 1960 Rolf Liebermann had left the North German Radio, where he had tried and failed to capture the European premiere of *Movements,* and taken over as administrator of the Hamburg State Opera, on whose behalf he was soon urging Stravinsky to write another opera. "If I live as long as Verdi and have his strength, I might well do it," the seventy-eight-year-old composer had replied, forgetting that at that age Verdi had already written more than half of *Falstaff,* his last opera. Now Liebermann had a better idea. He would take *The Flood* and stage it at the Hamburg Opera, perhaps in honor of Stravinsky's eightieth birthday in 1962. The fact that not a note of the music had yet been written seems not to have troubled him in the slightest. He had made up his mind that it would be a reasonable evening's entertainment; Günther Rennert would direct it and he would engage Marc Chagall, with his genius for religious imagery, to do the designs. As Stravinsky was in Paris for a few days at the end of November en route from Rome to Le Havre, Liebermann arranged for him to meet Chagall for tea at Nika Nabokov's apartment.

The creative meeting of these two giants of Russian art entered Stravinsky legend mainly because of the reasons why it never took place. On the day in question the Stravinskys had been lunching at the Boule d'Or with Souvtchinsky and Boulez's former flat-mate, François-Michel, and they had somehow managed to dispatch (according to Craft's reminiscence, though in the nature of the story there seems no reason to believe his statistics) two bottles of champagne, three of claret, two of vodka, and an unspecified amount of Calvados.[2] The Chagall meeting had been fixed for half past five. At half past six Vera Stravinsky phoned to say that her husband was in bed in a drunken stupor. "It is impossible to wake him." Craft was also drunk, and in the end Vera kept the appointment alone. "At two o'clock in the morning," Liebermann's account goes on,

> the phone rang. Stravinsky had woken up and with a terrible thirst. He wanted to booze with me. At his hotel, in his pajamas, Stravinsky was busying himself with two bottles of Dom Perignon on ice, waiting. I tried one last time to arrange matters. "Listen, Igor. Telephone Chagall or drop him a note." "Impossible," he snapped. "I don't want any decors by that *con*."[3]

The incident reflected a hostility on Stravinsky's part to the whole idea of staging *The Flood*. Liebermann was obviously thinking of it in operatic terms, while ever since his first discussions with Graff, Stravinsky had been trying to evade the stereotypes that impresarios and publicists were always trying to impose on works of uncertain or hybrid genre. He was also still resisting deadlines. Two months after the failed Paris meeting, he wrote to Liebermann from Hollywood reminding him that he had still not begun composing the music, that the work was not an opera but "a stage, theatrical work commissioned directly for television," and that it would have "narration and ballet but not much singing."[4] This touched on the contractual problem that had aroused Roth's fury back in the summer. Stravinsky did not have the right to assign the television rights in his music without his publisher's permission; and just as Roth had opposed the idea of a quick-profit recording of *The Rake's Progress* that would have spoilt its chances in the theatre, so he now pointed out that a twenty-year TV exclusivity for Sextant would seriously damage *The Flood* in live performance.[5] Liebermann was already a case in point. His Hamburg production would depend on local television, which the Sextant deal as originally proposed would have blocked. Roth wanted to reduce their exclusivity to five years, reserve the stage rights, and force Sextant to permit local television deals in conjunction with theatrical performances.[6] Before a note was composed and with the ink still wet on Craft's libretto, *The Flood* had become a promotional battleground.

Meanwhile the long break from serious composition at last drew to a close. After arriving in New York on 7 December, they were in Washington for a few days at the end of the year for a concert performance and recording of *The Nightingale* and *Oedipus Rex*, then back in New York for a week to record the Octet. There they also went to see Balanchine's dance version of *Monumentum* at City Center, a choreography done, Craft claimed, at his suggestion, but apparently without any direct participation from the composer.[7] "I never discussed this score with Balanchine," Stravinsky wrote on a cutting of a photograph in the *New York Herald Tribune*, which purported to show the two men studying the work together.[8] In his New York hotel, the St. Regis, he ran into Salvador Dalí, who had a suite on the same floor, and would ostentatiously emerge when the Stravinskys came along the corridor, ringing a little silver bell in order—he eventually had to explain—to attract attention to his long waxed moustaches.[9] Once before, in 1952, Dalí had proposed a ballet collaboration with Stravinsky.[10] Now he had an idea for what Craft mysteriously calls "a lucrative theatrical venture." Of its character, nothing is known, but it looks as if the enthusiasm (lucre notwithstanding) was entirely on the painter's side. Stravinsky was irritated by Dalí's gift of a book of his work with a line drawing and inscription describing himself as "Inconditionaliste Anti Neo-Clasique" [*sic*] and by Dalí's habit of whistling "Frère Jacques" loudly every time he returned to his room.[11] Perhaps it was precisely Dalí's "conditions" or lack of them that Stravinsky disliked. As for the anti-neoclassicism, that managed to be at once unshocking and rather pointedly insulting.

Back in Hollywood, in the second week of January, Stravinsky was soon immersed in more recordings, not all of them particularly to his liking. Having just done *The Nightingale,* he was now faced with the complete *Firebird,* which Columbia wanted as a flagship recording for their record-club subscription sales, but which to him was a mere pointless irrelevancy while he was trying to compose the last movement of his Basle cantata.[12] And how, he asked Souvtchinsky despairingly, "can one allow the composer of *Canticum sacrum, Agon, Threni,* and *Movements* to be fêted with *Firebird* and *Petrushka?*"[13] Here he was, juggling serial rotations for a funeral setting of a seventeenth-century prayer, while the great American public steeled itself to the "modernism" of the golden apples and Kashchey's magic garden; and then it would be the Symphony in Three Movements, *The Soldier's Tale,* the Violin Concerto, and only the re-recording of *Movements* with the youthful Charles Rosen—Margrit Weber having finally been abandoned—to indicate that Stravinsky the composer had not been completely ousted by Stravinsky the conductor and raconteur.

In spite of these distractions, the cantata was at last finished by the end of January, eight months earlier than he had promised Sacher as recently as the previous June. This would be a relief to the Swiss conductor, who had begun to get cold feet about the likely difficulty of the choral parts after hearing *Movements,* or at least hearing about it from Boulez. But Stravinsky himself had always really foreseen completion early in 1961, which was when he had told Libman he would be able to start thinking about *The Flood.* The "Prayer," unlike the "Narrative," was an essentially compact concept, sixty bars of slow vocal melody and polyphony supported by a tocsin of gongs, harp, piano, and double-bass, with comparatively little variation in texture. Behind it lay the idea of a devout epitaph for the fallen martyr, but Stravinsky probably also had in mind two dear friends who had died in December: their near neighbor the eccentric and of late somewhat decrepit Baroness d'Erlanger, and the art-loving Episcopalian minister, James McLane, whom Stravinsky had first met in Denver in 1935, and with whom in recent years he and Vera had been on regular dining terms. McLane had read out the Dekker prayer, in his notoriously loud preacher's voice, one evening at North Wetherly Drive. So it was the most natural thing in the world for Stravinsky to compose the music in part as a tribute to him, and then to dedicate the movement to his memory.

Within days of completing *A Sermon, a Narrative, and a Prayer,* he had begun sketching *The Flood.* Craft had made a skilful, subeditorial conflation of different components of the Chester and York plays, with elements of Genesis thrown in. At the start, God would be praised in a Latin *Te Deum;* a narrator would briefly remind the audience of the story of the Creation, after which the myth of the Fall would be related in the words of the mystery plays. Only then would the actual Flood be enacted. It was a radically different conception from Britten's children's opera *Noye's Fludde* (first staged at Aldeburgh in 1958), which was a straightforward and rather homely setting of the Noah story in the Chester play. Craft's text was much less a story than a kind of homily. Noah, as Stravinsky had suggested to Eliot, was both a second Adam and a prefiguring of Christ, at once Fall and Redemption, and the Flood itself was "also *The Bomb.*" Craft himself had already discussed some of these issues with Graff several months before; now, while Stravinsky worked on the setting of the *Te Deum* and the Creation narrative, Craft added a substantial section on the work to the new set of conversations, *Expositions and Developments,* the draft of which he had already announced as complete in October.

The conclusion to be drawn from all this is that not just the text, but the whole shape and even certain aspects of the character and timing of the eventual score were Craft's own work. His notes on his meeting with Graff, in New York in early May 1960, already go into detail on the subject and its treatment, and at some later stage he made additional notes including section timings, ideas for decor and camera shots, and even suggestions for orchestration and style models.[14] Of course, the mere fact that a document is in Craft's hand does not prove that he was its author. In mid-April 1960, when Stravinsky was briefing Libman for a contractual meeting with Graff (no doubt with Craft's help), he was still refusing to commit himself on the work's exact genre or even its subject matter, despite Sextant's having just announced in a press release that it would be Noah.[15] But he was clear that the form would be hybrid, with "narration, chorus, soloists, incidental choreographic movement." "The difficulty is," he went on, "that I now see the necessity of re-studying the various texts and of compiling something different than I had thought of before [. . .]. I will try to work with Robert Craft on the libretto [. . .] during our travels." So it looks as if Craft's meetings with Graff a fortnight later were the direct outcome of discussions with Stravinsky; and probably the later document is similarly in the nature of minutes of conversations with the composer. As for the account in *Expo,* this plainly reflects the collaborative nature of the work-in-progress.[16] The intensity of Craft's involvement explains his willingness, not to say his ability, to write in detail about a work at such an early stage of its composition, something Stravinsky had never permitted in the past—not even with *Threni* or *Movements.*

The main *Expo* text talks about *The Flood* somewhat evasively as if it were a work for the theatre. "Remember," it has Stravinsky say, "that I am planning the preliminaries of a theatre piece, and speaking purely in theatrical terms!" But later a rather coy footnote admits that the work is for television and so has to be kept "very simple as music."[17] Stravinsky had watched quite enough television to know that, when it came to musical style, nothing he would be capable of writing could conceivably be simple enough for that particular audience; but some concession had to be made, and the best way to make it was by stripping down the scenario to its simplest elements, emphasizing the "child's Bible" imagery, and drawing attention to the contemporary "relevance" of the story. These were questions that had come up in Craft's early conversations with Graff. Craft's own solution to the problem, which was to simplify by compression within a rapid montage of scenes, might suggest that he had as little idea about popular taste as his master. Had he made the story into a genuine pantomime, with a proper menagerie of animal costumes, comic turns, and popular songs or hymns slipped into the action; or had he, alternatively, turned the Noah plot into a miniature sitcom or a sentimental verismo melodrama along the lines of Menotti's *Amahl and the Night Visitors* (almost the only successful television opera ever written), there might have been some hope of success, even with a modern musical idiom. Menotti's music, after all, is modern, if not quite in Stravinsky's sense. But the real reason for the libretto taking the form it did in any case had nothing, at bottom, to do with such considerations. Rather, it was a way of accommodating the needs of the commission to the aging composer's growing tendency toward the reductive and the short-winded. Graff had wanted an hour-long ballet. Stravinsky, as we know from his dealings with the Festival of Faith and Freedom, thought he might manage half that length on the Seven Last Words—at, presumably, four minutes per "Word."[18] Craft's *Flood* text, similarly, is a four-minutes-per-Word sort of compilation, and in the end Graff had to resign himself to a less-than-half-hour score padded out into a one-hour program with documentary material and sponsors' ads.

Stravinsky at last started on the composition in early February, after recording the Symphony in Three Movements. Within a month he had written the short introduction, described in *Expo,* but not the score, as "Representation of Chaos" (as in Haydn's *Creation*); the *Te Deum,* with its curious serial plainchant, a device Stravinsky had used before, in *Threni;* and the much-compressed Creation story itself—part narrated, part sung by a pair of basses as the Voice of God—up to the naming of Adam and Eve: not quite four minutes of rapid-transit modernism rendered more palatable, if not more gripping, by the chunks of unmediated speech. By an odd coincidence, at this very moment Stravinsky was recording the most famous of all his narrated works, *The Soldier's Tale,* as well as the most recent of his modernistic ones, *Movements,* with Rosen. To judge from the result, the *Movements* sessions went smoothly; but there must have been some tremors on the way, since Vera noted enigmatically in her diary: "recording: bad, bad," and the pianist himself wrote self-deprecatingly a week or two later, regretting "that it was not possible to realize the performance that I had hoped."[19]

Stravinsky continued to make steady progress with *The Flood,* interrupted only by a ten-day visit to Mexico at the start of April, a trip made memorable as much by the all-night Good Friday vigil at the convent at Taxco as by the two performances he conducted of *The Rite of Spring*—a work he seldom risked these days.[20] By early May he had composed the brilliant episode of the fall of Lucifer from the York cycle, together with the ensuing melodrama, a mere fragment on the temptation of Eve, cutting abruptly to the Chester version of God's resolve to destroy mankind and his injunction to Noah to build an ark. He was still having to ward off the anxious optimism of his various entrepreneurs. Liebermann had it firmly in his head that *The Flood* was to be a full-length stage work, and he was soon, to Stravinsky's fury, advertising it as such in the Hamburg schedule for 1961–2, despite the composer's disclaimers about its length and his refusal to admit that it would be ready in time.[21] Graff, meanwhile, was innocently proposing a recording date in September, by which time Stravinsky would be in Europe at the start of his usual manic autumn touring schedule, and with the new work no more than two-thirds finished.[22] Even to get that far would involve composing the "Catalogue of the Animals" in Santa Fe, where they would be spending most of July, and much of the "Comedy" between Noah and his wife—ironically enough (since it concerns her refusal to come aboard)—on the boat to Stockholm at the start of September. None of this prevented Graff from continuing to hope that some parts of the score might be available for choreographing in August, to which Stravinsky tetchily instructed Libman to reply that "he now hoped to finish by January 1973."[23]

The mounting pressure over *The Flood* had a lot to do with the nature of the commission, but there was another factor that increased the general sense of urgency and the jockeying for position. In June 1962, Stravinsky was going to be eighty, and the musical institutions of the world were bracing themselves for a celebration from which few wanted to be excluded. In June 1961 he was conducting his music in the Los Angeles Festival: the *Symphony of Psalms* (which he had just recorded) and the Violin Concerto, which he was due to record at the end of the month.[24] A few days later, on the 11th, he attended another festival concert, which included Shostakovich's epic Eleventh Symphony and a violin concerto by another, slightly younger Soviet composer, Tikhon Khrennikov. Stravinsky went as much out of a sense of duty as from any interest in the music. In his diary, Craft reports him as having groaned and cursed throughout until, before the interval, he finally lost patience and left.[25] The next day, Stravinsky described the event in somewhat different terms to his Russian confidant, Souvtchinsky. The music, he insisted, "is incredible junk, but it was impossible for me to escape, especially as the previous day all these Soviet musicians had paid me a visit, we entertained them and they invited me to celebrate my eightieth birthday next year with them in Moscow (if I'm still alive). . . ."[26]

Describing the visit to North Wetherly Drive in the Soviet journal *Ogonyok* two months later, the wily Khrennikov implied that they had only discovered that Stravinsky was taking part in the festival when they arrived in Los Angeles, and that the invitation was issued more or less on the spur of the moment.[27] This was obviously a fiction. The propaganda value of bringing the most famous living Russian composer back to his native land in the year of his eightieth birthday was far too great to have occurred to the politically astute head of the Soviet Composers' Union (SSK) only as he chatted to Stravinsky in the green room of the Royce Hall. It was a deep-laid plan, a shot in the Cold War, and the dim and uncomplicated U.S. cultural authorities let it happen, did nothing to publicize their own pride that "the most famous living Russian composer" was actually an American until it was much too late, and then, as we shall see, produced a damp and carelessly packed squib in lieu of a fireworks display of their own.

The fact is that Stravinsky had been sounded out, casually and through various channels, well before June 1961. Of these channels, only traces now survive. In a letter to Yudina of January 1961, he remarked that "I should so much like to get to you this year, but it won't happen: too many commitments that I can't fulfil."[28] Yudina had written to him the previous spring about "the possibility of your coming as our guest, to your own country." Stravinsky annotated her letter and sent it to Souvtchinsky, who returned it and referred to it in his own next letter to the composer.[29] A year later, still only in May 1961, Nika Nabokov let slip that "someone has said that you're going to Moscow."[30] And that same month, the U.S. State Department, of all institutions, asked John Crosby whether Stravinsky—who was booked to appear with the Santa Fe Opera on a government-sponsored visit to Berlin and Warsaw in September—might be available to continue alone on a conducting tour of the Soviet Union. Stravinsky himself reported this idea to Goddard Lieberson with simple incredulity, but that was probably because of the suggestion that he go alone.[31] A general idea must have somehow got about that he was thinking of a Russian trip; but nobody had any very clear view of how it might happen.

He knew that the atmosphere in Moscow was less hostile to his music than at any time since the early thirties. He knew about the partial thaw under Khrushchev, and he knew about Leonard Bernstein's spectacular success with *The Rite of Spring* and the Concerto for Piano and Wind Instruments on his Soviet tour with the New York Philharmonic in 1959. From Yudina he had gathered not only that his music was being played in the Soviet Union, but that it included relatively "difficult" pieces like the Concerto for Two Solo Pianos and the Serenade, and that there were young (and less young) enthusiasts like Blazhkov who went to hear this music and were thirsting for scores and recordings. But he knew about the dark side as well, and like most White Russians he still feared the power and ruthlessness of the Communists, so violently revealed in Budapest a mere five years ago and still evident, for example, in the growing political tensions over Berlin. *"Zhutko"*—"terrifying"—is how he described the whole situation to Souvtchinsky when his Russian visitors had left: "terrifying to think about it, terrifying to peer into my eightieth year, terrifying the musical goings-on in Russia, terrifying the idea that they should celebrate 'their venerable musician' who happens to smile when he feels like throwing up."[32] He had said something similar, if less melodramatic, to a *Washington Post* reporter as recently as December 1960. "They're bad," he snapped. "Poor Shostakovich, the most talented, is just trembling all his life. Russia is a very conservative and old country for music. It was new just before the Soviets. Under Lenin they invited me. I couldn't go. Stalin never invited me."³³ All such remarks were reported, or misreported, in Moscow. In February, *Sovetskaya Kul'tura* ran a highly colored commentary that prompted Yudina to write in protest to Souvtchinsky, imploring him to tell Stravinsky not to say things that damaged his Russian admirers and impeded acceptance of his music.³⁴ In his *Ogonyok* article, Khrennikov claimed that when he confronted Stravinsky with the Washington interview, the master simply disowned the entire text, insisting that "I've never said anything bad either about Soviet music or about Soviet musicians. All these opinions were imputed to me in the interview by unscrupulous journalists."³⁵ We are here in the land of Kafka's *Trial:* somebody must have been telling tales about Igor S. But who, who says so, and for what reason? "What am I to do?" he asked Souvtchinsky imploringly, while the press, who had hung around North Wetherly Drive when Khrennikov went in and no doubt buttonholed him when he came out, announced the visit as signed and sealed.³⁶

Souvtchinsky did not hesitate. "Of course," he wrote modestly, "it's not for me to give you advice, but I think, and am convinced, that you must accept this invitation." He mused on its significance and what he somehow saw as its inevitability; it was already a fact of historic importance that would have "for the whole of Russian culture the most enormous consequences in every sphere" and "become a symbol of the liberation of a whole generation of Russian musicians." Souvtchinsky was in frequent touch with Yudina, and he sensed that she might have had some influence, however small, on the change of heart "in that terrible and inspired country." What did amaze him, he confessed, was the way the invitation had come from Khrennikov, with whose "music," he added in sardonic quotes, he was acquainted. "In Soviet Russia, with all its hierarchies," he assured Stravinsky, "I do not think that he would dare act on his own initiative without the approval of Shostakovich, from the top musical echelons. Yet your trip, and the celebrations in your honor, will not be to his [Shostakovich's] advantage. So clearly this is something stronger than him. . . ."³⁷

The curious thing about this rather complicated and profoundly ignorant advice is that it never seriously addresses what was for Stravinsky the most important issue of all: his own emotional response—the inner battle between his abrupt longing to see his native land once again, and his eternal loathing for the system that might take him there. Historic opportunities and the liberating of whole generations had never really been his thing, at least not since the wide-eyed days of his Ustilug conversations with the Polish doctor, Plekhanov's friend Bachnicki.³⁸ The simple fact was that he was a Russian, body and soul, who had not been home for nearly half a century. He was not remotely interested in Souvtchinsky's ridiculous speculations on who had to ask whom about inviting him. He wanted to go and he wanted to play his works for people who he knew wanted to hear them, but he was profoundly disturbed—as those around him quickly saw—by that collision between fear and desire that anyone will recognize who has ever had an unexpected opportunity to fulfil an ambition buried so deep that the very loss of its impossibility leaves a hole. Souvtchinsky apparently failed to notice all this because he himself had no wish, deep-seated or otherwise, to go back to Russia. For him, it was a purely intellectual conundrum, with an intellectual solution. "It isn't a question," he wrote later, "of my being pro-Soviet or anti-Soviet, but of the fact that I don't like to and cannot 'go back' to the past. The past becomes 'another state of being' and to go back is to my mind as forbidden as to look into the future."[39]

THEIR EUROPEAN landfall in 1961 was Göteborg in Sweden, from where they went by train to Stockholm and the same day, 9 September, flew on to Helsinki. It was by far their closest approach to Russian soil since before the war, and for Igor the closest to Leningrad since he had last left St. Petersburg in October 1912. They might well have been affected by this proximity even without the looming idea of a visit. Helsinki, like Oranienbaum and (near enough) St. Petersburg itself, lay on the Baltic coast and looked out over green islands and soft, barely saline waters. In the open-air market near the harbor you could buy mushrooms and arctic berries, exactly as you once could in St. Petersburg; and already in Soviet times passenger boats plied from there to Leningrad and back, so that it was hard to be in the more westerly city without hatching plans—invariably unfulfilled—for an excursion to the more easterly. You breathed the same air in the same climate; and everywhere, in the newspapers, in conversation, was a sense of the Soviet Union just along and across the gulf, closer than any of Finland's western neighbors. Dominating the old square was a statue of Tsar Alexander II on a horse.

So remote was Souvtchinsky from any sense of the reality of Soviet life that he had, with Stravinsky's somewhat skeptical permission, suggested to Yudina that she take advantage of the composer's visit to nearby Helsinki in order to meet him and discuss possible programs for the Soviet tour.[40] Yudina, of course, did not appear. Instead she sent back a letter, no more than hinting at the supreme tactlessness of the whole plan, and describing it to Souvtchinsky as "a remarkable example of your purity of heart and abstractness of spirit. . . . So near and yet so far, dear Pyotr Petrovich! Did you really think that I could just 'up and go' to Helsinki??!!"[41] But Pyotr Petrovich was not quite that naïve, he claimed. He had quite reasonably (in his picture of the Soviet musical hierarchies) assumed that Shostakovich would fix her a visa.[42] As for money, perhaps he supposed that in the U.S.S.R. the State paid all the bills. The failure, though it probably did not surprise Stravinsky, further undermined his confidence in the rightness of any decision to visit a country that would not grant even its leading musicians the most elementary freedom of movement. "Nice people?! And this is the country those Soviet obscurantists want to invite me to! But they wouldn't give Yudina a passport to come and see me in Helsinki. Thank you. I shall not go there."[43]

From Helsinki he had somewhat reluctantly made the necessary Sibelius pilgrimage and visited the Finnish master's wooden house at Järvenpäär, met his widow and daughter, and talked about his music, widely performed in English-speaking countries but routinely despised by modernists like Craft and, to some extent, Stravinsky himself, who nevertheless admitted to liking certain lyrical aspects of Sibelius's music—what he called "Italian-melody-gone-north."[44] Nostalgia may still have been working on him. Sibelius's music had been a presence in St. Petersburg before the revolution, and Stravinsky had probably heard him conduct his Third Symphony there with Rimsky-Korsakov in 1907.[45] But there was also an element of diplomacy, since he had been cited for the Wihuri-Sibelius award, which, unlike his earlier Sibelius medal, carried a substantial cash prize.

After his concert in Helsinki University Hall on the 12th of September, they flew back to Stockholm, where, on the 24th, Stravinsky conducted *The Rite of Spring* for what was to prove the last time. At the Royal Opera House, Ingmar Bergman's production of *The Rake's Progress* was in repertory, and the composer attended like royalty, receiving a standing ovation as he arrived in his box and again at the end. Whatever he may have feared about the performance itself, having recently seen Bergman's heavily, Nordically symbolic film *The Virgin Spring*, his fears were banished by the reality, which reminded this great enemy of "interpretation" that literal adherence to the text is in the end less important than an instinctive feeling for its spirit. Bergman was no apostle of *Texttreue*. He made significant cuts, reduced the three acts to two (with an interval after the street scene with Anne and Baba), and invented some modestly symbolic by-play of the kind that later audiences would take in their stride but which at that time could still seem high-handed and intrusive. Stravinsky nevertheless found the whole thing so moving and musicianly that he hardly seems to have noticed the retouchings.

Two days later, when he met Bergman himself at a dinner at the house of the Opera's administrator, Set Svanholm, he found Bergman intellectually able to defend his changes. He argued convincingly that the natural turning point of the opera—musically as well as scenically—was Baba's sarabande and the unveiling of her beard. It was almost as if he had read Stravinsky's very first letter to Auden, which talks of a two-act opera with "a Choreographic Divertissement in the first act's finale."[46] From this point in Bergman's staging, Craft noted, the colors became more somber and Swedish, reflecting the natural trajectory of the drama. The whole thing was as far as possible from the fake Italianism of Venice or the hectic pantomime bustle of the Met. It worked entirely on its own terms, and above all because it referred constantly to the music as the truest guide to what was actually—as opposed to superficially—taking place.[47]

Their flight to Berlin at the end of September brought them into a drastically different environment. Barely six weeks before, the East German government had slung a barbed wire fence along the boundary between East and West Berlin, and a week later had swiftly, and it seemed conclusively, turned it into a concrete wall. The political tension was almost palpable, emphasized by troop and tank movements, and by lines of guards with dogs and submachine guns. The three travellers were taken to look at the wall in a car provided by the mayor of West Berlin, Willy Brandt, an outing scarcely calculated to steady Stravinsky's nerves when he considered that this was the reality of the politics that had kept him from his native land for the past forty-four years. Perhaps he also reflected that in 1933, similarly, he had been in Germany only a few days after the political takeover that had eventually led to war.[48] Now, in September 1961, there were plenty of well-informed people who were predicting a similar outcome from the border confrontations in Berlin. Nicolas Nabokov, a friend of Brandt's, took Stravinsky on one side and did his best to talk him out of going to the Soviet Union at all, while others were suggesting he delay until the autumn and not give the Russians the benefit of his birthday publicity.[49] From Berlin they went on to Belgrade (Warsaw having long since fallen by the wayside)—their first direct experience of life in a Communist state. The gray drabness, the squalor, the sheer crumbling ugliness, were finally too much for them. "They have renounced all intentions," Craft wrote to Paul Horgan on the 10th of October, "ever to go to Russia."[50]

In such an atmosphere the Santa Fe Opera performances of Oedipus Rex and Persephone might have seemed about as relevant to either city as the Attic meadows and temples in which the two works are set. In fact they were a success, thanks in part at least to Stravinsky's insistence on changes in the cast that had played in Santa Fe in July.[51] From Belgrade, they reconnected with modern civilization in Zurich, where the composer was conducting The Soldier's Tale in a double bill with The Nightingale under the local music director, Victor Reinshagen. By the time they reached London in mid-October, Stravinsky must have felt more than ever like his soldier hero:

successful, by normal standards happy, but a stranger in strange lands, tormented by the forbidden desire to return home.

These days London was the intellectual focus of many of the concepts that lay behind his creative thinking. The attempts to form a collaboration with Eliot had failed, but the idea of *The Flood* had in a sense been his; and now there was a new plan for a setting of the mystical little two-stanza poem, "The dove descending breaks the air," that forms the entire fourth part of the last of the four quartets, *Little Gidding*. The original suggestion had come from a new venture called *The Cambridge Hymnal*, which had set itself the worthy if somewhat unrealistic task of raising the literary and musical tone of school assembly hymns.[52] For some reason, Stravinsky had ignored the original letter (of December 1960), and it is far from clear that even in London on this trip—though he dined with Eliot—he gave any commitment to write the hymn. Barely a month later he was telling a New Zealand press conference that "[Eliot's] words do not need music. I can find notes for Shakespeare because he wrote words for singing. Eliot's are for speaking."[53] Only when he got back to Hollywood in December did he change his mind and agree to compose the *Little Gidding* text in the form of "the standard, four-part hymn chorale."[54]

In fact the so-called *Anthem* that he wrote at New Year 1962 is neither hymn nor chorale, but an extremely tricky unaccompanied four-part motet that would suit a school assembly about as much as *Threni* would please a Rugby club dinner. That Stravinsky composed it at all is remarkable. He had always claimed to detest *a cappella* singing, yet "The dove descending" is the epitome of the kind of unaccompanied music you would not want to hear sung by any but the most expert, highly trained, small professional choir. When sung by such consorts—which of course exist and existed, especially in England—the piece can be intensely, concentratedly beautiful. When sung by anyone else, it can be simply a nightmare.[55]

A few days after the Eliot dinner, they were in Oxford for lunch with Isaiah Berlin. Robert Graves was there, too, perhaps at Craft's suggestion, and he enlivened the meal with his erudition on Alexander the Great, Plato, and, less predictably, the relative virtue of Protestants, Catholics, and Israelis as taxpayers[56]—though whether because, as often with Stravinsky, the subject of tax had come up, or because they had started discussing Israel, is unclear. Sir Isaiah and Nicolas Nabokov, who turned up after lunch, had recently been on a visit to that country, and they had come back with the outline of a commission from Ahron Propes, the director of the Israel Festival, linked to a proposal that Stravinsky should visit the festival in September 1962 to conduct the work. Nabokov, who knew his friend's ways, must have realized from the start that there was no chance of a new score being ready in so short a time. Perhaps he also knew, however, that Stravinsky had already half-formed the idea of writing a work to a text in Hebrew (a language of which he was completely ignorant), stimulated "by my discovery of Hebrew as sound."[57] Five months earlier the composer had asked Roth to get him a tape recording of a recent Cologne Radio performance of Schoenberg's marvelous setting of Psalm 130, *De Profundis*, an unaccompanied choral motet that not only has a biblical Hebrew text but is specifically dedicated to the then (1950) newly founded State of Israel.[58] This must surely have been the catalyst for Stravinsky's discovery. What would be more natural than to consult Berlin—a Hebraicist and, like Schoenberg, a long-standing Zionist—on suitable texts for a work with a similar object?

According to Craft, Berlin read them passages from the Bible in Hebrew, supplying literal translations as he went along. Berlin wanted Stravinsky to choose the Creation story, but Stravinsky, who had just been setting that episode in English in *The Flood*, was not strongly attracted by the idea. ("The music," he told Berlin, "would be longer than a British weekend.") A better choice for him was the story of Abraham and Isaac, which, as well as being "a very well-told tale," had the added advantage of being a symbolic account of the origin of the Israeli nation. Even so, no firm decision was made, and it was agreed that Berlin would provide a transliteration of the two narratives, together with a word-by-word translation, leaving Stravinsky to choose between them in due course.[59]

In London, Stravinsky conducted *Persephone* for a BBC studio recording and a few days later for a Sunday afternoon concert in the Festival Hall. They then set off on what could reasonably be described as a world tour. After a week's holiday in Egypt, they flew to Australia and New Zealand for three weeks of sightseeing and concert-giving, before polishing the whole circumnavigation off with a week in Tahiti at the start of December. Ten days later they were back in the air on their second trip of that year to Mexico City. At one point on the Australian flight Stravinsky told their pilot—half in jest, half in drink—"I feel like a planet."[60] Yet astonishingly this insane schedule for a man of seventy-nine, in indifferent health and with a potentially fatal blood condition, hardly seems to have troubled him beyond what could be counteracted by a day in bed and the tactical avoidance of unwanted visitors or unwelcome receptions or press conferences. Souvtchinsky later tried to explain it to Yudina. "When he's not composing he gets terribly bored; but for him travel is not merely amusement, or diversion, but also a kind of self-expression—a 'flight into the future.' What is more he says that it's more agreeable to fork out money for any kind of tour than to pay it to the American tax-man."[61] The real victim of this wanderlust was obviously Vera, who loathed provincial cities, was easily (for all her apparently effortless social grace and natural charm) bored by drab or run-of-the-mill people, and was a halfhearted sightseer. Her diaries are full of sour memos about such things, and occasionally the feeling would spill out onto postcards to close friends like Lawrence Morton, who would be disarmingly informed what hell it was being on tour with musicians.[62]

Vera was at least good at seeking oblivion when necessary. She would sleep on the interminable flights, while Craft fussed nervously with books and newspapers.[63] Stravinsky, who was a calm traveller these days as long as things went reasonably smoothly, had taken to working on minor compositional tasks while airborne. On the flight to Mexico just before Christmas, he completed a wind-band arrangement of the tango-like last piece of the *Cinq doigts* piano suite, and proceeded to conduct it in his concert in the Bellas Artes hall on the 20th of December, to a half-empty auditorium and a generally tepid reception.[64]

It was a depressing prelude to his celebratory year, but at least the negative feelings about Russia had for the time being dissipated. The official invitation had arrived in October. Craft had written to Libman from Melbourne the following month telling her to instruct Sol Hurok that he could now proceed to negotiate the "return," but for the autumn, rather than June.[65] Stravinsky's outburst a fortnight later over the Yudina visa looked like a passing squall, and moreover the United States had at last come up with its own piece of "official recognition" in the form of an invitation from President Kennedy's wife, Jacqueline, to "a dinner in your honor on or around your 80th birthday next June 5th."[66] At first Stravinsky actually declined this undeclinable invitation on the grounds of prior concert engagements.[67] But they were no more than a pretext. He had not yet agreed to Liebermann's proposal that he conduct his three "Greek" ballets (*Apollo, Orpheus, Agon*), in place of *The Flood* (to which he had never agreed), in Hamburg in June;[68] the South African trip in May would not interfere with a Washington dinner on June 18, his actual New Style birthday. He had simply taken against the whole empty charade, as he chose to regard it. "I don't see anything wrong with my telegram to Mrs. Kennedy," he told Nabokov;

> Am I a man of almost 80 years to fly all alone (notice, she did _not_ invite my wife) to Washington on the one day I would like to be with my family and friends. I want to add, too, that the Casals business there nauseated me—all publicity seeking and social climbing on the part of you know which American composers and conductors and violinists and . . . _No one_ in Washington has any real regard for my music—it is all for my name.[69]

It seems more likely that Nabokov had himself dropped a hint to Kennedy's personal assistant, Arthur Schlesinger, that Stravinsky's birthday ought not to be ignored especially since the Russians were ostentatiously honoring it.[70] At any rate, it was Schlesinger who now intervened with Nabokov, pointing out the awkwardness of Stravinsky's response and suggesting that he propose some more convenient date.[71] The dinner was duly fixed for the 18th of January, and Vera, Craft, and Nika were all invited, too.

JUST WHEN STRAVINSKY was telling Souvtchinsky that he refused to go to a country that denied its musicians visas, and Craft was telling Libman that he must at all costs go,[1] and Souvtchinsky was assuring the composer that he at least would never go,[2] a fifty-five-year-old woman whom none of them had ever met or even corresponded with picked up her pen in an apartment house on the Kryukov Canal in Leningrad.

> Dear Uncle Igor, I was very happy to learn that you intend to come to us in Russia next summer and celebrate your eightieth birthday here. So I made up my mind to write and tell you that not only your numerous admirers, but also your own flesh and blood, are looking forward to seeing you.[3]

The flesh and blood were, alas, no longer so numerous. Xenya Stravinsky had lost both her parents many years ago: her father, Yury—Igor's older brother—in 1941; her mother, Yelena, in 1948. Her older sister, Tanya, who had spent almost a year at her uncle's house in Nice in 1925, had died of cancer five years earlier, aged only fifty-two and already widowed, leaving a son named Roman. Xenya, too, had lost her husband, the father of her daughter, Yelena, but had remarried, and they all—she, her architect second husband, and Yelena and her husband together with their son, Igor—lived in a flat on the Kryukov Canal, not the old Stravinsky flat but a smaller one a few yards along the street. It was a melancholy little nucleus, but one all too typical of postwar Leningrad, heir to so much hardship and anxiety and forty years of moral and physical deprivation. Yet Xenya, excited by the thought of meeting the brilliant uncle about whom she had heard so much but whose existence might have been pursued on the planet Mars for all it ever had to do with her, uttered not a single word of complaint, merely adding laconically: "These are the sad facts of our life."

Her uncle replied promptly, but with that curious lack of effusiveness that typified his letters to all but his very closest friends and family—and even to them when he felt preoccupied by work or had nothing urgently personal to say. He was touched by everything Xenya had told him, he said, had no time to write at any length for the moment, but would do so soon. He was unable to come in the summer, but would possibly come later. Meanwhile he was sending photographs, and ordering copies of his conversation books for her from London.4 This curious guardedness toward a niece who had withheld nothing and demanded nothing might easily have affected her like a rejection, especially as the promised longer letter never materialized. Fortunately she had the good sense to understand that such a reply reflected a much wider ambivalence toward Russia, and also that the true way to his affections lay through his music, which—though she may not have known or analyzed it consciously—was the touchstone of his attitude to his native land. Like her mother, she herself was artistically more visual than musical, but she went to hear his music whenever she could, and the next time she wrote she reported on what she had heard.5 Still no second letter came back; but she did not reproach him, and did not lose hope that he would at last respond in kind.

Stravinsky's travels in the first month of 1962 were a tiny microcosm of the hectic schedule that he faced later in the year. On the 6th he conducted *The Soldier's Tale* suite in the Wilshire-Ebell Theater in a concert otherwise directed entirely by Craft. The next morning they flew to Toronto for a series of recordings for CBC,6 then on the 13th drove to Buffalo, from where they flew to Washington for three concert performances of *Oedipus Rex* and Ravel's *L'Heure espagnole* (conducted by Craft), and a recording of *Oedipus*.7 At the end of the month they were in New York to record *Renard* and *Ragtime,* done without the cimbalom parts because no adequate player could be found.8 It was on account of his Washington engagements that Stravinsky had accepted the invitation to dine with the President on the 18th, as if fitting in a lunchtime drink with a persistent concert agent. And one can almost sympathize with his cynical view of the proceedings, since it was transparently obvious that the invitation had been prompted by political considerations and had little to do with any celebratory attitude to him or his music. In general, the United States took little serious interest in her greatest composer citizen. Not a single American orchestra had proposed a full-scale birthday tribute, and indeed it was several years since he had been booked by any of the leading orchestras for a subscription concert. The attitude to him and his music in his adoptive country was nearly as benighted as it had for so long been in the Soviet Union, and in a way that was still more wounding, since it was a matter of pure aesthetic and commercial preference, backed up by no official doctrine or legal force.

The dinner itself illustrated perfectly the difficulty even relatively sophisticated politicians have in honoring great artists in a manner beyond the merely dutiful. Craft noted with a touch of scorn the political and in-house leavening among their fellow guests, who included Mrs. Kennedy's sister, Lee Radziwill, Helen Chavchavadze, and the Schlesingers, with only Nabokov, the Liebersons, and the Leonard Bernsteins to make the Stravinskys feel remotely at home.9 A well-thought-out evening would have run to at least a short concert of Stravinsky's music, but this dinner had been cooked up at the last minute with whatever came to hand. The composer himself thought the guests poorly chosen, and since there was a lot to drink and not much to do except drink it, he duly got drunk. But he could still observe his hosts. "She," he reported to Souvtchinsky, "is very striking and charming, he very quick on the uptake, but they both have very little connection with art, and I think that they invited me less for my music than for my age, and to steal a march on the Russians, *to whom*," he added mischievously, *"I shall not go."*10 The Kennedys were at their best as they stood with their guests of honor in the porch, waiting for the car to take them back to their hotel. They chatted easily and naturally for a quarter of an hour, the driver not having expected so early a departure. "Nice kids," Stravinsky remarked incongruously as they at last drove away.11

As for Russia, his latest reaction was obviously mere pique at being treated as Cold War fodder by those who had hitherto either abused his work or ignored it. Practically speaking, he was committed to going, provided that Hurok could extract satisfactory terms from the SSK. There was evidence of a more open attitude to his music in Moscow and Leningrad. Yudina had described in detail a concert of his chamber works at the Leningrad Composers' House in early January including the Serenade, Septet, Octet, Duo Concertant, the viola *Elegy*, and various songs; the composer Valerian Bogdanov-Berezovsky had made a twenty-minute speech, and the influx of people had been so great that the small concert hall of the Composers' House had nearly come apart at the seams.12 Admittedly Souvtchinsky had suddenly turned against the whole idea of the visit. He related a horror story told him by the novelist Nathalie Sarraute, who had been invited to Russia to lecture "in front of huge auditoria of five hundred people," had in fact found herself speaking to audiences of eight or nine, and had suddenly been assailed by feelings of terror at the alien and incomprehensible environment. Was it worth the risk, he asked, for Stravinsky to get mixed up in that world of obscurantists and imbeciles? At least put the trip off until 1963, when the ground would be prepared and the birthday celebrations over.13 But when Stravinsky replied in mid-March that it was now too late to back out, Souvtchinsky swung round behind him again and gave the visit his imprimatur.14 Craft meanwhile reported to Nabokov that the

Master was still changing his mind twice a day,[15] and there was a moment of sheer panic when a "hysterical" twenty-five-page letter arrived from Yudina in mid-April and Stravinsky confessed to Souvtchinsky that he could scarcely endure the mixture of blind adoration, provincialism, and what *Le Monde* had called "the jargon of cultural exchange," and that the whole trip was turning into a nightmare for him.[16] But this seems to have been his last significant wobble, and by the time they sailed for Le Havre en route for South Africa on the 8th of May nobody any longer seriously doubted that the visit would take place.

In the midst of all this agony, Stravinsky's latest completed work, *A Sermon, a Narrative, and a Prayer,* quietly had its premiere in distant Basle on 23 February (preceded by a public dress rehearsal on the 22nd). After all Sacher's anxieties—about the choir, the soloists' English,[17] the idiom in general—everything went smoothly, and the curious, unclassifiable score enjoyed something close to a triumph; in fact, the entire fifteen-minute work was encored. As for the press, it was almost the first opportunity European critics had had since before the war to give serious, concentrated attention to a major Stravinsky premiere without the intervention of the kind of distracting or even downright disruptive conditions that usually prevailed in Venice. The fat bundle of reviews that in due course landed on the North Wetherly Drive doormat might have been as much the product of Swiss tidiness and efficiency as the concert itself.

There were good reasons for this sudden wave of gravitas and sympathy. The fact, for instance, that several London newspapers sent critics to Basle instead of waiting for the British premiere in May simply reflected the appearance on the scene of a number of youngish writers with a genuine enthusiasm for and knowledge of new music, something frankly almost unknown in the British or American press before 1960.[18] Then again, in German-speaking Basle, the nearby German and Swiss critics naturally turned out in force and, as ever, engaged earnestly, if not always with flashing wit, with the loftiness of Stravinsky's intentions and thought. The reviews proclaim that the "thinking" musical world has at last got over its astonishment and—not to mince words—resentment at the serialization of the great master's technique. They mention it, but largely discount it as an aesthetic factor. The work is thought one of Stravinsky's most penetrable, most coherent, even most melodious. The debt to Webern is noticed but felt to have been fully absorbed, unlike the old stylistic references of neoclassicism. Above all, the spiritual message comes across as something intimate, direct, and personal, after the cool Latin rituals of the *Canticum sacrum* and *Threni* and the abstractions of *Movements*. People are touched by the beauty of the Dekker "Prayer" where they may have been merely impressed by that of the "Sensus spe" or the "Quomodo sedens." As he approaches eighty, it seems, the great composer is close to beatification. Only one (of course French) review attracts his wrathful marginalia for comparing his *Sermon* unfavorably, in intensity and grandeur, with Dallapiccola's *Canti di Prigionia*.[19] The rest is contented silence.

Less than three weeks after the premiere, Stravinsky put the finishing touches to *The Flood* and at once turned to the question of how the twenty-five-minute drama, with its odd mixture of speech, singing, and tone poem, might be rendered into visual language for the small screen. On the day that he completed the full score, the 14th of March, Balanchine arrived in Hollywood to discuss the production and choreography. They met on three consecutive days, and then again for two days a month later, and Craft took detailed notes, which he eventually published under the businesslike title: "Working Notes for 'The Flood.' "[20] In one sense these meetings were no different from the kinds of discussion they had had before *Orpheus* and *Agon;* in another sense they were utterly different, because at their core was a medium for which neither of the two artists had much sympathy or even a great deal of understanding. Balanchine had worked for television, but mainly on popular classics like *Coppelia, The Nutcracker,* and *The Magic Flute,* where the idiom was that of more or less conventional adaptation. Stravinsky had watched television but had never been near a studio except occasionally as conductor or interviewee. They seem to have approached the whole thing in much the way that an art-loving family might think about their next fancy-dress party. Ideas flowed, unchecked by any technical discipline or even any very coherent visual concept. When God says, "Let the dry earth appear," Stravinsky suggests showing photos of the moon, the sea, or the desert. Balanchine's idea for the Flood involves shiny black bituminous plastic made to wave and heave by the male dancers bobbing up and down on their knees underneath it, while the female dancers wallow on top like people drowning. In the Covenant, the dancers form the rainbow, "like an advertisement for Radio City."[21] All these inspirations have in common the fact that they would actually work well on a stage, where crudity of detail can be masked by lighting and distance. The idea that they might be televisual presumably comes from some vague notion that in the studio all things are possible and abstraction or surrealism are therefore appropriate genres. But this was to prove both technically and aesthetically a mistake.

The oddest feature of the initial discussions is that they apparently took place in the absence of both the designer, Rouben Ter-Arutunian, and the producer, Graff. These key figures in the visual presentation arrived some two weeks later, in time for the preliminary recording sessions at the end of March, which in fact consisted mainly of taping the music (from orchestral parts understandably littered with mistakes), together with interview material and rehearsal sequences, which Graff needed for the hour-long documentary program he planned to build round the performance itself. Graff had never expected more than twenty-five minutes of music, a length specified in his original letter of intent, but when he timed the recording and found that it lasted barely twenty-three minutes, he began to get cold feet about the amount of padding required, and he at once wrote to Stravinsky congratulating him on "composing such a vibrant, allusive and moving score" but inviting him to collaborate with Craft in lengthening it to "permit a dance presentation in excess of thirty minutes."[22] Whether Stravinsky took this suggestion seriously, or even calmly, is matter for speculation, but his joint reply with Balanchine, after their mid-April meetings, was measured but firm. No changes were needed. With a few extra pauses the work would last the full twenty-five minutes, and that was all that could be expected. Graff might (or might not) be pleased to learn that, after all the sour looks and sharp remarks whenever he had referred to the new work as a ballet, it had after all turned into . . . a ballet, or, to be exact, a "choreographic allegory." Balanchine therefore was to have "full power to carry out our mutual conception." The "chaos" prelude was neither curtain raiser nor credits music, but "already a part of the action." So there was no longer any need to show the conductor at all (which was just as well since, though Graff had no intention of admitting it, the recorded performance had been conducted by Craft).[23]

As far as anyone knows, this was Stravinsky's final contribution to *The Flood* before its TV premiere on 14 June. He had done his best to produce a score that would suit this strange and imponderable medium. In the latter stages of composition he had tinkered and adjusted, checked timings with Craft's help, thought hard about the role of the narrator and how what was heard would chime with what was seen. But he remained nervous and unsure about the result. "I hope," he wrote to Liebermann a week after finishing the score, "*The Flood* will not be *A Flop*."[24] Too much of it seemed to be outside his control. Even the recording, which Columbia were planning to issue simultaneously with the transmission, was being touched up in his absence. The spoken passages were being dubbed in in New York, and there were even a few fragments of music that Leonard Bernstein was being hauled in to re-record because the Hollywood tape was unsatisfactory.[25] None of this was being done "in the composer's presence," to use the formula Columbia were using for the commercial disc. In fact he took no part, and apparently not much interest, in the videotaping of the production itself in Manhattan in early June, by which time he was on the other side of the Atlantic. On the day of the transmission he was in Hamburg. If Robert Craft is to be believed, he never actually saw the program at all, but this, as we shall see, may not be quite correct.[26]

After finishing the score, he had not thought it worth embarking straight away on his next work, the commission for Israel. There were the planning and recording sessions to be got through, and then he was due to conduct at the World's Fair in Seattle in the third week of April. In any case, although he had finally settled on the Abraham story and had the Hebrew text to hand, he was still not confident enough of the pronunciation and accentuation to feel able to set the words to music.[27] So instead, in the vacant week in March, he fulfilled what was probably a request from Lawrence Morton for a piece to go into the Monday Evening Concert on the 26th, an extra event being put on with raised ticket prices in the hope of earning some badly needed cash for the series.[28]

There was no question of a new work. His idea was to make further arrangements of the *Cinq doigts* pieces, like the one he had done for Mexico, but this time for a mixed fifteen-piece ensemble including strings. Four of the eight pieces were ready in time for the concert and were duly played under Craft, though few heard them, the subscribers having apparently been frightened away by the thought of having to buy their tickets.[29] The remaining four pieces were added in the first week or so of April, and Stravinsky conducted the first complete performance of the *Eight Instrumental Miniatures,* as they were now called, in Toronto on the 29th. As before when transcribing his own music, he had been unable to resist the temptation to amplify and complicate. The *Miniatures* treat the *Cinq doigts* much as their composer had treated Gesualdo in adding voices to his defective motets. Two of the pieces have inner parts inserted in canon with the existing melody; others have free parts added, and one or two are radically recomposed and extended.[30] The whole set is a perfect model of Stravinsky's inability to perform mechanical tasks—inability, as it were, to go to sleep artistically; and like earlier self-transcriptions—the *Pastorale,* the Concertino—they offer a tiny key to his whole creative method.

ARRIVING in New York from Toronto at the start of May, they stayed for long enough to visit the spectacular exhibition of "Stravinsky and the Dance" put on in the Wildenstein Gallery under the patronage of Graff's wife, Marjorie, as a modest adjunct to the *Flood* production (which was trailed in the catalogue). They then fled to Europe. In Paris on 15 May, Isaiah Berlin called on them to discuss the Hebrew text for the work that the mayor of Jerusalem, Theodore Kollek, had with presumably intentional bathos referred to as "The Sacrifice of Sir Isaac."[31] But instead he suddenly found himself acting as agent for the whole contract with the State of Israel itself. Stravinsky no longer wanted to write a half-hour choral work, as originally mooted, but a piece for one or at most two solo voices lasting about fifteen minutes. He despaired of finishing in time for the 1963 festival and was insisting on 1964 (bullying him, Nabokov said, would not do the slightest good); and he wanted his fifteen-thousand-dollar fee to be net of all tax. Reporting this to Kollek, Berlin added that he was certain Stravinsky genuinely wanted "to do something for Israel" and was not about to double-cross the festival, as he had done Covent Garden over the *Rake* or Hamburg over *Movements*.[32] It seems not to have struck him as at all odd that he, a leading Oxford philosopher, should be talking dollars and delivery dates on someone else's behalf. The deal simply happened to combine two of his greatest passions: Israel and Stravinsky; and it offered him the chance, as he had once put it sycophantically in a letter to Craft, "to be secretly immortalised by the purely simple little piece of work that I have done with great hope and devotion."[33]

The next day Stravinsky lunched with Samuel Beckett, and discussed with him the relative pacing of words and music and the possibility of notating the tempo of a play.[34] It must have been the ritual motion of Beckett's plays, with their slow gait and long silences, that had intrigued Stravinsky for some years and led him to hint at a collaboration, through Goddard Lieberson, as long ago as 1956. Even so it is hard to believe that his supposed remark to Beckett, when they met again later in 1962, that "he would be honored to compose music for any opera that Beckett might wish to write," was any more than polite flattery.[35] That evening, Nabokov threw an advance eightieth-birthday dinner at Chez Laurent. Two days later they flew to Johannesburg.

This first and last visit to South Africa was another of those tours that, to the distant gaze, looked utterly pointless and even, in some ways, positively damaging. The animal-loving, zoo-addicted Stravinsky told Lillian Libman that he went because "he wanted to see the impalas in Kruger Park."[36] But Libman also hints that he had tried to get out of the tour by restricting the dates and upping his fee, and that it was Craft who implored her to accept the visit as agreed.[37] It was certainly a curious time for right-minded U.S. citizens to be insisting on touring South Africa, which had been the object of a unanimous United Nations censure motion for its racial policies a mere seven months before.[38] Stravinsky's hosts were, of course, the white authorities, specifically the South African Broadcasting Corporation, who would be programming concerts for white audiences only. When he enquired what arrangements there might be for him to conduct a concert for nonwhites, he was told that it would be permitted but that his fee would have to reflect the fact that there was very little money for such events.[39] This remarkable admission seems to have stung even the not instinctively humanitarian Stravinsky into a vengeful tactic. He undertook to perform for whatever the Bantu could raise and give it to a nonwhite charity. "I hope this makes them [the whites] mad," he told Libman optimistically: "Soak the whites and give to the nonwhites, but present it not as a 'color' problem, but as a question of rich and poor."[40] When they started rehearsing in Johannesburg for the first all-white concert, Stravinsky is supposed to have put it to an Afrikaner member of the orchestra that the choir and orchestra might conceivably be improved by a leavening of the best nonwhite musicians, and to have received the unblinking reply that indeed the nonwhite chorus was much better than the white one.[41] Such stories, if authentic, argue a change of heart by Stravinsky since the 1930s, when he seldom if ever risked a fee on a point of humanitarian (as opposed to musical) principle. Craft does claim, here and there, to have influenced him in the general direction of political liberalism. How this fits in with his own determination to go to South Africa, in the absence of what one might call strong pro-activist arguments on his part, is a little harder to fathom.

There were certainly those among Stravinsky's more politically engaged friends who thought he should not have gone. Isaiah Berlin, for one, was against the trip on principle; but he also had more specific grounds for anxiety. In Pretoria Stravinsky had apparently told Jewish reporters that the Israeli government had banned the performance of the *Symphony of Psalms* in Latin and that he had accordingly commissioned Berlin to oversee its translation into Hebrew. Now it was true, Berlin admitted, that the Israelis were inclined to make difficulties over sacred works like the Bach Passions that were openly offensive to Jews, and they were also still understandably touchy about works with German texts. But the idea that they might object to "any work not specifically offensive to Jewish national or religious sentiment" had not occurred to Berlin, and to suggest that he might himself be qualified to solve the problem merely compounded his surprise. But that, he sighed to Kollek, "is how the old boy carries on, and one might as well realize it. There is no serious harm in any of this, of course, except that I think things had better be cleared up now so that nobody is deluded or in any kind of false position on this subject."[42]

Stravinsky was not due in Israel until the end of August, and in between there was his actual eightieth birthday on the 18th of June to survive. He spent it in Hamburg, where he was conducting *Apollo* in the triple bill of his "Greek" ballets being given by the New York City Ballet a week after the birthday. The travellers arrived from Rome on the 17th to be greeted at the airport by a crowd of friends and photographers, and when Stephen Spender asked the composer if he was tired, he replied: "Not tired, just drunk." "The last time he was sober," Craft added, "was in Paris on March 17th."[43]

Meanwhile for the second time that year he missed a world premiere of one of his major works. *The Flood* was transmitted across the United States on 14 June, and millions of Americans tuned in in the hope of illumination or uplift or whatever it is that inspires people to watch television art shows who would never in their lives go to a concert, an opera, or an art gallery. Those that stayed tuned witnessed a curious mishmash of a presentation. The actual "dance drama" was prefaced by a disquisition, spoken in suitably orotund tones by the actor Laurence Harvey, on the flood myth in various cultures and on its symbolism for modern man, confronted as he was by the imminent threat of extinction by The Bomb. This was followed by a brief clip of the composer himself announcing in his idiosyncratic English that "I don't want to speak you more, I want to play you more," after which came the work itself. Then, once the music had finished, there was more documentary film, rehearsal sequences (including Stravinsky conducting), and biographical stills. As always on American TV, the bizarrely organized program was interrupted every ten minutes or so by advertisements from the program's adorably apt sponsors, Breck shampoo, whose music— naturally enough—was not close in style to Stravinsky's.

The show, which went by the title *Noah and the Flood*, was very widely reviewed throughout the States, and on the whole negatively, though many reviewers gave credit to CBS for backing even a failed attempt to bring culture to the philistine masses. There were plenty prepared to regard Stravinsky's work as a masterpiece ruined by the crudities of the medium. Others, especially among the professional TV critics, found the whole thing a tacky and patronizing shambles and simply admitted they could make nothing of the music. Some praised the brilliant visual inventiveness of Balanchine's and Ter-Arutunian's work on *The Flood* itself; others found it silly and stilted and made fun of the black plastic water, the invisible Ark, the for some reason rather morose lighting, and the camera work, which one reviewer thought "the worst since 'The Great Train Robbery.' "[44] Stravinsky may have been out of the country, but he read and kept the reviews, in at least one case apparently while still abroad. In reply to some mildly negative remarks by the *Tribune* critic, Paul Henry Lang, he exploded in a superbly malevolent telegram to that paper's editor, composed as usual, no doubt, with the help of his alter ego. "The only blight on my eightieth birthday," he raged, "is the realization my age will probably keep me from celebrating the funeral of your senile music columnist."[45] In this there was no small element of revenge. Lang it was who had attacked Craft's conducting and implicitly also his motives in his review of Stravinsky's New York concerts in January 1960.[46]

Today the *Flood* film (which has never been commercially released) seems an extremely archaic specimen, but the experiment it embodied is by no means to be despised, if only because it spawned one of the few genuinely entertaining works ever written in the angular, so-called serial style that so many composers thought compulsory in the sixties but few ever made their own. It also remains one of only a handful of musical works written for television that have survived either on or off the little box. It stands as a monument to the laudable but irrational and probably vain desire that from time to time afflicts the apostles of the mass media, to make the common man like difficult and uncongenial artifacts.

Stravinsky flew into New York from Hamburg a fortnight after the transmission, and immediately Graff set up a private showing of the film. For some unknown reason, it was cancelled at the last minute, but Graff rearranged it for a few days later, and it seems likely that Stravinsky attended.[47] It is true that he never expressed any opinion about the film publicly, and Craft has always maintained that he never saw it. But given the opportunities he certainly had, this seems frankly incredible, and it is much more probable that he saw it, hated it, but preferred not to denounce a production in which he could not deny involvement.

In the ensuing weeks, Stravinsky conducted a succession of open-air concerts, mainly of his popular early works—the nearest the main cities of the U.S.A. came to anything even faintly resembling a birthday celebration. Despite rain or the threat of rain, an audience of eleven thousand heard his Lewisohn Stadium concert in New York on the 12th of July, and five thousand his concert at Ravinia Park, Chicago, on the 21st. A few days later he conducted in the Hollywood Bowl. On all these occasions his own major contribution was the *Firebird* suite,[48] while Craft took charge of *The Rite of Spring*. At Santa Fe in August, also under the open skies, programs were naturally more adventurous and there was a systematic attempt at a Stravinsky Festival, with a whole series of talks about his music and staged performances of all his operas, including such marginal cases as *Mavra*, *Renard*, and *Persephone*, topped off with the concert premiere of *The Flood*, conducted by Craft in the auditorium of the city museum.[49] Alas, in the nature of things the only reports of this important premiere are by local journalists and "friendly" participants like Paul Horgan, whose whole account of the 1962 festival bubbles over with semi-official pride and loving complaisance.[50] As for balanced judgment, the work still at this stage eludes us.

In Santa Fe Stravinsky at last began his Israel commission, now firmly settled as *Abraham and Isaac*. He may have been drunk when he made the first sketches. Horgan relates how the composer, having imbibed too freely at the vernissage for Vera's latest exhibition, opted out of a dinner that evening, but later, when Horgan brought Vera back to the hotel, announced that "I came dronk, I slept one hour, I sent for some food, I have had supper, and then I have composed two bars!"[51] Admittedly if these bars were the first two of the work, the effort will not have been great since they contain only five notes for the violas; or perhaps "two bars" was simply his lay term for the more complex process of serial planning that always preceded actual composition of his late scores. Or, finally, "dronk" may even have been a fib to get free time for composing, so as to be able to assure his Israeli hosts that, while he may not have finished the work they had originally hoped to have that very year, he had at least started it.

They flew to Tel Aviv without returning home and with their many suitcases more than usually jam-packed for the three-week trip to the Soviet Union at the end of September. Musically the nine-day Israel visit was unremarkable; there were concerts in Haifa, Jerusalem, and Tel Aviv itself, given in heat so intense and an atmosphere so humid that their glasses steamed up and their evening clothes stuck to their bodies like wet swimming costumes.52 But like most visitors to the Holy Land, they were struck by the conflicting images in that troubled terrain: the shocking contrast between the biblical landscape of the mind and the shattered and often commercialized reality, with its sandbagged buildings and abandoned tanks, its factories and tourist trash, its soldiers and petty officials and assorted immigrants. At one point this "rough assembly," as Isaiah Berlin later called Israeli officialdom,53 made contact with Stravinsky's own past, when a group of Israelis descended from families at Ustilug presented him with a history of the Jewish community in that village of so many remote summers long past.54 Not least, perhaps, because he hoped to see Ustilug again for himself soon, he was visibly moved by the gift.

THERE WERE various opinions about why Stravinsky eventually decided to visit the Soviet Union, and nearly as many on the rights and wrongs of his doing so, but his and Vera's actual feelings as they landed at Sheremetevo Airport in Moscow on the 21st of September can only be guessed at. Craft, who of course went with them, was perfectly clear that the decision to go had been the composer's alone, motivated by curiosity and what Craft somewhat obscurely called the "desire for revenge."55 To come across an analysis that is at once so shrewd and so profoundly uncomprehending is disconcerting to say the least. Most of us are instinctively interested in our own past, but to call that interest "curiosity" is to reduce it to the status of a book we intend to read or a new neighbor we hope to meet; it is to treat Stravinsky's prewar refusals to return and his subsequent vilification of the Soviet Union entirely at face value, as lack of curiosity and genuine dislike, when it must have been obvious that fear, insecurity, and a passionate resentment gradually solidifying into a fixed and rigid intellectual position were really the active emotional ingredients. There was a kind of precedent that Craft knew all about. Stravinsky's cultivated ignorance and rejection of serialism for almost three decades had been symptomatic of the same reluctance to confront dangerous situations. When forced (by Craft himself) to face that danger, he did not so much overcome it as watch it dissolve in his own creative acids. But Craft, unfortunately, held no such key to the Russian question. On the contrary, Stravinsky's Russianness had always in a way been something outside his experience. After nearly thirteen years at Wetherly Drive he had still apparently made no serious attempt to learn the language in which Stravinsky thought his thoughts, conversed with his wife, and conducted his most intimate correspondence.⁵⁶ He seems to have preferred to keep such matters at arm's length, observing and assessing them under the spotlight of a sharp eye and mind, but not caring (or daring) to penetrate too deeply into the darkness beyond.

He quickly realized something that he admits he had not foreseen: that for both the Stravinskys, once they set foot on Russian soil, it was no longer a visit but a homecoming.⁵⁷ When Balanchine arrived in Moscow with the New York City Ballet, only a fortnight later as it happened, he made it very clear that he now regarded America as his home.⁵⁸ For the Stravinskys the situation, though factually the same, was for some reason psychologically more complex. Balanchine had an easy, unsentimental way of taking things as he found them. Stravinsky only pretended not to mind about the past, and his denial of Russia was plainly some kind of repression. When he landed at Sheremetevo and found himself engulfed by people speaking Russian, the waters broke through the floodgates and carried him into a region where his young American companion simply could not follow. To the latter, inevitably, there remained something distant and even threatening about these people who took possession of Stravinsky—with his seemingly absolute complicity—as if the last fifty years had been merely some unfortunate aberration. Between Craft and almost everything that was said stood his attractive, polished, omniscient, but when all was said and done official interpreter, Alexandra Alexandrovna Afonina; and between him and Stravinsky there now appeared another kind of threat, in the shape of the latter's niece Xenya.

Even though she had had no reply to her second letter, Xenya had decided to travel from Leningrad to Moscow to greet her uncle at the airport, encouraged by a Canadian interview she had heard on the radio, in which he had referred to the niece in Leningrad he had never met but already loved and was looking forward to meeting. At Sheremetevo, she waited nervously with Yudina behind the crowds of reporters and photographers and the official welcoming party led by Khrennikov, but at last found an opportunity to introduce herself to Vera, and then was somehow pushed forward with Yudina to meet her uncle. "I'm Xenya," she announced simply, as they kissed three times in the Russian style. Suddenly the stout

Yudina, to everyone's horror, went down heavily on one knee and kissed his hand. Stravinsky, embarrassed, kissed her hand in return and helped her to her feet.

Xenya had not intended to barge in on Stravinsky's tour, though she certainly hoped to invite him to visit her and her family in their Kryukov apartment. Gradually, though, she found herself being drawn into the family group. After the airport press conference, she accompanied them in Khrennikov's car to their hotel, the National, a grand former Tsarist establishment on Prospekt Marxa (just north of the Kremlin), drank vodka and Georgian champagne, and joined in the usual endless toasts, then was hauled off to the hotel restaurant with the Stravinskys, Craft, Afonina, and Hurok's Moscow representative, Ralph Parker. The next morning she went with them to their first rehearsal with the U.S.S.R. State Symphony Orchestra in the Great Hall of the Conservatoire, was taken on to a reception at the Dom Kompozitorov (the Composers' House), and was still in tow when they proceeded on a tour of the city, ending at the beautiful Novodevichy monastery. Craft was convinced that Afonina opposed this particular visit, and even Xenya noticed that it ran counter to their hosts' desire to show off the New Russia rather than the Old. But Stravinsky had not been in Moscow before, except for a brief carriage ride between trains when he was seven,[59] and he was determined to see the sights, from St. Basil's Cathedral to the hill from which Napoleon had himself first glimpsed the city.

The next day, Sunday, Xenya did not appear, not wanting to be in the way. But on Monday, when she presented herself at the National at the end of lunch, Stravinsky immediately demanded: "Why weren't you here yesterday?" "Well, I was afraid of being a nuisance." "Don't dare to talk like that, I want you to come every day. From now on you're licensed." They had been to *Boris Godunov* at the Bolshoi, and had kept a seat for her. So from then on, until they left Leningrad a fortnight later, Xenya was automatically included in almost everything. She sat in the Stravinskys' box at concerts, went with them to the theatre and opera, took meals with them, and even once or twice sat with her uncle in his hotel room while he was resting and the others had gone out. They talked about their families, and Xenya for the first time heard details of her cousins' grown-up lives and realized "how dear his children were to him, how much love and tenderness and concern he felt for them."[60] She sensed the same kind of affection in his attitude to her as well. It was as if they had known each other all her life and had merely been separated for a long time. She had of course expected something quite different. She had been afraid, at the airport, that he would be a "celebrity," and instead he had turned out to be, quite simply, her adored father's brother, with the same gestures, the same way of talking, the same manner. This "family blood" was so strong that she felt a vast joy, as if she had found someone very dear whom she had thought lost. By comparison, all the hullabaloo and glitter, the vortex of noise and bustle that enveloped him and into which she had been sucked willy-nilly, was no more than an interesting spectacle that she observed, so to speak, from the side. As she sat on the carpet that day in his hotel room, she looked at this infinitely dear, lovable sleeping old man, and was happy.[61]

ROBERT CRAFT was observing these strange new surroundings with a more skeptical, if not unsympathetic eye—the eye, though, of a superior nomad who had eaten better food in better hotels and was no stranger to the green-glass-bead tradition of travel in primitive lands. As a reasonable, civilized American—an admirer, admittedly, of the ethnic paraphernalia of *Pribaoutki* and *Les Noces*—he had been bemused by the useless basket of rustic debris thrust into his hands at the airport as a gift of welcome by the daughter of the poet Konstantin Balmont. But he quickly noticed that the Stravinskys' reaction to these things was by no means so rational or cosmopolitan. After barely a day in Moscow, they were starting to see things through Russian eyes, take pride in Russian achievements, believe in the supposed Soviet dream of social equality and universal happiness. Within two days the composer was slipping back into the despised Russian linguistic habit of diminutive forms for the names of objects as well as people.[62] He was saying agreeable things about Moscow's modern architecture, and even—if the newspapers were to be believed—about the Soviet press, about the Soviet Union, about Lenin himself. Perhaps he did not really tell *Komsomol'skaya Pravda* that "I know and love your newspaper, and often read it," or *Moskovskaya Pravda* that "in the United States I have tried hard to promote the great art of Russia—Glinka, Musorgsky, Rachmaninov, Scriabin, Prokofiev, Shostakovich: names as close and dear to me as the names of people I love."[63] He surely did tell the interpreter, Afonina, that "I'm so delighted by everything I've seen [. . .]. How remarkable that your government, with its vast building-program for the new Moscow, still takes such care of its ancient monuments!"[64] And he certainly more or less told Ida Vershinina that "I've seen a lot of cities, but Moscow has conquered me."[65] "All my life I've spoken Russian, thought in Russian," he said, "my whole makeup is Russian. Perhaps in my music it's not at once obvious, but it's there in the background, in its hidden nature."[66]

In fact the Russianness of his music rapidly became something of a motif of the Moscow concerts, of which there were four in all, with two different programs. At the very first rehearsal, in the Conservatoire, the visitors immediately noticed the completely different sound of the Russian orchestra in *The Rite of Spring*, which Craft was rehearsing and conducting in the first program.[67] Though much less familiar with the work than the average Western orchestra, the players were technically well in control of their music, while displaying a quite different set of priorities from those of the virtuoso American or European bands Stravinsky had come to know best. The steely brilliance of Chicago or New York was absent; intonation was wayward and generally regarded as of secondary importance, and the sound as a whole had a dry, thudding heaviness that recaptured for the composer something of the primitive menace of his original inspiration.[68] Some of these details are evident in the published recording taken from the two opening concerts on the 26th and 28th of September.[69] The eerie timbre of the Russian bassoon, so much more insinuating than that of the Western instrument, naturally imprints its character on the music from the outset. The string-playing consistently bears out Craft's implication that the players felt the music lyrically in a way that would scarcely occur to Western musicians, aware of Stravinsky's reputation for having rejected traditional expressive values. The rhythms have a convulsive violence in some ways more thrilling than the mechanistic precision of most American performances. In general, the non-Russian listener is suddenly more aware of the true ancestry of this most profoundly Russian of all late-Romantic masterpieces.

Pleased with his rehearsals, Stravinsky had reasonable hopes for the triple bill of his ballets—*Orpheus, Petrushka,* and *The Firebird*—which had been imported into Moscow's super-modern Palace of Congresses from the Leningrad Maly Theatre and which he was seeing on the 25th. He was blissfully unaware that, earlier that day, Yudina had telephoned Xenya from Leningrad, where she was putting together a Stravinsky exhibition, to warn her that the *Orpheus* was substandard and advising her to ensure that the composer got to the theatre too late to see it. Stravinsky was accordingly put to rest without an alarm clock; but when Xenya arrived at the hotel he had already left, and she herself barely reached the theatre in time for the start. She sat next to him and watched him in profile. To her relief, at the end of *Orpheus* he simply shrugged his shoulders and said he realized that the work (which was also in his own program the following evening) was quite unknown in Russia. But then as she glanced sidelong at him during *Petrushka,* she saw his brow darken and his mood change. She realized that what had looked good on the intimate stage of the Maly Theatre almost vanished in the huge spaces of the Kremlin palace. The crowd scenes were feeble and disorganized, the soloists barely visible. This time the composer was much less sympathetic. "They should be ashamed," he muttered. "Why couldn't they work it up properly? *Orpheus* I can understand—a new ballet—but this has been around for fifty years!" There was worse to come. Just before *Firebird,* Nikita Khrushchev entered the box opposite and, with the music already begun, there were shouts of "Viva Khrushchev" and some rhythmic chanting. Onstage, the Firebird (Safronova) appeared from above like a tiny dragonfly, and the whole production, supposedly based on the original dances and designs by Fokine and Golovine, looked tacky and unmagical. The music was almost unrecognizable. The last chord had barely died away when Stravinsky was on his feet. "Let me out, quick, quick . . . let's go!" he insisted, and hurried away without a thought for the dancers, musicians, and stagehands, all gathered in the wings, waiting hopefully for a word of thanks and a smile of reassurance from the great composer.[70]

His own concert in the Great Hall of the Conservatoire the next evening was a very different affair. The hall was of course packed, not just with politicians, diplomats, and the usual grandees, but with musicians of every stamp, young and old, from Shostakovich and Khachaturian down (or up) to the humblest and brightest students in the galleries. The atmosphere was tense with excitement. In some ways the program was curiously chosen: *The Rite of Spring*, conducted not by the composer but by his apparently inexplicable American assistant, while Stravinsky himself directed only *Orpheus* and *Ode*, works completely unknown in the Soviet Union and by all accounts of secondary importance. The first sounds of his own that Stravinsky had ever presented in person to a Russian audience were the soft, enigmatic brass chords that open the *Ode* in memory of Natalie Koussevitzky, while the second half of the program consisted entirely of *Orpheus*, a work that starts and ends very quietly and remains subdued for much of its half-hour duration. Even the *Song of the Volga Boatmen*, which Stravinsky added by way of encore, scarcely relieved the strangeness, with its harsh, brassy orchestration—an awkward modernization of a Tsarist image.

Yet it scarcely mattered. The audience had come to witness a living legend, not to cavil over this or that work or to notice the quality of what were, in fact, distinctive and in their way memorable performances. Everything was received with loud applause, and at the end they stood and cheered, and when, after numerous curtain calls, Stravinsky appeared in his overcoat, held up his hand, and told them, "You can't imagine how happy I am today," they clapped even louder.[71]

The second concert, two days later, went if anything even better, despite the fact that Stravinsky had felt unwell for much of the day and had taken opium washed down with whisky just before the concert, "to avoid any unpleasantness," as Xenya delicately put it. He was taken ill again in the interval, and she supposed that Craft would have to conduct *Orpheus* in the second half. "You don't know him," came the reply. "He's very tough. He'll be fine." And sure enough, after an extended interval lubricated by cups of coffee and slugs of cognac, Stravinsky duly stepped up and conducted

Orpheus with greater confidence than in the first concert, but without the encore and without the little speech.[72]

For the second pair of concerts, on the 2nd and 3rd of October, the orchestra was the Moscow Philharmonic, a generally younger and, Craft considered, better-drilled, brighter-sounding body of players;[73] and the program was more balanced, with *Petrushka* and the early *Fireworks* offset by the Symphony in Three Movements and the Capriccio for piano and orchestra (with Tatyana Nikolayevna as soloist). Admittedly, Stravinsky conducted only about twenty-two minutes of this music, by dint of reducing *Petrushka* to the old suite (starting with the "Tour de passe-passe"), and leaving the symphony and Capriccio to Craft. But once again nothing could puncture the Muscovites' enthusiasm for their lost master, whatever they may have thought about some of his music; once again they stood and cheered and threw flowers. It was, Xenya thought, to all intents and purposes a "farewell forever" from Moscow.[74] The next day they all flew to Leningrad.

In one obvious sense, the Moscow leg of the Soviet visit had been both the most detached and the most official. Moscow was the capital and the musical headquarters, and it was a city Stravinsky did not know. Leningrad would be the real homecoming, the more so because, for some unknown reason, Kiev (and hence any possibility of visiting Ustilug) had at the last minute been removed from the itinerary.[75] In Moscow he had met the cream and the dregs of Soviet music; he had met what Craft called the "plutocrat performers," Rostropovich, Gilels, Kogan, and Oistrakh,[76] conductors like Kondrashin and Rozhdestvensky (who had penned a sympathetic article in *Izvestiya*, comparing Stravinsky enthusiastically with Picasso and praising his conducting),[77] and of course a whole symphony of composers, the pillars of the Composers' Union, the real and for the most part irretrievable musical victims of the system that he had very publicly despised for thirty years and more. Actual Soviet music he had so far been spared, with the exception of Prokofiev's *War and Peace* at the Bolshoi. As for Shostakovich, Russia's sole unquestioned living master had been unable to greet Stravinsky personally at Sheremetevo because (by a profound and even rather beautiful irony) he had been taking part in the centenary celebrations of the Leningrad Conservatoire, an institution in which Stravinsky had not studied. They had eventually met at a dinner organized in the Metropole Hotel by Yekaterina Furtseva, the disconcertingly handsome minister of culture, who had sat between them in order, presumably, to ensure that communication stayed on an acceptably orthodox plane.[78]

She need hardly have worried. Shostakovich's independence of spirit was not of the kind that bred confidences with strangers, even (or perhaps especially) with one he so revered that, when he spoke to him, he stammered and trembled visibly. As for Stravinsky, he had once admired

Shostakovich's talent but had given up expecting work of (as he considered) high artistic caliber from him as long ago as 1935, when he had heard _Lady Macbeth of the Mtsensk District_ in New York. He knew about Shostakovich's stature in the Soviet Union, of course, and may even for a time have shared Souvtchinsky's fantasy about his political influence there, which would explain why, in Moscow, he kept asking his escort, Karen Khachaturian, "Where is Shostakovich?"[79] But the Furtseva dinner must have dispelled any such notion and in general confirmed once and for all the centralized, bureaucratic (rather than artistic) nature of the command structure in Soviet music. One by one, each of the composers present rose and spoke, acknowledging his own inadequacies (in the approved Stalinist tradition of the forced confession), and proposing a toast to the return of the prodigal, though without, for the most part, mentioning his music. In due course, Stravinsky himself spoke:

> A man has one birthplace, one fatherland, one country—he _can_ have only one country—and the place of his birth is the most important factor in his life. I regret that circumstances separated me from my fatherland, that I did not give birth to my works here and, above all, that I was not here to help the new Soviet Union create its new music. I did not leave Russia of my own will, even though I disliked much in my Russia and in Russia generally. Yet the right to criticize Russia is mine, because Russia is mine and I love it, and I do not give any foreigner that right.[80]

In a curious way this, too, was a kind of confession.

The Leningrad they drove into from Pulkovo airport was for most of the way unrecognizable as the St. Petersburg Stravinsky had last seen fifty years ago almost to the day. The city was like the old gentleman who had greeted him at the airport terminal and whom he had completely failed to recognize as his oldest and once upon a time greatest friend, Vladimir Rimsky-Korsakov. The outskirts had changed; the center was much the same, more decrepit, in some ways modernized (Volodya now wore a hearing aid and had shaved off his beard), but to the Western eye still decidedly dingy. The Italianate beauties of Rastrelli's Petersburg still nevertheless shone through the grayness of Soviet life, and Igor was soon recognizing buildings and streets and attaching their old names to them.

Leningrad, unlike Moscow, meant revisiting his own past. On the first full day, they drove out to Oranienbaum (long since renamed Lomonosov) and tried to imagine the location of the wooden dacha in which he had been born. They were not to know that the house had been pulled down almost thirty years before, and they could not discover that fact because neither Stravinsky nor his hosts had the slightest idea where it had been. Two days later they went to tea with Xenya and her husband in their Kryukov Canal flat. It was in the same long building as, and, Xenya assured them, identical in size and layout to, the former Stravinsky flat at no. 66—a statement they might not have accepted quite so readily if they had known more about Soviet housing policy (which by that time had allocated the old flat to no fewer than four separate households).[81] Outside his own staircase, two doors along the canal, Stravinsky stood and looked and said nothing, not daring to show any emotion. Nobody suggested mounting the stairs and knocking on the door of the second-floor flat. In the nearby theatre square he surveyed the Conservatoire on the one hand and the former Maryinsky Theatre—now the Kirov—on the other. Craft heard him mutter "Glazunov" as he caught sight of the one, and saw him beam with pleasure as he turned toward the other, and deduced from this that the Conservatoire had taught him to hate music as surely as the Maryinsky had taught him to love it.[82] Patient readers of this chronicle will know by now how false such an antithesis was. Stravinsky had never enrolled at the Conservatoire and never studied with Glazunov, as he himself (or perhaps his alter ego) had been at pains to inform the editor of the *Observer* only a few months before.[83] His sole connection with the Conservatoire had been through Rimsky-Korsakov, a teacher he revered, and two other Rimsky-Korsakov pupils, who probably did his own inner music no harm. As for the Maryinsky, he had certainly been much there and entirely to his musical advantage; but his *entrée* to the theatre had been by way of a musical influence he had never later wanted to overpraise: that of his own father.

Either Craft misheard, or Stravinsky was speaking for the microphones.

One other focus of his musical education had been the so-called Assembly of the Nobles, the elegant, pillared hall on the corner of Mikhailovsky Square (opposite the Europa Hotel, where they were now staying). Here he had attended the Ziloti, RMS, and Russian Symphony concerts, had sat with Rimsky-Korsakov in rehearsals, and had heard the first performance of his own *Scherzo fantastique* in January 1909. And it was to this same hall, now known as the Great Hall of the Leningrad Philharmonie (Filarmoniy), that he returned to conduct his two Leningrad concerts, on the 8th and 9th of October 1962. The program was such as might almost have been heard on the last occasion he had himself been in the hall, early in 1910. At that time *Fireworks* had just been premiered there, and *The Firebird* was nearing completion; it was these two works that he now conducted, apparently because the Leningrad Philharmonic—only the city's second orchestra— was unwilling to risk anything more recent. Craft conducted *The Fairy's Kiss*, more modern but, with its Tchaikovskian roots, not hugely more challenging. Yet even more than in Moscow, repertoire was of secondary importance. What mattered was the sense of homecoming and the unreserved enthusiasm of the welcome. "The first time I came to this hall," he reminisced from the podium, "was with my mother sixty-nine years ago. We sat over there in the right-hand corner. It was a concert under Napravnik in memory of Tchaikovsky, two weeks after his death. And today I'm conducting on this platform for the first time. It's a great occasion for me."[84] As in Moscow, this announcement was greeted with wild applause.

By contrast, the Composers' Union, where Yudina had been busy for weeks setting up her Stravinsky exhibition, was not a building—and certainly not an institution—that he would have stepped inside in Tsarist St. Petersburg. The Dom Kompozitorov, or Composers' House, occupied and still occupies a former mansion in Ulitsa Gertsen built in the 1840s by the architect of St. Isaac's Cathedral, Auguste Montferrand. In its Soviet incarnation, it provided a suitably melancholy headquarters for the anxious and often menial activity of composition in the second city of the U.S.S.R. Here, two days before his own concert, Yudina conducted Stravinsky round the exhaustive display of photographs and manuscripts that she had put together partly from family materials that he had either never seen before or had completely forgotten about. She then led him into the cramped but elegant concert hall for performances of his Octet and the Septet, a piece she had introduced to the Soviet Union in a concert the previous January— apparently Russia's first encounter with the serial or even proto-serial Stravinsky.

The atmosphere was very different from anything Stravinsky had encountered in his orchestral concerts. The audience consisted largely of musicians, not all of whom were necessarily sympathetic to the modernisms of the Septet especially, and some of whom undoubtedly felt at least a vestigial resentment against this colleague who had done so well by—as they might have put it—abandoning his native city. In the fourth row of the jam-packed and stuffy little hall Stravinsky felt hemmed in and soon retreated with his retinue to the back row, next to the exit, so that for a moment some of the audience thought he had simply left. After the concert, the director of the Composers' Union, Yevgeniya Vïkhodtseva, ushered him back into the exhibition room and mounted guard on the doorway, only permitting a select few to pass through to meet him. Many saw in all this a desire on his part to avoid contact with his Russian fellow musicians; yet it seems he had no such wish, knew nothing of Vïkhodtseva's activities, and had no idea that he was giving offense by seeming to distance himself from his less fortunate colleagues.[85]

As for the brief concert itself, it showed once more how hard it was for Soviet musicians, no matter how able, to come to terms with a complex music about whose background and discourse they knew nothing. The Octet, agilely performed by students, was almost entirely at the wrong speeds and kept pausing—Craft thought—at what had been changeover points on somebody's 78 recording.[86] Yudina tackled the difficult piano part in the Septet with great aplomb but little grasp of the music, which, Craft observed, sounded more or less incoherent. Yet she had for years been carrying on a lone fight in defense of Stravinsky's music, and she was that very night off to Moscow to play the Piano Concerto, before flying back to Petersburg for another performance of the Septet.[87]

THE STRAVINSKYS' own route back to the West was likewise by way of Moscow. They left Leningrad by train at midnight on the 9th of October 1962, and Xenya was at the Moscow Station, along with many others, to see them off. Inevitably they left behind them a trail of regrets. Letters had arrived at the Europa from family friends who remembered young Gima from St. Petersburg days and longed for some word from him, some assurance that he, too, remembered or at least acknowledged their part in his early life. Whether he replied to such communications we do not know, but perhaps at any rate he wrote to his cousin Inna Apollonskaya, the daughter of his father's brother Alexander and now eighty-eight years old, who remembered him as a child sitting at the piano in her father's house and playing his very first compositions, as she called them: "My frozen sweet" and "In the yard there stands a mop."[88] It was probably Inna who, according to Craft, had missed by one place the ballot for tickets for the Philharmonie concerts, but was found a seat at the last minute by Hurok's representative, Parker.[89]

There was also a short letter from Volodya Rimsky-Korsakov, regretting that they had had no chance of an intimate conversation, and enclosing a copy of a book he had written "as proof that I have done in my life as much as circumstances permitted."[90] In fact they had sat together at a dinner in the Composers' Union the day after Stravinsky's arrival; but to a Soviet citizen such occasions were not intimate and could not be treated as an opportunity to speak freely about the past or about any issue of a more than conventional or superficial character.[91] What, in any case, would Volodya have wanted to say? Would he have regretted the rift between them over Diaghilev and the *Khovanshchina* completion, or expressed remorse at his family's hostile attitude to Stravinsky's ballets at their first performances in St. Petersburg? It seems highly unlikely, in view of Stravinsky's recently published attack on Volodya's brother-in-law, Max Steinberg, of which the family can surely not have been wholly unaware.[92] Volodya's sister Nadezhda Steinberg certainly had not forgotten Stravinsky's ill-mannered treatment of her husband in Paris in 1925, which was quite sufficient grounds for her to refuse his invitation to the Philharmonie concert on 8 October.[93] It would have been nice to think that, through the Rimsky-Korsakovs, fifty years of silence and separation could be obliterated, friendship resumed, the thread of history retied. But to expect it would have been wishful thinking. Stravinsky, it seems, neither expected nor wished it.

In Moscow there was yet another dinner at the Metropole, at which Stravinsky and Shostakovich sat next to each other and talked—very edgily—about music. Shostakovich confessed his admiration for the *Symphony of Psalms,* and they discussed Mahler and Puccini, but trivially and without touching on each other's deeper attitudes.[94] The next day, they were summoned to the Kremlin to meet Khrushchev, just returned from a tour of irrigation works and hydroelectric installations in the Central Asian republics. It was a curious reminder of a not dissimilar meeting almost exactly thirty years before in the Palazzo Venezia in Rome. And just as in February 1933 Mussolini had impressed Stravinsky as a strong political leader, so Khrushchev now struck him not as a ruthless tyrant but as a man of extraordinary vision and organizational skill, with whom he could converse "as with a great artist, on questions of common concern."[95] "He is like a composer," the real composer confided to Craft as they drove to the airport, "showing you the score on which he is working, and of which he is very full and very proud."[96]

The most important score of all they did not discuss, but a mere ten days later it was revealed, unexpectedly, by the President of the United States. The Russians, he announced, had been constructing ballistic-missile launching pads and bomber bases in Cuba, within striking distance of "most of the major cities in the Western hemisphere." The U.S. navy was blockading Cuba. A convoy of Soviet supply ships was steaming westward and approaching the Caribbean. On the very day that Kennedy ordered the ships to be intercepted, Stravinsky flew from Rome to New York, and he was again in a plane, flying across the Caribbean to Caracas, when the crisis ended on the 28th of October. Thus, like a magus, the eighty-year-old composer spanned the troubled world; and, as he flew, he contemplated his latest work—the Hebrew story of the sacrifice of Isaac, prevented as the knife rose by the intervention of an angel.

STRAVINSKY LEFT the Soviet Union with every intention, it seems, of returning. Khrushchev, he told the Paris reporters at Orly, had invited him to spend time resting and working in the Crimea or the Caucasus. Craft was enthusiastic. Russia had made a bigger impression on him than any country he had visited, and he was eager to go back to teach, conduct, and generally spread the word about modern music in the West. It was obvious that the Stravinskys had both been profoundly moved by the visit. Aspects of their personalities that had lain buried under almost half a century of exile had welled to the surface, forced up by the recognition of a shared cultural, topographical, and linguistic heritage which all the grayness, deprivation, and falsehood of Soviet life were powerless to conceal. It no longer seemed so important that—as he had felt in 1949—"there is no discussion possible with people who are not free."[1] Face-to-face with individuals, he could form bonds even with those—like Khrennikov and Furtseva—part of whose job was to perpetuate that unfreedom, and could overlook the extent to which other contacts were inhibited by a fear that remained in large measure hidden and intangible.

Back in France, however, the shared Russianness seemed suddenly far off and perhaps even faintly absurd. In the Paris interviews—even as printed in the Russian-language press—he alluded to it in only a stereotyped way and talked much about the beauties of Moscow and Leningrad as if he were a space traveller just back from the moon. "I saw unforgettable things," he assured reporters, thereby studiously misrepresenting the place of memory in an event whose issue was not what could be, but what had been, forgotten or otherwise;[2] and when asked about the city of his childhood he confessed he had been happy to see it again but happiest of all to meet his niece and her family.[3] Questions about Soviet music and musicians were carefully avoided. In only a single rather longer interview, with the music critic Claude Samuel, did he risk what he plainly intended as an off-the-record remark about Khrennikov himself—"a good sort, but a servant of the old regime from the time of Stalin"—which unfortunately

Samuel included in the printed article and which soon inevitably came to its subject's attention.4 Having obviously failed to alert Samuel (himself the author of a well-informed book on Prokofiev) to his personal friendship with his erstwhile host, he was reduced to a squirming apology in which he pretended that Samuel was so ignorant and stupid as to have confused Khrennikov with Glazunov.5 It seems unlikely that the clever union secretary was deceived, but, being professionally at ease with façades, he accepted this one at its face value, and friendly relations were quickly resumed with barely a tremor.

Such contradictions and misunderstandings were, of course, in the nature of the situation, and they were no less severe for Soviet critics, who had somehow to reconcile their past denigration of Stravinsky with the new atmosphere of brotherly love and cordial artistic welcome. Musically, their difficulties were genuine enough. For thirty years before the late fifties, Stravinsky's music since *Petrushka* had gone largely unheard at least in the main Soviet concert halls and theatres; and when one recalls the panic-stricken reaction of French critics in the twenties and American critics in the thirties to what de Schloezer had called his "zigzag" evolution,6 it is scarcely surprising that post-thaw criticism in Moscow found itself at sea with works like *Orpheus* and *Ode* which, in their experience, were completely without context. *The Rite of Spring* they felt able to understand, for all its primitive, discordant violence—so loathsome to Stalinist taste—because its Russianism was patent and to some extent familiar, and the music could easily be heard as "a premonition of terrifying social cataclysms and the catastrophes of war."7 If anything they wanted the violence sensationalized, even sensualized, and they found Craft cold and too rational after Bernstein and Igor Markevitch, the only recent conductors of this work in Moscow.8 By the same token they found the Symphony in Three Movements easier to grasp than *Orpheus.* Its outer movements were "Russian" in the same sense as *The Rite;* and had not the composer himself admitted that the troubled times had left their mark on the music?9 *Orpheus,* by comparison, was cold-blooded and impassive, a masterly stylization, beautiful in places, but devoid of the violent tension and fury that went with the idea of ancient myth relived in the modern world.

The various arguments were nowhere more lucidly deployed than by Israel Nestyev in a long review of Stravinsky's Moscow concerts in *Sovetskaya muzïka.*10 Nestyev was a pillar of the Soviet cultural establishment, a senior research fellow at the Art History Institute, and the author of two quite different biographies of Prokofiev, tailored respectively to the American and Soviet markets.11 More to the point, he was a past scourge of Stravinsky—both his music and his person. He had once denounced the composer of *Orpheus* as "the shameless prophet of bourgeois modernism,"12 and only a few years before the 1962 visit he had launched a vicious assault on the *Canticum sacrum,* on its "tedious calculation and unbridled anarchy of sound." "In the *Canticum,*" he had concluded, "there is literally not a single natural inflection. It is a dead desert, barren and stony. . . . How ravaged, how emasculated must have been the soul of the composer capable of creating such dreadful music."[13]

In his 1962 review, Nestyev did not specifically retract these remarks; there being no serial music in any of the programs, the question could simply be avoided. Neither did he wholly acquit Stravinsky of past error. Instead the line now was that Stravinsky was too important a figure to be ignored, a great Russian composer whose best works were part of the "treasure-trove of world art." There were still things to regret. *Orpheus* was immaculate but cold, *Ode* was a deadly kind of musical Esperanto. The great works here were the *Rite* and—more guardedly—the symphony, with the Capriccio coming a good third: a jolly, colorful parody of early-twentieth-century keyboard virtuosity, without the poisonous malice of *Mavra* or (surprisingly enough) the little orchestral suites. Nestyev was in general conciliatory. "It is no secret," he admitted,

> that relations between Soviet criticism and Stravinsky have taken a not wholly normal course. Here there have been the most abrupt extremes: from unrestrained delight in the twenties to complete denial in the thirties and forties. While definitely not accepting the composer's aesthetic positions, we have not always taken the trouble to investigate his huge creative legacy, have not always managed carefully, thoughtfully to separate what was really valuable to us from all that was in decline, moribund, alien. In his turn, Stravinsky himself has more than once given cause for fair and pointed criticism, both in his work of recent years and in a number of printed remarks. In his long journey he has made many mistakes that have reflected the awkward zigzags of bourgeois art, and with many of his aesthetic aims we shall hardly ever agree . . .

It was not quite the ringing endorsement some might have hoped for, but it was at least, in the circumstances, a reasonably graceful compromise.

Alas, any hope that Stravinsky's visit might prove a major watershed in the liberalization of Soviet music, and of Soviet attitudes to his music in particular, was soon dashed. Performances of previously marginal works such as *The Nightingale, Les Noces,* and *The Soldier's Tale* did become more frequent and acceptable. But the situation remained volatile, unpredictable, and subject to the arbitrary dictates of Khrushchev's own uneducated tastes. Early in December he visited an exhibition of abstract and semi-abstract art in the Manège exhibition hall in Moscow and promptly let fly with a string of abusive remarks that were duly splashed over the front page of *Pravda*.[14] Suddenly once again fear was in the air. A conference was convened in the Kremlin in mid-December, guidelines were issued, tendencies denounced, individuals named. It was not that music was particularly under attack, but it was included by inference and association. Nicolas Nabokov was soon being assured by his Moscow literary connections that Khrushchev's outburst was significant only for visual artists;[15] but by late March he was hearing of purges that effectively put an end to his own intention to go to Russia, and by mid-April there were rumors that suspect musicians such as Yudina herself were being subjected to harassment and persecution.[16] As for Stravinsky, he stayed in touch with Khrennikov, but the prospect of a second visit quickly faded, as Souvtchinsky predicted it would.[17] Later in April, Khrennikov told Stravinsky that "your music is done here all the time now; hardly a concert goes by without something of yours."[18] But the hyperbole was transparent.

Gradually, the Soviet contact died away. The Christmas and birthday greetings continued. Xenya went on writing—newsy, informative, affectionate letters—but her uncle, irresistibly warm and loving in person, was a poor correspondent these days, and would reply only with brief postcards, or by way of a letter from Vera explaining at time-consuming length that he was too busy to write.[19] Yudina, curiously, did not write. At first it seemed that she felt a certain compunction over her failure to make close acquaintance with Stravinsky because of her extreme preoccupation with the Leningrad exhibition and rehearsals for the Septet.[20] Then it began to emerge that she considered that she had been specifically prevented from spending time alone with the Master, a thwarted desire that arose from her sense of a very intimate relationship with his music and her feeling that he, as an artist of genius, would understand and help alleviate her feeling of isolation. The odd thing was that she apparently blamed, not Mme. Vïkhodtseva, the Composers' Union, nor even the KGB, but Stravinsky's own entourage.[21] She had taken badly against Vera. "Forgive me," she wrote to Souvtchinsky, "but to sincerely get to like her was and is impossible for me—we're terribly different, and I'm not much accustomed to lying."[22] It had struck her forcibly that Mme. Stravinsky found other people superfluous and wearisome.[23] As for Craft, he was simply alien to the deeply spiritual Russian pianist and, in her opinion, completely out of place in Stravinsky's inner circle.[24] She thought of him as a mere counting machine, and dubbed him "Chislo-Craft"—"number-craft." The composer himself dwelt far above them all, in a kind of Goethesque empyrean; and yet even he had revealed frailties. Could it be, Yudina began to wonder, that his failure to communicate with her was simply due to his having no further need of her? Was this why, when she tried to telephone him in Milan, he was never available; or why, when she cabled him there, she received no reply?[25]

AFTER THE RETURN from Moscow, life resumed its normal exhausting pattern. There were concerts in Perugia and Rome, where the program included the old 1909 arrangement of Beethoven's "Song of the Flea," never previously conducted by its author; and, after New York, a pair of concerts in Caracas. Back in New York, Craft directed a semi-staged performance of *The Rake's Progress* in Carnegie Hall on 21 November, and then within days they were off to Toronto for a series of recording sessions culminating in Stravinsky's second (and final) taping of the Symphony in C— a performance so markedly different from his 1952 version with the Cleveland Orchestra as to undermine all his theories about recordings as authentic documents of the composer's wishes. Not until 4 December did they at last get back to North Wetherly Drive, after eight months of almost continuous absence on tour.

Stravinsky had already managed to start work on *Abraham and Isaac*. He had made some headway with it at Santa Fe in August, and he had taken it up again during a brief stay in Venice in September, between Israel and Russia. But it was probably only now, with three clear months at his disposal, that he was able to make fluent progress on what might well have proved an awkward creative task, in view of the opacity of the language and the technical intricacies it might entail. The unexpected fact is that composition seems to have come with relative ease. By the end of January 1963 the score was half-complete, and less than five weeks after that, on 3 March, it was finished. Considering that the music was once again utterly unlike anything that he or anyone else had written before, this was good going for a twelve-minute work. Any comparison one can think of breaks down. Britten's *Abraham and Isaac,* despite the weary jokes about the older composer shadowing the younger in subject after subject, is as different as can be in both style and treatment, while Schoenberg's *De Profundis,* which had probably suggested the idea of a Hebrew setting, is not remotely an influence musically.[26] In their various ways, both those composers had dramatized their setting of language. Stravinsky very studiously does not do so. He uses a single solo baritone with a spare chamber-orchestral accompaniment, and his narrative is even-paced and monotonous, ballad-like in that antique sense in which music has to carry the text as a horse carries a rider, without too much concern for route or destination and merely now and then pausing to crop a hedge or shy at a pig. This strange—and strangely affecting—idiom seems to arise directly from the (to the composer) strict incomprehensibility of the words. It owes almost nothing to the picturesque, eventful style of *The Flood,* with its graphic imagery and swift montage of dance movements. Whatever else it may be, *Abraham and Isaac* is not a dance work, and it is not graphic, one or two luminously symbolic moments notwithstanding. Its beauties are interior and esoteric, and they have to be teased out, like the number symbolisms in Bach's third *Clavierübung* or a motet by Ockeghem.

Not for the first time while working on some completely new kind of work, Stravinsky was embroiled in the fate of old ones. In Paris he had recently lunched—at whose behest is not clear—with the writer Jean Genet, and a few weeks later he had received a visit at North Wetherly Drive from the film director Joseph Strick, who was making a film of Genet's play *The Balcony.* A few days after that they were shown a rough cut of the film itself.[27] It seems to have been Strick's idea to invite Stravinsky to adapt his Octet and parts of *The Soldier's Tale* as music for this film, though something Genet himself had said in Paris might suggest that the idea was already in the air. Genet had remarked that Stravinsky's voice reminded him of "the sound of the percussion instruments in *Histoire du Soldat.*"[28] That would hardly explain why Strick thought the music right for a play set in a brothel during a revolution; but in any case the idea—or the cash incentive—pleased Stravinsky enough to persuade him to make the adaptation himself (early in 1963) and, in due course, have Craft conduct the result. For all his many brushes with the industry, *The Balcony* was the only feature film ever made that can accurately—if guardedly—claim to have a score by Stravinsky.[29]

Meanwhile, as an eightieth-birthday present, Boosey had given him the manuscript full score of *The Rite of Spring,* inherited by them along with the rest of the Éditions Russes archive in 1946, and the very copy from which Monteux had conducted the largely inaudible premiere in 1913. Stravinsky had recently been taking advantage of a U.S. revenue concession whereby the gift of a work of art, manuscript, or other object of value to a recognized national collection attracted a tax write-off equivalent to its full value. But for the priceless *Rite* holograph he had no such modest plans. He wanted to sell the manuscript, but in such a way as to avoid paying U.S. tax on the proceeds altogether, and for this he again needed the cooperation of his Swiss son, Theodore.

It seems somehow fitting that this infamous score should have become the object of a cloak-and-dagger operation that would eventually help provide sustenance for a whole army of starving New York lawyers. Even the gift of the score was less innocent and openhearted than it appeared. It was in fact made at Vera's suggestion; and Vera had suggested it because her husband had told her to. No sooner was the gift confirmed than Stravinsky instructed Boosey to send the score to Theodore, asking Theodore to explain to them that as he was short of money and his wife was sick (with a recurrence of her prewar tuberculosis), his father intended to make them a present of the manuscript to do with it whatever they chose.[30] It was true that Theodore was hard up, and that both Denise and their daughter, Kitty, were seriously ill. But needless to say, there was no genuine intention to make such a sumptuous gift to the Geneva Strawinskys, however needy they might be. Theodore's task would be to find a buyer, deposit the proceeds in his father's numbered Basle account, take his own commission, and keep his mouth shut. Meanwhile the composer would deduct the commission from his taxes under some other heading.

This matter was still in hand when another set of *Rite of Spring* manuscripts suddenly turned up in France. Souvtchinsky wrote to the composer about them just before Christmas.[31] It seemed that an elderly Paris collector by the name of André Meyer had recently bought a large volume of sketches for the ballet from Boris Kochno, who had presumably inherited it from Diaghilev, to whom Stravinsky had himself presented it—as recorded in an inscription on the title page—in October 1920, at the time of the Massine revival. Souvtchinsky was in seventh heaven over this incomparable document, and at once proposed that it be published in facsimile.[32] Obsessed as he was with what he called the "phenomenology of the creative process . . . the greatest secret of human genius," he saw instantly the unique value of such a manuscript of such a work. He wanted to have Boulez and Gilbert Amy make a full analysis of the sketches and present their findings in a critical introduction.[33] Stravinsky himself was predictably much less excited by the whole idea. He had completely forgotten about the sketches, and could not remember giving them away.[34] In any case, he had no time for such things.[35] As usual, he found the preoccupation with his old works— even the greatest of them—irritating to the extent that it might imply he was no longer the composer he had been, or even, to the slightly less well informed, that he was actually dead. Perhaps, again, he was mildly afraid of what the sketchbook might reveal. Had he not recently informed admirers of *The Rite of Spring* that no system of any kind had guided the work's composition, that "I had only my ear to help me. I heard and I wrote what I heard. I am the vessel through which *Le Sacre* passed"?[36] In such a mediumistic process, one might be tempted to ask what could possibly be the role of a sketchbook.

The climax of this sudden enthusiasm for *The Rite of Spring* came a few months later, when various performances were put on to mark the fiftieth anniversary of the premiere on the 29th of May 1913. Stravinsky had arrived in Hamburg by sea in mid-April after recording the *Symphony of Psalms* in Toronto at the end of March, and working briefly with Balanchine on his dance version of *Movements* in New York in the first week of April.37 After a fortnight preparing Günther Rennert's stage production of *The Flood* at the Staatsoper, they had flown to Budapest, and it was there, in the elegant Opera House where, half a century before, Monteux had conducted a *Firebird* so badly played that the composer had written him an insulting note, that they now witnessed a well-prepared, well-played and -staged production of the *Rite*. By the middle of May Stravinsky was in Paris, exactly as he had been in 1913. But this time he stayed only a few days before proceeding to London, where the eighty-eight-year-old Monteux himself was conducting *The Rite of Spring* in an Albert Hall concert on the actual anniversary, the 29th. Boulez's Paris commemoration, in the Théâtre des Champs-Élysées, was not until the 18th of June.

There can be no better illustration of the futility of much of Stravinsky's latter-day travel than this particular twelve-week excursion, which eventually took him to Dublin (where the radio choir and orchestra were so weak that Rufina had warned him the *Symphony of Psalms* might be beyond them38), back to Hamburg for a staging of *Oedipus Rex,* then on to Milan via Stockholm—a journey that recalls nothing so much as Chesterton's rolling English road.39 As ever, the artistic interest was variable. Stravinsky had never reconciled himself to Liebermann's idea of staging *The Flood* as an opera, and he disliked it in the event, finding the orchestral playing (under Craft) mediocre and what he called Rennert's "twenties Brechtian style" much too portentous for the music.40 When they got to London, there was the by now familiar socio-intellectual program, including lunch at Saltwood Castle with Kenneth Clark, dinner with Spender and Henry Moore at the Garrick Club, a trip to Harrow (in northwest London) to call on the painter-novelist David Jones, and a lunch at Isaiah Berlin's in Headington, Oxford, at which their main fellow guest was the philosopher Gilbert Ryle. As usual this looks much more like a Craft wish list than a Stravinsky one. Berlin, at any rate, realized that it was Craft rather than Stravinsky who wanted to meet the bluff, brilliant Ryle, and he had even doubted whether the Stravinskys would hit it off with him at all. He had, he told Nabokov, "acted with a kind of literary malice, and since a telegram was signed by Stravinsky and demanded the presence of Ryle, I first sent a telegram saying 'Why Ryle?' and then invited him: if they suffer, it will be no fault of mine."41

One thing the composer decidedly did not want to do was attend Monteux's *Rite of Spring* celebration on the 29th. Berlin had been asked—somewhat to his surprise—by Craft to get tickets for the Royal gala performance of *The Marriage of Figaro* at Covent Garden that evening, and there they all duly took their seats at the late starting time of eight-fifteen, by which time Monteux and Van Cliburn must have been well into Brahms's second piano concerto at the Albert Hall. Mozart's first act ended at about nine, Act 2 following, however, without an interval. At this point, Vera's probably less than wholly silent admonitions that they could not simply absent themselves from Monteux's *Rite* at last won the day, and all five of the distinguished party pushed their way out of their seats and past a protesting usherette—her protests dampened, probably, by Stravinsky's stage-whispered "We all have diarrhea."[42] Their taxi put them down at the Albert Hall at nine-thirty, just in time to catch the "Dance of the Earth," exactly halfway through the ballet. At the end, the composer was seen to be applauding ostentatiously from the front of his box, for all the world like Macavity, the Mystery Cat, establishing an alibi.[43] Sharp-eyed observers will not have failed to note that after the concert the Stravinskys took supper with Macavity's alter ego, Mr. T. S. Eliot.

As for Boulez's celebratory performance four weeks later, Stravinsky did not attend it at all, having not returned to Paris after leaving London for Dublin on 2 June. His absence was unfortunate, since the concert was one of the most spectacular ever heard in Paris, and it was one of two major events that year (the other was the Opéra production of Berg's *Wozzeck* in November) that established Boulez as a star conductor rather than a composer who also conducted. The program was astonishingly bold. It included alongside the *Rite* two of the most radical works from Stravinsky's early phase, the *Symphonies of Wind Instruments* and the rarely performed *Zvezdoliki* (which, as it happened, Stravinsky had recently recorded in Toronto), together with the recent, and difficult, *A Sermon, a Narrative, and a Prayer.* All this Boulez conducted, Souvtchinsky reported, like "some kind of super-Karajan (in the best sense of that 'complicated' term)." And Souvtchinsky added prophetically: "I'm afraid that anyone who starts conducting like that will soon stop composing."[44]

These days Souvtchinsky, who had been grumbling for years about Boulez's conducting ambitions, was gradually becoming more reconciled to the conflicts in the younger man's nature. He would still occasionally complain about Boulez's need—as he saw it—to be surrounded by yes-men.[45] Yet it was impossible to ignore the fact that hardly any other conductor of real stature could, or would, ever have conducted a Stravinsky program of this caliber. Stravinsky's own relations with Boulez had settled into a friendliness that was less intense, less perilous than before. They usually met when Stravinsky was in Paris, but they had not done so that year. Instead, Boulez had turned up in New York in April, and they had had a relaxed and enjoyable lunch. But Stravinsky remained wary of the Frenchman's attitude to his music—for him always the ultimate test of a musician's friendship. For a long time he had sensed that Boulez was quite uninterested in his latest work, and this seemed to be proved by the fact that he sometimes programmed late Stravinsky without so much as reporting the fact to its composer. He obviously conducted works like *Movements* and the *Sermon* out of a sense of duty or some feeling that it was a necessary part of his reputation to have them in his repertoire, but certainly not because he admired or liked them.⁴⁶ Of course, it was hard for Stravinsky— a lifelong scourge of star conductors—to accept that the composer he had regarded as the most gifted and serious of the postwar generation was rapidly becoming one, and one, moreover, who could not be counted on indefinitely to support the cause of his, Stravinsky's, music. But there was also another, more personal, factor, and this touched on the extent to which Boulez's success as a conductor might seem to reflect on the hopes of another aspirant with a special interest in Stravinsky and a home barely twenty doors down his street.

THERE HAD always been an intention that *Abraham and Isaac* would be ready for the 1963 Israel Festival, whether or not Stravinsky himself went there to conduct, or attend, the premiere. But when March came and the work was finished, it was plain that they could not go that year and that an unsupervised performance by any other likely conductor was out of the question. So at some point the whole event was deferred until 1964, and this time there was no talk (as had happened with *Movements*) of mounting an earlier performance outside Israel, which would have greatly agitated touchy sensibilities in Jerusalem and Tel Aviv.

The summer of 1963 was already, as usual, fully booked with largely unproductive activities, including a ten-day excursion from New York to Rio de Janeiro at the end of August—a flight of some twelve hours in each direction to conduct two concerts. Of course, Rio is paradise for the energetic sightseer. Nevertheless, if one sets Craft's elaborate and somewhat prosy description of the all-night *macumba* ceremony in the nearby hills, or his account of their dutiful but, at bottom, inexplicable visit to the niece of the late-nineteenth-century Brazilian novelist Machado de Assis, beside Vera's concise characterization of Rio as "a big bore" and her reference to "*macumba* and other boring events," one begins to feel the absurdity of these aging White Russians constantly engaged in a courtly progress through someone else's imaginary Who's Who in World Culture.⁴⁷ Yet another planned visit to Italy in the autumn seemed likely to fall into the same category. It was ludicrous, surely, to cross the Atlantic for the fourth time in a year merely to conduct a pair of concerts in Rome and Palermo. But when Nika questioned the trip, Craft explained that the Stravinskys now loathed Hollywood so much that almost any travel was a relief. At North Wetherly Drive Stravinsky slumped, he had few friends left, the film-star circuit had become deadly tedium, he could not drive, could barely walk, and in practice spent most of his time at home in the company of doctors and tax lawyers. Craft dreaded the day when conducting would no longer be possible for him. It would be something close to a death sentence.[48]

Composition under these circumstances was at best a fragmented pastime, and often a purely therapeutic one. In the nine days between returning home from Europe at the end of June and setting off once again for Santa Fe, via Chicago, there seemed no point in settling down to a brand-new work, whatever it might have been, and instead Stravinsky spent a few days making an arrangement for a mixed instrumental octet of the little string "Canzonetta" from Sibelius's incidental music to Jarnefelt's play *Kuolema* (of "Valse triste" fame). Of all his various transcriptions, this is in some ways the most bizarre, not in its musical procedures—which are better behaved than usual—but in the simple choice of work, a music one would have thought utterly remote from his own kind of discourse. The same could be said, of course, of *Pulcinella;* but there the material was given, whereas Stravinsky chose the Sibelius piece. The "Canzonetta" had evidently remained in his ears from an occasion in Toronto early in 1962, when it was played as the theme tune to a CBC broadcast concert conducted by Craft,[49] while the pretext for the arrangement seems to have been that Stravinsky had at last—two years after the first hint—been awarded the Wihuri-Sibelius Prize and wanted to make some gesture in return. The scoring (four horns, two clarinets, harp, and double bass) suggests, incidentally, that he might have envisaged performance in tandem with works like the Russian choruses, the *Berceuses du chat,* perhaps the *Epitaphium.* In fact the first performance was conducted by Craft on the 30th of September in a Monday Evening Concert that also included the *Eight Instrumental Miniatures* (whose scoring it hardly duplicates at all) and Schoenberg's Suite, op. 29, among other pieces. No wonder nobody really noticed, and the premiere has ever since been given as by Finnish Radio in March 1964.[50]

At Ravinia Park that July, it poured as it had done the previous year, reducing Stravinsky's audience to the three thousand or so who could sit under cover. But Santa Fe was dry and exceedingly hot, so hot and airless at that altitude, in fact, that they could hardly breathe.[51] Fortunately, Stravinsky for once had no conducting duties and could instead simply enjoy watching Craft work on a new production of Berg's incomplete *Lulu,* an opera that, perhaps because it used serial techniques, he now claimed to like better than *Wozzeck.*[52] In fact, it is supposed to have interested him so much that two months later he put his name to a letter (written, no doubt, by Craft) urging the director of Universal Edition, Alfred Schlee, to agree to have the score completed by the Berg expert George Perle, and offering to intercede if necessary with the composer's notoriously intractable widow.[53] The idea of Stravinsky—no lover of the Bergian *Jugendstil* and a sworn enemy of tamperers—going into battle for a scholarly completion of a post-Romantic Viennese masterpiece is so implausible that one wonders how much thought he gave as he appended his signature.

His own work in Santa Fe that year might have come from a different planet. He had started sketching a set of variations for orchestra, and by the time they left New Mexico on 19 August had got as far as an extraordinary variation for twelve solo violins, remorselessly patterned according to a serial grid, but sounding—as the platonic Stravinsky later put it—"like the sprinkling of very fine broken glass."[54] Everything about the writing was esoteric and almost elliptically concise, a kind of musical gasping for air. Yet short-breathed though it undoubtedly was, and to a considerable extent governed by mechanical processes, the music did not come easily, partly no doubt because of the lack of a supporting text. He probably made little progress with it during the few weeks they spent at Wetherly Drive that autumn. Meanwhile, as usual, rumors flew. Nabokov, who somehow knew that Stravinsky was writing an orchestral work, lobbied for it to be premiered in Berlin the following autumn during an extended stay that he was trying to set up for the composer in that beleaguered city.[55] Admittedly, his first idea had been that Stravinsky might arrange a set of Negro spirituals for Leontyne Price to sing there—a fantasy that suggests he was thinking more about his festival's theme ("Negro and Western art in the twentieth century") than about the composer's musical mentality.[56] William Glock, of the BBC, had meanwhile heard from somewhere that Stravinsky was writing a mass to be performed in the Sistine Chapel in memory of his friend Pope John XXIII, who had died in June. Could he have the British premiere?[57] Stravinsky replied curtly; there was no mass and no Vatican concert.[58] Nabokov he advised not to count on his current work (for the obvious reason that he was not confident of finishing it in time). But he added that he would have to conduct at least one concert in Berlin, otherwise "my tax lawyer will not permit me to come."[59]

It certainly would not have been surprising if memorial works had been brewing in Stravinsky's mind as 1963 drew toward its close. He had arrived at an age when telegrams announced deaths more often than births. Only a year before, Natalya Goncharova, the original designer of *Les Noces*, had died in a state of indigence in Paris, and soon afterwards Hans Rosbaud had succumbed to the cancer that had been killing him for four years. Then in October 1963, Jean Cocteau had died after a series of heart attacks. In sickness, as in health, Stravinsky had often been irritated by the master showman. In May, on first hearing of Cocteau's illness from a reporter in search of a get-well message, he had complained to the lunch table that "Cocteau can't even die without making a show of it."[60] The reality, though, upset him deeply and perhaps in too complex and personal a way for it to inspire anything in the way of a musical tribute.[61]

In the end they did go to Italy, for a pair of concerts in Sicily, and the original one in Rome, now transferred to the Gothic church of Santa Maria sopra Minerva. In Palermo, they witnessed an evil omen. An old woman stepped into the path of a bus and was horribly crushed to death.[62] The day after their concert there, Igor and Vera went by train to Catania, while Craft and Eugene Berman followed by car. While they were on the road, a series of rifle shots in Dallas, Texas, changed the course of American history. Only when they reached Catania did they hear the news of Kennedy's assassination; and only as the Rome train passed through Naples two days later did they learn from a newspaper billboard that Aldous Huxley had died on the same day, with news footage from Dallas still flickering on his television screen.

So in Rome, in a state of misery and extreme agitation, Stravinsky conducted a memorial mass after all: his own setting, dedicated to the memory of the young president, who was being buried at that very moment in Washington.

IN THE WHOLE OF 1963 the Stravinskys had spent less than five months at home in Hollywood, and in fact they did not return there in 1964 until early February. Whatever Craft might say about the depressive effect of West Coast life and Stravinsky's preference for travel, it was obvious that the incessant coming and going was bad for his health. Doctors who examined him after the Rio trip in September had found his polycythemia dangerously aggravated.[1] Friends in New York, where they as usual spent Christmas, were beginning to notice how much slower he had become, in both movement and speech, and there was a slightly melancholy air about him, as if he knew that his life was wrongly ordered but felt powerless to change it.[2] Death must have been on his mind: the deaths of close friends like Huxley and Cocteau, the very public death of Kennedy, and—year in year out— the annual death of his first wife and their beloved daughter, Mika. Françoise had written to him on the twenty-fifth anniversary of Mika's death. Exactly what she said we do not know because her letter has vanished from the composer's papers, but his reply indicates its flavor while guarding a certain ambiguity of its own. "Dearest Françoise," it says, "thank you, thank you, for your letter. A dreadful sadness never leaves me. I *entirely* share your sentiments. That's all I wanted to tell you today. I embrace you with all my heart."[3]

In recent months his relations with Françoise had grown perceptibly more affectionate, partly because, whereas Soulima was a poor correspondent (to some extent like his father), she wrote long, intelligent, and affectionate letters, addressing them to both Stravinskys and recommending books to Vera. After Cocteau's death in October, she had written her father-in-law an appreciation that was so moving and perceptive that he had filed it with a note on the envelope: "*Remarkable letter from Françoise* what she writes about Jean Cocteau!" and had written back that "I quite agree and admire your sagacity. Why do we see so little of each other!?!?!?"[4] He on his side had pleased Soulima and Françoise by giving their son, Johnny, a special eighteenth-birthday present that November, a ring with the Stravinsky coat of arms, "to be worn from now on. Bless you, dear. Love and kisses from your Grandfather."⁵ And the young man had replied with a charming and natural thank-you, a letter that cannot have failed to please, not least because it unaffectedly included Bob Craft in its greetings, something Stravinsky's children by no means invariably did.⁶ The composer probably in any case felt particularly warm toward the Urbana branch of his dynasty at this moment because from the Geneva branch there was little but depressing news. Denise's tuberculosis had responded slowly to treatment and had left her lame and weak, and meanwhile the twenty-six-year-old Kitty—perhaps in a bid for freedom from her adoptive home—had fallen into a relationship with a married man in Paris and had apparently severed all links with her family. Her grandfather's advice was sincere, to the point, and useless. "I must tell you," he wrote, "what is at the bottom of my heart: the urgent and absolute necessity *for you* to dominate your passions and not let yourself be dominated by them."⁷

This had come at a bad moment for him. He had not been home for more than two months, and was now, in mid-January, in the middle of a series of concerts with the Philadelphia Orchestra, four of them in Philadelphia itself, with a fifth to follow at the Lincoln Center in New York, the first time he had conducted in the new Philharmonic Hall. To make matters worse, Vera had stayed in her beloved New York, in their "marvelous apartment" in the Hotel Pierre,⁸ so was not on hand to salve his irritations. Twice he, Craft, and Lillian Libman drove the hundred and twenty miles to Manhattan and back, the second time returning in a blizzard so severe that they barely arrived in time for the concert, which in any case was played, for the same reason, to an audience in single figures.⁹ He was in no mood to reflect on the emotional troubles of a wayward granddaughter three thousand miles away. He had domestic worries of his own. For a long time it had been apparent that their little house in North Wetherly Drive was unsuitable for an ailing octogenarian who was becoming unsteady on his feet. The front door was reached by a steep, winding path with steps, and what you entered when you got to the top was still a one-bedroom house, despite the various bits that had been added on. In everyone's mind was the thought that, if Stravinsky ever needed a night nurse, there would be nowhere for her to sleep.¹⁰ But there was a solution, and by January 1964 it was close to realization. The late Baroness's considerably larger house at no. 1218, a few yards down the hill, was for sale, and though it had unsuitable aspects of its own, it answered the immediate need: it had space, and you came to it at street level.

The trouble was that Stravinsky did not want to move into it. He liked no. 1260 more than any of the innumerable houses and apartments he had occupied during his long life, and in any case both he and Vera now found

Hollywood itself so tedious that there hardly seemed much point in moving house without moving city. From distant Manhattan the whole idea must have appeared disheartening in the extreme. There was little comfort in the thought of going home, and yet, on all practical grounds, no serious alternative. So as soon as they were back in Hollywood in February, they proceeded with the purchase of the new house, signing contracts and putting down a deposit of five thousand dollars. Then on the actual day of the signing, the 3rd of March, Stravinsky received another kind of document altogether, a text from Auden for a new work he had decided to write in memory of the assassinated president.

In New York Stravinsky had worked, if spasmodically, on the set of orchestral variations he had started at Santa Fe. He had spent a good deal of time writing, then rewriting, the intricate music for woodwind that follows the second twelve-part variation (the one for violas and double-basses). But it could not be said that this patchwork of a score, begun on an impulse and with no sign of a commission, was going smoothly or with a clear sense of direction. One evening in January he had dined with Auden and, in the course of a bacchanalia exceptional even by their standards, had suggested the idea of a choral elegy in Kennedy's memory, probably for male voices, either unaccompanied or with mainly low-lying instruments. He even specified the kind of poem he wanted: "either six or nine stanzas of two long lines and one short." "I'm an old hand at this kind of thing," Auden said.[11] When it came, however, the poem turned out to be a haiku, a series of three-line stanzas of seventeen syllables each, and Stravinsky decided that it would go better with a solo voice accompanied by a trio of clarinets.[12] He (or, to be exact, the author of *Themes and Conclusions*) claimed later that he set the text first, and only then decided, on the basis of the contrapuntal patterns suggested by the vocal part, what kind of accompaniment to write.[13] Meanwhile, news of the *Elegy* had reached the press, still in the guise of a choral work that would, in a sense, be dedicated to the memory of all the various friends Stravinsky had recently lost.[14] "Journalists must listen under beds," his notoriously talkative poet wrote, knowing how the composer loathed publicity about work in progress.[15]

In fact, little or nothing was written before the end of March. First there was a brief trip to Cleveland for concerts and to record *Jeu de cartes* and the *Ode*. Then, when he got home, he found a commission waiting for him from Lincoln Kirstein for a short piece to mark the opening of the New York State Theatre in Lincoln Center the following month. It was not much: "a fanfare lasting thirty seconds to be played from the top balcony of the foyer to summon people into the Festspielhaus."[16] All the same Stravinsky's first, almost automatic response was negative. "If only you had asked me sooner," he wrote back.[17] With another tour coming up and his elegy to write, he needed every available minute. But even as he wrote, he knew the excuse was lame. The next trip—to Ann Arbor and Toronto—was well over a month away; the fanfare could be written in a morning, and the *Elegy* was hardly going to eat up more than a few days, even if—as is possible—he was still thinking in terms of a choral setting of the Auden, something relatively complicated and dense, with orchestra. In any case, he changed his mind about the fanfare probably even before licking the stamp on his reply to Kirstein, and two days later he wrote the mordant little piece for two trumpets that duly became the first music to be heard in the new theatre when it opened for a private gala preview by the City Ballet on 20 April, and that lasts precisely the thirty seconds specified by Kirstein.[18] Perhaps he was swayed by the fact that the opening program was to include *Agon* and the recent *Movements* ballet, which he had finally caught up with at City Center in December and had found—he told Souvtchinsky—simply "astounding."[19] Unfortunately he left no detailed account of the ballet apart from the obviously ghostwritten paragraphs in *Themes and Conclusions* (which falsely assert that he had not seen a public performance). But the ideas so well articulated there—of how the choreography had pointed up musical relationships, including rhythmic details and lyrical elements, of which he himself had been unaware—are no doubt broadly authentic.[20]

A week or so after composing the fanfare, he finally wrote the *Elegy for J.F.K.* It took him only two days, and having written it he somehow persuaded Lawrence Morton to include it in the Monday Evening Concert on 6 April, a program otherwise devoted entirely to piano music, songs, and unaccompanied choral music. None of the required musicians were on tap. Margery Mackay, a mezzo-soprano who was singing Schoenberg and Brahms, was a slow learner, and Stravinsky had in any case conceived the piece for baritone.[21] At the last minute they managed to book Richard Robinson—a reliable tenor with a good low register—who was singing elsewhere that evening but was able to arrive at the Fiesta Hall in time for the second half of the Monday Concert. He, the three clarinettists, and Craft actually rehearsed in an adjacent building during Palestrina's *Missa brevis*, then went straight on and gave what was, by all accounts, a perfectly respectable premiere, followed at once by a second performance.[22] The modest two-minute work—"much different than expected," Stravinsky told Nabokov[23]—was perhaps not the most spectacular tribute imaginable after so catastrophic a death, but it had at least an appropriate sense of urgency and a touching intimacy. "Ethereal music," he called it, and added, "I will publish it as it is."[24]

The orchestral variations still proceeded fitfully. He was calling them, he told Rufina Ampenoff with a certain air of defiance, "Some Variations."[25] He had three weeks on them (at least in theory) before his Toronto recordings in early May, and another three weeks when he got home, after which they had to set off yet again, this time for London, where Columbia had decided (because of the much less severe union conditions and therefore cheaper costs) to record *The Rake's Progress* for the second time. Stravinsky had also agreed, in a weak moment, to conduct his *Symphony of Psalms* and "Vom Himmel hoch" transcription at the Oxford Bach Festival that June. Lina Lalandi, the energetic Greek harpsichordist who had founded the festival the year before, had for months been bombarding him with more or less eccentric programming ideas. She had suggested coupling the *Symphony of Psalms* with the Octet, and more recently had come up with the bizarre proposal that Stravinsky conduct a Bach cantata by way of encore to the *Symphony*.[26] Stravinsky would respond to such suggestions with abusive epithets in the margins of Rufina Ampenoff's letters. But history does not relate exactly what he said when he arrived at the first rehearsal, in London on the 27th of June, and found that Lalandi, apparently unaware that the Bach transcription involved the choir, had not arranged copies or rehearsals for them.[27]

It was the difficult climax to a tense and exhausting month. The *Rake* sessions had also been marred by poor preparation and a sometimes ill-tempered atmosphere. Craft noted at the first session, in Abbey Road Studios on the 16th, that the singers had not previously sung together and the orchestra (the Royal Philharmonic) had never seen the music before.[28] The mood was described in more detail by the musicologist Oliver Neighbour in a letter to Lawrence Morton. Neighbour had gathered that communication between Craft and Stravinsky had at times been close to breakdown, "so that Craft did all the rehearsing, and then Igor would stump up and do the actual recording—often quite differently so that nobody knew what to expect, and Craft sat in a corner and shrugged."[29] They and the engineer, John McClure, were weary from the five-hour time change, and after the first sessions Stravinsky caught a cold that had him snuffling and croaking on the rostrum, while his bad leg impeded him in the walks to and fro. "You know, sometimes we do not speak, this *merdeux* leg and I," he confided to McClure. "He does not acknowledge my authority. He obeys someone else. I don't know who."[30]

Somehow the actual recording survived these troubles and emerged as a spirited, if not tremendously polished, document of at any rate somebody's view of the work. But Craft's own recording of Schoenberg's one-act opera *Von heute auf Morgen,* made as usual in time left over from the *Rake,* was a good deal less fortunate—not much better than a run-through of a difficult and intractable work in a style completely unfamiliar to the orchestra, if not to all of the singers.[31] At the end Craft was in a terrible state, and "poured out his woes at some length" to anyone who would listen.[32] Stravinsky told McClure, "My dear, they were all wonderful, the singers and the orchestra, and the music too I like very much and even I still like you. But you know? Let's never record it again. Twice is enough."[33] When they got to Oxford Town Hall on the 29th, Stravinsky's performances of the *Symphony of Psalms* and the Bach transcription rose above their technical limitations and achieved a grandeur and emotional intensity few had experienced in this music before. But Craft's opening performance of the Bach *Trauer-Ode*, "totally unrehearsed," was a disaster, and at one point actually broke down.[34]

Although they were due in Israel in mid-August for the long-delayed premiere of *Abraham and Isaac*, and thereafter in Berlin for the festival, they could not stay on in Europe, if only because Stravinsky and Craft were booked to appear for the third year running at Ravinia in July, and Craft was conducting a revival of *Lulu* at Santa Fe. Yet the interminable flights were clearly having a bad effect. These days the composer often used a wheelchair at airports, and even sometimes at railway stations. At best he walked with difficulty, invariably using a stick and often with help; his blood problems had by no means eased, he had temperatures, and he was frequently exhausted. He was prone, as he had always been, to passing infections. No sooner was he back in Los Angeles in early July than he contracted an ear infection. This seemed to clear up;[35] but in Chicago, where he and Craft arrived, without Vera, on 16 July, he was tired, in discomfort from the heat, and generally in a crotchety mood. When his grandson, Johnny, came to call on him and booked into the same hotel (the Ambassador East)—presumably at either his or Vera's suggestion—he refused either to see the young man or to talk to him on the telephone, and when he left the next day Johnny, not perhaps without a touch of youthful mischievousness, transferred his own sundry expenses to his grandfather's bill.[36]

Back in Hollywood, Stravinsky promptly wired Ahron Propes in Jerusalem and Nicolas Nabokov in Berlin to cancel both engagements, saying that his doctors were forbidding him to fly because of his ear infection.[37] This may or may not have been a prevarication. It would hardly have been unreasonable for his doctors to keep him at home simply on grounds of general exhaustion. But it would have made little difference. Propes responded at once with a masterfully self-contradictory cable, insisting that Stravinsky's health was the most important consideration but imploring him to come all the same, since the entire festival had been built round him, the orchestras had cancelled other dates for his benefit, prominent Jews from all over the world had been invited to Israel, etc., etc.[38] Nabokov grumpily pointed out that, while Israel had organized its festival around Stravinsky's personality, Berlin was basing itself on his music, conducted by him. "But I won't insist," Nika added disingenuously, "I love you too much."39

Stravinsky was genuinely touched by Propes's concern, and he wired back that after all he would come, a few days late, "because I feel how unhappy you are."40 But he held out against Berlin, telling Nabokov that they could perfectly well do *Abraham and Isaac* and all the other works without him, so long as they booked Craft.41 A few days later, he cabled the mayor of West Berlin, Willy Brandt, declining the city's invitation.42 By this time, as had now become usual in such cases, the press, having heard that Stravinsky was cancelling prominent engagements on grounds of health, were reporting his condition as more or less terminal. Souvtchinsky told the composer that he held Nabokov responsible for provoking the exaggerated reporting: "it's his style," he remarked.43 Nadia Boulanger wrote so anxiously that Stravinsky felt constrained to reassure her by explaining that his doctors had simply advised him not to fly "too often," a nuance that he had for some reason withheld from Nika.44 Greatly relieved, Nadia herself now urged him to go to Berlin after all, "for Nicolas's sake."45 Meanwhile Brandt wired very belated regrets at the composer's refusal, but he soon afterwards wired again his pleasure at the composer's acceptance.46 The brinkmanship had kept them all on the edge and had ensured that a massively abbreviated visit (Nabokov having originally wanted him for a month or two) would be taken as a concession on his, Stravinsky's, part. Yet at the end of it all, they not only flew to Israel in the third week of August, but they flew back to New York just over a week later, flew home a week after that, then after another fortnight yet again swooped across the ocean to Berlin, stayed ten days, then swooped back again. In the middle of all this, the master consulted one of his various West Coast medicos, who found his ears in perfectly good order.47

At Lod airport, Tel Aviv, they were greeted by a welcoming committee of Ruritanian impressiveness. The festival president, Jacob Tsur, made a long and slightly pompous speech and handed Vera an enormous bunch of flowers, which she swiftly passed on to Isaiah Berlin, who had himself flown in a day or two earlier. A children's orchestra played irrelevantly and almost inaudibly from a nearby balcony, but "the Stravinskys fortunately realized that this was in their honor, and waved graciously." After the composer's car had set off for Jerusalem, it was discovered that, instead of fourteen pieces of luggage, only thirteen had arrived, and the missing piece was naturally the one with all the scores and Vera's furs and jewelry. "Frantic calls to Paris, general *perepolokh* [commotion] until we all arrived in Jerusalem and it was discovered that nothing was missing as they had thirteen pieces of luggage in any case and not fourteen."48

They were to give two identical concerts, one in Jerusalem on the 23rd of August, the other in Caesarea the next day. The programming had been attended by all kinds of intricacies of a post-Holocaustian variety. The German baritone Dietrich Fischer-Dieskau, who was to sing *Abraham and Isaac* in Berlin, had been ruled out of the Jerusalem premiere on racial grounds, even though, as Sir Isaiah had assured Nabokov, "his record is spotless."[49] "Vom Himmel hoch" was being sung in Hebrew, and even the Latin of the *Symphony of Psalms* was, as threatened, being replaced by its Old Testament original out of consideration for local sensibilities. As for *Abraham and Isaac* itself, there was of course no difficulty with the text, and the music, in some ways Stravinsky's most hermetic so far, had troubled the substitute baritone, Ephraim Biran, more than it had the orchestra, who (under Craft's direction) took it in their stride.[50] For the audience, needless to say, it was quite another matter. "You should have seen the expression on the face of the minister of education," Isaiah Berlin told Nabokov, "when the first notes of *Abraham and Isaac* sounded."

> The mere appearance of this rough assembly, with a few absurd-looking German *Gelehrte* [intellectuals] sticking out from a rough forest of white and blue shirts and mops of rough white hair—like the editors of the *Readers Digest*—the whole "frontier" public: enter this extremely delicately constructed little porcelain figure, very slowly limping along towards the podium, pale, refined and sophisticated with no suspicion of any "narodnik" [populist] quality, in an audience soaked in it; with a lot of bewildered persons who had no idea what the sounds were meant to convey—and then, after he said "Shalom" loudly, applauding still more madly: it was touching, ridiculous, and very sweet . . .[51]

The multiple ironies of the situation were perhaps clearer to Berlin than to anyone there that night except Robert Craft. Craft had emerged from the plane at Lod with a wry smile that Berlin thought "the only genuine reaction seen on the airfield that afternoon."[52] It was not just the piquancy of so utterly esoteric a work being offered to a state so unsure of its place in modern culture; it was the delicious absurdity of its being offered by an ultra-civilized White Russian with (as Berlin knew perfectly well) anti-Semitism in his blood and an instinctive loathing for the petit-bourgeois mentality which, in the nature of things, still predominated in the young Israel. When Tsur pointed out at a press conference in the King David Hotel that the hotel was built on the site of Abraham's abortive sacrifice, it summed up, if only half-seriously, the banality of the idea of a biblical society in an age of international air travel. Invited to approve Israel's ban on the performance of Wagner, Stravinsky shrewdly dodged the reason for the ban while

With Craft (standing) and Pierre Boulez, in the control room during Craft's recording of Schoenberg's Serenade, op. 24, Hollywood, March 1957. Lawrence Morton is in the background.

With Darius and Madeleine Milhaud, Paris, 1957

With Pierre
Souvtchinsky, Paris,
October 1957

Rehearsing *Agon* with
Balanchine and the
rehearsal pianist,
Nicholas Kopeikine,
New York, December
1957

World premiere of
Threni, Scuolo di
San Rocco, Venice,
23 September 1958

With Robert Craft
at Paestum, October
1959

Conducting in the early sixties

With Lillian Libman listening
to the Craft rehearsal for the
Carnegie Hall *Rake's Progress*,
November 1962

Isaiah Berlin and Nicolas
Nabokov on the lawn of
Headington House, Oxford,
in the 1960s

With Robert Craft, 1962

With Vladimir Rimsky-
Korsakov at dinner in the
Leningrad Composers'
House, October 1962

Proposing a toast to the
Soviet Minister of Culture,
Yekaterina Furtseva, and to
Dmitry Shostakovich and his
wife, Irina, Hotel Metropole,
Moscow, 1962

With Tikhon Khrennikov on
Moscow television, September 1962

With his niece Xenya in the Kremlin
Theater, Moscow, September 1962

Applauding Pierre Monteux's
fiftieth-anniversary *Rite of Spring*
in the Royal Albert Hall, London,
May 1963; Robert Craft is in the
anteroom

In his studio at 1260 North Wetherly Drive, c. 1963

With Balanchine, Hollywood, 1966

With Milène, Hollywood,
1966 (photo: Arnold
Newman)

Orchestrating Bach, New
York, 1969

endorsing its effects: "In not playing Wagner, you are avoiding many very disagreeable things."[53] In the hotel restaurant after the concert, he kept handing Berlin (of all people) "drunken sheets with scrawls of note-like entities on them, meant to be half tango, half waltz, signed Igor Manteuffel."[54] "I shall always bear with me," Berlin concluded, "the image of I[gor] F[yodorovich]'s molten condition, liquid, vague, totally happy, tipsy, very different from anything in New York—he was much happier in Jerusalem, I thought." "Perhaps," he added optimistically, "he is all right in Hollywood."

That the next concert after Caesarea should have been in Berlin merely compounded these ironies. Fischer-Dieskau, for his part, had wanted to sing *Abraham and Isaac* in German, not of course for any political reason but on practical grounds. But that Stravinsky would not permit.[55] So the great baritone had to set himself to learn the Hebrew words phonetically, which he seems to have done without complaint and with fair accuracy, though he never did master the angular vocal line, with its awkward chromatic ornaments, which Stravinsky told a Paris interviewer he had composed in imitation of Arab chant.[56]

Despite the success of the one Berlin concert in which Stravinsky himself appeared (conducting *Renard* and the Capriccio, with Nikita Magaloff), his one-week stay was a mere torso of the extended residency that Nabokov had originally planned and that had been intended to bring prestige to the walled-off city and its festival while giving the over-travelled master the kind of rest Nika had constantly been urging him to take. Nabokov himself must have been tired out from the exertion and responsibility of organizing a festival with such complex political ramifications; and perhaps this partly explains a curious incident that marred the last day of Stravinsky's visit. Nika had a pretty young German secretary, who it seems may for some time have been also something more than a secretary, but who by now had tired of him in that less official role and, during the Stravinskys' Berlin stay, had attached herself to Craft. Craft himself gives various more or less self-congratulatory details about this brief affair;[57] but in any case its comic violent climax is not in question. At two o'clock in the morning after the *Abraham and Isaac* premiere, Nabokov rang Craft's hotel room and found himself speaking to his secretary. The next morning in the hotel lobby, he set about her with a bundle of rolled-up newspapers and had to be physically restrained by the hotel porters. Gasping as if from a mild heart seizure, he retreated to the Stravinskys' suite, from which he emerged some time later, with his dignity restored, to escort them to the airport for their flight to Paris.

The whole episode was a disconcerting reminder of Nabokov's behavior ten years earlier in Rome, when he had punched a doorman who refused to let Craft into Henze's *Boulevard Solitude* because he was incorrectly dressed.[58] To complete the coincidence, Henze was himself present at the Berlin premiere of *Abraham and Isaac,* and was actually photographed at a rehearsal, sharing a score with Nabokov.[59] The essential difference, of course, was that Nika had this time involved Stravinsky in a violent fracas that did not concern him in any way. Stravinsky had told him he had acted stupidly, and he freely admitted it, writing both to the composer and to Craft in abject apology.[60] Yet he spoke negatively to others about the composer's time in Berlin, and specifically about his conducting, not thinking, perhaps, that they in turn would transmit his comments to their subject. "I have just learnt," Stravinsky wrote to his Rome agent, Adriana Panni, a few weeks later, "of the very disagreeable things Nicolas Nabokov had told you about my last appearance for him in Berlin conducting *Renard* and the Capriccio. This is moreover not the first time (I'm told) that he has talked behind people's backs in such a way. But this time it greatly astonishes me, since everyone knows that I conduct my works better, much better, than plenty of other conductors."[61] One should at the same time perhaps not overpraise the motives of people who report such remarks back to their victims.

It was certainly true, in any case, that Stravinsky had slowed down in recent months. Souvtchinsky, who saw him in Paris on the way to Berlin, and again on the way back, found him much changed, stiffer and less mobile, and talking more slowly and sometimes almost inaudibly. He had been aware of tensions among the travellers, he hinted to Yudina. It had plainly become very difficult for the three of them to live together. Yet Stravinsky was obsessed with his new house and kept drawing its ground-plan for Souvtchinsky and describing its reconstruction. And he insisted: "I'm not old, but ill. You all have to understand that." Above all, his creative urge was apparently undiminished. He showed Souvtchinsky the draft score of the orchestral variations, now complete as far as the astonishingly athletic fugue-like tenth variation. Nothing could be less stiff or immobile. Yet he also talked pious nonsense about the inscriptions on Christ's shawls, and burst into tears as he said it. "These words and the way they were spoken," Souvtchinsky admitted, "shook me, overwhelmed me even. Who else could have said them?" But almost in the same breath, Stravinsky would be going on as usual about the iniquities of the American tax system.[62]

The main problem with the variations, and no doubt at bottom the reason why they were taking so long to finish, was still that nobody had commissioned them. Earlier in the year, he had even toyed with the idea of supplying (old) music for Dino de Laurentiis's film *The Bible,* and had actually signed an agreement to that effect which de Laurentiis had returned without endorsement, since it purported to transfer rights that were not Stravinsky's to sell. But in spite of the large fee involved, he had in any case decided to turn the project down, "because," as he told Rufina, "it will be more trouble, unpleasantness, and musical affliction than interest."[63] As ever, others wanted his old music, he was only interested in the new. Passing through New York on his way home from Berlin, he heard the Chicago Symphony Orchestra play Brahms, Debussy, and Bartók's *Miraculous Mandarin* in Carnegie Hall and was so impressed that he instantly wired his congratulations to the orchestra's conductor, Jean Martinon. Back in Hollywood early in October, he set to work on the third of the twelve-part variations, the one for wind instruments. Then, two or three days after completing this section on the 15th, he received a reply from Martinon, thanking him and inviting him to conduct in Chicago. The connection practically made itself. On the 26th, two days before completing the variations, Stravinsky wrote and offered Martinon the world premiere. A date in spring would be ideal, and they might combine the new work with *Persephone,* which he was expecting soon to record.

DURING THEIR brief sojourn in Hollywood in the first half of September, they had at last moved into their new house. But it was only when they returned from the Berlin trip a month later that, in arriving directly at no. 1218 instead of 1260, they felt properly "at home" there. The Baroness's house had been completely refurbished. As in all houses vacated by old ladies with a fondness for cats, the arrangements had been cluttered and inconvenient, gloomy, smelly, and somewhat the worse for wear. Now the clutter had been banished, the gloom expunged, and everything made new, modern, and, within the framework of the Stravinskys' own cosmopolitan impedimenta, sufficiently bourgeois. Vera had a room of her own, there were spare bedrooms and bathrooms, and the master's own studio was re-created, as nearly as possible though alas on the second floor, so that he had to negotiate an awkward staircase to get to it.[64] In due course, a new swimming pool would be installed.

For all the obvious comforts and conveniences, however, the Stravinskys were unhappy about the move. After twenty-three years, the composer had got used to the old house, and he must have felt, in his heart of hearts, that he was leaving it to die. Vera, though she loved her room, dreaded the sheer size of the new establishment; and in this she was not alone. Mrs. Gates— their dear, difficult Russian housekeeper and cook, Yevgenia Petrovna— was retiring, at least partly because she could not face the work of looking after the larger house. There would be other cooks and cleaners, a stream of factotums and helpers; but that in itself was something to fear, an element of the unknown, however kind, competent, and congenial such people might be individually. Like Parasha's mother in *Mavra,* they would need "to find a maid, who's cheap and strong and ill-paid," in a country notoriously hostile to the class divisions and differences of status on which the whole culture of servants had always depended.

Meanwhile, the domestic duties fell mainly on Vera. Igor was upstairs putting the finishing touches to his variations. Craft was busy writing in his flat over the old Erlanger garage behind the house. There is something slightly curious about all this writing, since you can hunt through newspapers, bibliographies, and lists of publications for those years and find almost nothing with Robert Craft's name on it. One might have supposed him to be writing some vast work of fiction, or perhaps the brilliant, belle-lettristic diaries that would indeed one day emerge from that talented and inventive pen; and he may well have been doing just that. But what he certainly was doing was writing for immediate publication under a name other than his own, exactly as Walter Nouvel and Roland-Manuel had done before the war. And needless to say, the name in question was one and the same.

Craft had been writing Stravinsky's prose for him for some time, but in the fifties this had usually been in the dialogue form under both their names. There had been, as we saw, the odd "letter to the editor"; but such things were relatively short and quite possibly written to Stravinsky's rough dictation, then tidied up. At the end of 1962, however, Craft had composed a four-thousand-word missive—an account of Stravinsky's daily routine—supposedly for Vera to translate and send to a Moscow cousin named Vladimir Petrov. Whether this was ever sent to anyone called Petrov may be doubted; at any rate the address on the letter was a false one. More to the point, the letter appeared in print (in *Musical America*) so promptly that it must have been forwarded to that journal's editor on the instant—surely the quickest publication of a private letter in the history of the free press.[65]

There is something rather touching about the pretense involved here. Craft makes no attempt to disguise his prosy English style, with its huge vocabulary and its love of literary periphrasis ("rich fricatives that would greatly increase an *avant-garde* writer's store of siphonic onomatopoeia").[66] Another article, allegedly by Vera, on the premiere of *The Rake's Progress* in Venice, was later transferred more or less bodily to Craft's own published diaries.[67] A second letter to "Petrov," dated February 1965, describes the new house.[68] Craft says in his autobiography that he wrote both letters at Vera's request,[69] though the commission would be hard to explain if Petrov were a real person, since Vera was a gifted letter-writer in her own language, and did in fact write a longish letter in Russian on the same subject to her step-niece, Xenya, soon afterwards.[70] There is no evidence or likelihood that this letter began life in Craft's English.

These are harmless little frauds in themselves, of course, but they began a trend that had its less innocent aspect. When the monthly music paper *Listen* published an acrimonious and rather spiteful article about Stravinsky by Vernon Duke (Vladimir Dukelsky) in the summer of 1964, an unremittingly vicious reply appeared in the form of a long letter bearing Stravinsky's signature in the journal's next issue, under the scurrilous title "A Cure for V.D.," a title the paper was careful to attribute to the composer himself.[71] But of course Stravinsky did not write the letter, and perhaps did not even know it had been written. When I asked Craft, in the course of a series of radio interviews, whether he was the author of the letter, he admitted he had sometimes written letters using Stravinsky's name, but claimed that the Dukelsky reply was actually the work of Lawrence Morton.[72] It is hard to know what to make of this claim, since one would think Morton—a byword for honesty and straightforwardness—incapable of so mean an act as to attack a fellow musician from the cover of an alias. Whoever wrote it, in any case, it did Stravinsky personal harm by showing him up as resentful and (no matter how theoretically just his defense, since Dukelsky had attacked him ad hominem, accusing him of a mercenary and opportunistic attitude to his art) in practice vindictive.

The attack on Menotti's *Last Savage* in a slightly earlier piece called "In the Name of Jean-Jacques" is more palatable, if only because it probably represents Stravinsky's opinion about that work, which he saw in New York in January 1964, whether or not he knew the subsequent "interview" had been written and published.[73] The same might be said of the long review of the English edition of Schoenberg's letters, a piece which first appeared under Stravinsky's byline in the London *Observer* in October.[74] Curiously enough, the authenticity of these and other writings seems hardly to have been questioned in print at the time, and they continue to be cited today as genuine by musicologists and others who ought by now to know better. But at least there was still then a Stravinsky—alert and working, however sickly—who might in theory have written them. This would not much longer be the case.

With the variations finished and, it seemed, successfully placed, Stravinsky certainly had no immediate intention of giving up writing music. But he needed commissions. He lived in fear of the time—plainly not far distant—when he would no longer be able to conduct, while his already grotesque medical bills continued to mount. When Nadia Boulanger wrote in early November conveying an offer of ten thousand dollars for a chamber work to celebrate the centenary of the Princesse de Polignac in 1965, he wired back regretting that for even a short piece these days he was asking not less than twenty-five thousand—roughly the equivalent of a high annual professional salary.[75] Nadia could have been forgiven for regarding this as a roundabout way of saying that he was no longer accepting commissions. But she would have been wrong. In fact, Stravinsky's West Coast lawyer, William Montapert, was already working on a draft contract for a requiem of a different kind and for a different kind of benefactress: a certain Helen Buchanan Seeger, who had died leaving money to Princeton University, some of which her son had decided to put toward a commission for a work in her memory.[76] Twenty-five thousand dollars was exactly the fee Stravinsky was demanding for this presumably not very short work; but there was another attraction, not shared by the Polignac tribute. Stanley Seeger was in no special hurry for his mother's requiem, and he was agreeing not to press for its completion. Considering how very little time Stravinsky would have for composition in the next several months, this was an essential condition, and one which Nadia was unable to meet.

What is clear about all this is that personal feeling either was not an issue, or was actually a negative one. Mrs. Seeger he had never met, whereas the Princesse de Polignac had been both a friend and a major patron. It has often been claimed that Stravinsky's numerous memorial pieces prove that he was preoccupied by death;[77] but in reality they suggest some kind of opposite. After his Funeral Song for Rimsky-Korsakov (1909) and possibly the *Symphonies of Wind Instruments* in memory of Debussy (1920), he composed hardly a single epitaph for a close friend or relation, and most of those he did write are brief and impersonal. Dylan Thomas and John F. Kennedy, though he was affected by their deaths, he had met precisely once each. As for the orchestral *Variations,* he seems to have decided to dedicate them to Aldous Huxley, to whom he certainly had been close, only when they were complete. The music, as he later explained to Nadia, had no connection with Huxley. "I was composing it during the months when dear Aldous was dying of throat cancer, so I naturally dedicated it to his memory. I am certain, anyway (and this doesn't discourage me), that this music would say nothing to him (or would even displease him), since what he liked was romantic and classical music, from which my composition is quite remote."[78] This is far indeed from the conventional idea of the memorial as spiritual image or evocation.

Nevertheless, within a few weeks he was prompted into something much closer to an elegiac tribute to, if not an intimate friend like Huxley, at least a good one and a sort of phantom collaborator (which Huxley never was), in the person of T. S. Eliot, who died in London on the 4th of January 1965. Stravinsky had gone to New York in December for the U.S. premiere of *Abraham and Isaac* on the 6th (conducted by Craft) and to record the *Elegy for J.F.K* and a batch of his early Russian songs. But he decided almost instantly on a memorial to the poet of "The Dove Descending" and *Sweeney Agonistes,* once floated by Kirstein as a possible ballet subject; and within barely a month of his return to Los Angeles on 11 January he had composed the four-minute *Introitus,* a doleful "Requiem aeternam" for tenors and basses with piano, harp, gongs, low strings, and a gently insistent tocsin of muffled drums.[79] The curious thing about this moving little work is the way it seems to have been suggested by other projects—for instance, by the original idea of the *Elegy for J.F.K,* which was to have been a low-lying piece for male chorus, or by the Princeton Requiem commission, which Seeger wanted to be a vocal work but Stravinsky, initially, did not. Like the *Elegy,* and also like *Abraham and Isaac,* it is essentially a single-line vocal setting—a monody—though it splits into two parts near the end. Musically it bears no resemblance at all to the spiky and mercurial *Variations,* which, from the singers' point of view, is probably just as well.

Having completed the *Introitus,* Stravinsky quickly decided to include it alongside the *Variations* in his Chicago concert on 17 April. So Martinon and his orchestra, thanks above all (presumably) to their brilliant Bartók in New York, were the unexpected recipients of two major Stravinsky premieres on the one program in the Windy City's picturesquely named Orchestra Hall. Craft conducted both works, the highly condensed *Variations* twice; the composer himself tottered to the rostrum only to direct the final item, the complete *Pulcinella,* looking, one reporter observed, "frighteningly frail."[80] In the past, when *Renard* and *Mavra* would appear on the same bill or the premiere of *Les Noces* would be swiftly followed by that of the Octet, critics had often reacted as if changes of style or simple muddles of chronology were smoke screens purposely devised by the composer to disrupt honest opinion of his work. But in sixties Chicago, it was more as if nobody even noticed the hardly less startling differences between these two latest products of his genius for renewal. One critic described them knowingly as "a logical, and fully artistic, development of the Stravinsky we have known for years, the natural—even inevitable—successors to the Symphony in three movements or his setting of the Mass," and went on to venture that "on the basis of three hearings of the 'Variations' [he had also attended a rehearsal], I am confident they will be in the repertory from now on."[81] Another admittedly liked the "Variations" ("brilliant [sic] alive in its acutely magnetic field of action"), but grumbled about the *Introitus.* "Either the music eluded me," she confided, "or the dull performance hid it," whereas the "Variations" were immaculately played, "in line with the composer's 'My music must be executed like a notary's certificate.' "[82]

Stravinsky seems to have felt such compliments to be not worth a great deal more than the invective his music had often attracted in the past. After his recent New York concerts, he had complained to Rufina Ampenoff about the abusive New York press for *Abraham and Isaac,* adding that "I really tried! Well, what can you do, it's not for everybody to have Benjamin Britten's success with the critics."[83] Yet the "abusive" New York press had included a perceptive and highly appreciative piece by Alan Rich in the *Herald Tribune,* linking the music's basically linear, melodic style in some detail to the folk-song elements of much older work such as *Les Noces*, while shrewdly observing the way in which Stravinsky had blended what Rich called "the constant angularity which is one of the earmarks of this style" with "the free rhapsodic coloratura of ancient Hebrew intonation, which in turn has cast its shadow on a great deal of the folk music of Eastern Europe."[84]

The fact is that Stravinsky was lucky to get such a positive, intelligent response to these arcane and alarmingly disparate little masterpieces. Few among his usual adherents received them with genuine—as opposed to ritual—affection. Isaiah Berlin had privately admitted to finding *Abraham and Isaac* "a kind of cuneiform,"[85] while Morton told Boulez that, having heard the *Variations* six times, he detected in them "many of the problems of an eighty-three-year-old master."[86] Boulez thought them "less aggravating than *Abraham and Isaac,* a biblical story I've always found profoundly repugnant and *widerlich* [repellent] [. . .] But there's nothing to get very worked up about in these variations; always canons and more canons and still more canons . . . and in between, Messiaen's *Chronochromie* with its epode and its eighteen strings in real parts: here the eighteen have come down to the sacred number twelve, and [Messiaen's] birds have disappeared, transformed—by whatever mythology—into canons. All this between ourselves! But when it comes to canon, I prefer Webern."[87]

It is not the least irony of these late pieces that they were generally rejected by that avant-garde which they seemed primarily designed to please. Fortunately, this is not necessarily any reflection on their intrinsic quality.

33

SMILING FOR THE CAMERA ▬

THAT FEBRUARY OF 1965, Stravinsky had been keeping company with two old associates who were both, quite independently, hoping to film him for television documentaries. David Oppenheim, the clarinettist and former repertoire director for Columbia Masterworks, had been trying to set up a documentary for the past three years, ever since Stravinsky had agreed to give him the exclusive right to film the Soviet visit. Alas, that was another of those rights Stravinsky was fond of selling or (in this case) giving away that turned out not to be his to sell or give, and Oppenheim had not in the end been able to film in Russia. The new project was better thought out and better funded. CBS themselves were now involved and there was money on the table, including (after some fairly hard-nosed negotiations) a decent slice for Robert Craft, who, after all, would be crucially involved as adviser and participant. Oppenheim not only intended to film Stravinsky on tour, but he planned to spirit him back to places of emblematic significance in his early life. It was a characteristic project of the new age of television: history caught in the act.[1]

A week after Oppenheim's visit to Wetherly Drive, Rolf Liebermann materialized with his own idea for a film of a somewhat more homely character. In certain ways it would hark back to the Graff NBC sessions in 1957, when Stravinsky's house and life had been taken over for a week by a film crew. Liebermann wanted his team to spend four or five days a little more discreetly in the new house that March, and he then planned to film Stravinsky in September in Hamburg, rehearsing and recording his latest works, the *Variations* and *Introitus*. Quite why the composer submitted to being followed around by film technicians for the better part of half a year is hard to explain. No doubt the money was a prime factor. CBS were paying him ten thousand dollars, with a twenty-five percent supplement for a repeat showing;[2] and presumably the EBU, Liebermann's paymasters, were offering something comparable. But it is hard not to suspect that Stravinsky was to some extent flattered by the attentions of what—as he knew from bitter personal experience—was above all a popular medium. He knew that the desire to record his movements for posterity was a recognition of his iconic significance to a mass of people who cared nothing about his music, but he also knew that he himself filmed well, that he was photogenic in motion or repose, and that the medium brought out in him a certain flair for facial and gestural theatre, a talent he considered he had inherited from his father. At any rate he enjoyed enough aspects of the process to be willing to endure its tiresomenesses, not least because both producers were musicians with a genuine knowledge of his work.

Liebermann moved in with his director, Richard Leacock, and Leacock's crew on the 16th of March, and they stayed five days, filming the composer in conversation with visitors and with Liebermann himself, using handheld cameras to obviate the old need for set-piece groupings, and achieving thereby a naturalness and intimacy that had evaded previous directors. The naturalness was, of course, to some extent spurious. Shots of Stravinsky at work on the *Introitus* would have been an obvious setup even if the work had not actually been finished a month before. The advantage of the technique was that, after a time, you forgot about the camera, and—perhaps with the help of a good meal and a bottle or two of wine—simply talked about the usual things in the usual way. Pierre Boulez was in Los Angeles to conduct his *Eclat* at a Monday Evening Concert on the 26th, and he came to lunch during the filming. Afterwards they talked about *Les Noces,* a score was produced, and Boulez drew attention to an oddity of the chords on the final page, where the bell-strokes occur at regular eight-beat intervals, with a single exception where what looks like a superfluous bar of silence brings the total to eleven beats. Boulez argued persuasively that the extra silent bar was a misprint and ought to be expunged, and Stravinsky—perhaps slightly the worse for drink, or else temporarily overawed by the power of logic— altered the score on camera. In a more lucid moment he might have gone to the piano and tried the passage out, as he had once done when Nadia Boulanger pointed out an inconsistency in the sequential writing in *Orpheus.*[3] The anomaly in *Les Noces* is part of a general asymmetry in the way the chords punctuate the ceremonious chimes of the four pianos, and it might have reminded Boulez of Stravinsky's remark about accidents in the *Poetics of Music,* to the effect that a composer "may draw profit from something unforeseen that a momentary lapse reveals to him."[4] Boulez's own analysis of *The Rite of Spring* had drawn attention to variable patterns of just this type;[5] but he could not reconcile himself to the glaring disruption in the simple series of eights at the end of *Les Noces.*[6]

Soon after Liebermann and his team left Wetherly Drive, the Stravinskys set out for Austin, Texas, where they were (all three of them) taking part in forums and discussions with students, and Craft was conducting a concert with the university orchestra. This whole event was the first of Oppenheim's set pieces. The composer was filmed arriving by plane from Dallas and being greeted by a posse of cowboys in stetsons. Later he conducted a master class with students playing his music and a seemingly spontaneous platform question-and-answer session which, as Charles Joseph (who examined the outtakes) has shown, was actually the object of many retakes for Oppenheim's benefit.[7] The cameras were also rolling in Chicago a fortnight later, for the premieres of the *Introitus* and *Variations,* though the orchestra itself could not be filmed, nor the concert recorded, because of a dispute with the Musicians' Union. Instead Oppenheim filmed Stravinsky with Craft in the car after a rehearsal, claiming that he had scored the *Variations* for the forces Chicago had told him would be available, and that he would have done it differently had he known the orchestra would have so many violas. This can only mean that he would have scored the second twelve-part variation (the one for ten violas and two double-basses) for twelve violas, since there is nothing in the viola writing otherwise to suggest self-limitation. The cameras also invaded Stravinsky's hotel room and perused the sketches for the *Variations,* while their composer tried to insist that the work's twelve-note row had come to him spontaneously as a melody and that he had only noticed its serial structure later on.[8] This recalls his remark about the *Epitaphium,* that its serial character was a chance, and unimportant, discovery made after half the first phrase had been composed.[9] Such claims would be more convincing if any of his works after *Threni* had had non-dodecaphonic themes, but as it is they look disconcertingly like a preemptive defense against the charge of intellectualism, and an attempt to fit these works into the serendipitous tradition of the *Poetics* so recently called into question by the *Noces* incident with Boulez.

From Chicago the CBS crew pursued him to New York, where he was recording the *Ebony Concerto* with Benny Goodman at the end of April; then at the start of May they sailed with him for Göteborg, in Sweden, from where they all flew via Copenhagen to Paris. There, Oppenheim filmed Stravinsky—drunk and crotchety, according to Mario Bois[10]—on the stage of the Théâtre des Champs-Elysées and in the stalls seat he had occupied on the first night of *The Rite of Spring.* A few days later they were in Vevey, on Lake Geneva, and two days after that, on the 17th of May, the entire outfit, including the composer and his wife, Robert Craft and Theodore Strawinsky, descended on the unsuspecting lakeside town of Clarens, looking for the very room in the very house, Les Tilleuls, in which in the winter of 1911–12 he had composed the greater part of his most famous work.[11]

The visit has been described in intimate detail by Craft in one of the best passages of his *Chronicle of a Friendship.*[12] Everything had of course been prearranged by Oppenheim, who had even found an old lady who had been a tenant at the same time as the Stravinsky family, who still lived in the house, and who—to season good fortune with coincidence—was called Rambert, like the best-remembered dancer in the original *Rite*. The film sequences of Stravinsky finding the house, mistaking the apartment, and forgetting that his tiny studio room had been on a lower floor, were thus to some extent theatre, though the composer himself had not been let in on the act, and his surprise and pleasure on reentering the studio were, according to Craft, genuine. By astonishing luck, there was a piano, and Stravinsky could sit down at it and, for the benefit of television, bash out the famous chord of the "Auguries of Spring." "I like this chord," he beams into the camera, and he repeats the story of Diaghilev's enquiry at a Venice runthrough, "How long will the chord last?" and his own reply, "Until it is done, my dea-rr."[13] But, as Craft rightly insists, something crucial eludes the reconstruction, something to do with the passage of more than half a century, two world wars, and the entire cultural environment in which that music was composed, in that tiny room by that same diminutive person. In some curious way the very precision and naturalness of modern film seem to limit one's picture of that time of silent movies and long-exposure photography, when Stravinsky was not yet the beaming celebrity of later years but an austere genius in the grip of a hitherto unknown idea. Try as it might, the medium could not dissolve its own essence.

A week after this voyage into the Swiss corner of his remote past, the Stravinskys flew from Paris to Warsaw, preceded by the CBS crew, who once again filmed their arrival at the airport.[14] Oppenheim had hoped for a visit to Ustilug, just across the River Bug, which these days formed Poland's border with the Soviet Union. But just as the Soviet authorities had been evasive about such a visit in 1962, so they refused—or at least withheld—permission in 1965, for reasons which might easily have been foreseen. In general, they did not allow foreigners to visit provincial areas, especially run-down, non-Russian ones, and they were of course jittery about border regions, whether or not of special strategic importance. The fact that Stravinsky would be coming with an American film crew would merely have compounded the impossibility in Soviet eyes. So his last chance of ever revisiting the happiest home of his early years, and the actual birthplace of the work that interested Oppenheim above all others, vanished in the fog of the Cold War.

The disappointment may not, in any case, have been too great. For Stravinsky nostalgia had always been tempered by fear, and the Ustilug of the sixties would, he knew perfectly well, be a very different place from the remote village of the Nosenkos and the Belyankins. "It's a tomb," he is supposed to have told Oppenheim, referring presumably to some country of his mind rather than whatever Ustilug may actually have become.[15] That the reality would have depressed him can hardly be doubted. Claudio Spies, with no knowledge of the place but a good knowledge of the man, thought that the whole experience would be too painful "and not really worth the risk of such strong emotion. But TV knows no risks."[16] Perhaps it was just as well that, for once, television did not call the shots.

Warsaw itself he had not seen since 1924, and though he had then arrived in late October and it was now late May, the gloom of Gomulka's Poland far outstripped the chill of those autumn days in the still-young republic. It was cold and rainy, the food was disgusting, and the shops were almost empty. In their hotel, the hot-water system was out of order.[17] The vaunted composers of the Polish avant-garde—Penderecki, Gorecki, Luto-slawski, and the rest—were all said to be at a festival in Germany, and at the reception at the Composers' Union the visitors met only friendly nonenti-ties, officials, academics.[18] As for the Warsaw Philharmonic Orchestra, its work displayed the same rawness of tone and phrasing, and the same easy-going attitude to intonation, that they had encountered with the orchestras in Moscow and St. Petersburg. This did not prevent it, any more than it had prevented them, from attacking *The Rite of Spring* with due vigor and a cer-tain primitive energy in their concerts on the 28th and 29th. Moreover, they acquitted themselves at least adequately in what was, as a matter of fact, the European premiere of the Huxley *Variations*. Both these works were con-ducted, of course, by Robert Craft. Stravinsky managed the *Symphony of Psalms* and, as usual, *The Firebird;* but the effort this cost him was all too apparent. Craft reported to Lillian Libman that his conducting had been "very vague," and Stravinsky himself told her that "I did not conduct well in Warsaw. I did not feel well. . . . I do not *see* well."[19] His left leg was more and more troublesome. Above all he felt weak and tired. When he attempted to conduct a fragment of the *Rite* with the Warsaw orchestra for the CBS cam-eras (the intention being to dub the takes onto footage of a production by the Warsaw ballet), he found it so difficult that in the end no take longer than a few bars could be filmed, and Oppenheim had to do the best he could with these brief cutaways.[20]

Their last port of call was Rome, where, on the 12th of June, Stravinsky received a papal decoration from Paul VI and sat near him, somewhat ner-vously, during a performance of the *Symphony of Psalms*. All the while, the cameras rolled. But the ordeal by celluloid was nearing its end, and by the time they flew into Kennedy Airport on the 14th the filming, as Spies reported to Lawrence Morton, was "mercifully finished."[21]

THEY GOT BACK to Hollywood on Stravinsky's eighty-third birthday, the 18th of June, to be greeted as ever by a pile of letters, among them a dis-tressing one from his daughter-in-law Françoise. Something had happened to cloud their mutual affection in the year since the incident of young Johnny and the Chicago hotel bill. The composer had been irritated, no doubt, by that trifling matter. But what had chiefly agitated his old, White Russian heart was the spectacle of this eighteen-year-old grandson behaving like a 1960s campus dropout, unkempt and bejeaned, with no obvious goal in life, more preoccupied with university counselling than with university lectures, and by all accounts making things difficult for his parents at home. Stravinsky wanted to settle money on both his grandchildren, but he not unnaturally felt that in doing so he was entitled to let the boy's mother know what he thought of his manners. He had treated Johnny to lunch in New York that October, then telephoned Françoise and favored her with his general opinion of her son.[22]

Françoise had not responded for several months, but then some chance remark triggered a fiercely maternal reaction. Someone had reported to her that her father-in-law was putting it about that her son only wanted to see him in order to cadge money off him. She was furious. Would he care to know what Johnny had told her about *him*? The young man had gone to Chicago hoping to see his grandfather, and what a depressing experience! He couldn't get through on the phone and wasn't allowed to see him. "My grandfather won't even put himself out to see his only grandson. I was to phone him the next day, but I lost my nerve. What an incredible family relationship! I'm shattered by it." Stravinsky's thoughts on the depravity of the young merely showed how out of touch he was. Either her son's problems were clinical or (more likely) they were fairly commonplace, and in neither case was the grandfather's intervention exactly helpful. As for the Soulima household, their affections were all firmly in place, thank you kindly. Like most mothers of only sons, Françoise was tormented by his every misery, his every insecurity, and she had suffered agonies of fear and anxiety on his account for the past two years. And as for the money, she enclosed a check for a hundred dollars and hoped to hear no more about it.[23]

So intimate an exchange would hardly count as material in an artist's life had it not already been aired—and in no very friendly context—by Robert Craft, who for some extraordinary reason calls Françoise's letter a "crucial document in the composer's biography."[24] Crucial it may be, but more as an example of Craft's own biographical methods than of anything out of the way in Stravinsky's behavior or his daughter-in-law's reaction. For Craft, the importance of the episode (which he misreports in a number of trivial but significant ways) lies in the lack of sympathy it reveals between the composer and his blood relations. But of course it actually reveals quite the opposite. It illustrates the pain of family ties that are close and highly strung; it shows, in case one had not realized, that an attachment existed between the two participants which these passing events were in some way felt to have disrupted. Milène had warned Vera not to raise the matter with Françoise, who was understandably rather touchy about it.[25] But by then it was too late; the composer had spoken and the damage was done.

In the cold light of day, Françoise realized she had gone too far. Three days later she wrote again, in a chastened tone. "I now tell myself that I risked giving you pain and this is an unbearable thought. Please bear in mind that I have been going through great anguish for long months. I embrace you very tenderly."[26] Quite apart from her anxieties about Johnny, she was tortured by the fear that Soulima, who had recently been experiencing blackouts during recital performances, was suffering from a brain tumor.[27] Craft, as usual, tries to give Vera the credit for explaining to Françoise the finer points of the composer's feelings; but he can only do this by ignoring Françoise's second letter and pretending that another one of a fortnight later was the relevant apology.[28] At the same time he maintains brusquely that the episode "effectively ended the relationship," a judgment frankly absurd in the face of Françoise's profoundly affectionate letters of the next two or three years to her father-in-law. If after that the relationship did, in a sense, come to an end, it was for other reasons and in other circumstances which will, in due course, be related. It is to these circumstances that Milène's much later testimony about Stravinsky having described Françoise speculatively as "a very unsympathetic person" truly refers.[29] The implication that he had previously, and lucidly, thought this is not the least of Craft's many and varied distortions in his account of Stravinsky's relations with his family.

Another, no less striking, concerns the affairs of the Geneva Strawinskys at this same period. In August 1964, according to Craft himself, Kitty had written to her adoptive parents accusing them of breach of confidence over her married lover, Pierre Théus, and had sent copies of the letter to her grandfather and to her aunt Milène and uncle Soulima.[30] Craft adds that Stravinsky was so angry with Theodore that he instructed him to stop interfering with Kitty and pointedly avoided telling him about "his next trip to Europe."[31] No trace of any such instruction has survived, and as for the secrecy about the trip, there was nothing particularly unusual about that, as Craft himself admits,[32] especially since they were in Paris for only two days on the way to Israel (a trip rearranged at short notice) and for only another three days on either side of Berlin, a trip that Stravinsky had intended to cancel. Craft then strongly implies that certain financial dispositions the composer made in Kitty's favor in September 1964 (parallel to the arrangements for Johnny referred to above) were in revenge for Theodore's supposed behavior, even though the relevant letter (which Craft quotes) expressly denies that the action has any connection with "the painful development in relations between Kitty and yourself," a wording that, moreover, carefully avoids apportioning blame.[33] Elsewhere Craft asserts that Stravinsky reduced Theodore's monthly allowance in the autumn of 1965, similarly, "as an act of reprisal for his and his wife's alleged harsh treatment" of Kitty (the "alleged" being, of course, a legal precaution, not an indication of any desire to imply doubt in the writer's mind).[34]

This whole set of allegations is so monstrous, so damaging and selective, at times so fallacious, and withal so private, that it seems astonishing today that it was ever dignified with publication. It is perfectly true that Henri Monnet, a Parisian lawyer friend whom Stravinsky asked to act as go-between in the matter of Théus's divorce, later informed him that Kitty had "preferred independent work in Geneva to more or less servile tasks for Theodore (or rather his wife)."[35] But Monnet had heard only Kitty's side of the story, and Kitty was for much of this time (January 1967) in a distraught and even somewhat hysterical state, unable to see beyond her own passionate feelings, inaccessible to reason, and, above all, eight months pregnant. Nowhere in Craft's account do we discover that Denise had for some time been seriously ill with arthritic tuberculosis, in constant pain, more or less unable to work, and mobile only with difficulty. Nobody would suggest that this gave her any right to treat her twenty-six-year-old daughter as a servant; but it would hardly be surprising or despicable if she had called on her for help, and had perhaps sometimes even done so too much or with too little concern for Kitty's own welfare. Why should such domestic troubles, of the sort that anybody who has had grown-up children or sick parents is perfectly familiar with, become the subject of ruthless and inaccurate dissection in print by an adoptive family member with privileged access to private documents and a reputation as a published essayist? Inaccurate? Craft's assertion that the reduction in Theodore's allowance was an act of reprisal is flatly refuted by the correspondence. Stravinsky had been making exceptional payments because of Denise's illness, but by the autumn of 1965 he was so worried about taxes that he felt unable to continue the allowance at the same level. In response, Theodore expressed only gratitude for past payments and accepted that they could not go on indefinitely. If any reprisal was intended, Stravinsky did not say so and Theodore did not notice: a curiously secretive, smiling sort of revenge, as befitted phantom hostilities.[36]

Since Theodore lived in Europe, it is to some extent possible to retrace his relations with his father and stepmother through their letters. What is much harder to unravel is the relationship with Milène, who still lived nearby and, when her father was at home, came to see him almost every day. She and Vera had always been on good, chatty terms. Milène would take her father for an afternoon drive, or she would sit and talk to him or help Vera choose curtains. The situation was on the surface easy and unconstrained. Milène was not clever in the intellectual sense, did not make sharp or witty remarks, but would talk pleasantly about nothing in particular, perhaps about her artifacts or Vera's paintings or the latest changes in the garden. But at some stage a certain tension crept into their friendship. It may have had something to do with André Marion, who still did secretarial work for Stravinsky but was once again without regular employment. Milène knew that Vera disliked André, and she had always suspected her stepmother of having undermined his position with her father because of Craft. Or it may have been something in Vera's attitude to Milène herself. Here one enters difficult waters. As we have seen, Robert Craft adored Vera and portrays her as practically without fault in her demeanor toward others, a woman physically and socially enchanting, unfailingly generous, trusting, altogether lovable and complete. In his picture of the Stravinsky household, it is invariably Vera who stands between the children and their difficult, preoccupied, impatient, often uncaring father, she who persuades him to act well toward them, to give them money or attention, to endure their demands and inadequacies.

Such a picture may be truthful as far as it goes, but it is not the whole truth. For one thing, the witness is suspect. Craft has often made exaggerated claims for Vera's tutelage. For instance, he once told me that Vera effectively brought up Stravinsky's children (in Paris in the twenties and thirties), a claim that is as demonstrably untrue as it is psychologically revealing, in that it suggests a need to see her as more satisfactory in all respects (including motherhood, which she never in fact essayed) than Katya Stravinsky.[37] On the other hand, Stravinsky may have been preoccupied, but he was not uncaring. His voluminous correspondence with his children is simply not that of a parent bullied into worrying about them; it shows genuine love and solicitude and a remarkable, if at times hectoring, attention to detail. There certainly were times when Vera interceded. Whether or not she was responsible, as Craft suggests, for putting pressure on her husband to invite Milène and Soulima to America after the war is hard to tell.[38] But if so, it must have been Vera herself who made the claim, since Craft was not yet a witness, and such letters as have surfaced are silent on the matter.

Vera Stravinsky was indeed a charming, sociable, openhearted woman. She had the knack, when you talked to her, of making you feel the most fascinating person in the world. But in the quiet of her boudoir, as we have seen, things were somewhat different. She would reflect with a sense of boredom on much that she had to endure. She detested, as any woman would, her husband's frequent drunkenness. She loved Bob and was terrified that he would abandon them. She often avoided their concerts, and one even wonders whether she cared all that much for her husband's music; at least, she left few if any penetrating or appreciative remarks about it, though she liked its success and often recorded ovations in her diary. In a legal deposition after her husband's death she admitted that she would be more interested in a diamond from Tiffany's than in the manuscript of *The Rite of Spring*.[39] When the two men in her life listened to gramophone records in the evening, she would make herself scarce. She liked clothes and boutiques, food and motor cars, New York and Paris. To a hostile judge these might seem the preferences of a shallow spirit; but just as possibly they were those of one who feared darkness and the abyss.

Soulima Stravinsky thought that Vera included her husband's children and their spouses among the "boring" things in life. They were conscious of being tolerated by her rather than liked. Perhaps, he reflected, she could have wished them to compliment her more: on her beauty, her clothes, her paintings, about which, in his opinion, she talked more than they strictly deserved.[40] Family life, in the sense in which they understood it, was not at all her natural element; she was wearied by the homely and the routine and would not have longed for these things—unlike the soldier in Stravinsky's *Tale*—if deprived of them. There is a hint of paranoia in Soulima's remarks about Vera, but it will not do to portray them, as Lillian Libman does in effect, as the stereotyped reaction of a boy in a fairy tale to his wicked stepmother.[41] After all, by 1965 Soulima had known Vera well for thirty-five years and been close to her for much of that time, including the first year of the war in Paris, when his mother was barely cold in the ground. If she had ever been going to seem like a fairy-tale stepmother, it would have been then. And if, much later, something happened to cool their relations in a more modest if eventually no less disastrous way, it would seem fair to keep an open mind, at the very least, about which of the two sides had changed and about who, if anyone, was to blame.

"TODAY I'M 83," Stravinsky wrote to Souvtchinsky on the 18th of June. "I don't know myself how to regard it: to be proud of the number or ponder on the ever nearer approach of nonexistence."[42] In fact he had little leisure to do either. A week later they were off again, this time to Muncie, Indiana, where he was booked to take part in a three-day Stravinsky festival at Ball State Teachers College, talking to students and attending their productions of *Oedipus Rex* and *The Soldier's Tale,* conducted by Craft. Yet again there was an open-air concert at Ravinia (on the 8th of July) and a pair of concerts in Vancouver on the 12th and 13th. In the latter part of August he was tied up with recording sessions in Hollywood and a concert in the Bowl, after which they were due back in Europe for filming with Liebermann in Hamburg and a concert in London.

To the world at large there was something miraculous in this victory of the creative spirit over the visibly fragile and decaying body. In Vancouver, "he walked to the podium looking frail and bent and old, leaning on a cane. But when the rehearsal began he seemed to become a different man. His whole length straightened until he stood on the tips of his toes with the arms uplifted, seeming to hover above the orchestra. His movements were sure and energetic as he moved the orchestra through . . . the *Firebird*."43 The transformation was, certainly, extraordinary.44 It was also to some extent a charade. Stravinsky was less and less capable of conducting music for which the orchestra seriously needed a conductor, and even in the recording studio it was becoming harder and harder to piece together whole performances from the fragmentary takes which often were the best he could manage. That August he stumbled through the *Variations,* but none of the takes could be used, and even Columbia never claimed that the published recording was by him. With simpler works like *The Fairy's Kiss* and *Pulcinella,* as we saw, usable takes by Stravinsky might be spliced together with "rehearsal" takes by Craft. But this was a more intricate task than might appear. In the rehearsal sessions, Craft would adopt his own speeds, which increasingly tended to be quicker than those of Stravinsky, who would then irritably refuse to adjust his own to match his assistant's. At the first *Pulcinella* session it was hot and uncomfortable and the atmosphere had been tense since Craft had kept them all waiting in the car on North Wetherly Drive and had then rehearsed the music at speeds guaranteed to boil the composer's blood. For the recording itself, Stravinsky duly adopted even slower tempi than usual, while Craft stood beside him trying desperately to indicate a faster beat to the orchestra. Unsurprisingly there was confusion, Stravinsky exploded in fury at one of the clarinettists, then turned on a horn player who was having routine problems with his instrument's tendency to "split," and when Craft rebuked him he spun round and shouted, "How dare you address me in this manner!" At that, Craft turned on his heel and stalked out.45

For a long time Craft had been sufficiently secure in his position not to hesitate to abuse Stravinsky if he felt himself slighted. He knew he was necessary to the composer, emotionally as much as practically. He records that at the end of this particular quarrel, Stravinsky sent him a note. "Dear Bob, whom I love, with my ardent longing for our former relations that gave me so much happiness. Maybe my age is spoiling everything? Excuse me this feeling never leaving my heart."46 The note, Craft claims, made him feel "more despicable" than ever, and one can well see why. Here he was forcing out of one of the great men of his day what amounted to a confession of utter dependency. Yet what a marvelous boost to his self-confidence! And surely to publish this humiliating little missive is hardly an act of contrition. It smacks rather of condescension, even (one might feel) self-congratulation. But then Craft was more than ever that summer casting himself as the composer's alter ego. Not only was he conducting Stravinsky's recordings, but he was writing his latest book for him. This fifth of the "conversation" volumes, eventually published in America as *Themes and Episodes*,[47] probably contains nothing written by Stravinsky himself, and possibly not much that he ever actually said. Half of the book is taken up with further extracts from Craft's diaries, and the rest consists of reprints of various letters and interviews which, for reasons already given, cannot seriously be regarded as authentic. Perhaps the short articles labelled "Contingencies" (renamed "Squibs" when they were published in revised form a few years later in England[48]) contain some genuine *obiter dicta*, like the remark about the purchase of a Renoir for $170,800 being "an example of a flagrant lack of respect for money."[49] But the program notes and book reviews are surely Craft's from start to finish, while of the material supposedly by Vera Stravinsky he has admitted in print that he wrote the letters to her cousin and has tacitly admitted that he wrote the review of the "Prima Assoluta" of *The Rake's Progress* by including it subsequently in his own *Chronicles of a Friendship*.[50]

Whatever Craft's motives in all this, straightforward self-promotion can hardly have been among them. After all, many of the best things in the book (and there are some very good things) were attributed to Stravinsky. And the same defense applies to the charge, frequently levelled in 1965, that the composer's "minders" were prolonging his concert career, against every consideration of his health and well-being, for reasons of their own. The fact is that Stravinsky's concerts did Craft's image as a conductor far more harm than good and they let him in for many predictable embarrassments and misunderstandings. That September (the 14th) they were due in London for a Festival Hall concert with the New Philharmonia Orchestra whose promoter, Robert Paterson, was firmly under the impression that the composer would himself be conducting *The Rite of Spring*, as well as *Pulcinella*, *Fireworks*, and the *Symphonies of Wind Instruments*. When Libman informed him in June that Craft would be conducting the *Rite*, Paterson's first, bizarre notion was that Stravinsky might conduct the work sitting down, and then, when that was rejected, he hinted darkly that the BBC (whose involvement was crucial to his budget) would not take the concert at all if Stravinsky did not conduct the *Rite*.[51] Weeks before the event, Paterson knew perfectly well that the *Rite* would be conducted by Craft, who would also (as he likewise knew) conduct the Huxley *Variations* in its British premiere. Yet nowhere in the publicity were these dispositions made clear, and even the program page of the printed program itself left them in doubt (they were announced at the end of each program note), so that when Craft stepped up after the opening *Fireworks* to conduct the famous ballet score, many in the audience were surprised not to see the composer reappear, and there were some mild expressions of disapproval. As for the *Variations,* even the program gave to understand that the composer would be conducting. In fact he only reemerged at the very end of the concert for the *Firebird* suite (*Pulcinella* and the *Symphonies of Wind Instruments* having long since been abandoned). None of this was strictly Craft's fault, but he naturally had to bear the brunt of the general annoyance. As it happened, the *Rite* was very poorly done, not helped by the testing of television lights during the "Jeu du rapt." Applause was tepid, considering the music, and there was much professional muttering at the bar during the interval. Almost as a matter of routine, Craft was blamed.

In Hamburg the previous week, he had conducted the *Introitus* and *Variations* for Leacock's film, and Stravinsky had himself rehearsed and conducted the Terpsichore variation from *Apollo,* a recording that would later be dubbed onto film of the very young Suzanne Farrell rehearsing the part with Balanchine.[52] Stravinsky had tried to postpone this leg of the European trip, but Liebermann had called his bluff by half-agreeing, insisting only that Craft come as planned to conduct the *Introitus,* since the choir was hard at work preparing it.[53] He obviously calculated that Craft would not make an extra journey to Hamburg on his own; and he was quickly proved right, for within four days Stravinsky had wired back that they were all coming after all.[54] So it turned out that not only could promoters not have Stravinsky without Craft, but they could no longer have Craft without Stravinsky. What Joan Peyser subsequently christened "Stravinsky-Craft, Inc." had at last become fully incorporated.[55] This was conclusively proved a few weeks later in Cincinnati, where Stravinsky had again been booked to conduct *The Rite of Spring* and to give a formal lecture in the local Corbett series. Lillian Libman claims that this unlikely concatenation had come about through an office error. But the truth is that it was no longer considered politic to refuse any such arrangement when setting up a contract, for fear that the booking might fall through altogether. In due course, Cincinnati learned (what they might have realized from the start) that the *Rite* would be conducted by Craft, and that he would also deliver the lecture. His subject would be "*The Rite of Spring:* Genesis of a Masterpiece," a major paper based on his recent study of the Meyer sketchbook in readiness for its forthcoming publication in facsimile. So seriously did he take this work that he actually flew home from New York in late September to collect the materials he needed to write it.[56] But alas for the hopes, already once blighted, of the Cincinnati Stravinskians. The lecture was not ready in time, and instead the audience had to make do with a question-and-answer session in which, after all, Stravinsky played the leading role and Craft for the most part sat on his hands.[57]

The one thing that Craft seems never to have done in Stravinsky's name is write his music, and yet the mere existence of the works of the 1950s and '60s is beyond question his greatest justification. Since July Stravinsky had been working spasmodically on his latest commission, which, as Stanley Seeger had written in February to remind him, was supposed to be a Requiem with a big "R."[58] The point about this curious insistence is that the draft contract drawn up by Montapert had specified "an original composition in the nature of a Sinfonia da Requiem," which seemed to imply a purely orchestral work, whereas Seeger was claiming that he had agreed to some but not all of the Requiem text being eliminated. In his reply, Stravinsky had affected not to notice this detail, and instead went on referring to a "Sinfonia da Requiem," though that, he added, would not be its title: "heaven forbid."[59]

Whether or not he seriously intended to force Seeger's hand on this issue is hard to decide. He had, after all, just composed a setting of the "Requiem aeternam" in the *Introitus,* and he may have felt that to compose another at his age might strike the angels as laboring the point. A month later he was still describing it to Nabokov as "a long-promised symphony for the orchestra of the youngsters at Princeton,"[60] and when he at last got down to serious composition in mid-July (after returning home from Vancouver) he worked on and off for several weeks at the purely wind-instrumental music of what eventually became the central interlude, with its exquisite chorales for quartets of flutes, horns, and kettledrums. These were the hottest weeks of the Los Angeles summer, and the domestic atmosphere was febrile, with Vera still without a regular cook, Craft working day and night to finish *Themes and Episodes,* and Stravinsky worried about his health and apprehensive about the coming recording sessions.[61] Yet no trace of these anxieties clouds the solemn radiance of the music, which like so much of his ritual thinking since the *Symphonies of Wind Instruments* and *Symphony of Psalms* (both of which it in some aspects resembles) seems to exist outside time and beyond dull care. Only when he got back to New York after the London concert and was able to settle down at the piano he had had moved into his room in the Pierre did he begin writing for voices, leaving out the "Requiem aeternam" itself and launching straight into the "Exaudi orationem meam," a line that had figured only covertly in the *Introitus, parlando,* and *sotto voce.* The closing "Requiem aeternam" he likewise omitted, replacing it with slow string chords.

They were back at North Wetherly Drive by the time he completed the "Exaudi" on the 10th of November. He had interrupted it briefly to toss off yet another epitaph, but one of a much less seraphic character, in memory of Pierre Monteux, who had died in July 1964, just over a year after the *Rite of Spring* anniversary concert at which Stravinsky had last set eyes on him. Somewhat perversely (since *Firebird* was the one early stage work of his whose first performance Monteux had not conducted), the piece was a short but spectacular canon for large orchestra on the theme of the "Coronation Scene" that ends that ballet—a kind of academic joke at the expense of the multiple repetitions the tune is subjected to in the original score. Why Stravinsky chose to commemorate his oldest musical collaborator at this moment and in so apparently dismissive a way is a good question, but one's instinct is that he wrote the piece first and only then decided to represent it as an *in memoriam*. As we saw, Stravinsky was not in the habit of writing epitaphs to close friends or associates. Monteux is not mentioned in the score, which simply calls the piece "Canon for Concert Introduction or Encore." Stravinsky sent it to Boosey and Hawkes on 8 November with a letter for Monteux's widow, saying we know not what.[62] A few weeks later, on 16 December, Craft conducted the first performance at a concert in Toronto, a concert Stravinsky did not attend.

34

FINAL CURTAIN

WHAT DID IT FEEL LIKE, a journalist had asked Stravinsky at his London press conference, to compose in old age? Did inspiration still come? Stravinsky's smile was irresistible. "For you," he teased, "I am somebody of old age. For myself, I am not of old age. I continue to live, and it is not my fault that I live eighty-three years."[1]

Inspiration still came. The *Requiem Canticles* was turning out to be a distillation of the austerities of the most recent serial works and the sacramental eloquence of scores as old as *Les Noces* and the *Symphonies of Wind Instruments*. It showed no trace of the disconnectedness and short breath that Lawrence Morton seems to have found in the *Variations*.[2] Its brevity was planned and coherent, concise rather than short-winded, and ideas continued to flow. By mid-December, when they again flew to New York, he had added an orchestral prelude to the "Exaudi" and the Interlude, and when they returned to Hollywood on 22 January he quickly finished the miniature "Dies irae" and "Tuba mirum" that he had been working on in his Manhattan hotel.

But still there was no letup in his performing schedule. There were recording sessions in late October and late November, and the New York trip, which took another six weeks out of his home life, was at least nominally for recording purposes, though in fact Stravinsky did not lift a baton while he was there. Instead he saw a good deal of Nabokov and of Soulima and Françoise, lunched with Kirstein, and met Balanchine to discuss his plans to choreograph the *Variations*.[3] Stravinsky had found a sponsor—a certain Jack Bomer—for a Russian-language recording of *Les Noces*, something he had never previously attempted, despite his repeated insistence that the work should only be sung in its original language.[4] But there had never been any intention that he should personally conduct the sessions. One idea had been for Craft to record them with Russian performers in Moscow.[5] In the end they were done under Craft in New York, in the composer's presence. Stravinsky's other New York recording that winter was made, by contrast, in his absence. He had been booked to record the Capriccio with the French pianist Philippe Entremont at the start of January. Then he suddenly remembered that when he and Entremont had recorded the Piano Concerto in New York eighteen months before, the sessions had been marked by aggravation and ill feeling; so this time he simply stayed away, and left Craft to conduct in his stead.[6] This presented Columbia with a problem which, not altogether surprisingly, they decided to get round by simply ignoring it and crediting Stravinsky in any case. But the composer would have none of it, "not only because it is extremely dangerous to pretend that I conducted the Capriccio but also because I don't want it."[7] He even objected to a photograph of himself with Entremont being used on the record sleeve, as if, he added, the two of them had ever made much music together. "The photograph with [Isaac] Stern was bad enough, as he never played the [Violin] Concerto before or since recording it and he had hardly done me the respect of learning it then." But at least he and the great violinist had "made music" together.

As for concerts, Vera had implored Lillian Libman not to pile up her husband's bookings in 1966, but Craft had been encouraging Paterson to arrange another European tour, and meanwhile they had concerts in a string of American cities—Minneapolis, Los Angeles, St. Louis, San Francisco, Rochester (at the Eastman School)—before again taking off for Europe in the second week of May. Paterson, for his part, was proposing dates in such exotic locales as Newcastle, East Berlin, Luxembourg, and Strasbourg. And to crown the whole trip, Stravinsky had agreed to conduct *Oedipus Rex* for Lina Lalandi, not just in Oxford, but also in the Athens Festival, with a performance in Lisbon to round things off.[8] The only consolation in the face of so daunting and apparently unnecessary a program was, as Vera confidently assured Lillian, that they would cancel everything anyway.[9] Stravinsky was looking frailer than ever, and what was in some ways worse, Craft was ill as well. In San Francisco in February he had conducted *The Rite of Spring* and the *Variations* in three consecutive concerts under sedation for a severe attack of flu, and by the time they reached New York in May he looked, Libman thought, like "someone who had spent several days in the company of a vampire."[10]

Nevertheless they duly got to Paris on the 12th of May, and ten days later they flew on to Athens, where, on the 26th, Stravinsky conducted *Oedipus Rex* with the London Symphony Orchestra in the Odeum of Herodes Atticus. The Lisbon performance followed on 1 June, and in the interval of the concert Stravinsky was presented with the Order of Santiago to add to the Doctorate of Humane Letters, which he had been unable to refuse at Rochester since it was handed to him without warning on the concert platform.[11] But Vera proved right about the remaining concerts. What was left of the Paterson tour, the concerts in Luxembourg and Strasbourg, were abandoned, ostensibly because Stravinsky had a cold, but in reality because they had decided as soon as they arrived in Paris from Lisbon that they could not face any more side trips. The Oxford Festival *Oedipus* went the same way. Instead they stayed in Paris, and Vera spent many hours in conversation with Kitty's lover, Théus, and with Kitty herself, now revealed to be pregnant. Milène, who knew all about the Strasbourg cancellation at least ten days before it "happened" (presumably because André had been instructed to unbook the hotel), was touched by Vera's devotion to "*ce pauvre* Théus," who had written her a tear-stained letter praising Vera's goodness of heart and her willingness to waste so much of her free time on their problems.[12]

The Athens and Lisbon concerts, like the London one the previous September, survived in the itinerary because the fees were too good to forgo. The cities themselves no longer attracted as tourist sites, as they once had done. These days, Stravinsky preferred to keep to his hotel, or make only short excursions, while Vera and Bob would take the occasional day trip without him—to Chartres from Paris, or to Corinth from Athens. There were those who noticed this tendency to abandon the ailing master, and drew sinister conclusions from it. Sometimes Stravinsky himself complained. "They leave me alone," he would grumble to Souvtchinsky, "they don't bother about me." But Souvtchinsky had his own way of explaining the situation. "Listen," he would say to Mario Bois of Craft, "this boy is insufferable but he's very interesting. They're lucky to have him. . . . He's young, intelligent, he distracts them, stimulates them, keeps them informed. . . . Look at old Igor, rebuffed, humiliated—it upsets me. But you know, I think he likes it. He's medieval man, and he's fond of the Devil . . ." And Bois had the wit to add that Craft had at least as much to endure with Stravinsky's foibles and tyrannies, day in, day out. One could almost say they needed and deserved one another. They were symbiotic. Even their humor was complementary, Craft's "redoubtable, biting, caustic . . . Stravinsky's clownish, Buster Keatonish, or else false-bottomed, subterranean, always unexpected, brief, with few words and much facial play."[13]

At the end of June they were due in New York for a Stravinsky Festival at the Lincoln Center organized by the composer Lukas Foss. Relations with Foss had improved in the three years since the publication of the American edition of *Dialogues and a Diary*, into which the platonic Stravinsky had slipped the inimitably lethal opinion that Foss's *Time Cycle* did not "require such strong criticism as that of the English newspaper that described it as 'appealing to teen-age taste' and called it 'an undergraduate parody of modern music from B to X (Boulez to Xenakis).' "[14] Foss wrote a pained letter, and the remark was expunged from all subsequent editions of the book.[15] But whatever his gifts as a composer, Foss turned out to be a brilliant organizer.[16] He had set up a superb festival of Stravinsky's music in its historical and contemporary contexts, with a dazzling team of conductors— Bernstein, Kondrashin, Ansermet, and, in the final concert, Stravinsky himself. And he had even put up a thousand dollars as an honorarium for Stravinsky's attendance at the opening concert on 30 June, which made it extremely hard for him to resist—as he conceivably might otherwise have done—the pleasure of hearing Bernstein conduct *The Rite of Spring* along-side a series of American works (including Copland's *Dance Symphony* and Revueltas's *Sensemayá*) supposedly showing its influence.

Stravinsky broadly approved of Bernstein's way with the *Rite,* though he did not much like his perspiring rostrum persona or some of the rhythmic mannerisms that went with it. In his box after the performance, he embraced Bernstein and remonstrated with him, good-humoredly, almost in a single gesture.[17] But he was much less anxious to hear Ansermet conduct *Persephone* in a pair of concerts entitled "Stravinsky and French Music" the following week. For all their apparent *rapprochement* in the late forties, he had never truly forgiven Ansermet for the *Jeu de cartes* affair before the war, and in particular he found it hard to overlook the conductor's remarks about his serial works in his recent, magisterial *Fondements de la musique dans la conscience humaine,* which purported to prove scientifically that atonality and serialism were contrary to the aesthetic laws under which the human brain perceives music. Ansermet had discussed in some detail the "bransle gai" in *Agon* as an example of "the absurdities [to which] the taste for learned and esoteric writing can lead."[18] Such defects appear, he had added,

> in most of the works Stravinsky has written since embarking squarely on a "learned" type of music, since passing from a music that was already learned but which responded to his sense of structural possibilities, to a music entirely thought out and "fabricated" on paper or at the piano by way of subtle combinations which belong in the domain of probability theory or the game of chess.[19]

The thought of this kind of criticism was quite enough to remind Stravinsky not only that he was conducting in the Hollywood Bowl on the 5th of July, but that it would obviously be quite impossible for him to get back to New York in time to attend Ansermet's second concert in Lincoln Center a week later. The day after the concert on the 12th, Ansermet wrote:

Lukas Foss told me that it was your wish that I should conduct these two concerts in your festival, which is why I accepted. I had hoped that it would be a chance to see you again. I'm very sad that this wasn't the case and that I have to leave for Geneva today.

Our old friendship carries more weight than any circumstance and we are both too near the end of our lives to forget it. I remain, with every wish for your health and happiness, your old Ansermet.[20]

Stravinsky did not reject the olive branch. "Your letter touched me," he replied.

We are both too old not to be thinking of the end of our days; and I wouldn't want to end those days weighed down by a painful enmity. Your letter relieves me of it completely [and] I am grateful to you.[21]

In the end, Igor and Vera returned to New York on the 14th, without Craft, who was in Santa Fe preparing Berg's *Wozzeck*. On the 15th they heard Foss conduct *The Soldier's Tale*, with Aaron Copland as Narrator, Elliott Carter as the Soldier, and John Cage as an "opéra-bouffe" Devil,[22] and a few days later they endured Larry Rivers's production of *Oedipus Rex*, which cast the hero as a heavyweight champion in a boxing ring. According to one newspaper account, Vera "stood up and booed," and she told the reporter: "It was a mishmash! But later, backstage, Larry Rivers asked me what I thought. I don't like to lie: I do it only to make somebody happy. So I said, 'Oh, I'm an old lady and very old-fashioned. Don't ask me.' "[23]

For Stravinsky's own concert on the 23rd, Craft reappeared as if by magic, having somehow evaded an airline strike and flown overnight from El Paso, arriving on the morning of the 22nd in time to rehearse *The Flood* and the Symphony in Three Movements, conduct the two works in the concert, then fly back to Santa Fe the next day.[24] The composer himself, helped to the rostrum by the pianist Paul Jacobs, conducted the *Symphony of Psalms*. It was a work that always made a profound effect when he directed it, even now that he was no longer able to command the performance in the fullest technical respect. Many—perhaps most—of the audience must have sensed that it would be his last appearance as a conductor in New York. It was a fitting end: "Alleluya. Laudate Dominum," in C major. Paul Horgan, who was convalescing after an operation and arrived at Philharmonic Hall in time for this one work, found the whole experience almost unbearably moving.

I was perhaps more than ordinarily susceptible in my weakened state; but it remains my conviction that that performance of *The Symphony of Psalms* . . . remains the summit of all musical performance which I have ever heard. His extraordinary vigour, his orchestral and auditory conception more acute than I had ever found it, and the glory of the writing itself— all brought me such exaltation as I had never known before in the concert room. This was not merely the gratification of the sensual pleasure one has in splendours of sound, or of the satisfaction for the intellectual faculty of detecting to the extent of one's ability the structure of such an abstraction as a masterpiece of music. It was rather to a communion of spirit wholly achieved by means of tonal art that one was lifted.[25]

One day in New York they dined at the Côte Basque with Elliott and Helen Carter. A man came up to their table, discreetly asked the composer for his autograph, then quietly returned to his own table. Stravinsky had not recognized him, though they had met before. It was Frank Sinatra.

STRAVINSKY had left for Europe in May with the *Requiem Canticles* almost but not quite complete. Since the Rochester trip in March he had written the "Rex tremendae," and when Francis Steegmuller arrived after Easter to interview him in connection with the Cocteau biography he was writing, the composer was hard at work on the "Lacrimosa," with its tearful, melismatic contralto solo. This particular piece is end-dated 27 April, but since the concluding sketch is written on a Hotel Pierre note-sheet, it seems possible that it was actually finished in May in New York: possible also that the "Libera me," which is undated but likewise sketched on a Pierre letterhead, was partly composed in Manhattan, though completed at the end of the month in Lisbon. There was no particular hurry, since Seeger had always agreed not to press for completion, and nobody seems to have envisaged a performance much before Stravinsky's eighty-fifth birthday in June 1967. Nevertheless, as soon as they got home on 25 July, he took up the instrumental postlude, with its clangor of bell chords so redolent, in their way, of the ceremonious chimes that conclude *Les Noces,* and within a fortnight or so he had completed the entire work. The final page of the *Requiem Canticles* is dated 13 August 1966.

Steegmuller, an urbane, cultivated New Yorker, had come with his young wife, the Australian writer Shirley Hazzard, who observed the household with a shrewd and attentive novelist's eye. She was struck by the absence of prominent relics in the Stravinskys' lives, considering the extent to which their conversation dwelt on the past. They talked with enthusiasm about Pushkin, about Russia, Diaghilev and Cocteau, Nijinsky and Ramuz. The house was comfortable but without conspicuous luxury, rather bourgeois in its furnishings, and dinner was excellent, cosmopolitan—with zakousky and endless Russian toasts, but the finest French wines, prosciutto, roast beef, first-class espresso, all enjoyed for their own sake, in no spirit of ostentation. As for their hosts, she was captivated by Vera's now somewhat corpulent beauty, her immense, rather prominent blue eyes, her expansive mouth, "her whole face radiant with feelings and expression." Like most people who met the composer for the first time, she was surprised, by how tiny he was and enchanted by his smile, which often seemed to burst out in childish pleasure at his own thoughts or those of his companions. He "leans forward with eyes beaming to make a point, looks [you] right in the eyes and listens, delighting in [the] interest of what he or [you] are saying." She thought him "very frail but no invalid," and he remarked that "my illness is thrombosis, not a heart attack, a *brain* attack. I ask my doctor, how long does it last? Not long, he said, but all your life." They were sick of California, Vera especially. Almost everyone they had known there had died or gone away. So why not go back to Paris? Steegmuller asked. "My husband loves to be where his things are, likes to be at home, where he's used to everything. When we were talking about our trip next month to Paris, I said we'll be ten days in Paris in May, then fourteen days there in June. He said "*Fourteen days*! Why so long?"[26]

HAVING COMPLETED the *Requiem Canticles* by mid-August, Stravinsky could not bear to wait ten months for its performance. Almost at once he suggested to Princeton that the first performance might be arranged for December,[27] and when this proved impossible he coolly proposed late September or early October, barely six weeks away.[28] They would be in Louisville for a concert on 17 September in any case, and could come on directly to New York, where Craft would be able to prepare and rehearse the work with the help of Claudio Spies, who held a visiting professorship at Princeton that year. Craft had again been pressing Paterson to arrange a European tour for October, and there were firm plans with Adriana Panni for a double-bill of *The Soldier's Tale* and *Renard* in Rome that same month, with designs by Eugene Berman and Giacomo Manzù. But Stravinsky had rejected everything, to the despair of Berman, who wrote querulously that "not since 1945 have my plans to work with you ever come off."[29] So October was clear, and Arthur Mendel (Stravinsky's old editor at AMP, now chairman of the Princeton music faculty) swallowed hard and bravely accepted the date. The premiere was fixed for 8 October in Princeton's McCarter Theatre.

"It will be another big flop," Stravinsky had assured Lawrence Morton just after finishing the score.[30] But he was reckoning without the circumstances and the special character of the music. It would, after all, be his first live East Coast premiere for almost seven years, and by far his most auspicious since, perhaps, the stage premiere of *Agon* or even the first *Orpheus*, nearly two decades before. For some years, moreover, his new works had in various ways been awkwardly skewed, toward their audience or their performers or both. *The Flood* had been a media failure, *Movements* had been a failure of communication in a barely adequate performance; *Abraham and Isaac* had aimed musically at the wrong audience, while the recent *Variations* and *Introitus* had simply been too short and too disparate to make a clear impact. Only *A Sermon, a Narrative, and a Prayer* had perhaps succeeded, and that had been far away and effectively out of earshot. Critics of Stravinsky's evolving serial method had had a field day; despite the brilliance of individual pages or movements, no single work, and certainly no group of works, had unmistakably clinched the issue of style and technique in his favor. They were an odd bunch of works, dislikable to many, to others evidence of failing powers and technical epigonism: the works of a master, no doubt, but masterworks, hardly.

From the start it seemed that *Requiem Canticles* would be different. Like the *Introitus*, but unlike his other memorial pieces, Stravinsky wrote it in a specifically elegiac spirit, pasting into the sketchbook as he went along obituaries of friends who died during its composition—an extraordinary reversal of his habitual refusal to associate his work with current events or feelings. Admittedly, the friends in question were not intimates of long standing, but rather a motley collection of more or less occasional calling or dining acquaintances, all of them as it happened famous: Varèse, whom they saw from time to time in New York; Giacometti, whom they had seen often in Paris since Souvtchinsky introduced them in 1957 and who had made a series of portrait drawings;[31] and Evelyn Waugh, whom Stravinsky admired but had met only once, in 1949. Stravinsky had certainly been upset by Giacometti's death the previous January, and he had told Souvtchinsky that he found it hard to accept (if for no other reason than that the sculptor was twenty years his junior).[32] But Waugh's death cannot possibly have affected him in any personal sense, and this fact leaves a slightly uncomfortable feeling that the pasting-in of newspaper cuttings and the inscribing of crucifixes was a self-conscious act, a gesture to the movie cameras of posterity, rather than a spontaneous token of grief. Another, less ungenerous, explanation is that Stravinsky found the detached tone of the printed obituaries useful precisely as a corrective to any tendency to personalize his Requiem setting, particularly in view of his own age and condition. He called them a "practical commentary," presumably for his own benefit.[33] They might suggest a poet who, before writing an epitaph, visits a graveyard to get himself into the right frame of mind.

Whether or not deliberately, the Princeton concert was planned in exactly the same lapidary spirit. It opened with Stravinsky conducting his Debussy memorial, the *Symphonies of Wind Instruments,* at an increasingly funereal tempo; then, after the three sacred choruses in their original Slavonic versions,[34] Craft conducted the *Variations* in memory of Huxley and two performances of the *Requiem Canticles* divided by the concert interval. Finally Stravinsky conducted his Mass. A note in the program requested the audience not to clap after the new work, out of respect, presumably, for its solemn, quasi-sacramental character—though applause seems to have been permitted after the other pieces, and Stravinsky was in fact given a standing ovation both at the start and the finish, led—according to Craft— by the tall figure of Robert Oppenheimer, the atom-bomb pioneer, whom the Stravinskys had met at Princeton seven years before. "Even his feet," Stravinsky had remarked, "are intelligent."[35] And Oppenheimer proved it by leaping to them and applauding ostentatiously as the composer mounted the McCarter podium.

Columbia had slated the new work for recording in New York three days after the premiere. It was a late-afternoon and evening session, and Stravinsky had doctors' appointments in the morning, then lunched with Isaiah Berlin, intending to arrive at the Manhattan Center in time for the first session at four o'clock. But something happened to change his mind, and Craft arrived at the studio alone and, according to some reports, evasive about the likelihood of Stravinsky's putting in an appearance at all. The plan, in any case, was for Craft to record the *Requiem Canticles* and *Variations,* scores which the composer himself was not technically able to conduct; but Stravinsky was down to record the Mass and the *Symphonies of Wind Instruments,* and it was also important to McClure, the producer, that he be there for at least part of Craft's sessions so that the recording could truthfully be described as "in the composer's presence." So at some point there were anguished phone calls between the studio and the Hotel Pierre, and in due course Stravinsky and his wife appeared, the composer "grim and silent," Vera angry and loquacious. They stayed only for a short time; Stravinsky did not conduct, and Craft somehow got all four works onto tape by himself, for the most part in the composer's absence.

To interpret these events now, after so many years, is almost impossible even with the help of eye and ear witnesses. Stravinsky was still smarting over the matter of the Entremont Capriccio recording, while, according to Craft, Vera was cross with Columbia for their condescending attitude in "allowing" him to record the new work on condition that Stravinsky direct the Mass.[36] Yet Columbia hardly needed this new version of the Mass, since they already had a perfectly good recording by the composer in their catalogue. It seems at least as likely that Vera was annoyed at her husband's being dragged to the studio as a kind of stooge, merely to authenticate

Craft's recordings. If so, she was not alone. Claudio Spies, who was present, had also taken umbrage at what he saw as the exploitation of the ailing composer, and not only in the recording studio, but on the concert circuit as well. A few weeks later he wrote to Lawrence Morton criticizing Craft's role in these activities and railing against the impending publication of *Themes and Episodes,* about which Stravinsky seems to have known nothing.[37] Spies had said these things to Craft's face at the recording session, and there had been a row. To some extent, he admitted, Stravinsky was perfectly aware of what was going on and acquiesced in it as the price of continued celebrity.[38] The real victim of the situation, in his opinion, was Vera; and Morton agreed, while preferring, on the whole, to distance himself from the entire argument, as if it were a family dispute and none of his business.[39] Morton's real attitude, as he claimed after Stravinsky's death but while Vera was still alive, was that there was nothing to be said openly against Craft that would not at the same time offend and injure the Stravinskys, something that he for one would never be prepared to do. "I came," he told Pierre Boulez, "to love these people very deeply." One day, when Vera too was dead, he would tell all.[40] But like the book on Stravinsky that he worked on for a decade or more before abandoning it in the cause of friendship and affection, this later project also was destined to remain an unfulfilled intention, the documents of which perhaps still lie buried in the vaults of the Special Collections archive of UCLA, not to be revealed until the day of judgment.

Within twenty-four hours of this unhappy recording session they were back in Hollywood, and five days after that Stravinsky put the finishing touches to a short song for voice and piano, which, according to one report, he had started before the *Requiem Canticles* but left to be completed after it "by way of insuring that the mass for the dead would not be his final work."[41] This was a good story, but not one that made a great deal of sense. Stravinsky was frail, certainly, but so he had been for some time, and there is no particular sign that he regarded the *Requiem Canticles* as his swan song. Two months later he was at work on the initial sketches for a new piece for orchestra.[42] As for the actual song, a setting of Lear's "The Owl and the Pussy-Cat," it hardly conjures up the picture of a lengthy or complicated gestation. Just as the poem pokes fun at a certain form of academic rhyming verse, so Stravinsky teases the mechanical aspects of serialism by fitting Lear's nonsense poem to a note-row of childlike plainness, in an unbroken quaver pulse, without bar lines, and with a single-line piano accompaniment that tracks (with one exception) through the same untransposed forms of the row. A fortnight after it was completed, Morton added it as a surprise item to the Monday Evening Concert on 31 October. This proved an even bigger risk than he had probably expected. Ingolf Dahl played the piano part, but the intended singer, Gloria Grace Prosper, fell ill two days before the concert, and her substitute, Peggy Bonini, struggled to master the mildly awkward, angular line and breathless phraseology of the three-minute song. She and Dahl rehearsed the day before the concert in the basement music room of the Stravinskys' house. The ailing composer sat grumpily in his pyjamas picking holes in her performance, and there were ill-tempered scenes and much brow-beating, hair-tearing, and arm-waving, not at all in the beatific spirit of the song, while Arnold Newman, who had been following Stravinsky round with a camera since the *Requiem Canticles* rehearsals, snapped away with merry indiscretion.[43] The actual premiere was adequate at best, and afterwards Stravinsky complained to Dahl, slurring his words but with all "the old strength, flash, conviction," that "everything is always too loud, too loud for me. More delicate—it should be like threads and it is like macaroni. On my piano upstairs, it is muted, you know, I can hear it right. It is like spiderwebs. One must speak *softly* in order to be understood *clearly*."[44]

Stravinsky did not take a seat in the audience, but positioned himself in the wings, not wishing, perhaps, to display his unease at the performance of his new work. From there, he listened with rapt attention as a twenty-one-year-old pianist by the name of Michael Tilson Thomas played the last, C minor, piano sonata of Beethoven. Afterwards, Thomas told Dorothy Crawford, they "sat together backstage and drank tea, while Stravinsky talked about the sonata."[45] He had loved Beethoven's music since the thirties, when he had listened to it obsessively as the spiritual basis of his own music in abstract classical forms and had countered Nouvel's loathing of the unchanging harmonies in the late A-flat sonata with the remark that "that's what's marvelous: that Beethoven didn't shun to go on and on and on with the same chord."[46] He might certainly have said the same about the Arietta of the C minor sonata. But more than that, it seems likely that he felt a special closeness—from behind his arras in the Leo S. Bing Center—to this music, which at times seems to ignore the ordinary concerns of the sublunary music lover and, as the platonic Stravinsky had himself observed in *Dialogues,* to address itself "not to the great unwashed, but to a select few, . . . to an intimate two or three, or perhaps only to the composer himself."[47]

FRAIL HE MAY have been, but Stravinsky was not yet ready to abandon the touring schedule that, one way and another, had kept him alert and in funds for the past forty years. Before the end of the year they had flown to Honolulu for a pair of concerts with the dreadful local orchestra but with another brilliant twenty-one year-old, Itzhak Perlman, as soloist in the Violin Concerto.[48] Later there were concerts in Columbus, Ohio, and Portland, Oregon. That Craft was the driving force behind this ever more alarming schedule can scarcely be doubted. He it was who promised Lina Lalandi the European premiere of the *Requiem Canticles* in return for repeat appearances in Athens and Oxford;[49] and he who announced to Igor Blazhkov that they would be back in the Soviet Union the following summer, including a visit to Kiev.[50] Paterson was booking yet another hair-raising European tour, including a London concert in March, visits to Liverpool, Newcastle, and Brighton, and a gala at the Paris Opéra, and meanwhile Peter Diamand, the director of the Edinburgh Festival, had got from someone the idea that the composer might come to Scotland to conduct the *Symphony of Psalms*. Every one of these European projects fell through, but the mere fact that they can have been contemplated—at least partly with Stravinsky's knowledge—is a measure of the determination to shut out the full implications of his age and condition, obvious though they increasingly were to friends, associates, and, most worryingly, potential customers.

As for whose determination was the strongest, that was a moot point. Craft told Lillian Libman that Stravinsky dreaded the day when he would no longer be able to conduct. But it was apparent that Craft himself feared it at least as much, not for the sake of his own career (which was hardly advanced by stand-in appearances in front of audiences who had paid high ticket prices to hear Stravinsky conduct, or even by movie work like the United Airlines publicity film for which Craft conducted a series of Stravinsky excerpts that December[51]), but for fear of the consequences for family life in the North Wetherly Drive household.[52] There were still times when the fears seemed groundless. In Chicago at the end of December, for a pair of concerts that were actually billed as his last appearances in that city, Stravinsky needed help onto the rostrum but once there managed at least to give the impression that he was fully in command. Nobody blamed him for the fact that, as one critic put it, he "did not make his exit with the kind of evening he deserved." The CSO, so brilliant in the *Variations* and *Introitus* eighteen months before, had taken a week's Christmas holiday, and the orchestra for the Stravinsky concert was a pickup, including some CSO players but also some who seemed to have no more than a passing acquaintance with even such music as *The Firebird* and the Shrovetide scene from *Petrushka*. There was a faint echo of bad feeling from the dispute over studio payments that had prevented the recording of the *Variations* concert. The players pointedly failed to rise for the composer as he limped to the podium. Yet Stravinsky seems to have noticed nothing untoward, and when the *Sun-Times* critic, Robert C. Marsh, described the orchestra, probably rightly, as "a miserable pickup band that was struggling merely to play the notes," Craft-Stravinsky fired off an unforgiving telegram to the paper's editor: "Wednesday's orchestra was a credit to Chicago. Your reviewer is a local disgrace."[53]

No one was suggesting that the substitute orchestra in Chicago was in any sense a reflection of Stravinsky's own failing powers. Yet there were distressing signs of a falling off in bookings, if not so much for that reason as because of the fear of cancellation. According to Libman, the Hollywood Bowl, where the master had conducted as recently as July, declined to engage him for 1967, and so did the Vancouver Festival.[54] In Miami, where he and Craft directed a single concert (their first ever in Florida) toward the end of February, the date clashed with the local Philharmonic Ball, and only about half the orchestra were prepared to make themselves available. Three days later, Stravinsky himself took to the floor of the International Ballroom of the Beverly Hills Hotel and conducted the same 1945 *Firebird* suite and the final tableau of *Petrushka* for—Libman tells us—less than half his usual fee of ten thousand dollars: not that it mattered, since the fee was never paid in any case.[55] Finally in March he reached what must have seemed almost the end of the road. After conducting *The Soldier's Tale* at the Seattle Opera "with a vigor that belied his years," as one reviewer put it, but in an "erratic" and "vague" manner, as Craft reported less indulgently to Libman on the telephone, he promptly cancelled until the late autumn all concerts that involved flying, on doctors' orders.[56] That finally ruled out any possibility of a European tour, but it also virtually eliminated bookings in the eastern half of the United States. In the second week of April, Craft took over an engagement in Lexington, Kentucky; concerts planned for St. Louis and Milwaukee later that month were quietly dropped; and after that there was not a single contracted booking but of course the usual optimistic clamor from distant impresarios who either did not hear the bush telegraph or preferred to ignore what they heard. Of all the various dates Stravinsky could have taken on at this moment, only one recommended itself as properly worthy of consideration, a Toronto concert in May that would involve only the physically undemanding *Pulcinella* suite, together with *Oedipus Rex* conducted by Craft, with an absolutely dependable orchestra and an organization that knew the maestro's needs and could be relied on to make him feel welcome.[57]

Stravinsky had been weak and, in a general sense, sickly for so long now that he was capable of interpreting quite severe attacks as nothing worse than bad days. There must have been some such episode in mid-March. His 1967 diary has not survived, and Vera's is silent about any specific illness but notes on 22 March that he is "better."[58] Only later, in the green room of Toronto's Massey Hall, did he confide to Craft that he thought he had had a stroke.[59] When they arrived in Toronto on 12 May, he looked so weak and ill that Libman, who met them at their hotel and went with them to rehearsals, had serious misgivings about CBC's intention to televise the concert and even, no doubt, about the concert itself.[60] Vera, too, was exhausted, and Craft was suffering from a kidney infection. But they all seemed to recover by the first rehearsal the next day, and there were grounds for hoping that all would be well for the concert itself on the 17th.

In a sense it was. The works were performed to a packed auditorium, there were scenes of wild enthusiasm and standing ovations, and at the end of his part of the program Stravinsky was presented with a medal by the chairman of the Canada Council. But when the critic of the Toronto *Globe and Mail* reported that "the performance of *Pulcinella* fell somewhat short of perfection, but the fault did not appear to lie with the conductor," he was being more diplomatic than candid.[61] In truth the orchestra's performance bore hardly any relation to the conductor's arm. For the most part, the players stuck to the tempi and nuances of Craft's rehearsing and did their best simply to ignore Stravinsky's beat. But in places where, all the same, a beat was essential, the result was scrappy and at times chaotic. Once or twice the performance came near to collapse. For the first and last time in his life, Stravinsky conducted sitting down, yet even so he had to steady himself for much of the time, Craft noticed, by gripping the podium rail with his left hand, which made properly nuanced conducting virtually impossible.[62] For a long time his beat had been unclear and erratic, his tempi unpredictable, his control a matter of presence rather than technique. But now he sat in front of the orchestra like a moving icon, a symbol of the music, no longer its master.

It was fifty-three years and one month since a reporter in Montreux had remarked of his debut performance in the scherzo of his E-flat symphony that "the fact that M. Stravinsky himself was conducting contributed in large measure to the success of the concert."[63] As with his first concert, so with his last.

35

A FAMILY AFFAIR

HOWEVER IT MAY have seemed in Toronto, Stravinsky had no immediate idea of retirement. For one thing, he still had an active recording contract. As recently as January, John McClure had sent a list of the works not yet recorded by Columbia and proposed a series of mopping-up sessions.[1] That same month, in Hollywood, Stravinsky had (for the second time) recorded his 1945 *Firebird* suite. Meanwhile the European concert tour that Robert Paterson had been arranging for that summer was still theoretically on, although Libman noted in January that the Stravinskys were "determined to make this a vacation trip."[2] Even after Toronto, she was still signing contracts for concerts the following winter, including a series of three with the visiting French National Orchestra. There was naturally a good deal of fantasy about such plans which often involved Craft, especially, in considerable personal inconvenience and embarrassment. As late as May 1968, he himself conducted a series of four concerts at Berkeley that had been advertised and sold out as being conducted by Stravinsky, even though all concerned except the paying public knew long in advance that he would not conduct, because he could not. Finally, the myth that Stravinsky was still composing died hard, even apparently among those who were close enough to him to know that it was not the case. In January 1968, Craft noted in his diary that Stravinsky had abandoned the piano work he had been sketching as he had "a bigger piece in mind." Six months later, Edwin Allen, a young librarian they had met in Santa Fe in 1961, who had recently been cataloguing the composer's books and acting as their driver and general in-house factotum, told the British musicologist Oliver Neighbour that the master's next work was going to be "for piano and instruments with a solo section."[3] By this time, Stravinsky's only work on staved paper was the instrumentation of songs by Hugo Wolf. Souvtchinsky had visited North Wetherly Drive in October 1967 and had seen, he told Yudina, the "new piano sketches (invention, sonata, variations)." "But can he write them?" he asked skeptically.[4]

The fact is that those who lived close to Stravinsky or who saw him frequently knew the true state of affairs, in whole or part, but found it desirable to prevaricate, or at least evade the issue. For one thing, his own spirits had to be kept up, in the face of creative, physical, and, in due course, mental decline. Then again, those whose lives were enmeshed with him and his work naturally had their own reluctance to stare into the abyss. Like wives in Brahmin India, they feared the collateral death, the moral suttee, that would accompany his demise. Finally, there was the question of tax deductions, so crucial to the household budget but justifiable only for as long as Stravinsky was seen to be professionally active. Thus a yawning gap opened up between the public and the private realities. In the public eye, though no longer musically visible or productive, Stravinsky remained almost until the day of his death the alert, active, sharp-witted observer of the cultural scene, the scourge of critics, the sparring partner of interviewers. In March 1971, less than five weeks before he died, the *New York Times* ran a sprightly, venomous riposte, allegedly by him, to Clive Barnes's review of the Béjart *Firebird* at the Brooklyn Academy of Music.[5] By this time, many no doubt suspected that the composer was not the author of everything printed under his name (Barnes's article shows that he knew but did not dare to say so openly, which may be what prompted the abusive reply to a review which, after all, was highly complimentary to Stravinsky's music).[6] But there were some, even in the trade, who did not want to see the nose on their face. Writing after the composer's death, B. H. Haggin talked about "the prose writing with which Stravinsky delighted those who found nothing to interest them in his recent music," referred specifically to a recent *New York Review of Books* article "in which Stravinsky commented with his usual perception and humor on the general New York scene," and finally described the composer's spat with Barnes as his "last public act," with which, he concluded, "Stravinsky earned the gratitude of his fellow artists and the admiration of us all."[7] If a specialist writer like Haggin was incapable of seeing through the deception, one should hardly expect his readers to have done so.

The private reality was that, for the final four years of his life, Stravinsky was physically decrepit, under constant medical supervision, increasingly in need of nursing, and on two or three occasions so terribly ill that his life was despaired of. Mentally, however, things were somewhat different. For a long time he remained sharp and aware; able to observe his own condition and treatment with dry, detached wit; lucid in reminiscence; voracious in reading and (with Craft) in listening to music, which, as the other faculties began gradually to fade, survived the longest of all his socio-intellectual pleasures. But his stamina and attention span were together shrinking. Though his reading ("still with a pack of dictionaries at hand," Lawrence Morton reported) was mainly in English, he was finding it more and more difficult to follow conversations in that language, especially on intellectual topics, and Vera would often have to translate into Russian for his benefit.[8] Socially, too, he had become short-winded, and more susceptible to the effects of drink. Dining at Wetherly Drive one evening that June, a few days before Stravinsky's eighty-fifth birthday, Morton found him well and in fine form for about an hour, but observed that "after 3 scotches and a glass of Haut-Brion he [fell] into a stupor."[9] The atmosphere had become afflicted and oppressive, as so often in houses where age and infirmity have taken up residence. Vera, with her high blood pressure, struggled to keep house in the frequent absence of good professional help. Returning to Hollywood from Santa Fe, where he was conducting Hindemith's *Cardillac* that summer, Craft was overwhelmed by the sense of their loneliness and fragility, and their utter dependence on him.[10]

Meanwhile the phlebotomies, electroencephalograms, and Roentgen treatments pursued their course, like the culmination of a thematic process that had begun with the fermented mare's milk of Igor's Pavlovka holidays six and a half decades before. And just as the youthful valetudinarian had reported with self-satisfaction on his intake of koumiss, so the octogenarian Stravinsky was rather pleased with his more scientific clinical data. "My blood is like purée," he announced matter-of-factly in the Toronto green room, and as for his brain, he was fascinated by the encephalogram, which reminded him of some "electronic score with unreadable avant-garde notation," and proud of the doctor's assurance that "no impairment whatever to your mental faculties has occurred."[11] Then abruptly in late August the long-running soap opera of his health turned into looming tragedy. On the 21st he was rushed to Cedars of Lebanon hospital with severe hemorrhaging from a stomach ulcer, and by the time Craft flew back from New York, where he had been recording Gesualdo and Stravinsky's *The Owl and the Pussy-Cat*, the composer had lost a huge quantity of blood and was suffering from an improbable syndrome of polycythemia and anemia, a combination of opposites like Theseus's "hot ice and wonderous strange snow."[12] But there was worse to come. For two months after his return home he suffered agonizing pain from what appeared to be gout in his left hand, aggravated by a recurrence of the ulcer, high temperatures, and an alarming tendency toward pneumonia. For the first time, those around him feared the worst. The barrage of medications, injections, X-rays, and solemn professional examinations and pronouncements began increasingly to resemble the comings and goings round the deathbed of a medieval emperor. Then on 2 November his left hand unexpectedly went black, and it was quickly realized that it had suffered a thrombosis, a straightforward side effect of the polycythemia. His gout, like Dylan Thomas's, had turned out to be a mirage—and a dangerous one at that, since (as with Thomas) the treatment for the condition was poisonous to his other, more threatening ailments.[13]

Gradually, through the month of November in the hospital and the month of December at home, Stravinsky returned to something resembling his normal shaky health. The ulcer healed and the thrombosis dispersed; but the doctor who had mistaken the blood condition for a pain in the joints, and had thereby come close to killing him, was not forgiven. All his life, Stravinsky had favored professional advisers who loved his music and waived their charges, and his health, his lawsuits, and, ironically, his finances had sometimes suffered accordingly. But never before had he turned on an adviser as he and Vera now turned on the unfortunate Max Edel, the Viennese Jew who had been their Hollywood physician since 1946. Edel was a classic example of the old-fashioned cultivated doctor with a personal touch and a beautiful bedside manner, a profound love of art and ideas, but a certain distaste for the technological intricacies of modern medicine. There is a hint of obstinacy in his gout diagnosis in the face of the hand's failure to respond to treatment; and when Vera consulted other doctors, he took umbrage and was promptly discharged. Robert Craft, who was fond of Edel, paints an affectionate portrait of him in his memoirs, but does not acquit him of the charge of medical incompetence.[14]

AT THE END of October, when the pain was at its height and before the correction to the diagnosis, Pierre Souvtchinsky had arrived at North Wetherly Drive on a short visit. It was his first trip to America, and the first time he had ever ventured onto an aeroplane. The two old friends had corresponded regularly throughout 1967, Stravinsky's contribution being almost his only late writings (apart from family letters) that can confidently be treated as authentic. Souvtchinsky had recently been involving himself in a minor squabble between Gilbert Amy, the new young musical director of the Domaine Musicale, and André Malraux, the French Minister of Culture, over who should mount the first Paris performance of the *Requiem Canticles,* a dispute eventually resolved by Stravinsky in Malraux's favor (despite a promise to Amy), probably because of the prestige of the actual event: the inaugural concert of the new Orchestre de Paris.[15]

Now another issue had arisen, this time one that would involve Souvtchinsky more directly. The facsimile publication of the *Rite of Spring* sketchbook, which had been his idea, was still going slowly ahead, delayed partly by indecision over the exact contents of the supplementary text.[16] But meanwhile a far larger and more ambitious project was being mooted: that of the systematic publication of Stravinsky's entire archive, insofar as it was publishable and of general interest. The idea for this project seems also to have originated with Souvtchinsky, and it was probably first discussed when Rufina came to see the composer in Paris in June 1966. That autumn, Libman was set to tidying up and reorganizing the hundred or more cardboard boxes of correspondence, manuscripts, photographs, contracts, newspaper cuttings, articles, concert programs, and assorted documents and scrapbooks that Stravinsky, an instinctive hoarder since childhood, had accumulated in more than half a century of exile.[17] No formal agreement had yet been struck, however, and it was only when Souvtchinsky himself put in his Hollywood appearance at the end of October 1967 that a contract was signed transferring publication rights to Boosey and Hawkes, and plans laid for the microfilming of the archive as the first step toward such publication.

Why did Souvtchinsky make this strenuous and, for him, somewhat frightening journey? It might seem a sufficient explanation that Stravinsky had been seriously, even dangerously, ill and might well not be able to travel to Europe again. Recently, he had made gifts of money to his oldest friend, whose wife, Marianna, had herself fallen ill two years before and had ever since been unable to work.[18] But perhaps all the same there was more to the visit than met the eye. Libman reported that Souvtchinsky's trip had been engineered by Craft to help boost the composer's morale.[19] Yet curiously enough Craft later alleged that Souvtchinsky only came to Hollywood, having refused all previous invitations, because he had been suborned by Rufina with the offer of a contract to edit the archives himself in return for obtaining Stravinsky's signed agreement to the publication.[20] The allegation goes still further. It hints that Stravinsky's condition was in some sense aggravated by Souvtchinsky's visit, that he signed the contract against his will, and that, having achieved his object, Souvtchinsky "promptly" (that is, too promptly) left Hollywood. As usual, Craft gives no source for this information, which can in fact only be understood in the light of subsequent disputes over the editorship of the archive. The idea that Boosey and Hawkes tricked Stravinsky into signing away his own publication rights without reimbursement by sending an old friend to work on him while he was at death's door is as ludicrous as it is revolting. But it requires only a moment's thought to realize that Craft could not have known about any such plot, even had it existed. Did Ampenoff tell him? Did Souvtchinsky? Craft later, he claims, told Ampenoff that Stravinsky's signature "would not hold up in court," since he could be shown to have been under sedation for the whole of Souvtchinsky's visit.[21] Ampenoff thereupon prepared a new contract and took it herself to New York, where Stravinsky duly signed it in October 1969. So why the Souvtchinsky "plot," and why the problem of sedation?

The row brewing over the archives was not the only dispute gathering about Stravinsky's bed of pain, nor was it by any means the most serious. A situation had arisen within and around the family that contained the seeds of a conflict that would long outlive its immediate cause. The material side of the problem had begun in all innocence early in 1962, at a time when Stravinsky's lawyers, William Montapert and his wife, Arminé, had been examining various methods of reducing his tax liability. It was the Montaperts who had explained to him that by donating autograph manuscripts to the Library of Congress (among other public archives) he could deduct for tax the full market value of the donation, and they who saved him, at the end of 1963, from a looming fiscal disaster brought about by an unexpectedly early ASCAP royalty payment of forty thousand dollars.[22] Stravinsky's loathing of the Internal Revenue Service was therefore not surprisingly equalled by his gratitude to the Montaperts. "The qualities of your service can be explained," he wrote to them in April 1963, "not only by your friendly feelings towards Vera and myself but also by [the] very exceptional skill in your work as my lawyers. You are artists in your field, devoted and creative artists."[23] The Montaperts had just crowned their artistry, in Stravinsky's opinion, by setting up a mining company in his and Vera's names, with the neat portmanteau title Verigor International and a stakeholding near Yuma, on the Arizona-California border.[24] Verigor held regular meetings and business dinners; but its mining activities were largely notional. The point was, as Stravinsky explained to his Paris publisher, that investments were not subject to tax, while income of course was. "You understand that, in America, if you extract minerals from the ground, they subsidize you, but if you extract music from your head, they tax you."[25] Perhaps there were minerals at Yuma and perhaps there weren't. Meanwhile, they had marked out the four corners of the holding and were planting a citrus grove.

A somewhat more covert aspect of Stravinsky's tax-avoidance regime was his numbered bank account with the Swiss Bank Corporation in Basle, which he used as a repository for European payments that he did not wish to come to the attention of the U.S. revenue service. Such accounts were of course illegal for U.S. citizens under federal law, and Montapert seems to have convinced the composer that in the event of his and Vera's simultaneous death, the Swiss money would be difficult to repatriate or would be in some other way a legal embarrassment. In April 1962, he persuaded them to sign a transfer of the entire numbered account into the names of his three children.[26] Later, his granddaughter Kitty's name was added to this document (as Mika's heir), and later still, at the end of 1965, the account was put into the sole name of Stravinsky's son-in-law, André Marion. According to Robert Craft, Stravinsky was unaware of this last change, which was made under Montapert's power of attorney. Craft points out that Montapert was an old acquaintance of André's and that it was André who had introduced him to Wetherly Drive, and he represents the manipulations in respect of the numbered account as an attempt on the part of the two men to misappropriate all or part of the Swiss money.[27] Craft's account of these transactions is characteristically self-assured, but like much of his work it is riddled with bias, error, supposition, and falsehood, and it suffers above all from what one might suppose to be a crippling disadvantage for any fair-minded reader—namely that he was in effect a party to the dispute that he purports to describe with such meticulous objectivity.

At the root of this developing quarrel was a simple fact to which Craft hardly ever alludes but which to many would be self-evident. Stravinsky was an extremely rich man in increasing but not yet terminal ill health, with three married children by his first wife, a second wife with no children, and an in-house surrogate son thought to exercise a strong and possibly grow-ing influence on both him and his wife. Such situations can be entirely manageable and fair to all parties, but they breed suspicion, and as old age advances, the suspicion increases. Craft had a reputation for blocking access to Stravinsky, and by the mid-sixties this tendency, which he has never denied, was affecting the composer's own family. As Stravinsky's health and mobility declined, it was natural for the two dominant people in his life to make decisions about whom he should see, when, and for how long. No less understandably, his own children feared and resented this state of affairs. They came to feel that Craft was exerting control by a form of censorship, whereby Stravinsky was told only those things that it was thought desirable he should know.[28] Messages were conveyed selectively, or not at all, and little by little Vera herself became perhaps unknowingly com-plicit in this process. Rightly, she protected her husband against intrusions on his work, well-being, or equanimity. And perhaps in the end she per-formed this function a shade too assiduously. Certainly her stepchildren thought so. She and Craft gradually assumed in their eyes the character of a hostile alliance cutting them off from their father. Vera was said to be putting it about that the children did not care about him, never telephoned or wrote, and hardly ever came to see him.[29] Worse still, she and Craft behaved in public as if they were in league. They would walk off together at airports, leaving Stravinsky to the tender mercies of his wheelchair atten-dant; or they would abandon him outside restaurants in the late evening and go window-shopping while he waited for a taxi.[30] Then there were the stories that they sometimes held hands and that Stravinsky had complained about it.[31]

Whatever the exact truth of such rumors, their mere possibility was enough to send a shiver down the family's collective spine. Stravinsky's monetary wealth, in the form of royalty income, equities, and bank deposits, was not vulnerable while he was still living; but as soon as he died it would pass to Vera. Under a will drawn up by the Montaperts themselves in 1960, the property was not even entailed to the children, but would pass to Vera in absolute ownership.[32] Later wills seem to have established the principle of a trust whereby the children (and Craft himself) would inherit on Vera's death. But meanwhile there was clearly nothing to prevent her, perhaps under pressure from Craft, from gradually disposing of or spiriting away the countless objects of art, books, manuscripts, and letters that were hung or shelved or stored at 1218 North Wetherly Drive. No proper inventory existed of these items, and even if there had been one, it would have been perfectly normal and proper for Vera to dispose of them to pay her husband's soaring medical bills. In short, Stravinsky's children feared her controlling hand and the hand that they were afraid controlled it, now that their father was apparently no longer in full command of the situation.

It must have been Stravinsky's attorney, Montapert, who alerted them—through André—to the fragility of their situation as their father's heirs, and presumably who also advised them on what steps to take. Exactly why he acted in this way is by no means obvious. That he sought his own financial advantage can hardly be doubted, but he may also—as the composer's lawyer—have believed, or at least been prepared to argue, that in using his power of attorney to transfer funds without the client's knowledge he was fulfilling the client's underlying intentions in the face of risks that, for obvious reasons, could not be explained to him. Broadly, the strategy appears to have been to make systematic withdrawals from the Swiss account in Montapert's own name and that of André Marion, under the protection of the illegality of the account and the composer's complete trust in him as a professional adviser. To what extent Marion acted with his wife's knowledge or that of his brothers-in-law is similarly unclear, though the fact that they never seem subsequently to have held his actions against him argues that they were broadly aware of the strategy, if not of the tactics. As for the Wetherly Drive Stravinskys, they obviously suspected nothing until a series of incidents during 1968 brought the whole matter into the open in such a way as to make a breach inevitable.

WHEN HE LEFT hospital at the end of November 1967, Stravinsky was weak and in poor spirits. For a long time he could neither work nor go out. When Craft was there, they would listen to music together; when he was away—for instance, conducting in New York in mid-December—the composer would grow bored and unsettled, deprived of this contact with the musical mind that he felt to be closest to his own. Then suddenly his health would seem to improve dramatically. Craft would find him talkative, and alert in memory and concentration, where previously he had been supine. Then again there would be a relapse. Toward Christmas he suffered what was probably another mild stroke, which depressed him once more, robbed him of clear speech, and left him drowsy and immobile. For the second time in as many months, his life seemed to hang by a thread.

Yet he himself was by no means ready to give up the struggle. He still fully intended to honor his conducting engagements in Oakland in February and Berkeley in May, and he was soon practicing and marking up scores with that in mind.[33] A European holiday was planned, and even a trip to Morocco to visit Ira and Ganya Belyankin, an idea originally mooted, then abandoned, a year earlier. Such projects would have struck anyone who saw Stravinsky that Christmas as pure make-believe; and indeed he did not conduct in San Francisco or anywhere else. But he did go to Oakland, sat in on rehearsals, and took a bow from the stage at the end of the concert; he was in San Francisco for the Berkeley series; and in between, he flew to Phoenix for *The Rake's Progress*, in Sarah Caldwell's latest staging—a trendy, multimedia affair very different from her Boston student production of fifteen years before. Any lingering question of flying to Switzerland in June, however, was rapidly abandoned when the maestro somehow dislocated a vertebra on his return from San Francisco and was confined to bed for a month, after which he was strapped into a corset so gross that he tore it off in a rage.[34]

Above all, he never renounced his intention of returning to composition. Not until January 1968 did he finally abandon the piano work he had been sketching before his illness, and even then he persuaded himself, as we saw, that he was putting it aside in favor of something bigger.[35] What this would have been is a matter for conjecture: perhaps the work for piano and instruments that Edwin Allen mentioned to Neighbour a few months later, or perhaps even the opera that Stravinsky mentions in his diary for April, and for which he says Craft agreed to write the libretto.[36] Craft himself never referred to this intention, but three days later he wrote to Igor Blazhkov that Stravinsky had again settled down to composition and was "full of projects and ideas."[37] Some of these were more modest. In his San Francisco hotel the following month, he started making arrangements for voice and ten instruments of the final two songs in the first volume, the so-called "Geistliche Lieder" ("Sacred Songs"), of the *Spanisches Liederbuch* by Hugo Wolf.[38]

Even when no longer able to put his hand to original work of his own, he lived up to his reputation for the utterly unpredictable. If he had suddenly produced a wind instrumentation of Isolde's "Liebestod," it would hardly have been more out of obvious character. Yet on closer study it is not hard to see what attracted him to these somewhat morose, *fin de siècle* lieder, which he had fallen for a few months earlier during a listening evening with

Craft.³⁹ In the first and much shorter of the two ("Herr, was trägt der Boden hier"), the accompaniment is cleanly divided into two distinct figures that never combine, and that he therefore scores antiphonally, the one always for wind (three clarinets and a pair of horns), the other always for strings. The long second song ("Wunden trägst du, mein Geliebter") splits less clinically; but the underlying idea is the same, of opposed colors and figures, sustained by multiple repetitions. Oddly enough, this might be a description of some piece by Stravinsky himself: the *Symphonies of Wind Instruments,* say, or *Threni.* It is as if he had taken hold of one aspect of Wolf's music, and changed it from an introverted late Romanticism into something frozen and iconic, by emphasizing its structure over its line. But no doubt the real attraction of these songs lay in their uncompromising treatment of the subject of sin and death, which Stravinsky wanted to ponder but no longer felt equal to dealing with creatively.⁴⁰

In one other respect these arrangements share an attribute that has run through Stravinsky's work like a vein of crystal: the quality of detachment from daily life and current affairs. While he was occupying himself with the crown of thorns and the blood of the Savior, the world seemed more than usually set on its own road to Calvary. In America, the assassinations of Martin Luther King and Robert Kennedy, campus disturbances, and anti-Vietnam War riots; in France, the *événements* of May and June; in Czechoslovakia, the Prague Spring and subsequent Soviet invasion; all these events made 1968 one of the most politically momentous years since the war. Insofar as Stravinsky's work or correspondence reflect any view on them, it is, if anything, a liberal one. But it is the passive liberalism of an old man whose mind is turning away from the Third World and toward the Next World. Invited by Stephen Spender and Isaiah Berlin to sign a letter in support of the Litvinov-Daniel appeal against the show-trial conviction of a group of dissident writers in Moscow, he complied apparently without hesitation, but then drew up a statement of his own (with, of course, Craft's help) which revealed a certain vagueness as to who these dissidents were and why they were important.⁴¹ A few months later, when Sol Hurok asked him to put his name to a letter in support of Hubert Humphrey for the Democratic presidential nomination, he declined on the grounds that he was supporting Eugene McCarthy—that is, the left-of-center, stop-the-Vietnam-War candidate.⁴² Yet when Bobby Kennedy, who was also campaigning against the war, was shot early in June, the assassination found no echo in the composer's letters, though both Françoise and Theodore expressed concern in letters to him.⁴³

Only after King's murder in April did he show any tremor of a creative response, in the form of "an extra instrumental prelude" intended for inclusion in a choreographed version of the *Requiem Canticles* that Balanchine was staging with the New York City Ballet in King's memory. Stravinsky started writing it on the 17th, a fortnight after the assassination, but gave up when he realized that he would not finish it in time for the performance on 2 May.[44] No sketches for this music survive, and Stravinsky never saw the ballet (which was danced only once), except possibly on a film that was sent to him soon after the performance.[45] But he seems officially to have approved of the idea. "I am honored," he wrote tactfully to Balanchine, "that my music is to be played in memory of a man of God, a man of the poor, a man of peace."[46] Whether this pious statement reflected his actual opinion of the choreographing of one of his religious works may be doubted. Craft, who also at most saw only the film, described it to Berman in terms that prompted him to reply that it "sounded ghastly."[47] Stravinsky himself never otherwise referred to it at all.

As the summer advanced and Stravinsky's vertebrae settled down, the idea of a Swiss holiday resurfaced. The composer's health was indeed astonishingly improved. It was true, as Lillian Libman observed, that the critics who attended the "Homage to Stravinsky" concert put on by Morton in the museum on 6 September remarked generally on his gaunt and decrepit appearance. But then, she goes on, they "had no way of knowing in detail the victories he had won during the preceding weeks," which she did know as she had been living with the Stravinskys since June.[48] The composer had come to hear Craft conduct the premiere of his Wolf arrangements, sung by Christina Krooskos, together with the original and revised scores of the *Symphonies of Wind Instruments,* and *Les Noces* in three different versions or part-versions, including the original chamber-orchestral score on which Stravinsky had worked with Ramuz in Morges in 1917 and the curious revision for pianola, harmonium, and cimbaloms, about which Diaghilev had grumbled to Ansermet in 1919.[49] What Stravinsky thought of the early versions of the ballet, which he had never previously heard, is not recorded; but he did not like the 1920 version of the *Symphonies,* which he had heard Craft conduct in Cincinnati in 1965, and he now took abruptly against the idea of publishing.[50] It was one of a number of things he would soon have an opportunity to discuss with the directors of Boosey and Hawkes.

Two days later they flew to New York, where as usual there was so much socializing that Stravinsky was showing signs of wear and tear by the time they boarded the plane for Zurich on the 24th.[51] They were staying in the Dolder, Zurich's grandest and best-placed hotel, set in a wooded park on the southwestern slopes of the Zurichberg, with long views of the lake and the city. "I don't want to go back to California," Stravinsky remarked, perhaps understandably, when he saw his suite in this luxurious establishment. And they were in fact yet again contemplating a permanent move to Switzerland, as Craft and Vera—who hated Los Angeles more than any of them did—had been at pains to inform their European friends.[52] Meanwhile they were booked in for what would prove to be, in a number of ways, one of their most expensive ever months in the country.

Although ostensibly a holiday, the Zurich trip was not without its business aspects. Above all, Stravinsky (or perhaps Craft: it becomes increasingly difficult from now on to decide who is in charge) was anxious to resolve the question of the publication of his archives. What exactly was the difficulty? From Stravinsky's point of view, it was partly financial. Whether or not he planned to sell any or all of the archives during his lifetime, the loss of the publication rights would certainly reduce their value. But it was his heirs for whom this was the greater worry. Craft was uneasy about the agreement already struck with Souvtchinsky and felt that the composer had been bamboozled into signing it. But Craft had quite another reason for disliking Souvtchinsky's editorship, which threatened to attenuate his own firsthand authority in the matter of Stravinsky documentation. Knowing no Russian, with limited German and no more than decent French, he could hardly present himself as sole editor of so polyglot an archive, though since Souvtchinsky had no English and quite lacked his detailed knowledge of the musical materials, Craft would obviously be involved in some editorial capacity, probably (as usual) without proper recognition. Souvtchinsky himself visited Stravinsky at the Dolder a few days after their arrival, but he was not present when Rufina Ampenoff turned up with a new contract letter, this time appointing Souvtchinsky as archive editor at an annual stipend of three thousand pounds, payable from Stravinsky's royalties.[53] Stravinsky, Craft maintains, did not want to sign this letter and only did so under pressure from Vera as a way of helping Souvtchinsky, even though—Craft adds somewhat illogically—he no longer wanted to publish the archives (he could, after all, simply have given Souvtchinsky the money, as he had done on at least one previous occasion).[54]

Theodore Strawinsky had already spent one day with his father at the Dolder and was expected again two days after the signing of the contract. He had found him, he told his cousin Xenya, "imprisoned in an armchair, waited on by nurses, but his reason intact, having to take things to make him sleepy."[55] On the day of the signing, Vera (or in some accounts Stravinsky himself) telephoned him in Geneva and asked him to bring with him the manuscript score of *The Rite of Spring*, which, it will be remembered, Booseys had presented to the composer in 1962 and sent to Theodore on his instructions, with a view to its sale.[56] Theodore had not in fact managed to sell it, but had deposited it in the Geneva branch of the Union Bank of

Switzerland. On 11 October he and Denise came to Zurich with the precious manuscript and handed it to its author in his hotel suite.

What followed imprinted itself in many different ways on the memories of those present in the Stravinsky suite that day. According to Vera Stravinsky, her husband had forgotten to give her a present for her name day, 30 September, and now remedied this oversight by presenting her with the manuscript of *The Rite of Spring*.[57] In one sense, it was an outrageously generous present even for an Orthodox Russian, for whom a name day was a festival at least as important as a birthday; but in another sense it was no present at all, since the manuscript would presumably become hers in any case when he died. But there was a subtler point at issue here. As befitted its violent and disordered past, this particular autograph enjoyed a unique status among those manuscripts that remained in Stravinsky's possession. It had never formed part of his archive, had never even crossed the Atlantic, and he had not set eyes on it since giving it to Diaghilev almost fifty years before. For its future owner, it was vital that it should pass out of its composer's hands before he died, in order that it not form part of his legacy, to be argued and fought over and its cash value dissipated into the pockets of tax men and lawyers.

Alas for Vera's present, nobody saw her husband give it to her, not even Robert Craft, though he later described the scene as if he had been there.[58] On the contrary, Theodore insisted that his father had asked Rufina Ampenoff to take the manuscript back to London with her for safekeeping, and she had only not done so because she had not wanted the responsibility.[59] Of course, from the family's point of view, it was just as important that the manuscript, with its potentially huge market value, remain part of Stravinsky's estate. But what did the composer himself care about such things? There he was in Switzerland, with the great manuscript no more than a few hours' drive away; he would have been less than human if he had not felt some curiosity about it, some impulse of possessiveness. Perhaps he phoned; or more likely Vera did, though hardly without his approval. Perhaps she put the idea into his head, from more or less innocent motives. When Theodore arrived with the manuscript, its creator looked on it, as he might have looked on an injured child, and a sudden fury seized him. Or perhaps he was already seething at the memory of what this music had cost him and how it had been treated by its first audience. According to Theodore, he had already contemplated some kind of inscription, some outburst, some release for the years of suppressed frustration.[60] But the words would no longer come. So Theodore and—reluctantly—Rufina helped him formulate his idea, first in Russian, then in French. At last he took a pen and wrote, in tidy, not at all distraught Russian, on the final page of the score: "May whoever listens to this music forever be preserved from the mockery of which I was the witness in Paris in the spring of 1913 at the premiere of the ballet production of "Le Sacre du printemps" in the Théâtre des Champs-Élysées. Igor Stravinsky. Zurich, 11th October 1968."[61]

Four days earlier, they had all—the Stravinskys, Craft, and Rufina—gone to Basle to inspect Stravinsky's other major Swiss asset, his numbered account in the Swiss Bank Corporation. The exact motive for this visit is even harder to establish than the sequence of events surrounding the retrieval of the *Rite of Spring* manuscript. According to Craft, it was Stravinsky himself who expressed a wish to visit the bank.[62] The composer's children were convinced on the other hand that the impulse came from Craft, who had become uneasy about the powers of attorney held by Montapert and André Marion.[63] Craft certainly suggests here and there that Stravinsky had become vaguely suspicious of Montapert's activities. But this is contradicted by events in Basle, where he removed André's name from the account and replaced it with Vera's, but did not cancel Montapert's power of attorney. Craft maintains that this was on the advice of the bank executive, whom he represents as in some unspecified way in league with Montapert. Stravinsky, he says, was so furious when he discovered that Vera did not have access to the account that he there and then tore up the agreement and demanded a new one.[64] Some of this is far-fetched, and Craft once again admits that he was not present for all the events he describes. Nevertheless, it seems quite possible that Stravinsky had not previously realized that his wife's name was not on the account, and that he was annoyed at the discovery. For him, no doubt, the point was largely symbolic, since Vera would have his money in any case.[65] But for her and Craft it was material, since with a power of attorney granted by her he could have immediate access to the money in the event of her or Stravinsky's death. This at least was what the children feared and what chiefly motivated their subsequent actions.[66]

In his deposition, Theodore referred to a letter that Stravinsky had supposedly signed in August 1968, in which he authorized Montapert to take steps to secure the Swiss money for the children, in the event that pressure be put on him to alter the account in Vera's and Craft's favor.[67] Theodore had seen this letter, and he told the investigating lawyers that it had removed any scruples he might have had about certain procedures Montapert intended to take using his power of attorney. It seems clear that at this stage, for various reasons, Stravinsky's children sincerely believed that their father was under Vera's and Craft's complete mental and physical control, brainwashed by them, effectively their prisoner. Unfortunately, the letter, which might show that Stravinsky himself feared this rather fantastic-sounding state of affairs, has never surfaced. The best that can be said for it (and it is quite a good best) is that it would explain many of the subsequent actions—often apparently extravagant and even paranoid—of the various *dramatis personae* in this closing act of the Stravinsky saga.

AFTER A MONTH in Zurich, they made up their minds against a permanent move to Switzerland, and instead, on 23 October, they flew to Paris. Three weeks later, having decided not to settle in France, either, they returned to New York. Craft kept Eugene Berman abreast of their thinking. The painter had favored Switzerland, was surprised by the switch to Paris, and astonished by the return to America, to the desert of Hollywood, with its "medical mediocrity," or still worse New York, with its atrocious climate. "All of a sudden," he wrote in November, "you all seem footloose and lost."[68] Vera, however, told Xenya that the idea of a Swiss move was a fantasy of Nabokov's; Switzerland was a "boring" country, and as for Paris, this had been a serious possibility, but her husband had eventually found that he could no longer enjoy the French capital. "Too many doctors," she explained enigmatically.[69]

But perhaps it was memories of *The Rite of Spring* as much as fear of French doctors that eventually told against Paris. Stravinsky had at last, reluctantly, gone to the Opéra to see Béjart's nine-year-old and by now famous staging of the ballet, with its notorious simulation of the sex act in the "Danse sacrale," and though he said little or nothing against the choreography, it is clear that the evening aroused disturbing memories. He had seen the work staged no more than once or twice since 1920. Yet "in the end," he said after the performance, "the embarrassing thing about this ballet is the music."[70]

Soon, in spite of everything, they were back at North Wetherly Drive, with little to show for their European excursion except a new Danish nurse, taken on in Paris, and a certain unease in family relations due to the changes to the Swiss signatories. Craft describes an agitated phone call from Montapert, and Vera refers to—without detailing—what she calls a "disagreeable conversation" with Soulima.[71] Even so, any deterioration in the family atmosphere seems to have been mild and purely temporary and probably did not reach Igor. Milène called in to see him often, sitting with him, talking in the relaxed, desultory way of routine sickbed visits, sometimes bringing food he liked. Soulima came down from Urbana for a few days. Theodore wrote from Geneva on the thirtieth anniversary of his mother's death, and received in return a brief but loving reply: "Deeply touched by your wish to be with me in feeling on this sad day. Thank you from the bottom of my heart."[72] In April 1969, his paternal feelings were firmly at the helm, and early that month he signed a deed transferring ownership of the citrus grove at Yuma to Milène and André, as trustees for his two sons and their wives.

Life at North Wetherly Drive returned in certain outward aspects to its old pattern. Morton, or Isherwood and Don Bachardy, would come to dinner. There would be visitors from farther afield: Alexei Haieff turned up from Salt Lake City, Goddard Lieberson from New York, Donald Mitchell, of Faber, from London. If there were no visitors, Stravinsky and Craft would often listen to music. But Stravinsky himself went out less and less, and there were constant health crises. One evening he felt ill at dinner, then fainted in the lavatory.[73] He slept for much of the day, attended by a rota of no fewer than four nurses. He was increasingly awkward and ill-tempered with the nurses; he threw pillows at them, and not in fun. Craft must have described these scenes in detail to Berman, who wrote back: "how dreadful to witness the continuous breakdown and disintegration of a loved person."[74] Xenya had hoped to come to Hollywood, but in March, at Vera's request, Milène wrote a discouraging letter.

> I was at first delighted . . . that you might take up Papa's and Vera's invitation to come to Los Angeles, but now I don't know when and how this will be possible as Papa is so ill. He was very sick after they got back from Paris, and now it's not even certain that they'll stay here. In December he had shingles, [which] lasted several weeks and has utterly defeated him. . . . He hardly eats, needs a huge amount of care. . . . There have been days when he hasn't spoken a single word. He can't walk and practically has to be carried. . . . Vera is exhausted. . . .[75]

In spite of all this, they were planning to return to Europe, since "all his friends are there, and here there's hardly anyone of interest to him." No wonder these friends expressed bewilderment. "What to think?" Souvtchinsky wrote to Morton. "Vera sends me a distress signal, but on the same day Bob tells Ampenoff that they'll be in Paris in May."[76]

Stravinsky still sometimes sat at the piano; and he was still writing notes on music paper. In Zurich he had drafted a partial and somewhat half-hearted three-voice setting of the Lord's Prayer, perhaps his last attempt at original composition.[77] And now, in April 1969, he settled down to transcribe the E minor Prelude from Book I of Bach's *Wohltemperierte Klavier* for string orchestra, and the two-part Fugue for clarinet-and-bassoon duet. Soon afterwards he made a similar transcription for strings of the C-sharp-minor Prelude from the same volume. That was on the 18th of April. Two days later, incredibly, they flew yet again to New York, and there, in his suite in the Hotel Pierre, he arranged the C-sharp minor Fugue for a quintet of clarinets and bassoons, and the B minor Prelude and Fugue, also from

Book I, for strings. Admittedly these arrangements were more in the nature of occupational therapy than practical work. Most sources do not list them among Stravinsky's transcriptions of other composers' music, they remain unpublished, and when Craft programmed them six months later in a Berlin Festival concert, he and Nabokov agreed that they were not performable as they stood, and withdrew them.[78]

Nevertheless the mere existence of these arrangements, with all their vagaries and confusions, is astonishing testimony to the resilience of the creative spirit. When incapable of almost any normal quotidian activity without help, he could still contemplate the intricate and solitary task of transferring music from one medium to another, and achieve it in a manner that was at least broadly coherent. On the 27th of April he attended a "Homage to Stravinsky" concert conducted by Craft at New York State University, Stony Brook. It was the last time he appeared in public. On 1 May he was photographed in his room at the Pierre working on Bach's B minor Fugue.[79] The following day he was taken into hospital with an embolism of the left leg, and during the next two days, in his already parlous physical condition, he underwent two major operations for the removal of enormous blood clots from the leg. Against all prognostications he survived, then promptly went down with pneumonia and was so weakened that Craft telephoned Milène in Los Angeles and told her to expect the worst.[80] It seemed impossible that he would reach his birthday in a month's time. Then just as suddenly, on the 26th of May, like the Emperor in *The Nightingale*, he sat up in bed, bid everyone a bright good morning, and demanded to be lifted out to continue work on the B minor Fugue.[81]

On 18 June 1969, his 87th birthday, he left hospital, and exactly three weeks later he was helped for the last time into a plane bound for Los Angeles.

36

A FINE AND PRIVATE PLACE ■

IT WAS NOT a happy gathering at 1218 North Wetherly Drive. Eugene Berman had heard from someone that life at the Hotel Pierre had reached "an apex of intolerable confusion and hysteria."[1] Now Vera was exhausted and depressed, hated Hollywood more than ever, and disliked the house as much as before. She still had no cook and no regular home help, and the stairs were too much for her. Craft was himself in a nervous and edgy state, and he was in any case thoroughly undomesticated and not at all disposed to skim round with a feather duster or a vacuum cleaner, or take a turn in the kitchen. Marilyn Stalvey, the regular secretary, was fully employed by him in that and related capacities; Edwin Allen, who had taken a sabbatical from his job as a college librarian and was living for the time being in the house, was more in the nature of a driver and factotum.[2]

Stravinsky, though out of hospital and just about well enough to travel, was still distressingly frail, unable to walk without support, and often too weak to talk above a whisper.[3] At times he scarcely recognized anyone except Vera and Craft. He could no longer work even on Bach arrangements, and his sole musical activity—almost his sole activity of any kind—was listening to the gramophone (particularly to late Haydn string quartets) with Craft. Twice during their first week in Hollywood he had to be taken back into hospital with respiratory troubles, and though a lung scan revealed no infection, Vera became unalterably convinced that his tuberculosis had resurfaced after lying dormant for thirty years. Stravinsky himself was skeptical. "The sickness," he whispered, "is in my soul."[4] But the subsequent medical records tended to confirm her fears.[5]

Milène came as before.[6] But the atmosphere had changed since the time when she could sit calmly with her father or chat easily with Vera. Vera's manner had for some reason become cool and unwelcoming, and her comportment more protective, as if her stepchildren were casual visitors whose appearance in the house was a nuisance that had to be endured. One day in August, Soulima called with Françoise to see his father and was shocked not only by the old man's condition but by the manner of their reception.

Prepared as we were by Milène, we did not expect the sight which faced us when we were admitted to his bedroom. He had lost so much weight that he seemed transparent. Vera and his nurse stayed by the sides of his bed all the time. I was allowed no more than ten minutes, in which I tried to express affection and concern. He looked like a ghost, his eyes so deeply sunk in a face which was but skin stretched on bones. Still he found the strength to bless me in Russian with a sign of the cross over my chest. We left in a state of utter desolation. To find him in such a condition was dreadful enough, but to find Vera so unsympathetic and unfriendly in times like this only added to our grief.[7]

Soulima does not ponder the reasons for this change, but one possible explanation must have crossed his mind. The day before their visit to Wetherly Drive, he and Françoise had met Milène and André at a motel in Cambria, a small coastal town halfway between San Francisco and Los Angeles, and had come to an agreement over tactics in the affair of Montapert and the Swiss account. They knew, of course, that André's power of attorney was being terminated and sensed that Montapert's position was also in doubt.[8] Vera had recently been grumbling to Milène about the lawyer's uncommunicativeness, and perhaps she had dropped some hint about his power of attorney and the question of access to the Swiss money. It appears that at Cambria an agreement was made to instruct Montapert to use his power to remove a substantial sum from the Swiss account, in order to place it beyond Vera's and Craft's reach.[9] Small wonder that, at Wetherly Drive the next day, Soulima felt ill at ease, troubled by his own scruples. The mutual suspicion had begun to verge on paranoia. Soulima looked around him and noticed that "the place was already empty of pictures and it was obvious that the move my father had opposed for so long, the final move to New York, was going to take place soon."[10] Craft speculates cynically that the object of the visit was to ascertain "how long [the composer] might last," and he claims, somewhat improbably in the circumstances, that Stravinsky feigned illness and stayed in bed, purely in order to curtail it. Warming to his theme, he adds that the visitors went past Vera's door "without speaking to her or even enquiring about her."[11]

By this time, if Craft is to be believed, Montapert's position as the Stravinskys' lawyer was already somewhat worse than precarious. In fact they had firmly made up their minds to discharge him. In his diary, Craft says that the immediate ground for Montapert's dismissal was his evasiveness over the rendering of financial accounts.[12] But in "Cher père" it turns out that he was fired because he was caught tapping the Stravinskys' phone. A friend of theirs, Laure Lourié, warned them that Montapert was tapping her phone and arranged to set him a trap by telephoning Vera, whereupon he obligingly gave himself away by repeating the contents of the call back to her.[13] The story is, of course, incredible as it stands. Vera herself later recalled that Montapert had voluntarily resigned both his brief and his power of attorney at a meeting with Craft in October 1969.[14] Sometime in September, he had gone to Basle and removed money from the composer's account, using his as-yet-uncancelled power. It seems reasonably clear that the intention was not the (obviously criminal) one of robbing the composer, but that of placing the money for the time being outside Vera's (and *a fortiori* Craft's) control. There is, as we have seen, circumstantial evidence that Montapert was acting with Stravinsky's at least partial knowledge.[15] Nevertheless, he was soon advised by independent lawyers that he was risking a charge of embezzlement, and he accordingly hastened to put the money back into the Swiss account. It was a race against time worthy of Hitchcock. Craft was conducting in Berlin early in October, and from there flew straight to Basle, where he was to meet Montapert on the 3rd and sign the audited accounts on behalf of Igor and Vera. Montapert had barely had time to reinstate the funds, while Craft, for his part, later claimed that he signed the papers without being given a chance to read them, which may have been a necessary fiction in the context of subsequent litigation, since his signature presumably amounted to an agreement that no irregularity had taken place, though he must surely have been aware that one had.[16]

Soulima was correct in his observation that a move to New York was being planned. Europe had not worked out; Los Angeles, quite apart from its social and cultural desolation, was impossibly remote from the first-rate doctoring the composer needed. In fact they had only returned there at all, Craft told Nabokov, in order to pack up the house and conclude various business transactions. They would be heading back to Paris in September and "camping at the Ritz."[17] On the 15th of that month, they drove in two separate cars to Los Angeles airport and took a midday flight to Newark, New Jersey. Milène, who drove one of the cars, kissed her father good-bye in the departure lounge, scarcely knowing if she would ever see him again. She did not. Edwin Allen, the other driver, then set off for New York in the Stravinskys' Lincoln sedan, which was packed to the gunwales. The house in North Wetherly Drive was closed up. For twenty-nine years Los Angeles had been the composer's home—the longest he had ever lived in one place; and now, though he had come to dislike the West Coast, and having said in Zurich that he did not want to go back there, at the last minute he announced that he did not want to leave it.[18] In his mind he may have echoed Othello's "here is my journey's end." In his body, whether he liked it or not, he had yet to find that end.

.   .   .

IN THE EVENT, they got no farther than the New York Plaza Hotel, overlooking Central Park on Fifth Avenue. Here Stravinsky's New York doctors performed their first office and refused him permission to cross the Atlantic. So Vera set off in search of an affordable apartment in Manhattan—a contradiction in terms, perhaps, but less so when one learns that at the Hotel Pierre in June the monthly bill, including meals and accommodation for nurses and secretaries, had amounted to three thousand dollars.[19] Craft, in any case, had told Kirstein that money was no object and that the only problem was "psychic."[20] He might, more kindly, have defined it as a question of suitability, so complex and intractable were Stravinsky's needs and those of his various attendants. In the end, no apartment was found, and instead they settled for a three-bedroom suite in the Essex House, a luxury establishment on Central Park South, which combined the virtues of a self-contained apartment (including a kitchenette and three bathrooms) with the facilities of a five-star hotel. Vera optimistically signed a two-year lease, and they moved in on 14 October 1969.

On the same day, Montapert's power of attorney was transferred to the Stravinskys' New York attorney, Arnold Weissberger. A lawyer who, in his spare time, liked to photograph his famous clients, Weissberger was a long-standing Stravinsky groupie who for years had acted as an unpaid agent and adviser on such matters as the placing of the premiere of The Rake's Progress and the negotiations over a commission for the Santa Fe Opera.[21] As a matter of fact, Weissberger's activities on Stravinsky's behalf had seldom if ever borne fruit, but his loyalty, unlike Montapert's, was beyond question, and he was to prove by far the shrewdest, most devoted, and most professional of all the composer's many legal advisers.[22] One of his first actions as Stravinsky's attorney was to draft a letter to André Marion requesting the dispatch of the composer's musical manuscripts, which had been left in a bank in Hollywood in André's name.[23] Weissberger was advising the formation, for tax purposes, of a freestanding corporation (Trapezoid) which would become the legal owner of the manuscripts, with shares held in appropriate proportions by the beneficiaries under Stravinsky's will. At the same time, the question of the publication of the archives had again come up. The day after the move to Essex House, Rufina Ampenoff arrived from London with a new contract appointing Craft and Souvtchinsky as co-editors.[24] It looks as if the arrival in New York and the appointment of a new lawyer were prompting an attempt to regularize the composer's possessions, material as well as artistic. The minute Weissberger heard about the Basle account, which Stravinsky had been shy of mentioning to him, he arranged for the money to be fully repatriated, regardless of the tax risk.[25]

It was at this point that certain facts relating to the most curious aspect of the Montapert affair came to light. It emerged that, although Stravinsky apparently believed that he had given the citrus grove jointly to his three children, with the Marions as trustees, the document he had signed in April had transferred the interest straightforwardly to the Marions.[26] It also appeared that André and Montapert had been taking advantage of their respective powers of attorney to pay themselves management fees on the Yuma account. Admittedly our information comes almost exclusively from Craft, who was the children's legal adversary, and from subsequent legal correspondence, which by its nature is adversarial. For example, it is incredible that the Marions can have wanted to acquire full ownership of the groves over their siblings' heads at a time when the whole thrust of the children's actions was to secure control of their father's estate as his morally entitled heirs. It does nevertheless seem that, at the time of the transfer, André—possibly unbeknownst to his wife—did not inform his brothers-in-law of the gift, a fact which only began to emerge some months later, when Vera asked Milène why the children had not thanked their father.[27] Montapert had a contract with Stravinsky for the management of the Swiss account, and it may be that the management fees he paid himself, as well as the fees drawn by André, were legitimate and aboveboard. All the same, it is hard to escape the feeling that Montapert was using the children's vulnerability, the composer's helplessness, and Vera's trusting nature as a means of securing for himself exorbitant payments from funds which he recognized to be unstable. As we saw, the children were terrified—not without reason, as the subsequent legal record shows—that their father's estate would effectively be appropriated by his second wife.[28] Stravinsky's will, the final version of which was drawn up by Weissberger in December 1969, left each of his children (including Mika's daughter, Kitty) two-ninths of his estate and Craft the remaining ninth. But Vera retained a lifetime interest in the entire estate, under a trust of which Weissberger was the sole trustee. Even if Vera had been completely blameless in regard to the children's mother, and even if Robert Craft had not existed, the family might well have felt uneasy about these arrangements. As it was, their behavior seems always to have assumed the worst possible outcome, and at times that led them into actions of a somewhat desperate appearance.

André's response to Weissberger's request for the dispatch of the manuscripts was initially to draw up an inventory with Montapert, but then in effect to decline to release them except in return for a general indemnity against legal proceedings in relation to any of his activities in connection with the Stravinskys' business affairs. Weissberger countered by withholding any such indemnity unless the manuscripts were first returned and the Yuma groves properly divided, but at the same time he put in place the necessary documents for a legal action, including a signed affidavit by the composer himself, in case André should fail to comply. There was probably an element of bluff in this otherwise heavy-handed proceeding, but if so it misfired badly. Instead of holding the affidavit pending instructions, Weissberger's representative filed it immediately with the Los Angeles court, Stravinsky was thus publicly in litigation with his son-in-law, and the suit was duly reported in the press. André soon released the manuscripts and the action was withdrawn. But the damage was done. Milène was bound in honor to stand by her husband, and that meant that to all intents and purposes her relations with her father were severed for good.[29]

Thereafter she was dependent for information about him on reports from others. In November, Theodore came from Geneva to visit his father, and from him she learnt that

> Papa's legs are completely paralysed, he can't walk and can't even stand without help. He sits in a wheelchair and hardly speaks, apparently not because he can't but out of sheer depression and gloom. His hearing is very bad, and he sleeps almost the whole day. His mind is still perfectly clear, but he can't altogether follow a conversation, being for the most part unable to connect its separate elements. He's well aware of this, and it causes him a lot of suffering. He's losing his memory badly, and forgets things that have just happened. Last winter, Soulima came to see him, but only a few days after he'd gone, Papa had completely forgotten his son's visit. . . .[30]

Paul Horgan's picture of the composer at about the same time is of a helpless but not yet senile old man. Conversation is essentially with Vera or Craft, but there are occasional interjections from Stravinsky. Nevertheless, Horgan's great affection for the Master cannot conceal the extreme dependency of his condition. The writer notices Edwin Allen's sensitivity in the observation of the old man's needs. Without any words exchanged, Allen lifts Stravinsky onto the sofa or back into his wheelchair. Stravinsky speaks so quietly that his words have to be relayed by Craft. Horgan kisses the old man because Craft tells him the kiss is desired. The scene is extremely touching.[31] Yet one cannot help contrasting this frail figure with the central character in Craft's reminiscences, who is still able to sign documents, instruct lawyers, berate newspaper editors, tease interviewers, and feign sleep or illness when his children come to visit him.

And come they still did, his sons at least. Theodore was in New York for two weeks in late November 1969, with a brief interlude to visit Soulima in Urbana. The following spring, Soulima called at the Essex House and as before had a distinctly frosty reception. Vera seemed to be angry about the visit and again made sure that she and a nurse were present throughout. "In less than a half-hour I was told to leave. I had not had a word alone with my father, not a chance for the slightest intimacy. . . . I left feeling that the situation was forever beyond my reach."[32] Theodore had been better received. His conversations with his father were brief, and probably one-sided, but with Vera he talked more. They were still on good terms personally, perhaps because Theodore was remote from the soured family atmosphere of recent months. He had not even heard about the citrus groves, and he claimed to know nothing about his father's will. He did know, of course, about the numbered account, and when Vera told him about their financial troubles, he raised an eyebrow and reminded her of the Basle deposit, as if unconscious of the objections to repatriating this money. Vera, for her part, was baffled by what she called her stepson's uncooperativeness. It seems that after talking to Soulima in Urbana Theodore returned to New York in a more guarded frame of mind and above all less sympathetic to Vera's protestations of poverty, which were beginning to sound like a pretext for the disposal of objects that were supposed, under Stravinsky's will, to be held in trust for her and for his children.

Whether or not Theodore and Soulima knew about Trapezoid is unclear. It was not a trust (whose purpose might have been to protect the manuscripts, paintings, and other valuables in the interests of all potential beneficiaries), but a corporation whose primary object was to permit their sale under favorable tax conditions. Within little more than three months of its formation, in October 1969, the manuscripts, which at last arrived in New York at the end of December, had been inventoried and valued by Sigmund Rothschild, whom Craft later claimed they had accepted only because they mistook him for a ballet specialist called Howard Rothschild.[33] The rest of the archives arrived in New York in March in a consignment of large cartons and were stored away in the cupboard in Craft's bedroom.[34] No wonder the children were anxious about their inheritance. Inadequately inventoried, their substance and extent largely unknown to outsiders, the manuscripts and other documents could in theory be plundered more or less at will by those with access to the Essex House apartment. Meanwhile, the Hollywood house had been cleared by Lillian Libman and Marilyn Stalvey, ready for sale. According to Libman, books and furniture were stored in a garage at Craft's family home in Kingston, New York, while the most valuable pictures and *objets d'art* came to the Essex House, where indeed they belonged.[35] To say that such things could be disposed of while their owner slept is not to say that they were. But the composer's heirs would have been less than human if they had not been perturbed by the dangerous possibilities of such a situation.

Meanwhile the principal actor in this evolving melodrama pursued his ever more remote and solitary existence. Fussed over by nurses and doctors, his mood and condition fluctuating from one day to the next, he was at once the center and the periphery of the social and business life of the apartment. On some days he would be well enough to go out. He would take a slow turn in Central Park with Lillian or the Danish nurse, Rita Christiansen, or Vera would take him for a drive. At other times he would receive visitors passively in bed, or at table when he got up, as he often did, to have breakfast or lunch. Very occasionally, they would all descend together to the Essex House restaurant. Nika Nabokov came often with his young fiancée, Dominique Cibiel; Elliott Carter would look in, or Sam Dushkin, or Lucia Davidova, or Francis and Shirley Steegmuller, who lived in New York when they were not away on Capri. One evening in December Auden came to dinner with Balanchine and Kirstein, got atrociously drunk on martinis, and disgusted everybody with his unwashed appearance and unkempt manners. In search of the lavatory, he tried several doors before finding the right one, an incident exaggerated (one hopes) by Craft's diagnosis of "a certain tactile dependency on the corridor walls."[36] The dinner was immortalized in photographs by Edwin Allen, which show Stravinsky, gaunt but reasonably alert, Balanchine turning toward Auden, the poet slumped and incapable, Vera stern and aloof. It might be the immediate aftermath of Auden's remark, apropos of nothing in particular, that "everybody knows that Russians are mad."[37] Theodore described his father's situation in a letter to Xenya.

> He can no longer walk at all, and he's indescribably frail and weak. In this condition, of course, he needs constant nursing. There are four nurses on duty in turn day and night—the nursing is first-class, and for this I'm grateful to Vera. But his chief misfortune is mental. He understands everything, and even sometimes makes witty remarks or jokes in general conversation, but he no longer remembers things. . . . He can't coordinate it all in his head—and he's perfectly conscious of the fact. It's tragic. And of course he no longer has or can have any power of decision in the daily affairs of life.[38]

Yet he could still take his old pleasure in good company. One evening at supper with Horgan, Allen, and the others, he turned benignly to Horgan, "lifted his glass—weakly at an angle so that its contents were almost tipped out—and with beautiful formal manners, he said, *'Pol, hier haben wir eine sehr gemütliche Gesellschaft.'* "[39]

In spite of everything, Vera and Craft were again itching to fly to Europe, the minute Igor was well enough. But there were days when his condition made such a prospect seem distant indeed. And meanwhile, the atmosphere in the apartment came increasingly to resemble something out of Dostoyevsky or the Book of Job. Craft himself, in Libman's not-unsympathetic portrait, was driven by a fear of the future and by the belief that, day in, day out, the world (mainly in the composite person of Stravinsky's children) was plotting his downfall. She pictures him sustained in his anxieties by the rumor-mongering of well-meaning friends of Vera's. Vera herself, understanding nothing of the household finances, worn out by present cares and blind to any in the future, was living her life through the daily fluctuations in her husband's mood and condition. Libman claims that it was she, and not Craft, who insisted on Vera being given a power of attorney like his, so that she could draw money if Stravinsky should suddenly die.[40] For a time in early April 1970 death actually seemed imminent. On the 6th he was taken into intensive care with pneumonia and symptoms of heart failure. He recovered quickly, but a week later he was back in intensive care with uremic poisoning. Obituarists' pens hovered. Theodore and Denise flew in from Geneva. But still the spirit would not yield. By the 29th he was back in the Essex House, listening to Schubert, Beethoven, and the lengthy, complex flute sonatina of Boulez. "Let's hope," the Master breathed, "he doesn't write a sonata."[41]

Four days later, remarkably, Stravinsky's doctor, Henry Lax, gave him permission to fly to Europe. He was perceptibly better, and as if to prove it he was throwing things at his nurses and generally behaving like a thwarted one-year-old.[42] Their first idea was to spend the summer at Ouchy, the little harbor town on the Swiss shore of Lake Geneva where Diaghilev and his company had gathered one summer more than half a century before, not far from the Stravinskys' old home at Morges. Then instead they decided to prefer France, and booked into the Hotel Royal at Évian-les-Bains, on the southern shore of the lake directly opposite Ouchy.[43] They arrived on 12 June. Not unlike the Dolder in Zurich, the Royal was and is a five-star hotel *grand-luxe* in flowered grounds and parkland slightly above the town and looking out across the lake toward the Jura and the low hills and vineyards of the Vaud. If Stravinsky had been more prone to nostalgia, and if his eyesight had deteriorated less, he might have scanned from his balcony almost the entire panorama of his early post-Russian life, from Lausanne to Clarens and back to Morges. Behind the hotel the ground rose steadily toward the Pays Gavot, beyond which lay in one direction Talloires and the Lac d'Annecy, where the Stravinsky family had spent three consecutive summers at the end of the twenties, and in the other direction Sancellemoz and the foothills of Mont Blanc. Along the lake toward Geneva, one arrived first at Thonon-les-Bains, where Stravinsky had come from Écharvines at the time of *The Fairy's Kiss* hoping to meet Ramuz, Auberjonois, and his other former Swiss collaborators, then eventually at Annemasse and the Château de Monthoux, where the Stravinskys and Belyankins had assembled for the last time in the summer of 1937. The landscape—Vaudois or

Savoyard—was a palimpsest of memories that appertained especially to the composer's first marriage. He came to it like a ghost, frail and translucent, or like the soldier in his own tale, returning from a new world to gather up the debris of the old.

Probably no such actual thoughts crossed his mind. Perhaps even, as Libman—who was with them for the first two or three weeks—suggests, he mostly neither knew nor cared where he was.[44] She relates how for the first few days he lay in bed, almost too weak to move, barely recognizing those around him. Theodore came from Geneva with Denise, but he found his father remote and uncommunicative. Craft, on the other hand, depicts the composer in top form, visiting the nearby church at Neuvecelle with them on the second day, crossing himself with holy water, then smoothing his hair with it.[45] Kitty arrives with her little daughter, and Rufina Ampenoff comes from London. As before, Stravinsky is the still center of all this coming-and-going, but at times he is well enough to participate. When Souvtchinsky comes from Paris for a few days, they all go for a drive round the lake to Montreux and Clarens, though even Craft admits that the composer takes little or no interest in Les Tilleuls and the rue Sacre du Printemps, and Souvtchinsky afterwards describes the whole atmosphere to Lawrence Morton as "sad and sinister."[46] His eighty-eighth birthday he celebrates by demanding to see his old *nyanya*, Berthe Essert, then with a celebratory lunch attended also by Theodore and Denise, at which he downs two large helpings of caviar and a cocktail of medicines topped off with vodka and champagne.[47]

The truth no doubt is that, while he was physically frailer than ever, his mood and spirits varied from day to day, to some extent according to whom he was with. Theodore came every few days, and he often found his father silent or disagreeable—the perennial lot of close family in the presence of the old and ill.[48] Soulima, though he spent at least part of the summer at Françoise's family home at Menet in the Auvergne, did not come, deterred perhaps by the difficulty of the journey and his troubled relations with Vera.[49] Finally, Xenya arrived from Leningrad via Paris and was shocked by what she saw. Vera had aged but was still modishly turned out: fashionable hairdo, white dress, huge red earrings, sky-blue eyelids. Uncle Igor sat slumped in an armchair near the French windows onto his balcony, incorporeal, vacant-eyed, like some creature from another planet. "He sat with us, but it was as if he wasn't there. When you spoke to him, his look would revive with an agonizing intensity, then after a brief reply in the softest of voices, would dissolve again and depart to some place of not-being."[50]

Xenya came with an invitation from the Soviet authorities. Stravinsky was known to be thinking of moving back to Europe. He should come and live in Russia, where he would be treated like a hero, permitted to live where he liked, and given the best medical treatment. Xenya knew, of course, that her uncle was no longer well enough to make such a decision, and she also knew that Craft would never agree to the move.[51] She hesitated to speak. But then Vera unexpectedly raised the issue with her. Where should they go next? France? No, Paris was too noisy and the doctors wouldn't make house visits out of town. Why not Russia? The question hung in the air without reply. And then . . . where should we bury him? "In Russia! He's Russian, and they wanted to ask him to go back for good. But if he's now too old to go, then let him return to the Russian soil." Vera had never even thought of it, but she was not averse to Xenya pursuing the matter with Moscow. Above all, she detested the idea of her Igor being buried in America, in particular Los Angeles, a city that had not even remembered his eighty-eighth birthday. "I thought of Venice," she went on. "Igor loved Venice so much, so many of his works were first played there, and Diaghilev is buried there."[52] A plot lay vacant at Ste. Geneviève-des-Bois, but Vera did not mention it.

IN SPITE of everything, at the end of the Évian season they went straight back to New York, as Vera had told Xenya they would.[53] They had again looked at houses in Switzerland, but they found nothing remotely suitable, and the Essex House lease still had more than a year to run. Their expenses, though, were enormous. Quite apart from the rent, they had annual medical costs (Craft reported) in the region of a hundred thousand dollars, and their sole income was royalties plus whatever they could raise from the sale of Stravinsky's manuscripts.[54] So Vera yet again set off in search of a cheaper apartment; and meanwhile the question of the archives—who might buy them, and how best to use them until they were sold—once more became an issue. At some time in October, Vera gave Francis Steegmuller, whose biography of Cocteau had just come out, authorization to research a life of her husband, making use of the archive materials in the Essex House.[55] Soon afterwards, on 2 December, the *New York Times* reported that the Stravinsky papers and manuscripts were being put on the market at an asking price of $3.5 million, and it hinted that both the Library of Congress and the Soviet Union were among those who had expressed interest.[56] On the very same day, Vera Stravinsky signed the escrow on an apartment at 920 Fifth Avenue at a price of twenty-seven thousand dollars.

Craft later maintained that the entire *Times* report was false, but had been planted by the sales agent, Lew Feldman, in order to excite market interest in the archive.[57] He added that on the day of the report he wrote to Theodore to explain this tactic, but that unfortunately Rufina Ampenoff had already seen the article and telephoned Geneva. As a result of this phone call, and before he received Craft's letter, Theodore wrote a letter of strong protest to his stepmother, while at the same time supposedly retaining a lawyer, a step that would of course effectively have ended direct personal relations between them.⁵⁸ To be exact, Theodore seems to have consulted a lawyer—not quite the same thing as retaining one—and he told Vera that he had done so.⁵⁹ Moreover, it is hard to see what difference Craft's letter could have made. Even if the *Times* article was an invention, it clearly indicated an intention to sell. Vera's reply to Theodore, which Craft publishes in extenso (and which he probably wrote), shows little willingness to understand the anxieties of the composer's heirs in such a situation. It treats the sale as inevitable and makes the fatuous insinuation that André Marion, in refusing to release the manuscripts, must also have meant to sell them. It complains of the children's neglect of their father and their financial reliance on him, and suggests, unbelievably in the circumstances, that it would be more normal for aging parents to be supported by than to support their middle-aged children.⁶⁰ Finally, it accuses Theodore of being more concerned about his own financial prospects than his father's health, though it also manages to upbraid him for thanking Vera for looking after the father so well, which rather suggests that any direct enquiry about Stravinsky's health would have been met with sarcasm.⁶¹

The exchange reveals something of the paranoia that had incurably infected the attitudes of both parties to the quarrel. At Christmas, Robert Craft sent Souvtchinsky a bulletin that mixed abuse of the children with a certain grim satisfaction at the likely impoverishment of all Stravinsky's heirs once doctors, lawyers, agents, and tax collectors had taken their cuts from any sale of the archive.⁶² Soon afterwards Vera cancelled the monthly payments to Theodore and Denise, and in March 1971 she also cancelled Kitty's allowance. Meanwhile the children were briefing lawyers on their own account, apparently on the assumption that Vera was or would soon be misappropriating royalties, the Swiss money, the *Rite of Spring* autograph, Trapezoid shares, and assorted paintings and sculptures.⁶³

Amid all these accusations and counter-accusations, the composer's vitality waxed and waned much as it had done for the past year. For obvious reasons, he was kept in ignorance of business matters and family squabbles, and actions in his name were almost certainly performed without his knowledge. His life moved from the bedroom to the dining room and back, with ever more infrequent excursions outside the apartment. Visitors came, and usually he received them or else lacked the force to refuse them. Elliott Carter dined at the Essex House one evening in December and they listened to *The Magic Flute*, "which [Stravinsky] particularly enjoyed, shaking his head and pointing out special beauties on the page."⁶⁴ Carlos Chávez came at the end of January and at one point in their conversation suddenly dropped to his knees in front of Stravinsky and almost wept, to Stravinsky's visible disquiet.[65] Nabokov called in regularly, and they listened to Beethoven string quartets together. At one point Stravinsky whispered: "This music is now so close to me, Nika . . . ah . . . so very close . . ." On another visit, when Nabokov and his young wife were leaving to dine with Vera and Craft, Stravinsky took his hand and said, "Nika, don't go away. Stay with me. Don't leave me *avec les femmes de chambres.*"[66] But when Nika asked routinely how he was, he suddenly turned on his old friend and snapped angrily: "You can see how I am, miserable."[67]

The new apartment was far from ready for human habitation. The elderly widow from whom they were buying it was slow to vacate and, when she did so, she left it in a dirty and decrepit condition.[68] Lillian Libman, who was taken on as a full-time factotum early in February, spent a good part of every day there, "smothered in rubble, plaster, paint—pleading with twenty or more workmen to rush their reconstruction of the apartment with which Mrs. Stravinsky had fallen in love after a five-minute tour because its three bedrooms provided a beautiful view of Central Park."[69] It promised, nevertheless, to suit them well, it would be cheaper to live in and a proper home, furnished with their own belongings out of storage in Kingston. What was more, as February turned into March, Stravinsky suddenly took a turn for the better. On the 3rd he was actually composing, seated at the piano and intensely engaged. At the Essex House a year before, Lillian had caught sight of him through the open bedroom door, with a score of Bach's *48* and a sheet of music paper on the piano desk. "He stared and stared at the paper for fully five minutes without moving a muscle or uttering a sound. Then he placed on the piano ledge a pencil he had been holding, took the paper and carefully tore it in half; and then he placed the two pieces together and tore them again in half, dropping the pieces on the floor."[70] But on this occasion he seemed to make progress. He announced that he had "had an idea beginning with a combination of *tierces* [thirds]." The next day he composed some more.[71]

Craft's account then peters out and we do not know what, if anything, was the outcome. But for a fortnight Stravinsky seems to have perked up and become more aware of his surroundings. Craft might once have claimed that the so-called Borborygms ("fragments of an interview") dated early March in *Themes and Conclusions* took advantage of this improvement, though he subsequently admitted to having written everything in the book himself, including these bizarre—some would say distasteful—discussions of the virtues of euthanasia and the latest treatments for blood deficiency and heart failure.[72] The real improvement was toward a greater cheerfulness and responsiveness. On the 15th they listened to Liszt symphonic poems and Stravinsky chuckled at the—as he seems to have felt—banality of much of the music (an occasion that became the subject of another Borborygm).[73] On the 16th he was photographed smiling at Vera and listening to her, their fingers touching. On the 17th he supposedly favored the *New York Review of Books* with his opinion on "the recent Warhol retrospective at the Tate."[74]

The next day, he was taken to hospital with pulmonary edema (water on the lungs), which was provoking dangerous bouts of coughing and unsettling his pulse. Nobody wanted him to go, and Libman protested.[75] But the doctor was adamant. For ten days the sick master lay in Lenox Hill Hospital with wires and tubes into and out of most of the usual apertures and some created for the purpose. Still he refused to give in. His wit retained a residual acuteness. When Vera complained about his constant rapping on the bed rails to attract her attention, he replied, "I want to be sure that *I* still exist." And when Rita, the nurse, tried to persuade him to swallow water with the argument that he was dehydrated, he complied with "Well, no one told me."[76] But sometimes his mind drifted into the past. He asked after his first wife, Katya, and when the nurse enquired how many children he had, he answered "four."[77]

Meanwhile the new apartment was emerging from its own brand of intensive care. Like its new occupant it had been plumbed and wired, unlike him it was being freshly repainted and newly furnished. On 29 March, when he was at last relieved of his fetters and taken home, it was to the Fifth Avenue flat that he went. He slowly toured the rooms, admired the new canary, expressed astonishment that he had suddenly become the owner of so seemingly luxurious an establishment.[78] It was his first city apartment since leaving Paris in 1939, and he must have known, in his heart, that the associations would be the same. For nearly a week he was well enough to enjoy the new surroundings. Then on the morning of 4 April something changed. At first they had difficulty waking him, then he awoke with renewed symptoms of edema. Again the doctor advised hospital, but this time Vera insisted that the necessary equipment be installed in the apartment.[79] Soon Stravinsky's bedroom had been converted into an intensive-care unit. But this time there was to be no wit and no regression. He lay as if suspended between life and death, neither eating nor drinking, breathing more and more faintly, a dead man kept alive by the overpowering desire of those around him that his astonishing life should not end. So great indeed was this desire that it turned to belief. On the 5th, Ed Allen went back to Middletown, Connecticut. Late that evening, Vera went to bed and slept; Rita Christiansen returned to the room she still kept at the Essex House. Robert Craft, after prowling around uncertainly for an hour or two, went back to his room at two o'clock and fell into a shallow sleep.[80]

Exactly how and at what moment Stravinsky died will never be known. Lillian Libman sat with him and the night nurse for a short time at about half past three. He was still breathing, but unevenly and barely audibly. She touched his legs and found them cold. She thought of calling Vera, but allowed the nurse to persuade her, somewhat irritably, that his condition was stable, and instead went back to her own bed, intending to read. It was a quarter past five when the nurse's young assistant came in and shook her out of her doze. She hurried to the bedroom, but Stravinsky was already dead. "What happened?" "He simply stopped breathing." *"When?"* "Just now." The intern, Dr. Berger, who had also been asleep in the next room, was already making tests and wanted Lillian present. Before leaving the room, Lillian closed Stravinsky's eyes. Then within minutes she was gently waking Vera, who understood instantly and sent her to tell Craft.[81]

Craft relates the story differently.[82] Lillian did, he acknowledges, wake him, but Stravinsky was still alive when he reached the bedroom, and Craft saw him die, "a simple cessation, without struggle." His eyes were still open and there was life in them, and a flicker of recognition. Lillian had not yet woken Vera, and Craft performed that office, haltingly and with a degree of pantomime: "He is very bad . . . dying . . . I think . . . No . . . he is dead." Together they sat holding his hands and kissing his cheeks and forehead. Then Vera ordered the mirrors to be covered, and left the room. Soon afterwards Rita arrived, closed the eyes, and embarked on the routine procedures that to the bereaved seem such an offense but that both symbolize and ensure the safe and unbroken continuity of life.

In the office, Lillian Libman was already steeling herself for the world's media. Craft went quietly to his room and began to write.

ACCORDING to the death certificate, Igor Stravinsky died of heart failure at twenty past five in the morning of 6 April 1971. No priest came, though it was the Tuesday in Holy Week, the kind of date that in life he would have recorded as suitable for the completion of some notable work. It was on a Tuesday in Russian Holy Week on precisely the same date forty-five years before that he had written to Diaghilev, asking forgiveness for past transgressions as a mark of his return to the Orthodox communion "out of extreme mental and spiritual need."[83] Such sentiments, however, were not Vera's, and they were certainly not Robert Craft's. The barbaric (as he thought) Orthodox funeral custom of an open coffin with an icon on the chest of the dead body and a prayer on its forehead was quietly ignored in favor of a sealed coffin, "for V's sake."[84] That evening in Campbell's funeral home on Madison Avenue, the bishop conducted a prayer service that Craft records merely as long and over-incensed. He was impressed, though, by the snowstorm that blew up as they set out for the service and by the rumbles of thunder that greeted the bishop's pronouncement of the name of the deceased.[85]

The funeral itself was set for Good Friday, the 9th, in the large funeral-home chapel. But it was even more than usually a rite of passage, for Stravinsky was not to be buried in New York, nor anywhere else in America, nor at Ste. Geneviève-des-Bois near his first wife and daughter, nor even in the Alexander Nevsky cemetery in Leningrad beside his father and younger brother. Instead he was to be flown to Venice and interred in the Russian corner of the island cemetery of San Michele, not far from the grave of Diaghilev, who had admittedly died in that city. Many asked: why Venice? Had he ever expressed a wish to be buried there? No, but it was a city he loved and the one in which he had stayed the longest and worked the best of any in Europe since the war. No fewer than five works of his had had their first performances there. The negative reasons probably remained unspoken. Neither Vera nor Craft would want to lay flowers on a grave in Los Angeles, or pick their way among the exiled princes and dispossessed Russian gentry of Ste. Geneviève-des-Bois to a sad group of consumptive Stravinskys. Leningrad was far out of reach, New York had meant nothing to the composer but hotels. Venice was beautiful, peaceful, and unspoilt, and Vera had been with him there through their happiest times. In due course she would lie there beside him. It was the choice of the living rather than the dead, and perhaps none the worse for that.

The Venetian funeral, on 15 April, was like a pageant by Carpaccio, one observer thought.[86] Crowds thronged the *campo* in front of the Dominican church of Santi Giovanni e Paolo and beneath Verrocchio's great equestrian statue of Bartolomeo Colleoni; many more hung from windows along the Rio dei Mendicanti and around the square, and the canal itself and the lagoon beyond swarmed with gondolas and *motoscafi* and launches and boats of every description. Banks of flowers lined the *campo* between the church and the landing stage. Inside the Gothic basilica a congregation of three thousand—family, friends, reporters, photographers and what Hofmannsthal happily called "the usual hangers-on"[87]—sat through a *Requiem* by Alessandro Scarlatti, a brief address by the mayor of Venice, some Andrea Gabrieli organ pieces, and a fairly speculative account of the master's own *Requiem Canticles* conducted by Craft, then stood for more than an hour while the archimandrite of Venice chanted with exquisite refinement the Greek Orthodox liturgy for the departed, seemingly undisturbed by the television cameras and the flashbulbs, the fidgeting and shuffling of his predominantly Catholic audience, and the noise of the crowd outside, which drifted up the nave from the open west door. At the end of the liturgy the Archimandrite beckoned to the composer's widow and the other members of his close family to come forward and kiss the coffin in farewell. Then the bier was wheeled back down the nave and through the *campo* to the waiting gondola that would serve as a hearse across the half-mile of open water to San Michele. From the island jetty, the pallbearers conducted the bier on its wheeled carriage through the elegant cloister of Coducci's early Renaissance church and along the gravel paths, through the various sectors of the great marine cemetery to the distant and as yet relatively uncluttered Orthodox section in the far corner of the burial ground.

There they buried the great composer to the sound of unaccompanied chanting such as must have rung in his ears at far-off *panikhida* services in the Nikolsky Cathedral of his childhood. The number of mourners was fewer now, though still considerable, and many that came without invitations were turned away—ineffectually, since the cemetery was public. After a brief ceremony, the coffin was lowered on ropes into the open grave. Vera walked unsteadily to the edge, threw in a handful of earth, and bowed to receive the Archimandrite's blessing and to kiss his ring. One by one the members of the family stepped forward and threw earth onto the coffin lid. All around, the paths were lined with friends and casual onlookers, and on the wall above the grave the photographers clicked and flashed, anxious to miss no furtive tear or anguished gesture.

Vera took Lillian's arm and, with Craft at her side, walked slowly and painfully back to the jetty.

37

BUT NONE DO THERE EMBRACE

THE TWIN FUNERALS of Stravinsky did not bring together the two sides of his divided family. For the New York ceremony, Theodore and Denise arrived from Geneva, Milène and André from Los Angeles, and Soulima and Françoise from Urbana, but they exchanged no words with Vera or Craft, who, perhaps partly to avoid such an encounter, had come very punctually to the funeral home and left for Florida that same evening. Theodore asked to see Vera, but she refused with the question: "Why didn't they come to see him when he was alive?"[1] apparently forgetting that Theodore, though he lived three and a half thousand miles away, had in the past two years made two separate visits to New York, been refused on another occasion, and seen his father many times in Zurich and Évian. By the time she reached Venice, she had relented sufficiently to ask Lillian to invite Theodore to a meeting; but this time he was unwilling to forget past refusals and told Lillian that "there could be no further contact 'except through representatives.' "[2] In the church, the stewards knew no better than to seat the "famigliari" in a single row, and there the cameras fixed them—Craft, Vera, Theodore, Milène, Soulima, John, Kitty, kept apart only by the benign, conciliatory figure of Nicolas Nabokov, their heads sunk in grief, a heartbreaking image of the incommunicability of sorrow and the contagiousness of anger.[3]

Could the quarrel have been resolved there and then? It was probably already too late. The composer's children had long since convinced themselves that, without deft legal footwork on their part, they could well end up without so much as a monogrammed handkerchief of their father's. And it is hard to insist that they were wrong. Ever since the archive sale had first been mooted in 1967, at a time when it was obvious that Stravinsky's active career was at an end, the question of ownership had assumed an importance that grew as his health deteriorated. The trouble had even begun several years earlier with Stravinsky's will of 1960, in which he left his entire estate to Vera, if she survived him for at least thirty days, and to his children only in the event that he outlived her. In that will his two executors were

Vera herself and William Montapert's lawyer wife, Arminé, who was already handling Stravinsky's tax affairs. The Montaperts must have warned André that if the composer died before Vera, his children would effectively be disinherited. And as we have seen, it was Montapert who, with power of attorney and for a substantial commission, transferred Stravinsky's illegal Swiss funds to the children's names, and who apparently later drew up a replacement will that reduced Vera's inheritance to a lifetime interest, with the children as heirs on her death. The final will of late 1969, the work of the lawyer who replaced Montapert, Arnold Weissberger, was in essence the same. Vera would inherit on the composer's death, but on her death the estate would be divided into nine equal parts, of which two would pass to each of his four children (including Mika's daughter, Kitty), and one to Robert Craft. The estate was to be held in trust for Vera, and the sole trustee (Weissberger) was empowered to "invade the principal of the trust and to distribute the same absolutely to or on behalf of my said wife . . . for any reason whatever, even though the principal of the Trust may thereby become exhausted." Perhaps more than anything else, it was this clause, which seemed to allow Vera to dispose of the children's future inheritance more or less as she chose, that sustained the bitterness and perpetuated the litigation for so many years after the composer's death.

It does appear that North Wetherly Drive had been caught napping by Montapert's activities. Vera was notoriously incapable of concentrating on such a thing as a legal document, and Craft, though by his own admission quarrelsome and pedantic by nature, had never involved himself in Stravinsky's legal or financial affairs, and when he eventually did so was inclined to talk as if his own dislike of his adversaries was enough to win the legal argument. With Weissberger in control, all this changed. He was unshakably loyal to the composer and his wife, and he was methodical, clever, and professional. It was surely at his suggestion that, while Stravinsky was still alive, Vera instructed Boosey and Hawkes to make a royalty payment of thirty-five thousand dollars directly into her account; and perhaps it was also actually Weissberger who initiated the newspaper report (in early December 1970) that the composer's archive was for sale at a price of three and a half million dollars and that the Soviet Union was a bidder.[4] Whether or not the lawyer encouraged Vera to remove art objects from the Essex House, objects were almost certainly removed. The situation was self-evidently fragile. The composer was alive but largely in ignorance of practical matters outside his own needs. The archive had been inadequately inventoried and was housed in a large number of boxes in the Essex House apartment, to which, for all practical purposes, Stravinsky's children had no access. For as long as he himself lived, his archive could in theory be plundered and sold, in whole or part, and his children were apparently powerless to prevent this. Fortunately for them, the market was stagnant, Stravinsky's household had other things on their minds, and for the time being no serious steps were taken.

Soon after the funeral, the children lodged a formal request that materials relating to them and their mother be removed from the archive and excluded from any sale. By August they had retained lawyers to try to force Weissberger to supply a proper inventory of the archive and a full financial accounting, and to challenge Vera's possession of the *Rite of Spring* manuscript. They had, indeed, little choice but to take some such action; and yet in doing so they committed themselves inexorably to years of expensive, wearying, morally and emotionally debilitating litigation. The New York Surrogate's Court has many of the attributes of Dickens's Court of Chancery, "which so exhausts finances, patience, courage, hope; so overthrows the brain and breaks the heart; that there is not an honourable man among its practitioners who would not give—who does not often give—the warning, 'Suffer any wrong that can be done you rather than come here!' "[5] It is a type of court that seems openly to serve the interests of lawyers above all else. Such decisions as it occasionally makes are subject to more or less interminable appeal and counter-appeal. Even where its demands are candidly ignored, there are invariably legal reasons to be advanced by attorneys who know as well as naughty schoolboys exactly how far it is safe to stretch cautious authority. Teams of lawyers will be dispatched to the ends of the earth with first-class tickets on executive flights to interview minor players who have little or nothing to reveal and perhaps no great desire to reveal it. Major players will be subpoenaed in remote Swiss hotels and subjected to days of examination and cross-examination for purposes that, when you read the transcripts and assess the outcomes, remain obscure. In December 1979 in the case of Stravinsky versus Stravinsky, the court at last, and with due solemnity, approved what it guardedly called a Stipulation of Settlement, set out precise percentages of ownership of the estate during Vera's lifetime and after her death, imposed new trustees from both sides, resolved a number of technical questions to do with property rights and the "invasion" of the trust, and secured for Craft a five-figure consultancy fee as musicologist to the estate. And yet in the following year, as Craft reported to Lawrence Morton, the litigation cost Vera Stravinsky two hundred thousand dollars.[6]

Weissberger knew all about the personal dimension to the dispute, though he never seems to have had much inkling of the children's point of view. He felt that they were motivated by hatred of Craft, whom they regarded as an evil influence on their father. He seems genuinely not to have considered that they had any claim on Stravinsky's estate, and he accepted without apparent question what he was told about their failure of affection toward their father and his lack of deep feeling for or interest in them.[7] Just what form this image took can be gleaned from the voluminous writings of Craft on the subject. Distraught as he himself undoubtedly was after Stravinsky's death, he chose, with almost unbelievable vulgarity, to characterize the children's grief as superficial and short-lived, and to publish this opinion within weeks in the *New York Review of Books*.[8] He quotes Milton: "Some natural tears they drop'd/But wip'd them soon. . . ."[9] Moreover, he told Weissberger that Stravinsky had rarely seen Milène and André "during the half of each year that he spent in California," which he knew perfectly well to be untrue.[10] But Weissberger wanted at all costs to avoid a will dispute, and that was why he preferred the device of "invading the Trust" to what in his view was the justifiable but risky procedure of cutting the children out altogether. In fact he greatly overrated the power of the invasion device, which, the minute he tried to implement it, on Vera's pleading, early in 1979, was successfully challenged by the opposing counsel as a breach of his trustee's duty "of ordinary care, diligence and prudence and of absolute impartiality among the several beneficiaries."[11] The so-called settlement was a direct outcome of this particular dispute, and that—as her subsequent costs indicate—was not in the least to Vera's liking.

Through all these long years the precious archive sat quietly in the apartment at 920 Fifth Avenue, even though it was nominally the property of the Trapezoid corporation, half of which belonged to the estate. Tax was duly paid on its valuation, but still it could not be sold to pay its own way. Some items, it is true, were disposed of. A number of sketches for *Oedipus Rex* were given to the sculptor Giacomo Manzù in return for the design of Stravinsky's gravestone. In October 1973, Vera sold a batch of seven manuscripts for two hundred thousand dollars, and two months later she at last managed to sell the *Rite of Spring* autograph full score, which her own lawyer told her she could not prove was hers rather than part of the archive. It was bought for two hundred and twenty thousand dollars by Stravinsky's old friend the Swiss conductor Paul Sacher, with money from his wife's Hoffmann–La Roche fortune.[12] The children promptly brought suit, a fresh accounting was ordered by the court, and a lengthy process instigated to discover assets of the estate. Allegations flew. André was accused of withdrawing money and appropriating books and documents that he had never returned. Vera was said to have secreted the repatriated Swiss money (nearly half a million dollars) and to have sold paintings against false invoices, along with other substantial depredations. Such allegations were never proved, but they did nothing to alleviate the atmosphere of mutual suspicion and recrimination. Meanwhile a court in France had supported Soulima's claim to a huge sum in undistributed French royalties, on the grounds that, since he had retained his French alongside his U.S. citizenship, he benefited from an ancient statute that exempted French citizens from claims in foreign courts. It was pointed out that, in taking U.S. citizenship, he had undertaken to relinquish all others. Thus a new suspicion was added to the old ones. Soon the children's lawyers were accusing Vera of misappropiating French monies, while Vera's lawyers counter-accused them of misrepresenting certain royalties as French in order to claim them. How either of these misdemeanors could actually have been committed was never explained. All that was necessary was to answer one charge with another.

Immediately after the settlement in December 1979, it emerged that the executors had been negotiating with UCLA for a sale of the archive under an agreement that, according to the children's lawyer James Higginson, involved the establishment of a Stravinsky Center with appointments for Robert Craft and Edwin Allen as archivists.[13] Unsurprisingly, the family objected. They had been grumbling for some time about Craft's uninhibited use of the archives in his recent book *Stravinsky in Pictures and Documents*.[14] Still more aggravatingly, he had recently published a candid selection of letters from Katya to Igor Stravinsky, letters that, through many intimate details, portrayed her as a sickly religious crank and a hopeless martyr to an unloving husband.[15] The trouble presumably was that the family could not sue on breach of copyright, since the ownership of the rights was itself in dispute; and meanwhile the court was slow—perhaps in effect powerless—to act on the questions of access and right of publication, supposedly fixed on a basis of equality by the settlement. Throughout 1980 and 1981 the arguments over this issue became increasingly strident. George Bobrinskoy, for the children, complained that not only were the family not being given access, but the archive was not even being properly maintained or adequately insured, and he urged the court to instruct the trustees to open the collection up for scholarly inspection.[16] In response, Craft wrote personally to Higginson and, calmly drawing a veil over his own recent acts of publication, begged him to support the closure of parts of the archive, on the grounds that freedom of access would reveal aspects of Stravinsky's personality, especially his anti-Semitism ("so shocking that Goebbels might have written some of it"), which would undoubtedly lead to a boycott of his music in the United States. He noted that Catherine's letters exposed Stravinsky's meanness and neglect, a fact already well known to his own *NYRB* readers. And he added a heartrending account of the possible damage to Soulima's marriage and the mental balance of his son if the composer's correspondence with his daughter-in-law were to come into the public domain.[17]

Despite all these arguments and counter-arguments, UCLA appeared to be winning the fight to purchase the archive. In May 1982, the *Los Angeles Times* reported that the New York Surrogate had awarded the collection to California in preference to a considerably higher offer by the University of Texas at Austin, apparently on the grounds of the close connection between Stravinsky and Los Angeles, though the report also hinted at dark rumors of a UCLA faculty post for Craft. The only snag was that UCLA were highmindedly insisting that they would only accept the archive if Stravinsky's heirs unanimously supported the sale, and since in fact the composer's children were unanimous in preferring Austin, yet another impasse appeared to have been reached.[18]

At this point the fate of so many of Dickens's Jarndyces caught up with the principal actress in the drama. On 17 September 1982, at the age of ninety-three, Vera Stravinsky died. For almost fifteen years she had set her face against the stepchildren she had formerly loved and with whose lives her own had once been so deeply enmeshed. Yet there had always been some feeling that the quarrel was not of her making, that she had tumbled into it because of a need to take sides, and perhaps out of loyalty to the young man who stood to lose most by her husband's death. And he had repaid her with his own love and dependability. It was true that the relationship had not been entirely untroubled. His numerous love affairs had not invariably delighted her, and one—perhaps the most serious—had almost caused a breach. An affair he had embarked on in 1968 with Stravinsky's Danish nurse, Rita Christiansen, resumed briefly soon after the composer's death, and in September she turned up in New York and revealed that she was expecting his child.[19] Even before this, Vera had half-expected that the pair would marry, and she had told Lillian that if this happened she would throw them both out and sell up.[20] Rita was equally determined to prise him away from Vera. It was a triangle, but of the kind schoolboys know as scalene—all its sides unequal. Rita had no chance. Craft duly married her in January 1972, but he no longer loved or even much liked her, and not long after giving him a son a few weeks later, she returned to Copenhagen with the baby, leaving her reluctant husband to continue his barely interrupted life with Vera in her Fifth Avenue apartment.

After Vera's death, the litigation dragged on, but it no longer mainly concerned apportionments under Stravinsky's will. Its principal focus now was on the sale of the archive and the question of publication. Vera had bought back the publication rights from Boosey and Hawkes in 1977, and Craft presumably inherited these along with the rest of her estate, not to mention heavy death duties and the expensive upkeep of the apartment, which he could neither sell nor (because of house cooperative rules on inherited tenancy) occupy.[21] But the rights would have to go with the archive, and since this would soon have to be rehoused and was in any case for sale on an increasingly active market, a degree of urgency had come into the equation. Craft's actions at about this time betray a trace of panic. The publication in rapid succession of three volumes of Stravinsky's correspondence, for instance, was undertaken with apparently scant regard for normal editorial standards of selection, organization, or textual accuracy, to say nothing of competence in translation, as long-suffering readers of the footnotes in the present biography will not need reminding.[22] During the same period, Craft must also have been writing his article "Cher père, chère Vera," an unrestrained attack on his legal opponents that, whatever may be said about its accuracy or fairmindedness, must rank high in the annals of sheer literary and documentary bad taste.[23] The Stravinsky family did their best to block all of these publications, in the end without success, perhaps because they were reluctant to face the likelihood of a further-protracted lawsuit involving the public airing of uncomfortable truths and half-truths. Instead they encouraged—perhaps (as Craft thought) commissioned[24]—an alternative account of the composer's life by a New York journalist by the name of John Kobler. Kobler completed his book, but when Craft, who has always been careful to see advance copies of significant texts on Stravinsky, noticed that the biography quoted extensively from the conversation books, in which it was assumed that he owned the copyright, he took legal action to block publication, and did in fact succeed in doing so, in a court judgment of August 1987. Three years later, by an irony that may or may not have struck Kobler as poetic, a quite different New York court awarded copyright in the conversation books to the composer's children.

In the summer of 1983 the entire Stravinsky archive was at long last sold to Paul Sacher in Basle. California and Texas had long since dropped out of the reckoning, but various New York institutions had continued to nourish the hope of raising funds to keep the papers in America. In March, when Sacher had offered three and a half million dollars, the court had given the New York Public Library, to which the archive had been moved that same month, a stay of execution to match the Swiss bid by the end of May. What now happened has been described by Sacher's agent in the negotiations, Albi Rosenthal.[25] The Stravinsky trustees at first let it be known at the beginning of June that, there having been no higher offer, they were proceeding with the sale to Basle. They then changed their minds and announced a decisive auction to be held in the presence of all interested parties on 20 June. The motive for this apparently somewhat underhand procedure seems to have been that the Pierpont Morgan Library in New York had meanwhile come forward on behalf of an anonymous private buyer with an offer of three and three-quarters million.[26] Although he must have been aware of this new bid, Rosenthal decided to turn the screw on the trustees and absent himself from the auction. Instead he sat nervously in his hotel room waiting in vain for a phone call from the Stravinsky lawyers. Only the next morning did a friend inform him that, according to a radio report, the auction had after all been indecisive. The day after that the lawyers themselves contacted him with a take-it-or-leave-it demand for five-and-a-quarter million dollars. After briefly resisting what must have felt very like blackmail, Sacher yielded, and on 23 June Rosenthal signed the contract on his behalf. Whether, had he attended the auction, he might have acquired the archive for less is something about which he chose not to speculate.

THUS, A CENTURY after their owner's birth, the long-fought-over documents of his extraordinary life—more than a hundred boxes of letters, postcards, contracts, programs, photographs, newspaper cuttings, and assorted trivia and memorabilia, and more than two hundred drawers of music manuscripts and sketches—made their way to the country of the rue Sacre du Printemps, there to be lodged in perpetuity in a newly converted house on the cathedral square in Basle, formerly the residence of the Catholic mystic Adrienne von Speyer and her husband, the Burckhardt scholar Walter Kägi, and already in 1983 the home of the manuscript full score of the famous ballet, which Sacher had bought from Vera Stravinsky in 1973.

The sale left the composer's heirs richer, but perhaps not remarkably happier. Robert Craft belabored the family in print, secure in the knowledge that they would not—indeed could not—reply in kind.[27] The legal squabbles continued, and for all I know continue still, though one by one the parties to the old disputes have found quieter resting places beyond the reach even of Manhattan lawyers. Theodore Strawinsky died in 1989, his brother, Soulima, in 1994; Françoise and Denise followed them to the grave, respectively, in 2002 and 2004. Kitty Yelachich, as she became after marrying her cousin Mikhail in 1978, also died in 2002. André Marion had died in 1983, but Milène, the composer's youngest child, has lived on in a remote western suburb of Los Angeles, quietly tending her roses and the delightful butterflies and birds she crafts out of colored stones and fossilized bone, and studiously avoiding disputes and public reminiscence. Of all Stravinsky's children, she remained closest to him, and perhaps in some ways she still resembles him, though in character more like her mother: shy, gently spoken, unassuming, but quietly self-contained. Her longevity, like his, might seem a triumph of the spirit over frail flesh, if such language were not entirely foreign to her nature, at least as it presents itself on casual acquaintance. He impressed those who knew him by his astonishing physical and mental vigor. In her, the resilience seems more passive, as if it might be possible to survive the gales of life by lifting your feet off the ground and simply floating.

Robert Craft has continued working into his eighties, his energy apparently unabated by the years of combat with enemies partly imaginary, partly not: Sancho Panza miraculously transformed into Don Quixote. Surviving the legacy, as he himself expressed it in the final part of his autobiography, has included recycling it: recording and re-recording Stravinsky's music, retracing and extending his travels, documenting and redocumenting his life. Like the shades in *Persephone,* he has often seemed to have "no other destiny than the endless rebeginning of the uncompleted gesture of life." Yet this does him an injustice. For, whatever the futility of the interminable litigations and the recurrent agony of his editorial work and personal animosities, one single fact remains that, for those who love Stravinsky's late music, will always outweigh those lesser frailties: that, without Robert Craft, there might have been no *Agon,* no *Canticum sacrum,* no *Requiem Canticles.*

As for the music whose mortal remains were carted off to the banks of the Rhine in boxes and packing cases, its immortal essence has amply repaid the debts it incurred in its creator's lifetime. Born of so many derivations and allusions, so many methods and traditions, it has grown into the one unquestioned staple of the modern repertoire, the body of work that, more than any other, stands as an icon of twentieth-century musical thought and imagery. Composers not yet conceived when Stravinsky died cleave to his music as if it could answer every question that might present itself to the creative spirit in times as troubled as his. Conductors who never contemplate Schoenberg and his school have taken Stravinsky to their repertory, if not always to their hearts. Theorists—even in his native Russia—pore over his music, expatiate on its grammar and aesthetics, and disagree about its meaning. That which is, designedly, repellent in twentieth-century music as a whole is repellent in his, too, but the unpleasantness is something sharp and invigorating, it grows on you as the taste of beer grows on an adolescent boy, and once the taste is there you can never recapture the time when it was not. Perhaps in any case Stravinsky's life shows why it could hardly have been otherwise. For ultimately this music that supposedly expresses nothing, and always seemed studiously, impenetrably deaf to the world around it, has turned out to be the most exact echo and the best response to those terrifying years that brought it into being.

Concerto for Two Solo Pianos, 1932–35. First performance: Paris, 21 November 1935. Published: Schott, 1936.

Jeu de cartes, ballet in three deals, 1935–6. First performance: New York, 27 April 1934. Published: Schott, 1937.

Praeludium, for jazz ensemble, 1936–7. First performance: Los Angeles, 19 October 1953. Published: Boosey and Hawkes, 1968.

Petit Ramusianum harmonique, for speaking and singing voice unaccompanied (words: Charles-Albert Cingria), 1937. First (private) performance: Paris, 24 September 1938. Published: in *Hommage à C.-F. Ramuz* (Lausanne: Porchet, 1938); also in I. Vershinina (ed.), *Igor Stravinsky: Vokal'naya Muzïka*, vol. 1 (Moscow: Sovetskiy Kompozitor, 1982).

Concerto in E-flat (Dumbarton Oaks), for chamber orchestra, 1937-8. First performance: Washington, D.C., 8 May 1938. Published: Schott, 1938.

Symphony in C, for orchestra, 1938–40. First performance: Chicago, 7 November 1940. Published: Schott, 1948.

Tango, for piano (originally planned for voice and instruments), 1940. First performance (arr. S. Dushkin for violin and piano): New York, 31 March 1941; (arr. F. Guenther for jazz orchestra): Philadelphia, 10 July 1941. Published (for piano): Mercury, 1941. Arrangement by Stravinsky for instrumental ensemble, 1953. First performance: Los Angeles, 19 October 1953. Published: Mercury, 1954.

Danses concertantes, for chamber orchestra, 1940–2. First performance: Los Angeles, 8 February 1942. Published: AMP, 1943; Schott.

Circus Polka, (1) for piano, 1941–2. Published: AMP, 1942. (2) arr. D. Raksin for circus band, 1942. First performance: New York, 9 April 1942. Published: AMP, 1948. (3) for orchestra, 1942. First performance: Cambridge, Mass., 13 January 1944. Published: AMP, 1944; Schott.

Four Norwegian Moods, for orchestra, 1942. First performance: Cambridge, Mass., 13 January 1944. Published: AMP, 1944; Schott.

Ode, elegiac chant in three parts for orchestra, 1943. First performance: Boston, 8 October 1943. Published: AMP/Schott, 1947.

Sonata for Two Pianos, 1942–4. First performance: Madison, Wisconsin, 2 August 1944. Published: AMP/Chappell, 1945.

Babel, cantata for narrator, male chorus, and orchestra (words: Genesis), 1944. First performance: Los Angeles, 18 November 1945. Published: Schott, 1953.

Scherzo à la russe, (1) for jazz band, 1943–4. First performance: Blue Network Radio, 5 September 1944. Published: Chappell, 1949; Schott. (2) for 2 pianos, 1943–4. Published: AMP, 1945. (3) for orchestra, 1945. First performance: San Francisco, 22 March 1946. Published: AMP/Chappell, 1945; Schott.

Scènes de ballet, for orchestra, 1944. First performance: Philadelphia, 27 November 1944. Published: Chappell, 1945; Boosey and Hawkes.

Elegy, for solo viola (or violin), 1944. First performance: Washington, D.C., 26 January 1945. Published: AMP/Chappell, 1945.

Symphony in Three Movements, for orchestra, 1942–5. First performance: New York, 24 January 1946. Published: AMP/Schott, 1946.

Ebony Concerto, for clarinet and jazz ensemble, 1945. First performance: New York, 25 March 1946. Published: Charling, 1946; Edwin H. Morris/Boosey and Hawkes.

Concerto in D, for string orchestra, 1946. First performance: Basle, 21 January 1947. Published: Boosey and Hawkes, 1947.

Orpheus, ballet in three scenes, 1946–7. First performance: New York, 28 April 1948. Published: Boosey and Hawkes, 1948.

Hommage à Nadia Boulanger ("Petit Canon pour la fête de Nadia Boulanger"), for two tenors (words: Jean de Meung), 1947. Published: Boosey and Hawkes/San Francisco Press, 1982 (in Clifford Caesar, *Igor Stravinsky: A Complete Catalogue*, p. 8).

Mass, for chorus and double wind quintet, 1944–8. First performance: Milan, 27 October 1948. Published: Boosey and Hawkes, 1948.

The Rake's Progress, opera in three acts (libretto: W. H. Auden and C. Kallman), 1947–51. First performance: Venice, 11 September 1951. Published: Boosey and Hawkes, 1951.

Cantata, for soprano, tenor, female chorus, and five instruments (words: anon. 15th–16th-century English), 1951–2. First performance: Los Angeles, 11 November 1952. Published: Boosey and Hawkes, 1953.

Septet, for clarinet, horn, bassoon, and piano quartet, 1952–3. First performance: Washington, D.C., 23 January 1954. Published: Boosey and Hawkes, 1953.

Three Songs from William Shakespeare, for mezzo-soprano, flute, clarinet, and viola, 1953. First performance: Los Angeles, 8 March 1954. Published: Boosey and Hawkes, 1954.

In Memoriam Dylan Thomas, for tenor, string quartet, and four trombones, 1954. First performance: Los Angeles, 20 September 1954. Published: Boosey and Hawkes, 1954.

Greeting Prelude, for orchestra, 1955. First performance: Boston, 4 April 1955. Published: Boosey and Hawkes, 1956.

Canticum sacrum ad honorem Sancti Marci Nominis, for tenor, baritone, chorus, and orchestra (words: Deuteronomy, Psalms, Song of Solomon, St. Mark's Gospel, and the First Epistle of St. John, Vulgate texts), 1955. First performance: Venice, 13 September 1956. Published: Boosey and Hawkes, 1956.

Agon, ballet for twelve dancers, 1953–7. First performance: Los Angeles (concert), 17 June 1957; New York (stage), 1 December 1957 (preceded by a private charity performance on 27 November). Published: Boosey and Hawkes, 1957.

Threni: id est Lamentationes Jeremiae Prophetae, for six soloists, chorus, and orchestra (words: Lamentations, Vulgate text), 1957–8. First performance: Venice, 23 September 1958. Published: Boosey and Hawkes, 1958.

Movements, for piano and orchestra, 1958–9. First performance: New York, 10 January 1960. Published: Boosey and Hawkes, 1960.

Epitaphium, for flute, clarinet, and harp, 1959. First performance: Donaueschingen, 17 October 1959. Published: Boosey and Hawkes, 1959.

Double Canon, for string quartet, 1959. First performance: New York, 20 December 1959. Published: Boosey and Hawkes, 1960.

Monumentum pro Gesualdo di Venosa (ad CD Annum), three Gesualdo motets recomposed for instruments, 1960. First performance: Venice, 27 September 1960. Published: Boosey and Hawkes, 1960.

A Sermon, a Narrative, and a Prayer, cantata for alto and tenor, speaker, chorus and orchestra (words: the Epistles of St. Paul and Acts of the Apostles [Authorized version], and Thomas Dekker), 1960–1. First performance: Basle, 23 February 1962. Published: Boosey and Hawkes, 1961.

The Flood, musical play for solo speakers and singers, chorus, and orchestra (words: Robert Craft, from Genesis [authorized version] and the York and Chester Miracle Plays), 1961–2. First performance: CBS TV (USA), 14 June 1962; first public performance: Santa Fe, 21 August 1962. Published: Boosey and Hawkes, 1963.

Anthem ("The dove descending breaks the air"), for chorus unaccompanied (words: T. S. Eliot), 1961–2. First performance: Los Angeles, 19 February 1962. Published: Faber and Faber (in *Expo*), 1962; Boosey and Hawkes.

Abraham and Isaac, sacred ballad for baritone and chamber orchestra (words: Genesis, Hebrew text), 1962–3. First performance: Jerusalem, 23 August 1964. Published: Boosey and Hawkes, 1965.

Elegy for J.F.K., for medium voice and three clarinets (words: W. H. Auden), 1964. First performance: Los Angeles, 6 April 1964. Published: Boosey and Hawkes, 1964.

Fanfare for a New Theatre, for two trumpets, 1964. First performance: New York, 20 April 1964 (private gala); first public performance: New York, 24 April 1964. Published: Boosey and Hawkes, 1968.

Variations Aldous Huxley in Memoriam, for orchestra, 1963–4. First performance: Chicago, 17 April 1965. Published: Boosey and Hawkes, 1965.

Introitus T. S. Eliot in Memoriam, for male chorus and chamber ensemble (words: from the "Requiem aeternam"), 1965. First performance: Chicago, 17 April 1965. Published: Boosey and Hawkes, 1965.

Canon for concert introduction or encore, for orchestra, 1965. First performance: Toronto, 16 December 1965. Published: Boosey and Hawkes, 1973.

Requiem Canticles, for contralto and bass, chorus, and orchestra (words: from the Missa pro defundis), 1965–6. First performance: Princeton University, 8 October 1966. Published: Boosey and Hawkes, 1967.

The Owl and the Pussy-Cat, for soprano and piano (words: Edward Lear), 1966. First performance: Los Angeles, 31 October 1966. Published: Boosey and Hawkes, 1967.

ARRANGEMENTS

TCHAIKOVSKY

Bluebird Pas de deux from *The Sleeping Beauty* (Act 3), arranged for small orchestra, 1941. First performance: New York, February 1941. Published: Schott, 1953.

J. S. SMITH

The Star-Spangled Banner, arranged for chorus and orchestra (various combinations), 1941. First performance: Los Angeles, 18 October 1941. Published: Mercury, 1941.

BACH

Chorale-Variations on "Vom Himmel hoch," arranged for chorus and orchestra, 1955–6. First performance: Ojai, California, 27 May 1956. Published: Boosey and Hawkes, 1956.

GESUALDO

Tres Sacrae Cantiones ("Da pacem Domine," "Assumpta est Maria," "Illumina nos"), completed for six, six, and seven voices, respectively, 1957–9. First performance: New York, 10 January 1960 ("Assumpta est Maria" only). Published: Boosey and Hawkes, 1957 ("Illumina nos") and 1960 (complete).

SIBELIUS

Canzonetta, op. 62a, arranged for eight instruments, 1963. First performance: Los Angeles, 30 September 1963. Published: Breitkopf and Härtel, 1964.

WOLF

Two Sacred Songs from the *Spanisches Liederbuch* ("Herr, was trägt der Boden hier," and "Wunden trägst du"), arranged for mezzo-soprano and ten instruments, 1968. First performance: Los Angeles, 6 September 1968. Published: Boosey and Hawkes, 1969.

BACH

Preludes and Fugues from *Das wohltemperierte Klavier*, in E minor, C-sharp minor, B minor (Book I) and F major (Book II), for wind and strings (various combinations), 1969. First performance: Neuchâtel, 18 January 2005. Unpublished (Boosey and Hawkes).

LIBRARY ABBREVIATIONS

(Specific collections are denoted by the name attached to the library identifier.)

BN	Bibliothèque Nationale, Paris
Columbia	Columbia University, New York City
HRC	Harry Ransome Center, University of Texas, Austin
LoC	Library of Congress, Washington, D.C.
NYPL	New York Public Library
PSS	Paul Sacher Stiftung, Basle
RGALI	Rossiyskiy gosudarstvennïy arkhiv literaturï i iskusstva (Russian State Archive of Literature and Art), Moscow
RGB	Rossiyskaya gosudarstvennaya biblioteka (Russian State Library), Moscow
SCNY	Surrogate's Court, New York County, 31 Chambers Street, NY 10007 (file no. 2749–71)
UCLA	Department of Special Collections, Research Library, University of California, Los Angeles

ENTR'ACTE: A HOUSE DIVIDED

1 H. G.Wells, *The Shape of Things to Come* (1933), book 1, chap. 13.
2 Quoted in J. E. Bowlt (ed.), *The Salon Album of Vera Sudeikin-Stravinsky* (Princeton: Princeton University Press, 1995), xv.
3 Maritain, *Art et scolastique* (Paris: Art Catholique, 1920), 9.

1 A GENTLE AND A FREE SPIRIT

1 See *SCS*, 514.
2 As Robert Craft does in *SSCII*, 492.
3 Letter of Prokofiev to Myaskovsky, 17 September 1934, in *PMP*, 427–8; English translation in Harlow Robinson (ed. and trans.), *Selected Letters of Sergei Prokofiev* (Boston: Northeastern University Press, 1998), 312. See also Prokofiev's letter of 6 September 1934 to Asafyev, in ibid., 137. Prokofiev does not exactly tell Myaskovsky that he saw Nouvel at Voreppe, but by mentioning the two authors and projects in the same sentence he strongly implies it. This is slightly obscured in the repunctuated English translation.

4 Letter of 25 February 1935 (PSS). The arguments, largely circumstantial, are too detailed to elaborate in full here. Nouvel certainly wrote Stravinsky's article "Diaghileff as I Knew Him" (the evidence is again in a letter from Katya, 4 March 1937 [PSS], wrongly dated 1935 in *SSCII*, 492, note 5). But for Haskell's book *Diaghileff: His Artistic and Private Life* (London and New York: Gollancz and Simon & Schuster, 1935), he provided only "a mass of carefully compiled notes," as Haskell acknowledges both in his introduction and on the title page. Craft finds a similarity of style between the two books, though (unless Haskell's acknowledgment is deliberately misleading) this is no argument for Nouvel's authorship of *Chron*. Similarities of content there certainly are, as one might expect. But Craft also, most bizarrely, suggests that oddities and archaicisms in the *English* translation of *Chron* are the fault of Nouvel (or whoever wrote the book). Incidentally, Stravinsky read excerpts to Katya at Sancellemoz in July 1935. "I'm so glad you read me what is written of your book," she wrote to him on the 26th, and later (6 August) she referred to Nouvel as "your faithful collaborator [sotrudnik]" (PSS).

5 After adopting "Soulima" as his professional Christian name in 1931, Svetik came to prefer it to the Russian diminutive of Sviatoslav, and while his family continued to call him "Svetik" or "Nini," new friends, including his French wife, knew him as Soulima. Henceforth, except sometimes in quotations, this book will follow suit.

6 Soulima Stravinsky, unpublished interview with Thor Wood, February 1977 (typed transcript in NYPL). I am grateful to Charles Joseph for bringing this interview to my attention. It is only fair to note, however, that Soulima is contrasting Nouvel's role with Robert Craft's in the conversation books and may therefore, more than forty years after the event, be affected by some bias against Craft.

7 The closure was by no means official. In August 1934 Frankfurt Radio had broadcast *The Rite of Spring*, conducted by Hans Rosbaud, and in November Erich Kleiber included the work in a public concert in Berlin. A memorandum of the German radio had stated on 27 July 1934 that "there was no racial or political objection to Stravinsky." Nevertheless a German tour, or regular German concert bookings, remained out of the question. See Joan Evans, "Stravinsky's Music in Hitler's Germany," *Journal of the American Musicological Society*, 56/3 (Fall 2003), 540.

8 See Katya's letter of 25 February 1935, referring to a (now lost or inaccessible) letter from her husband of 7 February (PSS). In fact no currency is specified, but since $150,000 would be a fantasy profit in the circumstances, I have assumed francs (the equivalent of $5,000–6,000). For information on Merovitch, see Gregor Piatigorsky, *Cellist* (New York: Doubleday, 1965), passim; also Merovitch's obituary in the *New York Times*, 9 August 1965 (he died on the 7th).

9 Stravinsky learnt about Merovitch's illness from Dushkin, who was in New York (telegram of 15 November 1935; letter of 26 November [PSS]).

10 *Milwaukee Wisconsin News*, 15 January 1935; *Town Crier*, 7 January 1935. The Arts Club reception and concert were on the 13th, the Milwaukee concert (with the Chicago Symphony Orchestra) on the 14th, and the three orchestral concerts in Chicago itself on the 18th, 19th, and 22nd. The Milwaukee concert seems to have been the first occasion on which the *Fairy's Kiss* excerpts, in their orchestral version, were formally billed as the Divertimento (see *SCS*, 660, note 85). On the 21st Stravinsky and Dushkin gave a recital in Minneapolis, a ten-hour train journey from Chicago, presumably returning overnight in time for the next day's concert.

11 Several critics noted a marked improvement in his conducting since 1925.

12 The only significant variation was that occasionally they gave only part of a whole program. In Toledo on the 23rd, for instance, they gave the second half of a concert whose first half was played by a quintet from Paris.

13   According to one reporter, Stravinsky uttered only two words in English at his first
      Chicago rehearsal: "red wine." He conducted the rehearsal in French. See Jack
      Diamond, "Stravinsky Likes His Wine Red; Talks to Orchestra," *Chicago News,*
      12 January 1935. But his English must have improved during the tour, if only because,
      by late March in Washington, he was speaking it enough to be frequently corrected. See
      SPD, 321, quoting the *Washington Post* of 24 March 1935.

14   Letter of 15 January 1935 (mistakenly dated 1934), Alexis Kall to Stravinsky (PSS). In the
      rejected ceremonious form of address, the word "you" *(vï)* is the polite second person
      plural, but elsewhere, and throughout their correspondence, Kall addresses Stravinsky
      in the intimate second person singular, as *tï.* For information on the hitherto unknown
      figures in Kall's list of former friends, see *PRKIII,* 555–6; also H. Colin Slim,
      "Unknown Words and Music, 1939–44, by Stravinsky," in D. Rosen and C. Brook (eds.),
      Words on Music: Essays in Honor of Andrew Porter on the Occasion of His 75th Birthday
      (Hillsdale, New York: Pendragon Press, 2004), 302–3. Fyodor Alexandrovich Luther
      was a schoolteacher who ran a literary discussion group attended by his pupils,
      including Kall, and possibly also by Stravinsky (who was presumably not one of them,
      as he went to a different school). According to Viktor Varunts (*PRKIII,* 555, note 7),
      "Bilibin" was not the well-known painter Ivan Bilibin, but his brother Alexander,
      though as Varunts notes that the painter brother also belonged to the Luther circle, the
      point would seem to be academic. The poet Ivan Oreus, who wrote under the nom de
      plume Konevskoy (not, pace Slim, the other way round), was tragically drowned in the
      summer of 1901 at the age of twenty-four, thus providing a probable latest date for
      Kall's first meeting with Stravinsky. On the pianist Nikolay Richter, Stravinsky's cousin
      Mikhail Yelachich, and Andrey Rimsky-Korsakov, see *SCS.* A group photograph of Kall,
      the Bilibin brothers, and Oreus, taken in 1898, is in *PRKIII,* following p. 432.

15   I am indebted to Colin Slim for much of the material on Kall's background, including
      the information that his former housemate, a well-known Hollywood con man called
      Michael Roomanoff, had committed suicide the previous month. The neighbors Kall
      mentions were the singer Nina Koshetz and a violinist by the name of Zhukovsky.

16   Letter of 19 January 1935, Stravinsky to Kall, in *PRKIII,* 558.

17   Letters of 22 January 1935 (misdated 1934), Kall to Stravinsky; 26 January, Stravinsky to
      Kall, in *PRKIII,* 559–61.

18   Letter of 2 March 1935, Stravinsky to Kall, in *PRKIII,* 571.

19   Merle Armitage, *Accent on Life* (Ames: Iowa State University Press, 1965), 176.

20   See the New York report in *Musical Times,* 76 (March 1935), 269. The orchestral pieces
      were interspersed with vocal items by Ponchielli, Bizet, Tchaikovsky, and others, sung
      by Gladys Swarthout and conducted by Frank Black.

21   According to the *Radio Guide,* however, the Stravinsky element in the program was
      limited by what were described as "the excessive demands of Stravinsky's publishers."

22   See Fernand Auberjonois, "Stravinsky, Fernand Auberjonois et les bisons," quoted in
      SNB, 369–70. At some time during this particular stay in New York, Stravinsky was
      also visited by Vera's husband, Sergey Sudeykin, in quest of work as a stage designer.
      See Vera's letter to Stravinsky of 19 February 1935, in *DB,* 70–1.

23   28 January 1936. See Laurel E. Fay, *Shostakovich: A Life* (Oxford and New York: Oxford
      University Press, 2000), 84–5.

24   *Novaya Zarya,* 14 February 1935 (quoted in *PRKIII,* 598, note 1).

25   Dagmar Godowsky, *First Person Plural* (New York: Viking, 1958), 213.

26   Ibid., 213–4. As always with Dagmar, a certain exaggeration has to be allowed for.
      Stravinsky was in Washington, taking his two 1935 visits together, for no more than five
      or six days in total, on two of which he had concerts. So the "scores" of parties Dagmar
      refers to can hardly have been more than half a dozen at the very outside. As for the

train journey, one wonders what had become of Dushkin. Finally, Craft claims that Dagmar did in fact become Stravinsky's mistress this time in New York (see *ImpLif*, 197), though if so it is extremely curious that Dagmar herself seems in effect to deny it.

27   Isabel Morse Jones, "Singing Scotsmen Appear; Stravinsky Tells Plans," *Los Angeles Times*, 19 February 1935.

28   Miguel de Reus, "Masterly Concert Puzzles L.A. Audience," *Illustrated Daily News*, 1 March 1935.

29   *Los Angeles Times*, 21 February 1935.

30   At that time the LAPO, like many American orchestras, contained a large number of European immigrants.

31   Florence Lawrence, "Philharmonic Throng Cheers Igor Stravinsky," *Los Angeles Examiner*, 22 February 1935.

32   Letter of 30 January 1935, in *PRKIII*, 562–3. Italicized words in English in the original.

33   Robinson's own phrase. See Edward G. Robinson and Leonard Spigelgass, *All My Yesterdays* (New York: Hawthorn Books, 1973), 147–8.

34   "Propositi di Strawinsky," *Gazetta del Populo* (Rome), 31 May 1935. For a detailed account of the MGM visit, including a group photograph of Stravinsky, Kall, and Merovitch with Stothart and the music staff, see William H. Rosar, "Stravinsky and MGM," in Clifford McCarty (ed.), *Film Music*, vol. 1 (New York: Garland, 1989), 108–22.

35   Charles Chaplin, *My Autobiography* (London: The Bodley Head, 1964), 429–30.

36   Letter of 17 November 1935 (PSS). Strecker had evidently outlined Chaplin's proposal in a letter to Stravinsky of 8 November which, unfortunately, seems not to have survived. In quoting Stravinsky's letter in *SPD*, 335, Craft misunderstands "je ne trouve pas ça du tout une idée utopique" in a sardonic sense; but in Stravinsky's vocabulary not to be utopian (i.e., impractical) was a virtue.

37   Chaplin, op. cit., 430. Chaplin says the dinner was at his house, but nothing else is known of such an occasion.

38   The text of his speech is reproduced in facsimile in *T&C*, facing 145.

39   *New York Times*, 16 March 1935; 28 April 1928.

40   *New York Times*, 5 February 1936.

41   Apart from a single matinee performance of *The Firebird*, in the Fokine choreography, which he conducted on the 21st.

42   The Chicago recital was to have been on the 29th. The trip was saved from complete pointlessness by a recital in Winnetka on the 27th.

43   Letter of 4 April, *CASIII*, 49–50.

44   Letter of 2 April 1935, in *DB*, 75.

2   THE POET OF MONTPARNASSE

1   See Vera's letters to Igor of 28 and 30 December 1934, in *DB*, 62, and Katya's of 29 December, in *PRKIII*, 550, and *DB*, 62, note 9.

2   See her letters to Igor in America, in *DB*, 61–75, passim.

3   See Milène to her father, letter of 16 January 1935; Katya to Igor, letter of 31 January 1935 (both PSS).

4   Vera to Igor, letter of 18 January 1935, in *DB*, 67. See also Katya's letters to Igor, January–February 1935, passim (PSS); and *Sfam*, 118.

5   Katya to Igor, letter of 11 February 1935, *PRKIII*, 568.

6   Ibid. Irina Terapiano was the sister of Igor Stravinsky's sister-in-law, Yelena Nikolayevna, the wife of his brother Yury. Craft (*SPD*, 256–7) misspells her name and—apparently quite unaware that she was Yury's sister-in-law—characterizes her

grotesquely as a "busybody" for having in 1925 intervened with Igor on his brother's behalf. Elsewhere Craft also uses Mika's "pleasant nature, good judgment . . . courage, maturity and independence" as a stick to beat her brothers, pointing out that it was Mika, not Theodore or Soulima, whom Stravinsky sent to Germany in May 1934 to bring out blocked funds. But Theodore had an emergency operation for peritonitis in mid-May, and Soulima was still convalescing from tuberculosis. In any event, a daughter is a much more effective emissary in such cases, being more likely to soft-talk her way past male guards.

7   Katya to Igor, *PRKIII*, passim.

8   See *SCS*, 531, which, however, mistakenly identifies Theodore as the subject of the diagnosis.

9   Concert of 11 September. This was the two composers' second and final meeting. Berg died fifteen months later.

10   Letter of 20 October 1934; see also Stravinsky's reply of 22 October (PSS).

11   Letter of 22 October (Akademie der Künste, Berlin).

12   Letter of 24 October, Scherchen to Stravinsky (PSS).

13   Letter of 24 October (Akademie der Künste).

14   See *SCS*, 13–14, 34–8.

15   See, for instance, her letter of 12 February 1935, in *DB*, 70.

16   But nothing, Katya thought, would induce Grisha to buy a new set of dentures, "even if he earned a million dollars" (letter of 28 February [PSS]).

17   See her letter to Igor of 30 January 1935, *DB*, 68. Other information is from Katya's letters of January and early February, passim.

18   See Vera's letter to Igor, 8 January 1935, *DB*, 66; also Katya's letter of the same date (PSS).

19   Letter of 16 February 1935 to Igor, in *PRKIII*, 568–9.

20   Letter of 24 February 1935, in *PRKIII*, 569–70.

21   Letter of 21 May 1935 to Igor, in *PRKIII*, 578–9.

22   Letter of 26 April 1935 (PSS).

23   Letter of 21 May.

24   Letter of 11 August 1935 to her husband (PSS). For an account of Ira's behavior on the eve of Mika and Yury's wedding, see Katya's letter of 12 October 1935 (PSS).

25   For this and further information on Mandelstam, see Ed Weeda, Introduction to *Yuriy Mandel'shtam: Sobraniye Stikhotvoreniy* (The Hague: Leuxenhoff, 1990). I am grateful to Stanislav Shvabrin for bringing this volume to my attention. See also Y. Terapiano, *Vstrechi* (New York: Izdatel'stvo imeni Chekhova, 1953), 122–5. Yury Mandelstam was apparently not related to his more famous namesake, Osip.

26   Letter of 22 August 1935, in *PRKIII*, 581–2.

27   The Russian Orthodox church-in-exile had recently split into pro- and anti-Moscow factions, the latter of which was compelled to find makeshift churches for its services. The Stravinskys adhered to this breakaway faction. See, for instance, *T&C*, 41.

28   Information kindly supplied to the author by Mika's younger sister, Milène Marion.

29   Letter to Igor, 13 June 1935 (PSS).

30   See Katya's letter to Igor, 15 May 1935, in *PRKIII*, 577.

31   Letter of 28 November 1934 (PSS). Stravinsky had spent three days in London, dining with Gollancz and his wife on the 26th and conducting the British premiere of *Persephone* at the Queen's Hall on the 28th.

32   "La Musique," *Vendredi*, 24 January 1936.

33   "La Musique," *Le Magazine d'aujourd'hui*, 1 May 1935.

34   *Chroniques de ma vie*, vol. 1 (Paris: Denoël et Steele, 1935), 106; *Chron*, 83. I have retranslated in this case in order to remain closer to the French text as cited by Marcel.

35 *Chron*, 91.
36 Stravinsky seems also to have been piqued by Romola Nijinsky's recently published biography of her husband, with its hostile and possibly mendacious portrait of the composer at Morges in 1916: *Nijinsky* (London: Gollancz, 1933), 306–9. See also *SCS*, 262–4.
37 *Chron*, 158: cf. *SCS*, 330–3.
38 "Les Concerts," *Le Temps*, 18 May 1935.
39 *Chron*, 282–3.
40 Ibid., 283–4, 286.
41 Ibid., 286.

3   GRAVES OF ACADEME

1 *Chron*, 193.
2 Soulima Stravinsky, interview with Thor Wood.
3 Ibid.; also letter of 14 November 1934, Willy Strecker to Stravinsky, referring to the death-mask request (PSS).
4 In *Dial* (42–3), Stravinsky claims that the double piano was specially built for work on the concerto; but it seems more likely that an existing instrument was commandeered. A letter from Katya of 14 August (PSS) suggests that the new piano was only installed in September.
5 *Dial*, 43.
6 Soulima Stravinsky, interview with Thor Wood.
7 The obvious exception, in the finale of Brahms's D minor Piano Concerto, pointedly excludes the soloist.
8 But Stravinsky already knew he was writing a concerto—if only with a small *c*—by 29 June 1935, when he mentioned the work in a letter to Ramuz; see Guisan (ed.), *C.-F. Ramuz, ses amis et son temps*, vol. 6 (Lausanne and Paris: La Bibliothèque des Arts, 1970), 272–3.
9 See Stuart Isacoff, "Musical Life with Father" (an interview with Soulima Stravinsky), *Keyboard Classics* (September/October 1981), 17–18.
10 Mann, *The Magic Mountain*, trans. H. T. Lowe-Porter (London: Secker & Warburg, 1946), 8. Mann's wife, like Stravinsky's, suffered from tuberculosis.
11 Ibid., 6.
12 In the main only Katya's letters to her husband appear to have survived. His to her, admittedly less frequent, can sometimes be glimpsed from the contents of her replies. She certainly corresponded with the rest of the family as well, but these letters, if they survive, remain in private hands.
13 Letter of 2 September 1935 (PSS).
14 Letter of 10 July 1935, Katya to Igor (PSS).
15 Letter of 16 May 1935, Katya to Igor (PSS).
16 Letter of 7 June 1935, Katya to Igor (PSS).
17 Letter of 28 May 1935, Katya to Igor (PSS).
18 Though he only abandoned it conclusively in late November: see his telegram to Dushkin of 25 November 1935 (PSS).
19 Letter of 17 September 1935 (PSS).
20 Rosenstiel, *Nadia Boulanger: A Life in Music* (London and New York: Norton, 1982), 259.
21 Much of my information about Stravinsky's teaching method at the École Normale comes from Maurice Perrin, "Stravinsky in a Composition Class," *The Score*, 20 (June 1957), 44–6. An undated letter from Nadia Boulanger to Stravinsky (PSS) indicates that she had also invited him to help with her summer teaching at the American

Conservatory at Fontainebleau. But Stravinsky, though he visited Nadia at Fontainebleau (for instance, in July 1935), seems never to have taught there.

22 "Novoye proizvedeniye I. F. Stravinskavo," *Posledniye Novosti*, 7 December 1935.

23 The actual first performance was an afternoon matinee, after which the whole was repeated in the early evening of the same day, with a third performance the following evening (the 22nd). Craft's mention of Polignac run-throughs on the 21st, 22nd, and 27th appears to be without foundation (see *SSCII*, 466), though the princess refers in an undated letter of (probably) 23 November (PSS) to "the *exposé* Nadia gave of it for me in my studio," which might mean a formal talk to an invited audience with, perhaps, a performance in whole or part, or a private tutorial for the princess's benefit. I am grateful to Sylvia Kahan for drawing this letter to my attention, and to Colin Slim for detective work on the dates.

24 The talk was published in *Conferencia* (the journal of the Université des Annales), 15 December 1935, 42–50, under the title "Quelques confidences sur la musique," with a number of analytical music examples which do, in fact, shed light on the work's conception, especially the emergence of the theme in the variation movement. The examples were also included in the program handout at the concert, but unfortunately the reprint of the article in White, *Stravinsky: The Composer and His Works* (London: Faber and Faber, 1979), 581–5, omits them.

25 *Le Figaro*, 3 December 1935.

26 *Vendredi*, 29 November 1935. Prokofiev wrote to Myaskovsky a few days later that "one is bound to feel he has constructed his work splendidly, but the themes are thin—not themes but themelets" (letter of 3 December 1935, in *PMP*, 443; Robinson, *Selected Letters of Prokofiev*, 317).

27 See *Chron*, 29; *Chroniques de ma vie*, vol. 1, 33. The acquired English sense of the word "trouvaille"—a "find"—is exactly Stravinsky's meaning.

28 Vittorio Tranquilli, "Strawinsky in prosa," *Il Piccolo di Trieste*, 23 April 1931.

29 *Vendredi*, 29 November 1935.

30 Stravinsky's letter of thanks to Pierné is dated 8 July: *SSCII*, 482. In his own letter of 14 July (PSS), Pierné refers to the *Firebird* premiere, but not to the anniversary.

31 "Ma candidature à l'Institut," *Le Jour*, 28 January 1936. A partial English translation is in *SSCII*, 485–6.

32 In his autobiography, the singer Doda Conrad asserts that Stravinsky only agreed to stand on condition that the visits be waived. But there is no sign of any such stipulation in his correspondence with Blanche or Pierné, and he certainly did pay calls. On 13 January, Katya wrote from Sancellemoz (where she had just arrived from Paris): "Obviously you are paying calls now . . . Tell me as much as you can about your latest visits" (PSS). Conrad's story is that the Princesse de Polignac set up a series of receptions in lieu of the visits, then, on the day of the election, held a final reception with the secret intention of announcing Stravinsky's victory. But everything about this tale is improbable. For one thing, it was evident several days before the ballot that such a victory was highly unlikely, a fact of which the worldly and well-connected princess would hardly have been unaware. For another, Conrad says that when Stravinsky failed to turn up at the reception, he telephoned him, and spoke to Katya, who told him that her husband was ill and had been advised by the doctor not to go out. Alas for this fable, Katya was in Sancellemoz on the 25th, *with* her husband, who had arrived there the previous day. See Doda Conrad, *Dodascalies: Ma chronique du XXe siècle* (Arles: Actes Sud, 1997), 133–4.

33 "Divertissements académiques," *La Dépêche de Toulouse*, 1 February 1936.

34 André Coeuroy, "Trois convois," *Gringoire*, 24 January 1936. I have failed to identify the review of *Les Noces* to which he refers.

35 Letter of 15 January 1936, Pierné to Stravinsky, with a postscript by Blanche (PSS).

36 See his reply of 15 January. Craft suggests (*SSCII*, 484) that Stravinsky ignored his wife's pleas that he withdraw; but her letter is dated the 18th, three days after the composer had made his instant decision.

37 "Le Sacre de l'automne," *Figaro*, 17 January 1936. Presumably "Guermantes" was a pseudonym.

38 "Ma candidature à l'Institut," loc. cit.

39 "How interesting and strange," Katya wrote on 28 May 1935, "that you are conducting such a program" (PSS). The concert was on the 29th.

40 *Chron*, 248–50.

41 See John Lowe, *Edward James: A Surrealist Life* (London: Collins, 1991), for more on this whole episode and the painful and very public divorce which followed.

42 Bernard Taper, *Balanchine* (Berkeley, Los Angeles, and London: University of California Press, 1987), 148.

43 Letter of 11 August 1935, quoted in *SSCII*, 312.

4   AN ENEMY OF DEMOCRACY

1 As stated by Ocampo herself, in her *Autobiografía* (Buenos Aires: Sur, 1979–84), vol. 6, 53.

2 Ibid., vol. 3, 21.

3 "El poeta de la arquitectur," in *Testimonios VII*, 140; quoted in Doris Meyer, *Victoria Ocampo: Against the Wind and the Tide* (New York: George Braziller, 1979), 97. I am indebted to Dr. Meyer's masterly study for much background information on Ocampo.

4 See her undated letter of July or early August 1934, sent from London (PSS).

5 Letter of 17 March 1936 (PSS).

6 On 4 April 1935, for instance, he had written to Theodore from New York that he was so obsessed and agonized by Katya's illness that he had completely forgotten about Theodore's birthday (PSS).

7 See Joan Evans, "Stravinsky's Music in Hitler's Germany," 543–4; also Evans, *Hans Rosbaud—A Bio-Bibliography* (New York: Greenwood, 1992), 29–30. Exactly what was planned for Frankfurt remains somewhat unclear. Evans mentions both the broadcast lecture-recital and a public concert organized by Gerhard Frommel's new-music workshop. Strecker had also tried to persuade Stravinsky to play the Capriccio under a local conductor called Wetzelberger, but he objected that he was too out of practice as a concerto soloist and instead proposed that he conduct Soulima in this or the Piano Concerto (letter of 1 February 1936 [PSS], published without the material on Soulima in *SSCIII*, 240).

8 Letter of 27 January 1936, in *SSCIII*, 239.

9 Letter of 26 February 1936 (PSS).

10 Letter of 4 March 1936 (PSS).

11 Quoted in *SPD*, 552. Craft was the first to pull together much of this information on Stravinsky's politics in the thirties, though the picture he paints is curiously unsympathetic to the intimate logic of the composer's worldview.

12 See *SCS*, 430, for an account of this incident.

13 Letter of 4 March 1936.

14 See his letter of 14 July 1936 to Yury Schleiffer-Ratkoff, a Russian friend living in Rome. Stravinsky had handed the book and medal to an aide, asking that there be no publicity. "However," he pointed out to Schleiffer, "I don't think this can be the reason for so complete a silence on the part of the Duce, who would usually always thank me on receiving music, books, or messages of congratulation from me" (PSS). Three months

later, he "joyfully" agreed to open his Naples concert on 29 November with the Fascist hymn, "Giovinezza," presumably played on a piano, since the concert was a joint recital with Soulima (13 October 1936, quoted in *SPD*, 552).

15   *SPD*, 328.

16   "Igor Strawinski nos habla de las orientaciones futuras de la música y de su arte," *La Nación*, 25 April 1936.

17   "Stravinsky es enemigo de la democracia," *Crítica*, 25 April 1936.

18   "Comentarios: Strawinsky y el materialismo," *Criterio*, undated cutting in PSS (May, 1936).

19   "Concepto deplorable," *El Liberal*, 6 May 1936.

20   José Gabriel, "Igor Strawinsky ha venido succionar el tesoro argentino," *Señales*, 6 May 1936.

21   From an interview by Danubio Torres Fierro, *Plural* (December 1975), quoted and translated by Doris Meyer, *Victoria Ocampo*, 115–6.

22   Undated note, presumably 24 or 25 April 1936 (PSS).

23   "Igor Strawinsky se presentó en el Teatro Colón," *La Nación*, 29 April 1936.

24   See Katya's letter of 18 March 1936 to her husband (PSS), also "Igor Strawinsky se presentó en el Teatro Colón," loc. cit. Nevertheless, Soulima's Buenos Aires appearances were not without incident. At one of his Buenos Aires recitals, the piano's music rack collapsed and Soulima crushed one of his fingers in the piano lid, according to his own account in his unpublished memoirs, *Are You the Son . . . ?* I am grateful to Soulima's son, John Stravinsky, for showing me this typescript.

25   Robert Craft's description in *SCF* (94), 229.

26   *La Prensa*, 18 May 1936.

27   In an undated note (PSS), Victoria upbraids herself for coming to Rio and letting down various people in Buenos Aires.

28   Letter of 25 February 1954 (PSS). I have been unable to identify the "G's" or, perhaps fortunately, the tenor.

29   Letter of 23 June 1936 (PSS).

30   *First Person Plural*, 216–7.

31   Letter dated June 1936 (PSS).

32   *First Person Plural*, 217.

33   *Chron*, 22.

34   *Expo*, 55.

35   *First Person Plural*, 218.

36   Ibid., 219–20. I have accepted Dagmar's account since, allowing for some mild exaggeration, it tallies—or at least does not conflict—with Stravinsky's own brief memoir and other known facts. Despite this breach, Stravinsky accepted membership of a committee of honor for a celebration, at the Metropolitan Opera House in July 1937, of the fiftieth anniversary of Hofmann's New York début.

37   *ImpLif*, 197.

38   Ibid., 115, 197; *SPD*, 331.

39   Craft, private communication. Ocampo, *Autobiografía*, vol. 4, 149–50.

40   Anne Ansermet, *Ernest Ansermet, mon père* (Lausanne: Payot, 1983), 73.

41   *Autobiografía*, vol. 5, 18.

42   Letter of 14 April 1936, in *DB*, 77.

43   Letter of 10 July 1936 (PSS).

44   *ImpLif*, 115–6. Vera's move seems to have been to an apartment with better heating. See Katya's letter to her husband, 18 March 1936 (PSS).

45   *ImpLif*, 115. Craft adds that photographs exist of them together in her hotel room at Wiessee.

46 See Vera's letter to Igor of 6 May 1936, in *DB*, 79. Craft suggests in a footnote that the rift was caused by Lourié's book on Koussevitzky. But that book came out in 1931, and while Stravinsky certainly disliked it and told Lourié so (see Lourié's letter of 21 April 1932 [PSS]), subsequent correspondence shows that they were back on a friendly footing in 1933 and 1934, if less close than before. Nor was the present breach final, as we shall see.

47 Letter of 6 June 1936, in *DB*, 81.

48 See Strecker's letters to Stravinsky of 6 July, 21 July, and 3 August 1936, respectively; also Stravinsky's letter of 1 August (all in *SSCIII*, 243–4). For more information on the whole affair, including the reviews cited here, see Joan Evans, " 'Diabolus triumphans': Stravinsky's *Histoire du soldat* in Weimar and Nazi Germany," in J. Daverio and J. Ogasapian (eds.), *The Varieties of Musicology: Essays in Honor of Murray Lefkowitz* (Warren, Michigan: Harmonie Park Press, 2000), 175–85.

49 *Sfam*, 124.

50 See Katya's letter of 20 July 1936 (PSS). Two months before (letter of 19 May), Katya had provided an almost comical history of her younger daughter's ailments. She had had her throat cauterized on the advice of her singing teacher, and she had been to a homeopath, who had diagnosed a weak liver, and problems with her sympathetic nervous system and circulation. That Milène is still alive and well in Los Angeles as I write—in January 2005—might seem one of the happier miracles of valetudinarianism.

51 See her letter of 17 January (PSS).

52 Letter of 20 February 1936, Balanchine to Stravinsky: *SSCII*, 314–5 (but wrongly dated 29 February). In *T&C*, 44 (*T&E*, 35), Stravinsky claims to have written a fragment of the final tableau on the boat to South America; but the statement cannot confidently be taken as authentic and (like other program-note details in that volume) may be an editorial assumption based on a study of the autograph materials.

53 Letter of 30 June 1936: *SSCII*, 315. Balanchine's letter (quoted ibid.) is dated 11 June.

54 Letter of 20 September 1935, in *SSCII*, 312, but inadequately translated. "Changerais-tu mon texte, que je m'inclinerais"—"Should you change my text, I should acquiesce." The reasonable assumption that this refers to the new ballet is Craft's.

55 *T&C*, 45. *T&E*, 36, has a slightly different wording of the same memoir.

56 See Katya's letter of 21 July 1936 (PSS). Her letters of February had revealed that Milène was also for a time roped in to help with the libretto, perhaps as a distraction from various unsuitable young men.

57 The letter has not survived but is quoted by Katya in her letter of 27 July to her husband (PSS).

58 *Le Jour*, 3 February 1938, quoted in White, *Stravinsky*, 394 (note).

59 Letter of 29 July 1936 (PSS).

60 See especially her letter of 13 April 1937 (PSS). "Malayev cannot be left alone at present, and he was in a sanatorium not long ago having tried to poison himself with phenobarbitone."

61 See Strecker's letter of 20 August 1936, partially quoted in *SSCIII*, 244–6, note 45.

62 The terms were conveyed by Dushkin in a letter of 2 August 1936. Stravinsky's acceptance (limiting the exclusivity to the U.S.A.) is dated 12 August. He had tried to insist (once again) on Theodore being engaged as designer, but this was refused, on the possibly genuine grounds that Theodore was not a member of the relevant trade union. See *SSCII*, 316–7.

63 See Katya's letter of 6 September 1936 (PSS).

64 For instance, by 17 September Strecker had 82 pages of score (up to fig. 92, the entry of the Joker in the second deal), but he did not yet have the third variation, which Stravinsky was still writing on the 18th. On 16 October he sent another 61 pages (up to

the Combat between Spades and Hearts), but the waltz-minuet was tipped in later, probably in November. Meanwhile Stravinsky had composed the ending of the whole ballet on 19 October.

65 Letter of 15 November 1936, *SSCIII*, 246.

66 See, for instance, Strecker's letter of 12 December 1936, and Stravinsky's reply of the 15th, in *SSCII*, 319–20. The score is prefaced by the moral from La Fontaine's "Les Loups et les brebis":

> ... *Il faut faire aux méchants guerre continuelle*
> *La paix est fort bonne de soi,*
> *J'en conviens; mais de quoi sert-elle*
> *Avec des ennemis sans foi?*

which seems a singularly inapt epigraph to a work in which good triumphs (in La Fontaine the wolves, having made a treaty with the sheep, gobble up the lambs and strangle the sheepdogs). But this may be a survival from the aborted collaboration with Cocteau.

67 *T&C*, 43, where the composer also claims a lifelong interest in card games, "ever since I learned *durachki* as a child" (note, as before, the slightly variant text in *T&E*, 34). His supposed enthusiasm for poker while writing *Jeu de cartes*, though, should be set beside his statement in *Expo* (136) that he could not gamble because "I hate to regret." A month after finishing the ballet he told an interviewer in Toronto (*Evening Telegram*, 4 January 1937) that he spent his evenings at the cinema or playing bridge, which (unlike poker) is not by its nature a gambling game.

68 The theme itself, halfway down the page, is circled in the same red crayon. See *SPD*, 332, for a facsimile reproduction of the page. Stravinsky often labelled his sketches ex post facto in this way.

69 He told Alberto Gasco, "I write music in the morning, devote the afternoons to less demanding activities, and play cards in the evening." See "Strawinsky e il Fascismo," in Gasco, *Da Cimarosa a Strawinsky* (Rome: Edizioni de Santis, 1939), 458.

70 Letter to Balanchine, 30 June 1936: *SSCII*, 315. This was, on my argument, before the subject was chosen, but that hardly affects the point.

5 DEATH DEALS ...

1 The matter is referred to in Katya's letters of January 1937. See also *SSCI*, 15, note 30. In the end Malayev did not go and the wine was delivered by the violinist Jeanne Gautier.

2 Lincoln Kirstein, "Working with Stravinsky," in M. Lederman (ed.), *Stravinsky in the Theatre* (New York: Da Capo, 1975), 137, 139–40.

3 *Toronto Evening Telegram*, 4 January 1937.

4 *Toronto Daily Star*, 4 January 1937.

5 *Newsweek*, 23 January 1937, 24.

6 Apart from in his General Motors radio concert in February 1935. Dushkin had been scheduled to play Stravinsky's Violin Concerto and the Mozart D major in the first set, with Webster programmed for the second set, but Dushkin was taken ill and Webster stood in at short notice. Rumor had it that Dushkin had damaged his left index finger in an all-night practice session on a new type of E string (see Milton Widder, "Igor Stravinsky—Small Body but a Giant Brain," *Cleveland Press*, 20 February 1937). He apparently had still not recovered by the second week.

7 *New York Herald Tribune*, 22 January 1937.

8 "Stravinsky Wins Stirring Ovation," *New York Times*, 22 January 1937.

9 *Newsweek*, 23 January 1937, 24. For details of the Philharmonic's conductor problems

during these years, see Howard Shanet, *Philharmonic: A History of New York's Orchestra* (New York: Doubleday, 1975); also Peter Heyworth, *Otto Klemperer: His Life and Times*, vol. 2 (Cambridge: Cambridge University Press, 1996).

10 Francis D. Perkins, *New York Herald Tribune*, 15 January 1937.

11 *New York Times*, 15 January 1937.

12 W. J. Henderson, *New York Sun*, 28 January 1937. The *Suite italienne* is based not on Tchaikovsky, but on the Pergolesi and Gallo borrowings in *Pulcinella*. The program did, however, also include the Tchaikovsky-based Divertimento.

13 Letter of 17 October 1949 to Ralph Hawkes (PSS). The sketches suggest that the title was added later (initially with the spelling "Preludium"), but they also show that the original scoring was close to that of the published 1953 version, notwithstanding the note in the printed score that "the string parts were added in June 1953." They were in fact merely revised at that time. The description "radio orchestra" is taken from an undated letter of Lawrence Morton to Nicolas Slonimsky (UCLA, Morton).

14 *Cleveland Press*, 20 February 1937.

15 Letters of Vera to Igor, 18 and 24 January 1937, *DB*, 83–5. See also Katya's letters of January in PSS.

16 Letter to Igor, 4 February 1937 (PSS).

17 Letter of 12 February 1937 (PSS). Ste Geneviève-des-Bois is in fact no more than thirty kilometers due south of the capital.

18 Letter of 15 February 1937, *DB*, 87.

19 The letters, from late February and early March, appear not to have survived, but are referred to in some detail in Katya's letters of the time (PSS).

20 See *SPD*, 334, for a transcript of the sketch.

21 Again the letter has not surfaced, but Strecker's reply of 3 February 1937 (PSS) alludes to it.

22 Letter of 8 March 1937, Copley to Dushkin (PSS).

23 See Katya's letters of 9 February and 16 March 1937 (PSS). On 5 March Stravinsky also wrote to Elizabeth Sprague Coolidge turning down a commission for a string quartet which he had previously accepted in principle. See her letter of 31 July and his of 15 August 1936 (PSS).

24 Dushkin travelled with his young wife, Louise.

25 Letter of 4 November 1936. Armitage envisaged that Stravinsky would actually work on the score while in Los Angeles.

26 The telegram and a copy of the undated draft contract are in UCLA, Morton.

27 Alexander Fried, "Stravinsky Likes Idea of Writing for Movies," *San Francisco Examiner*, 22 March 1937.

28 Alfred Frankenstein, "Just Where Is Stravinsky?," *San Francisco Chronicle*, 22 March 1937. Stravinsky refused to tell any of his interviewers what the script was about, but according to Craft the draft title was *The Knights of St. David* (see *SSCII*, 307, note 52).

29 André Frank, "Igor Stravinski va composer pour le cinéma," *L'Intransigeant*, 19 May 1937.

30 See, for example, Strecker's letter of 6 April 1937 (PSS).

31 D. Milhaud, "Le Respect de soi-même, de son art et le cinéma," *Figaro*, 19 January 1938.

32 Morros himself later abandoned music and, in the immediately postwar years, worked for the U.S.A. as a counterintelligence agent in the Soviet Union. See Morros, *My Ten Years as a Counter Spy* (New York: Viking, 1959).

33 See Dushkin's letter of 31 January 1938 to Stravinsky, quoted in *SSCII*, 310, note 59. For a brief account of the Robinson dinner see Gershwin's letter to Emily Paley quoted in Joan Peyser, *The Memory of All That* (New York: Billboard Books, 1998), 277 (but wrongly implying a January 1937 date for the letter and hence the dinner). Gershwin

notes that Stravinsky asked "if he and Dushkin could play for the group. They played seven or eight pieces superbly."

34 See Fairbanks's telegram of thanks, 20 March 1937, and an earlier, undated letter requesting the autograph (PSS). Stravinsky had met Fairbanks and Dietrich a few days before.

35 For an account of this lawsuit and some documentation, see *SSCII*, 250–2. A contemporary summary is in *Paris-Soir*, 6 May 1937, 13 (misdated 19 May in *SSCII*, which also gets the author's name wrong).

36 *Los Angeles Times*, 26 July 1936, quoted in Heyworth, *Otto Klemperer: His Life and Times*, vol. 2 (Cambridge: Cambridge University Press, 1996), 72.

37 As well as being a dancer and choreographer, Kosloff had studied violin with Leopold Auer in St. Petersburg.

38 Letter of 29 October 1936 to Stravinsky (PSS).

39 Florence Lawrence, "Petrouchka Has Brilliant Color, Carnival Spirit," *Los Angeles Examiner*, 13 March 1937.

40 See the photograph of this scene in *SPD*, 338.

41 Letter of 1 April 1937 (from Seattle) (UCLA, Kall).

42 "Erstens ist es anders, zweitens als man denkt," quoting the dictum of Wilhelm Busch. Letter of 19 April 1937 (UCLA, Kall).

43 Letter to his wife, 15 April 1937, in G. Skelton, ed., *Selected Letters of Paul Hindemith* (New Haven and London: Yale University Press, 1995), 103.

44 Kirstein, "Working with Stravinsky," 139.

45 See *SCS*, 467. In *Stravinsky and Balanchine* (New Haven and London: Yale University Press, 2002), 83 et seq., Charles Joseph proposes a much more specific collaboration, but his evidence is circumstantial. It depends, for instance, on the recollections of Vera Stravinsky, who was far away from Monte Carlo, where Balanchine was preparing *Apollo* in spring 1928, and it equates "discussion" of the music (which certainly took place the preceding winter) with actual production work, which Balanchine always did at rehearsal. Stravinsky himself was rather little in Nice (where he lived) in the first half of 1928. No doubt he attended one or two early sessions and he was certainly in Paris for the final rehearsals. Whether this adds up to a collaboration is a matter of opinion.

46 *Le Jour*, 4 March 1938.

47 George Balanchine, "The Dance Element in Stravinsky's Music," in Lederman (ed.), *Stravinsky in the Theatre*, 84.

48 Julian Seaman, "Music," *Daily Mirror*, 28 April 1937.

49 Winthrop Sargeant, "Stravinsky's *Card Party* Joyous Ballet Spectacle," *New York American*, 28 April 1937.

50 Letter to Willy Strecker, 20 May 1937.

51 "Stravinsky's *Card Party* Joyous Ballet Spectacle."

52 Rosenstiel (*Nadia Boulanger*, 274) states that Stravinsky "had appealed to Nadia," but gives no source. Correspondence between the two is lacking for this period, as they were both living in Paris.

53 See Nadia's telegram to the Blisses, 8 June 1937 (PSS).

54 Ibid.

55 Letter of 17 May 1937 (sold at Christie's, London, 29 June 1994, lot 124; Jonathan Stone kindly drew my attention to this substantial lot and allowed me to examine it before the sale).

56 8 June, part of the Exposition Internationale de Paris.

57 Letter of 20 June 1937, replying to Massine's of 17 June (PSS). The identity of the "gifted young writer" is unknown. Viktor Varunts suggests Yury Mandelstam (commentary on this letter in *PRKIII*, 630, note 1); but it is hard to imagine that intensely serious poet

working on a ballet scenario. Malayev is another, perhaps more obvious possibility. By late April he had recovered from his suicide attempt and was well enough to play tennis with Soulima, and even that most stressful of all ball games, croquet (letter of Katya to Igor, 27 April 1937 [PSS]).

58 Letter of 8 August 1937 (PSS).

59 Almost exactly at this time, Stravinsky also received a suggestion from Copley's assistant, Severin Kavenoki, for a theatre piece based on the recent series of frescoes by José Clemente Orozco, *The Epic of American Civilization*, in Dartmouth College, but Stravinsky turned it down on the grounds that "I feel incapable of writing a folklore ballet, whether American or otherwise" (letter of 4 September 1937) (NYPL, Kavenoki Archive).

60 Letter of 27 December 1937 (UCLA, Kall).

61 See *Sfam*, 133–5, for these and other details. The Château de Monthoux was, incredibly, demolished in 1990, but the library building still stands, not far from the church on its mound. The grounds are now a small municipal park, with a duck pond nearby.

62 *Sfam*, 136. Katya left for Sancellemoz early in September.

63 Letter of 28 July 1937, *SSCIII*, 123, but with the quoted phrase truncated.

64 Letter of 8 August 1937, *SSCII*, 306–8.

65 Cingria sent the text with his letter of 5 July, suggesting that any necessary cuts or changes be made by Theodore; see *SSCIII*, 121–3, but with the reference to Theodore conspicuously omitted.

66 *SPD*, 553.

67 See Joan Evans, "Some Remarks on the Publication and Reception of Stravinsky's *Erinnerungen*," *Mitteilungen der Paul Sacher Stiftung*, no. 9 (March 1996), 17–23, for these and other details. The first German-language edition soon came out, in the autumn of 1937. Dr. Evans notes that while the Bayreuth passages were restored in later German editions, the remarks on Jewish violinists have never been reinstated.

68 Another had been the German premiere of *Persephone* in Brunswick on 5 June, conducted by Ewald Lindemann. See Joan Evans, "Stravinsky's Music in Hitler's Germany," 555.

69 Hitler's speech on modern art in connection with the Munich Entartete Kunst exhibition in July had been reported in extenso in the August issue of the Fascist paper *Il musicista*. See Harvey Sachs, *Music in Fascist Italy* (London: Weidenfeld & Nicolson, 1987), 180.

70 Alfredo Casella, *Music in My Time*, trans. and ed. Spencer Norton (Norman: University of Oklahoma Press, 1955), 218.

71 This was of course a concert performance of *Jeu de cartes*. The European stage premiere was in Dresden on 13 October 1937.

72 Stravinsky seems definitely to have heard a rehearsal of the Schoenberg Suite (see, for instance, *SPD*, 635, note 98, and 643, note 17), but there is no hard evidence that he attended the actual concert.

73 M. Talalay, "Russkaya bogema v Positano," *Russkaya mïsl'*, 10 February 2000; quoted in *PRKIII*, 634, note 1.

74 Letter of 23 August 1937, in *PRKIII*, 633. One reason for including this quotation is in order to correct the startling mistranslation of it in *SSCII*, 263–4, note 6. Viktor Varunts suggests that Ira did not go to Positano (*PRKIII*, 643, note 3), but the evidence that she did is in several letters of Katya's and a telegram from her husband.

75 Letter of 18 September 1937 (PSS).

76 Letter of 13 September 1937 (PSS).

77 *SSCIII*, 253.

78 *CASIII*, 63–4.

79 Letter of 14 October 1937, *CASIII*, 65.

80   Letter of 15 October 1937, *CASIII*, 66. Their letters crossed, and Ansermet's change of mind came before he had read Stravinsky's reply to his original letter.

81   Letter of 19 October 1937, *CASIII*, 66–7. The London concert was on the 18th. Ironically, Stravinsky actually made two unmarked repeats in his performance, and these are preserved in his recordings (but not the published score) as follows: Berlin, 1938, bars 1–2 of fig. 202 repeated; Cleveland, 1964, figs. 99–106 and bars 1–2 of fig. 202 repeated. See White, *Stravinsky*, 397.

82   *Les Fondements de la musique dans la conscience humaine* (Neuchâtel: A la Baconnière, 1961).

83   Letter of 22 October 1937, *CASIII*, 67–70.

84   Letter of 19 October 1937.

85   *SSCI*, 227.

86   Anne Ansermet, *Ernest Ansermet, mon père*, 89.

87   See Berners's letter to Stravinsky, 25 November 1937, in *SSCII*, 157. Berners sprayed his pigeons with harmless colored pigments, which added, he said, "a tropical touch to this wintry country."

88   The London concerts were on 18 and 19 October, Amsterdam on 28 October, Naples on 13 November, French radio on 6 December, Tallinn on 13 December, and Riga on 16 December.

89   Letter to Stravinsky, 7 December 1937, in *PRKIII*, 639.

90   *L'Intransigeant*, 29 December 1937.

91   Letter to Dushkin of 4 January 1938.

6   … AND WINS

1   Letter of 3 December 1937 (PSS)

2   Letter of 20 March 1938 (PSS).

3   Letter of 23 April 1938 (Christie's, London, 29 June 1994, lot 124).

4   *DB*, 91–2, passim.

5   The *pneu* (Paris express letter by pneumatic tube) has not surfaced, but its contents can be gleaned from Lourié's reply of 23 December 1937 (PSS).

6   Letter of 10 September 1938 (PSS).

7   See *SCS*, 457; also *CherP*, 136.

8   See Theodore's letter to his father, 30 September 1938 (PSS).

9   Lourié sent Stravinsky birthday greetings on 18 June 1939. "Don't grumble at me for not writing," he added, "but I don't like empty phrases and a proper letter would use up a whole notepad" (*PRKIII*, 688–9). This might well be a veiled hint at the need for an explanation.

10   The Sérénade, an occasional series mainly devoted to music by living composers, had been started by the marquise in 1932.

11   For an account of the occasion (15 January 1938), see Prokofiev's letter of 29 January to Myaskovsky, in *PMP*, 454; English translation in Robinson, *Selected Letters of Prokofiev*, 322–3. Stravinsky's memory (*Mem*, 67) that he last saw Prokofiev in New York in 1937 is thus incorrect.

12   "Igor Strawinsky s'afflige de l'indifférence des milieux musicaux officiels à son égard," *L'Intransigeant*, 13 October 1937. In the same interview, he asserted emphatically (in the implied context of the recent death of Widor) that he would never again offer himself as a candidate for the Academy.

13   Review of *Jeu de cartes*, *Nouvelle Revue française*, 26e année, no. 292, 1 January 1938, 149.

14   See, for instance, René Simon, "Entendrons-nous bientôt des oeuvres de Stravinsky à l'Opéra?" *L'Intransigeant*, 19 March 1938.

15   As well as the concerto, Igor and Soulima recorded Mozart's Fugue in C minor, K. 426, which remains Stravinsky's only published recording of another composer's music, not counting his own arrangements.

16   Letter of 15 May 1938 (PSS); emphases hers.

17   Undated telegram (PSS). "Execution Concerto Dumbarton Oaks digne de l'oeuvre."

18   Letter of 15 May 1938 to Strecker (PSS). The comical confusion only arises because of the French word order and, of course, the telegraphic style.

19   Letter of 16 May 1938, Mildred Bliss to Nadia Boulanger: see J. Brooks, "Mildred Bliss Tells Nadia Boulanger to Think of Herself for Once," in Ralph P. Locke and Cyrilla Barr (eds.), *Cultivating Music in America: Women Patrons and Activists since 1860* (Berkeley, Los Angeles, and London: University of California Press, 1997), 209–13.

20   Letter of 31 May 1938, in *SSCIII*, 264, note 77.

21   Letter of 26 May 1938, *SSCIII*, 264–5. Bach's concertos were, of course, written for the Margrave of Brandenburg.

22   André Coeuroy, *Beaux-Arts*, 17 June 1938.

23   Robert Brussel, *Le Figaro*, 17 June 1938.

24   The Rosenthal concert was on 30 May rather than the 29th, the actual anniversary.

25   Coeuroy, op. cit.

26   *Vendredi*, 17 June 1938; *Posledniya novosti*, 21 June 1938; *NRF*, 26e année, no. 298 (1 July 1938), 152–3. The passage quoted is from the *NRF*.

27   *Vendredi*, 29 November 1935. Pelagius was a fifth-century British heretic who maintained that man could avoid sin and gain salvation through his own free will, and without divine grace.

28   *NRF*, 1 July 1938, 152–3.

29   Letter of 19 August 1938, quoted in Peter Sulzer (ed.), *Zehn Komponisten um Werner Reinhart*, vol. 1 (Winterthur: Stadtbibliothek Winterthur, 1979), 84.

30   Letter of 22 February 1938 (PSS). Dagmar's letters are mostly in German, Stravinsky's in French.

31   Letter of 16 May 1938 (PSS), emphases hers. Original in English.

32   See Stravinsky's letter to Strecker of 1 June 1938, in *SSCIII*, 267.

33   But not in 1910 at the time of *The Firebird*, as Stravinsky states in *Expo* (130). Claudel was in Prague throughout that period.

34   *SSCIII*, 194, note 1. See also *SPD*, 318.

35   P. Claudel, *Journal*, vol. 2 (Paris: Gallimard, 1969), 236, entry for 5 June 1938; Claudel's letter to Milhaud of 15 August 1938 is quoted in ibid., 1004, note 3.

36   *Le Figaro littéraire*, 26 March 1938. Stravinsky's annotated cutting is in PSS.

37   Letter of 9 June 1938, *SSCIII*, 194.

38   See their correspondence in *SSCIII*, 194–6.

39   Letter of 25 June 1938, *SSCIII*, 267–8.

40   See Paul Claudel and Jacques Madaule, *Connaissance et reconnaissance: Correspondance 1929–1954* (Paris: Desclée de Brouwer, 1996), 271–82.

41   "Manifeste aux intellectuels espagnols," in *Occident*, 10 December 1937, with a postscript indicating that "intellectuals who wish to associate themselves with this manifesto can send their signature to one of the following addresses" (including Claudel's own). The text names no names and claims to be politically neutral, but this would not have deceived its likely readers. See also Claudel's poem "Aux martyrs espagnols," in *Oeuvres complètes de Paul Claudel*, vol. 2 (Paris: Gallimard, 1952), 240–6, especially the passage beginning "L'heure du Prince de ce monde." I am grateful to Christopher Flood and Maryse Bazaud for their help in locating these texts.

42   For information on the exhibition and its background, I am indebted to A. Dümling

and P. Girth (eds.), *Entartete Musik: Dokumentation und Kommentar zur Düsseldorfer Ausstellung von 1938* (Düsseldorf: DkV, revised and expanded ed., 1993); also Michael Meyer, "A Musical Façade for the Third Reich," in Stephanie Barron, *"Degenerate Art": The Fate of the Avant-Garde in Nazi Germany* (Los Angeles: Harry N. Abrams, 1991), 171–82; and Joan Evans, "Stravinsky's Music in Hitler's Germany," 569–77. The main festival opened on 22 May, the exhibition on the 24th.

43   27 May 1938, *SSCIII*, 265. Bela Bartók, whose music was not in the exhibition, actually protested against its exclusion.

44   For a digest of this correspondence, see *SSCIII*, 267–71, passim, much of it in footnotes. As ever, the translations have to be treated with caution. See also *SPD*, 554–5.

45   Letter of 31 May 1938 to Jean Marx in the Ministry of Foreign Affairs in Paris: *SSCIII*, 267, note 83. In due course, a kind of disclaimer was issued by the German Foreign Office, to the effect that "neither the person nor the work of Igor Stravinsky as a whole was intended to be rejected on the basis of the exhibition." German text in Joan Evans, op. cit, 105–6.

46   Letter of 28 January 1939 (PSS). Strecker was echoing a statement by the critic Herbert Gerigk in that month's *Nationalsozialistischen Monatshefte* that "there existed no grounds for eliminating Stravinsky from German musical life." Only in 1940, after the fall of France, was he officially banned on account of his French citizenship. See "Notiz zu Strawinsky," in Dümling and Girth, *Entartete Musik*, 226; also Joan Evans, op. cit., 107–8.

47   Letter of 5 June 1939 to Strecker (PSS).

48   See *SCS*, 83–4.

49   Letter of 24 May 1938 (PSS). The following correspondence is all in the same file.

50   Letter of 28 June 1938 (PSS)

51   Letter to Stravinsky, 6 September 1938 (PSS).

52   Letter of 10 July 1938 (PSS).

53   Letters of 19 and 25 August 1938. Theodore and Denise were staying in Morges.

54   *DB*, 93.

55   See Cingria's letter to Stravinsky of 24 October 1938, *SSCIII*, 124; also 121–2, note 23.

56   Letter of 24 October.

57   *DB*, 93 (entry for 8 November); also Cingria's letter (undated, November or December 1938) to Stravinsky, *SSCIII*, 125. At risk of laboring the point, however, it needs restating that the Cingria letters in *SSCIII* are so chaotically mistranslated and so senselessly edited as to be nearly useless for practical purposes.

58   *DB*, 93 (entry for 21 November).

59   See Katya's and Theodore's letters of late November to Igor, in PSS; also *DB*, 93, passim, and *Sfam*, 141.

60   *SPD*, 640, note 187. The letter has not surfaced, but I have taken the poem to be the one published as no. 122 in Ed Weeda (ed.), *Yuriy Mandel'shtam: Sobraniye Stikhotvoreniy*, 93–4.

61   I assume this to be the "scene" referred to by Vera in her diary for 18 December 1938. See *DB*, 93, where the Russian word "skandal" is too mildly rendered as "difficulties."

62   Letter of 31 December 1938 (UCLA, Kall). Kall had written on the 9th (PSS).

63   *Sfam*, 143. In his unpublished memoirs *(Are You the Son . . . ?)*, Soulima implies that they were all in fact aware of the risk of infection, two respectable doctors having already asserted that the situation was beyond remedy.

64   Letter to Strecker, 1 February 1939, in *SSCIII*, 271.

65   I have broadly accepted Denise Strawinsky's account of Katya's death, though well aware of possible motives for romanticizing the scene. See *Sfam*, 144–5.

66   Craft notes in *SSCII*, 506, that Stravinsky left for Sancellemoz on the 15th of March. However, the Sancellemoz admission records show that he arrived on the 12th.

67   To be exact, Anna was ill for about a week before she died. Soulima's letter of 4 June to his father (PSS) refers to an "intestinal obstruction."

7   TO THE MAGIC MOUNTAIN

1   Soulima Stravinsky, *Are You the Son . . . ?*

2   Letter of 17 June 1939 (sold at Sotheby's, London, 18 November 1988, lot 470).

3   Matthew Arnold, "Dover Beach."

4   John Culhane, *Walt Disney's Fantasia* (New York: Abrams, 1983), 12, 108.

5   Culhane (op. cit., 135) describes a meeting in November 1938 at which Disney rejected the idea of commissioning new scores, on the grounds that "those guys don't work that way."

6   A copy of the contract is in PSS. Speiser claimed (letter of 14 January 1939) to have worked hard to push the fee up, for which his reward was to have his own percentage reduced, from 25 to just over 20. Of the $6,000, Speiser took $1,250, while ERM's U.S. agents, Galaxy, took $1,000, leaving the composer with $3,750. See *Expo*, 145–6, for Stravinsky's own account of these transactions.

7   As was all music by non-U.S. citizens at this time, since the U.S.A. had never signed the Berne Convention on copyright.

8   See Valérie Dufour, *Strawinsky à Bruxelles* (Brussels: Académie Royale de Belgique, 2003), 116–9; also Paul Collaer's letter of 18 April 1939 to Stravinsky, in ibid., 236–7, and Darius Milhaud's review in *La Revue musicale*, 20e année, no. 191 (May–June 1939), 69/309. On the failure of earlier performances to materialize, see *SCS*, 173.

9   Soulima noted down the relevant passages on a sheet of paper now in the New York Public Library. The Mozart is bars 37–8 of the Andante cantabile; the Haydn, for example, bars 17–25 of the Andante.

10   Letter of 15 March 1939, *SSCI*, 437.

11   Rosenstiel, *Nadia Boulanger*, 310.

12   Letter of 28 March 1939 (PSS). Other documents are in the E. W. Forbes Papers of the Harvard University Archives. Some additional published information is in Elliot Forbes, *A History of Music at Harvard to 1972* (Cambridge, Mass.: Harvard University, 1988). Craft states (in *SSCII*, 503) that Stravinsky had already been sounded out the previous autumn and had accepted in principle via Nadia. This is supported, however, by no surviving documents except possibly Forbes's ambiguous remark, in a letter of 21 March 1939 to Dean George H. Chase, that the decision had been delayed by the death of Stravinsky's wife and daughter, and that Nadia would be acting as intermediary.

13   Letter of about 21 April 1939 (UCLA, Kall).

14   See his letter of 29 July 1939 to Strecker (PSS). The Library of Congress purchase remained intact, as confirmed by the head of the Music Division, Harold Spivacke, in a letter of 7 July (PSS). It was the Chicago Symphony Orchestra commission that now seemed doubtful.

15   Curiously enough, Cingria had written an article for the *Nouvelle Revue française* on the same subject and with the same point of view as Souvtchinsky's, but graciously withdrew it. Souvtchinsky submitted his own article to the *NRF*, but it was rejected. See *SSCII*, 505–6.

16   *Courrier royal*, 4 January 1936.

17   Notes on a dinner at the Café Weber, 3 November 1938, reproduced in facsimile in Igor Stravinsky, *Poétique musicale*, ed. Myriam Soumagnac (Paris: Harmonique Flammarion, 2000), 159–62.

18   See Roland-Manuel's letter to Stravinsky, 24 March 1938, quoted in *SSCII*, 506–7, as if

it referred to the writing-up of notes for Harvard. Craft bases his discussion of this and other early texts in the collaboration on the assumption that Stravinsky already knew about the Harvard post in late 1938 and that Roland-Manuel was already preparing his texts in March 1939. But the evidence is against this. Stravinsky was only invited in late March 1939, and he did not accept even provisionally until 11 April, being uncertain until then that his doctors would let him do so. There is no significant evidence that Harvard were even considering him before February or March (see note 12, above), and no direct reference to the Harvard project in any outside correspondence, before Stravinsky's letter of about 21 April to Kall and Souvtchinsky's of 26 April to Stravinsky, which not only argues for Roland-Manuel as the better collaborator (in terms suggesting that the issue is still open), but also refers to Souvtchinsky having just shown Roland-Manuel the chapter headings, "which he liked very much." Craft's remark that Stravinsky's "in-principle acceptance had been conveyed to the university by Nadia Boulanger months earlier [than March 1939]" seems to be either speculation or a reminiscence of Vera Stravinsky's. Nadia was not in the U.S.A. between May 1938 and mid-January 1939, and she did not reach Boston until late February or early March. (In any case, why transmit such information by carrier? The telegram was in universal use.) It seems, therefore, that Roland-Manuel's 24 March letter must refer to his *RM* article. As for the *pensée*, as Craft calls it (ibid., 506), which Stravinsky scribbled on the back of the envelope of this letter, it may or may not have been written down at the time but in any case is not directly related to the Harvard lectures. It deals with the word as sound material, a topic not raised in the lectures.

19 Letter of 1 May 1939 (PSS). Nevertheless, Stravinsky's outline, written out at almost exactly this time, still refers in the first lecture to "8 lectures," though it only provides for six. See the free translation in *SSCII*, 511–5.

20 Souvtchinsky's letter is in *PRKIII*, 671. His recently discovered lecture drafts have been described and discussed by Valérie Dufour in two important articles: "La *Poétique musicale* de Stravinsky," *Revue de musicologie*, 89/2 (2003), 373–92; and "Strawinsky vers Souvtchinsky: Thème et variations sur la *Poétique musicale*," *Mitteilungenen der Paul Sacher Stiftung*, 17 (March 2004), 17–23.

21 See the photo in Strawinsky, *Poétique musicale*, ed. Soumagnac, 61.

22 *La Revue musicale*, 20e année, no. 191 (May–June 1939), 70/310-80/320 (unhelpfully, the pages are double numbered, for the issue and the year respectively).

23 Dufour, however, finds the influence of Souvtchinsky also in this interview, and it must be admitted that the text gives the impression of having been written out in advance in answer to a set of presubmitted questions. So perhaps Souvtchinsky planned this as well.

24 *Poet*, 53–5. The equivalent pages in the Soumagnac French edition are 98–9.

25 *La Revue musicale*, op. cit., 15/255–18/258.

26 *Poet*, 131–2; Soumagnac, 150–1. Valéry's "Première leçon du cours de poétique" is in Paul Valéry, *Oeuvres*, vol. 1 (Pléiade edition, Paris: Gallimard, 1957), 1340–58.

27 *Poet*, 13–15 (Soumagnac, 71–2); 61 (103).

28 Letter to Kall of (about) 21 April 1939 (UCLA, Kall).

29 Letter of 24 April 1939 (PSS).

30 Letter of 26 April, *PRKIII*, 671.

31 Letter of 28 April to Souvtchinsky, *PRKIII*, 672.

32 Letter of 23 May to Igor Stravinsky, *PRKIII*, 676–8.

33 Letter of 28 April.

34 Letter of 23 May.

35 Ibid. Souvtchinsky had heard from Roland-Manuel that Stravinsky was offended, but he does not say why. His letter of 3 May, however, will have arrived on the 4th or 5th, probably the day Roland-Manuel left Sancellemoz. It passes lightly over the Soulima

issue, saying "I love Svetik, but I love you more." Soulima himself remarked later that it was "not easy to resist the attractions of this intelligent, cultured, whimsical, enigmatic, truly Dostoyevskian character. It was easy to trust him and count on his loyalties. It was also most dangerous to do so, as I learned" *(Are You the Son . . . ?)*.

36 Letter of 25 May, *PRKIII*, 678–80.

37 4 June 1939 (PSS). This is the letter that includes an account of what turned out to be Anna Stravinsky's final illness.

38 These particular anecdotes are from Soulima Stravinsky, interview with Thor Wood, and *Are You the Son . . . ?* (in the memoir, the car at the funeral is Misia Sert's). No doubt the reminiscences are colored by subsequent events, but since the tone and content of the interview and memoir are not in general hostile to Vera, I have seen no reason to doubt their essential veracity.

39 Igor wrote to Souvtchinsky on 25 June that "I expect Vera on about the 10th at the latest," but Vera's PS to Igor's next letter of 9 July suggests that she was there by then. Both letters in PSS.

40 Stravinsky's letter of 8 July 1939 to Souvtchinsky (*PRKIII*, 698) is contradicted by Denise Strawinsky's memory (private communication). But see also *DB*, 104, note 2, supporting the composer.

41 Letter of 8 July to Souvtchinsky.

42 Ibid. Olivier Messiaen's short article, "Le rythme chez Igor Strawinsky" (*RM*, op. cit., 91/331–2/2), was to prove seminal for postwar analysis, but in any case it is hard to see from its sensitive and intelligent contents what Stravinsky can have disliked about it. The jab at de Schloezer, who did not contribute to the *Revue*, clearly implies that Stravinsky supposed he had been involved in planning the issue.

43 "Igor Strawinsky: Législateur du ballet," *RM*, op. cit., 81/321–90/330.

44 See Stravinsky's letter of 8 July to Souvtchinsky.

45 The claim that the reconciliation was due to Vera is Craft's: see *DB*, 104, note 2. See also Stravinsky's letter of 31 July 1939 to Theodore (PSS).

46 The movement was finished in short score on 19 July.

47 Letter of 20 April 1939, *PRKIII*, 670.

48 Letter of 24 August 1939, quoted in Soumagnac, 39, and "Diaghilev: Les Ballets Russes," exhibition catalogue (Paris: Bibliothèque Nationale, 1979), item 347. Strecker was at Sancellemoz on the 22nd, and the French mobilized part of their reserve on the 23rd. Soulima, though he still had a Nansen passport, had been enrolled as a reservist and now held a French "livret militaire."

49 Letter of "Monday" [28 August] 1939 (PSS).

50 Letter of 27 August (PSS). The Biennale was cancelled.

51 Letter of 29 August, quoted in Soumagnac, 39–40.

52 Some manuscripts had already been lodged with ERM the previous April: see M. F. Astrov, letter of 15 April 1939 to Stravinsky, *PRKIII*, 666. Unfortunately, the list enclosed by Astrov with his letter seems to have been lost.

53 Rosenstiel, *Nadia Boulanger*, 312.

54 See his letter of 13/15 September 1939 to Theodore (PSS).

55 Letter of 17 September 1939, in R. Mallet (ed.), *André Gide–Paul Valéry: Correspondance 1890–1942* (Paris: Gallimard, 1955), 517.

56 This and other details are in Rosenstiel, *Nadia Boulanger*, 313. I am not convinced, though, by Rosenstiel's view that "Paul Valéry enjoyed Stravinsky's company only when the composer was playing the piano and singing." This is not borne out by the various accounts of their meetings, and especially not by François Valéry's reminiscence, in a letter of 4 November 1946 to Stravinsky, of "that singular affinity in aesthetic rigor and at the same time that opposition of philosophical ideas. I can assure you that that opposition is not fundamental . . ." Quoted in Soumagnac, 43.

57 Letter of 6 October 1939, in M. Chimènes (ed.), *Francis Poulenc: Correspondance 1910–1963* (Paris: Fayard, 1994), 485.

58 See his letter of 21 September 1939 to James B. Conant, the Harvard president (Harvard University Archive).

59 Postcard of 16 September 1939 (PSS). On the 21st he wrote another postcard informing Theodore that he was "leaving in two hours. Departure fixed for tomorrow."

60 As related by Vera in her letter of 4 October to Stravinsky. See *DB*, 95; also 93, note 6.

8 THE POETICS OF SURVIVAL

1   Compare Forbes's letter of 11 December 1939 to Nadia Boulanger (Harvard University Archive) with his much later account to Lawrence Morton (letter of 4 April 1961: UCLA, Morton), which claims that after one night and a jolly dinner Stravinsky asked point-blank if they could stay. I have preferred the contemporary report. Forbes asked $250 a month in rent, but Stravinsky insisted on paying $300, then forgot, and there was an embarrassment the following January when Forbes had to remind him. See Forbes's letter to Stravinsky of 5 January 1940 (PSS).

2   Frederick Jacobi, Jr., "Harvard Soirée," *Modern Music* (October/November 1939), 47–8, reprinted in Carol J. Oja (ed.), *Stravinsky in* Modern Music (New York: Da Capo Press, 1982), 57–8.

3   Alexis Kall, "Stravinsky in the Chair of Poetry," *Musical Quarterly*, 26, no. 3 (July, 1940), 284.

4   Jacobi, op. cit., 48.

5   Winthrop P. Tryon, "Stravinsky on Composing," *Christian Science Monitor*, 2 November 1939; compare *Poet*, 62, 61.

6   Jacobi, op. cit., 48.

7   *SPD*, 642–3, note 13.

8   Lawrence Dame, "Harvard Lectures Resemble Concerts," *Boston Herald*, 28 April 1940.

9   See *SCS*, 358–9.

10 "With the Fire Bird's Heart," *Philadelphia Inquirer*, April 1940. See also Dagmar Godowsky's letter to Kall, 27 October 1939 (UCLA, Kall).

11 Walter Piston, "A Reminiscence," *Perspectives of New Music*, ix/2 and x/1 (1971), 6–7.

12 Most of this information is derived from her long letters of October–December 1939 to Stravinsky, in *DB*, 93–110.

13 See his letter of 21 November 1939 to Vera in *DB*, 103–4. Handwritten drafts (in French and Russian) are in UCLA, Kall.

14 See Vera's letters to Igor of 28 October and 23 November 1939, in *DB*, 99, 104–5. A draft of the letter to Theodore, mainly in Kall's hand but with an autograph conclusion in Stravinsky's, is in UCLA, Kall.

15 Letter of 11 December 1939 to Vera, in *DB*, 107–9.

16 Almost all the information in this paragraph is collated from Vera's letters to Stravinsky, and her diary for January 1940, as published in *DB*, 100–10. However, the diaries in their published form are a very far cry from the originals, preserved in PSS. As has previously been noted, Vera's diaries are hybrid, part engagement book, part journal. Many entries that Craft works into coherent, literate texts are actually no more than jotted names, with times and intentions—a dinner, a trip to Chartres, a visit to the cinema. Dinners will be preceded by shopping lists (with amounts paid) in the margins, or across the top or bottom of the page. Different inks and pencils, and varying weights and sizes of handwriting, indicate that the jottings were made at different times, as in any engagement diary. Craft's editing completely obscures these distinctions, often leaving the reader unaware that an "event" was actually no more than a plan. He even

sometimes aggravates this problem by adding events (for instance, concerts) that he happens to know took place, even though Vera doesn't mention them—thereby completely subverting the whole point of a published diary, which is its personal contemporaneity. Worst of all, he imports extensive material from elsewhere, without ever identifying it, except in the case of the many letters he quotes within the text (and a few entries from Igor's diaries). The diary for January 1940 is particularly rich in such additions. For instance, the sad parting with Ira Belyankin referred to here, though presumably authentic, is nowhere to be found in Vera's diaries. The entry for 4 January, about life onboard ship, is almost entirely imported, the reader can only guess from where (and will not ask unless he chance to consult the Russian-language originals in Basle). For what it's worth, the original Russian text may be translated: "At Gibraltar, we make an interminable stop and only leave at 2. Two fat Jewish ladies ask sleepily: 'Was ist das für eine Station?' ['What port is this?'']," which hardly coincides with *DB* at all. Add to this confusion of sources the misallocation of dates, the seemingly casual errors of translation, the more or less habitual change of verbal tense for the recording of events (past in the original, usually present in the book), and the subtly or unsubtly nuanced footnotes—all by now well-known features of Craft's editing—and you have a death trap for helpless, credulous researchers. In nevertheless using it as a source, I have always referred to the original diaries. All references to imported text are noted.

17 *DB*, 110.

18 Culhane, *Walt Disney's Fantasia*, 22. Stravinsky seems to have made no complaint about the changes to which his score had been subjected. Contrary to his account in *Expo*, 145–6, he did not see the finished film on this visit.

19 In Carnegie Hall on 6 and 7 January. The program consisted of the Second Symphony, the *Nutcracker* suite, and the Violin Concerto with Erica Morini as soloist. Stravinsky also conducted concerts of his own music *(Apollo, Petrushka, Jeu de cartes, and Firebird)* on 4 and 5 January.

20 See Godowsky, *First Person Plural*, 239–40, for a colorful account of this episode.

21 The Princess Mestcher*sky, now married to the American Freudian psychologist Pearce Baily. See *SPD*, 644, note 22.

22 Letter of 17 January 1940 to Soulima, quoted in *DB*, 110–11.

23 Quoted in *ASS*, 8.

24 *DB*, 111.

25 Letter of Frederick Stock to Stravinsky, 15 January 1940 (PSS).

26 See *SCS*, 88. The Bedford wedding, though, was a purely civil ceremony. The couple solemnized their marriage in church seven months later, on 14 October, in Los Angeles.

27 Unlike, that is, the Shepherd in *Oedipus Rex*. Stravinsky had arranged to contact Sudeykin in New York in January, but wrote to him from Pittsburgh on the 16th excusing himself for not having done so, on the (apparently false) grounds that he was ill after his New York concert (RGALI). A photograph of Stravinsky's handwritten note of the invented facts of Vera's divorce is in *ASS*, 9. See also Vera's diary entry for 27 August 1945, in *DB*, 133, and the present volume, chapter 12, note 6. By publishing irrefutable evidence that Igor and Vera were never lawfully married, Craft seems unintentionally to introduce a new and interesting complication into the legal battles between himself and the composer's children.

28 The Boston concert was on 6 March, the Cambridge one on 8 March.

29 *DB*, 112; *Christian Science Monitor*, 21 March 1940. But most of the material in *DB* is imported from some source other than the diary. See above, note 16.

30 *Christian Science Monitor*, 11 April 1940.

31 See his telegram of 17 January 1940 to Mildred Bliss (PSS). The New York program repeated that of Boston and Cambridge.

32 The Exeter concert was on 17 March, the Boston ones on 28, 29, and 30 March.

33 See Stravinsky's letter of 24 March 1940 to R. W. Bliss (PSS).

34 Letter of 23 March 1940 (PSS).

35 Undated letter of, probably, January 1940 (UCLA, Kall: original in English, emphases hers). Stravinsky had mentioned Forbes's good-looking daughter Betsy when he saw Dagmar in New York, which suggests an earlier rather than later meeting. Dagmar refers to this in her letter but does not mention Vera.

36 *DB*, 112, entry for 17 March. Unfortunately Vera does not record the exact nature of the "scene."

37 Ibid., 31 March.

38 Her letter to Kall of 25 March 1940 (UCLA, Kall) more or less claims as much, and probably truthfully.

39 Letter of 7 May 1940 (PSS). He had written to Soulima and Milène on the 3rd (family collection). The delay in writing to Theodore seems to reflect the fact that (as Igor grumbles in his letter to the other two) Theodore, unlike them, had not written to congratulate him on his remarriage. Yury Mandelstam's letter appears not to have survived.

40 Golubeff (1891–1958) was an American-born, Russian-educated musician, writer, and translator (of, for example, Pushkin) who had shared Kall's house in Los Angeles for a time and had undertaken agency work for Stravinsky on the West Coast (see Kall and Stravinsky's joint letter of authorization to him of 21 December 1939 in PSS). He translated *Renard* and an essay, "Pushkin, Poetry and Music," supposedly by Stravinsky but in all probability ghosted by Golubeff himself. See Slim, "Unknown Words and Music, 1939–44, by Stravinsky," 310 and note 42. The Pushkin essay is translated in White, *Stravinsky,* 588–91.

41 *DB*, 114. Much of the information in the following paragraphs is from this source, including some material (such as the phrase quoted here) apparently not to be found in the original diary.

42 Peter Heyworth was told by Robert Craft that Klemperer met the Stravinskys at the station and "immediately insisted on taking them on a tour of the area": *Otto Klemperer,* vol. 2, 105. But for various reasons this seems to me far-fetched.

43 See Stravinsky's letter to Natalya Koussevitzky, 18 June 1940 (the composer's fifty-eighth birthday) (LoC, Koussevitzky). English translation in Victor Yuzefovich, "Chronicle of a Non-friendship: Letters of Stravinsky and Koussevitzky," *Musical Quarterly,* 86 (2002), 784–5.

44 *T&C*, 51 (the point is missing from the earlier *T&E*, Craft presumably not having yet studied these particular sketches); also *SPD*, 368. The notation, curiously enough, is dated 19 October 1939.

45 Letter of Chávez to Stravinsky, 25 January 1941. But Craft (*SPD*, 367) says that the problem was caused by factory noise.

46 *Expo*, 72.

47 *DB*, 115.

48 Letter of 14 August 1940 (PSS). According to Soulima *(Are You the Son . . . ?),* he had himself secured Rieti's release from internment through the good offices of the local Prefet, a music lover who had befriended Soulima, lodged him in his own house, and provided him with a piano.

49 See Vera Stravinsky's letter of 19 August 1940 to Eleanor Schreiber, in *DB*, 116. Vera was asking Mrs. Schreiber, who lived in Zurich, to transmit money to Milène.

50 Letter to Theodore of 1 September 1940 (PSS).

51 17 August is the date on the sketch score of the symphony in PSS. However the autograph full score in the Library of Congress is dated 19 August.

52 W. E. Oliver, "Bolm Ballet Bowl Event," *Los Angeles Evening Herald and Express,* 28 August 1940.

53 Ibid. On the 20th, Mikhail Fokine, the ballet's original choreographer and nominal author of its scenario, had written to Stravinsky protesting at the use of his scenic and choreographic ideas in a reworked form by a choreographer so well acquainted with the original that he could not fail to steal from it. Stravinsky and Bolm replied by night letter (26 August [PSS]) that they were presenting only the 1919 suite, which obviously necessitated a fresh approach; in any case the work was in the public domain. As for the question of moral rights, they added, "we are surprised you lack confidence in us. . . ." Had Fokine attended the performance, he would have read in the program-book a description of the staging that began with the words: "Retaining the original fairy-tale and characters, [Bolm] has simplified the story . . ." and he would have remembered pointing out in his letter that "it isn't a fairytale turned into a ballet (there is no such fairytale), but a story based on the study and combination of a lot of fairytales." But he would still have gone home empty-handed.

54 The Nazi ban was announced by Peter Raabe, president of the Reichsmusikkammer, on 1 February 1940 (*Amtliche Mitteilungen der Reichsmusikkammer*, Jahrgang 7, no. 2, 15 February 1940, 8), though since he was glossing an earlier ban (18 September 1939) on the works of living enemy—including French—nationals (ibid., J. 6, no. 19, 1 October 1939, 57), it could be argued that Stravinsky had theoretically been banned from that date. Raabe simply took time to realize that Stravinsky was French.

55 Two days after this visit, he and Vera solemnized their marriage in a short ceremony in the Russian church on Micheltorena Street, Silverlake. See *DB*, 117, note 1.

56 He was in fact by no means unequivocally hostile. When *Fantasia* came up in conversation with Hindemith in New York the following January, Hindemith found the whole idea "truly unedifying," but added that "Igor appears to love it" (letter of 30 May 1941 to Willy Strecker, in Skelton, ed., *Selected Letters of Paul Hindemith*, 177).

57 The first public showing was in New York on 13 November 1940.

58 On 21 February 1941 the *New York Times* reported that *The Firebird* was one of several "new musical numbers" that Disney had in production, possibly for a second *Fantasia*. *Renard* and *Petrushka* were said to be "also under consideration."

59 Letter to Stone of 2 October 1940 (PSS).

60 Robert Craft has, however, suggested that the idea came from the violinist Sol Babitz, who was a jazz fan (private communication).

61 The sketch (in PSS) is dated 1–14 October 1940. In fact the provision of a concert arrangement for solo piano was one of the conditions of the agreement Stravinsky entered into with Mercury Music Corporation three months later (2 January 1941), after AMP had decided they did not want to publish the piece. According to a letter of 20 December 1940 from Leonard Feist, president of Mercury, to Stravinsky (PSS), he had heard about the Tango from Ernest Voigt of AMP. Mercury themselves hired an arranger and a writer, who duly produced a lyric but then decided to make himself awkward over terms. This difficulty was never resolved, and Mercury had to content themselves with publishing the piano arrangement.

62 For a brief period in the spring, he had thought of selling the symphony's dedication to the highest bidder, until he was called to order by his agent, Paul Stoes. See Stoes's letter of 29 March 1940 (PSS). In a letter of 14 April to the conductor of the Chicago Symphony Orchestra, Frederick Stock, Stravinsky claimed that he had always meant to dedicate the symphony to the CSO, but had merely delayed confirmation until the contract was signed.

63 Edward Barry, "Stravinsky's New Symphony Stirs Acclaim," *Chicago Daily Tribune*, 8 November 1940.

64 Eugene Stinson, "Music Views," *Chicago Daily News*, 8 November 1940.

65 See *SCS*, 419.

66 Edward Downes, "Igor Stravinsky: Plans and Views of a Tonal Giant," *Boston Evening*

Transcript, 21 October 1939. But at the first performance, the work was billed as "Symphony, C major."

9   A HOUSE IN THE HILLS

1   *DB*, 117.

2   Letter of 4 December 1940 (BN, Boulanger).

3   "Stravinsky is nuts about swing: 'I love swings, I love all kinds of swings. Now it is to the Harlem I go. It is so sympathetic to watch the negro boys and girls dancing' " (*New York World Telegram*, 15 January 1941). Whether or not Stravinsky still or ever spoke such English, it clearly suited interviewers to color their reports with picturesque details of the kind.

4   See Vera's letter to Kall, 4 January 1941 (UCLA, Kall); also *DB*, 117–8.

5   From Washington he also went to Baltimore to conduct (7 January). In *Expo* (80), Stravinsky claims to have worked from the piano score of the Tchaikovsky, but if so his aural memory of the original (last heard, presumably, in the twenties) must have been excellent, since his version is more a practical reduction of Tchaikovsky's score for a smaller orchestra (including piano) than a new arrangement. Only in the coda, where Tchaikovsky's string music is rescored for wind, are the differences in any way fundamental, while harmonic and rhythmic changes, of the *Pulcinella* or *Fairy's Kiss* variety, are entirely lacking.

6   He also conducted the performance on the 24th, but then he went down with flu again and missed the final performance on the 26th. On the 21st he had attended the premiere of Weill's *Lady in the Dark* and, according to *Expo* (66), went onstage at the end to shake Weill's hand.

7   *Dial*, 48.

8   Ibid.

9   Edwin Denby, "With the Dancers," *Modern Music* (March–April 1941), 197–8.

10   Henry Simon, "The Ballet Tangles Prettily with Stravinsky," *PM*, 23 January 1941. The headline writer, as so often, had read the article carelessly.

11   *Dial*, 48; see also *Conv*, 102.

12   Simon, op. cit.

13   Denby, op. cit., 198.

14   Letter of 23 January 1941, *SSCII*, 296, note 17. The letter has not surfaced in the Tchelitcheff file in PSS.

15   Taper, *Balanchine*, 321. Balanchine practiced what he preached; his later (1972) and presumably quite different ballet to this music was called, simply, *Violin Concerto*.

16   *DB*, 119: entry for 25 February.

17   See her letter to Olga Sallard, quoted without date in *SPD*, 644, note 24. Stravinsky's remark is in his letter of 10 April 1941 to Victoria Ocampo, quoted in ibid.

18   Letter to Dushkin, 29 December 1941, in *SSCII*, 311.

19   *Opera* (San Francisco), October 1946, quoted in *SPD*, 359.

20   Soulima Stravinsky, interview with Thor Wood.

21   *ImpLif*, 119.

22   Vera and Igor to Kall, 11 July 1941 (UCLA, Kall).

23   Acosta, *Here Lies the Heart* (London: André Deutsch, 1960), 118.

24   Compare *DB*, 123 (3 September), and Godowsky, *First Person Plural*, 243–4. *DB* calls Dagmar's contribution "explanations," but "to have things out" is perhaps a better rendering of the Russian verb "nagovorit'sya." Vera's remark that Dagmar contacted them "as if nothing had happened" indicates that she had been warned off, by either Igor or Vera herself, in New York. But the precise details are impossible to disentangle.

More intriguingly, there exists an English-language "summary" of the 1941 diary in Vera's hand that suggests that Dagmar rang to invite them to a cocktail party and only came round because Igor insisted, a curious echo of his supposed insistence that Vera and Katya Stravinsky meet in 1925. But the diary summaries are impossible to date and, therefore, to trust.

25 *DB*, 123, passim.

26 Letter of 11 March 1941 (PSS). Stravinsky had just supported Rieti's application for a post at the Curtis Institute.

27 Janssen's commission letter is dated 30 September 1941. Stravinsky was paid an immediate advance of $500 on a total fee of $1,500.

28 See Nadia's letter to him of 17 March 1941 (PSS).

29 See his letter of 10 April 1941 to Victoria Ocampo (PSS).

30 See Strecker's letter to Hans Gebhardt, 17 April 1941 (copy in PSS). Soulima became a French citizen only in 1947.

31 See Igor Stravinsky's letter of 29 July 1941 to Nadia Boulanger (BN, Boulanger); also *Sfam*, 150.

32 Letter of 20 June 1941 (PSS).

33 Undated letter (December 1941), Milhaud to Stravinsky (PSS).

34 Letter of Stravinsky to Milhaud, 27 September 1942 (PSS).

35 Letter of Milhaud to Stravinsky, 25 August 1943 (PSS).

36 See Milhaud's letters to Stravinsky of 21 January 1944 and 12 September 1944, respectively (PSS). Money and food parcels were also sent on Stravinsky's account by Vittorio and Elsie Rieti. See Igor Stravinsky's letter to Theodore, 20 June 1941; also Rieti to Stravinsky, 13 August 1941 (PSS).

37 Letter of 16 July 1941 (PSS). The performance was on the 10th. The orchestral arrangement was by a certain Felix Guenther, and it presumably differed from the later (1953) version published under the composer's own name. The violin arrangement was by Dushkin himself, done no doubt in collaboration with Stravinsky in New York early in the year, notwithstanding Robert Craft's claim that it was by Sol Babitz (see *ImpLif*, 128). The evidence that it was Dushkin's work is in Feist's letter to Stravinsky, 3 June 1941 (PSS). Babitz certainly did work with Stravinsky (on the Violin Concerto) in the fortnight or so between the composition of the Tango and Stravinsky's departure for the East Coast, and he may of course have drafted an arrangement at that time. But there is apparently no actual evidence that he did. Dushkin's recital was on 31 March 1941.

38 Howard Taubman, "Dushkin Presents Stravinsky Work," *New York Times*, 1 April 1941.

39 Letter to Koussevitzky, 25 December 1941 (LoC, Koussevitzky). English translation in Yuzefovich, "Chronicle of a Non-friendship," 790–1. After the U.S.A.'s declaration of war on Germany earlier that month it became harder for AMP to circumvent the blocking of their Schott account. Voigt managed this, in the end, by simply retaining Schott monies in an internal clients' account and releasing percentages to the various composers concerned, including Stravinsky.

40 Telegram of 11 August 1941 (PSS).

41 *Mem*, 99. The "information" in the new edition of the conversations (*MRC*, 234) that the arrangement was made in 1940 and conducted that August in the Hollywood Bowl is completely fictitious. Similarly, the theory in *SPD*, 368, that the idea came from Stravinsky's lawyer Aaron Sapiro does not hold water, as Sapiro only came on the scene in 1942. I am grateful to Colin Slim for confirming that the idea was Andersson's.

42 Letter to Leonard Feist, 14 August 1941 (PSS). Stravinsky had made his own copy of the first violin part, presumably as an aide-memoire, for his Hollywood Bowl concert in August 1940 (it is reproduced in facsimile in *ASS*, 13). But one cannot deduce from this that he had already at that time thought of rearranging the anthem.

43 Feist to Stravinsky, 19 August 1941 (PSS).

44 Letter of 19 September 1941 (PSS).

45 Isabel Morse Jones, *Los Angeles Times*, 15 October 1941.

46 See below, chapter 10.

47 *DB*, 125.

48 See Stravinsky's letter to Nadia Boulanger, 24 March 1942 (BN, Boulanger).

49 Quoted in Alfred Frankenstein, "Stravinsky in Beverly Hills," *Modern Music*, vol. 19, no. 3 (March–April 1942), 179; reprinted in *Stravinsky in Modern Music*, 69–71.

50 Ibid, 180.

51 "Stravinsky's Latest Work Introduced," *Los Angeles Times*, 9 February 1942.

52 "The Dance Element in Stravinsky's Music," in Minna Lederman (ed.), *Stravinsky in the Theatre*, 84; see also Stephen Walsh, *The Music of Stravinsky* (London: Routledge, 1988), 184–5.

53 Letter of 4 November 1941 (PSS).

54 See Katya's letter to Igor, 11 January 1935 (PSS).

55 Letter of 27 February 1946 (PSS).

56 Letter of 4 December 1941 (PSS).

57 See his letter to Dushkin, 29 December 1941, reporting the phone conversation, in *SSCII*, 311, and note 63.

58 Raksin, "Composer in Paradise," in Carol Merrill-Mirsky (ed.), *Exiles in Paradise* (Los Angeles: Hollywood Bowl Museum, 1991), 93–4. Stravinsky himself made the more familiar version for symphony orchestra later that same year, completing it on 5 October 1942. The autograph fair copy of the piano score, in the Library of Congress, is dated 15 February 1942.

59 Interview for Radio-Canada, Montreal (1945), quoted in Charles Joseph, *Stravinsky Inside Out* (New Haven and London: Yale University Press, 2001), 20.

60 Letter to Dushkin, 29 December 1941, op. cit.

61 I have précised the version in Taper, *Balanchine*, 177–8.

62 The Tchaikovsky reference is in figs. 5–6 (cf. Symphony no. 4, second movement, bar 118, etc.). The Schubert reference in *Danses concertantes* is at fig. 161. It seems, incidentally, to refute Joseph's suggestion (*Stravinsky Inside Out*, 20) that the idea for the Schubert parody was Balanchine's.

63 George Ritchie, "Circus Opens in Gay Splendor," *New York Sun*, 10 April 1942. Zorina appeared only on the opening night.

64 George Brinton Beal, "Stravinsky and the Elephants" (Boston Symphony Orchestra Concert Bulletin, 13–15 January 1944); quoted in White, *Stravinsky*, 413–4.

65 Letter of Ernest Voigt to Stravinsky, 3 June 1942. Stravinsky had sold Ringling the exclusivity, for circus performance only, for a year, and White (op. cit., 414) claims that it was in fact performed 425 times.

66 Nadia Boulanger, who saw him at Arthur Sachs's house in Santa Barbara that March, later recalled Stravinsky's pleasure in working on the elephant ballet. But this was probably pleasure at having earned a large sum for writing an enjoyable piece. Her assertion that "he would himself have paid to write this 'Circus Polka' " is pure fantasy. See Bruno Monsaingeon, *Mademoiselle: Conversations with Nadia Boulanger*, trans. R. Marsack (Manchester: Carcanet, 1985), 40.

67 A. Tansman, *Igor Stravinsky, The Man and His Music*, trans. T. and C. Bleefield (New York: Putnam, 1949), 251.

68 *Expo*, 77.

69 *SPD*, 371. The book also contains an excellent color reproduction of one page of the final composition draft: plate 12, facing p. 400.

70 Composer's statement in the program note for the first performance of the Symphony in Three Movements, New York, 24 January 1946.

71 *Dial*, 52. "Supposedly" because the authenticity of much of *Dial* is at least suspect. For

the first performance of the symphony in January 1946, Ingolf Dahl supplied a program note in which he hinted at, without specifying, a connection with the war, but two years later Stravinsky wrote to him denying that he had ever approved such an interpretation (letter of 9 February 1948, PSS).

72 Tom Chase, "Stravinsky Plans 'Puritan' National Anthem for Hub," unidentified Boston paper, 12 January 1944 (cutting in PSS).

73 See *DB*, 125–8, passim; also *SPD*, 360.

74 *SPD*, 325.

75 "Master Mechanic," *Time*, 26 July 1948, 46. The detail about the agent proves that the story is a fabrication.

76 See Rieti's letter to Stravinsky of 5 March 1942 (PSS). Rieti had previously mentioned the Bellini ballet in a letter of 13 August 1941. Stravinsky's letter of 10 March to Rieti strongly implies that the idea had not been his; see Franco Carlo Ricci, *Vittorio Rieti* (Naples and Rome: Edizioni Scientifiche Italiane, 1987), 407–9, also *SSCIII*, 279–80, note 4.

77 Letter to Ernest Voigt (AMP), 19 March 1942, in *SSCIII*, 279. In *Stravinsky and Balanchine* (New Haven: Yale University Press, 2002), 172, Charles Joseph refers to a vocal score Stravinsky had bought of Donizetti's *Linda di Chamonix*. "The composer chose fifteen excerpts, each carefully marked in the score." But the markings are those of a previous owner, cueing the part of Linda. There is no evidence of a particular intention on Stravinsky's part.

78 Telegram to Koussevitzky, 14 June 1942 (LoC, Koussevitzky): Yuzefovich, "Chronicle of a Non-friendship," 799.

79 Letter of 4 December 1941 (PSS).

80 *DB*, 125.

81 Ingolf Dahl, program note for the first performance of the Symphony in Three Movements, Boston, 24 January 1946.

10 TO EARN IS HUMAN

1 Letter of 25 July 1942 (PSS): in *SSCIII*, 283, but with the quoted passage omitted. This is the letter in which he announces the recent completion of the work (though the full score was not finished until 18 August).

2 Letter to Nicolas Nabokov, 5 October 1943, in *SSCII*, 369–70. The same point was made in the program note of the first performance, in Boston, January 1944, quoting Stravinsky. See Lawrence Morton, "Stravinsky at Home," in J. Pasler (ed.), *Confronting Stravinsky* (Berkeley, Los Angeles, London: University of California Press, 1986), 337. An early sketch in PSS is labelled "Danses norvégiennes."

3 *Expo*, 77n.

4 Pinning down Stravinsky's source is in fact rather more complicated than the actual music. In 1943 (letter of 5 October) he told Nabokov that he had found the collection in the library and that it was published by Hansen, whereas *The Norway Music Album*, which Morton (op. cit. 337–8) identifies as the only collection that contains all Stravinsky's tunes, and of which there are copies in both the public and the composer's libraries, was published by Oliver Ditson (Boston, 1881). Uwe Kraemer, on the other hand, found all but three of the tunes in a four-volume collection called *Norges Melodier*, which *is* a Hansen publication (Copenhagen and Leipzig, 1875–1924). Stravinsky told Craft (*Mem*, 99) that the collection had been picked up by Vera in a secondhand bookshop, but he did not identify it. Perhaps he borrowed the Hansen collection from the library then later found a secondhand copy of Ditson.

5 *Mem*, 99.

6   M. Bernard (ed.), *Pesni russkago naroda* (Moscow: Jurgenson, 1886). This source, like the *Norway Music Album*, was first identified by Morton (op. cit., 335–6). For an exhaustive account of Stravinsky's borrowings, complete with music examples, see *SRT*, 1623–47.

7   Letter of 15 July 1942 (PSS), emphases hers.

8   *Dial*, 42. Such remarks in the later conversation books often, though, look like conclusions from an analysis of the music or sketches, an activity foreign to Stravinsky but natural to Craft. Anthony Powers, a Boulanger pupil, tells me that piano duo (four hands on two pianos) was the standard medium for play-through in Nadia's analysis classes.

9   The manuscript materials are in PSS.

10 See his letter of 19 May 1941 to Nadia Boulanger (PSS). In *SSCI*, 239–41, the relevant text has been transposed as the second paragraph of his letter of 29 July, while two paragraphs from the 29 July letter are printed as paragraphs 2 and 4, respectively, of the letter of 19 May.

11 The *Polka* was completed on the 5th, the symphony movement, as it became, on the 15th.

12 *DB*, 127.

13 Mann, *Tagebücher, 1940–43* (Frankfurt: S. Fischer, 1982), 618.

14 *Expo*, 77. I am grateful to Jon Burlingame, a specialist in film-music history at the University of Southern California, for confirming from his own research in the Twentieth Century–Fox archives my hunch that the *Bernadette* idea was never more than a casual suggestion between friends. No evidence survives, he tells me, that Stravinsky was ever considered for the film by the studio itself.

15 *Expo*, 77n. In the novel, Rochester is riding home late one January afternoon when his horse slips on the ice and he is helped by Jane. Perhaps the intrusion of a hunting scene was a veiled protest on the part of Twentieth Century–Fox.

16 In February Aaron Copland was contracted instead and came to Hollywood. On 22 March he dined (with George Antheil) at the Stravinskys' house (*DB*, 127–8). For Copland's involvement in *North Star*, see Howard Pollack, *Aaron Copland: The Life and Work of an Uncommon Man* (London: Faber and Faber, 1999), 378–83.

17 *DB*, 127.

18 S. Bertensson and J. Leyda, *Sergei Rachmaninoff: A Lifetime in Music* (Bloomington: Indiana University Press, 2001), 374.

19 On Diamond's complicated relationship with Nadia, see Rosenstiel, *Nadia Boulanger*, 280–1.

20 *DB*, 128.

21 See *SCS*, 355.

22 *DB*, 130, note 3.

23 Stravinsky's letter of acceptance, 9 April 1943, is quoted in *SPD*, 645, note 37, but has not come to light in either PSS or the Library of Congress.

24 Slonimsky, *Perfect Pitch* (Oxford: Oxford University Press, 1988), 105. "Considering that Koussevitzky was himself a Jew," Slonimsky adds impishly, "born nearer to Odessa than I, the remark was fantastic in its rudeness."

25 *T&E*, 152, note 7. The remark was expunged from *T&C*, 228, the equivalent British edition of that text.

26 *DB*, 128. It is hard to resist adding that the word "Eulogy" suggests a pun on "Eule," the German for an owl.

27 Letter of 9 July 1943 (LoC, Koussevitzky). Yuzefovich's translator, Marina Kostalevsky, renders the crucial phrase "muzïka na lone prirodï" as "music at the heart of nature." See "Chronicle of a Non-friendship," 806–7.

28 Ernest Voigt had died in the spring.

29 *T&C*, 228–9. The book is credited solely to Stravinsky, while the American volume,

T&E, which includes extensive excerpts from Robert Craft's diaries, is naturally credited to both authors. As indicated elsewhere, however, both books are by Craft (though no doubt containing information supplied at various times by Stravinsky).

30 Letter of 11 October 1943 (LoC, Koussevitsky): Yuzefovich, "Chronicle of a Non-friendship," 813. The bars involved are the six before fig. 44, and the next six. The autograph full score is in the Library of Congress.

31 Night letter, 9–10 October 1943 (LoC, Koussevitzky): Yuzefovich, "Chronicle of a Non-friendship," 812.

32 Letter of 12 October 1943 (LoC, Koussevitzky): Yuzefovich, "Chronicle of a Non-friendship," 814. The letter of the 11th is also in LoC, with a copy in PSS. PSS also holds a slightly inaccurate handwritten draft of the 12 October letter.

33 The note (UCLA, Kall) is undated, and hard to date even speculatively, since St. Alexis's day is celebrated on different dates in the Eastern and Western churches (17 March and 17 July, respectively). "Song of the Bear" is the third of the *Three Children's Tales* (1916–17). I am grateful to Colin Slim for drawing my attention to this item and much else in the Kall Archive.

34 *SPD*, 357.

35 *DB*, 128, records a Warner Brothers lunch on 26 August 1943. But nothing came of it.

36 See Morton, op. cit., 335–6.

37 See his letter to Koussevitzky of 11 October 1943.

38 The AMP contract indicates that the arrangement had first been mooted, and commissioned, in 1941. See *SPD*, 660, note 62.

39 Nef had tried to book Stravinsky a year before, but at the time the composer had had no plans to come east. Nef wrote again on 30 September 1943, mentioning that he had been reading the *Poétique*; Stravinsky's letter of acceptance was written on the same day as his agreement to conduct *The Rite* in Boston, 11 October (PSS).

40 *Expo*, 141.

41 For a detailed account of the various *Rite of Spring* revisions, see Louis Cyr, "Le Sacre du printemps: petite histoire d'une grande partition," in F. Lesure (ed.), *Stravinsky: Etudes et témoignages* (Paris: J-C. Lattès, 1982), 89–147. A revised and updated English translation of this important article exists but has never been published. Cyr eventually came down in favor of 1922 for the first publication of the orchestral score of the *Rite*, but he admits that his argument is tenuous. The date usually given is 1921.

42 See Charles Joseph, *Stravinsky Inside Out*, 18–19, and *Stravinsky and Balanchine*, 175, for the latest perpetuations of this legend. *Stravinksy Inside Out* includes the well-known Boston police archive photograph of Stravinsky, taken in April 1940 when he applied for renewal of his temporary visa, with the caption: "Arrested in Boston, April 1940, for illegally arranging 'The Star-Spangled Banner.' " This same canard crops up in Tony Palmer's Stravinsky film *Once at a Border . . .* , and it still survives in Craft's commentary to the execrable omnibus edition of the conversations (*M&C*, 216). For a coolheaded account of the incident, see Nicolas Slonimsky, *Music Since 1900*, 4th ed. (London: Cassell, 1972), 779.

43 Letter to the *Christian Science Monitor*, 15 June 1944.

44 Compare this with the French text: "Car ce n'est pas l'art qui nous tombe du ciel avec un chant d'oiseau; mais la plus simple modulation correctement conduite est déjà de l'art, sans conteste possible," which, in the later published English text of *Poet*, becomes: "For it is not art that rains down upon us in the song of a bird; but the simplest modulation correctly executed is already art, without any possible doubt."

45 André Baltensperger, "Strawinskys 'Chicago Lecture' (1944)," *Mitteilungen der Paul Sacher Stiftung*, no. 5 (January 1992), 19–23.

46 *DB*, 130.

1   *DB*, 130.

2   Ibid. (entry for 31 March). Compare Stravinsky's letter of 6 April 1944 to Nadia Boulanger, telling her that he had found a copy and she need no longer look for one (BN, Boulanger).

3   Letter of 16 February 1944 (Rosenbach Library, Philadelphia).

4   The prelude was originally to have been composed by Hindemith, who, however, withdrew in August 1945, at which point Schoenberg was contracted. According to Craft, Schoenberg and Stravinsky asked to see each other's contract, to make sure the fees were equal (*SPD*, 646, note 39). But the dates argue against this. In any case Stravinsky's fee was $1,000, which Hugo Winter thought high, while Schoenberg, according to the copy of his contract which Shilkret sent to Aaron Sapiro, received $1,500. This, however, was a flat fee with no further rights, whereas Stravinsky retained a royalty on sales.

5   Tansman, *Igor Stravinsky*, 130.

6   Ibid., 131.

7   Telegram and letter of 11 April 1944, Winter to Stravinsky (PSS).

8   Whiteman had in fact supposedly tried to commission Stravinsky in 1925, the year after *Rhapsody in Blue*, but the composer had declined. See *SPD*, 373.

9   Letter of 17 April, Stravinsky to Winter (PSS).

10 *Mem*, 108.

11 Ibid.

12 For much detail on the sketches and composition sequence of the *Scherzo à la russe*, see H. Colin Slim, "Stravinsky's *Scherzo . . . à la russe* and its two-piano origins," in B. Haggh (ed.), *Essays on Music and Culture in Honor of Herbert Kellman* (Paris: Minerve, 2001), 518–37 (the ellipsis in the work title is a misprint). See also Christoph Flamm, preface to the Eulenburg edition of the two orchestral versions of the score (Mainz: Eulenburg, 1996). Curiously enough, amid much other information, Flamm does not identify the folk source of the music.

13 *Dial*, 53.

14 Letter of 17 February 1945 to Poulenc; in M. Chimènes (ed.), *Francis Poulenc: Correspondance*, 582.

15 See Stravinsky's letter of 4 June 1944 to Winter, and Rose's telegram of 8 June to Stravinsky (PSS).

16 Telegram, Winter to Stravinsky, 14 June 1944.

17 For details about Rose and his plans for *The Seven Lively Arts*, see John Schuster-Craig, "Stravinsky's *Scènes de Ballet* and Billy Rose's *The Seven Lively Arts*. The Abravanel Account," in S. Parisi (ed.), *Music in the Theater, Church, and Villa: Essays in Honor of Robert Lamar Weaver and Norma Wright Weaver* (Warren, MI: Harmonie Park, 2000). See also Stravinsky's correspondence with Winter in PSS, only patchily included in *SSCIII*, 296–9.

18 See David Drew, *Kurt Weill: A Handbook* (London and Boston: Faber, 1987), 416 and note. For the *Giselle* stipulation, see Alicia Markova, *Giselle and I* (London: Barrie and Rockliff, 1960), 103.

19 Letter of 27 June 1944, in *SSCIII*, 296. The new title had still not been found, however, by the time Stravinsky completed the work at the end of August. See his letter to Gretl Urban, 31 August 1944, in *SSCIII*, 298.

20 *DB*, 131.

21 See Winter to Stravinsky, 25 May 1944 (PSS).

22 Stravinsky to Winter, 4 June 1944, *SSCIII*, 294–5.

23   Edwin Denby, "Balanchine's 'Danses Concertantes,' " *New York Herald Tribune,*
     17 September 1944.

24   *DB,* 131. The concert was on the 26th of August, and the two musicians were apparently
     meeting for the first time.

25   Mandelstam had been transferred for a time from Drancy to a camp in the vicinity of
     Orleans, where he was visited by Soulima. The news of his death came eventually in a
     report from the Red Cross. See Weeda (ed.), *Yuriy Mandel'shtam: Sobraniye
     stikhotvoreniy,* xxi.

26   *Dial,* 50.

27   Schuster-Craig, op. cit., 289.

28   Letter to Stravinsky, 28 July 1944 (PSS).

29   See *SCS,* 363, 383. Arthur Prévost, the conductor and co-founder of the Brussels Pro
     Arte concerts, was Germain's brother.

30   Letter of 21 August 1944, which conveys Prévost's request (PSS).

31   *DB,* 131–2. But the published text glosses the original with a nonexistent "supposedly"
     (in case we miss the point of Vera's quotation marks) and omits the crucial "and,"
     which tells us that the professors and their wives were not even "supposedly" included
     among the most interesting people.

32   *SPD,* 645, note 30. According to Craft ("Pluralistic Stravinsky," *Stravinsky: Glimpses of a
     Life,* 306), Bukofzer had sent Stravinsky a copy of his *Speculum* article, "Speculative
     Thinking in Medieval Music," two years earlier, the effect of which Craft compares to
     that of Cingria and Handschin in the thirties. But there is not much evidence for this in
     Stravinsky's music in 1942, and since Craft was not yet on the scene, one wonders how
     he knows. Perhaps this is an example of speculative thinking in modern music.

33   Prévost gave the first performance of the *Elegy* in the Coolidge Auditorium at the
     Library of Congress (the theatre for which *Apollo* had been composed) in a concert in
     memory of Onnou on 26 January 1945. His unpublished recording of the piece, made
     four days later, reveals that he made an unmarked repeat of the first section, and also
     that the whole work stretched his technical resources (copy in the Library of Congress).
     Craft's attempt to redate the *Elegy* to the time of the *Danses concertantes* on graphological
     evidence (*SPD,* 372) is unfortunately at odds with all the other evidence including that
     of common sense.

34   *SPD,* 374; *Dial,* 53. See also Stravinsky's letter to Soulima of 12 December 1945 (private
     collection).

35   According to *DB,* 132, Denham telephoned on 2 November to invite Stravinsky to
     conduct.

36   Telegram to Stravinsky, 11 September 1944 (PSS).

37   Respectively: Louis Biancolli, *New York World Telegram,* 11 September 1944; John
     Martin, *New York Times,* 11 September 1944; Biancolli, op. cit. Biancolli thought the
     score bad, while denying it the excuse of not having been written for the dance, since he
     was under the impression that it had been.

38   Martin, op. cit.

39   Edwin Denby, *New York Herald Tribune,* 11 September 1944.

40   Denby, *New York Herald Tribune,* 17 September 1944.

41   *New York World Telegram,* 11 September 1944.

42   Letter of 17 September 1944 (PSS).

43   Rieti's letter of 14 September 1944 (PSS) and Stravinsky's reply of the 18th, in Ricci,
     Vittorio Rieti, 411–12.

44   Letter to Rieti, 18 September.

45   See Stravinsky to Winter, 8 October 1944, in *SSCIII,* 299, and Winter's letter of
     23 October (PSS).

46   Telegram of 30 November 1944 (PSS).

47 Telegram of 30 November 1944 (PSS).

48 Abravanel's account of the whole episode is in a letter to Eric Walter White, 28 February 1981 (HRC, White).

49 Ibid.

50 Anton Dolin, *Markova: Her Life and Art* (London: Allen, 1953), 242.

51 Letter to Abravanel, 4 December 1944 (HRC, White).

52 Howard Barnes, *New York Herald Tribune*, 8 December 1944.

53 *Time*, 18 December 1944, quoted in Schuster-Craig, op. cit., 289.

54 Letter to Vera Stravinsky, 15 December 1944 (PSS).

55 27 December 1944 (PSS).

56 Telegram from Abravanel to Stravinsky, 6 January 1945 (PSS).

57 *DB*, 128, entry for 21 May.

58 Compare *DB*, 131, with Vera's letter of 10 September 1944 (Rosenbach Library, Philadelphia). The ironic quotation marks in *DB* round the words "most beautiful" and "most famous" are not to be found in the original diary.

59 *DB*, 132.

60 N. Nabokov, *Old Friends and New Music* (London: Hamish Hamilton, 1951), 151.

61 Craft's first letter is dated 22 February 1944, Stravinsky's reply 27 February (PSS). See *SSCI*, 328, for a summary and excerpts.

62 Craft, "Encounter and Metamorphosis," in *Stravinsky: Glimpses of a Life*, 19–32.

63 Craft wrote on 29 March and 15 August 1944, but Stravinsky seems only to have answered the latter (19 August).

64 See Dorothy Lamb Crawford, *Evenings On and Off the Roof* (Berkeley: University of California Press, 1995), for this and much more information on Yates, Mullen, and the early history of the Roof concerts.

65 Ibid., 61, 64.

66 See note 2, above.

67 The fair copy of the Kyrie bears the copyright date 1944, that of the Gloria 1945 (PSS).

68 Craft, "Stravinsky—Relevance and Problems of Biography," in *Prejudices in Disguise* (New York: Knopf, 1974), 290–1.

69 Joseph, *Stravinsky Inside Out*, 74.

70 Ibid.

71 See Nadia Boulanger's letter to Stravinsky of 21 August 1944 (PSS).

72 *Expo*, 76–7. See also Craft, *Prejudices in Disguise*, 290.

73 Murrill, "Aspects of Stravinsky," *Music & Letters*, xxxii/2 (April 1951), 118–24.

12   DISTANT CLASHES OF ARMS

1 *New York Herald Tribune*, 2 February 1945. Later on there were side trips to Philadelphia, where he repeated his Chicago lecture and performed two-piano works with Vincent Persichetti, and (in early March) to Rochester and Montreal, where he conducted, of all things, Lalo's Cello Concerto, with Marcel Hubert as soloist.

2 Decca had already settled in 1943.

3 *DB*, 132.

4 See, for instance, his letter of 20 February 1942 to Ernest Voigt, urging AMP to acquire his works, as "I need a publisher . . ." (PSS).

5 Koussevitzky invited Stravinsky to his Carnegie Hall concert on 14 February, but Stravinsky declined as he was conducting *Apollo* for a broadcast later that evening. See his letter of 8 February 1945 (LoC, Koussevitzky): English translation in Yuzefovich, "Chronicle of a Non-friendship," 816. According to Vera's diary, Koussevitzky called on them on the 19th, the day before the AMP meeting (*DB*, 132).

6   Levy wired Stravinsky on 23 March 1945, inviting Stravinsky to telephone. There were then one or more meetings, after which Stravinsky summarized the position in a letter of 20 April (drafted, no doubt, by Sapiro) (PSS).

7   To recapitulate: *Petrushka* and *The Rite of Spring* enjoyed protection in countries signatory to the Berne Convention because ERM (in Berlin, the Russische Musikverlag) had copyrighted them in Germany, itself a signatory. Berne copyright in *Firebird*, on the other hand, had been established through legal action in the twenties (see *SCS*, 439–40). None of the three works had been protected in the U.S.A., which had never signed the convention, and of which their composer had not been a citizen.

8   Letter of Helen Jacobson to Sapiro, 27 July 1945 (PSS).

9   Letter of 14 August 1945 (PSS).

10 Lieberson to Stravinsky, 9 April 1945; Chase to Stravinsky, 22 June (PSS).

11 Letter of 18 December 1945 (PSS).

12 *The Prelude* (1850 text), Book X, 58–61.

13 Letter of 27 March 1945, in Chimènes (ed.), *Francis Poulenc: Correspondance*, 584–6 (phrase in internal quotes in English in the original).

14 "Strawinsky contre les imbéciles," *Carrefour*, 24 March 1945. Desormières had conducted the work twice.

15 "Un concert houleux," unidentified newspaper, March 1945 (cutting in PSS).

16 Sauguet, "Troisième festival Strawinsky," *La Bataille*, 22 March 1945.

17 Jolivet, "Assez de Strawinsky," *Noir et Blanc*, 4 April 1945; Nigg, "La querelle Strawinsky," *Combat*, 15 April 1945; Poulenc, "Vive Strawinsky," *Le Figaro*, 7 April 1945; Baudrier, "Lettre à Serge Nigg," unidentified newspaper, April 1945 (cutting in PSS).

18 Leibowitz, "Béla Bartók, ou la possibilité du compromis dans la musique contemporaine," *Les Temps modernes* (1947), 729.

19 Joan Peyser, *Boulez: Composer, Conductor, Enigma* (London: Cassell, 1976), 31.

20 "Schoenberg est mort," in *Relevés d'apprenti* (Paris: Éditions du Seuil, 1966), 271 (italics his). The article originally appeared as "Schoenberg Is Dead," in *The Score*, no. 6 (February 1952), 18–22. It appears retranslated into English in P. Boulez, *Stocktakings from an Apprenticeship*, trans. S. Walsh (Oxford: Oxford University Press, 1991), 209–14.

21 Letter of 18 August 1945 (PSS).

22 Lourié, "Neogothic and Neoclassic," *Modern Music*, 5 (1928), 3–8.

23 Letter of 25 April 1945, quoted in *SSCII*, 515–16.

24 See Schaeffner's letter of 1 September 1946 (PSS).

25 Radio Paris, 10 February 1944 (text in PSS).

26 The letter itself has not surfaced, but its contents can in general terms be deduced from Igor Stravinsky's letters to Soulima (30 March: private collection) and to Milhaud (23 May [PSS]), and Milhaud's to Poulenc of 19 June (private collection).

27 Letter of 23 May 1945 (PSS).

28 Letters of 3 January and 27 March 1945, passim: see Chimènes (ed.), *Francis Poulenc: Correspondance*, 577 (but with the information on Marcelle Meyer expunged), and 585 (originals: private collection).

29 Letter to Milhaud, 13 July 1945 (private collection).

30 See above, chapter 9, note 30.

31 Soulima's explanations are in *Are You the Son . . . ?*

32 The subject is first mentioned in Igor's letter to Theodore of 18 December 1945, which also indicates, however, that the Marions have already been invited and have accepted with enthusiasm (PSS).

33 Undated note, possibly a postscript to Bourdariat's letter of 25 April 1945, but dated by Myriam Soumagnac to February; see her preface to the *Poétique musicale*, 22. The chapter was, of course, largely the work of Souvtchinsky.

34 *Poet*, III, 110; Soumagnac, 137, 136.

35 Heyworth, _Klemperer_, vol. 2, 141.

36 Stravinsky wrote to Koussevitzky on 20 June that he had "just finished" the suite. See Yuzefovich, "Chronicle of a Non-friendship," 817. The letter is in English, which does not inhibit _SSCI_, 350, note 53, from rewording (and misdating) it.

37 Letter of 14 August 1945 (PSS).

38 The contract is dated 17 October 1945, and it specifies the exact lengths of the three movements.

39 Craft, "Discoveries in Stravinsky's Sketches," _The Moment of Existence_ (Nashville and London: Vanderbilt University Press, 1996), 272.

40 _Dial_, 51.

41 By 20 August, when he informed Gretl Urban of its completion. He told Rieti that the idea for a three-movement symphony was inspired by the latter's _Sinfonia tripartita_ (1944), which is dedicated to him. See Ricci, _Vittorio Rieti_, 166.

42 _The Billboard_, 29 September 1945; but the article carries the dateline 24 September.

43 _SPD_, 377. See also the correspondence between Sapiro and Woody Herman's agent, Herman Goldfarb, in PSS.

44 See Deakin's letter of 20 April 1945 to Stravinsky (PSS).

45 Telegram of 25 October 1945 (PSS).

46 Letter of 27 October 1945 (PSS). "Stinks" is in English in the original French text.

47 _DB_, 133. The ballet was choreographed by Todd Bollender and conducted by Emanuel Balaban.

48 _Dial_, 53.

49 Letter of 4 November 1945, in _SSCI_, 244.

50 David Hamilton, "Schoenberg on Records," _High Fidelity Magazine_ (September 1974), 70.

51 _Los Angeles Times_, 19 November 1945.

52 _Dial_, 106. Stein's account is in "Schoenberg and 'Kleine Modernsky,' " in Pasler (ed.), _Confronting Stravinsky_, 315. Stravinsky also claims that they "were in the recording studios on the same day," though there were probably no separate recording sessions and it was the concert that was taped. I have so far failed, however, to trace a copy of this recording, which is referred to by Morse Jones in her _LA Times_ review.

53 _Expo_, 78.

54 See his letter to Zirato of 8 December 1945, in _SSCII_, 437, note 6. The problem was that the _Symphony of Psalms_ also lacks violins and violas, so any normal orchestral filler (such as _Pulcinella_, which likewise has no clarinets) was ruled out. Stravinsky might equally have thought of his unperformed Kyrie and Gloria, each about the same length as the chorale, and scored within the available instruments. But from the start Stravinsky "heard" this music with children's voices on the soprano line; and in any case, he would not have expected a choir to learn so novel a work so quickly. Finally, he probably did not yet regard these pieces as complete. As early as March 1945, the (manuscript) full score of the _Symphonies of Wind Instruments_ had been among a group of scores he had asked Soulima to send from the Paris store; letter of 16 March (private collection).

55 _Expo_, 72.

56 See _ASS_, 16, for facsimiles of the two certificates. In ibid., 9, Craft implies that the divorce fraud was perpetrated in March 1940 at the time of their civil wedding, but in _SPD_, 635, note 91, he gives the date as 15 April 1945, and in _IVSPA_, as 5 August 1945. No evidence is adduced for any of these conflicting dates, but an entry in Vera's diary for 27 August 1945 is closest to the last date mentioned: "So as not to forget: I married Sud[eykin] on 11 February 1918 at Yalta. I divorced Sud[eykin] on 20 February 1920 at Tiflis" (_DB_, 133). See also above, chapter 8, note 27.

57 See _IVSPA_, 104, for a detailed account of these activities and a photograph of Vera in the gallery.

58 Sacher wrote on 30 December 1945; Stravinsky replied on 9 January that he could only accept if a maximum of twelve minutes' music was required (PSS).

59 Peter Hill, *Stravinsky: The Rite of Spring* (Cambridge: Cambridge University Press, 2000), 53.

13 ORPHEUS IN A NEW GUISE

1 In between, in New York the day after the Carnegie Hall concert, Szigeti recorded the early *Pastorale* in its version with wind quartet, under the composer's supervision. In the Carnegie concert, Claudio Arrau also played the Serenade in A.

2 See Winter's letters to Stravinsky of 24 February and 24 November 1944 (PSS).

3 Letter to Stravinsky, 8 April 1946 (PSS). "Humbleness" is in English in this otherwise Russian-language letter.

4 This may have been the occasion when, according to Craft, Haieff slept on the floor of the Stravinskys' compartment, since no other was available (*ImpLif*, 113). Craft places this on a journey from Los Angeles to New York, but Haieff apparently did not travel with the Stravinskys on any of their wartime or just-postwar transcontinental rail trips.

5 *DB*, 136; *ASS*, 26.

6 The San Francisco concerts included, on 22 March, the world premiere of the orchestral version of the *Scherzo à la russe*.

7 *New York Times*, 2 February 1945. See chapter 12; whatever might be said about individual pieces, the program (the Glinka, Tchaikovsky's second symphony, and Stravinsky's *Ode*, Piano Concerto, *Four Norwegian Moods*, and *Circus Polka*) undoubtedly lacked focus.

8 Letter to Stravinsky of 31 March 1946 (PSS).

9 Letter of 2 April (BN, Manziarly). Haieff's account is in his letter of 8 April (PSS).

10 Letter of 9 January 1946 (PSS).

11 See Berman's letter to Stravinsky of 7 February 1946 (PSS); also *DB*, 136. In a letter of 4 April to Theodore, Stravinsky says he has started work on the *Medea* music, which has to be ready by mid-July; but a postscript announces that the project has been called off, as they could not meet his terms (PSS).

12 Letter from Ralph Hawkes to Aaron Sapiro, 15 February 1946 (PSS).

13 See Stravinsky's letter of 7 April and Sacher's reply of 25 April; also chapter 37, note 12. Sacher offered 5,000 Swiss francs (about $1,200), on the grounds that Strauss had accepted this for *Metamorphosen* eighteen months before. He omitted to mention that the Strauss work is in twenty-three string parts and lasts half an hour.

14 See his letter to his son Theodore, 10 May 1946 (PSS).

15 Letter of 3 July 1946 (PSS).

16 See Stravinsky's correspondence with Massine in PSS.

17 The autograph score of the Concerto in D is dated 8 August 1946; the autograph score of the revised *Petrushka*, in the Pierpont Morgan Library, New York, is dated 14 October 1946.

18 "The man of talent is like a marksman who hits a target others cannot hit, but the man of genius is like a marksman who hits a target others cannot see." Bryan Magee, *The Philosophy of Schopenhauer* (Oxford: Oxford University Press, 1983), 171.

19 The contract letter is dated 7 May 1946 (*SSCI*, 265), but the proposal was probably brought by Balanchine in April.

20 The Stravinsky version is reproduced in facsimile in *DB*, 137; also in *Muzïkal'naya Akademiya*, no. 4 (1992), 190.

21 Taper, *Balanchine*, 220. They and Berman also discussed a possible new choreography for *Scènes de ballet*, but nothing came of it.

22 The notes, in Russian in Stravinsky's hand, are reproduced in Joseph, *Stravinsky and Balanchine*, 194 (originals in PSS).

23 Chapin, *Musical Chairs*, quoted in *SPD*, 347.

24 Letter of 17 January 1946 (PSS).

25 Letters of 25 April and 7 August 1946, respectively (PSS).

26 *Expo*, 38.

27 Letter of 11 April 1946 (BN, Boulanger).

28 Letter of 18 December 1945 (PSS). There had been a dispute between the two brothers over back payments of the rent on Denise's mother's flat in Paris.

29 See Païchadze's letter of 4 April 1946 to Stravinsky (PSS).

30 Letter of 25 October 1946 (PSS).

31 Sybille Bedford, *Aldous Huxley: A Biography. Volume Two: 1939–1963* (London: Chatto & Windus, 1974), 75.

32 *SCF* (94), 22.

33 Letter of 3 December 1947, quoted in Bedford, op. cit., 87.

34 *T&C*, 52; *T&E*, 46–7.

35 Taper, *Balanchine*, 221.

36 "On *Apollo* and *Orpheus*," *The Moment of Existence*, 295.

37 Stage directions printed in the score.

38 *T&C*, 53; *T&E*, 48. As usual the (inauthentic) texts of the two editions differ in many details.

39 N. Nabokov, *Old Friends and New Music*, 152. Stravinsky called it a "vielle," which Nabokov wrongly interprets as a viol. The medieval fiddle, played without vibrato, has a nasal, almost adenoidal sound.

40 *SPD*, 645, note 30. Bukofzer wrote on 8 April 1947.

41 *DB*, 138.

42 Quoted in Taper, *Balanchine*, 207.

43 *DB*, 139.

44 Craft, "Encounter and Metamorphosis," *Stravinsky: Glimpses of a Life*, 26.

45 The information that Stravinsky attended *Renard* rehearsals is in ibid., and also in *DB*, 139. By contrast, Todd Bollender, who danced the Fox, told Nancy Reynolds that Stravinsky did not attend any of the rehearsals (private communication from Dr. Reynolds, 2004).

46 The photograph was published in *AMC* under the misleading caption "Historic encounter." The admission that the two did not meet on this or any previous occasion is Craft's own, in *SSCI*, 331, note 8.

47 See Stravinsky's letter of 10 February 1947, replying to Craft's of 21 December, in *SSCI*, 329.

48 White's dating of the concerto's first performance to 27 January is an error, alas perpetuated by the present author in the Stravinsky work-list in *The New Grove* (2nd ed.).

49 See Stravinsky's letter of 25 January 1947 (misdated 1946), and Mrs. Bliss's telegram of 31 January (PSS).

50 Letter of 14 March 1947, *SSCIII*, 314.

51 Letter of 10 February 1947 (PSS).

52 Letter of 11 October 1946 (PSS).

53 Letter of 11 November 1946 (PSS).

54 Letter of 18 November 1946 (PSS). Messiaen was, of course, French, but it is not entirely clear from Stravinsky's letter whether he really thought him Belgian or was ironically pretending to think so.

55 Letter of 22 December 1946 (PSS).

56 This was noticed a few months later by Nicolas Nabokov, who, after spending some

time with Stravinsky in New York in early April 1947, wrote to Souvtchinsky that "I formed the impression he has something against you—some small irritation." See Yelena Pol'dyaeva, "Vtoroe pokoleniye," in A. Bretanitskaya (ed.), *Pyotr Suvchinskiy i ego vremya* (Moscow: Kompozitor, 1999), 186–7.

57 Letter of 19 April 1947, in *SSCI*, 245.

58 Sallard's letters are quoted by Craft in *DB*, 141, note 8, but the quotations (from otherwise inaccessible correspondence) are selective and patently hostile to Marion.

59 See his letter of 5 April 1947 replying to an enquiry of 31 March from Szigeti's agent, Herbert Barrett, about the possibility of a recording of the Divertimento (PSS).

60 I am grateful to Susan Palmer, archivist at the Sir John Soane's Museum in London, for confirming that the oils were never sent to Chicago.

61 This point was first made, as far as I know, by Lawrence Morton. See "Stravinsky in Los Angeles," in the program book of the *Festival of Music Made in Los Angeles* (Los Angeles: Los Angeles Philharmonic Association, 1981), 80–1.

62 Letter of 24 April 1947, Hawkes to Stravinsky (PSS). See also Stravinsky's reply of 11 May, in *SSCIII*, 315.

63 Letter of 23 June 1947, in *SSCIII*, 315.

64 Quoted in *SSCIII*, 109.

14 THE EYE OF THE NEEDLE

1 Letter to Stravinsky of 15 July 1947, in *SSCI*, 266.

2 Letter to Stravinsky of 16 October 1947, in *SSCI*, 269.

3 Letter to Stravinsky of 26 December 1947 (PSS). The letter is in *SSCI*, 269–70, but without the passage quoted.

4 As related to Christopher Isherwood. See Katherine Bucknell (ed.), *Christopher Isherwood: Diaries, Volume One: 1939–1960* (London: Vintage, 1997), 698.

5 Letter of 23 June 1947, in *SSCIII*, 315.

6 Letter of 26 September 1947, in ibid., 317.

7 Letter of 30 September 1947 (PSS).

8 See Spies's letter to Stravinsky of 17 March 1947 (PSS). Fine's performance was on 26 February.

9 Letter of 26 September.

10 The RCA contract was dated 8 July 1947.

11 See chapter 12.

12 Letter of 22 August 1947 (PSS). Stravinsky's contract was dated 28 May.

13 "A Run of Half Notes," *Los Angeles Times*, 9 November 1947.

14 Letter of 12 March 1948 (PSS).

15 Letter of 9 March 1949 (PSS).

16 See his letter to Stravinsky of 7 October 1947 (PSS).

17 Stravinsky to Hawkes, 7 October 1947 (PSS). The letter is in *SSCIII*, 318, but with the passage about Soulima omitted.

18 Letter of 7 October, *SSCIII*, 318.

19 Letter of 20 August 1947 (PSS).

20 Craft, unused material from interviews with the present author for the radio series, *Conversations with Craft* (BBC Radio 3, 1995), producer Andy Cartwright. Hereafter *CwC*.

21 Craft, "Encounter and Metamorphosis," in *Glimpses of a Life*, 27.

22 See Stravinsky's letter to Craft, 29 August 1947, together with Craft's commentary, in *SSCI*, 329–30.

23 *SSCI*, 329.

24 Letter of 5 September 1947, summarized in *SSCI*, 331.

25 Letter of 7 October 1947, *SSCI*, 331–2.

26 Letter of 7 October, *SSCI*, 332, which also quotes Craft's reply of 11 October.

27 Stravinsky to Craft, telegrams of 26 October and 4 November; Craft to Stravinsky, letter of 1 November (summary): *SSCI*, 333–4.

28 Letter of 10 December 1947, quoted in *SSCI*, 334–5.

29 Quoted in Charles Osborne, *W. H. Auden: The Life of a Poet* (London: Eyre Methuen, 1979), 225.

30 Alan Ansen, *The Table Talk of W. H. Auden* (Princeton: Ontario Review Press, 1990), 76–7.

31 Letter of 6 October 1947, in *SSCI*, 299.

32 Letter of 12 October 1947, in *SSCI*, 299.

33 *Mem*, 157.

34 Ansen, *Table Talk*, 17, 24.

35 *Mem*, 157.

36 *Mem*, 156.

37 *SCF* (94), 108.

38 Letter of 9 November 1947 (PSS). The letter is excerpted in *SSCIII*, 319–20, but with the Mozart request omitted.

39 As he told Albert Goldberg in an interview for the *Los Angeles Times*, 23 November 1947.

40 See Stravinsky's letter to Hawkes of 25 November 1947, in *SSCIII*, 320; also to Hawkes's assistant, Betty Bean, 10 December 1947 (in ibid. but the relevant passage omitted) and 12 January 1948 (ibid., 322). More curiously, he had previously asked Hawkes for music by Byrd (died 1623) and Purcell (died 1695) "as a sample of music in Hogarth's [born 1697] time" (see ibid., 319).

41 Letter of 5 October 1947, in *SPD*, 557.

42 Letter of 20 November 1947, in T. Page and V. W. Page (eds.), *Selected Letters of Virgil Thomson* (New York: Summit Books, 1988), 215–16.

43 Letter of 6 December 1947 (PSS).

44 Letter of 29 December 1947, quoted in *SPD*, 558, which also provides a useful summary of the whole affair.

45 *Poet*, 55. As it happens, the first English-language edition of the *Poetics* had just been published by Harvard University Press, translated by Arthur Knodel and Ingolf Dahl.

46 See Walsh, "Stravinsky's Symphonies: Accident or Design?" in C. Ayrey and M. Everist (eds.), *Analytical Strategies and Musical Interpretation* (Cambridge, Eng.: Cambridge University Press, 1996), 35–71, for a detailed examination of this topic.

47 Another possibility is that the prelude started life as an idea for a string quartet that Stravinsky had briefly toyed with writing for the Juilliard String Quartet. He had provisionally accepted the commission from William Schuman in July 1947; by January 1948 it had been put firmly into cold storage, but it was not actually cancelled until May 1950. See *SSCI*, 328, note 4, for relevant details.

48 Letter of 1 September 1946 (PSS). Leibowitz was a Polish Jew who settled in Paris in 1945, and who proselytized the work and method of Schoenberg (at that time largely ignored in France) through teaching, concerts, and two influential books, *Schoenberg et son école* (Paris: Janin, 1947) and *Introduction à la musique de douze sons* (Paris: L'Arche, 1949).

49 R. Leibowitz, "Two Composers: A Letter from Hollywood," *Partisan Review* (March 1948), 361–5.

50 Ibid., 365.

51 Letter of 24 November 1947, partly (mis)quoted in N. Nabokov, *Bagazh: Memoirs of a Russian Cosmopolitan* (New York: Atheneum, 1975), 171. The original is in the Nabokov Archive of HRC, Austin, Texas. Nabokov's story (in *Bagazh*, 172–3), of Craft having

failed to sign his postcard to Stravinsky and the latter asking Nabokov to track down its author, cannot as he claims belong to this Christmas visit, for reasons which will be obvious from the preceding narrative.

52 "Igor Stravinsky," *Atlantic Monthly* (November 1949), 21–7; reprinted in greatly expanded form in Nabokov, *Old Friends and New Music* (London: Hamish Hamilton, 1951), 139–67.

53 *Old Friends and New Music*, 155.

54 Ibid., 157.

55 Ibid., 148–51.

56 Letter of 3 October 1947, cited in *DB*, 142, note 4.

57 Letter of 17 December 1947 (PSS). For practical as well as political reasons, the planned festival was later moved to Munich, then eventually cancelled. Stravinsky notified Strecker in a letter of 23 March that he would not himself be coming.

58 Vera's letters of 2 and 7 January 1948, respectively, in *DB*, 143.

59 Stravinsky wrote to Koussevitzky on 15 March 1948 that they had cancelled their trip because of the risks. See Yuzefovich, "Chronicle of a Non-friendship," 822.

60 Letter of 13 January 1948, in *CASIII*, 86–7.

61 Night letter of 31 January, ibid., 99; *SSCI*, 231. For this whole January correspondence, see *CASIII*, 85–99, *SSCI*, 228–31 (Stravinsky's side only). Here and elsewhere the discrepancy of one day between the dates of night letters in *CAS* and those in *SSC* is apparently due to the fact that the editor of the former worked with the originals, which carry the date of receipt, while that of the latter worked from Stravinsky's drafts, which have the date of dispatch. In such cases, I have noted the date of dispatch. This also accounts for occasional textual discrepancies between the two editions.

62 Letter to Stravinsky, 1 February 1948, in *CASIII*, 100–1.

63 4 February 1948, *CASIII*, 102; *SSCI*, 232.

15 THE PROGRESS BEGINS

1 Letter of 16 January 1948, in *SSCI*, 304.

2 The attributions of these scenes in Paul Griffiths, *Igor Stravinsky: The Rake's Progress* (Cambridge, Eng.: Cambridge University Press, 1982), 14, are incorrect. An excellent, detailed account of the librettists' own collaboration is in Humphrey Carpenter, *W. H. Auden* (London: George Allen & Unwin, 1981), 352–7.

3 Ansen, *The Table Talk of W. H. Auden*, 76–7.

4 Letter of 28 January 1948, in *Mem*, 161.

5 Including, oddly enough, Robert Craft, who many years later questioned whether "irrational and emotionally indifferent acts hurtful to innocent others bring happiness to those who commit them?" ("Words for Music Perhaps," in *The Moment of Existence*, 24). But of course *The Rake's Progress* is specifically and deliberately a demonstration that they do not.

6 *SSCI*, 361.

7 See his letter to Auden of 18 October 1949, in *SSCI*, 309–10.

8 *SCF* (94), 1.

9 Letter of 9 March 1948, in *SSCI*, 338.

10 Craft's most vivid account of his background is in "Encounter and Metamorphosis," *Stravinsky: Glimpses of a Life*, 19–32. There is more detail but less entertainment in *ImpLif*, 3–56.

11 *SCF* (94), 6.

12 *DB*, 144. Craft's account of the episode is in "Encounter and Metamorphosis," 29.

13   *SCF* (94), 7.
14   A recording of the discussion is in the Library of Congress.
15   *New York Herald Tribune*, 12 April 1948.
16   *SCF* (94), 6.
17   Stravinsky's letter was published in the *New York Herald Tribune* on 18 April. Thomson's two reviews appeared in the *Tribune* on 12 and 18 April, respectively.
18   *DB*, 144.
19   Ansen, *The Table Talk of W. H. Auden*, 98. See also Edward Mendelson (ed.), *W. H. Auden and Chester Kallman: Libretti and Other Dramatic Writings by W. H. Auden* (London: Faber & Faber, 1993), xxiii. The idea was dropped.
20   Letter of 4 January 1948, in *SSCI*, 270.
21   *DB*, 144. The maquette and some of the cutouts are reproduced in *Stravinsky and the Theatre* (New York: New York Public Library, 1963), 43.
22   *T&C*, 53; *T&E*, 47.
23   *New York Times*, 28 April 1948.
24   *New York Herald Tribune*, 29 April 1948.
25   *New York Times*, 1 December 1957, quoted in *SPD*, 379.
26   In the poem "Musée des Beaux-Arts."
27   See *SCS*, 469 and 652, note 58.
28   Letter of 29 April 1948, in *SSCI*, 271.
29   Soulima was arriving on the 17th of June, which the composer had for many years celebrated as his New Style birthday. These days, though, he was celebrating it (correctly) on the 18th. See *SCS*, 539, for an explanation of Old and New Style dating.
30   Letter and telegram of 1 June 1948, in *SSCI*, 341.
31   Letter of 6 June, in ibid., 342.
32   Letter of 2 June, in ibid., 342.
33   *Sfam*, 150.
34   *DB*, 143.
35   *SSCI*, 343.
36   *SCF* (94), 8.
37   Craft, "Encounter and Metamorphosis," 31.
38   I am indebted to Robert Craft, both in his writings (passim) and in conversation, for much of the information in this paragraph.
39   February 1948.
40   *SCF* (94), 9–10; *DB*, 145.
41   "Encounter and Metamorphosis," *Stravinsky: Glimpses of a Life*, 32.
42   Letter of 4 August 1948 (PSS, emphases his). The letter is in *SSCIII*, 324, but with the quoted passage omitted.
43   Letter of 1 February 1948, *CASIII*, 101.
44   Letter to Erwin Stein (of Boosey and Hawkes), quoted in *SSCI*, 350.
45   F.A. [Franco Abbati], *Corriere della Sera*, 28 October 1948.
46   Quoted in *SSCI*, 350.
47   Letter of 27 November 1948, in *SSCI*, 351. Ansermet's letter, of 20 November, is in *CASIII*, 103–5.
48   *DB*, 145.
49   Letter of 8 October 1948, *SSCI*, 346.
50   Letter of 28 October 1948, *SSCI*, 348.
51   Letter of 8 October.
52   Stravinsky to Lieberson, letter of 5 June 1948; Lieberson to Stravinsky, letter of 15 June (PSS). According to Philip Stuart, Craft was nevertheless engaged by Lieberson to help edit the still-unreleased recording of *Ode*, "a task which Stravinsky himself was

prevented from undertaking by his RCA contract"; Stuart, *Igor Stravinsky—The Composer in the Recording Studio* (New York, Westport, and London: Greenwood Press, 1991), 11.

53 Letter of 7 October 1948 (PSS).
54 Letter of 10 December 1948 (PSS).
55 Night letter, 9 February 1948 (UCLA, Kall). I am grateful to Colin Slim for drawing my attention to the oddities of this communication.

16   A FAMILY HAPPY IN ITS OWN WAY

1 Letter to Craft of 8 October 1948, *SSCI*, 347.
2 See, respectively, Hawkes to Stravinsky, letter of 23 September 1948 (PSS), and Stravinsky to Auden, letter of 17 November 1948, *SSCI*, 306.
3 Letter of 15 October (PSS).
4 See Auden's letter of 23 November 1948 to Stravinsky, in *SSCI*, 307.
5 Nabokov's article, "The Atonal Trail—A Communication," is in *Partisan Review* 15 (May 1948), 580–5; Leibowitz's reply, in the form of a letter to the editor, is in *Partisan Review* 15 (August 1948), 943.
6 See *SCS*, 464–5.
7 Thomas Mann, *Tagebücher, 1940–43*, 952.
8 All quotations are from Theodor W. Adorno, *Philosophy of Modern Music*, trans. Anne G. Mitchell and Wesley V. Bloomster (London: Sheed and Ward, 1973).
9 Letter of 5 December 1949, quoted in Stuckenschmidt, *Arnold Schoenberg: His Life, World and Work*, trans. H. Searle (London: John Calder, 1977), 508.
10 See Stuckenschmidt, op. cit., 499–500 for a full account of the visits.
11 Letter of 7 January 1949 (PSS). Alexandre Tansman's *Igor Stravinsky* had been published in Paris in 1948.
12 *SSCI*, 357 (where the original text in PSS is slightly curtailed).
13 *SCF* (94), 13–14. The original final couplet, as set earlier in the cabaletta, had been "It shall not matter/What he may be." The substitute lines, not otherwise present, are "Time cannot alter/A loving heart" (extended to "An ever-loving heart" to fit the lead-up to the final top note).
14 See Stravinsky's telegram of 19 May 1948 to Koussevitzky (LoC, Koussevitzky): Yuzefovich, "Chronicle of a Non-friendship," 824.
15 That the initiative was Craft's is suggested by Stravinsky's letter to him of 3 November 1948, in *SSCI*, 349.
16 *SCF* (72), 8. The account in *SCF* (94), 14–16, is fuller, but the quoted remark is for some reason truncated. In general Craft's published diaries cannot automatically be accepted as contemporary with the events they describe, since they have appeared in several significantly variant forms (moreover, the description of the meeting in *Dial*, 91–2, though put into Stravinsky's mouth, is plainly based on Craft's diary notes).
17 Craft's entry for 21 February in *SCF* (94), 16, stating that the Piano Concerto was recorded on that day, is an error, apparently due to his habit of rewriting diary entries at a much later time. The concerto was not recorded until 1950.
18 Letter of 18 March 1949, in *SSCI*, 245–6.
19 W. H. Auden, "In Praise of Limestone," *Collected Poems* (New York: Vintage, 1991), 542.
20 *SCF* (94), 16.
21 Stravinsky to Craft, letter of 9 March 1949, in *SSCI*, 357–8.
22 The boxes had been dispatched by Soulima (by sea via the Panama Canal) before his own departure from Paris the previous summer.

23 *SSCI*, 358–9, and note 71.

24 *Bagazh*, 236.

25 Quoted in Laurel E. Fay, *Shostakovich: A Life* (New York: Oxford University Press, 2000), 173.

26 *Bagazh*, 238.

27 For a detailed account of the Waldorf conference, see Frances Stonor Saunders, *Who Paid the Piper?* (London: Granta Books, 1999), 45–56.

28 Letter of 3 April 1949 (PSS).

29 *DB*, 146. From this time until she returned to Switzerland in 1954, Madubo worked in Hollywood as a seamstress.

30 Soulima Stravinsky, interview with Thor Wood.

31 In such contexts, the term "children" should be taken to include children-in-law.

32 Letter of 27 April 1949, *SSCI*, 361.

33 *SSCI*, 332, note 13.

34 See variously *SCF* (94), 17–34; *CwC*; *DB*, 146–7.

35 *SSCI*, 409–10. Craft has suggested that the scoring was prompted by the range of the two lines, but the pun seems too obvious to ignore. The bulk of the materials sorted by Craft in 1949 are now in the Paul Sacher Stiftung in Basle, but some were given to the Library of Congress for purposes of tax deduction.

36 *SCF* (94), 34.

37 See above, chapter 2, note 33.

38 Isherwood, *Goodbye to Berlin* (London: Hogarth Press, 1939), 13.

39 Isherwood, *Lost Years: A Memoir 1945–1951*, ed. K. Bucknell (London: Vintage, 2001), 201, note 1.

40 Ibid., 201.

41 Ibid., 222–3.

42 Ibid., 203.

43 *SCF* (94), 29.

44 *SCF* (94), 22.

45 *SCF* (94), 28–9.

46 As usual, the different published editions vary, sometimes in significant respects. For instance, in *SCF* (72), 10, we read that "I. S. has not followed any science or philosophy of science since his reading of Bergson a half-century ago," which in *SCF* (94), 22, has become "I. S. has not followed any science or philosophy since his University of St. Petersburg years, at which time he was immersed in Kant." In *Lost Years*, 199, Isherwood likewise alleges that Craft's diaries "may in fact have been reconstructed . . . quite a long while after the event." Craft had relayed (*SCF* [72], 12) a story supposedly told by Isherwood at their first Farmers' Market meeting, about his having been struck off Chaplin's guest list for peeing on the sofa one evening when drunk, an incident Isherwood claims cannot have occurred until at least ten months later. Significantly, this anecdote no longer figures in *SCF* (94).

47 *Dial*, 168; *SCF* (94), 68.

48 Maria Huxley, letter to her son Matthew, quoted in Bedford, *Aldous Huxley, Volume 2, 1939 to 1963*, 121.

49 *SCF* (94), 48.

50 Ibid.

51 *SCF* (94), 18.

52 See, for instance, his letter of 19 July to Igor Markevitch, who had written to him on the 17th to inform him of the death of Elie Gagnebin, the Narrator in the original Lausanne *Soldier's Tale* (PSS).

53 *SCF* (94), 34.

54   *SCF* (94), 21.

55   The anecdotes here are from *CwC*.

56   *ASS*, 24.

57   Letter of 18 October 1949, *SSCI*, 309–10.

58   Stravinsky attended a performance of *Don Giovanni* by the visiting San Francisco Opera at the Shrine Auditorium on 31 October, when the trio was nearing completion.

59   "Une lettre de Stravinsky sur Tchaïkovsky," *Le Figaro*, 18 May 1922.

60   Letter of 24 October 1949, *SSCI*, 310.

61   *New York Herald Tribune*, 22 November 1949. In *ImpLif*, 109, note 133, Craft remarks that Berger complained that the concert was under-rehearsed. But Berger said nothing of the kind. The gist of his review is that "Mr. Craft sometimes attempts more than he can fulfil adequately. His Stravinsky readings last night offered, perhaps, more to people who know the works, and who took the concert in the spirit of a rehearsal at which to refresh their memory of the glorious instrumental inspirations in music they have come to love through the piano transcrip[tions]" (the final word is misprinted in the review).

62   Letter of 28 November 1949 (PSS).

63   Letter of 6 December, excerpted in *SSCI*, 369, note 94.

64   Undated letter (September 1949), quoted in *SSCI*, 364.

65   The acknowledged motive, as we have seen, was Soulima's need to make his own way outside his father's orbit. In *Are You the Son . . . ?*, however, he hints at other reasons, including the excessive competition for work among the army of accomplished musicians who infested Hollywood. He also alleges a less friendly attitude on Vera's part, and, generally, a "new situation in the household."

17   DEATH OF A PROPHET

1   Soulima Stravinsky, interview with Thor Wood; also *DB*, 147.

2   *Dial*, 106.

3   Robert Gross, "Gross at 69: A Fiddler Reminisces," *Calendar* (Los Angeles), 2 October 1983, 55.

4   *SCF* (94), 35.

5   Stravinsky is vague in *Dial* (103) about the occasion on which he and Krenek re-met, but since he certainly attended the twelve-note concert on 14 August (1949), at which Krenek made a speech, I am assuming that the meeting took place then. In *ImpLif*, 139–40, Craft seems to confirm this but misdates the event to September; cf. *DB*, 147, which implies that Vera went, too, though the original diary text merely records "Ebel [Wilshire Ebell] concert 12 tone."

6   George, Earl of Harewood, *The Tongs and the Bones*, quoted in Humphrey Carpenter, *Benjamin Britten: A Biography* (London: Faber and Faber, 1992), 298. Another possible explanation is that there was something odd about the performance Stravinsky had attended, which at any rate, as we saw in chapter 14, was of poor quality. Perhaps the orchestral part was entirely played on the piano, as in the *Così* to which he had taken Auden.

7   Letter of 15 December 1949, in *SSCI*, 369, but here retranslated from the Russian original in PSS. Presumably Nabokov relayed to Isaiah Berlin the version of this anecdote that Berlin later enjoyed telling. "Britten," Stravinsky is supposed to have said, "is a vonnnderrful . . . accompanist." As for "Auntie Britten," the vague suggestion conveyed in English is more specific in Russian, "tyotka" ("auntie") being a standard slang term for a "queer" or "gay."

8   See chapter 15, note 6, and related text.

9   See, for example, Carpenter, op. cit., 240–1 and 326–7, for remarks on Britten's gradual rejection of Auden's friendship.

10 *DB*, 147; see also Craft's letter to Hawkes, 27 December 1949, reproduced in facsimile in *SPD*, 441. Craft notes (page 442) that the letter was signed "Bob Craft" in Stravinsky's hand, in the desire to avoid direct communication with Hawkes. But the explanation is bizarre, since Stravinsky had written dozens of letters to Hawkes and would soon be writing more. The real reason is obviously that Stravinsky wrote Craft's name on the carbon copy as an aide-memoire as to who had actually signed the letter.

11 See Stein's letter of 20 December 1949 (PSS).

12 See Stravinsky's letter to Hawkes of 17 October 1949, in *SSCIII*, 329.

13 Letter of 20 December 1949 (PSS).

14 Letter of 3 January 1950 (PSS).

15 *SCF* (94), 35.

16 Ibid., 42; see also *DB*, 147.

17 *SCF* (94), 28. Many of the impressions in this paragraph are from *CwC*.

18 Letter of 28 November 1949, in *SSCI*, 273.

19 Presumably the idea was put forward in person in New York. It is referred to in Stravinsky's letter to Berman, 29 May 1950: "Kirstein had told me in a burst of enthusiasm that he would take it for City Center but is now playing dead" (PSS).

20 *SCF* (94), 36; but see also his letter to Berman, 7 June 1950 (PSS), in which he grumbles about Menotti's success.

21 *SCF* (94), 36.

22 Ibid.; see also Auden's undated (early March) note to Stravinsky containing the bidding sequence, in *SSCI*, 312–3.

23 *SPD*, 405.

24 Letters of 15 March, 15 and 22 April, respectively, all in PSS.

25 Letter of 4 June 1950 (PSS).

26 Letter to Hawkes, 20 May, in *SSCIII*, 331; also to Berman, 29 May 1950 (PSS).

27 In *Are You the Son . . . ?*, Soulima claims that John Kuypers, the head of the department at Urbana, had mentioned this possibility to Vera the previous summer and received a curt negative. Soulima himself only heard about the post from a Music Academy of the West colleague, who told Françoise about it on the beach at Santa Barbara and advised her to get Soulima to write quickly to Urbana. Another version of the story (told to me by Milène Marion) is that Kuypers had written to Vera, who had opened the letter and thrown it into the wastepaper basket.

28 *SCF* (94), 42.

29 Rimsky-Korsakov, *My Musical Life*, trans. Judah A. Joffe (London: Eulenburg, 1974), 46. For the cinema experience, see *SCF* (94), 43.

30 Letter of 23 June 1950 (PSS).

31 Letter of 6 July 1950, Auden and Kallman to Stravinsky. The remark quoted is in a postscript by Kallman omitted from *SSCI*, 314.

32 Stravinsky had written to Soulima in Paris on 25 March 1948, asking him to transfer 3,000 francs to Mrs. Sallard, "who is in dire need." In November 1950 she wrote to Vera that Soulima's wife had seemed cross at the North Wetherly Drive Stravinskys' failure to make a favorite of their little boy, Zizi; see *DB*, 150, note 9. The composer continued to make payments to Mrs. Sallard until the month of her death in a road accident in March 1961.

33 Letter of 4 June 1950 (PSS).

34 *DB*, 149 (with a photo).

35 *SCF* (94), 43.

36 Isherwood, *Diaries, Volume One: 1939–1960*, 426.

37 Letter to Ernst Roth, 20 September 1950 (PSS: the relevant passage is omitted from the letter as published in *SSCIII*, 335).

38 Ricketson eventually offered $5,000; see Betty Bean to Stravinsky, letter of 6 October 1950 (PSS).

39 See Ghiringhelli's letter of 9 June and Stravinsky's reply of 19 June 1950 (PSS).

40 Kirstein to Stravinsky, letter of 23 August 1950. Much of this enormous letter is printed in *SSCI*, 274–7.

41 Letter of 25 August 1950, 277–8.

42 *Apollo architectons* is not mentioned as such until Kirstein's letter of 26 August 1953 (*SSCI*, 285), but since he there refers to it as "the old idea," and the maturity of Apollo had been his initial suggestion (letter of 29 April 1948, *SSCI*, 271), I am assuming that the "architectons" slant had come up in early conversations.

43 Letters of 23 and 25 August respectively. Kirstein seems to be suggesting that *Sweeney* would be a separate project from the *Apollo* sequel; but this is one more aspect of his opportunism. Why lose a brilliant proposal just because it might not suit a preconception?

44 Stravinsky to Bean, letter of 6 November 1950, in *SSCIII*, 338.

45 See Stravinsky's letter to Soulima, 22 December 1950, quoted in *SSCIII*, 340, note 15.

46 Nabokov's letter to Stravinsky of 23 December 1950 is quoted in *SSCII*, 377; Stravinsky's reply of 2 January 1951 is in ibid.

47 Stravinsky had mentioned the Venice interest in a letter of 3 February 1948 to Soulima (private collection). The information about Hawkes is from *CwC*.

48 Letter to Stravinsky, 5 December 1950, in *SSCI*, 314.

49 See his letter of 26 January 1951; Stravinsky had told him about the Venice deal in a letter of the 24th (PSS).

50 Letter of 26 January.

51 Stravinsky's correspondence with Ghiringhelli is in PSS. For the threat of legal action, see Ghiringhelli's letter to Roth of 24 February (PSS).

52 Mentioned by Roth in his letter of 23 March to Stravinsky (PSS).

53 Telegram of 9 May 1951 (PSS).

54 Letter of 25 June, confirming his telegram of the 20th (PSS).

55 Letter of 9 February 1951 (PSS).

56 The first performance of *The Rake's Progress* at the Royal Opera was on 18 June 1979.

57 See his letter to Roth of 9 February 1951 (PSS).

58 Letter of 16 February 1951 (*SSCI*, 317), in reply to Auden's of 14 February addressed to Craft, quoted in *SCF* (94), 45, and also in *SPD*, 407, where it is incorrectly dated 16 February.

59 *SCF* (94), 1.

60 *SSCI*, 317, note 24.

61 In January 1948, Auden told Alan Ansen that "we're getting four thousand dollars for the libretto" (*Table Talk*, 95). It seems, however, that no contract survives, and we do not know exactly on what terms Auden agreed to write the libretto. The Boosey and Hawkes records indicate only that the librettists received $3,000 as an advance on royalties for their work. Under this agreement, copyright in the text remained with the publisher, another detail that Auden seems to have held against Stravinsky. I am grateful to Edward Mendelson and Andrew Kemp for their help in establishing these details.

62 Letter of 16 February to Auden, *SSCI*, 317. He had taken essentially the same line over the proposed deal with Central City; see his letter of 13 October 1950 to Betty Bean.

63 In a letter to Bean, 23 October 1950, he said that he was not renewing "for musical reasons" (PSS).

64 Letter to Stravinsky of 29 March 1951 (PSS).

65   Letter to Bean, 17 March 1951, in *SSCIII*, 342–3.

66   Letter of Sapiro to Roth, 15 May, and Roth's reply of 29 May 1951 (PSS).

67   Letter to Bean, 31 January 1952 (PSS).

68   See his letters to Stravinsky of 10 February and 25 July 1951, in *SSCI*, 316, 320.

69   Ebert to Stravinsky, telegram of 25 July 1951 (PSS).

70   Berman set out the problem in detail in his letter to Stravinsky of 14 April 1951, but years later he claimed that his participation had been vetoed by Auden, over Stravinsky's head. See Berman's letter to Craft, 24 May 1968 (PSS). On 14 July 1951 Ghiringhelli wired Stravinsky that Piper was unavailable, and on the same day Stravinsky wired back advising him to engage Balthus (PSS). Exactly when Ratto and Colciaghi were booked has proved hard to establish.

71   *SSCIII*, 192, note 16; also *SCF* (94), 45. Gide died on 19 February 1951, and the Stravinskys heard the news four days later during their journey through Texas.

72   News of Steinberg's death (in December 1946) came in a letter from the same Dmitry Borodin who had written to him about Yury's death in 1941. The letter also informed him of the death of Rimsky-Korsakov's eldest son Mikhail. Stravinsky replied on the 28th (PSS).

73   See Stravinsky's letter to Soulima, 17 April 1951, quoted in *SPD*, 650, note 96. Bolm had died on the 16th. Errazuriz died that same month, Koussevitzky on 4 June.

74   Quoted in *SCF* (94), 52–3.

75   "Influence or Assistance," in *Stravinsky: Glimpses of a Life*, 35. But Craft blatantly contradicts himself when he says that mention of Schoenberg's name was forbidden at North Wetherly Drive, yet explains Dushkin's embarrassment at meeting him at Mitropoulos's Schoenberg performance on the grounds that "he realized that I would mention the meeting to Stravinsky." Craft's tendency to exaggerate this problem may possibly be connected with a division in his own loyalties. Had things worked out differently, he might have ended up "Assisting Schoenberg" rather than Stravinsky.

76   Ibid., 36. See *SCF* (94), 38–40, for Craft's memorable account of this visit.

77   *SCF* (94), 49.

78   Ibid., 53–4.

79   Letter of 17 September 1951, in *SCF* (1994), 65–6 (dated original in PSS). See W. H. Auden and Norman Holmes Pearson, *Poets of the English Language* (5 volumes, New York: Viking, 1950).

18   THE TIME-TRAVELLER COMES ASHORE

1   *DB*, 151, note 2.

2   For an account of these first days in Italy, see *SCF* (94), 54–60.

3   Ibid., 60; letter to Elizabeth Mayer, quoted in Carpenter, *W. H. Auden*, 370.

4   *SCF* (94), 69. There was a second dress rehearsal on the 10th, conducted by Leitner.

5   "Stravinsky's 'Rake' Has Its Surprises," *New York Herald Tribune*, 30 September 1951.

6   *SCF* (94), 62–3; also *CwC*.

7   Quoted in *SCF* (94), 60.

8   " 'La carriera del libertino' non darà gloria a Stravinsky," Guido Pannain, *Il Tempo*, 12 September 1951.

9   Antonino Procida, " 'La carriera del libertino' di Igor Strawinsky alla Fenice," *Il Giornale*, 12 September 1951.

10   "La 'Carriera del libertino' di Strawinski accolta con successo al Festival musicale," *Corriere della sera*, 12 September 1951.

11   "Il Libertino di Strawinsky ha sposato la donna barbuta," *Oggi*, 20 September 1951.

12   John S. Weissmann and Gian Galeazzo Severi, respectively. These and other remarks

were collected at a press reception on the day of the premiere and quoted by Barrett McGurn in "Critics Say Stravinsky Opera Marks His Return to Melody," *New York Herald Tribune*, 12 September 1951.

13 *SCF* (94), 61; *CwC*.

14 *SCF* (94), 62; *CwC*.

15 Letter to Paul Gay, 23 September 1951, in Cingria, *Correspondance Générale*, vol. 4 (Lausanne: Éditions L'Age d'Homme, 1979), 319. But Cingria had written to Stravinsky from Ravenna on the 16th, recalling their meeting with pleasure but regretting that it was so brief. "We should have seen each other again, comforted each other in the things that matter, raked over the past a bit." He added: "That will happen, but in Switzerland when you come" (*SSCIII*, 130–1).

16 *T&C*, 57, where the memoir is signed "V. S." As usual in that volume, the text is actually by Craft, and reappears, substantially rewritten but with the same title, the same imagery, and the same verbal jokes, in *SCF* (94), 62–3.

17 See Eugenio Montale, *The Second Life of Art* (New York: Ecco Press, 1982), 249–50, for an account of the occasion, and *DB*, 153, for a photograph.

18 See *SCF* (94), 63–5, for these and other details of the Venetian holiday.

19 The contract is dated 24 August. The *Oedipus* recording, with Peter Pears in the title role, was unusual in that the German narrations (from the concert) were excised, and instead narrations in French by Cocteau himself were recorded in Paris the following May and spliced into the tape. See Stuart, *Igor Stravinsky: The Composer in the Recording Studio*, 36; also *SCF* (94), 82.

20 "Influence or Assistance?," *Stravinsky: Glimpses of a Life*, 38.

21 See *SCS*, 429. Craft (op. cit., 46) suggests that he may have heard Webern's early string quartet and the violin pieces, op. 7, which had been programmed with works of his own. Unfortunately he does not identify the concerts in question.

22 Krenek's concerto was in the same Donaueschingen program as the Boulez (6 October), while the Henze symphony was premiered on the 7th. The Südwestfunk kept recordings of the entire festival.

23 For his account of the origins of the festival, see *Bagazh*, 242–6. Nabokov claimed not to have known about the CIA funding for the CCF until the information began to leak out in the New York press in the mid-sixties, but he certainly did know that the agenda was specifically political and anti-Communist. See Frances Stonor Saunders, *Who Paid the Piper?*, and Ian Wellens, *Music on the Frontline* (Aldershot: Ashgate, 2002).

24 Stravinsky met Nabokov's assistant, Denis de Rougemont, in Geneva and informed him of his decision.

25 Information about this visit and Stravinsky's attitude to it is in two letters of Vera Stravinsky to Milène and André Marion, 15 and 31 October 1951, quoted in *DB*, 151. I have made my own deductions about the reasons for that attitude.

26 For these various incidents, see *SCF* (94), 67, and *DB*, 151.

27 Letter of 7 January 1949 (PSS).

28 *SCF* (94), 54.

29 Ibid., 67.

30 *SPD*, 415.

31 Kallman to Stravinsky, letter of 19 September 1951 (PSS). Kallman was in fact taken on as assistant director of the Milan *Rake*. For more details on the librettists' surely only half-serious ideas for additional scenes, see Kallman's note for Stravinsky's 1964 recording, reprinted in Edward Mendelson (ed.), *W. H. Auden and Chester Kallman: Libretti and Other Dramatic Writings by W. H. Auden*, 626–9.

32 See Kallman's letter of 27 January 1952, and Stravinsky's reply of 31 January (both PSS); emphases in the original.

33   Letter of Vera Stravinsky to the Marions, 23 November 1951, in *DB*, 151; also *SCF* (1994), 69.

34   On the 25th.

35   Letter of 28 November 1951, mostly in *SSCI*, 284–5, the rest PSS.

36   As noted in Stravinsky's letter of 8 January 1952 to Betty Bean, in *SSCIII*, 353. See also *SPD*, 204–5. He describes the libretto as "a celebration of Wisdom in a manner comparable to Ben Jonson's Masques." The text was eventually published in Mendelson (ed.), *W. H. Auden and Chester Kallman: Libretti*, 95–126.

37   See especially André Marion to Bean, 31 January 1952 (PSS).

38   *SCF* (94), 70.

39   In his letter to Craft of 20 September 1951, proposing further texts: see *SCF* (94), 65.

40   The theme and its inscription are reproduced in facsimile in *SSCI*, 251.

41   *SCF* (94), 71. The program was *The Soldier's Tale* (Suite), the Octet, *Dumbarton Oaks*, *Danses concertantes*.

42   Letter of 26 January 1952, quoted in Bedford, *Aldous Huxley*, vol. 2, 128. Other information in *SCF* (94), 70–1.

43   *SCF* (94), 72.

44   Letter of 21 January 1952 (PSS).

45   *SCF* (94), 72.

46   *Conv*, 21.

47   White, *Stravinsky*, 471.

48   Pace Robert Craft, "A Personal Preface," *The Score*, 20 (1957), 7–13. Joseph N. Straus even goes so far as to show how Webern's op. 22 influenced the canonic writing in "The maidens came," which, however, was essentially composed in July 1951, before Stravinsky had heard a note of Webern or looked at any score by him. See *Stravinsky's Late Music* (Cambridge, Eng.: Cambridge University Press, 2001), 22–6.

49   Luis Gongora, "Igor Strawinsky y el surrealismo," *La Noche* (Barcelona), 12 March 1936; also *Daily Mail*, 13 February 1913.

50   See *SCS*, 456.

51   Quoted in *SCF* (94), 72.

52   See Joseph N. Straus, *Stravinsky's Late Music*, 11–17, for a detailed technical assessment of the similarities and differences.

53   For further detail, see *SPD*, 422.

54   Craft notes that he drew Stravinsky's attention to this difficulty when he played it through on the piano on the 25th. See *SCF* (94), 72. Stravinsky subsequently added the two oboes of the final version, and divided the music between them and the flutes.

55   As revealed by his letters of 22 February to Betty Bean (*SSCIII*, 356) and Ernst Roth (also in *SSCIII*, but the relevant passage omitted).

56   This is my extrapolation from Craft's moving accounts in *SCF* (94), 72–3, and "Influence or Assistance?," *Stravinsky: Glimpses of a Life*, 38–9.

57   R. Leibowitz, "Two Composers: A Letter from Hollywood," *Partisan Review* (March 1948), 361–5.

58   *SCF* (94), 73, and "Influence or Assistance?," 39.

59   Letter to Roth of 10 March 1952, *SSCIII*, 358. See also *SCS*, 145, 242, and 607, note 16, where, however, the dating of the later Verlaine arrangement to 1951 is incorrect.

60   Once more, *SCF* (94), 73, is excellent on the changes, and Craft has a higher opinion of the outcome than I.

61   *SCF* (94), 73, entry for 13 March, already calls the work "Cantata." But the entry is suspect, and it was probably "corrected" for publication. There is no other evidence that Stravinsky had yet settled on either the title or the form of the finished work.

62   "Influence or Assistance?," *Stravinsky: Glimpses of a Life*, 49, note 2.

63 Ibid., 39; see also *ASS*, 39, which reproduces the page in facsimile. "Lob" is of course "love" rhymed with "Bob," but with hints of Russian ("lyublyu" = I love) and German ("lobe" = "praise").

19 COUNT ONE, COUNT TWO, COUNT TWELVE

1   Telegram of 15 December 1951 to Nabokov (PSS).
2   Letter of 2 January 1952. Nabokov had made a similar suggestion in a letter of 29 December (PSS).
3   Letter to Roth, 11 January 1952 (PSS).
4   Letter to Stravinsky, 6 March 1952 (PSS).
5   Letter to Stravinsky, 13 February 1952, quoted in *SSCII*, 383.
6   Letter of 21 March 1952 (PSS). Much of the relevant correspondence is in *SSCI*, 115–9, but in general so poorly and sometimes ineptly translated as to be better avoided. As for the drop curtain, it "showed an agonized Oedipus with eyes telescoping out of his head like those of a fiddler crab, gesticulating wildly in the direction of Jocasta. She, half clad, with crinkling, dangling hair and misshapen breasts grotesquely exposed, was wildly reaching toward Oedipus." Olin Downes, *New York Times*, 1 June 1952, quoted in Joan Evans, *Hans Rosbaud: A Bio-Bibliography* (New York: Greenwood Press, 1992), 55, note 134.
7   Jean Cocteau, *Journal d'un inconnu* (Paris: Bernard Grasset, 1953), 222–3.
8   Letter of 21 March.
9   Jean Cocteau, *Past Tense*, trans. R. Howard (London: Hamish Hamilton, 1987), 130.
10 Letter of 17 March 1952 (PSS).
11 *Past Tense*, 129.
12 Cocteau's scenario for the seven tableaux is reprinted in *Journal d'un inconnu*, 225–30.
13 *Past Tense*, 138.
14 Ibid., 140.
15 *SCF* (94), 75.
16 *DB*, 156.
17 *SCF* (94), 76–7; *Conv*, 71–3.
18 *SCF* (94), 75–7.
19 Undated letter, summer 1952, in *SSCIII*, 197.
20 Letter of 1 August 1952, in *SSCIII*, 197, note 1. There is some evidence, nevertheless, that Stravinsky's (or to be exact Souvtchinsky's) ideas about time in the *Poétique musicale* had been influenced by Sartre. Souvtchinsky's article "La Notion du Temps et la Musique," in the *Revue musicale* (May–June 1939), 70/310–80/320, bears two epigraphs on the subject of time from *La Nausée*.
21 For Cocteau's account of this reunion, see *Past Tense*, 145–6.
22 Ibid., 147.
23 *SCF* (94), 77.
24 J.-J. Nattiez and R. Piencikowski (eds.), *Pierre Boulez–John Cage: Correspondance et Documents* (Mainz: Schott, 2002), 210, letter of May 1952. Boulez told Jesús Aguilar that "Stravinsky did not attend the performance of *Structures 1a* in 1952. He was in Paris at the same moment, that's all" (see *Le Domaine Musical: Pierre Boulez et vingt ans de création contemporaine* [Paris: Fayard, 1992], 183–4 note). But this is merely to say that the two composers did not meet on that occasion.
25 *SCF* (94), 82. See also Stravinsky's letter to Nabokov, 9 February 1952, and Nabokov's reply of 15 February (PSS).
26 *Dial*, 107.

27 *SCF* (94), 82. A recording of Stravinsky's performance is available on CD, but no titters are audible.

28 *Past Tense*, 149.

29 *SCF* (94), 82. As an example of Craft's editorial technique, the account of this performance is worth examining. It first appeared in *SPD*, 419, credited as "from V.A.S.'s [Vera Arturovna Stravinsky's] diary," having been omitted from Craft's diary excerpts in *Dial*, *R&C*, and *SCF* (72), but then resurfaced as his in *SCF* (94). With touching naïveté, the latter text was modified from the former but not essentially changed.

30 *SSCIII*, 131, note 40.

31 *SCF* (94), 83.

32 Quoted in *SSCII*, 349–50, note 7. The program included another piece by Boulez, the *Étude à un son*.

33 Letter of 22 December 1946 (PSS).

34 Souvtchinsky sent him a note on the 14th of May: "I can't fail to be aware that you have something against me. Let our meeting depend entirely on your wishes." (PSS) But Stravinsky seems not to have replied.

35 *SCF* (94), 85. Other details of their itinerary are in *DB*, 156.

36 *SCF* (94), 86. The Canadian excursion may originally have been meant to extend as far as Vancouver, where Stravinsky had made a plan to visit the University of British Columbia to discuss his concert there in the autumn. See Slim, "Introduction" to *Annotated Catalogue of the H. Colin Slim Stravinsky Collection* (Vancouver: University of British Columbia, 2002), 6–8, for an account of the autumn visit.

37 Morton, "In praise of Stravinsky's new work," *Frontier*, November 1952, 21–2. Stravinsky found the "Lyke-wake Dirge," like all the other Cantata poems, in the Auden anthology. Craft told me in 1995 that he introduced Stravinsky to Britten's Serenade, but he did not say when.

38 Letter of 28 August 1952 to David Adams: *SSCIII*, 366.

39 *Mem*, 110.

40 Stravinsky's notation of the sixteen-note series is beautifully reproduced in *SPD*, plate 14.

41 Ibid., 422.

42 *SCF* (94), 74.

43 Richard Buckle and John Taras, *George Balanchine: Ballet Master* (London: Hamish Hamilton, 1988), 191–4.

44 See his letter of 11 November 1952 to Roth (PSS); also *CwC*.

45 See especially Adams's letter to Stravinsky of 19 September 1952 (PSS). Adams told me that Bean was fired at the instigation of Ralph Hawkes's brother, Geoffrey, who disliked her personally.

46 See his letter to Cuénod of 5 September 1952 (PSS), offering to pay an additional $100 out of his own pocket.

47 Mildred Norton, "All-Stravinsky concert," *Los Angeles Daily News*, 12 November 1952.

48 Goldberg, "Stravinsky Cantata Novel Experiment," *Los Angeles Times*, 12 November 1952.

49 Letter of 31 October 1952 (PSS).

50 Jay S. Harrison, "Talk With Stravinsky: Composer Discusses His Music," *New York Herald Tribune*, 21 December 1952.

51 Harrison, op. cit.

52 Norton, *Los Angeles Daily News*, 12 November 1952.

53 Roman text mine.

54 Telegram of 16 November 1952 (PSS).

55 Letter from Jakob Gimpel, *Los Angeles Daily News,* 24 November 1952.
56 Peter Yates on "Music," in *Arts and Architecture* (Los Angeles, February 1953).
57 "Lyrics of Hate," *Congress Weekly,* 19 January 1953.
58 Taruskin, *Defining Russia Musically* (Princeton: Princeton University Press, 1997), 459.
59 Letter of 3 December 1952 (PSS).
60 Letter of 10 December 1952, Igor to Vera Stravinsky, in *DB,* 160.
61 *New York Herald Tribune,* 22 December 1952.
62 "Stravinsky's Cantata Considered One of His Grander Vocal Works," *New York Herald Tribune,* 28 December 1952.
63 Joan Peyser, *Boulez: Composer, Conductor, Enigma* (London: Cassell, 1976), 97.
64 Specifically: "Trajectoires: Ravel, Stravinsky, Schönberg," *Contrepoints,* 6 (1949), 122–42; "Moment de J.-S. Bach," *Contrepoints,* 7 (1951), 72–86.
65 Peyser, op. cit., 97.
66 *Virgil Thomson by Virgil Thomson* (London: Weidenfeld and Nicolson, 1967), 402–3.
67 Letter to Cage, after 28 November 1951, in Nattiez and Piencikowski (eds.), *Pierre Boulez—John Cage: Correspondance et Documents,* 200.
68 *SCF* (94), 91. As we have seen, however, Craft's diaries cannot be trusted as wholly contemporary.
69 "Note to Tonight's Concert: Webern's Work Analyzed," *New York Herald Tribune,* 28 December 1952. Revised reprint as "Incipit" in Pierre Boulez, *Relevés d'apprenti* (Paris: Éditions du Seuil, 1966), 273–4; English retranslation by Stephen Walsh in *Stocktakings from an Apprenticeship* (Oxford: Oxford University Press, 1991), 215–16. For the various other transmogrifications of this short article, see ibid., 215, note.
70 Peyser, op. cit., 84; also 99.
71 Ibid., 97.
72 *SCF* (94), 89–90.
73 *The Table Talk of W. H. Auden,* 93.
74 *SCF* (94), 93.
75 Philip Hart, *Fritz Reiner* (Evanston, Ill.: Northwestern University Press, 1994), 147.
76 A photograph in Hart, op. cit., seems to illustrate this particular relationship.
77 Mayer's article (in *Esquire,* December 1953, 145, 209–13) is substantially excerpted in *SPD,* 416–18. Stravinsky's reply appeared in the February 1954 issue of the magazine, p. 14.
78 Elliott Carter told me that, after the second performance, Vera Stravinsky was overheard to remark to her husband, "I heard a lot of yawns tonight."
79 Olin Downes, "Rake's Progress Has U.S. Premiere," *New York Times,* 15 February 1953.
80 *SCF* (94), 97–8.
81 See the account in ibid., 98–9. It seems possible, however, that the dinner was engineered by Craft, who was attracted by Nuria Schoenberg.
82 Ibid., 99.

20 BRIEF ENCOUNTER

1 See Craft, "Stravinsky and Dylan Thomas," in *Stravinsky: Glimpses of a Life,* 52–60, for a useful, though not wholly reliable, memoir of the association.
2 Letter of 5 January 1953, Powell to Stravinsky (PSS).
3 See his letter of 16 January to Roth, *SSCIII,* 373–4.
4 "Stravinsky and Dylan Thomas," 54.
5 Vera had not made the Boston trip, but remained in Los Angeles.
6 *SCF* (94), 100. I have drawn on various versions of Craft's account, including *SCF* (72),

43; "Stravinsky and Dylan Thomas," and *Conv*, 77–8 (treating this as at least partly Craft's work). But see below in the main text.

7   J. M. Brinnin, *Dylan Thomas in America* (Readers Union edition, London: Dent, 1957), 180.

8   Notwithstanding Brinnin's suggestion, in ibid., 180–1, that Thomas did expect something of the kind.

9   Ibid., 181.

10 Letter of about 23 May 1953, in P. Ferris (ed.), *The Collected Letters of Dylan Thomas* (London: Dent, 1985), 888–9.

11 "Stravinsky and Dylan Thomas," 55.

12 Ibid.

13 *SCF* (72), 43; also *SCF* (94), 100.

14 For a very detailed, professional investigation of the cause of Thomas's death, see James Nashold and George Tremlett, *The Death of Dylan Thomas* (Edinburgh and London: Mainstream Publishing, 1997).

15 Telegram of 27 May 1953, Denis de Rougemont and Nicolas Nabokov to Stravinsky; André Marion to Nabokov, 29 May; Nabokov to Marion, 1 June (PSS).

16 Letter of 4 August 1953 (PSS). Balanchine's ex-wife was now married to the Columbia director.

17 Letter of 26 January 1954 (PSS). For a very fine, detailed account of this whole episode, see Doris Meyer, *Victoria Ocampo: Against the Wind and the Tide*, 152–69.

18 Letter to Stravinsky of 16 June 1953, in *Conv*, 79.

19 Letter of 22 June 1953 (HRC, Thomas).

20 Letter of 30 June to Robert Choate (dean of the Boston University College of Music), copy in HRC, Thomas.

21 *SCF* (94), 101. They first played the Septet reduction on the 28th June. See also Stravinsky's letter to Boosey and Hawkes, 21 July 1953, in *SSCIII*, 374–5.

22 See *ASS*, 40; also letter of 21 July to Boosey and Hawkes.

23 *SCF* (94), 106.

24 See the correspondence between Stravinsky and Acosta in PSS and the Rosenbach Library, Philadelphia.

25 28 July 1953 (PSS).

26 Letter of 9 August 1953 (PSS).

27 Telegram of 10 August 1953 (PSS).

28 See his letters of 17 December 1953 to Acosta, and 19 February 1954 to Acosta's agent, Margot Johnson, respectively (PSS). "The Diaghilev I Knew" is in *Atlantic Monthly* (November 1953), 33–6; "Le Diaghilev que j'ai connu" in *Le Figaro littéraire*, 21 November 1953.

29 See his letter to Boosey of 21 July (*SSCIII*, 374), and Boosey's reply, sending the score, of the 30th (PSS). "Never let the first performance of one of your operas be on the occasion of a diplomatic gala," Boosey advised, referring to the failure of *Gloriana* at its Covent Garden premiere the previous month.

30 *SCF* (94), 103–4.

31 Letter of 11 August 1953, *SSCIII*, 376.

32 Letter of 26 August 1953 (HRC, Thomas).

33 Letter of 26 August 1953, in *SSCI*, 285, but wrongly dated the 27th.

34 Letter of 27 August, in *SSCI*, 286, wrongly dated the 28th.

35 Letter of 28 August, partly in *SSCI*, 286, wrongly dated the 29th. The full text is in PSS.

36 Letter of 26 August, Stravinsky to Thomas (HRC, Thomas).

37 Letter to Stravinsky, 31 August 1953, in *SSCI*, 286–7.

38 F. de Lauze, *Apologie de la danse (1623)* (ed. Joan Wildeblood) (London: Frederic Muller, 1952).

39   Letter to Kirstein, 9 September 1953, in *SSCI*, 287. He later described it to David
      Adams as "a kind of symphony to be danced, without any blueprint for a plot" (letter of
      25 September 1953, PSS, partly in *SSCIII*, 377).

40   Letter of 22 September 1953, in *Conv*, 79–81: italics his.

41   Letter of 26 September 1953 (HRC, Thomas).

42   Letter of 27 October 1953; *Annotated Catalogue of the H. Colin Slim Stravinsky Collection*,
      279. This is the letter mentioned in *Conv*, 78, and wrongly dated 25 October, but not
      quoted.

43   For these and other details, see Nashold and Tremlett, *The Death of Dylan Thomas*,
      138–83. It should be added that Thomas's biographer Paul Ferris is skeptical about the
      diabetes theory and argues that Thomas died of hypoxia induced by an excessive dose of
      morphine. All agree, in any case, that while alcohol was part of the poet's trouble, it was
      not the direct cause of his death. See Ferris, *Dylan Thomas: The Biography*, new ed.
      (London: Dent, 1999), 299, 323–4.

44   Letter to Stravinsky, 22 September 1953, in *Conv*, 81.

45   Craft, "Stravinsky and Dylan Thomas," 57. Craft reports that the telegram arrived at
      nine a.m., but since Thomas died just after midday in New York (just after nine in Los
      Angeles), the news must have come later.

46   As we saw in chapter 5, the information in the published score that the string parts
      were added in 1953 is incorrect.

47   A facsimile fair copy of this sketch, dated December 1953, is in *ASS*, 42.

48   Richard RePass, *Musical Times*, 95 (1954), 205.

49   Soulima Stravinsky, interview with Thor Wood; also Soulima's memoirs, *Are you
      the Son . . . ?*

50   Letter of 11 October 1952 (PSS).

51   Letter of 17 November 1952 (PSS).

52   *CwC*.

53   For instance, he routinely and for the most part successfully recommended Theodore
      as cover designer for his scores.

54   According to Craft, Stravinsky wanted him to conduct the premiere of the Septet, and
      he would have done so had Thacher agreed *(CwC)*.

55   Ibid.

56   *SCF* (94), 107, entry for 2 January. Stravinsky got back to Los Angeles on 3 February.

57   Letter of 15 March 1954 (PSS).

21   COMPETITION OF THE GODS

1   Letter of 25 November 1952, Nabokov to Stravinsky (PSS).

2   Letter of 3 December 1952, *SSCII*, 386.

3   See his letter of 25 November. He remarried on 7 May 1953.

4   See Hans Werner Henze, *Bohemian Fifths: An Autobiography*, trans. Stewart Spencer
     (Princeton: Princeton University Press, 1999), 129–30, for a vivid account of the actual
     performance and one of several published accounts of the incident at the door. Other
     versions of the incident are in *SCF* (94), 108, and *ASS*, 44. See also Michael Steinberg's
     report in the *New York Times*, 9 April 1954.

5   *Bohemian Fifths*, 129.

6   *SCF* (94), 108.

7   *SPD*, 445, where, however, the work is given as a concerto by Karl Amadeus Hartmann.
     Spender told me in 1992 that it was the piece by Fricker.

8   *DB*, 172; *SCF* (94), 111.

9   *SCF* (94), 111–12.

10   Ibid., 108–12. More precise information is in *DB*, 172 (admittedly a volume edited by Craft), and here and there in contemporary correspondence.

11   Letter of 18 May 1954, in *DB*, 174.

12   As is confirmed by Igor's postcard of 1 June from Lisbon to Soulima. His letter of the previous day to Vera, in *DB*, 174, suggests that Milène went with him to London and that they were visited there by Theodore and Madubo, but this makes no sense (since Madubo was now living her own life in Switzerland), and I suspect a confused translation (the original is unavailable).

13   See his letter to Boosey and Hawkes of 21 July 1953, in *SSCIII*, 375–6.

14   See Craft, "Stravinsky in Albion," in *M&C*, 200, originally part of a lecture delivered to the Royal Philharmonic Society in London, 15 October 1998. Craft reported that the medal had gone missing at the time of Stravinsky's move to New York in 1969. But the baton had survived and was on display at the lecture.

15   Postcard of 1 June 1954, reproduced in *ASS*, 43.

16   Letter of 31 May 1954, in *DB*, 174.

17   *SCF* (94), 110.

18   Letter of 13 May 1954 (PSS).

19   Letter of 21 June 1954 (PSS).

20   See Piovesan's letter of 30 October, and Stravinsky's reply of 5 November (both PSS).

21   The sketches for the Postludium are dated, simply, June.

22   Stravinsky sent the original pair of songs to Douglas Gibson at Chester's on 15 June, then announced his decision to add the second pair in a letter of 18 August (PSS).

23   He announced the completion of the Balmont scoring in a letter to Roth, 7 July 1954. The new version of the *Podblyudniye* choruses is first mentioned in a letter to Gibson of 14 July, and they were sent on the 28th (PSS).

24   See Dorothy Lamb Crawford, *Evenings On and Off the Roof*, 104–5.

25   Letter of 14 July.

26   Letter of 13 August 1954, in *SSCI*, 289.

27   *SCF* (94), 110.

28   Program note for the dance premiere of *Agon*, New York, 1 December 1957, quoted in *SPD*, 429–30. A page of the draft is reproduced in facsimile in Irene Alm, "Stravinsky, Balanchine, and *Agon:* An Analysis Based on the Collaborative Process," *Journal of Musicology*, 7 (1989), 257–8.

29   See Kirstein's letter to Stravinsky of 31 August 1953, in *SSCI*, 287.

30   See his letter to Kirstein, 26 August 1954, where he gives the timing as twenty-six minutes. This is about four minutes too long. Balanchine recalled that they had "decided that the whole thing should last about twenty minutes." But this is a much later memory. See *101 Stories of the Great Ballets* (New York: Anchor Books, 1989), quoted in Irene Alm, op. cit., 256.

31   *DB*, 175. See also Craft, "Stravinsky and Dylan Thomas," in *Stravinsky: Glimpses of a Life*, 59.

32   Letter of 25 August 1954 (PSS).

33   See Crawford, *Evenings On and Off the Roof*, 310, note 104, quoting a memoir by the bassoonist Don Christlieb.

34   Ibid., 149.

35   Not all Stravinsky's friends were as "emotioned" by the occasion as he was (see Craft, "Stravinsky and Dylan Thomas," in *Stravinsky: Glimpses of a Life*, 58). Isherwood attended feeling ill with "pains in the penis, bladder and rectum," and found the *In Memoriam* "almost insultingly feeble—coming right after the magnificent voice of Dylan himself, on a record." But then, he adds, "how I loathe concerts," and admits that the audience "contained several people I dislike meeting." *Diaries, Volume One: 1939–1960*, 468.

36 *ImpLif*, 137–8.

37 *SCF* (94), 107.

38 Morton, "Stravinsky at Home," in Pasler (ed.), *Confronting Stravinsky*, 343–4.

39 See Stravinsky to Kirstein, letter of 13 August 1954, in *SSCI*, 289. Sacher's letter of 29 July (in PSS) is primarily a response to Stravinsky's congratulations on the success of the Glyndebourne *Rake's Progress* that month, which Sacher had conducted. Stravinsky probably regarded the commission as mere politesse.

40 Letter of 29 November 1954 (PSS).

41 Craft had conducted the new version of the *Podblyudniye* choruses, now retitled *Four Russian Peasant Songs*, at a Monday Evening on 11 October.

42 Letter of 6 November 1954, in *SSCIII*, 384.

43 Letter of 4 December 1954 (PSS).

44 Letter of 16 December 1954, in *SSCI*, 290.

45 *SCF* (94), 113. Craft writes as if he and Auden discussed the project in Stravinsky's absence, but *DB*, 177, suggests that they all dined together that evening. The actual diary is in truth much less clear in its layout than the neat text of *DB* implies (which may excuse *DB* for saying that Lucia Davidova came to tea, whereas the diary says they went to her apartment for tea). What probably happened is that Auden came early to discuss texts with Craft before the latter went out, as he indicates, to see Menotti's *Saint of Bleecker Street*. Later, Menotti came back to the Gladstone Hotel with Craft. Auden (and Kallman) meanwhile stayed to dinner. None of this matters much, of course, but it once again indicates the need to treat Craft's various texts with caution. For instance, it is impossible to decide from *SCF* or *DB* whether Stravinsky went to the Menotti or not, which is a matter of some slight biographical, and possibly musical, interest.

46 Stravinsky expressed his doubts in a letter to Munch of 9 February 1955, but all the same began composing on the 18th and sent the finished score to David Adams in Booseys' New York office on the 23rd. He had previously worked a two-part canon on the well-known tune in June 1951, when Samuel Barber asked him to harmonize the piece as a 75th-birthday present for Mary Curtis Bok. See *SSCIII*, 387–8, note 40, which includes a transcription of the canon. The *Greeting Prelude* was duly performed, alongside Milhaud's *Pensée amicale*, at the end of a Beethoven concert conducted in Boston by Monteux on 4 April 1955, the actual day of his eightieth birthday. The birthday pieces themselves were conducted by Munch.

47 *SCF* (94), 113; Isherwood, *Diaries*, 477.

48 *SCF* (94), 113.

49 For two separate but clearly related accounts of the meeting, see *Conv*, 90, and *SCF* (94), 119. If *SCF* is a genuine journal then it virtually proves Craft's authorship of this passage of *Conv* (unless Stravinsky read Craft's diary to refresh his own memory). If not, then it might derive from it. Neither of these possibilities is particularly encouraging in the troublesome matter of textual candor.

50 The contract is dated March 1955.

51 *SCF* (94), 121.

52 *SCF* (94), 123.

53 Letter of 14 May 1955, in *SSCIII*, 388–9. On the 13th he had written to Theodore asking him to find and send him a copy of the Vulgate, but on the 17th he wrote again that he had found a copy in Los Angeles (PSS).

22   AN ECHO CHAMBER BY CANDLELIGHT

1 Information from *DB*, 179, and note 7, and private communications from Milène Marion and Denise Strawinsky. Mrs. Marion recalled the applicant as a friend of

Edward James, but I have accepted the indication in *DB* that it was Barrie (who was in any case, no doubt, a friend of James).

2 "A Concert for Saint Mark," *The Score* (December 1956), 35–51.

3 Numerate readers will notice that this parallel falls down on the identity of the first and last domes. It would only work if St. Mark's had four main domes, rather than five. Significantly, when I asked Craft about the analogy standing in the nave of St. Mark's in 1995, he no longer seemed sure about it.

4 *Johannes Ockeghem* (London: Sheed & Ward, 1953); "The Treatment of Dissonance in Ockeghem," in E. Krenek (ed.), *Hamline Studies in Musicology*, 2 (Minneapolis: Burgess Publishing Co., 1945), 1–26.

5 *SCF* (94), 121-2; see also *ImpLif*, 140. Stravinsky confirmed the new title in a letter to Roth of 27 July: see *SSCIII*, 390.

6 Igor Stravinsky, "Foreword," in H. Eimert and K. Stockhausen (eds.), *Die Reihe, 2: Anton Webern* (2nd rev. Eng. edition, Bryn Mawr: Theodore Presser, 1959), vol. 7. The foreword is dated "June 1955" in Stravinsky's hand.

7 *H. Isaac: Choralis constantinus II*, ed. A von Webern, *DTÖ*, xxxii, Jahrgang xvi/1 (1909).

8 *SCF* (72), 64; the remark was retained in essence in *SCF* (94), but in a slightly altered context.

9 Craft, "Influence or Assistance?" in *Stravinsky: Glimpses of a Life*, 44. The article had first appeared under the title "Assisting Stravinsky," in *Atlantic Monthly* (December 1982), 69–74, but at that stage lacked the reference to Harold Bloom and gave the (slightly earlier) Septet as the starting point of the influence in question. Such modifications are entirely typical of Craft, and give some idea of his unreliability as a historical witness.

10 See his letter to Roth of 18 October 1955, in *SSCIII*, 392.

11 Letter to Roth, 18 October.

12 See his letter to Roth of 23 November 1955 (PSS); also Stravinsky's to Roth of 10 November, in *SSCIII*, 394.

13 Letter of 10 November.

14 Letters of 18 December and 25 November 1955, respectively; *SSCIII*, 395.

15 Letter of 10 November.

16 Letter of 31 October 1955 (PSS).

17 See Roth's letter to Stravinsky of 2 February 1956 (PSS).

18 As copied into Roth's letter of 2 February.

19 Letter of 11 February 1956 (PSS).

20 Letter from Piovesan to Roth, transmitted to Stravinsky by Roth in his letter of 14 February (PSS).

21 Or so Stravinsky reported in his letter to Roth of 25 February 1956 (PSS).

22 Letter to Roth of 1 May 1956, in *SSCIII*, 398–9.

23 See Roth's letter to Stravinsky of 25 April 1956; also Piovesan to Stravinsky, 7 May (PSS), quite forgetting his May 1954 idea of a shared concert.

24 See, respectively, Stravinsky's telegram of 16 May to Piovesan as copied into his letter of that date to Roth (*SSCIII*, 399–400); Piovesan's letters to Stravinsky of 6 and 10 June; and Stravinsky's telegram to Piovesan of 14 June (PSS).

25 The first occasion, a shared concert at Ojai in which Stravinsky conducted *Les Noces*, had just taken place that May. See below.

26 See Nabokov's letter to Stravinsky of 22 November 1955 (PSS). Craft had referred to the intention in a letter to Nabokov's son Ivan.

27 *SCF* (94), 123.

28 *DB*, 179–80. The quoted text is *sic* in the original diary, inexplicably altered to "Leave for Los Angeles, *hélas*" for the published version.

29 A photograph of the manuscript survives in UCLA, Morton (box 5), where it is described as "Lullaby for two flutes, for George and Mary Harris" and dated Christmas

Eve 1955. Craft, however, dates the arrangement to 15 May 1960 and says that it was made for the architect Perry Neuschatz, who had designed an extension to the North Wetherly Drive house the previous month, and who was an amateur recorder-player. See *IVSPA*, 131, and *SPD*, 464.

30 See *SSCI*, 396–7, for a summary of the relevant correspondence.

31 Letter of 27 February 1956, quoted in ibid., 397. The first two words (apparently too much for *SSC*) are in English in the otherwise French original.

32 See ibid., 397, for a list of the excerpts Stravinsky (or Craft) selected.

33 See de Lauze, op. cit., 155.

34 See Debussy's letter of 25 August 1912 to André Caplet, in F. Lesure (ed.), *Claude Debussy: Correspondance 1884–1918* (Paris: Hermann, 1993), 311.

35 *SCF* (94), 124.

36 Letters to Stravinsky, 4 and 10 April 1956 (PSS).

37 Letter of 18 April 1956 (PSS, partly quoted in *M&C*, xvi).

38 See her undated letter of "Friday," June 1956, referring to "your remarks yesterday." This can only have been the 22nd, so the recording was on the 21st.

39 Aldous Huxley, "Conversation with Stravinsky," in *Vogue*, 15 February 1953, 94–5, 127.

40 The full transcript is in PSS. A substantial excerpt is in *M&C*, 17.

41 Letter of "Friday."

42 *DB*, 180.

43 See his letter of 27 October 1953 to Edouard Svitalski, quoted in *DB*, 93, note 7.

44 *DB*, 179.

45 Letter of 19 August 1956 to Stravinsky (PSS).

46 *SCF* (94), 130–2. See also L. Morton, "Stravinsky in Los Angeles," 84.

47 *SCF* (94), 135; *DB*, 180.

48 *Sic* in the original. *DB*, 180, once again rewrites Vera's own English.

49 "Stravinsky in Los Angeles"; also "Stravinsky at Home," in Pasler (ed.), *Confronting Stravinsky*, 346.

50 "Stravinsky in Los Angeles," 84.

51 Letter of 19 August.

52 Telegram of 31 July 1956 to Boosey and Hawkes, in *SSCIII*, 401.

53 "Stravinsky at Home," 346.

54 *SCF* (94), 138.

55 The image is Craft's, from ibid.

56 *SCF* (94), 145; also *SPD*, plate 15 (following page 400), a photograph from 1957.

57 Letter of Kirstein to Stravinsky, 31 August 1953, in *SSCI*, 287.

58 Craft had conducted *Kontra-punkte* at a Monday Evening Concert on 20 February 1956, a concert Stravinsky almost certainly attended.

59 See *SCF* (94), 139, for an irresistible account of this visit, which Craft, the present author, and the radio producer Andy Cartwright retraced in January 1995 for the BBC Radio 3 series, *Conversations with Craft (CwC)*.

60 *SCF* (94), 145.

61 Letter of 1 May 1956, partly quoted in *SPD*, 434.

62 *SCF* (94), 162.

63 Franco Abbiati, "Strawinski dirige a Venezia il suo 'Canticum Sacrum,' " *Nuovo Corriere della sera*, 14 September 1956. See also *SCF* (94), 145–6.

64 P. Heyworth, "Stravinsky in Venice," *Observer*, 16 September 1956.

65 "Had the premiere performance taken place in the Fenice Theatre instead of in the Basilica," one critic suggested, "some sort of demonstration undoubtedly would have occurred." Christina Thoresby, "Stravinsky in Venice," *New York Times*, 15 September 1956.

66 *SCF* (94), 146; Craft talks about hundreds of people, but Stravinsky later told T. S. Eliot

that only a few still remained, seated at tables. See Stephen Spender, *Journals 1939–1983* (London: Faber, 1985), 184.

23   THE ETERNAL FOOTMAN HOLDS HIS COAT

1   Letter to Stravinsky of 3 November 1955 (PSS). Stein also wrote the first article about the *Canticum Sacrum:* see *Tempo*, 40 (Summer 1956), 3–5.

2   Robert-E. Dunand, "Une création à Venise: Canticum Sacrum d'Igor Strawinsky," *Le Courrier de Génève*, 26 September 1956.

3   *The Observer*, 16 September 1956.

4   Fred Goldbeck, "Le Cantique de Saint-Marc de Stravinsky," *Preuves*, no. 69 (November 1956).

5   Letter of 16 September 1956, in Chimènes (ed.), *Francis Poulenc: Correspondance*, 852–3. Stravinsky was in fact seventy-four at the time of the first performance. Poulenc, alas, would die ten years before reaching that age.

6   *SCF* (94), 146. What follows is much indebted to this volume.

7   He was certainly remarkably successful in concealing the attack from the concert audience. None of the reviews I have seen so much as mention the prolonged pause between the first and second movements, let alone any illness or general incapacity. Instead they draw attention to his economical style of conducting, perhaps significantly, since Stravinsky was normally active and athletic on the rostrum. According to the critic of the *Telegraf* (4 October), he "confined himself to essentials and simply gave the beat," while *Der Abend* of 3 October described him as "a very painstaking conductor, who avoids exhibitionism and is alive only to the orchestra." All reviews praise the playing, but I feel that Craft's reservations—to put it no more strongly—ring true. See *SCF* (94), 147.

8   See his letters of 11 and 23 October (PSS).

9   *CwC.*

10   *SCF* (94), 149.

11   Ibid.

12   Ibid., 162, 149.

13   Letter of 2 July 1956 (PSS).

14   See Souvtchinsky's letters of 11 November and 22 December 1946, quoted in chapter 13, above.

15   Evidence for this is circumstantial but convincing. In *Are you the son . . . ?*, Soulima remarks how easy it was to trust Souvtchinsky, and how dangerous. In May 1945, Stravinsky wrote to his pianist son (in Paris) that he had had three letters from Souvtchinsky, none of which so much as mentioned Soulima's name, an omission that—considering Souvtchinsky's pastoral role in the prewar dispute between father and son—was certainly strange. Many years later, Boulez told Jesús Aguila that Stravinsky had resented Souvtchinsky's treatment of Soulima over his alleged collaboration and that this was the cause of the breach between them. But Boulez adds, wrongly as we have seen, that the breach was healed by a meeting in 1952. See Aguila, *Le Domaine musical*, 45, note.

16   See above, chapter 19 and note 34.

17   P. Boulez, "Strawinsky demeure," in P. Souvtchinsky (ed.), *Musique Russe*, vol. 1 (Paris: Presses Universitaires de France, 1953), 221–2; English version taken (with small revisions) from the present author's translation of the subsequent Boulez collection, *Relevés d'apprenti*: see "Stravinsky Remains," in *Stocktakings From an Apprenticeship* (Oxford: Oxford University Press, 1991), 108.

18   Letter of 27 June 1953, in *SSCII*, 348 (the original is in BN Boulanger).

19 Souvtchinsky, "Introduction," in *Musique Russe,* vol. 1, 21–2 and note.

20 Letter of 27 June.

21 Aguila, *Le Domaine musical,* 43.

22 Souvtchinsky, "A propos d'un retard," *Cahiers de la Compagnie Madeleine Renaud—Jean-Louis Barrault,* 3 (1954), 7–24. See also Aguila, op. cit., 43–6.

23 Ibid., 53 et seq. The title "Domaine Musical" was introduced for the second season, starting in February 1955.

24 Letter of 23 March 1956 (PSS).

25 See his letter of 22 November 1955 (PSS).

26 *SCF* (1994), 151–2. The remark about the *Ode to Napoleon* was in fact made at dinner the next day.

27 See "Trajectoires: Ravel, Stravinsky, Schönberg," in *Contrepoints,* 6 (1949), 122-42; English translation by the present author in *Stocktakings From an Apprenticeship* (OUP, Oxford, 1991), 188–208.

28 *SCF* (1994), 152–7.

29 Ibid., 153. The French word for "boor" is "mufle," which Craft, however, misspells "mouffle." The conversation must have been in French as Souvtchinsky did not speak English, and one is mildly skeptical, therefore, about Craft's lengthy translations of his remarks, within quotation marks. With Boulez, Craft notes elsewhere (ibid., 151), the conversation had been bilingual, each speaking his own language. The impression of linguistic fluency conveyed by the Souvtchinsky transcripts is thus suspect, to say the least.

30 Aguila, *Le Domaine musical,* 43.

31 It is just possible, though extremely unlikely, that Craft himself knew about the letter, a copy of which had been sent to the composer by the denazification authorities in Paris (see above, chapter 9, note 30, and relevant text; also chapter 12, note 32). What is altogether more likely is that Craft came across it subsequently, probably after Stravinsky's death, when he was going through the archives and editing the composer's correspondence for publication. The first published reference to the letter is in *SSCI* (1982). By contrast, the earlier reports of the Souvtchinsky lunch in *R&C,* 191–9, and *SCF* (72), 61–5, omit all mention of Soulima, who admittedly was still alive at the time. But since he died in 1994, almost at the precise moment that *SCF* (94) came out, his death cannot have been the reason for the material's inclusion in that edition.

32 *SCF* (94), 153.

33 Letter of 28 March 1956 to Brigitte Manceaux, in Chimènes, 835–6, but first published in Hélène de Wendel (ed.), *Francis Poulenc: Correspondance 1915–1963* (Paris: Éditions du Seuil, 1967), 235–6. Poulenc does not, of course, refer expressly to the *Canticum Sacrum,* which was not yet known in March 1956. "Je continuerai," he writes, "à écrire *do mi sol do* et n'approuve pas Stravinsky qui se met des chapeaux trop jeunes pour son âge." Of course, Poulenc may have been "going about" saying this, as Craft put it in the original (but not the revised) edition of his chronicle, but if so, how did he—Craft—come to hear of it, not having been in France since 1952? See *SCF* (72), 62, where the text differs in many details from that of the 1994 edition. The original (1969) account of this conversation, in *R&C,* 191–9, tallies—apart from the usual tinkerings—with the 1972 text. The entry is not yet in the British edition of *Dial* (1968).

34 *SCF* (94), 157.

35 See his letter of 13 November 1956 to Craft (PSS).

36 Letter of 14 November 1956 to Theodore Strawinsky (PSS).

37 See Berman's letter of 23 October (PSS).

38 See, for instance, Poulenc's letter of 7 November 1956 to Milhaud (private collection).

39 See Stravinsky's medical diary, in *ASS,* 159; also Symonds's report in ibid., 157–8, and 155, note 2.

40 *SCF* (94), 158–9.

41 Craft was present, but has so far published no memoir of the meeting beyond the bald mention in *SCF* (94), 159.

42 *SCF* (94), 159. Tansman's letter has unfortunately not surfaced.

43 See above, chapter 17.

44 John Goldsmith (ed.), *Stephen Spender: Journals 1939–1983* (London: Faber and Faber, 1985), 183.

45 Stravinsky and Kirstein lunched together on 12 January and agreed that *Agon* would figure in the company's autumn season. See *SSCI*, 291, note 30.

46 Jay S. Harrison, "Stravinsky Is Conductor of His Own 'Persephone,' " *New York Herald Tribune*, 11 January 1957.

47 *SCF* (94), 163, 172.

48 Howard Taubman, "Music: Homage to a Living Master," *New York Times*, 11 January 1957.

24 TALKING THE BOOK

1 Letter of 24 May 1957 to John Andrewes (PSS: the letter is in *SSCIII*, 405, but without the passage quoted here).

2 Letter of "Friday" (June, 1956). See chapter 22, note 38.

3 PSS.

4 *M&C*, 18.

5 *SCF* (94), 151. The question and answer quoted figured eventually in *Conv*, 127, but appeared first in English in Igor Stravinsky, "Composing," in *Atlantic Monthly*, 199/6 (June 1957), 49.

6 For the first of these references, see *Conv*, 21; *Atlantic Monthly*, 49. The remark about Webern composing at the piano is in *Atlantic Monthly*, 48, and survived through the various other printings of these early questions, but was excised from *Conv*, 15 (see the question about "the musical idea").

7 Igor Stravinsky, "Foreword," *Die Reihe, 2: Anton Webern*, vii. The *juste de la musique* remark is in *Conv*, 127; *Atlantic Monthly*, 50.

8 This in spite of the fact that Stravinsky sent the definitive answer to Boulez on 13 May. See *SSCII*, 351, note 10.

9 Joan Peyser, *Boulez: Composer, Conductor, Enigma* (London: Cassell, 1976), 135, amplified by Boulez's remarks to me in a conversation of December 2002.

10 *SSCII*, 350.

11 The relevant letters, dated 28 January, 9 February, 17 February, and a postcard of 25 February, are all in PSS in the Craft collection.

12 Craft's letter is not accessible, but Boulez's postcard of 25 February makes its contents reasonably clear. "Please," it urges, "don't be shy [ne vous excusez pas] about conducting *Marteau*."

13 For confirmation of this account, see Dorothy L. Crawford, *Evenings On and Off the Roof*, 167–9.

14 *SSCII*, 350.

15 Letter of 15 March 1957, in *SSCII*, 392 (retranslated from the original in HRC, Nabokov). The "marvellously interesting" is also from this letter.

16 Letter of 12 May 1957, in *SSCI*, 259, but here retranslated from the original in BN (copy also in PSS).

17 Letter of 23 March 1956 (PSS).

18 Letter of 16 May 1957 (PSS).

19 Letter of 16 April 1957 (PSS).

20 Telegrams of 21 March, quoted in *M&C*, xviii, note 7.

21 Letter of 15 March.

22 See his letter to Adams of 3 May 1957, in *SSCIII*, 403.

23 See Joseph, *Stravinsky and Balanchine*, 260.

24 Letter of 22 May 1956 (PSS). Sacher had first proposed the commission, as we saw, on 29 July 1954, repeating the offer on 17 August 1955, 15 May 1956, and 4 April 1957.

25 Letter of 13 April 1957 (PSS).

26 Letters of 24 April (Sacher), 9 May (Stravinsky), and 15 May (Sacher), respectively. The Basle premiere of *Canticum sacrum* was on 16 May.

27 See chapter 22, note 7. The *DTÖ* publication is accompanied by a lengthy introduction by Webern: see H. Moldenhauer, *Anton von Webern: A Chronicle of His Life and Work* (London: Gollancz, 1978), 84–5, for a substantial quotation.

28 In the Monday Evening Concerts of, respectively, 4 February and 11 March. Stravinsky, as we saw, already knew the Couperin work from Hugues Cuénod's recording.

29 See *ASS*, 62–3, for a facsimile of the first seventeen bars of the transcript, with Stravinsky's added parts. Craft's account of the circumstances here and in *SPD*, 456–7, is self-effacing, but the motivation and necessary materials can only have come from him and through his efforts.

30 *SPD*, 456. See also Craft's preface to the Boosey and Hawkes edition of the three motets.

31 The edition is Glenn. E. Watkins (ed.), *Gesualdo di Venosa: Sacrae Cantiones für sechs und sieben Stimmen* (Hamburg: Ugrino Verlag, 1961), vol. 9. This commentary lists minor changes to the surviving parts of "Illumina nos" but none to the other two motets.

32 Letter of 20 May 1957, in *SSCIII*, 405.

33 See, respectively, Robert Graff's letter of 1 April 1957 to the Manhattan lawyer Arnold Weissberger, who was acting as Stravinsky's agent in the negotiations, proposing a fee of $3,500 plus a share of profits; and Stravinsky's letter of 3 May to Weissberger's partner, Aaron Frosch.

34 Letter of 4 July 1957, in *SSCIII*, 407.

35 See Charles M. Joseph, *Stravinsky Inside Out*, 169–70. Joseph prints the questions and answers, and notes that the corresponding text in Craft's *Present Perspectives*, 271–2 (now reprinted in *M&C*, vol. 18), is inaccurate. See Joseph, 289, note 4. In other ways, the present account is much indebted to Joseph's description, as well as to *SCF* (94), 165-6; *DB*, 184 and note 9; and *CwC*.

36 *CwC*.

37 Cf. Joseph, op. cit., 170.

38 *Diaries, 1939–1960*, 704–5.

39 Joseph, op. cit., 169.

40 "Stravinsky Honored at Festival Concert," *Los Angeles Times*, 19 June 1957.

41 "An Anniversary—An Evening of Stravinsky," *San Francisco Chronicle*, 23 June 1957.

42 See below, chapter 28, notes 4, 5, and related text.

43 Letter of 28 June 1957 (PSS).

44 Letter of 17 June 1957, excerpted in *SSCII*, 393. *Zuppa inglese*—"English soup"—is the Italian for the pudding known as "trifle."

45 Letter of 21 June, in *SSCII*, 394. Nabokov had written in English (presumably dictating to an anglophone secretary), and Stravinsky replied in the same language.

46 *SCF* (94), 159.

47 "Answers to 34 Questions: An Interview with Igor Stravinsky," *Encounter*, 9/1 (July 1957), 3–7. In the slightly earlier version of the interview in *Atlantic Monthly*, 199/6 (June 1957), 46–50, the same question figures but without the *Tenebrae* reference. David H. Smyth has shown that work on *Threni* began before the earliest dated sketch

(29 August). See "Stravinsky as Serialist: The Sketches for *Threni*," *Music Theory Spectrum*, 22, no. 2 (Fall, 2000), 206, note 5.

48 See Paul Horgan, *Encounters with Stravinsky: A Personal Record* (rev. ed., Middletown, Conn.: Wesleyan University Press, 1989), 49–57, for a firsthand account of this episode. "Mirandi" was Miranda Masocco's professional name, but it had stuck.

49 *SCF* (94), 166.

50 *ASS*, 160.

51 Stravinsky wrote to Arnold Weissberger on 17 August that "we are very much enjoying our staying in England and we have made many side trips in this beautiful country." *Annotated Catalogue of the H. Colin Slim Collection*, 303–4. But Craft notes in his diary that the Stravinskys soon became bored with the country and decided to go to London for the weekend (though he admittedly half-contradicts this suggestion in his 1994 "Postscript," where he recalls that they fell in love with the southwestern coastal region, and with the musicians they met there). See *SCF* (94), 167, 173.

52 The only document I have found of the "36 Answers" is an elaborate montage of typed pages and fragments, labelled "An interview with Stravinsky" and dated by Stravinsky "March '57." This is much worked over by Craft, with some insertions in Stravinsky's hand (PSS).

53 See *Conv*, 16–17.

54 *Conv*, 87, and note 1. But a comparison of this passage with its reprinted form in *M&C*, 156, gives yet another disconcerting insight into Craft's editorial method in general. In the later text the Modigliani anecdote is compressed and completely rephrased, and the footnote about the subsequently discovered portrait is partly rewritten and reattributed to Craft himself (as opposed to Stravinsky, writing in the first person). Worst of all, where Stravinsky had originally said of the portrait that "I regret to admit that it does resemble me," he is now made to say "I have not seen it." Craft thus either casts doubt on his own veracity or reveals Stravinsky as a liar, or both. Moreover, he seems to treat his readers as idiots who will swallow anything and themselves have no memory.

55 *Conv*, 38.

56 There is some speculation involved here. Nabokov was certainly in Paris, and they did, according to Craft (*ASS*, 64), discuss the possibility of an NDR concert in Venice. I have concluded from this that the idea of fusing the Venice and Hamburg commissions had already occurred to Nabokov, and that this possibility was raised in Paris. The NDR's formal letter of offer is dated 9 October 1957 (PSS).

57 See *SPD*, plate 15, following p. 400.

58 *Conv*, 17–18.

59 *ASS*, 64; *SCF* (94), 170. In *Conv*, 123, Stravinsky says that he changed the name because *Tenebrae* suggested a liturgical usage.

60 *Conv*, 116–17. A note by Ingolf Dahl in the Morton Archive of UCLA suggests that the flügelhorn part was inspired by an unnamed virtuoso bugler at a poetry and jazz concert in Los Angeles. Such a concert is mentioned in Vera Stravinsky's diary for 7 December 1957 (see *DB*, 190), but by that time the big flügelhorn solo in the "De Elegia Prima" had been written.

61 Stravinsky kept and annotated a cutting of a spiteful piece by the *New Yorker*'s Paris correspondent, which quoted a dismissive review by the *Figaro* critic, Bernard Gavoty (invariably nicknamed "Gavnoti" by Stravinsky, after the Russian word "govno," "shit"). The composer's marginalia are brutally expressive of his loathing for Parisian musical politics. He writes: "For a Lesbian, as she actually is, one could expect a little more subtlety. But let us not forget she is a friend of Goléa and Gavnoti" (cutting in HRC, Nabokov).

62 Goléa, *Rencontres avec Pierre Boulez* (Paris: Julliard, 1958), 196.

63 Quoted in Aguila, *Le Domaine Musical,* 189.

64 Denise Bourdet, *Le Figaro littéraire,* 19 October 1957, quoted in Aguila, op. cit., 189.

65 Jacques Schérer, *Le "Livre" de Mallarmé. Premières recherches sur des documents inédits* (Paris: Gallimard, 1957).

66 *SSCII,* 351–2.

67 *Conv,* 31–2.

25 HE HATH SET ME IN DARK PLACES

1 See Stravinsky's letter of 15 March 1957 to Nabokov, in *SSCII,* 393.

2 Letters of 17 August and 5 September 1957 to Arnold Weissberger (*Annotated Catalogue of the H. Colin Slim Collection,* 303–4; PSS).

3 Telegrams of 10 October 1957 (PSS). In the end the charity performance took place on the 27th of November.

4 See, for instance, Craft in *SCF* (94), 173, echoed by Joseph, *Stravinsky and Balanchine,* 256.

5 Kirstein's pushiness and sometimes transparent manipulativeness have been well described by Charles Joseph. See, for instance, *Stravinsky and Balanchine,* 182–3. Kirstein treated Stravinsky with a measure of deference, but from time to time the mask slipped.

6 See Weissberger's letter of 12 September. Weissberger also confirmed that the *Agon* staging was going ahead, another item of information Stravinsky would no doubt have preferred to receive from Kirstein himself.

7 See the marvelous series of photographs in Taper, *Balanchine,* 264-72. Taper, who was present, also noted down some of the composer's remarks. For instance, he observed that Diana Adams had "legs like the Solingen scissors trademark." See also Joseph, *Stravinsky and Balanchine,* 261–2.

8 Letter of 16 November 1957 (PSS).

9 What was tiresome about it is unclear. It may have been some feeling that Kirstein was neglecting him, but real evidence is lacking.

10 Telegram of 29 November (PSS).

11 28 November 1957.

12 "Three Sides of *Agon,*" *Evergreen Review* (Winter, 1959), reprinted in Edwin Denby, *Dance Writings* (London: Dance Books, 1986), 459–65.

13 *New York World Telegram,* 2 December 1957; cf. ibid., 11 September 1944.

14 *New York Herald Tribune,* 2 December 1957.

15 Letter of 9 December 1957, in *SSCI,* 291.

16 Quoted in Joseph, *Stravinsky and Balanchine,* 256.

17 See Roth's telegram of 27 December 1957 and Stravinsky's letter of 28 December in reply (PSS). The point was that Balanchine was to have staged *Agon* in Milan but was now ruling himself out. Writing to Stravinsky on 6 January, Roth grumbled that he had an unbreakable agreement with La Scala but hoped that, without Balanchine, they might themselves withdraw.

18 Letter of 10 January 1958 to Liebermann (PSS).

19 See Nabokov's letter of 12 February (PSS) and Stravinsky's reply of 19 February (HRC, Nabokov).

20 Letter of 19 March 1958 (HRC, Nabokov).

21 Letter of 27 March 1958 (PSS). Strictly speaking, these vacillations over the length of *Threni* are inexplicable, since they argue real uncertainty, not prevarication (for which no consistent motive is apparent). Stravinsky may have feared that the work would *seem* too long, but had then to admit that it could not be shortened.

22 The premiere of *Le Visage nuptial* was on 4 December 1957. After the performance, Boulez and Stockhausen sent Stravinsky a joint postcard from Cologne.

23 Letter of 23 December 1957 (PSS). Begun in Schoenberg's mid-twenties, *Gurrelieder* is a huge choral-orchestral work in a post-Wagnerian style, which took more than a decade to reach its final form.

24 Letter of 25 January 1958 (PSS).

25 Letter of 19 February, *SSCII*, 395.

26 Letter of 1 March (HRC, Nabokov).

27 Letter of 10 March (HRC, Nabokov).

28 Letter of 3 March, quoted in *SSCII*, 395.

29 Letter of 3 March (PSS).

30 Letter of 8 March, *SSCII*, 396.

31 Letter of 6 December 1957 (PSS).

32 Letters of 20 May 1958 to P. Huber and P. Sacher, respectively (PSS). Sacher had originally conveyed the proposal in his letter of 2 April. Basle University subsequently approached Britten, whose *Cantata Academica* is a setting of the text originally submitted to Stravinsky.

33 Letter of 11 March 1958, *SSCII*, 396–7.

34 Letter of 16 March, in *SSCII*, 397, but very misleadingly translated. The Russian epithet "tyotka" (literally "auntie," but also colloquially "pansy" or "queer") is applied to the pianist (whom Stravinsky assumed to be male), but interrogatively: not "Is the pederast Weber really taking on some serious expenditures?" (as if Stravinsky knew him already as both a pervert and a miser), but "He [the pianist, but also of course by implication Weber] must presumably be a pansy if Weber is taking on such serious expenses." Considering that such sentiments are likely to be heavily scrutinized by lawyers before going into print, it seems amazing that nobody could manage actually to translate the text accurately.

35 Letters of 21 and 29 March (PSS), quoted in *SSCII*, 397, 399.

36 Letter of 26 March; *SSCIII*, 414.

37 See Joseph N. Straus, *Stravinsky's Late Music*, 26–33, for a discussion of Krenek's influence and a reprint of the two charts; also Clare Hogan, " 'Threni:' Stravinsky's 'Debt' to Krenek," in *Tempo* 141 (June 1982), 22–9.

38 See Nabokov's letter to Stravinsky of 2 July 1958, in *SSCII*, 401.

39 Letter of 2 July (PSS). For fairly obvious reasons, the account of the Schuh meeting is omitted from *SSCII*.

40 See Schuh's letter of 11 November 1958 to Nabokov (HRC, Nabokov).

41 With designs by Caspar Neher. The libretto of *Rasputin's End* is by Stephen Spender.

42 *SPD*, 299. See also *SCF* (94), 189.

43 *SPD*, 437.

44 Letter of 21 June 1958 (PSS). I have left untranslated the nonexistent Russian adverb "ostil'no" in the final phrase. The funeral anecdote first appeared in print, as far as I know, in *Avec Stravinsky*, 22 (oddly, without the "we still have Glazunov"), and in English in *Conv*, 45. See also *SCS*, 112–3.

45 De Schloezer, "Chronique musicale," *Nouvelle Revue française*, 31 (1 July 1928), 104–8. Cf. *SCS*, 469, and note 58.

46 *SCF* (94), 178.

47 Craft, in *SCF* (94), 189, remembers it as a piano, but Stravinsky had asked Roth to get him "a small muted pianino (a spinet or an upright small piano)" (letter of 26 July, in *SSCIII*, 415), and Roth replied on 5 August that a "muted cembalo" was being installed.

48 So he claims in *SCF* (94), 189.

49 Craft's letters of September 1958 from Hamburg and Brussels are in PSS.

50 *SCF* (94), 176. Walpole's remark is in a letter of 15/16 August 1776 to the Countess of Upper Ossory: see W. S. Lewis (ed.), *The Yale Edition of Horace Walpole's Correspondence*, vol. 32 (London: Oxford University Press, 1965), 315.

51 Letter of 5 October 1958, quoted in *DB*, 193, note 3.

52 *Oedipus Rex* was performed without a speaker, apparently because of a mixup resulting from the death of Piovesan. *The Rite of Spring* was with the 1943 revision of the "Danse sacrale."

53 *SCF* (94), 180–1. An account of part of the conference is in Eugenio Montale, *Il Secondo mestiere: Arte, musica—società*, ed. G. Zampa (Milan: Arnoldo Mondadori, 1996), 389–92.

54 The letter is dated 21 September. Nabokov managed to get it back but, instead of destroying it, as Berlin presumably supposed, he kept it. It is now among his papers at UT Austin (HRC, Nabokov).

55 John Ruskin, *The Stones of Venice* (8th ed., London: George Allen, 1897), vol. 2, 303–22.

56 Montale, *Il Secondo mestiere*, 468, quoted also in *ASS*, 72–3. Montale's first trade ("mestiere") was, of course, that of one of Italy's leading poets.

57 Giuseppe Pugliese, "Le 'Lamentazioni' di Strawinsky," *Il Gazettino*, 24 September 1958.

58 " 'Threni' in Venice," *Observer*, 28 September 1958.

59 Undated note in UCLA, Morton.

60 Recordings were made of all the items in both of Stravinsky's 1958 Venice concerts, and released on Arkadia, 1CD 0062731.

61 Letter of 4 October 1958, in Chimènes (ed.), *Francis Poulenc: Correspondance*, 900.

62 Pugliese, op. cit.

63 Postcard of 2 October 1958 (UCLA, Morton).

64 See for instance *ImpLif*, 207. *DB*, 193, merely refers vaguely to "Boulez's concert."

65 Letter of 10 April 1958, Boulez to Stravinsky (PSS).

66 See for instance Roth's letter of 27 June (PSS).

67 Letter of 10 April.

68 The description is Souvtchinsky's, in his letter to Stravinsky of 17 June 1958 (PSS).

69 See Boulez's letter to Craft, 12 September 1958. Boulez had noticed that proper soloists were being rehearsed for the Venice premiere.

70 Private communication, December 2002.

71 *ImpLif*, 208.

72 Private communication from Boulez.

73 Clarendon (Bernard Gavoty), "Strawinsky a présenté ses 'Threni,' " *Le Figaro*, 17 November 1958.

74 This anecdote, and certain other elements of my description of the concert, are taken from an unsigned and undated contemporary account, "Tout ne s'est pas bien passé pour Stravinsky à Paris. Voici pourquoi"; in an unidentified periodical (cutting in PSS). The assumption that the Russian lady in question was Sonya Botkine is, however, mine, derived from the fact that she attended the concert and wrote to Stravinsky the following day regretting that she had tried but failed to speak to him (see *SPD*, 70–1). Most independent accounts of the concert agree that the audience reaction was friendly until Stravinsky declined to take a bow, though Craft implies in *SSCII*, 353, that Stravinsky refused to reappear because the audience had jeered his music. The fact that most newspaper reviews mention only the positive reaction tends to support the independent view, since in general newspaper critics do not wait to study the audience's behavior at the end of concerts they are having to review.

1   Letter of 14 November 1958 (PSS).
2   Letter of 16 September 1956 to Henri Hell, in Chimènes (ed.), *Francis Poulenc: Correspondance*, 852–3.
3   Letter of 15 November 1958, in R. Wangermée (ed.), *Paul Collaer: Correspondance avec des amis musiciens* (Sprimont: Mardaga, 1996), 436–7. Milhaud, in California, had not attended the Paris *Threni*, but he was plainly aware that it was taking place.
4   *Avec Stravinsky* (Monaco: Éditions du Rocher, 1958), 28, 18. For convenience, I quote the English text of this remark in *Conv*, 131.
5   Boulez, "D'une conjonction—en trois éclats," in *Avec Stravinsky*, 97–9. I have tried to improve my own translation (see *Stocktakings*, 219) for greater clarity in the present context.
6   See Goléa, *Rencontres avec Pierre Boulez* (Paris: Julliard, 1958), 10. It should perhaps be mentioned that no such browsing would actually have been possible, as the pages of a new copy of this volume were uncut. *Avec Stravinsky*, by contrast, had ready-cut pages.
7   See Souvtchinsky's letter of 19 December 1958 (PSS).
8   Letter of 25 November 1958 (PSS); English translation in *SSCII*, 354. The Rome concert included *Les Noces*, the Symphony in Three Movements, and *Scènes de ballet*.
9   See *Rencontres avec Pierre Boulez*, 195–6.
10 Letter of 19 December 1958 (PSS).
11 Letter of 26 December (PSS).
12 Letter of 30 December 1958 (HRC, Nabokov).
13 Letter of 25 January 1959 (PSS).
14 Letter of 8 January (PSS).
15 30 January and 1 February, respectively (PSS).
16 Letter of 26 February 1959 (PSS). Boulez told me that "Goléa could not accept the evolution of Stravinsky, and still less the fact that we were (Stravinsky and I) on friendly terms. He acted like a veteran of 45–46. And the veteran's mentality has never been particularly mine" (private communication, 9 November 2004).
17 Letter of 19 December.
18 Letter of 4 March 1959 (PSS).
19 Ibid.
20 A. Goléa, "Pariser Musikindustrie," *NZfM* (February 1959), 79–80.
21 As told to a press conference in Tokyo in April 1959. See *SCF* (94), 199.
22 Letter of 7 March 1959 (PSS).
23 Letter of, probably, 3 March 1959. The draft letter to the *NZfM* is dated 2 March, but the covering note, on a typed extract from the Goléa review, is undated (PSS).
24 Letter of 7 March.
25 Letters to Souvtchinsky of 9 March, and to Boulez of 10 March, in *SSCII*, 355–6.
26 See his letter to Souvtchinsky of 9 March.
27 Letter to Boulez of 6 March 1959 (PSS). The Stockhausen allegation is slightly mysterious, since Craft had been preparing a performance of *Zeitmasse* for its composer to conduct at a Monday Evening Concert the previous December (though the performance was cancelled as the flautist was ill). But Stravinsky had heard that Stockhausen had been talking in a similar vein about his music. See his letter of 9 March 1959 to Souvtchinsky. I have been unable to trace the attack on Boulez.
28 Letter of 19 March (PSS).
29 Letters of 19 March and 10 April, Boulez to Stravinsky. Stravinsky's prompt is dated 23 March (PSS).
30 I say this with all humility, toward the end of a half-million-word biography.
31 Letter of 23 February 1959 (PSS).

32   Letter of 23 March (PSS).

33   Letter of 1 April 1959 (PSS).

34   Crosby was communicating through Stravinsky's lawyer Arnold Weissberger. Weissberger's letter to Stravinsky with the offer of $20,000 is dated 27 February 1959 (PSS). Eliot wrote to the composer on 19 March referring to his own commission. See Craft, *ImpLif,* 211–12.

35   Letter of 19 March.

36   Letter of 8 April 1959 (PSS), quoted with some excisions in *ImpLif,* 212.

37   Letter of 21 May 1959, in ibid., 213.

38   See his letter to Eliot of 30 January 1958 (PSS).

39   Craft's "diary" note that *Avec Stravinsky* was published on the day of the *Agon* concert is another of those mistakes that support the view that the diary entries were often concocted at a later date. The first and only edition of *Avec Stravinsky* indicates on the final page—as usual with French publications—"Achevé d'imprimer . . . en Octobre MCMLVIII . . . Mise en vente: Novembre 1958." Some version of the conversation texts was nevertheless on sale at the October 1957 concert, but I have not been able to trace a copy. The German omnibus edition is *Igor Strawinsky—Leben und Werk—von ihm selbst* (Zurich/Mainz: Atlantis/Schott, 1957).

40   See "Dialoge: Igor Strawinsky—Robert Craft," *Melos,* 25 (February 1958), 49–59. A second instalment appeared (as "Neue Dialoge") in the September issue, 261–93.

41   The idea of updating *Chron* and adding the questions had been suggested by Herbert Weinstock of Alfred A. Knopf as early as March 1957 (letter of 21 March); the idea of a new book based on conversations was put forward by Ken McCormick, of Doubleday, in August 1957, in a letter to Stravinsky's lawyer-agent, Arnold Weissberger (see Weissberger's letter to Stravinsky of 30 August, in PSS).

42   The agreement with Doubleday is dated 31 March 1958. See also Eliot's letter to Stravinsky of 19 March 1958, quoted in part in *ImpLif,* 199.

43   See, for instance, Souvtchinsky's letter to Stravinsky of 22 February 1958 (PSS), and Peter du Sautoy's to Stravinsky of 11 April 1958 (PSS). The admission that Craft had written the journal for publication under Stravinsky's name is in his letter to Richard de la Mare (of Faber) of 9 June 1958. The composer, on the other hand, according to this letter, wanted Craft to change the person of the diarist and publish it under his own name (PSS).

44   Letter of 15 March 1958 (PSS).

45   Letter of 23 May. See note 43, above.

46   Joseph Bloch, in an unidentified 1959 journal (cutting in PSS).

47   *Conv,* 16. Strictly the remark is Craft's, but attributed to Stravinsky, who echoes it on page 18.

48   Alfred Frankenstein, "When Stravinsky Talks He Is Always Worth Hearing," *San Francisco Sunday Chronicle,* 19 July 1959.

49   Craft told me this himself, with understandable but revealing pride. I have not succeeded in tracing the remark in print.

50   Cf. *M&C.* Even the title of this edition (*Memories and Commentaries:* that of the completely different second volume of the original series) seems designed to throw a smoke screen over the past.

51   *Conv,* 125–6.

52   *Conv,* 48. The book also prints letters from Ravel, Dylan Thomas, and Jacques Rivière; but letters from Satie were excluded because of defamatory remarks they contained about Florent Schmitt, who was still alive during the editing process, though he died in August 1958, before publication.

53   Letter of 10 April 1959 (PSS). The final phrase is in English in the original.

54   Craft's latest account of the impression made by Kabuki is in *SCF* (94), 198–9.

However, the equivalent text in *Dial*, 190–1, is significantly different and attributes the reaction more specifically to Stravinsky himself (rather than the collective "we").

55 *ASS*, 164. The interview, from the English-language paper *The Mainichi*, is quoted in *SCF* (94), 202.
56 Letter of 8 April; see *ImpLif*, 212.
57 See *SCF* (94), 204–6, for a detailed and highly amusing account of the Noh experience.
58 Letter of 24 April 1959 (HRC, Nabokov).
59 *SCF* (94), 200.
60 "Stravinsky Concert Topping Festival Season Events," *The Mainichi*, 10 May 1959.
61 *ASS*, 164. See also *SCF* (94), 209.

27 A STRANGE CONCOCTION

1 On 6 April 1959.
2 Letter of 10 April (PSS).
3 *Mem*, 105–6.
4 Equivalent to just over $7,000 in the values of the day.
5 The French text remains unpublished. Stravinsky sent it to Souvtchinsky on 29 May, and a copy of this is in PSS.
6 See Stravinsky's letter to Souvtchinsky of 29 May 1959, actually a lengthy marginal gloss on a typed copy of the French text of Boulez's draft (PSS).
7 See Helmut Schmidt-Garre, "Scherchen und Boulez dirigieren in der Münchner Musica viva," *Melos*, 26 (April 1959), 116–17. The performance was on 6 March, the talk on the 5th. Boulez himself, forewarned now about Stravinsky's touchiness, brought the review to his attention in his letter of 9 May.
8 Letter of 6 June, quoted (in a different translation) in *SSCII*, 357.
9 Letter of 29 May.
10 Letter of 6 June 1959 (PSS).
11 Letter of 26 June (PSS).
12 On the 15th. The remainder of the concert (Bach's third orchestral suite, Schoenberg's *Accompaniment to a Film Scene*, and Mozart's Symphony in A major, K. 201) was conducted by Craft.
13 His slightly confusing account of the process is in *Mem*, 106–7.
14 Letter of 11 June 1959 (PSS). The concert was on the 8th.
15 See Gibson's letter of 8 June and Stravinsky's reply of the 10th (PSS).
16 *Encounters with Stravinsky*, 92.
17 For Horgan's full account of this episode, see ibid., 86–110.
18 Ibid., 97–8.
19 Ibid., 106–8.
20 "London Hears Threni," *New Statesman*, 13 June 1959, 824.
21 *Encounters with Stravinsky*, 93, 88.
22 *AMC*, 61.
23 *Encounters with Stravinsky*, 105.
24 30 July 1959.
25 Letter of Robert Craft to Glenn Watkins, 1 August 1959. See Watkins, "The Canon and Stravinsky's Late Style," in Pasler (ed.), *Confronting Stravinsky*, 234; also *Mem*, 106.
26 Letter of 15 August (PSS).
27 See Stravinsky's letters of 15 August and 8 September, also Liebermann's reply of 16 September (PSS).
28 Letter of 18 August, discussed in *AMC*, 53, 61–2. Libman thought that she owed the contact to Deborah Ishlon, or Bliss Hebert, the director of the Santa Fe *Anna Bolena*.

29 Letter to Graff of 2 August 1959 (PSS).

30 Letter of 6 August (PSS).

31 Letter of 16 August (PSS). The "new play" may have been a white lie. After *The Elder Statesman*, Eliot seems to have neither written nor projected anything for the stage.

32 See for instance his letter of 22 July to Souvtchinsky (PSS).

33 Letter of 11 August (PSS). The abbreviated letter to the *NZfM* is dated 4 August. Boulez explained to me that "Strobel was *not* interested in a polemical article about an event which took place in Paris, not in Germany, and many months before. There was already a row over a remark Stravinsky had made about German orchestras, which he had described as unable to play rhythmically, just as the Japanese could not distinguish between the consonants 'l' and 'r', and Strobel didn't want another polemic of this kind. So when he did the translation, he shortened and softened my text. And I agreed with him" (private communication, 9 November 2004).

34 Letter of 15 August, in *SSCII*, 358, but here retranslated.

35 Letter of 20 August (PSS).

36 Letter of 24 August, in *SSCII*, 358.

37 "Ein Brief von Pierre Boulez," *NZfM*, October 1959, 526. Craft's remark in *SSCII*, 358, that "the Copenhagen version was never published" is true only in the literal sense that it was published with relatively minor changes and of course in German (see below in the main text). In any normal sense of the words it is simply untrue, or at best grossly misleading.

38 Letters of 6 June, 26 June, 28 July (PSS).

39 Letter of 22 August (PSS).

40 Letter of 7 March 1959.

41 Letter of 23 August (PSS). The "Valkyries" were the female admirers who, according to Souvtchinsky, followed Boulez around.

42 Letter of 5 September (PSS).

43 Letter of 10 October, Souvtchinsky to Stravinsky (PSS).

44 See his letter of 23 February 1960 to Souvtchinsky, quoted in *SSCII*, 359, albeit in a confusingly edited text. Stravinsky was still in a rage with Goléa, and was simply incapable of understanding why the rest of the world was not in the same frame of mind.

45 *SCF* (94), 210–11.

46 See his letter to Stravinsky of 7 September (PSS).

47 For the Bernstein encounters, see *ASS*, 165 and note 21; *DB*, 194 and note 2.

48 See Craft's letter to Watkins of 19 June 1959, in "The Canon and Stravinsky's Late Style," 234. I am also indebted to Professor Watkins for his personal memories of this episode.

49 See his letter of 11 September 1959 (PSS). Watkins had previously sent his own realizations, which, moreover, Stravinsky had approved and declined to alter. It seems to have been Craft who persuaded the composer after all to make his own versions. See his letter to Watkins of 16 August 1959 (PSS).

50 Craft reported to Watkins on the 27th that the realizations were complete (PSS), and on the 29th Stravinsky announced them to Ernst Roth (*SSCIII*, 422).

51 Letter of 17 June 1959 (PSS). See also Marcelle Oury, *Lettres à mon peintre* (Paris: Perrin, 1965).

52 The draft of the full four-part double canon is dated 24 November 1959. Poulenc, on the other hand, wrote to Bois on 12 April 1960 that "I am quite inclined to set to music a new quatrain from the *Bestiaire*, for dear Dufy's memorial . . ." (see Chimènes [ed.], *Francis Poulenc: Correspondance*, 946). Bois's own account of the whole episode is in any case chronologically problematical. He says that Mme. Oury approached him because he was "close to Igor Strawinsky." Yet he himself had only met Stravinsky for the first

time in mid-September. Moreover, he has Poulenc's song arrive well before Stravinsky's canon, even though Stravinsky's two-part October draft already refers to Dufy. See Mario Bois, *Près de Strawinsky* (Paris: Marval, 1996), 81–2.

53 Most of these details are in Stravinsky's letter of 1 November 1959 to Souvtchinsky (PSS). Curiously, this London visit is passed over in silence by Craft (except, briefly, in *ImpLif*), and it is a blank in Vera's diary *(DB)* and (apart from the actual dates) in Stravinsky's medical diaries *(ASS)*.

54 Horgan's account is in *Encounters with Stravinsky*, 110–18.

55 *Times*, 10 November 1959. The anonymous review was by William Mann.

56 Letter of 19 November 1959. The body of the letter is in *SSCI*, 124, but the advice about foot baths is in a postscript that *SSC* omits.

57 *Dial*, 29–30.

58 Libman's assertion that *Movements* was recorded two days after the concert seems to be a mistake (*AMC*, 81). In a letter to Boulez of 13 January 1960 Stravinsky refers to a possible recording with Mrs. Weber in June, but there is no other evidence for this plan and John McClure told me that there was never a studio recording with her and Stravinsky. Instead she recorded the work with Ferenc Fricsay, whose idea the commission had been in the first place. Stravinsky recorded it in 1961 with Charles Rosen (see below, chapter 29).

59 Libman's own account, based on and therefore supported by her correspondence with Stravinsky and Craft in PSS, is in *AMC*, 61–85. Regrettably, this fascinating but—in matters of musical detail—error-prone memoir has always to be read in conjunction with Craft's vitriolic "review" of it in *SPD*, 569–93, a text that tells the reader more about its author than about the essential facts of the matter but which by that very token cannot be ignored as a psychological document in its own right.

60 *AMC*, 62–3.

61 For instance, to Craft on 26 January 1960 (PSS).

62 Libman first aired her complaints about Ishlon in a letter to Craft of 8 October 1959 (PSS). Later she accused her of withholding publicity photographs and taking unilateral decisions about program publicity.

63 *SCF* (94), 217. The postscript is candidly dated "1994."

64 The actual text in *DB*, 194, is roughly accurate (with Craft's usual editorial tinkerings), but obscures the previous omission with an invented first sentence.

65 *AMC*, 63.

66 *New York Herald Tribune*, 21 December 1959.

67 The other six-part Gesualdo motet completed by Stravinsky, "Da pacem, Domine," was listed in the program-book layout but not in the program notes, nor in any of the newspaper review program listings, and it is not mentioned in any review, even those that refer to "Assumpta est Maria." It seems fairly clear that it was not sung. The seven-part completion, "Illumina nos," was never in the program, pace Christian Goubault, *Igor Stravinsky* (Paris: Champion, 1991), 295.

68 Jay S. Harrison, "Robert Craft and His Unique Life," *New York Herald Tribune*, 20 December 1959.

69 *AMC*, 81.

70 "Stravinsky Conducts Own New Work at Town Hall," *New York Herald Tribune*, 11 January 1960.

71 Bois, *Près de Strawinsky*, 116.

72 *AMC*, 81.

73 Libman implies, however, that Stravinsky had in 1959 turned down a fee twice as large for a less demanding appearance with CBS's "chief rival." See *AMC*, 153.

74 As reported in the *New York Times* on 1 February 1960. The program was shown in CBS's "Leonard Bernstein and the Philharmonic" series on 31 January.

1   Jay S. Harrison, "Robert Craft and His Unique Life," *New York Herald Tribune,* 20 December 1959.

2   Letter of 23 March 1959 (private collection); emphasis in the original.

3   Soulima Stravinsky, interview with Thor Wood.

4   This and some other information in this paragraph is from private conversations in 2002 with John McClure, who succeeded David Oppenheim as Columbia's Director of Masterworks in 1959. McClure told me that he was not always personally present at routine tape-editing sessions.

5   The percussionist William Kraft told me in 2001 that he considered some, possibly all, of the edited *Petrushka* recording to have used takes conducted by Craft.

6   For instance, Stephen Spender, who told me in 1992 that he took Craft to one side during a visit to Kenneth Clarke at Saltwood Castle in 1963.

7   The Disney letter (consisting mainly of a quotation from the *Los Angeles Times,* and signed "A. G.") had appeared in the *Saturday Review* of 30 January 1960. Stravinsky's reply, dated 4 February 1960, appeared in the *Saturday Review* on 12 March, and was subsequently reprinted in *Expo,* 146, note 1.

8   For instance, the claim that he only visited Disney's studio once (false), and the (misleading) appeal to his Disney contract without mentioning the fact that the contract expressly gave Disney carte blanche to alter the score as he wished. Stravinsky may or may not have been upset by what he heard on his second visit, but he nevertheless sold Disney a similar option on three other works soon afterwards. See above, chapters 7 and 8.

9   Some of these reminiscences were scurrilous, and in particular certain remarks about Nijinsky's hereditary syphilis, which had to be excised after his widow's lawyers threatened to withdraw permission to print the long letter from the dancer that is the main feature of this memoir (see *Mem,* 38–40).

10 *Mem,* 65; cf. *SCS,* pp. 360, 449. Also *Mem,* 17–25, and Souvtchinsky's letter to Marya Yudina, 26 April 1960, partly printed in Bretanitskaya (ed.), *Pyotr Suvchinsky i ego vremya,* 335–6.

11 For example, in one draft of *Mem,* Stravinsky is made to say that after his father's death he moved to a room on another floor of the house. Another passage has Scriabin reporting to Stravinsky on the supposed brawl at the Moscow premiere of *The Rite of Spring.* Both these inventions are firmly crossed out in the draft.

12 *AMC,* 70.

13 Reported to Francis Steegmuller by Samuel Dushkin (Columbia, Steegmuller).

14 Private communication, 1992.

15 *SPD,* 424.

16 Private communication from Denise Strawinsky.

17 Letter of 12 June 1960, Etta Dahl to Lawrence Morton (UCLA, Morton).

18 Letter to Sheldon Meyer, 9 May 1962 (UCLA, Morton).

19 Letter to Boulez, 11 August 1971 (PSS).

20 Original in English, *sic.* The note was copied by Francis Steegmuller when he was researching a possible Stravinsky biography in about 1970, working with the composer's papers in his New York apartment. Since Steegmuller must have been reading many documents in the composer's hand, I trust his annotation "in IS's hand." The copy is in Columbia, Steegmuller, but the original has not surfaced among the composer's papers in PSS.

21 Letter of 28 October 1959 (PSS).

22 Letter of 6 September 1957. Not all the preceding communications survive, but their content can be deduced from those that do.

23 See especially the elaborate denunciation of the children in *CherP* reprinted most recently in *Stravinsky: Glimpses of a Life*, 130–201. For a veiled allusion to the Venice incident, see pp. 194–5, note 60.

24 See, for instance, his letter of 18 March 1961 (PSS).

25 See above, chapter 8. Stravinsky was also irritated with Theodore over his slowness in thanking Eugene Berman for recommending him as designer for *Mavra* at La Scala, Milan, early in 1960. "I'm afraid he will make enemies," he wrote to Denise on 17 February (PSS).

26 *AMC*, 164. See above, chapter 6. Craft notes that this revived Tobias idea was the suggestion of Stravinsky's Los Angeles friend, the Rev. James McLane. See *ImpLif*, 124.

27 The FFF's original letter is dated 5 February 1959; Stravinsky's proposal for a *Seven Last Words* is in his letter of 9 March. The entire brief correspondence is in PSS.

28 Letter of 29 January 1960 (PSS).

29 Sacher's letter is dated 15 February (PSS). Other details here are from *AMC*, 164–7. I consider Libman reliable in such matters, since her information comes substantially from correspondence and other documents, some of which also survive in PSS copies, while others (notably Craft's presumably handwritten letters to her) remain inaccessible.

30 See his letters to Libman of 16 and 23 April 1960 (PSS), also *AMC*, 167. Libman had had a meeting with Graff on the 18th.

31 Craft's notes for the meetings, on 4–6 May 1960, survive in PSS. See next chapter.

32 Letter of 5 July 1960 (PSS).

33 Letter of 1 March 1960 (PSS).

34 Craft told Watkins on 1 March that the *Monumentum* was finished, but four weeks later Stravinsky told Roth that he had "just" finished it, having written to Roth's assistant, Rufina Ampenoff, earlier in the month without mentioning the piece (letters of 28 and 10 March, respectively). The difference is probably between the sketch drafts and the fair copy (the score is dated, simply, March 1960). Gesualdo's birth year is disputed; see Vincis and Dal Molin, "Mo(nu)mentum di Carlo Gesualdo," 229, note 34.

35 So he claims in "Influence or Assistance?," *Stravinsky: Glimpses of a Life*, 44.

36 *Conv*, 24. Asked what he now felt about music as accompaniment to recitation (in connection with *Persephone*), Stravinsky had replied: "Sins cannot be undone, only forgiven."

37 Letter of 1 July 1960, in *SSCIII*, 425.

38 Letter to Paul Sacher, 25 June 1960 (PSS). He told Sacher he would finish in September 1961, but no doubt he was deliberately giving himself good leeway.

39 "Ich fühle Luft von anderen Planeten," from Georg's poem "Entrückung," set by Schoenberg in the vocal finale of his second string quartet.

40 Letter of 18 September 1959 (PSS). The likelihood, however, is that Stravinsky did not read the letter until his return home in mid-January.

41 Letter to Stravinsky of 23 September 1959 (PSS).

42 Letter of 5 September 1959 (PSS).

43 Letter to Souvtchinsky, 27 January 1960 (PSS).

44 See Horgan, *Encounters with Stravinsky*, 122–31, for a detailed account of these events. Horgan himself took the part of the Speaker in *Oedipus Rex*.

45 Letter of 30 March 1960 (PSS).

46 Letter of 19 September 1960 (PSS).

47 Letters of 27 January 1960 (PSS).

48 *ImpLif*, 245, note 4.

49 Bucknell (ed.), *Christopher Isherwood Diaries: 1939–1960*, 849 (entry for 25 March 1960).

50 Ibid., 866 (entry for 18 June).

51 Ibid., 849.

52   See *AMC*, 86–99, for Libman's account of the negotiations.

53   *AMC*, 116.

54   Or so one gathers from hints in *DB*. Libman does not mention problems with Alcazar. Vera's published diary refers to a row with Libman in Mexico about money, and reports "too much trouble with Libman, Alcazar." (*DB*, 201). But the first Libman reference is an editorial addition, while the second reads, in the original, "to much trouble," which may or may not be a spelling mistake.

55   *DB*, 201. The word "ever" is not in the original (so: worst of what?), but as the alteration in *DB* is by Craft it presumably does reflect his opinion that the Lima orchestra was the worst he had ever come across professionally.

56   Lawrence Morton told Souvtchinsky (letter of 19 November 1960, in UCLA, Morton), that the change of plan was due to the death of the conductor Dimitri Mitropoulos, but this looks like another invention of Craft's. Mitropoulos died in Milan on 2 November, and by the next day Stravinsky was telling Booseys' New York manager, David Adams, not only that they were returning early but that their boat tickets were booked and hotel dates confirmed (letter of 3 November 1960, in *SSCIII*, 427). This would have been smart work even for a close family bereavement.

57   *SCF* (94), 145.

58   "How I would like to live again in Paris," she had written to Lawrence Morton on 10 May 1960 (UCLA, Morton).

59   Goddard Lieberson had written to Aristotle Onassis in November 1957, suggesting that the shipping tycoon give Stravinsky a house in Monaco in return for a new ballet (see Joseph, *Stravinsky Inside Out*, 14). Nadia Boulanger approached Prince Rainier on the same subject at about the same time (letter to Stravinsky of 8 January 1958, in PSS). As late as January 1962 Craft was telling Nabokov that they were definitely buying a house in Monte Carlo (letter of 1 January: HRC, Nabokov). But they never did.

60   This time it was his publisher who was making the necessary enquiries. See Roth's letter to Stravinsky of 18 October 1960 (PSS).

29   SINKING THE ARK

1   Stravinsky's text is a slight paraphrase of part of the very first prayer of Dekker's first "birde," "The Dove": "A Prayer for a childe before he goeth to his study, or to schoole."

2   *SCF* (94), 234–5.

3   Liebermann, *Actes et entractes* (Paris: La Guilde du livre, 1976), 24–5. Stravinsky may have feared something in the manner of Chagall's ostentatious designs for the Ballet Theater *Firebird* in 1945; but when he remarks (in *Conv*, 102) that Chagall had done an ink portrait of him and given it to him "as a memento of our collaboration," he is embroidering slightly, since there was no collaboration, and the two only met for the first time in New York the following year.

4   Letter of 29 January 1961 (PSS).

5   Letter of 5 July 1960 to David Adams. Roth enclosed a copy of his reply to Adams, setting out the contractual position severely and in detail, with his letter of the same date to Stravinsky (PSS).

6   Letter to Graff, 3 November 1960, copy in PSS.

7   *SCF* (94), 219.

8   13 November 1960. The cutting is in PSS.

9   Horgan, *Encounters with Stravinsky*, 140.

10   As noted in Betty Bean's letter to Stravinsky of 28 January 1952 (PSS), and *SCF* (94), 71.

11   *ASS*, 96–7, with a facsimile of the inscription. Craft attributes the "Frère Jacques" story

to Horgan and even repeats it as a formal quotation from *Encounters with Igor Stravinsky*, but there is in fact no trace of it in any edition of that book.

12   See his letter of 28 January 1961 (PSS). The *Firebird* recording was eventually "chosen" as the record-club selection for June 1962. See Schuyler Chapin's letter to Stravinsky, 21 May 1962 (PSS).

13   Letter of 19 August 1961 (PSS). Stravinsky is complaining about the need to satisfy Soviet audiences, but in truth the situation with American audiences was not much different, as Stravinsky hints in his letter to Souvtchinsky of 28 January 1961, just after recording *The Firebird*.

14   These various documents survive in PSS. See Joseph, *Stravinsky Inside Out*, 150–1, for a brief survey of their contents.

15   See his letter of 16 April 1960 to Libman (PSS), abstracted in *AMC*, 165. The Sextant press release was dated 13 April.

16   *Expo*, 123–7.

17   *Expo*, 126, 127, note 1.

18   Letter of 9 March 1959 (PSS).

19   Letter to Stravinsky, 23 February 1961 (PSS). See also *DB*, 201.

20   Craft states (*SCF* [72], 110) that these were the last performances Stravinsky conducted of *The Rite*, but this is incorrect. He conducted it again in Stockholm on 24 September 1961, an occasion recorded in the revised 1994 edition of *SCF*, p. 248. For a detailed account of the Taxco visit, see ibid., 238–9.

21   See Stravinsky's letters to Liebermann of 9 February (PSS) and to Roth of 27 February 1961 (*SSCIII*, 429), respectively.

22   Letter of David Adams to Stravinsky, 17 April 1961 (PSS).

23   *Sic. AMC*, 169.

24   The *Symphony of Psalms* recording was never in fact released. For the concert on 5 June, Eudice Shapiro played the Violin Concerto, but for the recording at the end of June the soloist was Isaac Stern.

25   *SCF* (94), 240.

26   Letter of 12 June 1961 (PSS).

27   Tikhon Khrennikov, "Serdechnïy privet ot Stravinskogo," *Ogonyok*, August 1961.

28   Letter of 16 January 1961, in A. M. Kuznetsov (ed.), "Pis'ma I. F. Stravinskogo M. V. Yudinoy," *Nevel'skiy sbornik*, no. 3 (St. Petersburg: 1998), 40.

29   Yudina to Stravinsky, letter of 29 April 1960 (PSS). See also Souvtchinsky to Stravinsky, 12 May 1960 (PSS). Stravinsky sent a card of acknowledgment to Yudina with a covering note via Souvtchinsky, both dated 7 May: see Kuznetsov, op. cit, 39, and PSS, respectively.

30   Letter of 10 May (PSS).

31   Letter of 12 May 1961 (PSS).

32   Letter of 12 June 1961 (PSS).

33   "Stravinsky Shakes a Stick at Red Music, *Washington Post*, 24 December 1960.

34   Letter of 13–19 March 1961, in Bretanitskaya (ed.), *Pyotr Suvchinsky i ego vremya*, 346–8.

35   Khrennikov, "Serdechnïy privet ot Stravinskogo."

36   Letter of 12 June.

37   Letter of 16 June (PSS). On his Russian transcript of this letter kindly supplied to the present author, after the remark about Khrennikov needing Shostakovich's approval, the editor, the late Viktor Varunts, cannot contain his fury: "Can you beat this stupidity of Souvtchinsky's!"

38   In the mid-sixties, Stravinsky sent money to Bachnicki's daughter, who was in poor health and difficult circumstances in Warsaw.

39   Letter to Stravinsky, 18 December 1961 (PSS).

40   Letter of 28 August 1961, in Bretanitskaya (ed.), *Pyotr Suvchinsky i ego vremya*, 353. Souvtchinsky had sounded Stravinsky on this possibility in his letter of 15 August, to which Stravinsky had replied on the 19th (PSS).

41   Letter of 20 September 1961, in *Pyotr Suvchinsky i ego vremya*, 354–5. The Russian original reads literally; "Is it possible that you really thought that—to Helsinki—'sit and go'??!!" ('sel i poyekhal'), referring to the Russian custom of sitting in silence for a short time before leaving on a journey.

42   Letter to Yudina, 23 October 1961, in *Pyotr Suvchinsky i ego vremya*, 356–7.

43   Letter to Souvtchinsky, 10 December 1961 (PSS).

44   *SCF* (94), 242.

45   Rimsky-Korsakov's reaction is described in V. V. Yastrebtsev, *Reminiscences of Rimsky-Korsakov*, ed. and trans. Florence Jonas (New York: Columbia University Press, 1985), 420.

46   Letter of 6 October 1947, in *SSCI*, 299.

47   See *SCF* (94), 243–8, for Craft's detailed account of the production and the meetings with Bergman.

48   See *SCS*, 518.

49   *AMC*, 151.

50   *Encounters with Stravinsky*, 149. See also Craft's description in *SCF* (94), 249–50.

51   These changes were the subject of his long letter to Crosby of 17 August 1961 (PSS).

52   See the letter from Cambridge University Press to Stravinsky, 9 December 1960 (PSS).

53   *Wellington Evening Post*, 16 November 1961, quoted in *SPD*, 542.

54   Letter of 26 December 1961 to Eliot, *SPD*, 542–3.

55   Not surprisingly, the anthem was not used in the new hymnal, which instead includes an "Alleluya" arranged by Elizabeth Poston from the "Andantino" of *Les Cinq doigts*. See D. Holbrook and E. Poston (eds.), *The Cambridge Hymnal* (Cambridge: Cambridge University Press, 1967), no. 183. See also Stravinsky's remarks on the Mass in *Expo*, 77.

56   *SCF* (94), 253–4.

57   *T&C*, 59. The authenticity of the text is, of course, more than suspect, but in this particular case there are good reasons for accepting the factual basis.

58   Letter of 22 May 1961, in *SSCIII*, 431.

59   In his autobiography, Craft maintains that Stravinsky had already decided on the Abraham story that afternoon, but this is contradicted by Berlin's letter of 7 November (quoted in extenso on the same page of Craft's book), which shows that he sent both texts. Of course, Berlin may have got into a muddle, but this seems highly unlikely; or he may still have been angling for the Creation story, even in the knowledge that Stravinsky had rejected it, which would have been out of character and probably a waste of his time. By far the likeliest explanation is that Craft, for neither the first nor the hundredth time, has simply got things wrong. For what it is worth, Sir Isaiah Berlin told me in 1992 that the Abraham story was his choice (the "very well-told tale" was his phrase to me). He may indeed have selected it as one possibility, but there is no doubt that the final choice was Stravinsky's. See *ImpLif*, 228–9.

60   *SCF* (94), 272.

61   Letter of 21 May 1962 (RGB). The explanation was prompted by the 1962 trip to South Africa.

62   Postcard of 25 September 1961 from Stockholm (UCLA, Morton).

63   *AMC*, 114.

64   Craft reproduces a page of the fair-copy manuscript of this arrangement in *ASS*, 103, and states that it was made in Hollywood. Libman, 108, says that it was done on the Mexico flight on the 17th. The arrangement was not incorporated in the *Eight Instrumental Miniatures* of the following spring, but may well have been the trigger for it.

65 Letter of 24 November, cited in *AMC*, 151.
66 Letter of 21 November 1961, quoted in *SPD*, 653, note 122.
67 Letter of 9 December 1961, quoted in ibid.
68 Liebermann wrote with this firm proposal on 9 December. On the 13th Stravinsky counter-proposed that he conduct one ballet per evening (PSS).
69 Letter of 3 January 1962 (HRC, Nabokov). The "Casals business" was the concert Casals had given in the White House on 13 November with Alexander Schneider and Mieczyslaw Horszowski. Casals's biographer H. F. Kirk describes the concert as "one of the luminous cultural events of the Kennedy administration," but Stravinsky, whose music Casals disliked, was not invited. See Kirk, *Pablo Casals* (London: Hutchinson, 1974), 520.
70 Nabokov claims as much in *Bagazh*, 178.
71 Nabokov conveyed Schlesinger's request to Stravinsky in a letter of 26 December 1961 (PSS).

30 A GUEST IN HIS OWN COUNTRY

1   *AMC*, 152.
2   Letter of 18 December 1961 (PSS).
3   Letter of 18 December 1961, Xenya Stravinsky to Igor Stravinsky. See *SB*, 91.
4   Letter of 29 December, *SB*, 92.
5   Letter of 2 April 1962, *SB*, 94–5.
6   These included an interview with Vera, a conversation excerpt between Craft and Stravinsky, and a performance of the *Symphony of Psalms*.
7   The concerts were in the Lisner Auditorium on 19, 21, and 22 January. The recording was on the 20th.
8   The parts were recorded later and dubbed onto the original tape some time after 9 March, when McClure sent Stravinsky a disc of the cimbalom-less performances for checking.
9   *SCF* (94), 284.
10 Letter of 4 February 1962 (PSS); emphases his.
11 *SCF* (94), 285.
12 See Yudina's letter of 29 January 1962 to Souvtchinsky. Text omitted from Bretanitskaya, op. cit., but supplied to me by Viktor Varunts. The originals of Yudina's letters to Souvtchinsky were given by his widow to their author's executor, A. M. Kuznetsov, in 1988 (see Bretanitskaya [ed.], *Pyotr Suvchinsky i ego vremya*, 324, note).
13 Letter of 21 February (PSS).
14 Stravinsky to Souvtchinsky, 17 March, and Souvtchinsky's reply of the 25th (PSS).
15 Letter of 21 March (HRC, Nabokov).
16 Letter of 12 April to Souvtchinsky (PSS).
17 The soloists were Jeanne Deroubaix, Hugues Cuénod, and the narrator Derrick Olsen.
18 Stravinsky (or Craft) had already remarked on this change in a footnote in the recently published third volume of conversations, *Expo*, 111. But this cannot have been influenced by the *Sermon* reviews.
19 Jacques Lonchampt, *Le Monde*, 25–26 February 1962.
20 *Dial*, 72–80.
21 *Dial*, 78.
22 Letter of 2 April 1962 (PSS). The "letter of intent" was dated 21 April 1960 (PSS).
23 Letter of 15 April (PSS). Stravinsky wanted Graff (and Columbia) to use the formula "under the supervision of the composer," but Graff seems to have ignored this request.

24 Letter of 22 March 1962 (PSS: the italics are my version of Stravinsky's invariable habit of typing his work titles—and in this case "flop"—in Roman capitals).

25 See Stravinsky's letter of 6 April to Schuyler Chapin and John McClure (PSS).

26 *SPD*, 465.

27 Isaiah Berlin had sent the Abraham and Isaac text just before Christmas; see *SCF* (94), 279.

28 I deduce that Morton asked for a work because it was a pattern of the spring concerts of 1962 to celebrate Stravinsky's eightieth birthday with at least one work in every program, and this could also explain why the finished score of the *Eight Instrumental Miniatures* was dedicated to Morton, a gesture that both delighted and puzzled him, as he admitted to Sheldon Meyer, his editor at Oxford University Press. See chapter 28, note 18; also Dorothy Crawford, *Evenings On and Off the Roof*, 201.

29 Crawford, 201. The pieces performed at the 26 March concert were (in the *Cinq doigts* order) nos. 1, 7, 6, and 3, presumably in that order (nos. 1–4 of the *Eight Instrumental Miniatures*).

30 The canonic additions are discussed by Glenn Watkins in "Canon and Stravinsky's Late Style," in Pasler (ed.), *Confronting Stravinsky*, 235–7. Watkins had written to Stravinsky in January 1961 proposing himself to arrange some of the *Cinq doigts* for organ, but when Stravinsky made his own instrumentations, Watkins abandoned the organ version.

31 Letter to Isaiah Berlin, 30 January 1962 (copy in HRC, Nabokov).

32 The meeting is described in great detail in Berlin's letter of 21 May to Kollek (copy in HRC, Nabokov).

33 Letter of 7 November 1961, in *ImpLif*, 228.

34 *SCF* (94), 289. According to this version of Craft's diary, Beckett remarked that de Gaulle was "beginning to sound like Péguy." The reader interested in textual variants will be surprised to find that in earlier versions (*Dial*, 256; *SCF* [72], 154) it was the OAS of whom Beckett said this.

35 James Knowlson, *Damned to Fame: The Life of Samuel Beckett* (London: Bloomsbury, 1996), 500.

36 *AMC*, 109.

37 Ibid., 105.

38 Craft's autobiography omits all mention of the South African visit, depositing the travellers from Paris at Brazzaville (Congo) without explanation, before rediscovering them in Rome in the next paragraph. No doubt this was one of the sequences that suggested the book's title. See *An Improbable Life*, 256.

39 Letter of Anton Hartman to Lillian Libman, 10 February 1962 (PSS).

40 Letter of 16 February 1962 (PSS).

41 *SCF* (94), 291.

42 Letter of 5 June 1962 to Theodore Kollek (copy in HRC, Nabokov). Berlin had been alerted to Stravinsky's remarks by a report in the *Jewish Chronicle* for 1 June (" 'Strange Letter' to Stravinsky: Tour to Israel nearly cancelled"). It seems, nevertheless, that the *Symphony of Psalms* was indeed sung in Hebrew when Stravinsky conducted it in Israel in 1964. See below, chapter 32.

43 Spender, *Journals 1939–1983*, 238. The hyperbole was no doubt deliberate, unless Spender simply misheard. As it happened 17 May, when Stravinsky really had been in Paris, was the last time Spender had seen him, calling on him at the Hotel Berkeley and being treated to an imitation of the rhinoceros the composer now said he was going to South Africa to see (ibid., 227–8).

44 Jack Loughner, " 'Noah' Almost Got Drowned," *San Francisco News Call Bulletin*, 15 June 1962.

45 For Lang's review, see the *New York Herald Tribune*, 15 June 1962. The paper printed Stravinsky's telegram on the 24th in an inset to Lang's article of that Sunday ("Stravinsky Aims, Fires"), in which the critic naturally took the opportunity to enlarge on his previously quite moderately expressed opinion of *The Flood*. Lang had a few years previously attacked *The Poetics of Music* in a *Tribune* article, "The Position of Igor Stravinsky," of 18 March 1956.

46 See chapter 27.

47 Graff wrote to him on 29 June, and again on 2 July, informing him of the new date and time (PSS).

48 According to the archive listings at the Hollywood Bowl, this was the 1919 suite, but one cannot be confident about it. Stravinsky always preferred the 1945 revision. The concert was on 26 July.

49 On the 21st. In *ImpLif*, Craft says that he conducted the premiere on the 19th in Santa Fe Cathedral, in a concert that also included the *Cantata* conducted by Stravinsky. No other account mentions this performance, however.

50 *Encounters with Igor Stravinsky*, 150–66.

51 Ibid., 163.

52 *SCF* (94), 308.

53 Letter to Nicolas Nabokov, 7 September 1964 (HRC, Nabokov). Berlin is describing Stravinsky's second visit, at which he was present.

54 *SCF* (94), 307.

55 Letter of 4 August 1962 to Nabokov (HRC, Nabokov).

56 The contrast with Lawrence Morton, who was writing a book on Stravinsky, is instructive. Morton not only studied Russian, the better to understand Stravinsky's mind and music, but he also worked hard and successfully to improve his French, in order to correspond more intimately with Boulez (whose own English was as a matter of fact more than adequate).

57 *SCF* (94), 317.

58 R. Buckle, *George Balanchine: Ballet Master*, 232–3.

59 As recorded in his father's account book for 1890. See *PRKI*, 34. There had been a similar stop in 1883, but this would not have formed part of the then eleven-month-old Igor's memory (see ibid., 23).

60 *SB*, 124.

61 *SB*, 142. I have telescoped two hotel-room experiences described by Xenya, of which the second, in Leningrad, was the occasion for most of the thoughts here quoted. As for the Moscow conversation, according to Xenya it was occasioned by Vera's and Craft's absence at the Obratzova Puppet Theatre that afternoon, a performance that Craft claims they attended with the composer in the evening. By no means hostile to Xenya in the few passages where he notes her presence, Craft makes no mention of her ever having remained alone with her uncle. Compare *SCF* (94), 326, and *SB*, 122–5.

62 See *SCF* (94), 313, 317, 319.

63 "Igor' Stravinskiy: lyubite muzïky!" *Komsomol'skaya Pravda*, 27 September 1962; Y. Lidin and S. Razgonov, "I. F. Stravinskiy v Moskve," *Moskovskaya Pravda*, 26 September 1962. The former article ends with a facsimile of a supposedly (but clearly not) autograph text: "Bravo. Igor Stravinsky. Moskva krasavitsa [the beautiful] 1962."

64 A. Afonina, "Igor' Stravinskiy v Sovetskom Soyuze," *Sovetskaya Muzïka*, no. 1 (1963), 123–5, reprinted (without attribution) in *ISPS*, 201–6. In general the article is a balanced and unembroidered account of the visit.

65 I. Vershinina, "Vï ne predstavlyaye," *Ogonyok*, October 1962, 4–5. Stravinsky also told Vershinina (not, incidentally, to be confused with the fine Soviet musicologist Irina Vershinina) that his library in Hollywood contained a number of Soviet books that, he

implied, he had read with interest. No doubt such remarks arose from leading questions and were intended to please. But, though untruthful, they were probably uttered.

66 *Komsomol'skaya Pravda*, 27 September. "Makeup" is my translation of the difficult word "slog," whose dictionary meaning is "style." To a Russian "slog" is a much more inward quality—closer to "essence"—than the mere outward signals we associate with the word "style."

67 Craft says that the rehearsals and concerts took place in the Tchaikovsky Hall, but this seems to be an error of identification on his part.

68 *SCF* (94), 315.

69 Issued on Melodiya, 74321 33220 2.

70 This is a rough *précis* of the account in *SB*, 113–16, with additional details from *SCF* (94), 322.

71 *SB*, 118; *SCF* (94), 323.

72 *SB*, 121–2; *SCF* (94), 325–6.

73 *SCF* (94), 329.

74 *SB*, 132.

75 As late as 25 September, newspaper reports were mentioning Kiev as part of the itinerary, but an exchange in *SB* (106) between Stravinsky, Yury Shaporin, and the Ukrainian composer Konstantin Dankevich on the 22nd seems already to hint at some political infighting over the question. According to Xenya, Stravinsky himself badly wanted to go to Ukraine.

76 *SCF* (94), 330.

77 "S nadezhdoy na novïye vstrechi," *Izvestiya*, 30 September 1962.

78 A revealing photograph of this dinner is in *DB*, 208.

79 Quoted in Elizabeth Wilson, *Shostakovich: A Life Remembered* (Princeton: Princeton University Press, 1994), 375.

80 Quoted *verbatim* in *SCF* (94), 328.

81 *SCF* (94), 335.

82 Ibid.

83 Letter of 27 November 1961, reprinted in *Dial*, 131–2. See above, chapter 28, for support for the view that such letters were probably written by Craft.

84 *SB*, 159, where Xenya quotes the speech from memory. *SCF* (94), 337, gives a slightly different text. The concert to which Stravinsky refers took place on 18 November 1893 (NS), and included the second performance of the *Pathétique* symphony.

85 *SB*, 143–7.

86 *SCF* (94), 333.

87 Ibid., 333–4.

88 Letter of 6 October 1962 (PSS).

89 *SCF* (94), 332, 337.

90 Letter of 8 October (PSS).

91 The photograph of this dinner in *IVSPA*, 135, shows how little privacy they would have had, even apart from the interesting possibility of microphones in the chandeliers or the flower vases. Heads turn their way, cameras flash, and so forth. The meeting was a historic event.

92 *Mem*, 56.

93 *SCF* (94), 337.

94 See the references in *SCF* (94), 339, and Elizabeth Wilson, *Shostakovich Remembered*, 375.

95 "Igor Stravinsky: retour de Moscou," *L'Humanité*, 12 October 1962.

96 *SCF* (94), 341. One other parallel with the Mussolini association is the fact that eighteen months later, on 16 April 1964, Stravinsky cabled birthday greetings to Khrushchev. See

SPD, 470. Souvtchinsky was also for a time an admirer of the Soviet leader. "Do you not think that Khrushchev has been showing himself a very clever, farsighted politician?" he wrote to Stravinsky on 23 November 1962, a month after the Cuban missile crisis.

31   THE SACRE PAPERS

1   Quoted in SSCI, 358, note 71.
2   One Russian report even took this phrase as its headline. "Ya videl nezabïvaemïye veshchi," Smena, 13 October 1962.
3   Jacqueline Leulliot, "Igor Stravinsky à Paris," L'Aurore, 12 October 1962.
4   Claude Samuel, "Mi offrono una dacia," L'Europeo, 28 October 1962.
5   Letter to Khrennikov, 19 January 1963 (PSS). Stravinsky had heard about Khrennikov's reaction from Xenya's husband, Alexander Yakovlev, who had mentioned it in a letter to Craft. Samuel's Prokofiev, trans. Miriam John (London: Calder and Boyars, 1971), was originally published in French in 1960 (Paris: Éditions du Seuil).
6   See SCS, 366.
7   I. Nest'yev, "Vechera Igorya Stravinskogo," Sovetskaya Muzïka, no. 12 (December 1962), 92–5.
8   Ibid., 93.
9   See the program note for the first performance in New York, 24 January 1946.
10   Nest'yev, op. cit.
11   Sergei Prokofiev: His Musical Life (New York: Knopf, 1946); Zhizn Sergeya Prokof'yeva (Moscow: Sovetskiy Kompozitor, 1957).
12   Izvestiya, 7 January 1951, quoted in Boris Schwarz, Music and Musical Life in Soviet Russia 1917–1970 (London: Barrie and Jenkins, 1972), 354.
13   Sovetskaya muzïka, 1958, no. 2, quoted in Schwarz, "Stravinsky in Soviet Russian Criticism," Musical Quarterly, 48 (1962), 351.
14   See Schwarz, Music and Musical Life in Soviet Russia, 363.
15   Letter to Stravinsky of 13 February 1963 (PSS).
16   Respectively, Nabokov to Stravinsky, 31 March (PSS); Souvtchinsky to Stravinsky, 11 April (PSS); Souvtchinsky to Lawrence Morton, 16 April (UCLA, Morton). The main musician to suffer was, as usual, Shostakovich, whose Thirteenth Symphony, first performed in Moscow on 18 December 1962, was the object of petty censorship allegedly because of unacceptable aspects of the Yevtushenko poems it had set.
17   Letter to Stravinsky of 16 February 1963 (PSS).
18   Letter of 25 April 1963 (PSS).
19   Letter of May 1963 from Hamburg, quoted in SB, 169–70.
20   Letter to Souvtchinsky, 21 October 1962 (text omitted from Bretanitskaya [ed.], Pyotr Suvchinsky i ego vremya, but supplied to me by Viktor Varunts).
21   This is the clear, though not stated, implication of her letter to Souvtchinsky of 8 June 1963 (text omitted from Bretanitskaya, but supplied to me by Viktor Varunts).
22   Letter of 28 November 1962 (text omitted from Bretanitskaya, but supplied to me by Viktor Varunts).
23   Letter of 8 June.
24   Letters of 28 November 1962, 8 June 1963, respectively.
25   Letter to Souvtchinsky of 22 July 1963 (text omitted from Bretanitskaya, but supplied to me by Viktor Varunts).
26   Stravinsky continued to indicate De Profundis as a suitable model for the actual printing of the Hebrew text in Abraham and Isaac. See his letter of 11 March 1963 to Ernst Roth, in SSCIII, 440. As for Britten, Stravinsky wrote to David Adams on 15 February, while still at work on Abraham and Isaac, requesting scores of the War Requiem and A

Midsummer Night's Dream. In general, his interest in Britten's music survived the growing divide between their styles, whatever he may have said in company.

27 See *ImpLif*, 266. Mario Bois's statement (*Près de Strawinsky*, 94) that they went to see the finished film in Paris in December 1963 is inexplicable, not because they were not in Paris at that time, but because his account of Stravinsky's being shocked at the film's opening image—a mitred bishop in a brothel—cannot be squared with the fact that he had already seen the film and given permission for his music to be used. The Paris showing, if it took place, must have been in May 1963. What happened in December is that Bois saw the film with Souvtchinsky and Boulez, an outing described by Souvtchinsky in his letter to Stravinsky of 30 December 1963 (PSS).

28 *SCF* (94), 342.

29 In private conversation, however, Craft has claimed that he himself made the adaptations and that the composer was not involved: *CwC*, cf, *SPD*, 473. By an odd coincidence, an actual film of *The Soldier's Tale* was made only a few months later, with Brian Phelan as the Soldier, Robert Helpmann as the Devil, and Svetlana Beriosova as the Princess. But this time Stravinsky was not involved in any musical capacity, only as one party to the notoriously complicated rights arrangements with this particular work.

30 The gist of this information is in Stravinsky's letter of 10 November 1962 to Theodore (PSS). As usual with such dealings between father and son, the letter is in Russian.

31 Letter of 19 December 1962 (PSS).

32 Letter to Stravinsky of 7 January 1963. In this letter Souvtchinsky describes other manuscripts in Meyer's possession, including the score of Part I of *The Rite* (the copy Stravinsky had sent to Myaskovsky in the hope that he would proofread the score), one of the *Berceuses du chat* (with a dedication to Larionov), the *Petit ramusianum*, and Stravinsky's drawing of Bakst.

33 Letter to Stravinsky of 14 July 1963 (PSS).

34 Letter to Souvtchinsky of 25 December 1962 (PSS).

35 Letter of 19 January 1963 (PSS).

36 *Expo*, 147–8. He did not, all the same, expressly prohibit publication until early 1964, when he (or, to be exact, Craft) scribbled a marginal note on Rufina Ampenoff's request for approval (16 January), to the effect that he did not want the sketches to come out in his lifetime (the note is presumably a draft of a telegram). This abrupt refusal may somehow have been connected with Boulez. At any rate, when Souvtchinsky tried to persuade Stravinsky to change his mind, on the grounds that the sketches might not always be available, he studiously avoided mentioning Boulez, and instead proposed Amy and another young composer, Jean-Claude Eloy, to analyze the sketches under Craft's direction (letter of 10 February). Eventually, in October 1964, Stravinsky agreed to the publication on condition that Craft himself write the commentary and Boulez an introduction. "Why not, in the end? My own attitude to my first period has radically changed, as if it wasn't me who wrote it: my musical interests are now completely different—so let them come out, if it gives anyone legitimate pleasure." (Letter to Souvtchinsky of 10 October 1964; see *SSCI*, 398, note 1, for another translation.) All this documentation is in PSS.

37 The ballet first saw the light at City Center on 9 April, the day after Stravinsky sailed for Europe. The composer had attended a rehearsal on the 5th.

38 Letter of 1 April 1963 to Stravinsky (PSS).

39 There was also a concert in Zagreb, which prompted a diatribe against Craft's conducting by the *Frankfurter allgemeine Zeitung* critic Hans Heinz Stuckenschmidt (4 June 1963), and one in Bergen, which Craft had to conduct on his own, Stravinsky having at the last minute refused to travel to Norway.

40 Letter to Theodore Strawinsky, 28 May 1963 (PSS).

41 Letter to Nicolas Nabokov, 27 May 1963 (HRC, Nabokov).

42 Personal communication, Sir Isaiah Berlin.

43 See the second insert in this book for a photograph of the event.

44 Letter to Stravinsky, 26 June 1963 (PSS).

45 Letter to Stravinsky, 30 July 1963 (PSS).

46 Letter of Stravinsky to Souvtchinsky, 19 January 1963 (PSS).

47 *DB*, 213.

48 Letter of 13 October 1963 (HRC, Nabokov). Stravinsky's latest scheme to reduce his tax bill was to make an annual award to various composer and musicologist friends out of his ASCAP (performance rights) earnings. The original idea was for an eightieth-birthday university scholarship, but in the end he preferred to hand the cash directly to musicians in his own circle, such as Arthur Berger, Milton Babbitt, Ingolf Dahl, David Diamond, Lawrence Morton, and Sol Babitz. See especially David Adams's letter of 3 October 1963, and Stravinsky's reply of 4 October (PSS).

49 *SCF* (94), 281, entry for 13 January.

50 For instance, by White, *Stravinsky*, 551. Stravinsky seems not to have attended the Los Angeles premiere; see Lawrence Morton's letter to him of 2 October 1963 (PSS).

51 This was to be Stravinsky's last visit to Santa Fe. He routinely attributed his failure to return to problems with the altitude, but according to Paul Horgan it was rather due to a bad emotional atmosphere created, on this visit, by a youthful faction on the Santa Fe staff unsympathetic to Stravinsky and his music. See *Encounters with Igor Stravinsky*, 172–8.

52 Letter to Souvtchinsky, 23 July 1963 (PSS).

53 Letter of 21 October 1963 (LoC, Perle). Nothing came of this idea until Friedrich Cerha made his own realization, now accepted as standard, in the 1970s. However, Craft wrote to George Perle on 25 May 1964 that Stravinsky approved the idea of a Berg Society and agreed to be its president (PSS).

54 *T&C*, 63; *T&E*, 61, note 7.

55 Letter to Stravinsky, 24 October 1963 (PSS). Nabokov had originally made the Berlin proposal in a letter of 2 September, with many glossy details about the facilities that would be placed at Stravinsky's disposal.

56 Letter of 2 September (PSS). Stravinsky did not reject the spirituals out of hand but asked Nabokov to send them (letter of 6 October, *SSCII*, 409). Only then did Craft inform Nika (letter of 18 October: HRC, Nabokov) that Stravinsky felt the music to be too remote from his own preoccupations.

57 The enquiry was conveyed by Rufina Ampenoff in a telegram of 23 August 1963 (PSS).

58 Telegram to Ampenoff, 24 August (PSS). Stravinsky's Rome plan for the autumn had included a Vatican concert with his existing Mass on the program, but this had been fixed before the Pope's death and at his invitation (see Adriana Panni's letter to Stravinsky, 20 May 1963: PSS. Pope John died on 3 June). By August, however, he was refusing the Vatican concert, which it was intended to televise, and offering a studio filming of the Octet instead (see Panni to Craft, 5 August, and Stravinsky to Panni, 13 August). That same month, nevertheless, he was invested with a papal knighthood at a ceremony in Santa Fe Cathedral on the 18th, also of course on the authority of the late Pope. "Imagine my pride!" he wrote to Nadia Boulanger (see Monsaingeon, *Mademoiselle*, 83).

59 Letter of 2 November 1963, *SSCII*, 410.

60 *SCF* (94), 353.

61 A week after the death Stravinsky told Theodore that he was refusing interviews about Cocteau. He did, however, record a short tribute for Paris radio, which was broadcast on 20 January 1964; see *SSCI*, 125.

62 *SCF* (94), 379.

1   *DB*, 213.

2   See, for instance, Helen Carter's letter of 7 December 1963 from New York to Nicolas Nabokov: "The Stravinskys are here. . . . All the friends say that he has slowed up a great deal this year, and that he seems sad" (HRC, Nabokov).

3   Letter of 3 December 1963 (private collection); emphasis his. Only the date suggests that the "sadness" refers to Mika, the anniversary of whose death fell on 30 November. Stravinsky often replied in such terms to annual letters of condolence (most frequently from Nadia Boulanger) over the loss of his wife and daughter. Yet the present letter seems to hint also at some additional sorrow.

4   Letter of Françoise to Stravinsky, 28 October 1963 (PSS), and Stravinsky's reply of 3 November (private collection); emphasis his.

5   Undated letter of November 1963 (private collection).

6   Letter of 14 November 1963 (PSS).

7   Letter of 10 January 1964 (PSS); emphasis his.

8   *DB*, 213.

9   *DB*, 214, note 2, says "fewer than ten people." *SCF* (94), 391, gives the attendance as four, including the orchestra's resident conductor, Eugene Ormandy.

10   *SCF* (94), 399.

11   Ibid., 391–3.

12   Including, for some reason, the low E-flat clarinet, an instrument found only in military bands. Auden's haiku is not quite strict, according to the Japanese pattern of 5-7-5 syllables. Instead he varies the distribution of the seventeen syllables between the three lines of each verse, as he does also in other haikus of this period–"Symmetries & Asymmetries," "Ascension Day, 1964," "Lines for Elizabeth Mayer."

13   *T&C*, 61; *T&E*, 58. For once, the two texts differ only marginally, but by way of compensation the fragment of music ("the heavens are silent") is given in the wrong key in *T&E*, as if written for high E-flat clarinet transposing, rather than voice. I am grateful to David Matthews for drawing my attention to this peculiarity.

14   See, for instance, *Philadelphia Evening Bulletin*, 4 March 1964. It was presumably such reports that prompted William Glock to ask for the premiere of what he assumed would be a substantial choral-orchestral piece. See Rufina Ampenoff's letter to Stravinsky, 31 March 1964 (PSS). Other newspapers apparently reported that the piece was being written for Dietrich Fischer-Dieskau (letter of Nicolas Nabokov to Stravinsky, 10 April 1964). Nabokov was unaware that the work had by that time already been performed.

15   Letter of 6 March 1964 (PSS). The letter included minor textual changes and noted that the original final verse (the one beginning "When a just man dies") was mobile and could be placed at the start or in the middle. Stravinsky duly began with it, then repeated it at the end.

16   Kirstein to Craft, letter of 5 March 1964, in *SSCI*, 293.

17   Letter of 21 March, ibid.

18   The calculation of the number of quavers at metronome 144 is so exact that Stravinsky must have worked it out consciously. The first public performance of the fanfare opened the official NYCB first night on the 24th (I am grateful to Nancy Reynolds for confirming these dates from the State Theater programs).

19   Letter of 7 December 1963 (PSS).

20   *T&C*, 34; *T&E*, 24–5. The texts, however, differ in many details.

21   The published version for mezzo-soprano, with minor adjustments to the vocal line, was made after the first performance at the request of Cathy Berberian.

22   D. Crawford, *Evenings On and Off the Roof*, 215; *SCF* (94), 394. There had been a preliminary rehearsal on the morning of the day before. Stravinsky noted in his diary

that Lawrence Morton had asked that there be no applause. The performance, he added, "was very dignifying" (not "gratifying," as given in the published text in *ASS*, 174).

23 Letter of 18 April 1964, *SSCII*, 412.
24 *Newsweek*, 20 April 1964, 75.
25 Letter of 13 April 1964, *SSCIII*, 446.
26 Respectively: Ampenoff to Stravinsky, letter of 6 August 1963 (PSS), Stravinsky's reply of 10 August (*SSCIII*, 441), and Ampenoff's letter of 2 June 1964 (PSS), which Stravinsky returned with marginalia (printed as if it were a distinct letter in *SSCIII*, 448).
27 In his diary he wrote: "That is the organization of Mrs. Lalandi's Bach Festivals in Oxford. They did not even know that these Variations were with a chorus." *ASS*, 174 (original in English, PSS).
28 *SCF* (94), 394. The entry is wrongly dated 16 May (for 16 June).
29 Letter of 2 November 1964 (UCLA, Morton).
30 John McClure, "The Rake Again," *Gramophone*, vol. 42 (March 1965), 415.
31 In *ImpLif,* Craft recalls them as "four very good German singers, who had performed the opera many times in Hanover" (p. 273). But one of the four was the British soprano Heather Harper.
32 Letter of 2 November, Neighbour to Morton.
33 McClure, op. cit, 416.
34 *ImpLif,* 273. However, Stravinsky noted in his diary for 28 June that Craft had gone on to Oxford ahead of them because "he had a rehearsal for *Trauer-Ode* before me." See *ASS*, 175.
35 *ASS*, 175, Stravinsky's diary entry for 10 July.
36 The exact details are unclear. Craft, in his account of the incident, allows it to appear that Johnny charged his entire bill, plus some expenses for entertaining friends, but it seems to me likely that the composer expected to meet his grandson's room account (otherwise it is surely inconceivable that the eighteen-year-old student would have put up at a five-star hotel). According to Libman, 308, the extras were charged to the composer's account at her suggestion. See also Craft, *CherP*, most recently in *Stravinsky: Glimpses of a Life,* 148–9.
37 Telegram to Ahron Propes, 20 July 1964; to Nabokov, 22 July (PSS).
38 Telegram of 24 July (PSS).
39 Undated telegram of about 23 July (PSS).
40 Telegram of 24 July (PSS).
41 Letter of 24 July (PSS).
42 Telegram of 30 July 1964 (PSS).
43 Letter of 4 August 1964 (PSS).
44 Letter of 27 July, Boulanger to Stravinsky (PSS), and Stravinsky's reply of 30 July, in *SSCI*, 260.
45 Letter of 6 August (PSS).
46 The regretful telegram is dated 11 August; the countermanding text is an undated handwritten note (PSS).
47 *ASS*, 175.
48 Letter of Isaiah Berlin to Nicolas Nabokov, 7 September 1964 (HRC, Nabokov).
49 Letter of 27 May 1963 (HRC, Nabokov).
50 Without, however, quite the right complement of instruments. The orchestra, from Tel Aviv, lacked an alto flute, and since the local Jerusalem orchestra refused to lend their instrument, the part had to be played on a clarinet.
51 Letter of Berlin to Nabokov, 7 September.
52 Ibid.
53 Ibid.

54 A reference, presumably, to the Prussian military dynasty of the Manteuffels, and an interesting corrective to Stravinsky's remarks about Wagner.

55 See Ernst Roth's letter to Stravinsky of 11 February 1964 (PSS) and Stravinsky's reply of 16 February, in *SSCIII*, 443.

56 Nicole Hirsch, "Le nouveau Stravinsky," *L'Express*, 6 September 1964. See also *ImpLif*, 275.

57 See *ImpLif*, 275–6. Craft, as is his habit in this volume, vouchsafes the young lady's name.

58 See above, chapter 21.

59 The photograph is in *DB*, 215.

60 His letter to Stravinsky of 5 October 1964, citing the composer's reaction, is in PSS. He also there states his intention to write to Craft, though the letter itself is not on public view.

61 Letter of 13 January 1965, partially quoted (and misdated to the 11th) in *SSCII*, 416, note 81.

62 Letter of 19 October 1964 to Marya Yudina, in Bretanitskaya (ed.), *Pyotr Suvchinsky i ego vremya*, 376–8.

63 Letter of 8 August 1964, in *SSCIII*, 449, but here retranslated from the Russian. In refuting Libman's claim to have been involved in the negotiations, Craft states that de Laurentiis was "astonished" to receive Stravinsky's signed contract, "since he had never made any proposal at all" (*SPD*, 591, also quoting *AMC*, 177–8). The correspondence with Rufina Ampenoff makes it clear that de Laurentiis was and continued to be enthusiastic about the idea of Stravinsky's participation, and was still pestering her about it as late as November 1964 (see especially Ampenoff's letter to Stravinsky of 12 November: PSS). According to Libman, the fee would have been a million dollars subject to tax; Craft mentions no fee but denies that tax would have been payable (presumably because the project was based in Rome). Lawrence Morton told Oliver Neighbour in January 1965 that the fee would have been $250,000, and that Craft had talked Stravinsky out of accepting for the good of his health (letter of 15 January: UCLA, Morton). A copy of Stravinsky's signed letter of agreement with his agent for the project, Paul Kohner, is in the H. Colin Slim Stravinsky Collection, now in the Library of the University of British Columbia. See *Annotated Catalogue of the H. Colin Slim Stravinsky Collection*, 329–32.

64 In Britain this would be the first floor—the one above ground level.

65 "Stravinsky at Home," *Musical America* (January 1963), 10–11, reprinted in *T&E*, 64–75; *T&C*, 298–307. Libman refers to a row between Stravinsky and Craft supposedly provoked by Craft's release of "this private letter" to *Musical America* (*AMC*, 231). But she seems unaware of any actual issue of authorship.

66 *T&E*, 73. The text was significantly altered for the British reprint in *T&C*, 306.

67 Vera Stravinsky, "The Rake's Progress: 'La Prima Assoluta,' " in *T&E*, 51–4; *T&C*, 55–7. Compare *SCF* (94), 62–3.

68 *T&E*, 76–82; *T&C*, 308–13.

69 *ImpLif*, 260, 277, also reprinting both texts, but without the dates or address headings.

70 Letter of June 1965, in *SB*, 183–4.

71 Vernon Duke, "The Deification of Stravinsky," *Listen*, May-June 1964, 1–5; Stravinsky, "A Cure for V.D.," *Listen*, September-October 1964, 1–2.

72 *CwC*.

73 "Music: A Dialogue," *Show*, April 1964. Reprinted as "In the Name of Jean-Jacques!," in *T&E*, 97–101; and (edited) in *T&C*, 78–9.

74 "Schoenberg Speaks His Mind," *The Observer*, 18 October 1964, reprinted as "Schoenberg's Letters," in *T&E*, 132–8, and (much rewritten) *T&C*, 248–53. Morton told

Oliver Neighbour that the review "is of course Craft's work, though it does represent the master's feelings (Craft-induced)" (letter of 30 October 1964, UCLA Morton).

75 Nadia's first approach was in a letter of 7 November; when Stravinsky expressed interest but concern about the timetable (12 November); Nadia wrote again (14 November) offering $10,000 but little extra time. Stravinsky's ultimatum about money was wired on the 17th (PSS).

76 Seeger's original letter of commission is not in PSS, but Stravinsky's reply of 9 November 1964 (actually a reply to a reply) refers to Seeger's willingness to be patient and adds: "I can only work in my own tempo and under my own pressures" (PSS).

77 The most grotesque example is Heinz-Klaus Metzger's "Strawinsky und die Nekrophilie," in *Igor Strawinsky: Musik-Konzepte*, nos 34–5 (January, 1984), 99–106.

78 Letter postmarked 9 December 1966, in *SSCI*, 261, but there wrongly dated December 1964. The letter is a reply to a request in Nadia's of 4 December 1966, relayed from André Malraux, that he conduct a concert in Paris in honor of the Baudelaire centenary in 1967.

79 The work was completed on 17 February.

80 Claudia Cassidy, "On the Aisle," *Chicago Tribune*, 18 April 1965.

81 Robert C. Marsh, "2 Major Stravinsky Works Get World Premieres Here," *Chicago Sun-Times*, 18 April 1965.

82 Cassidy, op. cit.

83 Letter of 12 December 1964, *SSCIII*, 450–1.

84 Rich, "Stravinsky & Strauss?—It's Like Brando Reading Edgar Guest," *New York Herald Tribune*, 7 December 1964. One has always to remember that newspaper headlines are normally the work of harassed sub-editors.

85 Letter of 7 September 1964 to Nicolas Nabokov (HRC, Nabokov).

86 Morton to Boulez, 18 July 1965 (PSS).

87 Boulez to Morton, undated reply to the foregoing (probably October 1965) (PSS).

33 SMILING FOR THE CAMERA

1 Oppenheim told Charles Joseph that the idea of reviving the film project came not from him but from Stravinsky himself, after seeing a CBS documentary about Casals. See *Stravinsky Inside Out*, 177.

2 Charles Joseph's assertion (*Stravinsky Inside Out*, 176) that Stravinsky was paid $15,000 is slightly misleading. His flat fee stayed at $10,000, but with a $2,500 repeat fee and a $2,500 fee for Craft. See Arnold Weissberger's letter of 29 January 1965 to the composer (PSS).

3 After a rehearsal for the London Festival Hall concert in May 1954 at which he was to receive the RPS Gold Medal. Personal communication from John Carewe, who was present.

4 *Poet*, 55.

5 See "Stravinsky Remains," in *Stocktakings From an Apprenticeship*, 55–110.

6 And still cannot. When I talked to him in Paris in December 2002, he again referred to the *Les Noces* barrings as a mistake that needed correcting. There remains something doctrinaire about this point of view. In 1980 Boulez had written to Eric Walter White, in response to a footnote in the second edition of his *Stravinsky: The Composer and His Works* (p. 258), claiming to have checked the eight-counts in the manuscript and confirmed the error (letter of 1 February, HRC, White; I am very grateful to Jerry Young for bringing this letter to my attention). But in every autograph that I have seen, the counts are exactly as in the printed edition (that is, with the anomalous count of eleven).

The relevant manuscripts are in the British Library, loan deposit 75, 42–45: the autograph full score and vocal score, and an ensemble score without voices (mainly in Catherine Stravinsky's hand); also PSS. Boulez claims to have seen "a kind of 'particell,' " which suggests the vocal score in the BL, with accompaniment for piano four-hands. No other autograph of which I am aware fits this description.

7   *Stravinsky Inside Out*, 181–2.

8   I am again indebted to Charles Joseph for these details, which were not included in the film as shown. See *Stravinsky Inside Out*, 183–5.

9   *Mem*, 105.

10   *Près de Strawinsky*, 136–7.

11   *The Rite of Spring* was completed at the Hôtel du Châtelard, which alas by 1965 had been pulled down. Charles Joseph mistakenly calls Clarens a mountain village (*Stravinsky Inside Out*, 178).

12   *SCF* (94), 404–6.

13   See *SCS*, 184, quoting a different account of a story Stravinsky told on several occasions.

14   They had originally planned to go first to Bucharest, but this leg of the journey had been cancelled mainly on financial grounds. See *AMC*, 274.

15   Letter of Claudio Spies to Lawrence Morton, 1 May 1965 (UCLA, Morton).

16   Ibid.

17   *DB*, 216.

18   *SCF* (94), 414.

19   *AMC*, 200; italics and elision hers.

20   Ibid., 200, cf. *SCF* (94), 421, and Joseph, *Stravinsky Inside Out*, 178, 186–7. The inserts were cleverly done, with the supposed conductor giving leads in the right places.

21   Letter of 6 June 1965 (UCLA, Morton). Spies made this observation before the Rome concert, which had been arranged at the last minute by telephone to Warsaw. He knew (presumably from Craft) that television would be involved in Rome, but seems to have assumed it was a local station transmitting live. To confuse matters further, the CBS film represents the Rome concert as preceding the visit to Warsaw, which is made out to be the climax of the tour (and naturally of the film).

22   According to *DB*, 216, the lunch was on 4 October 1964. On the 25th, Stravinsky sent Soulima and Françoise a document for Johnny to sign when he came of age, in relation to the financial settlement. The phone conversation seems to have taken place that same month.

23   Letter of 7 June 1965 (PSS).

24   See *CherP*, 149.

25   Letter of 21 December 1964 (PSS).

26   Undated letter of 10 June 1965. The letter is marked "jeudi" (Thursday) and begins "I wrote to you on Monday" (i.e., the 7th). Soulima wrote on the same day, and the letters were probably sent in the same envelope.

27   The fear proved unfounded.

28   *CherP*, 150.

29   Ibid. Milène's recollection forms part of a lengthy deposition made under oath in 1977, and now on file in the New York Surrogate Court archives.

30   *CherP*, 151.

31   Ibid., 152.

32   Ibid., 193, note 50. Craft is apparently so anxious to belittle Stravinsky's affection for his elder son that he throws in extra "evidence" that actually weakens his point.

33   Letter of 2 September 1964 (PSS), quoted in ibid., 152.

34   *SSCIII*, 454, note 61, glossing Stravinsky's letter to Rufina Ampenoff of 8 November 1965.

35   Letter of 8 January 1967 (PSS).

36   See Stravinsky's letter to Theodore of 6 November 1965 and Theodore's reply of 15 November (PSS).

37   *CwC.*

38   *CherP*, 142–3.

39   Deposition, 6 March 1975 (SCNY).

40   *Are you the son . . . ?*

41   *AMC*, 237.

42   Letter of 18 June 1965 (PSS).

43   *Vancouver Sun*, 12 July 1965, quoted in *SPD*, 481.

44   I witnessed it myself two months later in London's Royal Festival Hall.

45   The story is related by Libman in *AMC*, 230, and vehemently contradicted in various details by Craft in *SPD*, 585–6. Craft maintains that the work in question was *The Fairy's Kiss*, and he insists that he was absent from the *Pulcinella* sessions, which is important only to the extent that he himself makes much of the point and uses the "mistake" to discredit Libman. There is, however, independent evidence that Libman was right. I have by and large accepted Craft's other factual corrections, while assuming that, since (for all his vituperative tone) he does not deny the story in essence, it must be broadly true. Ironically a brief clip from the *Pulcinella* session is included on the Columbia "Stravinsky in Rehearsal" disc, and shows the composer apparently in a cheerful mood. But John McClure still remembers the tempo differences between the two conductors in *Pulcinella*, and these are recorded in a brief exchange between him and Stravinsky on the rehearsal disc.

46   *SPD*, 586.

47   New York: Knopf, 1967.

48   In *T&C.*

49   *T&E*, 4; *T&C*, 19–20.

50   *SCF* (94), 62–3, replacing a much briefer account in *SCF* (72), 29. The most that can be said for Stravinsky's own contribution to the program notes is that in a few cases he gave brief written answers to factual questions put by Craft. See, for instance, the reproduction of a question-and-answer sheet on *Orpheus* in *ASS*, 123. A comparison of this page with *T&E*, 46–8 (*T&C*, 51–3), should give pause to anyone intending to quote the *Orpheus* program note as a sample of Stravinsky's thinking, let alone of his prose.

51   Libman to Paterson, 15 June 1965; Paterson to Libman, 17 June, 28 June (PSS).

52   For further details on this and other aspects of the Liebermann film, see Joseph, *Stravinsky Inside Out*, 172–4.

53   See Stravinsky to Liebermann, 19 July 1965, and Liebermann's reply of 2 August (PSS). According to Craft, Stravinsky again tried to cancel Hamburg when they arrived in New York on their way to Europe at the start of September, but Liebermann telephoned and persuaded him to go. See *ImpLif*, 283.

54   Telegram of 6 August (PSS).

55   Peyser, "Stravinsky-Craft, Inc.," *American Scholar* (Fall, 1983), 513–18.

56   See Stravinsky's letter of 24 September to Souvtchinsky (PSS).

57   See *AMC*, 252–5, for these and other details. Craft eventually delivered his lecture at Ohio State University in November 1966, and a version of it was published as the introduction to the facsimile publication of the sketches: Igor Stravinsky, *The Rite of Spring: Sketches 1911–1913* (London: Boosey and Hawkes, 1969).

58   Letter of 19 February 1965 (PSS).

59   Letter of 22 February (PSS). The sardonic reference is of course to Britten's work of that name. See also *T&C*, 98.

60   Letter of 21 March 1965, in *SSCII*, 417 (retranslated from the Russian original in HRC, Nabokov). Nabokov had been urging Stravinsky to accept a commission from Mstislav

Rostropovich for a work for cello and orchestra. See his letter of 17 March (PSS). Rostropovich, he claimed, was so desperate for a Stravinsky piece that he would "crawl on his knees" to get one. But Stravinsky confessed himself interested in neither Rostropovich nor his cello.

61 *AMC*, 202.

62 See his letters of 8 November to Rufina Ampenoff, in *SSCIII*, 454. The first of the two letters is in English, not Russian.

34 FINAL CURTAIN

1 In *ImpLif*, 283, Craft alleges that the film of this exchange was "inexcusably destroyed." But it exists and has been excerpted in various films, including János Darvas's *Igor Stravinsky: Componist* (2001), from which my quotation is taken. The journalist was Edward Greenfield, music critic of *The Guardian*.

2 Letter to Boulez, 18 July 1965 (PSS).

3 Soon afterwards Kirstein asked Stravinsky to write a piece as a "surprise present" for Balanchine. But nothing seems to have come of this. See Kirstein's letter of 26 February 1966, in *SSCI*, 294.

4 His own two recordings are in English.

5 See Stravinsky's letter of 27 July 1965 to John McClure (PSS).

6 *ImpLif*, 273, 284. Stravinsky had been ill in the night of the first ("champagne, probably"), but he seems to have recovered by the third, and was well enough to go to the theatre (*DB*, 219).

7 Letter of 27 October 1966 to McClure (PSS).

8 Lalandi had cleverly secured Stravinsky's agreement to succeed Albert Schweitzer as president of the Oxford Bach Festival by inviting him to write a short piece in Schweitzer's memory. Stravinsky declined to write the piece but (presumably) felt he could not also refuse the presidency. See Lalandi's letter to him of 25 December 1965 and his reply of 7 January 1966 (PSS).

9 *AMC*, 262.

10 Ibid.

11 *ImpLif*, 285.

12 Letter of 24 May 1966 (PSS).

13 Bois, *Près de Strawinsky*, 43.

14 *Dialogues and a Diary* (New York: Doubleday, 1963), 47.

15 Letter of 27 December 1963 (PSS).

16 Stravinsky to Souvtchinsky, letter of 10 September 1966 (PSS).

17 The accounts of this incident in *AMC*, 268, and *SCF* (94), 436, do not tally.

18 Ansermet, *Les Fondements de la musique dans la conscience humaine*, 502.

19 Ibid., 504.

20 Letter of 13 July 1966, in *CASIII*, 129. However, if Libman's account is correct, it was not the case that Stravinsky had proposed Ansermet. See *AMC*, 266–7, which suggests that Stravinsky would have vetoed the Swiss conductor if it had been within his power. Ansermet, on the other hand, waspishly told an interviewer that Stravinsky had deliberately programmed him to conduct *Persephone*, knowing him to have always avoided that work on principle because of its treatment of Gide's text. See Raymond Ericson, "At Odds in Their Eighties," *New York Times*, 3 July 1966. A cutting of this article (which also takes a stab at Stravinsky's conducting technique) is in PSS, but it seems unlikely that he read it at the time, in view of his amiable response to Ansermet's letter.

21 Letter of 15 July, in ibid., 132.

22 The composer's own phrase, in *R&C*, 43; *T&C*, 106. The interview as a whole—all clever wordsmithery and backstabbing—is patently the work of Craft, but the musical details were presumably given him by Stravinsky since he himself was not present. A few days later Cage visited Stravinsky at the Hotel Pierre in quest of a page of manuscript for a charity auction.

23 *Sunday Oregonian*, 19 February 1967, quoted in *SPD*, 476.

24 Once again it is impossible to reconcile the various timings of these events as related by Libman (*AMC*, 270–1) and Craft himself (*SCF* [94], 437–9, and *ImpLif*, 286). One would normally favor the protagonist in such cases, but since Craft gets the date of the concert wrong (in the autobiography, not in the diary), this seems even riskier than usual.

25 *Encounters with Stravinsky*, 181–2.

26 Shirley Hazzard's notes on the visit are in Columbia, Steegmuller.

27 See his letter of 16 August 1966 to Rufina Ampenoff, in *SSCIII*, 455–6.

28 See Arminé Montapert's letter of 27 August to the Princeton lawyers (PSS).

29 Letter of 16 August 1966 (PSS).

30 See Morton's letter of 20 August to Boulez (PSS).

31 See James Lord, "Stravinsky and Giacometti," in *SNB*, 376–81, with several reproductions.

32 Letter to Souvtchinsky of 24 January 1966 (PSS).

33 See Robert Craft's text introducing Arnold Newman's photographs of the *Requiem Canticles* sketchbook, in *Bravo Stravinsky* (Cleveland and New York: World Publishing Company, 1967), 48. Mysteriously, the obituary of Evelyn Waugh, though reproduced in Newman's book, is now missing from the sketchbook in PSS. I am grateful to David Smyth for pointing this out to me.

34 The *Credo* was given in a nominally revised version (1964), and billed as a first performance.

35 *ImpLif*, 216.

36 Ibid., 287; also *SCF* (94), 446–7.

37 See Spies's letter of 7 November 1966 to Lawrence Morton. Morton, however, seems to have distrusted Spies and regarded him as a troublemaker; see his letter of 14 June 1967 to Oliver Neighbour (UCLA, Morton).

38 Letter of 14 November to Morton (UCLA, Morton).

39 Letter to Spies, 11 November 1966 (UCLA, Morton).

40 Letter to Pierre Boulez, 11 August 1971 (PSS).

41 Walter Arlen, "Stravinsky Work Premiered," *Los Angeles Times*, 2 November 1966.

42 See the sketches reproduced in *SPD*, 484–5, and Arnold Newman's candid camera shots in *Bravo Stravinsky*, 13–21.

43 See *Bravo Stravinsky*, 62–7 (including a facsimile of the fair-copy autograph of "The Owl and the Pussy-Cat").

44 Quoted in Crawford, *Evenings On and Off the Roof*, 228.

45 Ibid., 228. Newman's photograph in silhouette of Stravinsky listening to the concert from behind a curtain (*Bravo Stravinsky*, 69) must have been taken during the Beethoven sonata. The piano lid is fully raised, which it would hardly have been for "The Owl and the Pussy-Cat."

46 Soulima Stravinsky, interview with Thor Wood.

47 *Dial*, 113.

48 The concerto was conducted by Craft, and Stravinsky conducted only the *Firebird* (apparently the 1919 suite, though printed programs are rarely dependable on such matters), and also apparently *Fireworks*. Vera noted that the orchestra was the worst they had had: see *DB*, 222.

49 Or so Lalandi told Rufina Ampenoff. See Ampenoff's letter of 28 November 1966 to Stravinsky (PSS).

50 See Xenya's letter to her uncle of 22 November, in *SB*, 190. Blazhkov had just phoned her with the news.

51 *AMC*, 176–7; *SCF* (94), 444–5.

52 *AMC*, 316–7.

53 Quoted in *AMC*, 310. See also Marsh, "Pick-Up Band Mars Stravinsky Concert," *Chicago Sun-Times*, 30 December 1966.

54 *AMC*, 317.

55 Ibid., 296.

56 *Seattle Post-Intelligencer*, 2 March 1967, quoted in *SPD*, 483; *AMC*, 315; letter of Craft to Ampenoff, 6 March 1967 (PSS).

57 *AMC*, 316–17.

58 *DB*, 223.

59 *SCF* (94), 452.

60 *AMC*, 317–18.

61 John Kraglund, "Stravinsky's Medal Is Icing on His Cake," *The Globe and Mail*, 18 May 1967.

62 *SCF* (94), 452.

63 *Messager de Montreux*, 17 April 1914. See *SCS*, 233, and 606, n. 103.

35   A FAMILY AFFAIR

1 Letter of 12 January 1967 (PSS). The works were: *Danses concertantes*, the *Firebird* suite (1945), the *Petrushka* suite, *The Song of the Nightingale, Abraham and Isaac*, Gorodetsky and Balmont songs, *Three Japanese Lyrics, Agon*, and *Song of the Volga Boatmen*.

2 Annotation on a letter from Rufina Ampenoff to Stravinsky, 31 January 1967.

3 *SCF* (94), 477 (entry for 24 January); Allen's remark is quoted by Neighbour in a letter of 7 July 1968 to Lawrence Morton (UCLA, Morton).

4 Letter of 8 April 1968, in Bretanitskaya (ed.), *Pyotr Suvchinsky i ego vremya*, 382–3. It confirms the reference in "Side Effects I" to "a set of pieces provisionally titled *Etudes, Inventions, and a Sonata*." See *R&C*, 54, *T&C*, 115; the article, dated October 1967, first appeared as "On Manners, Music, and Morality" in *Harper's Magazine*, February 1968.

5 Clive Barnes, "This Firebird Is for Burning," *New York Times*, 21 February 1971; Stravinsky's reply, dated 3 March, appeared in the *NYT*, 21 March, and was reprinted in *T&C*, 219–20. Curiously enough, the so-called Author's Foreword to *T&C*, which similarly carries Stravinsky's name, is dated 1 March 1971, two days earlier than the letter. But it could hardly, without mediumistic intervention, have been much later.

6 Barnes starts by talking about the impression left by Stravinsky's writing, "and that of his oddly literary alter ego, Robert Craft," as being that "of a querulous old man." The apparent solecism is surely deliberate. Barnes knew Craft to be in his forties.

7 B. H. Haggin, *A Decade of Music* (New York: Horizon Press, 1973), 206–7. See also Igor Stravinsky, "Rap Session," *New York Review of Books* (11 February 1971), 18–20, reprinted in *T&C*, 170–77. Incidentally, the last-dated interview in *T&C*, one of the so-called Borborygms (pp. 181–2), is supposed to have been conducted on the 1st and 2nd of April, by which time Stravinsky could speak only in whispers, could not concentrate on a conversation, or move without help. A borborygm is a tummy rumble.

8 *ImpLif*, 288.

9 Letter of 13 June 1967 to Boulez (PSS); also Morton to Neighbour, 14 June 1967 (UCLA, Morton).

10 *SCF* (94), 459.

11 Ibid., 452, 454.

12 Shakespeare, *A Midsummer Night's Dream*, V, i, 59.

13 For many details on the illness of autumn 1967, see *SCF* (94), 459–75, and *DB*, 223–5. Stravinsky's own diary for 1967, if he kept one, has not surfaced.

14 *ImpLif*, 127–8. See also *DB*, 225. A letter from Berman to Craft (31 January 1968) expresses relief at Edel's dismissal (PSS).

15 The performance took place in the Théâtre des Champs-Élysées on 14 November 1967. This was a particularly complicated moment in Parisian musical politics. Boulez had recently attacked Malraux for separating the state administration of music from that of the theatre and broadcasting and for handing music over to be run by the composer Marcel Landowski, whom Boulez considered a dyed-in-the-wool conservative. Boulez was now carrying out his threat to withdraw from active participation in French musical life, and had recently relinquished the directorship of the Domaine Musical to Amy. Stravinsky was hostile to Malraux, who had made it clear that he regarded music as an inferior art form and who moreover had not written to congratulate Stravinsky on his eighty-fifth birthday; but he seems to have felt unable (or so he told Souvtchinsky: letter of 20 July 1967 [PSS]) to oppose a request from so official a source. Amy had to content himself with a follow-up performance.

16 The sketchbook was at last published in 1969 with a short foreword by François Lesure, Craft's "Genesis of a Masterpiece" lecture from Ohio State University, and a supplementary booklet including Craft's "Commentary to the Sketches," a number of letters from Stravinsky to Roerich and Findeizen (in somewhat unreliable translations), the choreography directions from the printed four-hand piano reduction used by Stravinsky and Nijinsky in rehearsal, and a note by Craft on "The Performance of the 'Rite of Spring.' "

17 *AMC*, 282.

18 See for instance Stravinsky's letter to Souvtchinsky, 11 May 1967, informing him that he had asked Rufina Ampenoff to pay him $1,000 on the composer's account.

19 *AMC*, 322.

20 *CherP*, 157–8.

21 Ibid.

22 See Arminé Montapert's somewhat self-congratulatory letter of 17 December 1963 to the Stravinskys (PSS).

23 Letter of 21 April 1963 (PSS).

24 Arminé wrote on 17 March 1963, offering to act as official stockholder (as required by law), free of charge (PSS).

25 Mario Bois, *Près de Strawinsky*, 93.

26 The factual information about these agreements is taken from *CherP*, 156, there being no other accessible source.

27 Ibid., passim.

28 Early in 1967, Stravinsky wrote to Theodore grumbling about his uncommunicativeness, but Theodore sent a puzzled reply that they had written (about Kitty's pregnancy) but, receiving no reply, had concluded that his father had for some reason dropped them. Perhaps, he adds, their letters had got lost. See Stravinsky's letter of 28 January and Theodore and Denise's of 8 February, respectively (PSS).

29 See, for instance, Milène Marion's letter of 20 October 1969 to her brother Theodore (SCNY).

30 The former incident is recounted by Soulima Stravinsky in his memoir *Are You the Son . . . ?*; the latter was told to me by Elliott Carter, who witnessed it after a dinner at the Côte Basque in New York.

31 As reported by Dushkin to Francis Steegmuller (Columbia, Steegmuller).

32 A copy of this will is preserved in PSS.

33 *DB*, 225, entry for 10 January 1968.

34   *SCF* (94), 490; *AMC*, 334–5. Europe may, however, already have been postponed before the Berkeley concerts. See Craft's letter of 3 May to Rufina Ampenoff, referring to a plan to meet in Zurich in August to discuss the archive contract (PSS).

35   *SCF* (94), 477.

36   *ASS*, 179, diary entry for 23 April 1968.

37   Letter of 26 April 1968 (PSS).

38   In *SCF* (94), 458, note, Craft claims that the two Wolf arrangements were both made in the afternoon of 15 May, but this contradicts his note in *DB*, 227, that Stravinsky made them on the 15th, 16th, and 17th. In *SPD*, plate 26, a manuscript page of the second song is reproduced in facsimile with the information (again by Craft) that it was completed on 28 June.

39   *SCF* (94), 457–8.

40   Ibid., 458, note.

41   At least Craft's account in *SCF* (94), 476, shows that *he* was somewhat vague on the subject, which probably comes to much the same thing. Pavel Litvinov was not, as he states, a "condemned Soviet writer," but a physicist who (with Yuly Daniel's wife, Larisa) had appealed to world opinion to support the protest of a group of Soviet intellectuals against the imprisonment of the writers Alexander Ginsburg, Yury Galanskov, Alexei Dobrovolsky, and Vera Lashkova after a notorious "witch trial" in Moscow in early January 1968. Spender's telegram thanking Stravinsky for his support is dated 14 January; Stravinsky's own statement is dated the 16th. It should, however, be added that Craft's text for the Stravinsky statement differs significantly from the draft preserved in Stravinsky's Spender file in PSS. In particular, the composer there refers to "Pavel Litvinov and the condemned writers" (thereby distinguishing between them), and he adds: "Judging from the examples of their work that I have read, and from the new Soviet poets in general, the young Russian writers are among the most vital in the world," a passage Craft omits altogether. Exactly what Stravinsky had read is hard now to establish.

42   Hurok wired on 25 April, and Stravinsky wired back presumably on the same day (his Western Union copy is confusingly misdated the 24th). According to *SCF* (94), 484, Stravinsky later donated a monogrammed silver spoon to the McCarthy for President Committee. A fortnight later, McCarthy was nonetheless beaten to the nomination by Humphrey, who himself subsequently of course lost the election to Nixon.

43   See Theodore's letter of 8 June, Françoise's of 9 June, respectively (PSS).

44   *SCF* (72), 346, note 1. Curiously, this intriguing information was expunged from *SCF* (94).

45   Letter of Edward Bigelow to Stravinsky, 14 May 1968, quoted in Joseph, *Stravinsky and Balanchine*, 303.

46   Ibid., 302.

47   Letter to Craft, 24 May 1968 (PSS). Attempts to choreograph the *Symphony of Psalms* (for instance, by Béjart in 1962) had invariably been blocked by Boosey and Hawkes, presumably—though not provably—at the composer's behest. See, for instance, Rufina Ampenoff's letter to Stravinsky of 26 April 1962 (PSS); also Bois, *Près de Strawinsky*, 76–7.

48   *AMC*, 347.

49   See *SCS*, 282, 299. Craft had edited both scores for performance, and had intended to conduct them as part of a Harvard symposium in August, but had cried off supposedly because of Stravinsky's ill health. The Harvard performances had been conducted by Claudio Spies.

50   Private communication from Robert Craft.

51   *DB*, 227.

52   See, for instance, Berman's letters of 13 February and 5 May 1968 to Craft (PSS), and Souvtchinsky's to Yudina of 8 April, in Bretanitskaya (ed.), *Pyotr Suvchinsky i ego vremya,*

382–3. Craft's assertion in *CherP*, 194, note 58, that "Stravinsky at this time [i.e., in the month before 8 September 1968] had no intention of going to Switzerland at all" has charitably to be seen as a slip of memory which just happens to support his case against the family, since it supposedly gives the lie to André Marion's claim that Stravinsky had told Montapert that Vera and Craft were taking him to Switzerland "to change the status of the Swiss account in their favor." Stravinsky had in fact apprised Rufina Ampenoff of the Zurich plan in a letter of 3 May 1968 (PSS), and according to Libman (*AMC*, 347) the Dolder suite had been booked for a month before they flew to New York on 8 September.

53   Craft lists the dates of Stravinsky's main visitors at the Dolder in *CherP*, 154–5. According to this, Souvtchinsky left on 3 October; the contract letter was signed on the 9th (PSS).

54   *CherP*, 156–7. See also 195, note 61, where Craft pretends that the fact that the letter was typed by Ampenoff for Stravinsky's signature casts some unspecified doubt on its authenticity. In general, though, Craft's attempts to discredit Ampenoff are so transparent that it is hard to imagine any attentive reader being swayed by them.

55   Letter of 17 November 1968, in *SB*, 197.

56   See above, Chapter 31. In their respective depositions to lawyers in the subsequent litigation, Vera stated that her husband had made the call, Theodore that Vera had done so (copies of the depositions held in SCNY). In *CherP*, 158, Craft says that Stravinsky phoned.

57   Vera Stravinsky: deposition.

58   *CherP*, 159. Vera admitted that there had been no witnesses to the gift, and also that her diary entry recording the gift was written at a later date. See her deposition of March 1975.

59   Theodore Strawinsky: deposition. Craft pretends in *CherP* that Theodore himself had designs on the manuscript, but it is clear from all relevant correspondence and from Theodore's deposition that he regarded himself as merely the score's custodian.

60   Theodore Strawinsky: deposition.

61   The page is reproduced in facsimile in *SPD*, 76, but with a characteristically loose English translation of the inscription. Theodore misremembered the eventual text as being in French, but admits he was not present when it was finally written onto the score. See his deposition of 29 November 1976 (SCNY).

62   *CherP*, 155.

63   See, for example, Milène's letter of 20 October 1968 to Theodore (SCNY).

64   *CherP*, 155; *SCF* (94), 484–5.

65   Craft writes in *CherP* all the time as if he thinks that the fact of Marion's name on the Basle account made him the composer's heir. It is hard to believe that Craft really thinks this. Yet the alternative conclusion, that he is fabricating the whole assumption in order to represent Marion as a swindler, is even more incredible. See especially *CherP*, 155–6 and note 58.

66   See Milène's letter of 9 October to Theodore and Denise, and of 20 October to Theodore (SCNY).

67   This is my best guess as to the contents of the letter. The alternative assumption—that Stravinsky was removing the children's interest in the Swiss money, and that this gave them a green light to retaliate—is not borne out by Theodore's deposition, or by Milène's letter to him of 20 October 1969, in which she refers to the postscript in question.

68   Letters to Craft of 10 October and 15 November 1968, respectively (PSS).

69   Undated letter of December 1968, in *SB*, 200–1.

70   Bois, *Près de Strawinsky*, 78. Bois (73–9) gives an amusing history of Stravinsky's views on the idea of a sexually explicit *Rite of Spring* and the various strategies he employed to avoid seeing the Béjart production. According to Bois, Souvtchinsky thought the production a masterpiece and consistently stood between Stravinsky and an outright ban, but this is not consistent with Souvtchinsky's letter to the composer of 7/8 June

1965 (PSS): "Last night I went to the Opéra to hear *Les Noces, Renard,* and (with regret) the *Rite.* I shut my eyes, but even so the stage picture 'leaked in' and obstructed my listening. I shan't go again." Stravinsky's own supposed remark (*R&C*, 86; *T&C*, 143) that the production "belonged at the Folies-Bergères" is probably apocryphal. See also Valérie Dufour, *Strawinsky à Bruxelles,* 147–54.

71 *CherP,* 162–3; *DB,* 228 (entry for 30 December 1968).
72 Letter of 2 March 1969 (PSS).
73 *DB,* 228 (entry for 18 January).
74 Letter of 3 February 1969 (PSS).
75 Letter of 3 March 1969, in *SB,* 201–2.
76 Letter of 14 May 1969 (UCLA, Morton).
77 The sketch is reproduced in facsimile in *ASS,* 139.
78 *SCF* (72), 370. The entry was omitted from *SCF* (94). Stravinsky worked from the Czerny edition, sometimes including Czerny's dynamics and phrase marks. The many faults in transcription include errors of instrumental range, wrong accidentals, confused voice-leading, and at one point in the B minor Fugue an obviously unintentional seven-bar repeat. Stravinsky also arranged the F major Prelude and Fugue from Book II, probably later (the score is undated), since the hand is slightly shakier and the part-writing in the Prelude (for strings) more confused than before. Nevertheless the fugue, for three clarinets, is a minor stroke of genius, the swift three-part counterpoint responding marvelously to this utterly Stravinskian sonority. Craft's mention (*SPD,* 489) of an arrangement of the D minor Prelude and Fugue from Book II is a simple misreading for F major. The two keys have the same key signature.
79 See *SPD,* 488. He had finished arranging the corresponding prelude on the 27th of April.
80 *DB,* 228.
81 It must have been almost complete, since the arrangement is end-dated the 27th of May.

36   A FINE AND PRIVATE PLACE

1   Letter of Berman to Craft, 18 December 1969 (PSS).
2   See, for instance, Vera's letter to Souvtchinsky of 15 July 1969, partly quoted (in the form of a diary entry) in *DB,* 230.
3   Letter of Vera to Souvtchinsky, 15 July (PSS).
4   "Le mal est dans mon âme." See SCF (94), 501 (original in French).
5   *SPD,* 578.
6   According to her deposition, she visited him every day except at weekends, though Craft recalls, somewhat vaguely, that she made "a few token appearances." See *CherP,* 165.
7   Soulima Stravinsky, *Are you the son . . . ?*
8   According to *CherP,* 172, André was not formally notified of the cancellation until 30 September 1969, but this was probably no more than the dotting of the final "i."
9   *CherP,* 166–7.
10 *Are you the son . . . ?*
11 *SCF* (94), 502.
12 Ibid. See also *DB,* 230.
13 *CherP,* 166.
14 Letter to Weissberger, 30 August 1971 (SCNY).
15 See Chapter 35, note 67, and related main text.
16 *SCF* (94), 503. See also *CherP,* 171.

17 Letter of 23 July 1969 (HRC, Nabokov).

18 *AMC*, 353.

19 Lincoln Kirstein, letter of 25 June 1969 to Nicolas Nabokov (HRC, Nabokov). Kirstein actually gives this as a weekly figure, but Craft told Steegmuller, more believably, that it was monthly: letter of 8 August 1970 (Columbia, Steegmuller).

20 Kirstein to Nabokov, 25 June.

21 Weissberger published two volumes of his photographs: *Close-up* (New York: Arno Press, 1967) and *Famous Faces* (New York: H. N. Abrams, 1973).

22 By no means all Stravinsky's friends, nevertheless, approved of Weissberger. Eugene Berman, after itemizing (and exaggerating) the tale of the Stravinskys' recent woes, added: "Nor am I quite relieved to know IS and Vera now in the 'good hands' of Arnold Weissberger, this social wolf in whatever clothing he is wearing. He is a pretty sharp operator himself, and although he is, or was, familiar with some IS affairs in the past, I am afraid that his teeth are getting longer by the minute and his appetite bigger." Letter to Craft, 24 August 1969 (PSS).

23 *AMC*, 358. See also *CherP*, 172.

24 The contract, replacing the one brought by Souvtchinsky during Stravinsky's illness in the autumn of 1967, is dated 27 October 1969.

25 *CherP*, 171–2.

26 Craft again claims that Stravinsky signed this deed reluctantly and under pressure from Vera, and he describes an extraordinary pantomime in which Montapert is supposed to have turned up one lunchtime, unannounced and in a great rush, and forced Stravinsky to sign the deed while covering the relevant text with his hand. See *CherP*, 164.

27 *DB*, 230, note 2.

28 In February 1979, Weissberger, in his capacity as trustee, announced to Vera his intention to "invade the Principal of the Trust and to assign and transfer to you all of the Copyrights and such other assets of the Trust as I deem it desirable for you to have in the light of your intolerable situation" (letter of 28 February: SCNY). Stravinsky's will, drawn up by Weissberger, gave his trustees "sole and absolute discretion" to invade the trust "for any reason whatsoever" on Vera's behalf; but legally this was a less wide-ranging power than it sounds. The trustee's discretion in such cases, it transpired, "did not relieve him from obedience to the great principles of equity which are the life of every trust" (*Carrier v. Carrier,* 1919, quoted in George V. Bobrinskoy Jr. letter to Surrogate Millard L. Midonick, in the Surrogate's Court, New York, 7 September 1979).

29 I have accepted Libman's view that Stravinsky probably did not foresee the consequences of his affidavit and perhaps was not fully aware of its import. See *AMC*, 359–60. Weissberger obtained a medical opinion for 11 December 1969 that the composer was "in full possession of his mental faculties." See *CherP*, 200, note 91. But a clinical opinion is something very different from a psychological judgment, which requires intimate knowledge of the person.

30 Letter from Milène to Xenya Stravinsky, 30 December 1969, in *SB*, 206.

31 Horgan, *Encounters with Stravinsky*, 190 et seq.

32 *Are you the son . . . ?* Craft denied that this visit ever took place, and he also knocked a whole week off Theodore's November stay. See *CherP*, 167, 176.

33 Letter to Weissberger, 13 August 1971 (SCNY). Craft notes that Sigmund Rothschild could not read music or any foreign language, and had barely heard of Stravinsky, though why a ballet specialist should have been any better equipped to value music manuscripts is hard to comprehend. See ibid., and *SSCIII*, 513. The remarks about the appraisers in *DB*, 233 (entry for 5 January 1970), are incidentally nowhere to be found in Vera's actual diary and appear to be an editorial invention. In *AMC*, 360–1, Libman relates her day-return flight to Los Angeles on 28 December to collect the manuscripts.

34   *AMC*, 364.

35   *AMC*, 362.

36   "The Maker of Libretti," in *T&C*, 287. The article—in part an account of this and a subsequent dinner—is de facto attributed to Stravinsky, because the book is.

37   Quoted in *SCF* (94), 507. The group photograph is reproduced in *SPD*, 491, and there is another photograph, of Stravinsky and Balanchine in conversation, presumably on the same occasion, in *DB*, 232.

38   Letter of 27 January 1970, in *SB*, 206–7.

39   "This is a very cosy gathering we have here." *Encounters with Stravinsky*, 197.

40   *AMC*, 366–8.

41   *SCF* (72), 382. The passage was omitted from the 1994 edition.

42   *SCF* (94), 518.

43   In *CherP*, 176, Craft ascribes the change of plan to a recommendation from Lax, but in *ImpLif*, 294, note 42, the recommendation is said to have been Hurok's. The point is trivial but symptomatic of the difficulty Craft often seems to have in remembering details to which he apparently attaches importance. Libman told Steegmuller in July 1971 that Stravinsky himself did not want to go to Évian (or, presumably, Europe at all), and that they went because Craft wanted to go.

44   *AMC*, 371.

45   *SCF* (94), 519. Many of the other outings described by Craft were probably made without Stravinsky, a point that the author seems to leave deliberately vague.

46   Ibid., 523. See also Souvtchinsky's letter to Morton of 4 August 1970 (UCLA, Morton).

47   Ibid., 522.

48   In *CherP*, 176, Craft maintains that Stravinsky found Theodore's visits so tiring that he would go to bed and pretend to be asleep or ill when warned of his son's arrival.

49   Menet was in any case a seven-hour drive from Évian, and a no-less-complicated rail journey, added to which Françoise was, according to Soulima, in a state of nervous exhaustion and constantly on the verge of tears, for which reason the couple returned early to Urbana. Craft's implication that Soulima failed to visit his father out of pure negligence is at best an oversimplification. See *SCF* (94), 525–6.

50   *SB*, 214–15.

51   *SB*, 211.

52   *SB*, 223–4.

53   *SB*, 223. The well-known photographs by Lord Snowdon of Stravinsky at Évian were taken the day or two before they left.

54   Letter of 16 December 1970, in *SPD*, 496–7.

55   Steegmuller had been contemplating a book on Diaghilev, and presumably the idea of a Stravinsky biography came out of the discussion of his need to consult the composer's papers.

56   Donal Henahan, "Stravinsky Ready to Sell His Papers," *New York Times*, 2 December 1970.

57   *CherP*, 177–8.

58   The letter is summarized in *AMC*, 381–2.

59   This is clear from Vera's reply.

60   The point is hardly worth answering, but it should be noted that for well over twenty years Robert Craft was almost wholly dependent on financial support, in one form or another, from Stravinsky.

61   A draft of the letter, dated 15 December, is in *CherP*, 178–9.

62   Letter of 23 December 1970 (SCNY).

63   These and other items are listed in the family's objections to the Executors' accounting, filed in New York on the 20th of June 1975, but they relate either explicitly or implicitly mainly to transactions alleged to have taken place before Stravinsky's death (SCNY).

64 Tribute by Carter in *Perspectives of New Music,* ix/2 and x/1 (Spring/Summer–Fall/ Winter, 1971), 2.

65 *SCF* (94), 536.

66 *Bagazh,* 180. The "chambermaids" are presumably the nurses.

67 *SCF* (94), 536. Craft dates this incident to 12 February 1971, as does Nabokov the incident of the chambermaids.

68 *DB,* 236, note 6.

69 *AMC,* 380. Craft disputes Libman's account ("greatly exaggerated"), but it is broadly confirmed by *DB,* 237.

70 *AMC,* 366.

71 *SCF* (94), 538.

72 *T&C,* 178–81, cf. "Stravinsky: The Last Interview," in *New York Review of Books* (1 July 1971), 3–4. The fundamental lie of *Themes and Conclusions* might prompt the suspicion that the *SCF* account of Stravinsky's improvement at this period was partly designed to support the likelihood of his having written the articles. The problem with untruth, of course, is that it is logically self-perpetuating.

73 *T&C,* 182–4; cf. *SCF* (94), 539.

74 *T&C,* 184.

75 *SCF* (94), 539; *AMC,* 383.

76 *SCF* (94), 540–1.

77 Ibid., 540. Craft explains this away as a mishearing of "has" for "had," but it seems clear that the "four" is part of the reversion to the remote past, a reversion unwelcome to the diarist.

78 Strictly he had not, as the apartment had been bought in Vera's name. This was good sense, of course, but it neatly illustrates the children's fears about the possible switching of funds.

79 *SCF* (94), 543.

80 I have conflated the accounts in *SCF* (94), 544–5, and *AMC,* 384 and 19.

81 *AMC,* 19–21, amplified by Libman's verbal reminiscence to Francis Steegmuller at a lunch in New York on 26 July 1971. Steegmuller's notes are in Columbia, Steegmuller.

82 The accounts of Stravinsky's death in *SCF* (72), 409, and *SCF* (94), 545-6, actually differ in a number of significant and puzzling details. For instance, in 1972 the diary tells us that Craft alone held the dead man's hand and kissed his cheeks before Vera arrived, but by 1994 it is reporting that he and Vera sat together and performed these rites. Moreover, it seems highly unlikely that the kissing and hand-holding Craft describes would have taken place with the corpse's eyes open, as anyone who has witnessed death will surely confirm. It is also of note that in his earlier chronicle Craft describes the eye-recognition incident as occurring after the intern has pronounced death, but in the revised text the eyes are alive only before death, and there is no recognition. Libman at first thought Craft a "fiend" for writing and rewriting his account of the death eleven times "just after the event," but later changed her mind, realizing that "people express their feelings in different ways" (Columbia, Steegmuller). Certainly nobody could ever accuse Craft of an unfeeling attitude to Stravinsky's death, even if his descriptions may suggest too urgent a need to participate in it.

83 Letter of 6 April 1926, now in *PRKIII,* 184; also *SSCII,* 40. See *SCS,* 431 and 646, note 26.

84 *SCF* (94), 546.

85 *SCF* (94), 547.

86 Francis Steegmuller, "Burial in Venice," *The New Yorker* (1 May 1971), 102.

87 "Das gewöhnliche Bagagi": *Der Rosenkavalier,* Act 1.

1   *SCF* (94), 548–9.
2   *AMC*, 41.
3   One such photograph is reproduced in *AMC*, facing page 209.
4   See above, chapter 36, pp. 551, 555. In February Rothschild had valued the music manuscripts at $200,000. The following April, in Venice for the composer's funeral, Craft told Steegmuller that the whole archive had been valued at $500,000. Admittedly, valuations for tax or probate are likely to be well below market value. Boosey and Hawkes's control of publication rights was also probably an inhibiting factor on any sale. Not until 1977 did Vera buy back the rights, at the punitive price of $90,000.
5   *Bleak House,* chapter 1.
6   Letter of 18 May 1981 (UCLA, Morton).
7   This is apparent not only from correspondence, but also from his contribution to Tony Palmer's Stravinsky film, *Once at a Border . . . ,* including the unused outtakes, now in PSS.
8   Craft, "End of a Chronicle," *New York Review of Books* (1 July 1971), 4–14. See also *SCF* (94), 549.
9   *Paradise Lost,* xii, 641.
10 Letter of 1 August 1971 (SCNY)
11 Letter of 7 September 1979, George V. Bobrinskoy Jr. to Surrogate Millard L. Midonick, quoting case precedent. See above, chapter 36, note 28.
12 Sacher's wife, Maja Stehlin, was the widow of Emmanuel Hoffmann, a son of the founder of the pharmaceutical company. The other manuscripts were apparently the full score of the *Symphonies of Wind Instruments,* the short scores of the piano and violin concertos, the score of *Pulcinella,* the piano score of *Renard,* and the sketches for the Concerto in D for strings and *A Sermon, a Narrative, and a Prayer.*
13 Letter to Martin Garbus (Vera's lawyer), 14 May 1980 (SCNY).
14 Simon and Schuster, 1978. The book was nominally by Vera Stravinsky and Robert Craft, but the text and the selection of archival material appear to have been entirely Craft's work. The family had tried to block its publication, but without success.
15 "Catherine and Igor Stravinsky," *New York Review of Books* (22 November 1979), 33–6.
16 Letter of 9 January 1981 to Surrogate Millard L. Midonick (SCNY).
17 Letter of 10 February 1981 (copy in the possession of John Stravinsky).
18 Ken Sandler, "Stravinsky Archives: UCLA, Art Are Winners," *Los Angeles Times,* 15 May 1982.
19 For these and other details, see Craft, *ImpLif,* 302–5.
20 Notes by Francis Steegmuller of a conversation with Lillian Libman, 26 July 1971 (Columbia, Steegmuller). Libman also told Steegmuller that Vera disliked Rita.
21 *ImpLif,* 339.
22 *SSCI* (1982), *SSCII* (1984), and *SSCIII* (1985).
23 The essay first appeared in the collection, Robert Craft, *Present Perspectives* (New York: Knopf, 1984), 31–85. Craft told Morton (letter of 5 August 1983) that he had indemnified Knopf against legal action, but such indemnities are in any case enshrined in most standard book contracts. Craft's correspondence with Knopf (letter of 8 August 1983) merely asserts that he can prove that Kitty was not married when she had her baby, as if the rest of the essay were utterly devoid of questionable matter.
24 Letter to Lawrence Morton, 28 April 1983 (UCLA, Morton).
25 "The Paul Sacher Foundation at the Crossroads. The Purchase of the Igor Stravinsky Archive," in *Paul Sacher in Memoriam* (Paul Sacher Stiftung: Basel, 2000), 37–40.
26 As reported in the *New York Times* on 16 June. Since the trustees' letter announcing the auction was sent on the 13th, the connection seems fairly clear. According to an

unconfirmed report in the *New York Times* (24 June 1983), the unnamed bidder was the Morgan trustee and oil tycoon, Fred R. Koch.

27 As well as *CherP*, *DB* (published in 1985) should also be mentioned as a dumping ground for a large number of disagreeable asides about individual members of the Stravinsky family, many of them of only cursory relevance to the actual diaries, and some of them demonstrably false.

BIBLIOGRAPHY

PRINCIPAL SOURCES

AMC   Lillian Libman, *And Music at the Close: Stravinsky's Last Years* (London: Macmillan, 1972).

ASS   Robert Craft, *A Stravinsky Scrapbook 1940–1971* (London: Thames and Hudson, 1983).

CASIII   Claude Tappolet (ed.), *Correspondance Ansermet–Strawinsky (1914–1967)*, vol. 3 (Geneva: Georg, 1992).

CherP   Robert Craft, "Cher père, chère Vera," in *Stravinsky: Glimpses of a Life* (New York: St. Martin's Press, 1992).

Chron   Igor Stravinsky, *Chronicle of My Life* (London: Victor Gollancz, 1936).

Conv   Igor Stravinsky and Robert Craft, *Conversations with Igor Stravinsky* (London: Faber and Faber, 1959).

CwC   *Conversations with Craft.* A series of six radio interviews with Stephen Walsh (BBC Radio 3: Soundscape Productions, 1995); also outtakes.

DB   Robert Craft (ed.), *Dearest Bubushkin: The Correspondence of Vera and Igor Stravinsky, 1921–1954, with Excerpts from Vera Stravinsky's Diaries, 1922–1971*, trans. Lucia Davidova (London: Thames and Hudson, 1985).

Dial   Igor Stravinsky and Robert Craft, *Dialogues and a Diary* (London: Faber and Faber, 1968).

Expo   Igor Stravinsky and Robert Craft, *Expositions and Developments* (London: Faber and Faber, 1962).

ImpLif   Robert Craft, *An Improbable Life* (Nashville: Vanderbilt University Press, 2002).

ISPS   Viktor Varunts (ed.), *I. Stravinsky: Publitsist i sobesednik* (Moscow: Sovetskiy Kompozitor, 1988).

IVSPA   Vera Stravinsky, Rita McCaffrey, and Robert Craft, *Igor and Vera Stravinsky: A Photograph Album, 1921 to 1971* (London: Thames and Hudson, 1982).

M&C   Igor Stravinsky and Robert Craft, *Memories and Commentaries: New One-volume Edition* (London: Faber and Faber, 2002).

Mem   Igor Stravinsky and Robert Craft, *Memories and Commentaries* (London: Faber and Faber, 1960).

PMP   M. G. Kozlova and N. R. Yatsenzo (eds.), *S. S. Prokof'yev i N. Ya. Myaskovsky: Perepiska* (Moscow: Sovetskiy Kompozitor, 1977).

Poet   Igor Stravinsky, *Poetics of Music in the Form of Six Lessons*, trans. Arthur Knodel and Ingolf Dahl (Cambridge, Mass.: Harvard University Press, 1947).

PRK   Viktor Varunts (ed.), *I. F.Stravinsky: Perepiska s russkimi korrespondentami*.

Materialï k biografi, in three published volumes (Moscow: Kompozitor, 1997, 2000, 2003).

R&C Igor Stravinsky and Robert Craft, *Retrospectives and Conclusions* (New York: Knopf, 1969).

SB K.Yu. Stravinskaya, *O I. F. Stravinskom i evo blizkikh* (Leningrad: Muzïka, 1978).

SCF (72), Robert Craft, *Stravinsky: The Chronicle of a Friendship 1948–1971* (London: Gollancz, 1972).

SCF (94) Robert Craft, *Stravinsky: Chronicle of a Friendship.* Revised and Expanded Edition (Nashville and London: Vanderbilt University Press, 1994).

SCS Stephen Walsh, *Stravinsky, A Creative Spring: Russia and France 1882–1934* (vol. 1 of the present biography) (New York: Knopf, 1999; London: Jonathan Cape, 2000).

Sfam Theodore and Denise Strawinsky, *Stravinsky: A Family Chronicle 1906–1940,* trans. Stephen Walsh (London: Schirmer, 2004); edited translation of T. and D. Strawinsky, *Au coeur du foyer* (Bourg-la-Reine: Zurfluh, 1998), which in its turn incorporated a revised text from Theodore Strawinsky, *Catherine & Igor Stravinsky: A Family Album* (London: Boosey and Hawkes, 1973) (*CISFam* in *SCS*).

SNB *Strawinsky: Sein Nachlass. Sein Bild* (Basle: Kunstmuseum Basel in Zusammenarbeit mit der Paul Sacher Stiftung, 1984).

SPD Vera Stravinsky and Robert Craft, *Stravinsky in Pictures and Documents* (New York: Simon and Schuster, 1978).

SSCI, II, III Robert Craft (ed.), *Stravinsky: Selected Correspondence,* 3 vols. (London: Faber and Faber, 1982, 1984, 1985).

T&C Igor Stravinsky, *Themes and Conclusions* (London: Faber and Faber, 1972).

T&E Igor Stravinsky and Robert Craft, *Themes and Episodes* (New York: Knopf, 1967).

SECONDARY SOURCES

Acosta, M. de *Here Lies the Heart* (London: André Deutsch, 1960).

Adorno, T. W. *Philosophy of Modern Music,* trans. A. Mitchell and W. Bloomster (London: Sheed and Ward, 1973).

———. *Quasi una fantasia: Essays on Modern Music,* trans. R. Livingstone (London: Verso, 1992).

Aguila, J. *Le Domaine Musical: Pierre Boulez et vingt ans de création contemporaine* (Paris: Fayard, 1992).

Alm, I. "Stravinsky, Balanchine, and *Agon:* An Analysis Based on the Collaborative Process," *Journal of Musicology,* 7 (1989), 254–69.

Andriessen, L., and E. Schönberger. *The Apollonian Clockwork: On Stravinsky,* trans. J. Hamburg (Oxford and New York: Oxford University Press, 1989).

Ansen, A. *The Table Talk of W. H. Auden* (Princeton: Ontario Review Press, 1990).

Ansermet, A. *Ernest Ansermet, mon père* (Lausanne: Payot, 1983).

Ansermet, E. *Les Fondements de la musique dans la conscience humaine* (Neuchâtel: A la Baconnière, 1961).

Armitage, M. *Accent on Life* (Ames: Iowa State University Press, 1965).

Auberjonois, F. (ed.). "René Auberjonois (1872–1957): Lettres et souvenirs," *Études de lettres,* III/5 (Lausanne: Université de Lausanne, October–December 1972).

Auden, W. H. "Craftsman, Artist, Genius," *The Observer* (11 April 1971).

Auden, W. H., and N. H. Pearson (eds.). *Poets of the English Language* (5 volumes, New York: Viking, 1950).

Baltensperger, A. "Strawinsky's 'Chicago Lecture' (1944)," *Mitteilungen der Paul Sacher Stiftung*, no. 5 (January 1992), 19–23.

Barron, S. *"Degenerate Art": The Fate of the Avant-Garde in Nazi Germany* (Los Angeles: Harry N. Abrams, 1991).

Bedford, S. *Aldous Huxley: A Biography. Volume Two: 1939–1963* (London: Chatto & Windus, 1974).

Berger, A. "Stravinsky and the Younger American Composers," *The Score*, 12 (June 1955), 38–46.

———. *Reflections of an American Composer* (Berkeley: University of California Press, 2002).

Bernard, M. (ed.). *Pesni russkavo naroda* (Moscow: Jurgenson, 1886).

Bertensson, S., and J. Leyda. *Sergei Rachmaninoff: A Lifetime in Music* (Bloomington: Indiana University Press, 2001).

Bois, M. *Près de Strawinsky* (Paris: Marval, 1996).

Boretz, B. (ed.). "Stravinsky: A Composer's Memorial," *Perspectives of New Music*, ix/2 and x/1 (1971).

Boucourechliev, A. *Stravinsky*, trans. M. Cooper (London: Victor Gollancz, 1987).

Boulez, P. *Stocktakings From an Apprenticeship*, trans. S. Walsh (Oxford: Oxford University Press, 1991).

Bretanitskaya, A. (ed.). *Pyotr Suvchinskiy i evo vremya* (Moscow: Kompozitor, 1999).

Brinnin, J. M. *Dylan Thomas in America* (Readers Union edition, London: Dent, 1957).

Brooks, J. "Mildred Bliss Tells Nadia Boulanger to Think of Herself for Once," in Locke, R. P., and C. Barr (eds.) *Cultivating Music in America: Women Patrons and Activists since 1860* (Berkeley, Los Angeles, and London: University of California Press, 1997).

———. "Nadia Boulanger and the Salon of the Princesse de Polignac," *Journal of the American Musicological Society*, 46 (1993), 415–68.

Buckle, R., and J. Taras. *George Balanchine: Ballet Master* (London: Hamish Hamilton, 1988).

Burde, W. *Strawinsky: Leben, Werke, Dokumente* (expanded ed., Mainz: Schott, 1992).

Burt, F. "An Antithesis," *The Score*, 18 (December 1956), 7–17; *The Score*, 19 (March 1957), 60–74.

Carpenter, H. *W. H. Auden* (London: George Allen & Unwin, 1981).

Carr, M. *Multiple Masks: Neoclassicism in Stravinsky's Works on Greek Subjects* (Lincoln and London: University of Nebraska Press, 2002).

Carter, E. *The Writings of Elliott Carter*, ed. E. and K. Stone (Bloomington and London: Indiana University Press, 1977).

———. *Collected Essays and Lectures*, ed. J. Bernard (Rochester, N.Y.: University of Rochester Press, 1997).

Casella, A. *Music in My Time*, trans. S. Norton (Norman: University of Oklahoma Press, 1955).

Chaplin, C. *My Autobiography* (London: The Bodley Head, 1964).

Chimènes, M. (ed.). *Francis Poulenc: Correspondance 1910–1963* (Paris: Fayard, 1994); English trans. (of an earlier, less full edition) by Sidney Buckland, as *Francis Poulenc: Echo and Source* (London: Gollancz, 1991).

Claudel, P. *Journal* (Paris: Gallimard, 1969).

Claudel, P., and J. Madaule. *Connaissance et reconnaissance: Correspondance 1929–1954* (Paris: Desclée de Brouwer, 1996).

Cocteau, J. *Le Coq et l'arlequin* (Paris: Stock, 1979).

———. *Journal d'un inconnu* (Paris: Bernard Grasset, 1953).

———. *Past Tense*, trans. R. Howard (London: Hamish Hamilton, 1987).

Conrad, D. *Dodascalies: ma chronique du XXᵉ siècle* (Arles: Actes Sud, 1997).

Copland, A., and V. Perlis. *Copland 1900–1942* (London: Faber and Faber, 1984).

———. *Copland since 1943* (London and New York: Marion Boyars, 1992).

Corle, E. (ed.). *Igor Stravinsky* (New York: Duell, Sloan and Pearce, 1949).

Craft, R. (ed.). *Avec Stravinsky* (Monaco: Éditions du Rocher, 1958).

Craft, R. *Stravinsky: Glimpses of a Life* (New York: St.Martin's Press, 1992).

———. *Prejudices in Disguise* (New York: Knopf, 1974).

———. *Present Perspectives* (New York: Knopf, 1984).

———. *The Moment of Existence* (Nashville and London: Vanderbilt University Press, 1996).

———. *Small Craft Advisories* (New York: Thames and Hudson, 1989).

———. "A Personal Preface," *The Score*, 20 (1957), 7–13.

———. "A Concert for Saint Mark," *The Score* (December 1956), 35–51.

———. "A Note on Gesualdo's 'Sacrae Cantiones' and on Gesualdo and Stravinsky," *Tempo*, no. 45 (1957), 5–7.

———. "The Murderous Prince of Madrigalists," *High Fidelity*, 11/9 (September 1961), 54–6, 130–1.

Crawford, D. L. *Evenings On and Off the Roof* (Berkeley: University of California Press, 1995).

Cross, J. (ed.). *The Cambridge Companion to Stravinsky* (Cambridge: Cambridge University Press, 2003).

Cross, J. *The Stravinsky Legacy* (Cambridge: Cambridge University Press, 1998).

Culhane, J. *Walt Disney's Fantasia* (New York: Abrams, 1983).

de Lauze, F. *Apologie de la danse (1623)*, ed. J. Wildeblood (London: Frederic Muller, 1952).

Denby, E. *Dance Writings* (London: Dance Books, 1986).

Dolin, A. *Markova: Her Life and Art* (London: Allen, 1953).

Drew, D. *Kurt Weill: A Handbook* (London and Boston: Faber, 1987).

Druskin, M. *Igor Stravinsky: His Life, Works and Views*, trans. M. Cooper (Cambridge: Cambridge University Press, 1983).

Dufour, V. *Strawinsky à Bruxelles* (Brussels: Académie Royale de Belgique, 2003).

———. "La *Poétique musicale* de Stravinsky," *Revue de musicologie*, 89/2 (2003), 373–92.

———. "Strawinsky vers Souvtchinsky: Thème et variations sur la *Poétique musicale*," *Mitteilungen der Paul Sacher Stiftung*, no. 17 (March 2004), 17–23.

Duke, V. "The Deification of Stravinsky," *Listen* (May–June 1964), 1–5.

Dümling, A., and P. Girth (eds.). *Entartete Musik: Dokumentation und Kommentar zur Düsseldorfer Ausstellung von 1938* (revised and expanded ed., Düsseldorf: DkV, 1993).

Evans, J. "Stravinsky's Music in Hitler's Germany," *Journal of the American Musicological Society*, 56/3 (Fall, 2003), 525-94 (a much-expanded English version of "Die Rezeption der Musik Igor Strawinskys in Hitlerdeutschland," *Archiv für Musikwissenschaft*, XV/2 (1998), 91-109).

———. *Hans Rosbaud—A Bio-Bibliography* (New York: Greenwood, 1992).

———. " 'Diabolus triumphans': Stravinsky's *Histoire du soldat* in Weimar and Nazi Germany," in J. Daverio and J. Ogasapian (eds.), *The Varieties of Musicology: Essays in Honor of Murray Lefkowitz* (Warren, Michigan: Harmonie Park Press, 2000), 175–85.

———. "Some Remarks on the Publication and Reception of Stravinsky's *Erinnerungen*," *Mitteilungen der Paul Sacher Stiftung*, no. 9 (March 1996), 17–23.

Fay, L. E. *Shostakovich: A Life* (Oxford and New York: Oxford University Press, 2000).

Ferris, P. *Dylan Thomas: The Biography*, new edition (London: Dent, 1999).

———. (ed.) *The Collected Letters of Dylan Thomas* (London: Dent, 1985).

Fischer-Dieskau, D. *Echoes of a Lifetime*, trans. R. Hein (London: Macmillan, 1989).

Forbes, E. *A History of Music at Harvard to 1972* (Cambridge, Mass.: Harvard University, 1988).

Gasco, A. *Da Cimarosa a Strawinsky* (Rome: Edizioni de Santis, 1939).

Glock, W. *Notes in Advance* (Oxford and New York: Oxford University Press, 1991).

Godowsky, D. *First Person Plural* (New York: Viking, 1958).

Goldstein, M. "Zwei Briefe von Igor Stravinskij (Erstveröffentlichung)," *Musik des Ostens*, 7 (1975), 280–3.

Goléa, A. *Rencontres avec Pierre Boulez* (Paris: Julliard, 1958).

———. "Pariser Musikindustrie," *Neue Zeitschrift für Musik* (February, 1959), 79–80.

Goubault, C. *Igor Stravinsky* (Paris: Champion, 1991).

Graff, M. *Stravinsky and the Dance: A Survey of Ballet Productions, 1910–1962* (New York: Dance Collection of the New York Public Library, 1962).

Griffiths, P. *Stravinsky* (London: Master Musicians, Dent, 1992).

———. *Igor Stravinsky: The Rake's Progress* (Cambridge: Cambridge University Press, 1982).

Guisan, G. (ed.). *C.-F. Ramuz, ses amis et son temps*, vol. 6 (Lausanne and Paris: La Bibliothèque des Arts, 1970).

Haggin, B. H. *A Decade of Music* (New York: Horizon Press, 1973).

Hart, H. *Fritz Reiner* (Evanston, Illinois: Northwestern University Press, 1994).

Henze, H. W. *Bohemian Fifths: An Autobiography*, trans. Stewart Spencer (Princeton: Princeton University Press, 1999).

Heyworth, P. *Otto Klemperer: His Life and Times*, vol. 2 (Cambridge: Cambridge University Press, 1996).

Hill, P. *Stravinsky: The Rite of Spring* (Cambridge: Cambridge University Press, 2000).

Hogan, C. " 'Threni': Stravinsky's 'Debt' to Krenek," *Tempo*, 141 (June 1982), 22–9.

Holden, A. (ed.). *The Viking Opera Guide* (London: Viking Penguin, 1993).

Horgan, P. *Encounters with Stravinsky: A Personal Record* (rev. ed., Middletown, Connecticut: Wesleyan University Press, 1989).

Huxley, A. "Conversation with Stravinsky," *Vogue* (15 February 1953), 94–5, 127.

Ignatieff, M. *Isaiah Berlin: A Life* (London: Vintage, 2000).

Isacoff, S. "Musical Life with Father" (an interview with Soulima Stravinsky), *Keyboard Classics* (September/October 1981), 16–19.

Isherwood, C. *Diaries, Volume One: 1939–1960*, ed. K. Bucknell (London: Vintage, 1997).

———. *Lost Years: A Memoir 1945–1951*, ed. K. Bucknell (London: Vintage, 2001).

Joseph, C. M. *Stravinsky and the Piano* (Ann Arbor: UMI Research Press, 1983).

———. *Stravinsky and Balanchine* (New Haven and London: Yale University Press, 2002).

———. *Stravinsky Inside Out* (New Haven and London: Yale University Press, 2001).

———. "Stravinsky on Film," *Mitteilungen der Paul Sacher Stiftung* no. 6 (1993), 30–34.

Kahan, S. *Music's Modern Muse: A Life of Winnaretta Singer, Princesse de Polignac* (Rochester, N.Y.: University of Rochester Press, 2003).

Kall, A. "Stravinsky in the Chair of Poetry," *Musical Quarterly*, 26 no. 3 (July, 1940), 283–96.

Keller, H., and M. Cosman. *Stravinsky Seen and Heard* (London: Toccata Press, 1982).

Kirstein, L. *Thirty Years: Lincoln Kirstein's The New York City Ballet* (New York: Knopf, 1978).

———. *Three Pamphlets Collected* (New York: Dance Horizons, 1967).

Kuznetsov, A. M. (ed.). "Pis'ma I. F. Stravinskovo M. V. Yudinoy," *Nevel'skiy sbornik*, no. 3 (St. Petersburg: 1998), 39–44.

Lederman, M. (ed.) *Stravinsky in the Theatre* (New York: Da Capo, 1975).

Leibowitz, R. "Béla Bartók, ou la possibilité du compromis dans la musique contemporaine," *Les Temps modernes*, 2 (1947), 705–34.

———. *Schoenberg et son école* (Paris: Janin, 1947).

———. *Introduction à la musique de douze sons* (Paris: L'Arche, 1949).

———. "Igor Strawinsky, ou Le choix de la misère musicale," *Les Temps modernes*, 1 (1946), 1320–36.

———. "Two Composers: Schönberg and Stravinsky. A Letter from Hollywood," *Partisan Review* 15 (March 1948), 361–5.

Lesure, F. (ed.). *Stravinsky: Etudes et témoignages* (Paris: J-C. Lattès, 1982).

Levi, E. *Music in the Third Reich* (London: Macmillan, 1994).

Liebermann, R. *Actes et entractes* (Paris: La Guilde du livre, 1976).

Lourié, A. "Neogothic and Neoclassic," *Modern Music*, 5 (1928), 3–8.

Lowe, J. *Edward James: A Surrealist Life* (London: Collins, 1991).

Bibliography

Mallet, R. (ed.). *André Gide–Paul Valéry: Correspondance 1890–1942* (Paris: Gallimard, 1955).

Mann, T. *Tagebücher, 1940–43* (Frankfurt: S. Fischer, 1982).

Markova, A. *Giselle and I* (London: Barrie and Rockliff, 1960).

Massine, L. *My Life in Ballet*, ed. P. Hartnoll and R. Rubens (London: Macmillan, 1968).

Mayer, M "Igor Makes a Record," *Esquire* (December 1953), 144–5, 209–13.

Mendelson, E. (ed.). *W. H. Auden and Chester Kallman: Libretti and Other Dramatic Writings by W. H. Auden* (London: Faber & Faber, 1993).

Merrill-Mirsky, C. (ed.). *Exiles in Paradise* (Los Angeles: Hollywood Bowl Museum, 1991).

Messing, S. *Neoclassicism in Music* (Ann Arbor: UMI Research Press, 1988).

Meyer, D. *Victoria Ocampo: Against the Wind and the Tide* (New York: George Braziller, 1979).

Monsaingeon, B. *Mademoiselle: conversations with Nadia Boulanger*, trans. R. Marsack (Manchester: Carcanet, 1985).

Montale, E. *The Second Life of Art* (New York: Ecco Press, 1982).

———. *Il Secondo mestiere: Arte, musica—società*, ed. G. Zampa (Milan: Arnoldo Mondadori, 1996).

Morton, A. and H. *Monday Evening Concerts 1954–1971: The Lawrence Morton Years* (Los Angeles: Lawrence Morton Fund, 1993).

Morton, L. "Stravinsky in Los Angeles," program book of the *Festival of Music Made in Los Angeles* (Los Angeles: Los Angeles Philharmonic Association, 1981), 66–86.

Murrill, H. "Aspects of Stravinsky," *Music & Letters*, xxxii/2 (April 1951), 118–24.

Nabokov, N. *Old Friends and New Music* (London: Hamish Hamilton, 1951).

———. *Bagazh: Memoirs of a Russian Cosmopolitan* (New York: Atheneum, 1975).

———. "Stravinsky Now," *Partisan Review*, 11 (1944), 324–34.

———. "The Atonal Trail—A Communication," *Partisan Review* 15 (1948), 580–5.

Nashold, J., and G. Tremlett. *The Death of Dylan Thomas* (Edinburgh and London: Mainstream Publishing, 1997).

Nattiez, J.-J., and R. Piencikowski (eds.). *Pierre Boulez–John Cage: Correspondance et Documents* (Mainz: Schott, 2002).

Nest'yev, I. "Vechera Igorya Stravinskovo," *Sovetskaya Muzïka*, no. 12 (December 1962), 92–5.

Newman, A., and R. Craft. *Bravo Stravinsky* (Cleveland and New York: World Publishing Company, 1967).

Nichols, R. *Conversations with Madeleine Milhaud* (London: Faber and Faber, 1996).

Ocampo, V. *Autobiografía* (Buenos Aires: Sur, 1979–84).

Oja, C. J. (ed.). *Stravinsky in Modern Music* (New York: Da Capo Press, 1982).

Oliver, Michael. *Igor Stravinsky* (London: Phaidon, 1995).

Osborne, C. *W. H. Auden: The Life of a Poet* (London: Eyre Methuen, 1979).

Oury, M. *Lettres à mon peintre* (Paris: Perrin, 1965).

Page, T. and V. W. (eds.). *Selected Letters of Virgil Thomson* (New York: Summit Books, 1988).

Pasler, J. (ed.) *Confronting Stravinsky* (Berkeley, Los Angeles, London: University of California Press, 1986).

Perrin, M. "Stravinsky in a Composition Class," *The Score*, 20 (June 1957), 44–6.

Peyser, J. *The Memory of All That* (New York: Billboard Books, 1998).

———. *Boulez: Composer, Conductor, Enigma* (London: Cassell, 1976).

———. "Stravinsky-Craft, Inc.," *American Scholar* (Fall, 1983), 513–8.

Piatigorsky, G. *Cellist* (New York: Doubleday, 1965).

Pollack, H. *Aaron Copland: The Life and Work of an Uncommon Man* (London: Faber and Faber, 1999).

Prunières, H. (ed.). *La Revue musicale*, 20è année, no. 191 (May-June 1939) (Stravinsky issue).

Ricci, F. C. *Vittorio Rieti* (Naples and Rome: Edizioni Scientifiche Italiane, 1987).

Robinson, E. G., and L. Spigelgass. *All My Yesterdays* (New York: Hawthorn Books, 1973).

Robinson, H. (ed.). *Selected Letters of Sergei Prokofiev* (Boston: Northeastern University Press, 1998).

Rosar, W. H. "Stravinsky and MGM," in Clifford McCarty (ed.), *Film Music* (vol. 1, New York: Garland, 1989), 108–22.

Rosenthal, A. "The Paul Sachar Foundation at the Crossroads: The Purchase of the Igor Stravinsky Archive," in *Paul Sacher in Memorium* (Basel: Paul Sacher Stiftung, 2000), 37–40.

Rosenstiel, L. *Nadia Boulanger: A Life in Music* (London and New York: Norton, 1982).

Sachs, H. *Music in Fascist Italy* (London: Weidenfeld & Nicolson, 1987).

Saunders, F. S. *Who Paid the Piper?* (London: Granta Books, 1999).

Savenko, S. *Mir Stravinskovo* (Moscow: Kompozitor, 2001).

Scherliess, V. *Igor Strawinsky und seine Zeit* (Laaber: Laaber Verlag, 1983).

———. "*Inspiration* und *fabrication*: Beobachtungen zu Igor Strawinskys Arbeit an *The Rake's Progress*," in F. Meyer (ed.), *Quellenstudien II* (Winterthur: Amadeus, 1993), 39–72.

Schouvaloff, A., and V .Borovsky. *Stravinsky on Stage* (London: Stainer and Bell, 1982).

Schuster-Craig, J. "Stravinsky's *Scènes de Ballet* and Billy Rose's *The Seven Lively Arts*. The Abravanel Account," in S. Parisi (ed.), *Music in the Theater, Church, and Villa: Essays in Honor of Robert Lamar Weaver and Norma Wright Weaver* (Warren, Michigan: Harmonie Park Press, 2000), 285–9.

Schwarz, B. *Music and Musical Life in Soviet Russia 1917–1970* (London: Barrie and Jenkins, 1972).

———. "Stravinsky in Soviet Russian Criticism," *Musical Quarterly*, 48 (1962), 340-61.

Sessions, R. "Thoughts on Stravinsky," *The Score*, 20 (June 1957), 32–7.

Shanet, H. *Philharmonic: A History of New York's Orchestra* (New York: Doubleday, 1975).

Siohan, R. *Stravinsky*, trans. E. W. White (London: Calder and Boyars, 1965).

Skelton, G. (ed.). *Selected Letters of Paul Hindemith* (New Haven and London: Yale University Press, 1995).

Slim, H. C. *Annotated Catalogue of the H. Colin Slim Stravinsky Collection* (Vancouver: University of British Columbia, 2002).

———. "From Copenhagen and Paris: A Stravinsky Photograph-Autograph at the University of British Columbia," *Notes* 59/3 (2003), 542–55.

———. "Unknown Words and Music, 1939–44, by Stravinsky," in D. Rosen and C. Brook (eds.), *Words on Music: Essays in Honor of Andrew Porter on the Occasion of His 75th Birthday* (Hillsdale, New York: Pendragon Press, 2004), 300–19.

———. "Stravinsky's *Scherzo . . . à la russe* and its two-piano origins," in B. Haggh (ed.), *Essays on Music and Culture in Honor of Herbert Kellman* (Paris: Minerve, 2001), 518–37.

———. "A Stravinsky Holograph in 1936 for Juan José Castro in Buenos Aires," in C. Reardon and S. Parisi (eds.), *Music Observed: Studies in Memory of William C. Holmes* (Warren, Mich.: Harmonie Park Press, 2004), 447–58.

Slonimsky, N. *Music Since 1900* (4th ed., London: Cassell, 1972).

———. *Perfect Pitch* (Oxford: Oxford University Press, 1988).

Smyth, D. H. "Stravinsky as Serialist: The Sketches for *Threni*," *Music Theory Spectrum*, 22, no. 2 (Fall, 2000), 205–24.

———. "Stravinsky's Second Crisis: Reading the Early Serial Sketches," *Perspectives of New Music*, 37/2 (Summer 1999), 117–46.

Souvtchinsky, P. (ed.). *Musique Russe*, vol. 1 (Paris: Presses Universitaires de France, 1953).

———. *Un siècle de musique russe* (Arles: Actes Sud, 2004).

Spender, S. *Journals 1939–1983*, ed. J. Goldsmith (London: Faber, 1985).

Spies, C. "Impressions after an Exhibition," *Tempo*, no. 102 (1972), 2–9.

Steegmuller, F. *Cocteau* (London: Macmillan, 1970).

Straus, J. N. *Remaking the Past* (Cambridge, Mass., and London: Harvard University Press, 1990).

———. *Stravinsky's Late Music* (Cambridge: Cambridge University Press, 2001).

Stravinsky, I. "The Diaghilev I Knew," *Atlantic Monthly* (November 1953), 33–6.

———. "Foreword," in H. Eimert and K. Stockhausen (eds.), *Die Reihe, 2: Anton Webern* (2nd rev. Eng. edition, Bryn Mawr: Theodore Presser, 1959), vii.

———. "Quelques Confidences sur la musique," *Conferencia*, 15 December 1935; reprinted in White, *Stravinsky: The Composer and His Works*, 581–5.

———. *Leben und Werk—von ihm selbst* (Zurich/Mainz: Atlantis/Schott, 1957).

———. *Poétique musicale*, ed. Myriam Soumagnac (Paris: Harmonique Flammarion, 2000).

———. Introduction, in G. Watkins, *Gesualdo: The Man and His Music* (London: Oxford University Press, 1973).

Stravinsky, S. Unpublished interview with Thor Wood, February 1977 (typed transcript in New York Public Library).

Strawinsky, T. *Le Message d'Igor Strawinsky* (Lausanne: Librairie F. Rouge, 1948); trans. R. Craft and A. Marion, as *The Message of Igor Stravinsky* (London: Boosey and Hawkes, 1953).

Stuart, P. *Igor Stravinsky—The Composer in the Recording Studio* (New York, Westport and London: Greenwood Press, 1991).

Stuckenschmidt, H. H. *Arnold Schoenberg: His Life, World and Work*, trans. H. Searle (London: John Calder, 1977).

Sulzer, P. (ed.) *Zehn Komponisten um Werner Reinhart*, vol. 1 (Zurich: Stadtbibliothek Winterthur, Atlantis Musikbuch-Verlag, 1979).

Szigeti, J. *With Strings Attached* (London: Cassell, 1949).

Tansman, A. *Igor Stravinsky: The Man and His Music*, trans. T. and C. Bleefield (New York: Putnam, 1949).

Taper, B. *Balanchine* (Berkeley, Los Angeles and London: University of California Press, 1987).

Taruskin, R. "The Dark Side of Modern Music," *New Republic* (5 September 1988), 28–34.

———. *Stravinsky and the Russian Traditions: A Biography of the Works through "Mavra"* (Oxford: University Press, 1996).

———. *Defining Russia Musically* (Princeton: Princeton University Press, 1997).

Taruskin, R., and R. Craft. "Jews and Geniuses: An Exchange," *New York Review of Books*, 15 June 1989, 57–8.

Terapiano, Y. *Vstrechi* (New York: Izdatel'stvo imeni Chekhova, 1953).

Thomson, V. *Virgil Thomson by Virgil Thomson* (London: Weidenfeld and Nicolson, 1967).

Valéry, P. *Oeuvres*, vol. 1 (Pléiade edition, Paris: Gallimard, 1957).

Varunts, V. (ed.). *I. F. Stravinsky: Sbornik statey* (Moscow: Moskovskoy gosudarstvennoy konservatoriya, 1997).

Varunts, V. "Strawinsky protestiert . . . ," *Mitteilungen der Paul Sacher Stiftung*, no. 6 (March 1993), 35–7.

———. "A. Schoenberg—I. Stravinsky: khronika odnoy vrazhdï," in E. Y. Chigaryova and E. A. Dolenko (eds.), *Arnold Schoenberg: vchera, sevodnya, zavtra* (Moscow: Moskovskoy gosudarstvennoy konservatoriya, 2002), 142–77.

Vincis, C., and P. Dal Molin. "Mo(nu)mento di Carlo Gesualdo," *Acta Musicologica*, 76 (2004), 221–51.

Vlad, R. *Stravinsky* (2nd ed. London: Oxford University Press, 1967).

Walsh, S. *The Music of Stravinsky* (London: Routledge, 1988).

———. "Stravinsky's Symphonies: Accident or Design?" in C. Ayrey and M. Everist (eds.), *Analytical Strategies and Musical Interpretation* (Cambridge: Cambridge University Press, 1996), 35–71.

———. *The New Grove Stravinsky* (London: Macmillan, 2002).

Wangermée, R. (ed.). *Paul Collaer: Correspondance avec des amis musiciens* (Sprimont: Mardaga, 1996).

Weeda, E. (ed.). *Yuriy Mandel'shtam: Sobraniye Stikhotvoreniy* (The Hague: Leuxenhoff, 1990).

Wellens, I. *Music on the Frontline* (Aldershot: Ashgate, 2002).

White, E. W. *Stravinsky: the Composer and His Works* (London: Faber and Faber, 1979).

Wilson, E. *Shostakovich: A Life Remembered* (Princeton: Princeton University Press, 1994).

Yuzefovich, V. (ed.). "Chronicle of a Non-friendship: Letters of Stravinsky and Koussevistzky," trans. by Marina Kostalevsky, *Musical Quarterly*, 86 (Winter 2002), 750–884.

ILLUSTRATION CREDITS

Fondation Théodore Strawinsky, Geneva: family tea at the orangery; Catherine Stravinsky with her granddaughter (photograph: R. Heyd)

Paul Sacher Stiftung, Basel: Milène and Mika in the 1930s; Mika with her husband; with Victoria Ocampo; with Nadia Boulanger; in the Disney studios; with George Martin, Dagmar Godowsky, and Mercedes de Acosta; studying the score of *Persephone* (photograph: Ruth Orkin); opening scene of *The Rake's Progress* (photograph: Erio Piccagliani); with Jean Cocteau (photograph: Studio Lipnitzki); rehearsing *The Rake's Progress* (photograph: Erio Piccagliani); with Ernst Roth, Venice; with Craft and Pierre Boulez; with Darius and Madeleine Milhaud (photograph: Centre Culturel Américain); world premiere of *Threni* (photograph: Giacomelli, Venice); conducting in the early sixties; with Lillian Libman (photograph: Esther Brown); with Robert Craft, 1962; with Rimsky-Korsakov; proposing a toast; with Tikhon Khrennikov; with his niece Xenya; applauding Pierre Monteux's *Rite of Spring* (photograph: *Daily Mail*); in his studio at 1260 North Wetherly Drive; orchestrating Bach (photograph: Dominique Cibiel)

Getty Images: rehearsing *Ebony Concerto;* Christopher Isherwood and Aldous Huxley; with Balanchine, Hollywood, 1966 (photograph: Arnold Newman); with Milène, Hollywood, 1966 (photograph: Arnold Newman)

Martha Swope: rehearsing *Agon* with Balanchine

Lady Berlin: Isaiah Berlin and Nicolas Nabokov

No credit: Igor and Vera Stravinsky in Cincinnati (photograph: Eugene Goossens); studying the Symphony in C with Craft and Alexis Haieff; Stravinsky arrives in Venice for *The Rake's Progress*; Dylan Thomas at a book-signing (photograph: Jeff Towns / Dylans Bookstore); listening to Craft rehearsing the *Canticum Sacrum* (photograph: Columbia Records); with Pierre Souvtchinsky; with Robert Craft at Paestum (photograph: Robert Emmet Bright)

A NOTE ABOUT THE AUTHOR

STEPHEN WALSH is a critic and musicologist who has written and broadcast extensively on Stravinsky and other
aspects of twentieth-century music. He was for some years
a music critic with *The Observer,* and he has also reviewed
regularly for the London *Times,* the *Daily Telegraph, The Listener,* and most recently, *The Independent.* The first volume
of his biography of Igor Stravinsky, *A Creative Spring: Russia
and France, 1882–1934,* was published in 1999. He holds a
personal chair at Cardiff University.

A NOTE ON THE TYPE

This book was set in Scala, a typeface designed in 1988 by Martin Majoor and published in 1991 as the first serious text face by FontFont, a digital type foundry.

Composed by Creative Graphics,
Allentown, Pennsylvania
Printed and bound by Berryville Graphics,
Berryville, Virginia
Designed by Anthea Lingeman